SOCIAL RESEARCH METHODS

To Carole, Elyssa, and Sharyn,
for all their support all the time

SOCIAL RESEARCH METHODS

Qualitative and Quantitative Approaches

H. Russell Bernard

Sage Publications, Inc.
International Educational and Professional Publisher
Thousand Oaks ▪ London ▪ New Delhi

For information:

Sage Publications, Inc.
2455 Teller Road
Thousand Oaks, California 91320
E-mail: order@sagepub.com

Sage Publications Ltd.
6 Bonhill Street
London EC2A 4PU
United Kingdom

Sage Publications India Pvt. Ltd.
M-32 Market
Greater Kailash I
New Delhi 110 048 India

Printed in the United States of America

Library of Congress Cataloging-in-Publication Data

Bernard, H. Russell (Harvey Russell), 1940-
    Social research methods: Qualitative and quantitative approaches /
by H. Russell Bernard.
        p.   cm.
Includes bibliographical references and index.
    ISBN 0-7619-1403-X (cloth: alk. paper)
    1. Social science—Research—Methodology.   I. Title.
H62.B439   2000
300'.7'2—dc21   99-050458

This book is printed on acid-free paper.

            03   04   05   10   9   8   7   6   5   4   3

Acquiring Editor:	C. Deborah Laughton
Editorial Assistant:	Eileen Carr
Production Editor:	Astrid Virding
Editorial Assistant:	Karen Wiley
Designer/Typesetter:	Janelle LeMaster
Cover Designer:	Ravi Balasuriya

BRIEF CONTENTS

PART IV
DATA ANALYSIS

DETAILED CONTENTS

PART I
BACKGROUND TO RESEARCH

PART III
DATA COLLECTION

PART IV
DATA ANALYSIS

PREFACE

GOALS AND PHILOSOPHY

This book is an expansion of my *Research Methods in Anthropology* (Bernard 1994). In that book, my goal was to provide anthropology students with a general introduction to the excitement of social research. Naturally, the emphasis in that book was on methods that anthropologists are most likely to use in field research: participant observation, spot observation, decision modeling, and so on. But my larger goal was to make clear that there were no truly anthropological methods—that there were only research methods—and to help students of cultural anthropology develop an understanding of the key issues in sampling, measurement, and analysis.

In this book, my goals remain the same, but the audience is broader. I want to make the excitement of research clear to students across the social sciences—in sociology, education, political science, anthropology, social psychology, criminology, demography, nursing, education, social work. And I hope to make clear that some methods usually associated with anthropology are also useful to researchers in other disciplines.

There is, of course, an irreducible difference between those of us for whom the first principle of inquiry is that reality is constructed uniquely by each person and those of us who start from the principle that external reality awaits our discovery through a series of approximations. There is also an important (though not incompatible) difference between those of us who seek to *understand* human phenomena in relation to differences in beliefs and values and those of us who seek to *explain* human thought and behavior as the consequence of external forces.

But while the boundaries between the disciplines remain strong, those boundaries are no longer about methods—if they ever were. Whatever our epistemological differences, the actual methods by which we collect and analyze our data belong to everyone across the social sciences.

In short, all the methods belong to all of us.

WHAT'S IN THIS BOOK?

There are 16 chapters in this book, organized into four parts: (1) background to research, (2) designing research, (3) collecting data, and (4) analyzing data.

Part I, on the background to research, comprises three chapters: Chapter 1 covers the history of social science and introduces the competing philosophical positions in the field; Chapter 2 is about the logical foundations of social science research—the concepts of variables, measurement, and units of analysis; and Chapter 3 is about choosing research problems and searching the literature.

Chapter 1 addresses these questions: (1) What are the social sciences? (2) What are the intellectual roots of the social sciences? and (3) What good are the social sciences? Chapter 1 also introduces the complex issue of ethics in the social sciences, a subject dealt with throughout the book. My own position is strongly positivist, and this naturally influences my discussion of all these issues.

Chapter 2 introduces the vocabulary of social research. There's a lot of jargon, but it's the good kind. Important concepts deserve words of their own, and Chapter 2 is full of important concepts like reliability, validity, levels of measurement, covariation, and the controversial idea of operationism.

Chapter 3 is about choosing research problems and about searching the literature in preparation for collecting data. There is a profound difference between a social problem and a social *research* problem. Child abuse, infant mortality, the spread of HIV, teens carrying guns to school—these are social problems, and serious ones. Politicians, activists, members of the clergy, and social researchers can all contribute to solving these problems. But in my view, the most important contribution a social scientist can make to solving a social problem is to be right about what causes it. This requires ideas for research and familiarity with what has been done before. Learning the difference between a social problem and a social research problem is, I think, one of the most difficult tasks that social researchers face.

Selecting a research topic always involves an ethical issue. The operational test of whether a particular piece of research is ethical is whether social norms tolerate it, but this relativistic position has a serious flaw, which I address in this chapter.

Part II, on designing research, comprises two chapters. Chapter 4 is about the concepts and principles of experimental design, and Chapter 5 is about sampling. The experimental method is not a technique, but an entire approach to the development of knowledge. The experimental approach is as much part of the foundation of survey research in sociology as it is of laboratory research in psychology. The principle of random assignment in experiments, for example, has its analog in the principle of random sampling in survey research. Experiments on people involve special ethical issues, which I explore in this chapter as well.

Chapter 5 is about the various methods for getting samples, including, of course, simple and stratified random sampling, as well as nonrandom sampling methods (quota sampling, snowball sampling, purposive sampling, and convenience sampling). Together, Chapters 4 and 5 address two big questions in social research: (1) How can I be sure that my findings are valid? and (2) Given that my findings are valid, how far can I generalize them beyond the people (or countries, or court cases) I actually studied?

Including a chapter on sampling as part of research design reflects my own teaching style, but some instructors may assign Chapter 5 as part of data analysis (Chapters 14-16).

Part III is about the real how-to of collecting social science data. There are five chapters in this section: Chapter 6 deals with unstructured and semistructured interviewing and Chapter 7 with fully structured interviewing. Chapter 8 covers the development and use of scales. Chapter 9 is about the elusive yet highly effective method of participant observation. And Chapter 10 is about methods of direct and indirect observation.

Unstructured interviewing and semistructured interviewing, covered in Chapter 6, involve a minimum of control. In unstructured interviewing, the idea is to get people to open up and to let them express themselves in their own terms and at their own pace. Semistructured interviewing follows a written list of questions and topics that need to be covered in a particular order.

Focus groups—a kind of semistructured interview—are recruited to discuss a particular topic, like people's reaction to a television commercial or their attitudes toward a social service program. Survey researchers may use focus groups to help in designing a questionnaire and also to help interpret the results of surveys.

Response effects are a problem in all interviewing, from unstructured, hanging-out interviews to questionnaire-based telephone interviews. Response effects are measurable differences in interview data that are predictable from characteristics of respondents, interviewers, and environments. This chapter ends with a review of this important problem.

In structured interviews, covered in Chapter 7, people are asked to respond to as nearly identical a set of stimuli as possible. Questionnaires, for example, are fully structured interviews, as are methods like free listing, pile sorting, triad tests, sentence frames, paired comparisons, and rank-

ings and ratings. This chapter covers questionnaire design, improving response rates, the use of open-ended vs. closed-ended questions, asking questions about sensitive topics, using several interviewers in team research, and translating questionnaires from one language to another.

Chapter 8 is about the development and use of scales. A single question on a questionnaire is technically a scale if it lets you assign the people you're studying to categories of a variable. Many interesting variables in social science, however, are complex and can't easily be assessed with single indicators. This chapter covers methods for developing and testing composite measures of complex concepts. Methods covered include Guttman scales, Likert scales, semantic differential scales, and direct magnitude scales.

Chapter 9 is about participant observation, one of the four strategic methods of the social sciences, along with experiments, surveys, and archival research. Participant observation is popularly associated with cultural anthropology, but it has long been used across the social sciences. Participant observation turns field workers into instruments of data collection and data analysis. This requires certain skills, which include learning the local language, dialect, or jargon; developing explicit awareness; building memory; maintaining naïveté; learning to hang out and build rapport; maintaining objectivity; and learning to write clearly.

Chapter 10 covers direct and indirect observation. Direct observation involves watching people and recording their behavior on the spot; indirect observation involves gathering the archaeological residue of people's behavior. Some methods of direct observation include continuous monitoring (associated with behavioral assessment), spot observation (associated with time allocation studies), and experience sampling (for assessing moods and emotions as well as behaviors). Direct observation is reactive when people know that you are watching them (people can play to the observer), so some researchers use unobtrusive observation. This involves deception, which raises serious ethical issues.

Part IV comprises six chapters about analyzing data. Chapter 11 is an overview of the whole analysis enterprise. Different kinds of data—qualitative and quantitative—require different analytic methods, but analysis is always the same thing: the search for patterns in data and for ideas that help explain why those patterns are there in the first place. One of the most important concepts in all data analysis—whether we're working with quantitative or qualitative data—is the data matrix. This concept is introduced in Chapter 11.

Chapter 12 is the first of two chapters about the analysis of qualitative data. Actually, most of the recoverable information about human thought and behavior is naturally occurring text. This includes diaries, property transactions, recipes, correspondence, song lyrics, billboards, books, magazines, newspapers, artifacts, images, advertisements, and so on. Text analysis is not a single method. It includes interpretive analysis, narrative analysis, discourse analysis, the grounded theory approach, and content analysis. As in so many areas of social research, text analysis often involves a sensible blend of qualitative and quantitative methods.

Chapter 13 covers ethnographic decision modeling (including flow chart models and IF-THEN charts, and decision tables), the elicitation and display of folk taxonomies (including componential analysis), and analytic induction (including Boolean tests, which are a formalization of analytic induction). What these methods have in common is that they are based on some principles of systematic logic applied to qualitative data.

Chapters 14, 15, and 16 are an introduction to quantitative analysis in social research.

Univariate analysis involves getting to know data intimately by examining variables precisely and in detail. This is the focus of Chapter 14, which includes a discussion of frequency distributions and measures of central tendency, shape, and dispersion. I place a lot of emphasis on visual methods—things like box plots and histograms, pie charts, and polygons—for understanding "what's in there." Chapter 14 ends with a test for whether a sample mean is likely to represent the true mean of a population. This involves a discussion of the logic of hypothesis testing.

Bivariate analysis (Chapter 15) involves looking at associations between pairs of variables and trying to understand how those associations work. Chapter 15 covers *t*-tests, cross-tabs, chi-square, the principle of proportionate reduction of error, Fisher's exact test, gamma, correlation (Pearson's for interval data, Spearman's for rank-ordered data, and Eta for nonlinear relations), and regression. At the end of Chapter 15, I discuss some current (and recurring) questions in data analysis, including, What to do about outliers? Is it legitimate to shop for covariations by shotgunning? and Are tests of statistical significance really useful?

Chapter 16 is an introduction to the broad range of techniques available in multivariate analysis. This includes elaboration (teasing out the complexities in a bivariate relation by controlling for the effects of antecedent or intervening variables), partial correlation (a more direct way to control for the effects of a third or fourth or fifth variable on a relation between two variables), and multiple regression. Path analysis is introduced as a multiple regression method for causal models and discriminant function analysis as a method for classifying cases into categorical variables from ordinal and interval variables. Finally, I introduce some methods of data reduction, including factor analysis, multidimensional scaling, and cluster analysis.

There is no chapter devoted to ethics in this book because ethics is too important to deal with that way. It's part of everything we do in social science, and the topic of ethics is dealt with, at length, in several chapters.

Some Features of the Book

Opening objectives and introductions to the chapters. Each chapter begins with a page called "In This Chapter" that lays out all the major headings. This page repeats the material in the detailed Table of Contents for each chapter and makes it easier to understand, at a glance, what's coming. Right after this opening page, each chapter has an introduction that provides a quick review of the major issues.

Highlighted examples. I illustrate all the major points in the book with one or more examples. Some examples, though, seem to me to have exceptional pedagogic value, so I've set them off with a beginning indicator that looks like this

———————❖

and an ending indicator that looks like this

❖———————

Numbered steps. Methods like experiments, questionnaires, and participant observation are really complex processes rather than techniques. I've broken down these methods into a series of numbered, highlighted steps to make it easier to locate them for review.

Key concepts. All new terms appear in ***bold-faced type like this*** but only the first time they appear. Then, as a study aid, there is a page at the end of each chapter titled "Key Concepts in This Chapter." That page has all the bold-faced terms in the chapter, along with the page numbers on which the terms first appear.

Box Preface. 1
About Boxes

Boxes. You'll see some boxes, like this, throughout the book.

I use this device when I want to expand on, but don't want to interrupt the flow of, some key point and when I want to highlight some material.

For example, in Chapter 5, on sampling, I mention street-intercept surveys as one way to handle the problem of not having a sampling frame from which to choose survey respondents. Box 5.2 expands on this and points readers to examples of published studies in which the street-intercept method was used.

Another example is in Chapter 16 where I talk about data matrices. In Box 16.1, I point out the difference between symmetric and asymmetric matrices.

Summary and exercises. Following the Key Concepts page, there are two more study aids: a summary of the main points of the chapter, and a series of exercises for illustrating and nailing down some of the main points.

Further readings. Finally, each chapter ends with recommendations for further reading. These recommendations include classics in the literature on social science methods as well as recent examples that further illustrate some of the key points in each chapter. They are grouped by category so that readers can pursue topics of interest from the chapter.

ACKNOWLEDGMENTS

Anyone who has ever written a textbook knows that I really, really mean it when I say how grateful I am to a lot of people who have helped along the way—students, colleagues, editors, and production staff.

My thanks go to the many students over the years who shared with me their research methods problems and who offered trenchant advice in return on how best to teach the subject of research methods: Nanette Barkey, Timothy Brazill, Bryan Byrne, Domenick Dellino, John Dominy, Michael Evans, Mark Fleisher, Louis Forline, Lance Gravlee, Henry Green, Camilla Harshbarger, Fred Hay, Scott Hill, Shepherd Iverson, Jamie Jacobs, Jerry Jirimutu, David Kennedy, Robin Kennedy, Barbara Marriott, George Mbeh, Christopher McCarty, Isaac Nyamongo, David Price, Jorge Rocha, Gery Ryan, Gene Ann Shelley, Susan Stans, Kenneth Sturrock, Elli Sugita, Holly Williams, and Amber Yoder.

My thanks go to colleagues who provided much-needed advice on the predecessor to this book: Michael Chibnik (University of Iowa), Carole Hill (Georgia State University), Jeffrey Johnson and his student Dawn Parks (East Carolina University), Willett Kempton (University of Delaware), John Omohundro (SUNY at Potsdam), Aaron Podolefsky (University of Northern Iowa), Douglas Raybeck (Hamilton College), Paula Sabloff (University of Pennsylvania), Lynn Thomas (Pomona College), Roger Trent (California Department of Health Services), and Alvin Wolfe (University of South Florida).

Over the whole of my career, I've profited from lengthy discussions about research methods with Michael Agar, Stephen Borgatti, James Boster, Ronald Cohen, Roy D'Andrade, Linton Freeman, Sue Freeman, Linda Garro, Christina Gladwin, Marvin Harris, Jeffrey Johnson, Gretel Pelto, Pertti Pelto, the late Jack Roberts, A. Kimball Romney, Lee Sailer, the late Thomas Schweizer, Michael Trend, Susan Weller, Oswald Werner, and Douglas White. Other colleagues who have had a personal influence on my thinking about research methods include Ronald Burt, Michael Burton, Carol Ember, Melvin Ember, Eugene Hammel, Allen Johnson, Maxine Margolis, Ronald Rice, Peter Rossi, James Short, Harry Triandis, the late Charles Wagley, and Alvin Wolfe. Most of them knew that they were helping me talk and think through the issues presented in this book, but some may not have known, so I'd like to take this opportunity to say thanks to all of them.

Thanks go to the Alexander von Humboldt Fund and to my colleagues at the University of Cologne for their support in 1994-95. That support allowed me to read about research methods across the social sciences. My host during that year, Thomas Schweizer, encouraged my work on this book. Sadly, he did not live to see it published.

From 1988 to 1995, Pertti Pelto, Stephen Borgatti, and I taught the National Science Foundation Summer Institute on Research Methods in Cultural Anthropology, widely known as "methods camp" because the official name was just too long. Pelto wrote the pioneering methods text in cultural anthropology (1970; Pelto and Pelto 1978); my intellectual debt to him cannot be exaggerated. In particular, I've been influenced by his sensible combination of ethnographic and numerical data in social research.

Stephen Borgatti tutored me on the measurement of similarities and dissimilarities and has greatly influenced my thinking about the formal study of emically defined cultural domains. Readers will see references in this book to Borgatti's suite of computer programs, called ANTHRO-PAC. That package has made it possible for social scientists to do multidimensional scaling, hierarchical clustering, Likert scaling, Guttman scaling, and other computationally intensive data analysis tasks easily.

I am very much indebted to the following colleagues who gave their time to review the draft manuscript of this book and to offer detailed advice: W. Penn Handwerker (University of Connecticut), Charles Kadushin (CUNY), Paul Kim (Louisiana State University), Thomas Petee (Auburn University), Kwaku Twumashi-Ankrah (Fayetteville State University), and Paul Swank (University of Houston).

Handwerker and I collaborated on a book for teaching students the basics of statistical data analysis. He was there for me during the whole process of writing this book. Whether it was just to talk about how to present this or that method or to discuss the subtleties of multicollinearity, Penn never complained and never let up.

Marvin Harris, my colleague at the University of Florida, has helped me more than anyone to see the inextricable connection between method and theory. In particular, through discussions with him over the years, I have come to see the link between the positivist epistemology that I advocate for methods in social research and the materialist paradigm that he advocates for finding an swers to puzzles about aggregate human behavior.

My closest colleague, and the one to whom I am most indebted intellectually, is Peter Killworth, my research partner and friend for the past 28 years. Peter is a geophysicist at Southampton University, England. He shares my vision of an effective science of humanity. He appreciates the difficulties a naturalist like me encounters in collecting real-life data, in the field, about human behavior and thought. And he has made me understand, in turn, the difficulties a theoretical physicist like him encounters in trying to work with data that have been collected by deep-sea current meters, satellite weather scanners, and the like. Science—physical science, biological science, and social science alike—is messy. The results are never perfect, but the process of trying to do better is always exhilarating. That's the central lesson of this book, and I hope it comes through.

Textbook authors have special debts to editors and to members of the production staff. Those debts start accumulating even before the writing starts and continue to mount after the book is on the shelves. Mitch Allen, my editor (first at Sage Publications, now at AltaMira Press), guided me over the years and made many cogent suggestions for improving the prose, the epistemological arguments, and the organization of the material.

My editor for this book, and the person who guided me in expanding my anthropology methods text to a general methods text for the social sciences, is C. Deborah Laughton. Perfectionist and visionary are descriptors that come easily to mind. Without C. Deborah, this book would not have been thought of, much less written. My sincere thanks also go to Eileen Carr, Laughton's assistant. It was Carr who fielded two years of questions and found all the answers while I was holed up writing.

Producing a book takes a lot of teamwork—and a sense of humor. Kate Peterson did a superb job of copy editing the book (she worked with me by e-mail as if she were at the next desk, directing questions at me day and night) as did Astrid Virding, who was responsible for the complex task of coordinating the entire production process. Janelle LeMaster designed the lay-out and typeset the book, Kris Bergstad proofread the final product, Karen Wiley coordinated the manuscript preparation, and Ravi Balasuriya designed the cover.

I save for last the people who deserve my thanks more than any others. It's not just authors who give up vacations and weekends to write books. Whole families are brought into the art of abnegation. Thanks go to Elyssa and Sharyn for their uncompromising support and love, and thanks especially for understanding when I'd show up to visit with a laptop in tow and closet myself. And thanks to Carole Bernard for—well, for everything. Carole worked with me on this book through all its incarnations. Her editorial advice and deadly eye for detail has saved me from so many embarrassments that I've stopped counting. Much more important, she has lived through my writing this book. No one can possibly know, without firsthand experience, what it's like to live with someone who is writing a book like this one. I only know that I wouldn't want to do it.

H. Russell Bernard
Gainesville, Florida

PART 1

BACKGROUND TO RESEARCH

1 ABOUT SOCIAL SCIENCE

IN THIS CHAPTER:

❖ INTRODUCTION

This book is about research in the social sciences—that is, the sciences of human thought and human behavior. Our lives are profoundly affected by the social sciences. Our public schools are scenes of one experiment after another, as we search for better ways to help children learn. Those experiments are part of social science at work. Our cities are scenes of hundreds of programs designed, we hope, to help people develop their employment skills or gain access to health care or find shelter. All these programs are part of social science at work. We are bombarded with ads to buy this or that thing, to vote for this or that candidate, to give to this or that charity. Those ads, too, are part of social science at work.

THE SOCIAL SCIENCE SUCCESS STORY

We are always on the lookout for ways to extend and make our own lives and the lives of our children more comfortable. In the absence of any hard information about how to do those things, we quite naturally mystify the forces that make some people rich and some poor, make some people sick and others healthy, and make some people die young and others live a long time. From its beginnings in the sixteenth century, modern science has been demystifying those forces. Science is about the systematic creation of knowledge that provides us with the kind of control over nature—from the weather to disease to our own buying habits—that we have always sought.

Some people are very uncomfortable with this "mastery over nature" metaphor. When all is said and done, though, few people—not even the most outspoken critics of science—would give up the material benefits of science. For example, one of science's great triumphs over nature is antibiotics. We know that overprescription of those drugs eventually sets the stage for new strains of drug-resistant bacteria, but we also know perfectly well that we're not going to stop using antibiotics. We'll rely (we hope) on *more* science to come up with better bacteria fighters.

Air conditioning is another of science's triumphs over nature. In Florida, where I live, there is constant criticism of overdevelopment. But try getting middle-class people in my state to give up air conditioning for just one day in the summer and you'll find out in a hurry about the weakness of ideology compared to the power of creature comforts. If running air conditioners pollutes the air or uses up fossil fuel, we'll rely (we hope) on *more* science to solve those problems, too.

We are accustomed to thinking about the success of the physical and biological sciences, but not about the success of the social sciences. Ask 500 people, as I did recently in a telephone survey, to list "the major contributions that science has made to humanity" in the twentieth century and there is strong consensus. Many people list medical science and cures for diseases without hesitation, followed by things like space exploration, computers, nuclear power, satellite telecommunications, television, pacemakers, automobiles, artificial limbs, and transplant surgery.

In other words, the contributions of science are, in the public imagination, technologies—the things that provide the mastery over nature I mentioned.

Ask those same people to list "the major contributions that the social and behavioral sciences have made to humanity" and you get a long silence on the phone. This is followed by, "What do you mean?" Even after explaining that you want to know about the contributions of psychology, sociology, anthropology, economics, and political science, you get a raggedy list, with no consensus.

I want you to know, right off the bat, that social science is serious business and that it has been a roaring success, contributing mightily to humanity's global effort to control nature. Fundamental breakthroughs by psychologists in understanding the stimulus-response mechanism in humans, for example, have made possible the treatment and management of phobias, bringing comfort to untold millions of people.

The same breakthroughs have brought us wildly successful attack ads in politics and millions of adolescents becoming hooked on cigarettes from clever advertising. I never said you'd *like* all the successes of social science.

———————❖

Beginning in the 1840s, fundamental breakthroughs in sociology and anthropology have given us great understanding of how economic and political forces affect demography. One result is life insurance. Suppose I'm the life insurance company. You bet me that you will die within 365 days. I ask you a few questions: How old are you? Do you smoke? What do you do for a living? Then, depending on the answers (I've got all that fundamental knowledge, remember?), I tell you that the bet is your $235 against my promise to pay your heirs $30,000 if you die within 365 days. If you *lose the bet* and stay alive, I keep your $235. Next year, we go through this again, except that now I set your bet at $300.

This is simply spectacular human engineering at work, and it's all based on fundamental, scientifically developed knowledge about risk assessment. Another product of this knowledge is state lotteries—taxes on people who are bad at math.

In the late nineteenth century, Otto von Bismarck asked his minister of finance to come up with a pension plan that the government could provide for retired German workers. Based on sound social science data, the minister suggested that 65 would be just the right age for retirement. At that time, the average life expectancy in Germany was, of course, less than 65 and those workers who made it to 65 could expect only a few years on the government pension. In 1934, life expectancy was still less than 65 for men in the U.S. when the Social Security system was created, and Bismarck's magic number of 65 was adopted as the age of retirement.

Today, at the end of the twentieth century, life expectancy in the highly industrialized nations is close to 80—fully 30 years longer than at the beginning of the century—and social science data are being used more than ever in the development of public policy. How much leisure time should we have? What kinds of tax structures are needed to support a medical system that caters to the needs of 80-somethings?

Social Science Failures

If the list of successes in the social sciences is long, so is the list of failures. School busing to achieve racial integration was based on scientific findings in a report by James Coleman. Those findings were achieved in the best tradition of careful scholarship. They just happened to be wrong because the scientists involved in the study didn't anticipate "White flight"—a phenomenon in which Whites abandoned cities for suburbs, taking much of the urban tax base with them and driving the inner cities into poverty.

On the other hand, the list of failures in the physical and biological sciences is just as spectacular. In the Middle Ages, alchemists tried everything they could to turn lead into gold. They had lots of people investing in them, but it just didn't work. Cold fusion is still a dream that attracts a few hardy souls. And no one who saw the explosion of the Space Shuttle *Challenger* on national television will ever forget it.

There are some really important lessons in all this. First, science isn't perfect, but it isn't going away because it's just too successful at doing what people everywhere want it to do. Second, the sciences of human thought and human behavior are much, much more powerful than most people understand them to be. Third, the power of social science, like that of the physical and biological sciences, comes from the same source: the scientific method in which ideas, based on hunches or on formal theories, are put forward, tested publicly, and replaced by ideas that produce better results. And fourth, social science knowledge, like that of any science, can be used to enhance our lives or to degrade them.

WHAT ARE THE SOCIAL SCIENCES?

The social science landscape is pretty complicated. The main branches, in alphabetical order, are anthropology, economics, history, political science, psychology, social psychology, and sociology. Each of these fields has many subfields, and there are, in addition, many other disciplines in which social research is done. These include communications, criminology, demography, education, journalism, leisure studies, nursing, and social work, to name just a few.

> *Research is a craft. . . . It takes practice, and more practice.*

Over time, methods for research have been developed within each of these fields, but no discipline owns any method. You may not agree with my out-front, positivist epistemology, my enthusiasm for science as mastery over nature. Methods, however, belong to everyone. Anthropologists developed the method of participant observation. It continues to be the hallmark of that discipline, but today participant observation is used in all the social sciences. Sociologists developed the questionnaire survey. People still associate sociology with that method, but questionnaire surveys are used in all the social sciences today. Direct observation of behavior was developed in psychology. It's still used more in psychology (and animal ethology) than in other disciplines, but now that method belongs to the world, too.

No one is expert in all the methods available for research. But seasoned social scientists all know about the array of methods available to them for collecting and analyzing data. By the time you get through this book, you should have a pretty good idea of the range of methods used in the social sciences, and what kinds of research problems are best addressed by the various methods.

Research is a craft. I'm not talking analogy here. Research isn't *like* a craft. It *is* a craft. If you know what people have to go through to become skilled carpenters or makers of clothes, you have some idea of what it takes to learn the skills for doing research. It takes practice, and more practice.

⸺⸺❖

Have you ever known a professional seamstress? My wife and I were doing fieldwork in Ixmiquilpan, a small town in the state of Hidalgo, Mexico, in 1962 when we met Florencia. She made dresses for little girls—Communion dresses, mostly. Mothers would bring their girls to Florencia's house. Florencia would look at the girls and say, "Turn around . . . turn again . . . OK," and that was that. The mother and daughter would leave, and Florencia would start making a dress. No pattern, no elaborate measurement. There would be one fitting to make some adjustments, but that was it.

I was amazed at Florencia's ability to pick up a scissors and start cutting fabric without a pattern. Then, in 1964, we went to Greece and met Irini. She made dresses for women on the island of Kalymnos where I did my doctoral fieldwork. Women would bring Irini a catalog or a picture—from Sears or from some Paris fashion show—and Irini would make the dresses. Irini was more cautious than Florencia was. She made lots of measurements and took notes. But there were no patterns. She just looked at her clients, made the measurements, and started cutting fabric.

How do people learn that much? With lots of practice. And that's the way it is with research. Don't expect to do perfect research the first time out. In fact, don't ever expect to do perfect research. Just expect that each time you do a research project, you will bring more and more experience to the effort and that your abilities to gather and analyze data and write up the results will get better and better.

❖⸺⸺

SOME HISTORY OF METHODS IN SOCIAL RESEARCH

In the 1830s, when modern social science began, all the practitioners thought of themselves as belonging to one large enterprise: the application of the scientific method to the study of human thought and human behavior. By the 1930s, the social sciences had divided and formed separate departments in universities, and it was easy to distinguish all the disciplines from one another.

Partly, the distinctions were based on the kinds of questions people asked. Psychologists asked questions about the mind, anthropologists asked questions about culture, sociologists asked ques-

tions about society, and so on. But, to a large extent, distinctions among the social sciences were based on the methods people used in trying to answer research questions. Psychologists used laboratory experiments, sociologists used survey questionnaires, anthropologists trekked to the field to do something they called participant observation, economists built mathematical models, and historians hung out in archives and used special methods for assessing the credibility of documents.

> *Whether we use words or numbers,*
> *we might as well use them right.*

Today, despite the proliferation of departments and journals and professional organizations, we are coming full circle. More and more, social scientists recognize that we are part of the same enterprise. We continue to ask different questions about the same set of phenomena, but we now all have access to the same methods. No discipline owns survey research or participant observation or experiments. The theme of this book is that methods—all methods—belong to all of us. Whatever our theoretical orientation, whatever our discipline, a sound mix of qualitative and quantitative data is inevitable in any study of human thought and behavior. Whether we use words or numbers, we might as well use them right.

I use the term "social sciences" and not "social and behavioral sciences" because the latter is too big a mouthful. Actually, all of these disciplines are social and behavioral: They all deal with human behavior and thought at both the individual and group levels.

Some psychologists, for example, focus on individual thought and behavior, while others study group processes. Many sociologists and political scientists study groups of people (labor unions, firms, hospitals, churches, nations) and how those groups are organized and connected to one another, but many also study individual behavior (sexual preferences, consumer choices, responses to illness). They aggregate their data to understand societies, but they ask their questions of individual people. Anthropologists focus on cultures, but many are concerned with individuals. In-depth interviews produce rich data about the experiences that real people have being labor migrants, living with AIDS, making it as a single parent, or being a surgeon, a cop, or an intravenous drug user.

EPISTEMOLOGY: DIFFERENT WAYS OF KNOWING

The problem with trying to write a book about research methods (besides the fact that there are so many of them) is that the word "method" has at least three meanings. At the most general level, it means *epistemology,* or **the study of how we know things.** At a still general level, it's about strategic choices, like whether to do participant observation fieldwork, dig up information from libraries and archives, or run an experiment. These are *strategic methods,* which means that they **comprise lots of methods at once.**

At the specific level, method is about *technique*—**what kind** of sample to use, **whether to do** face-to-face interviews or use the telephone, **whether to use** an interpreter or learn the local language well enough to do your own interviewing, whether to use a Solomon four-group design or a static-group comparison design in running an experiment, and so on.

When it comes to epistemology, there are several key questions. One is whether you subscribe to the philosophical principles of *rationalism* or *empiricism.* Another is whether you buy the assumptions of the scientific method, often called *positivism* in the social sciences, or favor the competing method, often called *humanism* or *interpretivism.* These are tough questions, with no easy answers. I discuss them in turn.

Rationalism, Empiricism, and Kant

The clash between rationalism and empiricism is at least as old as ancient Greek philosophy. It is still a hotly debated topic in the philosophy of knowledge.

Rationalism is **the idea that human beings achieve knowledge because of their capacity to reason.** From the rationalist perspective, there are a priori truths, which, if we just prepare our minds adequately, will become evident to us. From this perspective, progress of the human intellect over the centuries has resulted from reason. Many great thinkers, from Plato to Leibniz, subscribed to the rationalist principle of knowledge. "We hold these truths to be self-evident . . . " is an example of assuming a priori truths.

The competing epistemology is *empiricism.* For empiricists, **the only knowledge that human beings acquire is from sensory experience.** David Hume (1711-76), for example, held that human beings are born with empty boxes for minds (the so-called *tabula rasa,* or **"clean slate"**) and that the boxes are filled with experiences throughout life. We see and hear and taste things, and, as we accumulate experience, we make generalizations; we come to understand what is true from what we are exposed to.

Immanuel Kant (1724-1804) proposed a way out, a third alternative. A priori truths exist, he said, but if we see those truths it's because of the way our brains are structured. The human mind, said Kant, has a built-in capacity for ordering and organizing sensory experience. This was a powerful idea that led many scholars to look to the human mind itself for clues about how human behavior is ordered.

Noam Chomsky for example, proposed that human beings can learn any language because humans have a universal grammar already built into their minds. This would account, he said, for the fact that material from one language can be translated into any other language. A competing theory was proposed by B. F. Skinner, a radical behaviorist. Humans learn their language, Skinner said, the way all animals learn everything, by operant conditioning, or reinforced learning. Babies learn the sounds of their language, for example, because people who speak the language reward babies for making the "right" sounds (see Skinner 1957; Chomsky 1972; Stemmer 1990).

The intellectual clash between empiricism and rationalism creates a dilemma for all social scientists. Empiricism holds that people learn their values and that values are therefore relative. I consider myself an empiricist, but I accept the rationalist idea that there are universal truths about right and wrong.

I'm not in the least interested, for example, in transcending my disgust with, or taking a value-neutral stance about, genocide in Germany of the 1940s or Bosnia and Rwanda of the 1990s. No one has ever found a satisfactory way out of this dilemma. As a practical matter, I recognize that both rationalism and empiricism have contributed to our current understanding of the diversity of human behavior.

Modern social science has its roots in the empiricists of the French and Scottish Enlightenment periods. The early empiricists of the period, like David Hume, looked outside the human mind, to human behavior and experience, for answers to questions about human differences. They made the idea of a mechanistic science of humanity as plausible as the idea of a mechanistic science of other natural phenomena.

In the rest of this chapter, I outline the assumptions of the scientific method and how they apply to the study of human thought and behavior in the social sciences today.

THE NORMS OF SCIENCE

The norms of science are clear. Science is "an objective, logical, and systematic method of analysis of phenomena, devised to permit the accumulation of reliable knowledge" (Lastrucci 1963:6). Three words in Lastrucci's definition—"objective," "method," and "reliable"—are especially important.

1. *Objective*. The idea of truly objective inquiry has long been understood to be a delusion. Scientists do hold, however, that *striving* for objectivity is useful. In practice, this means being explicit about our measurements, so that others can more easily find the errors we make. We constantly try to improve measurement, to make it more precise and more accurate, and we submit our findings to peer review—what Robert Merton called the "organized skepticism" of our colleagues.

2. *Method*. Each scientific discipline has developed a set of techniques for gathering and handling data, but there is, in general, a single scientific method. The method is based on three assumptions: (1) Reality is "out there" to be dis-covered, (2) direct observation is the way to discover it, and (3) material explanations for observable phenomena are always sufficient and metaphysical explanations are never needed.

3. *Reliable*. Something that is true in Detroit is just as true in Vladivostok and Nairobi. Knowledge can be kept secret by nations, but there can never be such a thing as "Venezuelan physics," "American chemistry," or "Kenyan geology."

Not that it hasn't been tried. From around 1935 to 1965, T. D. Lysenko, with the early help of Josef Stalin, succeeded in gaining absolute power over biology in what was then the Soviet Union. Lysenko developed a Lamarckian theory of genetics, in which human-induced changes in seeds would, he claimed, become inherited. Despite public rebuke from the entire non-Soviet scientific world, Lysenko's "Russian genetics" became official Soviet policy—a policy that nearly ruined agriculture in the Soviet Union and its European satellites well into the 1960s (Zirkle 1949; Joravsky 1970; see also Storer 1966, on the norms of science).

THE DEVELOPMENT OF SCIENCE

Early Ideas

The scientific method is barely 400 years old, and its systematic application to human thought and behavior is less than half that. Aristotle insisted that knowledge should be based on experience and that conclusions about general cases should be based on the observation of more limited ones. But Aristotle did not advocate disinterested, objective accumulation of reliable knowledge. Moreover, like Aristotle, all scholars until the seventeenth century relied on metaphysical concepts, like the soul, to explain observable phenomena. Even in the nineteenth century, biologists still talked about "vital forces" as a way of explaining the existence of life.

One ancient scholar stands out as a forerunner of modern scientific thinking—thinking that would eventually divorce science from studies of mystical phenomena. In his single surviving work, a poem titled *On the Nature of Things* (1995), Titus Lucretius Carus (first century B.C.) suggested that everything that existed in the world had to be made of some material substance. Consequently, if the soul and the gods were real, they had to be material, too (see Minadeo 1969). But Lucretius' work did not have much impact on the way knowledge was pursued, and even today, his work is little appreciated in the social sciences (but see Harris [1968] for an exception).

Exploration, Printing, and Modern Science

Skip to around 1400, when a series of revolutionary changes began in Europe—some of which are still going on—that transformed Western society and other societies around the world. In 1413, the first Spanish ships began raiding the coast of west Africa, hijacking cargo and capturing slaves from Islamic traders. New tools of navigation (the compass and the sextant) made it possible for adventurous plunderers to go farther and farther from European shores in search of booty.

These breakthroughs were like those in architecture and astronomy by the ancient Mayans and Egyptians. They were based on systematic observation of the natural world, but they were not generated by the social and philosophical enterprise we call science. That required several other revolutions.

Johannes Gutenberg completed the first edition of the Bible on his newly invented printing press in 1455. (Printing presses had been used earlier in China, Japan, and Korea, but lacked movable type.) By the end of the fifteenth century, every major city in Europe had a press. Printed books provided a means for the accumulation and distribution of knowledge. Eventually, printing would make organized science possible, but it did not by itself guarantee the objective pursuit of reliable knowledge any more than the invention of writing had done four millennia before (Eisenstein 1979; Davis 1981).

Martin Luther was born just 15 years after Gutenberg died, and the Protestant Reformation,

beginning in 1517, added much to the history of modern science. It challenged the authority of the Roman Catholic Church to be the sole interpreter and disseminator of theological doctrine. The Protestant affirmation of every person's right to interpret scripture required literacy on the part of everyone, not just the clergy. The printing press made it possible for every family of some means to own (and read) its own Bible. Universal literacy helped make possible the development of science as an organized activity.

Galileo

The direct philosophical antecedents of modern science came at the end of the sixteenth century. If I had to pick one single figure on whom to bestow the honor of founding modern science, it would have to be Galileo Galilei. His best-known achievement, of course, was his thorough refutation of the Ptolemaic geocentric (Earth-centered) theory of the heavens. But he did more than just insist that scholars *observe* things rather than rely on metaphysical dogma to explain them. He developed the idea of the experiment by causing things to happen (rolling balls down differently inclined planes, for example, to see how fast they go) and measuring the results.

Galileo was born in 1564 and became professor of mathematics at the University of Padua when he was 28. He developed a new method for making lenses and used the new technology to study the motions of the planets. He concluded that the sun (as Copernicus claimed), not the Earth (as the ancient scholar Ptolemy had claimed), was at the center of the solar system.

This was one more threat to their authority that church leaders didn't need at the time. They already had their hands full, what with breakaway factions in the Reformation and other political problems. The church reaffirmed its official support for the Ptolemaic theory, and in 1616 Galileo was ordered not to espouse either his refutation of it or his support for the Copernican heliocentric (sun-centered) theory of the heavens.

Galileo waited 16 years and published the book that established science as an effective method for seeking knowledge. The book's title was *Dialogue Concerning the Two Chief World Systems, Ptolemaic and Copernican,* and it still makes fascinating reading (Galilei 1967 [1632]). Between the direct observational evidence that he had gathered with his telescopes and the mathematical analyses that he developed for making sense of his data, Galileo hardly had to espouse anything. The Ptolemaic theory was simply rendered obsolete.

In 1633, Galileo was convicted by the Inquisition for heresy and disobedience. He was ordered to recant his sinful teachings and was confined to house arrest until his death in 1642. He nearly published *and* perished. (For the record, in 1992 Pope John Paul II apologized for the Roman Catholic Church's condemnation of Galileo.)

Bacon and Descartes

Two other figures are often cited as founders of modern scientific thinking: Francis Bacon (1561-1626) and René Descartes (1596-1650). Bacon is known for his emphasis on **induction, the use of direct observation to confirm ideas and the linking together of observed facts to form theories or explanations of how natural phenomena work.** Bacon correctly never told us how to get ideas or how to accomplish the linkage of empirical facts. Those activities remain essentially humanistic—you think hard.

To Bacon goes the dubious honor of being the first "martyr of empiricism." In March 1626, at the age of 65, Bacon was driving through a rural area north of London. He had an idea that cold might delay the biological process of putrefaction, so he stopped his carriage, bought a hen from a local resident, killed the hen, and stuffed it with snow. Bacon was right—the cold snow did

keep the bird from rotting—but he himself caught bronchitis and died a month later (Lea 1980).

Descartes didn't make any systematic, direct observations—he did neither fieldwork nor experiments—but in his *Discourse on Method* (1960 [1637]) and particularly in his monumental *Meditations* (1993 [1641]), he distinguished between the mind and all external material phenomena. He also outlined clearly his vision of a universal science of nature based on direct experience and the application of reason—that is, observation and theory (for more on Descartes's influence on the development of science, see Schuster 1977; Markie 1986; Hausman and Hausman 1997).

Newton

Isaac Newton (1643-1727) pressed the scientific revolution at Cambridge University. He invented calculus and used it to develop celestial mechanics and other areas of physics. Just as important, he devised the *hypothetico-deductive model of science* that combines both *induction* (empirical observation) and *deduction* (reason) into a single, unified method (Toulmin 1980).

In this model, which more accurately reflects how scientists actually conduct their work, it makes no difference where you get an idea: from data, from a conversation with your brother-in-law, or from just plain, hard, reflexive thinking. What matters is whether you can *test* your idea against data in the real world. This model seems rudimentary to us now, but it is of fundamental importance and was quite revolutionary in the late seventeenth century.

Science, Money, and War

The scientific approach to knowledge was established just as Europe began to experience the growth of industry and the development of large cities. Those cities were filled with uneducated factory laborers. This created a need for increased productivity in agriculture among those not en-gaged in industrial work.

Optimism for science ran high, as it became obvious that the new method for acquiring knowledge about natural phenomena promised bigger crops, more productive industry, and more successful military campaigns. The organizing mandate for the French Academy of Science (1666) included a modest proposal to study "the explosive force of gunpowder enclosed (in small amounts) in an iron or very thick copper box" (Easlea 1980:216).

As the potential benefits of science became evident, political support increased across Europe. More scientists were produced; more university posts were created for them to work in. More laboratories were established at academic centers. Journals and learned societies developed as scientists sought more outlets for publishing their work. Sharing knowledge through journals made it easier for scientists to do their own work and to advance through the university ranks. Publishing and sharing knowledge became a material

benefit, and the behaviors were soon supported by a value, a norm.

The norm was so strong that European nations at war allowed enemy scientists to cross their borders freely in pursuit of knowledge. In 1780, Reverend Samuel Williams of Harvard University applied for and received a grant from the Massachusetts legislature to observe a total eclipse of the sun predicted for October 27. The perfect spot, he said, was an island off the coast of Massachusetts.

Unfortunately, Williams and his party would have to cross Penobscot Bay. The American Revolutionary War was still on, and the bay was controlled by the British. The speaker of the Massachusetts House of Representatives, John Hancock, wrote a letter to the commander of the British forces, saying, "Though we are politically enemies, yet with regard to Science it is presumable we shall not dissent from the practice of civilized people in promoting it" (Rothschild 1981, quoted in Bermant 1982:126). The appeal of one "civilized" person to another worked. Williams got his free passage.

THE DEVELOPMENT OF SOCIAL SCIENCE

Newton and Locke

It is fashionable these days to say that social science should not imitate physics. As it turns out, physics and social science were developed at about the same time, and on the same philosophical basis, by two friends, Isaac Newton and John Locke (1632-1704). It would not be until the nineteenth century that a formal program of applying the scientific method to the study of hu-

manity would be proposed by Auguste Comte, Claude-Henri de Saint-Simon, Adolphe Quételet, and John Stuart Mill (more about these folks in a bit). But Locke understood that the rules of science applied equally to the study of celestial bodies (what Newton was interested in) and to human behavior (what Locke was interested in).

In his *Essay Concerning Human Understanding* (1996 [1690]), Locke reasoned that since we cannot see everything, and since we cannot even record perfectly what we do see, some knowledge will be closer to the truth than other knowledge. Prediction of the behavior of planets might be more accurate than prediction of human behavior, but both predictions should be based on better and better observation, measurement, and reason (see Nisbet 1980; Woolhouse 1996).

Voltaire, Condorcet, and Rousseau

The legacy of Descartes, Galileo, and Locke was crucial to the eighteenth-century *Enlightenment* and to the development of social science. Voltaire (François Marie Arouet, 1694-1778) was an outspoken proponent of Newton's nonreligious approach to the study of all natural phenomena, including human behavior (Voltaire 1967 [1738]). In several essays, Voltaire introduced the idea of a science to uncover the laws of history. This was to be a science that could be applied to human affairs and that *enlightened* those who governed so that they might govern better.

Other Enlightenment figures had quite specific ideas about the progress of humanity. Marquis de Condorcet (1743-94) described all of human history in 10 stages, beginning with hunting and gathering, and moving up through pastoralism, agriculture, and several stages of Western states. The 9th stage, he reckoned, began with Descartes

and ended with the French Revolution and the founding of the republic. The last stage was the future, reckoned as beginning with the French Revolution.

Jean-Jacques Rousseau (1712-78), by contrast, believed that humanity had started out in a state of grace, characterized by equality of relations, but that the rise of the state had corrupted all that and had resulted in slavery, taxation, and other evils. Rousseau was not, however, a raving romantic, as is sometimes supposed. He did not advocate that modern people abandon civilization and return to hunt their food in the forests. Instead, in his classic work *On the Social Contract*, Rousseau (1988) laid out a plan for a state-level society based on equality and agreement between the governed and those who govern.

The Enlightenment philosophers, from Bacon to Rousseau, produced a philosophy that focused on the use of knowledge in service to the improvement of humanity, or, if that wasn't possible, at least to the amelioration of its pain. The idea that science and reason could lead humanity toward perfection may seem like a rather naive notion to some people these days, but it was built into the writings of Thomas Paine and Jean-Jacques Rousseau and incorporated into the rhetoric surrounding rather sophisticated events like the American and French revolutions.

EARLY POSITIVISM: QUÉTELET, SAINT-SIMON, AND COMTE

The person most responsible for laying out a program of mechanistic social science was Auguste Comte (1798-1857). In 1824, he wrote: "I believe that I shall succeed in having it recognized . . . that there are laws as well defined for the development of the human species as for the fall of a stone" (quoted in Sarton 1935:10).

Comte could not be bothered with the empirical research required to uncover the Newtonian laws of social evolution that he believed existed. Comte was content to deduce the social laws and to leave "the verification and development of them to the public" (1875-77, III:xi; quoted in Harris 1968).

Not so Adolphe Quételet (1796-1874), a Belgian astronomer who turned his skills to both fundamental and applied social research. He developed life expectancy tables for insurance companies and, in his book *A Treatise on Man* (1969 [1842]), presented statistics on crime and mortality in Europe. The first edition of that book (1835) carried the audacious subtitle *Social Physics*, and, indeed, Quételet extracted some very strong generalizations from his data. He showed that, for the Paris of his day, it was easier to predict the proportion of men of a given age who would be in prison than the proportion of those same men who would die in a given year. "Each age [cohort]" said Quételet, "paid a more uniform and constant tribute to the jail than to the tomb" (1969 [1842]: viii).

Despite Quételet's superior empirical efforts, he did not succeed in building a following around his ideas for social science. But Claude-Henri de Saint-Simon (1760-1825) did, and he was apparently quite a figure. He fought in the American Revolution, became a wealthy man in land speculation in France, was imprisoned by Robespierre, studied science after his release, and went bankrupt living flamboyantly.

Saint-Simon had the audacity to propose that scientists become priests of a new religion that would further the emerging industrial society and would distribute wealth equitably. The idea was taken up by industrialists after Saint-Simon's death in 1825, but the movement broke up in the early 1830s, partly because its treasury was impoverished by paying for some monumental parties (see Durkheim 1958).

Saint-Simon was the originator of the so-called *positivist school* of social science, but Comte developed the idea in a series of major books. Comte tried to forge a synthesis of the great ideas of the Enlightenment—the ideas of Kant, Hume, and Voltaire—and he hoped that the new science he envisioned would help to alleviate human suffering. Between 1830 and 1842, Comte published a six-volume work, *The System of Positive Philosophy,* in which he proposed his famous "law of three stages" through which knowledge developed (see Comte 1974 [1855], 1975).

In the first stage of human knowledge, said Comte, phenomena are explained by invoking the existence of capricious gods whose whims can't be predicted by human beings. Comte and his contemporaries proposed that religion itself evolved, beginning with the worship of inanimate objects (fetishism) and moving up through polytheism to monotheism. But any reliance on supernatural forces as explanations for phenomena, said Comte, even a modern belief in a single deity, represented a primitive and ineffectual stage of human knowledge.

Next came the metaphysical stage, in which explanations for observed phenomena are given in terms of "essences" like the "vital forces" commonly invoked by biologists of the time. The so-called positive stage of human knowledge is reached when people come to rely on empirical data, reason, and the development of scientific laws to explain phenomena. Comte's program of positivism, and his development of a new science he called "sociology," is contained in his four-volume work *System of Positive Polity*, published between 1875 and 1877.

I share many of the sentiments expressed by the word "positivism," but I've never liked the word itself. I suppose we're stuck with it. Here is John Stuart Mill in 1866 explaining the sentiments of the word to an English-speaking audience: "Whoever regards all events as parts of a constant order, each one being the invariable consequent of some antecedent condition, or combination of conditions, accepts fully the Positive mode of thought" (p. 15) and "All theories in which the ultimate standard of institutions and rules of actions was the happiness of mankind, and observation and experience the guides . . . are entitled to the name Positive" (p. 69).

Mill thought that the word "positive" was not really suited to English, and he would have preferred to use "phenomenal" or "experiential" in his translation of Comte. I wish Mill had trusted his gut on that one.

Comte's Excesses

Comte wanted to call the new positivistic science of humanity "social physiology," but Saint-Simon had used that term. Comte tried out the term "social physics," but apparently dropped it when he found that Quételet was using it, too. The term "sociology" became somewhat controversial; language puritans tried for a time to expunge it from the literature on the grounds that it was a bastardization—a mixture of both Latin (*societas*) and Greek (*logo*) roots. Despite the dispute over the name of the discipline, Comte's vision of a scientific discipline that both focused on and served society found wide support.

Unfortunately, Comte, like Saint-Simon, had more in mind than just the pursuit of knowledge for the betterment of humankind. Comte envisioned a class of philosophers who, with support from the state, would direct all education. They would advise the government, which would be composed of capitalists "whose dignity and authority," explained John Stuart Mill, "are to be in the ratio of the degree of generality of their conceptions and operations—bankers at the summit, merchants next, then manufacturers, and agriculturalists at the bottom" (1866:122).

It got worse. Comte proposed his own religion; condemned the study of planets that were not visible to the naked eye; advocated burning most books except for a hundred or so of the ones that people needed to become best educated. "As his thoughts grew more extravagant," Mill tells us, Comte's "self-confidence grew more outrageous. The height it ultimately attained must be seen, in his writings, to be believed" (ibid.:130).

Comte attracted a coterie of admirers who wanted to implement the master's plans. Mercifully, they are gone (we hope), but for many scholars, the word "positivism" still carries the taint of Comte's outrageous ego.

The Activist Legacy of Comte's Positivism

Despite Comte's excesses, the idea that the scientific method is the surest way to produce effective knowledge (knowledge for control of events) and that effective knowledge could be used to bring about social reform and the improvement of human lives captured the imagination of many scholars. These were terrific ideas in the mid-nineteenth century and, as far as I'm concerned, they haven't lost any of their luster. They continue to motivate many social scientists, including me.

These days, positivism is often linked to support for whatever power relations happen to be in place. It's an astonishing turnabout, because historically, positivism was linked to social activism. *The Subjection of Women* (1869), by John Stuart Mill, advocated full equality for women. Adolphe Quételet, the Belgian astronomer whose study of demography and criminology carried the audacious title *Social Physics* (1969 [1835]), was a committed social reformer.

The legacy of positivism as a vehicle for social activism is clear in Jane Addams's work with destitute immigrants at Chicago's Hull House (1926), in Sidney and Beatrice Webb's attack on the British medical system (1910), in Charles Booth's account of the conditions under which the poor lived in London (1902), and in Florence Nightingale's (1871) assessment of death rates in maternity hospitals (see McDonald [1993] for an extended account of Nightingale's long-ignored work).

The central position of positivism as a philosophy of knowledge is that experience is the foundation of knowledge. We record what we experience visually, auditorily, and emotionally. The quality of the recording, then, becomes the key to knowledge. Can we, in fact, record what others experience? Yes, of course we can. Are there pitfalls in doing so? Yes, of course there are. To some social researchers, these pitfalls are evidence of natural limits to social science; to others, like me, they are a challenge to extend the current limits by improving measurement. The fact that knowledge is tentative is something we all learn to live with.

LATER POSITIVISM: THE VIENNA CIRCLE

Positivism has taken some interesting turns. Ernst Mach (1838-1916), an Austrian physicist, took Hume's arch-empiricist stance further than Hume might have done himself: If you could not verify something, insisted Mach, then you should question its existence. If you can't see it, it isn't there. This extreme stance led Mach to reject the atomic theory of physics because, at the time, atoms could not be seen.

The discussion of Mach's ideas was the basis for the foundation of a seminar group that met in Vienna and Berlin during the 1920s and 1930s. The group, composed of mathematicians, philosophers, and physicists, came to be known as the *Vienna Circle of logical positivists*. They were also known as logical empiricists, and when social scientists today discuss positivism, it is often this particular brand that they have in mind (see Mach 1976).

The term *logical empiricism* better reflects the philosophy of knowledge of the members of the Vienna Circle than does *logical positivism*. Unfortunately, Feigl and Blumberg used "logical positivism" in the title of their 1931 article in the *Journal of Philosophy* in which they laid out the program of their movement, and the name "positivism" stuck—again (L. D. Smith 1986).

The fundamental principles of the Vienna Circle were that knowledge is based on experience and that metaphysical explanations of phenomena were incompatible with science. Science and philosophy, they said, should attempt to answer only answerable questions. A question like "Is green or red a more beautiful color?" can be addressed only by metaphysics and should be left to artists.

In fact, the logical positivists of the Vienna Circle did not see art—painting, sculpture, poetry, music, literature, and literary criticism—as being in conflict with science. The arts, they said, allow people to express personal visions and emotions and are legitimate unto themselves. Since poets do not claim that their ideas are testable expressions of reality, their ideas can be judged on their own merits as either evocative and insightful, or not. Therefore, any source of wisdom (like poetry) that generates ideas and science, which tests ideas, are mutually supportive and compatible (Feigl 1980).

I find this eminently sensible. Sometimes, when I read a really great line of poetry, like Robert Frost's line from *The Mending Wall*, "Good fences make good neighbors," I think, "How could I *test* that? Do good fences *always* make good neighbors?" When sheepherders fenced off grazing lands in nineteenth-century Texas, keeping cattle out of certain regions, it started a range war. Listen to what Frost had to say about this in the same poem: "Before I built a wall I'd ask to know/ What I was walling in or walling out./ And to whom I was like to give offence." The way I see it, the search for understanding is a human activity, no matter who does it and no matter what epistemological assumptions they follow.

Understanding begins with questions and with ideas about how things work. When *do* fences make good neighbors? Why do women make less money, on average, for the same work as men? Why is Mexico's birth rate falling, but Mali's isn't? Why do Native Americans have such a high rate of alcoholism? Why do nation-states almost universally try to wipe out minority languages? Why do public housing programs often wind up as slums? If advertising can get children hooked on cigarettes, then why is public service advertising so ineffective in lowering the incidence of high-risk sex among adolescents?

Instrumental Positivism

The practice that many social scientists associate today with the positivist perspective in social science, however, is not the positivism of Auguste Comte, of Adolphe Quételet, of John Stuart Mill; nor is it even the logical positivism of the Vienna Circle. None of these is the tradition that so many today love to hate.

That honor belongs to what Christopher Bryant (1985:137) calls *instrumental positivism*. In his 1929 presidential address to the American Sociological Society, William F. Ogburn laid out the rules. In turning sociology into a science, he said, "it will be necessary to crush out emotion."

Further, "it will be desirable to taboo ethics and values (except in choosing problems); and it will be inevitable that we shall have to spend most of our time doing hard, dull, tedious, and routine tasks" (Obgurn 1930:10). Eventually, he said, there would be no need for a separate field of statistics because "all sociologists will be statisticians" (p. 6).

This kind of rhetoric just begged to be reviled. There were challenges to Ogburn's prescription, but, as Oberschall (1972:244) concluded, it was Ogburn's commitment to value-free science and to statistics that won the day.

We are all free, of course, to identify ourselves as humanists or as positivists, but it's much more fun to be both. The scientific component of social science demands that we ask whether our measurements are meaningful—"it is certainly desirable to be precise," said Robert Redfield (1948:148), "but it is quite as needful to be precise about something worth knowing"—but the humanistic component forces us to ask if we are pursuing worthwhile ends and doing so with worthwhile means.

In the end, the tension between science and humanism is wrought by the need to answer practical questions with evidence and the need to understand ourselves—that is, the need to measure carefully and the need to listen hard.

THE REACTION AGAINST POSITIVISM

No epistemological tradition has a patent on interesting questions like these or on good ideas about the answers to such questions.

Humanism

Humanism is an intellectual tradition that traces its roots to Protagoras' (485-410 B.C.) dictum that "man is the measure of all things," which

means that **truth is not absolute but is decided by human judgment.** Humanism has been historically at odds with the philosophy of knowledge represented by science.

Ferdinand C. S. Schiller (1864-1937), for example, was a leader of the European humanist revolt against positivism. He argued that since the method and contents of science are the products of human thought, reality and truth could not be "out there" to be found, as positivists assume, but must be made up by human beings (Schiller 1969 [1903]).

Wilhelm Dilthey (1833-1911) was another leader of the revolt against positivism in the social sciences. He argued that the methods of the physical sciences, while undeniably effective for the study of inanimate objects, were inappropriate for the study of human beings. There were, he insisted, two distinct kinds of sciences: the *geisteswissenschaften* and the *naturwissenschaften*—that is, the human sciences and the natural sciences. Human beings live in a web of meanings that they spin themselves. To study humans, he argued, we need to understand those meanings.

Humanists, then, do not deny the effectiveness of science for the study of nonhuman objects, but emphasize the uniqueness of humanity and the need for a different (that is, nonscientific) method for studying human beings. Similarly, scientists do not deny the inherent value of humanistic knowledge. To explore whether King Lear is to be pitied or admired as a pathetic leader or as a successful one is an exercise in seeking humanistic knowledge. The answer to the question cannot possibly be achieved by the scientific method. In any event, finding *the* answer to the question is not important. Producing many possible answers by carefully *examining* the question of Lear, however, leads to insight about the human condition. And that *is* important.

———————❖

Humanism is often used as a synonym for humanitarian or compassionate values and a commitment to the amelioration of suffering. Counting the dead *accurately* in Rwanda is one way—not the only way—to preserve outrage. We need more, not less, science, lots and lots more, and more humanistically informed science, to contribute more to the amelioration of suffering

and the weakening of false ideologies—racism, sexism, ethnic nationalism—in the world.

Humanism sometimes means a commitment to subjectivity—that is, to using our own feelings, values, and beliefs to achieve insight into the nature of human experience. Trained subjectivity is, of course, the foundation of clinical disciplines as well as the foundation of participant observation ethnography (see Berg and Smith [1985] for a review of clinical methods in social research). It isn't something apart from social science.

Humanism sometimes means an appreciation of the unique in human experience. Writing a story about the thrill or the pain of giving birth, about surviving hand-to-hand combat, about living with AIDS, about winning or losing a long struggle with illness—or writing someone else's story for them, as an ethnographer might do—is not an activity opposed to a natural science of experience. It *is* the activity of a natural science of experience.

❖———————

Hermeneutics

Hermeneutics originally referred to the close study of the Bible. In traditional hermeneutics, it is assumed that the Bible contains truths and that human beings can **extract those truths through careful study and exegesis. The hermeneutic tradition has come into the social sciences with the close and careful study of free-flowing texts. In** anthropology, for example, the texts may be myths or folktales. The hermeneutic approach would stress that the myths contain some underlying meaning, at least for the people who tell the myths, and that it is our job to discover that meaning. This same approach can be applied to the study of any body of texts, including sets of political speeches or doctor-patient interactions (Ricoeur 1981, 1991).

In fact, by extension, the term *hermeneutics* is now used to cover the study of free-flowing *acts* of people, construing those acts as if they were texts whose internal meaning can be discovered by proper exegesis. Portable camcorders should promote much more hermeneutic scholarship in the future, as researchers record people dancing, singing, interacting over meals, telling stories, and participating in events.

Phenomenology

Like positivism, *phenomenology* is **a philosophy of knowledge that emphasizes direct observation of phenomena.** Unlike positivists, however, phenomenologists seek to *sense* reality and to describe it in words, rather than numbers—words that reflect consciousness and perception. Phenomenology is part of the humanistic tradition that emphasizes the common experience of all human beings and our ability to relate to the feelings of others (see Veatch 1969).

The philosophical foundations of phenomenology were developed by Edmund Husserl (1859-1938), who argued that the scientific method, appropriate for the study of physical phenomena, was inappropriate for the study of human thought and action (see Husserl 1964 [1907]). Husserl's ideas were elaborated by Alfred Schutz, and Schutz's version of phenomenology has had a major impact in social science, particularly in psychology but also in anthropology.

When you study molecules, Schutz said, you don't have to worry about what the world "means" to the molecules (1962:59). But when you try to understand the reality of a human being, it's a different matter entirely. The only way to understand social reality, said Schutz, was through the meanings that people give to that reality. In a phenomenological study, the researcher tries to see reality through another person's eyes.

Phenomenologists try to produce convincing descriptions of what they experience rather than explanations and causes. Good ethnography—a narrative that describes a culture or a part of a culture—is usually good phenomenology, and there is still no substitute for a good story, well told, especially if you're trying to make people understand how the people you've studied think and feel about their lives.

ABOUT NUMBERS AND WORDS: THE QUALITATIVE/QUANTITATIVE SPLIT

The split between the positivistic approach and the interpretive-phenomenological approach pervades the human sciences. In psychology and social psychology, most *research* is in the positivistic tradition, while much *clinical* work is in the interpretivist tradition because, as its practitioners cogently point out, it works. In sociology, there is a growing tradition of interpretive research, but most sociology is done from the positivist perspective. In anthropology, most research is in the interpretivist tradition, but some anthropologists (including me) identify with the positivist epistemology.

Notice in that last paragraph the use of words like "approach," "perspective," "tradition," and "epistemology." Not once did I say that "research in X is mostly quantitative" or that "research in Y is mostly qualitative." That's because a commitment to an interpretivist or a positivist epistemology is independent of any commitment to, or skill for, quantification. Searching the Bible for statistical evidence to support the subjugation of women doesn't turn the enterprise into science.

By the same token, at the early stages of its development, any science relies primarily on qualitative data. Long before the application of mathematics to describe the dynamics of avian flight, qualitative, fieldworking ornithologists did systematic observation and recorded (in words) data about such things as wing movements, perching stance, hovering patterns, and so on. Qualitative description is a kind of measurement, an integral part of the complex whole that comprises scientific research.

As sciences mature, they come naturally to depend more and more on quantitative data and on quantitative tests of qualitatively described relations. But this never, ever lessens the need for or the importance of qualitative research in any science.

For example, qualitative research might lead us to say that "most of the land in Centerville is controlled by a minority." Later, quantitative research might result in our saying, "76% of the land in Centerville is controlled by 14% of the inhabitants." The first statement is not wrong. But the second statement confirms the first and carries more information as well. If it turned out that "54% of the land is controlled by 41% of the inhabitants," then the first part of the qualitative statement would still be true (more than 50% of the land is owned by less than 50% of the people), but the sentiment of the qualitative assertion would be rendered weak by the quantitative observations.

For social scientists whose work is in the humanistic, phenomenological tradition, quantification is inappropriate. And for those whose work is in the positivist tradition, it is important to remember that numbers do not automatically make any inquiry scientific. In Chapter 12, I'll discuss how texts—and pictures and other kinds of qualitative data—can be collected and analyzed by scholars who identify with either the positivist or the interpretivist tradition.

In the rest of this book, you'll read about methods for describing individuals and groups of people. Some of those methods involve library work, some involve controlled experiments, and some involve fieldwork. Some methods for studying people involve watching, others involve listening. Some result in words, others result in numbers. Never use the distinction between quantitative and qualitative as cover for talking about the difference between science and humanism. Lots of scientists do their work without numbers, and many scientists whose work is highly quantitative consider themselves humanists.

ETHICS AND SOCIAL SCIENCE

The biggest problem in conducting a science of human behavior is not selecting the right sample size or making the right measurement. It's doing those things ethically, so you can live with the consequences of your actions. I'm not exaggerating about this. Ethics is part of method in science, just as it is in medicine or business, or any other part of life. For while scholars discuss the fine points about whether a true science of human behavior is really possible, effective social science is being done all the time, and with rather spectacular, if sometimes disturbing, success.

The biggest problem in conducting a science of human behavior is not selecting the right sample size or making the right measurement. It's doing those things ethically.

In the mid-nineteenth century, when Quételet and Comte were laying down the program for a science of human affairs, no one could predict the outcome of elections, engineer the increased consumption of a particular brand of cigarettes, or help people through crippling phobias with behavior modification. We can do those things now. We can predict accurately the reduction in highway carnage that results from increasing the drinking age by one or two or three years. We can predict the number of additional suicides that result from each percentage point of unemployment.

Since the eighteenth century, every phenomenon (including human thought and behavior) to which the scientific method has been systematically applied, over a sustained period of time, by a large number of researchers, has yielded its secrets, and the knowledge has been turned into more effective human control of events. For all the jokes cracked about the mistakes made by economists, or about the wisdom of engineering cigarette purchases in the first place, the fact remains: We *can* do these things, we *are* doing these things, and we're getting better and better at it all the time.

It hardly needs to be pointed out that the increasing effectiveness of science over the past few centuries has also given human beings the ability to cause greater environmental degradation, to spread tyranny, and even to cause the ultimate, planetary catastrophe through nuclear war. This makes a science of humanity even more important now than it has ever been before.

Consider this: Marketers in a midwestern city, using the latest supercomputers, found that if someone bought disposable diapers at 5 p.m. the next thing he or she was likely to buy was a six-pack of beer. So they set up a display of chips next to the disposable diapers and increased snack sales by 17% (Wilke 1992).

We need to turn our skills in the production of such effective knowledge to important problems: hunger, disease, poverty, war, environmental pollution, family and intergroup violence, and racism, among others. Social science can play an important role in social change by predicting the consequences of ethically mandated programs and by refuting false notions (such as various forms of racism) that are inherent in most popular ethical systems.

Don't get me wrong here. The people who discovered that fact about the six-packs and the diapers are darned good social scientists. I'm not calling for rules to make them work on problems that *I* think are important. Scientists choose to study the things that industry and government pay for, and those things change from country to country and from time to time in the same country. In democracies and autocracies alike, science has to earn its support by producing useful knowledge. What "useful" means, however, changes from time to time even in the same society, depending on all sorts of historical circumstances.

Suppose we agreed that "useful" meant to save lives. Men are subject to prostate cancer and women are subject to breast cancer. Prostate cancer and breast cancer claim about the same number of lives each year—about 42,000 and 44,000, respectively, in 1996—but much more public money is spent on breast cancer research. AIDS is a terrible disease—still a nearly certain killer—but roughly the same number of people died in motor vehicle accidents in 1996 as died of AIDS (again, about 42,000 and 44,000, respectively). Should we spend the same amount of money on combating prostate cancer as we do on breast cancer? Should we spend the same amount of money on teaching safe driving as on teaching safe sex?

Do we really want to have statistics determine what we study? My guess is that all researchers want the freedom to put their skills and energies to work on what they think is important. Fortunately, that's just how it is, and, personally, I hope it stays just that way.

In the rest of this book, I deal with some of the methods we can use to make useful contributions. But *you* have to decide what those contributions will be, and for whom they will be useful.

KEY CONCEPTS

Epistemology, 8
Method as strategy, 8
Method as technique, 8
Rationalism, 8, 9
Empiricism, 8, 9
Positivism, 8
Humanism, 8, 18-19
Interpretivism, 8
Tabula rasa, 9
Induction vs. deduction, 12

Hypothetico-deductive model of science, 12
The Enlightenment, 14
Positivist school, 14-16
Vienna Circle, 17-18
Logical positivism/logical empiricism, 17-18
Instrumental positivism, 18
Hermeneutics, 19-20
Phenomenology, 20
The qualitative/quantitative split, 20-21

SUMMARY

- ❖ The social and behavioral sciences include psychology, social psychology, sociology, political science, economics, and anthropology.
  - ◆ In addition, many applied disciplines today use knowledge from all the social sciences and also contribute fundamental knowledge to the social sciences. Some of these applied disciplines include criminology and penology, nursing, social work, and education.

- ❖ The intellectual foundations of modern social sciences come from eighteenth-century Enlightenment philosophy, which included an activist commitment to knowledge as the basis for human progress and a commitment to empiricism in the pursuit of knowledge.
  - ◆ This led to the intellectual position known as positivism. Alternatives to positivism include various forms of humanism, including phenomenology and hermeneutics.

- ❖ Many social scientists today are asking legitimate questions about the scientific norms of objectivity and the universality of knowledge. Nevertheless, the social sciences have participated in the general success of science in the production of effective technologies that people want.
  - ◆ Opinion polls, auto and life insurance, and behavioral therapy are among the many successes of modern social science.

- ❖ As with all science, there is no guarantee that effective knowledge will be used for benign and not for malignant purposes, and so effective knowledge—whether in the physical, biological, or social sciences—creates ethical imperatives that are the focus of continuing discussion.

EXERCISES

1. Some people say that social science has little effect in the real world. Is there evidence to contradict this critique?

2. Explain the difference between the goals of humanists and those of positivists. Describe what you think might be the common ground for scholars in these camps. Is there common ground in their goals? In their epistemology? In their behavior?

3. Describe the difference between induction and deduction and the difference between rationalism and empiricism.

4. What does the saying "There's no such thing as value-free research" mean? Some scholars argue that, although value-free research is not possible, value-*neutral* research is. What do you think?

FURTHER READING

Epistemology. Good overviews are Dancy (1985), Grayling (1996), and Schweizer (1998). For more depth on Descartes, Leibniz, and other rationalists, see Cottingham (1988). For more depth on empiricism, see BonJour (1985). Don't neglect the original sources: Descartes (1993 [1641]), Hume (1978 [1739-40]), Kant (1966 [1787]), and Locke (1996 [1690]).

Philosophy of science. Must-read classics include Kuhn (1970) and Popper (1966, 1968). For general introductions to the philosophy of science and the philosophy of social science, see Hollis (1996) and Papineau (1996). For good overviews of postmodernism in the social sciences, see Hollinger (1994) and Rosenau (1992).

History of science. A wonderfully readable overview is Asimov (1989). A classic in the history of science is de Solla Price (1975). A good recent overview is Silver (1998). On the recent history of social science in the U.S., see Fisher (1993). On Galileo's life, see Fermi and Bernardini (1961) and Machamer (1998). For more on Francis Bacon's contributions to the development of science, see Weinberger (1985) and Wormald (1993). On Newton's contribution to the establishment of modern scientific thought and practice, see Christianson (1984) and Westfall (1993).

History of social science. For an overview of the history of the social sciences, see Gordon (1993) and R. Smith (1997). For an excellent discussion of the origins of social science, see McDonald (1993). And see McDonald (1994) for a discussion of the careers of the women founders of the social sciences.

Humanities and the sciences. For a discussion of the relation between the sciences and the humanities today, see Jones (1965) and Snow (1964). The ideas in these books are still current, after 35 years.

Interpretivism. To follow up on the interpretive and hermeneutic positions in the social sciences, see Dilthey (1989 [1883]), Geertz (1973), Kearney (1996), Rabinow and Sullivan (1987), Ricoeur (1981, 1991), and Weber (1978).

For a discussion of biblical hermeneutics, see Morgan and Barton (1988) and Prickett (1986). For a discussion of modern hermeneutical methods in the social sciences, see Agar (1982), Gubrium (1988), Kvale (1996), Packer and Addison (1989), and Ruby (1982).

Phenomenology. For historic works in phenomenology and psychology, see Husserl (1964 [1907]) and Schutz (1967). For overviews, see Kockelmans (1994), Lauer (1978), and Moustakas (1994).

Positivism. A brief version of the original formulation of positivism is reprinted in Comte (1988). For more on the history and philosophy of logical positivism, see Neurath (1973) and Sarkar (1996).

Ethics. Klockars and O'Connor (1979) discuss ethical issues in the use of human subjects for research. For a discussion of ethical issues in ethnography, see Appell (1978) and Fielding (1993), and for sociology, see Friedson (1984). McKenna (1995) discusses ethical issues that undergraduate students confront when doing social psychological research.

2 | THE FOUNDATIONS OF SOCIAL RESEARCH

IN THIS CHAPTER:

❖ INTRODUCTION

This chapter is about the fundamental concepts of social research: variables, measurement, validity, reliability, cause and effect, and theory. When you finish this chapter, you should understand the mutually supportive roles of data and ideas in the development of theory, along with the crucial role of measurement in science.

You should also have a new skill: You should be able to *operationalize* any complex human phenomenon, like "being modern" or "anomie" or "alienation" or "readiness to learn research methods"—that is, you should be able to reduce any complex variable to a set of measurable traits.

By the end of this chapter, though, you should also become hypercritical of your new ability at operationalizing. Just because you can make up measurements doesn't guarantee that they'll be useful or meaningful. However, the better you become at concocting clever measurements for complex things, the more critical you'll become of your own concoctions and those of others.

VARIABLES

A *variable* is something that can take more than one value, and those values can be words or numbers. If you ask people how old they are, the response might be "18" or "78." If you ask them their religion, the response might be "Methodist" or "Buddhist." The most common variables in social research are age, sex, ethnic affiliation, "race" (more about why that word is in quotes in just a minute), education, income, marital status, and occupation.

Others that you might see include blood pressure (in medical social science); number of children (lots of studies use this one); number of times married; distance from an airport (or a hospital, welfare agency, public library, bus stop); or level of support for various causes (a woman's right to an abortion, the distribution of clean needles to drug addicts, sex education for second graders, etc.).

> *A variable is something that can take more than one value, and those values can be words or numbers.*

Social research is based on defining variables, looking for associations among them, and trying to understand whether—and how—one variable causes another. Social science research, then, whether it's based on experiments or field observations or questionnaires, is about variables, not about people. Research affects people, though, so all research has an ethical component. I'll have more to say about this throughout the book.

Dimensions of Variables

Variables can be **unidimensional** or **multidimensional**. The distance from Boston to Denver can be expressed in driving time or in miles, but no matter which measure you use, you can express distance in just one dimension, with a straight line. You can see this in Figure 2.1.

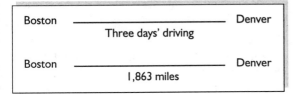

Figure 2.1 Two Ways to Measure Distance

If we add Miami, we have three distances: Boston-Miami, Boston-Denver, Denver-Miami. To express the relation among three cities, we have to use two dimensions. Look at Figure 2.2.

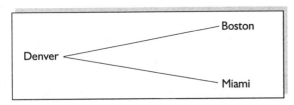

Figure 2.2 Three Points Create Two Dimensions

The two dimensions in Figure 2.2 are up-down and right-left, or North-South and East-West. If we add Nairobi to the exercise, we'd have to add a third dimension (straight through the paper at a slight downward angle from Denver—or do what Gerardus Mercator (1512-94) did to force a three-dimensional object (the Earth) into a two-dimensional picture. He managed to portray a sphere in two dimensions, but at the cost of distortion at the edges. This is why, on a map of the world, Greenland (an island of 840,000 square miles), looks the same size as China (a land mass of about 3.7 million square miles).

Unidimensional variables, like height, weight, birth order, age, and marital status, are relatively easy to measure. Stress, wealth, and political orientation, by contrast, are all multidimensional and more difficult to measure. To measure the annual income of various Americans, for example, you may have to account for salaries, Social Security, private pension funds, gifts, gambling winnings, tax credits, interest on savings, tips, food stamps, contributions from extended kin, and so on.

In Chapter 7, after we look at questionnaire design, I'll discuss the building of scales and how to test for unidimensionality of variables.

Dichotomous Variables: Race and Gender, for Example

Race and gender are examples of variables that are really complex but that appear to be simple. Their complexity is hard to measure so we measure them simply, as **dichotomous** variables, with two values each: Black/White, female/male.

We have learned a lot about the effects of racial discrimination in the United States by reducing the variable "race" to just two values. Any man in the United States who is labeled "Black" is eight times more likely to be the victim of homicide than any man labeled "White." Black babies are two and a half times more likely to die in infancy than are White babies. People labeled Black are three times more likely as people labeled White to be poor.

Still, there are many gradations of skin color besides black and white, so it's reasonable to ask whether people who are *more* black are more likely to be a victim of homicide, to die in infancy, to be poor, and so on. Around 1970, medical researchers began to find a relation in the United States between darkness of skin color and blood pressure among people labeled Blacks (see E. Boyle 1970; Harburg et al. 1978). The darker the skin, the higher blood pressure was likely to be.

Later, researchers began to find that education and social class were more important predictors of high blood pressure among Blacks than was darkness of skin color (see Keil et al. 1981; Keil et al. 1977). This meant that darker-skinned people were more likely to be the victims of discrimination: uneducated and poor. Poverty causes stress and poor diet, both of which are direct causes of high blood pressure.

This leads us to think about what we might learn if skin color were treated as a continuous variable rather than as a dichotomous one. Suppose that instead of coding people as "Black" or "White," we measured skin color with a reflectometer. We'd learn whether White schoolteachers react more negatively to darker-skinned Black children than to lighter-skinned Black children. We'd learn whether lighter Blacks live longer than do blacker Blacks.

Findings like these would illuminate the dynamics—the process—of racism: how it plays out, not just its consequences. We might be able to account for some of the variation in Black children's school scores as a function of teacher reaction to skin color. We might learn that skin color leads to discrimination and poverty and, finally, to lowered life expectancy.

If the benefits of such research are attractive, though, consider the risks. Racists might claim that our findings support their hateful ideas about the genetic inferiority of African Americans. Life insurance companies might start charging people's premiums based on amount of skin pigmentation. Even if the Supreme Court ruled against this practice, how many people would be hurt before the matter was adjudicated? As you can see, every research question has an ethical component.

❖

Gender is another dichotomous variable (male and female) that is more complex than it seems. We usually measure gender according to the presence of male or female sexual characteristics. Then we look at the relation between the presence of those characteristics and things like income, level of education, IQ score, amount of labor migration, attitudes to various social issues, aptitude for math, success in certain jobs, and so on.

But if you think about it, we're not interested in biological gender in most social research. We don't want to know whether primary or secondary sexual characteristics predict level of education or income. What we really want to know is how being *more* male or *more* female (socially and psychologically) predicts things like the ability to cope with widowhood, health status in old age, effectiveness in running a business, and so on.

Bem (1974, 1979) and Spence et al. (1974; Spence and Helmreich 1978; Spence 1991) developed scales that measure sex-role identity. The scales are called the BSRI (Bem Sex Role Inventory) and the PAQ (Personality Attribute Questionnaire).

The BSRI has two subscales, one that measures *instrumental* adaptive traits (that is, stereotypically masculine traits like "independent" and "assertive"), and one that measures *expressive* adaptive traits (that is, stereotypically feminine traits like "affectionate" and "sympathetic"). Hunt (1993) gave the BSRI to 57 undergraduate men and 72 undergraduate women at the University of Pennsylvania. Hunt's work confirms what other researchers had found before her: Androgynous people (those who score high on *both* sets of adaptive traits) score lowest on depression and highest on general measures of well-being and satisfaction with life.

Sundvik and Lindeman (1993) applied the BSRI to 257 managers (159 men and 98 women) of a government-controlled transportation company in Finland. Each of the managers had rated a subordinate on 30 dimensions—things like the ability to get along with others, independence in getting the job done, willingness to implement innovations. The sex-typed female managers (the women who scored high on "femaleness," according to the BSRI) rated their male subordinates more favorably than they rated their female subordinates. Similarly, the sex-typed male managers rated their female subordinates more favorably than they rated their male subordinates.

The bottom line is sex-typed managers discriminate against subordinates of the same sex. Sundvik and Lindeman conclude that "among persons whose self-concepts are formed on the basis of gender, both the queen bee and the king ape syndromes are alive and well" (ibid.:8).

After 25 years of research with the BSRI and the PAQ, we've learned a lot about the differences between men and women. One thing we've learned is that those differences are much more complex than a biological dichotomy would make them appear to be.

Dependent and Independent Variables

Recall the life insurance problem: The company predicts how long you will live, given your sex, age, education, weight, blood pressure, and a few other variables. They bet that you will *not die* this year. You take the bet. If you lose (and remain alive), the company takes your annual premium and banks it. If you win the bet (and die), the company pays your beneficiary.

For insurance companies to turn a profit, they have to win more bets than they lose. They can make mistakes at the individual level, but in the *aggregate* (that is, averaging over all people) they have to predict longevity from things they can measure.

Longevity, then, is the *dependent* variable, because it *depends on* sex, education, occupation, and so on. These are called *independent* variables, because they are logically prior to the dependent variable of longevity. How long you live doesn't have any effect on your sex. In our earlier example, blood pressure was the dependent variable. There is no way skin color depends on a person's blood pressure.

It's not always easy to tell whether a variable is independent or dependent. Do inner-city adolescent girls get pregnant because they are poor, or is it the other way around? Does the need for litigation stimulate the production of attorneys, or is it the other way around?

A lot of mischief is caused by failure to understand which of two variables depends on the other. Oscar Lewis (1961, 1965) described what he called a "culture of poverty" among slum dwellers in cities around the world. One of the things that characterizes this culture, said Lewis, is a low level of orientation toward the future, as indicated by poor people shopping every day for food and never buying large economy sizes of anything. Lewis's point was that truly poor people can't invest in soap futures by buying large boxes of it. He saw a low level of expressed orientation toward the future, then, as *dependent on* poverty.

Many people concluded wrongly from Lewis's work that poverty was dependent on a low level of future orientation. According to this topsy-turvy, victim-blaming reasoning, if poor people—Native Americans, inner-city African Americans, rural Appalachians—would just learn to save their money and invest in the future, then they could break the poverty cycle. Such reasoning may serve to create pointless programs to teach poor people how to save money they don't have, but it doesn't do much else.

In rural West Virginia, for example, many adolescents drop out of school and teen pregnancy is high. As Bickel et al. (1997) show, since the 1960s state policymakers have explained these behaviors as the consequences of a culture of poverty in which people become fatalistic and reckless. Actually, the behaviors that state policymakers want so much to change are driven by deteriorating economic and social conditions in rural communities. No amount of "educating" poor people about their bad habits will change the material circumstances that cause the culture of poverty.

The *educational model of social change* is another lesson in confusion about dependent and independent variables. The model is based on **the idea that thought causes behavior.** If you want to change people's behavior, the reasoning goes, then you have to change how they think: Teach women in India to use diaphragms to prevent unwanted pregnancies; teach Kenyans to use bed nets to prevent malaria; teach farmers across the world to wash their hands after handling manure and before preparing or ingesting food to prevent infectious diseases.

The educational model of social change creates a lot of employment for researchers and project workers, but it doesn't produce much in the way of desired change. This is because behavioral change (the supposed dependent variable) doesn't usually depend on education (the supposed independent variable). In fact, across the developing world, when women have access to well-paying jobs outside the home, they tend to lower their fertility. Once that happens, they encourage their daughters to stay in school longer. Jobs cause education across generations in this case, not the other way around. (I'll have more to say on fertility control and the educational model of behavioral change in Chapter 3, when I discuss the role of theory in the development of research questions.)

MEASUREMENT AND CONCEPTS

Variables are measured by their *indicators,* and indicators are defined by their *values.* Some variables, and their indicators, are easily observed and measured. Others are more conceptual. The difference is important.

Consider the variables race and gender again. If skin color can take one of two values (black or white), then to *measure* race you simply look at a person and decide which value to record. If you use secondary sexual characteristics as an indicator of gender, then to *measure* gender you look at a person and decide whether the person is female or male.

In other words, *measurement is deciding which value to record.* That decision is prone to error. Many people have ambiguous secondary sexual characteristics; many women wear men's clothes. Is Pat a man's name or a woman's? What about Chris? Leslie? Any of these indicators may mislead you into making the wrong measurement—marking down a male as female, or vice versa.

Improving measurement in science means lowering the probability of and the amount of error. Light-skinned African Americans who cease to identify themselves ethnically as Black persons count on those errors for what they hope will be upward economic mobility. Dark-skinned "Whites," like some Americans of Mediterranean descent, sometimes complain that they are being "mistaken for" Blacks and discriminated against.

Race and gender are concepts, or mental constructions. We have to make them up in order to study them. All variables are concepts, but some concepts, like height and weight, are easier to measure than others. Concepts like religious intensity, dedication to public service, willingness to accept new agricultural technologies, tolerance for foreign fieldwork, desire for an academic job, compassion, and jealousy are complex and much more difficult to measure.

Complex concepts are often called **constructs.** Our belief in the existence of such variables is based on our experience: Some people just seem more religiously intense than others, more jealous than others, more tolerant of foreign fieldwork than others, and so on.

We verify our intuition that conceptual variables exist by measuring them, or by measuring their results. Suppose you put an ad in the paper that says: "Roommate wanted. Easygoing, nonsmoker preferred." When people answer the ad you can look at their fingers and smell their clothes to see if they smoke. But you have to ask people a series of indicator *questions* to gauge their easygoingness.

Similarly, to predict who among a group of prisoners is predisposed to return to crime after release, you will want to measure that predisposition with a series of indicators. The indicators can be answers to questions on formal tests, answers to open-ended questions about plans for the future, or even directly observable facts—like whether someone has a strong family to which he or she will return after release from prison.

It is easier to measure some concepts than others, but all measurement is difficult. People have worked for centuries to develop good instruments for measuring things like temperature. And if it's difficult to measure temperature (a concept, after all, backed up by time-tested theories), how do you measure worker alienation or machismo? Measuring variables like these, that lack concrete indicators, is one of our biggest challenges in social science because these variables are mostly what we're interested in.

One of the most famous variables in social science is socioeconomic status (SES). Measuring it is no easy task. You can use income as one indicator, but there are many wealthy people who have low SES, and many relatively low-income people who have high SES. You can add level of education to income as an indicator, but that still won't be enough in most societies of the world to get at something as multidimensional as SES. You can add occupation, father's occupation, number of generations in a community, and so on, depending on the group you are studying, and you still might wind up dissatisfied with the result if your measure fails to predict some dependent variable of interest.

CONCEPTUAL AND OPERATIONAL DEFINITIONS

While most of the interesting variables in social science are concepts, some of our most important concepts are not variables. The concept of religion is not, by itself, a variable, but the concept of "professing to believe in a particular religion" is a variable. The concept of attitude is not a vari-

| | 5 | 10 | 15 | 20 | 25 | 30 | 35 | 40 | 45 | 50 | 55 | 60 | 65 | 70 | 75 | 80 | 85 | 90 | 95 | 100 |

Here is a line that represents age. Obviously, a person 1 year of age is a baby, and a person 100 years of age is old. Put a mark on the line where you think middle age begins and another mark where you think middle age ends.

Figure 2.3 An Instrument for Measuring What People Think "Middle Age" Means

able, but the concept of "supporting or not supporting the right of adults in the U.S. to own handguns" implies a variable with at least two attributes.

Conceptual Definitions

There are two ways to define variables—conceptually and operationally. *Conceptual definitions* are **abstractions, articulated in words, that facilitate understanding.** They are the sort of definitions we see in dictionaries, and we use them in everyday conversation to tell people what we mean by some term or phrase. *Operational definitions* consist of **a set of instructions on how to measure a variable that has been conceptually defined.**

Suppose I tell you that "Alice and Fred just moved to a spacious house." Nice concept. You ask: "What do you mean by 'spacious'?" and I say, "You know, it has lots and lots of space; the rooms are big and the ceilings are high."

If that isn't enough for you, we'll have to move from a conceptual definition of "spacious" to an operational one. We'll have to agree on what to measure: Do we count the screened-in porch and the garage or just the interior living space? Do we count the square footage or the cubic footage? That is, do we get a measure of the living surface, or some measure of the "feeling of spaciousness" that comes from high ceilings? Do we measure the square footage of open space before or after the furniture and appliances go in? If we had to agree

on things like this for every concept, ordinary human discourse would come to a grinding halt.

Science is not ordinary human discourse, however, and this, in my view, is the most important difference between the humanistic and the scientific (positivistic) approaches to social science. Humanistic researchers seek to maintain the essential feel of human discourse. Positivists focus more on specific measurement. I do not see these two styles as inimical to one another, but as complementary.

To get a feel for how complementary the two styles can be, ask some 50-year-old and some 20-year-old women and men to tell you how old you have to be to be middle-aged. You'll see immediately how volatile the conceptual definition of "middle age" is. If you ask people about what it means to "be middle-aged," you'll get plenty of material for an interesting paper on the subject. If you want to *measure* the differences between men and women and between older and younger people on this variable, you'll have to do more than just ask them. Figure 2.3 shows an instrument for measuring this variable.

Many concepts that we use in social research have volatile definitions: "power," "social class," "machismo," "alienation," "willingness to change," and "fear of retribution." If we are to talk sensibly about such things, we need clear, *intersubjective definitions* of them. In other words, while there can be no objective definition of middle age, we can at least agree on what we mean by middle age for a particular study and on how to measure the concept.

Complex variables are conceptually defined by reducing them to a series of simpler variables. The concept of "ethnic identity" is very complex. But if you state clearly that you mean to measure (1) "varying levels of overt expression of pride in ethnic heritage," (2) "varying levels of knowledge about ethnic foods," and (3) "varying levels of financial commitment to participation in ethnic heritage activities" in your conceptual definition, then at least others will understand what you're talking about when you say that people are "high" or "low" on ethnic identity.

Similarly, "machismo" might be characterized by "a general feeling of male superiority," accompanied by "insecure behavior in relationships with women." "Intelligence" might be conceptually defined as "the ability to think in abstractions and to generalize from cases." These definitions have something important in common: They have no external reality against which to test their truth value.

Conceptual definitions are at their most powerful when they are linked together to build theories that explain research results. Dependency theory, for example, links the concept of "control of capital" with those of "mutual security" and "economic dependency." The linkage helps explain why economic development often results in some groups winding up with less access to capital than they had before a development program. It is a theory, in other words, to explain why the rich nations of the world get richer and poor nations get poorer.

Conceptual definitions are at their weakest in the conduct of research itself, because concepts have no empirical basis—they have to be made up to study them.

There is nothing wrong with this. There are three things one wants to do in any science: (1) describe a phenomenon of interest; (2) explain what causes it; (3) predict what it causes. The existence of a conceptual variable is inferred from what it predicts—how well it makes theoretical sense out of a lot of data.

The Concept of Intelligence

The classic example of a conceptual variable is intelligence. Intelligence is anything we say it is. There is no way to tell whether it is really (1) the ability to think in abstractions and to generalize from cases, (2) the ability to remember long strings of unconnected facts, or (3) the ability to recite all of Shakespeare from memory. In the last analysis, the value of the concept of intelligence is that it allows us to predict, with varying success, things like job success, grade-point average, likelihood of having healthy children, and likelihood of being arrested for a felony, among other things.

The key to understanding the last statement is the phrase "with varying success." It is by now well known that measures of intelligence are culture bound; the standard U.S. intelligence tests are biased in favor of Whites and against African Americans because of differences in access to education and differences in life experiences. Further afield, intelligence tests that are designed for Americans may not have any meaning at all to people in radically different cultures.

There is a famous, perhaps apocryphal, story about some American researchers who were determined to develop a culture-free intelligence test based on manipulation and matching of shapes and colors. With an interpreter along for guidance, they administered the test to a group of Bushmen in the Kalahari Desert of South Africa. The first Bushman they tested listened politely to the instructions about matching the colors and shapes, and then excused himself.

He returned in a few minutes with half a dozen others, and they began an animated discussion about the test. The researchers asked the interpreter to explain that each man had to take the test himself. The Bushmen responded by saying how silly that was; they solve problems together, and they would solve this one like that, too. So, although the content of the test might have been culture free, the testing procedure itself was not.

This critique of intelligence *testing* in no way lessens the importance or usefulness of the *concept* of intelligence. The concept is useful, in certain contexts, because its measurement allows us to predict other things we want to know. And it is to actual measurement that we now turn.

Operational Definitions

Conceptual definitions are limited because, while they point us toward measurement, they don't really give us any recipe for measurement. Without measurement, we cannot make useful comparisons. We cannot tell whether Spaniards are more flamboyant than the British, or whether Catholicism is more authoritarian than Buddhism. We cannot evaluate the level of anger in an urban community over perceived abuses by the police of their authority, or compare the level of that anger to the anger found in another community in another city.

Operational definitions specify exactly what you have to do to measure something that has been defined conceptually. Here are four examples of operational definitions:

Intelligence: Take the Wechsler Adult Intelligence Scale (WAIS) and administer it to a person. Count up the score. Whatever score the person gets is his or her intelligence.

Machismo: Ask a man if he approves of women working outside the home, assuming the family doesn't need the money; if he says no, then give him a score of 1, and if he says yes, then score him 0. Ask him if he thinks women and men should have the same sexual freedom before marriage; if he says no, score 1, and score 0 for yes. Ask him if a man should be punished for killing his wife and her lover;

if he says no, score 1; score 0 for yes. Add the scores. A man who scores 3 has more machismo than a man who scores 2, and a man who scores 2 has more machismo than a man who scores 1.

Ethnic identity: Ask a sample of third-generation Chinese Americans who were born in San Francisco if they speak the language of their grandparents fluently. If yes, score 1. If no, score 0. Ask them if they eat at non-Chinese restaurants at least once a week. Score 1 for no, and 0 for yes. Ask them eight other questions of this type, and give them a score of 1 for each answer that signifies self-identification with their parents' heritage. Anyone who scores at least 6 out of 10 is an "identifier." Five or less is a "rejecter" of Chinese heritage or identity.

Support for trade barriers against Japan: Ask workers in a factory to complete the Support of Trade Barriers against Japan Scale. Add the four parts of the scale together to produce a single score. Record that score.

These definitions sound pretty boring, but think about this: If you and I use the same definitions for variables, *and if we stick to those definitions in making measurements,* then our data are strictly comparable:

We can tell if adults in city A have higher intelligence scores than do children in city B.

We can tell if members of one Hispanic group have higher machismo scores than members of another Hispanic group.

We can tell if members of an ethnic minority in city A have higher cultural identity scores than do members of the same ethnic minority in city B.

We can tell whether the average scores indicating level of support for trade barriers against Japan is greater among workers in the factory you studied than it is among workers in the factory I studied.

I find the ability to make such comparisons exciting, and not at all boring. But did you notice that I never said anything in those comparisons about ethnic identity per se, or intelligence per se, or machismo or support for trade barriers per se. In each case, all I said was that we could tell if the *scores* were bigger or smaller.

What's So Good about Operationism?

Operational definitions are strictly limited to the content of the operations specified. That's why I also didn't say anything about whether it was a good idea or a stupid one to make any of these measurements or comparisons. If the content of an operational definition is bad, then so are all conclusions you draw from using it to measure something.

This is not an argument against operationism in science. Just the opposite. Operationism is the best way to expose bad measurement. By defining measurements operationally, we can tell if one measurement is better than another. If the operational measurement of, say, machismo, seems silly or offensive, it may be because the concept is not very useful to begin with. No amount of measurement or operationism bails out bad concepts. The act of trying, though, usually *exposes* bad concepts and helps you jettison them.

> *If the content of an operational definition is bad, then so are all conclusions you draw from using it to measure something.*

Adhering to bad measurements is bad science and can have some bad consequences for people. In the 1960s, I was a consultant on a project that was supposed to help Chicano high schoolers develop good career aspirations. Studies had been conducted in which Chicano and Anglo high schoolers were asked what they wanted to be when they reached 30 years of age. Chicanos expressed, on average, a lower occupational aspiration than did Anglos. This led some social scientists to advise policymakers that Chicano youth needed reinforcement of career aspirations at home. (There's that educational model again.)

Contrary to survey findings, ethnographic research showed that Chicano parents had very high aspirations for their children. The parents were frustrated by two things: (1) despair over the cost of sending their children to college, and (2) high school counselors who systematically encouraged Chicana girls to become housewives and Chicano boys to learn a trade or go into the armed services.

The presumed relation between the dependent variable (level of career aspiration) and the independent variable (level of aspiration by parents for the careers of their children) was backward. The parents' level of career aspiration for their children didn't cause the children to have low aspirations. The children were driven to low aspirations by structural features of their environment. The parents of those children reflected this reality in order—they said explicitly to interviewers who bothered to ask—not to give their children false hopes.

The operational definition of the variable "parents' career aspirations for their children" was useless. Here's the operational definition that should have been used in the study of Chicano parents' aspirations for their children's careers:

Go to the homes of the respondents. Using the native language of the respondents (Spanish or English as the case may be), talk to parents about what they want their high school-age children to be doing in 10 years. Explore each answer in depth and find out why parents give each answer.

Ask specifically if the parents are telling you what they think their children *will* be doing or what they *want* their children to be doing. If parents hesitate, say, "Suppose nothing stood in the way of your [son] [daughter] becoming anything they wanted to be. What would you like them to be doing 10 years from now?"

Write down what the parents say and code it for the following possible scores: 1 = unambivalently in favor of children going into high-status occupations; 2 = ambivalent about children going into high-status occupations; 3 = unambivalently in favor of children going into low- or middle-status occupations.

Use Stricker's (1988) occupation scale to decide whether the occupations selected by parents as fitting for their children are high, middle, or low status. Be sure to take and keep notes on what parents say are the reasons for their selections of occupations.

Notice that taking an ethnographic—a so-called qualitative—approach did not stop us from being operational.

Operationism is often crude and simplistic, and that, too, can be its strength. Robert Wuthnow (1976) operationalized the concept of "religiosity" in 43 countries using UNESCO data on the number of books published in those countries and the fraction of those books classified as religious literature. Now *that's* crude. Still, Wuthnow's measure of "average religiosity" correlates with seven of eight indicators of modernity. For example, the higher the literacy rate in 1952, the lower the religiosity in 1972.

I have no idea what that means, but I think following up Wuthnow's work with more refined measurements—to test hypotheses about the societal conditions that support or weaken religiosity—is a lot more exciting than dismissing it because it was so audaciously crude.

The Problem with Operationism

Strict operationism creates a knotty philosophical problem. Measurement turns abstractions (concepts) into reality. Since there are many ways to measure the same abstraction, the reality of any concept hinges on the device you use to measure it. So, sea temperature is different if you measure it from a satellite (you get an answer based on radiation) or with a thermometer (you get an answer based on a column of mercury). Intelligence is different if you measure it with a Stanford-Binet test, a Kaufman Adolescent and Adult Intelligence Scale, or the Wechsler scales. If you ask a person in any of the industrialized nations, "How old are you?" or "How many birthdays have you had?" you will probably retrieve the same number. But the very concept of "age" in the two cases is different because different instruments (queries are instruments) were used to measure it.

This principle was articulated in 1927 by Percy Bridgman in *The Logic of Modern Physics* and has become the source of an enduring controversy. The bottom line on strict operational definitions is this: No matter how much you insist that intelligence is really more than what is measured by an intelligence test, that's all it can ever be. Whatever you think intelligence is, it is exactly and only what you measure with an intelligence test and nothing more.

If you don't like the results of your measurement, then build a better test, where "better" means that the outcomes are more useful in building theory, in making predictions, and in engineering behavior.

I see no reason to waffle about this, or to look for philosophically palatable ways to soften the principle here. The science that emerges from a strict operational approach to understanding variables is much too powerful to water down with backtracking. It is obvious that "future orientation" is more than my asking someone, "Do you buy large or small boxes of soap?" The problem is *you* might not include that question in your interview of the same respondent, unless I specify that I asked that question in that particular way.

Operational definitions permit scientists to talk to one another using the same language. They permit replication of research and the accumulation of knowledge about issues of importance. Consider the Attitudes Toward Women Scale, or AWS. The scale was developed by Janet Spence and Robert Helmreich in 1972 and was applied 71 times to samples of American undergraduate students between 1970 and 1995 (Twenge 1997). A lot has changed since 1972, and some of the items on the AWS might seem out of date, even quaint, today. In one item, respondents are asked how much they agree or disagree with the following statement: "Women should worry less about their rights and more about becoming good wives and mothers."

I wouldn't use that kind of wording if I were building an attitudes-toward-women scale today. But the fact is, the AWS has been applied across the U.S. in the same way for a quarter century. This operational definition of attitudes toward women makes it possible to track changes over time—and the results are illuminating. Attitudes toward women have become consistently more liberal/feminist over time, but men's support for women's rights has lagged behind women's support by about 15 years: Men's average score on the AWS in 1990 was about the same as women's average score in 1975 (Twenge 1997). (These data, remember, reflect the attitudes of college students—the quarter of the population whom we expect to be at the vanguard of social change.)

LEVELS OF MEASUREMENT

Whenever you define a variable operationally, you do so at some *level of measurement*. Most social scientists recognize the following four levels of measurement, in ascending order: nominal, ordinal, interval, and ratio. The general principle in research is this: Always use the highest level of measurement that you can. (This principle will be clear by the time you get through the next couple of pages.)

Nominal Variables

A variable is something that can take more than one value. The values of a *nominal variable* comprise **a list of names.** You can list religions, occupations, and ethnic groups; you can also list fruits, emotions, body parts, things to do on the weekend, baseball teams, rock stars—the list of things you can list is endless.

Think of nominal variables as yes-no questions, the answers to which tell you nothing about degree or amount. What's your name? In what country were you born? Are you healthy? On the whole, do you think the economy is in good shape? Is Mexico in Latin America? Is Bangladesh a poor country? Is Switzerland a rich country?

The following survey item is an operationalization of the nominal variable called "religious affiliation":

26a. Do you identify with any religion?
(check one)

☐ Yes   ☐ No

If you checked yes, then please answer question 26b.

26b. What is your religion (check one):
☐ Protestant
☐ Catholic
☐ Jewish
☐ Muslim
☐ Other religion
☐ No religion

This operationalization of the variable religious affiliation has two important characteristics: It is *exhaustive* and *mutually exclusive*. The famous "other" category in nominal variables makes the list exhaustive—that is, all possible categories have been named in the list—and the instruction to "check one" makes the list mutually exclusive. (More on this in Chapter 7 when we discuss questionnaire design.)

"Mutually exclusive" means that things can't belong to more than one category of a nominal variable at a time. We assume, for example, that people who say they are Catholic generally don't say they are Muslim. I say "generally" because life is complicated and variables that seem mutually exclusive may not be.

Most people claim just one religion, for example, but some citizens of Lebanon have one Catholic and one Muslim parent and may think of themselves as both Muslim and Catholic. Most people think of themselves as either male or female, but not everyone does. Most people think of themselves as a member of one so-called biological race or another, but more and more people think of themselves as belonging to two or more races. In fact, the U.S. Census for 2000 offers people the opportunity to check off more than one race, if they choose.

And when it comes to ethnic groups, the requirement for mutual exclusivity is just hopeless. There are people who identify themselves as ethnically, but not religiously, Jewish, and who simultaneously say that they are Chicanos; there are African Americans who identify simultaneously as American Indians; Filipino Americans who identify simultaneously as ethnic Chinese; and so on. Lots and lots of people think of themselves as members of more than one ethnic group.

If you let people check more than one attribute in a survey item that measures a nominal variable, you may wind up with a lot more categories than you bargained for: Chicano African Americans, Protestant agnostics, asexual homosexuals, and so on. This just reflects the complexity of real life, but remember that during data analysis, each *combination of attributes* will be treated as a separate category of the variable or it will be collapsed into one of the larger categories. More about this in Chapter 14.

The attributes of nominal variables can change over time. In the 1970s, surveys done in the U.S. typically asked people: "Are you (check one): Protestant, Catholic, Jewish, other religion, no religion." In the 1970s, there were very few people in the U.S. who considered themselves Muslims. By 1996, there were as many Muslims as there were Jews (about five million each).

Occupation is a nominal variable, but lots of people have more than one occupation. Even in one organization, like a hospital, people might have several job titles: pediatric oncology nurse and chief of nursing staff, for example. So, a list of occupations is a measuring instrument at the nominal level: You hold each respondent up against the list and see which occupation(s) he or she has.

Nominal measurement—naming things—is *qualitative measurement*. When you assign the numeral 1 to men and 2 to women, all you are doing is substituting one kind of name for another. Calling men 1 and women 2 does not make the variable quantitative. The number 2 happens to be twice as big as the number 1, but this fact is meaningless with nominal variables. You can't add up all the 1s and 2s and calculate the "average sex" any more than you can add up all the telephone numbers in the Chicago phone book and get the average phone number.

Assigning numbers to things makes it easier to do certain kinds of statistical analysis on qualitative data (more on this in Chapter 12), but it doesn't turn qualitative variables into quantitative ones.

Ordinal Variables

Like nominal variables, *ordinal variables* are **generally exhaustive and mutually exclusive,** but they have one additional property: Their **values can be rank ordered.** Any variable measured as high, medium, or low, like socioeconomic class, is ordinal. The three classes are, in theory, mutually exclusive and exhaustive. In addition, a person who is labeled "middle class" is lower in the social class hierarchy than someone labeled "high class" and higher in the same hierarchy than someone labeled "lower class." What ordinal variables do not tell us is how much more.

Scales of opinion—like the familiar *strongly agree, agree, neutral, disagree, strongly disagree* found on so many surveys—are ordinal measures. They measure an internal state, agreement, in terms of *less* and *more,* but not in terms of *how much* more.

This is the most important characteristic of ordinal measures: There is no way to tell how far apart the attributes are from one another. A person who is middle class might be twice as wealthy and three times as educated as a person who is lower class. Or she might be three times as wealthy and four times as educated. A person who "agrees strongly" with a statement may agree twice as much as someone who says he "agrees"—

or eight times as much, or half again as much. There is no way to tell.

Interval and Ratio Variables

Interval variables have all the properties of nominal and ordinal variables. They are an **exhaustive and mutually exclusive list of attributes,** and the **attributes have a rank-order structure.** They have one additional property, as well: The **distances between the attributes are meaningful.** Interval variables, then, involve true **quantitative measurement.**

The difference between 30° Celsius and 40° is the same 10° as the difference between 70° and 80°, and the difference between an IQ score of 90 and 100 is (assumed to be) the same as the difference between one of 130 and 140. On the other hand, 80° Fahrenheit is not twice as hot as 40°, and a person who has an IQ of 150 is not 50% smarter than a person who has an IQ of 100.

Ratio variables are **interval variables that have a true *zero point***—that is, a 0 that measures the absence of the phenomenon being measured. The Kelvin scale of temperature has a true zero: It identifies the absence of molecular movement, or heat.

The consequence of a true zero point is that measures have ratio properties. A person who is 40 years old is 10 years older than a person who is 30, and a person who is 20 is 10 years older than a person who is 10. The 10-year intervals between the attributes (years are the attributes of age) are identical. That much is true of an interval variable. In addition, however, a person who is 20 is twice as old as a person who is 10, and a person who is 40 is twice as old as a person who is 20. These, then, are true ratios.

While temperature (in Fahrenheit or Celsius) and IQ are nonratio interval variables, most interval variables in the social sciences are also ratio variables. In fact, it has become common practice in the social sciences to refer to ratio variables as interval variables and vice versa. This is not technically pure, but the confusion of the terms "interval" and "ratio" doesn't cause much real damage.

Some examples of ratio variables include age, number of years of education, number of times a person has changed residence, income in dollars or other currency, years married, years spent migrating, population size, distance in meters from a house to a well, number of violent crimes per hundred thousand population, number of dentists per million population, number of months since last employment, number of kilograms of fish caught per week, and number of hours per week spent in food preparation activities.

In general, *concepts* (like alienation, political orientation, and level of assimilation) are measured at the ordinal level. People get a high score for being "very assimilated," a low score for being "unassimilated," and a medium score for being "somewhat assimilated." When a concept variable like intelligence is measured at the interval level, it is likely to be the focus of a lot of controversy regarding the validity of the measuring instrument.

Concrete *observables*—things you can actually see—are often measured at the interval level. But not always. Observing whether a woman has a job outside her home is nominal, qualitative measurement based on direct observation.

A Rule about Measurement

Remember this rule: Always measure things at the highest level of measurement possible. Don't measure things at the ordinal level if you can measure them as ratio variables.

If you really want to know the price that people paid for their homes, then ask the price. Don't ask them whether they paid "less than $50,000, between $50,000 and $100,000, or more than

$100,000." If you really want to know how much education people have had, ask them how many years they went to school. Don't ask, "Have you completed grade school, high school, some college, four years of college?" These kinds of questions throw away information by turning interval variables into ordinal ones. As we'll see in Chapter 7, survey questions are pretested before going into a questionnaire. If people won't give you straight answers to straight questions, you can back off and try an ordinal scale. But why start out crippling a perfectly good interval-scale question by making it ordinal when you don't know that you have to?

> *Always measure things at the highest level of measurement possible. Don't measure things at the ordinal level if you can measure them as ratio variables.*

During data analysis you can lump interval-level data together into ordinal or nominal categories. If you know the ages of your respondents on a survey, you can divide them into "old" and "young"; if you know the number of calories consumed per week for each family in a study, you can divide the data into low, medium, and high. But you cannot do this trick the other way around. If you collect data on income by asking people whether they earn "up to $50,000 per year" or "more than $50,000 per year," you cannot go back and assign actual numbers of dollars to each informant.

Notice that "up to $50,000" and "more than $50,000" is an ordinal variable that *looks like* a nominal variable because there are only two attributes. If the attributes are rankable, then the variable is ordinal. "A lot of fish" is more than "a small amount of fish," and "highly educated" is greater than "poorly educated." Ordinal variables can have any number of ranks. For purposes of statistical analysis, though, ordinal scales with five or more ranks are often treated as if they were interval variables. More about this in Chapters 14 and 15.

UNITS OF ANALYSIS

One of the very first things to do in any research project is decide on the *unit of analysis*. In a case study, there is exactly one unit of analysis: the school, the hospital, the police squad, the sports team, the community, the church, the nation. Research designed to test hypotheses requires many units of analysis, usually a sample from a large population: organic farmers, Puerto Ricans living in Baltimore, women in the Teamsters Union, runaway children who are living on the street, children in Head Start programs, maternity nurses in private hospitals, people who go to chiropractors, Hispanic patrol officers in the U.S. Immigration and Naturalization Service who work on the border between the United States and Mexico.

Although most research in social science is about populations of people, many other things can be the units of analysis. You can focus on farms instead of farmers, on unions instead of union members, or on wars instead of warriors. You can study marriage contracts; folktales, songs, and myths; and countries, cultures, and cities.

Paul Doughty (1979), for example, surveyed demographic data on 134 countries to make a list of "primate cities." A country is said to have a primate city if its most populous city is at least three times larger than the next two cities combined. In Doughty's study, the units of analysis were countries rather than cities.

For each country, Doughty did the sums on the population of the three largest cities and coded whether the country had a primate city or not. He discovered that this characteristic of extreme concentration of population is associated with Latin America more than with any other region of the world.

Libraries are the units of analysis for the biannual Academic Libraries Survey in the U.S. For about 3,500 libraries at colleges and universities in the 50 states, Washington, D.C., the Virgin Islands, Guam, and Puerto Rico, the survey collects data on operating expenditures, number of employees, number of volumes, amount of interlibrary loan transactions, number of patrons, and average number of reference transactions per week. The National Center for Education Statistics keeps track of data about the 15,274 school districts in the U.S. For each district, variables include number of children, percentage of children enrolled, percentage of each major ethnic group, median value of homes, total amount of tax revenue available per student, and so on.

Mathews (1985) did a study of how men and women in a Mexican village tell a famous folktale differently. The tale is called *La Llorona* (The Weeping Woman) and is known all over Mexico. Mathews's research has to do with the problem of intracultural variation—different people telling the same story in different ways. She studied a sample of the population of *La Llorona* stories in a community where she was working. Each story, as told by a different person, had characteristics that could be compared across the sample of stories. One of the characteristics was whether the story was told by a man or a woman, and this turned out to be the most important variable associated with the stories, which were the units of analysis.

A Rule about Units of Analysis

Remember this rule: No matter what you are studying, always collect data on the lowest level unit of analysis possible.

Collect data about individuals, for example, rather than about households. If you are interested in issues of production and consumption (things that make sense at the household level), you can always package your data about individuals into data about households during analysis. But if you want to examine the association between female income and child spacing and you collect income data on households in the first place, then you are locked out. You can always *aggregate* data collected on individuals, but you can never *disaggregate* data collected on groups.

This rule applies whether you're studying people or countries. If you are studying relations among trading blocs in major world regions, then collect trade data on countries and pairs of countries, not on regions of the world.

The Ecological Fallacy

Once you select your unit of analysis, remember it as you go through data analysis, or you're likely to commit the dreaded *ecological fallacy*. This fallacy is also known as the Nosnibor effect, after Robinson (1950), who identified and described it. It comes from **drawing conclusions about the wrong units of analysis—making generalizations about people, for example, from data about groups or places.**

Suppose you do a consumer survey across a city. During your analysis, you notice that the neighborhoods that have the lowest average age also have the highest average dollar value of recent purchases of consumer electronics. You are tempted to conclude that young people are more interested in consumer electronics and purchase them more frequently than do older people.

But you could be completely wrong. The *neighborhoods* with lower average age may spend more on VCRs and such, but it may be the *older people* who are doing all the spending. It is usually not valid to take data gathered about neighborhoods and draw conclusions about neighbors. (For recent work on solving the ecological fallacy statistically, see King 1997.) And this brings us to the crucial issue of validity.

VALIDITY, RELIABILITY, PRECISION, AND ACCURACY

Validity

Validity refers to the **accuracy and trustworthiness of instruments, data, and findings in research.** Nothing in research is more important than validity.

The Validity of Instruments and Data

Are the instruments that were used to measure something valid? Are SAT and GRE (Graduate Record Exam) scores, for example, valid instruments for measuring the ability of students to get good grades? If they are, then are grades a valid measure of how smart students are? Is the question "Do you practice polytheistic fetishism?" a valid instrument for measuring religious practices? No, it isn't, because the concept of "polytheistic fetishism" is something that is meaningful only to specialists in the comparative study of religion.

Asking people that question is asking them to think in categories that are alien to their culture. Is the instrument "How long does it take you to drive to work each day?" a valid instrument for measuring the amount of time it takes people to drive to work each day? Well, that depends on how accurate you want the data to be. If you want the data to be accurate to within, say, 20 minutes on, say, 70% of occasions, then the instrument is probably valid. If you want the data to be accurate to, say, within 5 minutes on, say, 90% of occasions, then the instrument is probably not valid because people just can't dredge up the information you want at that level of accuracy.

The validity of data is tied to the validity of instruments. If questions asking people to recall their behavior are not valid instruments for tapping into informants' past behavior, then the data retrieved by those instruments are not valid, either.

The Validity of Findings

Assuming, however, that the instruments and data are valid, we can ask whether the findings and conclusions derived from the data are valid. Vietnamese Americans, Chinese Americans, and Japanese Americans comprise over 95% of all Americans of Asian ancestry. Those three groups generally get higher scores on the math part of the SATs than do other ethnic groups in the U.S.

Suppose that the SAT math test is a valid instrument for measuring the general math ability of 18-year-olds in the U.S. Is it valid to conclude that "Asians are better at math" than other people are? No, it isn't. That conclusion can be reached only by invoking an unfounded, racist assumption about the influence of certain genes—particularly genes responsible for epicanthic eye folds—on the ability of people to do math.

Reliability

Reliability refers to **whether or not you get the same answer by using an instrument to measure something more than once.** If you insert a thermometer into boiling water at sea level, it should register 212 ° Fahrenheit each and every time. Instruments can be things like thermometers and scales, or they can be questions that you ask people.

Like all other kinds of instruments, some questions are more reliable for retrieving information than others. "How many brothers and sisters do you have?" is a pretty reliable instrument. You almost always get the same response when you ask a person that question a second time as you get the first time. "How much is your parents' house worth?" is much less reliable. And "How old were you when you were toilet trained?" is just hopeless.

Precision

Precision is about the number of decimal points in a measurement. Suppose your bathroom scale works on a spring mechanism. When you stand on the scale, the spring is compressed. As the spring compresses, it moves a pointer to a number that signifies how much weight is being put on the scale. Let's say that you really, truly weigh 156.625 pounds, to the nearest thousandth of a pound.

If you have an old analog bathroom scale like mine, there are five little marks between each pound reading; that is, the scale registers weight in fifths of a pound. In terms of precision, then, your scale is somewhat limited. The best it could possibly do would be to announce that you weigh "somewhere between 156.6 and 156.8 pounds, and closer to the former figure than to the latter."

In this case, you might not be too concerned about the error introduced by lack of precision.

Whether you care or not depends on the needs you have for the data. If you are concerned about losing weight, then you're probably not going to worry too much about the fact that your scale is only precise to the nearest fifth of a pound. But if you're measuring the weights of pharmaceuticals, and someone's life depends on your getting the precise amounts into a compound, well, that's another matter.

Accuracy

Finally, *accuracy*. Assume that you are satisfied with the level of precision of the scale. What if the spring was not calibrated correctly (there was an error at the factory where the scale was built, or last week your overweight houseguest bent the spring a little too much), and the scale was off? Now we have the following interesting situation: The data from this instrument are valid (it has already been determined that the scale is measuring weight—exactly what you think it's measuring); they are reliable (you get the same answer every time you step on it); and they are precise enough for your purposes. But they are not accurate. What next?

You could see if the scale was always inaccurate in the same way. You could stand on it 10 times in a row, without eating or doing exercise in between. That way, you'd be measuring the same thing 10 different times with the same instrument. If the reading was always the same, then the instrument would at least be reliable, even though it wasn't accurate. Suppose it turned out that your scale was always incorrectly lower by five pounds. This is called *systematic bias*. Then, a simple correction formula would be all you'd need to feel confident that the data from the instrument were pretty close to the truth. The formula would be

True weight = Your scale weight + 5 pounds

The scale might be off in more complicated ways, however. It might be that for every 10 pounds of weight put on the scale, an additional half-pound correction has to be made. Then the **recalibration** formula would be

$$\text{True weight} = (\text{Your scale weight}) + (\text{Scale weight}/10)\,(.5)$$

or

$$(\text{Your scale weight}) \times (1.05)$$

That is, take the scale weight, divide by 10, multiply by half a pound, and add the result to the reading on your scale.

If an instrument is not precise enough for what you want to do with the data, then you simply have to build a more precise one. There is no way out. If it is precise enough for your research and reliable, but inaccurate in known ways, then a formula can be applied to correct for the inaccuracy.

The real problem, of course, is when instruments are inaccurate in unknown ways. The bad news is that this happens a lot. If you ask people how long it takes them to drive to work, they'll tell you. If you ask people what they ate for breakfast, they'll tell you that, too. Answers to both questions may be dead on target, or they may bear no useful resemblance to the truth. The good news is that respondent accuracy is one of the methodological questions that social scientists have been investigating for years and on which real progress continues to be made (Bernard et al. 1984; Sudman et al. 1996; Schwarz 1999).

Tests for Reliability

There are several tests for reliability:

1. *Interobserver reliability*. Suppose you set up an experiment to see whether five-year-old chil-

dren act more aggressively or more cooperatively in same-sex play groups or in mixed-sex play groups. You'll have several observers code the behavior of the children and you'll want them to achieve consistency in what they see and write down.

Or suppose you have a set of open-ended interviews about what it's like to break up after a relationship that's lasted more than a year. You'll want several people coding those interviews. In both cases—whether you're coding behavior or the content of text—you'll want your coders to achieve a high interobserver reliability score. I'll have more to say in Chapter 12 (on text analysis) about how to calculate that score.

2. *Test-retest reliability.* A reliable test of, say, ability in math or of interest in a particular occupation should give you more or less the same results each time you use it on the same person. When tests are developed, they are typically tested for reliability by giving them to a group of people then calling back those same people a week later to take the test again.

Many standardized tests have two *parallel forms.* When both forms are given to the same person, they should produce more or less the same results. "More or less" here means at least .80. Another test for reliability is the *split-half* test. This is used in the development of scales, about which *much* more in Chapter 8.

Determining Validity

You may have noticed that I just casually slipped in the statement that the scale had "already been determined" to be a valid instrument. How do we know that the scale is measuring weight? Maybe it's measuring something else. How can we be sure? Since we have to make concepts in order to study them, there is no direct way to evaluate the validity of an instrument for measuring a concept. Ultimately, we are left to

decide, on the basis of our best judgment, whether an instrument is valid or not.

We are helped in making that judgment by some tests for *face validity, content validity, construct validity,* and *criterion validity.*

Face Validity

Establishing *face validity* involves simply looking at the operational indicators of a concept and deciding whether or not, *on the face of it,* the indicators make sense. The indicators might be items on an opinion survey or they might be tests of knowledge and ability.

On the face of it, asking people, "How old were you when you were toilet trained?" is not a valid way to get at this kind of information. A paper-and-pencil test about the rules of the road is not a valid indicator of whether someone knows how to drive a car. But the paper-and-pencil test is a valid test for determining if an applicant for a driver's license can read road signs. These different instruments—the road test and the paper-and-pencil test—have face validity for measuring different things.

Face validity is based on consensus among researchers: If everyone agrees that asking people, "How old are you?" is a valid instrument for measuring age, then, until proven otherwise, that question is a valid instrument for measuring age.

Content Validity

Content validity is achieved when an instrument has appropriate content for measuring a complex concept, or construct. If you walk out of a test and feel that it was unfair because it tapped too narrow a band of knowledge, your complaint is that the test lacked content validity. Achievement tests—for assessing whether pilots are ready to fly solo and for assessing whether family therapists are ready to be licensed—are judged on their content validity.

Content validity is very, very tough to achieve, particularly for complex, multidimensional constructs. A test to measure the strength of "ethnic identity" among, say, second-generation Mexican Americans has to have content that deals with religion, language, political and economic values, sense of history, and gastronomy. Mexican Americans tend to be mostly Roman Catholic, but a growing number of Mexicans are now Protestants. The migration of a few million of these converts to the U.S. over the next decade will have an impact on ethnic politics—and ethnic identity—within the Mexican American population.

Some second-generation Mexican Americans speak almost no Spanish, while others are completely bilingual. While 54% of Mexican American households have incomes below $25,000 a year, about 18% have incomes above $50,000 a year. People with radically different incomes tend to have different political and economic values. Some Mexican Americans have roots in New Mexico that go back to before the British Pilgrims landed at Plymouth Rock, while others are recent immigrants. And for some second-generation Mexican Americans, cuisine is practically synonymous with identity, while for others it's no big deal.

A valid measure of ethnic identity, then, has to get at all these areas. People's use of Spanish inside and outside the home and their preference for Mexican or Mexican American foods are good measures of *some* of the content of Mexican American ethnicity. But if these are the only questions you ask, then your measure of ethnicity has low content validity.

"Life satisfaction" is another very complex variable, composed of several concepts—like "having sufficient income," "a general feeling of well-being," and "satisfaction with level of personal control over one's life." In fact, most of the really interesting things that social scientists study are complex constructs, things like "quality of life," "socioeconomic class," and "ability of teenagers to resist peer pressure to smoke."

Construct Validity

An instrument has high **construct validity** if there is a close fit between the construct it supposedly measures and actual observations made with the instrument. An instrument has high construct validity, in other words, if it allows you to infer that a unit of analysis (a person, a country, etc.) has a particular complex trait and if it supports predictions that are made from theory.

Scholars have offered various definitions of the construct of ethnicity, based on different theoretical perspectives. Does a particular measure of Mexican American ethnicity have construct validity? Does it somehow "get at" the various components of this complex idea? *You can only ask whether the measure actually measures the components if the construct is valid.* Lots of constructs in the social sciences—intelligence, ethnicity, machismo, feminism, being conservative—are controversial and so are the measures for those constructs.

To grasp the idea of construct validity, think of testing a hypothesis that's based on theory. You might be testing it with a questionnaire or an experiment. If you use a questionnaire, you test the hypothesis by asking people questions—about their attitudes, their behavior, their possessions, their health, and so on. If you use an experiment, you test the hypothesis by exposing some people to an intervention and comparing their responses (their attitudes, their behaviors, etc.) to those of others who have not been exposed to the intervention. In both cases—in surveys and in experiments—you try to relate your measure of some causal variables to your measure of an outcome variable.

The question is: Do your measures "get at"—that is, actually measure—the construct or constructs you are studying?

Asking people, "How old are you?" has so much face validity that you hardly need to ask whether the instrument gets at the construct of chronological age. Does the balance-of-payments deficit of a country "get at" its place in the global economy? Something as complex as "place in the global economy" can hardly be measured with a single indicator like "balance of payments."

Does the Wechsler IQ test measure intelligence? Intelligence is a highly complex construct, but then the Wechsler test is a highly complex instrument. The whole idea behind its development was to get at the complexity of the construct of intelligence. With so much controversy about the construct of intelligence, though, you can see that construct validity is sometimes very difficult to achieve. Lots of constructs in the social sciences are controversial. Getting people to agree that a particular measure has high construct validity requires that they agree that the construct is valid in the first place.

Suppose you test the hypothesis that uneducated and unskilled women who have steady, if low-paying, jobs are more likely to leave physically abusive relationships than are women who have no income other than welfare. This hypothesis comes from the theory that lower-class women in industrial (or industrializing) societies who are financially independent of men will, among other things, lower their fertility and get out of abusive situations. You gather the data and the results are mixed. Some women do leave those abusive relationships, some don't.

Now the problem is: Do you question the measure of financial independence (the construct), or do you question the hypothesis and the theory it comes from? Perhaps the theory was wrong. Or perhaps the measure had low construct validity.

Criterion Validity

An instrument has high **criterion validity** if there is a close fit between the measures it produces and the measures produced by some other instrument that is known to be valid. This is the gold standard test.

A tape measure, for example, is known to be an excellent instrument for measuring height. If you knew that a man in our culture wore shirts with 35″ sleeves and pants with a 34″ inseam, you could bet that he was over six feet tall and be right more than 95% of the time. On the other hand, you might ask: "Why should I measure his inseam length and sleeve length to know *most of the time, in general,* how tall he is, when I could use a tape measure and know *all of the time, precisely* how tall he is?"

Indeed. If you want to measure someone's height, then use a tape measure. Don't substitute a lot of fuzzy proxy variables for something that's directly measurable by known, valid indicators. But if you want to measure things like quality of life or socioeconomic class—things that don't have well-understood, valid indicators—then a complex measure will just have to do until something simpler comes along. (See Box 2.1.)

You can tap the power of criterion validity for complex constructs with the **known group comparison** technique. If you develop a scale to measure political ideology, you could try it out on members of the American Civil Liberties Union and on members of the Christian Coalition. Members of the ACLU should get high "left" scores, and members of the CC should get high "right" scores. If they don't, then there's probably something wrong with the scale. In other words, the known-group scores are the criteria for the validity of your instrument.

A particularly strong form of criterion validity is **predictive validity**—whether an instrument lets you predict accurately something else you're interested in. "Stress" is a complex construct. It occurs when people interpret events as threatening to their lives. Some people interpret a bad grade on an exam as a threat to their whole life, while others just blow it off. Now, stress is widely thought to produce a lowered immune response and increase the chances of getting sick. A really good *measure* of stress, then, ought to predict the likelihood of getting sick.

Remember the life insurance problem? You want to predict whether someone is likely to die

> **Box 2.1**
> **Ockham's Razor**
>
> There is a strong preference in science for simpler explanations and measures over more complicated ones. This is called the principle of *parsimony*. It is also know as *Ockham's razor,* after William of Ockham (1285-1349), a medieval philosopher who coined the dictum *"non sunt multiplicanda entia praeter necessitatem,"* or "don't make things more complicated than they need to be."

in the next 365 days to know how much to charge him in premiums. Age and sex tell you a lot. But if you know people's weight, whether they smoke, whether they exercise regularly, what their blood pressure is, whether they have ever had any of a list of diseases, and whether they test-fly experimental aircraft for a living, then you can predict—with a higher and higher degree of accuracy—whether they will die within the next 365 days. Each piece of data—each component of a construct you might call "lifestyle"—adds to your ability to predict something of interest.

The Bottom Line

The bottom line on all this is that while various forms of validity can be demonstrated, Truth, with a capital T, is never final. We are never dead sure of anything in science. We try to get closer and closer to the truth by better and better measurement. All of science relies on concepts whose existence must ultimately be demonstrated by their effects. You can ram a car against a cement wall at 50 miles an hour and account for the amount of crumpling done to the radiator by referring to a concept called "force." The greater the force, the more crumpled the radiator. You demonstrate the existence of intelligence by showing how it predicts school achievement or monetary success.

The Problem with Validity

If you suspect that there is something deeply, desperately wrong with all this, you're right. The whole argument for the validity (indeed, the very existence) of something like intelligence is, frankly, circular: How do you know that intelligence exists? Because you see its effects in achievement. And how do you account for achievement? By saying that someone has achieved highly because they're intelligent. How do you know machismo exists? Because men dominate women in some societies. And how do you account for dominance behavior, like wife beating? By saying that wife beaters are acting out their machismo.

In the hierarchy of construct reality, then, force ranks way up there (after all, it's got several hundred years of theory and experimentation behind it), while things like intelligence and machismo are pretty weak by comparison. And yet, as I made clear in Chapter 1, the social and behavioral sciences are roaring successes, on a par with the physical sciences in terms of the effects they have on our lives every day. This is possible because social scientists have refined and tested many useful concepts and measurements for those concepts.

Ultimately, the validity of any concept—force in physics, the self in psychology, modernization in sociology and political science, acculturation in anthropology—depends on two things: (1) the utility of the device that measures it, and (2) the collective judgment of the scientific community that a concept and its measure are valid. In the end, we are left to deal with the effects of our judgments, which is just as it should be. Valid measurement makes valid data, but validity itself depends on the collective opinion of researchers.

CAUSE AND EFFECT

Cause and effect is among the most highly debated issues in the philosophy of knowledge (see Hollis [1996] for a review), but if your measurements of two variables are valid, then you can be reasonably confident that one variable causes another if four conditions are met.

(1) The two variables *covary*—that is, **as scores for one variable increase or decrease, scores for the other variable increase or decrease as well.**

(2) The covariation between the two variables is not *spurious*.

(3) There is a *logical time order* to the variables. **The presumed causal variable must always precede the other in time.**

(4) A *mechanism* is available that explains how an independent variable causes a dependent variable. There must, in other words, be a *theory*.

Condition 1: Covariation

When two variables are related they are said to *covary*. Covariation is also called *correlation* or simply *association*.

Association is not a *sufficient condition* for claiming a causal relation between two variables, but it is a *necessary condition*. Whatever else may be needed to establish cause and effect, you can't claim that one thing causes another if they aren't related in the first place.

Here are a few interesting covariations taken from recent literature:

(1) Sexual freedom for women tends to increase with the amount that women contribute to subsistence (Schlegel and Barry 1986).

(2) When eyewitnesses are pressured, they are more likely to pick a suspect out of a police line-up than if they are left alone to make their decision (Steblay 1997).

(3) The more that people of all ages are exposed to violence on television, the more likely they are to show aggressive or antisocial behavior (Paik and Comstock 1994).

(4) When married men and women are both employed full time, they spend the same amount of time in the various rooms of their house—except for the kitchen (Ahrentzen et al. 1989).

(5) Ground-floor, corner apartments occupied by students at big universities have a much higher chance of being burglarized than other units in the same apartment bloc (Robinson and Robinson 1997).

It is usually better, for establishing cause and effect, if variables are strongly and consistently related, but this is not always the case. These days, for example, people all over the world are making decisions about whether or not to use (or demand the use of) a condom as a part of sexual relations. These decisions might be made on the basis of many simultaneous factors, all of which are weakly, but causally, related to the final decision.

Some factors might be the education level of one or both partners, the level of income of one or both partners, the availability and cost of condoms, the amount of time that partners have been together, the amount of previous sexual experience of one or both partners, whether either or both partners know anyone personally who has died of AIDS, and so on. Each independent variable may contribute only a little to the outcome of the dependent variable (the decision that is finally made), but the contribution may be quite direct and causal in nature.

Condition 2: Lack of Spuriousness

Just as weak correlations can be causal, strong correlations can turn out not to be. When this happens, the original correlation is said to be *spurious*. There is a spurious correlation between the number of firefighters at a fire and the amount of damage done: the more firefighters, the more the insurance claim. Do firefighters cause fire damage? We know better: Both the amount of damage and the number of firefighters are caused by the size of the blaze. We need to **control** for this third variable—the size of the blaze—to understand what's really going on.

Dellino (1984) found an inverse relation between perceived quality of life and involvement with the tourism industry on the island of Exuma in the Bahamas. When he controlled for the size of the community (he studied several on the island), the original correlation disappeared. People in the more congested areas were more likely to score low on the perceived-quality-of-life index whether or not they were involved with tourism, while those in the small, outlying communities were more likely to score high on the index. People in the congested areas were also more likely to be involved in tourism-related activities, because that's where the tourists go.

Mwango (1986) found that people who are illiterate in Malawi were much more likely than those who are literate to brew beer for sale from part of their maize crop. The covariation vanished when he controlled for wealth, which causes both greater education (hence, literacy) and the purchase, rather than the brewing, of maize beer.

The list of spurious relations is endless, and it is not always easy to detect them for the frauds that they are. A higher percentage of men get lung cancer than women, but when you control for the length of time that people have smoked, the gender difference in carcinomas vanishes. Pretty consistently, young people accept new technologies more readily than older people. But in many societies, the relation between age and readiness to adopt innovations disappears when you control for level of education. Urban migrants from tribal groups often give up polygyny in Africa and Asia, but both migration *and* abandonment of polygyny are often caused by a third factor: lack of wealth.

Your only defense against spurious covariations is vigilance. No matter how obvious a covariation may appear, discuss it with a disinterested colleague, or with several colleagues. Be sure that they are people who have no stake whatever in telling you what you'd like to hear. Present your initial findings in open colloquia and in class seminars at your university or where you work. Beg people to find potentially spurious relations in your work. You'll thank them for it if they do.

Condition 3: Precedence, or Time Order

Besides a nonspurious association, something else is required to establish a cause-and-effect relation between two variables: a *logical time order*. Just as firefighters don't cause fires—they show up *after* the blaze starts—a propensity for high blood pressure comes *after* the fact of being African American. Low scores on math aptitude tests come *after* gender.

Unfortunately, things are not always so clear-cut. Does adoption of new technologies cause wealth, or is it the other way around? Does urban migration cause dissatisfaction with rural life, or the reverse? Does consumer demand cause new products to appear, or vice versa? Does the growth in the number of lawsuits cause more people to study law so that they can cash in, or does overproduction of lawyers cause more lawsuits?

What about the increase in elective surgery in the U.S.? Does the increased supply of physicians cause an increase in elective surgery, or does the demand for surgery create a surfeit of surgeons? Or are both caused by one or more external variables, like an increase in discretionary income in the upper middle class, or the fact that insurance companies pay more and more of Americans' medical bills?

Figure 2.4 shows several forms of time order between two variables. Read Figure 2.4a as "*A* is *antecedent* to *B*." Read Figure 2.4b as "*A* and *B* are antecedent to *C*." And read Figure 2.4c as "*A* is antecedent to *B*, which is an *intervening variable* antecedent to *C*." A lot of data analysis in social science is about understanding and controlling for antecedent and intervening variables—about which much, much more in Chapters 15 and 16.

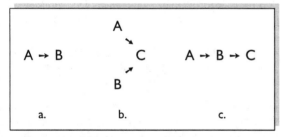

Figure 2.4 Time Order between Two or Three Variables

Condition 4: Theory

Finally, even when you have established nonspurious, consistent, strong covariation, as well as a logical time sequence for two or more variables, you need a *theory* that *explains* the association. Theories are good ideas about how things work.

One of my favorite good ideas in social science about how things work is called *cognitive dissonance theory* (Festinger 1957). It's based on the insight that (1) people can tell when their beliefs about what ought to be don't match their perception of how things really are, and (2) this causes an uncomfortable feeling. The feeling is called cognitive dissonance. People then have a choice: They can live with the dissonance (be uncomfortable); change the external reality (fight city hall); or change their beliefs (usually the path of least resistance, but not necessarily the "easy way out").

Dissonance theory helps explain why some people accept new technologies that they initially rejected out of fear for their jobs: Once a technology is entrenched, and there is no longer any chance of getting rid of it, it becomes easier to change one's ideas about what's good and bad than it is to live with dissonance. It explains why some men change their beliefs about women working outside the home: Economic necessity drives women into the work force and it becomes painful to hold onto the idea that that's the wrong thing for women to do.

On the other hand, some people leave their jobs rather than accept new technologies, and some men still are not supportive of women working outside the home—even when those men depend on their wives' income to make ends meet. These are examples of a general theory that fails to predict local phenomena. It leads us to seek more data and more understanding to predict when cognitive dissonance theory is insufficient as an explanation.

The literature is filled with good ideas for how to explain covariations. There is a well-known correlation between average daily temperature and the number of violent crimes reported to police (Anderson 1989; Cohn 1990). The association between temperature and violence, however, is neither as direct nor as simple as the correlational evidence might make it appear. Routine activity theory states that if you want to understand what people are doing, start with what they usually do. Social contact theory states that if you want to understand the probability for any event that involves human interaction, then start by mapping activities that place people in contact with one another. Both of these theories are examples of Ockham's famous razor (see Box 2.1).

Well, following routine activity theory, we find out that people are likely to be indoors, working, or going to school in air-conditioned comfort, during the hottest part of the day from Monday through Friday. Following social contact theory, we find that on very hot days, people are more likely to go out during the evening hours—which places them in more contact with one another. People also drink more alcohol during the evening hours. These facts, not temperature per se, may account for violence. Applying these theories, Cohn and Rotton (1997) found that more crimes of violence are reported to police on hot days than on cool days, but those crimes are, in fact, more likely to occur during the cooler evening hours than during the hottest part of the day.

Many theories are developed to explain a purely local phenomenon and then turn out to have wider applicability. Anthropologists have noticed, for example, that when men from polygynous African societies move to cities, they often give up polygyny. This consistent covariation is explained by the fact that men who move away from tribal territories in search of wage labor must abandon their land, their houses, and the shared labor of their kinsmen. Under those conditions, they simply cannot afford to provide for more than one wife, much less the children that multiple wives produce. The relation between urbanization and changes in marriage customs is explained by antecedent and intervening variables.

As you read the literature in social science, you'll see references to lots of theories. Contagion theory invokes a "copycat mechanism" to explain why suicides are more likely to come in batches when one of them is widely publicized in the press. Relative deprivation theory is based on the insight that people compare themselves to specific peer groups, not to the world at large. It explains why sociology professors don't feel all that bad about engineering professors earning a lot of money, but hate it if psychologists or anthropologists in their university get significantly higher salaries. World systems theory proposes that the world's economies and political bodies are part of a single capitalist system that has a core and a periphery and that each nation can be understood in some sense by examining its place in that system.

All such theories start with one or two *primitive axioms*—things that are simply defined and that you have to take at face value. The definition of cognitive dissonance is an example: When people have inconsistent beliefs, or when they perceive things in the real world to be out of whack with their ideas of how things should be, they feel discomfort. This discomfort leads people to strive naturally toward cognitive consonance.

Neither the fact of dissonance nor the need for consonance is ever explained. They are primitive axioms. *How* people deal with dissonance and *how* they try to achieve consonance are areas for empirical research. That people have reference groups to which they compare themselves doesn't get explained, either. It, too, is a primitive axiom, an assumption, from which you deduce some results. The results are predictions, or hypotheses, that you then go out and test.

The ideal in science is to deduce a prediction from theory and to test the prediction. That's the culture of science. The way social science really works much of the time is that you don't predict results, you *postdict* them. You analyze your data, come up with findings, and explain the findings after the fact.

There is nothing wrong with this. Knowledge and understanding can come from good ideas before you collect data or after you collect data. You must admit, though, there's a certain panache in making a prediction, sealing it in an envelope, and testing it. Later, when you take the prediction out of the envelope and it matches your empirical findings, you get a lot of points.

THE KALYMNIAN CASE: EXPLAINING WHY PEOPLE RISK THEIR LIVES

Here's an example of explaining findings after the fact. In my experience, it's pretty typical of how social scientists develop, refine, and change their minds about theories.

In my fieldwork in 1964-65 on the island of Kalymnos, Greece, I noticed that young sponge divers (in their 20s) were more likely to get the bends than were older divers (those over 30). (The bends is a crippling malady that affects divers who come up too quickly after a long time in deep water.) I also noticed that younger divers were more productive than very old divers (those over 45), but not more productive than those in their middle years (30-40).

As it turned out, younger divers were subject to much greater social stress to demonstrate their daring and to take risks with their lives—risks that men over 30 had already put behind them. The younger divers worked longer under water (gathering more sponges), but they came up faster and were consequently at higher risk of bends. The middle group of divers made up in experience for the shortened time they spent in the water, so they maintained their high productivity at lower risk of bends. The older divers were feeling the effects of infirmity brought on by years of deep diving, hence their productivity was lowered, along with their risk of death or injury from bends.

Of course, the real question was: What *caused* the young Kalymnian divers to engage in acts that placed them at greater risk?

My first attempt at explaining all this was pretty lame. I noticed that the men who took the most chances with their lives had a certain rhetoric and swagger. They were called *levedhis* by other divers and by their captains. I concluded that somehow these men had more *levedhia* and that that made them higher risk takers. In fact, this is what many of my informants told me. Young men, they said, feel the need to show their manhood, and that's why they take risks by staying down too long and coming up too fast.

The problem with this cultural explanation was that it just didn't explain anything. Yes, the high risk takers swaggered and exhibited something we could label "machismo." But what good did it do to say that lots of machismo caused people to dive deep and come up quickly? Where did young men get this feeling, I asked? That's just how young men are, my informants told me. I supposed that there could be something to this testosterone-poisoning theory, but it didn't seem adequate.

Eventually, I saw that the swaggering behavior and the values voiced about manliness were cultural ways to ratify, not explain, the high-risk diving behavior. Both the diving behavior and the ratifying behavior were the product of a third variable, called *platika*. (I was led to understanding this from materialist theory, which states that conditions in the infrastructural and structural sectors of society [the environment, the economy, the political system, etc.] take precedence over superstructural conditions [the culture].)

Divers traditionally took their entire season's expected earnings in advance, before shipping out in April for the six-month sponge fishing expedition in North Africa. By taking their money (*platika*) in advance, they placed themselves in debt to the boat captains. Just before they shipped out, the divers would pay off the debts that their families had accumulated during the preceding year. By the time they went to sea, the divers were nearly broke and their families started going into debt again for food and other necessities.

In the late 1950s, synthetic sponges began to take over the world markets, and young men on Kalymnos left for overseas jobs rather than go into sponge fishing. As divers left the island, and as living costs escalated, the money that the remaining divers commanded in advance went up. But with the price of sponge stable or dropping, due to competition with synthetics, the boat captains kept losing profits. Consequently, they put more pressure on the divers to produce more sponge, to stay down longer, and to take greater risks. This resulted in more accidents on the job (Bernard 1967, 1987).

Note that in all the examples of theory I've just given, the predictions and the post hoc explanations, I didn't have to quote a single statistic—not even a percentage score. That's because theories are qualitative. Ideas about cause and effect are based on insight; they are derived from either qualitative or quantitative observations and are initially expressed in words. *Testing* causal statements—finding out *how much* they explain rather than *whether* they seem to be plausible explanations—requires quantitative observations. But theory construction—explanation itself—is the quintessential qualitative act.

Chapter 2
Review

KEY CONCEPTS

Chapter 2
Summary

SUMMARY

❖ Social research is about variables—that is, about characteristics of people, countries, organizations, or other units of analysis—and how variables are related to one another.

❖ A controversial foundation of modern social research is operationism, which involves making absolutely explicit how measure variables are measured.
  ◆ The main advantage of operationism is that researchers can replicate one another's work and build cumulative knowledge.
  ◆ The main disadvantage of operationism is that it forces us to measure complex variables—like compassion, religiosity, and political orientation—using simple tools. There is, then, the risk of trivializing the process of research.
  ◆ On balance, more social scientists rely on operationism than criticize it, but this varies across the social science disciplines.

❖ Measurement in the social sciences can be at the nominal, ordinal, or interval/ratio level.
  ◆ Ratio variables have a true zero point.
  ◆ The rule is always to measure at the highest level of measurement possible. You can turn a variable measured at the ratio level into an ordinal or a nominal variable, but you can't go the other way.

❖ In developing measures for variables, researchers are concerned with the problems of reliability, validity, precision, and accuracy.
  ◆ Reliability is a necessary but insufficient condition for validity. Validity is never proven absolutely, but is a goal toward which we strive.
  ◆ Theory is explanation, which involves establishing an association between variables, eliminating the possibility that the association is spurious, establishing a logical time order, and developing a real-life mechanism that links the variables in a cause-effect relation.

EXERCISES

1. Ask 20 people a question that requires a self-report of behavior. For example, ask, "How many times during the last month have you cut class?" Then, ask the same people, "How many times during the last week have you cut class?" At the end of the interview, ask people to explain how they figured out what to say in answering your question. Did people think about and count up the actual incidents, or did they estimate the number of incidents? If they estimated, then ask them how they did that and try to understand the rules of inference they used.

   Calculate the per-week average for the one-month question and the average for the one-week question. Are the two averages the same?

2. Common wisdom has it that as people grow older, their idea of how old you have to be to be middle aged changes. To test this hypothesis, produce a copy of Figure 2.3 on a blank sheet of paper and use that instrument to collect some data from people of different ages.

3. Here is a list of adjectives, each of which is a concept that is of interest to social researchers. Try to conceptualize and operationalize these concepts that describe characteristics of individual people: poor, religious, macho, affluent, abusive. Suppose we want to array the countries of the world according to how much economic freedom and how much political freedom their citizens have. How can we conceptualize and operationalize economic and political freedom?

4. Using concrete examples, explain the characteristics of nominal, ordinal, and interval/ratio measurements. How would you measure each of the following, using at least two different levels of measurement? (a) age; (b) income; (c) family size.

5. Discuss the difference between validity and reliability. Why is it so hard to establish validity?

6. Ask some people if they consider themselves to be "politically liberal" or "politically conservative." Some people will find the question unanswerable, but some people will answer the question. Repeat this until you have data from 20 people. This question will create data at the nominal level of measurement. Next, ask those same 20 people who answered your first question whether they consider themselves very liberal (or very conservative), somewhat liberal (conservative), or mildly liberal (conservative). This will create some data at the ordinal level of measurement.

   Finally, ask those same 20 people a series of focused-issue questions. Here are a few examples: (a) Are you in favor of an adult woman's right to an abortion, entirely at her own discretion, or are you opposed to women having that right? (b) Are you in favor of the death penalty for premeditated murder or are you opposed to the death penalty for that crime? (c) Are you in favor of sending our troops to [fill in whatever country is in the news at the moment] to fight a ground war or are you opposed to sending troops?

These questions, or questions like them, will create data at the nominal level of measurement. Keep careful track of the reactions of your respondents and write up your findings. Among other things, you may find that people who say they are very conservative or very liberal fail to answer specific-issue questions in ways you might expect. Why is that?

FURTHER READING

The language and logic of social research. Paul Lazarsfeld and Donald Campbell are two of the most important methodologists in the history of social research. They and their colleagues and students have had an enormous impact on the language we use to describe the methods and logic of social research. Some classic works include Campbell and Overman (1988), Campbell and Stanley (1963), Cook and Campbell (1979), Lazarsfeld (1993), Lazarsfeld and Rosenberg (1955), and Merton and Lazarsfeld (1950). Gubrium and Holstein (1997) discuss the language of qualitative social research.

Operationism. The original statement of operationism (also called operationalism) is Bridgman (1927). The concept was taken up by many early methodologists, like Lundberg (1942, 1964). While I remain an advocate of operationism, many researchers today find it too confining. For a strong critique, see Lincoln and Guba (1985).

Measurement in the social sciences. There is a huge literature on measurement of particular variables in the social and behavioral sciences. The classic work on levels of measurement is by Stevens (1946). Authoritative texts on the theory of measurement in general include Blalock (1974), Coombs (1964), and Nunnally (1978). Lester and Bishop (1997) and Miller (1991) are resources for finding tests and scales that you can use or adapt for your own research. More about developing scales in Chapter 8.

Interrater reliability. There are several measurements for interrater reliability. One that is widely used is called kappa, from Cohen (1960). See Chapter 12 for details.

Construct validity. For further discussions of this and other subtle issues in validating measures and instruments, see the historic work by Campbell and Fiske (1959) and Fiske (1982).

Informant accuracy. The problem of informant accuracy is of interest to researchers across the social sciences. Health care behavior, alcohol consumption, and child abuse are just a few of the many areas of research in which informant accuracy plays a crucial role in the validity of data and findings. See Bernard et al. (1984) for a review of the problem. See Jackson and Nuttall (1997) on accuracy of reports of child abuse. See Tanur (1992) on the problem of respondent inaccuracies in survey research. See Ricci et al. (1995) for research on the accuracy of respondents in recalling their use of time. See Freeman et al. (1987) on some cognitive bases of informant inaccuracy.

The BSRI and the PAQ. The Bem Sex Role Inventory (BSRI) and the Spence/Helmreich Personality Attribute Questionnaire (PAQ) have been used in hundreds of studies. Note that these scales are used just as much for measuring characteristics of men as of women. For some recent uses of the BSRI with a variety of populations, see Burn et al. (1996), Chung (1996), Harris (1997), and Long and Martinez (1997). For recent uses of the PAQ, see Belansky and Boggiano (1994), Green and Kenrick (1994), Ruffing-Rahal et al. (1998), and Wark and Krebs (1996). Lippa (1991) is a good example of a study in which both the PAQ and the BSRI were used.

The AWS. See Spence and Hahn (1997) for recent work evaluating the change in American college students' attitudes toward women since 1972. See Twenge (1997) for a meta analysis of 71 studies in which the AWS was applied from 1972 to 1995.

The culture of poverty. On Lewis's ideas about the culture of poverty, see Harvey and Reed (1996) and Morris (1996).

Theory. For a general overview of how theory is constructed in the social sciences, see Stinchcombe (1968). See Harris (1979) for a discussion of the foundations of materialist theory in the social sciences. For further reading and more points of view, see Baert (1998), Barnes (1995), Craib (1997), Kincaid (1996), and Winch (1990). Each of the social sciences has developed a body of theory to account for, or explain, the particular phenomena on which it focuses. For example, see Cordella and Siegel (1996) and Henry and Einstadter (1998) in criminology, see Moody (1990) in nursing research, and see Mayadas et al. (1997) in social work.

3 PREPARING FOR RESEARCH

IN THIS CHAPTER:

❖ INTRODUCTION

This chapter is about some of the things that go on before data are collected and analyzed. First, I'll take you through the ideal research process and compare that to how research really gets done. I'll discuss the problem of choosing problems—how do I know what to study?—and I'll give you some pointers on how to scour the literature so you can benefit from the work of others when you start a research project.

I'll have a lot more to say about the ethics of social research in this chapter—choosing a research problem involves decisions that can have serious ethical consequences—and a lot more about theory, too. Method and theory, it turns out, are closely related.

THE IDEAL RESEARCH PROCESS

Despite all the myths about how research is done, it's actually a messy process that's cleaned up in the reporting of results. Figure 3.1 shows how the research process is supposed to work in the ideal world:

First, a theoretical problem is formulated.

Next, an appropriate site and method are selected.

Then, data are collected and analyzed.

Finally, the theoretical proposition with which the research was launched is either challenged or supported.

In fact, all kinds of practical and intellectual issues get in the way of this neat scheme. In the end, research papers are written so that the chaotic aspects of research are not emphasized, and the orderly inputs and outcomes are.

I see nothing wrong with this: It would be a monumental waste of precious space in books and journals to describe the *real* research process for every project that's reported. Besides, every seasoned researcher knows just how messy it all is, anyway. On the other hand, you shouldn't have to become a highly experienced researcher before you're let in on the secret of how it's really done.

A REALISTIC APPROACH

There are five questions to ask yourself about every research question you are thinking about pursuing. Most of these can also be asked about potential research sites and research methods. If you answer these questions honestly (at least to yourself), chances are you'll do good research every time. If you cheat on this test, even a teeny

bit, chances are you'll regret it. The questions, in no particular order, are

(1) Does this topic (or research site, or data-collection method) really interest me?

(2) Is this a problem that is amenable to scientific inquiry?

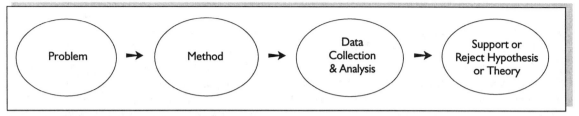

Figure 3.1 How Research Is Supposed to Work

(3) Are adequate resources available to investigate this topic? to study this population at this particular research site? to use this particular data-collection method?

(4) Will my research question, or the methods I want to use, lead to unresolvable ethical problems?

(5) Is the topic of theoretical or practical interest?

Personal Interest

The first thing to ask about any potential research question is: Am I really excited about this? Researchers do their best work when they are genuinely having fun, so don't do boring research when you can choose any topic you like.

Of course, you can't always choose any topic you like. In contract research, you sometimes have to take on a research question that a client finds interesting but that you find deadly dull. The most boring research I've ever done was on a contract where my co-workers and I combined ethnographic and survey research of rural homeowners' knowledge of fire prevention and their attitudes toward volunteer fire departments. This was in 1973. I had young children at home, and the research contract paid me a summer salary. It was honest work and I delivered a good product to the agency that supported the project. But I never wrote up the results for publication.

By comparison, that same year I did some contract research on the effects of coed prisons

on homosexuality among male and female inmates. I was very interested in that study, and it was much easier to spend the extra time and effort polishing the contract reports for publication (Killworth and Bernard 1974).

I've caught many students doing research for term projects, M.A. theses, and even doctoral dissertations simply out of convenience and with no enthusiasm for the topic. If you are not interested in a research question, then no matter how important other people tell you it is, don't bother with it. If others are so sure that it's a dynamite topic of great theoretical significance, let *them* study it.

The same goes for research populations. If you select a topic of interest, and then try to test it on a population in which you have no interest, your research will probably suffer. Some nursing researchers enjoy working in the maternity ward, while others are drawn to pediatric oncology. The maternity ward is filled with children being born, and the oncology ward with children who are facing death. It doesn't take much to imagine that some people who love working around newborns are going to be less than enthusiastic about doing research in pediatric oncology.

It doesn't matter whether you're going to do experiments, conduct a telephone survey, or do in-depth ethnographic interviews: Enthusiasm counts for a lot in the research business. Federal prisons and Wall Street banking firms are both complex organizations. But they are very, very different kinds of places to spend time in, so if you are going to study a complex organization, check your gut first and make sure you're excited about where you're going. It's really hard to conduct penetrating, in-depth interviews over a period of a several weeks to a year if you aren't interested in the lives of the people you're studying.

And if you think it's tough to run personal interviews on a topic you're bored with, try making up and administering a 10-page questionnaire on a topic of no interest to you. Or try designing an experiment in which you have to run subjects for months on end and where you have no personal stake in the results. It's not just deadly dull; it's a recipe for bad research.

You don't need any justification for your interest in studying a particular group of people or a particular topic. Personal interest is . . . well, personal. So ask yourself: Will my interest be sustained there? If the answer is no, then reconsider. Accessibility of a research site or the availability of funds for the conduct of a survey are pluses, but by themselves they're not enough to make good research happen.

Science vs. Nonscience

If you're really excited about a research topic, then the next question is: Is this a topic that can be studied by the methods of science? If the answer is no, then no matter how much fun it is, and no matter how important it seems, don't even try to make a scientific study of it. Either let someone else do it or use a different approach.

Consider a scholar who asks the empirical question "How often do derogatory references to women occur in the Old Testament?" So long as the concept of "derogatory" has been *intersubjectively* well defined, this question can be answered by applying the scientific method. You simply look through the corpus of data and count the instances that turn up. Recall that intersubjectiv-

ity means that **researchers agree on what constitutes an instance of some variable.** Intersubjectivity is a really useful concept because it eliminates the need for "objectivity," which everyone knows is impossible when dealing with conceptual variables like "derogatoriness."

But suppose the researcher asks: "Does the Old Testament offer support for unequal pay for women today?" This question is simply not answerable by the scientific method. It is no more answerable than the question "Is Rachmaninoff's music better than that of Tchaikovsky?" Or "Is it morally correct to mainstream slightly retarded children in grades K-6?" Or "Is Britain's parliamentary system or the U.S.'s presidential system a better form of democracy?" Or "Should the remaining hunting-and-gathering bands of the world be preserved just the way they are and kept from being spoiled by modern civilization?"

Whether or not a study is a scientific one depends first on the nature of the question being asked and *then* on the methods used.

I can't stress too often or too strongly that when I talk about using the scientific method I'm *not* talking about numbers. In science, whenever a research problem can be investigated with quantitative measurement, numbers are more than just desirable; they're required. On the other hand, there are many intellectual problems for which quantitative measures are not yet available. Those problems require qualitative measurement.

First-pass descriptions of processes (preparing for surgery, putting on makeup, setting the table for Thanksgiving), events (weddings, football games, art shows), or systems of nomenclature (kinds of trucks, ways to avoid getting AIDS, kinship terms, disease terms, ethnobotanical terms) require words, not numbers. Dorothy Holland and Debra Skinner (1987) asked some university women to list the kinds of guys there are. They got a list of words like "creep," "hunk," "nerd," "jerk," "sweetie pie," and so on. Then they asked some women, for each kind: "Is this someone you'd like to date?" The yes-no answers are nominal—that is, qualitative—measurement.

We'll get back to this kind of systematic, qualitative data collection in Chapter 7.

Resources

The next question to ask is whether adequate resources are available for you to conduct your study. There are three major kinds of resources: time, money, and people. What may be adequate for some projects may be inadequate for others. Be totally honest with yourself about this issue.

Time

Some social research projects can be completed in just a few days, while others take years. When anthropologists go off to do an ethnographic study of a culture that is very different from their own, they typically spend a year or more in the field—before they even get to the data analysis and write-up. Some experiments in social psychology can also take months or years to set up, especially in evaluation studies. By contrast, the data-collection phase of surveys and of some types of experiments might be completed in a matter of weeks.

> It makes no sense to select a topic that requires two semesters' work when you have one semester in which to do the research.

If you are doing research for a term project, the topic has to be something you can look at in a matter of a few months—and squeezing the research into a schedule of other classes, at that. It makes no sense to select a topic that requires two semesters' work when you have one semester in which to do the research. This effort to cram 10 gallons of water into a 5-gallon can is futile and quite common. Don't do it.

Money

Many things come under the umbrella of money. Equipment is essentially a money issue, as is salary or subsistence for you and other persons involved in the research. Funds for assistants, computer time, supplies, and travel all have to be calculated before you can actually conduct a major research project. No matter how interesting it is to you, and no matter how important it may seem theoretically, if you haven't got the resources to use the right methods, skip it for now.

Naturally, most people do not have the money it takes to mount a major research effort. That's why there are granting agencies. Writing proposals is a special craft. It pays to learn it early. Research grants for M.A. research are typically between $1,000 and $5,000. Grants for doctoral research are typically between $5,000 and $25,000. If you spend 100 hours working on a grant proposal that brings you $10,000 to do your research, that's $100/hr for your time. If you get turned down and spend another 100 hours rewriting the proposal, that's still $50 an hour for your time if you're successful. Where else can a student find interesting work at that kind of pay?

If your research requires the comparison of two panels of respondents using face-to-face interviews and you have only enough money to do telephone interviews, ask yourself if you can accomplish your research goal by using telephone interviews. If you can't, then can you accomplish it by cutting out the comparison and running the more expensive interviews on just one group? Ask yourself whether it's worthwhile pursuing your research if it has to be scaled down to fit available resources. If the answer is no, then find another topic.

People

"People" includes you and others involved in the research, as well as those whom you are studying. Does the research require that you personally do multiple regression? If it does, then are you prepared to acquire that skill? Does the research require access to or acceptance by a particular group of people, like ambulance paramedics? Do you have access to that group? Does the research require that you speak Haitian Creole? If so, are you willing to put in the time and effort to learn that language? If the research can be done with interpreters, are competent people available at a cost that you can handle?

Will the research require that you interview elite members of the society you are studying—like medical malpractice lawyers, plastic surgeons, Lutheran priests? Do you have access to these populations? Will you be able to gain their cooperation? Or will they tell you to get lost or, even worse, provide you with perfunctory answers to your questions. Better not to do the study in the first place than to wind up with useless data.

THE ETHICS OF SOCIAL RESEARCH

I wish I could give you a list of criteria against which you could measure the "ethicalness" of every research idea you ever come up with. Unfortunately, it's not so simple. The fact is, what is popularly ethical research today may become popularly unethical tomorrow, and vice versa.

During World War II, many social scientists worked for what would today be called the Department of Defense, and they were applauded as patriots for lending their expertise to the war effort. Twenty-five years later, during the Vietnam War, social scientists who worked for the Department of Defense were excoriated. Today, social scientists are again working for the Department of Defense. Is this simply because that's where the jobs are?

Perhaps. Times and popular ethics change. Here are two famous social science experiments that challenged the boundaries of ethics. Discussion about these experiments—one conducted in 1963, the other in 1971—continues to this day.

Milgram's Obedience Experiment

It's because times and popular ethics do change that Stanley Milgram was able to conduct his famous experiment on obedience (1963). Milgram duped people into thinking that they were taking part in an experiment on how well human beings learn under conditions of punishment. The subjects in the experiment were "teachers." The "learners" were Milgram's accomplices.

The so-called learners sat behind a wall, where they could be heard by subjects, but not seen. The subject sat at a panel of 30 switches. Each switch supposedly delivered 30 more volts than the last, and the switches were clearly labeled from "Slight Shock" (15 volts) all the way up to "Danger: Severe Shock" (450 volts). Each time the learner made a mistake on a word-recall test, the subject was told to give the learner a bigger shock.

Milgram paid each subject $4.50 up front (about $20 in 1999 dollars). That made the subjects feel obligated to complete the experiment in which they were about to participate. He also gave subjects a little test shock—45 volts (the second lever on the 30-lever panel). That made people believe that the punishment they'd be delivering to the so-called learners was for real.

As the learners made mistakes, they expressed greater and greater discomfort with the increasing electric shock level that they were supposedly enduring. They began pounding on the wall separating them from the subject and pleading to be let out of the experiment.

All those reactions by the learners were tape-recorded so that subjects would hear the same things. The experimenter, in a white lab coat, kept telling the subject to administer the shocks—saying things like: "You have no choice. You must go on." A third of the subjects obeyed orders and administered what they thought were lethal shocks. Many subjects protested, but were convinced by the researchers in white coats that it was all right to follow orders.

Until Milgram did his troubling experiments (he did many of them, under different conditions and in different cities), it had been very easy to scoff at Nazi war criminals, whose defense was that they were "just following orders." Milgram's experiment taught us that perhaps a third of Americans had it in them to follow orders until they killed innocent people.

Was Milgram's experiment unethical? Did his research subjects suffer emotional harm when they thought about what they'd done? If you were among Milgram's subjects who obeyed to the end, would you be haunted by this? This was one of the issues raised by critics at the time.

Of course, Milgram *debriefed* the participants. That's where you **make sure that people who have just participated in an experiment know that it had all been make-believe,** and you **help them deal with their feelings about the experiment.** Milgram tested over 369 people in his series of experiments (Milgram 1977b). A year after the experiments ended, he sent them each a copy of his report and a follow-up questionnaire. Ninety-two percent of them returned the questionnaire and 84% said that, after reading the report and thinking about their experience, they were glad or very glad to have taken part in the experiment. Fifteen percent said they were neutral about the whole thing, and about 1% said they were sorry or very sorry to have taken part (Milgram 1977a).

I doubt that the experiment would ever get by a Human Subjects Review Committee at any university in the United States today. Still, it was less costly, and more ethical, than the natural experiments carried out at My Lai, or Chatilla—the Vietnamese village and Lebanese refugee camps—whose civilian inhabitants were wiped out by American and Lebanese soldiers, respectively, "under orders." Those experiments, too, showed what ordinary people are capable of doing—except in those cases, real people really got killed.

Zimbardo's Stanford Prison Experiment

In 1971, Philip Zimbardo and his colleagues built a mock prison in the basement of the psychology building at Stanford University. They put an ad in the newspaper, asking for college student volunteers to participate in a study of prison life. They screened 75 young men and chose 21 whom they felt were the most mature and stable—people who could take the planned two weeks of role playing in the "Stanford County Prison."

These researchers had a rude shock ahead of them. "Most dramatic and distressing to us," they wrote at the end of the experiment, "was the ease with which sadistic behavior could be elicited from individuals who were not 'sadistic types' and the frequency with which acute emotional breakdowns could occur in men selected precisely for their emotional stability" (Haney et al. 1973:89).

The 21 recruits, all White men between ages 17 and 30, were told that if they were assigned to be prisoners, they should expect to go through a hard time for two weeks—no physical violence would be tolerated, but prisoners would give up privacy and other basic rights for the duration of the experiment. The participants would get $15 per day for their participation in the study (about $50 in 1999 dollars), and could quit at any time, but they would forfeit the money if they did so.

Once everyone was on board and fully briefed, the experimenters assigned 10 of the men randomly to be prisoners and 11 to be guards. The guards were issued uniforms, whistles, and nightsticks and were told they would serve on three-man, eight-hour shifts around the clock. Then everyone went home to wait.

When the time came for the experiment to begin, the Palo Alto City Police Department sent real officers to the homes of the "prisoners." The police handcuffed the prisoners and hustled them off to jail, sometimes in full view of neighbors. The prisoners were fingerprinted, placed in a detention cell, and then taken to the makeshift prison at Stanford University, where the guards were waiting. There, they were stripped and sprayed with what they were told was a delousing solution (it was really deodorant). They were issued smocks, with a number painted on the front and back, and no underwear. They were made to stand for mug shots in the humiliating uniforms and were given work assignments, exercise periods, and movie rights.

Then they were assigned, randomly, three at a time, to 6- × 9-ft cells. The cell doors shut.

Though no physical violence was allowed, the guards quickly became verbally abusive and learned to use every bit of the power they had. Prisoners had to ask permission to light a cigarette, read a novel, write a letter, go to the toilet—permission that some of the guards arbitrarily denied. When the prisoners were allowed to go to the toilet, they were blindfolded and handcuffed and led, publicly, from their cells by some guards. Some guards called the prisoners "girls," referring to the smock uniforms.

The prisoners became docile and passive. During the debriefing, after the experiment, some prisoners said they thought that the roles had been defined by size, with the larger men assigned the role of guard. In fact, the roles had been assigned randomly and there was no difference in the average weight of the guards and prisoners.

Some guards, of course, tried not to get into this abusive behavior pattern. But they immediately bought into the norm of never interfering with another guard whose behavior they didn't approve. They went along to get along.

By the second day, the guards had defined eating and sleeping time as privileges, and four of the prisoners had gone into what the experimenters diagnosed as "extreme emotional depression . . . and acute anxiety," accompanied by crying and rage (ibid. 1973:81). These four were released from the experiment, as was a fifth who had to be treated for a psychosomatic rash that covered parts of his body. Three times a day, the guards took the prisoners out of the cells for a count. On the first day, the counts lasted a few minutes. By the fifth day, the counts were lasting hours.

Five prisoners stuck it out. The warden of the prison held a hearing and asked each of the five if he would forfeit the money he was due if he was paroled and released early from the experiment. Three of them said they would. By the time of the so-called parole hearing, the prisoners were owed $75 apiece—about $250 today. When they were told that any decision to parole them would have to be discussed with the staff, each prisoner went quietly back to his cell.

They didn't have to. They could have just quit what had become a very painful experience. "Yet, so powerful was the control which the situation had come to have over them, so much a reality had this simulated environment become . . . they returned to their cells to await a 'parole' decision by their captors" (ibid. 1973:93).

After six days, then, there were still two prisoners who wanted to continue, but the experiment was stopped. The researchers decided that they couldn't ethically continue. Besides, they had already learned enough to support Milgram's conclusion: Otherwise good people can be induced by circumstances to do evil things.

In a way, though, Zimbardo's experiment is even more frightening than Milgram's, something that Zimbardo himself recognized (Zimbardo 1973). There were no men in white lab coats telling the guards that they had to harass their charges into acute anxiety, depression, and psychosomatic rashes. Everyone, guards and prisoners alike, knew at the outset that they could get out by just saying they wanted out. Instead, these folks all picked up the roles they were assigned and just played them to the hilt. The guards had the freedom to define their role any way they wanted to—and defined it by becoming abusive at the first opportunity they had. The prisoners who were emotionally disturbed in the first two days didn't ask to be released.

What Does It All Mean?

Just because times, and ethics, seem to change does not mean that anything goes. All the major professional associations across the social sciences have developed codes of ethics for the conduct of research, for teaching, and for practice. Appendix F has the Internet addresses for those associations and for the codes of ethics.

These documents are not perfect, but they cover a lot of ground and are based on the accumulated experience of thousands of researchers who have grappled with ethical dilemmas over the past 50 years. Look at those codes of ethics regularly during the course of any research project, both to get some of the wisdom that has gone into them and to develop your own ideas about how the documents might be improved.

Don't get trapped into nihilistic relativism. Cultural relativism is a great antidote for overdeveloped ethnocentrism, but it's a poor philosophy to live by, or on which to make judgments about whether to participate in particular research projects. Can you imagine, say, a social scientist today, defending the human rights violations of Nazi Germany as just another expression of the richness of culture? Would you feel comfortable defending, on the basis of relativism, the so-called ethnic cleansing in the 1990s of Kosovar Albanians in Yugoslavia, or of Tutsi by Hutus in Rwanda? Or of American Indians by immigrant Europeans a hundred years earlier?

There is no value-free science. Everything that interests you as a potential research focus comes fully equipped with risks to you and to the people you study. In each case, all you can do (and *must* do) is assess the potential human costs and the potential benefits. And when I say "potential benefits," I mean to you, personally, not just to humanity through the accumulation of knowledge.

Don't hide from the fact that you are interested in your own glory, your own career, your own advancement. It's a safe bet that your colleagues are interested in their career advancement, too. We have all heard of cases in which a scientist put his or her own career aggrandizement above the health and well-being of others. This is devastating to science and to scientists, but it happens when otherwise good, ethical people (1) convince themselves that they are doing something noble for humanity, rather than for themselves; and (2) consequently fool themselves into thinking that *that* justifies their hurting others.

When you make these assessments of costs and benefits, be prepared to come to decisions that may not be shared by all your colleagues. Remember the problem of the relation between darkness of skin color and various measures of life success (including wealth, health, and longevity)? Would you, personally, be willing to participate in a study of this problem? Some readers would, while others would not.

Suppose the study was likely to show that a small but significant percentage of the variation in earning power in the United States was predictable from (*not* caused by) darkness of skin color. Some would argue that this would be useful evidence in the fight against racism and would jump at the chance to do the investigation. Others would argue that the evidence would be used by racists to do further damage in our society and so the study should simply not be done lest the information it produces fall into the wrong hands.

There is no answer to this dilemma. Above all, be honest with yourself. Ask yourself: Is this ethical? If the answer is no, then skip it; find another topic. Once again, there are plenty of interesting research questions that won't put you into a moral bind.

THEORY: EXPLANATION AND PREDICTION

All research is specific. Whether you conduct ethnographic or questionnaire research, do content analysis or run an experiment, the first thing you do is *describe a process* or *investigate a relation* among some variables in a population. To get from description to theory is a big leap and involves asking: "What causes the phenomenon to exist in the first place?" and "What does this phenomenon cause?" Theory, then, is about explaining and predicting things.

It may seem odd to talk about theory in a textbook on research methods, but you can't design research until you choose a research question, and research questions depend crucially on theory. A good way to understand what theory is about is to pick a phenomenon that begs to be explained and to look at competing explanations for it. See which explanation you like best. Do that for a few phenomena and you'll quickly discover which paradigm you identify with. That will make it easier to pick research problems and to develop hypotheses that you can go off and test.

Here is an example of something that begs to be explained: Everywhere in the world, there is a very small chance that children will be killed or maimed by their parents. However, stepchildren have a higher chance of being killed by their parents than do biological children. That is, the chance that a child is killed by a parent is much higher if a child has one or more nonbiological parents than if the child has two biological parents (Lightcap et al. 1982; Daly and Wilson 1988). All those evil-stepparent folktales appear to be based on more than fantasy.

Alternative Paradigms for Building Theories

One explanation is that this is biological—in the genes, as it were. Male gorillas are known to kill off the offspring of new females they bring into their harem. Humans, the reasoning goes, have a bit of that instinct in them, too. They fight the impulse, but over millions of cases, it's bound to come out sometimes. This is called a *sociobi-ological* explanation.

Another explanation is that it's cultural. Yes, it's more common for children to be killed by nonbiological than by biological parents, but this kind of mayhem is more common in some cultures than in others. Furthermore, though killing children is rare everywhere, in some cultures mothers are more likely to kill their children, while in other cultures fathers are more likely to be the culprits in cases of child murder. This is because women and men learn different gender roles in different societies. So, the theory goes, we have to look at cultural differences for a true explanation of the phenomenon. This is called an *ideational* theory because it is based on what people think—on their ideas.

Yet another explanation is that, when adult men and women bring children to a second marriage, they know that their assets are going to be diluted by the claims the spouse's children have on those assets—immediate claims and claims of inheritance. This leads some of those people to harm their spouse's children from the former marriage. In a few cases, this causes death. This is a *materialist* theory.

Sociobiology, idealism, and materialism are *theoretical paradigms* or *theoretical perspectives*. They contain overarching rules for finding explanations of events. Each of these paradigms has many subtle variations.

Sociobiology, for example, is a cover term for a paradigm that stresses the biological basis of human behavior. Some variations of sociobiology are bioculturalism and biobehaviorism.

Idealism is a cover term for a paradigm that stresses internal states (attitudes, preferences, ideas, beliefs, values) as the basis for human behavior. Cultural explanations are idealist. Attitudinal explanations are idealist, too. Materialism is a cover term for a paradigm that stresses the primacy of structural and infrastructural forces—like the economy, power relations, the technology of production, demography, and environmental conditions—as the basis of human behavior.

Every time you want to explain a specific phenomenon, you apply the principles of your favorite paradigm and come up with a specific explanation. Why do Asian Americans have consistently high math scores on the SAT? The materialist perspective, the idealist perspective, and the sociobiological perspective generate different answers. Some scholars stress so-called Asian values (an ideational, or cultural, explanation), while others stress that the achieving behavior of Asian Americans is a reaction to racism (a materialist explanation). Neither of these explanations accounts for why the most discriminated-against minority in the U.S., Americans of African descent, have not done as well on standardized tests as Asian Americans have.

You hear a lot of stereotyped talk about this or that ethnic group being "naturally smart," but mostly you won't see any serious scientific explanations for achievement as something that's biologically based. Except when it comes to African Americans. About every 20 or 25 years since the beginning of the twentieth century, there have been dreadful, flawed academic studies purporting to show that biology—inferior genes—is the cause of low IQ scores by African Americans.

Every single time this has happened, the response by other academics has been swift and devastating to biological arguments about intelligence. And yet, the biological argument resurfaces every generation.

Now *that's* something that begs to be explained. What causes this periodic flight to biological explanations for social and economic inequality? It seems unlikely that the biological arguments advanced by some White academics is biologically driven behavior. Personally, I think a materialist explanation is more likely to be correct.

Why do women tend everywhere in the world to have nurturing roles? Can a change in material (economic, political, technological) conditions free women from their gender-typed roles? If you think that biology rules here, you'll be inclined to support biological theories about other phenomena as well. If you think economic and political forces cause values and behavior, then you'll be inclined to apply the materialist perspective in your search for explanations in general. If you think that culture—people's values—is of paramount importance, then you'll tend to apply the ideational perspective to come up with explanations.

Sociobiological, ideational, and materialist theories don't necessarily provide mutually exclusive explanations. Suppose that the materialist explanation for the greater likelihood of stepchildren to be battered has some merit. The explanation is appealing if we want to understand aggregate patterns—the big picture, as it were. But how would it play out on the ground? What would actually happen to cause some stepparents to harm their stepchildren?

We might theorize that stepparents who bring a lot of resources to a second marriage become personally frustrated by the possibility of having their wealth raided and diluted by their new spouse's children. Maybe the stepparent has competing obligations to biological children who are now with yet another family. Perhaps these frustrations cause some people to become violent. These ideational variables are, of course, testable.

Handwerker (1996b) found that stepparents in Barbados were, overall, no more likely to treat children violently than were biological parents. But the presence of a *stepfather* increased the likelihood that women battered their daughters and decreased the likelihood that women battered their sons. In the stepparent homes, women saw their daughters as potential competitors for resources available from their partner, and they saw sons as potential sources of physical protection and income.

And there was more. Powerful women (those who had their own sources of income) protected their children from violence, treated them affectionately, and elicited affection for them from their man. The probability that a son experienced an affectionate relationship with a biological father rose with the length of time the two lived together, but only for sons who had powerful mothers. Men battered powerless women and the children of powerless women, and powerless women battered their own children.

Is there a sociobiological basis for powerful spouses to batter powerless ones? Or is this all something that gets stimulated by material conditions, like poverty? Lots more research is needed on this fascinating question, but I think the points here are clear: (1) Different paradigms produce different answers to the same question, and (2) a lot of really interesting questions may have answers that are generated from several paradigms.

Idiographic vs. Nomothetic Theory

Theory comes in two basic sizes: elemental or *idiographic theory* and generalizing or *nomothetic theory*. An idiographic, or elemental, theory accounts for the facts in a single case. A nomothetic theory accounts for the facts in many cases. The more cases that a theory accounts for, the more nomothetic it is.

> *Idiographic theories explain a lot about a little; nomothetic theories explain less about a lot.*

When you first run into these concepts (which, despite the jargony sound of the words, have been in the dictionary for over a hundred years), it's easy to suppose that nomothetic is better than idiographic. But there's an exquisite trade-off:

Idiographic theories explain a lot about a little; nomothetic theories explain less about a lot.

The object, of course, is to develop theories that explain a lot about a lot. That's why I favor cultural materialism as the paradigm for building explanations: In my experience, it consistently produces theories that explain a lot about individual cases, and the knowledge it produces can be consistently aggregated into theories that explain more and more about clusters of cases.

A theory that explains why women in the U.S. earned 75 cents in 1998 for every dollar men earned is an idiographic theory. A theory that explains why women in all industrial societies earned less than men did in 1998 (controlling for currency differences, and differences in cost of living across countries) is more nomothetic. But it may not be immediately useful if what we need to know—because we are involved, say, in developing legislation on the matter—is why women in England or Sweden or Chile earn less than men.

The ratio of cents to the dollar is different in each of those countries because the political and economic realities of each country are different. A nomothetic theory that addresses the big picture is very interesting, and very important, but we often need explanations for the various cases just the same.

Most theory in the social sciences is, in fact, idiographic. Here are a few examples.

1. *The gender gap in U.S. presidential elections.* In 1920, when women got the vote in the U.S., politicians were afraid that women would swamp the polls and vote for things like child-support programs. For decades, neither of those fears materialized. Women were still only 34% of voters in 1954, and they were not voting in blocs for so-called women's issues.

In the 1990s, though, what those 1920s politicians predicted started coming true. The gender gap was an important part of Bill Clinton's victo-ries in both 1992 and 1996, as lots more women than men (59% vs. 41%) went to the polls and women voted overwhelmingly for Clinton and for programs traditionally associated with the Democratic Party.

Jeff Manza and Clem Brooks (1998) analyzed data from 11 presidential elections, from 1952 to 1992, to measure and explain the emerging gender gap. Their theory is that since (1) women are disadvantaged in the labor force (earning less than men do, hitting that glass ceiling in management, etc.), (2) women depend more on public sector jobs than men do, and (3) women need more help with child care and with welfare than men do, then (4) women's increasing participation in the labor force would naturally drive them toward the Democratic Party and away from the Republican Party in national elections.

A competing theory has women's political attitudes being raised by the women's movement, but as a materialist, I rather like Manza and Brooks's theory: Women's attitudes (and voting behavior) are explained by economic changes. (For more work on this issue, see Andersen and Cook 1985.)

2. *The case of the kitchen fires in India, also known as the "dowry death" phenomenon.* In 1977, the New Delhi police reported 311 deaths by kitchen fires of women, mostly young brides who were killed because their families had not delivered a promised dowry to the groom's family (Claiborne 1984). By 1987, the government of India reported 1,912 such dowry deaths of young women, and by 1994 the number was 5,199—over 14 per day (Thakur 1996). How to explain this phenomenon?

Gross (1992) theorizes that the phenomenon is a consequence of female hypergamy (marrying up) and dowry. Families that can raise a large dowry in India can marry off their daughter to someone of greater means. This has created a bidding war as the families of wealthier sons demand more and more for the privilege of marrying those sons.

Apparently, many families of daughters in India have gone into debt to accumulate the dowries. When they can't pay off the debt, some of the families of grooms have murdered the brides in faked "kitchen accidents," where kerosene stoves purportedly blow up. This gives the grooms' families a chance to get another bride whose families can deliver. (For more on this issue, see Van Willigen and Channa [1991] and Thakur [1996].)

3. *An idiographic theory derived entirely from ethnography.* Anthony Paredes has been doing research on the Poarch Band of Creek Indians in Alabama since 1971. When he began his research, the Indians were a remnant of an earlier group. They had lost the use of the Creek language, were not recognized by the U.S. government as a tribe, and had little contact with other Indians for decades. Yet, the Poarch Creek Indians had somehow maintained their identity.

Paredes wanted to know how the Indians had managed this. He did what he called "old-fashioned ethnography," including key-informant interviewing, and learned about a cultural revitalization movement that had been going on since the 1940s. That movement was led by some key people whose efforts over the years had made a difference. Paredes's description of how the Poarch Creek Indians held their cultural identity in the face of such odds is an excellent example of elemental, idiographic theory. As you read his account you feel you understand how it worked (see Paredes 1974, 1992).

So What's Wrong?

Nothing's wrong. Gross's intuitively appealing explanation for the kitchen fires in India rings true, but it doesn't explain why other societies that have escalating dowry don't have kitchen fires. Nor does it tell us why dowry persists in India despite its being outlawed since 1961, or why dowry—which, after all, only occurs in 7.5% of the world's societies—exists in the first place.

But Gross's theory is a first-class example of theory at the local level—where research begins. Manza and Brooks's theory about the rise of the gender gap in U.S. presidential elections seems plausible to me, but it doesn't explain why it took women in the U.S. so long to use their political power in presidential elections, and it doesn't tell us why women aren't putting Democrats into the U.S. House of Representatives and the Senate.

So what? Manza and Brooks's theory accounts for the facts on the ground in the case they deal with, and that's enough for a theory to do. Paredes's convincing theory of how the Poarch Creeks maintained their cultural identity doesn't tell us how other Native American groups managed to do this or why some groups did *not* manage it. Nor does it tell us anything about why other ethnic groups maintain or fail to maintain their identity in the U.S. or why ethnicity persists at all in the face of pressure from states on ethnic groups to assimilate. Fine. Others can try to make the theory more nomothetic.

In any science, much of the best work is at the idiographic level of theory making.

Nomothetic Theory

Nomothetic theories address questions like "So, what *does* account for the existence of dowry?"

Several theorists have tried to answer this question. Esther Boserup (1970) hypothesized that dowry should occur in societies where a woman's role in subsistence production is low. She was right, but many societies where women's productive effort is of low value do *not* have dowry.

Gaulin and Boster (1990) offered sociobiological theory that predicts dowry in stratified societies that have monogamous or polyandrous marriage. They tested their theory on Murdock and White's (1969) standard cross-cultural sample of 186 societies. Gaulin and Boster's theory works better than Boserup's—it misclassifies fewer societies—but still makes some mistakes. Fully 77% of dowry societies are, in fact, stratified and have monogamous marriage, but 63% of all monogamous, stratified societies do *not* have dowry.

Harris (1980), building on Boserup's model, hypothesized that dowry should occur in societies where women's role in subsistence production is low *and* where their value in reproduction is also low. In other words, if women are a liability in both their productive and reproductive roles, one should expect dowry as a compensation to the groom's family for taking on the liability represented by a bride who marries into a groom's family.

Adams (unpublished paper, 1993) operationalized this idea. He reasoned that, since women are less suited physically to handling a plow, societies with plow agriculture and high-quality agricultural land should find women's labor of low value. If those societies have high population density, then women's reproductive role should be of low value. Finally, in societies with both these characteristics, patrilocal residence would make accepting a bride a real liability and would lead to demand for compensation—hence, dowry.

Adams tested his idea on the same sample of 186 societies that Gaulin and Boster used, and Adams's theory makes about 25% fewer errors than Gaulin and Boster's in predicting which societies have dowry. There has thus been a succession of theories to account for dowry; each theory has done a bit better than the last and each has been based on reasoning from commonsense principles. That's how nomothetic theory grows.

A lot of comparative research is about testing nomothetic theory. If an idiographic theory accounts for some data in, say, India or Japan or England, then an obvious next step is to see how far the theory extends. Alice Schlegel and Herbert Barry (1986), for example, looked at the consequences of female contribution to subsistence. Their nomothetic theory predicts that women will be more respected in societies where they contribute a lot to subsistence than in societies where their contribution is low.

Of course, whether their theory is supported depends crucially on how Schlegel and Barry operationalize the concept of "respect." In societies where women contribute a lot to subsistence, say Schlegel and Barry, women will be spared some of the burden of pregnancy "through the attempt to space children" more evenly (ibid.:146). In such societies, women will be subjected to rape less often, they will have greater sexual freedom, they will be worth more in bride wealth, and they will have greater choice in selection of a spouse. Schlegel and Barry coded the 186 societies in the standard cross-cultural sample for each of those indicators of respect and their predictions were supported.

Now, a theory of why dowry exists is more nomothetic than is a theory about why dowry persists in, say, India or Greece. And a theory of why women are more respected in some societies than in others is more nomothetic than is a theory of why women in Finland hold more direct political power than do women in Japan. But *more* nomothetic is just the beginning.

As I said in Chapter 2, I really like Festinger's *cognitive dissonance theory* (1957). It's a brute of a theory: It has stimulated thousands of studies about how dissonance actually works to make people behave as they do. Immanuel Wallerstein's *world systems theory* (1974) divides all the world's countries into players in the international expansion of capitalism and accounts for the distribution of the world's nations into haves and have-nots (for more on this, see Hopkins et al. 1982). Competing explanations for inequalities in industrial development are *modernization theory* (Inkeles 1974), *achievement theory* (McClelland 1967), and *dependency theory* (Prebisch 1970).

Modernization theory and achievement theory are both derived from the ideational paradigm of theory building. McClelland tested children in various countries and found that their level of achievement motivation correlated with the level of industrial development of the countries. Modernization theorists find that there is a strong correlation between the level of industrial development and certain attitudes and values in populations. Modern—that is, industrially developed —countries contain people who think modern.

Dependency theorists and world systems theorists note a correlation between the level of a country's industrial development and various measures of its relation to the most developed industrial powers. World systems theory and dependency theory, then, derive from the materialist paradigm for theory building (see Black [1991] for a review of theories of development).

One More: The Second Demographic Transition

Let's do one more just to make sure it's clear. The second *demographic transition* is a big question that demands an explanation, and many scholars have tackled the problem (see Caldwell 1982; Handwerker 1989).

The first demographic transition happened at the end of the Paleolithic when humans began swapped agriculture for hunting and gathering as the main means of production. During the Paleolithic, population growth was very, very slow. But across the world, as people switched from hunting and gathering to agriculture, their populations fairly exploded.

The second demographic transition began in the late eighteenth century in Europe with industrialization and has been spreading around the world ever since. Today, Japan, Belgium, Italy, and other highly industrialized countries have **total fertility rates (the average number of children born to women during their entire lives)**, or TFRs, in the neighborhood of 1.3—that's about 38% below the 2.1 TFR needed in those countries just to replace the current population. In the last 30 years, some previously high TFR countries, like Barbados, Mauritius, and very recently, Mexico, have been through a major demographic transition.

Explaining why women in Mexico are having fewer children is idiographic, but predicting the conditions under which women in *any* underdeveloped country will start lowering their fertility rate is nomothetic. Handwerker's (1989) theory is that women in low-wage jobs encourage their daughters to get more education. And when women get sufficiently educated, their participation in the labor market becomes more effective (they earn more), freeing them from dependency on men (sons and husbands). As this dependency diminishes, women lower their fertility.

Handwerker's theory is nomothetic and materialist. It relies on material conditions forces to explain how preferences develop for fewer children and it does not rely on preferences (culture, ideas, values) to explain the level of a country's TFR. This difference has profound consequences. If you think that beliefs and attitudes are what make people behave as they do, then if you want to change people's behavior, the obvious thing to do is change their attitudes. This is the basis of the ***educational model of social change*** I mentioned in Chapter 2—the runaway best-seller model for change in our society.

Do you want to get students in American high schools to achieve more? Educate them about the importance of taking the most challenging courses. Want to get women in developing nations to have fewer children? Educate them about the importance of small families. Want to lower the rate of infectious disease in developing countries? Educate people about the importance of good hygiene. Want to get adolescents in Boston or Seattle or wherever to stop having high-risk sex? Educate them about the importance of abstinence or, if that fails, about how to take protective measures against sexually transmitted disease. Want to get people in the U.S. to use their cars less? Educate them about car pooling.

These kinds of programs rarely work—but they do work sometimes. You *can* educate people (through commercial advertising) about why they should switch from, say, a Honda to a Toyota, or from a Toyota to a Ford, but you can't get people to give up their cars. You *can* educate people (through social advertising) about using the pill as opposed to less effective methods of birth control, once people have decided to lower their fertility, but educational rhetoric doesn't influence the number of children that people want in the first place.

The closer a behavior is to the culture (or *superstructure*) of society, the easier it is to intervene culturally. Brand preferences are often superstructural, so advertising works to get people to switch brands—to change their behavior. But if people's behavior is rooted in the *structure* or *infrastructure* of society, then forget about changing their behavior by educating them to have better attitudes. For example, in poor countries, having many children may be the only security people have in their old age. No amount of rhetoric about the advantages of small families is going to change anyone's mind about the number of children they want to have. If you need a car because the only affordable housing is 30 miles

from your job, no amount of rhetoric will convince you to take the bus.

While I find materialist theories more powerful than ideational or sociobiological ones, they don't have to be nomothetic to be useful. The highly nomothetic demographic transition theory explains why Japan, a fully industrialized nation, has such a low TFR, but it doesn't predict what the consequences of that low TFR will be. For the time being, at least (until even bigger nomothetic theories are developed), we still need an idiographic theory for this.

Japan has about 125 million people—about half the population of the U.S.—living in an area about the size of Montana. The Japanese enjoy one of the highest average per capita incomes in the world. This is based on manufacturing products for export. The oil to run the factories that produce all those exports has to be imported. So does a lot of food to feed all those people who are working in the factories. The TFR of 1.3 in Japan makes it easy to predict that, in the next 20 or 30 years, Japan's industries will need to find lots of new workers to maintain productivity—and the lifestyle supported by that productivity.

Belgium and Italy—two other countries with comparable TFRs—have solved this problem by opening their borders to people from the formerly communist countries of eastern Europe. There are lots of people in Asia who are looking for work, but 97% of Japan's population is ethnically Japanese. Many Japanese don't like the idea of opening their borders to, say, Filipinos or North Koreans, so it will be a hard sell, in terms of domestic politics, for the government of Japan that proposes this solution to the problem of the coming labor shortage. Of course, Japan could recruit women more fully into the workforce, but many Japanese—particularly men—find this unappealing as well.

Obviously, something will have to give. Either Japan's productivity will drop, workers will be recruited from abroad, or Japanese women will be recruited into the high-paying jobs of Japan's industrial machine. Demographic transition theory, however, does not tell us which of these alternatives is the most likely. Ideational theorists, particularly scholars who are immersed in the realities of modern Japanese society and culture, will contribute their own ideas about which choice will win. What I'm hoping for is a nomothetic theory that explains this kind of choice in many countries, not just in one.

This is one of my current favorite topics to think about because it illustrates how important theory is in developing research questions, and it showcases the contributions of ideational and materialist perspectives, as well as the importance of idiographic and nomothetic theory.

There is no "list" of research questions. You have to use your imagination and your curiosity about how things work, and follow your hunches. Above all, never take anything at face value. Every time you read an article, ask yourself: "What would a study look like that would test whether the major assertions and conclusions of this article were really correct?" If someone says, "The only things students really care about these days are drugs, sex, and rock and roll," the proper response is, "We can test that."

A GUIDE TO RESEARCH TOPICS, ANYWAY

There may not be a list of research topics, but there are some useful guidelines. First of all, there are very few big-theory issues—I call them research *arenas*—in all of social science. Here are four of them: (1) the nature-nurture problem, (2) the evolution problem, (3) the internal-external problem, and (4) the superorganic social facts problem.

1. *The nature-nurture problem.* This one is quite familiar. Research on the extent to which cognitive abilities between men and women are the consequence of environmental factors (nurture) and genetic factors (nature) or the interaction between those factors is part of this research arena. So are studies of human response to signs of illness across cultures.

2. *The evolution problem.* Studies of how groups change from one kind of thing to another kind of thing are in this arena. Societies change very slowly through time, but at some point we say that a society has changed from, say, feudal to industrial. All studies of the differences between small societies—*gemeinschaften*—and big societies—*gesellschaften*—are in this arena. So are studies of inexorable bureaucratization as organizations grow.

3. *The internal-external problem.* Studies of the way in which behavior is influenced by values and by environmental conditions are in this arena. Studies of *response effects* (how people respond differently to the same question asked by a woman or by a man, for example) are in this arena, too.

4. *The social facts, or emergent properties, problem.* The name for this problem comes from Émile Durkheim's (1933 [1893]) argument that social facts exist outside of individuals and are not reducible to psychological facts. A great deal of social research is based on the assumption that people are influenced by social forces that *emerge* from the interaction of humans but that transcend individuals. Many studies of social networks and social support, for example, are in this arena, as

TABLE 3.1 Types of Studies

	Internal States	External States	Reported Behavior	Observed Behavior	Artifacts	Environment
Internal states	I	II	IIIa	IIIb	IV	V
External states		VI	VIIa	VIIb	VIII	IX
Reported behavior			Xa	Xb	XIa	XIIa
Observed behavior					XIb	XIIb
Artifacts					XIII	XIV
Environment						XV

are studies that test the influence of organizational forms on human thought and behavior.

Generating Types of Studies

Now look at Table 3.1. I have divided research topics (not arenas) into classes, based on the relation among various kinds of variables.

(1) *Internal states:* These include **attitudes, beliefs, values, and perceptions.** Cognition is an internal state.

(2) *External states:* These include **characteristics of people, such as age, wealth, health status, height, weight, and gender.**

(3) *Behavior:* This covers **what people eat, whom they communicate with, how much they work and play**—in short, everything that people do and much of what social scientists are interested in understanding.

(4) *Artifacts:* This includes **all the physical residue from human behavior**—radioactive waste, tomato slicers, sneakers, arrowheads, computer disks, Viagra, skyscrapers—everything.

(5) *Environment:* This includes **physical and social environmental characteristics.** The amount of rainfall, the amount of biomass per square kilometer, location on a river or ocean front—these are physical features that influence human thought and behav-

ior. Humans also live in a social environment. Living under a democratic vs. an authoritarian regime or working in an organization that tolerates or does not tolerate sexual harassment are examples of social environments that have consequences for what people think and how they behave.

Keep in mind that category (3) includes both reported behavior and actual behavior. A great deal of research has shown that about a third to a half of everything people report about their behavior is not true. (See Bernard et al. [1984] for a review of the literature on the informant accuracy problem.) If you ask children what they eat, they'll tell you, but their report may have no useful resemblance to what they actually eat (Johnson et al. 1996). If you ask people how many times a year they go to church, you're likely to get data that do not reflect actual behavior (Hadaway et al. 1993, 1998).

Some of the difference between what people say they do and what they do is the result of out-and-out lying. Most of the difference, though, is the result of the fact that people can't hang on to the level of detail about their behavior that is called for when they are confronted by social scientists asking them, for example, how often they go to church, or eat beef. Of course, what people *think* about their behavior may be precisely what you're interested in, but that's a different matter.

Most social research focuses on internal states and on reported behavior. But the study of humanity can be much richer, once you get the hang of putting together these five kinds of variables and conjuring up potential relations. Here are some examples of possible studies for each of the cells in Table 3.1.

Cell I. The interaction of internal states, like perceptions, attitudes, beliefs, values, and moods.

> Religious beliefs and attitudes about gun control in the U.S. (Flanagan and Longmire 1996).

> Support for Republican or Democratic Party politics in the U.S. and support for a woman's right to an abortion (DiMaggio et al. 1966).

> Relation between perceiving a common fate between humans and animals and preference for different conservation policy objectives (Opotow 1994; Liu et al. 1997).

Cell II. The interaction of internal states (perceptions, beliefs, moods, etc.) and external states (completed education, health status, organizational conditions).

> Health status and hopefulness about the future (Vieth et al. 1997).

> The relation between racial attitudes and the political context in different cities (Glaser and Gilens 1997).

Cell IIIa. The interaction between *reported* behavior and internal states.

> Perception of how well the economy is doing and reported voting behavior (Wlezien et al. 1997).

> Attitudes toward the environment and reported environment-friendly behavior (Minton and Rose 1997).

> Reported rate of church attendance and attitude toward premarital sex (Petersen and Donnenwerth 1997).

Cell IIIb. The interaction between *observed* behavior and internal states.

> Insider knowledge and stock-trading behavior (Guth et al. 1997).

> Differences in "locus of control" and various health problems like headaches and muscle pain (Saarijarvi et al. 1990; Scharff et al. 1995). (Locus of control is a widely used scale that measures the extent to which people feel they are in control of their own lives. A low score signals that a person feels that the locus of control for his or her life is "out there" in the hands of others.)

> Attitudes and beliefs about resources and actual behavior in the control of a household thermostat (Kempton 1987).

> The effect of increased overtime work on cognitive function in automotive workers, including attention and mood (Proctor et al. 1996).

Cell IV. The interaction of material artifacts and internal states.

> The effects on Holocaust Museum staff in Washington, D.C., of working with the physical reminders of the Holocaust (McCarroll et al. 1995).

> The ideas and values that brides and grooms in the U.S. share (or don't share) about the kinds of ritual artifacts that are supposed to be used in a wedding (Lowrey and Otnes 1994).

How children learn that domestic artifacts are considered feminine while artifacts associated with non-domestic production are considered masculine (Crabb and Bielawski 1994).

Physicians' attitudes toward television advertising of prescription drugs (Petroshius et al. 1995).

Cell V. The interaction of social and physical environmental factors and internal states.

The extent to which emotional health in Sweden is caused by organizational factors at work (Soderfeldt et al. 1997).

How culture influences the course of schizophrenia (Edgerton and Cohen 1994).

Personal experience of combat and political orientation of liberalism vs. conservatism (Grote et al. 1997).

The extent to which adopted children and biological children raised in the same household develop similar personalities (McGue et al. 1996).

Cell VI. How the interaction among external states relates to outcomes, like longevity or financial success.

The effects of things like age, sex, race, marital status, education, income, employment status, and health status on the risk of dying from the abuse of illegal drugs (Kallan 1998).

The interaction of variables like marital status, ethnicity, medical risk, and level of prenatal care on low birth weight (Abel 1997).

Cell VIIa. The relation between external states and *reported* behavior.

The likelihood that baby boomers will report attending church as they get older (Miller and Nakamura 1996).

Gender differences in self-reported suicidal behavior among adolescents (Vannatta 1996).

Cell VIIb. The relation between external states and *observed* behavior.

Health status, family drug history, and other factors associated with women who successfully quit smoking (Jensen and Coambs 1994). Note: This is also an example of Cell XIIb.

Cell VIII. The relation of physical artifacts and external states.

How age and gender differences relate to cherished possessions among children and adolescents from 6 to 18 years of age (Dyl and Wapner 1996).

Cell IX. The relation of external states and environmental conditions.

How the work environment contributes to heart disease (Kasl 1996).

How the outcome of psychoanalysis is affected by the kind of consulting room in which therapy takes place (Diaz de Chumaceiro 1996).

Relation of daily levels of various pollutants in the air and such things as violent crimes or psychiatric emergencies (e.g., Briere et al. 1983).

Cell Xa. The relation between behaviors, as *reported* by people to researchers.

The relation of self-reported level of church attendance and self-reported level of environmental activism among African Americans in Louisiana (Arp and Boeckelman 1997).

Cell Xb. The relation between behaviors, as *observed* by researchers.

> The relation of reports about recycling behavior and actual recycling behavior (Corral-Verdugo 1997).

> Also, see studies that compare the relation between reported and observed behaviors, for example, Skruppy (1993) comparing responses by frail elderly men to the Activities of Daily Living Scale with observations of those same men as they engage in activities of daily living, and studies that compare different ways to observe the same behavior directly, for example, Ebby et al. (1996) comparing two methods for direct observation of whether drivers going 60 mph are wearing their seat belts.
>
> Direct observation and comparison of behaviors are used in many fields, including psychology (in the assessment of behavioral disorders), education (in assessing learning disabilities), nursing (in assessing patients' dietary habits), political science (in assessing the bellicosity of nations toward one another), occupational sociology (in assessing ergonomics and performance), and so on. I'll discuss direct observation at some length in Chapter 10.

Cell XIa. The relation of *reported* behavior to specific physical artifacts.

> People who are employed view prized possessions as symbols of their own personal history, while people who are unemployed see prized possessions as having utilitarian value (Ditmar 1991).

Cell XIb. The relation of *observed* behavior to specific physical artifacts.

> Content analysis of top-grossing films over 31 years shows that "tobacco events" (which include the presence of tobacco paraphernalia, as well as characters talking about smoking or actually smoking)

are disproportionate to the actual rate of smoking in the population (Hazan et al. 1994).

Cell XIIa. The relation of *reported* behavior to factors in the social or physical environment.

> The relation of compulsive consumer behavior in young adults and whether they were raised in intact or disrupted families (Rindfleisch et al. 1997).

Cell XIIb. The relation of *observed* behavior to factors in the social or physical environment.

> People spend more or less time in a store and spend more or less money, depending on factors in the store environment (Sherman et al. 1997).

Cell XIII. The association of physical artifacts to one another and what this predicts about human thought or behavior.

> Comparing the favorite possessions of urban Indians (in India) and Indian immigrants to the U.S. to see whether certain sets of possessions remain meaningful among immigrants (Mehta and Belk 1991). This is also an example of Cell IV. Note the difference between expressed *preferences* across artifacts and the coexistence of artifacts across places or times.

Cell XIV. The probability that certain artifacts (relating, for example, to subsistence) will be found in certain physical or social environments (rain forests, deserts, shoreline communities).

> This area of research is mostly the province of archaeology.

Cell XV. How features of the social and physical environment interact and affect human behavioral and cognitive outcomes.

Social and physical environmental features of retail stores interact to affect the buying behavior of consumers (Baker et al. 1992).

The above list is only meant to give you an idea of how to think about potential covariations and, consequently, about potential research topics. Always keep in mind that covariation does not mean cause. Covariation can be spurious, the result of an antecedent or an intervening variable. (Refer to Chapter 2 for a discussion of causality, spurious relations, and antecedent variables.)

And keep in mind that many of the examples in the list above are statements about possible *bivariate relations*—that is, about **possible covariation between two things**. Social phenomena being the complex sorts of things they are, a lot of research involves *multivariate relations*—that is, **covariation among three or more things at the same time**.

For example, it's well known that people who call themselves religious conservatives in the U.S. are likely to support the National Rifle Association's policy on gun control (Cell I). But the association between the two variables (religious beliefs and attitudes toward gun control) is by no means perfect and is affected by many intervening variables.

I'll tell you about testing for bivariate relations in Chapter 15 and about testing for multivariate relations in Chapter 16. As in so many other things, you crawl before you run and you run before you fly.

THE LITERATURE SEARCH

The first thing to do after you get an idea for a piece of research is to find out what has already been done on it. It is impossible to overemphasize the importance of a thorough literature search. Without a truly heroic effort to uncover sources, you risk two things: wasting a lot of time going over already covered ground, and having your colleagues ignore your work because you didn't do your homework. Gottman and Levenson (1992), for example, studied the causes of divorce in the U.S. They went through nearly 1,200 published studies that contained the words "marital separation" or "divorce" and found just 4 that used a prospective, longitudinal design to predict separation and divorce. Now *that's* heroic.

Fortunately, with all the new *documentation resources* available, efforts like that are actually pretty easy. There are three main documentation resources: (1) people, (2) review articles and bibliographies, and (3) modern bibliographic search tools.

People

There is nothing useful, prestigious, or exciting about discovering literature on your own. Reading it is what's important, and you should not waste any time in finding it. Experts are great documentation resources. Begin by asking everyone and anyone who you think has a remote chance of knowing something about the topic you're interested in if they can recommend some key articles or books that will get you into the literature on your topic.

Use the network method to conduct this first stage of your literature review. If the people you know are not experts in the topic you're studying, ask them if they know personally any people who are experts. Then contact the experts by e-mail or even by phone.

Yes, by phone. Letters demand a written response and most people don't have the time to do that. E-mail is quick and cheap, but it also requires a written response and many scholars are just too busy to respond to requests for lists of articles and books. But most people will talk to you on the phone. A knowledgeable person in the field can give you three or four key citations over the phone right on the spot, and with the documentation resources I'm going to tell you about a little later, that's all you need to get you straight into the literature.

Review Articles

The *Annual Review* series is a good place to start reading. There are *Annual Review* volumes for sociology, psychology, and anthropology. Authors who are invited to publish in the series are experts in their fields; they have digested a lot of information and have packaged it in a way that gets you right into the middle of a topic in a hurry. Review articles in journals and bibliographies published as books are two other excellent sources.

Don't worry about review articles being out of date. The *Social Sciences Citation Index* (*SSCI*) and other documentation resources have virtually eliminated the problem of obsolescence in bibliographies and review articles. More about the *SSCI* below.

Bibliographic Search Tools

The overwhelming majority of the research in any discipline is published in hundreds upon hundreds of journals, some of which are short lived. A lot of descriptive data on social issues (crime, health care delivery, welfare) is published in reports from governments, industry, and private research foundations. No research project should

be launched (and certainly no request for funding of a research project should be submitted) until you have thoroughly searched these potential sources for published research on the topic you are interested in.

The bibliographic tools that I describe here are all available online and as paper products. Whether or not you use an online service, there is no way to overemphasize the importance of using the documentation tools described here when you are starting out on a research project.

A word of caution to new scholars who are writing for publication: Online literature searches make it easy for people to find articles only if the articles (or their abstracts) contain descriptive words. Cute titles on scientific articles hide them from people who want to find them in the indexing tools. If you write an article about illegal Mexican labor migration to the United States and call it something like "Whither Juan? Mexicans on the Road," it's a sure bet to get lost immediately, unless (1) you happen to publish it in one of the most widely read journals, and (2) it happens to be a blockbuster piece of work that everyone talks about and is cited in articles that *do* have descriptive titles.

Since most scientific writing is not of the blockbuster variety, you're better off putting words into the titles of your articles that describe what the articles are about. It may seem awfully dull, but descriptive, unimaginative titles are terrific for helping your colleagues find your work.

As formidable as the amount of information being produced in the world is, there is an equally formidable set of documentation resources for accessing information. If you have to use just one of these, then my choice is the *SSCI*.

The Social Sciences Citation Index

The Institute for Scientific Information, or ISI, produces the *SSCI*, the *Science Citation Index,* and the *Arts and Humanities Citation Index.*

These indexes, available in most major university libraries, and in many small college libraries, too, are important resources.

At the ISI, the staff pores over thousands of journals each year, entering into a computer the title, author, and reference for every article in each journal. The unique value of the citation indexes is that, in addition, the staff enters the *citations* in each article indexed—that is, they note all the references cited by each author of each article in each journal surveyed. The citations are alphabetized by the author's last name. So, if you know the name of an author whose work *should* be cited by anyone working in a particular field, you can find out, for any given year, who cited that author, and where.

For example, anyone writing on *locus of control* (whether people feel that they are in charge of their own destinies or are pawns of external forces) is going to cite one of Julian Rotter's classic papers (1966, 1990). Anyone writing about urban gangs in the U.S. is likely to cite William Foote Whyte's *Street Corner Society* (1981 [1943]) or Gerald Suttles's *The Social Order of the Slum* (1968).

In other words, you can search the literature *forward* in time—which means that older bibliographies, like those in the *Annual Review* series, are never out of date. If you run into a 1980 bibliography of research on ethnicity and consumer products, you can use it to determine the classic references up to that time, and then go to the *SSCI* to find out who has cited those references each year.

1989. Each of those references would also have a bibliography going back in time. But with the citation indexes, if you know of a single, classic article written in, say, 1978, you can find all the articles published *this year* in which that article was cited and then work backward from those.

The printed version of the *SSCI* has been available since 1959, and many libraries subscribe to it. The CD-ROM version has been available since 1987 and the online *SSCI* covers the social science literature back to 1992, with citations in that literature going back to 1972. Since it's been just eight years since 1992, you might think that the database is limited. Think again. The *SSCI* fully indexes about 1,700 of the world's leading social science journals and takes selected items from another 5,600 journals, across 54 social science disciplines. This produces a corpus of about 145,000 articles a year for indexing, and those articles contain about 2.5 million citations to references to literature.

OK, so 145,000 *sources* are only a good-sized fraction of all the significant social science papers published in the world each year. But over the eight years from 1992 to 1999, that means over a *million* articles indexed and, at 2.5 million citations a year, about *22 million citations* added to the literature. Even if the million articles indexed since 1992 don't include everything you need, the *authors* of those million articles almost certainly read—and cited—all the available work that you need. All it takes is systematic effort on your part to run that work down.

❖————

I want to make sure that you understand the power of this resource. Without the citation indexes, you can only search *backward* in time. If you have an article or book published in 1990, the references will go up to only, say, 1988 or

With the CD-ROM and online versions of the *SSCI,* you can search for articles by keyword, including the author's name, any word or words in the title, and so on. If your library doesn't have the online or CD-ROM version of the *SSCI,* don't be put off. I used the paper version of the *SSCI*

for 30 years, and if the online version vanished, I'd go back to the paper one in a minute. It's that good.

Other Documentation Databases

These days, documentation is a robust business, and there are many indexing and abstracting resources. Besides the *SSCI*, some of the most important resources for social scientist are CIS *Statistical Masterfile*, ERIC, NTIS, MEDLINE, PsycLIT, SOCIOFILE, LEXIS-NEXIS, and OCLC.

The CIS Statistical Masterfile

The CIS is the Congressional Information Service. The CIS indexes U.S. House and Senate hearings, reports entered into public access by submission to Congress, and testimony before congressional committees. All of these, of course, are in print and are available to the public. There are reports on health care, housing, transportation, agriculture, protection of the environment, nutrition, compensatory education, rural-urban migration, and many other social issues. These reports will help you locate research papers and primary data sources on the demographics of American ethnic groups, as well as basic demographic and economic data on other countries.

The CIS also produces the *American Statistical Index* (*ASI*), the *Statistical Reference Index* (*SRI*), and the *Index to International Statistics* (*IIS*). All are on CD-ROM as part of what's called the CIS *Statistical Masterfile*.

The *ASI* covers federal government publications other than those issued by Congress, and not including government agency journals (which are covered by the *Index to U.S. Government Periodicals*). The *SRI* is a selective guide to American statistical publications from private and state gov-

ernment sources. The *IIS* indexes statistical reports on particular countries or cities.

The CIS *Statistical Masterfile* contains abstracts for the reports that are indexed. You'll find abstracts of reports on the wages of Arizona farm workers; on the number of Native Americans attending public school in Maine, by grade; on health conditions and services across the world, 1970-2004 (from the World Health Organization); on income distribution and its relation to economic development and government policy (from the International Labor Organization).

The actual documents indexed and abstracted in the CIS *Statistical Masterfile* are all on microfiche. Larger libraries subscribe to the microfiche collection, along with the CD-ROM that contains the index and the abstracts. If your library doesn't have the microfiche collections, you can write to the agency or corporation that issued a particular listed report and get a copy.

The CIS does not index technical reports on contracts that are issued for research by federal agencies. Those reports are available through ERIC, NTIS, and MEDLINE.

ERIC

ERIC is a federally funded product of the Educational Resources Information Center. It began as a microfiche archive in 1966 and covers literature of interest to researchers in education. The online ERIC database corresponds to the *Current Index to Journals in Education* (*CIJE*), which covers 780 major social science journals, so a lot of the literature in ERIC is of interest to all social scientists. You can search the ERIC database by author, title, subject, or even by the name of the agency that sponsored the research. The ERIC database also includes a lot of gray literature—government reports and reports from private foundations and industries that contain useful information but can be tough to find.

NTIS

NTIS, the National Technical Information Service, indexes and abstracts federally funded research reports in all areas of science. The research that Peter Killworth and I did in the 1970s and 1980s testing our computer program for network analysis was supported by contracts from the Office of Naval Research. When you have a contract with a U.S. government agency, you generally produce a series of technical reports on the work you do as you go along. Those technical reports get logged in to the NTIS.

Many technical reports later get published as articles. But many don't. Some of the reports aren't published because they are too preliminary—"not ready for prime time," as it were. But lots of technical reports don't get published because they contain huge tables of basic data. That's not the stuff that journals can publish, but it may be treasure for another researcher. It used to be that reports on government contracts were filed and then shelved, never to be heard from again. But with the NTIS database, the public can now easily locate all that information.

The NTIS has technical reports from archaeological digs, from voter registration surveys, from consumer behavior surveys, from focus groups on attitudes about unprotected sex, from evaluations of new designs for low-cost housing, from laboratory experiments on how much people might be willing to pay for gasoline, from natural experiments to test how long people can stay in a submerged submarine without going crazy—if the federal government has funded it under contract, there's probably a technical report of it.

MEDLINE

MEDLINE is a product of the National Library of Medicine. It covers over 3,700 journals in the medical sciences—including the medical social sciences—and includes materials from the *International Nursing Index.* The online service, which began in 1991, had nearly 2 million citations at the end of 1998, with about 35,000 new entries added each month. The CD-ROM version of MEDLINE has abstracts of articles going back to 1966.

If you are working on anything that has to do with health care, MEDLINE is a must. Ask MEDLINE for articles from 1991 until now on "high-risk sexual behavior and adolescents" and it returns a list of over 30 items. Tell it to find articles in the last decade on "regimen compliance or compliance with regimen and malaria" and it returns abstracts for 20 articles.

PsycLIT

PsycLIT and PsycINFO are products of the American Psychological Association. The Jurassic version of these databases goes back to 1887, with about 50,000 new references and abstracts added each year. SOCIOFILE is a product of Sociological Abstracts, Inc. It covers about 2,000 journals dating from 1974 and also includes material from the *Social Planning/Policy and Development Abstracts* (SOPODA) database.

PsycLIT has excellent coverage of research methods, the sociology of language, occupations and professions, health, family violence, poverty, and social control. It covers the sociology of knowledge and the sociology of science, as well as the sociology of the arts, religion, and education. *SocioAbs* is a product of Sociological Abstracts, Inc., and *Social Sciences Abstracts* is a product of H. W. Wilson and Co. The former indexes and abstracts 250 English-language sociology journals. The latter indexes 350 English-language journals.

LEXIS/NEXIS

If your library has LEXIS/NEXIS, don't consider any literature search complete until you've used this system. The system started in 1973 as a way to help lawyers find information on cases. Today, the database contains the actual text of articles from nearly 14,000 news and business sources (including most of the major newspapers in the U.S.) and nearly 5,000 legal sources. At the end of 1998, there were over 1.5 billion documents and the system was adding about 9.5 million documents a day, including about 120,000 articles from the world's newspapers, magazines, and trade journals (LEXIS-NEXIS 1998). And don't forget the *New York Times* index if your library subscribes to that database.

OCLC

OCLS is the Online Computer Library Center. It is the world's largest library database. Over 25,000 libraries across the world catalog their holdings (in 370 languages) in OCLC. In 1998, the system had 37 million bibliographic records and was growing at about 2 million records a year. If you find a book or article in the *SSCI* or PsycLIT, for example, and your library doesn't have it, then OCLC will tell you which library does have it. Interlibrary loans depend on OCLC. In addition, OCLC publishes a database called ArticleFirst. This leviathan, which is updated daily, covers 12,500 journals in all fields, including many in the social sciences. Coverage is only from 1990, but as the database grows, it becomes more and more useful.

META-ANALYSIS

Meta-analysis involves piling up **all the quantitative studies ever done on a particular topic to assess quantitatively what is known about the size of the effect.** The pioneering work on meta-analysis (M. L. Smith and Glass 1977) addressed the question: Does psychotherapy make a difference? That is, do people who get psychotherapy benefit, compared to people who have the same problems and who don't get psychotherapy?

The problems in answering this question are well known. You have to control for type of therapy (that is, whether it's psychoanalytic therapy, behavioral therapy, cognitive therapy, etc.); whether the therapy is given individually or in groups; whether the therapy is offered in a public or private clinic—not to mention differences in

gender, ethnicity, age, and kinds of disorders. Still, with hundreds of assessment studies, Smith and Glass figured they could more or less control for all these variables.

More or less doesn't mean "nail down," but by 1996 there had been 63 meta-analyses of psychotherapy outcomes, so Matt and Navarro (1997) did a meta-analysis of the meta-analyses. "The good news for researchers, therapists, patients, and public health administrators, and managers of health care plans," they conclude, is that "the general effects of psychotherapy are overwhelmingly positive" despite all the problems involved in measurement (p. 26).

There are now thousands of meta-analyses—on everything from the effects of school-based drug prevention programs (Tobler and Stratton 1997) to gender differences on IQ tests (Snow and Weinstock 1990) to the predictive value of socio-economic status (or SES) on academic achievement in primary school and high school (White 1980) or the predictive value of the GRE (Graduate Record Exam) on grades in graduate school (Morrison and Morrison 1995).

Meta-analysis can be delightfully subversive. Morrison and Morrison (1995), for example, found that only 6.3% of the variance in graduate-level grade-point average is predicted by performance on the GRE quantitative and verbal exams. And White (1980) found that across a hundred studies up to 1979, SES explained, on average, an identical 6.3% of the variance in school achievement. The raw correlation across those hundred studies ranged from –.14 (yes, *minus* .14) to .97.

Meta-analysis forces you to become familiar with the literature on a particular topic, and it makes you aware of the research holes that need to be filled.

Meta-analysis has become a whole branch of research by itself in the last 20 years. I've listed the major reference works on meta-analysis in the Further Reading section at the end of this chapter. I just want to point out here, with an example, that meta-analysis can be a terrific way to look for important research topics. That's because meta-analysis forces you to become familiar with the literature on a particular topic, and it makes you aware of the research holes that need to be filled.

———————❖

Schutte and Hosch (1997) did a meta-analysis of mock jury studies about rape or child sexual abuse. In a mock jury study, participants are shown evidence of a defendant's guilt and inno-cence in a particular crime. The jury deliberates and renders a verdict. It's an attractive method because it mimics a real-world situation and because you can manipulate the experimental treatment—the crime, the various kinds of evidence for the defendant's guilt or innocence, the demographics of the jurors, and so on.

Schutte and Hosch scoured the literature. They began by searching the PsycINFO database from 1967 on for articles that contained *any* of the terms "sexual abuse," "child abuse," "rape," "sex," and "juror." They also posted requests on PSYLAW, an Internet discussion group for people interested in law and psychology. They then used the bibliographies from the articles they turned up to hunt for further references and kept on doing this iterative search until no new studies turned up that fit their criteria.

And what were the criteria? First, they only used reports that were based on studies of jury-eligible people. That meant excluding studies of people under 18 years of age and excluding studies of non-U.S. citizens (so all studies of Canadians and Britons, for example, were excluded). Second, they excluded studies in which respondents (mock jurors) were asked to rate a mock defendant's guilt on a Likert-type of scale of, say, 1 to 5. In real jury cases, defendants are judged guilty or not guilty, not "somewhat guilty" or "very guilty."

Schutte and Hosch wound up with 36 studies, 19 involving accusations of rape and 17 involving accusations of child sexual abuse. All these studies together comprise 9,813 participants (51% of whom were women) and a mean of 271 participants per study. This points up one of the strengths of meta-analysis: Even though the number of *studies* in such an analysis might be low, the number of *people* represented in those studies can be huge.

Across the 36 studies, women jurors were far more likely to vote for conviction than were men

(58.5% compared to 41.5%). This was hardly surprising, but the study did turn up something very interesting: 29 out of the 36 studies involved female victims and male defendants. Of the 7 studies in which females were the accused, every case was about child sexual abuse, and 3 of the 7 studies reported no difference in the probability that male or female mock jurors would vote to convict. This is just the sort of finding that sharp-eyed researchers latch on to when they're out shopping for interesting research gaps to fill.

Chapter 3
Review

KEY CONCEPTS

Ideal vs. real research process, 66-67

Intersubjectivity, 68

Resources for research, 69-70

Debriefing, 71

Experimental studies of obedience, 70-73

Explanation and prediction, 74-82

Paradigms for theory, 74-76

Sociobiology, 74-76

Idealism, 75-76

Materialism, 75-76

Idiographic theory, 76-78

Nomothetic theory, 76, 78-80

Gender gap, 77

"Dowry death," 77

Cognitive dissonance theory, 79

World systems theory, 79

Modernization theory, 79

Achievement theory, 79-80

Dependency theory, 80

Demographic transition, 80

Total fertility rate, 80

Educational model of social change, 80-81

Superstructure, 81

Structure, 81

Infrastructure, 81

The nature-nurture problem, 82

The evolution problem, 82

Gemeinschaften, 82

Gesellschaften, 82

The internal-external problem, 82

Response effects, 82

The emergent properties problem, 82-83

Internal and external states, 83

Reported vs. actual behavior, 83

Environment and artifacts, 83

Bivariate relations, 87

Multivariate relations, 87

Documentation resources, 87-92

Locus of control, 89

Online bibliographic tools, 88-92

Meta-analysis, 92-94

SUMMARY

❖ Research is idealized, but in the end, it gets done the way most things get done: by doing the best we can and by trying to do better next time.

❖ Researchers choose their problems for many reasons, including personal interest, availability of research funds, contractual obligations, and, of course, in order to build sound explanations for social and behavioral phenomena.

❖ The ethics dilemma in social research is profound. The operational test of whether a particular piece of research is ethical is whether social norms tolerate it.
  • This relativistic position, however, does not encourage absolute moral judgments. Ultimately, the choice is left to researchers, and the researchers are responsible for the consequences of their actions.
  • It is unlikely that either Milgram's or Zimbardo's experiments on obedience would be funded today, yet the lessons from their experiments continue to provide guidance on the responsibility of the individual for her or his actions.

❖ There are quite different approaches, or paradigms, to theory building in the social sciences. These paradigms guide us to search for different *kinds* of answers—biological, ideational, and material—to the same question.
  • The three main paradigms for explanation are sociobiology, idealism, and materialism.

❖ All research projects begin with a literature search. The bibliographic tools available today make it much easier than in the past to cover the literature thoroughly.
  • The *Social Sciences Citation Index,* the CIS *Statistical Masterfile,* ERIC, PsycLIT, NTIS, LEXIS-NEXIS, and OCLS are some of the online tools now available.
  • Many topics of research have been the subject of meta-analysis. Begin your assessment of the literature by reading any meta-analyses that may be available.

EXERCISES

1. If your library has some of the tools I've described here, then use those tools to build a bibliography for a research problem. Choose any topic you like, and then try to make the literature search exhaustive. This is a great way to learn about narrowing down your research *interests* into manageable research *problems.*

   If you're interested in gender differences, for example, the initial search for the string "gender differences" in PsycINFO returns a message that this topic is found under "human sex differences." Asking the machine for everything in the area of human sex differences returns a list of 9,999 references. In other words, you've maxed out the machine. Asking for "human sex differences" and "test taking" returns about 40 items. Asking for "human sex differences" and "child abuse" returns about 150 items.

   Building a database of references for a research topic of your choice is the best way to learn how to use the powerful bibliographic tools in your college library.

2. Use Table 3.1 to help you think up some research problems. Think about how you would operationalize the variables for each study you think up. Go to the library and see if you can find any studies on the research problems you come up with.

3. After reading this chapter, you should have more to say about the concept of value-free science and value-free research. The examples, though, have been experiments, not research based on questionnaires or on participant observation ethnography. Does questionnaire research done over the telephone pose any ethical problems? How about ethnographic research? Use the bibliographic tools in your library to find articles on these issues in social research ethics. Look up the problem of informed consent in psychological testing and in medical research. If you stop someone on the street to administer a questionnaire and he or she answers you, does that imply consent?

4. Use the bibliographic tools in your college library to find at least one example of social research that is based explicitly on the interpretivist paradigm. Then find an example of research based on the cultural materialist analysis paradigm, and another based on the sociobiological paradigm. Be sure that the three articles are reports of research, not theoretical discussions. Write a brief report describing the articles and then discuss the different approaches of taken by the authors.

FURTHER READING

More documentation resources. If you are interested in political science, start browsing through the *International Political Science Abstracts.* It has appeared annually since 1951 and is a good source of information on political movements. Of related interest, and quite useful, are the Gallup Poll reports, which have been published regularly since 1935. The *Index to International Public Opinion Research* (since 1978) provides similar data for other countries, mostly in western Europe and Japan.

Also of value are *Peace Research Abstracts Journal* (since 1970), *Sage Public Administration Abstracts* (since 1974), and *Sage Urban Studies Abstracts* (since 1973). The *Population Index* (since 1935) is a critical resource for basic demographic information about any country in which you are conducting research and for references to studies on migration, fertility, natality, health and welfare, and mortality.

Poverty and Human Resources Abstracts (since 1966) is particularly useful for finding research on immigration, ethnic and minority groups, aging and retirement, poverty and public policy, women's health and minority health, labor force participation, and similar social issues. Other documentation resources for social issues include *Sage Race Relations Abstracts* (since 1975), *Inventory of Marriage and Family Literature* (since 1971), and *Sage Family Studies Abstracts* (since 1979).

The *British Humanities Index* (since 1962) has good coverage of international folklore and ethnic minority studies and offers coverage of British journals that are not indexed in other publications. The *Film Literature Index* (since 1973) is an international quarterly journal that documents films, including documentaries of interest to scholars.

Since a lot of the really front-line research in any field is done by graduate students, no literature search is complete until you've gone through *Dissertation Abstracts.* That database includes titles going back to 1861, with full abstracts for dissertations from over 1,000 institutions since 1980.

If you are working in the area of criminal justice, you will want to consult the *Criminal Justice Periodical Index* (since 1975) as well as *Criminal Justice Abstracts* (since 1969).

Anthropological Index Online (http://lucy.ukc.ac.uk/AIO.html) is a must for anthropologists. AIO is the index to the periodicals in the Museum of Mankind library in the British Museum. It appears quarterly, from the Royal Anthropological Institute (RAI) in London, and is up-to-date. AIO covers a lot of journals and papers that other services do not cover, especially esoteric publications from Third World nations and from eastern Europe.

Since 1989, *Geographical Abstracts* has published regular volumes on human geography.

Agencies of the U.S. government publish a vast array of reports and data that are useful to social scientists. Just the statistical programs of the U.S. government had a budget of nearly $3 billion in 1998, and that was not counting the budget for the U.S. Census. Here is the Internet address for the U.S. Government Printing Office's list of agencies that had reports available online in 1999: http://www.access.gpo.gov/su_docs/dpos/

This master list of agencies will take you to all the major federal government databases and reports on housing, the elderly, alcohol and drug abuse, violence against women, Native American health, prisons, and hundreds of other topics.

Ethics. For a retrospective on the Stanford prison experiment, see McDermott (1993). For general reviews, see Boruch and Cecil (1983), Burgess (1989), Klockars and O'Connor (1979), Lyman (1989), and Weisstub (1998). Fluehr-Lobban (1996), Herrera (1996), and Wax (1996) discuss the difficult issue of informed consent and field research.

Theory. There are several, quite different, major approaches to theory building in the social sciences. For an overview of the social structural approach, see Blau (1975), Coser (1975), Merton (1968), Turner (1972), and Wellman and Berkowitz (1997 [1998]). For the symbolic interactionist approach, see Blumer (1969). For the materialist approach, see Harris (1979), and for the sociobiological approach, see Crawford and Krebs (1998) and Goldsmith (1991). For a critique of the sociobiological approach, see Sahlins (1976). For the social conflict paradigm of social theory, see Blalock (1989).

Meta-analysis. There are now thousands of meta-analyses available, so many, in fact, that there are summaries of them (meta-analyses of meta-analyses, as it were). Use the online bibliographic resources described here to see if someone has done a meta-analysis of the topic you're interested in.

For example, a search of "meta-analysis" and "bulimia" turns up Fettes and Peters (1992); a search for "meta-analysis" and "smoking" turns up Rooney and Murray (1996). For the original formulation of meta-analysis, see Glass (1976). For general works on meta-analysis, see Cook et al. (1992), Farley and Lehmann (1986), Guzzo et al. (1987), Hedges and Olkin (1985), Hunt (1997), Hunter and Schmidt (1990), Matt and Navarro (1997), Rosenthal (1984), and Wolf (1986).

PART II

RESEARCH DESIGN

4 RESEARCH DESIGN

EXPERIMENTS AND EXPERIMENTAL THINKING

IN THIS CHAPTER:

❖ INTRODUCTION

Early in this century, F. C. Bartlett went to Cambridge University to study with W. H. R. Rivers, an experimental psychologist. Rivers had been invited in 1899 to join the Torres Straits expedition and saw the opportunity to do comparative psychology studies of non-Western people (Tooker 1997:xiv). When Bartlett got to Cambridge, he asked Rivers for some advice. Bartlett expected a quick lecture on how to go out and stay out, about the rigors of fieldwork, and so on. Instead, Rivers told him: "The best training you can possibly have is a thorough drilling in the experimental methods of the psychological laboratory" (Bartlett 1937:416).

Bartlett found himself spending hours in the lab, "lifting weights, judging the brightness of lights, learning nonsense syllables, and engaging in a number of similarly abstract occupations" that seemed to be "particularly distant from the lives of normal human beings." In the end, though, Bartlett concluded that Rivers was right. Training in the experimental methods of psychology, said Bartlett, gives one "a sense of evidence, a realization of the difficulties of human observation, and a kind of scientific conscience which no other field of study can impart so well" (ibid.:417).

Whether you are doing questionnaire surveys, participant observation ethnography, or content analysis of texts, a solid grounding in the logic of the experimental method is one of the keys to good research skills. In this chapter, I discuss how experimental design and experimental thinking are used across the social sciences as a guide to better research on human thought and human behavior.

By the end of this chapter, you should understand the variety of research designs and how they are implemented in experiments, field research, and surveys. You should understand the concept of threats to validity and the various ways in which social scientists respond to those threats.

KINDS OF EXPERIMENTS

There are several ways to categorize experiments. First of all, there is the distinction between *random* and *nonrandom assignment* of participants, or *true experiments* vs. *quasi-experiments.* In true experiments, participants (or subjects) are assigned randomly, to either a *treatment group* or a *control group.* In quasi-experiments, subjects are selected rather than assigned.

Another way to categorize experiments is in terms of where they are done: in the laboratory or out in the world. Experiments in the lab offer greater control; *field experiments* offer greater realism. I distinguish two kinds of field experiments: *natural experiments* and *naturalistic experiments,* but the logic of experiments is the same no matter where they're done.

RANDOMIZED EXPERIMENTS

Whether you're studying people or pigeons, doing research in the laboratory or in the wild, the rules for the design of any true experiment in the social sciences are the same as they are for experiments in physics or agriculture. There are, of course, differences in experiments with humans vs. experiments with objects or pigeons or plants. These differences, though, involve important ethical issues like deception, informed consent, and withholding of treatment, not logic. More on these ethical issues later.

There are five steps to follow in a *classic experiment:*

(1) Formulate a hypothesis.
(2) Randomly assign participants to the intervention group or to the control group.
(3) Measure the dependent variable(s) in one or both groups.
(4) Introduce the treatment or intervention.
(5) Measure the dependent variable(s) again.

Later, I'll walk you through some variations on this five-step formula, including one very important variation that does not involve step 3 at all. But first, the basics.

Step 1. Before you can do an experiment, you need a research question that can be studied using the experimental approach. In other words, you need a clear hypothesis about the relation between some independent variable (or variables) and some dependent variable (or variables). Experiments thus tend to be based on *confirmatory* rather than *exploratory research* questions.

The testing of new drugs can be a simple case of one independent and one dependent variable. The independent variable might be, say, "taking vs. not taking" a drug. The dependent variable might be "getting better vs. not getting better." The independent and dependent variables can be much more subtle, of course. Taking vs. not taking a drug might be "taking more of or less of" a drug and getting better vs. not getting better might be "the level of improvement in high-density lipoprotein" (the so-called good cholesterol).

Move this logic to agriculture: Ceteris paribus (holding everything else—like amount of sunlight, amount of water, amount of weeding—constant), some corn plants get a new fertilizer and some don't. Then, the dependent variable might be the number of cobs per corn stalk or the number of days it takes for the ears to mature, or the number of grams of carbohydrates per ear.

Finally, move this same logic to human thought and human behavior: Ceteris paribus, police who take part in this new training program will be less aggressive in their arrests than will police who do not take part in it.

Things get more complicated, of course, when there are multiple independent (or dependent) variables. You might want to test two different training programs on police who come from three different ethnic backgrounds, for example. But the underlying logic for setting up experiments and for analyzing the results is similar across the sciences. When it comes to experiments, everything starts with a clear hypothesis.

Step 2. You need at least two groups, called the *treatment group* (or the *intervention group* or the *stimulus group*) and the *control group*. **One group gets the intervention (a new drug,**

for example, or exposure to a new method of teaching some subject), and the other group (the control group) doesn't. The treatment group (or groups) and the control group are involved in different *experimental conditions*.

In a true experiment, individuals are *randomly assigned* to either the intervention group or to the control group. This ensures that any differences between the groups are the consequence of chance and not of *systematic bias*. Some people in a population may be more religious, more wealthy, less sickly, or more prejudiced than others, but random assignment ensures that those traits are randomly distributed through the groups in an experiment.

Random assignment does not eliminate the possibility of selection bias altogether, but it makes differences between experimental conditions (groups) due solely to chance by taking the decision of who goes in what group away from the researcher. The principle behind random assignment will become clearer after you work through Chapter 5 on sampling, but the bottom line is this: Whenever you have the opportunity to assign subjects randomly in an experiment, do it.

Step 3. One or both groups are measured on one or more dependent variables. This is called the *pretest*.

Dependent variables in humans can be physical things like weight, height, number of leucocytes per milliliter of blood, or resistance to malaria. They can also be attitudes, psychological states, knowledge, or mental and physical abilities. The ratio of body fat to body mass, for example, is a typical variable in experiments that test the efficacy of weight-loss programs. A preliminary score on a vocabulary test might be the pretest in an

experiment to raise students' scores on the verbal part of the SAT.

Here are some social and psychological dependent variables I've seen recently in literature on experiments: attitude toward abortion, knowledge of mathematics among sixth graders, ability to function outside a hospital despite being clinically depressed, level of expressed racism, amount of self-esteem, level of perceived stress, and support for the distribution of needles to intravenous drug users. In short, the dependent variable in an experiment can be anything you think might change as a result of some intervention.

You don't always need a pretest. More on this in a bit, when we discuss threats to validity in experiments.

Step 4. The intervention (the independent variable) is introduced.

Step 5. The dependent variables are measured again. This is the *posttest*.

A Walkthrough

Here's a made-up example of a true experiment.

———————❖

Take 100 college women (18-22 years of age) and randomly assign 50 of them to each of two groups. Bring each woman to the lab and show her a series of flash cards. Let each card contain a single, three-digit random number. Measure how many three-digit numbers each woman can remember. Repeat the task, but let the members of one group hear the most popular rock song of the week playing in the background as they take the test. Let the other group hear nothing. Measure how many three-digit numbers people can remember and whether rock music improves or worsens performance on the task.

So, you think this is a frivolous experiment? It turns out that many college students, ages 18-22, study while listening to rock music. It also turns out that this drives their parents crazy. I'll bet that more than one reader of this book has been asked something like: "How can you learn anything with all that noise?" The experiment outlined here is designed to test whether students can, in fact, learn anything with all that noise.

There is plenty to criticize about this experimental design. Only women are involved and there are no graduate students, or high school students, either. Furthermore, there is no test of whether classic rock helps or hinders learning more than, say, New Wave, or rhythm and blues or country music or Beethoven. In fact, the experiment, as designed, doesn't even test whether people can learn anything important or useful when they listen or don't listen to rock music. The experiment tests only whether college-age women learn to memorize more or fewer three-digit numbers when the learning is accompanied by a single rock tune. The learning task is artificial.

On the other hand, a lot of what's really powerful about the experimental method is embodied in this example. Suppose that the rock music group does better on the task. We can be pretty sure that it's not because of their gender or their age or their education, but because of the music. Just sticking in more independent variables (for example, expanding the group to include men, graduate students, or high school students; playing different tunes; or making the learning task more realistic), without modifying the experiment's design to control for all those variables,

creates what are called *confounds*. They *confound* the experiment and **make it impossible to tell if the intervention is what really caused any observed differences in the dependent variable.** Good experiments test narrowly defined questions.

> *The kind of knowledge you get from a well-designed experiment can be verified or falsified by another experiment.*

What's really important about the experimental method is its epistemological power. When you do a good experiment, you *know* something at the end of it. It may not be much, but you really know it. In this case, for example, you know that women students at one school memorize or do not memorize three-digit numbers better when they listen to a particular rock tune.

I know this doesn't sound like much. Critics of experimental thinking in the social sciences say that it forces you to learn more and more about less and less, until finally you know everything there is to know about nothing.

Cute, but wrong. Think about it: The kind of knowledge you get from a well-designed experiment can be verified or falsified by another experiment. You can repeat the experiment at another school. If you get a different answer, then you need an explanation for this finding. Perhaps there is something about the student selection process at the two schools that produces the different results. Perhaps students at one school come primarily from working-class families, while students from the other school come from upper-middle-class families. Perhaps students from different socioeconomic classes grow up with different study habits, or prefer different kinds of music.

Conduct the experiment again, but this time include men. Conduct it again, and include two music conditions: a rock tune and a classical piece.

Continual replication and verification produce *cumulative knowledge.* That's the real power of experiments.

INTERNAL AND EXTERNAL VALIDITY

When a true experiment (with full control by the researcher) is carried out properly, the results have high *internal validity.* This means that changes in the dependent variables were probably *caused by*—not merely related to or correlated with—the treatment. This is why the experimental method is considered so powerful.

Consider the following experiment, designed to test whether offering people money produces fewer errors in an arithmetic task. Take two groups of individuals and ask them to solve 100 simple arithmetic problems. Tell one group's members that they will be given a dollar for every correct answer. Tell the other group nothing. Be sure to assign participants randomly to the groups to ensure equal distribution of skill in arithmetic. See if the treatment group (the one that gets the monetary rewards) does better than the control group.

This experiment can be embellished to eliminate confounds that threaten internal validity. Conduct the experiment a second time, with the same people, reversing the control and treatment groups. In other words, tell those in the former treatment group that they will not receive any financial reward for correct answers, and tell those in the former control group that they will receive a dollar for every correct answer. (Of course, give them a new set of problems to solve.)

This creates a whole new experiment, of course. You're no longer testing whether financial incentives motivate people to try harder in solving a set of arithmetic problems. Now you're also testing whether pulling financial incentives away

from people who are accustomed to getting them will affect their ability to solve those arithmetic problems.

Conduct the experiment many times, changing or adding independent variables. In one version of the experiment, you might keep the groups from knowing about each other. In another iteration, you might let each group know about the other's efforts and rewards (or lack of rewards). Perhaps, when people know that others are being rewarded for good behavior, and they themselves are not rewarded, they will double their efforts to gain the rewards (this is called the "John Henry effect"). Perhaps they just become demoralized and give up.

By controlling the interventions and the group membership you can build up a series of conclusions regarding cause and effect between various independent and dependent variables.

Controlled experiments, like good ethnography, have the virtue of high internal validity, but they have the liability of low *external validity.* It may be true that a reward of a dollar per correct answer results in significantly more correct answers for the groups you tested in your laboratory. But you can't tell whether a dollar is sufficient reward for all groups, or whether a quarter would be enough to create the same experimental results in some groups. Worst of all, you don't know whether the laboratory results explain anything you want to know about in the real world.

To test external validity, you might propose some kind of monetary reward for children in a dozen actual third-grade classrooms learning to do arithmetic—six classrooms in which, say, children earn a penny per correct answer and six in which there is no monetary incentive. If it turns out that the kids in the intervention classrooms get higher scores on arithmetic tests at the end of the year, then the next question is: How far do the results generalize? Just to the classrooms in the experiment? To all third graders in the school district? To all third graders in the state? In the country?

KINDS OF CONFOUNDS: THREATS TO VALIDITY

It's pointless to ask questions about external validity until you establish internal validity. In a series of influential publications, Donald Campbell and his colleagues identified the threats to internal validity of experiments (see Campbell 1957, 1979; Campbell and Stanley 1963; Cook and Campbell 1979). Here are seven of the most important confounds:

1. History

The *history confound* refers to **any independent variable, other than the treatment, that (1) occurs between the pretest and the posttest in an experiment and (2) affects the experimental groups differently.** Suppose you are doing a laboratory experiment, with two groups (experimental and control), and there is a power failure in the building. So long as the lights go out for both groups, there is no problem. But if the lights go out for one group and not the other, it's difficult to tell whether it was the treatment or the power failure that causes changes in the dependent variable.

In a laboratory experiment, history is controlled by isolating subjects as much as possible from outside influences. When we do experiments outside the laboratory, it is almost impossible to keep new independent variables from creeping in and confounding things.

❖

Recall the example of testing whether monetary incentives help third graders do better in arithmetic. Suppose that right in the middle of the school term during which the experiment was being conducted, the Governor's Task Force on Elementary Education issues its long-awaited report, and it contains the observation that arithmetic skills must be emphasized during the early school years. Furthermore, it says, teachers whose classes make exceptional progress in this area should be rewarded with 10% salary bonuses.

The governor accepts the recommendation and announces a request for a special legislative appropriation. Elementary teachers all over the state start paying extra attention to arithmetic skills. Even supposing that the students in the treatment classes do better than those in the control classes, how can we be certain that the magnitude of the difference would not have been greater had this historical confound not occurred?

2. Maturation

The *maturation confound* refers to the fact that **people in any experiment grow older, or get more experienced, while you are trying to conduct an experiment.** Consider the following experiment: Start with a group of teenagers on a

Native American reservation and follow them for the next 60 years. Some of them will move to cities, some will go to small towns, and some will stay on the reservation. Periodically, test them on a variety of dependent variables (their political opinions, their wealth, their health, their family size, etc.). See how the various experimental treatments (city vs. reservation vs. town living) affect these variables.

Here is where the maturation confound enters the picture. The people you are studying get older. Older people in many societies become more politically conservative. They are usually wealthier than younger people. Eventually, they come to be more illness prone than younger people. Some of the changes you measure in your dependent variables will be the result of the various treatments, and some of them may just be the result of maturation.

Maturation is sometimes taken too literally. Social service delivery programs "mature" by working out bugs in their administration. People "mature" through practice with experimental conditions and they become fatigued. We see this all the time in new social programs where people start out being all enthusiastic about innovations in organizations and eventually get bored or disenchanted.

3. Testing and Instrumentation

The *testing confound* occurs in laboratory and field experiments, when subjects get used to being tested for indicators on dependent variables. This quite naturally changes their responses. Asking people the same questions again and again in a longitudinal study, or even in an ethnographic study done over six months or more, can have this effect.

The *instrumentation confound* results from changing measurement instruments. Changing the wording of questions in a survey is essentially changing instruments. Which responses do you

trust, the ones to the earlier wording or the ones to the later wording? If you do a set of observations in the field, and later send in someone else to continue the observations, you have changed instruments. Which observations do you trust as closer to the truth: yours or those of the substitute instrument (the new field researcher)? In multiresearcher projects, this problem is usually dealt with by training all investigators to see and record things in more or less the same way. This is called increasing *interrater reliability*. (More on this in Chapter 12, on text analysis.)

4. Regression to the Mean

Regression to the mean is a confound that can occur when you study groups that have extreme scores on a dependent variable. No matter what the treatment is, over time you'd expect the extreme scores to become more moderate, just because there's nowhere else for them to go.

Suppose you're asked to evaluate a new reading program for third graders. To give the program a real workout, you choose children who scored in the bottom 10% of their class and you compare them to children in the top 10% of their class. You'll probably find that the bottom 10% shows improvement, but don't write home about this just yet. You'll also probably find that the top 10% shows some decrease in their performance.

What's going on? Well, those bottom 10-percenters have nowhere to go but up, and the top 10-percenters have nowhere to go but down. If you introduced no program at all, the kids at the extremes would have a statistical chance, just by random fluctuation, of getting scores that are more like the mean the next time you test them. By choosing groups that score at the extreme, you wind up not being able to tell if the new reading program caused the change in scores or if the change was just a statistical regression to the mean.

This same principle holds in the natural world. If men who are taller than 6′ 7″ marry women who are taller than 6′ 3″, then their children are likely to be (1) taller than average, and (2) closer to average height than either of their parents are. There are two independent variables (the height of each of the parents) and one dependent variable (the height of the children). We expect the dependent variable to "regress toward the mean," since it really can't get more extreme than the height of the parents.

I put that phrase "regress toward the mean" in quotes because it's really easy to misinterpret this phenomenon—to think that the "regressing behavior" toward the mean of an dependent variable is caused by the extreme scores on the independent variables. It isn't, and here's how you can tell that it isn't: Very, very tall children are likely to have parents whose height is more like the mean. One thing we know for sure is that the height of children doesn't cause the height of their parents. Regression to the mean is a statistical phenomenon—it happens in the aggregate and is not something that happens to individuals.

5. Selection of Participants

Selection bias in choosing subjects is **a major confound to validity in both quasi-experiments and natural experiments.** In laboratory experiments, you assign subjects at random, from a single population, to both treatment groups and control groups. This distributes any differences among individuals in the population throughout the groups, making the groups equivalent. This reduces the possibility that differences among the groups will cause differences in outcomes on the dependent variables, so selection is not a threat to the internal validity of the experiment.

Random assignment of participants to experimental conditions reduces the possibility of selection bias, but it doesn't eliminate the possibility altogether. Random assignment, then, maximizes

the chance for valid outcomes—outcomes that are not clobbered by hidden factors.

In natural experiments, we have *no control* over assignment of individuals to groups.

Question: Do victims of violent crime have less stable marriages than persons who have not been victims? Obviously, researchers cannot randomly assign subjects to the treatment (violent crime). It could turn out that people who are victims of this treatment are more likely to have unstable marriages anyway, even if they never experienced violence.

Question: Do migrants to cities from small towns engage in more entrepreneurial activities than stay-at-homes? If we could assign rural people randomly to the treatment group (those engaging in urban migration), we'd have a better chance of finding out. Since we cannot, selection is a threat to the internal validity of the experiment. Suppose that the answer to the question is yes. We could not know whether the treatment (migration) caused the outcome (greater entrepreneurial activity) or whether the outcome is the result of self-selection for migration by entrepreneurial personalities.

6. Mortality

The **mortality confound** refers to the fact that **individuals may not complete their participation in an experiment.** Suppose we follow two sets of married couples for five years. The couples in one group get free family counseling sessions once every three months. The other couples don't. During the first year of the experiment, we have 200 couples in each group. By the fifth year, 30 couples have dropped out of the treatment group and 130 of the 170 remaining couples (76%) are still married. In the control group, 50 couples have dropped out and 75 of the 150 remaining couples (50%) are still married. One conclusion is that lack of counseling caused those in the control group to get divorced at a faster rate than those in the treatment group.

But what of those 30 couples in the treatment group and the 50 couples in the control group who left? It could be that they were mostly still married or mostly divorced. In either case, this would affect the results of the experiment, but we just don't know. Mortality can be a serious problem in natural experiments if it gets to be a large fraction of the group(s) under study.

7. Diffusion of Treatments

The *diffusion of treatments* threat to validity occurs **when a control group cannot be prevented from receiving the treatment in an experiment.** This is particularly likely in quasi-experiments where the independent variable is an information program.

In a project with which I was associated a few years ago, African Americans in a group were given instruction on modifying their diet and exercise behavior to lower their blood pressure. Another group was randomly assigned from the population to act as controls—that is, group members would not receive instruction. The evaluation team measured blood pressure in the treatment group and in the control group before the program was implemented. But when they went back after the program was completed, they found that control group members had also been changing their behavior. They had learned of the new diet and exercises from the members of the treatment group.

CONTROLLING FOR THREATS TO VALIDITY

In what follows, I want to show you how the power of experimental logic is applied to real research problems. The major experimental designs are shown in Figure 4.1. The notation is pretty standard. X stands for some intervention—a stimulus or a treatment of a subject. R means that subjects are randomly assigned to experimental conditions—either to the intervention group that gets the treatment or to the control group that doesn't. Several designs include random assignment and several don't. O stands for observation. O_1 means that some observation is made at time 1, O_2 means that some observation is made at time 2, and so on.

"Observation" means measurement of some dependent variable, but as you already know, the idea of measurement is pretty broad. It can be taking someone's temperature or testing some-

one's reading skill. It can also be just writing down whether someone is smiling.

The Classic Two-Group Pretest-Posttest Design with Random Assignment

We begin with the classic experimental design, the *two-group pretest-posttest design with random assignment.* It is shown in Figure 4.1a. From a population of potential participants, some participants have been assigned randomly to a treatment group and a control group. Read across the top row of the figure. An observation (measurement) of some dependent variable or variables is made at time 1 on the members of group 1. That is O_1. Then an intervention is made (the group is exposed to some treatment, X). Then, another observation is made at time 2. That is O_2.

	Time 1		Time 2	
	Assignment	Pretest	Intervention	Posttest
Group 1	R	O_1	X	O_2
Group 2	R	O_3		O_4

Figure 4.1a The Classic Design: Two-Group Pretest-Posttest

	Time 1		Time 2	
	Assignment	Pretest	Intervention	Posttest
Group 1	R	O_1	X	O_2
Group 2	R	O_3		O_4
Group 3	R		X	O_5
Group 4	R			O_6

Figure 4.1b The Solomon Four-Group Design

	Time 1		Time 2	
	Assignment	Pretest	Intervention	Posttest
Group 1		O_1	X	O_2
Group 2			O_3	O_4

Figure 4.1c The Classic Design without Randomization

	Time 1		Time 2	
	Assignment	Pretest	Intervention	Posttest
Group 1	R		X	O_1
Group 2	R			O_2

Figure 4.1d The Campbell and Stanley Posttest-Only Design

	Time 1		Time 2	
	Assignment	Pretest	Intervention	Posttest
			X	O

Figure 4.1e The One-Shot Case Study Design

	Time 1		Time 2	
	Assignment	Pretest	Intervention	Posttest
		O_1	X	O_2

Figure 4.1f The One-Group Pretest-Posttest Design

	Time 1		Time 2	
	Assignment	Pretest	Intervention	Posttest
			X	O_1
				O_2

Figure 4.1g Two-Group Posttest-Only Design: Static Group Comparison

	Time 1		Time 2	
	Assignment	Pretest	Intervention	Posttest
		$O\ O\ O$	X	$O\ O\ O$

Figure 4.1h The Interrupted Time Series Design

Now look at the second row of the table. A second group of people is observed, also at time 1. Measurements are made of the same dependent variable(s) that were made for the first group. The observation is labeled O_3. There is no X on this row, which means that no intervention is made on this group of people. They remain unexposed to the treatment or intervention in the experiment. Later, at time 2, after the first group has been exposed to the intervention, the second group is observed again. That's O_4.

Random assignment of participants ensures equivalent groups, and the second group, without the intervention, ensures that several threats to internal validity are taken care of. Most important, you can tell how often (how many times out of a hundred, for example) any differences between the pretest and posttest scores for the first group might have occurred anyway, even if the intervention hadn't taken place.

Patricia Chapman and her colleagues (Chapman et al. 1997) are interested in developing effective ways to educate student athletes about sports nutrition. They had access to an eight-team girls' high school softball league in southern California. The participants were 14-18 years old. Chapman et al. assigned each of 72 players randomly to one of two groups. The girls in the treatment group got two 45-minute lectures a week for six weeks about things like dehydration, weight loss, vitamin and mineral supplements, and energy sources. The control group got no instruction.

Before the six-week program started, the researchers asked each participant to complete the Nutrition Knowledge and Attitude Questionnaire (Werblow et al. 1978) and also to list the foods each had consumed in the previous 24 hours. The nutrition knowledge-attitude test and the 24-hour dietary recall test were the *pretests* in this experiment. Then, when the six-week program was over, Chapman et al. gave the participants the same two tests. These were the *posttests*. The pretests provided baseline data and the posttests provided data for assessing whether the nutrition education program had made a difference.

The education intervention did make a difference—in knowledge, but not in reported behavior. The participants in both the treatment and control groups scored about the same on the knowledge-attitude test in the pretest. After they went through the lecture series, the participants in the treatment group scored about 18 points more (out of 200 possible points) than those in the control group. Before the program, the 36 girls in the control group reported an average 24-hour intake of 1,683 calories and those in the

treatment group reported an average of 2,054 calories.

	Time 1		Time 2	
	Assignment	Pretest	Intervention	Posttest
Group 1	R	O_1	X	O_2
Group 2	R	O_2		O_4

Figure 4.1a The Classic Design: Two-Group Pretest-Posttest.

As Chapman et al. point out, though, even 2,054 calories is not enough for adolescent females who are involved in competitive sports. After the intervention—after all those lectures—the reported 24-hour average caloric intake was 1,793 for the control group and 1,892 for the treatment group. In other words, if the intervention had any effect on behavior, it was to lower (and hence, worsen) the intake of these young female athletes. Chapman et al. point out that the results confirm the findings of other studies: For many adolescent females, the attraction of competitive sports is the possibility of losing weight.

This classic experimental design is used widely across the social sciences to evaluate programs. Abernethy and Cox (1994) used this design to test a program designed to help police manage their own anger more effectively during arrests. Kunovich and Rashid (1992) used this design to test their program for training freshman dental students in how to handle a mirror in a patient's mouth (think about it—it's not easy; everything you see is backward).

The Solomon Four-Group Design

The classic design has one important flaw: It is subject to testing bias. Differences between variable measurements at time 1 and time 2 might be the result of the intervention, but they also might be the result of people getting savvy about being watched and measured. Pretesting can, after all, sensitize people to the purpose of an experiment, and this, in turn, can change people's behavior. The *Solomon four-group design,* shown in Figure 4.1b, controls for this. Since there are no measurements at time 1 for groups 3 and 4, this problem is controlled for.

	Time 1		Time 2	
	Assignment	Pretest	Intervention	Posttest
Group 1	R	O_1	X	O_2
Group 2	R	O_3		O_4
Group 3	R		X	O_5
Group 4	R			O_6

Figure 4.1b The Solomon Four-Group Design

Larry Leith (1988) used the Solomon four-group design to study a phenomenon known to all sports fans as the "choke." That's when an athlete plays well during practice and then loses it during the real game, or plays well all game long and folds in the clutch when it really counts. It's not pretty.

Leith assigned 20 male students randomly to each of the four conditions in the Solomon four-group design. The pretest and the posttest were the same: Each participant shot 25 free throws on a basketball court. The dependent variable was the number of successful free throws out of 25 shots in the posttest. The independent variable—the treatment—was giving or not giving the following little pep talk to each participant just before he made those 25 free throws for the posttest:

Research has shown that some people have a tendency to choke at the free-throw line when shooting free throws. No one knows why some people tend to [exhibit] choking behavior. However, don't let that bother you. Go ahead and shoot your free throws. (Leith 1988:61)

What a wonderfully simple, utterly diabolic experiment. You can guess the result: There was a significantly greater probability of choking if you were among the groups that got that little pep talk, irrespective of whether they'd been given the warmup pretest.

The Solomon four-group design is very useful in evaluation research. From New York to Nairobi, for example, social workers, teachers, and researchers have been looking for ways to teach adolescents about the effective use of condoms in the prevention of sexually transmitted diseases and unwanted pregnancies. Interventions are usually some kind of teaching program administered in the classroom, and study after study shows that they don't work. Kvalem et al. (1996) evaluated one of these in-school programs. They had 124 classes of 16- to 20-year-olds, comprising a total of 2,411 students from Vestfold County in Norway. They assigned the classes randomly to the four conditions in the four-group design. I mention this study because the major finding was not that the program worked. It didn't. The major finding was a strong *interaction effect between the pretest and the intervention* on the reported use of condoms.

The pretest was an 80-item questionnaire about sexual behavior, use of condoms, and demographics. The posttest was the same questionnaire, sent 6 months and 12 months after the intervention. Of the four groups on the Solomon four-group design, the group that had both the pretest and the intervention had a higher likelihood of reporting condom use six months after

TABLE 4.1 The Solomon Four-Group Design Used by Dukes et al. (1995)

Group	N	Time 1	Intervention	Time 2
Group 1	97	Pretest (O_1)	DARE (X)	Posttest (O_2)
Group 2	96	Pretest (O_3)		Posttest (O_4)
Group 3	122		DARE (X)	Posttest (O_5)
Group 4	125			Posttest (O_6)

SOURCE: R. L. Dukes et al., "An Evaluation of DARE (Drug Abuse Resistance Education) Using a Solomon Four-Group Design with Latent Variables." *Evaluation Review* 19:409-35. Copyright © 1995 by Sage Publications. Reprinted by permission.

the intervention. Six months later, though, when the posttest was given again, the interaction effect had disappeared.

The study by Kvalem et al. is instructive. It shows clearly the importance of testing for the effects of pretesting in social and psychological experiments. And it shows clearly the importance of following up with a second posttest to make sure that any effects on the dependent variable have lasted. If Kvalem et al. had not done that second posttest, they might have been tempted to interpret the interaction effect as having policy implications: If you want to get adolescents to use condoms, combine a pretest with an educational intervention. Kvalem et al.'s second posttest questionnaire, sent to the participants after 12 months, stopped them from making that mistake

————❖————

Finally, consider the design used in evaluating the Colorado Springs, Colorado, DARE program. DARE (Drug Abuse Resistance Education) began in 1983 in Los Angeles and is now in elementary schools in 20 countries. In the DARE program, a trained police officer visits classrooms for a semester, teaching children to resist peer pressures and to stay away from alcohol, tobacco, and other

drugs. Richard Dukes and his colleagues evaluated the DARE program in the Colorado Springs elementary school system (Dukes et al. 1995).

For eight semesters, from 1990 to 1993, Dukes and his colleagues assigned half the 60 schools in the Colorado Springs school district to receive the DARE program. The other half of the schools were assigned to the control group—that is, they did not get the DARE program. Half the students in the DARE schools and half in the control schools were randomly chosen to take a pretest. This test measured the dependent variables that were supposed to be influenced by the DARE program: self-esteem, attitudes toward teachers and parents, attitudes toward the police, and self-reported behaviors regarding the consumption of alcohol, tobacco, and other drugs. At the end of each semester, all the students—in the DARE schools and in the control schools—took this same test.

In all, there were 440 classrooms in this experiment over the four years. The distribution of those classrooms to the four groups in the Solomon four-group design is shown in Table 4.1. (The reason that some conditions in the experiment have more classrooms than others is because some schools are bigger than others and have more classrooms than others. That's just the way the random assignment turned out. With more than 10,000 students in the study, though, there was no shortage of data in any on the conditions of the evaluation experiment.)

The results of this powerful evaluation design were mixed. On the one hand, students who went through the program reported increased self-esteem; greater resistance to peer pressure; stronger bonds with their families, teachers, and police; and lowered experimentation with alcohol, tobacco, and other drugs. With the Solomon four-group design, Dukes et al. determined that these positive effects were the result of the DARE curriculum and not the result of pretesting or simple maturation.

On the other hand, the effects didn't last: The intervention groups and the control groups became more like each other after a year. The educational model of social change remains appealing, but it is costly—DARE costs about $100 per student, plus about $50,000 per year for each police officer assigned to the program—and often ineffective because it doesn't address the structural causes of social problems.

The Two-Group Pretest-Posttest Design without Random Assignment

The term *quasi-experiment* refers to an experiment where participants are not assigned randomly to the control and the experimental condition. This compromise with design purity is often the best we can do and is shown in Figure 4.1c.

Michael Stitsworth (1989) tested 154 teenagers who spent a month in Japan as exchange students and 112 similar students who did not travel abroad. Obviously, Stitsworth couldn't just assign teenagers to be in the travel or no-travel groups, but he gave all the participants in the study—the treatment group and the control group—the California Psychological Inventory

(CPI) before the travel program got under way, again a month later when the travelers came home, and again four months after that.

	Time I		Time 2	
Assignment	Pretest	Intervention	Posttest
Group I		O_1	X	O_2
Group 2		O_3		O_4

Figure 4.1c The Classic Design without Randomization

The group that had traveled showed greater flexibility and independence after their experience, but the effect wasn't uniform. The effect was greatest on students who were the first members of their families to live overseas and on students who paid a high percentage of their own way. Curiously, students who had studied a foreign language for one or two semesters showed no personality changes, but those who had never studied a foreign language or who had studied for at least three semesters were greatly affected by the experience.

Campbell and Boruch (1975) show that lack of random assignment leads to problems. Suppose you invent a technique for improving reading comprehension among third graders. You select two third-grade classes in a school district. One of them gets the intervention and the other doesn't. Students are measured before and after the intervention to see whether their reading scores improve.

Suppose the children in one class are from wealthier homes, on average, than are the children in the other class, and suppose that the wealthier children test higher in reading comprehension at the end of the year than the poorer children. Would you be willing to bet, say, $300,000 on implementing the new reading comprehension program in all classes in the school district? Would you bet that it was the new program and not some confound, like socioeconomic class, that caused the differences in test scores?

If all the children, one at a time, were assigned randomly to the two groups (those who got the program and those who didn't), then this confound would disappear—not because socioeconomic status stops being a factor in how well children learn to read, but because children from poor and rich families would be equally likely to be in the treatment group or in the control group. Any bias that socioeconomic status causes in interpreting the results of the experiment would be distributed randomly and would, in theory, wash out.

But children come packaged in classrooms. It's physically impossible for a teacher to administer two separate programs in one classroom, so evaluation of these kinds of interventions are usually quasi-experiments because they have to be.

The Posttest-Only Design with Random Assignment

Look carefully at Figure 4.1d. It is the second half of the Solomon four-group design and is called the *Campbell and Stanley posttest-only design*. This design has a lot going for it. It retains the random assignment of participants in the classic design and in the Solomon four-group design, but it *eliminates pretesting*—and the possibility of a confound from pretest sensitization. When subjects are assigned randomly to experimental conditions (control or treatment group), a significant difference on O_1 and O_2 in the posttest-only design means that we can have a lot of confidence that the intervention, X, caused that difference (Cook and Campbell 1979).

Another advantage is the huge saving in time and money. There are no pretests in this design

	Time 1		Time 2	
	Assignment	Pretest	Intervention	Posttest
Group 1	R		X	O_1
Group 2	R			O_2

Figure 4.1d The Campbell and Stanley Posttest-Only Design

and there are only two posttests instead of the four in the Solomon four-group design.

McDonald and Bridge (1991) used this design in their study of how gender stereotyping by nurses affects how nurses care for patients. McDonald and Bridge asked 160 female medical-surgical nurses to read an information packet about a colostomy patient whom they would be attending within the next eight hours. The nurses were assigned randomly to one of eight experimental conditions:

(1) The patient was named Mary B. or Robert B. to produce *two patient-gender conditions.*

(2) Half the nurses read just a synopsis of the condition of Mary B. or Robert B., and half read the same synopsis as the fourth one in a series of seven. This produced *two memory-load conditions.*

(3) Finally, half the nurses read that the temperature of Mary B. or Robert B. had just spiked unexpectedly to 102°, and half did not. This produced *two patient-stability conditions.*

The three binary conditions combined to form eight experimental conditions in a *factorial design* (more on factorial designs in a little while).

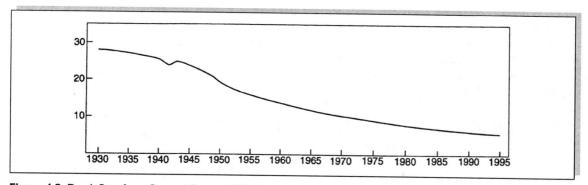

Figure 4.2 Death Rate from Cervical Cancer, 1930-95
SOURCES: B. Williams, *A Sampler on Sampling*, Figure 2.1, p. 17. Copyright © 1978, Lucent Technologies. Used by permission. Information after 1975 provided by the National Cancer Society web site.

> *The posttest-only design, with random assignment, is not used as much as it should be, despite its elegance, its delightful simplicity, and its low cost.*

Next, McDonald and Bridge asked nurses to estimate, to the nearest minute, how much time they would plan for each of several important nursing actions. Irrespective of the memory load, nurses planned significantly more time for giving the patient analgesics, for helping the patient to walk around, and for giving the patient emotional support when the patient was a man.

The posttest-only design, with random assignment, is not used as much as it should be, despite its elegance, its delightful simplicity, and its low cost. This is due partly to the appealing-but-mistaken idea that controlling the composition of experimental and control groups in experiments by matching subjects on key independent variables (age, ethnicity, etc.) is somehow better than randomly assigning subject to groups. It's also due partly to the nagging suspicion that pretests are essential.

The One-Shot Case Study Design

The **one-shot case study design** is shown in Figure 4.1e. It is also called the **ex post facto design** because a single group of individuals is measured on some dependent variable *after* an intervention has taken place. This design is widely used in culture change studies, where it is obviously impossible to manipulate the dependent variable. A researcher arrives in a community and notices that something important has taken place. A new exit on a highway produces more tourist traffic or an interstate highway has bypassed a town and tourism revenues have plummeted. The researcher tries to evaluate the experiment by interviewing people (O) and trying to assess the impact of the intervention (X).

	Time 1		Time 2
	Assignment	Pretest	Intervention	Posttest
			X	O

Figure 4.1e The One-Shot Case Study Design

With neither a pretest nor a control group, you can't be sure that what you observe is the result of some particular intervention. Despite this apparent weakness, however, the intuitive appeal of findings produced by one-shot case studies can be formidable.

In the 1950s, physicians began general use of the Pap test, a simple office procedure for determining the presence of cervical cancer. Figure 4.2 shows that since 1950, the death rate from cervical cancer in the U.S. has dropped steadily, from about 18 per 100,000 women to about 11 in 1970, to about 8.3 in 1980, and to about 6.5 in 1995. On the other hand, if you look only at the data *after* the intervention (the one-shot case study $X O$ design) you might conclude that the intervention (the Pap test) caused this drop in cervical cancer deaths. There is no doubt that the continued decline of cervical cancer deaths is, in some measure, due to the early detection provided by the Pap test, but by 1950, the death rate had already declined by 36% from 28 per 100,000 in 1930 (Williams 1978:16).

Never use a design of less logical power when one of greater power is feasible. If pretest data are available, use them. On the other hand, a one-shot case study is often the best you can do. Virtually all ethnography falls in this category, and as I have said before, nothing beats a good story, well told.

The One-Group Pretest-Posttest Design

The *one-group pretest-posttest design* is shown in Figure 4.1f. Some variables are measured (observed), then the intervention takes place, and then the variables are measured again. This takes care of some of the problems associated with the one-shot case study, but it doesn't eliminate the threats of history, testing, maturation, selection, and mortality. Most important, if there is a significant difference in the pretest and posttest mea-

surements, we can't tell if the intervention made that difference happen.

Time 1		Time 2	
Assignment	Pretest	Intervention	Posttest
	O_1	X	O_2

Figure 4.1f The One-Group Pretest-Posttest Design

Peterson and Johnstone (1995) used this design in testing the efficacy of a drug treatment program for 43 women inmates of a U.S. federal prison. The participants were volunteers who had a history of drug abuse, so there is no random assignment here. (Some scholars reject the idea that prisoners can ever volunteer freely for any such programs.) Peterson and Johnstone measured the participants' health status and perceived well-being before the program began and after the program had been running for nine months. They found that physical fitness measures were improved for the participants as was self-esteem, health awareness, and health-promoting attitudes.

The one-group pretest-posttest design is commonly used in evaluating training programs. The question asked is: Did the people who were exposed to this skill-building program (police officers, nurses, kindergarten teachers, high school algebra students, etc.) get any benefit out of it, and if so, how much?

The Two-Group Posttest-Only Design without Random Assignment

The *two-group posttest-only design without random assignment* is shown in Figure 4.1g. This design, also known as the *static group compari-*

son, improves on the one-shot ex post facto design by adding an untreated control group—an independent case that is evaluated only at time 2. The relation between smoking cigarettes (the intervention) and getting lung cancer (the dependent variable), for example, is easily seen by applying the humble ex post facto design with a control group for a second posttest.

In 1965, when the American Cancer Society (ACS) did its first big Cancer Prevention Study, men who smoked (that is, those who were subject to the intervention) were about 12 times more likely than nonsmokers (the control group) to die of lung cancer. There are no baseline data and no randomization of subjects to treatments, but the data are devastating.

	Time 1		Time 2	
	Assignment	Pretest	Intervention	Posttest
			X	O_1
				O_2

Figure 4.1g Two-Group Posttest-Only Design: Static Group Comparison

Once those ACS data were gathered, they became the baseline for a later study. By 1988, male smokers were about 23 times more likely than nonsmokers to die of lung cancer. In 1965, the relatively few women who smoked (compared to men) had not been smoking very long. Their risk was only 2.7 times that for women nonsmokers of dying from lung cancer. By 1988, though, women smokers were 12.8 times more likely than women nonsmokers to die of lung cancer. While men's risk had doubled (from about 12 to about 23), women's risk had more than quadrupled (from 2.7 to about 13) (National Cancer Institute 1997).

In true experiments run with the posttest-only design, participants are assigned at random to either the intervention or the control group. In the static group comparison design, the researcher has no control over assignment of participants. This leaves the static group comparison design open to an unresolvable validity threat. There is no way to tell whether the two groups were comparable at time 1, before the intervention, even with a comparison of observations 1 and 3. Therefore, you can only guess whether the intervention caused any differences in the groups at time 2.

Despite this, the static group comparison design is the best one for evaluating natural experiments, where you have no control over the assignment of participants, anyway. Jones and Badger (1991) used this design to assess the differences between 190 hearing children and 80 deaf children, ages 5-15, regarding internal human anatomy. Each child was presented with an outline drawing of a rear view of a human body and was asked to draw in and label internal body parts. Deaf children in every age group lagged behind their hearing counterparts in their knowledge of internal body parts because deaf children typically get less instruction in health education than do their hearing counterparts.

Lambros Comitas and I wanted to find out if the experience abroad of Greek labor migrants had any influence on men's and women's attitudes toward gender roles when they returned to Greece. The best design would have been to survey a group before the persons went abroad, then again while they were away, and again when they returned to Greece. Since this was not possible, we studied one group that had been abroad and another group that had never left Greece. We treated these two groups as if they were part of a static group comparison design (Bernard and Comitas 1978).

From a series of life histories with migrants and nonmigrants, we learned that the custom of giving dowry was under severe stress (Bernard and Ashton-Vouyoucalos 1976). Our survey confirmed this; those who had worked abroad were far less enthusiastic about providing expensive dowries for their daughters than were those who had never left Greece. We concluded that this was in some measure due to the experiences of migrants in (the former) West Germany.

Of course, there were threats to the validity of this conclusion: Perhaps migrants were a self-selected bunch of people who held the dowry and other traditional Greek customs in low esteem to begin with. But we had those life histories to back up our conclusion. Surveys are weak compared to true experiments, but their power is improved if they are conceptualized in terms of testing natural experiments and if their results are backed up with data from open-ended interviews.

❖———

Interrupted Time Series Design

The *interrupted time series design,* shown in Figure 4.1h, can be quite convincing. It involves **getting data from a series of points before and after an intervention and evaluating statistically whether the intervention has had an impact.**

Time 1		Time 2	
Assignment	Pretest	Intervention	Posttest
	O O O	X	O O O

Figure 4.1h The Interrupted Time Series Design

On November 3, 1991, Earvin "Magic" Johnson, a star basketball player for the Los Angeles Lakers, held a news conference and announced that he was HIV positive. AIDS had been in the news for 10 years by then, and poll after poll had shown that, despite government and media efforts to educate the public about AIDS, people generally believed AIDS to be a "gay disease." Philip Pollock (1994) treated those polls as a time series and Johnson's announcement as an interruption. Just as Pollock suspected, polls after Magic Johnson's announcement showed a clear change in public values and in the way people, at least across America, discussed AIDS (ibid.:444). If it had happened to Magic, it could happen to anyone.

The interrupted time series design is used to assess the effect of new laws. Until 1985, if two working spouses in Canada were married in January, then each of them paid full tax on their own income. But if they married in December, then one of them could claim the other as a dependent. The loophole was closed in 1986. Gelardi (1996) treated the new law as an interruption in a time series and found, just as we'd predict, a significant decrease in the percentage of marriages in December immediately after the new law took effect.

Gelardi found the same result when he examined times series data from England and Wales, where a similar change in the law had occurred in 1968. Bonham et al. (1992) found that Hawaii's 1987 tax of 5.25% on hotel rooms had no effect on rentals. In that case, the state simply made money and the hotel industry didn't suffer any loss.

And finally, this: In 1994, California adopted a "three strikes and you're out" law. Under the law, anyone convicted of a third felony receives a mandatory sentence of life in prison. Stolzenberg and D'Alessio (1997) used monthly data (a time series) from the 10 largest cities in California to test the effect of the law on violent crime and on petty theft. For the first few years, at least, the three-strikes law had no impact on crime rates for 9 of the 10 cities they looked at.

THOUGHT EXPERIMENTS

As you can see, it is next to impossible to eliminate threats to validity in natural experiments. However, there is a way to understand those threats and to keep them as low as possible: Think about research questions as if it were possible to test them in *true* experiments. These are called "thought experiments."

This wonderful device is widely taught in physical science. In 1972, I did an ethnographic study of scientists at Scripps Institution of Oceanography (Bernard 1974). Here's a snippet from a conversation I heard among some physicists there. "If we could only get rid of clouds, we could capture more of the sun's energy to run stuff on Earth," one person said. "Well," said another, "there are no clouds above the Earth's atmosphere. The sun's energy would be lots easier to capture out there."

"Yeah," said the first, "so suppose we send up a satellite, with solar panels to convert sunlight to electricity, and we attach a really long extension cord so the satellite was tethered to the Earth. Would that work?" The discussion got weirder from there, if you can imagine, but it led to a lot of really useful ideas for research.

Suppose your research question was whether Americans who own handguns are more likely to get shot than are Americans who don't own handguns. The experiment you'd have to set up is pretty macabre, but do the thought experiment nonetheless (no ethical issues are at stake in thinking). What experimental conditions would be required for you to be sure that both owning a handgun and having a high probability of getting shot were not caused by some third factor, like place of residence and exposure to violent crime?

Or suppose you wanted to know if small farms can produce organically grown food on a scale sufficiently large to be profitable. What would a true experiment to test this question look like? You might select some smallish farms with similar acreage and assign half of them randomly to grow vegetables organically. You'd assign the other half of the farms to grow the same vegetables using all usual technology (pesticides, fungicides, chemical fertilizers, etc.). Then, after a while, you'd measure some things about the farms' productivity and profitability and see which of them did better.

How could you be sure that organic or nonorganic methods of farming made the difference in profitability? Perhaps you'd need to control for access to the kinds of market populations that are friendly toward organically produced food (like university towns) or for differences in the characteristics of soils and weather patterns. Obviously, you can't do a true experiment on this topic, randomly assigning farmers to use organic or high-tech methods, but you *can* evaluate the experiments that real farmers are conducting every day in their choice of farming practices.

So, after you've itemized the possible threats to validity in your thought experiment, go out and look for natural experiments—societies, voluntary associations, organizations—that conform most closely to your ideal experiment. Then evaluate those natural experiments.

That's what Karen Davis and Susan Weller (forthcoming) did in their study of the efficacy of condoms in preventing the transmission of HIV among heterosexuals. Here's the experiment you'd have to conduct. First, get a thousand heterosexual couples. Make each couple randomly serodiscordant. That is, for each couple, randomly assign the man or the woman to be HIV positive. Assign each couple randomly to one of three conditions: (1) They use condoms for each sexual act, (2) they sometimes use condoms, or (3) they don't use condoms at all. Let the experiment run a few years. Then see how many of the couples in which condoms are always used remain serodiscordant and how many become seroconcordant—that is, they are both HIV positive.

Compare across conditions and see how much difference it makes to always use a condom.

Clearly, no one could conduct such an experiment. But Davis and Weller scoured the literature on condom efficacy and found 25 studies that met three criteria: (1) The focus was on serodiscordant heterosexual couples who said they regularly had penetrative sexual intercourse, (2) the HIV status of the subjects in each study had been determined by a blood test, and (3) there was information on the use of condoms. The 25 studies involved about a thousand subjects, and from this meta-analysis Davis and Weller established that consistent use of condoms reduced the rate of HIV transmission by over 85%.

TRUE EXPERIMENTS

True Experiments in the Lab

Laboratory experiments can test and clarify theories about how things work in the real world.

It has long been observed that fraternity hazing is difficult, dangerous, and painful—and produces people who come out of it supporting their tormentors. Remember Festinger's cognitive dissonance theory? Elliot Aronson and Judson Mills (1959) reasoned that people who go through severe initiation to get into a group *should* be more positive toward the group than are people who go through a mild initiation or no initiation. People who go through severe initiation, said Aronson and Mills, will convince themselves that the group is terrific even if they find out it's not all they expected it would be.

Aronson and Mills set up a laboratory experiment to test this idea. They recruited 63 college women for a discussion group that ostensibly was being formed to talk about psychological aspects of sex. To make sure that only mature people—people who could discuss sex openly—would make it into this group, some of the women would have to go through a screening test. Well, that's what they were *told*.

A third of the women did go through a pretty tough initiation. They were assigned randomly to a group that had to read a list of obscene words and some sexually explicit passages from some novels—aloud, in front of a man who was running the experiment. (It may be hard to imagine now, but those women who went through this in the 1950s must have been very uncomfortable.) Another third of the women were assigned randomly to a group that had to recite some nonobscene words that had to do with sex, and a third went through no screening at all.

Then, each participant listened in on a discussion that was supposedly going on among the members of the group she was joining. The "discussion" was actually a tape and it was as deadly boring as the experimenters could make it. The women were asked to rate the discussion on nine variables—things like dull-interesting, intelligent-unintelligent—from 0 to 15.

Those in the severe initiation condition rated the discussion higher than did the women in either the control group or the mild-initiation group. The differences were statistically very significant. We'll explore statistical significance in Chapter 15. For now, think of the outcome in the Aronson-Mills experiment as very unlikely to have occurred by chance. Since the women were assigned at random to the three groups, *something about the experiment* must have caused these women to form high opinions about what Aronson and Mills called "one of the most worthless and uninteresting discussions imaginable" (1959:179).

The women in the severe initiation condition had, after all, gone through a lot to join this wretched group. When they listened to the discussion and discovered how nonprurient it was, what did they do? They convinced themselves that the group was worth joining. Aronson and Mills's findings have been corroborated in other experiments (Gerard and Mathewson 1966).

Here's another laboratory classic. This one was stimulated by a real-world event. In 1963, in Queens, New York, Kitty Genovese was stabbed to death in the street one night. There were 38 eyewitnesses who saw the whole grisly episode from their apartment windows, and not one of them called the police. The newspapers called it "apathy," but Bibb Latané and John Darley had a different explanation. They called it *diffusion of responsibility* and they did an experiment to test their idea (1968).

Latané and Darley invited ordinary people to participate in a "psychology experiment." While the subjects were waiting in an anteroom to be called for the experiment, the room filled with smoke. If there was a single subject in the room, 75% reported the smoke right away. If there were three or more subjects waiting together, they reported the smoke only 38% of the time. People in groups just couldn't figure out whose responsibility it was to do something. So they did nothing.

True Experiments in the Field

When experiments are **done outside the lab, they are called** *field experiments.* Janet Schofield and her colleagues did a three-year ethnographic study of a middle school. During the first year, they noticed that African American and White children seemed to react differently to "mildly aggressive acts"—things like bumping in the hallway, poking one another in the classroom, asking for food, or using another student's pencil without permission. There appeared to be no overt racial conflict in the school, but during interviews, White students were more likely to report being intimidated by their African American peers than vice versa (Sagar and Schofield 1980:593).

To test their impression, Schofield and her colleagues did a field experiment. They randomly chose 40 Black and 40 White male students. Each student looked at a series of sketches depicting some mild aggressive act. One sketch, for example, showed a student poking another with a pencil in class. All the students saw the same sketches except that the race of the perpetrator and the race of the victim varied. After looking at the sketches, the students rated how well adjectives like "playful," "friendly," "mean," and "threatening" described the behavior of the perpetrator in the sketch (ibid.:594).

The result: The White children read more threat into the behaviors of Black children than vice versa. For subjects of this experiment, in this school, at least, the stereotype of the threatening Black male was already ingrained in Whites by middle school (Schofield and Anderson 1987:272).

Field experiments can produce powerful evidence for applications projects.

————————❖

Ronald Milliman (1986) conducted an experiment to test the effects of slow and fast music on the behavior of customers in a restaurant. First, Milliman played a number of instrumental pieces as background music. He asked 227 randomly chosen customers, "Do you consider the music playing right now as slow tempo, fast tempo, or in between?" From these data he identified slow music as 72 beats per minute or fewer, and fast music as 92 beats per minute or more.

Then, for eight consecutive weekends, Milliman played slow music and fast music on alternating nights. The first weekend, he played slow music on Friday night and fast music on Saturday night. The next weekend he reversed the order—just in case different kinds of people like to go out on Friday and Saturday nights. This procedure simulated assigning customers randomly to the different conditions of slow or fast music. Milliman used only instrumental music not to confound the experiment with *exogenous variables* like gender of vocalist, popularity of vocalist, and so on.

Milliman looked at the effect of the two music tempos on six dependent variables. Music tempo had no effect on five of those variables. It had no effect on the time it took for employees to take, prepare, and serve customers' orders. It had no effect on the number of people who decided to leave the restaurant before being seated (it was a popular restaurant, and there was usually a wait on weekends for a table). And it had no effect on the total dollar amount of food purchased.

Music tempo had a significant effect, however, on the amount of time that customers spent at their tables. With slow music, customers spent 56 minutes eating; with fast music, they spent only 45 minutes. For tables that were occupied those extra 11 minutes, the average bar tab was $30.47, about $9 more than the average bar tab per table in the fast-music treatment. Since the amount of food purchased was the same under both conditions, and since profits are much higher on bar purchases, the total profit margin per table was dramatically higher in the slow-music treatment.

❖————————

Marvin Harris and his colleagues (1993) conducted a field experiment in Brazil to test the effect of substituting one word in the question that deals with race on the Brazilian census. The demographers who designed the census had decided that the term *parda* was a more reliable gloss than the term *morena* for what English speakers call "brown," despite overwhelming evidence that Brazilians prefer the term *morena*.

In the town of Rio de Contas, Harris et al. assigned 505 houses randomly to one of two groups and interviewed one adult in each house. All respondents were asked to say what *cor* (color) they thought they were. This was the "free-choice option." Then they were asked to choose one of four terms that best described their *cor*. One group (with 252 respondents) was asked to select among *branca* (white), *parda* (brown), *preta* (black), and *amerela* (yellow). This was the "*parda* option"—the one used on the Brazilian census. The other group (with 253 respondents) was asked to select among *branca*, *morena* (brown), *preta,* and *amerela.* This was the "*morena* option," and is the intervention, or treatment in Harris's experiment.

Among the 252 people given the *parda* option, 131 (52%) identified themselves as *morena* in the free-choice option (when simply asked to say what color they were). But when given the *parda* option, only 80 of those people said they were *parda* and 41 said they were *branca* (the rest chose the other two categories). Presumably, those 41 people would have labeled themselves *morena* if they'd had the chance; not wanting to be labeled *parda,* they said they were *branca.* The *parda* option, then, produces more whites (*brancas*) in the Brazilian census and fewer browns (*pardas*).

Of the 253 people who responded to the *morena* option, 160 (63%) said they were *morena.* Of those 160, only 122 had chosen to call themselves *morena* in the free-choice option. So, giving people the *morena* option actually increases the number of browns (*morenas*) and decreases the number of whites (*brancas*) in the Brazilian census.

Does this difference make a difference? Social scientists who study the Brazilian census have found that those who are labeled Whites live about seven years longer than do those labeled non-Whites in that country. If 31% of self-described *morenas* say they are Whites when there is no *morena* label on a survey and are forced to label themselves *parda,* what does this do to all the social and economic statistics about racial groups in Brazil? (Harris et al. 1993).

NATURAL EXPERIMENTS

True experiments and quasi-experiments are *conducted* and the results are *evaluated* later. *Natural experiments,* by contrast, are **going on around us all the time. They are not conducted by researchers at all—they are simply evaluated.**

Here are four examples of common natural experiments: (1) Some employees in a company get expanded job responsibilities, while some do not; (2) some young people choose to migrate from small, isolated communities in northern Quebec to Montreal, while others stay put; (3) some second-generation, middle-class Mexican American students go to college, some do not; and (4) some cultures practice female infanticide, some do not.

Each of these situations constitutes a natural experiment that tests *something* about human behavior and thought. The trick is to ask, "What hypothesis is being tested by what's going on here?"

To evaluate natural experiments—that is, to figure out what hypothesis is being tested—you need to be alert to the possibilities and collect the right data. There's a really important natural experiment going on in an area of Mexico where I've worked over the years. A major irrigation system has been installed over the last 35 years in parts of a desert valley. Some of the villages affected by the irrigation system are populated entirely by Ñähñu (Otomí) Indians; other villages are entirely mestizo (as the majority population of Mexico is called).

Some of the Indian villages in the area are too high up the valley slope for the irrigation system to reach. I could not have decided to run this multi-million-dollar system through certain villages and bypass others, but the instant the decision was made by others, a natural experiment on the effects of a particular intervention was set in motion. There is a treatment (irrigation), there are treatment groups (villages full of people who get the irrigation), and there are control groups (villages full of people who are left out).

Unfortunately, I can't evaluate the experiment because I simply failed to see the possibilities early enough. Finkler (1974) saw the possibilities; her ethnographic study of the effects of irrigation on an Indian village in the same area shows that the intervention is having profound effects. But neither she nor I measured (pretested) things like average village wealth, average personal wealth, migration rates, alcoholism, and so on that I believe have been affected by the coming of irrigation. Had anyone done so—if we had *baseline data*—we would be in a better position to ask, "What hypotheses about human behavior are being tested by this experiment?" I can't reconstruct variables from 20 or 30 years ago. The logical power of the experimental model for establishing cause and effect between the intervention and the dependent variables is destroyed.

Some natural experiments, though, like the famous 1955 Connecticut speeding law, produce terrific data all by themselves for evaluation. In 1955, the governor of Connecticut ordered strict enforcement of speeding laws in the state. The object was to cut down on the alarming number of traffic fatalities. Anyone caught speeding had their driver's license suspended for at least 30 days. Traffic deaths fell from 324 in 1955 to 284 in 1956. A lot of people had been inconvenienced with speeding tickets and suspension of driving privileges, but 40 lives had been saved.

The question, of course, was whether the crackdown was the cause of the decline in traffic deaths. Campbell and Ross (1968) evaluated the experiment. They plotted the traffic deaths for all the years from 1951 to 1959 in Connecticut, Massachusetts, New York, New Jersey, and Rhode Island. Each of those states has more or less the same weather, and they all produced good data on traffic fatalities.

As it turned out, four of the five states experienced an increase in highway deaths in 1955, and all five states had a decline in traffic deaths the following year, 1956. If that was all you knew, you couldn't say that the governor's crackdown had had any effect. However, traffic deaths continued to decline steadily in Connecticut for the next three years (1957, 1958, 1959). They went up in Rhode Island and Massachusetts, went down a bit and then up again in New Jersey, and remained about the same in New York.

Connecticut was the only state that showed a consistent reduction in highway deaths for four years after the stiff penalties were introduced. Campbell and Ross treated these data as a series of natural experiments, and the results were convincing: Stiff penalties for speeders save lives.

Natural Experiments Are Everywhere

If you think like an experimentalist, you eventually come to see the unlimited possibilities for research going on all around you. Morrison et al. (1996), for example, took advantage of the fact that school boards establish cutoff dates for children going into kindergarten or first grade. Children who reach six years of age before, say, August 1, enter the first grade earlier than do children who are born after the same cutoff date. Since children from ages five to seven are going through an intense period of cognitive development, this sets up a really neat natural experiment: Are there short- and long-term impacts on cognitive skills of just missing or just making the cutoff?

There is a well-known hypothesis in psychology called the "goal-gradient" or "deadline" hypothesis. The hypothesis has been around since 1934, when Clark Hull showed that the closer rats came to food, the faster they went. In the 1970s, some of Eugene Webb's students at the Stanford Business School looked for naturally occurring tests of whether this hypothesis holds for humans.

The evidence is compelling: The number of plays in a football game is highest in the second quarter, next highest in the fourth quarter, and lowest in the first and third quarters, and trading goes up in the last two hours of the day at the New York Stock Exchange. When the trading day was extended from 3:00 p.m. to 3:30 p.m. in the 1970s, the rise in trading volume was *still* during the last two hours. Apparently, people, like rats, perform the most when they face a deadline (Webb and Weick 1983).

Cialdini et al. (1976) evaluated the natural experiment in pride that is conducted on most big university campuses every weekend during football season. Over a period of eight weeks, professors at Arizona State, Louisiana State, Ohio State, Notre Dame, Michigan, the University of Pittsburgh, and the University of Southern California recorded the percentage of students in their introductory psychology classes who wore school insignias (buttons, hats, T-shirts, etc.) on the Monday after Saturday football games. For 177 students per week, on average, over eight weeks, 63% wore some school insignia after wins in football vs. 44% after losses or ties. The difference is statistically significant.

On January 1, 1990, about 1,800 members of the United Mine Workers of America were given new health insurance coverage. Previously, they had not had any coverage for prescription drugs, but under the new plan they would pay $5 for each prescription drug, up to 10 prescriptions a year, for a maximum of $50. After that, all prescriptions were free.

Gianfrancesco et al. (1994) studied this natural experiment, using insurance claims data. The prescription costs for those who suddenly got the new benefits increased by 59% over the next three years. The costs of a control group (a matched sample of 1,800 people who had been covered by the plan since 1974) increased by 41% over the same period. Even after taking inflation out of the equation, there is still a powerful insurance effect. Greater coverage for prescription drugs produces greater use of prescription drugs. Does this produce better health? It's too early to tell, but this natural experiment and others like it are worth watching.

Notice that the data for evaluating these natural experiments came from direct observation (counting up the T-shirts with school colors) or from archives (records of stock trades or insurance claims).

Many natural experiments can be evaluated with data from survey questionnaires. Emotional pressures are among the predictors of alcoholism. Before 1975, all men 18 years old and older in the U.S. were subject to the military draft—a kind of lottery that determined who would spend at least two years in the armed services. Goldberg et al. (1991) reasoned that men who had been subject to the military draft were subject to more emotional pressures than those who weren't. Goldberg et al. evaluated this natural experiment with data on over 1,800 male respondents in the National Health Interview Surveys of 1977, 1983, and 1985.

As it turned out, men who had been eligible for the draft were not more likely to be heavy consumers of alcohol later in life than were men who had never been eligible for the draft. But, of course, the men who had been eligible for the draft were more likely to have served in the military, and *those* men were more likely to be heavy drinkers than were men who had not served.

NATURALISTIC EXPERIMENTS

The Small-World Experiment

In a *naturalistic* experiment, you **contrive to collect experimental data under natural conditions. You make the data happen, out in the natural world (not in the lab), and you evaluate the results.**

Consider this: You're having coffee near the Trevi Fountain in Rome. You overhear two Americans chatting next to you and you ask where they're from. One of them says he's from Sioux City, Iowa. You say you've got a friend from Sioux City and it turns out to be your new acquaintance's cousin. The culturally appropriate reaction at this point is for everyone to say, "Wow, what a small world!"

Stanley Milgram (1967) contrived an experiment to test how small the world really is. He asked a group of people in the midwestern United States to send a folder to a divinity student at Harvard University, but only if the subject *knew* the divinity student personally. Otherwise, he asked them to send the folders to an acquaintance whom they thought had a chance of knowing the "target" at Harvard.

The folders got sent around from acquaintance to acquaintance until they wound up in the hands of someone who actually knew the target—at which point the folders were sent, as per the instructions in the game, to the target. The average number of links between all the "starters" and the target was about five. It really *is* a small world.

Now, no one expects this experiment to actually happen in real life. It's contrived as can be and lacks control. On the other hand, it's compelling because it says *something* about how the natural world works. Tell people about Milgram's experiment and ask them to guess how many links it takes to get a folder between any two randomly chosen people in the United States. Most people

will guess a much bigger number than five. (Milgram's experiment, by the way, was the basis for the Broadway play "Six Degrees of Separation," as well as the movie of the same name that followed and the game "Six Degrees of Kevin Bacon," which has several Internet variations.)

The Lost-Letter Technique

Another of Milgram's contributions is a method for doing unobtrusive surveys of political opinion. The method is called the "lost-letter technique" and consists of "losing" a lot of letters that have addresses and stamps on them (Milgram et al. 1965).

The technique is based on two assumptions. First, people in many societies believe that they ought to mail a letter if they find one, especially if it has a stamp on it. Second, people will be less likely to drop a lost letter in the mail if it is addressed to someone or some organization that they don't like.

Milgram et al. (1965) tested this in an experiment in New Haven, Connecticut. They lost 400 letters in 10 districts of the city. They dropped the letters on the street, they left them in phone booths, they left them on counters at shops, and they tucked them under windshield wipers (after penciling "found near car" on the back of the envelope). Over 70% of the letters addressed to an individual or to a medical research company were returned. Only 25% of the letters addressed to either "Friends of the Communist Party" or "Friends of the Nazi Party" were returned. (The addresses were all the same post office box that had been rented for the experiment.)

By losing letters in a sample of communities, then, and by counting the differential rates at which they are returned, you can test variations in sentiment. Two of Milgram's students distributed anti-Nazi letters in Munich. The letters did not come back as much from some neighborhoods as from others, and they were thus able to pinpoint the areas of strongest neo-Nazi sentiment (Milgram 1969:68). The lost-letter technique has sampling problems and validity problems galore associated with it. But you can see just how intuitively powerful the results can be.

Three More Naturalistic Experiments

In a memorable experiment, elegant in its simplicity of design, Doob and Gross (1968) had a car stop at a red light and wait for 15 seconds after the light turned green before moving again. In one experimental condition, they used a new car, and a well-dressed driver. In another condition, they used an old, beat-up car, and a shabbily dressed driver. They repeated the experiment many times, and measured the time it took for people in the car behind the experimental car to start honking their horns. It won't surprise you to learn that people were quicker to vent their frustration at apparently low-status cars and drivers.

Piliavin et al. (1969) contrived an experiment to test what is called the "good Samaritan" problem. Students in the project rode a particular subway train in New York City. This particular express train made a 7.5-minute run; at 70 seconds into the run, a researcher pitched forward and collapsed. The team used four experimental conditions: The "stricken" person was either Black or White, and was either carrying a cane or a liquor bottle. Observers noted how long it took for people in the subway car to come to the aid of the supposedly stricken person, the total population of the car, whether bystanders were Black or White, and so on. You can conjure up the results. There were no surprises.

In a theatrical field experiment (done by psychologists and drama majors at a university),

Harari et al. (1985) tested whether men on a college campus would come to the aid of a woman being raped. These investigators staged realistic-sounding rape scenes and found that there was a significant difference in the helping reaction of male passersby if those men were alone or in groups.

Comparative Field Experiments

As an anthropologist, naturalistic field experiments appeal to me because they are excellent for comparative research—across cultures or even across time—and comparison is so important for developing theory.

Feldman (1968) did five field experiments in Paris, Boston, and Athens to test whether people in those cities respond more kindly to foreigners or to members of their own culture.

In one experiment, the researchers simply asked for directions and measured whether foreigners or natives got better treatment. Parisians and Athenians gave help significantly more often to fellow citizens than to foreigners. In Boston, there was no difference.

In the second experiment, foreigners and natives stood at major metro stops and asked perfect strangers to do them a favor. They explained that they were waiting for a friend, couldn't leave the spot they were on, and had to mail a letter. They asked people to mail the letters for them (the letters were addressed to the experiment headquarters), and simply counted how many letters they got back from the different metro stops in each city. Half the letters were unstamped.

In Boston and Paris, between 32% and 35% of the people refused to mail a letter for a fellow citizen. In Athens, 93% refused. Parisians treated Americans significantly better than Bostonians treated Frenchmen on this task. In fact, in the case where Parisians were asked to mail a letter that was stamped, they treated Americans significantly better than they treated other Parisians! (So much for *that* stereotype.)

In the third experiment, researchers approached informants and said, "Excuse me, sir. Did you just drop this dollar bill?" (or other currency, depending on the city). It was easy to measure whether or not people falsely claimed the money more from foreigners than from natives. This experiment yielded meager results.

In the fourth experiment, foreigners and natives went to pastry shops in the three cities, bought a small item and gave the clerk 25% more than the item cost. Then they left the shop and recorded whether the clerk had offered to return the overpayment. This experiment also showed little difference among the cities, or between the way foreigners and locals are treated.

And in the fifth experiment, researchers took taxis from the same beginning points to the same destinations in all three cities. They measured whether foreigners or natives were charged more. In neither Boston nor Athens was a foreigner overcharged more than a local. In Paris, however, Feldman found that "the American foreigner was overcharged significantly more often than the French compatriot in a variety of ingenious ways" (1968:11).

Feldman collected data on more than 3,000 interactions and was able to draw conclusions about cultural differences in how various peoples respond to foreigners as opposed to other natives. Some stereotypes were confirmed, while others were crushed.

Bochner has done a series of interesting experiments on the nature of Aboriginal-White relations in urban Australia (see Bochner [1980:335-40]

for a review). These experiments are clever, inexpensive, and illuminating, and Bochner's self-conscious critique of the limitations of his own work is a model for field experimentalists to follow. In one experiment, Bochner put two classified ads in a Sydney paper:

> Young couple, no children, want to rent small unfurnished flat up to $25 per week. Saturday only. 759-6000.

> Young Aboriginal couple, no children, want to rent small unfurnished flat up to $25 per week. Saturday only. 759-6161. (Bochner 1972:335)

Different people were assigned to answer the two phones, to ensure that callers who responded to both ads would not hear the same voice. Note that the ads were identical in every respect, except that in one of the ads the ethnicity of the couple was identified, while in the other it was not. There were 14 responses to the ethnically nonspecific ad and 2 responses to the ethnically specific ad (3 additional people responded to both ads).

In another experiment, Bochner exploited what he calls the "Fifi effect" (Bochner 1980: 336). The Fifi effect refers to the fact that urbanites acknowledge the presence of strangers who pass by while walking a dog and ignore others. Bochner sent a White woman and an Aboriginal woman, both in their early 20s and similarly dressed, to a public park in Sydney. He had them walk a small dog through randomly assigned sectors of the park, for 10 minutes in each sector.

Each woman was followed by two observers, who gave the impression that they were just out for a stroll. The two observers *independently* recorded the interaction of the women with passersby. The observers recorded the frequency of smiles offered to the women, the number of times anyone said anything to the women, and the number of nonverbal recognition nods the women received. The White woman received 50 approaches, while the Aboriginal woman received only 18 (Bochner 1971:111).

There are many elegant touches in this experiment. Note how the age and dress of the experimenters were controlled, so that only their ethnic identity remained as a dependent variable. Note how the time for each experimental trial (10 minutes in each sector) was controlled to ensure an equal opportunity for each woman to receive the same treatment by strangers. Bochner did preliminary observation in the park, and divided it into sectors that had the same population density, so that the chance for interaction with strangers would be about equal in each run of the experiment and he used two independent observer-recorders.

As Bochner points out, however, there were still design flaws that threatened the internal validity of the experiment (1980:337). As it happens, the interrater reliability of the two observers in this experiment was nearly perfect. But suppose the two observers shared the same cultural expectations about Aboriginal-White relations in urban Australia. They might have quite reliably misrecorded the cues that they were observing.

Reactive and unobtrusive observation alike tell you *what* happened, not *why*. It is tempting to conclude that the Aboriginal woman was ignored because of active prejudice. But, says Bochner, "perhaps passersby ignored the Aboriginal . . . because they felt a personal approach might be misconstrued as patronizing" (ibid.:338).

In Bochner's third study, a young White or Aboriginal woman walked into a butcher's shop and asked for 10 cents' worth of bones for her pet dog. The dependent variables in the experiment were the weight and quality of the bones. (An independent dog fancier rated the bones on a 3-point scale, without knowing how the bones were obtained, or why.) Each woman visited seven shops in a single middle-class shopping district.

In both amount and quality of bones received, the White woman did better than the Aboriginal, but the differences were not statistically significant—the sample was just too small, and so no conclusions could be drawn from that study alone. Taken all together, though, the three studies done by Bochner and his students comprise a powerful set of information about Aboriginal-White relations in Sydney. Naturalistic experiments have their limitations, but they often produce intuitively compelling results.

ARE FIELD EXPERIMENTS ETHICAL?

Field experiments come in a range of ethical varieties, from innocuous to borderline to downright ugly. I see no ethical problems with the lost-letter technique. When people mail one of the lost letters, they don't know that they are taking part in a social science experiment, but that doesn't bother me. Personally, I see no harm in the experiment to test whether people vent their anger by honking their car horns more quickly at people they think are lower socioeconomic class. These days, however, with road rage an increasing problem, I do not recommend repeating Doob and Gross's experiment.

Randomized field experiments, used mostly in evaluation research, can be problematic. Suppose you wanted to know whether fines or jail sentences are better at changing the behavior of drunk drivers. One way to do that would be to randomly assign people who were convicted of the offense to one or the other condition and watch the results. Suppose one of the subjects whom you didn't put in jail kills an innocent person. Similarly, is it fair to randomly deny some people the benefits of a new drug just to study the effects of not having it? The ethical problems associated with *withholding of treatment* are under increasing scrutiny (see, e.g., Wertz 1987; De Leon et al. 1995).

There is a long history of debate about the ethics of *deception* in psychology and social psychology (see Korn [1997] for a review). On balance, some deception is clearly necessary—certain types of research just can't be done without it. When you use deception, though, you run all kinds of risks—not just to research subjects but to the research itself. These days, college students (who are the subjects for most social psych experiments) are very savvy about all this and are on the lookout for clues as to the "real" reason for an experiment the minute they walk in the door.

If you don't absolutely need deception in true behavioral experiments, that's one less problem you have to deal with. If you decide that deception is required, then understand that the responsibility for any bad outcomes is yours and yours alone.

The experiments by Piliavin et al. (1969) and Harari et al. (1985) on whether people will come to the aid of a stricken person or a woman being raped are real problems. Some of the participants (who neither volunteered to be in an experiment nor were paid for their services) might still be wondering what happened to that poor guy on the subway whom they stepped over in their hurry to get away from an uncomfortable situation—or that woman whose screams they ignored. In laboratory experiments, at least, subjects are debriefed—told what the real purpose of the study was—to reduce emotional distress. In the guerrilla theater type of field experiment, though, no debriefing is possible.

Even debriefing has its dark side. People don't like to find out that they have been duped into being part of an experiment, and some people may suffer a terrible loss of self-esteem if they do find out and conclude that they acted badly. How would *you* feel if you were one of the people who failed to respond to a rape victim, and then were told that you were just part of an experiment—that no real rape ever took place, and thank you very much for your help?

If you think some of these cases are borderline, consider the study by West et al. (1975) on whether there is a little larceny in us all.

The Watergate Experiment

In the Watergate affair, men loyal to then President Richard Nixon broke into the headquarters of the Democratic National Committee at the Watergate Hotel in Washington, D.C., to photograph documents pertinent to the 1972 election campaign. Their bungling of the job, and the subsequent cover-up by Nixon and his staff at the White House, led to the unprecedented resignation of the president of the United States from office in 1974. Soon thereafter, West et al. conducted their experiment.

They confronted 80 different students with a proposition to burglarize a local advertising firm. Subjects were randomly assigned to one of four conditions. In the first condition, subjects were told that the job was to be committed for the Internal Revenue Service. The IRS, it seemed, needed to get the goods on this company to bring them to trial for tax evasion. If the subjects were caught in the act, then the government would guarantee immunity from prosecution. In the second condition, subjects were told that there was no immunity from prosecution.

In the third condition, subjects were told that another advertising agency had paid $8,000 for the job and that they (the subjects) would get $2,000 for their part in it. (Remember, that was

$2,000 in 1979—about $8,000 today.) Finally, in the fourth condition, subjects were told that the burglary was being committed just to see if the plan would work. Nothing would be taken from the office.

Understand that this was not a "let's pretend" exercise. Subjects were not brought into a laboratory and told to imagine that they were being asked to commit a crime. This was for real. Subjects met the experimenter at his home or at a restaurant. They were all criminology students at a university and knew the experimenter to be an actual local private investigator. The private eye arranged an elaborate and convincing plan for the burglary, including data on the comings and goings of police patrol cars, aerial photographs, blueprints of the building—the works.

> The key ethical issue in the conduct of all social research is whether those being studied are placed at risk by those doing the studying.

The subjects really believed that they were being solicited to commit a crime. Just as predicted by the researchers, a lot of them agreed to do it in the first condition, where they thought the crime was for a government agency and that they'd be free of danger from prosecution if caught. What do you suppose would happen to *your* sense of self-worth when you were finally debriefed and told that you were one of the 36 out of 80 (45%) who agreed to participate in the burglary in the first condition? (See Cook [1975] for a critical comment on the ethics of this experiment.)

The key ethical issue in the conduct of all social research is whether those being studied are placed at risk by those doing the studying. This goes for field research—including surveys, ethnographies, and naturalistic experiments—as much as it does for laboratory studies. All universities in the U.S. have long had Institutional Review Boards, or IRBs. These are internal agencies whose members review and pass judgment on the ethical issues associated with all human subjects research, including biomedical and psychosocial. The concept of informed consent has developed and matured over the years. All researchers are asked by the IRBs to describe clearly and precisely what steps will be taken to ensure that human subjects will be protected from harm. And not just physical harm. Research subjects should not experience emotional harm or financial harm, either.

Experiments with human subjects, both laboratory and field experiments, pose unique threats of harm that survey research or ethnographic research don't share. A great many experiments, as we have seen, involve deception—fooling subjects into thinking that an experiment is about one thing when it really is about something else entirely. Research subjects in these experiments may experience a loss of self-esteem when they find out that they've been duped.

If an experiment requires deception, make sure a debriefing session is a routine part of the design. At the debriefing, the true goal of the experiment is divulged. Subjects are told why deception was required, are thanked for their cooperation, and are given the opportunity to talk about any problems they may have with their participation in the experiment. The idea is to help people feel good about their cooperation in a scientific experiment rather than foolish about their having been hoodwinked.

TABLE 4.2 Three-Way, $2 \times 2 \times 2$, Factorial Design

		Variable 2	Variable 3	
			Attribute 1	Attribute 2
Variable 1	Attribute 1	Attribute 1	1,1,1 Condition 1	1,1,2 Condition 2
		Attribute 2	1,2,1 Condition 3	1,2,2 Condition 4
	Attribute 2	Attribute 1	2,1,1 Condition 5	2,1,2 Condition 6
		Attribute 2	2,2,1 Condition 7	2,2,2 Condition 8

FACTORIAL DESIGNS: MAIN EFFECTS AND INTERACTION EFFECTS

Most experiments involve analyzing the effects of several independent variables at once. A *factorial design* **lays out all the combinations of all the categories of the independent variables.** That way you know how many subjects you need, how many to assign to each condition, and how to run the analysis when the data are in.

It is widely believed that a good laugh has healing power. Rotton and Shats (1996) developed an experimental design to test this. They recruited 39 men and 39 women who were scheduled for orthopedic surgery. The patients were assigned randomly to one of nine groups—eight experimental groups and one control group. The patients in the eight treatment groups got to watch a movie in their room the day after their surgery.

There were three variables: choice, humor, and expectancy. The participants in the high-choice group got a list of 20 movies from which they chose 4. The participants in the low-choice group watched a movie that one of the people in the high-choice group had selected. Half the subjects watched humorous movies, and half watched action or adventure movies. Before watching their movie, half the subjects read an article about the benefits of humor, while half read an article about the healthful benefits of exciting movies.

Figure 4.3 is a branching tree diagram that shows how these three variables, each with two attributes, create the eight logical groups for Rotton and Shats's experiment. Table 4.2 shows the same eight-group design, but in a format that is more common. The eight nodes at the bottom of the tree in Figure 4.3 and the sets of numbers in the eight boxes of Table 4.2 are called *conditions*.

Condition 1 (group 1): They had a choice. They saw a humorous movie. They had been led to expect that humor has healing benefits.

Condition 2 (group 2): They had a choice. They saw a humorous movie. They had been led to expect that excitement has healing benefits.

Condition 3 (group 3): They had a choice. They saw an action movie. They had been led to expect that humor has healing benefits.

Condition 4 (group 4): They had a choice. They saw an action movie. They had been led to expect that excitement has healing benefits.

Condition 5 (group 5): They didn't have a choice. They saw a humorous movie. They had been led to expect that humor has healing benefits.

Condition 6 (group 6): They didn't have a choice. They saw a humorous movie. They had been led to expect that excitement has healing benefits.

Condition 7 (group 7): They didn't have a choice. They saw an action movie. They had been led to expect that humor has healing benefits.

Condition 8 (group 8): They didn't have a choice. They saw an action movie. They had been led to expect that excitement has healing benefits.

The dependent variables in this study included a self-report by patients on the amount of pain they had and a direct measure of the amount of pain medication they took. All the patients had access to a device that let them administer more or less of the analgesics that are used for controlling pain after orthopedic surgery.

In assessing the results of a factorial experiment, researchers look for **main effects** and **interaction effects**. **Main effects are the effects of each independent variable on each dependent variable. Interaction effects are effects on dependent variables that occur as a result of interaction between two or more independent variables.** In this case, Rotton and Shats wanted to know the effects of humor on postoperative pain, but they wanted to know the effect in different contexts: in the context of choosing the vehicle of humor or not, in the context of being led to believe that humor has healing benefits or not, and so on.

As it turned out, being able to choose their own movie had no effect when patients saw action films. But patients who saw humorous films and who had not been able to make their own choice of film gave themselves more pain killer than did patients who saw humorous films and had been able to make the selection themselves (Rotton and Shats 1996).

We'll look at how to measure these effects when we take up ANOVA, or analysis of variance, in Chapter 15.

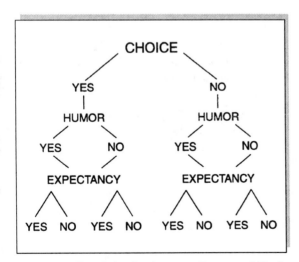

Figure 4.3 The Eight Conditions in Rotton and Shat's (1996) 2 × 2 × 2 Design

KEY CONCEPTS

Chapter 4
Summary

SUMMARY

❖ The experimental method is not one single technique, but an approach to the development of knowledge. In experiments, researchers try to control the effects of confounds to understand the effects of particular independent variables on outcomes. In other words, they try to maximize the internal validity of experiments.

- The well-known threats to validity include history, maturation, testing, regression to the mean, selection bias, so-called mortality of subjects (referring to the subjects of experiments dropping out), and diffusion of treatment.

- Different experimental designs control for various threats to validity. Among the widely used designs are
  — Two-group, pretest-posttest design with random assignment
  — Solomon four-group design
  — Two-group pretest-posttest design without random assignment
  — Posttest-only design with random assignment
  — One-shot case study design
  — One-group pretest-posttest design
  — Two-group posttest-only design, also called the static group comparison
  — Interrupted time series design

- Some designs are more effective than others, but it is not possible to use the most effective designs in all situations.

❖ You don't necessarily need a laboratory to carry out a true social science experiment. Many experiments are conducted in the field.

- Natural experiments, quasi-experiments, and naturalistic experiments are based on field research rather than on laboratory research.

❖ Social and behavioral experiments raise particularly serious ethical problems. Even with proper debriefing, participants in experiments may experience loss of self-esteem. The need, or lack of need, for deception in social research is a matter of continuing debate.

❖ Most experiments involve analyzing the effects of several independent variables at once. A factorial design lays out all the combinations of all the categories of the independent variables. This sets up a blueprint for systematic data analysis.

- In assessing the results of a factorial experiment, researchers look for main effects and interaction effects. Main effects are the effects of each independent variable on each dependent variable. Interaction effects are effects on dependent variables that occur as a result of interaction between two or more independent variables.

EXERCISES

1. For a random sample of students on your campus, count the number who are wearing school colors—clothes, insignia, and so on—on Mondays following sports wins vs. Mondays following sports losses. This replicates the study I discussed earlier by Cialdini et al. (1976). See Chapter 5 about taking a random sample.

2. Suppose you were designing an experiment to test whether a new diet plan, coupled with a motivational seminar, helped obese people lose weight. This is a plan developed by a major food manufacturer, so there's plenty of money behind it and you can design the experiment with whatever resources you think are needed. For example, you can have a large number of participants and a control group, you can have random assignment, you can pay participants, and so on. Write up the design and discuss how you plan to address various threats to the validity of the experiment, including regression to the mean, the John Henry effect, maturation, history, and so on.

3. Look through your local newspaper and find a report of some innovative social program, such as prison reform, a program to provide jobs to young people during school vacations, or a proposal for a new welfare system. Describe how you would evaluate the success of the innovative program. First, briefly describe the innovative program. Next, specify the key dependent variable that the program seeks to affect. Finally, describe how you would measure the dependent variable and how you would assess whether the program had any effect on that variable.

4. A local government agency has awarded you a contract to evaluate a program it has had in place for two years. The program is a day care center for children of working mothers in a predominantly Spanish-speaking area of a major city in the Southwest. When the program was proposed, its advocates claimed that the cost, in dollars, would be less than the cost of welfare payments to the women who couldn't work because they had no place to leave their children. Now, two years later, the data are in and the bottom line is that it costs much more to keep each child than it would cost to close the day care center and return to the system of direct welfare payments to the mothers.

   Advocates for the center claim that there are many more concerns than just "the bottom line," but they are having a hard time articulating those concerns. Design an evaluation research effort that addresses all the concerns, *except the fiscal ones,* of the parties in this situation.

5. Assume that you have developed a study technique that you believe will result in students scoring higher on this exam. You test the technique with the following design:

$$RO_1 \quad X \quad O_2$$
$$RO_3 \quad \quad O_4$$

   List all the predictions you can make. If it turns out that O_4 is greater than O_1, what will you conclude? Describe the confounds to internal validity in this experiment. Be sure to distinguish between internal and external validity.

FURTHER READING

Research design. The Solomon four-group design is named for Richard Solomon (see Solomon 1949; Solomon and Lessac 1968). The Campbell and Stanley posttest-only design is named for Donald Campbell and Julian Stanley (1963). For more on this elegant but little-used design, see Oliver and Berger (1980). See Stewart et al. (1993) for an example of how the posttest-only design was used in testing the health benefits of exercise in 50- to 65-year-olds. See Reiss and Dyhdalo (1975) for a modified posttest-only design used in testing the results of replacing rigid seating arrangements in classrooms with open seating.

For a general review of principles of experimental design, with up-to-date articles and a focus on clinical research, see Kazdin (1998). There are many texts that focus on problems of research design in particular fields. For nursing research, for example, see Brink and Wood (1998). See Reichardt and Mark (1998) for a review of quasi-experimental design, including interrupted times series. For a discussion of the general time series experimental design, see Glass et al. (1979).

See Lincoln and Guba (1985), especially Chapters 9 and 11, and all of Maxwell (1996) for discussions of design issues in qualitative social research.

Thought experiments. Thought experiments may be a playful device for coming up with ideas in science, but the whole notion of thought experiments as the source of ideas is the subject of intellectual debate in the philosophy of science. For more on the philosophic foundations of thought experiments in science, see Horowitz and Massey (1991) and Sorensen (1992). For a discussion of thought experiments in social psychology, see Tindale and Vollrath (1992).

Natural experiments. Economists have long treated changes in corporate insurance policies and changes in tax laws as natural experiments that can be evaluated. See Anderson and Meyer (1998) and Eissa (1995) for examples. Some educational and developmental psychologists treat schooling as a natural experiment—a naturally occurring intervention in the cognitive development of children. For example, Morrison et al. (1996) looked at differences in psychological skills of children who just made the cutoff date for entry into first grade and children who just missed the cutoff. (This ubiquitous part of public school administration in the U.S. means that children who are barely six years old and children who are almost seven years old wind up in the same first-grade class.) Oettingen et al. (1994) treated the unification of the East and West Berlin school systems as a natural experiment on the educational development of Berlin children.

Diffusion of responsibility. Latané and Darley's 1968 work on diffusion of responsibility and moral disengagement was extended in a series of experiments by Shotland and Straw (1976) and recently by Bandura et al. (1996).

Ethics of research. There is a growing literature on the ethics of research, including many case studies of ethical issues that arise in relation to the study of particular populations. Hoagwood et al. (1996), for example, present case studies on ethical issues in the study of children and adolescents who have mental disorders. See Kimmel (1996) for an overview of ethical issues in behavioral research (including research involving nonhuman animals).

The issue of deception in psychological experiments has received a lot of attention in recent years—including experiments to assess its effects on the data collected in experiments that require deception. Nicks et al. (1997) studied the history of the use of deception in psychology. Taylor and Shepperd (1996) show the potential impact of deception on data quality (and also see Oliansky 1991).

Ortmann and Hertwig (1997) called for outlawing all forms of deception in psychology experiments. See comments on their work by Kimmel (1998) and by Broeder (1998) in support of deception under limited circumstances, and see Ortmann and Hertwig's response (1998).

5 | SAMPLING

IN THIS CHAPTER:

❖ INTRODUCTION

Informant accuracy, data validity, and even ethical issues (like whether it's all right to deceive people in conducting experiments) are all measurement problems in research. The other big class of problems involves sampling: Given that your measurements are credible, how much of the world do they represent? How far can you generalize the results of your research?

The answer depends, first of all, on the kind of data in which you're interested. There are two kinds of data of interest to social scientists: individual data and cultural data. These two kinds require different approaches to sampling.

WHAT ARE SAMPLES AND WHY DO WE NEED THEM?

Individual data are about **attributes of individuals in a population.** Each person has an age, for example; each person has an income; and each person has preferences for things like products, political positions, and characteristics for a mate. If the idea in collecting data is to estimate the average age or income or preference in a larger population—that is, to estimate some *population parameters*—then a scientifically drawn, unbiased sample is a must. By "scientifically drawn," I mean random selection of cases so that every unit of analysis in your study has an equal chance of being chosen for study. Barring that (since it's often impossible to choose a true random sample), I mean a sample where the probability of inclusion is known for each case.

Cultural data are different. Cultural data require experts. If you want to understand a process—like how people in a factory work group decide on whether to lodge a complaint to management, or how police in a squad car determine whether to stop someone on the street—then **you want people who can offer expert explanations and who represent the intracultural variation that we find in all societies.** It's one thing to ask: "How many people did you stop on the street for questioning last week?" This requires an answer about individual behavior. It's another thing to ask: "How do people in your squad decide whether to stop someone for questioning on a street patrol?" This requires cultural experts.

All social scientists are interested in both kinds of data. An anthropologist may ask people: "How many cows did *you* give to your in-laws as bride price when you got married?" They may also ask key informants (experts), "So, why do men who get married around here deliver cows to their in-laws?"

Individual-attribute data require *probability sampling*; **cultural data require** *nonprobability sampling*. Probability sampling is by far the best known kind of sampling in the social sciences, so we'll begin with it. This will take us into a discussion of probability theory, variance, and distributions. As we go through that material, remember that Freud's ideas about the unconscious, Skinner's ideas about operant conditioning, and Piaget's ideas about stages of cognitive development were all based on intensive study of a relatively small number of cases and not on a survey of a random sample of anything.

This is not an argument against random sampling. Far from it. It's just a reminder that there are lots of ways to conduct scientific research. When the project calls for random sampling, it pays to get that right, too. Whether the population consists of 16,886 households in a town, the 4,643 records of residential property transactions between 1970 and 1999 in that same town, or the 40,000 members of the National Cattlemen's Beef Association, it takes less time and less money to study a sample of them than it does to study all of them.

If samples were just easier and cheaper to study but failed to produce useful data, there wouldn't be much to say for them. A study based on a random sample, however, is often better than one based on the whole population.

WHY THE U.S. STILL HAS A CENSUS

Estimates of many segments of the population of the U.S., for example, would be more accurate if they were based on good samples instead of on a census. The General Accounting Office estimated that, in 1990, the Bureau of the Census failed to count 5.3 million people, mostly African Americans and Hispanics (*New York Times,* August 25, 1991, sec. 1, p. 23). This means, among other things, that statistics about the incidence of everything from criminal behavior to AIDS among African American men are artificially high.

Lots of things can go wrong with counting. Heads of households are responsible for filling out and returning the census forms, but only 63% of the mailed forms were returned in 1990 (that's down, by the way, from 78% in 1970). The Bureau of the Census had to hire and train half a million people to track down all the people who had not been enumerated in the mailed-back forms.

Some people wound up being counted twice. Some college students were counted twice, for example, because their parents had counted them on the mailed-back census form. Then, on census day, some of those same students were tracked down again by enumerators who canvassed the dorms. Meanwhile, lots of other people (like illegal immigrants and people living in places to which the census takers would rather not go) were not being counted at all.

The Bureau of the Census publishes adjustments to the census figures based on samples, and every so often there is serious talk of replacing the census with estimates based on samples. The U.S. Constitution, however, in Article I, Section 2, *requires* that the government conduct an "Enumeration" (with a capital E) of the population every 10 years to apportion seats in the House of Representatives to the states.

There's also a serious political issue: If sampling produced higher estimates of the number of citizens who are, say, homeless or who are migrant farm workers, this would benefit only certain states. It would also benefit the Democratic Party over the Republican Party, since more poor people vote the Democratic ticket. In 1999, the Supreme Court of the United States held that, at least for the big *decennial census,* the word "Enumeration" means going out and counting noses. So, for the moment, we're stuck with a census and all its inaccuracies.

IT PAYS TO TAKE SAMPLES AND TO STICK WITH THEM

If you are doing all the work yourself, it's next to impossible to interview more than a few hundred people. Even a small, county school system might have 500 employees, including teachers, administrators, and staff. You'd need several interviewers to reach all those people within a reasonable amount of time. Interviewers may not use the same wording of questions; they may not probe equally well on subjects that require sensitive interviewing; they may not be equally careful in recording data on field instruments and in coding data for analysis. And, as you'll see in the section on telephone interviewing, in Chapter 7, some interviewers actually falsify data.

Most important, you have no idea how much error is introduced by these problems. A well-chosen sample, interviewed by people who have similarly high skills in getting data, has a known chance of being incorrect on any variable. (Careful, though: If you have a project that requires multiple interviewers and you try to skimp on personnel, you run a big risk. Overworked or poorly trained interviewers will cut corners; see Chapter 7.) Furthermore, studying an entire population may pose a history threat to the internal validity of your data. If you *don't* add interviewers it may take you so long to complete your research that events intervene that make it impossible to interpret your data.

You're interested in how the nursing staff at a midsize, private hospital feels about a reorganization plan. You decide to survey all 210 nurses on the staff, using a structured, 10-minute personal interview. You know that it's tough to track some nurses down—they are very busy and sometimes don't have even 10 minutes to stop and chat; they change shifts, forcing you to find them at four in the morning—but you have three months for the

research and you figure you can do the survey a little at a time.

Two months into your work, you've gotten 160 interviews on the topic—only 50 to go. Just about that time, the hospital announces that it has been bought out by a big health maintenance corporation—one that's traded on the New York Stock Exchange. All of a sudden the picture changes. Your "sample" of 160 is biased toward those people whom it was easy to find, and you have no idea what *that* means. And even if you could now get those remaining 50 respondents, their opinions may have been radically changed by the new circumstances. The opinions of the 160 respondents who already talked to you may have also changed.

Now you're really stuck. You can't simply throw together the 50 and the 160 interviews; you have no idea what that will do to your results. Nor can you compare the 160 and the 50 as representing the nursing staff's attitudes before and after the buyout. Neither sample is unbiased with regard to what you are studying.

If you had taken a ***random sample*** of 60 people in a single week early in your project, you'd now be in much better shape, because you'd know the potential sampling error in your study. If historical circumstances (the surprise buyout, for example) require it, you could interview the same sample of 60 again (in what is known as a ***panel study***), or take another representative sample of the same size and see what differences there are before and after the critical event. In either case, you are better off with the sample than with the whole population.

By the way, there is no guarantee that a week is quick enough to avoid the problem described here. It's just less likely to be a problem. Less likely is better than more likely.

WHAT KINDS OF SAMPLES ARE THERE?

There are eight major kinds of samples. Four of them—simple random, systematic random, stratified random, and cluster samples—are based on the principles of probability theory. The other four—quota, purposive/judgment, convenience/haphazard, and snowball samples—are not. *Probability samples* are representative of larger populations and they increase external validity in any study.

The general rule is this: If your objective is to generalize about individual characteristics from a sample to a population, then use probability sampling whenever you can; use *nonprobability sampling* methods when you really, really can't do probability sampling. There are some research problems that simply demand nonprobability sampling. If your objective is to generalize about cultural data (rather than about individual characteristics), then use one of the appropriate methods for nonprobability sampling. More about them later.

PROBABILITY SAMPLING

Probability samples are based on taking a given number of units of analysis from a list, called a *sampling frame,* which represents some *population* under study. In a probability sample, or *unbiased sample,* each individual has exactly the same chance as every other individual of being selected.

In 1970, while the United States was engaged in a very unpopular war in Vietnam, men were selected to serve in the military by a supposedly random draw. Three hundred sixty-six capsules (one for each day of the year, including leap year) were put in a drum and the drum was turned to mix the capsules. Then dates were pulled from the drum, one at a time. All the men whose birthdays fell on the days that were selected were drafted.

When enough men had been selected to fill the year's quota, the lottery stopped. Men whose birthdays hadn't been pulled were safe until the following year when the lottery would be run again. It turned out that men whose birthdays were in the later months had a better chance of being drafted than men whose birthdays were earlier in the year. This happened because the drum wasn't rotated enough to thoroughly mix the capsules (Williams 1978). Not a good sampling technique.

Sampling Frames

If you can get it, the first thing you need for a good sample is a good *sampling frame.* (I say "if you can get it" because a lot of social research is done on populations for which no sampling frame exists. More on this later.) A sampling frame is a list of units of analysis *from which* you take a sample and *to which* you generalize.

A sampling frame may be a telephone directory, the tax rolls of a community, or a census of a community that you do yourself. In the U.S., the city directories (published by R. L. Polk and Company) are often adequate sampling frames. The directories are available for many small towns at the local library or chamber of commerce. Professional survey researchers in the U.S. often purchase samples from firms that keep up-to-date databases just for this purpose.

For many projects, though, especially projects that involve field research, you have to get your own census of the population you are studying. A census of a factory or a hospital or a small town gives you the opportunity to walk around a community and to talk with most of its members at least once. It lets you be seen by others, and it gives you an opportunity to answer questions, as well as to ask them. It allows you to get information that official censuses don't retrieve. A list of the employees at a plant, for example, probably won't have information on all the variables that you need for your research.

A census of a community of actors gives you a sampling frame from which to take many samples during a research project. It also gives you a basis for comparison if you go back to the same community later.

Simple Random Samples

To get a *simple random sample* of 200 out of 640 professors in a university, you number each individual from 1 to 640 and then take a random grab of 200 out of the numbers from 1 to 640. The easiest way to take random samples is with a computer. All full-featured program packages for statistical analysis have built-in random-number generators. Some of the most popular include SAS®, SPSS®, SYSTAT®, KWIKSTAT®, STATA®, and STATMOST®. (Internet addresses for all these programs are given in Appendix F.) You can also take a random sample with a table of random numbers, like the one in Appendix A, taken from the RAND Corporation's volume *A Million Random Digits with 100,000 Normal Deviates* (1965). The book has no plot or characters, just a million random numbers—a few of which have been reprinted in Appendix A.

Just enter the table anywhere. Since the numbers are random, it makes no difference where you start (see Box 5.1). Read down a column or across a row. The numbers are in groups of five, in case

---

> ### Box 5.1
> ### On Being Truly Random
>
> If you always enter Appendix A at the same spot, the numbers cease to be random! Entering the table more or less haphazardly, however, is good enough. Things have gotten a bit tougher with modern technology. Programmable calculators come with a built-in routine for generating random numbers, as do all statistical packages. The problem is, they use a "seed" (a starting number) from which to start a series of random numbers. If you never change the seed, that's the same thing as always entering Appendix A at the same spot.

---

you ever want to take samples up to 99,999 units. If you are sampling fewer than 10 units in a population, then look just at the first digit in each group. If you are sampling 10-99 units, then look just at the first two digits, and so on.

Throw out any numbers that are too big for your sample. Say you are taking 300 sample minutes from a population of 5,040 daylight minutes in a week during November in Atlanta, Georgia. (You might do this if you were trying to describe what a family did during that week.) Any three-digit number larger than 300 is automatically ignored. Just go on to the next number in the table. Ignore duplicate numbers, too.

If you go through the table once (down all the columns) and still don't have enough numbers for your sample, then go through it again, starting with the second digit in each group, and then the third. If you began by taking numbers in the columns, take them from rows. You probably won't run out of random numbers for rough-and-ready samples if you use Appendix A for the rest of your life.

When you have your list of random numbers, then whoever goes with each one is in the sample. Period. If there are 1,230 people in the population, and your list of random numbers says that you have to interview person number 212, then do it. No fair leaving out some people because they are members of the elite and probably wouldn't want to give you the time of day. No fair leaving out people you don't like or don't want to work with. None of that.

> A common form of meddling with samples is when door-to-door interviewers find a sample selectee not at home and go to the nearest house for a replacement.

In the real world of research, of course, random samples are tampered with all the time. (And no snickering here about the "real world" of research. Social research is at least a $10 billion a year industry in the U.S. alone—and that's real enough for most people.) A common form of meddling with samples is when door-to-door interviewers find a sample selectee not at home and go to the nearest house for a replacement. This can have dramatically bad results.

Suppose you go out to interview between 10 a.m. and 4 p.m. The average number of children among people who are home between 10 a.m. and 4 p.m. is higher than the average of all families. People who are home during the day tend to be old, sick, or mothers with several small children.

Of course, those same people are home in the evening, too, but now they're joined by all the single people home from work, so the average family size goes down. As Tom Smith, director at the National Opinion Research Center, says, going to the nearest at-home household for a replacement interview introduces systematic bias into your data because you tend to replace nonrespondents with people who are like respondents rather than with people who are like nonrespondents (1989:53).

Telephone survey researchers typically call back three times before replacing a member of a sample. When survey researchers suspect (from prior work) that, say, 25% of a sample won't be reachable within, say, three call-backs, they increase their original sample size by 25% so the final sample will be both the right size and representative. The reason we know this is because researchers report these kinds of compromises when they publish their results. You should, too.

Systematic Random Sampling

Most people don't actually do simple random sampling these days; instead, they do something called *systematic random sampling* because it is much, much easier and more economical to do. If you are dealing with an unnumbered sampling frame of 43,288 (the student population at the University of Florida in 1999), then simple random sampling is nearly impossible. You would have to number all those names first. In doing systematic random sampling, you need a random start and a *sampling interval*, N. You enter the sampling frame at a randomly selected spot (using Appendix A again) and take every Nth person (or item) in the frame.

In choosing a random start, you need only to find one random number in your sampling frame. This is usually easy to do. If you are dealing with 43,288 names, listed on a computer printout at 400 to a page, then number 9,457 is 257 names down from the top of page 24.

The sampling interval depends on the size of the population and the number of units in your sample. If there are 10,000 people in the population, and you are sampling 400 of them, then after you enter the sampling frame (the list of

10,000 names) you need to take every 25th person ($400 \times 25 = 10,000$) to ensure that every person has at least one chance of being chosen. If there are 640 people in a population, and you are sampling 200 of them, then you would take every 4th person. If you get to the end of the list and you are at number 2 in an interval of 4, just go to the top of the list, start at 3, and keep on going.

Periodicity and Systematic Sampling

I said that systematic sampling *usually* produces a representative sample. When you do systematic random sampling, be aware of the **periodicity** problem. Suppose you're studying a big retirement community in southern Florida. The development has 30 identical buildings. Each has six floors, with 10 condominiums on each floor, for a total of 1,800 condos. Now suppose that each floor has one big corner condo that costs more than the others and attracts a slightly more affluent group of buyers. If you do a systematic sample of every 10th condo, then, depending on where you entered the list of condos, you'd have a sample of 180 corner condos or no corner condos at all.

David and Mary Hatch (1947) studied the Sunday society pages of the *New York Times* for the years 1932-42. They found only stories about weddings of Protestants and concluded that the elite of New York must therefore be Protestant. Cahnman (1948) pointed out that the Hatches had studied only June issues of the *Times*. It seemed reasonable. After all, aren't most society weddings in June? Well, yes. Protestant weddings. Upper-class Jews married in other months, and the *Times* covered those weddings as well.

You can avoid the periodicity problem by doing simple random sampling, but if that's not possible, another solution is to make two systematic passes through the population using different sampling intervals. Then you can compare the two samples. Any differences should be attributable to sampling error. If they're not, then you might have a periodicity problem.

Sampling from a Telephone Book

Systematic sampling is fine if you know that the sampling frame has 43,288 elements. What do you do when the size of the sampling frame is unknown? A big telephone book is an unnumbered sampling frame of unknown size. To use this kind of sampling frame, first determine the number of pages that actually contain listings. To do this, jot down the number of the first and last pages on which listings appear. Most phone books begin with a lot of pages that do not contain listings.

Suppose the listings begin on page 30 and end on page 520. Subtract 30 from 520 and add 1 ($520 - 30 + 1 = 491$) to calculate the number of pages that carry listings.

Then note the number of columns per page and the number of lines per column (count all the lines in a column, even the blank ones).

Suppose the phone book has three columns and 96 lines per column (this is quite typical). To take a random sample of 200 nonbusiness listings from this phone book, take a random sample of 400 page numbers (yes, 400) out of the 491 page numbers between 30 and 520. Just think of the pages as a numbered sampling frame of 491 elements. Next, take a sample of 300 column numbers. Since there are three columns, you want 300 random choices of the numbers 1, 2, 3. Finally, take a sample of 300 line numbers. Since there are 96 lines, you want 300 random numbers between 1 and 96.

Match up the three sets of numbers and pick the sample of listings in the phone book. If the first random number between 30 and 491 is 116, go to page 116. If the first random number between 1 and 3 is 3, go to column 3. If the first random number between 1 and 96 is 43, count down 43 lines. Decide if the listing is eligible. It may be a blank line or a business. That's why you generate 400 sets of numbers to get 200 good listings.

Telephone books don't actually make good sampling frames—too many people have unlisted numbers (which is why we have random digit dialing; see Chapter 7). But since everyone knows what a phone book looks like, it makes a good example for learning how to sample big, unnumbered lists of things, like the list of orthopedic surgeons in California.

Stratified Random Sampling

Stratified random sampling ensures that key subpopulations are included in your sample. You divide a population (a sampling frame) into subpopulations (subframes), based on key independent variables, and then take a random (unbiased) sample from each of those subpopulations. You might divide the population into men and women, or into rural and urban subframes—or into key age groups (18-34, 35-49, etc.) or key income groups. As the main sampling frame gets divided by key *independent* variables, the subframes presumably get more and more homogeneous with regard to the key *dependent* variable in the study.

In 1996, for example, representative samples of adult voters in the U.S. were asked the following question:

Which comes closest to your position? Abortion should be

*Legal in   Legal in   Illegal in   Illegal in
all cases   most cases   most cases   all cases*

Across all voters, 60% said that abortion should be legal in all (25%) or most (35%) cases and only 36% said it should be illegal in all (12%) or most (24%) cases. (The remaining 4% had no opinion.)

These facts hide some important differences across religious, ethnic, gender, political, and age groups. Among Catholic voters, 59% said that abortion should be legal in all (22%) or most (37%) cases; among Jewish voters, 91% said that abortion should be legal in all (51%) or most (40%) cases. Among registered Democrats, 72% favored legal abortion in all or most cases; among registered Republicans, 45% took that position (Ladd and Bowman 1997:44-46). Sampling from smaller chunks (by age, gender, etc.) ensures not only that you capture the variation but that you also wind up understanding how that variation is distributed.

This is called *maximizing the between-group variance* and *minimizing the within-group variance* for the independent variables in a study. It's what you want to do in building a sample because it reduces sampling error and thus makes samples more precise.

This sounds like a great thing to do, but you have to know what the key independent variables are. Shoe size is almost certainly not related to what people think is the ideal number of children to have. Gender and generation, however, seem like plausible variables on which to stratify a sample. So, if you are taking a poll to find what people think is the ideal number of children, you might divide the adult population into, say, four generations: ages 15-29, 30-44, 45-59, and over 59.

With two genders, this creates a *sampling design* with eight strata: men 15-29, 30-44, 45-59, and over 59; women 15-29, 30-44, 45-59, and over 59. Then you take a random sample of people from each of the eight strata and run your poll. If our hunch about the importance of gender and generation is correct, we'll find the attitudes of men and the attitudes of women more homogeneous than the attitudes of men and women thrown together.

Table 5.1 shows the distribution of gender and *age cohorts* for the U.S. in 1997.

TABLE 5.1 Gender and Age Cohorts for the United States, 1997

Age Cohort	Male	Female	Total
15-29	28,276 (13%)	27,173 (13%)	55,449 (26%)
30-44	32,222 (15%)	35,516 (17%)	67,738 (32%)
45-59	22,103 (10%)	23,287 (11%)	45,390 (21%)
> 59	18,753 (9%)	25,378 (12%)	44,131 (21%)
Total	101,354 (47%)	111,354 (53%)	212,708 (100%)

NOTE: Numbers are in thousands. Numbers in parentheses are percentages of the total population 15 and older.

SOURCE: *Statistical Abstract of the United States* (U.S. Census Bureau 1998, Table 16).

A *proportionate stratified random sample* of 2,400 respondents would include 360 men between the ages of 30 and 44 (15% of 2,400 = 360), but 408 women between the ages of 30 and 44 (17% of 2,400 = 408), and so on.

Watch out, though. We are accustomed to thinking in terms of gender on questions about family size, but gender-associated preferences are changing rapidly in late industrial societies, and we might be way off base in our thinking. Separating the population into gender strata might just be creating unnecessary work. Worse, it might introduce unknown error. If your guess about age and gender being related to desired number of children is wrong, then using Table 5.1 to create a sampling design will just make it harder for you to discover your error.

Here are the rules on stratification:

(1) If differences on a dependent variable are large across strata like age, sex, ethnic group, and so on, then stratifying a sample is a great idea.

(2) If differences are small, then stratifying just adds unnecessary work.

(3) If you are uncertain about the independent variables that could be at work in affecting your dependent variable, then leave well enough alone and don't stratify the sample. You can always stratify the *data* you collect and test various stratification schemes in the analysis instead of in the sampling.

Disproportionate Sampling

Disproportionate stratified random sampling is appropriate whenever an important subpopulation is likely to be underrepresented in a simple random sample or in a stratified random sample. Suppose you are doing a study of factors affecting grade-point averages among college students. You suspect that the independent variable called "race" has some effect on the dependent variable.

Suppose further that 5% of the student population is African American and that you have time and money to interview 400 students out of a population of 8,000. If you took 10,000 samples of 400 each from the population (replacing the 400 each time, of course), then the average number of African Americans in all the samples would approach 20—that is, 5% of the sample.

But you are going to take *one* sample of 400. If that sample turned out to be entirely representative of the population, it would contain just 20 (5%) African Americans. To ensure that you have sufficient data on African American students and on White students, you put the African Americans and the Whites into separate *strata* and draw two random samples of 200 each. The African Americans are disproportionately sampled by a factor of 10 (200 instead of the expected 20).

The National Maternal and Infant Health Survey was conducted in 1988. Sugarman et al. (1994) used birth certificates dated July 1–December 31, 1988, from 35 Native American health centers as their sampling frame and selected 1,480 eligible mothers for the study of maternal and infant health. Without disproportionate sampling, Native Americans, who comprise just 8/10 of 1% of the population, would be underrepresented in any national survey in the U.S.

Rosabeth Kanter (1977) outlined a theory of tokens in work groups. According to Kanter's theory, women who are hired as tokens experience a lot of stress because so much is expected of them. Does Kanter's token theory apply to African Americans? Jackson et al. (1995) tested this with data on 167 African American leaders in the U.S. Specifically, Jackson et al. tested the relation between proportional representation of African Americans in various elite occupations and the amount of stress that they suffer in those occupations. The lower the representation of African Americans in any occupation, the more symptoms of stress Jackson et al. expected to find.

The sample frame was a list, organized into sectors, of over a thousand prominent African Americans in business, government, academe, entertainment, journalism, religion, the judiciary, literature, and so on. Jackson et al. used a random sample of 15–20 persons from each institutional sector, for a total sample of 260 potential respondents. (Excluding 23 respondents who had died or were otherwise unreachable at the time of the study, the response rate was 167/237 = 70%.)

Some of the sectors have a much higher representation of African Americans than do others, but the sample design called for about the same number of interviews in each sector. This disproportionate random sampling procedure ensured that there would be a minimum number of respondents in each of the cells of the research design.

Weighting Results

One popular method for collecting data about daily activities is called "experience sampling" (Csikszentmihalyi and Larson 1987). You give a sample of people a beeper. They carry it around and you beep them at random times during the day. They fill out a little form about what they're doing at the time. (We'll look at these kinds of methods in Chapter 10.)

Suppose you want to contrast what people do on weekends and what they do during the week. If you beep people, say, eight times during each day, you'll wind up with 40 reports for each person for the five-day workweek but only 16 forms for each person for each two-day weekend because you've sampled the two strata—weekdays and weekends—proportionately.

If you want more data points for the weekend, you might beep people 12 times on Saturday and 12 times on Sunday. That gives you 24 data points, but you've disproportionately sampled one stratum. The weekend represents 2/7, or 28.6% of the week, but you've got 64 data points and 24 of them, or 37.5%, are about the weekend. Before comparing any data across the strata, you need to make the weekend data and the weekday data statistically comparable.

This is where *weighting* comes in. Multiply each weekday data point by 1.50 so that the 40 data points become worth 60 and the 24 weekend data points are again worth exactly 2/7 of the total.

You should also weight your data when you have unequal response rates in a stratified sample. Suppose you sample 200 men and 200 women for a survey in a factory that employs 60% women and 40% men. Of the 400 potential respondents, 178 men and 163 women respond to your questions. If you compare the answers of men and women on a variable, first, weight each man's data by 178/163 = 1.09 times each woman's data on that variable.

That takes care of the unequal response rates. Then weight each woman's data as counting 1.5 times each man's data on the variable. That takes care of the fact that there are half again as many women employees as there are men.

This seems complicated because it is. In the BC era (before computers), researchers had to work very hard to use disproportionate sampling. Fortunately, these days weighting is a simple procedure available in all major statistical analysis packages.

Cluster Sampling and Complex Sampling Designs

Cluster sampling is a way to sample populations for which there are no convenient lists or frames. It's also a way to minimize travel time in reaching scattered units of data collection. Cluster sampling is based on the fact that people act out their lives in more or less natural groups, or "clusters." They live in geographic areas (like counties, precincts, and states), and they participate in the activities of institutions (like schools, churches, brotherhoods, and credit unions). Even if there are no lists of people whom you want to study, you can sample areas or institutions and locate a sample within those clusters.

For example, there are no lists of schoolchildren in large cities, but children cluster in schools. There *are* lists of schools, so you can take a sample of them, and then sample children within each school selected. The idea in cluster sampling is to narrow the sampling field down from large, heterogeneous chunks to small, homogeneous ones that are relatively easy to sample directly.

❖

In Chapter 4, I mentioned a study that Lambros Comitas and I did comparing Greeks who had returned from West Germany as labor migrants with Greeks who had never left their country (Bernard and Comitas 1978). There were no lists of returned migrants, so we decided to locate the children of returned migrants in the Athens schools and use them to select a sample of their parents. The problem was, we couldn't even get a list of schools in Athens.

So we took a map of the city and divided it into small bits by laying a grid over it. Then we took a random sample of the bits and sent interviewers to find the school nearest each bit selected. The interviewers asked the principal of each school to identify the children of returned labor migrants. (It was easy for the principal to do, by the way. The principal said that all the returned migrant children spoke Greek with a German accent.) That way, we were able to make up two lists for each school: one of children who had been abroad, and one of children who had not. By sampling children randomly from those lists at each school, we were able to select a representative sample of parents.

This two-stage sampling design combined a cluster sample with a simple random sample to select the eventual units of analysis.

❖

Anthony and Suely Anderson (1983) wanted to compare people in Bacabal County, Brazil, who exploited the babassu palm with those who didn't. There was no list of households, but they did manage to get a list of the 344 named hamlets in the county. They divided the hamlets into those that supplied whole babassu fruits to new industries in the area and those that did not. Only 10.5% of the 344 hamlets supplied fruits to the industries, so the Andersons selected 10 hamlets randomly from each group for their survey. In other words, in the first stage of the process they stratified the clusters and took a disproportionate random sample from one of the clusters.

Next, they did a census of the 20 hamlets, collecting information on every household and particularly whether the household had land or was landless. At this stage, then, they created a sampling frame (the census) and stratified the frame into land-owning and landless households. Finally, they selected 89 landless households randomly for interviewing. This was 25% of the stratum of landless peasants. Since there were only 61 landowners, they decided to interview the entire population of this stratum.

Sampling designs can involve several stages. If you are studying Haitian refugee children in Miami, you could take a random sample of schools, but if you do that, you'll almost certainly select some schools in which there are no Haitian children. A three-stage sampling design is called for.

In the first stage, you would make a list of the neighborhoods in the city, find out which ones are home to a lot of refugees from Haiti, and sample those districts. In the second stage, you would take a random sample of schools from each of the chosen districts. Finally, in the third stage, you would develop a list of Haitian refugee children in each school and draw your final sample.

Al-Nuaim et al. (1997) used multistage stratified cluster sampling in their national study of adult obesity in Saudi Arabia. In the first stage, they selected cities and villages from each region of the country so that each region's total population was proportionately represented. Then they randomly selected districts from the local maps of the cities and villages in their sample. Next, they listed all the streets in each of the districts and selected every third street. Then they chose every third house on each of the streets and asked each adult in the selected houses to participate in the study.

Probability Proportionate to Size

The best estimates of a parameter are produced in samples taken from clusters of equal size. When clusters are not equal in size, then samples should be taken *PPS*—with *probability proportionate to size.*

Suppose you had money and time to do 800 household interviews in a city of 50,000 households. You intend to select 40 blocks, out of a total of 280, and do 20 interviews in each block. You want each of the 800 households in the final sample to have exactly the same probability of being selected.

Should each block be equally likely to be chosen for your sample? No, because census blocks never contribute equally to the total population from which you will take your final sample. A block that has 100 households in it *should* have twice the chance of being chosen for 20 interviews as a block that has 50 households, and half the chance of a block that has 200 households.

When you get down to the block level, each household on a block with 100 residences has a 20% (20/100) chance of being selected for the sample; each household on a block with 300 residences has only a 6.7% (20/300) chance of being selected.

PPS sampling is called for under three conditions: (1) when you are dealing with large, unevenly distributed populations (such as cities that have high-rise and single-family neighborhoods); (2) when your sample is large enough to withstand being broken up into a lot of pieces (clusters) without substantially increasing the sampling error; and (3) when you have data on the population of many small blocks in a population and can calculate their respective proportionate contributions to the total population.

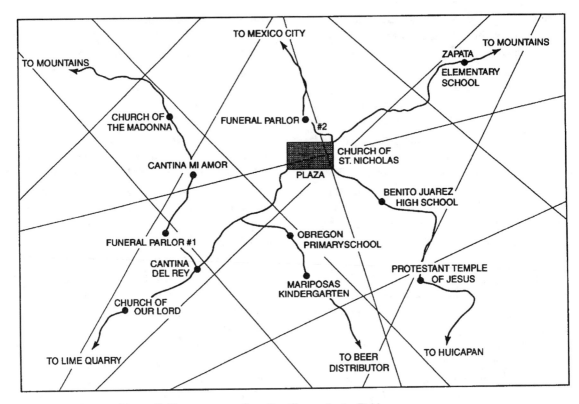

Figure 5.1 Creating Maximally Heterogeneous Sampling Clusters in the Field

PPS Samples in the Field

What do you do when you don't have neat clusters and neat sampling frames printed out on a computer by a reliable government agency? The answer is to place your trust in randomness and create maximally heterogeneous clusters from which to take a random sample.

Draw or get a map of the area you are studying. Place 100 numbered dots around the edge of the map. Try to space the numbers equidistant from one another, but don't worry if they are not. Select a pair of numbers at random and draw a line between them. Now select another pair of numbers (be sure to replace the first pair before selecting the second), and draw a line between them. In the unlikely event that you choose the same pair twice, simply choose a third pair. Keep doing this, replacing the numbers each time. After you've drawn about 50 lines, you can begin sampling.

> *What do you do when you don't have neat clusters and neat sampling frames printed out on a computer by a reliable government agency? Place your trust in randomness.*

Notice that the lines drawn across the map (see Figure 5.1) create a lot of wildly uneven spaces. Since you don't know the distribution of population density in the area you are studying, this technique maximizes the chance that you will properly survey the population, more or less PPS. By creating a series of (essentially) random chunks of different sizes, you distribute the error you might introduce by not knowing the density, and that distribution lowers the possible error.

Number the uneven spaces created by the lines and choose some of them at random. Go to those spaces, number the households, and select an appropriate number at random. Remember, you want to have the same number of households from *each* made-up geographic cluster, no matter what its size. If you are doing 400 interviews, you would select 20 geographic chunks and do 20 interviews or behavioral observations in each.

My colleagues and I used this method in 1986 to find out how many people in Mexico City knew someone who died in that city's monster earthquake the year before (Bernard et al. 1989). Instead of selecting households, though, my interviewers went to each geographic chunk we'd selected and stopped the first 10 people they ran into on the street at each point. This is called a *street-intercept survey* (see Box 5.2).

Handwerker (1993) used a map sampling method in his study of sexual behavior on Barbados. In his variation of map sampling, you generate 10 random numbers between 0 and 360 (the degrees on a compass). Next, put a dot in the center of a map that you will use for the sampling exercise, and use a protractor to identify the 10 randomly chosen compass points. You then draw lines from the dot in the center of the map through all 10 points to the edge of the map and interview people (or observe houses, etc.) along those lines. (See Duranleau [1999] for an empirical test of the power of map sampling.)

If you use this technique, you may want to establish a sampling interval (like every fifth case, beginning with the third case). If you finish interviewing along the lines and don't have enough cases, you can take another random start, with the

---

Box 5.2
Intercept Surveys

Street intercept surveys are can produce highly reliable, unbiased samples. K. W. Miller et al. (1997) ran a public health survey in an urban African American neighborhood and found that the street-intercept method produced more representative distributions of age and sex than the random-digit-dialing method.

A variant of the street-intercept method, called the *mall-intercept survey,* is used widely in market research. McLain and Sternquist (1991) collected 176 questionnaires from shoppers in several malls and found that consumers who display strong American ethnocentrism are no more likely to buy U.S.-made products than are shoppers who score low on ethnocentrism. (See Bush and Hair [1985] and Hornik and Ellis [1988] for more on mall-intercept methods.)

---

same or a different interval and start again. Be careful of periodicity, though.

Camilla Harshbarger (1995) used another variation of map sampling in her study of farmers in North West Province, Cameroon. To create a sample of 400 farmers, she took a map of a rural community and drew 100 dots around the perimeter. She used a random number table to select 50 pairs of dots and drew lines between them. She numbered the points created by the crossing of lines, and chose 80 of those points at random. Then, Harshbarger and her field assistants interviewed one farmer in each of the five compounds they found closest to each of the 80 selected dots. (If you use this dot technique, remember to include the points along the edges of the map in your sample, or you'll miss households on those edges.)

Of course, there are times when a random, representative sample is out of the question. After she did those interviews with 400 randomly selected farmers in North West Province, Cameroon, Harshbarger set out to interview Fulani cattle herders in the same area. Here's what Harshbarger wrote about her experience in trying to interview the herders:

> It was rainy season in Wum and the roads were a nightmare. The graziers lived very far out of town and quite honestly, my research assistants were not willing to trek to the compounds because it would have taken too much time and we would never have finished the job. I consulted X and he agreed to call selected people to designated school houses on certain days. We each took a room and administered the survey with each individual grazier.
>
> Not everyone who was called came for the interview, so we ended up taking who we could get. Therefore, the Wum grazier sample was not representative and initially that was extremely difficult for me to accept. Our team had just finished the 400-farmer survey of Wum that *was* representative, and after all that work it hit me hard that the grazier survey would not be. To get a representative sample, I would have needed a four-wheel-drive vehicle, a driver, and more money to pay research assistants for a lengthy stay in the field. Eventually, I forgave myself for the imperfection. (Personal communication)

The lessons here are clear: (1) If you are ever in Harshbarger's situation, you, too, can forgive yourself for having a nonrepresentative sample; and (2) even then, like Harshbarger, you should feel bad about it.

Maximizing Between-Group Variance: The Wichita Study

Whenever you do multistage cluster sampling, be sure to take as large a sample as possible from the largest, most heterogeneous clusters. The larger the cluster, the larger the between-group variance; the smaller the cluster, the higher the within-group variance. Counties in the United States are more like each other on any variable (income, race, average age, etc.) than states are; towns within a county are more like each other than counties are; neighborhoods in a town are more like each other than towns are; blocks are more like each other than neighborhoods are. In sampling, the rule is: Maximize between-group variance.

———————❖

What does this mean in practice? Following is an actual example of multistage sampling from John Hartman's study of Wichita, Kansas (Hartman 1978; Hartman and Hedblom 1979:160ff.). At the time of the study, in the mid-1970s, Wichita had a population of about 193,000 persons over age 16. This was the population to which the study team wanted to generalize. The team decided that it could afford only 500 interviews. There are 82 census tracts in Wichita, from which the researchers randomly selected 20. These 20 tracts then became the actual population of their study. We'll see in a moment how well their actual study population simulated (represented) the study population to which they wanted to generalize.

Hartman and Hedblom added up the total population in the 20 tracts and divided the population of *each tract* by the total. This gave the percentage of people that each tract, or cluster, contributed to the new population total. Since the researchers were going to do 500 interviews, each tract was assigned that percentage of the interviews. If there were 50,000 people in the 20 tracts, and one of the tracts had a population of 5,000, or 10% of the total, then 50 interviews (10% of the 500) would be done in that tract.

Next, the researchers numbered the blocks in each tract and selected blocks at random until they had enough for the number of interviews that were to be conducted in that tract. When a block was selected it stayed in the pool, so that in some cases more than one interview was to be conducted in a single block. This did not happen very often, and the team wisely left it up to chance to determine this.

This study team made some excellent decisions that maximized the heterogeneity (and hence the representativeness) of its sample. As clusters get smaller and smaller (as you go from tract to block to household, or from village to neighborhood to household), the homogeneity of the units of analysis within the clusters gets greater and greater. People in one census tract or village are more like each other than people in different tracts or villages. People in one census block or barrio are more like each other than people across blocks or barrios. And people in households are more like each other than people in households across the street or over the next hill.

This is very important. Most researchers would have no difficulty with the idea that they should only interview one person in a household because, for example, husbands and wives often have similar ideas about things and report similar behavior with regard to kinship, visiting, health care, child care, and consumption of goods and services. Somehow, the lesson becomes less clear when new researchers move into clusters that are larger than households.

But the rule stands: Maximize heterogeneity of the sample by taking as many of the biggest clusters in your sample as you can, and as many of the next biggest, and so on, always at the expense of the number of clusters at the bottom where homogeneity is greatest. Take more tracts or villages, and fewer blocks per tract or barrios per village. Take more blocks per tract or barrios per village, and fewer households per block or barrio. Take more households and fewer persons per household.

Many survey researchers say that, as a rule, you should have no fewer than five households in a census block. The Wichita group did not follow this rule but only had enough money and person power to do 500 interviews, and the researchers wanted to maximize the likelihood that their sample would represent faithfully the characteristics of the 193,000 adults in their city.

The Wichita study group drew two samples—one main sample and one alternate sample. Whenever the researchers could not get someone on the main sample, they took the alternate. That way, they maximized the representativeness of their sample because the alternates were chosen with the same randomized procedure as the main respondents in their survey. They were not forced to take "next-door neighbors," when a main respondent wasn't home. (This kind of "winging it" in survey research has a tendency to clobber the representativeness of samples. In the U.S., at least, interviewing only people who are at home during the day produces results that represent women with small children, shut-ins, telecommuters, and the elderly—and not much else.)

Next, the Wichita team randomly selected the households for interview within each block. This was the third stage in this multistage cluster design. The fourth stage consisted of flipping a coin to decide whether to interview a man or a woman in households with both. Whoever came to the

TABLE 5.2 Comparison of Survey Results and Population Parameters for the Wichita Study by Hartman and Hedblom (1979) (in percentages)

	Wichita in 1973	Hartman and Hedblom's Sample for 1973
White	86.8	82.8
African American	9.7	10.8
Chicano	2.5	2.6
Other	1.0	2.8
Male	46.6	46.9
Female	53.4	53.1
Median age	38.5	39.5

SOURCE: *Methods for the Social Sciences: A Handbook for Students and Non-specialists* (Contributions in Sociology, No. 37), Greenwood Press; an imprint of Greenwood Publishing Group, Inc. Copyright © 1979 by John J. Hartman and Jack H. Hedblom, p. 165. Reproduced with permission of Greenwood Publishing Group, Inc., Westport, Conn.

door was asked to provide a list of those in the household over 16 years of age. If there was more than one eligible person in the household, the interviewer selected one at random, conforming to the decision made earlier on sex of respondent.

Table 5.2 shows how well the Wichita team did.

All in all, they did very well. In addition to the variables shown in the table here, the Wichita sample was a fair representation of marital status, occupation, and education, although on this last independent variable there were some pretty large discrepancies. For example, according to the 1970 census, 8% of the population of Wichita had less than eight years of schooling, but only 4% of the sample had this characteristic. Only 14% of the general population had completed one to three years of college, but 22% of the sample had that much education.

All things considered, though, the sampling procedure followed in the Wichita study was a model of technique, and the results show it. Whatever they found out about the 500 people they interviewed, the researchers could be very confident that the results were generalizable to the 193,000 adults in Wichita.

In sum: If you don't have a sampling frame for a population, try to do a multistage cluster sample, narrowing down to natural clusters that do have lists. Sample heavier at the higher levels in a multistage sample and lighter at the lower stages.

HOW BIG SHOULD A SAMPLE BE?

There are two things you can do to get good samples. You can ensure *sample accuracy* by making sure that every element in the population has an equal chance of being selected—that is, you can make sure the sample is unbiased. You can ensure *sample precision* by **increasing the size of** unbiased samples. We've already discussed the importance of making samples unbiased. The next step is to decide how big a sample needs to be.

Sample size depends on (1) the heterogeneity of the population or chunks of population (strata or clusters) from which you choose the elements, (2) how many population subgroups (that is, independent variables) you want to deal with simultaneously in your analysis, (3) the size of the phenomenon that you're trying to detect, and (4) how precise you want your *sample statistics* (or *parameter estimators*) to be.

1. *Heterogeneity of the population.* When all elements of a population have the same score on some measure, a sample of 1 will do. Ask a lot of people to tell you how many days there are in a week and you'll soon understand that a big sample isn't going to uncover a lot of heterogeneity. But if you want to know what the average ideal family size is, you may need to cover a lot of social ground. People of different ethnicities, religions, incomes, genders, and ages may have very different ideas about this. In fact, these independent variables may interact in complex ways.

2. *Number of subgroups in the analysis.* Remember the *factorial design* problem in Chapter 4 on experiments? We had three independent variables, each with two attributes, so we needed eight groups ($2^3 = 8$). It wouldn't do you much good to have, say, one experimental subject in each of those eight groups. If you're going to analyze all eight of the conditions in the experiment, you've got to fill each of the conditions with some reasonable number of subjects.

The same principle holds when you're trying to figure out how big a sample you need for a survey. In the example above about stratified random sampling, we had four generations and two genders—which also produced an eight-cell design.

If all you want to know is a single proportion—like what percentage of people in a population approve or disapprove of something—then you need about 100 respondents to be 95% confident, within plus or minus 3 points, that your sample estimate is within 2 standard deviations of the population parameter (more about confidence limits, normal distributions, standard deviations, and parameters in a minute). But if you want to know whether retired widowers who have less than $3,000 per month in total income have different opinions from, say, working, married mothers who have more than $3,000 per month in total income, then you'll need a bigger sample.

3. *Size of the subgroup.* If the population you are trying to study is rare and hard to find, and if you have to rely on a simple random sample of the entire population, you'll need a very large initial sample. Just under 2% of Florida's population is 85 and older, so a random sample of 1,600 survey respondents is likely to turn up around 32 people in that age group. If you are doing a telephone survey using random digit dialing, you may have to make 10,000 calls before you get 100 people in that age group who are willing and able to participate in a survey.

A needs assessment survey of people over age 75 in Florida, in fact, took 72,000 phone calls to get 1,647 interviews—about 44 calls per interview (Henry 1990:88). This is because only 6.5% of Florida's population was over 75 at the time of the survey. By contrast, the monthly Florida survey of 600 representative consumers takes about 5,000 calls (about 8 per interview). That's because just about everyone in the state who is 18 and older is a consumer and is eligible for the survey (Christopher McCarty, personal communication).

The smaller the difference on any measure between two populations, the bigger the sample you need to detect that difference. Suppose you suspect that Blacks and Whites in a prison system have received different sentences for the same crime. Henry (1990:121) shows that a difference of 16 months in sentence length for the same crime would be detected with a sample of just 30 in each racial group (if the members of the sample were selected randomly, of course). To detect a

difference of three months, however, you need 775 in each group.

4. *Precision.* This one takes us into sampling theory.

PROBABILITY DISTRIBUTIONS

Sampling theory is partly about *probability distributions,* which come in a variety of shapes. Suppose the numbers from 1 to 100 are a population of elements—things from which you want to choose a sample. If you choose a number from 1 to 100 at random, then each number (or element) has a uniform probability of being chosen. These elements have a *uniform probability distribution.* The characteristic shape of a uniform distribution is a rectangle, shown in Figure 5.2a. The items in the population (in this case, a list of numbers from 1 to 100) are listed along the x-axis. Each number has a 1/100 (1%) probability of being selected, and this probability (.01) is shown on the y-axis.

Figure 5.2b shows an *exponential distribution.* Exponential distributions **describe many phenomena that happen through time.** In some sports, games that are tied at the end of a certain amount of time are sent into sudden-death overtime. The number of minutes it takes for a team to score the winning goal in these sports forms an exponential distribution like the one in Figure 5.2b. As the minutes drag on (the horizontal x-axis along the bottom), the probability of a team scoring a winning goal (the vertical y-axis) goes up.

But the probability doesn't go up steadily. It goes up exponentially. The longer it takes, the

faster the probability rises that one team will score in the next minute.

Figure 5.2c shows a *bimodal distribution.* Suppose the x-axis in Figure 5.2c is age and the y-axis is the probability of answering yes to the question "Did you like the beer commercial shown during the Superbowl yesterday?" The bimodal distribution shows that people in their 20s and people in their 60s liked the commercial, but others didn't.

Figure 5.2d shows two *skewed distributions.* A distribution can be skewed to the right or to the left. The schematic figure on the right in Figure 5.2d looks like the percentage of people on welfare across the United States. That percentage is skewed to the right. (If you want to see the actual distribution of this variable, take a look at Figure 14.6.) The schematic figure on the left in Figure 5.2d looks like the percentage of people across the United States who own their own homes. That distribution is skewed to the left. (The actual distribution is shown in Figure 14.7.)

Figure 5.3 shows three variations of a symmetric distribution—that is, distributions for which the mean and the median are the same. The one on the left is *leptokurtic* (from Greek, meaning "thin bulge") and the one on the right is *platykurtic* (meaning "flat bulge"). The curve in the middle is the famous bell-shaped, normal distribution.

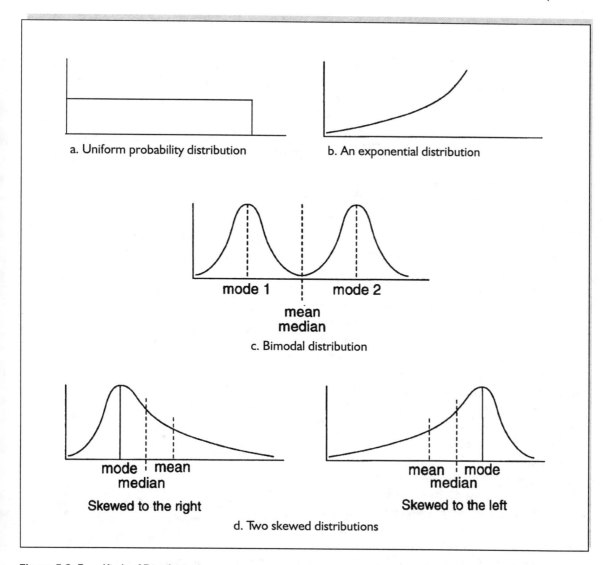

a. Uniform probability distribution

b. An exponential distribution

mode 1　　mode 2

mean
median

c. Bimodal distribution

mode ┆ mean
median

Skewed to the right

mean ┆ mode
median

Skewed to the left

d. Two skewed distributions

Figure 5.2 Four Kinds of Distributions

The Normal Curve and z-Scores

The so-called *normal distribution* is generated by a formula that can be found in many introductory statistics texts. The distribution has a mean of 0 and a *standard deviation* of 1 (if you are not familiar with standard deviations and standard scores, see Chapter 14).

Appendix B is a table of *z-scores,* or *standard scores.* These scores are the number of standard deviations from the mean in a normal distribution, in increments of 1/100th of a standard deviation. For each z-score, beginning with 0.00 standard deviations (the mean) and on up to 3.09 standard deviations (on either side of the mean),

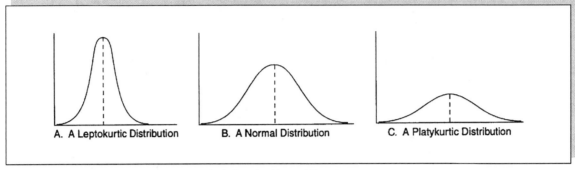

Figure 5.3 Three Symmetric Distributions Including the Normal Distribution

Appendix B shows the percentage of the physical area under the curve of a normal distribution.

We see from Appendix B that 34.13% of the area under the curve is 1 standard deviation above the mean and another 34.13% is 1 standard deviation below the mean. Thus, 68.26%—usually rounded to 68%—of all scores in a normal distribution fall within 1 standard deviation of the mean. We also see from Appendix B that 95.44% of all scores in a normal distribution fall within 2 standard deviations and that 99.7% fall within 3 standard deviations. This is shown graphically in Figure 5.4.

If 95.44% of the area under a normal curve falls within 2 standard deviations from the mean, then 95% should fall within slightly less than 2 standard deviations. Appendix B tells us that 1.96 standard deviations above and below the mean account for 95% of all scores in a normal distribution. And, similarly, 2.58 standard deviations

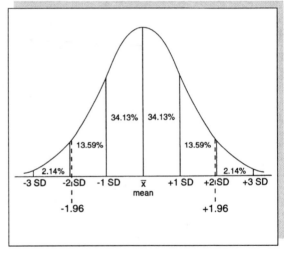

Figure 5.4 The Normal Curve and the First, Second, and Third Standard Deviations

account for 99% of all scores. This is also shown graphically in Figure 5.4.

THE CENTRAL LIMIT THEOREM

According to the *central limit theorem,* if you take many samples of a population, and if the samples are big enough, then

(1) the mean and the standard deviation of the sample means will approximate the true mean and standard deviation of the population; and

TABLE 5.3 All Samples of 2 from 5 Elements

Sample	Mean	Cumulative Mean
NY and LA	(17 + 25.7)/2 = 21.35	21.35
NY and ID	(17 + 12)/2 = 14.50	17.93
NY and FL	(17 + 14.9)/2 = 15.95	17.26
NY and IA	(17 + 10.7)/2 = 13.85	16.41
LA and ID	(25.7 + 12)/2 = 18.85	16.90
LA and FL	(25.7 + 14.9)/2 = 20.30	17.47
LA and IA	(25.7 + 10.7)/2 = 18.20	17.57
ID and FL	(12 + 14.9)/2 = 13.45	17.06
ID and IA	(12 + 10.7)/2 = 11.35	16.42
FL and IA	(14.9 + 10.7)/2 = 12.80	16.06

$$\bar{x} = 160.6/10 = 16.06$$

(2) the distribution of sample means will approximate a normal distribution.

We can demonstrate both parts of the central limit theorem with some examples.

Part A of the Central Limit Theorem

Consider the following data from five U.S. states: New York, Louisiana, Idaho, Florida, and Iowa. These five states had poverty rates in 1994 of 17%, 25.7%, 12%, 14.9%, and 10.7%, respectively. That is, 17% of the population of the state of New York lived below the official poverty line in 1994, 12% of the population of Idaho lived below the poverty line, and so on. These five numbers sum to 80.3 and their average is 16.06.

There are 10 possible samples of two elements in any population of five elements. All 10 samples for the five states in our example are shown in the left-hand column of Table 5.3. The middle column shows the mean for each sample. And the right-hand column shows the *cumulative mean.*

Notice that the mean of the means for all 10 samples of two elements—that is, the mean of the *sampling distribution*—is 16.06%, which is *ex-* *actly the actual mean* of the five states in the population. In other words, the mean of all possible samples of size 2 is equal to the parameter that we're trying to estimate.

The distribution of the five actual poverty rates is shown in Figure 5.5a. It is highly skewed. The distribution of the 10 sample means for the five poverty rates is shown in Figure 5.5b. This distribution looks more like the shape of the normal curve: It's got that telltale bulge in the middle.

Part B of the Central Limit Theorem

Table 5.4 shows the percentage of people living below the poverty line in 1994 for each of the 50 states in the U.S. and the District of Columbia. Figure 5.6 shows the distribution of the 51 data points in Table 5.4. The range is quite broad, from 7.6% to 25.7%, and the distribution is skewed to the right. Ten states have less than 10% of their population living below the official poverty line; there's a bulge of 25 states in the 10%-15% range; and then there is a tail going off to the right, with Washington, D.C., New Mexico, and Louisiana all above 20%.

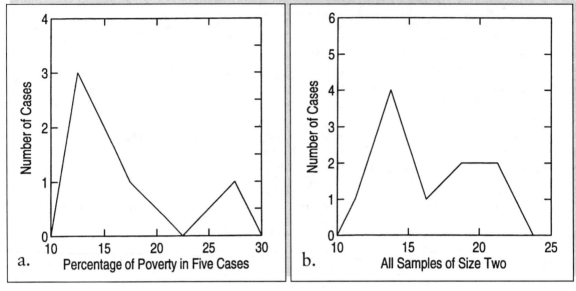

Figure 5.5 Five Cases and the Distribution of Samples of Size 2 from Those Cases

The actual mean of the data in Table 5.4—the parameter we want to estimate—is 13.23%. There are 2,349,060 samples of size 5 that can be taken from 51 elements. I used a random-number generator to select 15 samples of size 5 from the data in Table 5.4 and calculated the mean of each sample. Table 5.5 shows the results.

Even in this small set of 15 samples, the mean is 13.515—quite close to the actual mean of 13.23. Figure 5.7a shows the distribution of these samples. It has the look of a normal distribution straining to happen. Figure 5.7b shows 100 samples of 5 from the 51; the strain toward the normal curve is unmistakable.

The problem, of course, is that in real research, we don't get to take 15 or 100 samples. We have to make do with one. And it's very clear that any of those samples of 5 in Table 5.5 could be off by a lot. They range, after all, from less than 10 to almost 18. That's a very big spread when the real average we're trying to estimate is 13.23.

Figure 5.7c shows what happens when we take 30 samples of size 30 from the 51 elements in Table 5.4. Not only is the distribution pretty normal looking, the range of the 30 samples is between 12.38 and 14.22—that is, within plus or minus 1 point of the true mean.

We are much closer to answering the question: How big does a sample have to be?

THE STANDARD ERROR AND CONFIDENCE INTERVALS

The *standard deviation* is a measure of how much the scores in a distribution vary from the mean score. The larger the standard deviation, the more dispersion (see Chapter 14).

The mean of a population (what we want to estimate), is symbolized by μ, the Greek lowercase letter mu (pronounced "myoo").

TABLE 5.4   Persons in the United States below the Poverty Line, 1994

State	Percentage in Poverty	State	Percentage in Poverty
Alabama	16.4	Montana	11.5
Alaska	10.2	Nebraska	8.8
Arizona	15.9	Nevada	11.1
Arkansas	15.3	New Hampshire	7.7
California	17.9	New Jersey	9.2
Colorado	9.0	New Mexico	21.1
Connecticut	10.8	New York	17.0
Delaware	8.3	North Carolina	14.2
Washington, D.C.	21.2	North Dakota	10.4
Florida	14.9	Ohio	14.1
Georgia	14.0	Oklahoma	16.7
Hawaii	8.7	Oregon	11.8
Idaho	12.0	Pennsylvania	12.5
Illinois	12.4	Rhode Island	10.3
Indiana	13.7	South Carolina	13.8
Iowa	10.7	South Dakota	14.5
Kansas	14.9	Tennessee	14.6
Kentucky	18.5	Texas	19.1
Louisiana	25.7	Utah	8.0
Maine	9.4	Vermont	7.6
Maryland	10.7	Virginia	10.7
Massachusetts	9.7	Washington	11.7
Michigan	14.1	West Virginia	18.6
Minnesota	11.7	Wisconsin	9.0
Mississippi	19.9	Wyoming	9.3
Missouri	15.6		

Average = 13.23
Standard deviation = 4.05

SOURCE: *Statistical Abstract of the United States* (U.S. Census Bureau 1996, Table 735).

The standard deviation of the mean of a population is symbolized by σ, the Greek lowercase letter sigma.

The mean of a *sample* is signified by $\bar{x}$ (read: x bar), and the standard deviation of the mean of a sample is written as SD or just s. (For a full discussion of how to calculate the standard deviation and the mean of a sample, see Chapter 14.)

The standard deviation of the mean of a sampling distribution is the **standard error** of the mean, or *SE*. The formula for calculating *SE* is

$$SE = \frac{SD}{\sqrt{n}} \qquad \text{(Formula 5.1)}$$

where n is the sample size.

In a sample of 100 people, we find the average income is $26,400 with a standard deviation of $4,000. The standard error of the mean is

$$\$26,400 \pm \frac{4,000}{\sqrt{100}} = \$26,400 \pm \$400$$

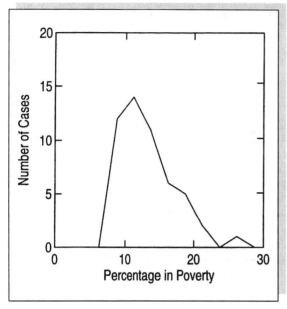

Figure 5.6 Percentage in Poverty, United States

TABLE 5.5	15 Means from Samples of Size 5 Taken from the 51 Elements in Table 5.4

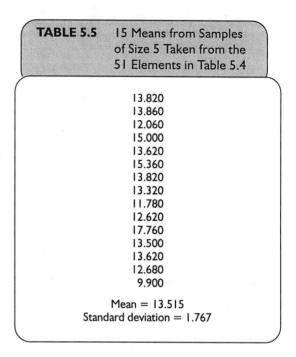

13.820
13.860
12.060
15.000
13.620
15.360
13.820
13.320
11.780
12.620
17.760
13.500
13.620
12.680
9.900

Mean = 13.515
Standard deviation = 1.767

Do the calculation:

$$\$26,400 + \$400 = \$26,800$$
$$\$26,400 - \$400 = \$26,000$$

We know from Figure 5.4 that 68.26% of all samples of size 100 from this population will produce an estimate that is between 1 standard error above and 1 standard error below the mean—that is, between $26,000 and $26,800. The 68.26% *confidence interval,* then, is $400.

We also know from Figure 5.4 that 95.44% of all samples of size 100 will produce an estimate of ± 2 standard errors, or between $25,600 and $27,200. The 95.44% confidence interval, then, is ± $800.

You won't often see confidence levels of .9544 (or 95.44%) in the social science literature. Instead, most researchers report nice round confidence intervals, like 95% or 99%. If you look carefully at Appendix B, you'll see that 95% of the area under a normal curve conforms to a z-score of 1.96 and that a z-score of 2.00 con-

forms to 95.44% of the area under a normal curve.

The z-score that conforms to 99% of the normal curve is 2.58, and a z-score of 3.00 conforms to 99.7% of the curve. (You'll run into these numbers a lot as you learn to do data analysis.) This is shown in Figure 5.4, where we see that 95% of all samples of size 100 will produce an estimate of ±1.96 standard errors, and 99% will produce an estimate of 2.58 standard errors.

The figures of 1.96 and 2.58 standard errors represent *alpha levels* of .05 and .01, or what's left over in the *critical region* of the normal curve after 95% or 99% of all samples have been accounted for. If we do the sums for the example, we see that the 95% confidence limits are

$$\$26,400 \pm 1.96 \, (\$400) = \$25,616 \text{ to } \$27,184$$

and the 99% confidence limits are

$$\$26,400 \pm 2.58 \, (\$400) = \$25,368 \text{ to } \$27,432$$

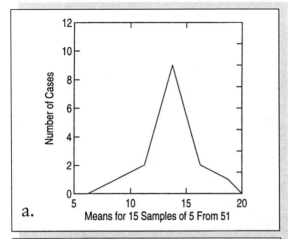

a.

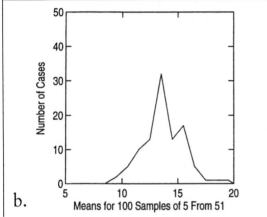

b.

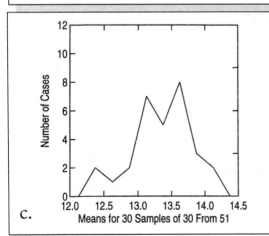

c.

Figure 5.7 Visualizing the Central Limit Theorem: The Distribution of Sample Means Approximates a Normal Distribution

---

Box 5.3
What Confidence Limits Are and What They Aren't

If you say that the 95% confidence limits for the estimated mean income are $25,616 to $27,184, this does not mean that there is a 95% chance that the true mean, μ, lies somewhere in that range. The true mean may or may not lie within that range and we have no way to tell. What we can say, however, is that

(1) if we take a very large number of suitably large random samples from the population (we'll get to what "suitably large" means in a minute); and

(2) if we calculate the mean, $\bar{x}$, and the standard error, *SE*, for each sample; and

(3) if we then calculate the confidence intervals for each sample mean, based on ±1.96 *SE*; then

(4) 95% of these confidence intervals will contain the true mean, μ.

Our "confidence" in these 95% or 99% estimates comes from the power of a random sample and the fact that (by the central limit theorem) sampling distributions are known to be normal irrespective of the distribution of the variable whose mean we are estimating (see Box 5.3).

Now we are really close to answering the question about sample size. Suppose we want to get the standard error down to $200 instead of $400. We need to solve the following equation:

$$SE = \frac{SD}{\sqrt{n}} = \frac{4,000}{20} = \$200$$

Solving for *n*:

$$\sqrt{n} = \frac{4,000}{200} = 20 \qquad n = 20^2 = 400$$

In other words, to reduce the standard error of the mean from $400 to $200, we have to increase the sample size from 100 to 400 people.

Suppose we increase the sample to 400 and we still get a mean of $26,400 with a standard deviation of $4,000. The standard error of the mean would then be $200, and we could estimate, with 95.44% confidence, that the true mean of the population was between $26,000 and $26,800. With just 100 people in the sample, the 95.44% confidence limits were $25,600 and $27,200. As the standard error goes down, we get narrower—that is, more precise—confidence limits.

Let's carry this forward another step. If we wanted to get the standard error down to $100

and the 95.44% confidence interval down to $200 from $400, we would need a sample of 1,600 people. There is a pattern here. To cut the 95% confidence interval *in half*, from $800 to $400, we had to *quadruple* the sample size from 100 to 400. To cut the interval *again in half*, to $200, we'd need to *quadruple* the sample size again, from 400 to 1,600.

There is another pattern, too. If we want to increase our confidence from 95% to 99.7% that the true mean of the population is within a particular confidence interval, we can raise the multiplier in Formula 5.1 from 2 standard deviations to 3. Using the confidence interval of $400, we would calculate

$$\sqrt{n} = 3 \times \frac{4,000}{400} = 30 \qquad n = 30^2 = 900$$

We need 900 people, not 400, to be about 99% confident that our sample mean is within $400, plus or minus, of the parameter.

SMALL SAMPLES: THE *t* DISTRIBUTION

Samples of 100, 400, and 1,600 are large, but I've been vague on what the minimum number is for a "large" sample. In social research, we often have to use small samples. You might be able to run a *survey* with hundreds of respondents, but direct observation in fieldwork and lab experiments usually have to be based on samples of 20 or fewer research participants.

What we need is a distribution that is a bit more forgiving than the normal distribution. Fortunately, just such a distribution was discovered by W. S. Gossett, an employee of the Guinness brewery in Ireland. Writing under the pseudonym of

"Student," Gossett described the distribution known as Student's *t*. It is based on a distribution that takes into account the fact that small samples have a bigger chance of misestimating the parameter of a continuous variable.

The *t* distribution is found in Appendix C. Figure 5.8 shows graphically the difference in the two distributions. The shorter curve has tails extending out 4 standard deviations, while the taller one has all the characteristics of a true normal distribution: 3 standard deviations from the mean contain 99.7% of all sample means.

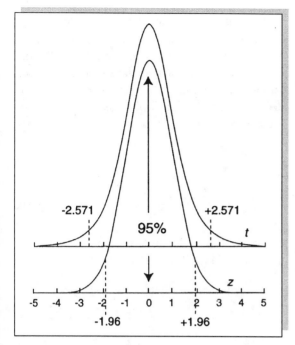

Figure 5.8 Variability in a t Distribution and a Normal Distribution

The confidence interval for small samples, using the *t* distribution, is

$$\bar{x} \pm t_\alpha/2 \; \frac{SD}{\sqrt{n}}$$

where alpha (α) is the confidence interval you want. If you want to be 95% confident, then α equals .05. Since half the scores fall above the mean and half below, we divide alpha by two and get .025.

Look up what's called the *critical value* of *t* in Appendix C. In the column for .025, we see that the value is 2.571 with 5 degrees of freedom. Degrees of freedom are one less than the size of the sample, so for a sample of six we need a *t* statistic of > 2.571 to attain 95% confidence. (The concept of degrees of freedom is described further in Chapter 14 in the section on *t*-tests.)

So, with small samples—which, for practical purposes, means less than 30 units of analysis—we use Appendix C (for *t*) instead of Appendix B (for *z*) to determine the confidence limits around the mean of our estimate. You can see from Appendix C that for large samples—which, in practical terms, means 30 or more—the difference between the *t* and the *z* statistics is negligible (see Box 5.4).

The Catch

Suppose that instead of estimating the income of a population with a sample of 100 we use a sample of 10 and get the same result: $26,400 and a standard deviation of $4,000. For a sample this size, we use the *t* distribution. With 9 degrees of freedom and an alpha value of .025, we have a *t*-value of 2.262. For a normal curve, 95% of all scores fall within 1.96 standard errors of the mean. The corresponding *t*-value is 2.262 standard errors. Substituting in the formula, we get

$$\$26{,}400 \pm 2.262 \; \frac{\$4{,}000}{\sqrt{10}} = \$23{,}539 \text{ to } \$29{,}261$$

But there's a catch. With a large sample (greater than 30), we know from the central limit theorem that the sampling distribution will be normal even if the population isn't. Using the *t* distribution with a small sample, we can calculate the confidence interval around the mean of our sample *only under the assumption that the population is normally distributed*.

In fact, looking back at Figure 5.6, we know that the distribution of the real data is not perfectly normal. It is somewhat *skewed* (more about skewed distributions in Chapter 14). In real research, we'd never take a sample from a set of just 51 data points—we'd do all our calculations on the full set of the actual data. When we take samples, it's because we don't know what the distribution of the data looks like. And that's why sample size counts.

ESTIMATING PROPORTIONS

And now for proportions. What we've learned so far about estimating the mean of continuous variables (like income and percentages) is applicable to the estimation of proportions as well.

In February 1998, President Bill Clinton had a job-approval rating of 68%, according to an ABC poll. The poll included 1,021 respondents and had, as the media say, a "margin of error of plus or minus 3 points." This job-approval rating of 68% means that 694 of the 1,021 people polled said that they approved of the job Clinton was doing.

Once again, we have a point estimate, but we'd like to know what the confidence interval is for the point estimate of 68%. From the central limit theorem again, we know that whatever the true proportion of Clinton approvers, the estimates of that proportion will be normally distributed if we take a large number of samples of 1,021 people. The formula for determining the 95% confidence limits of a point estimator is

$$P \text{ (the true proportion)} = 1.96\sqrt{PQ/n} \quad \text{(Formula 5.2)}$$

We use an italicized letter, *P*, to indicate the true proportion. Our estimate is the regular uppercase P and Q is 1 − P. Table 5.6 shows what happens to

the square root of PQ as the true value of *P* goes up from 10% to 90% of the population.

TABLE 5.6	Relation of P and Q and $\sqrt{PQ}$	
If the value of P is really	Then PQ is	And the square root of PQ is
.10 or .90	.09	.30
.20 or .80	.16	.40
.30 or .70	.21	.46
.40 or .60	.24	.49
.50	.25	.50

We can use our own estimate of *P* in the equation for the confidence limits. Substituting .68 for P and .32 (1 − .68) for Q, we get

$$P = P \pm 1.96 \sqrt{(.68)(.32)/1,021} = .0286$$

which reads: "We are 95% confident that the true proportion of people who approve of President Clinton's job performance in the U.S. at the time this poll was conducted was between 65.14% and 70.86%." Rounding to the nearest whole number, we get that "68% with a margin of error of plus or minus 3 points" that ABC News reported. It's really plus or minus 2.86 points, but rounding *up* to 3 points is conservative—it widens the confidence limits—and it's easier to understand.

Suppose we want to estimate P to within plus or minus 2 percentage points instead of 2.86 and we still want to maintain the 95% confidence level. We substitute in the formula as follows:

$$P = P \pm 1.96 \sqrt{(.68)(.32)/n} = .02$$

Now we solve for n:

$$n = (1.96)^2 (.68)(.32)/(.02)^2$$

$$n = (3.842)(.68)(.32)/.0004 = 2,090$$

Generalizing, then, the formula for "sample size when estimating proportions in a large population" is

$$n = z^2 (P)(Q)/(\text{confidence interval})^2 \quad \text{(Formula 5.3)}$$

where z is the area under the normal curve that corresponds to the confidence limit we choose. When the confidence limit is 95%, then z is 1.96. When the confidence limit is 99%, then z is 2.58. And so on.

If we start out fresh and have no prior estimate of P, we follow Table 5.6 and set P and Q to .5 each. (This maximizes the size of the sample for any given confidence interval or confidence level.) If we want a sample that produces an estimate of a proportion with a confidence interval of 2 percentage points and we want to be 95% confident in that estimate, we calculate

$$n \text{ (sample size)} = (1.96)^2 (.5)(.5)/(.02)^2 = 2,401$$

Estimating Proportions in Samples for Smaller Populations

This general formula, 5.3, is *independent of the size of the population.* Florida has a population of about 14 million. A sample of 400 is .000029 of 14 million; a sample of 2,402 is .00017 of 14 million. Both percentages are microscopic. A sample of 400 from a population of 1 million gets you the same confidence level and the same confidence interval as you get with a sample of 400 from a population of 14 million.

Often, though, we want to take samples from relatively small populations. The key word here is "relatively." When Formula 5.2 (or 5.3) calls for a sample that turns out to be 5% or more of the total population, we apply the *finite population correction.* The formula (from Cochran 1977) is

$$n' = \frac{n}{1 + (n - 1/N)} \quad \text{(Formula 5.4)}$$

where n is the sample size calculated from Formula 5.3, n' (read: n prime) is the new value for the sample size, and N is the size of the total population from which n is being drawn.

Here's an example. Suppose you are sampling the 540 female students at a small college to determine how many have ever participated in extreme sports. How many of those women do you need to interview to ensure a 95% probability sample, with a 5% confidence interval?

Answer: Since we have no idea what the percentage is that we're trying to estimate, we set P and Q at .5 each in Formula 5.2. Solving for n (sample size), we get

$$n = (1.96)^2 (.5)(.5)/(.05)^2 = 384.16$$

which we round up to 385.

Then we apply the finite population correction:

$$n' = \frac{385}{1 + (384/540)} = 225$$

This is still a hefty percentage of the 540 people in the population, but it's a lot smaller than the 384 called for by the standard formula (see Box 5.5).

Another Catch

All of this discussion has been about estimating single parameters, whether proportions or means. You will often want to measure the interaction among several variables at once. Suppose you study a population of wealthy, middle-class, and poor people. That's 3 kinds of people. Now add two sexes, male and female (that makes 6 kinds of people) and two colors, Black and White (that makes 12 kinds). If you want to know how all those independent variables combine to predict, say, average number of children desired, the sampling strategy gets more complicated.

Sampling is one of the trickiest parts of social research. I recommend strongly that you consult an expert in sampling if you are going to do complex tests on your data. (For excellent coverage of all the basics in sampling theory and sample design, see Sudman [1976] and Jaeger [1984].)

**Box 5.5
Settling for Bigger
Confidence Intervals**

If we were willing to settle for a 10% confidence interval, we'd need only 82 people in this example, but the trade-off would be substantial. If 65 out of 225, or 29%, reported that they had participated in one or more extreme sports, we would be 68% confident that from 24% to 34% really did, and 95% confident that 19% to 39% did. But if 24 out of 82 (the same 29%) reported having participated in extreme sports, we'd be 68% confident that the true figure was between 19% and 39%, and 95% confident that it was between 9% and 49%. With a spread like that, you wouldn't want to bet much on the sample statistic of 29%.

Anthropologists, epidemiologists, and others who work with small populations often face this problem. Anthropologists work around it by relying on long-term ethnography—combining qualitative and quantitative approaches. Epidemiologists may use special statistical treatments appropriate to small samples.

NONPROBABILITY SAMPLING

If your objective is to estimate a parameter or a proportion from a sample to a larger population, and if your research calls for the collection of data about attributes of individuals (whether those individuals are people or Boy Scout troops or episodes of a sitcom), then the rule is simple: Collect data from an unbiased sample. If you know that you *ought* to use a random, unbiased sample and you have the means to *get* an unbiased sample, and you still choose to use a nonprobability sample, then expect to take a lot of flak.

There are, however, two quite different circumstances under which nonprobability samples are exactly what are called for.

(1) Despite our best efforts, it is often impossible to do probability sampling under real research conditions. In these cases, use a nonprobability sample and *document the bias*. That's all there is to it. No need to agonize about it.

(2) As I mentioned at the beginning of this chapter, when you are collecting cultural data, as contrasted with data about individual experience, then expert informants, not randomly selected respondents, are what you need. (See Box 6.1 for more on this distinction. And for a detailed discussion of on selecting expert informants, see Chapter 9.)

There are several nonprobability sampling methods that are appropriate under different circumstances. These include *quota sampling, purposive sampling* (also called *judgment sampling*), *convenience sampling* (also called *haphazard sampling*), and *snowball sampling*.

Quota Sampling

In quota sampling, you decide on the subpopulations of interest and on the proportions of those subpopulations in the final sample. If you are going to take a sample of 400 full-time employed adults in a city, you might decide that, since gender is of interest to you as an independent variable, and since women make up about half the population, then half your sample should be women and half should be men. Perhaps half of each gender quota should be older than 40 and half should be younger; maybe half of each of those quotas should be self-employed and half should be salaried. How you design a quota sample depends, like any sampling problem, on what's important for your study.

When you are all through designing a multistage quota sample, you go out and fill the quotas. You look for, say, five self-employed females who are over 40 years of age and who are self-employed and for five salaried males who are under 40. And so on. Quota sampling resembles stratified probability sampling with an important difference: Respondents are not chosen randomly. Instead, interviewers choose members of the sample on the spot.

Commercial polling companies use quota samples that are fine-tuned on the basis of decades of research. Organizations like Gallup, Roper, and Harris have learned how to train interviewers not to choose respondents who are pretty much like themselves; not to select only people whom they would enjoy interviewing; not to avoid people whom they would find obnoxious or hostile; not to avoid people who are hard to contact (busy people who are hardly ever home, or people who work nights and sleep days); and not to favor people who are eager to be interviewed.

The result is quota samples that are *not unbiased* but that often do a good job of reflecting the population parameters of interest. In other words, quota sampling is an art that often approximates the results of probability sampling at less cost and less hassle than strict probability sampling.

Often, but not always. Back in 1948, pollsters predicted, on the basis of quota sampling, that Thomas Dewey would beat Harry Truman in the U.S. presidential election. The *Chicago Tribune* was so confident of those predictions that it printed an edition announcing Dewey's victory— while the votes were being counted that would make Truman president.

Half a century later, quota sampling is just as dangerous. In the general election in Britain in 1992, four different polls published on the day of the election put the Liberal Party, on average, about 1 point ahead of the Conservative Party. All the polls were based on quota sampling. The Conservatives won by 8 points. In fact, from 1992 to 1997, political polls using quota samples in Britain systematically overestimated the support for the Liberals (Curtice and Sparrow 1997).

Quota sampling is also used in the study of cultural data, but here the operation and the rationale are entirely different. Anthropologists often speak of choosing "key informants"—people who are knowledgeable about particular domains of life in a culture—and of focusing their attention on those people. We can extend the idea of *a* key informant, to a *set* of key informants—people who are chosen in a quota sample to represent the variation in domains of a culture.

For example, if you want to know about how Little League baseball functions in the life of American families, you wouldn't ask people who have never played the game or who have never had children who played the game. But there is plenty of intracultural variation even among Little League players and parents of players. Open-ended interviews with four or five really knowledgeable people will produce the relevant cultural data. For data on how individuals feel about the level of competitiveness in Little League, or on the prevailing opinion with regard to Little League as preparation for later life, 30 or 40 open-ended interviews will produce the appropriate data.

Purposive or Judgment Sampling

In judgment sampling, you decide the purpose you want informants (or communities) to serve, and you go out to find some. This is somewhat like quota sampling, except that there is no overall sampling design that tells you how many of each type of informant you need for a study.

Kimberly Mahaffy (1996) was interested in how lesbian Christians deal with the cognitive dissonance that comes from being rejected by mainstream Christian churches. Mahaffy sent letters to gay Christian organizations, asking them to put an ad for potential respondents in their newsletters. She sent flyers to women's bookstores and to lesbian support groups, asking for potential respondents to get in touch with her.

Eventually, Mahaffy got 163 completed questionnaires from women who fit the criteria she had established for her research, including 44 from women who self-identified as born-again or evangelical Christians. Mahaffy could not possibly have gotten an unbiased sample of lesbian Christians, but the corpus of data that she collected from her respondents had all the information she needed to answer her research questions.

Moreover, in judgment sampling it's not even necessary to decide up front what *kinds* of units of analysis to study. I used purposive sampling in my study of the Kalymnian (Greek) sponge-fishing industry (Bernard 1987). I knew I had to interview sponge merchants, boat owners, and divers, but my first interviews taught me that I had to interview people whom I had never considered: men who used to be divers but who had quit, gone to Australia as labor migrants, and returned to their island.

There are many good reasons for using purposive samples. They are used widely in **pilot studies** before testing a hypothesis with a representative sample. Pound et al. (1993) developed a questionnaire to measure the satisfaction of caregivers of people who had suffered a stroke. They did the pilot test of the questionnaire on 23 people—caregivers of patients whose names were taken straight out of hospital registration lists. Samples don't get much more purposive than this, and they don't get much more appropriate, either.

Purposive samples are also used in the selection of a few cases for intensive study. Researchers don't usually pull research sites—communities, hospitals, school systems—out of a hat. They rely on their judgment to find one that reflects the things they are interested in. Life history research and qualitative research on special populations (drug addicts, trial lawyers, shamans) rely on judgment sampling.

Hays (1984) went through the obituary section of a local newspaper and interviewed a purposive sample of survivors. She found that three-fourths

TABLE 5.7 Characteristics of Residents in Shostack and Campagna's (1991) Sample Homes and All of the Homes in the State of New Jersey in 1988

Characteristics	Residents in Sample Homes (percentage)	Residents in All 450 Homes (percentage)
Male	43	42
Female	57	58
Under 50 years of age	19	31
50 and over	81	69
White	89	88
Non-White	11	12

SOURCE: Adapted from A. E. Shostack and G. P. Campagna, *Adult Residential Care Journal* 5. Copyright © 1991. Reprinted by permission of Plenum Publishing Corporation.

of those who died at age 65 or older had surviving children or siblings living close enough to provide support and one-fourth didn't. Barroso (1997) studied a purposive sample of 14 men and 6 women in the Tampa, Florida, area, all of whom had lived with AIDS for at least three years.

Judgment sampling is also used in studying critical cases. Polling companies try to identify communities across the United States that have voted for the winner in the past, say, six presidential elections. Then they poll those few communities that meet the criterion. Choosing key informants in ethnographic research is a kind of critical-case sampling. It would be pointless to select a handful of people randomly from a population and try to turn them into trusted key informants (for more on ethnography, see Chapter 9).

Purposive sampling can be applied to any units of analysis, just like probability sampling. In the mid-1960s, in a movement known as "mainstreaming," publicly supported psychiatric hospitals across the U.S. were closed and their residents were released to live in their own communities. A private board-and-care industry has grown up to accommodate these patients, as well as people who suffered from physical disorders. Shostack and Campagna (1991) were interested in the conditions and needs of these board-and-care homes in New Jersey, and in the needs of the residents of those homes—things like whether residents had opportunities for recreation, whether residents were being prepared for life outside the home, and so on.

Working alone and without financial support, Shostack and Campagna were not able to cover the entire state. They approached the welfare boards of five New Jersey counties, and those boards arranged for interviews with the operators of 17 homes in their jurisdictions. Table 5.7 compares the age, sex, and racial distribution of the residents in Shostack and Campagna's purposive sample with that of the 450 homes in the entire state.

This is an interesting example of nonprobability cluster sampling. Shostack and Campagna identified appropriate board-and-care *homes* and then interviewed the operators of those homes. Shostack and Campagna are careful to note that theirs is a judgment sample, not an unbiased sample. They had a very good sample for an exploratory study, however, especially one that involved just two researchers. Their detailed findings about the institutional needs of the low-income frail elderly and the low-income mentally ill who live in privately run board-and-care homes deserve careful reading.

Most purposive samples are pretty small (ethnographic studies are usually based on 30-60 interviews, plus participant observation), but purposive sampling is not just for small samples. Ackerman and Gondolf (1991) had some ideas they wanted to test about differences between ACOAs (adult children of alcoholics) and non-ACOAs. ACOAs are said to be disproportionately represented in the human services field. They went to 62 human development conferences in 38 states across the U.S. and handed out 50 questionnaires to anyone who was around after the keynote address. Ackerman and Gondolf got back 1,630 usable questionnaires, or about half of the 3,275 questionnaires they handed out.

One of the questions they asked was: "When you were growing up, did you have a parent who drank too much?" Ackerman and Gondolf randomly selected 500 respondents who answered yes and 500 who answered no to construct their sample of ACOAs and non-ACOAs for data analysis. The ACOAs were much more likely to have witnessed child abuse and spouse abuse than were non-ACOAs, and as adults, the ACOAs had a much higher divorce rate than did non-ACOAs. Ackerman and Gondolf concluded that the data from their purposive sample support the suggestion of clinicians that people who have an alcoholic parent are more likely to have other indicators of a tough family life.

If you think Ackerman and Gondolf had a big purposive sample, consider the work of Kail et al. (1995). They studied female drug addicts who

traded sex for money or drugs and female addicts who didn't. The team of researchers had a purposive sample of over 9,000 female drug addicts who were not in treatment. Prostitutes were more likely than nonprostitutes to share needles with others and were less likely to use new needles or to clean old needles before each episode. The sample of female drug addicts was not unbiased; it was, in fact, *intentionally* biased to get answers to questions of practical importance.

Convenience or Haphazard Sampling

Convenience sampling is nothing more than grabbing whoever will stand still long enough to answer your questions. It is useful for exploratory research, to get a feel for "what's going on out there," and for pretesting questionnaires to make sure that the items are unambiguous and not too threatening. In other situations, convenience sampling can be just plain dangerous.

If you ask students at the library how they feel about some current campus issue, you may get different answers than if you ask students who are playing cards in the cafeteria. If you only do interviews around noon, when it is convenient for you, you'll miss all those people for whom noon is not a convenient hour. If you want to know the effect of a new road on some peasants and you only interview people who come to town on the road, you'll miss all the people who live too far off the road for it to do them any good.

It is not necessary to list all the ways that your own prejudices can inflict mortal damage on a convenience sample. Just remember that all samples are representative of *something*. The trick is to make them representative of what *you* want them to be. That's the difference between purposive and convenience sampling.

Still, convenience samples are useful in many situations. Pilot studies are often done with convenience samples. S. Miller et al. (1997) wanted to get a handle on sources of conflict between certified nurse-midwives and physicians who are in collaborative practices. Miller et al. posted a copy of their survey on an electronic bulletin board maintained by a school of nursing and got a convenience sample of 78 nurse-midwife respondents.

The data from these respondents produced a list of common sources of conflict in collaborative practices between nurse-midwives and physicians. We wouldn't put much stock in the fact that a specific *percentage* of the nurse-midwives report conflict with their physician partners over billing of insurance companies for services, but the *list* of conflicts is very instructive because it is the basis for more in-depth research.

Sometimes, convenience samples are all that's available, and you just have to make do. Studies of the homeless in America, for example, are usually done with convenience samples, for obvious reasons. (Burnam and Koegel [1988], however, showed that probability samples are better than convenience samples for estimating how many people actually sleep on the street.) Matthey et al. (1997) compared various tests for identifying major depression among Arabic-speaking and Vietnamese-speaking women in Australia. They interviewed a convenience sample of a few women from each group about the cultural appropriateness of each of the tests. Shih (1997) studied a convenience sample of 35 Taiwanese and Chinese American patients who went through cardiac surgery. Shih interviewed the patients in the intensive care unit during their recovery, clearly a case where a convenience sample is called for.

Snowball Sampling

In snowball sampling, you locate one or more key individuals and ask them to name others who would be likely candidates for your research. Snowball sampling is used in studies of social networks, where the object is to find out who people know and how they know each other. It is used in studies of difficult-to-find populations. E. Miller (1986), for example, used the method to locate female petty criminals and prostitutes in her study of street women.

But "difficult to find" doesn't just mean "people who'd rather not be exposed." It also means any small population for which it is impossible to construct a sampling frame. Richardson (1988), for example, used snowball sampling to locate single or divorced women who were in long-term relationships (a year or more) with married men. A national survey in Britain of 1,997 adults failed to turn up a single self-identified vegan; Beardsworth and Keil (1992) used snowball sampling to find and interview 76 vegetarians in Britain, including 18 strict vegans.

Kadushin (1968) laid out the snowball method for the study of elites. Using key informants and documents, you first construct a preliminary list of elites. These might be "people in this town whose opinions really count" or "living artists whose work everyone wants to buy" or "fellow physicians whose opinions you trust when it comes to adopting a new drug." The elite group can range from very local (a single high school) to international (opinion makers).

Once you have a preliminary list, you show it to several people who are on the list and ask them to name others who they think should be on the list. The process continues until the list becomes "saturated"—that is, until no new names are offered. Elites are easy to find, but hard to interview. Snowball interviewing can be a way out of that problem. Doors open when one member of an elite group passes you on to another.

Ostrander (1980) used snowball sampling to locate informants in her study of class consciousness among upper-class women in a midwestern U.S. city. She selected her first informant by looking for someone who had graduated from an elite women's college, was listed in the social register, was active in upper-class clubs—and who would talk to her. At the end of the interview, she asked the informant to "suggest another woman of your social group, with a background like yours, who might be willing to talk to me."

David Griffith and his colleagues used two snowball samples in their study of food preferences in Moberly, Missouri. They chose an initial "seed" household in a middle-income neighborhood and asked a man in the house to name three people in town with whom he interacted on a regular basis. The first person cited by the informant lived in a lower-income neighborhood across town. That person, in turn, named other people who were in the lower-income bracket.

After a while, the researchers realized that, though they'd started with a middle-income informant who had children at home, they were getting mostly lower-income, elderly people in the snowball sample. So they started again, this time with a seed from an elite, upper-middle-income neighborhood. By the time they got through, Griffith et al. had a well-balanced sample of 30 informants with whom they did in-depth interviews (reported in Johnson 1990:78).

If you are dealing with a relatively small population of people who are likely to be in contact with one another, then snowball sampling is an effective way to build an exhaustive sampling frame. But in a large population, people who are better known have a better chance of being named in a snowball procedure than people who are less well known. In large populations, then, every person does not have the same chance of being included in a snowball sample.

AND FINALLY

Particularly in ethnographic research, you learn in the field, as you go along, to select the units of analysis (people, court records, etc.) that will provide the information you need. This is what Russell Belk and his colleagues (1988) did in their detailed ethnographic study of buyers and sellers at a swap meet. When you study a process, like bargaining over goods, and you're doing the research in the field, in real time (not under simulated conditions in a lab), then selecting informants who meet certain criteria is the right thing to do.

> *Good measurement is the key to internal validity, and representative sampling is the key to external validity.*

The credibility of research results comes from the power of the methods used in measurement and sampling. Good measurement is the key to internal validity, and representative sampling is the key to external validity. Well-done nonprobability sampling is actually part of good measurement. It contributes to credibility by contributing to internal validity. When someone reads a research report based on really good measurement of a nonprobability sample, they come away thinking, "Yep, I believe those conclusions about the people who were studied in that piece of research."

That's plenty. If you want the credibility of your conclusions to extend beyond the group of people (or countries, organizations, or comic books) you studied, then either (1) repeat the study one or more times with nonprobability samples, or (2) use a probability sample.

Chapter 5 Review

KEY CONCEPTS

SUMMARY

❖ There are two kinds of data of interest to social scientists: individual data and cultural data. These two kinds of data require different approaches to sampling.

- Individual data are about attributes of individuals in a population. To estimate the parameters of these attributes in a population requires probability sampling.
- Cultural data require experts, which means relying on nonprobability sampling.

❖ There are several ways to take probability samples.

- Simple random sampling involves generating a list of random numbers and applying that list to a numbered sampling frame. (Most researchers actually take systematic, rather than simple, random samples.)
- Stratified random samples are used to ensure that key subpopulations are included in a study. Disproportionate stratified random sampling is used to ensure that important, but relatively small, subpopulations are included in a sample.
- Cluster sampling is used when there is no overall sampling frame. Cluster sampling is based on the fact that people live in natural clusters (counties, states, etc.) and they participate in the activities of institutions (schools, churches, credit unions, etc.).
- The best estimates of a parameter are produced in samples taken from clusters of equal size. When clusters are not equal in size, then samples should be taken PPS—with probability proportionate to size.

❖ Sample size depends on (1) the heterogeneity of the population from which you choose the elements, (2) how many population subgroups you want to deal with simultaneously in your analysis, (3) the size of the phenomenon that you're trying to detect, and (4) how precise you want your parameter estimators to be. Precision involves sampling theory.

- Sampling theory is based on the normal distribution and the central limit theorem. According to the central limit theorem, if you take many samples of a population, and if the samples are big enough, then (1) the mean and the standard deviation of the sample means will approximate the true mean and standard deviation of the population, and (2) the distribution of sample means will approximate a normal distribution.
- Sample precision refers to the size of the standard error you are willing to tolerate. As the standard error goes down, the confidence limits become more precise.

❖ It is often impossible to do strict probability sampling under real research conditions. In these cases, use a nonprobability sample. Also, when you are collecting cultural data, rather than individual-attribute data, random sampling is inappropriate. Some types of nonprobability sampling are quota sampling, purposive/judgment sampling, convenience/haphazard sampling, and snowball sampling.

- In quota sampling, you decide on the subpopulations of interest and on the proportions of those subpopulations in the final sample. Quota sampling resembles stratified probability sampling, but respondents are not chosen randomly. Many commercial polling companies use quota samples that are fine-tuned on the basis of decades of research.

- In purposive, or judgment, sampling you decide the purpose you want the units of analysis (people, communities, countries) to serve. This is somewhat like quota sampling, except that there is no overall sampling design that tells you how many of each type of informant you need for a study.

- Convenience, or haphazard, sampling means grabbing whoever will stand still long enough to answer your questions. It is useful for exploratory research, to get a feel for "what's going on out there," and for pretesting questionnaires to make sure that the items are unambiguous and not too threatening. Pilot studies are often done with convenience samples.

- In snowball sampling, you locate one or more key individuals and ask them to name others who would be likely candidates for your research. Snowball sampling is used in studies of social networks, where the object is to find out who people know and how they know each other. It is used in studies of difficult-to-find populations.

EXERCISES

1. Assume that in a sample of 400 respondents, chosen properly from a population of 300,000, 22% said that they came from a family in which at least one of their parents had been an immigrant, and 78% said that both of their parents had been born in this country. How closely do these data describe the population parameter?

2. Consider a study in which we will do 150 interviews in a town of 23,000 inhabitants. There are neighborhoods in the town, and we want an unbiased sample that represents all of the neighborhoods. One of the neighborhoods, with 12,000 residents, is much larger than the other four. If we do a PPS sample (one that takes account of the different sizes of the neighborhoods), then what is the probability that any individual in the big neighborhood will wind up in our sample?

3. Answer the following questions about sampling:
   a. What is the danger in systematic random sampling?
   b. Why are telephone books usually poor sampling frames?
   c. What is a stratified, random, disproportionate sample?
   d. Why do we sample more heavily among hierarchically higher (more heterogeneous) units than among lower (more homogeneous) ones?
   e. What is the relation among "parameter," "estimator," and "sampling error"?
   f. What are the two ways in which sampling error is reduced?

4. Here's an experiment you can run to show that the mean of many samples of any given size approaches the true mean of a population. Collect 100 well-worn pennies and make a list of their dates of issue (1949, 1976, 1994, etc.). Add up the 100 dates and divide by 100 to get the average date of issue.

   Throw the pennies into a bag and shake well. (Use a big bag, like from the supermarket, so you can shake and mix the pennies really well.) Now reach into the bag and, without looking, take a sample of 5 pennies. Calculate the average date of issue of those 5 pennies and put them back in the bag. This is called sampling with replacement. Repeat this 14 more times and plot the 15 average dates, just as I plotted the 15 scores in Figure 5.7a.

   Run the experiment again, but this time don't put the pennies back in the bag after each grab. This is sampling without replacement. Compare the results of the two experiments. Consider the implication of these results for estimating parameters of populations of people with samples that are done with or without replacement.

5. A multinational corporation asks you to survey its 840 midlevel managers. There are 590 men and 250 women in the cohort of managers. You decide to take a stratified random sample of 100 from each of the gender groups. What is the sampling weight for each of the strata? Hint: Find the probability, p, of sampling each man and each woman, given that you are sampling 100 of each. The weight is the inverse of p, or $1/p$.

FURTHER READING

The U.S. Census. For more on the undercount problem, see Choldin (1994), Hogan (1992), and U.S. Senate (1993). See Edmonston and Schultze (1995) for a discussion of problems in modernizing the U.S. Census. See Light and Lee (1997) for problems in measuring ethnicity and race in the U.S. Census.

Sampling theory. There are many excellent books on sampling theory. The classic, by Kish (1965), was reissued in 1995. Sudman (1976) is thorough and is more readable. Scheaffer et al. (1990) is a useful textbook with lots of examples. Henry (1990) is a brief and useful introduction to elements of sampling. Williams (1978) is lots of fun (yes, fun) and very useful. The central limit theorem is dealt with in many statistics textbooks. See, for example, Hogg and Tanis (1997). For a review of statistical problems associated with complex surveys (in which multiple samples are used), see Brogan (1998).

In the end, compromises have to be made to get credible samples of some hard-to-count populations. Burnam and Koegel (1988) discuss thoroughly their design for a probability sample of the homeless in Los Angeles.

Nonprobability sampling for individual data. For further discussion of the advantages and disadvantages of nonprobability sampling, see Lennon et al. (1995).

On problems associated with quota sampling, see Marsh and Scarbrough (1990) and Curtice and Sparrow (1997). Braunstein (1993) used geographic and quota sampling in a study of IV drug users who were neither institutionalized nor under treatment.

For a critical discussion of techniques in snowball sampling, see Biernacki and Waldorf (1981) and Watters and Biernacki (1989). For reviews of problems and more examples of snowball sampling, see Sarantokos (1996) on locating same-sex couples; see Brent (1994) on locating people who abandoned Protestant fundamentalism; and see Rothbart et al. (1982) on locating very specific populations—like Mexican American veterans of the Vietnam War.

See Killoran (1984) for an example of purposive sampling applied to content analysis of a Canadian women's magazine. See Sque and Payne (1996) for an example of purposive sampling in the study of relatives of organ donors in England.

Westermeyer (1996) discusses the use of convenience sampling in a study of alcoholism among older Native Americans.

Nonprobability sampling for cultural data. Recently, anthropologists have been working on methods for identifying and selecting cultural informants. See Johnson (1990) for a discussion of how to use snowball sampling and other nonprobability sampling methods to identify key informants. See Romney et al. (1986) for a discussion of cultural consensus theory and how the theory can be applied to finding informants who are knowledgeable about a particular cultural domain. And, in particular, see Handwerker and Wozniak (1997) for a discussion of the difference between life experience data and cultural data and how this difference affects sampling and sample size.

PART III

DATA
COLLECTION

6 INTERVIEWING

UNSTRUCTURED AND SEMISTRUCTURED

IN THIS CHAPTER:

❖ INTRODUCTION

The concept of "interviewing" covers a lot of ground, from totally unstructured interactions, through semistructured situations, to highly formal interactions with respondents. Interviewing is done on the phone, in person, by mail—even by computer. This chapter is about unstructured and semistructured face-to-face interviewing, including the management of focus groups.

Unstructured interviewing is used across the social sciences as the front end to the development of questionnaires and, in cultural anthropology, as one of the main methods for collecting data. Unstructured interviewing goes on during the course of an ordinary day of participant observation, in offices, factories, patrol cars, hospital wards—just about anywhere. Semistructured interviewing, or in-depth interviewing, is another of the main data-collection methods in ethnography, and it's also one of the main methods for collecting household survey data. Semistructured interviews follow a general script and cover a list of topics, but are also open ended.

There is a vast literature on how to conduct effective interviews: how to gain rapport, how to get people to open up, how to introduce an interview, and how to end one. You can't learn to interview by reading about it, but after you read this chapter and practice some of the techniques described, you should be well on your way to becoming an effective interviewer. You should also have a pretty good idea of how much more there is to learn, and be on your way to exploring the literature.

INTERVIEW CONTROL

There is **a continuum of interview situations based on the** *amount of control* **we try to exercise over people's responses** (Dohrenwend and Richardson 1965; Gorden 1975; Spradley 1979). These different types of interviews produce different types of data that are useful for different types of research projects and that appeal to different types of researchers. For convenience, I divide the continuum of interviews into four large chunks: informal, unstructured, semistructured, and structured.

Informal Interviewing

At one end there is *informal interviewing,* characterized by **a total lack of structure or control.** The researcher just tries to remember con-

versations heard during the course of a day "in the field." This requires constant jotting and daily sessions in which you sit at a computer, typing away, unburdening your memory and developing field notes. If you're doing participant observation fieldwork, then informal interviewing is the method of choice at the beginning, when you're just settling in and getting to know the lay of the land. It is also used throughout ethnographic fieldwork to build greater rapport and to uncover new topics of interest that might have been overlooked.

When it comes to interviewing, never mistake the adjective "informal" for "lightweight." This is hard, hard work. You have to remember a lot, you have to duck into private corners a lot (so you can jot things down), and you have to use a lot of deception (to keep people from knowing that you're really at work, studying them). Informal interviewing can get pretty tiring.

> When it comes to interviewing, never mistake the adjective "informal" for "lightweight."

Still, in some kinds of research, informal interviewing is all you've got. Mark Connolly (1990) studied *gamines,* or street children, in Guatemala City and Bogotá, Colombia. These children live, eat, and sleep on the street. Hanging out and talking informally with these children was the only way that Connolly could do this research.

Unstructured Interviewing

Next comes *unstructured interviewing,* one of the two types covered in this chapter. There is nothing at all informal about unstructured interviewing, and nothing deceptive, either. You sit down with another person and hold an interview. Period. Both of you know what you're doing, and there is no shared feeling that you're just engaged in pleasant chit-chat.

Unstructured interviews are **based on a clear plan that you keep constantly in mind, but are also characterized by a minimum of control over the respondent's responses** (see Box 6.1 on the difference between informants and respondents). The idea is to get people to open up and let them express themselves in their own terms, and at their own pace. A lot of what is called *ethnographic interviewing* is unstructured. Unstructured interviewing is used in situations where you have lots and lots of time—like when you are doing long-term fieldwork and can interview people on many separate occasions.

Semistructured Interviewing

In situations where you won't get more than one chance to interview someone, *semistructured interviewing* is best. It has much of the freewheeling quality of unstructured interviewing, and requires all the same skills, but semistructured interviewing is based on the use of an *interview guide.* This is **a written list of questions and topics that need to be covered in a particular order.**

This is the kind of interview that most people write about—the kind done in professional surveys. The interviewer maintains discretion to follow leads, but the interview guide is a set of clear instructions—instructions like this one: "Probe to see if informants (men and women alike) who have daughters have different values about dowry and about premarital sex than do people who have only sons."

Formal, written guides are an absolute must if you are sending out several interviewers to collect data. But even if you do all the interviewing on a project yourself, you should build a guide and follow it if you want reliable, comparable qualitative data.

Semistructured interviewing works very well in projects where you are dealing with managers, bureaucrats, and elite members of a community—people who are accustomed to efficient use of their time. It demonstrates that you are fully in control of what you want from an interview but leaves both you and your respondent to follow new leads. It shows that you are prepared and competent but that you are not trying to exercise excessive control over the respondent (see Box 6.1).

Structured Interviewing

Finally, in fully *structured interviewing,* people are asked to respond to as nearly identical a set of stimuli as possible. One variety of structured interviewing involves use of an *interview*

Box 6.1
About Informants and Respondents

Anthropologists use the word "informant" while sociologists use "respondent" when they refer to someone being interviewed. I like Levy and Hollan's (1998) distinction: When people describe their culture, they are informants. When they talk about their own characteristics, their own beliefs (opinions, preferences, values, ideas), and their own experiences and behavior, they are respondents.

The difference is important. Everyone is knowledgeable about themselves, and so everyone can be a respondent. Not everyone can be an equally good informant. Some people are clearly more competent than others to talk about the culture of some group. The group can be "everyone who speaks German"—that is, the *Deutschsprachige Welt,* which covers much of Switzerland; parts of Italy, Belgium, Poland, Hungary, and Namibia; and all of Austria, in addition to Germany.

It can be the national culture of Navajos or Singaporeans or Americans. It can be an ethnic subculture within a national culture (Ashkenazi Jewish Puerto Ricans, Lebanese Barbadians, Pakistani Kenyans). It can be the local culture of New York City (which has dozens of even-more-local ethnic cultures—and even neighborhood cultures). It can be the culture of an occupation: stockbrokers, long-haul truckers, commercial fishermen, minor league baseball players.

If you want to know about the lived experience of individuals, you need a *nonrandom sample of respondents.* You choose those respondents because they offer insight into something that they are best able to talk about—their own lives. If you want to know the proportion of African American and White high school seniors in Minneapolis and Atlanta who date cross-racially, then you need a *random sample of respondents.* If you want to know the rules of Australian rugby, or when to genuflect in a Roman Catholic Mass, or how to be an effective nonviolent protester, you need people who can speak knowledgeably about those things—that is, *key informants.*

And if you want to test whether a majority of people in a population are likely to have substantially the same culture as the culture described by a key informant, then you need four or five key informants, none of whom knows each other well.

Suppose you work with a key informant who tells you that it is the custom among non-Orthodox Jews in the U.S. to have an open casket and period of viewing of the body before funeral services are conducted, but that some people don't follow this custom. If you want to know the actual proportion of funerals in which this custom is practiced, you'd need data on a representative sample of funerals. If you want to know the proportion of non-Orthodox Jews who think that an open casket is the correct thing to do, then, again, you need a representative sample of non-Orthodox Jews.

Of course, there is no law against using respondents as informants and vice versa. Survey respondents are often asked open-ended questions about their occupation or other aspects of their culture.

schedule, an explicit set of instructions to interviewers who administer questionnaires orally. Instructions might read, "If the informant says that she or he has at least one daughter over 10 years of age, then ask questions 26b and 26c. Otherwise, go on to question 27."

Self-administered questionnaires are a kind of structured interview. Other structured interviewing techniques include pile sorting, frame elicitation, triad sorting, and tasks that require informants to rate or rank order a list of things. I'll deal with structured interviews in Chapter 7.

UNSTRUCTURED INTERVIEWING

Unstructured interviewing is truly versatile. It is used by scholars who identify with the hermeneutic tradition and by those who identify with the positivist tradition (see Chapter 1). It is used in studies that require only textual data and in studies that require both textual and numerical data. Field ethnographers may use it to develop formal guides for semistructured interviews, or to learn what questions to include, in the native language, on a highly structured questionnaire (see Werner and Schoepfle [1987] for a good discussion of this). I say that field ethnographers *may* use unstructured interviewing in developing structured interview schedules because unstructured interviewing also stands on its own.

When you want to know about the *lived experience* of fellow human beings—what it's like to survive hand-to-hand combat, how you get through each day when you have a child dying of leukemia, how it feels to make it across the border into Texas from Mexico only to be deported 24 hours later—you just can't beat unstructured interviewing.

Unstructured interviewing is excellent for building initial rapport with informants, before moving to more formal interviews, and it's perfect for talking to informants who would not tolerate a more formal interview. The personal rapport you build with close informants in long-term fieldwork can make highly structured interviewing—and even semistructured interviewing—feel somehow "unnatural." In fact,

really structured interviewing can get in the way of your ability to communicate freely with key informants.

But not always. Some people want very much to talk about their lives, but they really don't like the unstructured interview format. I once asked a fisherman in Greece if I could have a few minutes of his time to discuss the economics of small-scale fishing.

I was about five minutes into the interview, treading lightly—you know, trying not to get too quickly into his finances, even though that's exactly what I wanted to know about—when he interrupted me: "Why don't you just get to the point?" he asked. "You want to know how I decide where to fish, and whether I use a share system or a wage system to split the profits, and how I find buyers for my catch, and things like that, right?" He had heard from other fishermen that these were some of the topics I was interviewing people about. No unstructured interviews for him; he was a busy man and wanted to get right to it.

A Case Study of Unstructured Interviewing

Once you learn the art of probing (which I'll discuss in a little while), unstructured interviewing can be used for studying sensitive issues, like sexuality, racial or ethnic prejudice, or hot political topics. I find it particularly useful in studying conflict. In 1972-73, for example, I went to sea on two different oceanographic research vessels (Bernard and Killworth 1973, 1974). In both cases, there was an almost palpable tension between the scientific personnel and the crew of the ship. Through both informal and unstructured interviewing on land between cruises, I was able to establish that the conflict was predictable and regular. Let me give you an idea of how complex the situation was.

In 1972-73, it cost $5,000 a day to run a major research vessel, not including the cost of the science. (The cost is about four times that today.) The way oceanography works, at least in the United States, is the chief scientist on a research cruise has to pay for both ship time and for the cost of any experiments he or she wants to run. To do this, ocean scientists compete for grants from institutions like the U.S. Office of Naval Research, NASA, and the National Science Foundation.

The spending of so much money is validated by publishing significant results in prominent journals. It's a tough, competitive game, and one that leads scientists to use every minute of their ship time. As one set of scientists comes ashore after a month at sea, the next set is on the dock waiting to set up their experiments and haul anchor.

The crew, consequently, might get only 24 or 48 hours shore leave between voyages. That can cause some pretty serious resentment by ships' crews against scientists. And that can lead to disaster. I found many documented instances of sabotage of expensive research by crew members who were, as one of them said, "sick and tired of being treated like goddam bus drivers." In one incident, involving a British research vessel, a freezer filled with Antarctic shrimp, representing two years of data collection, went overboard during the night. In another, the crew and scien-

tists from a U.S. Navy oceanographic research ship got into a brawl while in port (*Science* 1972:1346-47).

The structural problem I uncovered began at the top. Scientists whom I interviewed felt they had the right to take the vessels wherever they wanted to go, within prudence and reason, in search of answers to questions they had set up in their proposals. The captains of the ships believed (correctly) that *they* had the last word on maneuvering their ships at sea. Scientists, said the captains, sometimes went beyond prudence and reason in what they demanded of the vessels.

For example, a scientist might ask the captain to take a ship out of port in dangerous weather because ship time is so precious. This conflict between crew and scientists was apparently mentioned by Charles Darwin in his diaries from HMS *Beagle*—and then promptly ignored. This problem will certainly play a role in the productivity of long-term space station operations.

Unraveling this conflict at sea required participant observation and unstructured (as well as informal) interviewing with many people. No other strategy for data collection would have worked. At sea, people live for long periods of time in close physical quarters, and there is a common need to maintain good relations for the organization to function well.

It would have been inappropriate for me to have used highly structured interviews about the source of tension between the crew and the scientists. Better to steer the interviews around the issue of interest and to let informants teach me what I needed to know. In the end, no analysis was better than that offered by one engine room mechanic, who told me "these scientist types are so damn hungry for data, they'd run the ship aground looking for interesting rocks if we let them."

❖———

Getting Started

There are some important steps to take when you start interviewing someone for the first time. First of all, assure people of anonymity and confidentiality. Explain that you simply want to know what *they* think, and what *their* observations are. If you are interviewing someone whom you have come to know over a period of time, explain why you think his or her opinions and observations on a particular topic are important. If you are interviewing someone chosen from a random sample, and whom you are unlikely to see again, explain how he or she was chosen and why it is important that you have the person's cooperation to maintain representativeness.

If people say that they really don't know enough to be part of your study, assure them that their participation is crucial and that you are truly interested in what they have to say (and you'd better mean it, or you'll never pull it off). Tell everyone you interview that you are trying to learn from *them*. Encourage them to interrupt you during the interview with anything they think is important. And always ask for permission to *record* personal interviews *and to take notes*. This is vital. If you can't take notes, then, in most cases, the value of an interview plummets. (See below, on using a tape recorder and taking notes.)

Keep in mind that people who are being interviewed know that you are shopping for information. There is no point in trying to hide this. If you are open and honest about your intentions, and if you are genuinely interested in what people have to say, many people will help you.

This is not always true, of course. When Colin Turnbull went out to study the Ik in Uganda, he found a group of people who had apparently lost interest in life and in exchanging human kindnesses. The Ik had been brutalized, decimated, and left by the government to fend for themselves on a barren reservation. They weren't impressed with the fact that Turnbull wanted to study their culture. In fact, they weren't much interested in anything Turnbull was up to and were anything but friendly (Turnbull 1972).

Letting the Informant or Respondent Lead

If you can carry on "unthreatening, self-controlled, supportive, polite, and cordial interaction in everyday life" then interviewing will come easy to you, and informants will feel comfortable responding to your questions (Lofland 1976:90). No matter how supportive you are as a person, though, an interview is never really like a casual, unthreatening conversation in everyday life. In casual conversations, people take more or less balanced turns (Spradley 1979), and there is no feeling that somehow the discussion has to stay on track or follow some theme (see also Merton et al. 1956; Hyman and Cobb 1975). In unstructured interviewing, you keep the conversation focused on a topic, while giving the respondent room to define the content of the discussion.

The rule is: Get people on to a topic of interest and get out of the way. Let the informant provide information that he or she thinks is important.

During my research on the Kalymnian sponge fishermen in Greece, I spent a lot of time at Procopis Kambouris's *taverna*. (A Greek *taverna* is a particular kind of restaurant.) Procopis's was a favorite of the sponge fishermen. Procopis was a superb cook, he made his own wine every year from grapes that he selected himself, and he was as good a teller of sea stories as he was a listener to those of his clientele. At Procopis's *taverna* I was able to collect the work histories of sponge fishermen: when they'd begun their careers, the training they'd gotten, the jobs they'd held, and so on. The atmosphere was relaxed (plenty of retsina wine and good things to eat), and conversation was easy.

As a participant observer, I developed a sense of camaraderie with the regulars, and we exchanged sea stories with a lot of flourish. Still, no one at Procopis's ever made the mistake of thinking that I was there just for the camaraderie. They knew that I was writing about their lives and that I had lots of questions to ask. They also knew immediately when I switched from the role of participant observer to that of ethnographic interviewer.

———————❖

One night, I slipped into just such an interview/conversation with Savas Ergas. He was 64 years old at the time and was planning to make one last six-month voyage as a sponge diver during the coming season in 1965. I began to interview Savas on his work history at about 7:30 in the evening, and we closed Procopis's place at about 3 a.m. During the course of the evening, several other men joined and left the group at various times, as they would on any night of conversation at Procopis's. Savas had lots of stories to tell (he was a living legend and he played well to a crowd), and we had to continue the interview a few days later, over several more liters of retsina.

At one point on that second night, Savas told me (almost offhandedly) that he had spent more than a year of his life walking the bottom of the Mediterranean. I asked him how he knew this, and he challenged me to document it. Savas had decided that there was something important that I needed to know, and he maneuvered the interview around to make sure I learned it.

This led to about three hours of painstaking work. We counted the number of seasons he'd been to sea over a 46-year career (he remembered that he hadn't worked at all during 1943 because of "something to do with the war"). We figured conservatively the number of days he'd spent at sea, the average number of dives per trip, and the average depth and time per dive. We joked about the tendency of divers to exaggerate their exploits and about how fragile human memory is when it comes to this kind of detail.

It was difficult to stay on the subject, because Savas was such a good raconteur and a perceptive analyst of Kalymnian life. The interview meandered off on interesting tangents, but after a while, either Savas or I would steer it back to the issue at hand. In the end, discounting heavily for both exaggeration and faulty recall, we reckoned that he'd spent at least 10,000 hours—about a year and a fourth, counting each day as a full 24 hours—under water and had walked the distance between Alexandria and Tunis at least three times.

The exact numbers really didn't matter. What did matter was that Savas Ergas had a really good sense of what *he* thought I needed to know about the life of a sponge diver. It was I, the interviewer, who defined the focus of the interview, but it was Savas, the respondent, who determined the content. And was I ever glad he did.

❖———————

PROBING

The key to successful interviewing is learning how to probe effectively—that is, to stimulate a respondent to produce more information, without injecting yourself so much into the interaction

that you only get a reflection of yourself in the data. Suppose you ask a suburban housewife, "Have you ever worked outside the home?" and she says, "Yes." The next question (the probe) is,

"What did you do?" Suppose the answer is, "Oh, lots of different things." Your next response should not be "Waitress? Sales? Construction?" but "Like what, exactly? Could you tell me some of the places where you've worked?"

There are many kinds of probes that you can use in an interview. (In what follows, I will draw on the important work by Kluckhohn [1945], Merton et al. [1956], Kahn and Cannell [1957], Whyte [1960; Whyte and Whyte, 1984], Dohrenwend and Richardson [1965], Gorden [1975], Hyman and Cobb [1975], Warwick and Lininger [1975], Reed and Stimson [1985], and on my own experience and that of my students.)

The Silent Probe

The most difficult technique to learn is the *silent probe,* which consists of just **remaining quiet and waiting for an informant to continue.** The silence may be accompanied by a nod, or by a mumbled "umhmm" as you focus on your note pad. The silent probe sometimes produces more information than does direct questioning. At least at the beginning of an interview, informants look to you for guidance as to whether or not they're on the right track. They want to know whether they're "giving you what you want." Most of the time, especially in unstructured interviews, you want the informant to define the relevant information.

Some informants are more glib than others and require very little prodding to keep up the flow of information. Others are more reflective and take their time. Inexperienced interviewers tend to jump in with verbal probes as soon as an informant goes silent. Meanwhile, the informant may be just reflecting, gathering thoughts, and preparing to say something important. You can kill those moments (and there are a lot of them) with your interruptions.

Glibness can be a matter of *cultural,* not just personal, style. Gordon Streib (1952) reports that he had to adjust his own interviewing style radically when he left New York City to study the Navajo in the 1950s. Streib, a New Yorker himself, had done studies based on semistructured interviews with subway workers in New York. Those workers uniformly maintained a fast, hard-driving pace during the interviews—a pace with which Streib, as a member of the culture, was comfortable.

But that style was entirely inappropriate with the Navajo, who were uniformly more reflective than the subway workers (Streib, personal communication). In other words, the silent probe is sometimes not a probe at all; being quiet and waiting for an informant to continue may simply be appropriate cultural behavior.

On the other hand, the silent probe is a high-risk technique, which is why beginners avoid it. If an informant is genuinely at the end of a thought and you don't provide further guidance, your silence can become awkward. You may even lose your credibility as an interviewer. The silent probe takes practice to use effectively. But it's worth the effort.

The Echo Probe

Another kind of probe consists of **simply repeating the last thing someone has said and asking them to continue.** This *echo probe* is particularly useful when an informant is describing a process or an event. "I see. The goat's throat is cut and the blood is drained into a pan for cooking with the meat. Then what happens?" This probe is neutral and doesn't redirect the interview. It shows that you understand what's been said so far and encourages the informant to continue with the narrative. If you use the echo probe too often, though, you'll hear an exasperated informant asking, "Why do you keep repeating what I just said?"

The Uh-huh Probe

You can **encourage an informant to continue with a narrative by just making affirmative comments, like "Uh-huh," "Yes, I see," "Right, uh-huh," and so on.** Matarazzo (1964) showed how powerful this *neutral probe* can be. He did a series of identical, semistructured, 45-minute interviews with a group of informants. He broke each interview into three 15-minute chunks. During the second chunk, the interviewer was told to make affirmative noises, like "uh-huh," whenever the informant was speaking. Informant responses during those chunks were about a third longer than during the first and third periods.

The Tell-Me-More Probe

This may be the most common form of probe among experienced interviewers. Respondents give you an answer and you probe for more by saying: "Could you tell me more about that?" Other variations include "Why exactly do you say that?" and "Why exactly do you feel that way?" You have to be careful about using stock probes like these. As Converse and Shuman (1974:50) point out, if you get into a rut and repeat these probes like a robot, don't be surprised to hear someone finishing up a nice long discourse by saying, "Yeah, yeah, and why *exactly* do I feel like that?" (From personal experience, I can guarantee that the mortification factor only allows this sort of thing to happen once. The experience lasts a lifetime.)

The Long-Question Probe

Another way to induce longer and more continuous responses is by making your questions longer. Instead of asking, "How do you plant a home garden?" ask, "What are all the things you have to do to actually get a home garden going?" When I interviewed sponge divers on Kalymnos, instead of asking them, "What is it like to make a dive into very deep water?" I said, "Tell me about diving into really deep water. What do you do to get ready, and how do you descend and ascend? What's it like down there?"

Later in the interview, of course, or on another occasion, I would home in on special topics. But to break the ice and get the interview flowing, there is nothing quite as useful as what Spradley (1979) called the "grand tour" question.

This does not mean that asking longer questions or using neutral probes necessarily produces *better* responses. They do, however, produce *more* responses, and, in general, more is better. Furthermore, the more you can keep informants talking, the more you can express interest in what they are saying and the more you build rapport. This is especially important in the first interview you do with someone whose trust you want to build (see Spradley 1979:80). There is still a lot to be learned about how various kinds of probes affect what informants tell us.

Threatening questions—questions asking for sensitive information—should be short, but should be preceded by a long, rambling run-up: "We're interested in the various things that people do these days in order to keep from getting diseases when they have sex. Some people do different kinds of things, and some people do nothing special. Do you ever use condoms?" If the respondents says "Yes," "No," or "Sometimes," *then* you can launch that series of questions about why, why not, when, with whom, and so on. The wording of sensitive questions should, in general, be supportive and nonjudgmental (see Wiederman et al. 1994; Catania et al. 1996).

Probing by Leading

After all this, you may be cautious about being really directive in an interview. Don't be. Many researchers caution against "leading" an informant. Lofland (1976), for example, warns against questions such as "Don't you think that . . . ?" and suggests asking, "What do you think about . . . ?" He is, of course, correct. On the other hand, any question an interviewer asks leads an informant. You might as well learn to do it well.

Consider this leading question that I asked a Ñähñu Indian: "Right. I understand. The compadre is *supposed* to pay for the music for the baptism fiesta. But what happens if the compadre doesn't have the money? Who pays then?" This kind of question can stop the flow of an informant's narrative stone dead. It can also produce more information than the informant would otherwise have provided. At the time, I thought the informant was being overly "normative." That is, I thought he was stating an ideal behavioral custom (having a compadre pay for the music at a fiesta) as if it were never violated.

It turned out that all he was doing was relying on his own cultural competence—"abbreviating," as Spradley (1979:79) called it. The informant took for granted that the anthropologist knew the "obvious" answer: If the compadre didn't have enough money, well, then there might not be any music.

My interruption reminded the informant that I just wasn't up to his level of cultural competence; I needed him to be more explicit. He went on to explain other things that he considered obvious but that I would not have even known to ask about. Someone who has committed himself to pay for the music at a fiesta might borrow money from another compadre to fulfill the obligation. In that case, he wouldn't tell the person who was throwing the fiesta. That might make the host feel bad, like he was forcing his compadre to go into debt.

In this interview, in fact, the informant eventually became irritated with me because I asked about so many things that he considered obvious. He wanted to abbreviate a lot and to provide a more general summary; I wanted details. I backed off and asked a different informant for the details. I have since learned to start some probes with "This may seem obvious, but . . ."

Directive probes (leading questions) may be based on what an informant has just finished saying, or may be based on something an informant told you an hour ago, or a week ago. As you progress in long-term research, you come to have a much greater appreciation for what you really want from an interview. It is perfectly legitimate to use the information you've already collected to focus your subsequent interviews.

This leads researchers from informal to unstructured to semistructured interviews, and even to completely structured interviews like questionnaires. When you feel as though you have learned something important about a group and its culture, the next step is to test that knowledge—to see if it is idiosyncratic to a particular informant or subgroup in the culture or if it can be reproduced in many informants.

Baiting: The Phased-Assertion Probe

A particularly effective probing technique is called **phased assertion** (Kirk and Miller 1986), or **baiting** (Agar 1996:142). This is when you **act like you already know something to get people to open up.**

I used this technique in a study of how Ñähñu Indian parents felt about their children learning to read and write Ñähñu. Bilingual (Spanish-Indian) education in Mexico is a politically sensitive issue (Heath 1972), and when I started asking about it, a lot of people were reluctant to talk freely.

In the course of informal interviewing, I learned from a schoolteacher in one village that some fathers had come to complain about the teacher trying to get the children to read and write Ñähñu. The fathers, it seems, were afraid that studying Ñähñu would get in the way of their children becoming fluent in Spanish. Once I heard this story, I began to drop hints that I knew the reason parents were against children learning to read and write Ñähñu. As I did this, the parents opened up and confirmed what I'd found out.

Every journalist (and gossip monger) knows this technique well. As you learn a piece of a puzzle from one informant, you use it with the next informant to get more information, and so on. The more you seem to know, the more comfortable people feel about talking to you and the less people feel they are actually divulging anything. *They* are not the ones who are giving away the "secrets" of the group.

Phased assertion also prompts some informants to jump in and correct you if they think you know a little but that you've "got it all wrong." In some cases, I've purposely made wrong assertions to provoke a correcting response.

Verbal Respondents

Some informants try to tell you *too much*. They are the kind of people who just love to have an audience. You ask them one little question and off they go on one tangent after another, until you become exasperated. Converse and Shuman (1974:46) recommend "gentle inattention"— putting down your pen, looking away, leafing through your papers. Nigel King (1994:23) recommends saying something like: "That's very interesting. Could we go back to what you were saying earlier about . . . ?"

You may, however, have to be a bit more obvious. New interviewers, in particular, may be reluctant to cut off informants, afraid that doing so is poor interviewing technique. In fact, as William Foote Whyte notes, informants who want to talk your ear off are probably used to being interrupted. It's the only way their friends get a word in edgewise. But you need to learn how to cut people off without rancor. "Don't interrupt *accidentally* . . . ," Whyte said, "learn to interrupt *gracefully*" (1960:353, emphasis his). Each situation is somewhat different; you learn as you go in this business.

Nonverbal Respondents

One of the really tough things you run into is someone telling you "I don't know" in answer to lots of questions. In qualitative research projects, where you choose respondents precisely because you think they know something of interest, the "don't know" refrain can be especially frustrating. Converse and Schuman (1974:49) distinguish four kinds of don't-know response: (1) I don't know (and frankly I don't care); (2) I don't know (and it's none of your business); (3) I don't know (actually, I do know, but you wouldn't be interested in what I have to say about that); and (4) I don't know (and I wish you'd change the subject because this line of questioning makes me really uncomfortable). There is also the (I wish I could help you but) I really don't know response.

Sometimes you can get beyond this, sometimes you can't. You have to face the fact that not everyone who volunteers to be interviewed is a good respondent. Sometimes you just have to take "don't know" for an answer and cut your losses by going on to someone else.

The Ethics of Probing

Are these tricks of the trade ethical? I think they are, but using them creates some responsibilities to your respondents.

First, there is no ethical imperative in social research more important than seeing to it that you do not harm innocent people who have provided you with information in good faith. The problem, of course, is that not all respondents are innocents. Some people commit wartime atrocities. Some practice infanticide. Some are HIV positive and, out of bitterness, are purposely infecting others. Do you protect them all?

Are any of these examples more troublesome to you than the others? These are not extreme cases, thrown in here to prepare you for the worst, "just in case." They are the sort of ethical dilemmas that field researchers confront all the time.

Second, the better you get at making people open up, the more responsible you become that they don't later suffer some emotional distress for having done so. Informants who divulge too quickly what they believe to be secret information can later come to have real regrets, and even loss of self-esteem. They may suffer anxiety over how much they can trust you to protect them in the community.

It is sometimes better to stop an informant from divulging privileged information in the first or second interview and to wait until both of you have built a mutually trusting relationship. If you sense that an informant is uncomfortable with having spoken too quickly about a sensitive topic, end the interview with light conversation and reassurances about your discretion. Soon after, look up the informant and engage in light conversation again, with no probing or other interviewing techniques involved. This will also provide reassurance of trust.

Remember: The first ethical decision you make in research is whether to collect certain kinds of information at all. Once that decision is made, *you* are responsible for what is done with that information, and *you* must protect people from becoming emotionally burdened for having talked to you.

LEARNING TO INTERVIEW

It's impossible to eliminate reactivity and subjectivity in interviewing, but like any other craft, you will get better and better at interviewing the more you practice. It helps a lot to practice in front of others and to have an experienced interviewer monitor and criticize your performance. Even without such help, however, you can improve your interviewing technique just by paying careful attention to what you're doing. Harry Wolcott (1995:102) offers excellent advice on this score: Pay as much attention to your own words as you do to the words of your respondents.

Wolcott also advises: Keep interviews focused on a few big issues (1995:112). More good advice from one of the most accomplished ethnographers around. Here's a guaranteed way to wreck

rapport and ruin an interview: A respondent asks you, "Why do you ask? What does that have to do with what we're talking about?" You tell her: "Well, it just seemed like an interesting question—you know, something I thought might be useful somehow down the road in the analysis."

Here you are, asking people to give you their time and tell you about their lives and you're treating that time with little respect. If you can't imagine giving a satisfactory answer to the question "Why did you ask *that*?" then leave *that* out.

Do not use your friends as practice informants. You cannot learn to interview with friends because there are role expectations that get in the way. Just when you're really rolling, and getting into probing deeply on some topic that you both know about, they are likely to laugh at you or tell you to knock it off.

Practice interviews should not be just for practice. They should be done on topics you're really interested in and with people who are likely to know a lot about those topics. Every interview you do should be conducted as professionally as possible and should produce useful data (with plenty of notes that you can code and file and cross-file).

The Importance of Language

Most anthropology students, and an increasing number of sociology and social psychology students, do research outside their own country. If you are planning to go abroad for research, find persons from the culture you are going to study and interview them on some topic of interest. If you are going to Turkey to study women's roles, then find Turkish students at your university and interview them on some related topic.

It is often possible to hire the spouses of foreign students for these kinds of "practice" interviews. I put "practice" in quotes to emphasize again that these interviews should produce data of interest to you. If you are studying a language that you'll need for research, these practice interviews will help you sharpen your skills at interviewing in that language.

Even if you are going off to the interior of the Amazon, this does not let you off the hook. It is unlikely that you'll find native speakers of Yanomami on your campus, but you cannot use this as an excuse to wait until you're out in the field to learn general interviewing skills. Interviewing skills are honed by practice. Among the most constructive things you can do in preparing for field research is to practice conducting unstructured and semistructured interviewing.

Pacing the Study

Two of the biggest problems faced by researchers who rely heavily on semistructured interviews are boredom and fatigue. Even small projects may require 30-40 interviews to generate sufficient data to be worthwhile. Most field researchers collect their own interview data, and asking the same questions over and over again can get pretty old. Gorden (1975) studied 30 interviewers who worked for 12 days doing about two tape-recorded interviews per day. Each interview was from one to two hours long.

The first interview on each day, over all interviewers, averaged about 30 pages of transcription. The second averaged only 25 pages. Furthermore, the first interviews, on average, got shorter and shorter during the 12-day period of the study. In other words, on any given day, boredom made the second interview shorter, and over the 12 days, boredom (and possibly fatigue) took its toll on the first interviews of each day.

Of course, in many projects you won't conduct all your interviews in 12 days. Nevertheless, the lesson is clear. Plan each project in advance and calculate the number of interviews you are going to get. Pace yourself. Don't try to bring in all your interview data in a short time. Spread the project out, if possible.

But not always. When you are studying patterns of behavior that have been stable for some time, spreading the interviews out is a good thing to do. If you are studying people's reactions to hot issues, spreading out a project over a long period of time creates a serious "history" confound (see Chapter 4).

Here's the trade-off: The longer a project takes, the less likely that the first interviews and the last interviews will be valid indicators of the same things. In long-term, participant observation fieldwork (like six months to a year), I recommend going back to your early informants and interviewing them a second time. See whether their observations and attitudes have changed, and if so, why.

PRESENTATION OF SELF

How should you present yourself in an interview? As a friend? As a professional? As someone who is sympathetic or as someone who is nonjudgmental? It depends on the nature of the project. When the object is to collect comparable data across respondents, then it makes no difference whether you're collecting words or numbers—cordial-but-nonjudgmental is the way to go.

That's sometimes tough to do. You're interviewing someone on a project about what people do to help the environment and your respondent says: "All those eco-Nazis want is to make room for more owls. They don't give a damn about real people's jobs." That's when you find out whether you can probe without injecting your feelings into the interview. Professional interviewers (the folks who collect the data for the General Social Survey, for example) learn to maintain their equilibrium and move on (see Converse and Schuman 1974).

Some situations are so painful, however, that it's impossible to maintain a neutral facade. Gene Shelley interviewed 72 people in Atlanta who were HIV positive (Shelley et al. 1995). Here's a typical comment by one of Shelley's informants: "I have a lot of trouble watching all my friends die. Sometimes my whole body shuts down inside. I don't want to know people who are going to die. Some of my friends, there are three or four people a week in the obits. We all watch the obits."

How would *you* respond? Do you say: "Uh-huh. Tell me more about that"? Do you let silence take over and force the respondent to go on? Do you say something sympathetic? Shelley (personal communication) reports that she treated each interview as a unique situation and responded as her intuition told her to respond—sometimes more clinically, sometimes less, depending on her judgment of what the respondent needed her to say. Good advice.

Sometimes you have to go even further, beyond sympathetic response, all the way to intervention. Christine Webb (1984) interviewed women who had been through a hysterectomy. Webb is a nurse and researcher who also has personal experience as a gynecology patient. As a nurse, she was bound by hospital regulations not to initiate treatments on her own. As a researcher, she was expected to remain neutral. But as she listened to women talk about how they were treated with indifference or arrogance by their male physicians, Webb couldn't justify keeping her knowledge and advice to herself. "I felt," she said, "that my responsibilities to the women justified the risk that the doctors might disapprove of what I was doing" (ibid.:255).

Webb reminds us that doctors "control not only nurses' more regular work with patients but also what nursing research is carried out, and how and by whom it is done" (p. 254), so "disapproval" by the doctors might have meant the end of her research. There are times when you just have to make your choice and stand your ground.

On Just Being Yourself

In 1964, when we were working on the island of Kalymnos, my wife Carole would take our two-month-old baby for daily walks in a carriage.

Older women would peek into the baby carriage and make disapproving noises when they saw our daughter sleeping on her stomach. Then they would reach into the carriage and turn the baby over, explaining forcefully that the baby would get the evil eye if we continued to let her sleep on her stomach.

Carole had read the latest edition of *The Common Sense Book of Baby and Child Care* (the classic "baby book" by Dr. Benjamin Spock). We carried two copies of the book with us—in case one fell out of a boat or something—and Carole was convinced by Dr. Spock's writings that babies who sleep on their backs risk choking on their own mucous or vomit. Since then, of course, medical opinion—and all the baby books that young parents read nowadays—have flip-flopped about this issue several times. At the time, though, not wanting to offend anyone, Carole listened politely and tried to act nonjudgmental.

One day, enough was enough. Carole told off a woman who intervened and that was that. From then on, women were more eager to discuss child-rearing practices in general, and the more we challenged them, the more they challenged us. There was no rancor involved, and we learned a lot more than if Carole had just kept on listening politely and had said nothing. Of course, this was informal interviewing in the context of long-term participant observation. If we had offended anyone, there would have been time and opportunity to make amends—or at least come to an understanding about cultural differences.

Little Things Mean a Lot

Little things are important in interviewing, so pay attention to them. How you dress and where you hold an interview, for example, tell your respondent a lot about you and what you expect. The "interviewing dress code" is: Use common sense. Proper dress depends on the venue. Showing up with a backpack or an attaché case, wearing jeans or a business suit—these are choices that should be pretty easy to make, once you've made the commitment to accommodate your dress to different circumstances.

The same goes for venue. I've held interviews in bars, in business offices, in government offices, on ferry boats, on beaches, in homes. I can't give you a rule for selecting the single *right* place for an interview, since there may be several right places. But some places are just plain wrong for certain interviews. Here again, common sense goes a long way.

USING A TAPE RECORDER

Don't rely on your memory in interviewing; use a tape recorder in all structured and semistructured interviews, except where people specifically ask you not to. Tapes are a permanent record of primary information that can be archived and passed on to other researchers. (Remember, I'm talking here about formal interviews, not the hanging-out interviews that are part of ethnographic research. More on *that* in Chapter 9.)

If you sense some reluctance about the tape recorder, leave it on the table and don't turn it on right away. Start the interview with chit-chat and when things get warmed up, say something like, "This is really interesting. I don't want to trust my memory on something as important as this; do you mind if I record it?" Charles Kadushin (personal communication) hands a microphone with a shut-off switch to respondents to hold. Rarely, he says, do respondents actually use the switch, but giving people control over the interview shows that you take them very seriously.

Sometimes you'll be taping an interview and things will be going along just fine and you'll sense that a respondent is backing off from some sensitive topic. Just reach over to the recorder and ask the respondent if she or he would like you to turn it off. Harry Wolcott (1995:114) recommends leaving the tape recorder on, if possible, when the formal part of an interview ends. Even though you've finished, Wolcott points out, your respondent may have more to say.

Recording Equipment: Machines, Tapes, Batteries, Etc.

The best field-recording technology available today is digital audiotape, or DAT. The fidelity is terrific but the best part is that there is no distortion when you make copies of your tapes for archiving. It's just like making copies of a word processor document: You get every byte in every copy. The downside is the cost of this light, reliable, portable, high-fidelity technology—about $700 in 1999.

Because of their cost, and also because DAT can last longer than batteries do (more on batteries below), most interviewers opt for analog tape recording (the kind that everyone is familiar with). Highly rated field machines were selling for around $350 in 1999. These machines are professional equipment—the sort you'd want for linguistic fieldwork (when you're straining to hear every phoneme) or for high-quality recording of music. If you are not investing in professional-level equipment, there are many very good field recorders that cost less than $200.

For simple recording of interviews, though, especially in a language you understand well, you can get away with a good, basic cassette machine for under $50. (Buy two of them. When you skimp on equipment costs, and don't have a spare, the probability rises that you'll need one at the most inconvenient moment.) Just be sure to use a good, separate microphone (around $20). Some people like wearing a levalier microphone—the kind you clip to a person's lapel or shirt collar—but many people find them intrusive.

I prefer an omnidirectional microphone (good ones cost a bit more), because they pick up voices from anywhere in a room. Sometimes, people get rolling on a subject and they want to get up and pace the room as they talk. Want to kill a really great interview? Tell the respondent who's on a roll to please sit down and speak directly into the mike. Good microphones come with stands that keep the head from resting on any surface, like a table. Surfaces pick up and introduce background noise into tapes. If you don't have a really good stand for the mike, you can make one easily with some rubbery foam (the kind used in making mattresses).

No matter what you spend on a tape recorder, never, ever skimp on the quality of tapes. Use only cassettes that are put together with screws so you can open them up and fix the tape when (inevitably) they jam or tangle. And don't use thin, long-playing tapes. Transcribing involves listening, stopping, and rewinding—often hundreds of times per tape. Thin tape (the kind that runs for two hours or more) just won't stand up to this kind of use.

Bruce Jackson (1987:145), a very experienced field worker in folklore, recommends taking brand new tapes to a studio and getting them bulk erased before recording on them for the first time. This cuts down on the magnetic field noise on the new tape. Jackson also recommends running each tape through your machine three or four times on fast forward and fast reverse. All tapes stretch a bit, even the best of them, and this will get the stretch out of the way.

Test your tape recorder before every interview. And do the testing at home. There's only one thing worse than a recorder that doesn't run at all. It's one that runs but doesn't record. Then your informant is sure to say at the end of the interview: "Let's run that back and see how it came out!" (Yes, that happened to me. But just once. And it needn't happen to anyone who reads this.)

Good tape recorders have battery indicators. Want another foolproof way to kill an exciting interview? Ask the informant to "please hold that thought" while you change batteries. When batteries get slightly low, throw them out. Edward Ives (1995) recommends doing all recording on batteries. That guarantees that, no matter what kind of flaky or spikey current you run into, *your* recordings will always be made at exactly the same speed.

Particularly if you are working in places that have unstable current, you'll want to rely on batteries to ensure recording fidelity. Just make sure that you start out with fresh batteries for each interview. (You can save a lot of battery life by using house current for all playback, fast forward, and rewind operations, reserving the batteries only for recording.) If you prefer household current for recording, then carry along a couple of long extension cords so you have a choice of where to set up for the interview.

Good tape recorders come with voice activation (VA). When you're in VA mode, the recorder turns on only if there is noise to record. During long pauses (while an informant is thinking, for example), the recorder shuts off, saving tape. Holly Williams (personal communication), however, recommends against using the VA mode. It doesn't save much tape and she finds that the long breaks without any sound make transcribing tapes much easier. You don't have to shut the machine off and turn it on as many times while you're typing.

Transcribers

It can take from six to eight hours to transcribe one hour of tape, depending on how closely you transcribe, how clear the tape is, and how proficient you are in the language. It may not be necessary to fully transcribe interviews. If you are using life histories to describe how families in some community deal with prolonged absence of fathers, then you *must* have full transcriptions to work with. And you can't study cultural *themes,* either, without full transcriptions. But if you want to know how many informants said they had helped their adult children with a down payment on a house, you may be able to get away with only partial transcription. You may even be as well off using an interview guide and taking notes.

If you transcribe your interview tapes, invest in a transcription machine. These machines cost around $300. You use a foot pedal to start and stop the machine, to back up and to fast forward, and even to slow down the tape so you can listen carefully to a phrase or a word. A transcription machine and a good set of earphones will save you many hours of work because you can keep both hands on your keyboard all the time.

Whether you do full transcriptions or just take notes during interviews, try to tape your interviews anyway. You may need to go back and fill in details in your notes.

Tape Is Not a Substitute for Taking Notes

Finally, never substitute tape for note taking. A lot of very bad things can happen to tape, and if you haven't got backup notes, you're out of luck. Don't wait until you get home to take notes, either. Take notes during the interview *about* the interview. Did the informant seem nervous or evasive? Were there a lot of interruptions? What were the physical surroundings like? How much probing did you have to do? Take notes on the contents of the interview, even though you get every word on tape.

A few informants, of course, will let you use a tape recorder but will balk at your taking notes. Don't assume, however, that informants will be offended if you take notes. Ask them. Most of the time, all you do by avoiding note taking is lose a lot of data. Informants are under no illusions about what you're doing. You're interviewing them. You might as well take notes and get people used to it, if you can.

FOCUS GROUPS

Focus groups are recruited to discuss a particular topic—like people's reaction to a television commercial or their attitudes toward a social service program. The method derives from work by Paul Lazarsfeld and Robert Merton in 1941 at Columbia University's Office of Radio Research. A group of people listened to a recorded radio program that was supposed to raise public morale prior to America's entry into World War II.

The listeners were told to push a red button whenever they heard something that made them react negatively. When they heard something that made them react positively, they were to push a green button. The reactions were recorded automatically by a primitive polygraph-like apparatus. When the program was over, an interviewer talked to the group of listeners to find out why they had felt positively or negatively about each message they'd reacted to (Merton 1987).

The commercial potential of Lazarsfeld and Merton's pioneering work was immediately clear. The method of real-time recording of people's reactions, combined with focused interviewing of a group, is today a mainstay in advertising research. MCI, the long-distance phone company, used focus groups to develop its initial advertising when it was just starting out. MCI found that customers didn't blame AT&T for the high cost of their long-distance phone bills; they blamed themselves for talking too long on long-distance calls. MCI came out with the advertising slogan

"You're not talking too much, just spending too much." The rest, as they say, is history (Krueger 1994:33).

Whole companies now specialize in focus group research, and there are manuals on how to recruit participants and how to conduct a focus group session (Stewart and Shamdasani 1990; Krueger 1994; Vaughn et al. 1996; Morgan 1997; Morgan and Krueger 1998).

Why Are Focus Groups So Popular?

The focus group method was a commercial success from the 1950s on, but it lay dormant in academic circles for more than 20 years. This is probably because the method is virtually devoid of statistics. Since the late 1970s, however, interest among social researchers of all kinds has boomed as researchers have come to understand the benefits of combining qualitative and quantitative methods.

Focus groups do not replace surveys, but rather complement them. Many survey researchers today use focus groups as the front end to designing questionnaires. Do the questions seem arrogant to respondents? Appropriate? Naive? A focus group can discuss the wording of a particular question or offer advice on how the whole questionnaire comes off to respondents.

Focus groups are also used to help interpret the results of surveys. A representative sample of Californians might be asked what they think about the three-strikes law (that's the law that, since 1994, has sent people to prison for life, without parole, if they are convicted of a third felony of any kind). Then a series of focus groups would be convened to find out *why* people feel as they do and *how* they arrive at these feelings.

But focus groups are not just adjuncts to surveys. If you want to know *why* people feel as they do about something; the mental steps they went through to decide which candidate to support or which product to buy; why they like or don't like some program, like their company's health plan; or the reasons behind some complex behavior, then a series of focus groups can provide a tremendous amount of credible information.

Two Cases of Focus Groups

Knodel et al. (1984), for example, used focus groups to study the fertility transition in Thailand. They held separate group sessions for married men under age 35 and married women under age 30 who wanted three or fewer children. They also held separate sessions for men and women over 50 who had at least five children. This gave them four separate groups. In all cases, the participants had no more than an elementary school education.

Knodel et al. repeated this four-group design in six parts of Thailand to cover the religious and ethnic diversity of the country. The focus of each group discussion was on the number of children people wanted and why.

Thailand has recently undergone fertility transition, and the focus group study clearly illuminated the reasons for the transition. "Time and again," these researchers report, "when participants were asked why the younger generation

wants smaller families than the older generation had, they responded that nowadays everything is expensive" (ibid.:302).

People also said that all children, girls as well as boys, needed education to get the jobs that would pay for the more expensive, monetized lifestyle to which people were becoming accustomed. It is, of course, easier to pay for the education of fewer children. These consistent responses are what you'd expect in a society undergoing fertility transition.

Ruth Wilson and her co-workers (1993) used focus groups in their study of acute respiratory illness (ARI) in Swaziland. They interviewed 33 individual mothers, 13 traditional healers, and 17 health care providers. They also ran 33 focus groups, 16 male groups and 17 female groups. The groups had from 4 to 15 participants, with an average of 7.

Each individual respondent and each group was presented with two hypothetical cases. Wilson et al. asked their respondents to diagnose each case and to suggest treatments. Here are the cases:

Case 1. A mother has a one-year-old baby girl with the following signs: coughing, fever, sore throat, running or blocked nose, and red or teary eyes. When you ask the mother, she tells you that the child can breast-feed well but is not actively playing.

Case 2. A 10-month-old baby was brought to a health center with the following signs: rapid/difficult breathing, chest indrawing, fever for one day, sunken eyes, coughing for three days. The mother tells you that the child does not have diarrhea but has a poor appetite.

Many useful comparisons were possible with the data from this study. For example, mothers attributed the illness in case 2 mostly to the weather, heredity, or the child's home environment. The male focus groups diagnosed the child in case 2 as having asthma, fever, indigestion, malnutrition, or worms.

Wilson et al. (1993) acknowledge that a large number of individual interviews make it easier to estimate the degree of error in a set of interviews. However, they conclude that the focus groups provided valid data on the terminology and practices related to ARI in Swaziland. Wilson and her co-workers did, after all, have 240 respondents in their focus groups, they had data from in-depth interviews of all categories of persons involved in treating children's ARI, and they had plenty of participant observation in Swaziland to back them up.

Note two very important things about the Knodel et al. and Wilson et al. studies. First, they didn't run *a focus group*; they ran *a series of groups*. Each of the groups was chosen to represent a subgroup in a factorial design, just as we saw with experiments in Chapter 4 and with survey sampling in Chapter 5. Second, each of the groups was homogeneous with respect to certain independent variables—again, just as we saw with respect to experimental and sampling design.

The principle of *factorial design* is an essential part of focus group methodology. Knodel et al., for example, had two age groups and two genders, so they wound up with four groups: young (under 35) married men and young (under 30) women who wanted three or fewer children; men over 50 and women over 50 who had at least five children. They repeated this series of four groups in six places across the country, for a total of 24 groups.

The focus group method is becoming widely used in basic and applied research. Morgan (1989) ran focus groups with widows to find the factors that made it easier for some to cope with bereavement than others; Mein and Winkleby

(1998) studied what low-income Hispanic women in San Jose, California, think are risk factors in heart attacks; and Pramualratana et al. (1985) used focus groups to explore ideal marriage age among men and women in Thailand.

Focus groups on some topics—like teen smoking—are now so frequent that meta-analyses are possible. Goldman and Glantz (1998) analyzed the results of 186 focus groups, involving over 1,500 children, on the effectiveness of antismoking campaigns in Massachusetts and California.

And focus groups are an excellent way to start any evaluation project. Packer et al. (1994) work for the Jewish Vocational Service (JVS) in Chicago. JVS is a nonprofit, nonsectarian agency that offers a variety of job-training and job-placement programs. Packer et al. used focus groups to help assess client satisfaction with the agency's programs.

Are Focus Groups Valid?

Ward et al. (1991) compared focus group and survey data from three studies of voluntary sterilization (tubal ligation or vasectomy) in Guatemala, Honduras, and Zaire. Ward et al. report that, "overall, for 28% of the variables the results were similar" in the focus group and survey data. "For 42% the results were similar but focus groups provided additional detail; for 17% the results were similar, but the survey provided more detail. And in only 12% of the variables were the results dissimilar" (p. 273).

In the Guatemala study, 97% of the women surveyed reported no regrets with their decision to have a tubal ligation. The "vast majority" of women in the focus groups also reported no regrets. This was counted as a "similar result." Ten percent of the women surveyed reported having had a tubal ligation for health reasons. In the focus groups, too, just a few women reported health factors in their decision to have the operation, but they provided more detail and context, citing such things as complications from previous pregnancies.

This is an example of where the focus group and survey provide similar results, but where the focus group offers more detail. Data from the focus groups and the survey confirm that women heard about the operation from similar sources, but the survey shows that 40% of the women heard about it from a sterilized woman, 26% heard about it from a health professional, and so on. Here, the survey provides more detail, though both methods produce similar conclusions.

In general, though, focus groups—like participant observation, in-depth interviews, and other systematic qualitative methods—should be used for the collection of data about content and process and should not be relied on for collecting data about personal attributes or for estimating population parameters of personal attributes. The belief that a woman has or does not have a right to an abortion is a personal attribute, like gender, age, annual income, or religion. If you want to estimate the proportion of people in a population who believe that a woman has a right to an abortion, then focus groups are not the method of choice.

A proportion is a number and if you want a good number—a valid one, a useful one—then you need a method that produces exactly that. A survey, based on a representative sample, is the method of choice here. But if you want information about content—about *why* people think a woman should or should not have the right to an abortion—then that's just the sort of thing a focus group can illuminate.

Focus Group Size, Composition, and Number

Focus groups typically have 6-12 members, plus a moderator. A popular size is 7 or 8 people.

If a group is too small, it can be dominated by one or two loudmouths; if it gets beyond 10 or 12, it gets tough to manage. However, smaller groups are better when you're trying to get really in-depth discussions going about sensitive issues (Morgan 1992). Of course, this assumes that the group is run by a skilled moderator who knows how to get people to open up and how to keep them opened up.

The participants in a focus group should be more or less homogeneous and, in general, should not know one another. Richard Krueger, a very experienced focus group moderator, says that "familiarity tends to inhibit disclosure" (1994:18). It's easy to open up more when you get into a discussion with people whom you are unlikely ever to see again (sort of like what happens on long air flights).

Obviously, what "homogeneous" means depends on what you're trying to learn. If you want to know why a smaller percentage of middle-class African American women over 40 get mammograms than do their White counterparts, then you need a group of middle-class African American women who are over 40.

Running a Focus Group

The group moderator gets people talking about whatever issue is under discussion. Leading a focus group requires the combined skills of an ethnographer, a survey researcher, and a therapist. You have to watch out for people who want to show off and close them down, without coming on too strongly. You have to watch out for shy people and draw them out, without being intimidating.

Tips on how to do all this, and a lot more, are in *The Focus Group Kit*, a series of six how-to books (Morgan and Krueger 1998). Don't even think about getting into focus group management without going through this kit.

In a focus group about sensitive issues like abortion or drug use, the leader works at getting the group to gel and getting members to feel that they are part of an understanding cohort of people. If the group is run by an accomplished leader, one or more members will eventually feel comfortable about divulging sensitive information about themselves. Once the ice is broken, others will feel less threatened and will join in. Moderators should not be known to the members of a focus group, and in particular, focus group members should not be employees of a moderator. Hierarchy is not conducive to openness.

In running a focus group, remember that people will disclose more in groups that are supportive and nonjudgmental. Tell people that there are no right or wrong answers to the questions you will ask and emphasize that you've invited people who are similar in their backgrounds and social characteristics. This, too, helps people open up (Krueger 1994:113).

Above all, don't lead too much and don't put words in people's mouths. In studying nutritional habits, don't ask focus group members why they eat or don't eat certain foods; do ask them to talk about what kinds of foods they like and dislike and why. In studying political preferences, don't ask, "Why don't you like Senator X?" but do ask people to explain what they like or dislike about various politicians. Your job is to keep the discussion on the topic. Eventually, people will hit on the nutritional habits or the politicians that interest you, and you can pick up the thread from there.

Analyzing Data from Focus Groups

You can analyze focus group data with the same techniques you would use on any corpus of text: field notes, life histories, open-ended interviews, and so on. As with all large chunks of text, you have two choices for very different kinds of analysis. You can do formal content analysis, or you can do qualitative analysis. See Chapter 12 (on text analysis) for more about this.

As with in-depth interviews, it's best to tape record (or videotape) focus groups. This is a bit tricky, though, because tapes are hard to understand and transcribe if two or more people talk at once. A good moderator keeps people talking one at a time. Don't hide the recorder or the microphones. Someone is sure to ask if they're being recorded, and when you tell them yes—which you must do—they're sure to wonder why they had to ask.

If you are just trying to confirm some ideas or to get a general notion of the how people feel about a topic, you can simply take notes from the tapes and work with your notes. Most focus groups, however, are transcribed. The real power of focus groups is that they produce ethnographically rich data. Only transcription captures a significant part of that richness. But be prepared to work with a lot of information. Any single hour-and-a-half focus group can easily produce 50 pages or more of text.

Many focus groups have two staff members: a moderator and a person who does nothing but jot down the name of each person who speaks and the first few words he or she says. This makes it easier for a transcriber to identify the voices on a tape. If you can't afford this, or if you feel that people would be uncomfortable with someone taking down their names, you can call on people by name, or mention their name when you respond to them. Things can get rolling in a focus group (that's what you want), and you'll have a tough time transcribing the tapes if you don't know who's talking.

RESPONSE EFFECTS

Response effects are measurable differences in interview data that are predictable from characteristics of informants, interviewers, and environments. As early as 1929, Rice showed that the political orientation of interviewers can have a substantial effect on what they report their respondents told them. Rice was doing a study of derelicts in flophouses and he noticed that the men contacted by one interviewer consistently said that their down-and-out status was the result of alcohol; the men contacted by the other interviewer blamed social and economic conditions and lack of jobs. It turned out that the first interviewer was a prohibitionist and the second was a socialist (cited in Cannell and Kahn 1968:549).

Since Rice's pioneering work, hundreds of studies have been conducted on the impact of things like race, sex, age, and accent of both the interviewer and the informant; the source of funding for a project; the level of experience respondents have with interview situations; whether there is a cultural norm that encourages or discourages talking to strangers; and whether the question being investigated is controversial or neutral (Cannell et al. 1979; Schuman and Presser 1981; Bradburn 1983).

Katz (1942) found that middle-class interviewers got more conservative answers in general from lower-class respondents than did lower-class interviewers, and Robinson and Rhode (1946) found that interviewers who looked non-Jewish and had non-Jewish-sounding names were almost *four times more likely* to get anti-Semitic answers to questions about Jews than were interviewers who were Jewish looking and who had Jewish-sounding names.

Hyman and Cobb (1975) found that female interviewers who took their cars in for repairs themselves (as opposed to having their husbands do it) were more likely to have female respondents who report getting their own cars repaired. And Zehner (1970) found that when women in the United States were asked by women interviewers about premarital sex, they were more inhibited than if they were asked by men. Male respondents' answers were not affected by the gender of the interviewer.

By contrast, William Axinn (1991), a demographer, found that women in Nepal were better than men as interviewers. In the Tamang Family Research Project, the female interviewers had significantly fewer "don't know" responses than did the male interviewers. Axinn supposes this might be because the survey dealt with marital and fertility histories.

Robert Aunger (1992), an anthropologist, studied three groups of people in the Ituri forest of Zaire. The Lese and Budu are horticultural, while the Efe are foragers. Aunger wanted to know if they shared the same food avoidances. He and three assistants, two Lese men and one Budu man, interviewed a total of 65 people. Each of the respondents was interviewed twice and asked the same 140 questions about a list of foods.

Aunger identified two types of errors in his data: forgetting and mistakes. If informants said in the first interview that they did not avoid a particular food but said in the second interview that they did avoid the food, Aunger counted the error as forgetfulness. If informants reported in interview 2 a different type of avoidance for a food than they'd reported in interview 1, then Aunger counted this as a mistake.

Even with some missing data, Aunger had over 8,000 pairs of responses in his data (65 *pairs* of interviews, each with up to 140 responses), so he was able to look for the causes of discrepancies between interview 1 and interview 2. About 67% of the forgetfulness errors and about 79% of the mistake errors were correlated with characteristics of informants (gender, ethnic group, age, etc.).

However, about a quarter of the variability in what informants answered to the same question at two different times was due to characteristics of the interviewers (ethnic group, gender, native language, etc.).

And consider this: About 12% of variability in forgetting was explained by interviewer experience. As the interviewers interviewed more and more informants, the informants were less likely to report "no avoidance" on interview 1 and some avoidance on interview 2 for a specific food. In other words, interviewers got better and better with practice at drawing out informants on their food avoidances.

Of the four interviewers, though, the two Lese and the Budu got much better, while the anthropologist made very little progress. Was this because of Aunger's interviewing style, because informants generally told the anthropologist different things than they told local interviewers, or because there is something special about informants in the Ituri forest? We'll know when we add variables to Aunger's study and repeat it in many cultures, including our own.

The Deference Effect

When people tell you what they think you want to know, not to offend you, that's called the *deference effect* **or the** *acquiescence effect.* Aunger may have experienced this in Zaire. In the United States, the answers you get to questions about race, gender, and ethnicity probably depend a lot on the race of the interviewer and the respondent. As early as 1954, Hyman showed the potential of race-of-interviewer effects in interviews. In 1971, Schuman and Converse reported

that African Americans tailored their responses not to offend White interviewers.

When the questions are about race, the deference effects works for African Americans interviewing Whites by telephone, too. In 1989, Douglas Wilder, an African American, ran against Marshall Coleman, who is White, for the governorship of Virginia. Preelection polls showed that Wilder was way ahead, but in the end, he won by a slim margin. When White voters were asked whom they would vote for, they were more likely to claim Wilder as their choice if the interviewer was African American than if the interviewer was White.

This effect accounted for as much as 11 percentage points of Wilder's support (Finkel et al. 1991). This finding has serious consequences for the future of election polls in the United States, as more and more elections involve competition between White and African American candidates.

Reese et al. (1986:563) tested the deference effect in a telephone survey of Anglo and Mexican American respondents. When asked specifically about their cultural preference, 58% of Hispanic respondents said they preferred Mexican American culture over other cultures, irrespective of whether the interviewer was Anglo or Hispanic. Just 9% of Anglo respondents said they preferred Mexican American culture when asked by Anglo interviewers, but 23% said they preferred Mexican American culture when asked by Hispanic interviewers.

Questions about gender and gender roles produce response effects, too. When you ask people how most couples actually divide child care, men are more likely than women to say that men and women share this responsibility—if the interviewer is a man (Kane and Macaulay 1993:11).

Do women have too much influence, just the right amount of influence, or too little influence in today's society? When asked this question by a male interviewer, men are more likely to say that women have too much influence; when asked the same question by a female interviewer, men are more likely to say that women have too little influence.

And similarly for women: When asked by a female interviewer, women are more likely to say that men have too much influence than when asked by a male interviewer (Kane and Macaulay 1993:14-15). Lueptow et al. (1990) found that women gave more liberal responses to female interviewers than to male interviewers on questions about gender roles. Men's attitudes about gender roles were, for the most part, unaffected by the gender of the interviewer—except that highly educated men gave the most liberal responses about gender roles to female interviewers.

"It appears," said Lueptow et al., "that educated respondents of both sexes are shifting their answers toward the socially desirable positions they think are held by female interviewers" (p. 38). Attitudes about gender roles sure are adaptable.

Questions that aren't race related are not affected much by the race or the ethnicity of either the interviewer or the respondent. The Center for Applied Linguistics conducted a study of 1,472 bilingual children in the United States. The children were interviewed by Whites, Cuban Americans, Chicanos, Native Americans, or Chinese Americans. Weeks and Moore (1981) compared the scores obtained by White interviewers with those obtained by various ethnic interviewers and

it turned out that the ethnicity of the interviewer didn't have a significant effect.

> *Identifying sources of bias is better than not identifying them, even if you can't eliminate them.*

Whenever you have multiple interviewers, keep track of the race, ethnicity, and gender of the interviewer and test for response effects. Identifying sources of bias is better than not identifying them, even if you can't eliminate them.

Threatening Questions

In general, if you are asking someone a nonthreatening question, slight changes in wording of the question won't make much difference in the answers you get. Peterson (1984) asked 1,324 people one of the following questions: (1) How old are you? (2) What is your age? (3) In what year were you born? or (4) Are you 18-24 years of age, 25-34, 35-49, 50-64, 65 or older? Then Peterson got the true ages for all the respondents from reliable records.

There was no significant difference in the accuracy of the answers obtained with the four questions. (However, almost 10% of respondents refused to answer question 1, while only 1% refused to answer question 4, and this difference *is* significant.) On the other hand, if you ask people about their alcohol consumption, whether they ever shoplifted when they were children, whether they have family members who have had mental illness, or how many sexual partners they've had, then even small changes in the wording can have significant effects on informants' responses. (See Catania et al. [1996] for recent work on how to increase response to questions about sexual behavior.)

The Expectancy Effect

In 1966, Robert Rosenthal conducted an experiment. At the beginning of the school year, he told some teachers at a school that the children they were about to get had tested out as "spurters." That is, according to tests, he said, those particular children were expected to make significant gains in their academic scores during the coming year. Sure enough, those children did improve dramatically—which was really interesting, because Rosenthal had matched the spurter children and teachers at random.

The results, published in a widely read book called *Pygmalion in the Classroom* (Rosenthal and Jacobson 1968) established once and for all what experimental researchers across the sciences had long suspected. There is an *expectancy effect*. The expectancy effect is "**the tendency for experimenters to obtain results they expect, not simply because they have correctly anticipated nature's response but rather because they have helped to shape that response through their expectations**" (Rosenthal and Rubin 1978:377).

In 1978, Rosenthal and Rubin reported on the "first 345 studies" that were generated by the discovery of the expectancy effect. The effect is largest in animal studies (perhaps because there is no danger that animals will go into print rejecting findings from experiments on them), but it is likely in all experiments on people. As Rosenthal's first study proved, the effect extends to teachers, managers, therapists—anyone who makes a living creating changes in the behavior of others.

Expectancy is different from distortion. The distortion effect comes from seeing what you want to see, even when it's not there. The expectancy effect involves creating the objective results we want to see. We don't distort results to conform to our expectations as much as we make the expectations come true.

Strictly speaking, then, the expectancy effect is not a response effect at all. But for field workers, it is an important effect to keep in mind. If you are studying a school system, a large hospital, or a prison for a year or more, interacting daily with a few key informants, your own behavior can affect theirs in subtle (and not so subtle) ways.

ACCURACY

An important, but too often overlooked, response issue concerns the accuracy of data obtained from interviews. Even when respondents tell you the absolute truth, as they see it, in response to your questions, there is still the question of whether the information they give you is accurate.

A lot of survey research is about mapping opinions and attitudes. When people tell you that they *approve of* the job a politician is doing, when they tell you that they *support* sex education in public schools or that they *prefer* a particular brand of beer to some other brand, they are talking about internal states, and you pretty much have to take their word for such things.

When we ask people on a survey to report on their actual behavior, however (How long does it take you to drive to work? How many beers do you drink each day?), or about their environmental circumstances (How many acres of land do you currently have in soybeans? How many hours per day is the TV on in your house?), we can't just assume respondent accuracy.

We read survey results in the newspaper all the time: High-school students are smoking less marijuana than they did a decade ago; Americans are going to church more often than they did a decade ago; single men and women in their 20s, especially college graduates, are using condoms more than they did five years ago as a result of the AIDS epidemic.

In back of such findings are questions like the following:

Circle one answer:

How often do you smoke marijuana?
  Never
  Very occasionally
  About once a month
  About once a week
  More than once a week

How often do you go to church?
  Never
  Very occasionally
  About once a month
  About once a week
  More than once a week

How often do you use a condom when you have sex with someone for the first time?
  Never
  Occasionally
  Usually
  Always

La Pierre Discovers the Problem

Can we trust such data? The problem was articulated clearly in 1934 by Richard La Pierre, who was interested in the relation between attitude and behavior. Accompanied by a Chinese couple, La Pierre traveled a total of 10,000 miles by car, crossing the United States twice between 1930 and 1932 (La Pierre 1934).

The three travelers were served in 184 restaurants (were refused in none), and were refused accommodation in only 1 out of 66 hotels. Six months after the experiment ended, La Pierre sent a questionnaire to each of the 250 establishments where the threesome had stopped. One of the things he asked was, "Will you accept members of the Chinese race as guests . . . ?" Ninety-two percent replied no.

By today's standards, La Pierre's experiment was crude. There was no control group. La Pierre might have surveyed another 250 establishments from the towns they had visited but did not patronize. There was attrition in response. La Pierre might have used a "two-wave" survey approach to increase the response rate. There was no way to tell whether the people who answered the survey (and claimed that they wouldn't serve Chinese) were the same ones who had actually served the threesome. And La Pierre did not mention in his survey that the Chinese would be accompanied by a White man.

Still, La Pierre's experiment was terrific for its time. It established a major focus of research on the relation between attitudes and behavior (see Deutscher 1973) and on informant accuracy in reporting behavior.

A long list of studies now shows that a fourth to a half of what informants say about their behavior is inaccurate (Killworth and Bernard 1976; Bernard et al. 1984). This finding shows up in studies of what people say they eat, who they say they talked to on the phone, how often they claim to have gone to the doctor, and so on. It shows up in the most unlikely (we would have thought) places: In the 1961 census of Addis Ababa, 23% of the women underreported the number of children they had! Apparently, people there didn't count babies who die before reaching the age of two (Pausewang 1973:65).

Johns (1994) did a meta-analysis of 11 studies in which (1) respondents reported on the number of days they were absent from a job, and (2) the researcher was able to check the accuracy of those self-reports against actual job records. The correlation between respondent reports and job records ranged from .30 to .92, with an average of .57, which means that about a third of the variance in the job records ($.57^2 = .32$) is predicted by the respondent reports.

Why People Are Inaccurate Reporters of Their Own Behavior

There are many reasons for people to report inaccurate data about matters of externally verifiable fact, like whether they were hospitalized in the last year, as opposed to matters of opinion, like whether they think that the monarchy in England should be abolished. Here are four:

(1) People usually try to answer all your questions, once they agree to be interviewed— even if they don't remember what happened, don't want to tell you, don't understand what you're after, or don't know.

(2) People's memories simply fail them, though some behaviors are easier to remember than others. Cannell et al. (1961) found that people's ability to remember their stays in the hospital was related to the length of time since their discharge, the

length of their stay, the level of threat of the illness that put them in the hospital, and whether or not they had surgery. And Cannell and Fowler (1965) found that people report accurately 90% of all overnight hospital stays that happened six months or less before being interviewed.

(3) People simply want to mislead you to create a good impression. People overreport socially desirable behavior and underreport socially undesirable behavior. Adolescent boys tend to exaggerate, and adolescent girls tend to minimize, reports of their own sexual experience (see Catania et al. 1996). University professors surely report watching less TV than they actually watch.

(4) People may report what they *suppose* happened, rather than what they actually saw. Freeman et al. (1987) asked people in their department to report on who attended a particular colloquium. People who were *usually* at the department colloquium were mentioned as having attended the particular colloquium—even those who hadn't attended. This is an example of D'Andrade's (1974) theory that people think in terms of "what goes with what," even if this creates errors in reporting factual events (also see Shweder and D'Andrade 1980).

Reducing Errors: Jogging Informants' Memories

Sudman and Bradburn (1974) distinguish two types of memory errors. The first is simply forgetting things, like a visit to the city, the purchase of a product, or attendance at an event. The second type is called "forward telescoping." This is when someone reports that something happened a month ago when it really happened two months ago. (Backward telescoping is rare.) There are five things you can do to increase the accuracy of self-reported behavior. These methods won't eliminate all the error, but they will definitely eliminate some error. Less error is better.

1. *Cued recall*. People are asked to consult records, such as bank statements, telephone bills, and college transcripts. Having people consult their records does not always produce the results you might expect. Horn (1960) asked people to report their bank balance. Of those who did not consult their records, 31% reported correctly. Those who consulted their records did better, but not by much. Only 47% reported correctly (reported in Bradburn 1983:309). Still, there is much psychological evidence that cuing stimulates greater recall of things like word pairs and the message content of television commercials (Otani and Whiteman 1994; Gunter et al. 1997), so cued recall *should* increase recall of behavior.

2. *Aided recall*. People are given a list of possible answers to a question and asked to choose among them. Aided recall increases the number of events recalled, but also appears to increase the telescoping effect (Bradburn 1983:309).

3. *Bounded recall*. People are interviewed periodically, reminded what they said last time in answer to a question, and asked about their behavior since their last report. Bounded recall corrects for telescoping but does not increase the number of events recalled and, in any event, is only useful in studies where the same informants are interviewed again and again.

4. *Landmarks*. This involves establishing a personal landmark—like being in an auto accident, having surgery, getting married, filing for bankruptcy, becoming a grandparent, graduating from college—and asking people to report on things that have happened since then. Loftus and Mar-

burger (1983) found that landmarks help reduce forward telescoping.

If you ask people to recall incidents during, say, the last two years in which they were victims of crime, they are likely to mention incidents that happened three and four years ago. Being victimized by crime is something people remember rather well, but people are terrible at bracketing events during a two-year interval.

If you tell people to think about landmark events, they can more accurately report events (like having been robbed or raped) in relation to those landmarks. Means et al. (1989) asked people to recall landmark events in their lives going back 18 months from the time of the interview. Once the list of personal landmark events was established, people were better able to recall hospitalizations and other health-related events.

5. *Restricted time*. To increase the accuracy of recall, Sudman and Schwarz (1989) advocate keeping the recall period short. They asked people, "How many times have you been out to a restaurant in the last three months?" and "How many times have you been out to a restaurant in the last month?" The per-month average for the one-month question was 55% greater than the per-month average for the three-month question.

The Social Desirability Effect

Finally, new research shows that how you word questions about behavior can have a dramatic effect on respondent accuracy. Hadaway et al. (1998) polled members of a large Protestant church on a Monday about attendance at Sunday school the previous day. Of the 181 people who claimed to have been in Sunday school, Hadaway et al. had counted (yes, gone there on Sunday and counted) 115. Head-count experiments like this one typically produce estimates of church attendance that are 55%-59% of what people report (T. W. Smith, 1998).

> *How you word questions about behavior can have a dramatic effect on respondent accuracy.*

To get around this *social desirability effect,* Presser and Stinson (1998) tried asking the question differently. Major surveys like the Gallup Poll and the General Social Survey ask something like: "How often do you attend religious services?" and give the respondent some choices like "once a week, once a month, seldom, never."

The Survey Research Center at the University of Maryland, however, called people on Monday and asked respondents to list everything they did from "midnight Saturday to midnight last night." Direct questions—"How often do you go to church?"—produced estimates of 37%-45%. Asking people to list their activities produced an estimate of 29%. This is a 28%-50% *difference* in reported behavior and is statistically very significant.

The problem of informant accuracy remains an important issue and a fruitful area for research in social science methodology. Sudman and Schwarz (1989) conclude that people estimate rather than enumerate many behaviors. If you ask about a rare behavior that occurred recently, people are likely to remember the actual event. They won't remember the event if you ask about the frequency or amount of a behavior that occurs often, especially if you ask them to think about a common event over a period going back months. Instead, people are likely to use some "inference rules."

For example, if you ask people, "How many [sticks] [cans] of deodorant did you buy in the last six months?" they start thinking, "Well, I usually buy deodorant about twice a month in the summer, and about once a month the rest of the year. It's now October, so I suppose I must have bought 10 deodorants over the last six months," and then they say, "10," and that's what you write down.

I hope to see a lot more research about the *rules of inference* that people use when they respond to questions about their behavior.

Chapter 6
Review

KEY CONCEPTS

Chapter 6
Summary

SUMMARY

❖ There is a continuum of interview situations based on the amount of control we try to exercise over people's responses.

- In informal interviewing, the researcher just tries to remember conversations heard during the course of a day. This requires constant jotting and daily sessions in which jottings are turned into extended field notes. Informal interviewing is used in ethnographic fieldwork to build rapport and to uncover new topics of interest.

- Unstructured interviewing involves actual interviewing but is characterized by a minimum of control over the respondent's responses. The idea is to get people to open up and to let them express themselves in their own terms and at their own pace. A lot of what is called ethnographic interviewing is unstructured. Unstructured interviewing is used in situations where you have lots and lots of time and can interview people on more than one occasion.

- Semistructured interviewing has much of the freewheeling quality of unstructured interviewing but is based on the use of an interview guide. This is a written list of questions and topics that need to be covered in a particular order.

- In structured interviews, people are asked to respond to as nearly identical a set of stimuli as possible. Interview schedules and questionnaires are fully structured interviews.

❖ The key to successful interviewing is learning how to probe effectively—that is, to stimulate a respondent to produce more information, without injecting yourself so much into the interaction that you get only a reflection of yourself in the data. Learning the art of probing takes practice.

- The most difficult technique to learn is the silent probe. Other forms of probing include the echo probe, the tell-me-more probe, the long-question probe, the phased-assertion probe, and probing by leading.

- The better you learn the art of probing, the better you get at making people "open up" and the more responsible you become that they don't later suffer some emotional distress for having done so.

- Successful interviewing takes a variety of skills. It may require that you learn a specialized vocabulary, or even a new language. You also have to learn to pace a set of interviews to avoid boredom and fatigue. Presentation of self is another important part of interviewing.

❖ Interviewing produces a huge amount of data. Whenever possible, use a tape recorder in all structured and semistructured interviews, except where people specifically ask you not to.

- The best field-recording technology available today is digital audiotape. A good, omnidirectional microphone helps keep the interview spontaneous.

- It can take six-eight hours to transcribe one hour of tape. If you transcribe your interview tapes, invest in a transcription machine.

❖ Focus groups are recruited to discuss a particular topic—like people's reaction to a television commercial or their attitudes toward a social service program. Focus groups complement surveys. Survey researchers may use focus groups to help in designing a questionnaire. A focus group can discuss the wording of a particular question, for example, or offer advice on how the whole questionnaire comes off to respondents. Focus groups are also used to help interpret the results of surveys.

  ◆ Focus groups typically have 6-12 members, plus a moderator. The participants in a focus group should be more or less homogeneous and, in general, should not know one another.

  ◆ You can analyze focus group data with the same techniques you would use on any corpus of text: field notes, life histories, open-ended interviews, and so on.

❖ Response effects are measurable differences in interview data that are predictable from characteristics of informants, interviewers, and environments.

  ◆ When people tell you what they think you want to know, not to offend you, that's called the deference effect or the acquiescence effect.

  ◆ The distortion effect comes from seeing what you want to see, even when it's not there. The expectancy effect involves creating the objective results we want to see.

  ◆ An important, but often overlooked, response effect is inaccuracy in self-reports of behavior. This may come from people trying to answer questions even when they don't know the answer, from simple inaccurate memory, from the social desirability effect (people wanting to project a desirable image of themselves), or even from simple lying.

  ◆ Interviewers use cued recall, aided recall, bounded recall, landmarks, and time restriction to help respondents report behavior accurately.

EXERCISES

1. The only way to learn how to interview is to do it. Interviewing has to have a purpose. You can't interview someone "just for practice." So pick a topic about which you'd really like to know more—something that you want to write up into a research paper—and interview several people about that topic.

   Some people like to start off with antiseptic, uncontroversial topics because they think it will be easier to get respondents to open up. I find that the opposite is true. It takes pretty high-level interviewing skills to get people to pour out details about things that are common and ordinary and uncontroversial.

   To get an idea of how hard it is to get details in an interview, start by trying to get someone's life history. You can begin with a favorite aunt or uncle, or a family friend who is much older than you. As you set up your tape recorder, tell the person that you'd like them to start at the beginning and give you as much detail as possible about each event they describe in their life.

   Once you get started, don't be surprised if the first thing your respondent says is something like: "I was born in Canton, Ohio, in 1940. I went to Manning High School and when I graduated I joined the army." That's about as bare-bones as it can get. Now it's your job to get the details.

   Ask people to tell you about their earliest memories and follow the threads you get from that. Ask them to name their friends in grade school and high school and ask if they know what those friends are doing now. Follow those leads, too. Ask about their first date and movies and music they remember from when they were kids. Did they dance? If so, what were the names of the dances they did back then?

   This is just the beginning, but you get the idea. Don't let a life history take less than two hours of solid interviewing. If it takes more than one sitting, then just go with the flow. If you're lucky, it will take you five hours, not two. By the time you repeat this exercise with your second respondent, you'll be asking questions you'd never thought of before and moving the interview along with some of the techniques I discussed earlier.

2. Get a team of five or six people together to learn about running a focus group. Have the team read *The Focus Group Kit*, by Morgan and Krueger (1998). Decide on a topic together. Focus groups about consumer products seem to work well, assuming that everyone in the group has experience with the products. Take turns being the moderator of the group. Try to keep the conversation going for an hour. Have one member of the group videotape each session so that you can all learn from the experience, no matter who is the moderator.

3. Do a computer bibliographic search for the term "response effect." What are gender-of-interviewer and race-of-interviewer effects? Are there differences in these effects for telephone interviews vs. face-to-face interviews?

FURTHER READING

Focus groups. The single most useful reference work on all aspects of focus groups—from recruiting participants to moderating a session to analyzing the results—is *The Focus Group Kit*, by Morgan and Krueger (1998). These scholars distill years of experience and wisdom in their series of six short books.

Many other works, however, are very useful because they contain lots of practical suggestions on the details of running a focus group. Should a focus group room have windows? Should focus groups be videotaped? How can a focus group moderator deal with a person who tries to hog the discussion? See Goldman and McDonald (1987), Greenbaum (1998), and Templeton (1994).

Two journals have devoted whole special issues to focus groups: *Qualitative Health Research*, Vol. 5, No. 4; and the *Journal of Cross-Cultural Gerontology*, Vol. 10, No. 1. See Morgan (1996) for an overview of the literature on the focus group method. And see Weinberger et al. (1998) for a cautionary tale about reliability (or lack thereof) when multiple coders work on focus group data.

Interviewing. There are many texts on specialized interviewing technique, including clinical interviewing (e.g., Edinburg et al. 1975), social work interviewing (Kadushin 1972), personnel interviewing (Uris 1988), and legal interviewing (Shaffer and Elkins 1997). For overviews of interviewing method, see Bingham et al. (1959), Garrett and Zaki (1982), and Hyman and Cobb (1975). McCracken (1988) discusses the special techniques used in long interviews. Some recent texts on interviewing include Kvale (1996) and Rubin and Rubin (1995). Once you get started reading about interviewing, you'll find the literature huge and full of practical hints.

Respondent accuracy. The early work of Marquis and Cannell (1969) and Cannell et al. (1979) shows how researchers began treating the respondent accuracy problem as an example of a response effect in interviewing. There is now an extensive literature on respondent accuracy, on everything from self-reports of drug and alcohol use to self-reports of visits to doctors. For some recent examples, see Widom and Morris (1997) on the accuracy of adults in recalling episodes of childhood abuse, see McGovern et al. (1998) on the accuracy of low-income women in recalling whether they had gone in for mammography or a Pap smear, and see Payne et al. (1995) on the accuracy of college students in recalling their ACT scores.

Response effects and survey mode effects. See Sudman and Bradburn (1974) for the definitive review of early work. See Schwarz (1999) for an important review of how the wording of questions shapes the answers of respondents. A recent example of the experimental survey approach is Catania et al.'s (1996) study of how the gender of the interviewer and different wording of questions affect responses to surveys about sexual behavior. For other recent work on questions about sexuality, see Morris (1993) and Wiederman et al. (1994).

See Bradburn and Sudman et al. (1979), Sudman and Bradburn (1982), Tanur (1992), and Wentland and Smith (1993) for entry into the voluminous evidence on response effects in surveys. Consult the journal *Public Opinion Quarterly (POQ)* for the latest research on how to improve the results of survey research. *POQ* covers such topics as the costs and benefits of various types of surveys, the advantages and disadvantages of various ways of asking the same question, the advantages and disadvantages of different survey modes, and so on.

Singer and Presser (1989) is a compilation of some of the best articles from *POQ* on response effects. A lot has been published in the past decade, though. For example, see Aquilino (1994), Fowler et al. (1998), Narayan and Krosnick (1996), and Schober and Conrad (1997).

7 STRUCTURED INTERVIEWING

IN THIS CHAPTER:

❖ INTRODUCTION

This chapter is about the construction and administration of structured interviews. In a structured interview, every respondent or informant is exposed to the same stimuli. The most familiar kind of structured interview is the questionnaire. A questionnaire may be self-administered or it may be administered over the phone or in person, but in all cases the questions posed to respondents are the same.

The stimuli in a structured interview may be straightforward questions or complex scales, as in a questionnaire. The stimuli may also be carefully constructed vignettes, lists, clips of actual music or video, a set of photographs, a table full of physical artifacts, or a garden full of plants. The idea is to control the input that triggers each person's responses so that the output can be reliably compared. If you walk 50 employees through an automobile assembly plant and ask each of them to name 30 kinds of machines, you've done a piece of structured interviewing.

I'll cover two broad categories here of methods for structured interviewing: questionnaires and a range of methods used in cultural domain analysis. We begin with questionnaires and survey research. I review some of the important lessons concerning the wording of questions, the format of questionnaires, the management of survey projects, and the maximizing of response rates. (Refer to Chapter 6 again for more discussion of response effects.)

QUESTIONNAIRES AND SURVEY RESEARCH

Survey research is a major industry in all the industrialized countries of the world. Japan developed a survey research industry soon after World War II. (See Passin [1951] for a discussion of this fascinating story.) India, South Korea, Jamaica, Greece, Mexico, and many other countries have since developed their own survey research capabilities, either in universities, in the private sector, or in both (and see Box 7.1).

In the United States, the top 50 market research companies employed over 50,000 people in 1996, including at least 5,000 professional social scientists. Those companies had revenues of $5.5 billion (Honomichl 1997). Add the international corporations, like Gallup and Roper, that conduct public opinion polls; add the federal and state survey research agencies; and add university-based survey bureaus (like the National Opinion Research Center at the University of Chicago, the Institute for Social Research at the University of Michigan, and the Social Research Center at the University of Illinois).

The industry began its modern development in the mid-1930s when quota sampling was first applied to voting behavior studies and to determining the characteristics of listeners to various radio programs, readers of various magazines, and purchasers of various products. Then, as now, survey research helped advertisers target their messages more profitably.

Studies of American soldiers in World War II provided massive opportunities for social scien-

---

Box 7.1
Survey Research in Non-Western Societies

Is survey research really feasible everywhere? Perhaps not everywhere, but it's a more widely used method than you might think, and has been for a long time. Gordon Streib did survey research among the Navajo in 1950 and had only a 2% refusal rate. Streib says that this was because the Navajo were able to put his role as a survey researcher into meaningful perspective. The Navajo had, of course, been studied by many anthropologists, but when Streib (a sociologist) began his survey they said to him, "We wondered what you were doing around here. Now we know that you have a job to do like other people" (Streib, personal communication; see also Streib 1952).

In the 1950s, Stycos (1955, 1960:377) did a five-island study of fertility patterns in the Caribbean. Across the world, refusal to be interviewed is linked to the perceived threat of the questions being asked, the length of the interview, and the education level of the respondents (respondents with low education refuse more often). Stycos's face-to-face survey took from 1.5 to 6 hours and contained sensitive questions about sexual experiences in and out of marriage—and his respondents had much less education than typical American and British respondents. Typical refusal rates for face-to-face interviews in the U.S. and Britain run between 5% and 20%, but Stycos got a 2% refusal rate.

Ari Nave (1997) recently studied ethnic identity in Mauritius. Nave used a combination of face-to-face, mailed, and telephone interviews to get a representative sample (see the section When to Use What, page 237 in this chapter, for details). Akhtar (1996) used a multistage, stratified random sample of 3,500 households in Karachi, Pakistan, to study the differential school drop-out rate of boys and girls.

---

tists to refine their skills in taking samples and in collecting and analyzing survey data (Stouffer 1947-50). The continued need for consumer behavior data in the private sector and the developing need by government agencies for information about various "target populations" (poor people, African Americans, Hispanics, users of public housing, users of private health care, etc.) have stimulated the growth of the survey research industry.

FACE-TO-FACE, SELF-ADMINISTERED, AND TELEPHONE INTERVIEWS

There are three methods for collecting survey questionnaire data: personal, *face-to-face interviews; self-administered questionnaires;* and *telephone interviews.* Self-administered questionnaires are usually mailed to respondents, but they may also be dropped off and picked up later or they may be given to people in a group all at once. Self-administered questionnaires can also be programmed into a computer.

Each of the data-collection methods has its own advantages and disadvantages. There is no conclusive evidence that one method of administering questionnaires is better, overall, than the others. Your choice of a method will depend on your own calculus of things like cost, convenience, and the nature of the questions you are asking.

Personal, Face-to-Face Interviews

Face-to-face administration of questionnaires offers some important advantages, but it has some important disadvantages as well.

Advantages of Face-to-Face Interviews

1. They can be used with people who could not otherwise provide information—respondents who are illiterate, blind, bedridden, or very old, for example.

2. If a respondent doesn't understand a question in a personal interview, you can fill in, and, if you sense that the respondent is not answering fully, you can probe for more complete data.

Carry a notebook that tells you exactly how to respond when people ask you to clarify an unfamiliar term. If you use more than one interviewer, be sure each of them carries a copy of the same notebook. Good interview schedules are pretested to eliminate terms that are unfamiliar to intended respondents. Still, there is always someone who asks, "What do you mean by 'income'?" or "How much is 'a lot'?"

3. You can use several different data-collection techniques with the same respondent in a face-to-face survey interview. Part of the interview can consist of open-ended questions; another part may require the use of visual aids, such as graphs or cue cards; and in still another, you might hand the respondent a self-administered questionnaire booklet and stand by to help clarify potentially ambiguous items. This is a useful technique for asking really sensitive questions in a face-to-face interview.

4. Personal interviews at home can be much longer than telephone or self-administered questionnaires. An hour-long personal interview is relatively easy, and even two- and three-hour interviews are common. It is next to impossible to get respondents to devote two hours to filling out a questionnaire that shows up in the mail, unless you are prepared to pay well for their time, and it requires exceptional skill to keep a telephone interview going for more than 20 minutes, unless respondents are personally interested in the topic.

Note, though, that street-intercept or mall-intercept interviews, while face to face, usually have to be very quick. (See Chapter 5, on sampling, for more on street-intercept and mall-intercept surveys.)

5. Face-to-face respondents get one question at a time and can't flip through the questionnaire to see what's coming. If you design an interview to start with general questions (how people feel about using new technologies at work, for example) and move on to specific questions (how people feel about using a particular new technology), then you really don't want people flipping ahead.

6. With face-to-face interviews you know who answers the questions.

Disadvantages of Face-to-Face Interviews

1. They are intrusive and *reactive.* It takes a lot of skill to administer a questionnaire without

subtly telling the respondent how you hope he or she will answer your questions. Other methods of administration of questionnaires may be impersonal, but that's not necessarily bad. Furthermore, the problem of reactivity increases when more than one interviewer is involved in a project.

2. Personal interviews are costly in both time and money. In addition to the time spent in interviewing people, locating respondents in a representative sample may require going back several times. In urban research especially, count on making up to a half dozen callbacks to get the really hard-to-find respondents.

By the way, it's really important to keep going back to land those hard-to-get interviews. Survey researchers sometimes use the *sampling by convenient replacement* technique, which just means **going next door or down the block and picking up a replacement for an interviewee who happens not to be home when you show up.** This keeps the sample size honest, but as I mentioned in Chapter 5, it can produce some deadly bias. This is because, as you replace nonresponders with conveniently available respondents, you tend to homogenize your sample and make it less and less representative of all the variation in the population you're studying.

3. The experience of fieldworking anthropologists is that the number of people whom individual researchers can contact personally in a year, without any research assistants, is around 200. Of course, that's if you are working in the kind of place that anthropologists often go—places where transport is a problem. Sociologists working in major cities in Europe or North America can do more, but it gets really, really tough to maintain a consistent, positive attitude long before you get to the 200th interview. With mailed and telephone questionnaires you can survey thousands of respondents.

4. Personal interview surveys conducted by lone researchers over a long period of time run the risk of being overtaken by events. A war breaks out, a volcano erupts, or the government decides to cancel elections and imprison the opposition. It sounds dramatic, but these sorts of things are actually quite common across the world. Far less dramatic events can make the responses of the last 100 people you interview radically different from those of the first 100 to the same questions. If you conduct a questionnaire survey over a long period of time in the field, it is a good idea to reinterview your first few respondents and check the stability (reliability) of their reports.

Self-Administered Questionnaires

Self-administered questionnaires also have some clear advantages and disadvantages.

Advantages of Self-Administered Questionnaires

1. Mailed questionnaires put the post office to work for you in finding respondents. If you cannot use the mail (because sampling frames are unavailable, because you cannot expect people to respond, or because you happen to be in a country where mail service is unreliable), you can use cluster and area sampling (see Chapter 5), combined with the *drop and collect* technique. This involves **leaving a questionnaire with a respondent and going back later to pick it up.** In either case, self-administered questionnaires allow a single researcher to gather data from a large, representative sample of respondents, at relatively low cost per datum.

Here is a list of things that people say they'd like to see in their high school. For each item, check how you feel __this__ high school is doing.

	WELL	OK	POORLY	DON'T KNOW
1. High quality instruction	——	——	——	——
2. Good pay for teachers	——	——	——	——
3. Good mix of sports and academics	——	——	——	——
4. Preparation for college entrance exams	——	——	——	——
5. Safety	——	——	——	——
6. Music program	——	——	——	——
7. Good text books	——	——	——	——

Figure 7.1 A Battery Item in a Questionnaire (batteries can consist of many items)

2. All respondents get the same questions with a self-administered questionnaire. There is no worry about interviewer bias.

3. You can ask more complex questions with a self-administered questionnaire than you can in a personal interview. Questions that involve a long list of response categories, or that require a lot of background data are hard to follow orally, but are often challenging to respondents if worded right.

4. You can ask long **batteries** of otherwise boring questions on self-administered questionnaires that you just couldn't get away with in a personal interview. Look at Figure 7.1. Imagine trying to ask someone to sit still while you recited, say, 30 items and asked for their response.

5. Response effects are absent in self-administered questionnaires that arrive by mail. Questions about sexual behavior (including family planning) and scales that measure attitudes toward women or men or members of particular ethnic/racial groups are particularly susceptible to response effects based on variation in gender, age, race, or ethnicity. The perceived sexual orientation of the interviewer, for example, affects how supportive respondents are of homosexuality (Kemph and Kasser 1996).

Respondents may be more willing to report socially undesirable behaviors and traits in self-administered questionnaires (and in telephone interviews) than they are in face-to-face interviews. They aren't trying to impress interviewers, and anonymity gives people a sense of security, which produces more reports of things like premarital sexual experiences, constipation, arrest records, alcohol dependency, interpersonal violence, and so on (Hochstim 1967; Bradburn 1983).

This does not mean that *more* reporting of behavior means more *accurate* reporting. We know better than that now. But, as I've said before, more is usually better than less. If Chicanos report spending 12 hours per week in conversation with their families at home, while Anglos (as White, non-Hispanic Americans are known in the American Southwest) report spending 4 hours, I wouldn't want to bet that Chicanos *really* spend 12 hours, on average, or that Anglos *really* spend 4 hours, on average, talking to their families. But I'd find the fact that Chicanos reported spending three times as much time talking with their families pretty interesting.

> *More reporting of behavior does not always mean more accurate reporting.*

6. Self-administered questionnaires can be programmed into a computer, or even given automatically by e-mail. (You may see this called CAI in the social research literature, for *computer-assisted interviewing.*) Respondents take quickly to this format—it's used a lot in market research—and often find it to be a lot of fun. Fun is good because it cuts down on fatigue. Fatigue is bad because it sends respondents into robot mode and they stop thinking about their answers (O'Brien and Dugdale 1978; Barnes et al. 1995).

In 1988, I ran a computer-based interview study as part of an ongoing project to estimate the size of uncountable populations. One member of our team, Christopher McCarty, programmed a laptop to ask respondents in Mexico City and Jacksonville, Florida, about their acquaintanceship networks. (Actually, "laptop" is not quite the right word for the computer we used. In those days, a portable computer was one that fit under an airline seat—just barely. They were known as lug-ables.) Those respondents said they

enjoyed the experience. "Wow, this is like some kind of computer game," one respondent said.

In some cases, computer-based interviews may produce more honest answers about sensitive topics than do traditional paper-and-pencil tasks. Peterson et al. (1996) randomly assigned two groups of 57 Swedish Army veterans to fill out the Beck's Depression Inventory (Beck et al. 1961). One group used the pencil-and-paper version, while the other used a computer-based version. Those who used the computer-based version had significantly higher mean scores on sensitive questions about depression.

Disadvantages of Self-Administered Questionnaires

Despite these advantages, there are some hefty disadvantages to self-administered questionnaires.

1. You have no control over how people interpret questions on a self-administered instrument. There is always the danger that, no matter how much background work you do, no matter how hard you try to produce culturally correct questions, respondents will be forced into making culturally inappropriate choices in closed-ended questionnaires.

2. If you are not working in a highly industrialized nation, or if you are not prepared to use Dillman's total design method (discussed below), you are likely to see response rates of 20%-30% from mailed questionnaires. It is entirely reasonable to analyze the data statistically and to offer conclusions about the correlations among variables among those who responded to your survey. But response rates like these are unacceptable for drawing conclusions about larger populations.

3. Even if a questionnaire is returned, you can't be sure that the respondent who received it is the person who filled it out.

4. Mailed questionnaires are prone to serious sampling problems. Sampling frames of addresses are almost always flawed, sometimes very badly. For example, if you use a phone book to select a sample, you miss all those people who don't have phones or who choose not to list their numbers. Face-to-face administration of questionnaires is often based on an area cluster sample, with random selection of households within each cluster. This is a much more powerful sampling design than most mailed questionnaire surveys can muster.

5. In some cases, you may want a respondent to answer a question without the respondent knowing what's coming next. This is impossible in a self-administered questionnaire.

6. Self-administered questionnaires are simply not useful for studying nonliterate or illiterate populations, or for studying people who can't see. Some new technologies, like voice recognition software, are coming along that will address this problem.

Telephone Interviews

It wasn't too long ago that telephone surveys were considered a poor substitute for face-to-face surveys, but this has changed completely in recent years (Taylor 1997). In fact, *telephone interviewing* has become the most widely used method of gathering survey data across the industrialized nations of the world where so many households have their own phones.

Administering questionnaires by phone has some very important advantages.

Advantages of Telephone Interviews

1. Research has shown that, in the United States at least, answers to many different kinds of questions asked over the phone are as valid as those to questions asked in person or through the mail (Dillman 1978).

2. Phone interviews have the impersonal quality of self-administered questionnaires and the personal quality of face-to-face interviews. Hence, telephone surveys are unintimidating (like self-administered questionnaires), but allow interviewers to probe or to answer questions dealing with ambiguity of items (like personal interviews).

3. Telephone interviewing is inexpensive and convenient to conduct. It's not without effort, though. Professional survey organizations routinely do at least three callbacks to numbers that don't answer, and many survey researchers insist on 10 callbacks to make sure that they get an unbiased sample. As it is, in most telephone surveys, you can expect 30%-40% refusals. You can also expect nearly 100% sample completion, because it's relatively easy to replace refusers with people who will cooperate, but remember to keep track of the refusal rate and to make an extra effort to get at least some of the refusers to respond so you can test whether cooperators are a biased sample.

4. Using *random digit dialing* (RDD), you can reach almost everyone who has a phone. In the U.S., that means you can reach almost everybody. One recent survey found that 28% of completed interviews using RDD were with people who had unlisted phone numbers (Taylor 1997:424). There are huge regional differences, though, in the availability of telephones (see below, in the

section on the disadvantages of telephone interviewing).

5. Unless you do all your own interviewing, interviewer bias is an ever-present problem in survey research. It is relatively easy to monitor the quality of telephone interviewers' work by having them come to a central place to conduct their operation. (If you don't monitor the performance of telephone interviewers, though, you invite cheating. See below.)

6. There is no reaction to the appearance of the interviewer in telephone surveys, although respondents do react to accents and speech patterns of interviewers. Oskenberg et al. (1986) found that telephone interviewers who had the lowest refusal rates had higher-pitched, louder, and clearer voices. And, as with all types of interviews, there are *gender-of-interviewer* and *race-of-interviewer effects* in telephone interviews, too. Respondents try to figure out the race or ethnicity of the interviewer and then tailor responses accordingly.

In the National Black Election Study, 872 African Americans were polled before and after the 1984 presidential election. Since interviewers were assigned randomly to respondents, some people were interviewed by a White person before the election and an African American after the election. And vice versa: Some people were interviewed by an African American before the election and a White person on the second wave.

Darren Davis (1997) looked at data from this natural experiment. When African American interviewers in the preelection polls were replaced by White interviewers in the postelection surveys, African Americans were more likely to say that Blacks don't have the power to change things, that Black people can't make a difference in local or national elections, that Black people cannot form their own political party, and that Whites are not responsible for keeping Blacks

down—very powerful evidence of a race-of-interviewer effect.

7. Telephone interviewing is safe: You can talk on the phone to people who live in urban neighborhoods where many professional interviewers (most of whom are women) would prefer not to go. Telephones also get you past doormen and other people who run interference for the rich.

Disadvantages of Telephone Interviewing

The disadvantages of telephone surveys are obvious.

1. If you are doing research in Haiti or Bolivia or elsewhere in the developing world, telephone surveys are out of the question, except for some urban centers, and then only if your research is about relatively well-off people. Nave (1997) was able to combine telephone and door-to-door interviewing with mailed questionnaires to study the rate of intermarriage across ethnic groups in Mauritius (see Box 7.1).

Even in highly industrialized nations, not everyone has a telephone. About 94% of all households in the United States have telephones. This makes *national* surveys a cinch to do and highly reliable. But the distribution of telephones is uneven, which makes some *local* surveys impossible to do by phone.

In Westchester County, New York, for example, the median per capita income is over $35,000 per year and over 98% of all households have phones. The 2% of households that don't have phones in Westchester County are rental properties. In Coconino County, Arizona, the median per capita income is less than $15,000 per year and about 75% of all housing units—owner-occupied and rentals alike—have phones. Be very certain about the demographics of the area you're thinking of studying before deciding on a telephone survey. If having a telephone is associated with having a certain amount of income and/or membership in an ethnic group, as it is in Coconino County, Arizona, then a telephone interview of that population will produce statistically ungeneralizable results.

2. Telephone interviews must be relatively short, or people will hang up. There is some evidence that once people agree to give you their time in a telephone interview, you can keep them on the line for a remarkably long time (up to an hour) by developing special "phone personality" traits. Generally, however, you should not plan a telephone interview that lasts for more than 20 minutes.

3. And finally, this: It has long been known that, in an unknown percentage of occasions, hired interviewers willfully produce inaccurate data. When an interviewer who is paid by the completed interview finds a respondent not at home, the temptation is to fill in the interview and get on to the next respondent. This saves a lot of calling back and introduces garbage into the data.

Unless there is continual monitoring, it's particularly easy for interviewers to cheat in telephone surveys—from failing to probe, to interviewing unqualified respondents, to fabricating an item response, and even to fabricating whole interviews. Kiecker and Nelson (1996) hired 33 survey research companies to do eight interviews each, ostensibly as "mop-up" for a larger national market survey. The eight respondents were plants—graduate students of drama, for whom this must have been quite a gig—and were the same eight for each of the surveys. Of the 33 interviewers studied, 10 fabricated an entire interview, 32 fabricated at least one item response, and all 33 failed to record responses verbatim.

The technology of telephone interviewing has become very sophisticated. *Computer-assisted telephone interviewing* (CATI) makes it harder to do things like ask questions out of order, but a determined cheater on your interviewing team can do a lot of damage. The good news is that once you eliminate cheating (with monitoring), the main thing left that can go wrong is inconsistency in the way interviewers ask questions. Unstructured and structured interviews each have their own advantages, but for structured interviews to yield reliable results, they have to be really, really structured. That is, the questions have to be read verbatim so that every respondent is exposed to the same stimulus.

Repeated verbatim readings of questions is boring to do and boring to listen to. When respondents (inevitably) get restless, it's tempting to vary the wording to make the interview process seem less mechanical. This turns out to be a bigger problem in face-to-face interviews (where interviewers are generally working alone, without any monitoring) than in telephone interviews. Presser and Zhao (1992) monitored 40 trained telephone interviewers at the Maryland Survey Research Center. For the 5,619 questions monitored, interviewers read the questions exactly as worded on the survey 91% of the time. Training works.

Still, no matter how much you train interviewers. . . . Johnstone et al. (1992) studied 48 telephone interviews done entirely by women and found that female respondents elicited more sympathy while male respondents elicited more joking. Men, say Johnstone et al., may be less comfortable than women are with being interviewed by women and wind up trying to subvert the interview by turning it into teasing or banter.

Sampling for telephone surveys is also aided by computer. There are companies that sell telephone numbers for surveys. The numbers are chosen to represent businesses or residences and to represent the varying saturation of phone service in different calling areas.

Even the best sample of phone numbers, though, may not be enough to keep you out of trouble. During the 1984 election, Ronald Reagan's tracking poll used a list of registered voters, Republicans and Democrats alike. The poll showed Reagan comfortably ahead of his rival, Walter Mondale, except on Friday nights. Registered Republicans, it turned out, being wealthier than their counterparts among Democrats, were out Friday nights more than Democrats were, and simply weren't available to answer the phone (Begley et al. 1992:38).

WHEN TO USE WHAT

There is no perfect data-collection method. However, self-administered questionnaires are preferable to personal interviews when three conditions are met: (1) You are dealing with literate respondents; (2) you are confident of getting a high response rate (at least 70%); and (3) the questions you want to ask do not require a face-to-face interview or the use of visual aids such as cue cards, charts, and the like. Under these circumstances, you get much more information for your time and money than from the other methods of questionnaire administration.

When you really need complete interviews—answers to all or nearly all the questions in a particular survey—then face-to-face interviews are the way to go. Caserta et al. (1985) interviewed recently bereaved respondents about adjustment to widowhood. They interviewed 192 respondents, 104 in person, at home, and 88 by mailed questionnaire. Both groups got identical questions.

On average, 82% of those interviewed at home three-four weeks after losing their husband or wife answered any given question. Just 68% of those who responded to the mailed questionnaire answered any given question. As Caserta et al. explain, the physical presence of the interviewer helped establish the rapport needed for asking sensitive and personal questions about the painful experience of bereavement (1985:640).

If you are working in a highly industrialized country, and if a very high proportion (at least 80%) of the population you are studying has its own telephones, then consider doing a phone survey whenever a self-administered questionnaire would otherwise be appropriate.

If you are working alone or in places where the mail and the phone system are inefficient for data collection—as is often the case with anthropologists and epidemiologists, and is sometimes the case for sociologists and social psychologists—the drop-and-collect technique is a good alternative.

Finally, there is no rule against using more than one type of interview. Mauritius, an island nation in the Indian Ocean, is an ethnically complex society. Chinese, Creoles, Franco-Mauritians, Hindus, Muslims, and other groups make up a population of about a million. Nave (1997) was interested in how Mauritians maintain their ethnic group boundaries, particularly through their choices of whom to marry. A government office on Mauritius maintains a list of all people over age 18 on Mauritius, so it was relatively easy for Nave to get a random sample of the population.

Contacting the sample was another matter. Nave got back just 347 out of 930 mailed questionnaires, but he was able to interview another 296 by telephone and face to face, for a total of 643, or 69% of his original sample.

USING INTERVIEWERS

There are several advantages to using multiple interviewers in survey research. The most obvious is that you can increase the size of the sample. Multiple interviewers, however, introduce several disadvantages, and whatever problems are associated with interviewer bias are increased with more than one interviewer.

Just as important, multiple interviewers increase the cost of survey research. If you can collect 100 interviews yourself and maintain careful quality control in your interview technique, then hiring one more interviewer would probably not improve your research by enough to warrant both spending the extra money and worrying about quality control. Recall that for estimating population proportions or means, you have to quadruple the sample size to halve the sampling error. If you can't afford to hire three more interviewers (besides yourself), and to train them carefully so that they at least introduce the *same* bias to every interview as you do, you're better off running the survey yourself and saving the money for other things.

This only goes for surveys in which you interview a random sample of respondents to estimate a population parameter. If you are studying the experience of a group of people, or are after cultural data (as in "How are things usually done around here?"), then getting more interviews is better than getting fewer, whether you collect the data yourself or have it collected by others.

Training Interviewers

If you hire interviewers, be sure to train them—and monitor them throughout the research. A colleague used a doctoral student as an interviewer in a project in Atlanta. The senior researcher trained the student, but listened to the interview tapes that came in. At one point, the interviewer asked a respondent: "How many years of education do you have?" "Four," said the respondent. "Oh," said the student researcher, "you mean you have four years of education?" "No," said the informant, bristling and insulted, "I've had four years of education beyond high school." The informant was affluent; the interview was conducted in his upper-middle-class house; he had already told the interviewer that he was in a high-tech occupation. So monitor interviewers.

If you hire a *team* of interviewers, you have one extra chore besides monitoring their work. You need to get them to act as a team. Be sure, for example, that they all use the same probes to the various questions on the interview schedule. Especially with open-ended questions, be sure to do random spot checks, during the survey, of how interviewers are coding the answers they get. The act of spot-checking keeps coders alert. When you find discrepancies in the way interviewers code responses, bring the group together and discuss the problem openly.

Billiet and Loosveldt (1988) found that asking interviewers to tape all their interviews produces a higher response rate, particularly to sensitive questions about things like sexual behavior. Apparently, when interviewers know that their work can be scrutinized (from the tapes) they probe more and get informants to open up more.

Carey et al. (1996) studied the beliefs of 51 newly arrived Vietnamese refugees in upstate New York about tuberculosis (TB). The interviews consisted of 32 open-ended questions on beliefs about symptoms, prevention, treatment, and the social consequences of having TB. The two interviewers in this study were bilingual refugees who participated in a three-day workshop to build their interview skills. They were told about the rationale for open-ended questions and about techniques for getting respondents to open up and provide full answers to the questions. The training included a written manual (this is very important) to which the interviewers could refer during the actual study. After the workshop, the trainees did 12 practice interviews with Vietnamese adults who were not in the study.

William Axinn ran the Tamang Family Research Project, a comparative study of villages in Nepal (Axinn 1991). Axinn and his co-workers trained a group of interviewers using the *Interviewer's Manual* from the Survey Research Center at the University of Michigan (1976). That manual contains the distilled wisdom of hundreds of interviewer-training exercises in the United States, and Axinn found the manual useful in training Nepalese interviewers, too.

Axinn recruited 32 potential interviewers. After a week of training (five days at eight hours a day, and two days of supervised field practice), the 16 best interviewers were selected, 10 men and 6 women. The researchers hired more interviewers than they needed and after three months, 4 of the interviewers were fired. "The firing of interviewers who clearly failed to follow protocols," said Axinn et al., "had a considerable positive effect on the morale of interviewers who had worked hard to follow our rules" (1991:200). No one has accused Axinn of overstatement.

Who to Hire

In general, when hiring interviewers, look for professional interviewers first. Next, look for people who are mature enough to accept the need for rigorous training and who can work as part of a team. If need be, look for interviewers who can handle the possibility of going into some rough neighborhoods and who can answer the many questions that respondents will come up with in the course of the survey.

If you are running a survey based on personal interviews in a developing country, consider hiring college students, and even college graduates, in the social sciences. "Social sciences," by the way, does not mean the humanities. In Peru, sociologists Donald Warwick and Charles Lininger found that "some students from the humanities . . . were reluctant to accept the 'rigidities' of survey interviewing." Those students felt that "as educated individuals, they should be allowed to administer the questionnaire as they saw fit in each situation" (1975:222).

Students from sociology, however, are likely to be experienced interviewers and will have a lot to contribute to the design and content of questionnaires. It is very important in those situations to remember that you are dealing with colleagues who will be justly resentful if you treat them merely as employees of your study. By the same token, college students in developing nations are almost certain to be members of the elite who may find it tough to establish rapport with peasant farmers or the urban poor (Hursh-César and Roy 1976:308).

Make It Easy for Interviewers to Do Their Job

If you use interviewers, be sure to make the questionnaire booklet easy to use. Leave enough space for interviewers to write in the answers to open-ended questions—but not too much space. Big spaces are an invitation to some interviewers to develop needlessly long answers (Warwick and Lininger 1975:152).

Also, use two different typefaces for questions and answers; put instructions to interviewers in capital letters and questions for respondents in normal type. Figure 7.2 is an example.

> 5. INTERVIEWER: CHECK ONE OF THE FOLLOWING
> ☐ R HAS LIVED IN CHICAGO MORE THAN FIVE YEARS.
>   SKIP TO QUESTION 7.
> ☐ R HAS LIVED IN CHICAGO LESS THAN FIVE YEARS.
>   ASK QUESTION 6 AND CONTINUE WITH QUESTION
> 6. Could you tell me where you were living five years ago?
> 7. Where were you born?

Figure 7.2 Using Two Different Typefaces in a Survey Instrument
SOURCE: Adapted from D. P. Warwick and C. A. Lininger, *The Sample Survey: Theory and Practice*, p. 153, 1975.

CLOSED- VS. OPEN-ENDED:
THE PROBLEM OF THREATENING QUESTIONS

The most often asked question about survey research is whether *forced-choice* (also called closed-ended) or *open-ended* items are better. Schuman and Presser (1979) tested this. They asked one sample of people this question: "Please look at this card and tell me which thing you would most prefer in a job." The card had five items listed: (1) high income, (2) no danger of being fired, (3) working hours are short with lots of free time, (4) chances for advancement, and (5) the work is important and gives a feeling of accomplishment. Then they asked another sample the open-ended question: "What would you most prefer in a job?"

About 17% of the respondents to the closed-ended question chose "chances for advancement" and over 59% chose "important work." Fewer than 2% of the respondents who were asked the open-ended question mentioned "chances for advancement," and just 21% said anything about "important" or "challenging" or "fulfilling" work.

When the questions get really threatening, the problem gets worse. Masturbation, alcohol consumption, and drug use are reported with 50%-100% greater frequency in response to open-ended questions (Bradburn 1983:299). For reporting these kinds of behavior, people are apparently least threatened when they can offer their own answers to open-ended questions on a self-administered questionnaire, rather than being forced to choose among a set of fixed alternatives (for example, once a month, once a week, once a day, several times a day), and are most threatened by a face-to-face interviewer (Blair et al. 1977).

Recently, Ivis et al. (1997) found that at least one pretty embarrassing question was better asked in a closed-ended format—over the phone. People in their survey were asked: "How often in the last 12 months have you had five or more drinks on one occasion?" Then, later in the interview, they were asked the same question, but were given nine fixed choices: (1) every day, (2) about once every other day, . . . (9) never in the last year.

The closed-ended format produced significantly more positive responses. Many people in the industrialized countries have become accustomed to telephone surveys and are comfortable with the anonymity of those surveys. Notice that the anonymity of telephone surveys lets the interviewer, as well as the respondent, off the hook. You can ask people things you might be squeamish about if the interview were face-to-face, and respondents feel that they can divulge very personal matters to disembodied voices on the phone.

Experiments are continuing on the efficacy of survey format (self-administered, face-to-face, telephone) and question format (open- vs. closed ended), and the jury is still out (see Wentland and Smith 1993). Overall, since closed-ended items are so efficient, most survey researchers prefer them to open-ended questions and use them whenever possible.

But there is no rule that prevents you from mixing question types. Many survey researchers use the open-ended format for really intimidating questions and the fixed-choice format for everything else, even on the phone. Even if there are no intimidating questions in a survey, it's a good idea to stick in a few open-ended items. The open-ended questions break the monotony for the respondent, as do tasks that require referring to visual aids (like a graph).

The responses to fixed-choice questions are unambiguous for purposes of analysis. Be sure to take full advantage of this and *precode fixed-choice items* on a questionnaire. Put the codes right on the instrument so that computer input of the data is made as easy (and as error free) as possible.

QUESTION WORDING AND FORMAT

There are some well-understood rules that all survey researchers follow in constructing questionnaire items. Here are 15 of them.

1. *Be unambiguous.* If respondents can interpret a question differently from the meaning you have in mind, they will. In my view, this is the source of most response error in closed-ended questionnaires.

> A simple question like
> *"How often do you visit a doctor?"*
> can be very ambiguous.

The problem is not easy to solve. A simple question like "How often do you visit a doctor?" can be very ambiguous. Are acupuncturists, chiropractors, chiropodists, and public clinics all doctors? If you think they are, you'd better tell your respondents that, or you leave it up to them

to decide. If you are working some parts of the southwestern U.S., people may be visiting native curers and herbalists. Are those practitioners doctors? In Mexico, many community clinics are staffed by nurses. Does "going to the doctor" include a visit to one of those clinics?

If you ask: "How long have you lived in New York?" does "New York" include the 13 million people who live in the urban sprawl, or just the 7.5 million who are residents of the city's five boroughs? And how "near" is "near Detroit"?

Words like "lunch," "community," "people," and hundreds of other innocent lexical items have lurking ambiguities associated with them, and phrases like "family planning" will cause all kinds of mischief. Half the respondents in the 1985 General Social Survey were asked if they agreed that there was too little spending for "assistance to the poor," while half were asked if there was too little spending for "welfare." A whopping 65% agreed with the first wording, while just 19% agreed with the second (T. W. Smith 1987:77).

Even the word "you," as Payne pointed out in 1951, can be ambiguous. Ask a nurse at the clinic, "How many patients did you see last week?" and you might get a response like "Who do you mean, me or the clinic?" Of course, if the nurse is filling out a self-administered questionnaire, she'll have to decide for herself what you had in mind. Maybe she'll get it right; maybe she won't.

2. Use a vocabulary that your respondents understand, but don't be condescending. This is a difficult balance to achieve. If you're studying a narrow population (sugar cane cutters, midwives, race car drivers, pediatric nurses), then proper ethnography and pretesting with a few respondents will help ensure appropriate wording of questions.

But if you are studying a more general population, even in a small town of just 3,000 people, then things are very different. Some respondents will require a low-level vocabulary; others will find that vocabulary insulting. This is one of the reasons often cited for doing personal interviews: You want the opportunity to phrase your questions differently for different segments of the population. Realize, however, that this poses risks in terms of reliability of response data.

3. Remember that respondents must know enough to respond to your questions. You'd be surprised at how often questionnaires are distributed to people who are totally unequipped to answer them. I get questionnaires in the mail all the time asking for information I simply don't have.

Most people can't recall with any acceptable accuracy how long they spent in the hospital last year, how many miles they drive each week, or whether they've cut back on their use of electricity. They *can* recall whether they own a television, have ever been to Cairo, or voted in last year's election, and they can tell you whether they *think* they are well paid, or *believe* the current chief of

police is doing a better job than his predecessor at cleaning up the staffing problem at the county jail.

4. Make sure there's a clear purpose for every question you ask in a survey. When I say "clear purpose," I mean clear to respondents, not just to you. And once you're on a topic, stay on it and finish it. Respondents can get frustrated, confused, and annoyed at the tactic of switching topics and then coming back to a topic that they've already dealt with on a questionnaire. Some researchers do exactly this just to ask the same question in more than one way and to check respondent reliability. This underestimates the intelligence of respondents and is asking for trouble—I have known respondents to sabotage questionnaires that they found insulting to their intelligence.

You can (and should) ask questions that are related to one another at different places in a questionnaire, so long as each question makes sense in terms of its placement in the overall instrument. For example, if you are interviewing labor migrants, you'll probably want to get a labor history—by asking where the respondent has worked during the past few years. Later, in a section on family economics, you might ask whether a respondent has ever sent remittances and from where.

As you move from one topic to another, put in a transition paragraph that makes each shift logical to the respondent. For example, you might say: "Now that we have learned something about the kinds of food you like, we'd like to know about. . . ." The exact wording of these transition paragraphs should be varied throughout a questionnaire.

5. Pay careful attention to contingencies and filter questions. Many question topics contain several contingencies. Suppose you ask people if they are married. If they answer no, then you probably want to ask whether they've ever been married.

You may want to know whether they have children, irrespective of whether they are married or have ever been married. You may want to know what people think is the ideal family size, irrespective of whether they've been married, plan to be married, have children, or plan to have children.

You can see that the contingencies can get very complex. The best way to ensure that all contingencies are accounted for is to build a *contingency flow chart* like that shown in Figure 7.3 (Sirken 1972; Sudman and Bradburn 1982).

6. Use clear scales. There are some commonly used scales in survey research, things like *excellent-good-fair-poor, approve-disapprove, oppose-favor, for-against, good-bad, agree-disagree,* and *better-worse-about the same.* Just because these are well known, however, does not mean that they are clear and unambiguous to respondents.

To cut down on the ambiguities associated with these kinds of scales, explain the meaning of each potentially ambiguous scale when you introduce it. With self-administered questionnaires, use 5 scale points rather than 3, if you can. For example, use *strongly approve-approve-neutral-disapprove-strongly disapprove,* rather than *approve-neutral-disapprove.* This will give respondents the opportunity to make finer-grained choices. If your sample is large enough, you can distinguish during analysis among respondents who answer, say, "strongly approve" and "approve" on some item.

For smaller samples, you'll have to aggregate the data into three categories for analysis. Self-administered questionnaires allow the use of 7-point scales, like the semantic differential scale shown in Figure 7.4. Telephone interviews usually require 3-point scales. (See below for more on how to construct scales.)

7. Try to package questions in self-administered questionnaires (as shown earlier in Figure 7.1). This is a way to get a lot of data quickly and easily, and, if done properly, it will prevent respondents

from getting bored with a survey. For example, you might say, "Please indicate how close you feel to each of the persons on this chart" and provide the respondent with a list of relatives (mother, father, sister, brother, etc.) and a scale (very close, close, neutral, distant, very distant, etc.).

Be sure to make scales unambiguous (if you are asking how often people think they do something, don't say "regularly" when you mean "more than once a month"), and limit the list of activities to no more than seven. Then introduce a question with a totally different format, to break up the monotony and to keep the respondent interested.

Packaging is best done in self-administered questionnaires. If you use these kinds of lists in a personal interview, you'll have to repeat the scale for at least the first three items or activities you name, or until the respondent gets the pattern down. This can get very tiring for both interviewers and respondents.

8. If you want respondents to check just one response, then be sure to *make the possible responses to a question exhaustive and mutually exclusive.* Here is an example (taken from a questionnaire I received) of what *not* to do:

How do you perceive communication between your department and other departments in the university? [check one]

There is much communication_____
There is sufficient communication_____
There is little communication_____
There is no communication_____
No basis for perception_____

The "no basis for perception" response took care of making the item exhaustive. You can always make questionnaire items like this one exhaustive by giving respondents the option of saying some variant of "don't know"—like "no basis for perception." Some researchers feel that

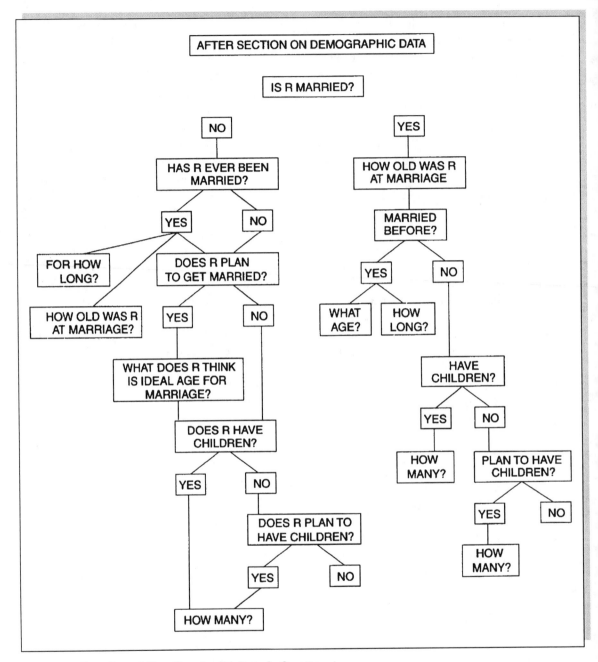

Figure 7.3 Flow Chart of Filter Questions for Part of a Questionnaire

this just gives respondents a lazy way out—that people need to be made to work a bit. If there is a good chance that some of your respondents really won't have the information you ask for, then I think the "don't know" option is too important to leave out. In consumer preference

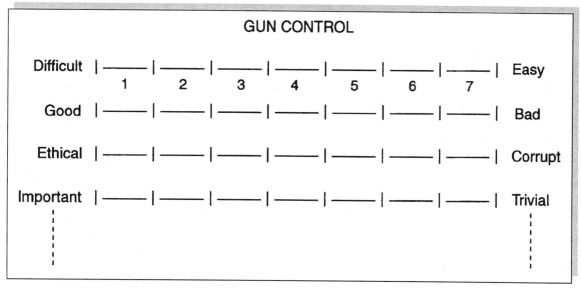

Figure 7.4 A 7-Point Semantic Differential Scale

surveys, though, where you actually give someone a taste of a cracker and ask them to tell you if they like it, the "don't know" option is a bad idea.

The problem for me on this item was that I wanted to check both "little communication" and "sufficient communication." For me, at least, these two categories were not mutually exclusive—I didn't think there was a lot of communication, and I wasn't at all bothered by that—but the author of the survey asked me to "check one."

9. *Keep unthreatening questions short.* Questions that are likely to intimidate respondents should have long preambles to lessen the intimidation effect. The questions themselves, however, should contain as few words as possible.

10. *Always provide alternatives, if appropriate.* Suppose people are being asked to move off their land to make way for a new highway. The government offers to compensate people for the land, but people are suspicious that the government won't evaluate fairly how much compensation landowners are entitled to. If you take a

survey and ask, "Should the government offer people compensation for their land?" respondents can answer yes or no for very different reasons. Instead, let people check whether they agree or disagree with a set of alternatives, like "The government should offer people compensation for their land" and "An independent board should determine how much people get for their land."

11. *Avoid loaded questions.* Any question that begins "Don't you agree that . . . " is a **loaded question.** Sheatsley (1983) points out, however, that asking loaded questions is a technique you can use to your advantage, on occasion, just as leading or baiting informants can be used in unstructured interviewing. A famous example comes from Kinsey's landmark study of sexual behavior of American men (Kinsey et al. 1948). Kinsey asked men, "How old were you the first time you masturbated?" This made respondents feel that the interviewer already *knew* about the fact of masturbation, and was only in search of additional information.

12. *Don't use **double-barreled questions**.* Here is one I found on a questionnaire: "When did you leave home and go to work on your own for the first time?" There is no reason to assume, of course, that someone had to leave home to go to work or that they necessarily went to work if they left home.

Here is another bad question:

Please indicate if you agree or disagree with the following statement:

Marijuana is no more harmful than tobacco or alcohol, so the personal use of marijuana should be legal.

Suppose a respondent agrees (or disagrees) with the first part of the statement—the assertion that marijuana is no more harmful than tobacco or alcohol. He or she may agree or disagree with the second part of the statement. If respondents answer yes or no, how do you know if they are indicating agreement with both parts of it or just one part? Which part? How can you tell? You can't. That's why it's a bad question.

13. *Don't put false premises into questions.* I once formulated the following question for a survey in Greece: "Is it better for a woman to have a house and cash as a dowry, or for her to have an education and a job that she can bring to the marriage?" This question was based on a lot of ethnographic work in a community, during which I learned that many families were sinking their resources into getting women educated and into jobs and offer-

ing this to eligible bachelors as a substitute for traditional material dowries.

My question, however, was based on the false premise that all families respected the custom of dowry. The question did not allow respondents to state a third alternative—namely, that they didn't think dowry was a custom that ought to be maintained in any form, traditional or modern. In fact, many families were deciding to reject the dowry custom altogether—a fact that I missed for some time because I failed to pretest the item (see Pretesting, below).

14. *Don't take emotional stands in the wording of questions.* Here's an example of the sort of question you see on surveys all the time—and that you should never ask: "Should the legislature raise the drinking age to 21 in order to reduce the carnage among teens on our highways?" Another example of a bad question is: "Don't you agree with the President when he says . . . ?"

15. *When asking for opinions on controversial issues, specify the referent situation as much as possible.* Instead of asking "Do you approve of abortion?" ask "Under what conditions do you approve of abortion?" Then give the respondent as exhaustive a list of circumstances as possible to check. If the circumstances are not exclusive (rape and incest are not necessarily exclusive, for example), then let respondents check as many circumstances as they think appropriate.

TRANSLATION AND BACK TRANSLATION

All the tips given here about writing good survey questions continue to apply when you are working in another culture. They are just a lot more difficult to implement because you have to deal

with phrasing questions properly in another language as well. The best way to deal with this is through *back translation*.

First, write any questionnaire in your native language, paying attention to all the lessons of this chapter. Then have the questionnaire translated by a bilingual person who is a native speaker of the language you a working in. Work closely with the translator, so that he or she can fully understand the subtleties you want to convey in your questionnaire items.

Next, ask another bilingual person, who is a native speaker of *your* language, to translate the questionnaire back into that language. This back translation should be almost identical to the original questionnaire you wrote. If it isn't, then something was lost in one of the two translations. You'd better find out which one it was and correct the problem. This is what Axinn et al. (1991) did in their study of fertility in Nepal. In fact, they cross-checked the meaning of each question in the back translation against the original and went through the whole exercise several times until they were satisfied that questions in Nepalese were sensible.

The Delphi Technique

Back translation is widely used to produce multiple versions of standardized scales, but another method, called the *Delphi technique,* also works well. The Ennis Value Orientation Inventory was developed by Catherine Ennis and her co-workers (1990) to assess the goals of physical education teachers. Teachers who are oriented toward self-actualization, for example, argue that personal growth and the development of self-esteem are the real goals of sports in the curriculum. By contrast, teachers who are highly oriented toward social responsibility think that students should learn to align their own needs with those of the larger group and that sports in the curriculum can help students achieve this goal. Ennis developed her inventory for use in the U.S.

Chen et al. (1997) wanted to use the scale to compare the value orientation of physical education teachers in the U.S. and China. First, they translated the 90-item instrument into Mandarin Chinese. (There are eight major Chinese languages, but Mandarin is the lingua franca for the nation, and all educated people speak and write Mandarin.) Next, they sent the English and Chinese versions of the instrument to a panel of eight experts. All eight had completed their university education and their professional training in physical education in China. All eight were either teaching physical education at universities in the U.S. (and had doctorates) or were completing their doctoral studies in the U.S. These were, then, experts in the field of study (physical education) who could judge the adequacy of the Chinese translation from English into Chinese.

Each member of the panel inspected each of the 90 items on the two versions of the inventory. They rated each item on a scale of 1 to 5 for consistency between the English and the Chinese. Giving an item a 5 meant that they thought the Chinese and English were *highly consistent,* while giving an item a 1 meant they thought the items were *inconsistent.*

Panelists wrote comments and suggestions right on the rating sheet about any items they thought needed work. Then they sent the package back to Ennis and Chen. If the mean score for an item was below 4.00 (near the top of the 5-point consistency scale), Ennis and Chen incorporated the panelists' suggestions and rewrote the Chinese version of the item. (They left the English version alone since that scale had been already been validated.) Then they sent the package back to the panelists for another round.

The process continued for four rounds until every one of the 90 items had a consistency score of at least 4.00. Now *that's* a translation.

THE RESPONSE RATE PROBLEM

Mailed questionnaires can be very, very effective, but there is one problem with them that all survey researchers watch for: getting enough of them back. In 1936, the *Literary Digest* sent out 10 million straw poll ballots in an attempt to predict the winner of the presidential election. They got back 2.3 million ballots and predicted Alf Landon over Franklin Delano Roosevelt in a landslide. Roosevelt got 61% of the vote.

Now, you'd think that 2.3 million ballots would be enough for anyone, but two things caused the *Digest* debacle. First, they selected their sample from automobile registries and telephone books. In 1936, this favored richer people, who tend to be Republican. Second, the 2.3 million ballots were only 23% of the 10 million sent out. The low response rate biased the results in favor of the Republican challenger since those who didn't respond tended to be poorer and less inclined to participate in surveys (Squire 1988).

❖

Table 7.1 is an example of *nonresponse bias* based on Rosnow and Rosenthal's (1997) analysis of data published by William Cochran in 1977 (p. 360). In that study, 3,116 fruit growers were sent questionnaires (about their farming practices), and one of the questions was about how many trees they owned. By luck, the real number of trees owned by each grower was known from other data.

The survey had three waves. By the end of the third wave, 1,839 (59%) of the 3,116 growers had not responded. Each successive wave produced responses from growers who owned fewer and fewer trees. The 59% of the growers who never responded had 290 trees each, compared to 456 trees for the growers who responded in the first wave. The 1,277 respondents had an average of 385 trees each—6 trees more than the actual average of 329 trees for the 3,116 growers in the population.

We know, then, that the enthusiastic respondents in the first wave had a lot more trees than others who responded in the second and third waves. What about their answers to all the socioeconomic and opinion questions on the survey? Were those answers somehow affected by the number of trees they had? We don't know, and that's the problem.

TABLE 7.1 An Example of Nonresponse Bias in Surveys

	First Wave	Second Wave	Third Wave	Total Nonrespondents	Total Population
Number of respondents	300	543	434	1,839	3,116
Proportion of the population	.10	.17	.14	.59	1.00
Mean number of trees per respondent	456	382	340	290	329

SOURCE: R. L. Rosnow and R. Rosenthal, *People Studying People: Artifacts and Ethics in Behavioral Research*, p. 92. Copyright © 1997, W. H. Freeman and Company. Reprinted by permission.

How to Adjust for Nonresponse

Skip to 1991. The American Anthropological Association (AAA) sent questionnaires to a sample of 1,229 members. The sample was stratified into several cohorts who had received their Ph.D. degrees beginning in 1971-72 and 1989-90. The 1989-90 cohort comprised 306 then-recent Ph.D.s. The idea was to find out what kinds of jobs those anthropologists had.

The AAA got back 840 completed questionnaires, or 68% of the 1,229, and the results of the survey were reported in the *Anthropology Newsletter* in May 1991. The response rate is not high for this kind of survey, where the respondents are being asked for information from their own professional organization. (The U.S. Office of Management and Budget demands a minimum 75% response rate from survey contract researchers [Fowler 1984:48] and, as we saw earlier, this is not an excessive demand.)

Now, 41% of those responding from the 1989-90 cohort said they had academic jobs. The *Anthropology Newsletter* didn't report the response rate by cohort, but suppose that 68% of the 1989-90 cohort—the same percentage as applies to the overall survey—sent back their questionnaires. That's 208 out of 306 responses. The 41% who said they had academic jobs would be 85 of the 208 respondents; the other 123 had nonacademic jobs.

Suppose that everyone who didn't respond (32%, or 98 out of 306) got nonacademic jobs. (Maybe that's why they didn't bother to respond.) In that case, 98 + 123 = 221 out of the 306 people in the cohort, or 72%, got nonacademic jobs that year—not the 59% (100% – 41%) as reported in the survey.

It's unlikely, of course, that *all* the nonresponders were in nonacademic jobs. To handle the problem of nonresponse, the AAA might have run down a random grab of 10 of the nonresponders and interviewed them by telephone. Suppose that 7 said they had nonacademic jobs. You'll recall from Chapter 5 on sampling that the formula for determining the 95% confidence limits of a point estimator is

$$P \text{ (the true proportion)} = 1.96 \sqrt{PQ/n} \quad \text{(Formula 7.1)}$$

which means that

$$1.96 \sqrt{(.7)(.3)/10} = .28$$

The probable answer for the 10 holdouts is .70 ± .28. Somewhere between 42% and 98% of the 98 nonresponders from the 1989-90 cohort probably had nonacademic jobs. We guess that from 41 to 96 of those 98 nonresponders had nonacademic jobs. We can now make a reasonable guess: 123 of the responders plus 41-96 of the nonresponders = 164-219 of the 306 people in the cohort, or 54%-71%, probably had nonacademic jobs.

Low response rate can be a disaster. People who are quick to fill out and return mailed questionnaires tend to have higher incomes and consequently tend to be more educated than the later respondents. Any dependent variables that covary with income and education, then, will be seriously distorted if you get back only 50% of your questionnaires. And what's worse, there is no accurate way to measure nonresponse bias. With a lot of nonresponse, all you know is that you've got bias but you don't know how to take it into account.

IMPROVING RESPONSE RATES: DILLMAN'S TOTAL DESIGN METHOD

Fortunately, a lot of research has been done on increasing response rates to mailed questionnaires. Yammarino et al. (1991) reviewed 184 controlled experiments, done between 1940 and 1988, on maximizing the return of mailed questionnaires, and Don Dillman, of the Survey Research Laboratory at Washington State University, has synthesized the research on maximizing return rates and has developed what he calls the "total design method" of mail and telephone surveying (Dillman 1978, 1983; Salant and Dillman 1994).

Professional surveys done in the United States following Dillman's method achieve an average return rate of around 73%, with many surveys reaching 85%-90% response. In Canada and Europe, around 79% of personal interviews are completed, and the response rate for mailed questionnaires is around 75% (Dillman 1978, 1983). Of course, those numbers are for the usual kinds of surveys about consumer behaviors, political attitudes, and so on. What happens when you ask people really threatening questions? In the Netherlands, Nederhof (1985) conducted a mail survey on attitudes toward suicide and achieved a 65% response rate. Pretty impressive.

The average response rate for face-to-face interviews in the United States was between 80% and 85% during the 1960s, but fell to less than 70% in the early 1970s (American Statistical Association 1974). It has apparently recovered somewhat, as more is learned about how to maximize cooperation by potential respondents.

Willimack et al. (1995), for example, report a refusal rate of 28% for face-to-face interviews in the annual Detroit Area Study conducted by the University of Michigan. They also report that giving people a gift-type ballpoint pen (a small, nonmonetary incentive) *before* starting a face-to-face interview lowered refusal rates and increased the completeness of responses to questions. The bottom line is that, with everything we've learned over the years, the gap between the response rate to personal interviews and mailed questionnaires is now insignificant.

This does not in any way reduce the value of personal interviews, especially for anyone working in developing nations. It does mean, however, that if you are conducting *mailed* survey research in the United States, Canada, Western Europe, Australia, New Zealand, or Japan, you should use Dillman's method.

STEPS IN DILLMAN'S METHOD

Step 1. *About professionalism.* Mailed questionnaires must look thoroughly professional. Jaded, hard-bitten, oversurveyed people simply don't respond to amateurish work. Fortunately, with today's word processing, making attractive questionnaire booklets is easy. Use standard-size paper: 8.5″ × 11″ in the U.S. and slightly longer, A4 paper, in the rest of the world. Several researchers have found that light green paper produces a higher response rate than white paper (Fox et al. 1988). I wouldn't use any other colors until controlled tests are made.

You must be thinking: "Controlled tests of *paper color*?" Absolutely. It's because social scientists have done their homework on these little things that a response rate of over 70% is now routine—provided you're willing to spend the time and money it takes to look after all the little things. Read on and you'll see how small-but-important those "little things" are.

Step 2. *Front and back covers.* Don't put any questions on either the front or back covers of the booklet. The front cover should contain a title that provokes the respondent's interest and some kind of eye-catching graphic design. By "provoking interest" I don't mean "threatening." A title like "The Greenville Air Quality Survey" is fine. "Polluted Air Is Killing Us" isn't.

Graphic designs are better than photographs on survey covers. Photos contain an enormous amount of information and you never know how respondents will interpret the information. If a respondent thinks a photo contains an editorial message (in favor of or against some pet political position), then the survey booklet goes straight into the trash.

The front cover should also have the name and return address of the organization that's conducting the survey.

The back cover should contain a *brief* note thanking the respondent and inviting open-ended comments about the questionnaire. Nothing else.

Step 3. *Question order.* Pay careful attention to question order. Be sure that the first question is directly related to the topic of the study (as determined from the title on the front of the booklet), that it is interesting and easy to answer, and that it is nonthreatening. Once

respondents start a questionnaire or an interview, they are very likely to finish it. Introduce threatening questions well into the instrument, but don't cluster them all together.

Put general socioeconomic and demographic questions at the end of a questionnaire. These seemingly innocuous questions are threatening to many respondents who fear being identified (Sudman and Bradburn 1982). Once respondents have filled out a questionnaire, they are unlikely to balk at stating their age, income, religion, occupation, and so on.

Step 4. *Formatting.* Construct the pages of the questionnaire according to standard conventions. Use upper-case letters for instructions to respondents and mixed upper and lower case for the questions themselves. Never allow a question to break at the end of a page and continue on another page. Mailed surveys have to look good and be easily readable or they get tossed out.

Use plenty of paper; don't make the instrument appear cramped. Line answers up vertically rather than horizontally, if possible. This, for example, is not so good:

Strongly approve   Approve   Neutral   Disapprove   Strongly disapprove

This is better:

Strongly approve
Approve
Neutral
Disapprove
Strongly disapprove

It pays to spend time on the physical format of a questionnaire. The general appearance, the number of pages, the type of introduction, and the amount of white (or green) space—all can affect how people respond, or whether they respond at all. Once you've gone to the expense of printing up hundreds of survey instruments, you're pretty much stuck with what you've got.

Use lots of open space in building schedules for personal interviews, too. Artificially short, crowded instruments only result in interviewers missing items and possibly in annoying respondents (imagine yourself sitting for 15 minutes in an interview before the interviewer flips the first page of an interview schedule).

Step 5. *Length.* Keep mailed questionnaires down to 10 pages, with no more than 125 questions. Beyond that, response rates drop (Dillman 1978). Herzog and Bachman (1981) recommend splitting questionnaires in half and alternating the order of presentation of the halves to different respondents to test for response effects of questionnaire length.

It is tempting to save printing and mailing costs and to try to get more questions into a few pages by reducing the amount of white space in a self-administered questionnaire. Don't do it. Respondents are never fooled into thinking that a thin-but-crowded questionnaire is anything other than what it seems to be: a long questionnaire that has been forced into fewer pages and is going to be hard to work through.

Step 6. *The cover letter.* A one-page cover letter should explain, in the briefest possible terms, the nature of the study, how the respondent was selected, who should fill out the questionnaire (the respondent or the members of the household), who is funding the survey, and why it is important for the respondent to send back the questionnaire. ("Your response

to this questionnaire is very important. We need your response because . . .")

The one thing that increases response rate more than any other is university sponsorship (Fox et al. 1988). University sponsorship, though, is not enough. If you want a response rate that is not subject to bias, be sure to address the cover letter directly and personally to the respondent—no "Dear Respondent" allowed—and sign it using a blue ballpoint pen. Ballpoints make an indentation that respondents can see—yes, some people do hold those letters up to the light to check. This marks the letter as having been individually signed.

The cover letter must guarantee confidentiality, and it must explain the presence of an identification number (if there is one) on the questionnaire. Some survey topics are so sensitive that respondents will balk at seeing an identification number on the questionnaire, even if you guarantee anonymity. In this case, Fowler (1984) recommends eliminating the identification number (thus making the questionnaire truly anonymous) and telling the respondents that they simply cannot be identified.

Enclose a printed postcard, with the respondent's name on it, and ask the respondent to mail back the postcard *separately* from the questionnaire. Explain that this will notify you that the respondent has sent in the questionnaire so that you won't have to send the respondent any reminders later on. Fowler found that people hardly ever send back the postcard without also sending back the questionnaire.

Step 7. *Packaging.* Package the questionnaire, cover letter, reply envelope, and postcard in another envelope for mailing to the respondent. Type the respondent's name and address on the mailing envelope. Avoid mailing labels. Use first-class postage on the mailing envelope and on the reply envelope. Some people respond better to real stamps than to metered (even first-class-metered) postage. Hansley (1974) found that using bright commemorative stamps increased response rate.

Step 8. *Inducements.* What about sending people money as an inducement to complete a survey? Mizes et al. (1984) found that offering respondents a dollar to complete and return a questionnaire resulted in significantly increased returns, but offering respondents five dollars did not produce a sufficiently greater return to warrant using this tactic. In 1984, five dollars was close to the value of many respondents' time for filling out a questionnaire. This makes responding to a survey more like a strictly economic exchange and, as Dillman pointed out, makes it easier for people to turn down (1978:16).

Inflation will surely have taken its toll by this time (sending people a dollar in the mail to answer a survey can't possibly buy as much response today as it did in the 1980s), but the point is clear: There is a Goldilocks solution to the problem of how much money to send people as an incentive to fill out and return a survey. If you send people too much money or too little, they throw the survey away. If you send them just the right amount, they are likely to fill out the survey and return it. This finding was confirmed recently by Warriner et al. (1996). They offered people in Ontario, Canada $2, $5, or $10 to send back a mailed survey. Factoring in all the costs of follow-up letters, the $5 incentive produced the most returns for the money.

First-class postage and monetary incentives may seem expensive, but they are cost-effective because they increase the response rate. Whenever you think about cutting corners in a survey, remember that all your work in designing a representative sample goes for nothing if your response rate is low. Random samples cease to be representative unless the people in it respond. Also remember that small monetary incentives may be insulting to some people. This is a cultural and socioeconomic class variable that only you can evaluate in your specific research situation.

Step 9. *Contact and follow-up.* Pay careful attention to contact procedures. Send a letter to each respondent explaining the survey and informing the respondent that a questionnaire will be coming along soon. Send a postcard reminder out to all potential respondents a week after sending out the questionnaire. Don't wait until the response rate drops before sending out reminders. Some people hold onto a questionnaire for a while before deciding to fill it out or throw it away. A reminder after one week stimulates response among this segment of respondents.

Send a second cover letter and questionnaire to everyone who has not responded two weeks later. Finally, four weeks later, send another cover letter *and questionnaire,* along with an additional note explaining that you have not yet received the respondent's questionnaire and stating how important it is that the respondent participate in the study. Heberlein and Baumgartner (1978, 1981) found that sending a second copy of the questionnaire increases response rate 1%-9%. Since there does not appear to be any way to predict whether the increase will be 1% or 9%, the best bet is to send the extra questionnaire.

When you send out the second copy of the questionnaire, send the packet by certified mail. House et al. (1977) showed that certified mail made a big difference in return rate for the second follow-up.

Does All This Really Make a Difference?

❖

Thurman et al. (1993) were interested in the attitudes and self-reported behaviors of people who admit to drunk driving. Using Dillman's total design method, they sent out questionnaires to a national sample of 1,310 and got back 765, or 58%. Not bad for a first pass.

Unfortunately, for lack of time and money, Thurman et al. couldn't follow through with all the extra mailings. Of the 765 respondents, 237 said they were nondrinkers. This left 525 eligible questionnaires for analysis.

Of the 525 respondents who said they were consumers of alcohol, 133 admitted driving while drunk in the past year. Those 133 respondents provided data of intrinsic interest, but the 765 people who responded from the nationally representative sample of 1,310 may be a biased sample on which to base any generalizations. I say "may be" a biased sample because there is no way to tell. And that's the problem.

> *The last interview you get in any survey . . . is always the most costly and it's almost always worth it.*

Mainieri et al. (1997) also used Dillman's method in their survey about "green" (environmentally friendly) buying behavior among middle-class people in Los Angeles. Mainieri et al. mailed out 800 questionnaires and got back 201, or 25%. They sent follow-up postcards to all sample addresses 10 days after the first mailing, but, running out of time and money, they didn't follow through after that and were forced to report results based on a 25% response rate.

The bottom line: The last interview you get in any survey—whether you're sending out questionnaires, doing a phone survey, or contacting respondents for face-to-face interviews—is always the most costly and it's almost always worth it. If you really care about representative data, you won't think of all the chasing around you have to do for the last interviews in a set as a nuisance but as a necessary expense of data collection. And you'll prepare for it in advance by establishing a realistic budget of both time and money.

PRETESTING AND LEARNING FROM MISTAKES

There is no way to emphasize sufficiently the importance of *pretesting* any survey instrument you prepare. No matter how much you do to prepare a culturally appropriate questionnaire, it is absolutely guaranteed that you will have forgotten something important or that you will have

poorly worded one or more vital elements. These glitches can be identified only by pretesting.

If you are building a self-administered questionnaire, bring in at least 6-10 pretest respondents and sit with them as they fill out the entire instrument. Encourage them to ask questions about each item. Your pretest respondents will make you painfully aware of just how much you took for granted, no matter how much ethnographic research you did or how many focus groups you ran before making up a questionnaire.

For face-to-face interviews, do your pretesting under the conditions you will experience when the survey is under way for real. If respondents are going to come to your office, then pretest the instrument in your office. If you are going to respondents' homes, then go to their homes for the pretest.

Never use any of the respondents in a pretest for the main survey. If you are working in a small community, where each respondent is precious (and you don't want to use up any of them on a pretest), take the survey instrument to another community and pretest it there. This will also prevent the pretest respondents in a small community from gossiping about the survey before it

actually gets under way. A "small community," by the way, can be "the 27 students from Taiwan at your university" or all the residents of a small town.

Use all your interviewers in any pretest of a face-to-face interview schedule, and be sure to do some of the pretesting yourself. After the interviewers have done the pretests, bring them together for a discussion on how to improve the survey instrument. As you conduct the actual survey, ask respondents to tell you what they think of the study and of the interview they've just been through.

At the end of the study, bring all the interviewers back together for an evaluation of the project. If it is wise to learn from your mistakes, then the first thing you've got to do is find out what the mistakes are. If you give them a chance, your respondents and interviewers will tell you.

CROSS-SECTIONAL AND LONGITUDINAL SURVEYS

Most surveys are *cross-sectional*. The idea is to **measure some variables at a single time.** Of course, people's attitudes and reported behaviors change over time, and you never know if a single sample is truly representative of the population. Many surveys are conducted again and again to monitor changes and to ensure against picking a bad sample. **Multiple cross-sectional polls use** *longitudinal design*. The daily—even hourly—tracking polls in presidential elections are an extreme example, but in the United States, Canada, Great Britain, Germany, Japan, Israel, and other industrialized countries some questions have been asked of representative samples for many years.

The Gallup Poll, for example, has been asking the following question since 1974: "Do you approve or disapprove of the way Congress is han-

dling its job?" If you think that Americans back then thought better of Congress than they do today, think again. In April 1974, just 30% of Gallup's representative sample of Americans said they approved of the way Congress was doing its job. In October 1997, the number was 36%. In between, the approval rating ranged from a high of 42% (in September 1987) to a low of 18% (in March 1992). At no time since 1974 did 50% or more of Americans approve of the way Congress was doing its job.

The Gallup Poll has been asking Americans to list "the most important problem facing this country today" for about 60 years. The data track the concerns of Americans about unemployment, the quality of education, drugs, street crime, the federal deficit, taxes, health care costs, poverty, racism, AIDS, abortion, and so on. In March 1992, 67% of Gallup's sample said that unemployment was the most important problem in America. In July 1996, just 9% gave that answer. Of course, in 1992, the U.S. was in a recession, while in 1996 the country was experiencing a booming economy.

No surprises here. Still, these data are important because they were collected with the same instrument. People were asked the same question again and again over the years. After several generations of effort, longitudinal survey data have become a treasured resource in the highly industrialized nations.

Panel Studies

Multiple cross-sectional surveys have their own problems. If the results from two successive samples are very different, you don't know if it's because people's attitudes or reported behaviors have changed, or the two samples are very different, or both. To deal with this problem, survey researchers may use the powerful panel design. In a *panel study*, you **interview the exact same people over again.** Panel studies are like true experiments: Randomly selected participants are tracked for their exposure or lack of exposure to a series of interventions in the real world.

To understand this feature of panel studies, consider the work of Jennings and his colleagues (Jennings 1987; Jennings and Markus 1984; Jennings et al. 1991). In 1965, they began a 17-year panel study of American high school seniors. In the first wave of the Youth Parent Socialization Panel Study (YPSPS), they interviewed 1,669 students—a stunning 99% of the sample for the study.

In 1972, when the panelists were around 25 years old, the researchers interviewed 1,348 (80.8%) of the students from the original panel.

By 1982, when the third and final wave of the YPSPS was done, the 1,135 original panel members (68%) who were interviewed were about 35 years old. Jennings was able to track how political orientation changed as the students matured, controlling for things like occupation, education, and other variables (see Jennings et al. 1991; Jennings 1987).

The computer data files from the whole study were deposited with the Inter-University Consortium for Political and Social Research (ICPSR) at the University of Michigan so that researchers can do secondary and comparative analysis (Jennings et al. 1991). (The ICPSR maintains and distributes a huge archive of computer files from social research projects conducted all over the world.)

We can think of involvement in the antiwar and civil rights movements of the 1960s as "interventions" in a classic experiment because the data from all three waves of the YPSPS are from interviews with the same respondents. Sherkat (1998; Sherkat and Blocker 1994) reanalyzed the YPSPS data, looking specifically at (1) the factors that accounted for whether those 1965 high school seniors had been involved in antiwar and civil rights protests, and (2) the factors that affected how political attitudes changed as those baby boomers matured.

In 1968, the U.S. government began the Panel Study on Income Dynamics (PSID) with a representative sample of about 7,000 households. Every year since then, the PSID has reinterviewed the members of the original panel. The PSID has also followed the members of the original households as they moved out and began their own homes (Hill 1992). The data from the PSID are also on file at the ICPSR and have been used in many studies, including research on chronic poverty in the U.S. (Rodgers and Rodgers 1993), studies of the gender gap in wages (Ashraf 1996), and studies of the real cost of the so-called marriage tax (Alm and Whittington 1996).

There are things that only a longitudinal panel design can uncover, and panel studies don't have to be big, national affairs. Griffin (1991) evaluated the effects of automating the work of bank tellers at a big firm in the southwestern United States. In the new system, each teller would have an online terminal. The object was to enhance job performance and job satisfaction at the same time by speeding up routine tasks (like deposits and withdrawals) and giving tellers more autonomy and responsibility. For example, before the intervention, tellers had to get a manager's signature for withdrawals over $100. With the new computer system, tellers could authorize any withdrawal on their own. After all, they could see right at their terminals if a customer had the funds to cover any particular withdrawal.

Griffin measured job satisfaction, job performance, and commitment to the organization at four different times. At time 1, in May, just before the new system went in, Griffin collected questionnaire data from 923 of the 1,047 tellers in the 36 banks that were going to get the system, and from 45 of the 48 tellers in the banks who were going to be left out.

At time 2, in September, after the system was functioning smoothly, Griffin reinterviewed 861 of the 923 tellers who had participated at time 1. At time 3, two years later, he interviewed 790 of the original sample; and finally, at time 4, four years after the intervention, he interviewed 526 of the original sample.

Satisfaction and commitment increased dramatically at time 2—immediately after the new system went in—but dropped back to their preintervention levels by time 4. On the other hand, job *performance* scores were the same at time 2 as at time 1, but increased dramatically by time 3 (two years out) and continued to increase at time 4 (four years out).

But here's the real point of this story: If Griffin had taken measures of satisfaction and perfor-

mance only at times 1 and 2, he would have found that redesigning those tellers' jobs enhanced their satisfaction, but not their performance. If he had taken measures at times 1 and 4, he would have learned that computerization of the tellers' jobs enhanced their performance, but not their job satisfaction. But by taking four measurements and by following the tellers through time, Griffin showed that the tellers' increased job satisfaction was ephemeral and that it takes quite a while before actual increased performance shows up.

Respondent Mortality

Panel studies may suffer from what's called the *respondent mortality* problem. This is where **people drop out between successive waves of the panel survey.** If this happens, and the results of successive waves are very different, you can't tell if that's because of (1) the special character of the drop-out population, (2) real changes in the variables you're studying, or (3) both. For example, if dropouts tend to be male or poor, your results in successive waves will overrepresent the experiences of those who are female or affluent.

Respondent mortality is not always a problem. Roger Trent and I studied riders on the Morgantown, West Virginia "People Mover," an automated transport system that was meant to be a kind of horizontal elevator. You get on a little railway car (they carry only 8 seated and 12 standing passengers), push a button, and the car takes you to your stop—a block away or eight miles across town. The system was brought on line a piece at a time between 1975 and 1980. Trent and I were tracking public support as the system went more places and became more useful (Trent and Bernard 1985). We established a panel of 216 potential users of the system when the system opened in 1975 and reinterviewed the members of that panel in 1976 and 1980 as more and more pieces of the system were added.

All 216 original members of the panel were available during the second wave and 189 were available for the third wave of the survey. Note, though, that people who were unavailable had moved out of Morgantown and were no longer potential users of the system. What counted in this case was maintaining a panel large enough to represent the attitudes of people in Morgantown about the People Mover system. The respondents who stayed in the panel still represented the people whose experiences we hoped to learn about.

Sometimes, panels can be teased out of multiple-wave surveys. Cramer (1996) studied job satisfaction at a British aerospace engineering company. When you study job satisfaction, you pretty much have to guarantee anonymity to respondents if you want to get back any useful data, so Cramer couldn't simply set up a panel and interview them across time. He sent out 1,522 questionnaires to a cross section of the employees at the firm and got back a respectable 1,074, or 71%. In the cover letter that went with the questionnaire, Cramer invited respondents to give the first two letters of their forename, the first two letters of their mother's forename, and the day of the month of their mother's birthday.

In the second wave, Cramer got back 1,068 (71% again) of 1,500 questionnaires. He was able to identify 295 people in the firm who had participated in both waves. Of course, we don't know whether the 295 people who completed both questionnaires represent the work force, but under the circumstances, Cramer did the best he could.

SOME SPECIALIZED SURVEY TECHNIQUES

Factorial Surveys

In a *factorial survey,* respondents are presented with *vignettes* that describe hypothetical social situations and are asked for their judgments about those situations. Here is a typical vignette from a survey conducted by the developer of the method, Peter Rossi (Rossi and Nock 1982):

> You find yourself discussing [your personal life] with a [Black] [male] who is [younger than] you. He is [working class] and is someone who [shares your general religious beliefs]. He is someone who [works where you do] and [generally doesn't vote].
>
> How likely is this to happen to you (circle one)?

Highly likely   I   2   3   4   5   6   7   Highly unlikely

You can make substitutions for each of the bracketed phrases in the vignette. So, another vignette might hypothesize that you are "discussing [business problems] with a [Hispanic] [female] who is [the same age as] you, [wealthy] and is [an atheist], [unemployed], and [generally votes Republican]."

Obviously, each dimension in this situation (socioeconomic class, age, religion, etc.) can have several alternatives. Several thousand vignettes would be needed to cover all the possible combinations, and no survey respondent could deal with all of them. In a factorial survey, however, vignettes like these are created by randomly combining the criteria and giving each respondent a unique questionnaire to deal with.

Over many respondents, a large sample of the combinations of variables in a complex social situation can be dealt with. If 400 respondents each respond to 100 vignettes, you get 40,000 unique judgments to analyze. This technique combines the internal validity features of a randomized experiment with the external validity features of a sample survey. It reduces the size of samples needed for investigating multidimensional phenomena by sampling both situations and people (Rossi and Nock 1982).

Miller et al. (1991) used the factorial survey method to measure perceptions of appropriate prison sentences for felons who had been convicted of 50 typical crimes, ranging from petty theft to murder. Here is one of the vignettes:

> Victor J., a White, employed sewing-machine operator, was convicted of intentionally shooting his friend, Laura L., a housewife. The victim required two weeks' hospitalization. In the last five years, the offender has not been arrested or convicted. The offender claims to have been taking drugs at the time. Victor J. was sentenced to 10 years in prison.
>
> The sentence given was . . .

| Much too low | Low | About right | High | Much too high |

The independent variables in this study combined to form 61,025 vignettes, but each of the 774 respondents in the survey only needed to see 50 randomly selected vignettes. It turns out that people's perception of the seriousness of any given crime (and what the appropriate punishment should be) depends only partly on the consequences of the crime itself. It also depends partly on characteristics of the victim, partly on characteristics of the criminal, and partly on characteristics of the respondent (like whether the respondent had been the victim of a crime).

The General Social Survey, or GSS, is a nationally representative survey of about 1,600 adults. (It's run every year by the National Opinion Research Center at the University of Chicago.) Each respondent in the 1986 GSS saw seven vignettes about poor families to test public opinion about welfare. Jeffry Will (1993) analyzed the GSS vignette data. Here's one of the vignettes that respondents saw:

> This family has four children, the youngest is 6 months old, living with their mother. The mother is divorced. The mother has a college degree and is unemployed and not looking for work because she has no ready means of transportation. The father has remarried and is permanently disabled. The family is likely to face financial difficulties for a couple of years. Her parents cannot afford to help out financially. The family has $1,000 in savings. All in all, the family's total income from other sources is $100 per week.
>
> What should this family's weekly income be? Include both the money already available from sources other than the government and any public assistance support you think this family should get.

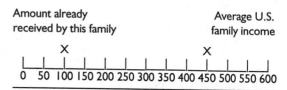

SOURCE: J. A. Will, "The Dimensions of Poverty: Public Perceptions of the Deserving Poor." *Social Science Research*, p. 322. Copyright © 1993, Academic Press, Inc. Reprinted with permission.

There are 10 variables in this vignette (number of children, marital status of the mother, how much savings the family has, the total income of the family, etc.) with 1,036,800 possible combinations. That seems just about right to me. The calculus for any individual's opinion about how much money to award the deserving poor on welfare is really that complicated. If the 1,600 respondents in the GSS saw seven vignettes each, then the survey captured

(1,600 people) (7 vignettes) (10 variables) = 112,000

combinations, which is a sample of about 11% of all the factors that probably go into people's opinion on this issue.

The results of that survey were very interesting. Respondents awarded people who were looking for work a lot more than they awarded people who weren't looking for work. But mothers got only an extra $6 per week for seeking work, while fathers got over $12. And if mothers were unemployed because they wouldn't take minimum-wage jobs, they had their allotments reduced by $20 per week, on average, compared to what people were willing to give mothers who were working full time. (For comparison, it took about $150 in 1998 to buy what $100 bought in 1986.)

The factorial survey combines the validity of randomized experiments with the reliability of survey research and lets you measure subtle differences in opinion.

Time Budgets and Diaries

Time budget surveys have been done all over the world to track how ordinary human beings spend most of their days (Szalai 1972). The idea is to learn about the sequence, duration, and frequency of behaviors and about the contexts in which behaviors take place. Some researchers ask respondents to keep diaries; others conduct "yesterday interviews," in which respondents are asked to go over the last 24 hours and talk about everything they did. Some researchers combine these methods, collecting diaries from respon-

dents and then following up with a personal interview.

Susan Shaw (1992) used time budgets to compare the family activities of mothers and fathers in eastern Canada. She studied 46 middle- and working-class couples who had children living at home. All the fathers were employed full time. Among the mothers, 12 were employed full time, 9 were employed part time, and 25 were full-time homemakers. Both parents kept time diaries for one day during the week and for one day on a weekend.

Then, both parents were interviewed, separately, for one-two hours in their homes. For each activity that they had mentioned, parents were asked if they considered the activity to be work or leisure, and why.

Shaw calculated the amount of time that each parent reported spending with their children—playing with them, reading to them, and so on. The results are in Table 7.2.

The husbands of the 12 women who were employed full time spent an average of 71 minutes per day with their children. The husbands of the 25 full-time homemakers spent just 23 minutes a day with their children. The 12 full-time employed mothers reported spending 97 minutes of each day, on average, with their children—more than the 71 minutes spent by their husbands with the children, but a lot less than the 241 minutes per day that full-time homemakers reported spending with their children. For these middle- and working-class families in eastern Canada, at least, fathers spend a lot more time with their children when their wives work full time. It would be very interesting to see if this finding holds up in other places.

TABLE 7.2 Average Amount of Time That Fathers and Mothers Report Spending with Children, by the Mother's Employment Status

Mother's Employment Status	N	Time with Children per Day (in minutes)	
		Mothers	Fathers
Employed full time	12	97	71
Employed part time	9	144	52
Full-time homemaker	25	241	23
Total	46		

SOURCE: S. Shaw, "Dereifying Family Leisure: An Examination of Women's and Men's Everyday Experiences and Perceptions of Family Time," p. 279, *Leisure Studies* 14. Copyright © 1992, Taylor and Francis. Reproduced by permission.

Like all instruments for collecting self-reports about behavior, time budgets and diaries are subject to **demand characteristics** and other sources of inaccuracy. Some data reported by Niemi (1993) from studies in Finland give us a taste of the problem.

(1) In one study, respondents were asked: How many hours did you work at your main work last week, possible overtime included? (Domestic work is not included in work time.) Respondents also kept diaries for two days in which they recorded all their activities at 10-minute intervals.

These data were scaled up to reflect annual rates. (To scale up the data for one week to a year, you simply multiply results by 52; to scale up data from one day to a year, you multiply each data point by 365. That way, you can compare the results from a week's worth of survey data to two days' worth of diary data.)

The results? Respondents recorded in their diaries working 2.4% fewer hours per week than they reported in the survey. Men reported half of 1% more hours; women reported 4.8% more. Men in agriculture reported 25% more work time

than they recorded, and women in agriculture reported 43% more work time.

(2) In a second study, Niemi compared time-diary data with data from this question: How often do you engage in physical exercise during the summer/wintertime? (This included outdoor recreation, walking and bicycling, organized sports, hunting or fishing, or collecting mushrooms —a broad swath of activities.)

Men reported about 7.4% more minutes per day of physical exercise than they recorded in their diaries. Women reported about 50% more. In fact, women reported exercising about 19% more minutes per day than men reported, but women recorded about 17% fewer minutes per day of physical exercise than men did.

(3) In a third study, respondents were asked: How many times do you think you have visited the library during the past six months? The same respondents kept daily diaries and the two kinds of data were converted to annual rates.

In this case, men and women alike report over 70% more library visits than they record in their diaries.

The discrepancies, as I pointed out in Chapter 6, can be due to many things. Women in Finland may understand that question about physical exercise differently than men do and may be including a lot more of their daily activities in that category than men do. The data from the question about library visits are hardly shocking: People inflate their association with socially desirable activities to make themselves look good. And people in some occupations (like managerial positions) may be subtly trained to more accurately estimate their work time than are people in other occupations (like agriculture).

Michaelson (1985) showed that giving people a checklist increased the number of child care behaviors they reported in "yesterday interviews." Diaries and time budget interviews, particularly with the aid of checklists, appear to be more accurate than 24-hour recall of activities. A lot of work remains to be done on testing the accuracy of activity diaries against data from direct observation. In Chapter 10, we'll look at methods for direct observation and measurement of behavior.

Randomized Response

Randomized response is a technique for estimating the amount of some socially negative behavior in a population—things like shoplifting, extramarital sex, child abuse, and being hospitalized for emotional problems. The technique was introduced by Stanley Warner in 1965 and is particularly well described by Williams (1978:73). It is a simple, fun, and interesting tool. Here's how it works.

First, you formulate two questions, A and B, that can be answered yes or no. One question, A,

is the question of interest (say, "Have you ever shoplifted?"). The possible answers to this question (either yes or no) do not have known probabilities of occurring. That is what you want to find out.

The other question, B, must be innocuous and the possible answers (again yes or no) must have known probabilities of occurring. For example, if you ask a respondent to toss a fair coin and ask, "Did you toss a heads?" then the probability of the respondent answering yes or answering no is 50%. If the chances of being born in any given month were equal, then you could ask respondents, "Were you born in April, May, or June?" and the probability of getting a yes would be 25%. Unfortunately, births are seasonal, so the coin-toss question is preferable.

Let's assume you use the coin toss for question B. You ask the respondent to toss the coin and to note the result *without letting you see it*. Next, have the respondent pick a card, from a deck of 10 cards, where each card is marked with a single integer from 1 to 10. The respondent does not tell you what number he or she picked, either. The secrecy associated with this procedure makes respondents feel secure about answering question A (the sensitive question) truthfully.

Next, hand respondents a card with the two questions, marked A and B, written out. Tell respondents that if they picked a number between 1 and 4 from the deck of 10 cards, they should answer question A. If they picked a number between 5 and 10, they should answer question B.

That's all there is to it. You now have the following: (1) Each respondent knows he or she answered yes or no and which question the respondent answered; (2) you know *only* that a respondent said yes or no but not which question, A or B, was being answered.

If you perform this procedure with a sufficiently large, representative sample of a population, and if respondents cooperate and answer all questions truthfully, then you can calculate the percentage of the population that answered yes to question A. Here's the formula:

$$P_{A \text{ or } B} = (P_{A+} \times P_A) + (P_{B+} \times P_B) \qquad \text{(Formula 7.2)}$$

The percentage of people who answer yes to *either* A or B equals (the percentage of people who answer yes to question A) times (the percentage of times that question A is asked) plus (the percentage of people who answered yes to question B) times (the percentage of times question B is asked).

The only unknown in this equation is the percentage of people who answered yes to question A, the sensitive question. We know, from our data, the percentages of yes answers to *either* question. Suppose that 33% of all respondents said yes to *something*. Since respondents answered question A only if they chose a number from 1 to 4, then A was answered 40% of the time and B was answered 60% of the time. Whenever question B was answered, there was a 50% chance of it being answered yes because that's the chance of getting a heads on the toss of a fair coin. The problem now reads

$$.33 = X(.40) + .50(.60) \text{ or}$$
$$.33 = .40X + .30$$

which means that X equals .08. That is, given the parameters specified in this experiment, if 33% of the sample says yes to either question, then 8% of the sample answered yes to question A.

There are two problems associated with this technique. First, no matter what you say or do, some people will not believe that you can't identify them and will therefore not tell the truth. Bradburn et al. (1979) report that 35% of known offenders would not admit to having been convicted of drunken driving in a randomized response survey. Second, like all survey techniques, randomized response depends on large, representative samples. Since the technique is time-consuming to administer, this makes getting large, representative samples difficult.

Still, the evidence is mounting that for some sensitive questions, when you want the truth, the randomized response method is worth the effort.

———❖

Dalton et al. (1996) asked two groups of professional auctioneers six very sensitive questions about seriously illegal practices. I mean, these were rough questions, like "Have you ever engaged in self-dealing without disclosure?" and "Have you ever engaged in the use of a phantom bid?"

An example of self-dealing without disclosure would be getting your spouse or one of your employees to bid secretly on merchandise you wanted. Phantom bids are bids that the auctioneer acknowledges but that aren't real. You bid $50 for something; the auctioneer recognizes your bid and immediately signals that he has a bid of $60. You up your bid to $70. But the $60 bid was just a gimmick to get you to raise your bid.

One group ($N = 74$) was asked these questions straight out, in the usual way, on a written survey. The other group ($N = 67$) was asked using the randomized response technique. In the conventional survey, 15% of the auctioneers admitted to self-dealing without disclosure and 12% admitted to having engaged in phantom bids. On the randomized response survey, 46% admitted self-dealing and 36% admitted phantom bids. The results across the six questions were pretty consistent: About three times more people admitted these behaviors than did so when responding to a conventional survey.

❖———

If that makes you nervous about auctions, then think about this: Buchman and Tracy (1982) asked two samples of accountants, "Have you ever, whether because of time pressure or other reasons, indicated in any way on the audit working papers that you examined all supporting documents and minor additions (or other increases) to fixed assets, when in fact you did not?" Just 2.6% of the accountants who got asked that question in the usual paper-and-pencil questionnaire way said yes but over 13% said yes when they were asked that question with the randomized response technique.

Scheers and Dayton (1987) gave a standard questionnaire to 194 undergraduates in a large university. The students were asked if they'd ever lied to avoid an exam, lied to avoid a term paper, purchased a term paper, obtained an illegal copy of an exam, or copied answers on an exam. Scheers and Dayton asked 184 other students the same questions, but with the second sample they used the randomized response method. Across all grade-point averages, more students admitted to these behaviors in the randomized response test than in the questionnaire. A lot more. The difference in the rate of admission was as high as 83% (for purchasing a term paper).

Goodstadt et al. (1978) used randomized response to estimate drug use among 800 high school students. No surprise here, either: Randomized response turned up significantly more drug use than was estimated by the usual self-report survey method.

Every time I read in the newspaper that self-reported drug use among adolescents has dropped by such-and-such an amount since whenever-the-last-self-report-survey-was-done, I think about how easy it is for those data to be utter nonsense. And I wonder why the randomized response technique isn't more widely used. Of course, the answer is that it's hard work and all that work produces exactly one number: the percentage of tax cheats or drug users or whatever you're studying. But still . . .

Dietary Recall

Studies of diet and human nutrition rely on informants to recall what they've eaten over the past 24 hours or what they usually eat for various meals. These 24-hour recall tests, or dietary recall interviews, are a specialized kind of structured interview. For an overview of methods, see Pelto et al. (1989). For recent examples, see C. Smith et al. (1996), Chapman et al. (1997), Schoenberg (1997), and Melnik et al. (1998).

CULTURAL DOMAIN ANALYSIS

Cultural domain analysis comprises a set of structured interviewing methods including free lists, pile sorts, triad tests, paired comparisons, and rankings and rating scales. These methods are used in social psychology and cognitive anthropology to study how people in a group think about cultural domains—that is, lists of things that somehow "go together." These can be lists of plants, animals, occupations, symptoms of illness, ways to have sex, and so on. All these things have some physical reality, but people in different cultures may interpret physical reality differently.

The spectrum of colors, for example, has a single physical reality that you can see on a machine. Several Native American peoples, however, identify a color we might call "grue." The word (which is actually used by linguists who study this phenomenon) covers all the colors across the physical spectrum of green and blue.

This does not mean that people who use a word that we gloss as "grue" fail to *see* the difference between things that are the color of grass and things that are the color of a clear sky. They just *label* chunks of the physical spectrum of colors differently than we do. If this seems exotic to you, get a list of, say, 100 lipstick colors and ask college women and men to describe all those colors. You may find, as I have, that most women recognize (and can name) many more colors than do most men.

The structured interviewing methods used in cultural domain analysis are widely used in market research to understand differences in the meaning of symbols to various populations. What do people in various ethnic groups, for example, associate with various options on a new car—options like a sun roof, leather seats, and passenger-side airbags? Two things make these structured interviewing methods very productive for fieldworking social researchers. First, they are fun to use and informants find them fun to respond to. Second, ANTHROPAC software (Borgatti 1992a, 1992b) makes it easy to collect and analyze data using these techniques.

Free Listing

Free listing is a deceptively simple but powerful technique. In free listing, you ask informants to "list all the *X* you know about" or "what kinds of *X* are there?" where *X* might be movie stars, brands of computers, or kinds of motor vehicles.

————❖————

You'd be surprised at how much you can learn from a humble set of free lists. Henley (1969) asked 21 adult Americans (students at Johns Hopkins University) to name as many animals as they

could in 10 minutes. She f
variety of expertise when i
animals. In just this small g
(which didn't even represer
Johns Hopkins University, n
timore or of the United States), the lists ranged in length from 21 to 110, with a median of 55.

In fact, those 21 people named 423 different animals, and 175 were mentioned just once. The most popular animals for this group of informants were dog, lion, cat, horse, and tiger, all of which were named by more than 90% of informants. Only 29 animals were listed by more than half the informants, but 90% of those were mammals. By contrast, among the 175 animals named only once, just 27% were mammals.

But there's more. Previous research had shown that the 12 most commonly talked about animals in American speech are bear, cat, cow, deer, dog, goat, horse, lion, mouse, pig, rabbit, and sheep. There are $N(N-1)/2$, or 66, possible unique pairs of 12 animals (dog-cat, dog-deer, horse-lion, mouse-pig, etc.). Henley examined each informant's list of animals, and for each of the 66 pairs found the difference in order of listing.

That is, if an informant mentioned goats 12th on her list, and bears 32nd, then the distance between goats and bears, for that informant, was $32 - 12 = 20$. This distance was standardized: It was divided by the length of the informant's list, and multiplied by 100. Then Henley calculated the mean distance, over all the informants, for each of the 66 pairs of animals.

The lowest mean distance was between sheep and goats (1.8). If you named sheep, then the next thing you named was probably goats, and if you named goats, then next thing you named was probably sheep. The common expression about "separating the sheep from the goats" was originally a metaphor for separating the righteous from the wicked and has more recently become a metaphor for separating the strong from the weak. The first meaning of the metaphor is first tioned in the Old Testament of the Bible (Ezekiel 34:17), and then again around 600 years later in the New Testament (Matthew 25:31-46).

Henley's respondents were neither shepherds nor students of Western biblical lore, but they all knew that sheep and goats somehow "go together." Free lists tell you *what goes with what,* but you need to dig to understand *why.* Cats and dogs were only 2 units apart in Henley's free lists—no surprise there, right?—while cats and deer are 56 units apart. Deer, in fact, are related to all the other animals on the list by at least 40 units of distance, except for rabbits, which are only 20 units away from deer.

Robert Trotter (1981) reports on 378 Mexican Americans who were asked to name the *remedios caseros,* or home remedies, they knew, and what illnesses each remedy was for. Informants listed a total of 510 remedies for treating 198 illnesses. However, the 25 most frequently mentioned remedies (about 5% of the total) made up about 41% of all the cases, and the 70 most frequently mentioned illnesses (about 36%) were 84% of the cases.

Trotter's free list data reveal a lot about Mexican American perceptions of illness and home cures. He was able to count which ailments were reported more frequently by men and which by women, which ailments were reported more frequently by older people and by younger people, which by those born in Mexico and those born in the United States, and so on.

Free listing is often a prelude to cluster analysis and multidimensional scaling, which we'll get to in Chapter 16. But consider what John Gatewood (1983b) learned from *just* a set of free lists. He asked 40 adult Pennsylvanians to name all the trees they could think of. Then he asked them to

check the trees on their list that they thought they could recognize in the wild. Thirty-seven people (out of 40) listed "oak," 34 listed "pine," 33 listed "maple," and 31 listed "birch." I suspect that the list of trees and what people say they could recognize would look rather different in, say, Wyoming or Mississippi. We could test that.

Thirty-one of the 34 who listed "pine" said they could recognize a pine. Twenty-seven people listed "orange," but only four people said they could recognize an orange tree (without oranges hanging all over it, of course). On average, the Pennsylvanians in Gatewood's sample said they could recognize half of the trees they listed. Gatewood calls this *the loose talk phenomenon.* He thinks that many Americans can name a lot more things than they can recognize in nature.

Does this loose talk phenomenon vary by gender? Suppose, Gatewood says, we ask Americans from a variety of subcultures and occupations to list other things besides trees. Would the 50% recognition rate hold?

Gatewood and a group of students at Lehigh University interviewed 54 informants, all university students, including 27 men and 27 women. The informants free listed all the musical instruments, fabrics, hand tools, and trees they could think of. Then the informants were asked to check off the items in each of their lists that they thought they would recognize in a natural setting.

Gatewood chose musical instruments, with the idea that there would be no gender difference in number of items listed or recognized; he thought that women might name more kinds of fabrics than would men and that men would name more kinds of hand tools than would women. He chose the domain of trees to see if his earlier findings would replicate. All the hypotheses were supported (Gatewood 1984).

Romney and D'Andrade asked 105 American high school students to "list all the names for kinds of relatives and family members you can think of in English" (1964:155). They were able to do a large number of analyses on these data. For example, they studied the order and frequency of recall of certain terms, and the productiveness of modifiers, such as "step-," "half-," "-in-law," "grand-," "great," and so on. They assumed that the nearer to the beginning of a list that a kin term occurs, the more salient it is for that particular informant. By taking the average position in all the lists for each kin term, they were able to derive a rank-order list of kin terms, according to the variable's "saliency."

They also assumed that more salient terms occur more frequently. So, for example, "mother" occurs in 93% of all lists and is the first term mentioned on most lists. At the other end of the spectrum is "grandson," which was mentioned only by 17% of the 105 informants, and was, on average, the 15th, or last, term to be listed. They found that the terms "son" and "daughter" occur on only about 30% of the lists. But remember, these informants were all high school students. It would be interesting to repeat Romney and D'Andrade's experiment on many different American populations. We could then test the saliency of English kin terms on the many subpopulations.

Finally, free listing can be used to find out where to concentrate effort in applied research—that is, as part of a rapid assessment approach. In a project on which I consulted, interviewers asked people on the North Carolina coast how they viewed the possibility of offshore oil drilling. One of the questions was: "What are the things that make life good around here?"

The researchers decided to ask this question after some informal interviews in seven small, seaside towns. People kept saying what a "nice little town this is" and "what a shame it would be if things changed around here." Informants had no difficulty with the question, and after just 20 interviews, the researchers had a list of over 50 "things that make life good around here." The researchers chose the 20 items mentioned by at least 12 informants and explored the meaning of those items further (Institute for Coastal and Marine Resources et al. 1993).

The humble free list has many uses. Use it a lot.

The True-False/Yes-No and Sentence Frame Techniques

Another common technique in cultural domain analysis is called the *sentence frame* or *frame elicitation* method (see also Chapter 12 on text analysis). The method produces true-false or yes-no data.

The frame elicitation method has been used a lot in anthropology to study the distribution of beliefs about the causes of and cures for illnesses (Fabrega 1970; D'Andrade et al. 1972). Linda Garro (1986) used the frame elicitation method to compare the knowledge of curers and noncurers in Pichátaro, Mexico. She used a list of 18 illness terms and 22 causes, based on prior research in Pichátaro (Young 1978). The frames were questions, like "Can _____ come from _____?" Garro substituted names of illnesses in the first blank, and things like "anger," "cold," "overeating," and so on in the second blank. (ANTHROPAC has a routine for building questionnaires of this type.) This produced an 18×22 yes-no matrix for each of the informants. The matrices could then be added together and submitted to analysis by multidimensional scaling (see Chapter 16).

James Boster and Jeffrey Johnson (1989) used the frame substitution method in their study of how recreational fishermen in the United States categorize ocean fish. They asked 120 fishermen to consider 62 belief frames, scan down a list of 43 fish (tarpon, silver perch, Spanish mackerel, etc.), and pick out the fish that fit each frame. Here are a few of the belief frames:

The meat from _____ is oily tasting.

It is hard to clean _____ .

I prefer to catch _____ .

That's $43 \times 62 = 2,666$ judgments by each of 120 informants, but informants were usually able to do the task in less than half an hour (J. Johnson, personal communication). The 62 frames, by the way, came straight out of ethnographic interviews where informants were asked to list fish and to talk about the characteristics of those fish.

Gillian Sankoff (1971) studied land tenure and kinship among the Buang, a mountain people of northeastern New Guinea. The most important unit of social organization among the Buang is the *dgwa,* a kind of descent group, like a clan. Sankoff wanted to figure out the very complicated system by which men in the village of Mambump identified with various *dgwa* and with various named garden plots.

The Buang system was apparently too complex for bureaucrats to fathom, so, to save administrators a lot of trouble, the men of Mambump had years earlier devised a simplified system that they presented to outsiders. Instead of claiming that they had ties with one or more of five different *dgwa,* they each decided which of the two largest *dgwa* they would belong to, and that was that as much as the New Guinea administration knew.

To unravel the complex system of land tenure and descent, Sankoff made a list of all 47 men in the village, and all 140 yam plots that they had used over the recent past. Sankoff asked each man to go through the list of men and identify which *dgwa* each man belonged to. If a man belonged to more than one, then Sankoff got that information, too. She also asked her informants to identify which *dgwa* each of the 140 garden plots belonged to.

As you might imagine, there was considerable variability in the data. Only a few men were uniformly placed into one of the five *dgwa* by their peers. But by analyzing the matrices of *dgwa*

membership and land use, Sankoff was able to determine the core members and peripheral members of the various *dgwa.*

She was also able to ask important questions about intracultural variability. She looked at the variation in cognitive models among the Buang for how land use and membership in descent groups were related. Sankoff's analysis was an important milestone in our understanding of the measurable differences between individual culture and shared culture. It supported Goodenough's (1965) notion that cognitive models are based on shared assumptions but that ultimately they are best construed as properties of individuals.

Techniques like true-false and yes-no tests that generate nominal-level data are easy to construct, especially with the use of a computer program like ANTHROPAC, and can be administered to a large number of informants. Frame elicitation in general, however, can be quite boring, both to the informant and to the researcher alike. Imagine, for example, a list of 25 animals (mice, dogs, antelopes, . . .), and 25 attributes (ferocious, edible, nocturnal, . . .).

The structured interview that results from such a test involves a total of 625 (25×25) questions to which an informant must respond—questions like "Is an antelope edible?" "Is a dog nocturnal?" "Is a mouse ferocious?" People can get pretty exasperated with this kind of silliness. So be careful about cultural relevance when doing frame elicitations and true-false tests. It is essential to have a good ethnographic grounding in the local culture to select domains, items, and attributes that make sense to people.

Triad Tests

In a ***triad test,*** you show people three things and tell them, "Choose the one that doesn't fit," "Choose the two that seem to go together best," or "Choose the two that are the same." The things can be photographs, actual plants, or 3×5 cards with names of people on them. (Respondents often ask, "What do you mean by things being 'the same' or 'fitting together'?" Tell them that you are interested in what *they* think that means.) By doing this for all triples from a list of things or concepts, you can explore differences in cognition among individuals, and among cultures and subcultures.

Suppose you ask a group of Americans to "choose the item that is least like the other two" in each of the following triads:

Whale	Dolphin	Moose
Shark	Dolphin	Moose

All three items in the first triad are mammals, but two of them are sea mammals. A few people would choose "dolphin" as the odd item because "whales and mooses are both big mammals and the dolphin is smaller." Most people I know, however, would choose "moose" as the most different. In the second triad, many of the same people who chose "moose" in the first triad will choose "shark" because moose and dolphins are both mammals, and sharks are not.

But some people who chose "moose" in triad 1 will choose "moose" again because sharks and dolphins are sea creatures, while moose are not. Giving people a judiciously chosen set of triad stimuli can help you understand interindividual similarities and differences in how people think about the items in a cultural domain.

The triad test was developed in psychology (see Kelly 1955; Torgerson 1958) and has long been used in cognitive studies across the social sciences. Kirk and Burton (1977) used it to study personality traits, and Alvarado (1996) used it to test consensus among U.S. undergraduates about the meaning of various facial expressions.

Romney and D'Andrade (1964) presented people with triads of American kinship terms and asked them to choose the term that was most *dissimilar* in each triad. For example, when they presented informants with the triad "father, son, nephew," 67% selected "nephew" as the most different of the three items. Twenty-two percent chose "father" and only 2% chose "son." Romney and D'Andrade asked people to explain why they'd selected each item on a triad. For the triad "grandson, brother, father," for example, one informant said that a "grandson is most different because he is moved down further" (p. 161). There's a lot of cultural wisdom in that statement.

By studying which pairs of kinship terms their informants chose most often as being similar, Romney and D'Andrade were able to isolate some of the salient components of the American kinship system (components such as male vs. female, ascending vs. descending generation, etc.). They were able to do this, at least, for the group of informants they used. Repeating their tests on other populations of Americans, or on the same population over time, would yield interesting comparisons.

Lieberman and Dressler (1977) used triad tests to examine intracultural variation in ethnomedical beliefs on the Caribbean island of St. Lucia. They wanted to know if cognition of disease terms varied with bilingual proficiency. They used 52 bilingual English-Patois speakers, and 10 monolingual Patois speakers. From ethnographic interviewing and cross-checking against various informants, they isolated nine disease terms that were important to St. Lucians.

Here's the formula for finding the number of triads in a list of N items:

$$\text{The number of triads in } N \text{ items} = \frac{N(N-1)(N-2)}{6} \quad \text{(Formula 7.3)}$$

In this case, N is 9, so there are 84 possible triads.

Lieberman and Dressler gave each of the 52 bilingual informants two triad tests, a week apart: one in Patois and one in English. (Naturally, they randomized the order of the items within each triad, and also randomized the order of presentation of the triads to informants.) They also measured how bilingual their informants were, using a standard test. The 10 monolingual Patois informants were simply given the triad test.

The researchers counted the number of times that each possible pair of terms was chosen as most alike among the 84 triads. (There are $N(N - 1)/2$ pairs or $(9 \times 8)/2 = 36$ pairs.) They divided the total by seven (the maximum number of times that any pair appears in the 84 triads). This produced a similarity coefficient, varying between 0.0 and 1.0, for each possible pair of disease terms. The larger the coefficient for a pair of terms, the closer in meaning are the two terms. They were then able to analyze these data among English-dominant, Patois-dominant, and monolingual Patois speakers.

It turned out that when Patois-dominant and English-dominant informants took the triad test in English, their cognitive models of similarities among diseases was similar. When Patois-dominant speakers took the Patois-language triad test, however, their cognitive model was similar to that of monolingual Patois informants.

This is a very interesting finding. It means that Patois-dominant bilinguals manage to hold on to two distinct psychological models about diseases and that they switch back and forth between them, depending on what language they are speaking. By contrast, the English-dominant group displayed a similar cognitive model of disease terms, irrespective of the language in which they are tested.

The Balanced Incomplete Block Design for Triad Tests

Typically, the terms that go into a triad test are generated by a free list, and typically the list is much too long for a triad test. There are 84 stimuli in a triad test containing 9 items. But with just 6 more items, the number of decisions an informant has to make jumps to 455. At 20 items, it's a mind-numbing 1,140.

Free lists of illnesses, ways to prevent pregnancy, advantages of breast-feeding, places to go on vacation, and so on easily produce 60 items or more. Even a selected, abbreviated list may be 20 items.

This led Burton and Nerlove (1976) to develop the *balanced incomplete block design,* or BIB, for the triad test. BIBs take advantage of the fact that there is a lot of redundancy in a triad test. Suppose you have just four items, 1, 2, 3, 4, and you ask informants to tell you something about *pairs* of these items (for example, if the items were vegetables, you might ask, "Which of these two is less expensive?" or "Which of these two is more nutritious?" or "Which of these two is easier to cook?"). There are exactly 6 pairs of four items (1-2, 1-3, 1-4, 2-3, 2-4, 3-4), and the informant sees each pair just once.

But suppose that instead of pairs you show the informant triads and ask which two out of each triple are most similar. There are just four triads in four items (1-2-3, 1-2-4, 2-3-4, 1-3-4), but each item appears $(N - 1)(N - 2)/2$ times, and each pair appears $N - 2$ times. For four items, there are $N(N - 1)/2 = 6$ pairs; each pair appears twice in four triads, and each item on the list appears three times.

It is all this redundancy that reduces the number of triads needed in a triad test. If you want each pair to appear just once (called a "lambda 1" design) instead of seven times in a triad test involving nine items, then, instead of 84 triads, only 12 are needed. If you want each pair to appear just twice (a "lambda 2" design), then 24 triads are needed. For analysis, lambda 2 designs are much better than lambda 1s. Table 7.3 shows the lambda 2 design for nine items. For 10 items, a lambda 2 design requires 30 triads; for 13 items, it requires 52 triads; for 19 items, 114 triads; and for 25 items, 200 triads. In literate societies, most

TABLE 7.3   Balanced Incomplete Block Designs for Triad Tests Involving 9 and 10 Items

For 9 items, 24 triads are needed, as follows: Items		For 10 items, 30 triads are needed, as follows: Items	
1, 5, 9	1, 2, 3	1, 2, 3	6, 8, 9
2, 3, 8	4, 5, 6	2, 5, 8	7, 10, 3
4, 6, 7	7, 8, 9	3, 7, 4	8, 1, 10
2, 6, 9	1, 4, 7	4, 1, 6	9, 5, 2
1, 3, 4	2, 5, 9	5, 8, 7	10, 6, 7
5, 7, 8	3, 6, 8	6, 4, 9	1, 3, 5
3, 7, 9	1, 6, 9	7, 9, 1	2, 7, 6
2, 4, 5	2, 4, 8	8, 10, 2	3, 8, 9
1, 6, 8	3, 5, 7	9, 3, 10	4, 2, 10
4, 8, 9	1, 5, 8	10, 6, 5	5, 6, 3
3, 5, 6	2, 6, 8	1, 2, 4	6, 1, 8
1, 2, 7	3, 4, 9	2, 3, 6	7, 9, 2
		2, 4, 8	8, 4, 7
		4, 9, 5	9, 10, 1
		5, 7, 1	10, 5, 4

SOURCE: M. L. Burton and S. B. Nerlove, "Balanced Design for Triad Tests." *Social Science Research*, p. 5. Copyright © 1976, Academic Press. Reprinted by permission.

informants can respond to 200 triads in less than 15 minutes.

Unfortunately, there is no easy formula for choosing *which* triads in a large set to select for a BIB. Fortunately, Burton and Nerlove (1976) worked out various lambda BIB designs for up to 21 items and Borgatti (1992a) has incorporated BIB designs into ANTHROPAC. You simply tell ANTHROPAC the list of items you have, select a design, and tell it the number of informants you want to interview. ANTHROPAC then prints out a randomized triad test, one for each informant. (Randomizing the order in which the triads appear to informants eliminates "order effects"—possible biases that come from responding to a list of stimuli in a particular order.)

Boster et al. (1987) used a triad test and a pile sort in their study of the social network of an office. There were 16 employees, so there were 16 "items" in the cultural domain ("the list of all the people who work here" is a perfectly good domain). A lambda 2 test with 16 items has 80 distinct triads. Informants were asked to "judge which of three actors was the most different from the other two."

Triad tests are easy to create with AN-THROPAC, easy to administer, and easy to score, but they can only be used when you have relatively few items in a cultural domain. Also, people sometimes find triad tests to be boring. Use the triad test method when you have just a few items in a domain. Use the pile sort method to look at the cognitive organization of a large cultural domain. I find that informants easily handle lambda 2 triad tests with 9-15 items, and pile sorts with 40-60 items.

Pile Sorts

Typically, *pile sorts* are done with cards or slips of paper. Each card has the name of a thing or a concept written on it. Once again, the items are gleaned from a free list that defines a cultural domain. Informants are asked to "sort these cards into piles, putting things that are similar together in a pile."

Two questions that informants often ask are: "What do you mean by 'similar'?" and "Can I put something in more than one pile?" The answer to the first question is, "Well, whatever *you* think is similar. We want to learn what you think about these things. There are no right or wrong answers."

The easy answer to the second question is no, just because there is one card per item and a card can only be in one pile at a time. This answer cuts off a lot of information, however, because informants can think of items in a cultural domain along several dimensions at once. For example, in a pile sort of consumer electronics, an informant might want to put a VCR in one pile with TVs (for the obvious association) and in another pile with camcorders (for another obvious association) but might not want to put camcorders and TVs in the same pile. You can make up a duplicate card on the spot if you want, and fortunately, the ANTHROPAC software makes easy work of handling this during analysis. An alternative is to ask the informant to do *multiple pile sorts* of the same object.

The P-3 Game

In a series of papers, John Roberts and his co-workers used pile sorts and rating tasks to study how people perceive various kinds of behaviors in games (see, e.g., Roberts and Chick 1979; Roberts and Nattrass 1980). One "game," studied by Roberts et al. (1981), is pretty serious: searching for foreign submarines in a P-3 airplane. The P-3 is a four-engine, turboprop, low-wing aircraft that can stay in the air for long periods of time and cover large patches of ocean. It is also used for search-and-rescue missions. Making errors in flying the P-3 can result in career damage and embarrassment at least, and injury or death at worst.

Roberts et al. isolated 60 named pilot errors, through extensive unstructured interviews with navy pilots of the P-3. (This is the equivalent of extracting a free list from your interviews.) Here are a few of the errors: flying into a known thunderstorm area; taking off with the trim tabs set improperly; allowing the prop wash to cause damage to other aircraft; inducing an autofeather by rapid movement of power-level controls. The researchers asked 52 pilots to do an unrestricted pile sort of the 60 errors and to *rate* each error on a 7-point scale of seriousness.

They also asked their informants to rank a subset of 13 errors on four criteria that were chosen on the basis of unstructured interviews: (1) how much each error would "rattle" a pilot, (2) how badly each error would damage a pilot's career, (3) how embarrassing each error would be to commit, and (4) how much "fun" it would be to commit each error. Flying into a thunderstorm on purpose, for example, could be very damaging to a pilot's career, and extremely embarrassing if he had to abort the mission and turn back in the middle. But if the mission turned out to be successful, then taking the risk of committing a very dangerous error would be a lot of fun for pilots who are "high self-testers" (Roberts, personal communication).

Inexperienced pilots rated "inducing an autofeather" as more serious than did highly experienced pilots. Inducing an autofeather is more embarrassing than it is dangerous and is the sort of error that experienced pilots just don't make. On the other hand, as the number of air hours increased, so did pilots' view of the seriousness of "failure to use all available navigational aids to determine position." Roberts et al. suggested that inexperienced pilots might not have had enough training to assess the seriousness of this error correctly.

The Lumper and Splitter Problem

Most researchers use the *free pile sort* method (also called the **unconstrained pile sort** method), where informants are told that they can make as many piles as they want, so long as they don't make a separate pile for each item or lump the items into one pile. Like the triad test, the free pile sort presents a common set of stimuli to informants. But here, the informants manage the information and put the items together as they see fit. The result is that some informants will make many piles, others will make few. This is known as the *lumper-splitter problem* (Weller and Romney 1988:22).

In a pile sort of animals, for example, some informants will put all the following together: giraffe, elephant, rhinoceros, zebra, wildebeest. They'll explain that these are the "African animals." Others will put giraffe, elephant, and rhino in one pile, and the zebra and wildebeest in another, explaining that one is the "large African animal" pile and the other is the "medium-sized African animal pile."

Some informants will have singleton piles, explaining that each singleton is unique and doesn't go with the others. It's fine to ask informants why they made each pile of items, but wait until they finish the sorting task so you don't interfere with their concentration. And don't hover over informants. Find an excuse to walk away for a couple of minutes after they get the hang of it.

Pile Sorts with Objects

Although pile sorts are typically done with cards or slips of paper, they can also be done with objects. James Boster (1987) studied the structure of the domain of birds among the Aguaruna Jívaro of Peru. He paid people to bring him specimens of birds, and he had the birds stuffed. He built a huge table out in the open, laid the birds on the table, and asked the Aguaruna to sort the birds into groups.

Carl Kendall led a team project in El Progreso, Honduras, to study beliefs about dengue fever (Kendall et al. 1990). Part of their study involved a pile sort of the nine most-common flying insects in the region. They mounted specimens of the insects in little boxes and asked people to group the insects in terms of "those that are similar." Some anthropologists have used photographs of objects as stimuli for a pile sort.

Borgatti (1992b:6) points out that asking someone to sort photographs of objects (or actual objects) rather than cards with the names of object can produce different results. Imagine sorting 30 photographs of automobiles (sports cars, pickup trucks, minivans, etc.). Seeing the photos, you might classify the vehicles on the basis of physical form or function. If you sorted cards with stimuli like "Alpha Romeo coupe," "Dodge minivan," "Mercedes sedan," and so on, you might do the sort on other criteria, like price, prestige, desirability. "If you are after shared cultural beliefs," says Borgatti, "I recommend keeping the stimulus as abstract as possible" (ibid.).

Pile Sorts and Taxonomic Trees

Pile sorting is an efficient method for generating *taxonomic trees* (Werner and Fenton 1973). Simply hand informants the familiar pack of cards, each of which contains some term in a cultural domain. Informants sort the cards into piles, according to whatever criterion makes sense to them. After the first sorting, informants are handed each pile and asked to go through the exercise again. They keep doing this until they say that they cannot subdivide piles any further. At each sorting level, informants are asked if there is a word or phrase that describes each pile.

Perchonock and Werner (1969) used this technique in their study of Navajo animal categories. After an informant finished doing a pile sort of animal terms, Perchonock and Werner built a branching tree diagram (like the one shown in

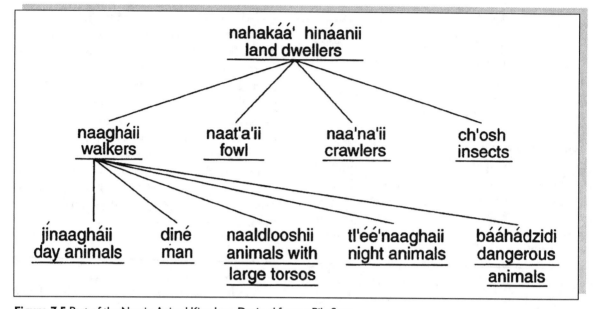

Figure 7.5 Part of the Navajo Animal Kingdom, Derived from a Pile Sort

SOURCE: N. Perchonock and O. Werner, "Navajo Systems of Classification: Some Implications of Food." *Ethnology* 8. Copyright © 1969. Reprinted by permission.

Figure 7.5) from the data. They would ask the informant to make up sentences or phrases that expressed some relation between the nodes. They found that informants intuitively grasped the idea of tree representations for taxonomies. (For more about folk taxonomies, see Chapter 13.)

Pile Sorts and Networks

I've used pile sorts to study the social structure of institutions such as prisons, ships at sea, and bureaucracies, and also to map the cognitively defined social organization of small communities. I simply hand people a deck of cards, each of which contains the name of one of the people in the institution, and ask informants to sort the cards into piles, according to their own criteria. The results tell me how various components of an organization (managers, production workers, advertising people; guards, counselors, prisoners;

seamen, deck officers, engine room personnel; or men and women in a small Greek village) think about the social structure of the group. Instead of "what goes with what," I learn "who goes with who."

Informants usually find pile sorting fun to do. Asking informants to explain why people appear in the same pile produces a wealth of information about the cognitively defined social structure of a group.

Rankings

Rank ordering produces interval-level data, though not all behaviors or concepts are easy to rank. Hammel (1962) asked people in a Peruvian village to rank order the people they knew in terms of prestige. By comparing the lists from different informants, Hammel was able to determine that the men he tested all had a similar view of the social hierarchy. Occupations can easily be rank ordered on the basis of prestige, or lucrativeness.

Or even accessibility. The instructions to respondents would be, "Here is a list of occupations. Please rank them in order, from most likely to least likely that your daughter will have this occupation." Then ask respondents to do the same thing for their sons. (Be sure to assign people randomly to doing the task for sons or daughters first.) Then compare the average ranking of accessibility against some independent variables and test for intracultural differences among ethnic groups, genders, age groups, and income groups.

Weller and Dungy (1986) studied breast-feeding among Hispanic and Anglo women in southern California. They asked 55 informants for a free list of positive and negative aspects of breast- and bottle-feeding. Then they selected the 20 most frequently mentioned items in this domain and converted the items to neutral, similarly worded statements. A few examples: "A way that doesn't tie you down, so you are free to do more things"; "A way that your baby feels full and satisfied"; "A way that allows you to feel closer to your baby."

Next, Weller and Dungy asked 195 women to rank the 20 statements. The women were asked which statement was most important to them in selecting a method of feeding their baby, which was the next most important to them, and so on. In the analysis, Weller and Dungy were able to relate the average rank order for Hispanics and for Anglos to independent variables like age and education.

Paired Comparisons

The method of *paired comparisons* is an alternative way to get rank orderings of a list of items in a domain. If you have a list of 14 items, there are $N(N-1)/2$, or $14(13)/2 = 91$, pairs of items. You write out a list of all the pairs (A and B, A and C, . . . , B and C, . . . , F and J, etc.). Show informants each pair and ask them to circle the item that conforms to some criterion. You might say: "Here are two animals. Which one is the more ____?" where the blank is filled in by "vicious" or "wild" or "smarter" or some other descriptor. You could ask informants to choose the "illness in this pair that is more life threatening," "the food in this pair that is better for you," or "the crime in this pair that you're most afraid of."

In a list of 14 items, each item appears 13 times (A and B, A and C, A and D, etc., down through A and N). To find the rank order of the list for each informant, you simply count up how many times each item "wins"—that is, how many times each item was circled. If cancer is on a list of illnesses, and the criterion is "life threatening," you expect to find it circled each time it is paired with another illness—except, perhaps, when it is paired with AIDS. Since this is so predictable, it's not very interesting. It gets really interesting when you have illnesses like diabetes and high blood pressure on your list and you compare the average rank ordering among various ethnic groups.

The paired-comparison technique has a lot going for it. People make one judgment at a time, so it's much easier on them than asking them to do a rank ordering of a list of items. Also, you can use paired comparisons with nonliterate informants by reading the list of pairs to them, one at a time, and recording their answers. Weller and Dungy (1986) did that in their study of breast-feeding.

Like triad tests, paired comparisons can only be used with a relatively limited number of items in a domain. With 20 items, for example, informants have to make 190 judgments. Fortunately, there are BIB designs for paired comparisons, just as there are for triad tests (see above). ANTHRO-

PAC produces individual paired-comparison tests and lets you select a BIB design.

Rating Scales

Everyone is familiar with *rating scales*—all those *agree-disagree, approve-disapprove* instru-ments that populate the surveys we've been filling out all our lives. Rating scales are powerful data generators. They are so powerful and so ubiqui-tous that they deserve a whole chapter—which comes up next.

KEY CONCEPTS

Chapter 7
Summary

SUMMARY

❖ There are two broad categories of methods for structured interviewing: questionnaires, used in survey research, and a range of methods used in cultural domain analysis. There are three methods for collecting survey questionnaire data: (1) personal, face-to-face interviews; (2) self-administered questionnaires; and (3) telephone interviews.

  ◆ There is no perfect data-collection method. Self-administered questionnaires are preferable when you are dealing with literate respondents; you are confident of getting a response rate of at least 70%; and the questions you want to ask do not require the use of visual aids such as cue cards, charts, and the like.

  ◆ Face-to-face interviews are preferred when you need answers to all or nearly all the questions in a particular survey.

  ◆ Telephones are widely used in countries where at least 80% of the population has its own telephone.

❖ Multiple interviewers allow a larger sample, but any problems associated with interviewer bias are increased with more than one interviewer. If you hire interviewers, use professionals if you can. Be sure to train all interviewers—and monitor them throughout the research.

❖ Experiments continue on the efficacy of open- vs. closed-ended questions. Since closed-ended items are so efficient, most survey researchers prefer them to open-ended questions and use them whenever possible. There is no rule against mixing question types.

❖ There are well-understood rules that all survey researchers follow in constructing questionnaire items. Some important rules include

  • Questions must be unambiguous.

  • The vocabulary must be appropriate to the respondents.

  • There must be a clear purpose for every question.

  • Scales and filter questions must be clear and well packaged.

  • Never use loaded or double-barreled questions.

❖ Survey instruments can be translated using the back translation method. This may be combined with the Delphi technique.

❖ Low response rate hurts the validity of surveys. There are ways to adjust in the data analysis phase of research for nonresponse bias, but it's much better to increase response rate in the first place.
  ◆ Dillman's total design method requires paying attention to many details, but it can increase response rate dramatically.

❖ Always pretest survey instruments, and never use any of the respondents in a pretest for the main survey.

❖ Surveys can be cross-sectional or longitudinal. Daily tracking polls in presidential elections in the U.S. are an extreme example of longitudinal surveys. Randomly selected panels are an especially powerful form of longitudinal survey. Because the same people are interviewed again and again, randomly selected panel studies share many features of true experiments.
  ◆ Some specialized methods include factorial surveys, based on vignettes; time budgets and diaries; dietary recall; and the randomized response technique.

❖ Cognitive studies of cultural domains involve methods like free listing, pile sorting, triad tests, sentence frames, paired comparisons, and rankings and rating scales.
  ◆ Pile sorts are also used in building taxonomic trees and in network studies.

EXERCISES

1. A survey research firm has landed a contract to run a statewide survey on the question "What should be done with the $4 billion the state will receive from the tobacco settlement?" The survey will be done by mailed questionnaire. Write the cover letter for this questionnaire.

2. For this next exercise, get a group of two or three students together. Replicate Henley's (1969) study: Ask 30-40 people to free list all the animals they can think of in one minute. Analyze the lists to discover the most popular animals and also to see if there are clear packaging effects in how people remember animals. Look for clumpings of domestic animals, pets, wild animals, birds, fishes, and so on. If you have access to the AN-THROPAC software (Borgatti 1992a, 1992b), you can use it to analyze lists like these very quickly.

3. What's wrong with each of these questionnaire items?

   Do you agree or disagree that the United States shouldn't construct the proposed new antiballistic-missile system?

   ( ) Agree   ( ) Disagree

   Where do you get most of your information about current events in the nation and the world?

   ( ) Radio   ( ) Newspapers   ( ) Magazines

   Why do you think big cars are a bad thing for America?

   Why did you decide to go to college?

   ( ) I had a thirst for more knowledge.

   ( ) I wanted to get a better understanding of the world.

   ( ) I was too lazy to get a job.

   Do you agree or disagree that the trouble with welfare is that people get too comfortable and don't want to go back to work, so the government should institute some job-training programs for people on welfare and then set a limited amount of time in which they can learn work skills and get a job?

   ( ) Agree   ( ) Disagree

   Many people these days have come to see marijuana as being far less harmful than tobacco and they urge that its use be made legal. Do you agree or disagree with those people?

   ( ) Agree   ( ) Disagree

At what age were you toilet trained?

( ) Before six months

( ) Betwen six months old and nine months old

( ) Between nine months old and one year old

( ) Between one year old and one and a half years old

( ) Between one and a half years old and two years old

( ) Between two years old and three years old

( ) Older than three years old

( ) Not applicable

How much money do you make? $ _____/_____.

4. We've all spent a good part of our lives on the phone, but good telephone interviewing skills are not easy to come by. Here's one way. Get four or five students together, all of whom agree to be part of a training group. Use any published telephone survey for this exercise. Have each person in the group interview *one other* person on the phone. Don't allow people to interview each other.

   You don't need to run a whole interview. Five minutes' worth will do. Tape-record each interview. Then get together in a group and listen to the interviews together. You'll quickly hear the mistakes that others make and they will quickly hear yours. Soon enough, though, you'll start hearing your own mistakes.

   Be sure to have everyone sign an agreement that lays out the details of this exercise. Specify clearly that the interviews will be recorded. Specify clearly that everyone in the group will hear all the interviews. Decide among yourselves whether you want to keep or destroy the tapes when the exercise is over and put whatever you decide into the agreement. Clear the agreement with your school's Institutional Review Board (IRB). If your school receives any federal funds, you've got an IRB, the function of which is to judge the ethical and legal standing of research proposals.

FURTHER READING

Questionnaire design. For more on the design of questions, see Foddy (1993) and Schuman and Presser (1981). Compared to research on response effects due to age, sex, race, and so on, surprisingly little research has been done on the differences between open-ended and forced-choice survey questions. See Converse (1984) for an interesting discussion of the history of this problem. See Chyba (1993) for examples of the questionnaires used in the National Health Interview Surveys. See Schwarz (1999) for a discussion of how the form of a question can influence the response.

Telephone interviews. For step-by-step instructions on planning and conducting telephone interview studies, consult Frey (1989) and Lavrakas (1993).

Computer-assisted interviews. Ferriter (1993) compared psychiatric social histories done by people and by computer. He found fewer discrepancies with known facts about the patients' lives in the data from the computer-assisted interviews. Apparently, some people, at least, are more willing to be candid about events in their lives when they are interviewed by a machine than when they are interviewed by a live human being. This finding is corroborated by Turner et al. (1998). For some cautions about computer-assisted interviews, see Bloom (1998).

Interviewer training. For more on this problem, see Cannell et al. (1975), Groves and Mathiowetz (1984), Mathiowetz and Cannell (1980), and Oskenberg et al. (1986). See Marcus et al. (1994) for an example of how researchers incorporated systematic training of interviewers into a study of public attitudes toward smoking.

Response rates. For more on response rates in questionnaires, see Yammarino et al. (1991:628). For a detailed analysis of nonresponse in a major survey, see Monaco et al. (1997).

Translation and back translation. Abdel-Khalek (1998) reports on the use of back translation to develop a useful Arabic version of the Beck Depression Inventory. Bravo et al. (1993) report on the use of back translation in converting the DISC (Diagnostic Interview Schedule for Children) into Spanish.

Factorial survey. For more examples of the factorial survey design, see Byers and Zeller (1998) on whether respondent characteristics (like gender or political party affiliation) affect people's judgment about the seriousness of elder abuse, Hunter and McClelland (1991) on evaluating the relative seriousness of sexual harassment behaviors, and Love and Thurman (1991) on assessing what people think is the relative health risk of various behaviors.

Randomized response. The randomized response technique is attractive for asking sensitive questions. Wimbush and Dalton (1997), for example, used this method to assess the rate of theft among employees who have ready access to cash (or supplies or merchandise that can be converted easily to cash). Still, people can still cheat with the randomized response technique. Clark and Desharnais (1998) discuss a method for avoiding this problem.

Time budgets. Michaelson's (1985) book on the time budgets of employed women in Toronto is very useful because it contains his entire survey instrument. Bishop and Syme (1995) studied the relation between people's perceived time budget and their perceived quality of life in Australia. Tiefenthaler (1997) compared the reported time budgets of mothers and fathers in the Philippines.

Delphi technique. Campostrini and McQueen (1993) used the Delphi technique to build an index that would measure risk of exposure to HIV from sexual behaviors. The Delphi method is used across the social sciences to identify desirable outcomes in applications. White et al. (1997), for example, used the method to identify the successful elements in marriage and family therapy. Pollard and Tomlin (1995) used the 50 state teachers of the year in the U.S. as a Delphi panel to establish and prioritize the areas of education that they thought were most in need of change over the next 10 years.

Cultural domain analysis. For further reading, consult Weller and Romney (1988) and Werner and Schoepfle (1987), and for handling the actual chores of data collection and analysis, consult the ANTHROPAC software (Borgatti 1992a, 1992b).

Triad tests and **paired comparisons.** These tests are widely used in cognitive studies. For an example of how they are used to study children's cognitive development, see Callanan et al. (1994). See Alvarado (1994) for use of these methods in the study of how people recognize emotions in faces.

Pile sorts. For detailed instructions on conducting pile sorts, triad tests, and other systematic methods for collecting cultural domain data, see Weller and Romney (1988). Trotter and Potter (1993) used pile sorts in assessing the risk of AIDS among Navajo teenagers. Hines (1993) argues for combining pile sorts, triad tests, and so on with questionnaire surveys in cross-cultural social psychology.

8 | SCALES AND SCALING

IN THIS CHAPTER:

◈ INTRODUCTION

This chapter is about building and using composite measures. I'll cover five kinds of composite measures: (1) indexes, (2) Guttman scales, (3) Likert scales, (4) semantic differential scales, and (5) direct magnitude scales. The first four are the most commonly used in social research today. The fifth, magnitude scaling, is less common, but it's very interesting, and it will give you an idea of the clever things that are going on in the field of scaling these days. First, though, some basic concepts of scaling.

SIMPLE AND COMPLEX SCALES

Simple Scales: Single Indicators

A *scale* is **a device for assigning units of analysis to categories of a variable.** The assignment is usually done with numbers, and questions are used a lot as scaling devices. Here are three typical scaling questions:

(1) How old are you?

You can use this question to assign individuals to categories of the variable "age." In other words, you can *scale* people by age. The number that this first question produces has ratio properties (someone who is 50 is twice as old as someone who is 25).

(2) How satisfied are you with your classes this semester? Are you satisfied, neutral, or unsatisfied?

You can use this question to assign people to one of three categories of the variable "satisfied." That is, you can *scale* them according to how satisfied they are with their classes. Suppose we let *satisfied* = 3, *neutral* = 2, and *unsatisfied* = 1. Someone who is assigned the number 3 is more satisfied

than someone who is assigned the number 1. We don't know if that means 3 times more satisfied or 10 times or just marginally more satisfied, so this scaling device produces numbers that have ordinal properties.

(3) Do you consider yourself to be Protestant, Catholic, Jewish, Muslim, some other religion? Or do you consider yourself as having no religion?

This scaling device lets you assign individuals to—that is, *scale them* by—categories of the variable "religious affiliation." Let *Protestant* = 1, *Catholic* = 2, *Jewish* = 3, *Muslim* = 4, and *no religion* = 5. The numbers produced by this device have nominal properties. You can't add them up and find the average religion.

These three questions have different content (they tap different concepts), and they produce numbers with different properties, but they have two very important things in common. All three questions are devices for scaling people and in all three cases the respondent is the principal source of measurement error.

When you use your own judgment to assign units of analysis to categories of a scaling device, *you* are the major source of measurement error. In other words, if you assign individuals by your own observation to the category "male" or "female," then any mistakes you make in that assignment (scaling people by sex) are yours.

The same is true no matter what the unit of analysis is. Suppose you have a list of 100 countries and your job is to assign each to a category of government (parliamentary republic, constitutional monarchy, dictatorial monarchy, military dictatorship, etc.). For each country, you have some literature—scholarly books and articles, stories from the *New York Times,* reports from the U.S. State Department, and so on. You read each of these, looking for clues about the nature of governance, and assign a number (1, 2, 3, etc.) to each country. Each country is a unit of analysis and is scaled on the nominal variable called "predominant type of government."

Later, in the analysis, you might ask a question like "Are democracies less likely to go to war with one another than, say, dictatorships?" Any mistakes you make in assigning the countries to a category of government will affect the relations you find (or don't find) in your analysis.

Complex Scales: Multiple Indicators

So, a single question on a questionnaire is technically a scale if it lets you assign the people you're studying to categories of a variable. A lot of really interesting variables in social science, however, are complex and can't easily be assessed with single indicators. What single question could you ask people to measure the amount of stress they are experiencing? Their overall political orientation, from far left to far right? How much they value physical attractiveness compared to other characteristics in potential marriage partners? How prejudiced they are against Asian immigrants on the job?

We try to measure complex variables like these with complex instruments—that is, instruments that are made up of several indicators. In fact, these instruments are what we *usually* call scales.

A standard social science concept is "socioeconomic status," or SES. It is often measured by combining measures of income, education, and occupational prestige. Each of these measures is an operationalization of the concept SES, but none of the measures, by itself, captures the complexity of the idea of "socioeconomic status." Each indicator captures a piece of the concept, and together the indicators produce a single measurement of SES.

> *Composite measures, or complex scales, are used when single indicators won't do the job.*

Now, by Ockham's razor, we would never use a complex scale to measure something when a simple scale will do. Suppose you ask people some questions to find out how they feel about growing old. If their income alone predicts their responses to the growing-old attitude questions, then there's no point in making the scale more complex. Often, though, a complex measure of SES predicts attitudes better than single indicators do.

One more time, then: The function of *single indicator* scales is **to assign units of analysis to categories of a variable.** The function of *composite measures,* or complex scales, is exactly the same, but they are **used when single indicators won't do the job.**

INDEXES

The most common composite measure is a *cumulative index*. This is **made up of several items, all of which count the same.** Indexes are everywhere. The Dow Jones Industrial Average is an index of the prices of 30 stocks that are traded on the New York Stock Exchange. The U.S. Consumer Price Index is a measure of how much it costs to buy a fixed set of consumer items in the United States. We use indexes to measure people's health risks: the risk of contracting HIV, of getting lung cancer, of having a heart attack, of giving birth to an underweight baby, of becoming an alcoholic, of suffering from depression, and on and on.

And, of course, we use indexes with a vengeance to measure cognitive and physical functions. Children in the industrial societies of the world begin taking intelligence tests, achievement tests, and tests of physical fitness practically from the first day they enter school. Achievement indexes—like the SAT, ACT, and Graduate Record Exam (GRE)—affect the lives of everyone in our society, to the point where there is a thriving industry devoted to helping children and adolescents do well on these tests.

Indexes can be *criterion referenced* or *norm referenced*. You probably already know about these two methods for scoring indexes. If you've ever taken a test where the only way to get an A was to get at least 90%, you've had your knowledge of some subject assessed by a criterion-referenced index. If you've ever taken a test where getting an A required that you score in the top 10% of the class—even if the highest grade in the class was 78%—then you've had your knowledge of some subject assessed by a norm-referenced index.

Standardized tests (whether of achievement, performance, or personality traits) are usually norm referenced: Your score is compared to the norms that have been established by thousands of people who took the test before you.

How Indexes Work

Multiple-choice exams are cumulative indexes, and since we're all familiar with these beasts, they're a good vehicle for understanding how indexes work. The idea is that asking just one question about the material in a course would not be a good indicator of students' knowledge of the material. Instead, students typically are asked a bunch of multiple-choice questions.

Taken together, the reasoning goes, all the questions measure how well a student has mastered a body of material. If you take a test that has 60 multiple-choice questions and you get 45 correct, you get 45 points, one for each correct answer. That number, 45 (or 75%), is a cumulative index of how well you did on the test.

Note that in a cumulative index, it makes no difference *which* items are assigned to you. In a test of just 10 questions, for example, there are obviously just 10 ways to get one right—but there are 45 ways to get two right, 120 ways to get three right, and so on. Students can get the same score of 80% on a test of 100 questions and miss entirely different sets of 20 questions. This makes cumulative indexes *robust*—they **provide many ways to get at an underlying variable** (in the case of an exam, the underlying variable is knowledge of the material).

On the other hand, stringing together a series of items to form an index doesn't guarantee that the composite measure will be useful—any more than stringing together a series of multiple-choice questions guarantees that a test will fairly assess a student's knowledge of, say, sociology or political science.

We pretend that (1) knowledge is a *unidimensional* variable; (2) a fair set of questions is chosen to represent knowledge of some subject; and therefore, (3) a cumulative index is a fair test of the knowledge of that subject. We know that the system is imperfect, but we pretend in order to get on with life.

We don't have to pretend. When it comes to scaling units of analysis on complex constructs—like scaling countries on the construct of freedom or people on the construct of political conservatism—we can test the unidimensionality of an index with a technique called Guttman scaling.

GUTTMAN SCALES

In a *Guttman scale,* as compared to a cumulative index, **the measurements for the items have a particular pattern indicating that the items measure a unidimensional variable.** To understand the pattern we're looking for, consider the following three questions.

(1) How much is 124 plus 14?
(2) How much is 1/2 + 1/3 + 1/5 + 2/11?
(3) If $3x = 133$, then how much is x?

If you know the answer to question 3, you probably know the answer to questions 1 and 2. If you know the answer to question 2, but not to 3, it's still safe to assume that you know the answer to question 1. This means that, in general, "knowledge about basic math" is a unidimensional variable.

Suppose you're studying worker alienation in a factory. Is alienation a unidimensional variable? After running a focus group and talking to some of the union leaders, you decide on three indicators of alienation: signing a recent petition against new work rules, calling in sick a lot, and having filed a grievance against management in the past year. You look at each worker in the factory and assign her or him one point for each of these three indicators.

In a cumulative index, a worker who has any two points (it doesn't matter which two) is more

alienated than a worker who has just one or no points. There are three ways to score two points: You could have indicators 1 and 2, or indicators 2 and 3, or indicators 1 and 3. To test whether the indicators you've identified form a unidimensional, or Guttman, scale, set up a table like Table 8.1. It's not pretty.

Respondents 1, 2, and 3 scored positive on all three items. The next three respondents (4, 5, and 6) signed the petition and call in sick regularly, but haven't filed any grievances in the past year. Respondent 7 signed the petition, but did not call in sick and did not file a grievance. And respondents 8 and 9 have no alienation points on this scale. They have not signed the petition, have not called in sick a lot, and have not filed a grievance. So far so good.

The next three (10, 11, 12) called in sick, but have neither signed a petition nor filed a grievance. The next three (13, 14, 15) have filed grievances, but have neither signed the petition nor called in sick a lot. Finally, respondent 16 signed the petition and filed a grievance, but does not tend to call in sick.

If we had data from only the first nine respondents, the data would form a perfect Guttman scale. For those first nine respondents, in other words, the three behaviors (signing a petition, calling in sick, and filing a grievance) are indicators of a unidimensional variable, worker alienation.

TABLE 8.1 An Index That Scales with a Guttman Coefficient of Reproducibility Less Than 0.90

Respondent	Signed a Petition	Called in Sick a Lot	Filed a Grievance
1	+	+	+
2	+	+	+
3	+	+	+
4	+	+	−
5	+	+	−
6	+	+	−
7	+	−	−
8	−	−	−
9	−	−	−
10	−	+	−
11	−	+	−
12	−	+	−
13	−	−	+
14	−	−	+
15	−	−	+
16	+	−	+

The Coefficient of Reproducibility

Unfortunately, we've got those other seven respondents to deal with. For whatever reasons, respondents 10-16 do not conform to the pattern seen in respondents 1-9. The data for respondents 10-16 are "errors" in the sense that their data diminish the extent to which the index of alienation forms a perfect scale. To test how closely any set of index data reproduces a perfect scale, apply Guttman's *coefficient of reproducibility,* or CR. The formula for Guttman's CR is

$$CR = 1 - \text{No. errors} / \text{No. entries} \qquad \text{(Formula 8.1)}$$

Given the pattern in Table 8.1, we don't expect to see those minus signs in column 1 for respondents 10, 11, and 12. If the data scaled according

to our hypothesis, then anyone who called in sick a lot and didn't file a grievance should have signed a petition, as is the case with respondents 4, 5, and 6. *Those* respondents have a score of 2. It would take three corrections to make cases 10, 11, and 12 conform to the hypothesis (you'd have to replace the minus signs in column 1 with pluses for respondents 10, 11, and 12), so we count cases 10, 11, and 12 as having one error each.

We don't expect to see the plus signs in column 3 for respondents 13, 14, and 15. If our hypothesis were correct, anyone who has a plus in column 3 should have all pluses, and a score of 3 on alienation. If we give respondents 13, 14, and 15 a scale score of 3 (for having filed a grievance), then those three cases would be responsible for *six* errors—you'd have to stick two pluses in for each of the cases to make them come out according to the hypothesis. (Yes, you could make it just three, not six, errors, by sticking a minus sign in column 3. Some researchers use this scoring method, but I prefer the more conservative method of scoring more errors. Keeps you on your toes.)

Finally, we don't expect that minus sign in column 2 of respondent 16's data. That case creates just one error (you only need to put in one plus to make it come out right). All together, that makes 3 + 6 + 1 = 10 errors in the attempt to reproduce a perfect scale. For Table 8.1, the CR is

$$1 - (10/48) = .79$$

which is to say that the data come within 21% of scaling perfectly. By convention, a coefficient of reproducibility of .90 or greater is accepted as a significant approximation of a perfect scale (Guttman 1950). I'm willing to settle for around .85, especially with the conservative method for scoring errors, but .79 just isn't up to it, so these data fail the Guttman test for unidimensionality.

Some Examples of a Guttman Scale

Christopher Mooney and Mei-Hsien Lee (1995) studied the history of abortion law reform. The 1973 *Roe v. Wade* decision by the U.S. Supreme Court affirmed a woman's right to abortion during the first six months, though allowing states to ban it during the final trimester. This decision didn't just happen all at once.

Before 1973, abortion was outlawed in all 50 states, but it was legal in some states when carrying the fetus to term was a threat to the woman's life. Beginning in the 1950s, various groups began working to get states to enact regulation reform and to make abortion legal under more and more circumstances. The first state in this era to enact regulation reform was Mississippi in 1966. By the time the *Roe v. Wade* decision came down, 17

other states had enacted some kind of legislation reforming the regulation of abortion.

Mooney and Lee (1995) found that the laws in these 18 states formed a perfect Guttman scale, based on four successively more liberal conditions. In addition to cases involving threats to the woman's life, abortion would be legal (1) when the pregnancy resulted from rape or incest, (2) when the fetus was defective or there was a risk to the woman's physical health, (3) when there was a threat to the woman's mental health, and (4) whenever a woman decided she wanted one.

Table 8.2 shows the data. When you collect data on cases, you don't know what (if any) pattern will emerge, so you pretty much grab cases and code them for traits in random order. If you grabbed cases in chronological order, for example, you wouldn't see the perfect pattern of pluses and minuses in Table 8.2.

When you have the data in a table, the first thing to do is arrange the pluses and minuses in their "best" order—the order that conforms most to the perfect Guttman scale—and compute the CR. We look for the trait that occurs most frequently (the one with the most pluses across the row) and place that one at the bottom of the matrix. Then we look for the next-most-frequent trait, and put it on the next-to-the-bottom row of the matrix.

We keep doing this until we rearrange the data to take advantage of whatever underlying pattern is hiding in the matrix. Then we count up the "errors" in the matrix and compute Guttman's coefficient of reproducibility. For these 18 states and four traits, the coefficient is a perfect 1.0, and all 18 cases can be ranked on the degree of permissiveness regarding abortion.

Obviously, if a state allows abortion on demand, it allows it in all specific cases, so it gets a scale score of 4. If a state allows abortion in cases where the woman's mental health is at risk, then it allows abortion in cases where the woman's physical health is at risk and in cases of rape or

TABLE 8.2 A Guttman Scale of Abortion Law during the 1960s and 1970s for 18 States in the United States

State	Year of Reform	Rape or Incest	Defect in Fetus or Threat to Woman's Physical Health	Threat to Woman's Mental Health	On Demand	Scale Score on Permissiveness
MS	1966	+	−	−	−	1
AR	1969	+	+	−	−	2
FL	1972	+	+	−	−	2
GA	1968	+	+	−	−	2
CA	1967	+	+	+	−	3
CO	1967	+	+	+	−	3
NC	1967	+	+	+	−	3
MD	1968	+	+	+	−	3
DE	1969	+	+	+	−	3
KS	1969	+	+	+	−	3
NM	1969	+	+	+	−	3
SC	1970	+	+	+	−	3
VA	1970	+	+	+	−	3
OR	1969	+	+	+	−	3
AK	1970	+	+	+	+	4
HI	1970	+	+	+	+	4
NY	1970	+	+	+	+	4
WA	1970	+	+	+	+	4

SOURCE: Constructed from data in C. Z. Mooney and M.-H. Lee, "Legislating Morality in the American States: The Case of Pre-Roe Abortion Regulation Reform." *American Journal of Political Science* 39: 599-627. Copyright © 1995. Reprinted by permission of the University of Wisconsin Press.

incest, so it gets a scale score of 3; and so on. (The actual work of arranging the data and counting the errors is done by computer. See, for example, ANTHROPAC, in Appendix F.)

What this means is that when it came to abortion, permissiveness during the 1960s and early 1970s in the U.S. was a unidimensional variable. That's nice to know, but there's more. The scale scores in Table 8.2 have a Spearman's rank-order correlation of .44 with the year of reform, and this correlation was statistically significant (see Chapter 15 for more on correlation). This is support for the theory of incremental policy reform in political science.

According the theory, as pressure builds for some reform, one or two states lead the way with tentative steps. Other states hang back and watch the results. Then there is a rush of states that follow and the steps are less tentative. Finally, all the states that are going to take the steps have done so and the process goes back to a slow pace again, as the remaining states hang back and assess the situation some more.

The process is evident in Table 8.2. Mississippi led off with a small step in 1966. By 1970, 17 states had enacted reform, but it would take two more years before the 18th state, Florida, would join, and that state reversed the trend to more and more liberal reform by enacting less permissive legislation than the 10 states before it had done.

Kelloway and Barling (1993) were interested in measuring the amount of participation by workers in their unions. This is an area of research with a long history, and Kelloway and Barling wanted to establish a unidimensional scale of union participation so they could use that scale in other research. They tested seven items on three groups of union members in Canada: 551 members of a national union of airline employees; 229 members of the clerical and technical staff of a university; and 323 unionized members of the faculty and staff at two other universities in Ontario, who responded to two waves of a survey, six months apart.

Kelloway and Barling tested a set of seven items as a possible Guttman scale for the variable "participation in union activities." The seven items were, in decreasing order of difficulty:

(1) Hold union office
(2) Serve on union committees
(3) Attend union meetings
(4) Talk to union leaders
(5) Vote in union elections
(6) Vote in other votes
(7) Read union literature

These seven items scaled in all three groups with a coefficient of reproducibility >.90. And in the group that was tested twice, the CR was stable. Multiple tests, across different groups in different parts of the country and repeated twice over six months, give the Kelloway and Barling scale of union participation credibility.

DeWalt (1979) used Guttman scaling to test his index of material style of life in a Mexican farming community. He scored 54 informants on whether they possessed eight material items (a radio, a stove, a sewing machine, etc.) and achieved a remarkable CR of .95. This means that, *for his data,* the index of material style of life is highly reliable and differentiates among informants.

An early example of a Guttman scale is the Bogardus Social Distance Scale, developed by Emory Bogardus in 1925. Of course, since Guttman didn't describe his method for testing the unidimensionality of a scale until 1944, the Bogardus scale is not usually called a Guttman scale, but a Guttman scale it is, nevertheless.

Bogardus showed people names of ethnic groups and asked them, for each group, which of the following seven opinions they agreed with most: "I would be willing to accept members of this group: (1) as kin through marriage; (2) as personal friends; (3) as neighbors; (4) as co-workers; (5) as citizens of their country; (6) only as visitors to their country; 7) under no condition, not even as visitors to my country." Some version of this scale has been used in dozens of studies over the years, so there is now a substantial literature on racial and ethnic distance (see Owen et al. 1981; McAllister and Moore 1991).

Data Scale, Variables Don't

Remember, only data scale, not variables. If the items in a cumulative index form a Guttman scale with 0.90 CR or better, we can say that, *for the sample we've tested,* the concept measured by the index is unidimensional. That is, the items are a composite measure of one, and only one, underlying concept. DeWalt's data show that, for the informants he studied, the concept of "material style of life" is unidimensional (at least for the indicators he used).

I want to make it absolutely clear that the unidimensionality of an index is *sample dependent.* The Guttman technique is a way to test whether unidimensionality holds for a particular set of data. An index must be checked for its Guttman scalability each time it is used on a population. My hunch is that DeWalt's material style of life scale has its analog in nearly all societies. The particular list of items that DeWalt used in rural Mexico won't scale in a middle-class neighborhood of Chicago, but *some* list of material items will scale there. You just have to find them.

The way to do this is to code every household in your study for the presence or absence of a list of material items. The particular list could emerge from focus groups or from participant observation or from informal interviews. Then you'd use a program like ANTHROPAC to sort out the matrix, drop some material items, and build the material index that has a *CR* of 0.90 or better.

Indexes That Don't Scale

Indexes that do not scale can still be useful in comparing populations. Dennis Werner (1985) studied psychosomatic stress among Brazilian farmers who were facing the uncertainty of having their lands flooded by a major dam. He used a 20-item stress index developed by Berry (1976).

Since the index did not constitute a unidimensional scale, Werner could not differentiate among his informants (in terms of the amount of stress they were under) as precisely as DeWalt could differentiate among his informants (in terms of their quality of life). But farmers in Werner's sample gave a stress response to an average of 9.13 questions on the 20-item test, while Berry had found that Canadian farmers gave stress responses on an average of 1.79 questions. It is very unlikely that a difference of such magnitude between two *populations* would occur by chance.

LIKERT SCALES

Perhaps the most commonly used form of scaling is attributed to Rensis Likert (1932). Likert introduced the ever-popular 5-point scale that we talked about in Chapter 7 on questionnaire construction. Recall that a typical question might read as follows:

> Please consider the following statements carefully. After each statement, circle the answer that most reflects your opinion. Would you say you agree a lot with the statement, agree a little, are neutral, disagree a little, or disagree a lot with each statement?

The 5-point scale might become 3 points or 7 points, and the *agree-disagree* scale may become *approve-disapprove, favor-oppose,* or *excellent-bad,* but the principle is the same. These are all *Likert-type scales.*

I say "Likert-type scales" rather than just "Likert scales" because Likert did more than just introduce a format. He was interested in measuring internal states of people (attitudes, emotions, orientations), and he realized that most internal states are multidimensional. "Political orientation," for example, has an economic dimension, a domestic policy dimension, a foreign policy dimension, and what we might label a "personal behavior" dimension. Likert was after a way to tease apart the various dimensions and to see which dimensions hung together.

A person who is fiscally liberal on matters of domestic policy—favoring government-supported health care, for example—may be quite conservative on matters of foreign policy—against involvement in foreign military actions under almost any circumstances. Someone who is liberal on matters of foreign policy—favoring economic aid for all democracies that ask for it—may be quite conservative on matters of personal behavior—against equal protection under the law for homosexuals.

The "liberal or conservative on matters of personal behavior" dimension is also complicated. There's no way to assign people to a category of this variable by asking one question. People can have live-and-let-live attitudes about sexual preference and extramarital sex, and be against a woman's right to an abortion on demand.

Of course, there are packaging effects. People who are conservative on one dimension of political orientation are *likely* to be conservative on other dimensions, and people who are liberal on one kind of personal behavior are *likely* to be liberal on others. Still, no single question lets you scale people in general on a variable as complex as "attitude toward personal behavior," let alone "political orientation." That's why we need composite scales.

Steps in Building a Likert Scale

Likert's method was to take a long list of possible scaling items for a concept and find the subsets that measured the various dimensions. If the concept was unidimensional, then one subset would do. If it was multidimensional, then several subsets would be needed. Here are the steps in building and testing a Likert scale.

Step 1. Identify and label the variable you want to measure. This is generally done by induction—that is, from your own experience (Spector 1992:13). After you work in some area of research for a while, you'll develop some ideas about the variables you want to measure. The people you talk to in focus groups, for example, may impress you with the idea that "people are afraid of crime around here," and you decide to scale people on the variable "fear of crime."

You may observe that some people love to poke around for hours in malls, while others prefer picking up the telephone to buy all their clothes and gifts. Some people seem to have a black belt in shopping, while others would rather have root canal surgery than set foot in a mall. The task is, then, to scale (measure) people on a variable you might call "shopping orientation" with all its multidimensionality. You may need a subscale for "shopping while on vacation," another just for "car shopping," and another for "shopping for clothing that I really need." (The other way to identify variables is by deduction. This generally involves analyzing similarity matrices, about which more in Chapter 16.)

Step 2. Write a long list of indicator questions or statements. This is usually another exercise in induction. Ideas for the indicators can come from reading the literature on whatever research problem has captured you, from personal experience, from ethnography, from reading newspapers, from interviews with experts.

Free lists are a particularly good way to get at indicators for some variables. If you want to build a scaling device for the concept of "attitudes toward growing old," you could start by asking a large group of people to "list things that you associate with growing old" and then you could build the questions or statements in a Likert scale around the items in the list.

Be sure to use both negative and positive indicators. If you have a statement like "One of the great things about this university is the emphasis on consistently winning sports teams," then you need a negatively worded statement for balance, like "One of the bad things about this university is the emphasis they put on sports."

And don't make the indicator items extreme. Here's a badly worded item: "The emphasis on sports is the most terrible thing that has ever happened here." Let your respondents tell *you* where they stand by giving them a range of response choices (*strongly agree-strongly disagree*). Don't bludgeon people with such strongly worded scale items that they feel forced to reduce the strength of their response.

In wording items, all the cautions from Chapter 7 on questionnaire design apply: Remember who your respondents are and use *their* language. Make the items as short and as uncomplicated as possible. No double negatives. No double-barreled items. Here is a terrible item:

On a scale of 1 to 5, how much do you agree or disagree with the following statement: "People should speak English and give up any language they brought with them when they came to this country."

People can agree or disagree with both parts of this statement, or agree with one part and disagree with the other.

When you get through, you should have four or five times the number of items you think you'll need in your final scale. If you want a scale of, say, 6 items, use 25 or 30 items in the first test (DeVellis 1991:57).

Step 3. Determine the type and number of response categories. Some popular response categories are *agree-disagree, favor-oppose, helpful-not helpful, many-none, like me-not like me, true-untrue, suitable-unsuitable, always-never,* and so on. Most Likert scale items have an odd number of response choices: three, five, or seven. The idea is to give people a range of choices that includes a midpoint.

The midpoint usually carries the idea of neutrality—neither agree nor disagree, for example. An even number of response choices forces informants to "take a stand," while an odd number of choices lets informants "sit on the fence."

There is no best format. But if you ever want to combine responses into just two categories (*yes-no, agree-disagree, like me-not like me*), then it's better to have an even number of choices. Otherwise, you have to decide whether the neutral responses get collapsed with the positive answers or the negative answers—or thrown out as missing data.

Step 4. Test your item pool on some respondents. Ideally, you need at least 100—or even 200—respondents to test an initial pool of items (Spector 1992:29). This will ensure that (1) you capture the full variation in responses to all your items, and (2) the response variability represents the variability in the general population to which you eventually want to apply your scale.

Step 5. Conduct an *item analysis* to find the items that form a unidimensional scale of the variable you're trying to measure. More on item analysis coming up next.

Step 6. Use your scale in your study and run the item analysis again to make sure that the scale is holding up. If it does, then look for relations between the scale scores and the scores of other variables for persons in your study.

Item Analysis

Item analysis is the key to building scales. The idea is to find out, among the many items you're testing, which need to be kept and which should be thrown away. The set of items that you keep should tap a single social or psychological dimension. In other words, the scale should be unidimensional.

In the next few pages, I'm going to walk through the logic of building scales that are unidimensional. Read these pages very carefully. At the end of this section, I'll advocate using *factor analysis* to do the item analysis quickly, easily, and reliably. No fair, though, using factor analysis for scale construction until you understand the logic of scale construction itself.

There are three steps to doing an item analysis and finding a subset of items that constitute a unidimensional scale: (1) scoring the items, (2a) taking the *interitem correlation* and (2b) *Cronbach's alpha,* and (3) taking the *item-total correlation.*

1. Scoring the Responses

The first thing to do is make sure that all the items are properly scored. Assume that we're trying to find items for a scale that measures the strength of support for formal training in research methods among sociology students. Here are two potential scale items:

Training in multivariate statistics should be required for all undergraduate students of sociology.

1	2	3	4	5
Strongly disagree	Disagree	Neutral	Agree	Strongly agree

Sociology undergraduates don't need training in multivariate statistics.

1	2	3	4	5
Strongly disagree	Disagree	Neutral	Agree	Strongly agree

You can let the big and small numbers stand for any direction you want, but you must be consistent. Suppose we let the bigger numbers (4 and 5) represent support for training in multivariate statistics and let the smaller numbers (1 and 2) represent lack of support for that concept. Respondents who circle *strongly agree* on the first item get a 5 for that item. Respondents who circle *strongly agree* on the second item get scored as 1.

2a. Taking the Interitem Correlation

Next, test to see which items contribute to measuring the construct you're trying to get at, and which don't. This involves two calculations: the intercorrelation of the items and the correlation of the item scores with the total scores for each informant. Here are the scores for three people on three items, where the items are scored from 1 to 5.

	Item 1	Item 2	Item 3
Person 1	1	3	5
Person 2	5	2	2
Person 3	4	1	3

To find the *interitem correlation,* we would look at all pairs of columns. There are three possible pairs of columns for a three-item matrix:

	Pair 1		Pair 2		Pair 3	
	Item 1	Item 2	Item 1	Item 3	Item 2	Item 3
	1	3	1	5	3	5
	5	2	5	2	2	2
	4	1	4	3	1	3
Σ_d (sum of the differences)	8		8		4	
Σ_d / max_d	0.67		0.67		0.33	
$1 - (\Sigma_d / max_d)$	0.33		0.33		0.67	

A simple measure of how much these pairs of numbers are alike or unalike involves, first, adding up their *actual differences,* Σ_d, and then dividing this by the total *possible differences,* $\max_d$.

In the first pair, the actual difference between 1 and 3 is 2; the difference between 5 and 2 is 3; the difference between 4 and 1 is 3. The sum of the differences is $\Sigma_d = 2 + 3 + 3 = 8$.

For each item, there could be as much as 4 points difference—in pair 1, someone could have answered 1 to item 1 and 5 to item 2, for example. So for three items, the total possible difference, $\max_d$, would be $4 \times 3 = 12$. The actual *difference* is 8 out of a possible 12 points, so items 1 and 2 are $8/12 = 0.67$ *different,* which means that these two items are $1 - (\Sigma_d / \max_d) = 0.33$ *alike.* Items 1 and 3 are also 0.33 alike, and items 2 and 3 are 0.67 alike.

Items that measure the same underlying construct should be related to one another. If I answer "strongly agree" to the statement "Training in multivariate statistics should be required for all undergraduate students of sociology," then (if I'm consistent in my attitude and if the items that tap my attitude are properly worded) I should strongly disagree with the statement "Sociology undergraduates don't need training in multivariate statistics." If everyone who answers "strongly agree" to the first statement answers "strongly disagree" to the second, then the items are perfectly correlated.

2b. Cronbach's Alpha

Cronbach's alpha is a statistical test of how well the items in a scale are correlated with one another. One of the methods for testing the unidimensionality of a scale is called the *split-half reliability* test. If a scale of, say, 10 items were undimensional, all the items would be measuring parts of the same underlying concept. In that case, any 5 items should produce scores that are more or less like the scores of any other 5 items. Like this:

	A Score on items 1-5	B Score on items 6-10
Person 1	x_1	y_1
Person 2	x_2	y_2
Person 3	x_3	y_3
.	.	.
.	.	.
.	.	.
Person N	x_n	y_n
	Total for A	Total for B

There are many ways to split a group of items into halves (see Box 8.1), and each split will give you a different set of totals. On average, though, the totals for all possible split-half tests should be fairly similar. Cronbach's **coefficient alpha** tests this.

Box 8.1
Split Halves and
the Combinations Rule

To select n elements from a set of N elements, paying no attention to the ordering of the elements, the formula is

$$\frac{N!}{n!\,(N-n)!} \qquad \text{(Formula 8.2)}$$

There are 252 ways to select 5 elements from a group of 10 elements, so there are 252 ways to split a group of 10 items into two groups of 5 each. For 20 items, there are 184,756 possible splits of 10 each. Cronbach's alpha provides a way to get the average of all these split-half calculations directly.

The formula for Cronbach's alpha is

$$\alpha = N\rho/[1 + \rho(N - 1)] \qquad \text{(Formula 8.3)}$$

The symbol ρ (the Greek letter rho) in the formula stands for the average correlation among all pairs of items being tested.

By convention, a good set of scale items should have a Cronbach's alpha of 0.80 or higher. Be warned, though, that if you have a long list of scale items, the chances are good of getting a high alpha coefficient. An interitem correlation of just .14 produces an alpha of .80 in a set of 25 items (DeVellis 1991:92).

Eventually, you want an alpha coefficient of 0.80 or higher for a *short* list of items, all of which hang together and measure the same thing. Cronbach's alpha will tell you if your scale hangs together, but it won't tell you which items to throw away and which to keep. To do that, you need to identify the items that do not discriminate between people who score high and people who score low on the total set of items.

3. Finding the Item-Total Correlation

First, find the total score for each person. Add up each respondent's scores across all the items. Suppose there are 50 items in your item pool, and you test those items on 200 people. Your data will look like this:

	Item 1	Item 2	Item 3 . . .	Item 50
Person 1	x	x	x	x
Person 2	x	x	x	x
Person 3	x	x	x	x
.	.	.	.	.
.	.	.	.	.
.	.	.	.	.
Person 200	x	x	x	x

where the xs are the scores for each person on each item. For 50 items, scored from 1 to 5, each person could get a score as low as 50 (by getting

a score of 1 on each item) or as high as 250 (by getting a score of 5 on each item). In practice, of course, each respondent in a survey will get a total score somewhere in between.

A rough-and-ready way to find the items that discriminate well among respondents is to divide the respondents into two groups, the 25% with the highest total scores and the 25% with the lowest total scores. Look for the items that the two groups have in common. Those items are *not discriminating* among informants with regard to the concept being tested. Items that fail, for example, to discriminate between people who strongly favor training in methods (the top 25%) and people who don't (the bottom 25%) are not good items for scaling people in this construct. Throw those items out.

There is a more formal way to find the items that discriminate well among respondents and the items that don't. This is the ***item-total correlation***. Here are the data you need for this:

	Total Score	Item 1	Item 2	Item 3 . . .	Item 50
Person 1	x	x	x	x	x
Person 2	x	x	x	x	x
Person 3	x	x	x	x	x
.	.	.	.	.	.
.	.	.	.	.	.
.	.	.	.	.	.
Person N	x	x	x	x	x

With 50 items, the total score gives you an idea of where each person stands on the concept you're trying to measure. If the interitem correlation were perfect, then every item would be contributing equally to our understanding of where each respondent stands. Of course, some items do better than others. The ones that don't contribute a lot will correlate poorly with the total score for each person. Keep the items that have the highest correlation with the total scores.

You can use any statistical analysis package to find the interitem correlations, the alpha coefficient, and the item-total correlations for a set of preliminary scale items. Your goal is to get rid of items that detract from a high interitem correlation and to keep the alpha coefficient above 0.80. (For an excellent step-by-step explanation of item analysis, see Spector 1992:43-46.)

TESTING FOR UNIDIMENSIONALITY WITH FACTOR ANALYSIS

Factor analysis is a technique for data reduction. If you have 30 items in a pool of potential scale items, and responses from a sample of people to those pool items, factor analysis lets you reduce the 30 items to a smaller set—say, 5 or 6. Each item is given a score, called its factor loading. This tells you how much each item "belongs" to each of the underlying factors. (See Chapter 16 for a brief introduction to factor analysis and Comrey [1992] for more coverage.)

If a scale is unidimensional, there will be a single, overwhelming factor that underlies all the variables (items) and all the items will "load high" on that single factor. If a scale is multidimensional, then there will be a series of factors that underlie sets of variables. Scale developers get a large pool of potential scale items (at least 40) and ask a lot of people (at least 200) to respond to the items. Then they run the factor analysis and select those items that load high on the factor or factors (the underlying concept or concepts) they are trying to understand.

Patricia Morokoff and her colleagues at the University of Rhode Island used factor analysis to develop a scale of sexual assertiveness in women (Morokoff et al. 1997). Morokoff et al. hypothesized three dimensions to this variable: (1) Women varied in their ability to initiate wanted sex, (2) women varied in their ability to refuse unwanted sex, and (3) women varied in their ability to protect themselves from pregnancy and sexually

transmitted disease (by demanding that the man use a condom).

Morokoff et al. made up several questionnaire items for each of nine sexual behaviors in women: kissing, touching of breasts, touching by partner of genitals, touching of partner's genitals, receiving oral sex, performing oral sex, vaginal intercourse, anal intercourse, and protecting themselves against pregnancy or disease by asking a partner to use a condom. For each behavior, the questionnaire items covered the three dimensions and the presence or absence of pressure.

For example, for kissing, when the woman was *not* under a lot of external pressure to give in, Morokoff et al. had items like "I feel comfortable refusing to kiss a partner when I don't want to" and "If a partner wants to kiss and I don't want to, we do it anyway." For kissing when the woman *is* under a lot of external pressure to give in, they had items like "If a partner pressures me to kiss him after I have refused, I continue to refuse" and "If I refused to kiss a partner and he continued to pressure me, I would give in."

There were similar items for touching of genitals, vaginal intercourse, demanding the use of a condom, and so on. All in all, they had 112 items about self-reported sexual behavior. The items were rated by respondents on a 5-point scale: *never, sometimes (about 25% of the time), about 50% of the time, usually (about 75% of the time), and always (100% of the time).* Morokoff et al. also had 24 items about attitudes, and these, too, were rated on a 5-point scale: *disagree strongly, disagree, mixed, agree somewhat, agree strongly.*

TABLE 8.3 Sexual Assertiveness in Women Scale

Initiation
 1. I begin sex with my partner if I want to.
 2. I let my partner know if I want my partner to touch my genitals.
 3. I wait for my partner to touch my genitals instead of letting my partner know that's what I want. (R)
 4. I wait for my partner to touch my breasts instead of letting my partner know that's what I want. (R)
 5. I let my partner know if I want to have my genitals kissed.
 6. Women should wait for men to start things like breast touching. (R)

Refusal
 7. I give in and kiss if my partner pressures me, even if I already said no. (R)
 8. I put my mouth on my partner's genitals if my partner wants me to, even if I don't want to. (R)
 9. I refuse to let my partner touch my breasts if I don't want that, even if my partner insists.
10. I have sex if my partner wants me to, even if I don't want to. (R)
11. If I said no, I won't let my partner touch my genitals even if my partner pressures me.
12. I refuse to have sex if I don't want to, even if my partner insists.

Protection against pregnancy-STD
13. I have sex without a condom or latex barrier if my partner doesn't like them, even if I want to use one. (R)
14. I have sex without using a condom or latex barrier if my partner insists, even if I don't want to. (R)
15. I make sure my partner and I use a condom or latex barrier when we have sex.
16. I have sex without using a condom or latex barrier if my partner wants. (R)
17. I insist on using a condom or latex barrier if I want to, even if my partner doesn't like them.
18. I refuse to have sex if my partner refuses to use a condom or latex barrier.

SOURCE: P. J. Morokoff et al., "Sexual Assertiveness Scale (SAS) for Women: Development and Validation." *Journal of Personality and Social Psychology* 73:790-804. Copyright © 1997 by the American Psychological Association. Reprinted with permission.

The full 136-item test was given to 260 women. The results (a matrix of 260 women by 136 responses) was factor analyzed. The analysis isolated 42 items that loaded .45 or higher on each of the three factors: 17 items for the "initiation" factor, 14 items for the "refusal" factor, and 11 items for the "pregnancy-STD prevention" factor (the condom factor).

Morokoff et al. next gave the 42-item questionnaire to an entirely different sample of 136 women. They used factor analysis and item-total correlation on the results of the second sample to winnow the 42 items down to just 18, with 6 items for each of the three subscales. Table 8.3 shows the 18-item scale they wound up with.

Items that are reverse coded are indicated by (R). Notice that in all three subscales, half the items are reverse coded. In other words, the same concepts are tested with items that are worded positively and with items that are worded negatively. The factor loadings for each of these 18 items were all above .55 in two separate studies.

Morokoff et al. went on to test their scale on over 1,600 women and confirmed that they could measure three distinct factors—dimensions—of sexual assertiveness in women: initiation, refusal, and pregnancy-STD prevention. Consistently, women reported being less assertive in refusing unwanted sex and in demanding the use of a condom when they anticipated a negative reaction from their partners (Morokoff et al. 1997:802).

❖————

SCALES GET SIMPLER AND MORE WIDELY USED OVER TIME

Notice how the scale that Morokoff and her colleagues developed got simpler as it went through a couple of tests. They started with 136 items. These were reduced to 61 (the ones that scored over .45 on the first factor analysis). They removed 19 of those 61 items that were redundant (they were more or less rewordings of the same thing). The remaining 42 items were reduced to 18 in the next phase of the research when they gave the test to the next sample.

Morokoff et al. wound up giving the test to more than 1,600 women in a total of seven surveys, including year-later follow-up surveys on some of the women who were in the earlier samples. This allowed Morokoff et al. to test whether their scale was reliable, or had *test-retest reliability,* and whether it predicted other variables of interest. For example, the longer a respondent was in a relationship, the less assertive she was likely to be in refusing unwanted sex.

As scales get used more and more, they tend to shrink in size. Quite naturally, researchers err on the side of caution when they make and test scales—no sense in leaving out some items that may be important until you know that you can do without them. But as researchers test and retest scales, they determine that some items are redundant. They publish these results so that other researchers can use the simpler versions of tests. The original Michigan Alcoholism Screening Test (MAST), for example, has 25 items (Selzer 1971). Pokorny et al. (1972) showed that their 5-item Brief-MAST instrument was about as effective as the longer original. Both the MAST and the Brief-MAST instruments continue to be used in research and in screening populations for alcoholism.

The original, 1970, version of the Attitudes Toward Women Scale (AWS) had 55 items

(Spence and Helmreich 1972). By 1973, Spence et al. had tested and formulated a 25-item AWS, and by 1978, Spence and Helmreich published a 15-item version. Jean Twenge (1997) did a meta-analysis of 71 samples of American undergraduates who had responded to one or another version of the AWS. Over those 25 years, men and women alike have been responding with increasingly liberal/feminist answers to the items on the AWS, with (not surprisingly) women scoring consistently higher than men. Twenge's analysis, though, shows that these results are just as strong with the 15-item AWS as with the 25-item and 55-item tests.

Successful scales get validated on many different populations over time. A scale developed to assess, say, the social support network of elderly, urban Euro-American women may be modified to assess the same variable for elderly, rural Hispanic women. Then it may get used, and validated, for a population of old, rural African American men, and so on. Henderson et al. (1981), for example, developed a 50-item test of social support (called the ISSI, or Interview Schedule for Social Interaction) on respondents in Canberra, Australia. Undén and Orth-Gomér (1989) tested and validated a much reduced version of the scale on Swedish men who were at risk for heart disease.

That widely used MAST I mentioned earlier? It has a version that's just for the elderly. It's called the MAST-G, where "G" stands for "geriatric version" (DeHart and Hoffmann 1997). The ATWSA (Galambos et al. 1985) is an adaptation for adolescents of Spence and Helmreich's (1972) famous AWS.

A widely used intelligence test is the WAIS-R, or Wechsler Adult Intelligence Scale-Revised. Some of the questions in that test are culturally appropriate only for Americans. Pugh and Boer (1989) tested some alternative questions to make the WAIS-R appropriate for Canadians.

> Do a thorough search for existing scales before launching out on your own to build new scales from scratch.

Each of these revalidations and reformulations, if successful, winds up in the literature, so it pays to do a thorough search for existing scales before launching out on your own to build new scales from scratch.

SEMANTIC DIFFERENTIAL SCALES

I've always liked the semantic differential scaling method. It was developed in the 1950s by Charles Osgood and his associates at the University of Illinois and has become an important research tool in psychology (Osgood et al. 1957; Snider and Osgood 1969). It has also been used by thousands of researchers across the social sciences, and with good reason: The semantic differential test is easy to construct and easy to administer.

Osgood was interested in how people interpret things—inanimate things (like artifacts or monuments), animate things (like persons or the self), behaviors (like incest, buying a new car, or shooting a deer), and intangible concepts (like gun control or literacy). Of course, this is exactly what Likert scales are designed to test, but instead of asking people to rate questionnaire items about things, Osgood tested people's feelings differently: He gave them a *target item* and a list of *paired adjectives* about the target. The adjective pairs could come from reading of the literature or from focus groups or from ethnographic interviews.

Figure 8.1 is an example of a semantic differential test. The target is the concept of "abortion on demand." If you were taking this test right now, you'd be asked to place a check on each line, depending on your reaction to each pair of adjectives.

With a Likert scale, you ask people a series of questions that get at the target concept. With a semantic differential scale, you name the target concept and ask respondents to rate their feelings toward it on a series of variables. The semantic differential is usually a 7-point scale, as I've indicated in the first adjective pair above. (You can leave out the numbers and let people respond to the visual form of the scale.) Your score on this test would be the sum of all your answers to the 14 adjective pairs.

Osgood and his associates did hundreds of replications of this test, using hundreds of adjective pairs, in 26 different cultures. Their factor analyses showed that in every culture there are three major kinds of adjectives. The most important (the ones that account for most of the variation in people's responses) are *adjectives of evaluation* (good-bad, difficult-easy, etc.), followed by *adjectives of potency* (strong-weak, dominant-submissive), and *adjectives of activity* (fast-slow, active-inactive, sedentary-mobile).

Figure 8.1 A Semantic Differential Scale to Test How People Feel about the Concept of "Abortion on Demand"

NOTE: The dimensions in this scale are useful for measuring how people feel about many different things.

In the semantic differential test above, you could substitute "late-twentieth-century America," "words that describe me," "land reform," or "having a cold" for "abortion on demand." As the target changes, of course, you have to make sure that the adjective pairs make sense. The adjective pair indoor-outdoor works for lots of targets (kinds of music, hobbies, even famous persons), but it's not appropriate for others (patio furniture, preservation of wilderness, hang gliding).

SOME OTHER SCALES

The Cantril Ladder of Life

There are many interesting variations in the construction of scales. Hadley Cantril (1965) devised a 10-rung *ladder of life,* shown in Figure 8.2. People are asked to list their concerns in life (financial success, healthy children, freedom from war, etc.). Then they are shown the ladder and are told that the bottom rung represents the worst possible situation, while the top rung represents the best. For each of their concerns, they are asked to point out where they are on the ladder right now, where they were five years ago, and where they think they'll be five years from now.

Note that the ladder of life is a *self-anchoring scale.* Respondents are asked to explain, in their own terms, what the top and bottom rungs of the ladder mean to them.

In the late 1980s, the Hamilton Psychiatric Hospital in Hamilton, Canada, reassessed its basic mission. The goals of the hospital with regard to schizophrenics changed from long-term residential care, to treatment, rehabilitation, and re-integration. Over the next few years, 35 clients (mostly men) were relocated into supervised boarding homes or nursing homes in nearby communities. These clients had lived in the hospital for an average of nearly 14 years.

Two years into the program, Kirkpatrick et al. (1996) assessed the global well-being of the clients. During the interviews, the clients were shown a picture of a ladder and were told that the bottom rung represented the "worst life I could expect," while the top rung represented the "best life I could expect." They were asked where they would put their life when they were living in the hospital and during the past month. They were also asked to estimate where they would put their life a year from now. The longer the men had lived

outside the hospital, the higher their global satisfaction with life tended to be.

The ladder of life is a useful prop for interviewing nonliterate people. Hansen and McSpadden (1993), for example, used the technique in their studies of Zambian and Ethiopian refugees in Zambia and the United States. In Zambia, Hansen actually constructed a small wooden lad-

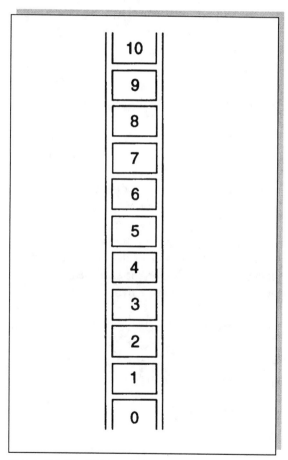

Figure 8.2 The Ladder of Life

SOURCE: H. Cantril, *The Pattern of Human Concerns.* Copyright © 1965 by Rutgers, The State University. Reprinted by permission of Rutgers University Press.

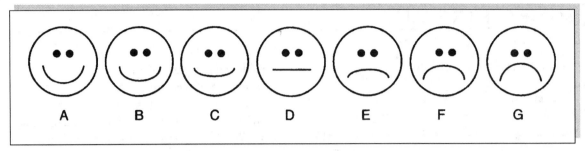

Figure 8.3 The Faces Scale

SOURCE: F. M. Andrews and S. B. Withey, *Social Indicators of Well-Being: Americans' Perceptions of Life Quality*, Appendix A, p. 13. Copyright © 1976. Reprinted by permission of Plenum Publishing Corporation.

der and found that the method worked well. McSpadden used several methods to explore how Ethiopian refugees adjusted to life in the U.S. Even when other methods failed, McSpadden found that the ladder of life method got people to talk about their experiences, fears, and hopes (ibid.).

Be careful, though, to tell respondents exactly what you want when you use this kind of visual prop. Jones and Nies (1996) used Cantril's ladder to measure the importance of exercise to elderly African American women. Well, at least Jones and Nies thought that's what they were measuring. The mean for the ladder rating was about 9 on a scale of 1 to 10. Respondents thought they were being asked how important exercise is, not how important exercise is to them, personally. The researchers failed to explain properly to their respondents what the ladder was supposed to measure, and even devout couch potatoes are going to tell you that exercise is important if you ask them the general question.

The Faces Scale

Another interesting device is the *faces scale* shown in Figure 8.3. It's a 7-point (or 5-point, or 9-point) scale with stylized faces that change from joy to gloom. The meaning of the faces in Figure 8.3 may, in fact, be universal (Ekman et al. 1969).

This scaling method was developed by Kunin in 1955 to measure job satisfaction, and has been widely used for this ever since (P. C. Smith et al. 1969; Brief and Roberson 1989; Wanous et al. 1997). Physicians and psychologists use this scale as a prop when they ask small children to describe pain (Belter et al. 1988; Bieri et al. 1990), but the prop is just as useful for interviewing adults about their satisfaction with things like health care (Pound et al. 1993) or life in general (Andrews and Withey 1976). Respondents are told: "Here are some faces expressing various feelings. Which face comes closest to how you feel about X?"

Pound et al. (1993) interviewed 99 primary caregivers of stroke patients. Respondents were asked to check the face that "best sums up how satisfied you are with the hospital in general." The results of this single measure correlated very highly with two four-item scales of satisfaction with the hospital staff and hospital services.

The idea of "hospital services" is pretty complex. It includes things like the quickness with which the ambulance arrived when you called, the politeness of staff during the outpatient phase after release from the hospital, and lots of other things. You can make up a scale that contains separate items for each of these things: How satisfied are you with X, Y, and Z?

But you might leave out some key items, and a key item for one person might be trivial to another. That's why it's good to have an overall measure in addition to measures of the components of a complex concepts. The faces scale is a really good device for capturing general feelings about really complex things.

You can use the faces scale to score how people feel about their access to health care, the safety of their neighborhood, media coverage of some big event—or even a list of consumer items (brands of beer, titles of current movies, etc.).

MAGNITUDE SCALING

Most scales in the social sciences are *category scales*. The semantic differential is usually a 7-point scale. Likert-type scales are often 5-point scales. The idea is to give people a range of options from which to choose. Whatever they choose is recorded as the measurement, for a particular object, for a particular person. A typical survey question asked of people coming out of a newly released film is: "On a scale of 1 to 5, about how much did you like the movie you just saw?" So, if a person checks 4, they get recorded as having a measurement of 4 for that movie.

The measurement is an ordinal category, and it's a compromise. People have much more finely graded opinions about things like movies (and everything else) than a 1-5 scale captures. And when you ask people a question that gives them a fixed number of choices, you have to be affecting their responses. How do you know, for example, that a particular attitude should be measured on a 5-point scale while some other attitude should be measured on a 7-point scale?

Some researchers believe that you can measure the actual magnitude of people's impressions, feelings, and attitudes. The method they use is called *magnitude scaling* and is based on research from psychophysics.

Magnitude Scaling and Psychophysics

Researchers in psychophysics have shown (in hundreds of experiments) that people can make very accurate proportional judgments about visual, auditory, and other sense stimuli. These experiments led to what's called the "power law" in psychophysics. It looks like this:

$$\psi = R = kS^b$$

where the Greek letter ψ (psi, pronounced "sigh") is perception of the magnitude of some physical stimulus (like a light or a tone), R is what people *say* is the magnitude of the stimulus, and S is the physical stimulus itself (for example, the intensity of the tone in decibels). The exponent b is the power to which you have to raise people's responses to make R and S identical, and k is some constant (Lodge 1981:13).

Suppose you tell people that the brightness value of some light is 50 points and then show them a light that is twice as bright. If the exponent b were exactly 1.00, then, averaging over a lot of people, R would be 100. If people's responses to proportional differences in physical stimuli are proportional responses, then you don't have to

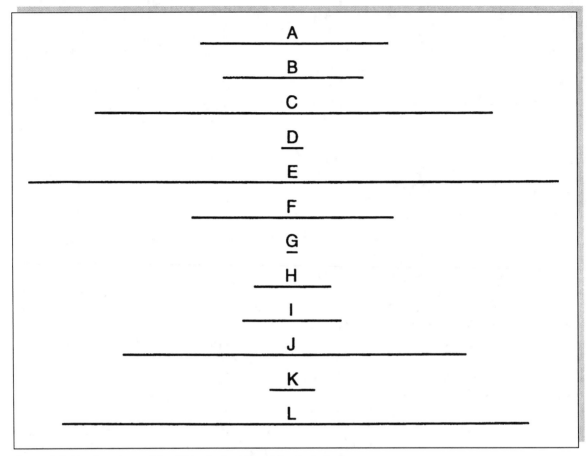

Figure 8.4 Line Lengths as a Visual Stimulus for Direct Magnitude Scaling
SOURCE: M. Lodge, *Magnitude Scaling: Quantitative Measurement of Opinions*, p. 9. Copyright © 1981 by Sage Publications.

adjust *S* with an exponent. Over the years, researchers in psychophysics have discovered the proportionality exponents for many stimuli.

Figure 8.4 is a visual stimulus, from Milton Lodge's book on magnitude scaling (1981:9).

It turns out that the proportionality exponent for this stimulus is 0.988. Lodge told 375 people that line A has a length of 50 (not 50 inches or millimeters or miles, just 50) and asked them to say how long they thought each of the other lines were. The correlation between the average of their guesses about the length of each line and the actual length of each line was .988.

Now line A is actually about 50 mm. Hardly anyone can look at line A and tell you it's 50 mm, but if you tell people that line A has a value of 50, most of the time they'll tell you that line E has a value of 100. Line J is actually 98 mm, or 1.96 times as long as line A, but people round off and get the proportion almost dead on (the *almost* part is why the proportionality exponent is "only" 0.988 and not 1.00). Line G is 2 mm long, so it's 1/49th the length of line E. Most people give line G a 1 if you tell them that line E is 50. In other words, with a little error, people mostly get the proportions right. (You can test this yourself.)

Hundreds of experiments with many sense stimuli (the intensity of light, loudness of sound, pressure on the body, etc.) led to the formulation by Stevens (1957) of that power law: Equal physical stimulus ratios produce equal subjective ratios.

If you ask people to rate, on a 1-5 scale, how long those lines are in Figure 8.4, you get less accurate subjective measurements. With only five categories to play with (short, medium short, medium, medium long, long), people give lines D and G a 1 (short) and they give lines E and L (and perhaps C) a 5 (long). Categorical measurement reduces the correlation between the average perceived line length and the actual line length for each line.

Magnitude Scaling of Constructs

The big question, though, is this: Does the power law for physical stimuli (like line lengths, light intensity, etc.) translate into better measurement for subjective things, like attitudes? In 1977, the possibility of magnitude scaling of opinions was tested on the National Crime Victimization Survey. The 54,000 respondents saw subsets of 25 from a list of 204 crimes. Here are the instructions to the respondents:

I would like to ask your opinion about how serious YOU think certain crimes are. The first situation is "A person steals a bicycle parked on the street." This has been given a score of 10 to show its seriousness. Use this first situation to judge all others. For example, if you think a situation is 20 TIMES MORE serious than the bicycle theft, the number you tell me should be around 200, or if you think it is HALF AS SERIOUS, the number you tell me should be around 5, and so on. There is no upper limit. Use ANY number so long as it shows how serious YOU think the situation is. If YOU think something is not a crime, give it a zero.

The respondents then saw a list of 25 crimes, things like

(1) A person using force, robs a victim of $10. The victim struggles and is shot to death.
(2) A person steals property worth $10,000 from outside a building.
(3) A person disturbs the neighborhood with loud, noisy behavior.

And so on. As it turns out, many respondents find magnitude scaling easy to do, and it appears that, for some stimuli, subjective responses do obey some version of the power law. For example, across repeated national studies in the U.S., on average, people think a crime of theft is twice as serious as another crime of theft if the dollar amount stolen in one crime is about 13 times greater than the dollar amount stolen in another crime (Lodge 1981:22).

Two political scientists, Valerie Sulfaro and Mark Crislip (1997), hypothesized that, with the collapse of the Soviet Union, Americans would have to realign their ideas about who the "enemies" are out there. Sulfaro and Crislip asked 145 undergraduates to rate 19 countries (including 1 fictitious country, the United Arab Republic) on a 7-point scale. The end points of the scale were labeled *most hostile* and *least hostile* to the United States.

Respondents practiced direct magnitude estimation by doing that line-length exercise I described. The correlation between the students' estimation of the line lengths and the actual line lengths was more than .99. With this practice session behind them, the students moved on to estimating, by direct magnitude scaling, the

TABLE 8.4 Standardized Hostility/Friendliness Scores for 19 Countries

Country	Line Lengths	Categorical Estimates
Canada	1.24	1.36
Australia	1.24	1.32
Britain	1.15	1.17
Mexico	.78	.65
India	.51	.76
Japan	.23	.35
Saudi Arabia	.52	.21
Israel	.38	.29
Germany	.35	.30
France	.19	.85
Panama	−.03	.03
United Arab Republic	−.29	−.41
PRC (China)	−.32	−.23
Bosnia	−.35	−.84
Russia	−.40	−.29
Nicaragua	−.52	−.72
Serbia	−.42	−.81
Cuba	−1.11	−1.29
Iraq	−3.15	−2.67

SOURCE: V. A. Sulfaro and M. S. Crislip, "How Americans Perceive Foreign Policy Threat: A Magnitude Scaling Analysis." *Political Psychology* 18. Copyright © 1997. Reprinted with permission of Blackwell Publishers.

amount of hostility they thought various countries had toward the U.S.

Sulfaro and Crislip used France as their reference point for this exercise. They showed respondents a line whose length represented the amount of hostility that France has toward the U.S. Respondents then drew lines representing how much hostility they thought the other 18 countries (Britain, Iraq, Panama, etc.) had toward the U.S. Each country wound up with two average scores, one for the categorical estimate (on a scale from 1 to 7) of hostility, and one for the line-drawing exercise. Sulfaro and Crislip converted these average scores into standard scores. The results are shown in Table 8.4.

I'll show you how to compute standard scores in Chapter 14, when we get to quantitative data analysis. In this case, positive standard scores tell you how friendly each country is perceived to be toward the U.S., relative to the average for all countries; negative scores tell you how hostile each country is perceived to be, relative to the average for all countries. The entries in Table 8.4 are in standard deviations above and below the mean. Canada, Australia, and Britain are more than 1 standard deviation higher on friendliness (the opposite of hostility). Cuba and Iraq are more than 1 standard deviation below the mean.

The correlation between these two measures of perceived hostility to the U.S. is a whopping .96, but notice the difference in the score for France on the line lengths and categorical estimates. When France is evaluated categorically, it is not directly compared to any other country. In this condition, France gets a very low hostility-toward-the-U.S. score: .85 is nearly a full standard deviation above the mean, almost the same as Britain. When France's hostility toward the U.S. is evaluated *relative to that of other countries,* then France scores far, far below Britain—the same as Japan.

Magnitude scaling is relatively little used in the social sciences. It produces some excellent results, but it is complicated to administer (respondents don't always understand what they're supposed to do) and the data are a bit harder to analyze than are categorical data. (For one thing, you need to calculate geometric means rather than arithmetic means of the measure of subjective stimuli. This involves taking the natural logarithm of each measure, taking the average of the logs, and then exponentiating the result to get back to where you started. Not exactly straightforward.)

On the other hand, one of the most widely used scales in the social sciences today is the Social Readjustment Rating Scale (SRRS). In developing the first version of the scale in 1967, Holmes and Rahe showed people a list of 43 life events that require some getting used to—some readjustment. They told respondents that getting married recently had a value of 500 points and they asked people to rate each of the other 42 events. Events included a range of things, from the death of a spouse to retirement to taking on a large mortgage, and so on. To get their original scores for

the 43 life events, Holmes and Rahe simply averaged the magnitude ratings from 394 respondents, and divided by 10 (that just cut down the size of the scale numbers).

The SRRS is really an index. If you were married recently, you'd get 50 points for that; if you had recently been fired, you'd get 47 points; if you were experiencing a change in your sleeping habits, you'd get 16 points for that; and so on. Then you'd add up all your points. The SRRS is a composite measure for assessing people on a complex variable. The idea is that the more readjustment you've got buffeting your life, the more likely you are to have other problems—like health problems, or problems keeping friends.

> *With much easier-to-use computer programs available for data analysis these days, magnitude scaling is going to come into its own. It's got a lot of appeal.*

Over the years, the SRRS has been adapted for use in many languages and for many research problems. It was developed with a modified version of the magnitude scaling method. I think that with much easier to use computer programs available for data analysis these days, magnitude scaling is going to come into its own. It's got a lot of appeal.

AND FINALLY

There are thousands of published scales. Whatever you're interested in, the chances are good that someone has developed and tested a scale to measure it. Of course, scales are not automatically portable. A scale that measures stress among Bar-

badian women may not measure stress among Ghanaian men.

Still, it makes sense to seek out any published scales on variables you're studying. You may be able to adapt the scales to your needs, or you may get ideas for building and testing an alternative scale. Just because scales are not perfectly transportable across time and cultures doesn't mean those scales are useless to you. For a start on looking for scales that you can adapt, consult Delbert Miller's *Handbook of Research Design and Social Measurement* (5th ed., 1991).

*Chapter 8
Review*

KEY CONCEPTS

Chapter 8
Summary

SUMMARY

❖ A scale is a device for assigning units of analysis to categories of a variable. The assignment is usually done with numbers, and questions are used a lot as scaling devices.

♦ A single question on a questionnaire is technically a scale if it lets you assign the people you're studying to categories of a variable. A lot of really interesting variables in social science, however, are complex and can't easily be assessed with single indicators.

❖ The most common composite measure is a cumulative index. These are made up of several items, all of which count the same.

♦ A test in which the only way to get an A is to get at least 90% is a criterion-referenced index. A test in which getting an A requires that you score in the top 10% of the class is a norm-referenced index.

❖ A Guttman scale is a unidimensional index. That is, the items are a composite measure of one, and only one, underlying concept.

♦ The unidimensionality of an index is sample dependent. If the items in a cumulative index form a Guttman scale, then the concept measured by the index is unidimensional, but only for the sample tested.

❖ Likert scales are the best-known and most widely used scales. A true Likert scale is more than just a format for asking questions. It is a series of items that have been shown to be indicators of an underlying, unidimensional concept.

♦ Multidimensional concepts are often measured with complex Likert scales that have several subscales, each of which comprises indicators of a unidimensional concept.

♦ Likert scales are tested through a procedure called item analysis. This involves taking the interitem correlation and calculating Cronbach's alpha as a measure of scale reliability. Computers make it easy to use factor analysis to test the unidimensionality of scales.

❖ With a Likert scale, you ask people a series of questions that get at the target concept. In a semantic differential scale, you name the target concept and ask respondents to rate their feelings toward it on a series of variables.

❖ Most scales use ordinal categories, but people have more finely graded opinions than, say, a 1-5 scale captures. Magnitude scaling adapts methods from psychophysics to measure attitudes more directly and at a higher level of measurement.

❖ Other scales include Cantril's ladder of life and the faces scale.

EXERCISES

1. This exercise is on the history of scale development. Many scales have changed over the years. It's very instructive to pick an old scale and follow it through its evolution to a modern form. The Wilson-Patterson Conservatism Scale, for example, was developed in the 1960s in New Zealand (Wilson and Patterson 1968). It was modified for use in the U.S. by Bahr and Chadwick (1974). Later, Collins and Hayes tested a short version of the scale (1993).

   Document the history of a widely used scale. Here are some you might choose from: the Locus of Control Scale (Rotter 1966), the Social Readjustment Scale (Holmes and Rahe 1967), the Authoritarian Personality Scale (Adorno et al. 1950), and the Bem Sex Role Inventory (Bem 1974).

2. Try building a Likert scale to test how serious colleges students are about their education. This may sound like an easy thing to do, but it isn't. Get together with a small group of students and work on this together. What questions would you ask students if you wanted to scale them on how serious they were about their education? Would the amount of time they claim to spend in the library, or the amount of time they claim to spend partying, be useful data? How about what they want to do with their lives after they get their bachelor's degree?

   Once you have a list of questions about attitudes and behaviors, follow the rest of the steps outlined in this chapter, including the item analysis, to get your scale down to a small number of items. Of course, you can substitute any value or orientation you like for this exercise. If measuring how serious students are about their education is too close for comfort, then try that shopping orientation variable I mentioned earlier.

3. Get together with a group of other students and decide on a set of target items for a semantic differential test. The items can types of jobs (forest ranger, family physician, insurance salesperson, etc.), names of colors (blue, red, yellow, pink, etc.), names of countries (France, Venezuela, Zambia, etc.), kinds of music (reggae, jazz, country, classical, etc.). Build copies of Figure 8.1 on your word processors and print out a series of semantic differential tests, one for each target item. Choose adjective pairs that make sense for the target items you are studying. For each target item, calculate the mean, across the respondents, of each adjective pair.

FURTHER READING

Scale development. For a general overview of the theory of measurement and scaling, see Coombs (1964), Nunnally (1978), and Torgerson (1958).

For recent examples of how researchers develop and test scales, see Gatz and Hurwicz (1990) (a scale that measures depression in old people), Handwerker (1996a) (a scale for measuring family violence across cultures), Heatherton and Polivy (1991) (a scale that measures self-esteem), Koeske and Koeske (1989) (a scale for measuring job burnout), Morris et al. (1990) (a scale for self-assessment by old people on seven dimensions), Sellers et al. (1997) (a scale that measures the strength of racial identity in African Americans), Simpson and Gangestad (1991) (a scale that measures willingness to engage in uncommitted sexual relations), and Watt and Ewing (1996) (a scale that measures levels of sexual boredom).

Scales and indexes. I've mentioned a few widely used scales: Rotter's Locus of Control (Rotter 1966; and see P. B. Smith et al. [1995] for a massive cross-cultural comparison of data using Rotter's scale), the Bem Sex Role Inventory (Bem 1974), Holmes and Rahe's Social Readjustment Scale (Holmes and Rahe 1967), and Spence and Helmreich's (1972) Attitudes Toward Women Scale.

There are thousands of scales and indexes available for measuring attitudes and psychological states. There is no point in trying to make up a new scale if one already exists that has been tested. Delbert Miller's *Handbook of Research Design and Social Measurement* (1991) always seems hopelessly out of date, yet it remains the best place to start looking for published scales. It's a treasure-house full of useful information.

Guttman scaling. Sonn et al. (1996) found that a set of nine activities of daily living formed a nearly perfect Guttman scale for their sample of 382 elderly men and women in Göteborg, Sweden. The activities are cleaning the house, shopping, transportation, cooking, bathing, dressing, going to the toilet, getting in and out of bed, and eating. Mikolic et al. (1997) found, in a laboratory experiment, that escalation of responses to persistent annoyance conformed to a Guttman scale. People start with requests for termination of the annoyance. This is followed by impatient demands, complaints, angry statements, threats, harassment, and abuse.

Likert scaling. For extensive discussions of how to construct and test a Likert scale, see DeVellis (1991) and Spector (1992).

Semantic differential. For recent uses of the semantic differential test, see Adams-Webber (1997) (psychology), Cooker and White (1993) (education), Leunes et al. (1996) (social psychology), and Ohanian (1990) (marketing).

Magnitude scaling. For further examples of direct magnitude scaling, see Orth and Wegener (1983).

9 PARTICIPANT OBSERVATION

IN THIS CHAPTER:

❖ INTRODUCTION

This chapter is about the skills required for doing participant observation ethnography. What I have to say about participant observation is naturally colored by my own experience as an anthropologist. That experience includes fieldwork in places that take several days to get to, where the local language has no literary tradition, and where the chances of coming down with a serious illness are nontrivial. It also includes the study of an elite blue-collar work group (the men and women who run oceanographic research vessels), acculturation among European ethnics in the U.S. (Greek Americans in Tarpon Springs, Florida), and the effects of word processors on the organization of work in six cultures.

These days, in fact, cultural anthropologists are more likely to study army platoons (Killworth 1997), consumer behavior (Sherry 1995), gay culture in major cities (Herdt 1992; Murray 1992), or the mean streets of big cities (Bourgois 1995; Fleisher 1998) than they are to study isolated tribal peoples.

While participant observation in small, rather isolated communities has some special characteristics, the techniques and skills that are required seem to me to be pretty much the same everywhere.

WHAT IS PARTICIPANT OBSERVATION?

Participant observation **usually involves fieldwork, but not all fieldwork is participant observation.** Goldberg et al. (1994) interviewed 206 prostitutes and collected saliva specimens (to test for HIV and for drug use) during 53 nights of fieldwork in Glasgow's red light district. This was serious fieldwork, but hardly participant observation. Nor is participant observation the same thing as ethnography. Inconsiderately, *ethnography* is **both the process of collecting descriptive data about a culture and it's the product of all that work.** The product is usually an article or a book, sometimes a film. And there is nothing particularly qualitative about participant observation or ethnography.

So much for what participant observation isn't. Here's what it is: Participant observation is one of those *strategic methods* I talked about in Chapter 1—like experiments, surveys, or archival research. It puts you where the action is and lets you collect data—any kind of data you want, qualita-

tive or quantitative, narratives or numbers. It has been used for generations by positivists and interpretivists alike.

As it turns out, a lot of the data collected by participant observers are qualitative: texts of open-ended interviews that have been taped and transcribed; field notes taken while watching and listening to people in natural settings; photographs of the content of people's houses; audiotapes of people telling folk tales; videotapes of people making canoes, getting married, having an argument.

But lots of data collected by participant observation field workers are based on quantitative measurements: direct observation and recording of behavior, questionnaires, pile sorts. Whether your data consist of numbers or words, whether you consider yourself an interpretivist or a positivist, participant observation lets you in the door so you can collect life histories, attend rituals, and talk to people about sensitive topics.

Participant observation involves going out and staying out, learning a new language (or a new dialect of a language you already know), and experiencing the lives of the people you are studying as much as you can. Participant observation is about stalking culture in the wild—establishing rapport and learning to act so that people go about their business as usual when you show up. If you are a successful participant observer you will know when to laugh at what people think is funny, and when people laugh at what you say, it will be because you *meant* it to be a joke.

But participant observation is not about *going native.* It's about immersing yourself in a culture and learning to remove yourself every day from that immersion so you can intellectualize what you've seen and heard, put it into perspective, and write about it convincingly. Participant observation is the most ethically problematic of social research methods, because it's thoroughly manipulative.

If this sounds a bit raw, I mean it to come out that way. Only by confronting the stark truth about participant observation—that, like everyday life everywhere, it involves deception and constant *impression management*—can we hope to conduct ourselves ethically in fieldwork.

When it's done right, participant observation turns field workers into instruments of data collection and data analysis. The implication is that better field workers are better data collectors and better data analyzers. And the implication of *that* is that participant observation is not an attitude or an epistemological commitment or a way of life. It's a craft, like running so-called subjects in lab experiments or digging through historical archives or building and administering questionnaire surveys. As with all crafts, becoming a skilled artisan at participant observation takes practice.

SOME BACKGROUND AND HISTORY

Bronislaw Malinowski (1884-1942) didn't invent participant observation, but he is widely credited with developing it as a serious method of social research. A British social anthropologist (born in Poland), Malinowski went out to study the people of the Trobriand Islands, in the Indian Ocean, just before World War I. When the war broke out, he was prevented from returning to England for three years.

He made the best of the situation, though. Here is Malinowski describing his methods:

Soon after I had established myself in Omarkana, Trobriand Islands, I began to take part, in a way, in the village life, to look forward to the important or festive events, to take personal interest in the gossip and the developments of the village occurrences; to

wake up every morning to a new day, presenting itself to me more or less as it does to the natives. . . . As I went on my morning walk through the village, I could see intimate details of family life, of toilet, cooking, taking of meals; I could see the arrangements for the day's work, people starting on their errands, or groups of men and women busy at some manufacturing tasks.

Quarrels, jokes, family scenes, events usually trivial, sometimes dramatic but always significant, form the atmosphere of my daily life, as well as of theirs. It must be remembered that the natives saw me constantly every day, they ceased to be interested or alarmed, or made self-conscious by my presence, and I ceased to be a disturbing element in the tribal life which I was to study, altering it by my very approach, as always happens with a newcomer to every savage community. In fact, as they knew that I would thrust my nose into everything, even where a well-mannered native would not dream of intruding, they finished by regarding me as a part and parcel of their life, a necessary evil or nuisance, mitigated by donations of tobacco. (1961 [1922]: 7-8)

Ignore the patronizing rhetoric about the "savage community" and "donations of tobacco." (We've learned to live with this part of our history in anthropology. Knowing that all of us, in every age, look quaint to those who come later, has made it easier.) Focus instead on the amazing, progressive (for that time) method that Malinowski advocated: Spend lots and lots of time in studying a culture, learn the language, hang out, do all the everyday things that everyone else does, become inconspicuous by sheer tenaciousness, and stay aware of what's really going on. Strip away the colonialist underpinnings of the rhetoric and Malinowski's discussion of participant observation is as powerful today as it was three-quarters of a century ago.

Actually, by the time Malinowski went to the Trobriands, *Notes and Queries on Anthropology*—the fieldwork manual produced by the Royal Anthropological Institute of Great Britain and Ireland (RAI)—was in its fourth edition. The first edition came out in 1874 and the last edition (the sixth) was reprinted five times until 1971.

That final edition of *Notes and Queries* is must reading for anyone interested in learning about anthropological field methods. Ignore the antiquated language and the vestiges of paternalistic colonialism—"a sporting rifle and a shotgun are . . . of great assistance in many districts where the natives may welcome extra meat in the shape of game killed by their visitor" (RAI 1951:29)—and *Notes and Queries* is full of useful, late-model advice about how to conduct a census; how to handle photographic negatives in the field; what

questions to ask about sexual orientation, infanticide, food production, warfare, art. The book is just a treasure.

Anthropologists continue to make the most consistent use of participant observation, but the method has very, very deep roots in sociology. Beatrice Webb was doing participant observation—complete with note taking and informant interviewing—in the 1880s, and she wrote in detail about the method in her 1926 memoir (Webb 1926).

Just about then, the long tradition in sociology of urban ethnography—the "Chicago school"—began at the University of Chicago under the direction of Robert Park and Ernest Burgess (see Park et al. 1925). This tradition has never paid any respect at all to disciplinary boundaries. One of Park's students was his son-in-law, the anthropologist Robert Redfield, who pioneered community studies in Mexico.

A young anthropologist from Harvard, William Lloyd Warner, just back from extensive fieldwork with Aborigine peoples in Australia (Warner 1937) was also influenced by Park and launched one of the most famous American community study projects of all time, the Yankee City series (Warner and Hunt 1941; Warner 1963). (Yankee City was the pseudonym for Newburyport, Massachusetts.) In 1929, sociologists Robert and Helen Lynd published the first of many ethnographies about Middletown. (Middletown was the pseudonym for Muncie, Indiana.)

Some of the time-honored ethnographies that came out of the early Chicago School include Harvey Zorbaugh's *The Gold Coast and the Slum* (1929) and Clifford Shaw's *The Jack-Roller* (1930). These ethnographies, by sociologists, still make terrific reading. In *The Jack-Roller*, a 22-year-old named Stanley tells his own life story about what it was like to grow up as a juvenile delinquent in early-twentieth-century Chicago. This was a pioneering effort in life history research.

Becker et al.'s *Boys in White* (1961) is also still a great read. (It's about the student culture of medical school in the 1950s.) The tradition continues today in the many students of students of students from that tradition and in the pages of the journal *Contemporary Ethnography,* which began in 1972 under the title *Urban Life and Culture.* (See L. Lofland [1983] and Bulmer [1984] for more on the history of the Chicago school of urban ethnography.)

In fact, participant observation today is absolutely ubiquitous in the social sciences. It has been used in recent years by political scientists (Fenno 1990; Glaser 1996); social psychologists (Weisfeld and de Olivares 1992; A. B. Smith and Inder 1993); students of management (Gummesson 1991; Weick 1995; Watson 1996); researchers in nursing (De Valck and Van de Woestijne 1996; Woodgate and Kristjanson 1996), education (Woods 1986, 1996; Hammersley 1990; Rovegno and Bandhauer 1997), social work (Lawler and Hearn 1997), and expert systems engineering (Meyer 1992); and by legions of sociologists (see Denzin and Lincoln 1994).

Among the wonderful results of all this is a continually growing body of literature about participant observation itself. There are highly focused studies, full of practical advice, and there are poignant discussions of the overall *experience* of fieldwork (Wolcott 1995; Agar 1996; C. D. Smith and Kornblum 1996).

FIELDWORK ROLES

Fieldwork can involve three very different roles: (1) *complete participant,* (2) *participant observer,* and (3) *complete observer.* The first role involves deception—becoming a member of a group without letting on that you're there to do research. The third role involves following people around and recording their behavior with little if any interaction. This is part of direct observation, which we'll take up in the next chapter.

By far, most ethnographic research is based on the second role, that of the participant observer. Participant observers can be insiders who observe and record some aspects of life around them, or they can be outsiders who participate in some aspects of life around them and record what they can.

In 1965, I went to sea with a group of Greek sponge fishermen in the Mediterranean. I lived in close quarters with them, ate the same awful food that they did, and generally participated in their life—as an outsider. I did not dive for sponges, but spent most of my waking hours studying the behavior and the conversation of the men who did. The divers were curious about what I was writing in my notebooks, but they went about their business and just let me take notes, time their dives, and shoot movies (Bernard 1987). I was a *participating observer.*

Similarly, when I went to sea in 1972 and 1973 with oceanographic research vessels, I was part of the scientific crew, there to watch how oceanographic scientists, technicians, and mariners interacted and how this interaction affected the process of gathering oceanographic data. There, too, I was a participating observer (Bernard and Killworth 1973).

Gene Shelley (1992) studied people who suffer from end-stage kidney disease. She spent hundreds of hours in a dialysis clinic, observing, listening, chatting, interviewing, and taking notes on all aspects of the patients' lives. She did not pretend she was a nurse. Nor did she go through dialysis herself. She, too, assumed the middle role: the participating observer.

Circumstances can sometimes overtake the role of mere participating observer. William Kornblum was doing fieldwork with a group of Boyash (gypsies) in France. One night, the camp was attacked by a rival group and Kornblum found himself on the front line. As Kornblum explained the situation, the woman of the house where he was living "had no sympathy for the distinction between participant and observer. She thrust a heavy stick in my hand shoved me toward the door" (1989:1).

Mark Fleisher (1989) studied the culture of guards at a federal penitentiary in California, but as an insider—an *observing participant*. Researchers at the U.S. Bureau of Prisons asked Fleisher to do an ethnographic study of job pressures on guards—called correctional officers, or COs, in the jargon of the profession—in a maximum-security federal penitentiary. It costs a lot to train a CO, and there was an unacceptably high rate of COs leaving the job after a year or two. Could Fleisher look into the problem?

Fleisher said he'd be glad to do the research and asked when he could start "walking the mainline"—that is, accompanying the COs on their rounds through the prison. He was told that he'd be given an office at the prison and that the guards would come to his office to be interviewed.

Fleisher said he was sorry, but he'd have to have the run of the prison. He was told that only sworn COs could walk the prison halls. So Fleisher went to training camp for six weeks and became a sworn federal correctional officer. Then he began his year-long study of the U.S. Penitentiary at Lompoc, California. In other words, he became an observing participant in the culture he was studying. Note, though, that Fleisher never hid what he was doing. When he went to USP-Lompoc, he told everyone that he was an anthropologist doing a study of prison life.

Barbara Marriott (1991) studied how the wives of U.S. Navy male officers contributed to their husbands' careers. Marriott was herself the wife of a retired captain. She was able to bring the empathy of 30 years' full participation to her study. She, too, took the role of observing insider, and like Fleisher, she told her informants exactly what she was doing.

Some field workers start out as participating observers and find that they are drawn completely into their informants' lives. This happened to Kenneth Good when he went to study the Yanomami Indians in the Amazon. He learned Yanomami, married a Yanomami woman, and wound up staying in the forest for 13 years (Good 1991). (Good and his wife, Yarima, moved to the U.S., but after a few years, Yarima returned to the Yanomami.)

Marlene Dobkin de Rios, another anthropologist, did fieldwork in Peru and married the son of a Peruvian folk healer, whose practice she studied (Dobkin de Rios 1981). Jean Gearing (1995) is another anthropologist who married her "best informant" on the island of St. Vincent. There are many examples of anthropologists going native. Is this good or bad? There are no pat answers.

Complete observation, or direct observation, is a potent method for gathering data. If you stand in a school yard counting the number of aggressive acts between same-sex and opposite-sex pairs of playmates, that's field research, but it's direct observation, not participant observation.

Direct observation can be done as a part of long-term ethnographic fieldwork. In 1949, John Roberts and a Zuñi interpreter took turns sitting in one of the rooms of a Zuñi house, simply dictating their observations into a tape recorder. This went on for five days. The data from this landmark study produced an entire book, rich in detail about Zuñi life (Roberts 1965 [1956]). People let Roberts park in their homes for five days because Roberts was a participant observer of Zuñi life and had gained his informants' confidence.

How Much Time Does It Take?

It's common to spend a year or more doing participant observation fieldwork. Anthropologists do this all the time, but so do sociologists and other social scientists. From 1970 to 1975, William Bainbridge (1978) studied a satanic cult called the Process Church of the Final Judgment. Bainbridge pretended to be a "depressive piano tuner" and convinced the members of the church that he himself was a believer (1992:31). (See Chapter 10 for a discussion of the ethics of disguised observation.)

Ruffing-Rahal (1993) acted as facilitator for a wellness group of older women. As a participant observer, Ruffing-Rahal took field notes on 75 of these weekly meetings in an attempt to identify core themes of well-being. Salisbury et al. (1993) spent two and a half years studying how disabled children were treated at one elementary school.

A lot of participant observation studies are done, however, in a matter of a few months. Yu (1995) spent four months as a participant observer in a family-run Chinese restaurant, looking at differences in the conceptions that Chinese and non-Chinese employees had about things like good service, adequate compensation, and the role of management.

Applied ethnographic research is often done in just a few weeks. Applied researchers usually don't have the luxury of doing long-term participant observation fieldwork, and may use *rapid assessment* procedures, instead. Rapid assessment of agricultural or medical practices may include participant observation.

Basically, **rapid assessment means going in and getting on with the job of collecting data without spending months developing rapport.** This means going into a field situation armed with a list of questions that you want to answer and perhaps a checklist of data that you need to collect. Chambers (1991) advocates what he calls *participatory*

rural appraisal. In *participatory mapping,* for example, he **asks people to draw maps of villages and locate key places on the maps.**

In *participatory transects,* he **borrows from wildlife biology and systematically walks through an area, with key informants, observing and asking for explanations of everything he sees along the transect.** He engages people in group discussions of key events in a village's history and asks them to identify clusters of households according to wealth. In other words, as an applied anthropologist Chambers is called on to do rapid assessment of rural village needs, and he takes the people fully into his confidence as research partners. This method is just as effective in organizations as in small villages.

At the extreme low end, it is possible to do useful participant observation in just a few days. Assuming that you've wasted as much time in laundromats as I did when I was a student, you could conduct a reasonable participant observation study of one such place in a week. You'd begin by bringing in a load of wash and paying careful attention to what's going on around you.

After two or three nights of observation, you'd be ready to tell other patrons that you were conducting research and that you'd appreciate their letting you interview them. The reason you could do this is because you already speak the native language and have already picked up the nuances of etiquette from previous experience. Participant observation would help you intellectualize what you already know.

In general, though, participant observation is not for the impatient. Gerald Berreman studied life in Sirkanda, a Pahari-speaking village in north India. Berreman's interpreter-assistant, Sharma, was a Hindu Brahmin who neither ate meat nor drank alcohol. As a result, villagers did neither around Berreman or his assistant. Three months into the research, Sharma fell ill and Berreman hired Mohammed, a young Muslim schoolteacher, to fill in.

When the villagers found out that Mohammed ate meat and drank alcohol, things broke wide open and Berreman found out that there were frequent intercaste meat and liquor parties. When villagers found out that the occasional drink of locally made liquor was served at Berreman's house, "access to information of many kinds increased proportionately" (Berreman 1962:10). Even then, it still took Berreman six months in Sirkanda before people felt comfortable performing animal sacrifices when he was around (ibid.:20). It took Daniel Wolf three years just to get into the Rebels, a brotherhood of outlaw bikers, and another couple of years riding with them before he had the data for his doctoral dissertation (Wolf 1990).

The amount of time you spend in the field really makes a difference in what you're likely to find. Raoul Naroll compared ethnographies based on a year or more in the field with those based on less than a year. He found that anthropologists who stayed in the field for at least a year were more likely to report on sensitive issues like witchcraft, sexuality, and political feuds (Naroll 1962). Ethnographers who have done very long-term participant observation—that is, a series of studies over decades—find that they eventually get data about social change that is simply not possible to get in any other way (Foster et al. 1979).

The bottom line: You can do highly focused participant observation research in your own language, to answer specific questions about your own culture, in a matter of weeks or months. How do middle-class, second-generation, Mexican American women make decisions on which of several brands to select when they go grocery shopping? If you are a middle-class Mexican American woman, you can probably find the answer to that question, using participant observation, in a few weeks, because you have a wealth of personal experience to draw on.

But if you're starting out fresh, and not a member of the culture you're studying, count on taking three months or more, under the best conditions, to be accepted as a participant observer—that is, as someone who has learned enough to learn.

VALIDITY—AGAIN

There are at least five reasons for insisting on participant observation in the conduct of scientific research about cultural groups.

First, as I've stressed, participant observation makes it possible to collect different kinds of data. Participant observation field workers have witnessed births, interviewed violent men in maximum-security prisons, stood in fields noting the behavior of farmers, trekked with hunters through the Amazon forest in search of game, and pored over records of marriages, births, and deaths in village churches and mosques around the world.

It is impossible to imagine a complete stranger walking into a birthing room and being welcomed to watch and record the event or being allowed to examine any community's vital records at whim. It is impossible, in fact, to imagine a stranger doing any of the things just mentioned, or the thousands of other intrusive acts of data collection that anthropologists, sociologists, and other field workers engage in all the time. What makes it all possible is participant observation.

Second, participant observation reduces the problem of *reactivity,* of **people changing their behavior when they know that they are being**

studied. As you become less and less of a curiosity, people take less and less interest in your comings and goings. They go about their business and let you do such bizarre things as conduct interviews, administer questionnaires, and even walk around with a stopwatch, clipboard, and camera. Phillipe Bourgois (1995) spent four years living in El Barrio (the local name for Spanish Harlem) in New York City. It took him a while, but eventually he was able to keep his tape recorder running for interviews about dealing crack cocaine and even when groups of men bragged about their involvement in gang rapes.

Bottom line: Presence builds trust. Trust lowers reactivity. Lower reactivity means higher validity of data.

Nothing is guaranteed in fieldwork, though. When Le Compte told children at a school that she was writing a book about them, they started acting out in "ways they felt would make good copy" by mimicking characters on popular TV programs (Le Compte et al. 1993).

Third, participant observation helps you formulate sensible questions, in the native language. Have you ever gotten a questionnaire in the mail and said to yourself, "What a dumb set of questions"? If a social scientist who is a member of your own culture can make up what you consider to be dumb questions, imagine the risk *you* take in making up a questionnaire in a culture very different from your own! Remember, it's just as important to ask sensible questions in a face-to-face interview as it is on a survey instrument.

Fourth, participant observation gives you an intuitive understanding of what's going on in a culture and allows you to speak with confidence about the meaning of data. It lets you make strong statements about cultural facts that you've collected. It extends both the internal and the external validity of what you learn from interviewing and watching people. In short, participant observation helps you understand the *meaning* of your observations. Here's a classic example.

In 1957, N. K. Sarkar and S. J. Tambiah published a study, based on questionnaire data, about economic and social disintegration in a Sri Lankan village. They concluded that about two-thirds of the villagers were landless. The British anthropologist Edmund Leach (1967) did not accept that finding. He had done participant observation fieldwork in the area and knew that the villagers practiced patrilocal residence after marriage. By local custom, a young man might receive *use* of some of his father's land even though legal ownership might not pass to the son until the father's death.

In assessing land ownership, Sarkar and Tambiah asked whether a "household" had any land, and if so, how much. They defined an independent household as a unit that cooked rice in its own pot. Unfortunately, all married women in the village had their own rice pots. So, Sarkar and Tambiah wound up estimating the number of independent households as very high and the number of those households that owned land as very low. Based on these data, they concluded that there was gross inequality in land ownership and that this characterized a "disintegrating village" (the title of their book).

> *Qualitative and quantitative data inform each other and produce insight and understanding in a way that cannot be duplicated by either approach alone.*

Don't conclude from Leach's critique that questionnaires are "bad" while participant observation is "good." I can't say often enough that participant observation makes it possible to collect quantitative survey data or qualitative interview data from some sample of a population. Qualitative and quantitative data inform each other and produce insight and understanding in a way that cannot be duplicated by either approach alone. Whatever data-collection methods you choose, participant observation maximizes your chances for making valid statements.

Fifth, many research problems simply cannot be addressed adequately by anything except participant observation. If you want to understand how a local court works, you can't very well disguise yourself and sit in the court room unnoticed. The judge would soon spot you as a stranger, and after a few days, you would have to explain yourself. It is better to explain yourself at the beginning and get permission to act as a participant observer. In this case, your participation consists of acting like any other local person who might sit in on the court's proceedings.

After a few days, or weeks, you would have a pretty good idea of how the court worked: what kinds of crimes are adjudicated, what kinds of penalties are meted out, and so forth. You might develop some specific hypotheses from your qualitative notes—hypotheses regarding covariations between severity of punishment and independent variables other than severity of crime. Then you could test those hypotheses on a sample of courts.

Think this is unrealistic? Try going down to your local traffic court and see whether defendants' dress or manner of speech predicts variations in fines for the same infraction. The point is, getting a general understanding of how any social institution or organization works—the local justice system, a hospital, a ship, or an entire community—is best achieved through participant observation.

ENTERING THE FIELD

Perhaps the most difficult part of actually doing participant observation fieldwork is making an entry. There are five rules to follow.

1. *There is no reason to select a site that is difficult to enter when equally good sites are available that are easy to enter* (see Chapter 3). In many cases, you *will* have a choice—among equally good school districts, communities, hospitals, political precincts, or cell blocks. When you have a choice, take the field site that promises to provide easiest access to data.

2. *Whenever it's appropriate, go into the field with plenty of written documentation about yourself and your project.* Being "appropriate" means that whenever you are going to a foreign country or whenever you are studying a mainstream organization like a school or a corporation or a shopping center, you have one or more letters of introduc-

tion from your university, your funding agency, or your client if you are doing contract research. Letters from universities should spell out your affiliation, who is funding you, and how long you will be at the field site. Be sure that those letters are in the language spoken where you will be working, and that they are signed by the highest academic authorities possible.

Letters of introduction should not go into detail about your proposed research. Have a separate document describing your proposed work and present it to gatekeepers who ask for it, along with your letters of introduction.

Of course, if you study an outlaw biker gang, like Daniel Wolf did, forget about letters of introduction (Wolf 1991).

3. *Don't try to wing it, unless you absolutely have to.* There is nothing to be said for "getting in on your own." Use personal contacts to help you

make your entry into a field site. Charles Gall-meier spent nearly a year traveling with and studying the Summit City Rockets, a pseudonym for a minor league hockey team in the U.S. Midwest. Gallmeier got permission to travel and hang out with the team because his father was a respected sports writer who had spent 25 years covering the league (Gallmeier 1991).

When I went to the island of Kalymnos, Greece, in 1964, I carried with me a list of people to look up. I collected the list from people in the Greek American community of Tarpon Springs, Florida, who had relatives on Kalymnos. When I went to Washington, D.C., to study how decision makers in the bureaucracy used (or didn't use) scientific information, I had letters of introduction from colleagues at Scripps Institution of Oceanography (where I was working at the time).

If you are studying any hierarchically organized community (hospitals, police departments, universities, school systems, etc.), it is usually best to start at the top and work down. Find out the names of the people who are the gatekeepers and see them first. Assure them that you will maintain strict confidentiality and that no one in your study will be personally identifiable. In some cases, starting at the top can backfire, though. If there are warring factions in a community or organization, and if you gain entry to the group at the top of *one* of those factions, you will be asked to side with that faction.

Another danger is that top administrators of institutions may try to enlist you as a kind of spy. They may offer to facilitate your work if you will report back to them on what you find out about specific individuals. This is absolutely off limits in research. If that's the price of doing a study, you're better off choosing another institution. In the two years I spent doing research on communication structures in federal prisons, no one ever asked me to report on the activities of specific inmates. But other researchers have reported experiencing

this kind of pressure, so it's worth keeping in mind.

4. *Think through in advance what you will say when ordinary people (not just gatekeepers) ask you: What are you doing here?* Who sent you? Who's funding you? What good is your research and whom will it benefit? Why do you want to learn about people here? How long will you be here? How do I know you aren't a spy for _____? (where the blank is filled in by whoever people are afraid of). The rules for presentation of self are simple: Be honest, be brief, and be absolutely consistent. In participant observation, if you try to play any role besides yourself, you'll just get worn out (Jones 1973).

But understand that not everyone will be thrilled about your role as a researcher. Terry Williams studied cocaine use in after-hours clubs in New York. One club he went to turned out to be having "gay night" when he showed up. "I thought," said Williams, "I would take advantage of the situation for sociological purposes, making comparisons between heterosexual and homosexual cocaine users." He goes on:

> I was wearing black leather (the fashion in New York at the time), not realizing the role of black leather in the gay community. I noticed a group of men sitting in a corner and moved toward them inconspicuously, or so I thought, until I was eight or ten feet away. One of them stared up at me and I, of course, looked toward him. His sleeves were rolled past his elbows, revealing purple and red tattoos on both arms.
>
> After looking at me for a few seconds, he walked over and offered to buy me a drink, asking if this was my first time there. I explained that I had been there before and informed him that I was a researcher and just wanted to talk to as many people as possible. He grew red in the face and said to his companions in a loud voice, hands on hips, head

cocked to one side: "Hey, get a load of this one. He wants to do research on us. You scum bag! What do we look like, pal? Fucking guinea pigs?" (Williams 1996:30)

After that experience, Williams became, as he said, "more selective" in whom he told about his real purpose in those after-hours clubs.

5. *Spend time getting to know the physical and social layout of your field site.* It doesn't matter if you're working in a small town, an urban enclave, a hospital, or a police precinct. Walk it and map it. Write down notes about how it *feels* to you. Is it crowded? Do the buildings or furniture seem old or poorly kept? Are there any distinctive odors?

You'd be surprised how much information comes from asking people about little things like these. If you are working in a really large area, you may not be able to map it, but you should walk as much of it as possible, as early as possible in your fieldwork. If you are studying a group that has no physical location (like a social movement), it still pays to spend time "mapping" the social scene (Schatzman and Strauss 1973). This means getting down the names of the key players and charting their relations.

In fact, a really good preliminary activity in any participant observation project is to make as many maps and charts as possible—kinship charts of families, chain-of-command charts in organizations, maps of offices or malls or whatever physical space you're studying, charts of who sits where at meetings, and so on.

Another good thing to do is to take a census of the group you're studying as soon as you can. Be careful, though. Taking a census can be a way to gain rapport in a community (walking around and visiting every household can have the effect of giving you credibility), but it can also backfire if people are afraid you might be a spy. Michael Agar (1980b) reports that he was branded as a Pakistani spy when he went to India, so his village census was useless.

THE SKILLS OF A PARTICIPANT OBSERVER

To a certain extent, participant observation must be learned in the field. The strength of participant observation is that you, as a researcher, become the instrument for data collection and analysis through your own experience. Consequently, you have to experience participant observation to get good at it. Nevertheless, there are a number of skills that you can develop before you go into the field.

Learning the Language

Unless you are a full participant in the culture you're studying, being a participant observer makes you a freak. Here's how anthropologists looked to Vine Deloria (1969:78), a Sioux writer:

Anthropologists can readily be identified on the reservations. Go into any crowd of people. Pick out a tall gaunt white man wearing Bermuda shorts, a World War II Army Air Force flying jacket, an Australian bush hat, tennis shoes, and packing a large knapsack incorrectly strapped on his back. He will invariably have a thin, sexy wife with stringy hair, an I.Q. of 191, and a vocabulary in which even the prepositions have eleven syllables. . . . This creature is an anthropologist.

Now, 30 years later, it may be the anthropologist's husband who jabbers in 11-syllable words, but the point is still the same. The most important thing you can do to stop being a freak is to speak the language of the people you're studying—and speak it well. Raoul Naroll (1962:89-90) once surveyed ethnographies and found that anthropologists who spoke the local language were statistically more likely to report data about witchcraft than were those who didn't. His interpretation was that local-language fluency improves your rapport, and this, in turn, increases the probability that people will tell you about witchcraft.

Does the credibility of our data depend on control of the local language? In 1933, Paul Radin, one of Franz Boas's students, complained that Margaret Mead's work on Samoa was superficial because she wasn't fluent in Samoan (Radin 1966 [1933]: 179). Fifty years later, Derek Freeman (1983) claimed that Mead had been duped by her adolescent informants about the extent of their sexual experience because she didn't know the local language.

According to Brislin et al. (1973:70), Samoa is one of those cultures where "it is considered acceptable to deceive and to 'put on' outsiders. Interviewers are likely to hear ridiculous answers, not given in a spirit of hostility but rather sport." Brislin et al. call this the *sucker bias,* and warn field workers to watch out for it. Presumably, knowing the local language fluently is one way to become alert to and avoid this problem.

When it comes to doing effective participant observation, learning a new jargon in your own language is just as important as learning a foreign language. Peggy Sullivan and Kirk Elifson studied the Free Holiness Church, a rural group of Pentecostals whose rituals include the handling of poisonous snakes (rattlers, cottonmouths, copperheads, and water moccasins). They had to learn an entirely new vocabulary:

Terms and expressions like "anointment," "tongues," "shouting," and "carried away in the Lord" began having meaning for us. We learned informally and often contextually through conversation and by listening to sermons and testimonials. The development of our understanding of the new language was gradual and probably was at its greatest depth when we were most submerged in the church and its culture. . . . We simplified our language style and eliminated our use of profanity. We realized, for example, that one badly placed "damn" could destroy trust that we had built up over months of hard work. (Sullivan and Elifson 1996:36)

How to Learn a New Language

In my experience, the way to learn a new language is to learn a few words and to say them brilliantly. Yes, you should study the grammar and vocabulary and so on, but the key to learning a new language is saying things right, even just a handful of things. This means capturing not just the pronunciation of words, but also the intonation, the use of your hands, and other nonverbal cues that show you are really, really serious about the language and are trying to look and sound as much like a native as possible.

When you say the equivalent of "hey, howya doin'" in any language—Zulu or French or Arabic—with just the right intonation, people will think you know more than you do. They'll come right back at you with a flurry of words, and you'll be lost. That's just fine. Tell them to slow down—again, in that great accent you're cultivating.

Consider the alternative: You announce to people, with the first, badly accented word out of your mouth, that you know next to nothing about the language and that they should therefore speak to you with that in mind. When you talk to someone who is not a native speaker of your language, you make an automatic assessment of how large their vocabulary is and how fluent they are. You adjust both the speed of your speech and your vocabulary to ensure comprehension. That's what Zulu and Arabic speakers will do with you, too. The trick is to act in a way that gets people into pushing your limits of fluency and into teaching you cultural insider phrases.

As you articulate more and more of those phrases like a native, people will increase the rate at which they teach you by raising the level of their discourse with you. They may even compete to teach you the subtleties of their language and culture. When I was learning Greek in 1960 on a Greek merchant ship, the sailors took delight in seeing to it that my vocabulary of obscenities was up to their standards and that my usage of that vocabulary was suitably robust.

In 1964-65, I spent a year on the island of Kalymnos in the Aegean Sea, collecting data for my doctoral thesis, and although I studied modern Greek as part of my graduate training at the University of Illinois, my accent, mannerisms, and vocabulary were heavily influenced by the experiences I had actually using the language.

When I went to teach at the University of Athens in 1969, my colleagues there were delighted that I wanted to teach in Greek, but they had some cognitive dissonance about my accent. How to reconcile the fact that an educated foreigner spoke reasonably fluent Greek with a rural, working-class accent? It didn't scan, but they were very forgiving. After all, I *was* a foreigner, and the fact that I was making an attempt to speak the local language counted for a lot.

So, if you are going off to do fieldwork in a foreign language, try to find an intensive summer course in the country where that language is spoken. Not only will you learn the language (and the local dialect of that language), you'll make personal contacts, find out what the problems are in selecting a research site, and discover how to tie your study to the interests of local scholars. You can study French in France, but you can also study it in Montreal, Martinique, or Madagascar.

You can study Spanish in Spain, but you can also study it in Mexico, Bolivia, or Paraguay.

You'd be amazed at the range of language courses available at universities these days: Ulithi, Aymara, Quechua, Nahuatl, Swahili, Turkish, Amharic, Basque, Eskimo, Navajo, Zulu, Hausa, Amoy. If the language you need is not offered in a formal course, try to find an individual speaker of the language who would be willing to tutor you in a self-paced course.

When Not to Mimic

The key to understanding the culture of loggers, lawyers, bureaucrats, schoolteachers, or ethnic groups is to become intimately familiar with their vocabulary. Words are where the cultural action is. My rule about mimicking pronunciation changes, though, if you are studying an ethnic or occupational subculture in your own society and the people in that subculture speak a different dialect of your native language. In this situation, mimicking the local pronunciation will just make you look silly. Even worse, people may think you're ridiculing them.

Building Explicit Awareness

Another important skill in participant observation is what Spradley (1980:55) called *explicit awareness* of the little details in life. Try this experiment: The next time you see someone look at their watch, go right up to them and ask them the time. Chances are they'll look again because when they looked the first time they were not *explicitly aware* of what they saw. Tell them that you are a student conducting a study and ask them to chat with you for a few minutes about how they tell time.

Many people who wear analog watches look at the *relative positions* of the hands, and not at the numbers on the dial. They subtract the current time (the position of the hands now) from the time they have to be somewhere (the image of what the position of the hands will look like at some time in the future), and calculate whether the difference is anything to worry about. They never have to become explicitly aware of the fact that it is 3:10 p.m. People who wear digital watches may be handling the process somewhat differently.

Kronenfeld et al. (1972) report an experiment in which informants leaving several different restaurants were asked what the waiters and waitresses (as they were called in those gender-differentiated days) were wearing, and what kind of music was playing. Informants agreed much more about what the waiters were wearing than about what the waitresses were wearing. The hitch: None of the restaurants had waiters at all, only waitresses.

Informants also provided more detail about the kind of music in restaurants that did not have music than they provided for restaurants that did have music. Kronenfeld speculated that, in the absence of real memories about things they'd seen or heard, informants turned to cultural norms for what must have been there (that is, "what goes with what") (D'Andrade 1973).

You can test this yourself. Pick out a large lecture hall where a male professor is not wearing a tie. Ask a group of students on their way out of a lecture hall what color tie their professor was wearing. Or observe a busy store clerk for an hour and count the number of sales she rings up. Then ask her to estimate the number of sales she handled during that hour.

You can build your skills at becoming explicitly aware of ordinary things. Get a group of colleagues together and write separate, detailed descriptions of the most mundane, ordinary things you can think of: making a bed, doing laundry, building a sandwich, shaving (face, legs, underarms), picking out produce at the supermarket, and so on. Then discuss one another's descriptions and see how many details others saw that

you didn't and vice versa. If you work carefully at this exercise you'll develop a lot of respect for how complex, and how important, the details of ordinary life are.

Building Memory

Even when we are explicitly aware of things we see, there is no guarantee that we'll remember them long enough to write them down. Building your ability to remember things you see and hear is crucial to successful participant observation research.

Try this exercise: Walk past a store window at a normal pace. When you get beyond it and can't see it any longer, write down all the things that were in the window. Go back and check. Do it again with another window. You'll notice an improvement in your ability to remember little things almost immediately. You'll start to create mnemonic devices for remembering more of what you see. Keep up this exercise until you are satisfied that you can't get any better at it.

Here's another one. Go to a church service, other than one you're used to. Take along two colleagues. When you leave, write up what you each think you saw, in as much detail as you can muster and compare what you've written. Go back to the church and keep doing this exercise until all of you are satisfied that (1) you are all seeing and writing down the same things, and (2) you have reached the limits of your ability to recall complex behavioral scenes.

Try this same exercise by going to a church service with which you *are* familiar and take along several colleagues who are not. Again, compare your notes with theirs, and keep going back and taking notes until you and they are seeing and noting the same things. You can do this with any repeated scene that's familiar to you: a bowling alley, a fast-food restaurant, and so on. Remember, training your ability to see things reliably does not guarantee that you'll see thing accurately. But unless you become at least a reliable instrument of data gathering, you don't stand much of a chance of making valid conclusions.

Bogdan (1972:41) offers some practical suggestions for remembering details in participant observation. If, for some reason, you can't take notes during an interview or at some event, and you are trying to remember what was said, *don't talk to anyone* before you get your thoughts down on paper. Talking to people reinforces some things you heard and saw at the expense of other things.

Also, when you sit down to write, try to remember things in historical sequence, as they occurred throughout the day. As you write up your notes you will invariably remember some particularly important detail that just pops into memory out of sequence. When that happens, jot it down on a separate piece of paper (or tuck it away in a separate little note file on your word processor) and come back to it later, when your notes reach that point in the sequence of the day.

Another useful device is to draw a map—even a rough sketch will do—of the physical space where you spent time observing and talking to people that day. As you move around the map, you will dredge up details of events and conversations. In essence, let yourself walk through your experience. You can practice all these memory-building skills now and be much better prepared if you decide to do long-term fieldwork later.

Maintaining Naïveté

Try also to develop your skill at being a novice—at being someone who genuinely wants to learn a new culture. This may mean working hard at suspending judgment about some things. David Fetterman made a trip across the Sinai Desert with a group of Bedouins. One of the Bedouins, says Fetterman (1989:33),

> Shared his jacket with me to protect me from the heat. I thanked him, of course, because I appreciated the gesture and did not want to insult him. But I smelled like a camel for the rest of the day in the dry desert heat. I thought I didn't need the jacket. . . . I later learned that without his jacket I would have suffered from sunstroke. . . . An inexperienced traveler does not always notice when the temperature climbs above 130 degrees Fahrenheit. By slowing down the evaporation rate, the jacket helped me retain water.

Maintaining your naïveté will come naturally in a culture that's unfamiliar to you, but it's a bit harder to do in your own culture. Most of what you do "naturally" is so automatic that you don't know how to intellectualize it.

If you are like many middle-class Americans, your eating habits can be characterized by the word "grazing"—that is, eating small amounts of food at many, irregular times during the course of a typical day, rather than sitting down for meals at fixed times. Would you have used that kind of word to describe your own eating behavior? Other members of your own culture are often better informants than you are about that culture, and if you really let people teach you, they will.

If you look carefully, though, you'll be surprised at how heterogeneous your culture is and how many parts of it you really know nothing about. For example, I'm a "ham" (amateur) radio operator. When CB radio buffs start learning to be hams they make a lot of mistakes. They think that their experience with CB radios will transfer to ham radio and are usually surprised at how little they know about all the etiquette for over-the-air interaction that ham operators take for granted.

CBers feel awkward at first. Their jargon isn't right, and they don't share any of the ham lore. Try studying to become a ham operator and see for yourself what it takes to learn to act properly in that culture. Or find some other part of your own culture that you don't control and try to learn it. That's what you did as a child, of course. Only this time, try to intellectualize the experience. Take notes on what you learn about *how to learn,* on what it's like being a novice, and how you think you can best take advantage of the learner's role. Your imagination will suggest a lot of other nooks and crannies of our culture that you can explore as a thoroughly untutored novice.

When Not to Be Naive

The role of naive novice is not always the best one to play. Humility is inappropriate when you are dealing with a culture whose members stand to lose a lot by your incompetence. Michael Agar (1973, 1980a) did field research on the life of heroin addicts in New York City. His informants made it plain that Agar's ignorance of their lives wasn't cute or interesting to them.

Even with the best of intentions, Agar could have given his informants away to the police just by being stupid. Under such circumstances, you shouldn't expect your informants to take you under their wing and teach you how to appreciate their customs. Agar had to learn a lot, and very quickly, to gain credibility with his informants.

There are situations where your expertise is just what's required to build rapport with people. Anthropologists have typed documents for illiterate people in the field and have used other skills (from coaching basketball to dispensing antibiotics) to help people and to gain their confidence and respect. If you are studying highly educated people, you may have to prove that you know a

fair amount about research methods before they will deal with you. Agar (1980b:58) once studied an alternative lifestyle commune and was asked by a biochemist who was living there: "Who are you going to use as a control group?" In my study of ocean scientists (Bernard 1974), several informants asked me what computer programs I was going to use to do a factor analysis of my data.

Building Writing Skills

The ability to write comfortably and clearly is one of the most important skills you can develop as a participant observer. Ethnographers who are not comfortable as writers produce few field notes and little published work. If you have any doubts about your ability to sit down at a typewriter or word processor and pound out thousands of words, day in and day out, then try to build that skill now, before you go into the field for an extended period.

The way to build that skill is to team up with one or more colleagues who are also trying to build their expository writing ability. Set concrete and regular writing tasks for yourselves, and criticize one another's work on matters of clarity and style. There is nothing "Mickey Mouse" about this kind of exercise. If you think you need it, do it.

Good writing skills will carry you through participant observation fieldwork, writing a dissertation, and finally, writing for publication. Don't be afraid to write clearly and compellingly. The worst that can happen is that someone will criticize you for "popularizing" your material. I think ethnographers should be criticized if they take the exciting material of real people's lives and turn it into deadly dull reading.

Hanging Out, Gaining Rapport

It may sound silly, but just *hanging out* is a skill, and until you learn it you can't do your best work as a participant observer. Remember what I said at the beginning of this chapter: Participant observation is a *strategic* method that lets you learn what you want to learn and apply all the data-collection methods that you may want to apply.

When you enter a new field situation, the temptation is to ask a lot of questions to learn as much as possible as quickly as possible. There are many things that people can't or won't tell you in answer to questions. If you ask people too quickly about the sources of their wealth, you are likely to get incomplete data. If you ask too quickly about sexual liaisons, you may get thoroughly unreliable responses.

Hanging out builds trust, or *rapport,* and trust results in ordinary conversation and ordinary behavior in your presence. Once you know, from hanging out, exactly what you want to know more about, and once people trust you not to betray their confidence, you'll be surprised at the direct questions you can ask.

In his study of Cornerville, William Foote Whyte wondered whether "just hanging on the street corner was an active enough process to be dignified by the term 'research.' Perhaps I should ask these men questions," he thought. He soon realized that "one has to learn when to question and when not to question as well as what questions to ask" (1989:78).

Philip Kilbride studied child abuse in Kenya. He did a survey and focused ethnographic interviews, but "by far the most significant event in my research happened as a byproduct of participatory 'hanging out,' being always in search of case material." While visiting informants one day, Kilbride and his wife saw a crowd gathering at a local secondary school. It turned out that a young mother had thrown her baby into a pit latrine at the school. The Kilbrides offered financial assistance to the young mother and her family in exchange for "involving ourselves in their . . . misfortune." The event that the Kilbrides had witnessed became the focus for a lot of their research activities in the succeeding months (Kilbride 1992:190).

The Ethical Dilemma of Rapport

If all this gaining rapport seems a little manipulative, it's because it is. My favorite super-honest story about manipulating others comes from E. E. Evans-Pritchard, one of the most famous anthropologists of all time.

Evans-Pritchard wanted to study witchcraft among the Azande. He decided to "win the good will of one or two practitioners and to persuade them to divulge their secrets in strict confidence" (1958 [1937]: 151). Strict confidence? He was planning on writing a book about all this. Anyway, progress was slow, and while he felt that he could have "eventually wormed out all their secrets" he turned his attention to other matters.

A few months later, he hit on another idea: His personal servant, Kamanga, was initiated into the local group of practitioners and "became a practising witch-doctor" (ibid.:151). With the full knowledge of his tutor, named Badobo, Kamanga reported every step of his training to his employer. In turn, Evans-Pritchard used the information "to draw out of their shells rival practitioners by playing on their jealousy and vanity."

Evans-Pritchard analyzed the situation carefully. Kamanga's tutor knew that anything he told Kamanga would be tested with rival witch-doctors. The tutor, then, couldn't lie to Kamanga, but he could certainly withhold the most secret material. Evans-Pritchard remained undeterred. "Armed with preliminary knowledge," he said, "nothing can prevent [an ethnographer] from driving deeper and deeper the wedge if he is interested and persistent" (ibid.:152).

Still, Kamanga's training was so slow that Evans-Pritchard nearly abandoned his inquiry into witchcraft. Providence intervened. A very prominent witch-doctor, named Bögwözu, showed up from another district. Evans-Pritchard offered him a very high wage if he'd take over Kamanga's training and teach Kamanga everything. "I explained to [Bögwözu] that I was tired of Badobo's wiliness and extortion, and that I expected my generosity to be reciprocated by the equipment of Kamanga with something more than esoteric knowledge of a witch-doctor's technique" (ibid.).

Evans-Pritchard was the wily one. He kept paying Badobo to tutor Kamanga, but he *knew* that Badobo would be very jealous of Bögwözu. Here is Evans-Pritchard going on about his deceit and the benefits of this tactic for ethnographers:

> The rivalry between these two practitioners grew into bitter and ill-concealed hostility. Bögwözu gave me information about medicines and magical rites to prove that his rival was ignorant of the one or incapable in the performance of the other. Badobo became alert and showed himself no less eager to demonstrate his knowledge of magic to both Kamanga and to myself. They vied with each other to gain ascendancy among the local practitioners. Kamanga and I reaped a full harvest in this quarrel, not only from the protagonists themselves but also from other witch-doctors in the neighborhood, and even from interested laymen. (ibid.:153)

Objectivity

Finally, *objectivity* is a skill, like language fluency, and you can build it if you work at it. Some people build more of it, others less. More is better.

If an objective measurement is one made by a robot—that is, a machine that is not prone to the kind of measurement error that comes from having opinions and memories—then no human being can ever be completely objective. We can't rid ourselves of our experiences, and I don't know anyone who thinks it would be a good idea even to try.

We can, however, become aware of our experiences, our opinions, our values. We can hold our field observations up to a cold light and ask whether we've seen what we wanted to see, or what is really out there. The goal is not for us, as humans, to become objective machines; it is for us to achieve objective—that is, accurate—knowledge by transcending our biases.

Laurie Krieger, an American woman doing fieldwork in Cairo, studied physical punishment against women. She learned that wife beatings were less violent than she had imagined and that the act still sickened her. Her reaction brought out a lot of information from women who were recent recipients of their husbands' wrath. "I found out," she says, "that the biased outlook of an American woman and a trained anthropologist was not always disadvantageous, as long as I was aware of and able to control the expression of my biases" (1986:120).

Colin Turnbull held objective knowledge as something to be pulled from the thicket of subjective experience. Fieldwork, said Turnbull, involves a self-conscious review of one's own ideas and values—one's self, for want of any more descriptive term. During fieldwork you "reach inside," he observed, and give up the "old, narrow, limited self, discovering the new self that is right and proper in the new context." We use the field experience, he said, "to know ourselves more deeply by conscious subjectivity." In this way, he concluded, "the ultimate goal of objectivity is much more likely to be reached and our understanding of other cultures that much more profound" (Turnbull 1986:27).

Many phenomenologists see objective knowledge as the goal of participant observation. Danny Jorgensen, for example, advocates complete immersion and *becoming the phenomenon* you study. "Becoming the phenomenon" Jorgensen says, "is a participant observational strategy for penetrating to and gaining experience of a form of human life. It is an objective approach insofar as it results in the accurate, detailed description of the insiders' experience of life" (1989:63). In fact, many ethnographers have become cab drivers or exotic dancers, jazz musicians, or members of satanic cults to do participant observation fieldwork.

If you use this strategy of full immersion, Jorgensen says, you must be able to switch back and forth between the insider's view and that of an analyst. To do that—to maintain your objective, analytic abilities—Jorgensen suggests finding a colleague with whom you can talk things over regularly. That is, give yourself an outlet for discussing the theoretical, methodological, and emotional issues that inevitably come up in full participation field research. It's good advice.

Objectivity and Neutrality

Objectivity does not mean (and has never meant) *value neutrality.* No one asks Cultural Survival, Inc. to be neutral in documenting the violent obscenities against indigenous peoples of the world. No one asks Amnesty International to be neutral in its effort to document state-sanctioned torture. We recognize that the power of the documentation is in its objectivity, in its chilling irrefutability, not in its neutrality.

Claire Sterk, an ethnographer from the Netherlands, has studied prostitutes and intravenous drug users in mostly African American communities in New York City and Newark, New Jersey. Sterk was a trusted friend and counselor to many of the women with whom she worked. In one two-month period in the late 1980s, she attended the funerals of seven women she knew who had died of AIDS. She felt that "every researcher is affected by the work he or she does. One cannot remain neutral and uninvolved; even as an outsider, the researcher is part of the community" (1989:99).

At the end of his second year of research on street life in El Barrio, Phillipe Bourgois's friends and informants began telling him about their experiences as gang rapists. Bourgois's informants were in their mid- to late 20s then, and the stories they told were of things they'd done as very young adolescents, more than a decade earlier. Still, Bourgois says, he felt betrayed by people whom he had come to like and respect. Their "childhood stories of violently forced sex," he says, "spun me into a personal depression and a research crisis" (1995:205).

In *any* long-term field study, be prepared for some serious tests of your ability to remain a dispassionate observer. Powdermaker (1966) was once confronted with the problem of knowing that a lynch mob was preparing to go after a particular Black man. She was powerless to stop the mob and fearful for her own safety.

I have never grown accustomed to seeing people ridicule the handicapped, though I see it every time I'm in Mexico and Greece, and I recall with horror the death of a young man on one of the sponge diving boats I sailed with in Greece. I knew the rules of safe diving that could have prevented that death; so did all the divers and the captains of the vessels. They ignored those rules at a terrible cost. I wanted desperately to *do* something, but there was nothing anyone could do.

Objectivity and Indigenous Research

Objectivity gets its biggest test in *indigenous research*—that is, when you study your own culture. Barbara Meyerhoff worked in Mexico when she was a graduate student. Later, in the early 1970s, when she became interested in ethnicity and aging, she decided to study elderly Chicanos. The people she approached kept putting her off, asking her, "Why work with us? Why don't you study your own kind?" Meyerhoff was Jewish. She had never thought about studying her own kind, but she launched a study of poor, elderly Jews who were on public assistance. She agonized about what she was doing and, as she tells it, never resolved whether it was anthropology or a personal quest.

Many of the people she studied were survivors of the Holocaust. "How, then, could anyone look at them dispassionately? How could I feel anything but awe and appreciation for their mere presence? . . . Since neutrality was impossible and idealization undesirable, I decided on striving for balance" (Meyerhoff 1989:90).

There is no final answer on whether it's good or bad to study your own culture. Plenty of people have done it, and plenty of people have written about what it's like to do it. On the plus side, you'll know the language and you'll be less likely to suffer from culture shock. On the minus side, it's harder to recognize cultural patterns that you live every day and you're likely to take a lot of things for granted that an outsider would pick up right away.

If you are going to study your own culture, start by reading the experiences of others who have done it so you'll know what you're facing in the field (Messerschmidt 1981; Stephenson and Greer 1981; Fahim 1982; Altorki and El-Sohl 1988).

GENDER, PARENTING, AND OTHER PERSONAL CHARACTERISTICS

By the 1930s, Margaret Mead had already made clear the importance of gender as a variable in data collection (see Mead 1986). Gender has at least two consequences: It limits your access to certain information, and it influences how you perceive others.

In all cultures, you can't ask people certain questions because you're a [woman] [man]. You can't go into certain areas and situations because you're a [woman] [man]. You can't watch this or report on that because you're a [woman] [man]. Even the culture of social scientists is affected: Your credibility is diminished or enhanced with your colleagues when you talk about a certain subject because you're a [woman] [man] (Scheper-Hughes 1983; Golde 1986; Whitehead and Conaway 1986; Altorki and El-Solh 1988; Warren 1988).

Sara Quandt, Beverly Morris, and Kathleen DeWalt spent months investigating the nutritional strategies of the elderly in two rural Kentucky counties (Quandt et al. 1997). According to De-Walt, the three women researchers spent months interviewing key informants, and never turned up a word about the use of alcohol. "One day," says DeWalt:

The research team traveled to Central County with Jorge Uquillas, an Ecuadorian sociologist who had expressed an interest in visiting the Kentucky field sites. One of the informants they visited was Mr. B, a natural storyteller who had spoken at length about life of the poor during the past sixty years. Although he had been a great source of information about use of wild foods and recipes for cooking game he had never spoken of drinking or moonshine production.

Within a few minutes of entering his home on this day, he looked at Jorge Uquillas, and said, "Are you a drinking man?" (Beverly whipped out the tape recorder and switched it on.) Over the next hour or so, Mr. B talked about community values concerning alcohol use, the problems of drunks and how they were dealt with in the community, and provided a number of stories about moonshine in Central County. The presence of another man gave Mr. B the opportunity to talk about issues he found interesting, but felt would have been inappropriate to discuss with women. (DeWalt et al. 1998:280)

On the other hand, feminist scholars recently have made it clear that gender is a negotiated idea. What you can and can't do if you are a man or a woman is more fixed in some cultures than in others, and in all cultures there is a lot of individual variation in gender roles. While men or women may be "expected" to be this way or that way in any given place, the variation in male and female attitudes and behaviors within a culture can be tremendous.

All participant observers confront their personal limitations and the limitations imposed on them by the culture they study. When she worked at the Thule relocation camp for Japanese Americans during World War II, Rosalie Wax did not join any of the women's groups or organizations. Looking back after more than 40 years, Wax concluded that this was just poor judgment.

I was a university student and a researcher. I was not yet ready to accept myself as a total person, and this limited my perspective and my understanding. Those of us who instruct future field workers should encourage them to understand and value their full range of being, because only then can they cope intelligently with the range of experience they will encounter in the field. (1986:148)

Beside gender, we have learned that being a parent helps you talk to people about certain areas of life and get more information than if you were not a parent. My wife and I arrived on the island of Kalymnos, Greece, in 1964 with a two-month-old baby. As Joan Cassell says, children are a "guarantee of good intentions" (1987:260), and wherever we went, the baby was the conversation opener. But be warned: Taking children into the field can place them at risk. More on risk in the section on surviving fieldwork.

Being divorced has its costs. Nancie González found that being a divorced mother of two young sons in the Dominican Republic was just too much. "Had I to do it again," she says, "I would invent widowhood with appropriate rings and photographs" (1986:92).

Even height may make a difference: Alan Jacobs once told me he thought he did better fieldwork with the Maasai because he's 6′ 5″ than he would have if he'd been, say, an average-sized 5′ 10″.

Personal characteristics make a difference in fieldwork. Being old or young lets you into certain things and shuts you out of others. Being wealthy lets you talk to certain people about certain subjects and makes others avoid you. Being gregarious makes some people open up to you and makes others shy away. There is no way to eliminate the "personal equation" in participant observation fieldwork, or in any other scientific data-gathering exercise, for that matter, without sending robots out to do the work. Of course, the robots would have their own problems. In all sciences, the personal equation (the influence of the observer on the data) is a matter of serious concern and study (Romney 1989).

SEX AND FIELDWORK

It is unreasonable to assume that single, adult field workers are all celibate, yet the literature on field methods is nearly silent on this topic. When Evans-Pritchard was a student, just about to head off for Central Africa, he asked his major professor for advice. "Seligman told me to take ten grains of quinine every night and keep off women" (Evans-Pritchard 1973:1). As far as I know, that's the last we heard from Evans-Pritchard on the subject.

Colin Turnbull (1986) tells us about his affair with a young Mbuti woman, and Dona Davis (1986) discusses her relationship with an engineer who visited the Newfoundland village where she was doing research on menopause. In Turnbull's case, he had graduated from being an asexual child in Mbuti culture to being a youth and was expected to have sexual relations. In Davis's case, she was expected not to have sexual relations, but she also learned that she was not bound by the expectation. In fact, Davis says that "being paired off" made women more comfortable with her because she was "simply breaking a rule everyone else broke" (1986:254).

Recently, several anthologies have been published in which researchers discuss their own sexual experiences during participant observation fieldwork (Kulick and Willson 1995; Lewin and Leap 1996). The rule on sexual behavior in the field is this: Do nothing that you can't live with, both professionally and personally. Be even more conscious of the possible fallout, for you and for your partner, than you would in your own community. Eventually, you will be going home. Will that affect your partner negatively?

Proscriptions against sex in fieldwork are silly, because they don't work. But understand that this is one area that people everywhere take very seriously.

SURVIVING FIELDWORK

The title of this section is the title of an important book by Nancy Howell (1990). All researchers—whether they are anthropologists, epidemiologists, or social psychologists—who expect to do fieldwork in developing nations should read Howell's book. Howell surveyed 204 anthropologists about illnesses and accidents in the field, and the results are sobering. The maxim that "anthropologists are otherwise sensible people who don't believe in the germ theory of disease" is apparently correct (Rappaport 1990).

One hundred percent of anthropologists who do fieldwork in south Asia reported being exposed to malaria, and 41% reported contracting the disease. Eighty-seven percent of anthropologists who work in Africa reported exposure, and 31% reported having had malaria. Seventy percent of anthropologists who work in south Asia reported having had some liver disease.

Among all anthropologists, 13% reported having had hepatitis A. I was hospitalized for six weeks for hepatitis A in 1968 and spent most of another year recovering. Glynn Isaac died of hepatitis B at age 47 in 1985 after a long career of archaeological fieldwork in Africa. Typhoid fever is also common among anthropologists, as are amoebic dysentery, giardia, ascariasis, hookworm, and other infectious diseases.

Accidents have injured or killed many field workers. Fei Xiaotong, a student of Malinowski's, was caught in a tiger trap in China in 1935. The injury left him an invalid for six months. His wife died in her attempt to go for help. Michelle Zimbalist Rosaldo was killed in a fall in the Philippines in 1981. Thomas Zwickler, a graduate student at the University of Pennsylvania, was killed by a bus on a rural road in India in 1985. He was riding a bicycle when he was struck. Kim Hill was accidentally hit by an arrow while out with an Ache hunting party in Paraguay in 1982 (Howell 1990: passim).

Five members of a Russian-American team of researchers on social change in the Arctic died in 1995 when their *umiak* (a traditional, walrus-hide Eskimo boat) was overturned by a whale (see Broadbent 1995). The researchers were three Americans (two anthropologists, Steven McNabb and Richard Condon, and a psychiatrist, William Richards) and two Russians (one anthropologist, Alexander Pika, and the chief Eskimo ethnographic consultant to the project, Boris Mumikhpykak). Nine other Eskimo villagers also perished in that accident. I've had my own unpleasant brushes with fate, and I know many others who have had very, very close calls.

What can you do about the risks? Get every inoculation you need before you leave, not just the ones that are required by the country you are entering. Check your county health office for the latest information from the Centers for Disease Control about illnesses prevalent in the area you're going to. If you go into an area that is known to be malarial, take a full supply of antimalarial drugs with you so you don't run out while you're out in the field.

When people pass around a gourd full of *chicha* or *pulque* or palm wine, decline politely and explain yourself if you have to. You'll probably insult a few people, and your protests won't always get you off the hook, but even if you only lower the number of times you are exposed to disease, you lower your risk of contracting disease.

After being very sick in the field, I learned to carry a supply of bottled beer with me when I'm going to visit a house where I'm sure to be given a gourd full of local brew. The gift of bottled beer is generally appreciated and heads off the embarrassment of having to turn down a drink I'd rather not have. It also makes plain that I'm not a teetotaler. Of course, if you are a teetotaler, you've got a ready-made get-out.

If you do fieldwork in a remote area, consult with physicians at your university hospital for information on the latest blood-substitute technology. If you are in an accident in a remote area and need blood, a nonperishable blood substitute can buy you time until you can get to a clean blood supply. Some field workers carry a supply of sealed hypodermic needles with them in case they need an injection. Don't go anywhere without medical insurance and don't go to developing countries without evacuation insurance. It costs about $60,000 to evacuate a person by jet from central Africa to Paris or Frankfurt. It costs less than $50 a month for insurance that will cover it.

Fieldwork in remote areas isn't for everyone, but if you're going to do it, you might as well do it as safely as possible. Candice Bradley is a Type I diabetic who does long-term fieldwork in western Kenya. She takes her insulin, glucagon, blood-testing equipment, and needles with her. She arranges her schedule around the predictable, daily fluctuations in her blood-sugar level. She trains people on how to cook for her, and she lays in large stocks of diet drinks so that she can function in the relentless heat without raising her blood sugars (Bradley 1997:4-7).

With all this, Bradley still had close calls—near blackouts from hypoglycemia—but her close calls are no more frequent than those experienced by other field researchers who work in similarly remote areas. The rewards of foreign fieldwork can be very great, but so are the risks.

THE STAGES OF PARTICIPANT OBSERVATION

In what follows, I will draw on three sources of data: (1) a review of the literature on field research; (2) conversations with colleagues during the last 30 years, specifically about their experiences in the field; and (3) five years of work, with the late Michael Kenny, directing National Science Foundation (NSF) field schools in cultural anthropology and linguistics.

During our work with the field schools (1967-71), Kenny and I developed an outline of *researcher response* in participant observation fieldwork. Those field schools were 10 weeks long and were held each summer in central Mexico. One school was held in the interior of the Pacific Northwest. In Mexico, students were assigned to Ñähñu-speaking communities in the vicinity of Ixmiquilpan, Mexico. In the Northwest field school, students were assigned to small logging and mining communities in the Idaho panhandle. In Mexico, a few students did urban ethnography in the regional capital of Pachuca, while in the Northwest field school, a few students did urban ethnography in Spokane, Washington.

What Kenny and I found so striking was that the stages we identified in the 10-week field experiences of our students were the same across all these places. Even more interesting—to us, anyway—was that the experiences our students had during those 10-week stints as participant observers apparently had exact analogs in our own experiences with year-long fieldwork.

1. Initial Contact

During the initial contact period, many long-term field workers report experiencing a kind of euphoria as they begin to move about in a new culture. It shouldn't come as any surprise that people who are attracted to the idea of living in a new culture are delighted when they begin to do so.

But not always. Here is Napoleon Chagnon's recollection of his first encounter with the Yanomami: "I looked up and gasped when I saw a dozen burly, naked, sweaty, hideous men staring at us down the shafts of their drawn arrows! . . . had there been a diplomatic way out, I would have ended my fieldwork then and there" (Chagnon 1983:10-11).

The desire to bolt and run is more common than we have admitted in the past. Charles Wagley, who would become one of our discipline's most accomplished ethnographers, made his first field trip in 1937. A local political chief in Totonicapán, Guatemala, invited Wagley to tea in a parlor overlooking the town square. The chief's wife and two daughters joined them. While they were having their tea, two of the chief's aides came in and hustled everyone off to another room. The chief explained the hurried move to Wagley:

> He had forgotten that an execution by firing squad of two Indians, "nothing but vagrants who had robbed in the market," was to take place at five p.m. just below the parlor. He knew that I would understand the feelings of ladies and the grave problem of trying to keep order among brutes. I returned to my ugly pensión in shock and spent a night without sleep. I would have liked to have returned as fast as possible to New York. (Wagley 1983:6)

Finally, listen to Rosalie Wax describe her encounter with the Arizona Japanese internment camp that she studied during World War II. When she arrived in Phoenix it was 110°. Later that day, after a bus ride and a 20-mile ride in a GI truck, across a dusty landscape that "looked like the skin of some cosmic reptile," with a Japanese American who wouldn't talk to her, Wax arrived at the Gila camp. By then it was 120°. She was driven to staff quarters, which was an army barracks divided into tiny cells, and abandoned to find her cell by a process of elimination.

> It contained four dingy and dilapidated articles of furniture: an iron double bedstead, a dirty mattress (which took up half the room), a chest of drawers, and a tiny writing table—and it was hotter than the hinges of Hades. . . . I sat down on the hot mattress, took a deep breath, and cried. . . . Like some lost two-year-old, I only knew that I was miserable. After a while, I found the room at the end of the barrack that contained two toilets and a couple of wash basins. I washed my face and told myself I would feel better the next day. I was wrong. (Wax 1971:67)

2. Culture Shock

Even among those field workers who have a pleasant experience during their initial contact period (and many do), almost all report experiencing some form of depression and shock soon thereafter (within a week or two). One kind of shock comes as the novelty of the field site wears off and there is this nasty feeling that research has to get done. Some researchers (especially those on their first field trip) may also experience feelings of anxiety about their ability to collect good data.

A good response at this stage is to do highly task-oriented work: making maps, taking censuses, doing household inventories, collecting genealogies, and so on. Another useful response is to make clinical, methodological field notes about your feelings and responses in doing participant observation fieldwork.

Another kind of shock is to the culture itself. *Culture shock* is an uncomfortable stress response and must be taken very seriously. In serious cases of culture shock, nothing seems right. You may find yourself very upset at a lack of clean toilet facilities, or people's eating habits or their child-rearing practices. The prospect of having to put up with the local food for a year or more may become frightening. You find yourself focusing on little annoyances—something as simple as the fact that light switches go side to side rather than up and down may upset you.

This last example is not fanciful, by the way. It happened to a colleague of mine, and I once became infuriated with the fact that men didn't shake hands the way "they're supposed to." You may find yourself blaming everyone in the culture, or the culture itself, for the fact that your informants don't keep appointments for interviews.

Culture shock commonly involves a feeling that people really don't want you around (this may, in fact, be the case). You feel lonely and wish you could find someone with whom to speak your native language. Even with a spouse along in the field, the strain of using another language day after day, and concentrating hard so that you can collect data in that language, can be emotionally wearing.

A common personal problem in field research is not being able to get any privacy. Many people across the world find the Anglo-Saxon notion of privacy grotesque. When we first went out to the island of Kalymnos in Greece in 1964, my wife and I rented quarters with a family. The idea was that we'd be better able to learn about family dynamics. Women of the household were annoyed and hurt when my wife asked for a little time to be alone. When I came home at the end of each day's work, I could never just go to my family's room, shut the door, and talk to my wife about my day, or hers, or our new baby's. If I didn't share everything during waking hours with the family we lived with, they felt rejected.

After about two months of this, we had to move out and find a house of our own. My access to data about intimate family dynamics was curtailed. But it was worth it because I felt that I'd have had to abort the whole trip if I had to continue living in what my wife and I felt was a glass bowl all the time. As it turns out, there is no word for the concept of privacy in Greek. The closest gloss translates as "being alone," and connotes loneliness.

I suspect that this problem is common to all English-speaking researchers who work in developing countries. Here's what M. N. Srinivas, himself from India, wrote about his work in the rural village of Ramapura, near Mysore:

> I was never left alone. I had to fight hard even to get two or three hours absolutely to myself in a week or two. My favorite recreation was walking to the nearby village of Kere where I had some old friends, or to Hogur which had a weekly market. But my friends in Ramapura wanted to accompany me on my walks. They were puzzled by my liking for solitary walks. Why should one walk when one could catch a bus, or ride on bicycles with friends. I had to plan and plot to give them the slip to go out by myself. On my return, however, I was certain to be asked why I had not taken them with me. They would have put off their work and joined me. (They meant it.) I suffered from social claustrophobia as long as I was in the village and sometimes the feeling became so intense that I just had to get out. (1979:23; used by permission)

Culture shock subsides as researchers settle in to the business of gathering data on a daily basis, but it doesn't go away because the sources of annoyance don't go away.

Unless you are one of the very rare people who truly go native in another culture (in which case it will be very difficult for you to intellectualize your experience), you will cope with culture shock, not eliminate it. You will remain conscious of things annoying you, but you won't feel like they are crippling your ability to work. Like Srinivas, when things get too intense, you'll have the good sense to leave the field site for a bit rather than try to stick it out.

3. Discovering the Obvious

In the next phase of participant observation, researchers settle into collecting data on a more or less systematic basis (see Kirk and Miller 1986). This is sometimes accompanied by an interesting personal response, a sense of discovery where you feel as if informants are finally letting you in on the "good stuff" about their culture. Much of this "good stuff" will later turn out to be commonplace. You may "discover," for example, that women have more power in the community than meets the eye or that there are two systems for dispute settlement—one embodied in formal law and one that works through informal mechanisms.

A concomitant to this feeling of discovery is sometimes a feeling of being in control of dangerous information, and a sense of urgency about protecting informants' identities. You may find yourself going back over your field notes, looking for places that you might have lapsed and identified an informant, and making appropriate changes. You may worry about those copies of field notes you have already sent home, and even become a little worried about how well you can trust your major professor to maintain the privacy of those notes.

This is the stage of fieldwork when you hear anthropologists start talking about "their" village, and how people are, at last, "letting them in" to the secrets of the culture. The feeling has its counterpart among all long-term participant observers. It often spurs researchers to collect more and more data; to accept every invitation, by every informant, to every event; to fill the days with observation, and to fill the nights with writing up field notes. Days off become unthinkable, and the sense of discovery becomes more and more intense.

This is the time to take a serious break.

4. The Break

The midfieldwork break, which usually comes after three or four months, is a crucial part of the overall participant observation experience for long-term researchers. It's an opportunity to get some distance, both physical and emotional, from the field site. It gives you a chance to put things into perspective, think about what you've got so far, and what you need to get in the time remaining. Use this time to collect data from regional or national statistical services; visit with colleagues at the local university and discuss your findings; visit other communities in other parts of the country. And be sure to leave some time to just take a vacation, without thinking about research at all.

Your informants also need a break from you. "Anthropologists are uncomfortable intruders no matter how close their rapport," notes Charles Wagley. "A short respite is mutually beneficial. One returns with objectivity and human warmth restored. The anthropologist returns as an old friend" who has gone away and returned, and has thereby demonstrated his or her genuine interest in a community (Wagley 1983:13). The same goes for sociologists, or any other researchers doing participant observation. Everyone needs a break.

5. Focusing

After the break, you will have a better idea of exactly what kinds of data you are lacking, and your sense of problems will also come more sharply into focus. The reason to have a formally prepared design statement *before* you go to the field, of course, is to tell you what you should be looking for. Nevertheless, even the most focused research design will have to be modified in the field. In some cases, you may find yourself making radical changes in your design, based on what you find when you get to the field and spend several months actually collecting data.

There is nothing wrong or unusual about this, but new researchers sometimes experience anxiety over making any major changes. The important thing at this stage is to focus the research and use your time effectively rather than agonizing over how to save components of your original design.

6. Exhaustion, the Second Break, and Frantic Activity

After seven or eight months, some participant observers start to think that they have exhausted their informants, both literally and figuratively. That is, they may become embarrassed about continuing to ask informants for more information. Or they may make the supreme mistake of believing that their informants have no more to tell them. The reason this is such a mistake, of course, is that the store of cultural knowledge in any culturally competent person is enormous— far more than anyone could hope to extract in a year or two.

At this point, another break is usually a good idea. You'll get another opportunity to take stock, order your priorities for the time remaining, and see both how much you've done and how little. The realization that, in fact, informants have a great deal more to teach them and that they have precious little time left in the field sends many investigators into a frenetic burst of activity during this stage.

7. Leaving the Field

The last stage of participant observation is leaving the field. When should you leave? Steven Taylor, a sociologist at the Center for Human Policy, says that when he starts to get bored writing field notes, he knows it's time to close down and go home. Taylor recognizes that writing field notes is time-consuming and tedious, but it's exciting, too, when you're chasing down information that plugs directly into your research effort (Taylor 1991:243). When it stops being exciting, it's time to leave the field.

Don't neglect this part of the process. Let people know that you are leaving and tell them how much you appreciate their help. The ritual of leaving a place in a culturally appropriate way will make it possible for you to go back, and even to send others.

Participant observation is an intensely intimate and personal experience. People who began as your informants may become your friends as well. In the best of cases, you come to trust that they will not deceive you about their culture, and they come to trust you not to betray them—that is, not to use your intimate knowledge of their lives to hurt them. (You can imagine the worst of cases.) There is often a legitimate expectation on both sides that the relationship may be permanent, not just a one-year fling.

For many long-term participant observation researchers, there is no final leaving of "the field." I've been working with some people, on and off, for 35 years. Like many anthropologists who work in Latin America, I'm godparent to a child of my closest research collaborator. From time to time, people from Mexico or from Greece will call my house on the phone, just to say hi and to keep the relationship going.

Or their children, who happen to be doing graduate work at a university in the U.S., will call and send their parents' regards. They'll remind you of some little event they remember when they were seven or eight and you came to their parents' house to do some interviewing and you spilled your coffee all over yourself as you fumbled with your tape recorder. People remember the darndest things. You'd better be ready when it happens.

Many field workers have been called on to help the children of their informants get into a college or university. This is the sort of thing that happens 20 years after you've "left" the field. The fact is, participant observation fieldwork can be a lifetime commitment. As in all aspects of ordinary life, you have to learn to choose your relationships well. Don't be surprised if you make a few mistakes.

ETHNOGRAPHIC INFORMANTS

When we conduct questionnaire surveys, we know how to choose an unbiased sample of *respondents*. In any large aggregate of people, there are bound to be serious differences of opinion and behavior. A random sample ensures that these differences (even if you don't know what they might be) are represented in your data. (The logic for this was explored in Chapter 5.)

Ethnography, on the other hand, is about understanding people's lived experiences. This kind of information requires a few knowledgeable and articulate informants rather than an unbiased sample of people. Ethnography is also about *emic explanations* of how things work—why people think they are poor, why they think some ethnic groups are successful and others aren't, why they think women earn less for the same work than men do, what they think people can do to prevent or treat colds. This kind of information, too, requires a few key informants.

An important question for participant observation ethnography then, is: Are a few informants *really* capable of providing adequate information about a culture? The answer is: Yes, but it depends on choosing good informants and asking them things they know about. In other words, we select ethnographic informants for their competence rather than for their representativeness.

There are really two kinds of ethnographic informants: people who are highly competent in particular areas of a culture and *key informants,* or **people who are generally competent, highly articulate, and for whatever reason of their own, ready and willing to walk you through their culture and show you the ropes.** I'll deal first with finding key informants. Then, I'll walk you through the cultural consensus model (Romney et al. 1986), a formal method for identifying the small number of people you need to produce reliable and valid data about focused domains of culture.

Key Informants

Key informant interviewing is an integral part of ethnographic research. Good key informants are people you can talk to easily, who understand the information you need, and who are glad to give it to you or get it for you. Pelto and Pelto (1978:72) advocate training informants "to conceptualize cultural data in the frame of reference" that you, the researcher, use.

In some cases, you may want to just listen. But when you run into a really great informant, I see no reason to hold back. Teach the informant about the analytic categories you're developing and ask whether the categories are correct. In other words, encourage the informant to become the ethnographer. (For a thoughtful presentation of another perspective, see Wolcott [1999].)

I've worked with Jesús Salinas for 37 years. In 1971, I was about to write an ethnography of his culture, the Ñähñu of central Mexico, when he mentioned that he'd be interested in writing an ethnography himself. I dropped my project and taught him to read and write Ñähñu.

Over the next 15 years, Salinas produced four volumes about the Ñähñu people—volumes that I translated and from which I learned many things

that I'd never have learned had I done the ethnography myself. For example, Ñähñu men engage in rhyming duels, much like the "*dozens*" of African Americans. I could not have even asked the questions in Ñähñu that would have retrieved the information about those rhyming duels in Salinas's work (see Bernard and Salinas 1989).

Just as Salinas has influenced my thinking about Mexican Indian life, Salinas's ethnography was heavily influenced by his association with me. We've discussed analytic categories over the years and have argued over interpretation of observed facts. When I think about all this, it seems somehow insulting to call Salinas my informant. Then I remember that I've been his informant as well, telling him what he wanted to know about anthropology and linguistics and about how people in my culture look at data about cultures. I wish there were a better-sounding word than "informant." Some researchers, like Oswald Werner (1996), have taken to using the word "consultant."

Finding Key Informants

One of the most famous key informants in the ethnographic literature is Doc in William Foote Whyte's *Street Corner Society* (1981 [1943]). Whyte studied "Cornerville," an Italian American slum neighborhood in a place he called "Eastern City." Whyte asked some social workers if they knew anyone who could help him with his study. One social worker told Whyte to come to her office and meet a man whom she thought could do the job. When Whyte showed up, the social worker introduced him to Doc and then left the room. Whyte nervously explained his predicament and Doc asked him, "Do you want to see the high life or the low life?" (Whyte 1989:72).

Whyte couldn't believe his luck. He told Doc he wanted to see all he could, learn as much as possible about life in the neighborhood. Doc told him, "Any nights you want to see anything, I'll take you around. I can take you to the joints—the gambling joints. I can take you around to the street corners. Just remember that you're my friend. That's all they need to know. I know these places and if I tell them you're my friend, nobody will bother you. You just tell me what you want to see, and we'll arrange it. . . . When you want some information, I'll ask for it, and you listen. When you want to find out their philosophy of life, I'll start an argument and get it for you" (ibid.).

Doc was straight up; he told Whyte to rely on him and to ask him anything, and Doc was true to his word all through Whyte's three years of fieldwork. Doc introduced Whyte to the boys on the corner; Doc hung out with Whyte and spoke up for Whyte when people questioned Whyte's presence. Doc was just spectacular. (See also Whyte and Whyte [1984] for a wonderful retrospective by Whyte about his fieldwork.)

Doc may be famous, but he's not unique. He's not even rare. All successful ethnographers will tell you that they eventually came to rely on one or two key people in their fieldwork.

What was rare about Doc is how quickly and easily Whyte teamed up with him. It's not easy to find informants like Doc. When Jeffrey Johnson began fieldwork in a North Carolina fishing community, he went to the local marine extension agent and asked for the agent's help. The agent, happy to oblige, told Johnson about a fisherman whom he thought could help Johnson get off on the right foot.

It turned out that the fisherman was a transplanted northerner; he had a pension from the navy; he was an activist Republican in a thoroughly Democratic community; and he kept his fishing boat in an isolated moorage, far from the village harbor. He was, in fact, maximally differ-

ent from the typical local fisherman. The agent had meant well, of course (Johnson 1990:56).

In fact, the first informants with whom you develop a working relationship in the field may be "deviant" members of their culture. Agar (1980b:86) reports that during his fieldwork in India, he was taken on by the *naik,* or headman of the village. The *naik,* it turned out, had inherited the role, but he was not respected in the village and did not preside over village meetings. This did not mean that the *naik* knew nothing about village affairs and customs; he was what Agar called a "solid insider," and yet somewhat of an outcast—a "marginal native," just like the ethnographer was trying to be (Freilich 1977). If you think about it, Agar said, you should wonder about the kind of person who would befriend an ethnographer.

> *Ethnographic fieldwork stands or falls on building mutually supportive relations with a few key people.*

In my own fieldwork (at sea, in Mexican villages, on Greek islands, in rural communities in the United States, and in modern American bureaucracies), I have consistently found the best informants to be people who are cynical about their own culture. They may not be outcasts (in fact, they are always solid insiders), but they say they *feel* somewhat marginal to their culture, by virtue of their intellectualizing of and disenchantment with their culture. They are always observant, reflective, and articulate. In other words, they invariably have all the qualities that I would like to have myself.

Don't choose key ethnographic informants too quickly. Allow yourself to go awash in data for a while, and play the field. When you have several prospects, check on their roles and statuses in the community. Be sure that the key informants you select don't prevent you from gaining access to other important informants (that is, people who won't talk to you when they find out you're so-and-so's friend). Since good ethnography is, at its best, a good story, find trustworthy informants who are observant, reflective, and articulate—who know how to tell good stories—and stay with them. In the end, ethnographic fieldwork stands or falls on building mutually supportive relations with a few key people.

Informants Sometimes Lie

Don't be surprised if informants lie to you. Jeffrey Johnson, a skilled boat builder, worked in an Alaskan boat yard as part of his field study of a fishing community. At one point in his fieldwork, two other ethnographers showed up, both women, to conduct some interviews with the men in the boat yard. "The two anthropologists had no idea I was one of *them*," Johnson reports, "since I was dressed in carpenter's overalls, with all the official paraphernalia—hammer, tape measure, etc. I was sufficiently close to overhear the interview and, knowing the men being interviewed, recognized quite a few blatant lies. In fact, during the course of one interview, a captain would occasionally wink at me as he told a whopper of a lie" (personal communication).

This is not an isolated incident. A Comox Indian woman spent two hours narrating a text for Franz Boas. The text turned out to be nothing but a string of questions and answers. Boas didn't speak Comox well enough to know that he was being duped, but when he found out he noted it in his diary (Rohner 1969:61). Nachman (1984), drawing on his own experience with the Nissan of New Guinea, offers interesting insights into the problem of informants lying to anthropologists.

This sort of thing can happen to anyone—whether you're a nurse, a sociologist, or a political scientist—who does participant observation ethnography.

Selecting Culturally Specialized Informants

The search for formal and systematic ways to select focused ethnographic informants—people who can help you learn about particular areas of a culture—has been going on for a very long time. In 1957, Marc-Adelard Tremblay was involved in a Cornell University survey research project on poverty in Nova Scotia. He wanted to use ethnographic informants to help the team's researchers design a useful questionnaire, so he made a list of some roles in the community he was studying—things like sawmill owners, doctors, farmers, bankers—and chose informants who could talk to him knowledgeably about things in their area of expertise. Tremblay had no external test to tell him whether the informants he selected were, in fact, the most competent in their areas of expertise, but he felt that on-the-spot clues made the selection of informants valid.

Michael Robbins and his colleagues studied acculturation and modernization among the Baganda of Uganda, using a more formal method to select informants who might be competent on this topic (Robbins et al. 1969). First, they ran a survey of households in a rural sector, asking about things that would indicate respondents' exposure to Western culture. Then they used the results of the survey to select appropriate informants.

Robbins et al. had 80 variables in the survey that had something to do with acculturation, and they ran a factor analysis to find out which variables package together. We'll look a bit more at factor analysis in Chapter 16. For now, think of factor analysis as a way to reduce those 80 variables to just a handful of underlying variables

TABLE 9.1 Agreement between Informants and Survey Data in Seven Villages

Questions Asked of Informants	Correlation with Questionnaire Data
Number of men from this town who are workers in Ciudad Industrial	.90
Percentage of houses made of adobe	.71
Percentage of households that have radios	.52
Percentage of people who eat eggs regularly	.33
Percentage of people who would like to live in Ciudad Industrial	.23
Percentage of people who eat bread daily	.14
Percentage of people who sleep in beds	.05

SOURCE: J. Poggie, Jr., "Toward Quality Control in Key Informant Data," *Human Organization* 31:26-29. Copyright © 1972, Society for Applied Anthropology. Reprinted with permission.

around which individual variables cluster. It turned out that 14 of the original 80 variables clustered together in one factor. Among those original variables were being under 40 years of age, drinking European beer, speaking and reading English, having a Western job, and living in a house that has concrete floors and walls.

Robbins et al. called this cluster the "acculturation factor." They chose informants who had high scores on this factor and interviewed them about acculturation. Robbins et al. reversed Tremblay's method. Tremblay used key informants to help him build a survey instrument; Robbins et al. used a survey to find key informants.

In any given domain of culture, some people are more competent than others. In our culture, some people know a lot about the history of baseball; some people can name the actors in every sitcom since the beginning of television in the 1940s. Some people are experts on medicinal plants; others are experts on cars and trucks. John Poggie (1972) did an early study of informant competence. He selected one informant in each of seven

Mexican communities. The communities ranged in size from 350 to 3,000 inhabitants. The informants were village or town presidents, judges, or (in the case of agricultural communities) the local commissioners of communal land. Poggie asked these informants questions about life in the communities, and he compared the answers with data from a high-quality social survey.

For example, Poggie asked the seven informants: "How many men in this town are workers in Ciudad Industrial?" In his survey, Poggie asked respondents if they had ever worked in Ciudad Industrial. (Ciudad Industrial is a fictitious name of a city that attracted many labor migrants from the communities that Poggie studied.) The correlation between the answers given by Poggie's expert informants and the data obtained from the survey was .90.

Poggie also asked, "What percentage of the houses here are made of adobe?" This time the correlation between the informants and the survey was only .71. Table 9.1 shows the seven questions Poggie asked, and how well his informants did when their answers were compared to the survey.

Overall, informants produced answers most like those in the survey when they were asked to respond to questions about things that are publicly observable. The survey data are not necessarily more *accurate* than the informants' data. But as the questions require informants to talk about things inside people's homes (such as what percentage of people eat eggs), or about what people think (what percentage of people would *like* to work in Ciudad Industrial), informants' answers look less and less like those of the survey.

Poggie concluded that "there is little reason to believe that trust and rapport would improve the reliability and precision concerning what percentage sleep in beds, who would like to live in the new industrial city, or what percentage eat bread daily" (1972:29).

THE CULTURAL CONSENSUS MODEL

The idea that people can be more competent or less competent in various areas of their culture has led to formal tests of new methods for selecting focused ethnographic informants. James Boster (1985, 1986) walked 58 Aguaruna Jívaro women (in Peru) through a garden that had 61 varieties of manioc. He asked the women, "*Waji mama aita?*" ("What kind of manioc is this?") and calculated the likelihood that all possible pairs of women agreed on the name of a plant. Since Boster had planted the garden himself, he knew the true identification of each plant. Sure enough, the more that women agreed on the identification of a plant, the more likely they were to know what the plant actually was. In other words, as cultural consensus increased, so did cultural competence.

This makes a lot of sense. Suppose you give a test about the rules of baseball to two groups of people: a group of rabid baseball fans and another group (Americans, Canadians, Mexicans, Dominicans, etc.) who never watch the game. You'd expect that (1) the serious baseball fans will agree more among themselves about the answers to your test questions than will the nonfans, and (2) the serious fans will get the answers right more often than the nonfans. These outcomes are expected because of the relation between cultural consensus and cultural competence.

Boster's experiment and the hypothetical baseball experiment are pretty much like any test you might take in a class. The instructor makes up both the test and an answer key with the (supposedly) correct answers. Your job is to match your answers with those on the answer key.

But what if there were no answer key? That's exactly what happens when we ask people to tell us the uses of various plants, to list the sacred sites in a village, or to rate the social status of others in a community. We are not asking people for their opinions, attitudes, beliefs, or values. We ask informants to rate the social status of others in their community because we want to *know* the social status of all those people. The problem is, we don't have an answer key to tell whether informants are accurate in their reporting of information.

Romney et al. (1986) developed a formal method, called the **cultural consensus model,** to **test informant competence without having an answer key.** The theory behind the technique makes three assumptions:

(1) You test only those informants who share a common culture. Any variation you find among informants is the result of *individual* differences in their knowledge, not the

TABLE 9.2	Answers by Four Students to a 40-Question True-False General Knowledge Test

Informant

No. 1   1 1 1 0 0 1 0 0 0 0 1 1 1 0 0 0 0 1 1 0 0 1 0 1 1 0 1 1 0 1 1 1 1 0 1 0 1 1 0 1 0 1

No. 2   0 1 1 0 0 1 0 0 1 1 1 0 1 1 0 0 1 1 1 0 1 1 1 0 0 1 1 1 1 1 1 0 0 0 1 0 0 1 0 1

No. 3   0 1 0 0 0 1 0 0 1 1 1 0 1 1 0 0 1 1 1 0 0 0 1 0 0 1 1 1 1 0 1 0 1 0 1 0 0 1 0 0

No. 4   0 1 1 1 0 0 0 1 0 0 0 0 0 0 0 0 1 0 1 0 0 0 0 0 0 1 1 1 0 1 1 0 1 1 0 0 1 0 0

SOURCE: A. K. Romney et al., "Culture as Consensus: A Theory of Culture and Informant Accuracy." Reproduced by permission of the American Anthropological Association from *American Anthropologist* 88:24, June 1986. Not for further reproduction. NOTE: 1 = true; 0 = false.

result of their being members of subcultures.

(2) Informants give their answers to your test questions independently of one another.

(3) All the questions in your test come from the same "cultural domain." A test that asks about kinship and Australian-rules football would be a poor test. People can be competent in one domain and incompetent in another. The cultural consensus method must be used *only* for identifying people who are knowledgeable about a particular domain.

To use the consensus technique, simply give a sample of informants a test that asks them to make some judgments about a list of items in a cultural domain. You can use true-false and yes-no questions. An example of a true-false question in fieldwork might be: "You can get [pneumonia] [diarrhea] [*susto*] from being [overweight] [tired] [scared] [in the room with a sick person]." Some other typical test questions might be: "The highest paid teacher in this district earns $72,000" or "A field goal is worth 7 points." You can also use multiple-choice questions or even open-ended,

fill-in-the-blank questions. (See Appendix F for information about ANTHROPAC, a set of programs that includes models for handling cultural consensus data.)

For the test to reliably distinguish cultural competence among informants, it's best to have about 40 test items and about 40 informants. As an example, Table 9.2 shows the answers of four informants to a 40-question true-false test about "general knowledge" for Americans (things like who starred in some classic movies). The 1s are items to which a student answered "true" (or yes), and the 0s are items to which a student answered "false" (or no).

Table 9.3 shows the *number* of matches between informants, the *proportion of matches* (the number of matches divided by the number of items in the test), and the proportion of matches *corrected for guessing*. (This correction is necessary because anyone can guess the answers to any true-false test item half the time. The program package ANTHROPAC has a built-in error-correction routine for consensus analysis.)

The three matrices in Table 9.3 are called *similarity matrices* because the entries in each matrix give some direct estimate of how similar

TABLE 9.3 Matches, Proportions of Matches, Proportions of Corrected Matches, and Competency Scores for the Data in Table 9.2

Informant	Matrix I: Number of Matches				Matrix II: Proportion of Matches				Matrix III: Proportion of Corrected Matches				Competency Score for Student	
	1	2	3	4	1	2	3	4	1	2	3	4		
No. 1	—	27	25	22	—	.675	.625	.550	—	.35	.25	.10	1	.48
No. 2	27	—	34	21	.675	—	.850	.525	.35	—	.70	.05	2	.61
No. 3	25	34	—	23	.625	.850	—	.575	.25	.70	—	.15	3	.61
No. 4	22	21	23	—	.550	.525	.575	—	.10	.05	.15	—	4	.32

SOURCE: A. K. Romney et al., "Culture as Consensus: A Theory of Culture and Informant Accuracy." Reproduced by permission of the American Anthropological Association from *American Anthropologist* 88:24, June 1986. Not for further reproduction.

any pair of informants is (see Chapters 11, 15, and 16 for more on similarity matrices). Look at Matrix I, the one called "number of matches." Informants 1 and 2 have 27 matches. If you look along the first two rows of Table 9.2 and count, you'll see that on 27 out of 40 test questions, informants 1 and 2 answered the same. When informant 1 said "false" (0), then informant 2 said "false" (0) and when informant 1 said "true" (1), then informant 2 said "true" (1).

Now look at Matrix II, "proportion of matches." This shows that informants 1 and 2 were 67.5% similar, because 2/40 = .675. Finally, look at Matrix III, "proportion of corrected matches." After correcting for the possibility that some of the similarity in Matrix II between informants is because they guessed the same answers when they didn't really know the answers, we see that informants 1 and 2 are .35 alike, while informants 2 and 3 are .70 alike. Informants 2 and 3 are twice as similar to one another as informants 1 and 2 are to one another.

Look down the last column of Matrix III. Informant 4 is not like any other informant. That is, informant 4's answers to the 40 questions were

practically idiosyncratic compared to the answers that other informants gave.

We can use this information to compute a competency score for each informant. To do this, run a factor analysis on the matrix of corrected matches. (The ANTHROPAC program does all this automatically. You don't need to understand factor analysis to read the rest of this section. For an introduction to factor analysis, see Chapter 16.) If the three conditions I've listed for the model have been met, then the first factor in the solution should be at least three times the size of the second factor. If it is, this means that (1) the first factor is *knowledge* about the domain (because agreement equals knowledge under conditions of the model), and (2) the individual factor scores are a measure of knowledge for each person who takes the test.

At the far right of Table 9.3, we see that informants 2 and 3 have the highest factor scores (.61). They are also the students who got the highest of the four scores in the general knowledge test. You can use the consensus test on any group of informants, for any cultural domain. Pile sorts, triad tests, paired comparisons, ratings, and rankings

---

Box 9.1
Testing the Cultural Consensus Model

The cultural consensus model makes a lot of sense, but it may be a bit of a stretch to imagine that you can find the answer key to a test under certain conditions. You can test this. Get the results from any multiple-choice test in any class that has at least 40 students and run the consensus analysis available in ANTHROPAC. Correlate the first factor score for each student against the score that each student actually got on the test. If the exam was a fair test of students' knowledge, you'll get a correlation of over .90 and the answers of the students who have the highest first-factor scores (knowledge scores) will mirror the professor's answer key at least 90% of the items.

The cultural consensus model is an important contribution to social science methods. It means that, under the conditions of the model (informants share a common culture; informants answer test questions independently of one another; the questions in the test come from a single cultural domain), you can throw away the answer key and retrieve it from the agreement matrix across students.

If you can retrieve an etically correct answer key, then you can apply the model (cautiously, of course, always cautiously) to tests of emic data, like people's ideas about who hangs out with whom in an organization or who, in rank order, people think are the greatest [male golfers] [female country vocalists] [women of science] [military men] of all time.

---

all produce data that can be subjected to consensus analysis, as do true-false tests and multiple choice tests (see Box 9.1).

I want to stress that if you are doing general descriptive ethnography, and you're looking for all-around good informants, the cultural consensus method is *not* a substitute for the time-honored way that ethnographers have always chosen key informants: luck, intuition, and hard work by both parties to achieve a working relationship based on trust. The cultural consensus method, though, is very useful for finding highly competent people who can talk about well-defined areas of cultural knowledge.

A Handy Shortcut

Weller and Romney (1988), two of the developers of the cultural consensus model, have determined the number of informants you need to produce valid and reliable data about particular cultural domains, given that the three conditions of the model are more or less met. (I say "more or less" because the model is very robust, which means that it produces very similar answers even when its conditions are more or less, not perfectly, met.)

Table 9.4 shows those numbers: Just 10 informants, with an average competence of .7, have a 99% probability of answering each question on a true-false test correctly, with a confidence level of .95. Only 13 informants, with a relatively low average competence of .5, are needed if you want a 90% probability of answering each question on a test correctly, with a confidence level of .95.

Weller and Romney (1988) also showed that you can use the simple Spearman-Brown Prophesy formula, available in many general statistical packages, as a proxy for the full consensus method (the one that involves doing a factor

TABLE 9.4 Minimal Number of Informants Needed to Classify a Desired Proportion of Questions with a Specified Confidence Level for Different Levels of Cultural Competence

	Average Level of Cultural Competence				
Proportion of Questions	.5	.6	.7	.8	.9
.95 confidence level					
.80	9	7	4	4	4
.85	11	7	4	4	4
.90	13	9	6	4	4
.95	17	11	6	6	4
.99	29	19	10	8	4
.99 confidence level					
.80	15	10	5	4	4
.85	15	10	7	5	4
.90	21	12	7	5	4
.95	23	14	9	7	4
.99	30	20	13	8	6

SOURCE: S. C. Weller and A. K. Romney, *Structured Interviewing*, p. 77. Copyright © 1988 by Sage Publications.

analysis on the informant-by-informant agreement matrix, etc.) when you have interval-level data. Table 9.5 shows the results: If you interview 10 informants whose responses correlate .49, then the aggregate of their answers is likely to correlate .95 with the true answers.

Paying Informants

Should you pay informants? It all depends. If you are studying elites in your own culture, then payment is inappropriate. If you are studying elites in an African village, then payment may be mandatory. Be sensitive to the situation and be prepared to pay people a reasonable, negotiated fee for their time and information if circumstances require it.

William Foote Whyte was a colleague of Allan Holmberg's at Cornell University during the 1950s when Holmberg was conducting action research at Hacienda Vicos in the Peruvian highlands. Holmberg took over the hacienda when the local *patrón* failed to pay his government fees. Holmberg immediately declared the Indian serfs on the hacienda free of their obligations to the *patrón* and then studied what happened.

According to Whyte, "Holmberg did not pay Indian informants, but he was most generous in allowing other researchers access to his field site. One summer," Whyte tells us, "a group of well-financed psychologists and psychoanalysts moved in and paid informants willing to tell their life stories and describe their dreams. Having discovered that their information had a commercial value," Whyte said, "naturally Vicosinos thereafter sought to charge researchers the going rate" (Whyte and Whyte 1984:109).

Whyte did not recommend paying informants in general, but felt that "if the informant is not wealthy and has to make a financial sacrifice to talk with us, then clearly some material compensation is needed" (ibid.).

| **TABLE 9.5** | Agreement among Individuals and Estimated Validity of Aggregating Their Responses for Different Sample Sizes | | | | |

	Validity				
Agreement	.80	.85	.90	.95	.99
.16	10	14	22	49	257
.25	5	8	13	28	148
.36	3	5	8	17	87
.49	2	3	4	10	51

SOURCE: S. C. Weller and A. K. Romney, *Structured Interviewing*, p. 77. Copyright © 1988 by Sage Publications.

In today's market-oriented economy, information is a commodity and often has a price. Personally, I think researchers should pay for information whenever they can and whenever it's appropriate. If we pay people nothing (or almost nothing) and then sell what we learn from them at a value-added price when we return from the field, we deny our informants a fair share of the value of the information. The problem, of course, is to decide what a fair price should be. Obviously, it will vary with circumstances—yours and your informant's. As a student, you can afford to pay less than when you are a paid professional. Don't be surprised if your informants know that and charge you more as your own wealth increases.

Note that in the last paragraph I took it for granted that you'd be going back to your field sites during your professional career. Paying informants a just, negotiated fee when you're a student will only make it easier for you to go back later. Professional researchers get paid for what they know—for their *culture,* in other words. If we sell our culture, we shouldn't expect others to give it away, particularly poor people who need all the material support they can get.

ABOUT FIELD NOTES

The difference between fieldwork and field experience is field notes.

Plan on spending two-three hours, every working day of a participant observation study, writing up field notes, working on your diary, and coding interviews and notes. Ralph Bolton asked 34 anthropologists about their field note practices; they reported spending anywhere from an hour and a half to seven hours a day on write-up (1984:132).

Remember that it takes twice as long to write up notes *about* a tape-recorded interview as it does to conduct an interview in the first place. You have to listen to a recorded interview at least once before you can write up the essential notes from it, and then it takes as long again to get the notes down. Actually *transcribing* a tape takes about six-eight hours for each hour of interview—and that's if the recording is clear, the interview is in your own language, and you have a transcribing machine with a foot pedal. Don't even try to transcribe taped interviews without one of those machines (they cost about $200) unless you are conducting an experiment to see how long it takes

---

Box 9.2
On Being Obsessive

Actually, there are two radically different styles when it comes to writing field notes. Some people like to immerse themselves completely in the local culture and concentrate on the experience. They write up field notes when and as they find the time. Most ethnographers advocate writing up field notes every day, while you are still capable of retrieving detail about the day's events and interactions. I've done both and, like Miles and Huberman (1994), I'm convinced that obsessiveness about writing field notes is the way to go.

---

to get frustrated with transcribing. (More about taping and tape recorders back in Chapter 6.)

All participant observation ethnographers I've talked to agree that it's best to set aside a time each day for working on your notes. Don't sleep on your notes, either. That is, don't write up notes in the morning from the previous day's jottings. You'll forget a lot of what you would like to have in your notes if you don't write them up in the afternoon or evening each day. The same goes for your own thoughts and impressions of events. If you don't write them up every day, while they are fresh, you'll forget them (see Box 9.2).

This means that you shouldn't get embroiled in a lot of activities that prevent you from writing up field notes. There are plenty of exceptions to this rule. Here's one. You are studying how families create culture by telling and retelling certain stories. You sit down to write up the day's field notes and you get a call from a key informant who tells you to come right over to meet her father, who is leaving in the morning and wants to tell you himself the story she had told you earlier

about his experience playing poker on the battlefield during World War II. You couldn't possibly turn that one down. Just keep in mind, though, how easy it is to let doing *anything except writing notes* become the norm rather than the exception.

Create many small notes rather than one long, running commentary. If you write your notes on a computer, make many separate files—one for each day is fine—rather than adding to the same humongous file day after day. The advantage is that you can name your notes by their date of creation. That way, the computer will present the notes to you in chronological order so you can always find a particular day's (or week's) notes. Many small files are also easier to handle when you get to text management and retrieval programs.

How to Write Field Notes

The method I present here for making and coding field notes was developed and tested by the late Michael Kenny and me, between 1967 and 1971, when we ran those NSF-supported field schools in cultural anthropology I described earlier in this chapter. Kenny and I relied initially on our own experience with field notes, and we borrowed freely from the experience of many colleagues. The method we developed—involving jottings, a diary, a daily log, and three kinds of formal notes—was used by 40 field school participants in the United States and in Mexico and by others since then. Some years later, after microcomputers came on the scene, my students and I began to think about using machines to help manage textual data (Bernard and Evans 1983).

Two things can be said about the method I'm going to lay out here: (1) It works, and (2) it's not the only way to do things. If you do field research, you'll develop your own style of writing notes and you'll add your own little tricks as you go along. Still, the method described here will help you work systematically at taking field notes, and it will allow you to search through them quickly and easily to look for relations in your data. I wish I had used this method when I was doing my own M.A. and Ph.D. fieldwork—and I wish laptops and database management systems had been available then, too.

THE FOUR TYPES OF FIELD NOTES: JOTTINGS, THE DIARY, THE LOG, AND THE NOTES

Jottings

Field *jottings*—or what Roger Sanjek calls *scratch notes* (1990:96)—are what get you through the day. Human memory is a very poor recording device, especially for the kind of details that make the difference between good and so-so ethnographic research. Keep a note pad with you at all times and make field jottings on the spot. This applies to both formal and informal interviews in bars and cafés, in homes and on the street.

> Keep a note pad with you at all times and make field jottings on the spot. . . . Remember: If you don't write it down, it's gone.

It also applies to things that just strike you as you are walking along. Jottings will provide you with the trigger you need to recall a lot of details that you don't have time to write down while you're observing events or listening to an informant. Even a few key words will jog your memory later. Remember: If you don't write it down, it's gone.

Of course, there are times when you just can't take notes. Morris Freilich did research with the Mohawks in Brooklyn, New York, and on the Caughnanaga Reservation, 10 miles south of Montreal, in the 1950s. He did a lot of participant observation in a bar, and as Freilich tells it, every time he pulled out a notebook his audience became hostile. So, Freilich kept a small notebook in his hip pocket and would periodically duck into the men's room at the bar to scribble a few jottings (Freilich 1977:159).

William Sturtevant used stubby little pencils to take furtive notes; he found the technique so useful, he published a note about it in the *American Anthropologist* (1959). When Hortense Powdermaker did her research on race relations in Mississippi in 1932, she took surreptitious notes on sermons at African American churches. "My pocketbook was large," she said, "and the notebook in it was small" (1966:175).

Every field worker runs into situations where it's impossible to take notes. It is always appropriate to be sensitive people's feelings, and it is sometimes a good idea to just listen attentively and leave your notebook in your pocket. You'd be surprised, though, how few of these situations there are. Don't talk yourself into not jotting down a few notes on the incorrect assumption that people won't like it if you do.

The key is to take up the role of researcher immediately when you arrive at your field site, whether that site is a peasant village in a developing nation or a corporate office in Chicago. Let people know from the very first day you arrive that you are there to study their way of life. Don't try to become an inconspicuous participant rather than what you really are: an observer who wants to participate as much as possible. Participant observation means that you try to *experience* the life of your informants to the extent possible; it doesn't mean that you try to melt into the background and *become* a fully accepted member of a culture other than your own.

It's usually impossible to do that anyway. After four decades of coming and going in Indian villages in Mexico, I still stick out like a sore thumb and have yet to become the slightest bit inconspicuous. Be honest with people and keep your note pad out as much of the time as possible. Ask your informants for their permission to take notes while you are talking with them. If people don't want you to take notes, they'll tell you.

Or they may ask to see your notes. A student researcher in one of our field schools worked in a logging camp in Idaho. He would write up his notes at night from the jottings he took all day. Each morning at 6:00 a.m., he nailed the day's sheaf of notes (along with a pen on a string) to a tree for everyone to look at. Some of the men took the time to scribble helpful (or amusing, or rude) comments on the notes. If you use this technique, watch out for the "CNN effect." That's when people tell you things they want to tell everyone because they know you're going to broadcast whatever they say. This is a disaster if you're trying to make everybody around you feel confident that you're not going to blab about them.

Even when people get accustomed to your constant jottings, you can overdo it. Emerson et al. (1995:23) cite the following field note from an ethnographer who was studying divorce negotiations:

On one occasion when finishing up a debriefing . . . [the mediator] began to apply some eye make-up while I was finishing writing down some observations. She flashed me a mock disgusted look and said, "Are you writing *this* down too!" indicating the activity with her eye pencil.

The Diary

Notes are based on observations that will form the basis of your publications. A *diary,* on the other hand, is personal. It's a place where you can run and hide when things get tough. You absolutely need a diary in ethnography project. It will help you deal with loneliness, fear, and other emotions that make fieldwork difficult.

A diary chronicles how you feel and how you perceive your relations with others around you. If you are really angry at someone, you should write about it—in your diary. Jot down emotional highs and lows while they're happening, if you can, and write them up in your diary at the end of the day. Try to spend at least half an hour each day pouring out your soul to a diary. Later on, during data analysis, your diary will become an important professional document. It will give you information that will help you interpret your field notes and will make you aware of your personal biases.

The important thing about a diary is just to have one and to keep it separate from your other field notes. Franz Boas got engaged to Marie Krackowizer in May 1883, just three weeks before beginning his first field trip. It was a grueling 15 months on Baffin Island and at sea. Boas missed German society terribly, and though he couldn't mail the letters, he wrote about 500 pages to his fiancée. Here is an excerpt from this extraordinary diary:

December 16, north of Pangnirtung. My dear sweetheart. . . . Do you know how I pass these long evenings? I have a copy of Kant with me, which I am studying, so that I shall not be so completely uneducated when I return. Life here really makes one dull and stupid. . . . I have to blush when I remember that during our meal tonight I thought how good a pudding with plum sauce would taste. But you have no idea what an effect privations and hunger, real hunger, have on a person. Maybe Mr.

Kant is a good antidote! The contrast is almost unbelievable when I remember that a year ago I was in society and observed all the rules of good taste, and tonight I sit in this snow hut with Wilhelm and an Eskimo eating a piece of raw, frozen seal meat which had first to be hacked up with an axe, and greedily gulping my coffee. Is that not as great a contradiction as one can think of? (Quoted in Cole 1983:29)

February 16. Anarnitung . . . I long for sensible conversation and for someone who really understands me! Unfortunately, this time I did not bring a book to read, so I cannot help myself. I read all the advertisements and everything else on one page of the *Kölnische Zeitung* [a magazine]. In four days I shall have been away eight months. I have heard from none of you for four and a half months. (ibid.:42)

When Malinowski was trapped in the Trobriand Islands during World War I, he too, missed his fiancée and European society and occasionally lashed out at the Trobrianders in his diary (Malinowski 1967:253-54).

Fieldwork in another culture is an intense experience. And don't think that you have to be stranded in the Arctic or in Melanesia for things to get intense.

Your diary will give you an outlet for writing things that you don't want to become part of a public record. Publication of Malinowski's and Boas's diaries has helped make all field workers aware that they are not alone in their frailties and self-doubts.

The Log

A *log* is **a running account of how you plan to spend your time, how you actually spend your time, and how much money you spent.** A good log is the key to doing systematic fieldwork and to collecting both qualitative and quantitative data on a systematic basis.

A field log should be kept in bound books of blank, lined pages. There are schedule-planning computer programs, of course, but I suspect they will never take the place of a big, clunky logbook for field research. Don't use a skimpy little notebook for your log, like the kind you might keep in your pocket for jottings. Use a book around 6″ × 8″ in size, or one even larger.

Each day of fieldwork, whether you're out for a year or a week, should be represented by a double page of the log. The pages on the left should list what you *plan* to do on any given day. The facing pages will recount what you *actually* do each day.

Begin your log on pages 2 and 3. Put the date on the top of the even-numbered page to the left. Then, go through the entire notebook and put the successive dates on the even-numbered pages. By doing this in advance, even the days on which you "do nothing," or are away from your field site, will have double log pages devoted to them.

The first day or two that you make a log you will use only the right-hand pages where you keep track of where you go, who you see, and what you spend. Some people like to carry their logs around with them. Others prefer to jot down the names of the people they run into or interview, and enter the information into their logs when they write up their notes in the evening. Keep an alphabetized file of 25-word profiles on as many people you meet as you can.

This can be on index cards or on a database. The file will make it much easier to remember who you're dealing with. Before you go into any second or third interview, look up the key biographical information you have about the person (palmtop computers are perfect for this sort of thing). During the first couple of minutes of the interview, work in a comment that shows you remember some of those key bio-facts. You'll be surprised how far that'll take you.

Jot down the times that you eat and what you eat (especially if you are doing fieldwork in another culture), and write down who you eat with and how much you spend on all meals away from your house. You'd be surprised, too, at how much you learn from this.

After a day or two, you will begin to use the left-hand sheets of the log. As you go through any given day, you will think of many things that you want to know but can't resolve on the spot. Write those things down in your jot book or in your log. When you write up your field notes, think about who you need to interview, or what you need to observe, regarding each of the things you wondered about that day.

Right then and there, open your log and commit yourself to finding each thing out at a particular time on a particular day. If finding something out requires that you talk to a particular person, then put that person's name in the log, too. If you don't know the person to talk to, then put down the name of someone whom you think can steer you to the right person.

Suppose you're studying a school system. It's April 5th and you are talking to MJR, a fifth-grade teacher. She tells you:

> The new head of the school board we hired is a real suit; you know, a real executive type . . . thinks everything has to be done like he used to do it when he ran whatsit before he retired. I guess he's bored and has to find somebody's life to run, but geez, why did he have to pick us [teachers]. . . . He's driving us crazy with silly paperwork.

Write a note to yourself in your log to ask other teachers about this issue. Make a note to bring this topic up when you get to interview the new head of the school board.

Later on, when you're writing up your notes, you may decide not to interview the school board head until after you have accumulated more data about how other teachers feel about him. On the left-hand page for April 23rd you note: "target date for interview with school board head." On

the left-hand page of April 10th you note: "make appointment for interview on 23rd with school board head." For April 6th you note: "need more interviews with teachers about life since new guy was elected to school board."

As soon as you think that you need to know how much money parishioners contributed to the church you're studying, or the difference in price between wine sold in the store and wine sold in the restaurant you're studying, commit yourself *in your log to a specific time* when you will try to resolve the questions. Whether the question you think of requires a formal appointment, a direct and personal observation, or an informal interview in a bar, write the question down on one of the left-hand pages of your log.

Don't worry if the planned activity log you create for yourself winds up looking nothing like the activities you actually engage in from day to day. Frankly, you'll be lucky to do half the things you think of to do, much less do them when you want to. The important thing is to fill those left-hand pages, as far out into the future as you can, with specific information that you need, and specific tasks you need to perform to get that information.

This is not just because you want to use your time effectively, but because the process of building a log forces you to think hard about the questions you really want to answer in your research and the data you really need. You will start any field research project knowing some of the questions you are interested in. But those questions may change; you may add some, and drop others—or your entire emphasis may shift.

The right-hand pages of the log are for recording what you actually accomplish each day. As I said, you'll be appalled at first at how little resemblance the left-hand and the right-hand pages have to one another.

Remember, good field notes do not depend on the punctuality of informants or your ability to do all the things you want to do. They depend on your systematic work over a period of time. If some informants do not show up for appointments (and often they won't), you can evaluate whether or not you really need the data you thought you were going to get from them. If you do need the data, then put a note on the left-hand page for that same day, or for the next day, to contact the informant and reschedule the appointment.

If you still have no luck, you may have to decide whether it's worth more of your time to track down a particular person or a particular piece of information. Your log will tell you how much time you've spent on it already and will make the decision easier. There's plenty of time for everything when you think you've got months stretching ahead of you. But you only have a finite amount of time in any fieldwork project to get useful data, and the time goes very quickly.

Field Notes

There are three kinds of notes: notes on method and technique, ethnographic or descriptive notes, and notes that discuss issues or provide an analysis of social situations.

Methodological Notes

Methodological notes **deal with technique in collecting data.** If you work out a better way to keep a log than I've described here, don't just *use* your new technique; write it up in your field notes and publish a paper about your technique so others can benefit from your experience. If you find yourself spending too much time with marginal people in the culture, make a note of it, and discuss how that came to be. You'll discover little tricks of the trade, like the "uh-huh" technique, discussed in Chapter 6. (Remember that? It's where you learn how and when to grunt encouragingly to keep an interview going.) Write up

notes about your discoveries. Mark all these notes with a big "M" at the top—M for "method."

Methodological notes are also about your own growth as an instrument of data collection. Collecting data is always awkward when you begin a field project, but it gets easier as you become more comfortable in a new culture. During this critical period of adjustment, you should intellectualize what you're learning about doing fieldwork by taking methodological notes.

When I first arrived in Greece in 1960, I was invited to dinner at "around 7 p.m." When I arrived at around 7:15 (what I thought was a polite 15 minutes late), I was embarrassed to find that my host was still taking a bath. I should have known that he really meant "around 8 p.m." when he said "around 7." My methodological note for the occasion simply stated that I should not show up for dinner before 8 p.m. in the future.

Some weeks later, I figured out the general rules for timing of evening activities, including cocktails, dinner, and late-night desserts in the open squares of Athens. Robert Levine has studied the psychology of time by asking people around the world things like, "How long would you wait for someone who was late for a lunch appointment?" On average, Brazilians say they'd wait 62 minutes. On average, says Levine (1997:136), "Americans would need to be back at their office two minutes *before*" the late Brazilian lunch was just getting under way.

When I began fieldwork with the Ñähñu people of central Mexico in 1962, I was offered *pulque* everywhere I went. (*Pulque* is fermented nectar from the maguey cactus.) I tried to refuse politely; I couldn't stand the stuff. But people were very insistent and seemed offended if I didn't accept the drink. Things were particularly awkward when I showed up at someone's house and there were other guests there. Everyone enjoyed *pulque* but me, and most of the time people were too poor to have beer around to offer me.

At that time, I wrote a note that people "felt obliged by custom to offer *pulque* to guests." I was dead wrong. As I eventually learned, people were testing me to see if I was affiliated with the Summer Institute of Linguistics (SIL), an evangelical missionary group (and, of course, nondrinkers of alcohol) that had its regional headquarters in the area where I was working.

The SIL is composed of many excellent linguists, who produce books and articles on the grammar of the nonwritten languages of the world and translations of the Bible into those languages. There was serious friction between the Indians who had converted to Protestantism and those who remained Catholic. It was important for me to disassociate myself from the SIL, so my methodological note discussed the importance of conspicuously consuming alcohol and tobacco to identify myself as an anthropologist and not as a missionary.

Nine years later I wrote:

> After all this time, I still don't like *pulque*. I'm sure it's unhealthy to drink out of the gourds that are passed around. I've taken to carrying a couple of six-packs of beer in the car and telling people that I just don't like *pulque*, and telling people that I'd be pleased to have them join me in a beer. If they don't offer me beer, I offer it to them. This works just fine, and keeps my reputation of independence from the SIL intact.

Eight years later, in 1979, I read that William Partridge had a similar predicament during his work in Colombia (Kimball and Partridge 1979:55). Everywhere Partridge went, it seems, people offered him beer, even at 7:00 in the morning. He needed an acceptable excuse, he said, to avoid spending all his waking hours getting drunk.

After a few months in the field, Partridge found that telling people, "*Estoy tomando una pastilla*" ("I'm taking a pill") did the trick. Locally, the pill referred to in this phrase was used in treating venereal disease. Everyone knew that you didn't drink alcohol while you were taking this pill, and the excuse was perfect for adding a little virility boost to Partridge's reputation. Partridge used his knowledge of local culture to get out of a tough situation.

Methodological notes, then, have to do with the conduct of field inquiry itself. You will want to make methodological notes especially when you do something silly that breaks a cultural norm. If you are feeling particularly sheepish, you might want to write those feelings into your diary where no one else will see what you've written, but you don't want to waste the opportunity to make a straightforward methodological note on such occasions, as well.

Descriptive Notes

Descriptive notes are the meat and potatoes of fieldwork. Most notes are descriptive and are from two sources: watching and listening. Interviews with informants produce acres of notes, especially if you use a tape recorder and later write down large chunks of what people say. Observations of processes, like feeding children, building a house, making beer, and so on, also produce a lot of notes. Descriptive field notes may contain birth records that you've copied out of a local church registry, or they may consist of summary descriptions of a village plaza or an urban shopping mall or any environmental characteristics that you think are important.

The best way to learn to write descriptive field notes is to practice doing it with others who are also trying to learn. Get together with one or more partners and observe a process that's unfamiliar to all of you. It could be a church service other than one you've seen before, or it could be an occupational process that you've not witnessed. (I remember the first time I saw plasterers hang ceilings. They do it on stilts.)

Whatever you observe, try to capture in field notes the details of the behavior and the environment. Try to get down "what's going on." Then ask informants who are watching the ceremony or process to explain what's going on, and try to get notes down on their explanation. Later, get together with your research partner(s) and discuss your notes with one another. You'll find that two or three people see much more than just one sees. You might also find that you and your partners saw the same things but wrote down different subsets of the same information.

————————❖

Gene Shelley studied people who suffer from end-stage kidney disease. Most patients are on hemodialysis. Some are on peritoneal dialysis. The "hemo" patients go to a dialysis center, several times a week, while the "pero" patients perform a dialysis (called continuous ambulatory peritoneal dialysis, or CAPD) on themselves several times a day.

Here are three descriptive notes from Shelley's research (1992 and unpublished notes produced here with permission of the author). Along the top of each note are codes. First, there's a delimiter (the dollar sign) that marks the beginning of each note. This lets you pack all the notes together in one big file if you want to and still lets a computer text management program know where notes begin and end. Next is a unique number that identifies the note in a continuing sequence, starting with 0001. Next is the date.

Then come some *topical codes*. Shelley used a modified version of the *Outline of Cultural Materials* (Murdock 1996), but you can make up your own topical codes. We'll talk about that when we get to text analysis in Chapter 12. And finally, there's an indicator of the person to whom Shelley attributes the information.

$ 615 8-16-89: 757.3; Dr. H

Dr. H explains that in peritoneal dialysis you exchange 2 liters of fluid several times a day (based on body size). Women do it about 3 times and men about 4 times because of larger body size. People mostly do a "dwell" for about 8 hours overnight while they sleep (fluid is inflowed into peritoneal cavity and allowed to sit there overnight). Then they do peritoneal dialysis when they wake up and another time or two during the day. Peritoneal dialysis patients are pretty close to being healthy. They have to take medication but you cannot tell them from healthy people, he says.

$ 742 8-30-89: 57.3, 757.5; Nurse Ralph B

CAPD training takes about a week to 10 days. During this time, the patient comes in every day and receives training. Ralph thinks that when the whole family comes in for the training, the patients do better. They have about 20 CAPD patients right now. Ralph said there are 3 types of CAPD patients: (1) those patients who are already on hemo and in pretty good shape, usually well-motivated. (2) those who are late getting started and are in trouble (medically) and are hurriedly trying to learn the procedure. (It takes 2 weeks to get a catheter inserted and then have it heal. Since this surgery is viewed as "elective surgery," it can be bumped and rescheduled.) Only after surgery and healing can the training take place. (3) those who have lost a kidney which was transplanted. They are just waiting for another kidney and they view CAPD as temporary and are not that motivated to learn it because they think they won't be on it long.

$ 876 12-6-89: Waiting Room 571; 580; 580.7; 580.1; 264; 12;

While waiting to talk to Dr. H, I sat in the hemodialysis waiting room. I watched and listed to patients (and waiting family) who were waiting to get on the dialysis machines. They were talking about how sometimes the staff is rough with them when putting the needles in to get the vein access. One guy said the needle went once "right into his bone." Another guy said "the girl had to try 7 times" to get his blood and he was about to hit her. (The nurse said at the time, "I know this hurts.") Another woman threatened physical harm to technicians who draw blood roughly. One patient mentioned that sometimes they have to get different vein access sites (i.e., the groin or the top of the foot). They were all talking, not always to anyone in particular (but sometimes they were). They were talking in a way so that everyone in the room could be in the conversation if they wanted to.

It's good practice to use cryptic codes for places and informant names and to keep the codebook of names and locations physically separate from your field notes. You never know what would embarrass or hurt someone if your data fall into the wrong hands. William Partridge studied cannabis use in highland Colombia. He recorded interviews with cannabis growers separately from all his other notes and kept the only copy of those notes in a locked trunk. The interview texts were identified only by a letter code (Kimball and Partridge 1979:174).

When you finish writing up your field notes for the day, go back and fill in the topical codes. Code field notes as you go along. Miles and Huberman are right: "Coding is hard, obsessive work. It is not nearly as much fun as getting the good stuff in the field" (1994:63). As the pile of uncoded field notes grows, it gets harder and harder to be obsessive.

Furthermore, as I'll have occasion to say a few more times, coding is what most of qualitative data analysis really is. By the time you've coded your field notes, you've established the themes that need to be indexed and the patterns that need to be located and thought about. Spending a lot of time coding notes is not Mickey Mouse work. It's analysis.

Analytic Notes

You will write up fewer *analytic notes* than any other kind. This is where you **lay out your ideas about how you think the culture you are studying is organized.** Analytic notes can be about relatively minor things. When I finally figured out the rules for showing up on time for evening functions in Greece, that was worth an analytic note. And when I understood the rules that governed the naming of children, that was worth an analytic note, too.

As I said in Chapter 2, in the section on theory, it took me almost a year to figure out why the casualty rate among Kalymnian sponge divers was going up while the worldwide demand for natural sponges was going down. When it finally made sense, I sat down and wrote a long, long analytic field note about it. Recently, after thinking about the problem for some years, I finally understood why bilingual education in Mexico does not result in the preservation of Indian languages (it's a long story; see Bernard 1992). As the ideas developed, I wrote them up in a series of notes.

In her research on kidney patients, Shelley (1992) noticed that African Americans were far more likely to be on hemodialysis than on peritoneal dialysis, or CAPD. In her analytic notes, she explains that White physicians tend to assign African American patients to hemodialysis because CAPD is very demanding and the physicians, who are White, don't trust Black patients to handle properly the chores involved.

Analytic notes are the product of a lot of time and effort and may go on for several pages. They are often the basis for published papers, or for chapters in dissertations and books. They will be the product of your understanding, and that will come about through your organizing and working with descriptive and methodological notes over a period of time. Don't expect to write a great many analytic notes, but write them all your life, even (especially) after you are out of the field.

IS PARTICIPANT OBSERVATION SCIENCE?

For many researchers, participant observation is a humanistic method, not a scientific one. It is the strategic method that produces experiential knowledge, that lets you talk from the gut about what it feels like to plant a garden in the high Andes or dance all night in a street rave in Seattle.

From my traditional, positivist perspective, participant observation is also a scientific method, and a brawny one at that. It produces effective knowledge—knowledge for moving the levers of the world.

It is used in the development and testing of new consumer products: John Lowe reports on how he and a team of participant observers at the Cultural Analysis Group figured out why consumers avoided automated, credit card gasoline purchases when that technology first appeared on the pumps in the early 1990s (*Wall Street Journal,* August 4, 1993).

It is used in understanding high-technology work operations: Brigitte Jordan reports on how she and her team of ethnographers at Xerox Corporation determined the information flow and the hierarchy of interactions in the operations room of a major airline at a metropolitan airport (Jordan 1992b).

And it is used in the development of explanations for important human problems: Nancy Scheper-Hughes developed a nomothetic theory, based on participant observation, that accounts for the tragedy of infant mortality in northeast Brazil and the direct involvement of mothers in their infants' deaths (1992).

THE FRONT EDGE OF SOCIAL SCIENCE: COMBINING METHODS

More and more social researchers these days have learned what a powerful method participant observation is at all stages of the research process. The method stands on its own, but it is also increasingly part of a mixed-method strategy, as researchers combine qualitative and quantitative data to answer questions of interest.

Laura Miller (1997), for example, used a mix of ethnographic and survey methods to study gender harassment in the U.S. Army. Keeping women out of jobs that have been traditionally reserved for men is *gender* harassment; asking women for sex in return for a shot at one of those jobs is *sexual*

harassment. (Gender harassment need not involve sexual harassment, or vice versa.)

Miller spent nearly two years collecting data at eight Army posts and at two training centers in the U.S. where war games are played out on simulated battlefields. She lived in Somalia with U.S. Army personnel for 10 days, in Macedonia for a week, and in Haiti for six days during active military operations in those countries. Within the context of participant observation, she did unstructured interviewing, in-depth interviewing, and group interviewing. Her group interviews were spontaneous: over dinner with a group of high-ranking officers; sitting on her bunk at night, talking to her roommates; in vehicles, bouncing between research sites, with the driver, guide, protocol officer, translator, and guard (Miller, personal communication).

Now, "forms of gender harassment" in the U.S. Army turn out to be one of those cultural domains that people recognize and think about, but for which people have no ready list in their heads. You can't just ask people: "List the kinds of gender harassment." From her ethnographic interviews, though, Miller was able to derive what she felt was just such a list, including

(1) *resistance* to authority (hostile enlisted men ignore orders from women officers);

(2) *constant scrutiny* (men pick up on every mistake that women make and use those mistakes to criticize the abilities of women in general);

(3) *gossip and rumors* (women who date many men are labeled "sluts," women who don't date at all are labeled "dykes," and any woman can easily be unjustly accused of "sleeping her way to the top");

(4) *outright sabotage* of women's tools and equipment on work details; and

(5) *indirect threats* against women's safety (talking about how women would be vul-

nerable to rape if they were to go into combat).

This list emerges from qualitative research—hanging out, talking to people and gaining their trust, and generally letting people know that you're in for the long haul with them. If you are trying to develop programs to correct things that are wrong with a program, then this list, derived entirely from participant observation, is enough. An education program to counter gender harassment against women in the U.S. Army must include something about each of the problems that Miller identified.

While ethnographic methods are enough to *identify* the problems and processes, ethnography can't tell you *how much* each problem and process counts. Yes, enlisted Army men can and do sabotage Army women's tools and equipment on occasion. How often? Ethnography can't help with that one. Yes, men do sometimes resist the authority of women officers. How often? Ethnography can't help there, either.

Fortunately, Miller also collected questionnaire data—from a quota sample of 4,100 men and women, Whites and Blacks, officers and enlisted personnel. In those data, 19% of enlisted men and 18% of male noncommissioned officers (like sergeants) said that women should be treated exactly like men and should serve in the combat units just like men, while just 6% of enlisted women and 4% of female noncommissioned officers agreed with this sentiment. You might conclude, Miller says, that men are more supportive than women are of equality for women in combat roles. Some men with whom Miller spoke, however, said that women should be given the right to serve in combat *so that, once and for all, everyone will see that women can't cut it.*

Are men really what Miller called "hostile proponents" of equality for women? Could that be why the statistics show so many more men in favor of women serving in combat units? Miller went back to her questionnaire data: About 20% of men in her survey said that women should be assigned to combat units just like men were—but almost to a man they also said that putting women into combat units would reduce the military's effectiveness.

Notice the constant feedback between ethnographic and survey data here. The ethnography produced ideas for policy recommendations and the content for a questionnaire. The questionnaire data illuminated and validated many of the things that the ethnographer learned during participant observation, but those same survey data produce anomalies—things that didn't quite fit with Miller's intuition as an ethnographer.

And sure enough, the numerical analysis showed that her concept of "hostile proponent of equality" was correct. This subtle concept advances our understanding considerably of how gender harassment against women works in the U.S. Army. (See Harrell and Miller [1997] for an example of how survey research was combined with focus group interviews to study gender-related issues in the U.S. military.)

Chapter 9 Review

KEY CONCEPTS

Participant observation, 318-319, 324-328
Ethnography, 318, 345-346
Strategic methods, 318
Going native, 319, 322
Impression management, 319
Fieldwork roles, 321-322
Complete participant, 321
Participating observer and observing
    participant, 321, 322
Complete observer, 321, 322
Direct observation, 321, 322
Rapid assessment, 323
Participatory rural appraisal, 323
Participatory mapping, 323
Participatory transects, 323
Reactivity, 324-325
Sucker bias, 329
Explicit awareness, 330-331
Naïveté, 332-333
Hanging out, 333-334

Gaining rapport, 334-335
Objectivity, 335-337
Becoming the phenomenon, 336
Value neutrality, 336
Indigenous research, 336-337
Researcher response, 341
Culture shock, 342-343
The privacy problem, 342-343
Respondents, 345
Emic explanations, 345
Key informants, 346-348
Cultural consensus model, 350-355
Jottings, or scratch notes, 357-358
Daily diary, 358-359
Daily log, 359-360
Methodological notes, 361-362
Descriptive notes, 362-364
Topical codes, 363
Analytic notes, 364, 365

SUMMARY

❖ Participant observation is one of the strategic methods of the social sciences, along with experiments, surveys, and archival research.

  ◆ Participant observation turns field workers into instruments of data collection and data analysis. It involves establishing rapport and learning to act so that people go about their business as usual when you show up.

  ◆ Participant observation involves deception and impression management. The ethical imperative looms as large for participant observers as it does for experimentalists.

❖ While participant observation is most associated with cultural anthropology, it has a long history and is used across the social sciences.

  ◆ The Chicago school of sociology, beginning in the 1920s under Robert Park and Ernest Burgess, was based on an ethnographic approach. It continues today in monographs and in the pages of the journal *Contemporary Ethnography*.

❖ It's common to spend a year or more doing participant observation fieldwork. Many participant observation studies are done in a few months or even less.

  ◆ Applied ethnographic research is often done in just a few weeks using methods known collectively as rapid assessment procedures, including participatory mapping and participatory transects. These methods are effective in villages or in organizations.

❖ One of the strengths of participant observation is its emphasis on validity. Participant observation lowers the reactivity problem in the collection of observational data.

❖ Participant observation requires certain skills. These include learning the local language, dialect, or jargon; developing explicit awareness; building memory; maintaining naiveté; learning to hang out and build rapport; maintaining objectivity; and learning to write clearly.

  ◆ Learning to hang out and develop rapport involves skills that are highly manipulative. This raises special ethical concerns for participant observers.

  ◆ Objectivity does not mean value neutrality. When Amnesty International documents state-sanctioned torture, we recognize the power of the documentation in its objectivity, not in the neutrality of the data collectors.

❖ Personal characteristics are important variables in participant observation. Gender, sexual orientation, race, ethnicity, and marital status all color in some way our access to data and the way we interpret data.

- Feminist scholars have made it clear that gender is a negotiated idea. What you can and can't do if you are a man or a woman is more fixed in some cultures than in others, and in all cultures there is a lot of individual variation in gender roles.

❖ There are seven stages of emotional response in projects based on participant observation fieldwork: (1) initial contact; (2) culture shock; (3) discovering the obvious; (4) the break; (5) focusing; (6) exhaustion, the second break, and frantic activity; and (7) leaving.

❖ Key informant interviewing is an integral part of ethnographic research. Good informants are people you can talk to easily, who understand the information you need, and who are glad to give it to you or get it for you.
  - Find trustworthy informants who are observant, reflective, and articulate and stay with them. Ethnographic fieldwork stands or falls on building mutually supportive relations with a few key people.

❖ The difference between fieldwork and field experience is field notes.
  - There are four types of field notes: jottings, the diary, the log, and the notes. There are three types of notes: methodological notes, substantive notes, and analytic notes.
  - Diaries are essential. Your diary will give you an outlet for writing things that you don't want to become part of a public record. The log is the key to collecting both qualitative and quantitative data on a systematic basis.

❖ Participant observation is a powerful method that stands on its own, but it is also increasingly part of a mixed-method strategy, as researchers combine qualitative and quantitative data to answer questions of interest.

EXERCISES

1. This exercise is designed to help you develop skills in taking field notes and in intellectualizing the idea of participant observation. For the next two weeks, take field notes about going to class. Eventually, you want to be able to write a descriptive paper about the act of going to class and the meaning of going to class to different kinds of people. Do men and women act differently in class? Do they sit differently? Do they position themselves in the lecture hall differently? Do people act differently at 8 a.m. and at 3 p.m.? How about in large lecture classes vs. small classes?

   You'll find that there's a lot to this little exercise. You'll have to interview students who attend a variety of classes, including classes that you'd never consider taking, and you'll have to do some observing of classes in which you aren't enrolled. This will require asking professors for permission to sit in, and asking them to sign informed consent forms. Be sure you code your field notes from your observations. If several students in your class are doing this exercise, get together with them and compare your note-taking and note-coding tactics.

2. This next exercise is designed to help you build your skills at becoming explicitly aware of everyday things. Get a group of three or more students together and make a list of some mundane, everyday activities—things like making a bed, doing laundry, building a sandwich, shaving (face, legs, underarms), picking out produce at the supermarket. Pick three things and have everyone in the group write one-page descriptions of those things. The idea is to just sit down and think through the details and write up, from memory, how you go about, say, doing your laundry. Then, get the group together to read and discuss each other's descriptions. Look specifically for details that everyone writes down about a particular activity and for details that only one person writes down about the same activity.

3. Tomorrow night you're going to write down a simple list of your day's activities, so tomorrow when you wake up, remember to think about everything you do all day. The idea is to remember as many details as you can about what you did, what you ate, where you went, and whom you met all day.

   The day after tomorrow, carry a little notepad with you and jot down everything you do, what you eat, where you go, whom you meet. The object of this exercise is to make you painfully aware of the limitations of memory and why it's a good idea to jot down notes, even if they're just reminders and not full of detail.

4. Make a map of some physical space where you spend time. It can be the cafeteria, a lounging area, your apartment, a laundromat, a public park, and so on. The idea is to learn to make maps to scale. This involves, among other things, learning to walk so that your pace is constant. My pace is 30.5 inches on flat ground. Your pace will tend to lengthen when you walk downhill and to decrease when you walk uphill, but with practice, you can learn to adjust for these differences and keep your pace constant.

5. The object of this next exercise is to write a paper on a specialized craft by interviewing one key informant. The craft can be computer repair or shoe repair. Harriers and glaziers have very specialized knowledge. The problem in a complex society is not finding people who have specialized craft knowledge. The problem is finding people who will talk to you openly about their knowledge. Pick one area of specialized craft knowledge and interview at least three people who control that knowledge.

Take careful *methodological* notes during the interview about the dynamics of the interaction. Some people are better cultural informants than are others. How can you tell?

FURTHER READING

Participant observation. There are many excellent books, by scholars across the social sciences, about the craft of participant observation. Among these are Agar (1996), Behar (1996), Bogdan (1972), Bruyn (1966), Cassell and Symon (1994), Fenno (1990), Fetterman (1998), Gummesson (1991), Junker (1960), Spradley (1980), Whyte and Whyte (1984), Wolcott (1995), and Woods (1986). For thorough introductory overviews of participant observation, see DeWalt et al. (1998) and Stewart (1998).

Field notes. The fullest treatment of field notes is Sanjek (1990). Atkinson (1992) discusses different ways of reading field notes.

Rapid assessment. For an introduction to rapid assessment in medical anthropology, see Scrimshaw and Hurtado (1987); for rapid assessment procedure in agricultural research, see Shaner et al. (1982).

Learning a field language. For lots of good hints about learning a field language, see Burling (1984).

Selecting ethnographic informants. Johnson (1990) devotes an entire book to this subject. Many ethnographers, however, discuss how they met their key informants. See, for example, the memorable discussion by Whyte (1981 [1943]; Whyte and Whyte 1984).

Dangerous fieldwork. Participant observation ethnography can be dangerous. On surviving fieldwork in general, including coming back healthy from unhealthy environments, see Howell (1990). For studies of ethnographers who work in violent situations, see Lee (1995) and Nordstrom and Robben (1995).

"You can observe a lot just by watching."
Yogi Berra (1964; see Berra and Garagiola 1998)

10 DIRECT AND INDIRECT OBSERVATION

IN THIS CHAPTER:

❖ INTRODUCTION

Interviewing people gets at information about their attitudes and values and what they think they do. When you want to know what people actually *do,* however, there is no substitute for watching them or studying the physical traces their behavior leaves behind. This chapter is about direct observation (watching people and recording their behavior on the spot) and indirect observation (gathering the archaeological residue of human behavior).

We begin with the two most important methods for direct observation, continuous monitoring and spot sampling of behavior. Then we take up unobtrusive observation (and the ethical issues associated it) and, finally, indirect observation.

STRATEGIES FOR DIRECT OBSERVATION

There are two general strategies for direct observation of behavior. You can be obvious and *reactive,* or you can be **unobtrusive** and **nonreactive.** In reactive observation, people know that you are watching them and may play to their audience—you. Thus, there is always a danger in reactive observation that you will record what people want you to see, and not the behavior that goes on when you're not there.

In unobtrusive observation, you study people's behavior without their knowing it. This eliminates the problem of informants playing to the audience, but it automatically involves serious ethical questions. We'll get to some of those problems later in this chapter.

CONTINUOUS MONITORING

In *continuous monitoring,* or CM, you watch a person, or group of people, and record their behavior as faithfully as possible. The technique was developed in the field of management and is used today in all the social sciences—in laboratory studies and in studies of naturally occurring behavior as well (see Box 10.1).

The earliest example of CM is attributed to Charles Babbage, the nineteenth-century mathematician who invented the computer. He studied the behavior of workers in a factory and determined that a pound of number 11 straight pins (5,546 of them) should take exactly 7.6892 hours to make (Niebel 1982:4).

In 1911, F. B. Gilbreth studied bricklayers. He looked at things like where masons set up their pile of bricks and how far they had to reach to retrieve each brick. From these studies, he was able to make recommendations on how to lessen worker fatigue, increase morale, and raise productivity through conservation of motion.

Box 10.1
Continuous Monitoring across the Social Sciences

Organizational researchers use CM to evaluate the performance of professionals such as teachers and lawyers in actual classroom and courtroom settings (Medley and Mitzel 1958; Mileski 1971; Rosenshine and Furst 1973) and for assessing employee-employer interactions (Sproull 1981). Educational researchers use CM to study teacher-pupil interaction (Guilmet 1979; Meh 1996) and children's behavior (Raver and Peterson 1988), and CM is at the core of animal ethology studies (Hutt and Hutt 1970; Lehner 1996; Sullivan 1990). In sociology and social psychology, CM in the field has been used to study police-civilian interactions (Reiss 1971; McCall 1978; Sykes and Brent 1983), how people eat (Stunkard and Kaplan 1977), and how people use architectural space (Bechtel 1977).

CM is also widely used in psychology for the behavioral assessment of everything from anxieties and phobias (Dadds et al. 1994) to social support in families (Liotta et al. 1985), and it is used in nursing research to assess the behavior of long-term patients in hospitals and nursing homes (Algase et al. 1997).

Before Gilbreth, the standard in the trade was 120 bricks per hour. After Gilbreth published, the standard reached 350 bricks per hour (Niebel 1982:24). Of course, not everybody was thrilled with these new standards, but studies like those of Gilbreth were the beginning of what is today called *scientific management, time and motion research,* and *human factors engineering.* The method of continuous monitoring of behavior is still used in assessing work situations (Chadsey-Rusch and Gonzalez 1988; Drury 1990; Frank et al. 1997).

Continuous Monitoring and Children

CM is particularly useful in studying children—in classrooms and on playgrounds, in clinical settings, and in homes. Self-administered questionnaire surveys are practically useless with children: The young ones can't read them or fill them out, and the older ones won't put up with them. Personal interviews are useful but don't tell you what children actually do with their time.

You can do *participant* observation with children (see Fine and Sandstrom [1988] for tips on how to do this), but the attractive thing about studying children by CM is that, unlike adults, children seem not to be bothered by the presence of researchers. Children don't usually change their behavior when they're being studied, and when they do, they're pretty obvious about it. Most researchers report that, after a time, children go about their business and ignore researchers, note pads, stopwatches, video cameras, and other gadgets. (See Pellegrini [1996] for methods of studying children's behavior under natural conditions. See Longabaugh [1980] for a review of the uses of direct observation in cross-cultural psychology.)

One Boy's Day

On April 26, 1949, eight observers took 30-minute turns following Raymond Birch, a seven-year-old, as he went through his day—from the time he got up at 7:00 a.m. until he was asleep again at 8:33 p.m. Raymond lived in a small town—population 725—in the Midwest. Roger Barker and Herbert Wright (1951) called this a "field study in psychological ecology." As part of a larger community study of children, the eight field workers spent six months observing grades 1 and 2 in the local public school before following Raymond.

By then, the observers were well known around town. In fact, four of them were from the town. At approximately one-minute intervals, they recorded Raymond's vocalizations and body movements, as well as their own on-the-spot impressions of Raymond's perceptions, motives, and feelings. As Barker and Wright recognized, "Behavior without motives, feelings, and meanings is of little significance" (ibid.:8). Some of the behavior was interaction with the observer. No sense in pretending the observer wasn't part of the picture. They got everything.

At the end of each 30-minute session, the field workers used their notes and dictated to a tape recorder, getting down as much detail as they could remember. (Remember, this was 1949. Tape recorders weighed around 30 pounds then and were anything but portable.) Another member of the team listened to the narrative and made notes on ambiguities in the record. The listener queried the observer about any points in question.

Both the queries and the answers were recorded and the final narrative—the book *One Boy's Day*—reflects everything the team could come up with. They're never going to make a movie of this book, but it's a phenomenal piece of naturalistic research. Figure 10.1 shows an excerpt from Barker and Wright's study—an excerpt that covers just five minutes of Raymond Birch's day.

The Zapotec Children Study

Douglas Fry used CM to study aggressive play among Zapotec children (1990). From 1981 to 1983, Fry did 18 months of participant observation fieldwork in La Paz and San Andrés, two small, Zapotec-speaking villages just four miles apart in the Valley of Oaxaca, Mexico. During the last five months of his research, Fry did direct, continuous monitoring of 24 children (three-eight years old) in each village. Before that, he visited almost all the households in the villages several times so that children had become accustomed to him when he began his intensive observation.

Fry describes his data-collection procedures clearly:

> The formal focal sampling observations were conducted between May and September of 1983. They represent each day of the week and encompass the daylight hour. Most observations (84%) were conducted within family compounds, although children were also observed in the streets, town squares, school yards, fields, and hills. I alternated sampling between the two communities on a weekly to biweekly basis. A total of 588 observations were conducted, resulting in an average of approximately 12 observations for each focal child ($M = 12.25$, $SD = 6.21$). On average, each focal child was observed for just over 3 hours ($M = 3.13$ hours, $SD = 1.39$ hours), resulting in a total of 150 hours of observation time for the entire sample. [Note: It is common in scientific papers to report means and standard deviations; hence the M and SD figures in this paragraph.]
>
> Focal observations were narrated into a tape recorder carried in a small backpack or recorded on paper using a shorthand system. I recorded a running commentary of the behaviors engaged in by the focal child, using behavior elements defined in the previously developed ethogram. I moved with a focal child in order to maintain continuous visual contact (Altmann 1974), but did not remain so close as to interfere with actions or unduly attract the child's attention. Whenever a focal child engaged in any type of antagonistic behavior, the specifics of

After school

3:15. Raymond climbed on his bicycle.

Very slowly he started to ride away from the school with Roy holding onto the carrier over the back wheel.

Roy called out to Jimmy Olson, who was going by, "Look at Jimmy's old, big, long raincoat."

Raymond asked, "What you got your raincoat on for, Jimmy?"

Jimmy immediately took the raincoat off and said, "There," rather self-satisfied and as if to please Raymond.

Roy slowed down a little and Raymond sped up, leaving Roy behind with Jimmy and some of the others.

3:16. Raymond continued on his way alone. He rode slowly and carefully down to the corner of the square.

He saw Mr. Howard coming.

He got off his bike.

He stepped off the curb and started pushing his bike across the street.

About in the middle of the street he met Mr. Howard and said, "Hello, Mr. Howard," in a pleasant way.

Mr. Howard responded warmly, "Well, hi, sir. How are you getting along?"

He passed Raymond and went on his way.

3:17. Raymond remounted his bike.

He rode on across the intersection to the sidewalk in front of the courthouse.

He kicked the front wheel of the bike up over the curb. He bit his lower lip as he made the effort.

He walked the bicycle to the bottom of the front steps leading up to the courthouse lawn.

Raymond practically carried the bicycle up the steps (See Plate 21.) The bicycle was heavy and it took many grunts, groans, and puffs to get it up the flight of six or eight steps. Raymond did this efficiently and quickly.

He immediately mounted the bike, almost before he had gotten past the top step.

3:19. He rode back and forth near the top of the steps on the walk.

Without dismounting, he paused momentarily.

Looking very intent, he rode around the trees, between benches, crisscrossing the sidewalk.

It looked as if he were putting on a performance for me.

He scrutinized the pedals as he rode by me.

Raymond began to ride somewhat faster as he zigzagged along the sidewalk.

Then he rode up the sidewalk to the main courthouse entrance, using only one hand to steer.

With a sidelong glance, he looked at me shyly but proudly. The restrained smile that came and went fleetingly seemed to indicate that he was quite proud of his one-hand riding but did not want to show it.

He barely missed some trees and benches as he made a very sharp turn.

Figure 10.1 Five Minutes of Observation

SOURCE: R. Barker and H. F. Wright, *One Boy's Day: A Specimen Record of Behavior,* pp. 278-80, 1951, Harper & Brothers.

the interaction were noted, including identity of the interactant(s) and any facial expressions or gestures. For instance, interactions such as the following were recorded: Focal boy punches, pushes sister of 3-year-old while laughing (sister does nothing in response). (Fry 1990:326-27)

Like Barker and Wright's study of a single focal child, Fry's study is in the tradition of *ethology,* or *behavioral biology.* Most ethologists study nonhuman animals (everything from moths to fish to chimpanzees), but there is increasing interest across the social sciences in the study of natural human behavior and in the methods of ethology (see Eibl-Eiblsfeldt [1989] for the definitive resource on human ethology).

It is standard practice in ethology to develop an *ethogram,* or **list of behaviors,** for a species being studied. Fry developed his ethogram of Zapotec children by watching them in public places before beginning his study of focal individuals. Based on 150 hours of focal child observation, Fry's data contain 764 episodes of what he calls "play aggression" and 85 episodes of "serious aggression."

Play aggression is a punch, kick, tackle, etc., accompanied by smiles, laughs, and playfaces. Serious aggression are episodes accompanied by low frowns, bared teeth, fixated gazes, and crying. Fry found that when girls initiated serious aggression, it was almost always with other girls (93% of cases). But when boys initiated serious aggression, it was just as likely to be with girls as with other boys.

Observing Grownups in the Field

I don't want to give the impression that direct observation is only for watching kids. A lot of really interesting research is done across the social sciences by following adults around and watching what they do. Pearson (1990) studied the energy expenditure of 145 Samoan men and women in Western Samoa, American Samoa, and Honolulu. He wanted to know if urbanization changed the Samoans' lifestyle as measured by their energy intake and expenditure. He interviewed his informants and asked them to recall their activities over the past 24 hours, noting each activity and probing during the interview to help people remember them.

> A lot of really interesting research is done across the social sciences by following adults around and watching what they do.

To check the **24-hour recall** data, he did continuous monitoring of 47 men, while a female assistant monitored 43 women. They accumulated a total of 825 hours of observation, with their subjects in direct view 92% of the time. The estimates of active energy expenditure from direct observation data of men were 33%-80% lower than the estimates from the recall data. The estimates for women were 27%-53% lower. Women did better than men in recalling their activities, but both men and women were way off the mark, particularly in recalling their light-to-moderate work of the previous day. Pearson's work makes it clear that recall is not a good substitute for observation.

Studying Shoppers

Murtagh (1985) used CM to understand how people use arithmetic in grocery shopping. He recruited 24 adults in Orange County, California, for his study. Each informant wore a tape recorder while shopping at a supermarket and was accompanied by two researchers. As the informants went about their shopping, they talked into the tape recorder about how they were deciding which product to buy, what size to choose, and so on.

One observer mapped the shopper's route through the store and recorded the prices and amounts of everything purchased. The other researcher kept up a running interview with the shopper, probing for details. Murtagh was aware of the potential for reactivity in his study. But he was interested in understanding the way people thought through ordinary, everyday arithmetic problems, and his experiment was a good way to generate those problems under natural conditions.

In a similar experiment, Titus and Everett (1996) gave 63 people a list of 21 actual items to buy in a grocery store. The shoppers wore small tape recorders and talked about their experiences and their decisions as they went through the store, finding the items on the list. Here are a few actual snippets of the shoppers' monologues as they went through the store, putting the 21 items into their grocery carts:

> *Shopper 42.* Picnic supplies, plastic wrap, dog food. I don't think we need anything here. I see bread, candy. Doesn't look like I need that. Bleaches, liquid detergents. I need some dishwashing detergent.

> *Shopper 31.* Bouillon cubes . . . let's try with soup. It's a soup base.

> *Shopper 02.* The powdered milk. I'm going to go right up here to baking needs. It may be there. But it's not. (Titus and Everett 1996:272, 274, 276)

Titus and Everett transcribed and analyzed the taped monologues of the shoppers. This is a case of continuous monitoring of behavior by the subjects themselves, and it yielded some very interesting findings. As they went through the store, consumers made a lot of errors—they would go down this aisle or that, thinking they'd find a particular product and soon realize that they were on the wrong track. A lot of these errors were the result of consumers simply not sharing the culture of the store managers regarding what goes with what.

Using a Tape Recorder

Many CM researchers record their observations on audiotape. This has a lot of advantages: It's less tedious than writing, it lets you focus your eyes on what's going on, it lets you record details later that might be left out of an on-the-spot written description, it avoids the limitations of a checklist, and it lets you get information about context as well as about the behavior you're studying. Here's what a transcription looks like:

> Alex has turned left down the aisle for paper products. The next item on his list is dinner napkins. He stops and looks down the aisle. Around midway down the aisle there are four people stopped, all looking at products on the shelves. They are blocking the aisle. Alex stares at this for a few seconds, like he's trying to assess the situation. He does a 180 and heads back this way, skipping the napkins and going on to the pork roast.

Using a tape recorder like this gets you plenty of contextual data, but there are trade-offs. If you want measurements from those qualitative data, you have to code them—that is, you have to listen to the tapes, over and over again, and decide what behaviors to code for each of the people you observe. Coding on the spot (by using a behavioral checklist or by inputting codes into a "palmtop" computer) produces immediately useful, quantitative data. You can't code on the fly *and* talk into a recorder at the same time, so you need to decide what kind of data you need and why you need them before you choose a method.

If you are trying to understand a behavioral *process,* then focus on qualitative data. If you need measurements of *how much* or *how often* people engage in this or that behavior, then focus on quantitative data.

Continuous Monitoring and Reactivity

Does direct observation distort behavior? We know that **people tell interviewers what they think interviewers want to hear (the *deference effect*) and that people answer interview questions in ways that make them look good (the *social desirability effect*).**

Are there analogous effects in continuous monitoring of behavior? Joel Gittelsohn and his co-workers (1997) tested this in their CM study of child care practices in rural Nepal. Over the course of a year, 10 trained field workers observed behavior in 160 households. Each home was visited seven times. Except for a three- to four-hour break in the middle of the day, the field workers observed a focal child, two to five years of age, and all the caregivers of that child, from 6:00 a.m. until 8:00 p.m. This study, then, involved both children and adults.

The observers coded for over 40 activities, including health-related behaviors, feeding activities, and various kinds of social interactions (punishment, affection, etc.). The rate of some behaviors changed a lot over the course of the year. On average, across 1,101 observations, the number of times per day that a caregiver served food to a child without asking the child if he or she wanted it fell by half.

The observers also coded each time they were interrupted by one of the people whom they were observing (and what the interruption was about: light conversation, being asked for favors or medicine). This allowed Gittelsohn et al. to track reactivity across the seven household visits. Reactivity was noticeable during the first visit and then fell off dramatically. This study shows clearly that (1) reactivity exists, and (2) it goes away rather quickly when indigenous observers stay on the job over time (Gittelsohn et al. 1997).

This does not mean that only indigenous observers can melt into the background. Even obtrusive participant observers from a foreign culture can build up rapport so that people become less likely to change their behavior.

CODING CONTINUOUS MONITORING DATA

Go to a shopping mall and record the interaction behavior of 30 mother-child pairs for five minutes each. Record carefully the number of children each mother has and her interaction with each child. Try to find out whether interaction patterns are predictable from (1) the number of children a mother has to cope with, (2) the ages of the children, (3) the perceived socioeconomic class or ethnicity of the family, or (4) some other factors.

This exercise is instructive, if not humbling. It's a real challenge to code for socioeconomic class and ethnicity when you can't talk to the people you observe. Do this with at least one colleague so you can both check the reliability of your coding.

In hypothesis-testing research, where you already know a lot about the people you are studying, you go out to observe armed with a coding scheme worked out in advance. The idea is to record any instances of behavior that conform to the items in the scheme. This allows you to see if your hunches are correct about conditions under which certain behaviors occur. In some studies, you might be interested in noting instances of aggressive vs. submissive behavior. In other cases, those variables might be irrelevant.

Coding Schemes

Over the years, researchers have developed *coding schemes* for using direct observation in many different situations—in lab studies of interactions between married couples, in classroom studies of teacher effectiveness, in worker-management negotiations, and so on. If you decide to do CM, take a look at some of these coding schemes (I've listed a few in the Further Reading section at the end of this chapter) and see whether you can use one of them.

Just as with attitude scales and surveys (in Chapters 7 and 8), there's no point in reinventing the wheel. If others have developed and tested a good system for coding behaviors of interest to you, use it. Don't feel that somehow it's more prestigious or morally better for you to make up everything from scratch. Knowledge grows when researchers can compare their data to the data others have collected using the same or similar instruments.

Figure 10.2 shows the basic coding scheme for *interaction process analysis,* a system developed 50 years ago by Robert F. Bales in his research on communications in small groups (Bales 1950).

Although the Bales coding scheme was worked out a very long time ago, it continues to be tested for validity and to be used in research to this day. Papini et al. (1988), for example, brought parents and their adolescent children to a lab and asked them to engage in a standard task. Papini et al. used the Bales scheme to assess how the children acted out pubescence.

Lindman et al. (1987) videotaped the interactions of college men who drank alcohol in a group setting. Some of the men were selected because they were nominated by peers as aggressive drinkers, and some were selected because they were nominated by their peers as nonaggressive drinkers. Lindman et al. coded the videotape in 10-second intervals, using the 12 categories of the Bales scheme. These data showed that, as the men drank, the aggressives tended not to address other aggressives but to address the group as a whole. Lindman et al. suggest that the tendency to become aggressive when drinking may be a stable personality trait.

This kind of work doesn't only have to be done in a lab setting. Stewart (1984) audiotaped 140 doctor-patient interactions in the offices of 24 family physicians and assessed the interactions with Bales's interaction process analysis. Ten days later, Stewart interviewed the patients at their homes to assess satisfaction and compliance. That is, were the patients satisfied with the care they'd gotten and were they taking the pills they'd been told to take? Sure enough, when physicians are coded as engaging in many patient-centered behaviors, patients report higher compliance and satisfaction.

One of the best things about the interaction process analysis system is that the 12 behaviors shown in Figure 10.2 are recognizable in practically any culture. Any act of communication can be identified as being one of those 12 categories. A more detailed outline for coding interpersonal relations was developed by Bales and Cohen (1979). A complete course on how to use their system is available in their book, aptly titled *SYM-LOG,* which stands for "systematic multiple level observation of groups" (see Crespi [1993] and Hare and Hare [1997]).

CM is used widely in educational research to track student-teacher interactions and to assess teacher effectiveness. Amidon and Flanders (1967) developed a coding scheme for this kind of work that has been used and adapted ever since (see Amidon and Hough 1967; Flanders 1970; Devet 1990; Calhoun 1994). Figure 10.3 shows the original Amidon/Flanders scheme.

Hops et al. (1995) developed a complex coding system called LIFE—Living in Familial Environments—for studying the behavior of naturally occurring interactions among family members. Hops et al. argue that direct observation, while tough to do, lets you identify specific behaviors that require intervention.

Make no mistake about this: CM is tough to do. It takes several months of intensive training for observers to become adept at using complex coding schemes. It used to be that observers had to code behaviors with pen and paper, and this, I

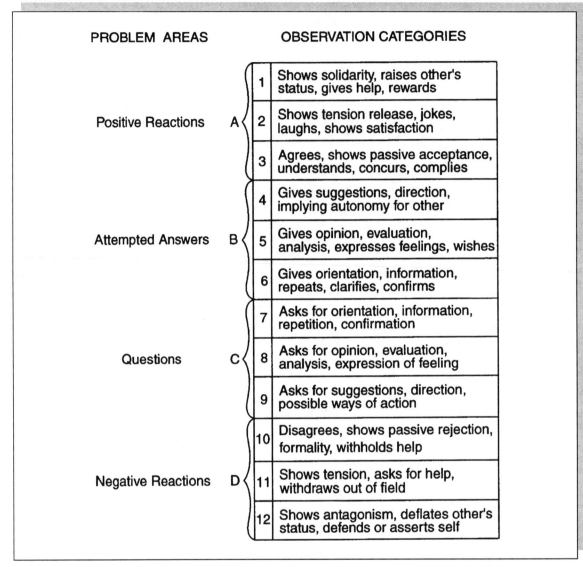

PROBLEM AREAS | OBSERVATION CATEGORIES

Positive Reactions A
1 Shows solidarity, raises other's status, gives help, rewards
2 Shows tension release, jokes, laughs, shows satisfaction
3 Agrees, shows passive acceptance, understands, concurs, complies

Attempted Answers B
4 Gives suggestions, direction, implying autonomy for other
5 Gives opinion, evaluation, analysis, expresses feelings, wishes
6 Gives orientation, information, repeats, clarifies, confirms

Questions C
7 Asks for orientation, information, repetition, confirmation
8 Asks for opinion, evaluation, analysis, expression of feeling
9 Asks for suggestions, direction, possible ways of action

Negative Reactions D
10 Disagrees, shows passive rejection, formality, withholds help
11 Shows tension, asks for help, withdraws out of field
12 Shows antagonism, deflates other's status, defends or asserts self

Figure 10.2 Categories for Direct Observation
SOURCE: R. F. Bales, *Interaction Process Analysis: A Method for the Study of Small Groups*, p. 9, 1950, Addison-Wesley.

think, is what made direct observation relatively rare in social research. These days, though, behavioral coding is typically done with hand-held computers called palmtops. Commercially available software lets you program any key to mean "initiates conversation" or "reciprocates affect" or any behavioral code you want. (See Appendix F for information about this technology.)

The more complex the coding system, of course, the longer it takes for observers to learn how to use it accurately and reliably. The new computer systems, though, are making it easier

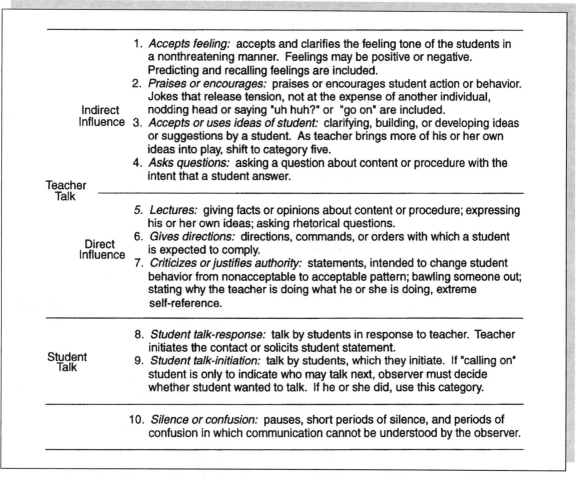

1. *Accepts feeling:* accepts and clarifies the feeling tone of the students in a nonthreatening manner. Feelings may be positive or negative. Predicting and recalling feelings are included.

2. *Praises or encourages:* praises or encourages student action or behavior. Jokes that release tension, not at the expense of another individual, nodding head or saying "uh huh?" or "go on" are included.

Indirect Influence 3. *Accepts or uses ideas of student:* clarifying, building, or developing ideas or suggestions by a student. As teacher brings more of his or her own ideas into play, shift to category five.

4. *Asks questions:* asking a question about content or procedure with the intent that a student answer.

Teacher Talk

5. *Lectures:* giving facts or opinions about content or procedure; expressing his or her own ideas; asking rhetorical questions.

Direct Influence 6. *Gives directions:* directions, commands, or orders with which a student is expected to comply.

7. *Criticizes or justifies authority:* statements, intended to change student behavior from nonacceptable to acceptable pattern; bawling someone out; stating why the teacher is doing what he or she is doing, extreme self-reference.

Student Talk

8. *Student talk-response:* talk by students in response to teacher. Teacher initiates the contact or solicits student statement.

9. *Student talk-initiation:* talk by students, which they initiate. If "calling on" student is only to indicate who may talk next, observer must decide whether student wanted to talk. If he or she did, use this category.

10. *Silence or confusion:* pauses, short periods of silence, and periods of confusion in which communication cannot be understood by the observer.

Figure 10.3 The Amidon/Flanders Scheme for Coding Categories of Interaction in the Classroom
SOURCE: E. J. Amidon and J. B. Hough, *Interaction Analysis: Theory, Research, and Application,* 1967, Addison-Wesley.

for field workers to code behavior on the fly, so I think we'll see renewed interest in CM. (One of the problems in the use of direct observation is the need for reliable coding by several researchers of the same data. We'll take up measures of intercoder reliability in Chapter 12 on text analysis. The problem of testing intercoder reliability is the same, whether you're coding text or behavior.)

COMPARATIVE RESEARCH: THE SIX CULTURE STUDY

Broad, general coding schemes are particularly useful for comparative research. Whether you're comparing sessions of psychotherapy groups, interaction sessions in laboratory experiments, or the natural behavior of people in field studies, using a common coding scheme really pays off because you can make direct comparisons across cases and look for generalization.

—————❖

The most important comparative study of children ever was run by Beatrice and John Whiting between 1954 and 1956. In the Six Culture Study, field researchers spent from 6 to 14 months in Okinawa, Kenya, Mexico, the Philippines, New England, and India. They made a total of some 3,000 five-minute (continuous monitoring) observations on 67 girls and 67 boys between the ages of 3 and 11.

Observations were limited to just five minutes because they were so intense, produced so much data, and required so much concentration and effort that researchers would have become fatigued and lost a lot of data in longer sessions. The investigators wrote out, in clear sentences, everything they saw children doing during the observation periods and also recorded data about the physical environment and others with whom children were interacting.

The data were sent from the field to Harvard University for coding according to a scheme of 12 behavior categories that had been worked out in research going back some 15 years before the Six Culture Study began. The behavioral categories were the following: seeks help, seeks attention, seeks dominance, suggests, offers support, offers help, acts socially, touches, reprimands, assaults sociably, assaults not sociably, and symbolic aggression (frightens, insults, threatens with gesture, challenges to compete). (Full details on the use of the Whiting scheme are published in Whiting et al. [1966]. See Whiting and Whiting [1973] for a discussion of their methods for observing and recording behavior.)

On average, every 10th observation was coded by two people, and these pairs of "coding part-

ners" were rotated so that coders could not slip into a comfortable pattern with one another. Coders achieved 87% agreement on children's actions; that is, given a list of 12 kinds of things a child might be doing, coders agreed 87% of the time. They also agreed 75% of the time on the act that precipitated a child's actions, and 80% of the time on the effects of a child's actions (Whiting and Whiting 1975:55).

The database from the Six Culture Study consists of approximately 20,000 recorded acts, for 134 children, or about 150 acts per child, on average.

Very strong conclusions can be drawn from this kind of robust database. For example, Whiting and Whiting (1975:179) note that nurturance, responsibility, success, authority, and casual intimacy "are types of behavior that are differentially preferred by different cultures." They conclude that "these values are apparently transmitted to the child before the age of six." They found no difference in amount of nurturant behavior among boys and girls three to five years of age. After that, however, nurturant behavior by girls increases rapidly with age, while boys' scores on this trait remain stable.

By contrast, reprimanding behavior starts out low for both boys and girls and increases with age equally for both sexes, across six cultures. The older the children get, the more likely they are to reprimand anyone who deviates from newly learned cultural rules. "Throughout the world," the Whitings conclude, "two of the dominant personality traits of children between seven and eleven are self-righteousness and bossiness" (1975:184). Anyone who grew up with an older sibling already knows that, but the Whitings' demonstration of this cross-cultural fact is a major scientific achievement.

❖—————

TECHNOLOGY AND CONTINUOUS MONITORING

Even with a fixed coding scheme, an observer in a CM situation has to decide among alternatives when noting behavior—whether someone is acting aggressively, or just engaging in rough play, for example. Recording behavior on film or video lets several analysts study the behavior stream and decide at leisure how to code it. (It also makes your data available for coding by others, now and in the future. Human ethologists, like Irenäus Eibl-Eiblsfeldt [1989], have amassed hundreds of *kilometers* of film and videotape of ordinary people doing ordinary things across the world.)

In 1958, William Soskin, a psychologist, and Vera John, an anthropologist, got several pairs of people—young married couples at a resort—to wear voice transmitters 14-16 hours a day for two weeks. This was before spy-size transmitters. The contraptions were $1.5'' \times 2.5'' \times 5''$ and were worn on a shoulder strap. A one-foot-long antenna, attached to the strap, stuck up from the shoulder blade, and the couples carried a battery pack that was changed daily. The couples' conversations were recorded on tape.

The couples weren't meant to be inconspicuous and (in a stroke of luck) the resort manager not only gave permission for the experiment, he announced at dinner one night why the couples were wearing the apparatus (Soskin 1963; Soskin and John 1963). The data from this experiment make clear how much we miss when we take notes of real conversations. There is a violent argument in the data and moments of joy and tenderness.

Videotape has made CM easier. In the 1970s, Marvin Harris and his students installed videotape cameras in the public rooms of several households in New York City. Families gave their permission, of course, and were guaranteed legal control over the cameras during the study and of the videotapes after the cameras were removed. Teams of observers monitored the equipment from remote locations. Later, the continuous verbal and nonverbal data were coded to study regularities in interpersonal relations in families.

Dehavenon (1978), for example, studied two Black and two White families for three weeks and coded their nonverbal behavior for such things as compliance with requests and the distribution and consumption of foods in the households. Dehavenon's data showed that the amount of authoritarianism in the four families correlated perfectly with income differences. The lower the family income, the more superordinate behavior in the home (p. 3).

One would hypothesize, from participant observation alone, that this was the case. But *testing* this kind of hypothesis requires the sort of quantified data that straightforward, direct observation provides. (See Sharff [1979] and Reiss [1985] for two more studies of households using the Harris videotapes.)

As video cameras have gotten smaller, easier to use, and less expensive, more field researchers have been using this technology for close examination of behavior streams. Heath (1986), for example, studied interactions between patients and physicians, and Jordan has used videotape to study birthing events across cultures (1992a; see also Jordan and Henderson 1993).

Video is also used in studies of consumer behavior. Observers at Planmetrics, a marketing research firm, videotaped 70 volunteer parents, for over 200 total hours, as the volunteers diapered their babies. The research was done on contract with Kimberly-Clark, manufacturer of Huggies, a brand of disposable diapers. The cameras were not hidden, and after a while people just went about their business as usual, according to Steven Barnett, an anthropologist who led the study.

Close observation showed that many parents could not tell whether their babies needed a diaper change, so the researchers recommended that the diapers contain an exterior chemical strip that changed color when the baby was wet. The observers also noticed that parents were powdering their babies' legs and that parents were treating the red marks left by the diaper gathers as if the marks were diaper rash. The firm recommended that the gathers be redesigned so that there would be no more red marks (Associated Press, October 1, 1985; *Wall Street Journal,* September 4, 1986, p. 29).

SPOT SAMPLING AND TIME ALLOCATION STUDIES

Time allocation (TA) studies are based on *spot sampling,* or *time sampling,* a technique in which **a researcher simply appears at randomly selected places, and at randomly selected times, and records what people are doing when they are first seen** (Gross 1984). There is usually no attempt at continuous monitoring of a behavior stream, although Pederson (1987) combined random spot sampling with 15-minute continuous monitoring of behavior.

The idea behind spot sampling is simple and appealing: If you sample a sufficiently large number of representative acts, you can use the percentage of *times* people are seen doing things (working, playing, resting, eating) as a proxy for the percentage of *time* they spend in those activities.

Time sampling was pioneered by behavioral psychologists in the 1920s. Influenced by John B. Watson's (then) revolutionary behaviorist approach to psychology, W. C. Olson (1929) sought to measure the behavior of nervous habits in normal children by taking repeated short samples under the most natural conditions possible. Leonard H. C. Tippett introduced spot sampling of the behavior stream in 1934 in his study of the fraction of time that textile workers actually spent working at their machines (Drury 1990:51).

Over the years, time sampling, like CM, has been used by psychologists, anthropologists, and researchers in nursing, education, and other fields to assess the actual behavior of people in various laboratory and natural settings. Shore et al. (1995), for example, used spot sampling to assess various aspects of care in a nursing home. Shore et al. confirmed (as others have found) that residents of the home spend most of their time (about 85%) alone and not engaged in social activity. Furthermore, the staff of the home spent most of their time (about 67%) interacting with one another or in solitary activities and not interacting with the residents.

Reactivity in Time Allocation Research

In CM, getting around the reactivity problem involves staying with the program long enough to get people accustomed to your being around. Eventually, people just get plain tired of trying to manage your impression and they act naturally. In TA research, the trick is to catch a glimpse of people in their natural activities before they see you coming on the scene—before they have a chance to modify their behavior.

Richard Scaglion (1986) did a TA survey of the residents of Upper Neligum, a Samakundi Abelam village in the Prince Alexander mountains of East Sepik Province in Papua New Guinea. "It is not easy," he says, "for an anthropologist in the field to come upon an Abelam unawares. Since I did not want to record 'greeting anthropologist' as a frequent activity when people were first observed, I often had to reconstruct what they were doing immediately before I arrived" (p. 540).

Borgerhoff-Mulder and Caro (1985) coded the observer's judgment of whether people saw the observer first, or vice versa, and compared that to whether the Kipsigis (in Kenya) they were studying were observed to be active or idle. People were idle significantly more often when they spied the observer coming before the observer saw them.

Did people become idle when they saw an observer approaching? Or was it easier for idle folks to see an observer before the observer saw them? Borgerhoff-Mulder and Caro found that people who were idle were sitting or lying down much more often than were people who were active. People at rest may be more attentive to their surroundings than those who are working and would be judged more often to have seen the researcher approaching.

Sampling Problems

There are five questions to ask when drawing a sample for a TA study: (1) Whom do I watch? (2) Where do I go to watch them? (3) When do I go there? (4) How often do I go there? and (5) How long do I spend watching people when I get there? (Gross 1984). Allen Johnson's study (1975) of the Machiguenga is instructive.

The Machiguenga are horticulturalists in the Peruvian Amazon. They live along streams, in small groups of related families, with each group comprising about 10-30 people, and subsist primarily from slash-and-burn gardens. They supplement their diet with fish, grubs, wild fruits, and occasional monkeys from the surrounding tropical forest. Johnson spent 14 months studying the Machiguenga in the community of Shimaa.

Johnson's strategy for selecting people to study was simple: Because all travel was on foot, he decided to sample all the households within 45 minutes of his own residence. This produced a convenience sample of 13 households totaling 105 persons. Since the Machiguenga live along streams, each time Johnson went out he walked either upstream or downstream, stopping at a selected household along the route. Which hour of the day to go out and which houses to stop at were determined by using a table of random numbers, like the one in Appendix A of this book.

Thus, Johnson used a nonrandom sample of all Machiguenga households, but he randomized the times that he visited any household in his sample. This sampling strategy sacrificed some external validity, but it was high on internal validity. Johnson could not claim that his sample of households *statistically* represented all Machiguenga households. His 14 months' worth of experience in the field, however, makes his claim for the representativeness of his data credible.

That is, if Johnson's data on TA in those 13 households seem to him to reflect time allocation in Machiguenga households generally, then they probably do. But we can't be sure. Fortunately, randomizing his visits to the 13 households, and making a lot of observations (3,945 of them, over 134 different days during the 14-month fieldwork period), gives Johnson's results a lot of *internal* validity. So, even if you're skeptical of the external validity of Johnson's study, you could repeat it (in Shimaa or in some other Machiguenga community) and see whether you got the same results.

Regina Smith Oboler (1985) did a TA study among the Nandi of Kenya. She was interested in differences in the activities of adult men and women. The Nandi, Oboler said, "conceptualize the division of labor as sex segregated. Is this true in practice as well? Do men and women spend

TABLE 10.1 Number of Observations to Estimate the Frequency of an Activity to within a Fractional Accuracy

True Frequency of Activity f	Number of Observations Needed to See the Activity at a Particular Fraction of Accuracy							To See Activities at Least Once with 95% Probability
	.05	.10	.15	.20	.30	.40	.50	
0.01	152,127	38,032	16,903	9,508	4,226	2,377	1,521	299
0.02	75,295	18,824	8,366	4,706	2,092	1,176	753	149
0.03	49,685	12,421	5,521	3,105	1,380	776	497	99
0.04	36,879	9,220	4,098	2,305	1,024	576	369	74
0.05	29,196	7,299	3,244	1,825	811	456	292	59
0.06	24,074	6,019	2,675	1,505	669	376	241	49
0.07	20,415	5,104	2,268	1,276	567	319	204	42
0.08	17,671	4,418	1,963	1,104	491	276	177	36
0.09	15,537	3,884	1,726	971	432	243	155	32
0.10	13,830	3,457	1,537	864	384	216	138	29
0.15	8,708	2,177	968	544	242	136	87	19
0.20	6,147	1,537	683	384	171	96	61	14
0.25	4,610	1,152	512	288	128	72	46	11
0.30	3,585	896	398	224	100	56	36	9
0.40	2,305	576	256	144	64	36	23	6
0.50	1,537	384	171	96	43	24	15	5

SOURCE: H. R. Bernard and P. D. Killworth, "Sampling in Time Allocation Research." *Ethnology* 32:211, 1993. Reprinted with permission.

their time in substantially different or similar types of activities?" (p. 203).

Oboler selected 11 households, comprising 117 people, for her TA study. Her sample was not random. "Selecting a random sample," she said, " . . . even for one *kokwet* (neighborhood) would have made observations impossibly difficult in terms of travel time" (p. 204). Instead, Oboler chose a sample of households that were matched to social and demographic characteristics of the total population and within half an hour's walking distance from the compound where she lived.

Oboler divided the daylight hours of the week into 175 equal time periods and gave each period (about two hours) a unique three-digit number. Then, using a table of random numbers, she chose

time periods to visit each household. She visited each household four times a week (on different days of the week) during two weeks each month and made nearly 1,500 observations on those households during her nine months in the field.

Oboler found that, for her sample of observations, adult men spend around 38% of their time "in activities that might reasonably be considered 'work' by most commonly used definitions of that term" (p. 205). Women in her sample spent over 60% of their time working.

Table 10.1 shows the number of spot observations necessary to estimate the frequency, *f*, of an activity to within a fractional accuracy. It also tells you how many observations you need if you want to compare time estimates.

Here's how to read the table. Suppose people spend about 5% of their time eating. This is shown in the first column as a frequency, f, of 0.05. If you want to estimate the frequency of the activity to within 20%, look across to the column in the center part of the table under 0.20. If you have 1,825 observations, and your data say that people eat 5% of the time, then you can safely say that the true percentage of time spent eating is between 4% and 6%. (Twenty percent of 5% is 1%. Five percent, plus or minus 1%, is 4%-6%.) (For the formula used to derive the numbers in Table 10.1, see Bernard and Killworth [1993].)

Suppose you do a study of the daily activities of families in a community and your data show that men eat 4% of the time, while women eat 6% of the time. If you have 300 observations, then the error bounds of the two estimates overlap considerably (about 0.02-0.06 for the men and 0.04-0.08 for the women).

You need about 1,800 observations to tell whether 0.06 is really bigger than 0.04 comparing across groups. It's the same for activities: If women are seen at leisure 20% of their time and caring for children 25% of their time, then 1,066 observations are required to tell if women really spend more time caring for children than they do at leisure.

Oboler had 1,500 observations. It is clear from Table 10.1 that her findings about men's and women's leisure and work time are not accidents. An activity seen in a sample of just 256 observations to occur 40% of the time can be estimated actually to occur between 40%, plus or minus 15% of 40%, or between 34% and 46%. Since men are seen working 38% of the time and about half of Oboler's 1,500 observations were of men, her finding is solid.

Nighttime Sampling

Virtually all spot sampling studies of behavior are done during the daylight hours, between 6 a.m. and 7 p.m. In Johnson's case, this was explicitly because "travel after dark is hazardous, and because visiting at night is not encouraged by the Machiguenga" (Johnson 1975:303). However, Scaglion (1986) showed the importance of nighttime observations in TA studies.

When Scaglion did his TA study of the Abelam in 1983, there were 350 people in the village, living in 100 households. Scaglion randomly selected two households each day, and visited them at randomly selected times, throughout the day and night. Now, if your sampling strategy demands that you be somewhere at 3 a.m., this will cut down considerably on the number of observations you can make. You have to sleep sometime! Nevertheless, Scaglion managed to make 153 observations in one month of work.

Scaglion used a recording scheme composed of 13 categories of activities: sleeping, gardening, idle, cooking and food preparation, ritual, visiting, eating, hunting, construction, personal hygiene, child care, cleansing and washing, and craftswork. Among his findings were that only 74% of Abelam activities during nighttime hours were coded as "sleeping." Seven of the nine observations that he coded as "ritual" occurred after dark. Half of all observations coded as "hunting" occurred at night, and six out of eight observations coded as "visiting" were nocturnal.

Had he done his TA study only during the day, Scaglion would have overestimated the amount of time that Abelam people spend gardening by about a fourth. His data show that gardening takes up about 26% of the Abelam's daylight hours, but only 20% of their total waking time in each 24-hour period.

Of course, it may not always be possible to conduct TA studies at night. Johnson, you'll remember, made a point of the fact that the Machiguenga discourage nighttime visiting. Scaglion, on the other hand, worked among a people who "go visiting at unusual hours, even when their prospective host is likely to be sleeping."

ı fact, rather enjoyed showing up at
1983 to observe households in the
ge. "In 1974-75," he said, "when I
was still quite a novelty . . . I was frequently
awakened by hearing 'Minoa, mine kwak?' ('Hey,
you, are you sleeping?'). This study allowed me
to return old favors by visiting people in the late
night hours to be sure *they* were sleeping"
(p. 539).

Coding and Recording
Time Allocation Data

Sampling is one of two problems in TA research. The other is measurement. How do we
know that when Oboler recorded that someone
was "working," we would have recorded the same
thing? If you were with Johnson when he recorded that someone was engaged in "hygiene
behavior," would you have agreed with his assessment? Every time? You can see the problem.

It gets even more thorny. Suppose you work
out a coding scheme that everyone agrees with.
And suppose you train other observers to see just
what you see (Rogoff [1978] achieved a phenomenal 98% interobserver agreement in her
study of nine-year-olds in Guatemala). Or, if you
are doing the research all by yourself, suppose you
are absolutely consistent in recording behaviors
(that is, you never code someone lying in a ham-
mock as sleeping when they're just lounging
around awake).

Even if all these reliability problems are taken
care of, what about observation validity? What do
you do, for example, when you see people engaged in multiple behaviors? A woman might be
holding a baby and stirring a pot at the same time.
Do you code her as engaged in child care or in
cooking? (Gross 1984:542). If someone saw that
you were lying down reading, and you were

studying for an exam, should they record that you
were working or relaxing?

Do you record all behaviors? Do you mark one
behavior as primary? This last question has important implications for data analysis. There are
only so many minutes in a day, and the percentage
of people's time that they allocate to activities has
to add up to just 100%. If you code multiple
activities as equally important, then there will be
more than 100% of the day accounted for. Most
TA researchers use their intuition, based on participant observation, to decide which of the multiple simultaneous activities they witness to record as the primary one, and which as secondary.

The best solution is to record *all* possible behaviors you observe in the order of their primacy,
according to your best judgment at the time of
observation. Use a check sheet to record behaviors
and use a separate check sheet for each observation you make, even if it means printing up 1,000
sheets for a TA study, and hauling them home
later. As you can see from Table 10.1, 1,000 spot
observations is enough for most TA studies.

> *Be paranoid about data.*
> *Those horror stories you've heard*
> *about lost data? They're true.*

If you can afford it, consider using the palmtop
recording technology I mentioned earlier. (More
about this in Appendix F on resources for research.) If you hand-code your original observations, then enter the data into a laptop while
you're still in the field, as a precaution against loss
of the original data sheets. Be paranoid about
data. Those horror stories you've heard about lost
data? They're true.

EXPERIENCE SAMPLING

The *experience sampling* method, or ES, **mixes random spot observation and informant recall.** People carry beepers that are programmed to signal informants at specified times. When the beeper goes off, informants fill in a form they carry around about what they're doing, who they're with, or what they're feeling at the moment. Alternatively, they might write an entry into a diary or talk into a small tape recorder and describe their actions, feelings, and surroundings, in their own words. They might even call a number and report, live, to a telephone interviewer.

The point is to combine the power of random spot checks with the relative ease of having people report on their own behavior. The thought is that the inaccuracy of recall data is mitigated by having people record on paper, or talk about, what they're doing on the spot. A lone investigator can only be in one place at a time, but with those beepers, you can collect spot-observation behavioral data from lots of people at once.

Using portable technology in behavioral observation goes back to that pioneering study by Soskin (1963). In those days, the technology was clunky—people were asked to walk around with big transmitters and separate battery packs and such. But these days, what with teeny beepers and easy data entry, ES has come into its own. Csikszentmihalyi and Larson (1987) have demonstrated the reliability of ES in a number of studies. Figure 10.4 shows the ES form used by Csikszentmihalyi and Larson (1987) in their study of daily life among adolescents.

———————❖

Wong and Csikszentmihalyi (1991) used ES in their study of gender differences in affiliation motivation—that is, differences in how men and women establish and maintain relationships with others. They recruited 170 high-achieving students from two suburban high schools in Chicago. The students (68 boys and 102 girls) filled out a background questionnaire about demographic information and family relationships. They also filled out the Personality Research Form, which, among other things, measures "affiliateveness"—how motivated people are to "win friendships and maintain association with others" (Jackson 1984:6).

Each student carried around a beeper for a week and received seven to nine random pages per day, between 7:00 a.m. and 10:00 p.m. on weekdays and between 9:00 a.m. and 12:00 noon on weekends. Whenever the beeper went off, students filled out an ES form, which asked them, (1) If you had a choice, who would you be with? (2) Who are you with? (3) What are you thinking about? and (4) What are the main things you're doing?

The researchers met with each student before the study got under way to explain how the beepers worked and to practice filling out the ES form. The forms were bound in 5.5″ × 8.5″ pads of 15 sheets each. (I really like the fact that Wong and Csikszentmihalyi tell us about the size of those pads in their article. That's just the kind of detail you need if you want to go out and do this kind of work. By the way, 5.5″ × 8.5″ is the size you get if you fold an ordinary 8.5″ × 11″ piece of paper in half.)

Three experienced coders tackled the open-ended questions (questions 3 and 4). They coded 20 forms each and discussed the differences in their codes. Then they coded 60 forms and had interrater agreement between 90% and 95%. After that, they just coded the forms and kept

APPENDIX: EXPERIENCE-SAMPLING FORM

Date: _____ Time Beeped: _____ am/pm Time Filled Out _____ am/pm

As you were beeped........
What were you thinking about? _____
Where were you? _____
What was the MAIN thing you were doing? _____
What other things were you doing? _____
WHY were you doing this particular activity? ☐ I had to   ☐ I wanted to do it   ☐ I had nothing else to do

	not at all		somewhat			quite			very
How well were you concentrating?	0	1	2	3	4	5	6	7	8	9
Was it hard to concentrate?	0	1	2	3	4	5	6	7	8	9
How self-conscious were you?	0	1	2	3	4	5	6	7	8	9
Did you feel good about yourself?	0	1	2	3	4	5	6	7	8	9
Were you in control of the situation?	0	1	2	3	4	5	6	7	8	9
Were you living up to your own expectations?	0	1	2	3	4	5	6	7	8	9
Were you living up to expectations of others?	0	1	2	3	4	5	6	7	8	9

Describe your mood as you were beeped:

	very	quite	some	neither	some	quite	very	
alert	0	o	•	—	•	o	0	drowsy
happy	0	o	•	—	•	o	0	sad
irritable	0	o	•	...	•	o	0	cheerful
strong	0	o	•	—	•	o	0	weak
active	0	o	•	—	•	o	0	passive
lonely	0	o	•	·	•	o	0	sociable
ashamed	0	o	•	—	•	o	0	proud
involved	0	o	•	—	•	o	0	detached
excited	0	o	•	—	•	o	0	bored
closed	0	o	•	—	•	o	0	open
clear	0	o	•	—	•	o	0	confused
tense	0	o	•	...	•	o	0	relaxed
competitive	0	o	•		•	o	0	cooperative

Did you feel any physical discomfort as you were beeped:

Overall pain or discomfort	none		slight			bothersome			severe
	0	1	2	3	4	5	6	7	8	9

Please specify: _____

Who were you with?

☐ alone   ☐ friend(s) How many? _____   ☐ female   ☐ male
☐ mother   ☐ strangers   ☐ other _____
☐ father   ☐ sister(s) or brother(s)

Indicate how you felt about your activity:

	low								high
Challenges of the activity	0	1	2	3	4	5	6	7	8	9
Your skills in the activity	0	1	2	3	4	5	6	7	8	9

	not at all								very much
Was this activity important to you?	0	1	2	3	4	5	6	7	8	9
Was this activity important to others?	0	1	2	3	4	5	6	7	8	9
Were you succeeding at what you were doing?	0	1	2	3	4	5	6	7	8	9
Do you wish you had been doing something else?	0	1	2	3	4	5	6	7	8	9
Were you satisfied with how you were doing?	0	1	2	3	4	5	6	7	8	9
How important was this activity in relation to your overall goals?	0	1	2	3	4	5	6	7	8	9

If you had a choice......
Who would you be with? _____
What would you be doing? _____
Since you were last beeped has anything happened or have you done anything which could
have affected the way you feel?
Nasty cracks, comments, etc.

Figure 10.4 Appendix from Csikszentmihalyi and Larson (1987)

SOURCE: M. Csikszentmihalyi and R. Larson, "Validity and Reliability of the Experience-Sampling Method." *Journal of Nervous and Mental Disease* 175:526-36. [Special issue: Mental disorders in their natural settings: The application of time allocation and experience-sampling techniques in psychiatry]. Copyright © 1987, Lippincott Williams & Wilkins. Reprinted with permission.

checking regularly with one another to make sure that they were able to keep up the high level of agreement.

This study yielded a lot of interesting results. Girls reported about twice as many thoughts about interpersonal relations as did boys. Regardless of how high students scored on the affiliation scale, the female students spent more time with friends and less time alone than did boys. Just as you'd expect, girls who scored higher on the affiliation scale (meaning they liked being with others) actually spent more time in social interactions (talking and hanging out with friends, going to parties, etc.) than did girls who scored low on that scale.

No surprise there. But differences in affiliation orientation had no effect on the amount of time that boys spent in social interactions. Boys were more likely than girls to be loners, no matter how much they liked being with others.

And even more interesting: Boys who scored high on the affiliation scale felt worse than boys who scored low, regardless of whether they were with friends or alone. According to Wong and Csikszentmihalyi, if boys like to develop interpersonal relationships, they are ambivalent about themselves. Highly affiliative girls think of themselves as influential, while influential boys are more likely to be aggressive than affiliative. These findings emerge from data about how people actually spend their time and about how people feel about themselves and others. The combination is tough to beat.

A FEW FINAL WORDS ON REACTIVE OBSERVATION

Where does all this leave us? Well, first of all, I don't want to give the impression that direct observation data are automatically accurate. Lots of things can clobber the accuracy of directly observed behavior. Observers may be biased by their own expectations of what they are looking for or by expectations about the behavior of women or men or any ethnic group (Kent et al. 1977; Repp et al. 1988).

On the other hand, while it's impossible to eliminate all observer bias, there is a lot of evidence that training helps make people better—more reliable and more accurate—observers (Kent et al. 1977; Hartmann and Wood 1990). We do the best we can. Just because a "perfectly aseptic environment is impossible," said Clifford Geertz, doesn't mean we "might as well conduct surgery in a sewer" (1973:30).

On balance, though, direct observation does provide more accurate results than do reports of behavior. McCann et al. (1997) studied 12 behaviors of Alzheimer's patients in a nursing home. The staff reported on the amount of each behavior for each of 177 patients, while trained observers actually counted a sample of the behaviors using a time sampling method I'll tell you about later in this chapter.

You can guess the result: Reports by the staff were way off the mark. If you want to know, say, whether, wandering happens *more often* than, say, unconnected speech among Alzheimer's patients, then staff reports might be enough. But if you want to know *how often* those behaviors actually occur, then nothing short of direct observation will do.

If you are unfamiliar with the direct, reactive observation approach to data gathering, you may feel awkward about walking around with a clipboard (and perhaps a stopwatch) and writing down what people are doing—or with beeping people and asking them to interrupt what they're doing to help you get some data.

This is a reasonable concern, and direct observation is not for everyone. It's not a detached method, like sending out questionnaires and waiting for data to be delivered to your doorstep. It is not a fun method, either. Hanging out, participating in normal daily activities with people, and writing up field notes at night is more enjoyable than monitoring and recording what people are doing.

But many field workers find that direct observation allows them to address issues that are not easily studied by any other method. Grace Marquis (1990) studied a shanty town in Lima, Peru. Children in households that kept chickens were at higher risk for getting diarrhea than were other children. The chickens left feces in the homes, and the feces contained an organism that causes diarrhea. Continuous monitoring showed that children touched the chicken droppings and, inevitably, touched their mouths with their hands. It was hard, tedious work, but the payoff was serious.

Direct observation may also seem overly time-consuming. Actually, random spot-checking of behavior is a cost-effective and productive way to use *some* of your time in any field project. When you're studying a group that has clear boundaries (an organization, like a hospital or a police precinct, or a public school), you can get very fine-grained data about people's behavior from a TA study, based on random spot checks. More important, as you can see from Table 10.1, with proper sampling you can generalize to large populations (whole school districts, an entire aircraft manufacturing plant, even cities) from spot checks of behavior, in ways that no other method allows.

You may be concerned that a strictly observational approach to gathering data about human behavior fails to capture the *meaning* of data for the actors. This, too, is a legitimate concern. A classic example is the observation that a wink can be the result of getting a speck of dust in your eye or a conscious act of conspiracy. And that's just a wink. People can engage in any of thousands of behaviors (skipping a class, wearing a tie, having their navel pierced) for many, many different reasons. Knowing the meaning of behavior is essential to understanding it.

On the other hand, one of our most important goals in science is to constantly challenge our own ideas about what things mean. That's how theories develop, are knocked down, and gain in their power to explain things. Why shouldn't we also challenge the theories—the explanations—that the people we study give us for their own behavior?

Ask people who are coming out of a church, for example, why they just spent two hours there. Some common responses include "to worship God," "to be a better person," "to teach our children good values." Hardly anyone says, "to dress up and look good in front of other people," "to meet potential golf partners for Sunday afternoon," "to maximize my ability to meet potential mates whose ethnic and social backgrounds are compatible with my own." Yet, we know that these last three reasons are what *some* people would say if they thought others wouldn't disapprove.

Finally, you may have some qualms about the ethics of obtrusive observation. It cannot be said too often that every single data-collection act in the field has an ethical component, and a field worker is obliged every single time to think through the ethical implications of data-collection acts. Personally, I have less difficulty with the potential ethical problems of obtrusive, reactive observation than I do with any other data-collection method, including participant observation. In obtrusive observation, people actually see you (or a camera) taking down their behavior, and they can ask you to stop. Nothing is hidden.

In participant observation (the method you might think of as the least problematic from an ethical perspective), we try to put people at ease, make them forget we're really listening hard to what they're telling us, and get them to "open up." When I do ethnographic fieldwork, I'm constantly aware that people are taking me into their confidence and I'm always a bit nervous about the responsibility that puts on me not to abuse that confidence.

On the other hand, the method that presents the most ethical problems is unobtrusive, nonreactive direct observation.

DISGUISED FIELD OBSERVATION

In *disguised field observation,* a researcher pretends to actually join a group and proceeds to record data about people in the group. It is the ultimate in participant observation—where the participation is so complete that informants do not know that the ethnographer is watching them. This presumes, of course, that the ethnographer can blend in physically and linguistically with the group he or she is studying.

In 1960, John H. Griffin, a White journalist, underwent drug treatment to temporarily turn his skin black. He traveled the southern United States for about a month, taking notes on how he was treated and received. His book, *Black Like Me* (1961), was a real shocker. It galvanized a lot of support by Whites in the North for the then fledgling civil rights movement. Clearly, Griffin engaged in premeditated deception in gathering the data for his book. But Griffin was a journalist; scientists don't deceive their informants, right?

Pseudopatients Check into a Psychiatric Hospital

Wrong. Everyone knows that you can get psychiatrists to disagree in court with one another about the diagnosis and prognosis of a defendant. David Rosenhan was interested in this instability of psychological diagnoses and particularly in the possibility that psychiatric hospitals might create an environment conducive to certain kinds of diagnoses. He recruited seven confederates who, like him, would check themselves into psychiatric hospitals and observe how they were treated.

The eight *pseudopatients* (three women and five men) called a total of 12 psychiatric hospitals in the U.S. and asked for an appointment to be evaluated for admission. (After they were released from one hospital, some of the researchers checked into another; hence the 12 hospitals for 8 patients.) During their admission interviews, the pseudopatients reported hearing voices. The voices said "empty," "hollow," and "thud."

That was it. No other symptoms. The putative patients gave false names and occupations (they couldn't very well mention their real occupations since three of them were psychologists and one was a psychiatrist), but otherwise acted normally and answered questions about themselves truthfully. In the end, these field workers were all admitted to the various hospitals. One of the pseudopatients was diagnosed as manic-depressive, but all the rest were diagnosed as schizophrenics.

They were model patients. They accepted medications—which they secretly flushed down the toilet—and obeyed orders from the staff. This was tough work. The pseudopatients were not allowed to divulge what they were up to just because they were tired of (or exasperated with) the experiment. If they wanted out, they had to convince the hospital staff to release them. The idea was to act normally long enough to be diagnosed as ready for release. And eventually, they were released (it took them between one week and seven weeks of confinement to achieve this)—diagnosed as "schizophrenia in remission" or as "asymptomatic" or as "improved" (Rosenhan 1973, 1975). The common implication in all these release diagnoses is not that the patient has been cured but that she or he is still a schizophrenic.

Rosenhan's study makes wonderful reading. The "patients" took notes. Some staff members wrote this up as "note-taking behavior"—a clear sign of schizophrenia. A nurse at one hospital unbuttoned her blouse to adjust her bra—in front of a room full of male patients. The researcher who reported this incident said he felt that the nurse just didn't think of the men in that room as human beings. To her, those men were patients, with no humanity, sexual or otherwise.

A senior psychiatrist, with a group of young physicians, pointed to some patients who were waiting outside the cafeteria. It was half an hour before lunch. The senior psychiatrist explained that this was an example of the "oral-acquisitive" behavior one expects in patients with schizophrenia. It hadn't occurred to these psychiatrists, said Rosenhan, that there isn't much else to do in a psychiatric institution beside eat (Rosenhan 1973:253).

While none of the doctors, nurses, and attendants at these hospitals had a clue about what was going on, some of the real patients saw through the charade. One actually accused the field worker of being an undercover journalist.

Critiques of Rosenhan's Study

Despite all this, Rosenhan's study met with fierce criticism. Spitzer (1976) pointed out that the diagnosis "in remission" is hardly ever used in the discharge of real schizophrenics. Of 300 schizophrenic patients discharged at the New York State Psychiatric Institute in 1974, Spitzer found that not one was released with a diagnosis of "in remission." He corroborated this by checking with 12 other hospitals in New York, California, and Georgia. Only a handful of patients were ever released from those hospitals as schizophrenics in remission.

In Rosenhan's study, the staff were fooled into letting people into the hospitals, but, asks Spitzer, so what? Wouldn't people showing up at an emergency room complaining of intense stomach pains be diagnosed as suffering from gastritis? The duped psychiatrists, said Spitzer, had no way of knowing that the pseudopatients were lying. Eventually, those same duped psychiatrists diagnosed that rarest of events, "schizophrenia in remission" (Spitzer 1976:461). Rosenhan's data, said Spitzer, are a testimony to the diagnostic skills of the staff at the hospitals where Rosenhan and his fellow pseudopatients did their fieldwork.

Rosenhan's study raises some serious issues. Was it ethical to dupe the hospital workers like that? Perhaps not, but the U.S. Equal Employment Opportunity Commission (EEOC) sends fake job seekers—African American, Hispanic, and White—to apply for advertised jobs at companies suspected of racial discrimination (Sharpe 1998). The EEOC uses data from these field experiments to bring court cases against offending businesses. People across the political spectrum have quite different ideas about whether this is just a dose of the same medicine that offenders dish out (which seems fair), or entrapment (which seems foul).

Does this mean that ethics are simply a matter of political orientation and opinion? In the abstract, most people answer this question with a strong no. But when things get concrete—when the fortunes and reputations of real people are at stake—the answer becomes less clear for many people.

Doesn't the weakness of Rosenhan's research design make his results a bit suspect? Perhaps, but Rosenhan's study also made mental health workers—from psychiatrists to nurses to social workers—conscious of the power of labeling. Once you get tagged officially as "crazy," the label tends to stick. People start treating you the way they think people in your condition ought to be treated. The price of this knowledge was deceit.

This kind of deception, by the way, is used in legal research to test for discrimination. So-called testers—Black and White, male and female pseudoclients—are sent out by various government agencies to apply for jobs, to rent apartments, or to buy homes. The U.S. Supreme Court has ruled that this practice is legal in the pursuit of fair housing (Ayres 1991:823). Ayres conducted a field experiment, sending pseudobuyers to car dealerships in the Chicago area. The results were clear. Across more than 400 attempts by pseudoclients to buy cars, White men got lower final offers than White women, and Whites got lower final offers than African Americans. Among African Americans, men got lower final offers than women.

But if you think deceiving the staff of psychiatric hospitals or the staff of car dealerships is something, read on.

The Tearoom Trade Study

Without telling his subjects that he was doing research, Laud Humphreys (1975) observed hundreds of homosexual acts among men in St. Louis,

Missouri. Humphreys's study produced very important results. The men involved in this "tearoom trade," as it is called, came from all walks of life, and many were married and living otherwise straight lives. Humphreys made it clear that he did not engage in homosexual acts himself, but played the role of the "watch queen," or lookout, warning his informants when someone approached the rest room. This deception and unobtrusive observation, however, did not cause the storm of criticism that accompanied the first publication of Humphreys's work in 1970.

That was caused by Humphreys having taken his research a step further. He jotted down the license plate numbers of the men who used the rest room for quick, impersonal sex, and got their names and addresses from motor vehicle records. He waited a year after doing his observational work, and then, on the pretext that they had been randomly selected for inclusion in a general health survey, he interviewed 100 of his research subjects in their homes.

Humphreys was careful to change his car, his hair style, and his dress. According to him, his informants did not recognize him as the man who had once played watch queen for them in public toilets. *This* is what made Humphreys's research the focus of another debate, that is still going on, about the ethics of nonreactive field observation.

Five years after the initial study was published, Humphreys himself said that he had made a mistake. He had endangered the social, emotional, and economic lives of his research subjects. Had his files been subpoenaed, he could not have claimed immunity. He decided at the time that he would go to jail rather than hurt his informants (Humphreys 1975).

Everyone associated with Humphreys agreed that he was totally committed to protecting his informants. He was very concerned with the ethics of his research, as any reader of his monograph can tell. Humphreys was an ordained Episcopal priest who had held a parish for more than a decade before going to graduate school. He was active in the civil rights movement in the early 1960s and spent time in jail for committing crimes of conscience. His credentials as an ethical person, conscious of his responsibilities to others, were in good order.

But listen to what Arlene Kaplan Daniels had to say about all this, in a letter to Myron Glazer, a sociologist and ethnographer:

> In my opinion, no one in the society deserves to be trusted with hot, incriminating data. Let me repeat, *no one.* . . . We should not have to rely on the individual strength of conscience which may be required. Psychiatrists, for example, are notorious gossipers [about their patients]. . . . O.K., so they mainly just tell one another. But they *sometimes* tell wives, people at parties, you and me. [Daniels had done participant observation research on psychiatrists.] And few of them would hold up under systematic pressure from government or whatever to get them to tell. . . . The issue is not that a few brave souls *do* resist. The issue is rather what to do about the few who will not. . . . There is *nothing* in our training—any more than in the training of psychiatrists, no matter what they say—to prepare us to take up these burdens. (Quoted in Glazer 1975:219-20; emphasis in original)

Researchers who conduct the kinds of studies that Humphreys did invoke several arguments to justify their use of deception.

(1) It is impossible to study such things as homosexual encounters in public rest rooms in any other way.

(2) Disguised field observation is a technique that is available only to researchers who are physically and linguistically indistinguishable from the people they are studying. In other words, to use this technique, you must be a member of the larger culture, and thus, there is no real ethical question involved, other than whether you, as an individual, feel comfortable doing this kind of research.

(3) Public places, like rest rooms, are, simply, public. The counterargument is that people have a right to expect that their behavior in public toilets will not be recorded, period. (Koocher 1977)

Sechrest and Phillips (1979) take a middle ground. They say that "public behavior should be observable by any means that protect what might be called 'assumed' privacy, the privacy that one might expect from being at a distance from others or of being screened from usual views" (p. 14). This would make the use of binoculars, listening devices, peepholes, and periscopes unethical. Casual observation, on the other hand, would be within ethical bounds.

Some social scientists (Erikson 1967) take the position that disguised observation should never be used as a data-gathering technique by social scientists.

My own position is that the decision to use deception is up to you, provided that the risks of detection are your own risks and no one else's. If detection risks harm to others, then don't even consider disguised participant observation. Recognize, too, that it may not be possible to foresee the potential harm that you might do using disguised observation. This is what leads scholars like Erikson to the conclusion that the technique is never justified.

GRADES OF DECEPTION

But is all deception equally deceitful? Aren't there *grades of deception*? In the 1960s, Edward Hall and others (Hall 1963, 1966; Watson and Graves 1966) showed how people in different cultures use different body language to communicate—that is, they stand at different angles to one another, or at different distances when engaging in serious vs. casual conversation. Hall called this different use of space *proxemics*. He noted that people learn this proxemic behavior as part of their early cultural learning, and he hypothesized that subcultural variations in spatial orientation often leads to breakdowns in communication, isolation of minorities, and so on.

This observation by an anthropologist set off a flurry of research by social psychologists that continues to this day. Early on, Aiello and Jones (1971) studied the proxemic behavior of middle-class White and lower-class Puerto Rican and Black schoolchildren. They trained a group of elementary school teachers to observe and code the distance and orientation of pairs of children to one another during recess periods.

Sure enough, there were clear cultural and gender differences. White children stand much farther apart in ordinary interaction than do either Black or Puerto Rican children. The point here is that the teachers were natural participants in the system. The researchers trained these natural participants to be observers, to cut out any reactivity that outsiders might have caused in doing the observation.

Scherer (1974) studied pairs of children in a schoolyard in Toronto. He used only lower-class Black and lower-class White children in his study, to control for socioeconomic effects. Scherer adapted techniques from photogrammetry (making surveys by using photographs). He mounted a camera in a park adjacent to the schoolyard.

Using a telephoto lens, he took unobtrusive shots of pairs of children who were at least 30 meters away.

This got rid of the reactivity problem. Then Scherer devised a clever way to measure the average distance between two children, and did his analysis on the quantitative data. Scherer found no significant differences in the distance between pairs of White or Black children.

Unobtrusive observation is used in environmental studies to assess the walking speed of people in cities as opposed to rural areas (Levine and Bartlett 1984), indoors vs. outdoors (Rotton et al. 1990), in cities of various sizes (Walmsley and Lewis 1989; Levine 1997), and so on. Rotton et al. (1990), for example, timed 80 men and 80 women who were walking in either a climate-controlled mall that contained 46 stores or in an open-air shopping center of 44 stores.

As in most studies of this type, they marked off 50-ft. strips of pavement or floor space and stationed themselves where they could watch and time people who were traversing those strips. (By the way, conventional wisdom has it that heat causes lethargy and slows people down. Despite its popularity, this stereotype is not supported by systematically collected evidence.)

I don't consider these field studies of children and of pedestrians to have been unethical. The subjects of the study were observed in the course of their ordinary activities, out in the open, in truly public places. Despite the making of unobtrusive observations, or the taking of surreptitious pictures, the deception involved was passive—it didn't involve "taking in" the subjects of the research, making them believe one thing to get them to do another. I don't think that any real invasion of privacy occurred.

The Micturition Study

Contrast these studies with the work of Middlemist et al. (1976). They wanted to measure the length of time it takes for men to begin urinating, how long men continue to urinate, and whether these things are affected by how close men stand to each other in public toilets. (*Why* they wanted to know these things is another story.)

At first, the investigators simply pretended to be grooming themselves at the sink in a public toilet at a university. They tracked the time between the sound of a fly being unzipped and urine hitting the water in the urinal as the time for onset; they also noted how long it took for the sound of urine to stop hitting the water in the urinal, and counted this as the duration of each event. They noted whether subjects were standing alone, next to someone, or one or two urinals away from someone.

In general, the closer a man stood to another man, the longer it took him to begin urinating and the shorter the duration of the event. This confirmed laboratory research showing that social stress inhibits relaxation of the urethral sphincter in men, thus inhibiting flow of urine.

Middlemist et al. decided to control the independent variable—how far away another man was from each subject. They placed "Being Cleaned" signs on some urinals, and forced unsuspecting men to use a particular urinal in a public toilet. Then a confederate stood next to the subject, or one urinal away, or did not appear at all. The observer hid in a toilet stall next to the urinals and made the measurements. The problem was, the observer couldn't hear flies unzipping and urine hitting the water from inside the stall—so the researchers used a periscopic prism, trained on the area of interest, to make the observations directly.

Personally, I doubt that many people would have objected to the study if Middlemist and his colleagues had just lurked in the rest room and done simple, unobtrusive observation. But when they contrived to make men urinate in a specific place; when they contrived to manipulate the dependent variable (urination time); and, above all, when they got that periscope into the act, that changed matters. This is a clear case of invasion of privacy by researchers, in my view.

In a severe critique of the research, Koocher (1977:120) said that "at the very least, the design seems laughable and trivial." Middlemist et al. (1977:123) defended themselves, saying that "we believe . . . that the pilot observation and the experiment together constitute an example of well-controlled field research, adequate to test the null hypothesis that closeness has no effect" on the duration of urination among males in public rest rooms. Actually, Middlemist et al.'s study *design* was anything but trivial. In fact, it was quite elegant. But is knowing what they found out worth using the method they chose?

Passive Deception

Passive deception involves **no experimental manipulation of informants to get them to act in certain ways.** Humphreys's first, strictly observational, study (not the one where he used a pretext to interview people in their homes) involved passive deception. He made his observations in public places where he had every right to be in the first place. He took no names down, and there were no data that could be traced to any particular individual. Humphreys observed felonies, and that fact makes the case more complex. But in my mind, at least, he had the right to observe others in public places, irrespective of whether those observed believed that they would or would not be observed.

Many social scientists, including anthropologists and social psychologists, use passive deception in their field research. I have spent hours pretending to be a shopper in a large department store and have observed mothers who are disciplining their children. I have played the role of a strolling tourist on Mexican beaches (an easy role to play, since that was exactly what I was), and recorded how American and Mexican families occupied beach space. I have surreptitiously clocked the time it takes for people who were walking along the streets of Athens (Greece), New York City, Gainesville (Florida), and Ixmiquilpan (Mexico) to cover 10 meters of sidewalk at various times of the day. I have stood in crowded outdoor bazaars in Mexico, watching and recording differences between Indians and non-Indians in the amount and kinds of produce purchased.

I have never felt the slightest ethical qualm about having made these observations. In my opinion, passive deception is ethically aseptic. Ultimately, however, the responsibility for the choice of method, and for the practical, human consequences of using a particular method, rests with you, the individual researcher. You can't foist off that responsibility on "the profession," or on some "code of ethics."

Are you disturbed by the fact that Humphreys did his research at all, or only by the fact that he came close to compromising his informants? As you answer that question for yourself, you'll have a better idea of where *you* stand on the issue of disguised field observation.

INDIRECT OBSERVATION: BEHAVIOR TRACE STUDIES

Think of trace studies as behavioral archaeology. Do people in different cultures really have a different sense of time? There's a lot of ethnographic evidence about this phenomenon, but can we measure it? Can we tell if people in, say, New York are more punctilious about time than are people in, say, Atlanta?

Well, you can't just ask people to explain their "sense of time," but Levine and Bartlett (1984) used a clever trace method to get at the problem. They went to 12 cities in six countries and noted the time on 15 randomly chosen bank clocks. They measured the difference between the time shown on those clocks and the time reported by the local telephone company in each city. Japan had the most accurate public clocks, off by an average of just 34 seconds. U.S. clocks were off by an average of 54 seconds, followed by those in Taiwan (off by 1 min., 11 sec.), England (1 min., 12 sec.), Italy (1 min., 30 sec.), and Indonesia (3 min., 9 sec.).

> Think of trace studies as
> behavioral archaeology.

The statistically significant deviations from "real time" found on those clocks is archaeological evidence—physical traces—of clock-setting behavior in those countries, and this is presumably evidence of a difference in how people feel about things like time and punctuality in those countries. After all, real people had actually set those 15 clocks in each city—we're talking about behavior here, not reports of behavior—and real people were responsible for making sure that the clocks were adjusted from time to time. Levine and Bartlett looked at whether differences in the average deviation of the clocks from the real time predicted differences in the rate of heart disease.

They don't. The country with the lowest rate of heart disease, Japan, has the most accurate clocks and the fastest overall pace of life (as measured by several other indicators). Apparently, according to Levine and Bartlett, it's possible in some cultures to be hard *working* without being hard *driving*.

Sechrest and Flores (1969) recorded and analyzed bathroom graffiti in a sample of men's public toilets in Manila and Chicago. They wanted to examine attitudes toward sexuality in the two cultures. The results were striking. There was no difference in the percentage of graffiti in the two cities that dealt with heterosexual themes. But fully 42% of the Chicago graffiti dealt with homosexuality, while only 2% of the Manila graffiti did, showing a clear difference in the two cultures regarding level of concern with homosexuality.

Gould and Potter (1984) did a survey of used up (not smashed up) automobiles in five Providence, Rhode Island, junkyards. They calculated that the average use-life of American-made cars is 10.56 years, irrespective of how many times cars change hands. This is a good deal longer than most Americans would guess. Gould also compared use-life against initial cost and found that paying more for a car doesn't affect how long it will last. Interesting and useful findings.

In their classic book *Unobtrusive Measures,* Webb et al. (1966) identified a class of measures based on erosion. Administrators of Chicago's Museum of Science and Industry had found that the vinyl tiles around an exhibit showing live, hatching chicks needed to be replaced about every six weeks. The tiles around other exhibits lasted for years without having to be replaced. Webb et al. suggested that this erosion measure (the rate of wear on vinyl tiles) might be a proxy for a direct measure of the popularity of exhibits. The faster the tiles wear out, the more popular the exhibit (p. 37).

Weighing the Evidence

Dean Archer and Lynn Erlich (1985) report a method for studying confidential records when you want to know only aggregate outcomes and don't need data about individuals. They had a hypothesis that sensational crimes (with a lot of press coverage) result in increased sales of handguns. The police would not allow them to see the handgun applications, so they asked a member of the police staff to put the permits into envelopes, by month, for three months prior to and three months after a particular sensational crime. Then they weighed the envelopes, and converted the weight to handgun applications. To do this, they got a chunk of blank applications and found out how many applications there were per ounce.

The technique is very reliable. The correlation between the estimates of researchers and the actual weights of the envelopes was .99, and in a controlled experiment, researchers were able to tell the difference of just one sheet of paper in 15 out of 18 tries. Real data can be messy, though. Lots of handgun applications have addenda attached, for example. The correlation between researchers' estimates and the true number of handgun applications across six months was .94.

Archer and Erlich suggest that the weight method can be used to study things like drunk driving arrests, the influx of psychiatric patients to a clinic, the number of grievance filings in a company, the number of abortion referrals, and the number of complaints against agencies.

The Garbage Project

The largest and most important trace measure research ever attempted is the ongoing Garbage Project, headed by archaeologist William Rathje at the University of Arizona.

Since 1973, Rathje and his associates have studied the current consumer behavior patterns of Tucson, Arizona (and, in 1978-79, Milwaukee, Wisconsin), by analyzing the garbage from a representative sample of residents.

In 1988, about 6,000 residents of Tucson were sent flyers, explaining that they were selected to be part of a study of recycling behavior. Their garbage would be studied, the flyer explained, and confidentiality was assured, but if they didn't want to be part of the study, residents could send in a card and they would be removed from the list. About 200 people returned the cards and opted out of the study (Wilson Hughes, personal communication. And see Hughes [1984] for a detailed review of the methodology of the Garbage Project.)

By studying the detritus of ordinary people, researchers on the Garbage Project have learned interesting things about food consumption and waste among Americans. Squash is the favored baby food among Hispanics in the United States, and 35% of all food from chicken take-out restaurants is thrown away (Rathje 1992). You can accurately estimate the population of an area by weighing only the plastic trash. Children, it turns out, generate as much plastic trash as adults do (Edmondson 1988).

Early in the Garbage Project, researchers expected that people would not waste much beef during a shortage, but exactly the opposite happened in 1973. Two things were shown to be responsible for this finding. First, as the shortage took hold, the price of beef rose, and people started buying cheaper cuts. Some residents did not know how to prepare those cuts properly, and this created more waste; others found that they didn't like the cheaper cuts, and threw out more than they usually would have; and cheaper cuts have more waste fat to throw out to begin with. Second, as the price continued to rise, people started buying greater quantities of beef, perhaps as a hedge against further price hikes. Inevitably, some of the increased purchases spoiled from lack of proper storage (Rathje 1984:17).

Rathje found the same pattern of consumer behavior during the sugar shortage of 1975. He reasoned that whenever people changed their food buying and consuming habits drastically, there would be at least a short-term increase in food loss. Conversely, when people use foods and ingredients that are familiar to them, they waste less in both preparation and consumption.

This led Rathje to compare the food loss rate among Mexican Americans and Anglos. "The final results of Mexican-American cooking," Rathje said, "can be extremely varied— chimichangas, burritos, enchiladas, tacos, and more—but the basic set of ingredients are very few compared to standard Anglo fare. Thus, Mexican-American households should throw out less food than Anglo households" (Rathje 1984:17-18). In fact, this is exactly what Rathje found in both Tucson and Milwaukee.

Pros and Cons of Trace Studies

The most important advantage of trace studies is that they are nonreactive, so long as the people you are studying are kept in the dark about what you are doing. What happens when people are told that their garbage is being monitored? Rittenbaugh and Harrison (1984) compared data from an experimental group (people who were told that their garbage was being monitored) and a control group (people who were not told). There was no difference in the refuse disposal behavior of the experimental and control groups—with one important exception. The number of empty bottles of alcoholic drinks that showed up was significantly lower when people knew that their garbage was being monitored.

Where did the extra bottles go? Buried in the back yard? Stuffed in the trash cans of neighbors who were not in the sample? It remains a mystery.

In addition to being nonreactive, behavior trace studies yield enormous amounts of data that can be standardized, quantified, and compared across groups and over time (Rathje 1979). Moreover, traces reflect some behaviors more accurately than informant reports of those behaviors. If you want to know what people eat, for instance, you're better off examining their garbage than asking them what they eat, and if you want to know about their long-distance calling behavior, you're better off looking at their phone bills than asking them (Bernard et al. 1984; see D'Andrade 1973, 1974; Romney et al. 1986; and Freeman et al. 1987 for work on the causes of inaccuracy).

Trace studies have plenty of problems, however. Early in the Garbage Project, it became apparent that garbage disposals were going to be a serious problem. The researchers constructed a subsample of 32 households, some of which had disposals, some of which did not. They studied these 32 households for five weeks and developed a "garbage disposal correction factor" (Rathje 1984:16).

As the project went on, researchers learned that some families were recycling all their aluminum cans, while others were throwing theirs in the trash. This made it difficult to compare households regarding their consumption of soft drinks and beer. Some families had compost heaps that they used as fertilizer for their vegetable gardens. This distorted the refuse count for those families. Garbage Project researchers had to develop correction factors for all of these biases, too (see Harrison 1976).

As with much unobtrusive research, the Garbage Project raised some difficult ethical problems. To protect the privacy of the households in the study, no addresses or names of household members are recorded. All personal items, such as photographs and letters, are thrown out without being examined. The hundreds of student sorters who have worked on the project have signed pledges not to save anything from the refuse they examine. All the sampling, sorting, and data analysis procedures are approved by the Human Subjects Research Committee of the University of Arizona.

The Garbage Project receives consistent coverage in the press, both nationally and locally in Tucson. In 1984, after 10 years of work, Hughes reported that "no public concern over the issue of personal privacy has been expressed, and community response has been supportive" (Hughes 1984:42). With proper safeguards, trace measures can be used to generate useful data about human behavior.

Chapter 10 Review

KEY CONCEPTS

Continuous monitoring, 376-382, 386-388
Direct observation, 376, 382, 385, 395-396
Indirect observation, 376, 403-406
Reactive observation, 376, 395-396
Nonreactive observation, 376, 405
Unobtrusive observation, 376, 399, 401, 406
Scientific management, 377
Time and motion research, 377
Human factors engineering, 377
Ethology, or behavioral biology, 379-380
Ethogram, 379-380
24-hour recall, 380
Deference effect, 381

Social desirability effect, 381
Coding schemes, 382-385
Interaction process analysis, 383
Time allocation studies, 388-392
Spot sampling, 388
Time sampling, 388
Experience sampling, 392-395
Disguised field observation, 397-400
Pseudopatients, 397
Grades of deception, 400-402
Proxemics, 400-401
Passive deception, 402
Behavior trace studies, 403-406

SUMMARY

❖ When you want to know what people actually do, there is no substitute for watching them or studying the physical traces their behavior leaves behind. Direct observation involves watching people and recording their behavior on the spot; indirect observation involves gathering the archaeological residue of human behavior.

❖ In continuous monitoring, or CM, you watch a person, or group of people, and record their behavior. The technique was developed in the field of management and is used today across the social sciences.
  ◆ CM is particularly useful in studying children—in classrooms and on playgrounds, in clinical settings and in homes.
  ◆ CM is widely used in clinical research. Field researchers use CM to track shopping behavior.
  ◆ CM is hard work and is highly reactive, but it produces very important data about behavior. The database from the Six Culture Study, for example, consists of about 20,000 recorded acts, for 134 children. Strong conclusions can be drawn from this kind of robust database.

❖ Data from CM must be coded. Researchers have developed coding schemes for interactions between married couples, for studies of teacher-pupil interaction, for worker-management negotiations, and so on.
  ◆ Videotape has made CM easier. As video cameras have gotten smaller, easier to use, and less expensive, more field researchers have been using this technology for close examination of behavior streams.

❖ Time allocation, or TA, studies are based on spot sampling. The researcher simply appears at randomly selected places, and at randomly selected times, and records what people are doing when they are first seen.
  ◆ If you sample a large, unbiased number of acts, then the percentage of *times* people are seen doing things is an unbiased estimated of the percentage of *time* they spend in those activities.
  ◆ Nearly all spot sampling studies of behavior are done during the daylight hours, between 6 a.m. and 7 p.m.

❖ Besides issues of sampling, TA studies have special coding problems. If someone saw that you were lying down reading, and you were studying for an exam, should they record that you were working or relaxing?
  ◆ Record *all* possible behaviors you observe in the order of their primacy, according to your best judgment at the time of observation and use a separate check sheet for each observation.

❖ Experience sampling, or ES, combines the power of random spot checks with the relative ease of having people report on their own behavior.
  ◆ People carry beepers and fill in a form about what they're doing, who they're with, or what they're feeling at the moment the beeper goes off.
  ◆ A single investigator can only be in one place at a time, but with beepers, you can collect spot-observation behavioral data from lots of people at once.

❖ In disguised field observation, a researcher pretends to actually join a group, and proceeds to record data about people in the group.
  ◆ Some of the most interesting and important studies in the social sciences have been done using disguised field observation, but this method raises very serious ethical concerns.
  ◆ There are grades of deception in research. Unobtrusive observation is used in environmental studies to measure the walking speed of people in cities and rural areas. Compare this passive deception to sending pseudopatients to a hospital to test the diagnostic skills of the staff.

❖ You can observe behavior indirectly by examining the traces of it that people leave behind. Everything from telephone bills to garbage creates indirect indicators of real human behavior. Think of this as behavioral archaeology.
  ◆ Behavior trace studies are nonreactive and often yield enormous amounts of data that can be standardized, quantified, and compared across groups and over time.

EXERCISES

1. Give some shoppers a tape recorder and ask them to go around a grocery store looking for the following list of items. These are the same items that Titus and Everett (1996) used in their study of shoppers:

Cooking oil	Apple juice
Tomato paste	Maple syrup
Household dyes	Whipped nondairy topping
Dishwashing liquid	Frozen waffles
Grated cheese	Peanut butter
Powdered soft drink mix	Cream cheese
Furniture polish	Limes
Charcoal	Canned tuna
Powdered milk	Marshmallows
Vinegar	Frozen turkey
Bouillon cubes	

Analyze the results to see if there are global strategies that people use to find their way through an unfamiliar environment.

Repeat this in a different kind of store—like an office supply store—to see how different products might produce different wayfinding strategies. Remember to ask permission from the manager of any store in which you want to do some systematic observation. Offer to provide the manager with a copy of your report. Be sure that the shoppers you work with have given written, informed consent regarding their participation in this exercise.

2. David Barash (1972) found that students who eat alone in a cafeteria are more likely to choose a table next to a wall, while students in groups are equally likely to sit at a wall table or a table in the middle of the room. He also found that loners look up about twice as much as do people in groups. Freidenberg and Cimbalo (1996) repeated and confirmed the results of Barash's experiment.

Now it's your turn. As they did, make your observations between 11:30 a.m. and 1:30 p.m. on seven consecutive weekdays. Map the tables in a cafeteria (you'll be able to do this if you've completed the map-making exercise in Chapter 9) and record whether singles or groups (count the number of people in groups) choose a wall or a center table.

To count people looking up, choose a random person from each group and do continuous monitoring for five minutes. Think of wall tables and middle tables as being conditions in an experiment. If there are more wall tables (or middle tables), then remember to weight your counts when you do the analysis. For more on human ethology experiments about how people use and manage personal space, see Barash (1973, 1974, 1977).

3. There are 1,440 minutes in a day, so there are 10,080 minutes in a week. If you sleep eight hours a day, then cut the 10,080 minutes down by a third, or 3,360 minutes. If you sleep 7.5 hours a day, then cut the 10,080 minutes down by 3,150 minutes, and so on.

Take a random sample of 204 minutes from the minutes of all nonsleeping time in your week. Then, on each of those 204 minutes, jot down what you're doing. Nobody else is going to see this, so be ruthlessly honest about the exercise. As Table 10.1 shows, with 204 observations you can say, with great confidence, that an activity that occurs 7% of the time in your data, actually occurred between 3.5% and 10.5% of the time in your life during those seven days.

One of the problems you'll face in this exercise is deciding how to code all the various activities you write down. You'll wind up with things like "getting a candy bar from the vending machine at Arbuth Hall" and "having breakfast." Do you code both of those observations as "eating behavior" or do you code the first as "snacking" and the second as "eating"? Or do you code the first one as "acquiring food" and only the second as "eating"?

FURTHER READING

Deception in research. The "simulated client method" is becoming widely used in studies of health care delivery, especially in developing nations. See Huntington and Schuler (1993), Igun (1986), and Kafle et al. (1996).

Continuous monitoring. See Bakeman and Gottman (1997) and Bakeman and Quera (1995) for useful summaries of methods for observing interactions and for analyzing interaction data. Pellegrini (1996) provides a comprehensive discussion of methods for observing children in their natural world. Also see Blurton-Jones (1972), Borich and Klinzing (1984), McGrew (1972), and Vaughn and Horner (1997). For an example of CM in clinical assessment of children, see Mian et al. (1996).

Among the most important early studies of workers were those done by Frederick W. Taylor (1911). His methods of scientific management became known as "Taylorism," but Taylorism now connotes a kind of ruthless extraction of productivity by regulating every second of a worker's time (see Waring 1991; Jurgens et al. 1993).

Bales's coding scheme. The Bales coding system is the most widely used in direct observation studies. It is relatively simple to learn and it is very general—that is, it can be used in many different applications. See Allen et al. (1989).

Other coding systems. For a general overview of how direct observation is used in clinical assessment, see Foster and Cone (1986) and Foster et al. (1988). Some other coding schemes include the Eyberg Child Behavior Inventory (Eyberg 1992) for assessing problem behaviors in children and behavioral problems in child-parent interactions, and the Code for Instructional Structure and Student Academic Performance (Greenwood et al. 1985) for assessing pupil-teacher interactions.

Some other coding schemes that have been developed over the years are by Matsumoto et al. (1991) for studying nonverbal behavior, by Longabaugh (1963) for studying interpersonal exchange, by Hill (1978) for classifying the responses of counseling therapists to their clients, by Thomas et al. (1987) for assessing disruptive behavior among children on a playground, by Roberts et al. (1991) for classifying the behaviors of participants in mutual-help psychotherapy groups, and by Brown et al. (1996) for charting the social interactions of children.

Time sampling studies. Much of the fundamental work on time sampling was done in ethology, or animal behavior studies. The standard discussion is Altmann (1974). See Saudargas and Zanolli (1990) for an example of TA research in a classroom situation. See Sykes et al. (1993) for a time sampling study of people drinking in public bars.

Experience sampling. This method is becoming very popular in psychology and social psychology for assessing moods and behaviors in many different populations. For some recent examples, see Asakawa and Csikszentmihalyi (1998) and Rusting and Larsen (1998).

Unobtrusive observation and unobtrusive measures. The classic references for unobtrusive measures are Sechrest (1979) and Webb et al. (1966). Data from archival sources, like newspapers, are unobtrusive. See Chapter 12 of this book for more on methods of text analysis. Sagberg et al. (1997) unobtrusively observed taxi drivers in Oslo, Norway, whose cabs had antilock brakes. Those drivers compensated by driving closer to the car in front of them than did drivers whose cars lacked the special brakes. Gottschalk (1997) reviews his work on unobtrusive measures for psychological states and traits.

Proxemics. Kenner and Katsimaglis (1993) observed 648 people in a city in Australia get into a taxi. Men, women, and young children consistently chose different seats. Albas (1991) experimentally manipulated the distance that an interviewer stood from 70 women undergraduates at a Canadian university and documented the negotiation of a comfortable distance by the respondents.

PART IV

DATA ANALYSIS

11 INTRODUCTION TO QUALITATIVE AND QUANTITATIVE ANALYSIS

IN THIS CHAPTER:

❖ INTRODUCTION

This is the first of six chapters about analyzing data. In this chapter, we begin with the basics—what analysis is, how to store and manage data, and how to use matrices, tables, and flow charts to present the results of data analysis. Then we move on, in Chapters 12 and 13, to methods for analyzing qualitative data.

I think you'll be surprised at how many different kinds of data and how many different kinds of analysis are qualitative. Two of the best-known methods for analyzing qualitative data are grounded theory and content analysis. These methods are called qualitative because the primary data they deal with are all text. We'll take these methods up next, in Chapter 12. In Chapter 13, I'll introduce you to other qualitative methods of data analysis, including ethnographic decision modeling, componential analysis, taxonomic analysis, and Boolean analysis. These methods are qualitative in the sense that they are based entirely on nonnumerical data.

Finally, in Chapters 14, 15, and 16 I'll introduce you to the basics of quantitative analysis, including univariate, bivariate, and multivariate analysis.

QUALITATIVE/QUANTITATIVE

By a quirk of English grammar, the phrase "qualitative data analysis" is delightfully ambiguous. Unless someone spells it out in lots of words, you never know if he or she means the "qualitative analysis of data" or the "analysis of qualitative data." And, of course, the same goes for "quantitative data analysis." Table 11.1 lays out the possibilities.

Cell A is the qualitative analysis of qualitative data. Interpretive studies of texts, like transcriptions of interviews, are of this kind. You focus on and name themes in texts. You tell the story, as you see it, of how the themes are related to one another and how characteristics of the speaker or speakers account for the existence of certain themes and the absence of others. You may deconstruct the text, look for hidden subtexts, and, in general, try to let your audience know—using the power of good rhetoric—the deeper meaning or the multiple meanings of the text.

Cell D refers to numerical or statistical analysis of numerical data. Lots of useful data about human behavior come to us as numbers. Closed-ended questions in surveys produce numerical data. So do national censuses. Organizations, from businesses to charities to zoos, produce numerical data, too—data about the socio-economic characteristics of people who use their products or services, data about how often they have to replace managers and secretaries, and on and on.

Cell B is the qualitative analysis of quantitative data. This can involve the search for patterns using visualization methods, like multidimensional scaling and hierarchical clustering. (We'll get to these methods in Chapter 16.) Cell B is also about the search for, and the presentation of, *meaning* in the results of quantitative data processing. It's what quantitative analysts do after they get through doing the work in cell D. With-

	Data	
TABLE 11.1 Qualitative/Quantitative Data Analysis		
Analysis	_Qualitative_	_Quantitative_
Qualitative	A	B
Quantitative	C	D

out the work in cell B, cell D studies are sterile and vacuous.

Which leaves cell C, the quantitative analysis of qualitative data. This involves turning the data from words or images into numbers. Scholars in communications, for example, tag a set of television ads from Mexico and the U.S. to test whether consumers are portrayed as older in one country than in the other. Political scientists code the rhetoric of a presidential debate to look for patterns and predictors. Archaeologists code a set of artifacts to produce emergent categories or styles, or to test whether some intrusive artifacts can be traced to a source.

Most quantitative analysis in the social sciences involves reducing people (as observed directly or through their texts) to numbers; most qualitative analysis involves reducing people to words—_your_ words about the meaning of _their_ words or actions or artifacts. I say "most" because a lot of analysis these days, qualitative and quantitative, involves visualization of data: not just looking for patterns in data, but showing the patterns as maps, networks, and matrices.

It's pretty obvious, I think, that each kind of data—qualitative and quantitative—and each kind of data reduction—qualitative and quantitative—is useful for answering certain kinds of questions. Skilled social researchers can do it all.

WHAT'S ANALYSIS?

Analysis **is the search for patterns in data and for ideas that help explain why those patterns are there in the first place.** The way I see it, analysis is ultimately all qualitative. It starts before you collect data—you have to have some ideas about what you're going to study—and it continues throughout the research effort. As you develop ideas, you test them against your observations; your observations may then modify your ideas, which then need to be tested again; and so on. Don't look for closure in the process. If you're doing it right, it never stops.

> _Analysis starts before you collect data— you have to have some ideas about what you're going to study._

Most methods for quantitative analysis— things like factor analysis, cluster analysis, regression analysis, and so on—are really methods for data processing. They are powerful tools, in other words, for finding patterns in data. Interpreting those patterns is up to you. Interpretation—telling us what findings mean, linking your findings to the findings of other research—starts with ideas in your head and comes out in words on paper. It's a pretty qualitative exercise.

Don't worry about getting ideas, either. Once you have data in your hands, words or numbers, your hardest job will be to sort through all the ideas you get and decide which ones to test. And don't worry about seeing patterns in your data or about not being able to come up with causal explanations for things you see in the course of an interviewing project or one based on participant observation. It can happen very fast, often in a matter of hours or days after starting any research project, so be suspicious of your pet ideas and continually check yourself to make sure you're not inventing or at least not embellishing patterns.

Seeing patterns that aren't there happens all the time in research, qualitative or quantitative, just from eagerness and observer expectations. If you are highly self-critical, your tendency to see patterns everywhere will diminish as the research progresses. But the problem can also get worse if you accept uncritically the folk analyses of articulate or prestigious informants. It is important from a humanistic standpoint to seek the emic perspective and to document folk analyses (Lofland 1971). In some cases, those analyses may be correct. But it is equally important to remain skeptical, to retain an etic perspective, and not to "go native" (Miles and Huberman 1994:216).

The Constant Validity Check

As research progresses—as your interviews or survey questionnaires or field notes or experiment data pile up—try consciously to switch back and forth between these two perspectives, the emic and the etic. Check yourself from either buying into the folk explanations or rejecting them without considering their possible validity. Checking yourself during research is not hard to do; it's just hard to remember to do it systematically. Here are some guidelines.

(1) If you are interviewing people, look for consistencies and inconsistencies among knowledgeable informants and find out why those informants disagree about important things.

(2) Whenever possible, check people's reports of behavior or of environmental conditions against more objective evidence.

(3) Be open to negative evidence rather than annoyed when it pops up. When you run into a case that doesn't fit your theory (a middle-class suburban teenager who doesn't like hanging out at malls, for example), ask yourself whether it's the result of (a) normal *intracultural variation,* (b) your lack of knowledge about the range of appropriate behavior, or (c) a genuinely unusual case.

(4) As you come to understand how something works, seek out alternative explanations from key informants and from colleagues, and listen to them carefully. American folk culture, for example, holds that women left the home for the work force because of something called "feminism" and "women's liberation." That's a popular emic explanation. An alternative explanation is that feminist values and orientations are supported, if not caused, by women being *driven* out of their homes and into the work force by the hyperinflation during the 1970s that drove down the purchasing power of their husbands' incomes (Margolis 1984). Both the emic, folk explanation and the etic, materialist explanation are interesting for different reasons.

Respondent	Age	Sex	Education	Natal Household Size	Current Household Size	Ethnicity
1	27	2	3	6	4	3
2	31	1	2	3	2	1
3	.	.	.	.	.	.
4	.	.	.	.	.	.
.	.	.	.	.	.	.
.	.	.	.	.	.	.
.	.	.	.	.	.	.
.	.	.	.	.	.	.
.	.	.	.	.	.	.

a. Profile matrix of persons by variables

	Age	Sex	Education	Natal Household Size	Current Household Size	Ethnicity
Age	—					
Sex		—				
Education			—			
Natal Household Size				—		
Current Household Size					—	
Ethnicity						—

b. Proximity matrix of the variables (columns) in Figure 11.1a

Figure 11.1 Two Kinds of Matrices: Profiles and Proximities

(5) Try to fit extreme cases into your theory, and if the cases won't fit, don't be too quick to throw them out. It is always easier to throw out cases than it is to reexamine your own ideas, but the easy way out is hardly ever the right way in research.

DATA MATRICES

One of the most important concepts in all data analysis—whether we're working with quantitative or qualitative data—is the *data matrix*. There are two basic kinds of data matrices: *profile matrices* and *proximity matrices*. Figure 11.1 shows what these two kinds of matrices look like.

Profile Matrices

Most analysis in the social sciences is about how properties of things are related to one another. We ask, for example, "Does how much money a family has affect the SAT scores of its children?"

TABLE 11.2 Profile Matrix for Two Cases and Six Variables

	Variable					
Respondent	How Much Spent	Gender	Age	Years in School	Where Born	How Many in House
1	67	M	34	12	Chicago	5
2	19	F	60	16	Tuscaloosa	1

"Does having been sexually molested as a child influence whether a woman will remain in a physically abusive marriage?" "Does the per capita gross national product of a nation affect the probability that it will go to war with its neighbors?"

This is called *profile analysis.* You start with series of *things*—units of analysis—and you measure a series of *variables* for each of those things. This produces a profile matrix, or, simply, a data matrix. A data matrix is a table of cases and their associated variables. Each unit of analysis is *profiled* by a particular set of measurements on some variables.

Suppose you interview 100 people outside a supermarket. You record six pieces of information about each person: (1) how much they say they've spent, (2) their gender, (3) their age, (4) how many years they went to school, (5) where they were born, and (6) how many people live with them in their house or apartment.

These data produce a 100 × 6 (read: "100 by 6") profile matrix.

Each of the 100 cases (cases are people here) in your data file is characterized, or profiled, by those six pieces of information. Table 11.2 shows the profiles for two cases.

Respondent 1 reported spending $67.00, is male, is 34 years old, graduated high school (12 years of school), was born in Chicago, and lives in a household with four other people. Respondent 2 reported spending $19.00, is female, is 60 years old, graduated college (16 years of school), was born in Tuscaloosa, Alabama, and lives alone.

The units of analysis in a profile matrix are often respondents to a questionnaire, but they can also be things, like countries, prisons, churches, supermarkets, schools, folktales, marriage contracts, or even time periods (1980, 1981, 1982, . . . 1991). If you know the number of hospital beds per million people and the average per capita income for each of 50 countries, you can construct a 50-country-by-2-variable profile matrix. If you know, for each of 100 prisons, the number of violent incidents per year, the number of guards per 100 inmates, and the average number of dollars spent on job training per year per inmate, you can construct a 100-prison-by-3-variable profile matrix.

You can create a profile matrix from questionnaire data, and you can create a matrix from a set of coded texts or a set of coded artifacts. (More about this in Chapter 12.)

Proximity Matrices

Profile matrices contain measurements of variables for a set of items. *Proximity matrices* contain **measurements of relations, or proximities, between items.** If the measurements in a proxim-

Box 11.1
Converting Profile Matrices
into Similarity Matrices

You can convert a profile matrix into a proximity matrix. You can, for example, compare pairs of rows or pairs of columns of a profile matrix to see how similar they are. If you compare rows, you find out how similar the units of analysis are to one another. If you compare columns, you find out how similar the variables are to one another.

ity matrix tell *how close* things are to each other, then you have a ***similarity matrix***. If the measurements in a proximity matrix tell *how far apart* things are from each other, then you have a ***dissimilarity matrix*** (see Box 11.1).

If you've ever read one of those tables of distances between cities that you see on road maps, you've had experience with a dissimilarity matrix. The bigger the number in the cells, the more "dissimilar" two cities are. In this case, dissimilarity means that the larger the number in

any cell, the farther apart two cities are on the map.

If you've had a course in statistics and seen a correlation matrix, then you've had experience with a similarity matrix. The bigger the number in each cell—the higher the correlation—the more alike two things are.

Figure 11.1b shows a similarity matrix of variables. Imagine the list of variable names stretching several feet to the right, off the right-hand margin of the page, and several feet down, off the lower margin. That is what would happen if you had, say, 100 variables about each of your respondents. For each and every pair of variables in the matrix of data, you could ask: Are these variables related?

We'll need the concept of a proximity matrix when we get to multivariate analysis in Chapter 16.

> *If you've ever read one of those tables of distances between cities on a road map, you've had experience with a dissimilarity matrix.*

PRESENTING RESULTS IN MATRICES AND TABLES

An important part of all analysis, qualitative and quantitative, is the production of visual displays. Laying out your data in table or matrix form, and drawing your theories out in the form of a flow chart or map, helps you understand what you have. These are also potent ways to communicate your ideas to others (Miles and Huberman 1994). Learning to build and use qualitative data matrices and flow charts requires practice, but

you can get started by studying examples published in research journals.

❖

Van Maanen et al. (1982), for example, compared a traditional commercial fishing operation in Gloucester, Massachusetts, with a modern opera-

TABLE 11.3 Contemporary Forms of Commercial Fishing

	Traditional Fishing (e.g., Gloucester, MA)	Modern Fishing (e.g., Bristol Bay, AK)
Social organization		
Backgrounds of fishermen	Homogeneous	Heterogeneous
Ties among fishermen	Multiple	Single
Boundaries to entry	Social	Economic
Number of participants	Stable	Variable
Social uncertainty	Low	High
Relations with competitors	Collegial and individualistic	Antagonistic and categorical
Relations with port	Permanent, with ties to community	Temporary, with no local ties
Mobility	Low	High
Relations to fishing	Expressive (fishing as lifestyle)	Instrumental (fishing as job)
Orientation to work	Long term, optimizing (survival)	Short term, maximizing (seasonal)
Tolerance for diversity	Low	High
Nature of disputes	Intraoccupational	Transoccupational
Economic organization		
Relations of boats to buyers	Personalized (long term, informal)	Contractual (short term, formal)
Information exchange	Restrictive and private	Open and public
Economic uncertainty	Low (long term)	High (long term)
Capital investment range	Small	Large
Profit margins	Low	High
Rate of innovation	Low	High
Specialization	Low	High
Regulatory mechanisms	Informal and few	Formal and many
Stance toward authority	Combative	Compliant

SOURCE: J. Van Maanen et al., "An Occupation in Transition: Traditional and Modern Forms of Commercial Fishing." *Work and Occupations* 9:193-216. Copyright © 1982 by Sage Publications.

tion in Bristol Bay, Alaska. Table 11.3 shows what they found in the analysis of their qualitative field notes. Simple inspection of Table 11.3 gives you an immediate feel for the results of Van Maanen et al.'s descriptive analysis.

The social organization of the traditional fishing operation is more homogeneous, more expressive, and more collegial than that of the modern operation, but profits are lower. Based on the qualitative analysis, Van Maanen et al. were able to state some general, theoretical hypotheses regarding the weakening of personal relations in technology-based fishing operations. This is the

kind of general proposition that can be tested by using fishing operations as units of analysis and their technologies as the independent variable.

Donna Birdwell-Pheasant (1984) wanted to understand how differences in interpersonal relations change over time in the village of Chunox, Belize. She questioned 216 people about their relations with members of their families over the years, and simulated a longitudinal study with data from a cross-sectional sample. She checked the retrospective data with other information gathered by questionnaires, direct observations, and semistructured interviews. Table 11.4 shows

TABLE 11.4 Birdwell-Pheasant's (1984) Matrix of Criteria for Assigning Values to Major Relationships between People in Her Study

Values of Relationships	Major Types of Relationships			
	Ascending Generation	Siblings	Spouse	Descending Generation
Absent	Parents deceased, migrated permanently, or estranged	Only child; siblings deceased, migrated permanently, or estranged	Single or widowed; spouse migrated or permanently estranged	No mature offspring; all offspring deceased, migrated permanently, or estranged
Attenuated	Does not live with parents or participate in work group with parent; does visit and/or exchange food	Does not live with siblings or participate in work groups with them; does visit and/or exchange food	Separation, but without final termination of union; e.g., temporary migration	Offspring do not live with parents or participate in work group with them; do visit and/or exchange food
Coordinate	Participates in work group with parents, sharing decision-making authority	Participates in work group with siblings under parents' authority or works with siblings only, sharing decision making	Married; in charge of own sex-specific domain with minimal interference from partner	Participates in a work group with offspring, sharing decision-making authority
Subordinate	Participates in work group with parent; parent makes decisions	Participates in work group of siblings; other sibling(s) make decisions	Individual's normal control within sex-specific domain is interfered with by spouse	Dependent, elderly parent, unable to work
Superordinate	Makes decisions for dependent, elderly parent who is unable to work	Participates in work group with siblings; makes decisions for group	Interferes with spouse's normal controls within sex-specific domain	Heads work group that includes one or more mature offspring; makes decisions for group

SOURCE: D. Birdwell-Pheasant, "Personal Power Careers and the Development of Domestic Structure in a Small Community." Reproduced by permission of the American Anthropological Association from *American Ethnologist* 11: 699-717. November 1984. Not for further reproduction.

the analytic framework that emerged from Birdwell-Pheasant's work.

Birdwell-Pheasant identified five kinds of relations: absent, attenuated, coordinate, subordi-

nate, and superordinate. These represent the rows of the matrix in Table 11.4. The columns in the matrix are the four major types of family relations: ascending generation (parents, aunts, un-

TABLE 11.5 Family History of Haitian Migrants to Miami

Year	Jeanne	Anna (mother)	Lucie (sister)	Charles (brother)	Marc (adopted son)	Helen (aunt)	Hughes & Valerie (cousins)	No. in Household
1968	+							1
1971	+	+	+	+				4
1975	+	+	+	+	+			5
1976	+	+	−	−	+			3
1978	+	+	−	+	+		*	4
1979	+	+	−	+	+	+	*	5
1982	+	+	−	−	+	−	*	4

SOURCE: S. M. Fjellman and H. Gladwin, "Haitian Family Patterns of Migration to South Florida," *Human Organization*, 44:307. Copyright © 1985, Society for Applied Anthropology. Reprinted with permission.

cles, etc.), siblings, spouse, and descending generation (children, nephews and nieces, etc.).

Birdwell-Pheasant then went through her data and "examined all the available data on Juana Fulana and decided whether, in 1971, she had a coordinate or subordinate relationship with her mother (e.g., did she have her own kitchen? her own wash house?)." (In Latin America, Juan Fulano and Juana Fulana are the male and female equivalents of "so-and-so"—as in "Is so-and-so married?")

Birdwell-Pheasant repeated the process, for *each* of her 216 informants, for *each* of the four relations in Table 11.4, and for *each* of the years 1965, 1971, 1973, 1975, and 1977. This required 216(4)(5) = 4,320 decisions. Birdwell-Pheasant didn't have data on all possible informant-by-year-by-relation combinations, but by the time she was through, she had a database of 742 "power readings" of family relations over time and was able to make some very strong statements about patterns of domestic structure over time in Chunox. This is an excellent example of the use of qualitative data to develop a theory, and the conversion of qualitative data to a set of numbers for testing that theory.

Stephen Fjellman and Hugh Gladwin (1985) studied the family histories of Haitian migrants to the United States. Fjellman and Gladwin found an elegant way to present a lot of information about those histories in a simple chart. Table 11.5 shows one chart for a family of four people in 1982.

This Haitian American family began in 1968 when Jeanne's father sent her to Brooklyn, New York, to go to high school. The single plus sign for 1968 shows the founding of the family by Jeanne. Jeanne's father died in 1971, and her mother, sister, and brother joined her in New York. Jeanne adopted Marc in 1975, and in 1976 she and her mother moved with Marc to Miami. Lucie and Charles remained together in New York. The two minus signs in the row for 1976 indicate that Jeanne's sister and brother were no longer part of the household founded by Jeanne.

Two years later, in 1978, Lucie got married and Charles joined Jeanne's household in Miami. Also in 1978, Jeanne began saving money and applying for visas to bring her cousins Hughes and Valerie to Miami. The asterisks show that these two people are in the process of joining the household. In 1979, Anna's sister, Helen joined the family and in 1982 Charles went back to New York to live again with Lucie.

There is a lot of information in this chart, but the detail is gone. We don't know why Jeanne went to the United States in 1968; we don't know why Charles left Jeanne's household in 1976 or why he rejoined the group in 1978. Fjellman and Gladwin present seven of these family history charts in their article and they provide the historical detail in vignettes below each chart. Their purpose in reducing all the historical detail to a set of pluses and minuses, however, is to allow us to see the *patterns* of family growth, development, and decay.

PRESENTING RESULTS: CAUSAL MAPS/FLOW CHARTS

Causal maps represent theories about how things work. They are **visual representations of ideas that emerge from studying data, seeing patterns, and coming to conclusions about what causes what.** Causal maps do not have to have numbers attached to them, although that is where causal modeling eventually leads. After all, it is better to know *how much* one thing causes another than to know simply that one thing *does* cause another. With or without numbers, though, causal models are best expressed as a *flow chart*.

A causal flow chart consists of a set of boxes connected by a set of arrows. The boxes contain descriptions of states (like being the youngest child, owning a tractor, being Catholic, or feeling angry), and the arrows tell you how one state leads to another. The simplest causal map is a visual representation of the relation between two variables

$$A \rightarrow B$$

which reads: "A leads to or causes B."

Of course, real life is usually much, much more complicated than that. Look at Figure 11.2. It is Stuart Plattner's *algorithm,* based on intensive interviews and participant observation at produce markets in St. Louis, for how merchants decide what stock to buy. An algorithm is a set of ordered rules that tell you how to solve a problem—like "find the average of a list of numbers" or, in this case, "determine the decisions of produce merchants." (The capital Q in Figure 11.2 stands for "quantity.")

Read the flow chart from top to bottom and left to right, following the arrows. At the beginning of each week, the merchants seek information on the supply and cost of produce items. After that, the algorithm gets complicated. Plattner notes that the model may seem "too complex to represent the decision process of plain folks at the marketplace." However, Plattner says, the chart "still omits consideration of an enormous amount of knowledge pertaining to qualities of produce at various seasons from various shipping areas" (1982:405).

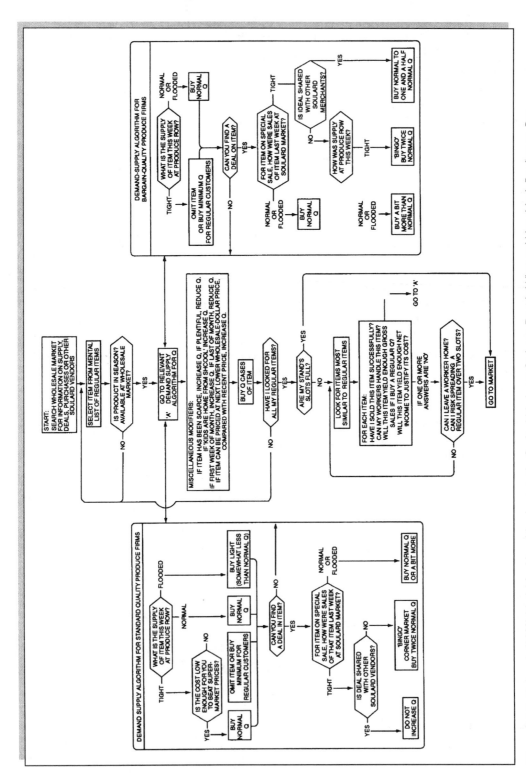

Figure 11.2 Plattner's (1982) Model for How Merchants in the Soulard Market in St. Louis Decide What and How Much Produce to Buy

SOURCE: S. Plattner, "Economic Decision Making in a Public Marketplace." Reproduced by permission of the American Anthropological Association from *American Ethnologist* 9:404. May 1982. Not for further reproduction.

NOTE: Q = quantity.

DATABASE MANAGEMENT

Whether you collect texts or questionnaire data, run lab experiments or observe behavior in the wild, you need a way to store and manage all the data. Long before you try to analyze the data, long before try to find patterns in your data, you absolutely must have it packed away in some convenient form. Shoe boxes full of questionnaires or transcripts just won't cut it. That's where *database management,* or DBM, comes in. It's easy, once you get the hang of it.

Actually, we use DBM all the time. If someone asks you to suggest a French restaurant in San Francisco that costs less than $75.00 per person, you search through your database of restaurants, limiting yourself to those you know in San Francisco (the first criterion). Then you look through *that* list for the French restaurants and pull out only those that also satisfy the second criterion. Finally, you look through *that* list and see if any of them cost less than $75.00 per person (the third criterion).

When you look up books in your school library, you're using a DBM system. Each book has a computer record that contains information on author, title, date of publication, and so on. So, if you want a book on statistical methods used in criminology, you could use the *logical expression* "statistics AND crim*." The * (asterisk) is a commonly used "wildcard." In this case, it would mean "find me all the books that are about statistics and about anything that starts with crim, like criminology, criminals, crime, and so on."

To use a database manager, you need to understand two basic concepts: *records* and *fields.* **A record is the unit whose characteristics you want to retrieve. The fields are the characteristics.** Think of all the CDs you own as the units. Each CD then becomes a record. The descriptive fields for each record might be artist, title, publisher, date of release, and a series of topics that tell things about the CD. If you have 1,000 CDs, then you have 1,000 records in the database.

You can use DBM software, like FileMaker™ or Microsoft Access™ to manage information about paper notes, photos and slides, collections of artifacts, collections of news clippings—in short, any collection of *things.*

In fact, anything you can list is a candidate for DBM. Code your photographs and make each one a record in a database. Then ask the database, "Which photos are about palm oil?" or "Which photos are about old men in the plaza?" or "Which are about market sellers *and* about meat *and* about servants making purchases for others?" (see Box 11.2).

Local newspapers provide important information for ethnographers. Once you start clipping all the interesting stories, you soon wind up with hundreds of pieces. Just number them and code them for the topics that are germane to your research. Then, later, ask the database: "Which clippings are about property disputes between siblings?"

If you collect folk songs, you'll quickly develop a collection of several hundred, even several thousand. If you have the lyrics typed into a computer, you can use a text management program to look for recurrent words and themes. But if you've got a collection of several hundred audiotapes, you can use a database manager. If you collect artifacts, you can catalog them, index them for variables, and manage the information in a DBM system. Once you get accustomed to setting up databases, you'll wonder how you ever got along without them.

Text Management Systems

If you do 100 semistructured interviews and each interview takes an hour and a half, you'll

---

Box 11.2
Using DBM Concepts to Handle Paper Copies of Texts

If you have paper copies of interview transcripts (from research you or someone else did before computers), you can use database management concepts to analyze the information. Just number the notes, starting with 00001. Consider each note a record and create appropriate descriptive fields. As with all field notes, you'll have one for the name of the informant, another for the place, another for the date, and several for the topics covered in each note. Some notes may get 1 or 2 topical codes; others may need 10. Be sure to define enough topical codes when you design your database. Ten codes are usually enough.

Once you've defined the fields, it takes about two or three minutes per note to enter the codes. That means only about 30-50 hours of work at the computer to enter codes for 1,000 pages of field notes. Once that's done, you can ask questions like "Which notes are about religion and also about political factionalism but not about generational conflict?" When you ask your DBM system for information like this, you'll get back answers like "The information you want is on pages 113, 334, 376, 819, 820, and 1,168." You simply flip through the "database" of field notes on your lap. As you do, you will see the entire page of each field note and you'll get a feel for the context.

By the way, the same basic concepts of DBM that are used in handling quantitative data are used in handling artifacts. You can use a database manager to enter data from a set of questionnaires just as easily as you can use it to enter data about books in your library or any other long list of things.

---

wind up with about 3,000 pages of transcripts. Suppose you want to ask this enormous database: "Which pieces of the texts are about migration and about females who are under 30 years of age?" To answer this question with an ordinary database program, you'd have to code every chunk of text with the age and gender of the informant.

Relational database management is a concept that applies here. In a relational database, you'd have one file with information about the respondents you've interviewed and another file that contains information about their transcripts.

These files are *related* to one another, so when you ask: "Which pieces of text are about migration and about females under 30?" the program

(1) rushes off to find all the chunks of text that you've tagged for migration,

(2) makes a temporary list of those chunks,

(3) looks at each chunk in the temporary list and finds the respondent's name or code, and

(4) looks up the respondent in the respondent information file.

If the respondent is not female, or is not a female under 30, the program drops the chunk of text from the temporary list. When the program finishes, it tells you whether any of the chunks of text conform to all the criteria you listed in your question. Asking questions like this about 3,000 records takes a couple of seconds.

Modern text management software, like NUD*IST and ATLAS/ti (see Appendix F), are relational database managers with special capabilities. They let you code chunks of text and find all the chunks that fit a set of criteria ("Find me chunks of text where people talked about sports AND breaking up."). They also let you build networks of codes and produce reports and diagrams of how codes are related to one another in a set of texts.

More about all this in Chapter 12 when we get to text analysis. Now, on to the nuts and bolts of data analysis.

Chapter 11
Review

KEY CONCEPTS

SUMMARY

❖ Different kinds of data require different analytic methods. The adjectives "quantitative" and "qualitative" are ambiguous when they are used with the phrase "data analysis."

 ◆ There are four meanings to account for: the qualitative analysis of qualitative data, the quantitative analysis of quantitative data, the qualitative analysis of quantitative data, and the quantitative analysis of qualitative data.

❖ Analysis is the search for patterns in data and for ideas that help explain why those patterns are there in the first place.

 ◆ The constant validity check involves (a) looking for consistencies and inconsistencies among knowledgeable informants and finding out why those informants disagree about important things, (b) checking people's reports of behavior or of environmental conditions against more objective evidence, (c) being open to negative evidence rather than annoyed when it pops up, and (d) looking for alternative explanations from key informants and from colleagues.

❖ One of the most important concepts in all data analysis—whether we're working with quantitative or qualitative data—is the data matrix. There are two basic kinds of data matrices: profile matrices and proximity matrices.

 ◆ Profile matrices show properties (in columns) of things (in rows). Profile analysis is about how properties of things are related to one another.

 ◆ Proximity matrices contain measurements of relations between items. Measurements of how close things are to each other produce a similarity matrix. Measurements that show how far apart things are from each other form a dissimilarity matrix.

❖ An important part of all analysis is the production of visual displays. Laying out your data in table or matrix form, and drawing your theories out in the form of a flow chart or map, helps you understand what you have.

 ◆ Causal maps, or flow charts, are visual representations of ideas that emerge from studying data, seeing patterns, and coming to conclusions about what causes what. Causal maps do not have to have numbers attached to them.

❖ Long before you try to analyze the data, you absolutely must have it packed away in some convenient form. This is the role of database management systems.

 ◆ Database management systems involve two basic concepts: records and fields. A record is the unit whose characteristics you want to retrieve. The fields are the characteristics.

❖ Modern text management software are specialized database managers. They let you code chunks of text and find all the chunks that fit a set of criteria. ("Find me chunks of text where people talked about sports AND breaking up.")

  ◆ Some text management software let you build networks of codes and produce reports and diagrams of how codes are related to one another in a set of texts.

EXERCISES

1. Write a brief essay on the idea that quantitative analysis in social research involves reducing people to numbers, while qualitative analysis involves reducing people to words.

2. Why are the phrases "qualitative data analysis" and "quantitative data analysis" ambiguous?

3. What is a causal flow chart? How is it different from a matrix display of relations among variables?

4. Explain the concepts behind database management. How are text analysis packages related to database management systems?

FURTHER READING

Chapter 11 is an overview of the data analysis section of this book. Most of the methods mentioned in this chapter are covered in detail in the next five chapters. For example, you'll find further reading about content analysis and grounded theory at the end of Chapter 12, along with exercises in text analysis. You'll find further reading about methods based on the analysis of proximity matrices at the end of Chapter 16, along with exercises for multivariate analysis and further reading on one variety of causal modeling, path analysis. See Appendix F for information on text analysis packages.

12 QUALITATIVE DATA ANALYSIS I

TEXT ANALYSIS

IN THIS CHAPTER:

❖ INTRODUCTION

Texts are everywhere. Most of the recoverable information about human thought and behavior is naturally occurring text. Diaries, property transactions, recipes, correspondence, song lyrics, billboards—not to mention books, magazines, and newspapers—these are the archaeological residue of literate societies around the world.

And there's more—lots and lots more. *Artifacts* (clothing, buildings, computer programs) and *images* (television ads, slasher films, family photo albums) are texts. *Behaviors* (crossing a busy street, giving a university lecture, laying out a garden) and *events* (church ceremonies, homecoming games, blind dates) are texts. They come to us raw, in qualitative form. We can study them raw or we can code them—turn them into variables—and study the relations among the variables. Both approaches can produce insight and under-standing.

ABOUT TEXTS

A lot of texts are available as machine-readable archives. The entire corpus of U.S. Supreme Court opinions is available online through LEXIS-NEXIS™. Electronic text centers at universities across the world are bringing together hundreds of machine-readable corpora: the holy writ of the world's religions, all of Shakespeare's work, all the ancient Greek and Latin plays and epics, U.S. Civil War newspapers, letters of delegates to Congress (1774-89), and the Watergate hearings are texts.

The list goes on and on. Conversions of text corpora to online databases proceeds at a breathtaking pace. The Human Relations Area Files (HRAF), for example, consists of over a million pages of ethnographic text on 350 societies around the world. All the data on a 60-culture sample from that database are now available on CD-ROM, and the entire million-page corpus of texts will be on the Internet in the next few years.

Scholars of social change have lots of longitudinal quantitative data available (the Gallup Poll for the last 50 years, the Bureau of Labor Statistics surveys for the last couple of decades, and base-ball statistics for over a hundred years are just a few of the best-studied data sets), but longitudinal text data are produced naturally all the time. For a window on American popular culture, take a look at the themes dealt with in country music and in *Superman* comics over the years.

Or look at sitcoms and product ads from the 1950s and the 1990s. Notice the differences in, say, the way women are portrayed or the things people think are funny in different eras. In the 1950s, Lucille Ball created a furor when she dared to continue making episodes of the *I Love Lucy* show while she was pregnant. Now think about almost any episode of *Seinfeld*. Or scan some of the recent episodes of popular soap operas and compare them to episodes from 30 years ago. Today's sitcoms and soaps contain much more sexual innuendo.

How much more? If you really wanted to measure that, you could code a representative sample of exemplars (ads, sitcoms, soaps) from the 1950s and another representative sample from the 1990s, and compare the codes. That's content analysis. Interpretivists, on the other hand, might be more interested in understanding the meaning across time of concepts like "flirtation," "deceit," "betrayal," "sensuality," and "love," or the narrative mechanisms by which any of these concepts are displayed or responded to by various characters. Text analysis is for everyone.

Text analysis is not a single method or even a single approach. Some of the major traditions of text analysis include hermeneutics (interpretive analysis), narrative analysis, discourse analysis, the grounded theory approach, and content analysis.

HERMENEUTICS/INTERPRETIVE ANALYSIS

Modern *hermeneutics* derives from *biblical hermeneutics* (also called *biblical exegesis*). In the Western tradition of exegesis, the Old and New Testaments are assumed to contain eternal truths, put there by an omnipotent creator through some emissaries—prophets, writers of Gospels, and the like. The idea is **to continually interpret the words of those texts to understand their meaning and their directives.**

Formal rules for biblical exegesis were developed by the early Talmudic scholars, about a hundred years after the death of Jesus. For example, one of the rules was that "the meaning of a passage can be derived either from its context or from a statement later on in the same passage." Another was that "when two verses appear to contradict one another, a third verse can be discovered which reconciles them."

The 13 rules for interpreting Scripture remain to this day part of the morning service among Orthodox Jews. In the eighteenth and nineteenth centuries, New Testament scholars used hermeneutic reasoning to solve what was called the "synoptic problem"—that is, to determine the order in which the four Gospels were written (see Farmer [1976] and Stein [1987] for detailed histories of the problem).

The method of close interpretation of text has been extended from biblical studies to many other areas. Constitutional law, for example, is a form of hermeneutics. (The word "hermeneutics," by the way, comes from Hermes—he of the winged hat—messenger of the gods, whose job it was to interpret the will of the gods to humans.) In the United States, for example, we assume that the writers of the Constitution had some things in mind when they penned each phrase. We take it as our task to interpret and to extract that meaning in light of current circumstances. It is exegesis that produces different interpretations across time about the legality of slavery, abortion, women's right to vote, the government's ability to tax income, and so on.

Extending Hermeneutics to All Kinds of Texts

In social science, the hermeneutic method has been extended to the study of all kinds of texts, including images, conversations—even song lyrics. Herzfeld (1977), for example, studied renditions of the *khelidonisma,* or swallow song, sung in modern Greece as part of the welcoming of spring. Herzfeld collected texts of the song from ancient, medieval, and modern historical sources and recorded texts of current-day renditions in several locations across Greece. His purpose was to show that inconsistencies in the texts come not from "some putative irrationality in the processes of oral tradition" but are, in fact, reflections of structural principles that underlie the rite of passage for welcoming spring in rural Greece.

To make his point, Herzfeld looks for anomalies across renditions—like "March, my good March" in one song compared to "March, terrible March" in another. Herzfeld claims that the word "good" is used ironically in Greek where the referent is a source of anxiety.

Is March a subject of symbolic anxiety for Greek villagers? Yes, says Herzfeld, it is, and we can tell that it is because of widely observed practices like avoidance of certain activities during the *drimata* (the first three days of March). Herzfeld supports his analysis by referring to the *drimes,* a word that denotes the first three days of August, which are associated with malevolent spirits. Since March is the transition from winter to summer and August is the transition from summer to winter, Herzfeld concludes that there is symbolic danger associated with these mediating months. He finds support for this analysis in the fact that February is never referred to with an unequivocally good epithet.

This is hermeneutic analysis: the search for meanings and their interconnection in the expression of culture. The method for doing this kind of analysis requires deep involvement with the culture, including an intimate familiarity with the language, so that the symbolic referents emerge during the study of those expressions—as in the study of texts here. You can't see the connections among symbols if you don't know what the symbols are and what they are supposed to mean.

Holly Mathews (1992) collected 60 tellings of *La Llorona* (The Weeping Woman), a morality tale told across Mexico. Here is one telling, which Mathews says is typical:

La Llorona was a bad woman who married a good man. They had children and all was well. Then one day she went crazy and began to walk the streets.

Everyone knew but her husband. When he found out he beat her. She had much shame. The next day she walked into the river and drowned herself. And now she knows no rest and must forever wander the streets wailing in the night. And that is why women must never leave their families to walk the streets looking for men. If they are not careful they will end up like La Llorona. (p. 128)

In another telling, La Llorona kills herself because her husband becomes a drunk and loses all their money. In yet another, she kills herself because her husband is seen going with other women and La Llorona, in disbelief, finally catches him paying off a woman in the streets.

Mathews found that men and women tended to emphasize different things in the story, but the woman always winds up killing herself, no matter who tells it. The morality tale succeeds in shaping people's behavior, she says, because "the motives of the main characters draw upon culturally shared schemas about gendered human nature" (ibid.:129).

Men, according to Mathews's understanding of the cultural model in rural Mexico, view women as sexually uncontrolled. Unless they are controlled, or control themselves, their true nature will emerge and they will begin (as the story says) to "walk the streets" in search of sexual gratification. Men, for their part, are viewed by women as sexually insatiable. Men are driven, like animals, to satisfy their desires, even at the expense of family obligations. In her grammar of La Llorona tales, Mathews shows that women have no recourse but to kill themselves when they cannot make their marriages work.

Mathews goes beyond identifying the schema: She offers an explanation of where key parts of the schema come from. Most marriages in the village where Mathews did her research (the state of Oaxaca) are arranged by parents and involve some exchange of resources between the families. Parents usually won't take back a daughter if she wants out of a marriage (once serious resources, like land, are exchanged, there's no turning back), so "the only option perceived to be open to a woman who wants to terminate her marriage is suicide" (ibid.:150). Mathews shows, in other words, how structural features in the society lead to perceptions, which lead to particular behavior—the inclusion of suicide by the woman in virtually all tellings of the La Llorona tale.

NARRATIVE AND PERFORMANCE ANALYSIS

In *narrative analysis,* the goal is **to discover regularities in how people tell stories or give speeches.** Dennis Tedlock (1985), for example, translated the *Popol Vuh,* a sixteenth-century Quiché Maya manuscript that had been written out by Francisco Ximénez, a Spanish missionary of the time. The *Popol Vuh* was one of those big epics, like the *Iliad* or *Beowulf,* that were meant to be narrated. Is it possible, Tedlock asked, to analyze the text and figure out how to narrate it today as performers would have done in ancient times?

In doing the translation of the *Popol Vuh,* Tedlock had relied on Andrés Xiloj, a modern speaker of Quiché. Xiloj had not been trained to read Maya, but he was literate in Spanish and he made the transition quickly. "When given his first chance to look at the *Popol Vuh* text," Tedlock reported, Xiloj "produced a pair of spectacles and began reading aloud, word by word" (1987:145).

As was true of many medieval manuscripts in Europe, Ximénez's rendition of the *Popol Vuh* was more or less an undifferentiated mass of text with almost no punctuation. We take punctuation for granted, but its widespread use is actually pretty recent (it was promoted by publishers after the invention of the printing press to make books easier to read and more appealing to potential customers). Without punctuation, there were no clues in Ximénez's manuscript about how a performer might have used intonational contours or variations in timing in reciting the epic.

What Tedlock did was record oral narratives (speeches, prayers, songs, stories), not just casual speech, from modern speakers of Maya. He looked for "patterns in the wording that have analogs in the ancient text" and noted how these patterns were enunciated (Tedlock 1987:147). Then he devised special punctuation symbols for marking pauses, accelerations, verse endings, and so on and applied these to the *Popol Vuh.*

Tedlock made systematic comparison across other ancient texts to look for recurrent sound patterns that signify variations in meaning. (Think of how we use rising intonation at the end of sentences in English to signify a question, and how some people in our society use the same intonation in declarative sentences at the beginning of phone conversations when the object is to jar someone's memory, as in: "Hi, this is Mary? I was in your intro class last semester?")

In making these systematic comparisons, Tedlock found that Quiché Maya verse has the same structure as ancient Middle Eastern texts—texts that predate Homer. In fact, he concluded it is the same structure found in all living oral traditions that have not yet been influenced by writing.

DISCOURSE ANALYSIS

Discourse analysis involves **the close study of naturally occurring interactions.**

————❖

Howard Waitzkin and his colleagues (1994:32) taped 336 encounters involving older patients and primary care internists. (The physicians included some in private practice, some who worked in a teaching hospital, and some who worked both in private practice and in hospital outpatient departments.)

Waitzkin et al. randomly chose 50 of these encounters for intensive study. They had each of the 50 encounters transcribed, verbatim—with all the "uhs," and pauses, and whatnot that occur in real discourse—and two research assistants checked the accuracy of the transcriptions against the original tape.

During the interpretation phase, research assistants read the transcripts and noted the ones that dealt with aging, work, gender roles, family life, leisure, substance use, and socioemotional problems—all areas in which the researchers were interested at the time. The assistants read through the transcripts and tagged instances where either the doctors or the patients "made statements that conveyed ideological content or expressed messages of social control" (ibid.:328).

To illustrate their interpretive approach to discourse analysis, Waitzkin et al. go through two texts in detail. They use the same method as that used in biblical exegesis: A chunk of text is laid out, followed by commentary involving all the wisdom and understanding that the commentators can bring to the effort. For example, Waitzkin et al. produce this snippet of interaction between a doctor (D) and his patient (P), an elderly woman with heart disease who has come in for a follow-up:

> P: Well I should—now I've got birthday cards to buy. I've got seven or eight birthdays this week—month. Instead of that I'm just gonna write 'em and wish them a happy birthday. Just a little note, my grandchildren.
> D: Mm hmm.
> P: But I'm not gonna bother. I just can't do it all, Dr. —.
> D: Well.
> P: I called my daughters, her birthday was just, today's the third.
> D: Yeah.
> P: My daughter's birthday in Princeton was the uh first, and I called her up and talked with her. I don't know what time it'll cost me, but then, my telephone is my only connection.

Waitzkin et al. comment:

> At no other time in the encounter does the patient refer to her own family, nor does the doctor ask. The patient does her best to maintain contact, even though she does not mention anything that she receives in the way of day-to-day support. Compounding these problems of social support and incipient isolation, the patient recently has moved from a home that she occupied for 59 years. (ibid.:330-31)

When they get through presenting their running commentary on the encounter, Waitzkin et al. interpret the discourse:

> This encounter shows structural elements that appear beneath the surface details of patient-doctor

communication. . . . Contextual issues affecting the patient include social isolation; loss of home, possessions, family, and community; limited resources to preserve independent function; financial insecurity; and physical deterioration associated with the process of dying. . . . After the medical encounter, the patient returns to the same contextual problems that trouble her, consenting to social conditions that confront the elderly in this society.

That such structural features should characterize an encounter like this one becomes rather disconcerting, since the communication otherwise seems so admirable. . . . The doctor manifests patience and compassion as he encourages a wide-ranging discussion of socioemotional concerns that extend far beyond the technical details of the pa-

tient's physical disorders. Yet the discourse does nothing to improve the most troubling features of the patient's situation. To expect differently would require redefining much of what medicine aims to do. (ibid.:335-36; used by permission)

Waitzkin et al. make clear that alternative readings of the same passage are possible and advocate, as part of their method, the systematic archiving, in publicly available places, of texts on which analysis is conducted. When the project was over, Waitzkin et al. filed the transcripts with University Microfilms International so that other researchers could use the data for later analysis.

GROUNDED THEORY

The *grounded theory* approach is a set of techniques for (1) identifying categories and concepts that emerge from text, and (2) linking the concepts into substantive and formal theories (Glaser and Strauss 1967; Strauss and Corbin 1990). The approach was developed by sociologists and has a long history in ethnographic case studies (Becker et al. 1961; Agar 1979, 1980a). Journals such as *Qualitative Health Research, Qualitative Sociology,* and the *Journal of Contemporary Ethnography* are major outlets for this type of research.

Today, grounded theory is used across the social sciences to examine topics in, for example, public health (Hitchcock and Wilson 1992; Yamamoto and Wallhagen 1998), social welfare (Lazzari et al. 1996), clinical and counseling psychology (Rennie 1994; Blustein et al. 1997), gerontology (Tomita 1998; Young 1998), business

administration (Locke 1996; Fox-Wolfgramm et al. 1998), drug abuse (Morgan and Joe 1996), and criminology (Ward et al. 1998).

The mechanics of grounded theory are deceptively simple:

(1) Produce transcripts of interviews and read through a small sample of text.
(2) Identify potential *analytic categories*— that is, potential *themes*—that arise.
(3) As the categories emerge, pull all the data from those categories together and compare them.
(4) Think about how categories are linked together.
(5) Use the relations among categories to build theoretical models, constantly checking the models against the data—particularly against negative cases.

(6) Present the results of the analysis using *exemplars*—that is, **quotes from interviews that illuminate the theory.**

The key to making all this work is called *memoing*. Throughout the grounded theory process, you keep running notes about the coding and about potential hypotheses and new directions for the research. Grounded theory is an *iterative process* by which you, the analyst, become more and more *grounded* in the data. During the process, you come to understand more and more deeply how whatever you're studying really works.

Coding Themes

The heart of grounded theory is identifying themes in texts and coding the texts for the presence or absence of those themes. Coding turns free-flowing texts into a set of nominal variables (what statisticians mean, by the way, when they use the phrase "qualitative data"). In a set of texts about the experience of divorce, people do or do not talk about what to do about pension funds, they do or do not talk about how their children are taking it, they do or do not talk about their relations with their former in-laws, and so on.

Where do you stop? There is practically no end to the number of themes you can isolate for any text. When I was in high school, my physics teacher put a bottle of Coca-Cola on his desk and challenged our class to come up with interesting ways to describe that bottle. Each day for weeks that bottle sat on his desk as new physics lessons were reeled off, and each day new suggestions for describing that bottle were dropped on the desk on the way out of class.

I don't remember how many descriptors we came up with, but there were dozens. Some were pretty lame (pour the contents into a beaker and see if the boiling point was higher or lower than that of sea water) and some were pretty imaginative (cut off the bottom and test its magnifying power), but the point was to show us that there was no end to the number of things we could describe (measure) about that Coke bottle, and the point sunk in. I remember it every time I try to code a text.

Inductive and Deductive Coding

Grounded theory research is mostly based on *inductive coding,* or *"open" coding*. **The idea is to become grounded in the data and to allow understanding to emerge from close study of the texts.** That's why Barney Glaser and Anselm Strauss (1967), the originators of this approach, called it the *discovery* of grounded theory. The whole idea is to discover patterns of behavior or thought in a set of texts.

Content analysis (which we'll take up in the next section) is mostly based on *deductive coding*. In doing deductive analysis of text, you **start with a hypothesis before you start coding. The idea is to test whether your hypothesis is correct.** Inductive research is what you do when you're in the *exploratory* or *discovery phase* of any research project, whether your data are words or numbers. Deductive research is what you do in the *confirmatory* stage of any research project, no matter what kind of data you have. There is no point in talking about which is better. They're both terrific if you use them to answer appropriate questions.

For inductive research, like grounded theory, a lot of people start out by just reading the texts and underlining or highlighting things as they go. Strauss and Corbin (1990:68) recommend using actual phrases—the words of real people—to name themes. This is called *in vivo coding*. In my study of how ocean scientists interact with people in Washington, D.C., who are responsible for ocean policy (Bernard 1974), I kept hearing the word "brokers." Scientists and policymakers alike used this word to describe people whom they trusted to act as go-betweens, so "broker" became one of the code themes for my field notes.

Finding Themes

Whether you use actual words from the people you study or make up your own codes, you'll want to use a computer to help you actually code your texts.

In the very, very beginning of this kind of grounded analysis, I recommend getting your hands on the texts and marking them up with a highlighter pen. This is the ocular scan method, otherwise known as eyeballing. In this method, you live with your data, handle them, lay them out all over your floor, read them over and over again, tack bunches of them to a bulletin board, and eventually get a feel for what's in them. This is followed by the interocular percussion test—which is where you wait for patterns to hit you between the eyes.

This may not seem like a very scientific way of doing things, but for sheer fun and analytic efficiency, I still think that pawing and shuffling through your texts and thinking about them is the best way to start. Once you have a feel for the themes and the relations among themes in a set of texts, then I see no reason to struggle bravely on without a computer. Of course, if you start with thousands of interviews, or if you are working on a big project that has several sites and many subprojects, integrating material can be done only by computer.

> *For sheer fun and analytic efficiency, pawing and shuffling through your texts and thinking about them is the best way to start.*

Spradley (1979:199-201) offered some very good advice for noticing themes. Look for evidence, he said, of social conflict, cultural contradictions, informal methods of social control, things that people do in managing impersonal social relationships, methods by which people acquire and maintain achieved and ascribed status, and information about how people solve problems. Each of these arenas is likely to yield major themes in cultures.

Willms et al. (1990) and Miles and Huberman (1994) suggest starting with some general themes derived from reading the literature and adding more themes and subthemes as you go. This is somewhere between inductive and deductive coding. You have a general idea of what you're after and you know what at least some of the big themes are, but you're still in a discovery mode, so you let new themes emerge from the texts as you go along.

Ryan and Weisner (1996) used a computer to help them shop for themes in texts. They asked fathers and mothers of adolescents in Los Angeles: "Describe your children. In your own words, just tell us about them." Ryan and Weisner used a computer program to generate a list of all the unique words in the corpus of texts and the number of times each word was used by mothers and by fathers. Mothers, for example, were more likely to use words like "friends," "creative," "time," and "honest"; fathers were more likely to use words like "school," "good," "lack," "student," "enjoys," "independent," and "extremely." Ryan and Weisner used this information as clues for themes that they would use later in actually coding texts.

No matter how you actually *do* inductive coding—whether you start with paper and highlighters or use a computer to paw through your texts; whether you use in vivo codes or use numbers or make up little mnemonics of your own; whether you have some big themes in mind to start or let all the themes emerge from your reading—by the time you identify the themes and refine them to the point where they can be applied to an entire corpus of texts, a lot of interpretive analysis has already been done. Miles and Huberman say simply: "Coding is analysis" (1994:56).

Making a Codebook

Theme codes should be easy to remember and easy to use. Private codes tend to disappear from your memory quickly when you're not using them (you'll never remember the codebook for any project a year after you've completed it), so be sure to write up a detailed codebook in case you forget what "A5" or "EMP" or whatever abbreviations you dreamed up at the time you did the coding mean. You can use numbers or words as theme codes, but make sure that your codebook is in plain English (or Spanish, etc.).

You can use numbers or words as codes. Whatever you do, though, don't get too picky. Coding is supposed to be data *reduction* not proliferation. Mathew Miles was involved in a major ethnographic project to evaluate six schools. The researchers each developed their own codes. The list of codes quickly grew to 202 categories of actors, processes, organizational forms, and efforts. Each of the six researchers insisted that his or her field site was unique and that the highly specialized codes were all necessary. It became impossible for anyone to use the unwieldy system and they just stopped coding altogether (Miles 1983:123).

———————❖—————

Kurasaki (1997) studied the ethnic identity of *sansei,* third-generation Japanese Americans. She interviewed 20 people and used a grounded theory approach to do her analysis. She started with seven major themes: (1) a sense of history and roots, (2) values and ways of doing things, (3)

biculturality, (4) sense of belonging, (5) sense of alienation, (6) self-concept, and (7) worldview. As the analysis progressed, she split the major themes into subthemes. So, for example, she split the first theme into (1) sense of having a Japanese heritage and (2) sense of having a Japanese American social history.

As the coding progressed further, she eventually decided to combine two of the major themes (sense of belonging and sense of alienation) and wound up with six major themes and a total of 18 themes. Kurasaki assigned her own numerical codes to each of the themes—1.1 for the first subtheme in macrotheme 1, 7.2 for the second subtheme in macrotheme 7, and so on—and used those numbers to actually code her transcribed interviews. Her codebook is shown in Table 12.1.

Shelley (1992) studied the social networks of people who had end-stage kidney disease. The traditional therapy is hemodialysis, a blood-cleaning process that requires hooking people up to a machine for several hours every other day. Shelley reasoned that people whose lives depend on those hemodialysis machines will come to have very restricted social networks. Patients who are treated with other therapies, like organ transplants or portable dialysis technology, are able to work and travel and should not have restricted networks.

Shelley used the *Outline of Cultural Materials* (Murdock 1996), or OCM, as the basis of her coding scheme and applied those codes to her field notes and interviews. (See below, in the Cross-Cultural Content Analysis section, for more about the OCM.) Table 12.2 shows a part of her codebook—the adaptation of OCM code 757 (medical therapy).

Every society in the world has some ways to deal with illness, some therapies that are culturally appropriate. Obviously, not many societies have categories for HIV blood test results or hemodialysis. Shelley simply added decimal points to the basic OCM code for medical therapy. The

TABLE 12.1 Kurasaki's (1997) Coding Scheme for Her Study of Ethnic Identity among *Sansei* in California

First-Order Category	Second-Order Category	Numeric Code
Sense of history and roots	Sense of having a Japanese heritage	1.1
	Sense of having a Japanese American social history	1.2
Values and ways of doing things	Japanese American values and attitudes	2.1
	Practice of Japanese customs	2.2
	Japanese way of doing things	2.3
	Japanese American interpersonal or communication styles	2.4
	Japanese language proficiency	2.5
Biculturality	Integration or bicultural competence	3.1
	Bicultural conflict or confusion	3.2
Sense of belonging	Sense of a global ethnic or racial community	4.1
	Sense of interpersonal connectedness with same ethnicity or race of others	4.2
	Sense of intellectual connectedness with other ethnic or racial minorities	4.3
	Searching for a sense of community	4.4
Sense of alienation	Sense of alienation from ascribed ethnic or racial group	5.1
Self-concept	Sense of comfort with one's ethnic or racial self	6.1
	Searching for a sense of comfort with one's ethnic or racial self	6.2
Worldview	Social consciousness	7.1
	Sense of oppression	7.2

SOURCE: K. S. Kurasaki, "Ethnic Identity and Its Development among Third-Generation Japanese Americans." Ph.D. diss., Department of Psychology, DePaul University, 1997. Reprinted with permission.

TABLE 12.2 Shelley's (1992) Adaptation of the OCM (Murdock 1996) for Her Study of Renal Disease Patients

757.1	Transplantation
757.2	Hemodialysis
757.3	CAPD (peritoneal dialysis)
757.4	Home dialysis
757.5	Adjustment to dialysis
757.6	Compliance with medical regime
757.7	Machinery involved in dialysis
757.8	Medicines
757.9	Medical test results
757.91	HIV test results

SOURCE: Data reproduced with permission of the author.

TABLE 12.3 Nyamongo's (1998) Codebook: How Gusii Respond to Malaria

Column	Code	Variable Description and Variable Values
1-3	RESP_ID	Informant number, from 001 to 035
4-11	NAME	Name of the informant
12-13	AGE	Age in years as reported by the informant
14-18	GENDER	1 = female, 2 = male
19-32	OCC	Occupation of the informant. This is a nominal variable. The possible scores are housewife (1), farmer (2), retired worker (3), security guard (4), teacher (5), student (6), artisan (7), village elder (8), and n.a. if the informant reported no occupation
33	SES	Socioeconomic status is an ordinal variable measured by presence of the following in the homestead: 1 = grass-thatched house; 2 = iron-sheet-roofed, dirt-floor house; 3 = iron-sheet-roofed, cemented-floor house; 4 = semipermanent house; 5 = permanent house; 9 = information not available
	.	
	.	
41	CAUSE1	If mosquito is mentioned by informant as the cause of malaria. 1 = yes, 0 = no
42	CAUSE2	If eating sugarcane, ripe bananas, and roast green maize are mentioned by informant as the cause of malaria. 1 = yes, 0 = no
43	CAUSE3	If causes other than CAUSE1 and CAUSE2 are given. 1 = yes, 0 = no
	.	
	.	
48	CTRL1	What should be done to reduce malaria cases? 1 = keep compound clean, 0 = other
49	CTRL2	What should be done to reduce malaria cases? 1 = take medicine for prophylaxis, 0 = other
50	CTRL3	What should be done to reduce malaria cases? 1 = use net or spray or burn coil, 0 = other
51	CTRL4	What should be done to reduce malaria cases? 1 = nothing can be done, 0 = other
52	DIAG	Diagnosis of illness by the informant. 1 = malaria, 0 = other illness
53	FACTOR1	Does cost influence whether people use home management or hospital-based care? 1 = yes, 0 = no
54	FACTOR2	Does duration of sickness influence whether people use home management or hospital-based care? 1 = yes, 0 = no
55	FACTOR3	Is intensity (severity) a factor influencing whether people use home management or hospital-based care? 1 = yes, 0 = no
56	HELP1	Type of support given to informant by family or friends. 1 = buying medicine, 0 = other
	.	
	.	

TABLE 12.3 Continued

Column	Code	Variable Description and Variable Values
75	SYM1	If the informant mentions headache as a symptom. 1 = yes, 0 = no
.		
.		
.		
80	SYM14	If the informant mentions child has unusual cries as a symptom. 1 = yes, 0 = no
81	SYM15	Other—if not one of SYM1 through SYM14. 1 = yes, 0 = no.
91	TREAT11	Did the informant report using pills bought over the counter as the first treatment resort? 1 = yes, 0 = no
.		
.		
.		
96	TREAT21	Second treatment resort. The values are the same as for TREAT11, Column 91
.		
.		
119	WITCH	If the informant mentions that witchcraft may be implicated if patient has malaria. 1 = yes, 0 = no
120	YESDIAG	Does the coder think the informant made the right diagnosis based on the informant's stated symptoms? 1 = yes, 0 = no
121	COST	Cost of receiving treatment from private health care provider in Kenyan shillings, from 0001 to 9999. 9999 = information not available

SOURCE: Data reproduced with permission of the author.

OCM code 759 refers to "medical personnel." You can create 759.1 for midwives, 759.2 for physicians, 759.3 for acupuncturists, and the like. Code 231 is for practices relating to the keeping of livestock. If you are studying a farming community, you might use 231.1 to refer to data on the keeping of goats and 231.2 to refer to data about pigs.

Nyamongo (1998) did semistructured interviews with 35 Gusii people in Kenya about how they responded to various symptoms associated with malaria. In addition to using a grounded theory approach to develop the theme codes, Nyamongo wanted to do statistical analysis of his data. Table 12.3 shows his codebook. (Nyamongo did all the interviewing in Gusii—a language spoken by about two million people in Kenya—and all the interviews were transcribed in Gusii, but he coded the transcripts using English themes and English-looking mnemonics.)

Notice the difference between Nyamongo's and Kurasaki's codebooks. In addition to some basic information about each respondent (in his columns 1-33), Nyamongo coded for 24 themes.

TABLE 12.4 Part of the Data Matrix from Nyamongo's Analysis of 35 Gusii Texts

Person	Age	Sex	Occupation	SES	...	CTRL1	...	CAUSE1	...	HELP1	...	WITCH	...
1	48	M	Retired worker	2		1		1		0		0	
2	58	M	Farmer	1		0		1		0		1	
3	68	M	Clan elder	1		1		1		0		1	
.	.	.	.	.		.		.		.		.	
.	.	.	.	.		.		.		.		.	
.	.	.	.	.		.		.		.		.	
33	54	F	Teacher	2		1		1		0		0	
34	57	F	Artisan	2		0		0		0		0	
35	26	F	Housewife	1		1		1		0		1	

Those 24 themes, however, were nominal variables. He coded occupation, for example, as one of eight possible types. Notice that he used words, not numbers, for those occupations and that one possible entry was "n.a." This is a common abbreviation used in research for "information not available."

The code SYM1, in column 75, stands for "symptom 1" and refers to whether or not an informant mentioned headache in his or her narrative as a symptom of malaria. Nyamongo coded for whether people mentioned any of 14 symptoms, and he added a 15th code, SYM15 (in column 81) for "other." When you break up a list of things into a series of yes/no, present/absent variables, like Nyamongo did with CAUSE and SYM, and so on, this turns nominal variables into a series of *dummy variables.* Thus, Nyamongo's codebook has a total of 88 theme *variables* (including all the dummy variables), even though he coded for just 24 *themes* (symptoms, treatments, etc.).

Table 12.4 shows a piece of the *data matrix* produced by Nyamongo's coding of the 35 narratives.

❖——————

Building Conceptual Models by Memoing

Once you have a set of themes coded in a set of texts, the next step is to identify how themes are linked to each other in a theoretical model (Miles and Huberman 1994:134-37).

Memoing is a widely used method for recording relations among themes. In memoing, you **continually write down your thoughts about what you're reading. These thoughts become information on which to develop theory. Memoing is taking field notes on observations about texts.**

Strauss and Corbin discuss three kinds of memos: *code notes, theory notes,* and *operational notes* (1990:18, 73-74, 109-29, 197-219). **Code notes describe the concepts that are being discovered in "the discovery of grounded theory." In theory notes, you try to summarize your ideas about what's going on in the text. Operational notes are about practical matters.**

Once a model starts to take shape, start shopping for negative cases—cases that don't fit the pattern. Suppose you comb through a set of narratives from women in the labor market. Some women say that they got upset with their last job and quit. You find that most of the women who did this have husbands who earn a pretty good living. Now you have a take-this-job-and-shove-it category. Is there a case in which a woman says, "You know, I'd be outta this crummy job in a minute if I didn't have two kids at home to take care of"? Don't wait for that case to come to you. Go looking for it.

Negative cases either disconfirm parts of a model or suggest new connections that need to be made. In either case, negative cases need to be accommodated when you present your results. Negative case analysis is discussed in detail by Becker et al. (1961:37-45), Strauss and Corbin (1990:108-109), Lincoln and Guba (1985:309-313), Dey (1993:226-33), and Miles and Huberman (1994:271).

Displaying Concepts and Models

So, how do you actually build those models and what do they really look like? Here's a step-by-step example.

———————❖

Kearney et al. (1995) interviewed 60 women who reported using crack cocaine an average of at least once weekly during pregnancy. The semistructured interviews lasted from one to three hours and covered childhood, relationships, life context, previous pregnancies, and actions during the current pregnancy related to drug use, prenatal care, and self-care. Kearney at al. coded and analyzed the transcripts as they went. As new topics emerged, investigators asked about the topics in subsequent interviews. In this way, they linked data collection and data analysis in one continuous effort.

Kearney et al. coded the data first for the general topics they used to guide the interviews. Later, they would use these codes to search for and retrieve examples of text related to various interview topics. Next, team members reread each transcript searching for examples of social psychological themes in the women's narratives. Each time they found an example, they asked: "What is this an example of?" The answers suggested substantive categories that were refined with each new transcript.

Kearney et al. (1995) looked at how substantive categories were related. They recorded their ideas about these interactions in the forms of memos and developed a preliminary model. With each subsequent transcript, they looked for negative cases and pieces of data that challenged their emerging model. They adjusted the model to include the full range of variation that emerged in the transcripts.

To begin with, Kearney et al. identified five major categories, which they called VALUE, HOPE, RISK, HARM REDUCTION, and STIGMA MANAGEMENT. (Capital letters are often used for code names in grounded theory research, just as in statistical research.) Women valued their pregnancy and the baby-to-be in relation to their own life priorities (VALUE); women expressed varying degrees of hope that their pregnancies would end well and that they could be good mothers (HOPE) and they were aware that cocaine use posed risks to their fetus but they perceived that risk differently (RISK). Women tried in various ways to minimize the risk to the fetus (HARM REDUCTION) and they used various stratagems to reduce social rejection and derision (STIGMA MANAGEMENT).

By the time they had coded 20 interviews, Kearney et al. realized that the categories HARM REDUCTION and STIGMA MANAGEMENT were components of a more fundamental category that they labeled EVADING HARM. After about 30 interviews had been coded, they identified and labeled an overarching psychological process they called SALVAGING SELF that incorporated all five of the major categories. By the time they'd done 40 interviews, Kearney et al. felt they had reached *theoretical saturation,* which means that they were **not discovering new categories or relations among categories.** Just to make sure, they conducted another 20 interviews and confirmed the saturation.

Figure 12.1 shows the graphic model that Kearney et al. produced to represent their understanding of how the process worked. Kearney et al. described in rich detail each of the major categories they discovered, but notice how each of the substantive themes in their model is succinctly defined by a quote from a respondent.

When the steps of the grounded theory approach are followed, models or theories are produced that are, indeed, *grounded* in the text. These models, however, are not the final product of the grounded theory approach. In their original formulation, Glaser and Strauss (1967) emphasized that the building of grounded theory models is a step in the research process. The next, of course, is to confirm the validity of a model by testing it on an independent sample of data. Kearney et al. checked the validity of their model by presenting it to knowledgeable respondents (pregnant drug users), to members of the project staff, and to health and social service professionals who were familiar with the population.

Using Exemplar Quotes

Beside displaying models, one of the most important methods in grounded theory text analysis is the presentation of **direct quotes from respondents that lead the reader to understand quickly what it took you months or years to figure out.** You choose segments of text—verbatim quotes from respondents—as exemplars of concepts and theories or as exemplars of exceptions to your theories (those superimportant negative cases).

This technique looks easy, but it's not. You have to choose the exemplars very carefully because your choices constitute your analysis, as far as the reader is concerned, and you have to avoid what Lofland (1971) called the two great sins of qualitative analysis to use the exemplar quote technique effectively.

The first sin, excessive analysis, involves the all-too-familiar practice of jargony writing and the avoidance of plain English to say plain things. If you analyze a batch of data and conclude that something simple is going on, don't be afraid to say so. There is absolutely nothing of scientific value to be gained from making straightforward things complicated.

> *If you analyze a batch of data and conclude that something simple is going on, don't be afraid to say so.*

Compare these two sentences:

(1) The more generations that people from various ethnic groups are in the U.S., the less likely they are to speak anything but English.

(2) Over an expanding number of generations, people of ethnic heritage in the U.S. become, probabilistically, less likely to adhere to their traditional linguistic symbol systems.

The formal term to describe the second sentence is "yucky."

The second sin consists of avoiding doing any analysis on your own—being so gun-shy of theory and jargon that you simply fill up your papers and books with lengthy quotes from people and offer no analysis at all. Data do not speak for themselves. You have to develop your ideas (your analysis) about what's going on, state those ideas

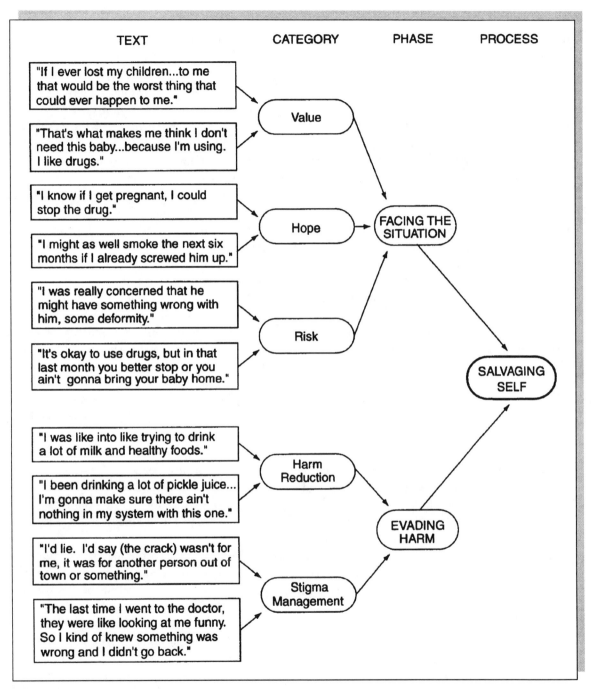

Figure 12.1 Relation of Themes/Categories in Kearney et al.'s (1995) Analysis of How Pregnant Drug Users Viewed Their Own Behavior

SOURCE: M. H. Kearney et al., "Salvaging Self—A Grounded Theory of Pregnancy on Crack Cocaine." *Nursing Research* 44:208-13. Copyright © 1995, Lippincott Williams & Wilkins. Reprinted with permission.

clearly, and illustrate them with selected quotes from your respondents.

Katherine Newman (1986), for example, collected life history material from 30 White, middle-class American women, ages 26-57, who had suffered severe losses of income as a result of divorce. Newman discovered and labeled two groups of women, according to her informants' own accounts of which period in their lives had the greatest effect on how they viewed the world. Women whose adolescent and early married years were in the 1960s and early 1970s seemed to be very different from "women of the Depression" who were born between 1930 and 1940.

These women had grown up in two very different socioeconomic and political environments; the differences in those environments had a profound effect on the shaping of people's subjective, interpretive, and symbolic views of the world, and, according to Newman's analysis, this accounted for differences in how her informants responded to the economic loss of divorce. Newman illustrated her analytic finding with quotes from her informants.

One woman said:

> I grew up in the '30s on a farm in Minnesota, but my family lost the farm during the Depression. Dad became a mechanic for the WPA, after that, but we moved around a lot. I remember that we never had any fresh fruits or vegetables during that whole time. At school there were soup lines and food handouts. . . . You know, I've been there. I've seen some hard times and it wasn't pleasant. Sometimes when I get low on money now, I get very nervous remembering those times.

By contrast, "women of the '60s" felt the economic loss of divorce but tended to stress the value of having to be more self-reliant, and the importance of friends, education, and personal autonomy over dependence on material things.

Newman illustrated this sentiment with quotes like the following:

> Money destroyed my marriage. All my husband wanted was to accumulate more real estate. We had no emotional relationship. Everything was bent toward things. Money to me now is this ugly thing.

Newman found differences in the way women in the two age cohorts dealt with kin support after divorce, the way they related to men in general, and a number of other things that emerged as patterns in her data. For each observation of a patterned difference in response to life after divorce, Newman used selected quotes from her informants to make the point.

Here's another example, from the study I did with Ashton-Vouyoucalos (1976) on Greek labor migrants. Everyone in the population we were studying had spent five years or more in (the former) West Germany and had returned to Greece to reestablish their lives. We were interested in how these returned migrants felt about the Greece they returned to, compared with the Germany they left.

Before doing a survey, however, we collected life histories from 15 persons, selected because of their range of experiences. Those 15 returned migrants were certainly no random sample, but the consistency of their volunteered observations of differences between the two cultures was striking. Once we noticed the pattern emerging, we laid out the data in tabular form, as shown in Table 12.5. The survey instrument that we eventually built reflected the concerns of our informants.

In reporting our findings, Ashton-Vouyoucalos and I referred to the summary table and illustrated each component with selected quotes from our informants. The issue of gossip, for example (under "negative aspects of Greece" in Table 12.5), was addressed by Despina, a 28-year-old woman

TABLE 12.5 Summary of Repatriates' Ambivalent Statements about Greece

Negative Aspects of Greece

Economic

(1) Wages are low.
(2) Few jobs are available, especially for persons with specialized skills.
(3) Working conditions are poor.
(4) Inflation is high, especially in the prices of imported goods.

Sociocultural

(1) People in general (but especially public servants) are abrupt and rude.
(2) The roads are covered with rubbish.
(3) Everyone, even friends and relatives, gossips about each other and tries to keep each other down.
(4) People of the opposite sex cannot interact easily and comfortably.

Political

(1) The government is insecure and might collapse with ensuing chaos or a return to dictatorship.
(2) Fear of actual war with Turkey creates a climate of insecurity.

Negative Aspects of Germany

Economic

(1) Economic opportunities are limited because a foreigner cannot easily open up a private business.
(2) People are reluctant to rent good housing at decent prices to migrant workers.

Sociocultural

(1) One feels in exile from one's home and kin.
(2) Life is limited to house and factory.
(3) The weather seems bitterly cold and this furthers the sense of isolation.
(4) Migrants are viewed as second-class citizens.
(5) Children may be left behind in Greece, to the sometimes inadequate care of grandparents.
(6) Lack of fluency in German puts Greek workers at a disadvantage.
(7) Parents must eventually choose between sending their children to German schools (where they will grow away from their parents) or to inadequate Greek schools in German cities.
(8) Factory routines are rigid, monotonous, and inhuman and sometimes the machinery is dangerous.

Political

(1) Migrants have no political voice in Germany or in their home country while they are abroad.

SOURCE: H. R. Bernard and S. Ashton-Vouyoucalos, "Return Migration to Greece." *Journal of the Steward Anthropological Society* 8:31-51, 1976. Table reproduced with permission from the *Journal of the Steward Anthropological Society.*

from Thrace. Despina was happy to be back in Greece, but she said:

Look, here you have a friend you visit. Sooner or later you'll wear or do something she doesn't like. We have this habit of gossiping. She'll gossip behind your back. Even if it's your sister. In Germany, they don't have that, at least. Not about what you wear or what you eat. Nothing like that. That's what I liked.

> **Box 12.1**
> **Content Analysis Doesn't Have to Be Complicated to Be Effective**
>
> Maxine Margolis (1984) did ethnohistorical research on the changing images of women in the United States. She used the *Ladies Home Journal*, from 1889 to 1980, as an archival database, and asked a simple question: Do ads in the *Ladies Home Journal* for household products show homemakers or servants using those products (Margolis, personal communication)?
>
> From historical data, Margolis knew that the large pool of cheap servant labor in U.S. cities—labor that had been driven there by the Industrial Revolution—was in decline by about 1900. The readers of the *Ladies Home Journal* in those days were middle-class women who were accustomed to employing household servants. Margolis's counts showed clearly the transformation of the middle-class homemaker from an employer of servants to a direct user of household products.
>
> Margolis took a random sample of her database (two years per decade of the magazine, and two months per year, for a total of 36 magazines), but she did not have to devise a complex tagging scheme. She simply looked for the presence or absence of a single, major message. It is very unlikely that Margolis could have made a mistake in coding the ads she examined. Servants are either portrayed in the ad or they aren't. So, by defining a nominal variable, and one that is easily recognized, Margolis was able to do a content analysis that added an interesting dimension to her historical ethnographic work on changing images of middle-class urban women.

By the way, the translation of Despina's comment has been doctored to make it sound a bit more seamless than it did in the original. I've seen thousands of really interesting quotes in ethnographic reports, and common sense says that most of them were fixed up a bit. I don't see anything wrong with this. In fact, I'm grateful to writers who do it. Unexpurgated speech is terrible to read. It's full of false starts, run-ons, fragments, pauses, filler syllables (like "uh" and "y'know"), and whole sentences whose sole purpose is to give speakers a second or two while they think of what to say next. If you don't edit that stuff, you'll bore your readers to death.

There is a case to be made for *recording* people's statements verbatim, but that's different from *reporting* those statements. Obviously, if you are doing linguistic or narrative analysis, you need to record *and* report verbatim material.

CONTENT ANALYSIS

While grounded theory is concerned with the *discovery of hypotheses* from texts, **content analysis** is concerned with *testing hypotheses,* usually, but not always, quantitatively. This requires

(1) creating a set of codes;
(2) applying those codes systematically to a set of texts;
(3) testing the reliability of coders when more than one applies the codes to a set of texts;

(4) creating a unit-of-analysis-by-variable matrix from the texts and codes; and

(5) analyzing that matrix statistically with methods like those laid out in Chapters 14, 15, and 16 (see Box 12.1).

The "texts" don't have to be written. Cowan and O'Brien (1990) had some ideas about the roles of men and women in slasher films. They wanted to know, for example, whether men or women were more likely to be survivors, and what other personal characteristics accounted for those who got axed and those who lived. The corpus of texts in this case was 56 slasher movies.

These movies contained a total of 474 victims, who were coded for gender and survival. Conventional wisdom about slasher films, of course, holds that victims are mostly women and slashers are mostly men. While slashers in these films were, in fact, mostly men, it turned out that victims were equally likely to be male or female. Surviving as a female slasher victim, however, was strongly associated with the absence of sexual behavior and with being less physically attractive than nonsurviving females. The male nonsurvivors were cynical, egotistical, and dictatorial. Cowan and O'Brien conclude that, in slasher films, sexually pure women survive and that "unmitigated masculinity" ends in death (1990:195).

The methodological issues associated with content analysis are all evident here. Does the sample of 56 films used by Cowan and O'Brien justify generalizing to slasher films in general? Did the coders who worked on the project make correct judgments in deciding things like the physical attractiveness of female victims or the personality and behavioral characteristics of the male victims? These two issues in particular, sampling and coding, are at the heart of content analysis.

Sampling in Content Analysis

There are two components to sampling in content analysis. The first is identifying the *corpus* of texts; the second is identifying the units of analysis *within* the texts. If you collect 40 or 50 life histories, then you naturally analyze the whole corpus. But when the units of data run into the hundreds or even thousands—like all television commercials that ran during prime time in August 1997, all front-page stories of the *New York Times* from 1887 to 1996, all campaign speeches by Bill Clinton and Bob Dole during the 1996 presidential campaign—then a representative sample of records must be made.

Gilly (1988) did a cross-cultural study of gender roles in advertising. She videotaped a sample of 12 hours of programming in Los Angeles (U.S.), Monterrey (Mexico), and Brisbane (Australia), from 8 a.m. to 4 p.m. on Tuesday and from 7 p.m. to 11 p.m. on Wednesday. To control for seasonal variation between the hemispheres, the U.S. and Mexico samples were taken in September 1984, while the Australia sample was taken in February 1985. There were 617 commercials: 275 from the U.S., 204 from Mexico, and 138 from Australia.

Because of her research question, Gilly used only adult men and women who were on camera for at least three seconds or who had at least one line of dialogue. There were 169 women and 132 men in the U.S. ads; 120 women and 102 men in the Mexican ads; and 52 women and 49 men in the Australian ads.

Waitzkin and Britt (1993:1121) did an interpretive analysis of 50 encounters between patients and doctors by randomly selecting texts from 336 audiotaped encounters. Nonquantitative text analysis is often based on purposive sampling. Trost (1986) thought the relationship between teenagers and their families might be affected by five different dichotomous variables. To test this idea, he intentionally selected five cases from each of the 32 possible combinations of the five variables and conducted 160 interviews.

Nonquantitative studies in content analysis may also be based on extreme or deviant cases, cases that illustrate maximum variety on variables, cases that are somehow typical of a phenomenon, or cases that confirm or disconfirm a hypothesis. Even a single case may be enough to display something of substantive importance, but Morse (1994) suggests using at least six participants in studies where you're trying to understand the essence of experience and carrying out 30 to 50 interviews for ethnographies and grounded theory studies.

Once a sample of texts is established, the next step is to identify the basic, nonoverlapping units of analysis. This is called *unitizing* (Krippendorf 1980) or *segmenting* (Tesch 1990). The units may be entire texts (books, interviews, responses to an open-ended question on a survey) or segments (words, word-senses, sentences, themes, paragraphs). If you want to compare across texts—to see *whether or not certain themes occur*—the whole text (representing a respondent or an organization) is the appropriate unit of analysis.

When the idea is to compare the *number of times a theme occurs* across a set of texts, then you need to break the text down into smaller chunks—what Kortendick (1996) calls *context units*—each of which reflects a theme.

Coding in Content Analysis

With a set of texts in hand, the next steps are to develop a codebook and actually code the text. Up to this point, this is what's done in grounded theory analysis.

❖

Consider Elizabeth Hirschman's (1987) work on how people sell themselves to one another in personal ads. From her reading of literature on the theory of resources, Hirschman thought that she would find 10 kinds of resources in personal ads: love, physical characteristics, educational status, intellectual status, occupational status, entertainment services (nonsexual), money status, demographic information (age, marital status, residence), ethnic characteristics, and personality info (not including sexual or emotional characteristics).

Hirschman formulated and tested specific hypotheses about which resources men and women would offer and seek in personal ads. She selected 20 test ads at random from the *New York Magazine* and *The Washingtonian* and checked that the 10 kinds of resources were, in fact, observable in the ads. Sexual traits and services were less than 1% of all resources coded. This was 1983-84, but even then, ads with explicit references to sexual traits and services were more common in other periodicals than in *The Washingtonian* and *New York Magazine*.

Hirschman next gave 10 men and 11 women the list of resource categories and a list of 100 actual resources ("young," "attractive," "fun loving," "divorced," "32-year-old," etc.) gleaned from the 20 test ads. She asked the 21 respondents to match the 100 resources with the resource category that seemed most appropriate. This exercise demonstrated that the resource items were *exhaustive* and *mutually exclusive*: **No resource items were left over, and all of them could be categorized into only 1 of the 10 resource categories.**

When she was confident her codebook worked, Hirschman tested her hypotheses. She sampled approximately 100 female-placed ads

TABLE 12.6 Measuring Simple Agreement between Two Coders on a Single Theme

Coders	Units of Analysis (documents/observations)									
	1	2	3	4	5	6	7	8	9	10
Coder 1	0	1	0	0	0	0	0	0	1	0
Coder 2	0	1	1	0	0	1	0	1	0	0

and 100 male-placed ads from each magazine—a total of 400 ads. A male and a female coder, working independently (and unaware of the hypotheses of the study), coded 3,782 resource items taken from the 400 ads as belonging to 1 of the 10 resource categories. The coding took three weeks. This is not easy work.

Hirschman was concerned with *intercoder reliability*—that is, making sure that coders saw the same thing when they coded those ads. She gave the data to a third coder, who identified discrepancies between the first two coders. Of 3,782 resource items coded, there were discrepancies (theme contrasts) on 636 (16.8%) and one of the coders failed to code 480 items (12.7%). Hirschman resolved the theme contrasts herself. She checked the omissions against the ads to see if the coder who had made an assignment had done so because the resource was, in fact, in the ad. This was always the case, so the 480 resource items omitted by one coder were counted as if they had been assigned to the ad by both coders.

The results? Men were more likely than women to *offer* monetary resources; women were more likely than men to *seek* monetary resources. Women were more likely than men to offer physical attractiveness. Washington, D.C., and New York City are supposed to be hip places, yet the way men and women wrote those personal ads in 1983-84 conforms utterly to traditional gender role expectations. It would be really interesting to repeat this study today with the same magazines.

Are the stereotypes of how men and women market themselves to one another today very different from what they were in 1983-84?

Intercoder Reliability

It is quite common in content analysis to have more than one coder mark up a set of texts. The idea is to see whether the constructs being investigated are shared—whether multiple coders reckon that the same constructs apply to the same chunks of text. There is a simple way to measure agreement between a pair of coders: You just line up their codes and calculate the percentage of agreement. This is shown in Table 12.6 for two coders who have coded 10 texts for a single theme, using a binary code, 1 or 0.

Both coders have a 0 for texts 1, 4, 5, 7, and 10, and both coders have a 1 for text 2. These two coders agree a total of 6 times out of 10: 5 times that the theme, whatever it is, does not appear in the texts and 1 time that the theme does appear. On 4 out of 10 texts, the coders disagree. On text 9, for example, coder 1 saw the theme in the text, but coder 2 didn't. Overall, these two coders agree 60% of the time.

The total observed agreement, though, is not a good measure of intercoder reliability because people can agree that a theme is present or absent

TABLE 12.7 Calculating Kappa for the Data in Table 12.6

		Coder 2		
		Yes	No	Coder 1 Total
Coder 1	Yes	1	1	2
	No	3	5	8
Coder 2 total		4	6	10

in a text just by chance. To adjust for this possibility, many researchers use a statistic called Cohen's kappa (Cohen 1960), or κ.

Cohen's Kappa

Kappa is a statistic that **measures how much better than chance the agreement is between a pair of coders on the presence or absence of binary (yes/no) themes in texts.** Here is the formula for kappa:

$$\kappa = \frac{\text{Observed} - \text{Chance}}{1 - \text{Chance}} \qquad \text{(Formula 12.1)}$$

When κ is zero, agreement is what might be expected by chance. When κ is negative, the observed level of agreement is less than what you'd expect by chance. And when κ is positive, the observed level of agreement is greater than what you'd expect by chance.

Table 12.7 shows the data in Table 12.6 rearranged so that we can calculate kappa.

We know the observed agreement: Coder 1 and coder 2 agreed that the theme was present in the text 1 time and they agreed that the theme was absent 5 times, for a total of 6, or 60% of the 10 texts. To find the probability that both coders would see the theme in these 10 texts just by chance, we multiply the proportions of the texts in which each coder saw the theme and multiply that product by the number of times they *could have* seen the theme, which in this case is 10. So,

the probability that the two coders *did see* the theme in these 10 texts just by chance is

$$(2/10) \times (4/10) \times 10 = 0.80$$

The probability that two *do not* see the theme in these 10 texts just by chance is

$$(8/10) \times (6/10) \times 10 = 4.80$$

Adding these together and dividing by 10—the number of times the two coder could have agreed by chance—gives

$$(0.80 + 4.80)/10 = 0.56$$

Now we can calculate kappa using Formula 12.1:

$$\kappa = \frac{.60 - .56}{1 - .56} = .0909$$

In other words, the 60% agreement between the two coders for the data in Table 12.6 is about 9% better than we'd expect by chance. Whether we're talking about agreement between two psychologists identifying aggressive behaviors in a child or agreement between two qualitative sociologists identifying the existence of a theme in a text, 9% better than chance is nothing to write home about.

Carey et al. (1996) asked 51 newly arrived Vietnamese refugees in New York State 32 open-ended questions about tuberculosis (TB). Topics included knowledge and beliefs about TB symptoms and causes, as well as beliefs about susceptibility to the disease, prognosis for those who contract the disease, skin-testing procedures, and prevention and treatment methods. The researchers read the responses and built a code list based simply on their own judgment. The initial code book contained 171 codes.

Then, Carey et al. broke the text into 1,632 segments. Each segment was the response by one of the 51 respondents to one of the 32 questions. Two coders independently coded 320 of the segments, marking as many of the themes as they thought appeared in each segment. Segments were counted as reliably coded if both coders used the same codes on it. If one coder left off a code or assigned an additional code, then this was considered a coding disagreement.

On their first try, only 144 (45%) out of 320 responses were coded the same by both coders. The coders discussed their disagreements and found that some of the 171 codes were redundant, some were vaguely defined, and some were not mutually exclusive. In some cases, coders simply had different understandings of what a code meant. When these problems were resolved, a new, streamlined codebook was issued, with only 152 themes, and the coders marked up the data again. This time they were in agreement 88.1% of the time.

To see if this apparently strong agreement was a fluke, Carey et al. tested intercoder reliability with kappa. The coders agreed perfectly ($\kappa = 1.0$) on 126 out of the 152 codes that they'd applied to the 320 sample segments. Only 17 (11.2%) of the codes had final κ values < 0.89. As senior investigator, Carey resolved any remaining intercoder discrepancies himself (Carey et al. 1996).

How much intercoder agreement is enough? As with so much in real life, the correct answer, I think, is: It depends. It depends, for example, on the level of inference required. If you have texts from single mothers about their efforts to juggle home and work, it's easier to code for the theme "works full time" than it is to code for the theme "enjoys her job."

It also depends on what's at stake. X-rays are texts, after all, and I'd like a pretty high level of intercoder agreement if a group of physicians were deciding on whether a particular anomaly meant my going in for surgery or not. In text analysis, the standards are still evolving. Many researchers are satisfied with kappa values of around .70, while others like to shoot for .80 and higher (Krippendorf 1980; Gottschalk and Bechtel 1993).

CROSS-CULTURAL CONTENT ANALYSIS: THE HUMAN RELATIONS AREA FILES

The most important archive of ethnographic materials is the Human Relations Area Files (HRAF), located at Yale University. HRAF is a million-page database, collected from more than 7,000 books and articles, on 350 cultural groups around the world.

The pages are coded by professionals at HRAF. The coders use the *Outline of Cultural Materials,* or OCM, a massive codebook that was developed by George Peter Murdock (1996) specifically to organize texts about cultures and societies of the world. The OCM codebook provides cross-cultural researchers from across the social sciences with a way to handle materials from very different sources about very different societies and a way to test hypotheses about human behavior across cultures.

> *HRAF turns the ethnographic literature into a database for content analysis and cross-cultural tests of hypotheses.*

There are 79 main codes in the OCM, in blocks of 10, from 10 to 88. Code 13, for example, covers geography. Within code 13, there are seven subthemes, labeled 131, 132, . . . 137, covering topics like climate, topography, flora and fauna, and so on. Code 40 is about machines, with codes 401-407 for specific things like household appliances and agricultural machinery. Other major codes are for themes like recreation, family, government, social problems, death, sex, religion, education, growth and development, and so on.

Every 10th page that a coder at HRAF handles is *recoded* independently by someone else, so that they maintain an intercoder reliability of 75%. This means that no more than 25% of the codes on any given page would be different if different coders at HRAF handled that page. Furthermore, the coders are 90% reliable in coding for the first two digits in the 79 major themes. That is, if a coder labels a sentence 765 (mourning), then 90% of the time other coders label the same sentence 765, or 764 (funerals) or 766 (deviant mortuary practices).

On average, each page contains five different codes. The archive that was produced up to 1992 (about 800,000 pages of materials) is available on microfiche. Since 1993, the archive has been produced electronically and it is now available on the Internet. About 100 university libraries around the world subscribe to the HRAF Internet files, and the file is growing at about 40,000 pages a year, including about 15,000 pages of material on a worldwide, 60-culture sample from the microfiche archive. You can search the archive for every reference to any of the 350 cultures that are covered or for every reference to particular OCM codes—things like 177 (culture contact), 266 (cannibalism), 294 (clothing manufacture), 579 (brawls, riots, and banditry), 757 (medical therapy), 854 (infant care), and so on.

HRAF turns the ethnographic literature into a database for content analysis and cross-cultural tests of hypotheses. The database is used by psychologists, political scientists, sociologists, and anthropologists alike.

Doing Cross-Cultural Text-Based Research

There are five steps in doing an HRAF study (Otterbein 1969):

(1) State a hypothesis that requires cross-cultural data.

(2) Draw a representative sample of the world's cultures from the 350 in the files.

(3) Find the appropriate OCM codes in the sample.

(4) Code the variables according to whatever conceptual scheme you've developed in forming your hypothesis.

(5) Run the appropriate statistical tests and see if your hypothesis is confirmed.

Sampling and Coding

Note that steps 3 and 4 refer to different kinds of codes. If an HRAF analyst codes a particular paragraph as 445, this means the paragraph is about service industries. The code 445 does not tell you which service industry is involved. You have to read the paragraph and convert the primary ethnographic material into usable codes for statistical analysis. You might use 1 = retail, 2 = entertainment, 3 = financial, and so on, depending on your particular research problem.

Suppose you have an idea that highly militaristic societies need to replace a lot of young people who are lost in wars and are therefore likely to outlaw abortion. You'd look through the HRAF archive for paragraphs marked 726, which refers to warfare, and for paragraphs marked 847, which refers to abortion and infanticide. Then you'd decide exactly how to code those paragraphs.

For militarism, for example, you might use a simple scale, like high/low, or you might find sufficient data to code involvement in warfare from 1 to 3 (*rare or never, sometimes, often*). You might code abortion as permitted/prohibited or you might find sufficient data to code its acceptability on a scale of 1 to 3 (*prohibited under all conditions, accepted under some conditions, permitted at the discretion of the mother*).

In the end, in content analysis as in all research, *you* have to make the measurements.

As researchers from across the social sciences have used the HRAF, they've read through the primary materials and actually coded variables that were germane to their particular studies. Reliable codes for perhaps 500 variables have been published for all the societies in the Murdock-White sample. Two journals, *Ethnology* and *Cross-Cultural Research,* print the variable codes used by cross-cultural researchers who publish papers in those journals.

Codes for 300 variables have been published on diskette by HRAF Press for a 60-society sample, and Barry and Schlegel (1980) published codes for several hundred variables on a 186-society sample developed by Murdock and White (1969). The *World Cultures Journal* has published most of the Barry and Schlegel codes on diskette.

(Most researchers today use the 186-society Murdock and White sample.)

All this facilitates the development and testing of hypotheses about cross-cultural regularities. Barber (1998), for example, used some of these published codes to test hypotheses about the social environmental correlates of homosexuality. The frequency of male homosexual activity was low in hunting-and-gathering societies and increased with the complexity of agricultural production. Reports of male homosexuality were also more likely for societies in which women had no control over their own sexuality (which corresponds with increased reliance on complex agriculture).

Other Problems

Besides sampling and coding, there are other problems to keep in mind when using the HRAF. You may not always find information where you expect it to be. David Levinson (1989) has done cross-cultural research on family violence. He asked the coders at HRAF how they would code family violence (which is not one of the categories in the OCM). They said that they would classify it under code 593 (family relations) or code 578 (in-group antagonisms).

Levinson scoured the files for references to those codes, and found quite a lot of useful information. He coded whether or not a society was reported to exhibit family violence, what kind of violence was reported (child abuse, abuse of the elderly, etc.), and how severe the violence was. Later, however, just by browsing through the files, Levinson noticed that wife beating was usually coded under 684, sex and marital offenses (personal communication).

Many societies, it turns out, only exhibit (or are reported to have) wife beating in cases of adultery or suspicion of adultery. The lesson for conducting a cross-cultural study is pretty clear: There is no substitute for reading the ethnographies and looking for new clues on how to code variables.

There is also no substitute for reliable data. When we use textual reports of field researchers, we depend on the skill of the person who made the original observations. He or she may have interviewed incompetent respondents or even people who just flat-out lied. Ethnographers may be biased in recording their data. These and other problems were discussed in a pioneering work by Raoul Naroll in 1962, and cross-cultural researchers have since done many studies on data quality control (see Rohner et al. 1973; Levinson 1978).

Divale (1976) tested the long-standing notion that female status increases with societal complexity. He used two independent measures of female status, compared against a measure of societal complexity, and found a relation between these two variables—in the opposite direction from what everyone expected. According to the data, the higher the complexity of the society, the *lower* the status of women.

Divale then controlled for the effects of data quality control variables. He limited his database to ethnographies written by investigators who had spent at least a year in the field and who spoke the native language fluently. When he controlled for these factors, the unexpected inverse relation between female status and societal complexity vanished! In these ethnographies, high female status is reported at all levels of societal complexity, while low status is reported primarily among less complex societies.

Despite some problems, research using HRAF continues to illuminate theoretically interesting problems. Carol Ember (1975, 1978) showed that 62% of hunter-gatherers are patrilocal, 16% are matrilocal, and 16% are bilocal (the rest show a variety of rare postmarital residence types). The tendency of hunter-gatherers to be bilocal was predicted by three factors: level of depopulation, size of community, and stability of rainfall in their area. Ember's theory for this is that fluctuating rainfall leads to fluctuations in the presence of fauna. If you have a protein resource problem, you have to keep the group size down. To do this, you have to have some flexibility in moving males and females around.

In other words, you have to go where the meat is and not insist on following marriage residence rules. Furthermore, in small communities, there is a statistically greater chance that at any moment there will be too few men or too few women available for marriage according to a rigid residence rule. If, for example, you insisted that women leave the group, then, in extreme cases, this might lead to a group becoming so small that it was no longer viable.

COMBINING GROUNDED THEORY AND CONTENT ANALYSIS APPROACHES

By now, you must be thinking: "Why not combine the power of inductive and deductive methods—grounded theory and content analysis in a single study?"

Actually, a lot of researchers do just that. Kurasaki's (1997) analysis of ethnic identity among third-generation Japanese Americans and Nyamongo's (1998) analysis of how Gusii in Kenya respond to and think about malaria are both examples of combining qualitative and quantitative approaches to the analysis of interview texts.

———————❖

Agar's (1979, 1980a, 1983) long-term work with young adult drug users shows clearly the evolution of methods from qualitative to quantitative—from grounded theory to content analysis. Agar began by transcribing three interviews with each of three informants. In the 1979 article, Agar describes his initial, intuitive analysis. He pulled all the statements that pertained to informants' interactions or assessments of other people. He then looked at the statements and sorted them into piles based on their content. He named each pile as a theme and assessed how the themes interacted.

Agar found that he had three piles. The first contained statements where the informant was expressing negative feelings for a person in a dominant social position. The second pile emphasized the other's knowledge or awareness. The third small cluster emphasized the importance of change or openness to new experiences.

From this intuitive analysis, Agar felt that his informants were telling him that those in authority were only interested in displaying their authority unless they had knowledge or awareness; knowledge or awareness comes through openness to new experience; most in authority are close to new experience or change.

In his second article (1980a), Agar systematically tested his intuitive understanding of the data. He used all the statements from a single informant and coded the statements for their role type (kin, friend/acquaintance, educational, occupational, or other), power (dominant, symmetrical, subordinate, or undetermined), and affect (positive, negative, ambivalent, or absent). Agar realized that he could analyze the covariations among role type, power, and affect; he could examine the distribution of the themes as they occur throughout the text; or he could simply count the number of statements in the different categories.

Agar restricted his analysis to check his earlier primary finding: that for a given informant, a particular negative sentiment is expressed toward those in dominant social roles. He found that out of 40 statements coded as dominant, 32 were coded negative and 8 were coded positive. For the 36 statements coded as symmetrical, 20 were coded positive and 16 negative, lending support to his original theory.

Next, Agar looked closely at the deviant cases—the eight statements where the informant expressed positive affect toward a person in a dominant role. These counterexamples suggested that the positive affect was expressed toward a dominant social other when the social other possessed, or was communicating to the informant, knowledge that the informant valued.

Finally, Agar (1983) developed a more systematic questionnaire to further test his hypothesis with an independent set of data for one of his informants. He selected 12 statements, 4 from each of the control, knowledge, and change themes identified earlier. Some statements came directly from the informant. Others he made up. Then he selected eight roles from the informant's transcript (father, mother, employer, teacher, friend, wife, co-worker, and teammate). Each role term was matched with each statement, and the informant was asked if the resulting statement was true, false, or irrelevant. (In no case did the informant report "irrelevant.") Agar then took the responses and compared them to what his hypotheses suggested.

The results both met and did not meet his expectations. On balance, there seemed to be general support for his hypothesis, but discrepancies between Agar's expectations and his results suggested areas for further research.

COMPUTERS AND TEXT ANALYSIS

The panorama with regard to text-processing software is changing quickly. Like early word processors and database managers, the first generation of text processors was designed to help us do what we already did. Word processors started out as simple text editors. Today's word processors let us do things that even million-dollar printing presses couldn't do 60 years ago—things like checking your grammar and spelling on the fly, using built-in voice-recognition software to create text from audiotape; the list goes on and on.

The first generation of text analysis programs made light work of chores like coding and finding the right quotes with which to illuminate a point in an article. Text processors today still do coding and retrieving, but more and more we find features that help with building conceptual models, linking concepts into networks, and producing numerical text-by-variable matrices.

The grounded theory approach, including iterative coding, analysis by constant memoing, and the production of on-screen maps of how codes are tied together, has been the inspiration for two of the most widely used software packages in text

analysis, NUD*IST and ATLAS/ti (for a detailed review of both programs, see Lewis 1998). In fact, 17 of the 24 text analysis packages reviewed by Weitzman and Miles (1995:316-25) have some provision for writing memos on the fly and retrieving them during analysis.

Eventually, text analysis software will have built-in modules for doing everything I've covered in this chapter—including a battery of tests for assessing intercoder reliability—as well as many other qualitative methods, like those covered in the next chapter: ethnographic decision modeling, Boolean analysis, taxonomies, and componential analysis.

Voice recognition software will also become part of the text analysis package. This will cut down the time it takes to produce a clean transcript of an hour-long interview from about eight hours to around two hours, and this will make all forms of text analysis—narrative analysis, discourse analysis, grounded theory analysis of interviews—more and more attractive. Text analysis is only just coming into its own. It's going to be very exciting.

KEY CONCEPTS

Text analysis, 438
Hermeneutics, or interpretive analysis,
   439-400
Biblical hermeneutics, 439
Exegesis, 439
Narrative analysis, 441
Discourse analysis, 442-443
Grounded theory, 443-456
Analytic categories, 443
Themes, 443
Exemplars, 444
Memoing, 444, 450
Iterative process, 444
Inductive coding, or "open" coding, 444
Deductive coding, 444
Exploratory phase, or discovery phase,
   of research, 444

In vivo coding, 444
Confirmatory phase of research, 444
Dummy variables, 450
Data matrix, 450
Code notes, 450
Theory notes, 450
Operational notes, 450
Theoretical saturation, 451-452
Content analysis, 456-461
Unitizing text, or segmenting text, 458
Context units in text, 458
Mutually exclusive codes, 458
Exhaustive codes, 458
Intercoder reliability, 459-460
Kappa, 460-461
Cross-cultural research, 461-464

SUMMARY

❖ Most of the recoverable information about human thought and behavior is naturally occurring text.
  ◆ Examples of texts include diaries, property transactions, recipes, correspondence, song lyrics, billboards, books, magazines, newspapers, artifacts, images, behaviors, and events.
  ◆ Many texts are available today in machine-readable form. Computer-aided text analysis is becoming an increasingly important component of modern social science research.

❖ Text analysis is not a single method. Some of the major traditions of text analysis include hermeneutics (interpretive analysis), narrative analysis, discourse analysis, the grounded theory approach, and content analysis.
  ◆ Hermeneutics originally referred to biblical exegesis, but has been extended in the social sciences to the study and interpretation of all kinds of texts.
  ◆ In narrative analysis, the goal is to discover regularities in how people tell stories or give speeches.
  ◆ Discourse analysis involves the close study of naturally occurring interactions, like physician-patient encounters.

❖ The grounded theory approach is a set of techniques for identifying categories and concepts that emerge from text and linking the concepts into substantive and formal theories.
  ◆ The heart of grounded theory is identifying themes in texts and coding the texts for the presence or absence of those themes. Coding turns free-flowing texts into a set of variables.
  ◆ Grounded theory research is mostly based on inductive or "open" coding. The idea is to become grounded in the data and to allow understanding to emerge from close study of the texts. Theme codes should be easy to remember and easy to use.
  ◆ Themes in grounded theory are linked to one another in a theoretical model. This is achieved through constant memoing, which involves continually writing down your thoughts about what you're reading. Memoing is taking "field notes" on observations about texts.
  ◆ The results of grounded theory research are presented through exemplars and in visual displays.

❖ While grounded theory is concerned with the discovery of hypotheses from texts, content analysis is concerned with testing hypotheses, usually quantitatively.
  ◆ The texts used in content analysis may be movies or television ads or other image-based data.
  ◆ Sampling is an important issue in content analysis since the idea is to generalize to a corpus of texts.
  ◆ It is common in content analysis to have more than one coder mark up a set of texts. The results are tested for intercoder reliability.
  ◆ Comparative research, using the Human Relations Area Files, is a content analysis on the corpus of ethnographic literature.

❖ Increasingly, social researchers are combining the inductive power of grounded theory and the deductive power of content analysis.

❖ Text-processing software is developing quickly. New technologies, like voice recognition software, are making text analysis an increasingly important component of social research.

EXERCISES

1. Ask six people to tell you a commonly known fairy tale: Cinderella, Little Red Riding Hood, The Three Little Pigs, and so on. (See Dundes [1982] for an example of how folklorists compare renditions of the same tale.) Tape-record and transcribe the six tellings. This will give you an appreciation for what transcription really takes, and it will give you six replications of a narrative cultural artifact. Describe differences in the six tellings.

   If possible, form a research group of five or more students so that the group winds up with 30 or more tellings of the same fairy tale. Working together, develop a codebook and analyze the data using a grounded theory approach or a content analysis approach. (It's easier on everyone if 15 students each collect and transcribe two tellings of the same fairy tale.)

2. Working together in a group of five or more students, collect at least 30 narratives from people about what it's like to have a cold. Ask each respondent to tell you about what causes colds; how they treat colds; how they prevent colds. Ask all respondents to tell you about the consequences of having a cold and how they feel when they have a cold. Working together, develop a codebook and analyze these data using a content analysis approach or a grounded theory approach.

3. Videotape a five-minute dialogue between any two people and analyze the dialogue using a discourse approach. A good way to generate the data is to give two people a hot political or other topic to discuss. The topic can be local (something going on at your school), national, or international. It just has to be something that both parties know about and want to talk about. In particular, analyze the turn-taking behavior of the two parties. Do they give each other equal time? Does one party interrupt more often than the other? Does one party use put-down language more than the other?

   Develop a codebook of themes for the dialogue and code the entire five minutes. Ask another student to code the video of the dialogue, using the codebook you've developed. Measure the difference between the two codings of the same dialogue.

4. Replicate one of the content analysis studies described in this chapter. For example, replicate Hirschman's (1987) study of personal ads, Cowan and O'Brien's (1990) study of slasher films, or Gilly's (1988) study of gender roles in television ads. Replicating one of these studies (or any published study based on classic content analysis) is an excellent way to learn about sampling and coding issues.

FURTHER READING

Hermeneutics and interpretive social science. There is an enormous literature on treating the observable world—behavior, objects, words, images—as texts that can be interpreted. The effort to interpret text goes by several names in the social sciences. Some key references include Geertz (1973, 1983) on interpretive studies, Dilthey (1989 [1883], 1996) on hermeneutics, and Becker and McCall (1990) on symbolic interactionist studies.

Literary text analysis. Segre (1988) is an introduction to the full range of methods in literary text analysis.

Narrative analysis. See Hanks (1989) for a review of studies of narrative, and see Riessman (1993) for an introduction to narrative analysis.

Discourse analysis. For an overview of discourse-centered methods, see Farnell and Graham (1998). On gender issues in discourse, see Tannen (1994) and Wodak (1997).

Grounded theory. The original formulation of the method (Glaser and Strauss 1967) is still useful, but later works are easier to read and more practically oriented. See Charmaz (1990), Lincoln and Guba (1985), Lonkila (1995), and Strauss (1987). Strauss and Corbin (1990) and Dey (1993) are especially useful. For some recent examples of grounded theory research, see Fox-Wolfgramm et al. (1998), Hunt and Ropo (1995), Irurita (1996), Kearney et al. (1994), Kearney et al. (1995), Sohier (1993), Wilson and Hutchinson (1996), Wright (1997), and Young (1998).

The mechanics of coding texts. Scholars have different styles when it comes to actually coding texts. See Agar (1996), Bogdan and Biklen (1992), Lincoln and Guba (1985), Lofland and Lofland (1995), Miles and Huberman (1994), Sandelowski (1995), Strauss and Corbin (1990), and Taylor and Bogdan (1998).

Intercoder reliability. There are many ways to calculate intercoder reliability. The earliest measure of intercoder agreement for two coders using binary (yes/no or 1/0) themes is Scott's pi (Scott 1955). Scott's measure was generalized by Krippendorf (1980:147-54) for multiple coders and for metric data.

The most widely used measure in the field today is Cohen's kappa (Cohen 1960). Fleiss (1971) and Light (1971) expanded kappa to handle multiple coders. Kappa can be used for binary data, when coders tag text for themes that are either present or absent. For data on continuous variables, the appropriate statistic is the ICC, or intraclass correlation coefficient (Robinson 1957; Fleiss 1981). See Elder et al. (1993:45) for a discussion of how to calculate the ICC. See Holsti (1969) for several other measures.

READINGS

Computers and text analysis. For pioneering work on the use of computers in text analysis, see Kelly and Stone (1975), Stone et al. (1966), and Zuell et al. (1989). For discussions of epistemological issues involved in using computers for the qualitative analysis of texts, see Kelle et al. (1995) and Fielding and Lee (1998). Reviews of software and reviews articles about text analysis are found in the *Cultural Anthropology Methods Journal* (now *Field Methods*), *Qualitative Sociology,* and *Computers and the Humanities.*

Computer programs. For a discussion of the theory behind Atlas/ti, see Muhr (1991). For a discussion of how NUD*IST was developed, see Richards and Richards (1991). Other popular programs include The Ethnograph and Code-A-Text. For current information on these programs, go to http://www.scolari.com, then click on "Software." A very good basic program for coding text and retrieving exemplars is EZ-Text. This program was developed by the Centers for Disease Control, an agency of the U.S. government, and is, therefore, free of charge. Go to http://www.cdc.gov/nchstp/hiv_aids/software/ez-text.htm.

13 | QUALITATIVE DATA ANALYSIS II
MODELS AND MATRICES

❖ INTRODUCTION

In Chapter 12, I focused on the analysis of texts—analyses that require identifying and organizing themes. In this chapter, I focus on an entirely different set of formal, qualitative analyses: ethnographic decision models; folk taxonomies, or taxonomic analysis; componential analysis; and Boolean analysis. What these methods have in common is that they are based on some principles of systematic logic. More about this as we move along. Let's get right to the first method: ethnographic decision modeling.

ETHNOGRAPHIC DECISION MODELS

Ethnographic decision models (EDMs) are **quali-tative, causal analyses that predict what kinds of choices people will make under specific circum-stances.** Ethnographic decision modeling has been used to study how fishermen decide where to fish (Gatewood 1983a) or what price to place on their products (Gladwin 1971; Quinn 1978), and how people decide on which treatment to use for an illness (Young 1980). Recently, I've used EDMs to study how people decide whether to recycle aluminum cans and whether to ask for paper or plastic bags at the grocery (Bernard et al. 1999).

Here's the idea behind decision models. Suppose I could ask a farmer some questions, none of which is, "What did you plant last year?" When I'm done, I make a prediction about what the farmer planted. *Then* I ask the farmer what crop he or she planted and I get it right most of the time. In fact, Christine Gladwin has modeled the planting and credit-seeking decisions of farm-ers in Malawi, Guatemala, the United States, Mexico, and Peru and typically predicts those decisions with 80%-90% accuracy (Gladwin 1976, 1980, 1983, 1989, and personal commu-nication).

> *Even if ethnographic decision models "simply" predict behavior, that would make them a very important part of any field worker's tool kit.*

As with all cognitive research methods, there is a question as to whether decision models simply predict behavior or whether they also reflect the way people think about things. The jury is still out on that one. But even if EDMs "simply" predict behavior, that would make them a very important part of any field worker's tool kit (see Box 13.1).

Prediction of a dependent variable (like plant-ing corn instead of some other crop) from some independent variables (like a farmer's financial condition, or family size) is the goal of statistical analysis, which is the subject of the next few chapters. But ethnographic decision modeling is based on asking questions, sorting out some logi-cal rules about how the questions have to be ordered, and laying out the order in a picture—like a *tree diagram*—or in writing. It is, in other words, entirely qualitative.

> ## Box 13.1
> ### Decision Making and Decision Models in the Social Sciences
>
> Ethnographic decision modeling was developed in anthropology, but the study of decision making and the statistical modeling of decisions are major areas of research across the social sciences.
>
> In health care, for example, Fortney et al. (1998) studied why people decide to seek or not to seek treatment for depression, Fenton et al. (1997) studied why schizophrenics take or don't take their prescribed medicines, and Salazar and de Moor (1995) studied factors affecting the decision by working women to get a mammogram.
>
> In counseling, Amundson (1995) developed a model of how people make career decisions. In organizational behavior, MacColl (1995) used existing literature to develop a model of Japanese corporate decision making and then tested his model on interview data from Japanese managers.

How to Build an EDM

Gladwin (1989) lays out the steps to building an EDM. The first thing you have to do is decide which decision you are studying and what the alternatives are in that decision. I'll use the decision "to make your 8 a.m. class or not" as an example.

A grand tour ethnographic question like "Tell me about why people go to class or skip 8 a.m. classes" will get you a lot of information about the alternatives and the reasons for the alternatives, especially from expert informants. The major alternatives are: Get up and go to class, get up and do something else, sleep in. The "get up and do something else" alternative consists of a list: Lounge around, watch old soaps on the tube, study for an exam later in the day, and so on.

To make your ethnographic knowledge about the decision more formal—that is, to build an EDM—track down Alex, a respondent who has an 8 a.m. class and ask, "Did you make your 8 a.m. class today?" When he answers, ask him, "Why [did] [didn't] you go to that class?" Suppose he says, "I went to class today because I *always* go to class unless I'm sick." Ask him: "Were you sick this morning?" Record his answer and draw a tree diagram (also called a *dendrogram*), like the one in Figure 13.1, to represent his decision.

Figure 13.1 accounts perfectly for Alex's decision. It has to; it contains nothing more than the information from the ethnographic interview with Alex.

Now go to your second respondent, Sheila, who says that yes, she went to her 8 a.m. class. Why? "It's a really tough class," she says. "If I miss one of those classes, I'll never catch up."

Every reason for your respondents' decisions becomes a question you can ask. Use what you learned from your interview with Alex and ask Sheila: "Do you *always* go to class?" Sheila says that she sometimes skips early classes if those classes are really easy and she needs to study for an exam in another class later in the day. Ask her: "Were you sick this morning?" If she says no, draw the diagram in Figure 13.2.

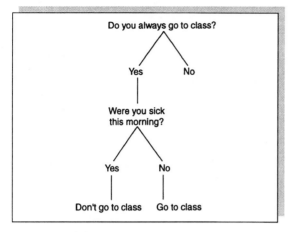

Figure 13.1 An Ethnographic Decision Model after Interviewing One Informant (Alex)

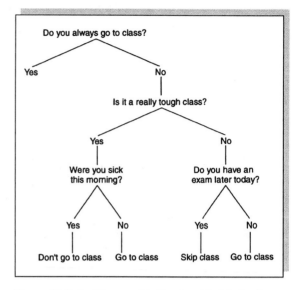

Figure 13.2 An Ethnographic Decision Model after Interviewing Two Informants (Alex and Sheila)

Your third respondent, Brad, says that no, he didn't go to class this morning; no, he doesn't always go to class; yes, he skips class when he's sick; no, he wasn't sick this morning; no, he didn't have an exam later in the day; no, his 8 a.m. class isn't tough; but he was out very late last night and just didn't feel like going to class this morning. Figure 13.3 combines all the information we have for Alex, Sheila, and Brad.

In fact, we don't know if Sheila was out late last night, and if she had been, whether that would have affected her decision to go to class early this morning. We can find out by going back and asking Sheila the new question. We could also go back and ask Alex if he had an exam later in the day and if he'd been out late last night.

But we won't. In practice, it is very difficult to go back to informants and ask them all the questions you accumulate from EDM interviews. Instead, the usual practice is to build a composite diagram, like the one in Figure 13.3, and push on. We also won't ask Brad what he *would* have done if he'd had a really tough 8:00 a.m. class and had been out late the night before. In building EDMs, we deal only with people's reports of their actual, most recent behavior.

Eventually, you'll stop getting new decisions, reasons, and constraints. In a homogeneous culture, this should not require more than about 20 informants. In a heterogeneous culture, you may have to interview a hundred informants before you stop getting lots of new information (Gladwin 1989:26). What's a homogeneous culture? That's an empirical question, but building a model for the decision on your campus to go to early classes will probably not require more than 20 informants.

Building an EDM that accounts for this particular decision at small, private schools and at gigantic state schools in the United States may take twice that many informants. As the student culture gets more complex (heterogeneous), the sample size needed to find a stable decision model goes up and up. Accounting for the decisions of students in New York City and Sussex, England, will require more interviews. Add Mexico City and the number may double again. Add Cameroon . . .

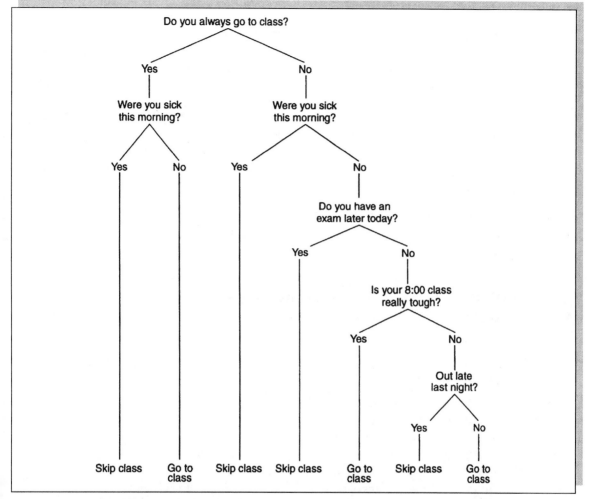

Figure 13.3 An Ethnographic Decision Model after Interviewing Three Informants (Alex, Sheila, and Brad)

Testing an EDM

Figure 13.3 may account for all the decisions of your next several informants, but eventually you'll run into an informant who says she doesn't always go to class, she wasn't sick this morning, she doesn't have a tough class at 8 a.m., she wasn't out late last night, and she still didn't make her early class today. Why? Because she just didn't feel like it.

Now, you can always build a model complex enough to account for every decision of every respondent. A model with 20 different sets of ordered reasons can, trivially, account for the decisions of 20 informants. But suppose you can model the decisions of 18 out of 20 informants with just a handful of ordered rules. That's 90% prediction. Is it worth building a complicated model, with a long list of rules, to account for the last 10%?

The whole idea of models is to make them parsimonious and to test them. You want to account for many outcomes using just a few rules. So, when you stop getting new reasons or constraints from EDM interviews, try to build a model that accounts for at least 80% of the decisions with the fewest number of rules. Then—and here's the important part—test your model against an entirely new group of informants.

> *The whole idea of models is to make them parsimonious and to test them. You want to account for many outcomes using just a few rules.*

The interview for the second group of informants is rather different. You ask them all the questions in your model (that is, you probe for all the reasons and constraints for the decision that your first group taught you), and then you guess what their decision was. In our example, you'd interview 20 or 30 new informants, all of whom have 8 a.m. classes, and you'd ask each one: Do you always go to class? Were you sick this morning? Were you out late last night? and so on, exhausting all the questions from your model. If your model works, you'll be able to *predict* the decisions of the informants in the second group from their answers to the model's questions.

REPRESENTING COMPLICATED MODELS WITH TABLES AND IF-THEN CHARTS

James Young's EDM: Decision Tables

James Young (1980) studied how Tarascan people in Pichátaro, Mexico, choose one of four possible ways to treat an illness: Use a home remedy, go to a native curer, see a *practicante* (a local, nonphysician practitioner of modern medicine), or go to a physician. From his ethnographic work, Young believed that the decision to use one or another of these treatments depended on four factors:

(1) how serious an illness was perceived to be (gravity);

(2) whether a home remedy for the illness was known;

(3) whether the informant had faith in the general efficacy of a mode of treatment for a particular illness; and

(4) the accessibility (in terms of cost and transportation) of a particular mode of treatment.

The choice situations emerged from structured interviews with eight men and seven women, who were asked:

> If you or another person in your household were ill, when—for what reasons—would you [consult] [use] _____ instead of [consulting] [using] _____?

Young used this question frame to elicit responses about all six possible pairs of treatment alternatives: home remedy vs. a physician, curer vs. home remedy, and so on. To check the validity of the statements made in the interviews, Young collected case histories of actual illnesses and their treatments from each of the 15 informants.

Next, Young completed interviews with 20 informants using a series of "what if . . ." questions to generate decisions, under various combinations of circumstances, regarding the selection of treatments for illnesses. For example, informants were asked:

TABLE 13.1 Young's (1980) Decision Table for How Pichatareños Choose an Initial Method of Treating an Illness

	Rule								
	1	2	3	4	5	6	7	8	9
Conditions									
1 Gravity	1	1	1	2	2	2	3	3	3
2 Known home remedy	Y	N	N	Y	N				
3 "Faith"		F	M	(F)	F	M	F	M	(M)
4 Accessibility								N	Y
				X					
		X			X		X		
			X			X		X	
									X

...atment Decisions in a Tarascan Town." Reproduced by permission of the American ...hnologist 7:106-31, 1980. Not for further reproduction.

...moderately serious, 3 = grave; 2 Known home remedy row: Y = yes, N = no; ...favors medical treatment; 4 Accessibility row: Y = money and transportation available, ...vailable.

...s a very grave —sure, they're left over. They ...efore, and they ...fited the illness ...you think they on the previous .... are going to do?

This vignette combines the condition of a serious illness (level 3 on gravity in Tables 13.1 and 13.2), with lack of accessibility (no money), and a known remedy that can be applied at home. Young used the three levels of gravity, two possible conditions of knowing a remedy (yes and no), and two possible conditions of accessibility (yes and no) in making up his vignettes, which meant that he had to make up eight of them. Each vignette was presented to each informant for a response. Tables 13.1 and 13.2 show the *decision tables* for Young's data.

From these qualitative data, collected in structured interviews, Young developed his decision model, for the initial choice of treatment. The model, containing nine decision rules, is shown in Table 13.1. Rule number 1, for example, says that if the illness is not serious and there is a known home remedy, then treat the illness yourself. Rule number 9 says that for grave illnesses there is an implicit understanding that physicians are better (hence the M in parentheses), so if there is money, then go to a physician.

Rule number 9 also says that for the few cases of very grave illnesses where physicians are commonly thought not to be effective, apply rule number 7 and go to a curer. The blank cells in Table 13.1, for example, in the Accessibility row, indicate irrelevant conditions. In rule number 1, for example, there is no question about accessibility for home remedies because they cost little or nothing and everyone has access to them.

TABLE 13.2 Young's (1980) Decision Table Showing How Pichatareños Choose a Method of Treating an Illness When Their First Choice Doesn't Work

					Rule						
	1	2	3	4	5	6	7	8	9	10	11
Conditions											
0 Preceding choice	ST	ST	ST	ST	C-P	C-P	C	P	Dr	Dr	Dr
1 Current gravity		1-2	3	3	1	2-3	2-3	2-3			
3 "Faith"	F	M	M	(M)							M
4 Accessibility			N	Y		Y	N	N		N	Y
Choices											
a Self-treatment					X						
b Curer	X							X	X	X	
c Practicante		X	X				X				
d Physician				X		X					X

SOURCE: J. C. Young, "A Model of Illness Treatment Decisions in a Tarascan Town." Reproduced by permission of the American Anthropological Association from *American Ethnologist* 7:106-31, 1980. Not for further reproduction.

NOTE: 0 Preceding choice row: ST = self-treatment, C = curer, P = *practicante*, Dr = physician; 1 Current gravity row: 1 = nonserious, 2 = moderately serious, 3 = grave; 3 "Faith" row: F = favors folk treatment, M = favors medical treatment; 4 Accessibility row: Y = money and transportation available, N = either money or transportation not currently available.

Sometimes, of course, the treatment selected for an illness doesn't work, and another decision has to be made. Table 13.2, with 11 decision rules, shows Young's analysis of this second stage of decision making. Young's entire two-stage model is based on his sense of emerging patterns in the data he collected about decision making. The question, of course, is: Does it work?

Young tested his model against 489 treatment choices gathered from 62 households over a six-month period. To make the test fair, none of the informants in the test was among those whose data were used in developing the model. Table 13.3 shows the results of the test. There were 157 cases covered by rule number 1 from Table 13.1 (first-stage decision), and in every single case informants did what the rule predicted. Informants did what rule number 6 of the first-stage decision model predicted 20 out of 29 times.

Overall, for the first stage, Young's decision rules predict about 94% of informants' reported behavior. After removing the cases covered by rules 1 and 4 (which account for half the cases in the data, but which could be dismissed as commonsense, routine decisions and not in need of any pretentious "analysis"), Young's model still predicts almost 83% of reported behavior. Even for the second stage, after first-stage decisions fail to result in a cure, and decisions get more complex and tougher to predict, the model predicts an impressive 84% of reported behavior.

Ryan and Martínez's EDM: IF-THEN Charts

Gery Ryan and Homero Martínez (1996) studied how mothers in San José, Mexico, decide what treatment to use when their children have diarrhea. They built an EDM on interviews with 17 mothers who had children under age five, asking each mother what she did the last time her

TABLE 13.3 Test Results of Young's (1980) Decision Model of How Pichatareños Choose a Treatment Method When They Are Ill

Table	Rule	Self-Treatment	Curer	Practicante	Physician	Total	Percentage Correct
	1	157				157	
	2		4			4	
	3			5		5	
	4	67			(1)	68	
	5		8			8	
	6	(2)		20	(7)	29	
	7		8			8	
	8		(2)	4	(2)	8	
	9			(2)	11	13	94
5	1		19			19	
	2		(1)	28	(6)	35	
	3		(3)	6		9	
	4			(2)	22	24	
	5	3	(1)			4	
	6	(2)	(2)	(1)	24	29	
	7	(1)		3	(2)	6	
	8		2	(1)		3	
	9	(1)	7			8	
	10					0	
	11				7	7	83

SOURCE: J. C. Young, "A Model of Illness Treatment Decisions in a Tarascan Town." Reproduced by permission of the American Anthropological Association from *American Ethnologist* 7:106-31, 1980. Not for further reproduction.

NOTE: Numbers in parentheses are the errors (cases not predicted) by the model. Overall prediction: 91%.

child had diarrhea. Then they asked why she had used this treatment or series of treatments.

Ryan and Martínez knew from living in San José that mothers in the village used seven different treatments: giving the child one or more of the following: (1) tea, (2) homemade rice water, (3) medication from the pharmacy (their informants told them, "if you can say it, you can buy it"), (4) a carbonated beverage, or (5) a commercially produced oral rehydration solution; (6) manipulating the child's body (massaging the child's body, pinching the child's back); and (7) taking the child to the doctor. Ryan and Martínez went systematically through the treatments, asking each mother why she had used X instead of A, X instead of B, X instead of C, and so on down through the list.

Mothers in San José listed the following factors for choosing one treatment modality over another:

Duration of the episode

Perceived cause (from worms, from *empacho*, from food, etc.)

Whether there was mucous in the stool

TABLE 13.4 Decision to Take the Child to the Doctor

Mother	Doctor	Days	Cause	Muc	Blood	Smell	Freq	Loose	Fever	Color	Mouth	Eyes	Vomit	Gland
1	N	2	C	Y	N	Y	Y	Y	Y	A	Y	Y	N	N
2	N	20	E	Y	N	Y	Y	Y	N	A	Y	Y	N	N
3	Y	8	T	N	N	Y	Y	Y	Y	N	Y	Y	N	N
4	Y	8	C	Y	N	Y	N	Y	Y	V			Y	Y
5	N	3	P	Y	N	Y	Y	Y	Y	A	Y	Y	N	Y
6	N	3	L	N	N	Y	Y	Y	N	B	Y	Y	N	N
7	Y	8	D	Y	N	Y	Y	Y	N	A	Y	Y	N	N
8	N	1	D	N	N	Y	Y	Y	N	A			N	N
9	N		C	Y	N	N	Y	Y	N	B	Y	Y	N	N
10	N	3	O	N	N	Y	Y	Y	N	A	Y	Y	N	N
11	N	2	C	N	N	N	N	N	N	A			N	N
12	N		C	N	N	Y	Y	Y	N	A	Y	Y	N	N
13	N	4	C	N	N	Y	N	N	N	A	Y	Y	N	N
14	Y	4	E	N	N	Y	Y	Y	Y	V	Y		N	N
15	Y	3	I	Y	Y	Y	Y	Y	Y	A	Y	Y	Y	N
16	N	2	C	Y	N	N	Y	Y	N	V	Y	Y	N	N
17	N	7	E	N	N	N	Y	Y	N	A	N	N	N	N

SOURCE: G. W. Ryan and H. Martínez. Data used with permission of the authors.

NOTE: Cause: C = food, D = teething, L = worms, T = dirt, E = *empacho*, P = parasites, I = indigestion, O = other; color: A = yellow, V = green, B = white, N = black.

Whether there was blood in the stool

Whether the stools smelled bad

Whether the stools were frequent or not

Whether the stools were loose or not

Whether the child had fever

Color of the stool

Whether the child had a dry mouth

Whether the child had dry eyes

Whether the child was vomiting

Whether the child had swollen glands

Table 13.4 shows the data from the 17 women in Ryan and Martínez's original sample and the decision to take the child to the doctor (the eighth treatment modality). Read the table like this: Mother no. 1 said that her child's last episode of diarrhea lasted two days and was caused by bad food. The stools contained mucous, but did not contain blood. The stools smelled bad, were frequent and loose. The child had a fever, the stools were yellow. The child had dry mouth and dry eyes, but was not vomiting and did not have swollen glands. The codes for cause and color are from Spanish (see the legend just below the table).

Table 13.4 makes it clear that mothers took their children to the doctor if the child had blood in the stool, had swollen glands, or was vomiting, or if the diarrhea had lasted more than seven days. None of the other factors played a part in the final decision to take the child to the doctor.

But remember: There were seven different treatments, and mothers would try several treatments in any given episode. Ryan and Martínez looked at the pattern of circumstances for all seven treatments and built a model that accounted for all the treatment decisions made by the 17 mothers. Their model had just six rules and three constraints.

Figure 13.4 shows their model as a series of IF-THEN statements. Notice the constraints: For a woman to choose a modern medication, she had to know about it and it had to be cheap and easy to obtain. The constraints to the rules are derived from ethnographic interviews. So was the observation that mothers distinguished between curative and palliative treatments—things that stopped the diarrhea and things that just made the child feel better during the episode. The model *postdicted* (accounted for) 89% of the treatments that the 17 mothers had reported.

Ryan and Martínez interviewed 20 more women. This time they asked the women all the questions inherent in the model. That is, they asked each of the 20 women: "In your child's last episode of diarrhea, did the stools have blood in them? Did the child have swollen glands? What caused the diarrhea?" and so on. The IF-THEN model in Figure 13.4 accounted for 84% of the *second* group's treatment decisions.

I expect to see EDMs applied to lots of important social behaviors in the near future. Gery Ryan, Steven Borgatti, and I have applied the method to study the decision to recycle or not recycle the aluminum beverage cans people have in their hands hundreds of times a year. This study, like all ethnographic decision studies, is based on asking people to think about the most recent behavioral event. In this case, the study was based on the question "Think about the last time you had an aluminum beverage can in your hands. . . . What did you do with it?"

FOLK TAXONOMIES (TAXONOMIC ANALYSIS)

There are about 6,000 languages spoken in the world today. Speakers of all those languages—English, Russian, Japanese, Navajo, Thai, Hausa, Inuit—name things in the natural world. Scholars have been interested for a very long time in how people organize their knowledge of the natural world (see Henderson and Harrington [1914] for a really spectacular early example).

In the 1950s, anthropologists began systematically to collect lists of local names for plants and animals and producing *folk taxonomies*—that is, **hierarchical, taxonomic graphs to represent how people organize their knowledge of plants and animals.** These ethnobotanical and ethnozoological taxonomies don't necessarily mirror scientific taxonomies, but then, the whole point of what became known as *ethnoscience* is to understand cultural knowledge on its own terms.

Scientific taxonomies for plants and animals recognize six primary levels of distinction (phylum, class, order, family, genus, and species) and lots of in-between levels, as well (infraorder, superorder, subclass, etc.), but folk taxonomies of plants and animals across the world are generally limited to five or, at most, six levels. Figure 13.5 (from D'Andrade 1995) shows a piece of the folk taxonomy of *creatures* for native speakers of English.

Covert Categories

There's a lot of information in Figure 13.5. First, note the six culturally appropriate levels of hierarchical distinction:

Rule 1

IF   child has blood stools OR
child has swollen glands OR
child is vomiting

THEN   take child to doctor.

Rule 2

IF   diarrhea is caused by *empacho*

THEN   give physical treatment.

Rule 3

IF   previous rules do not apply OR
there is no cure with the *empacho* treatment

THEN   give the highest-preferred curing treatment that meets constraints.

Rule 4

IF   previous treatment did not stop diarrhea

THEN   compare the two highest treatments of remaining options.

4.1

IF   one is a curing remedy AND
meets its constraints

THEN   give this treatment.

4.2

IF   both or neither are curing remedies AND
each meets its respective constraints

THEN   give the highest-ranked preference.

Rule 5

IF   the previous treatment did not stop the diarrhea AND
the episode is less than 1 week

THEN   repeat rule 4.

Rule 6

IF   the episode has lasted more than 1 week

THEN   take the child to a doctor.

Constraints

IF   you know how to make ORS (oral rehydration solution) AND
your child will drink ORS

THEN   give ORS.

IF   you know a medication that works for diarrhea AND
you have it in the house

THEN   give the pill or liquid medication.

IF   you know of a medication that works for diarrhea AND
it is cheap AND
it is easy to obtain

THEN   give the pill or liquid medication.

Figure 13.4 Ryan and Martínez's (1996) Decision Model as a Series of IF-THEN Rules

SOURCE: G. W. Ryan and H. Martínez, "Can We Predict What Mothers Do? Modeling Childhood Diarrhea in Rural Mexico," *Human Organization*, 55:47-57. Copyright © 1996, Society for Applied Anthropology. Reprinted with permission.

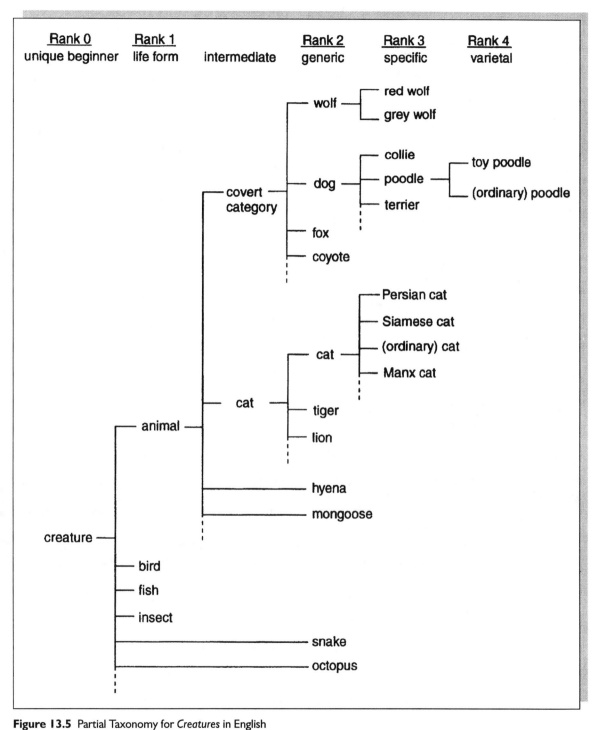

Figure 13.5 Partial Taxonomy for *Creatures* in English

SOURCE: R. G. D'Andrade, *The Development of Cognitive Anthropology*, p. 99. Copyright © 1995, Cambridge University Press. Reprinted by permission.

(1) There is a unique beginner, which is, by definition, a single term that names the cultural domain.

(2) This is followed by a small number of life forms (animals, fish, insects, etc.).

(3) Then there is an intermediate level, which can (but need not) include *covert categories.*

(4) Next comes the generic level, (5) the specific level, and finally, (6) the varietal level.

Next, note that the generic level of animals in English contains words for things that are at the species level in scientific nomenclature. Wolf, coyote, and dog, for example, are all members of the genus *Canis* (species *lupus, latrans,* and *familiaris,* respectively). The specific level in the folk taxonomy contains names for things that are at the subspecies level in scientific taxonomy.

Now note the covert category that remains unnamed (that's why it's called "covert," or hidden). It contains wolves, foxes, dogs, coyotes, and some other things (see the dashed line extending down from coyote, indicating that the covert category contains more than what's listed in the figure). If you press speakers of English about this, some will say that all those things are "canines" or "in the dog family." Foxes actually comprise the genus *Vulpes* and are not in the genus *Canis* at all. But since many speakers of English classify foxes and wolves in the category of "things in the dog family," a folk taxonomy of English ethnozoological nomenclature will respect that.

The intermediate category of "cat" is not covert. How can you tell? As D'Andrade says, you can say "Look at that cat!" if you're talking about a tiger, but it's weird to say "Look at that dog!" if you're pointing to a fox, so "cat" is a named intermediate category.

One more thing about Figure 13.5: Look at how D'Andrade has placed octopus and snake. The horizontal lines show that D'Andrade has classified these creatures as *nonaffiliated generics.* They might be classified as life forms, but as D'Andrade points out, there are many nonaffiliated generics in the ocean, including clams, lobsters, seahorses, jellyfish, and of course, octopi.

It was quickly recognized that folk taxonomies could be developed not only for ethnobotanical and ethnozoological knowledge but also for cultural knowledge of any *cultural domain.*

We Use Folk Taxonomies All the Time

Cultural domains are easy to recognize. Just ask people to list things (remember the free-listing technique from Chapter 7?), and if lots of people can respond easily, you've probably gotten hold of a culturally relevant domain. Some domains (like animals and plants) are very large and inclusive, while others (like children's games or brands of beer) are relatively small.

> *If lots of people can list things easily, you've probably gotten hold of a culturally relevant domain.*

Some lists (like the list of terms for members of a family, or the names of all the current Major League Baseball teams) are highly consensual; they are agreed on by all native speakers of a language. Other lists (carpenters' tools, kinds of fabric) represent highly specialized knowledge. Many lists (for example, the greatest left-handed baseball pitchers of the twentieth century) are a matter of heated debate.

We use folk taxonomies all the time to order our experience and guide our behavior. Remember that wayfinding experiment from Chapter 10 where Titus and Everett (1996) watched people find their way around a grocery store?

Try this yourself: Walk into any large super-market and study how the merchandise is assembled and laid out. There are frozen foods, meats, dairy products, canned vegetables, soaps and cleansers, household gadgets, and so on. Once you get the hang of it, take someone with you to the same supermarket—someone who has never shopped there before—and ask them to find peanut butter. As they make their way around the store, get them to talk about what they're doing. A typical response goes like this:

Well, let's see, milk and eggs are over there by that wall, and the meat's usually next to that, and the canned goods are kind of in the middle, with the soaps and paper towels and stuff on the other side, so we'll go right in here, in the middle. No, this is the soap aisle, so let's go over to the right. Sure, here's the coffee, so it's got to be on this aisle or the next, with cans of things like ravioli and stuff you can eat for lunch right out of the can.

It isn't very long before any competent member of U.S., Canadian, or British culture will find the peanut butter. Not everything is so clear. Shredded coconut and walnuts are often shelved with flour in the U.S. because they are used in baking, while other nuts—cashews and peanuts, for example—may be shelved somewhere else, like with the snacks. Matzohs (unleavened bread boards eaten primarily by Jews) and litchi nuts (a Chinese dessert food) are sometimes shelved in American supermarkets together under "ethnic foods," but may be shelved in separate "Jewish foods" and "Oriental foods" sections if local populations of those groups are sufficiently large.

Spradley (1979) reported that he once called the St. Paul, Minnesota, police department and said he needed to find the case number of a robbery that had been committed at his house. Two bicycles had been stolen from his garage in the middle of the night, while he was asleep. The police had investigated, but Spradley's insurance company needed the case number to process the claim. When Spradley told the police that he needed the case number for a "robbery," they quite naturally transferred his call to the robbery unit. But they couldn't help him because, according to their rules, robberies are acts committed with a gun, and where there is a face-to-face encounter between the criminal and the victim.

Spradley was transferred to burglary, but after another frustrating conversation he was transferred to the juvenile division. It seems that any theft of bicycles is handled by that division in St. Paul, and Spradley finally got his case number. Spradley observed that if he had understood the police culture, he "would have begun with a simple question: What part of the police department has records of bicycles stolen from a garage when no one is present?" (p. 142). If he'd known the native (police) taxonomy of crimes, he'd have asked the right question and gotten taken care of right away.

How to Make a Taxonomy: Lists and Frames

In building a folk taxonomy, many researchers combine the free-listing technique I described in Chapter 7 and the *frame elicitation* technique developed by Frake (1964), Metzger and Williams (1966), and D'Andrade et al. (1972). (See also Chapter 7 on structured interviewing.) Start with the frame:

What kinds of _____ are there?

where the blank is "cars," "trees," "saddles," "snow," "soldiers"—whatever you're interested in understanding. This frame is used again and again, until an informant says that the question is silly.

For example, suppose you asked a native speaker of American English, "What kinds of foods are there?" You might get a list like carbs, proteins, fruits, vegetables, snacks, and junk. (You'll probably get a slightly different set of labels if you ask a native speaker of British English this same question.)

Next, you ask: "What kinds of carbs [proteins] [fruits] [etc.] are there?" The answer for carbs might be bread, potatoes, rice, pasta, and so on.

So you extend the search: "What kinds of breads [potatoes] [rice] [etc.] are there?"

Finally, when you ask, "What kinds of spaghetti are there?" you might be told: "There are no kinds; they just are what they are." Of course, if you are dealing with a specialist in pasta culture, you might be told about the various sizes and shapes of spaghetti and the various blends of different kinds of wheat.

Once you have a list of lexical items in a domain, and once you've got the basic divisions down, the next step is to find out about overlaps. Some foods, like peanuts, get classified as snacks and as protein sources by different people—or even by the same person at different times.

The point is, there is no codified set of rules for dividing the domain of foods in American culture. The only way to map this is to construct folk taxonomies from information provided by a number of people and to get an idea of the range of variation and areas of consistency in how people think about this domain. You can learn about the possible overlaps in folk categories by using the substitution frames:

Is _____ a kind of _____ ?

Is _____ a part of _____ ?

Once you have a list of terms in a domain, and a list of categories, you can use this substitution frame for all possible combinations. Are marshmallows a kind of carb? A kind of protein? A kind of snack or junk food? This can get really tedious, but discovering *levels of contrast*—that *magenta* is a kind of *red*, that *cashews* are a kind of *nut*, that *alto* is a kind of *sax*, or that *ice cream* is a kind of *dessert*—just takes plain hard work. Unless you're a child, of course, in which case all this discovery is just plain fun.

A common way to display folk taxonomies is with a branching tree diagram. Figure 13.6 shows a tree diagram for part of a folk taxonomy of passenger cars. I elicited this taxonomy in Morgantown, West Virginia, from Jack in 1976.

Things to Look For in Folk Taxonomies

There are four important points to make about the taxonomy shown in Figure 13.6:

(1) *Interinformant variation* is common in folk taxonomies. That is, **different people may use different words to refer to the same category of things.** Sometimes, in fact, terms can be almost idiosyncratic. Jack distinguished among what he called "regular cars," "station wagons," and "vans." The term "regular cars" is not one seen in automobile ads, or heard from a salesperson on a car lot.

(2) Category labels do not necessarily have to be simple lexical items, but may be complex phrases. The category labeled "4-wheel drive" vehicles in Figure 13.6 was sometimes called "off-road vehicles" in 1976, or even "vehicles you can go camping in or tow a horse trailer with." Jack said that Jeep station wagons were both wagons and 4-wheel-drive cars you can go camping in. Remember, I elicited this taxonomy in 1976, long before the advertising industry came up with the concept of a "sport utility vehicle." In 1998, I asked some people to list "types of cars." The term "utes" showed up and I flat-out

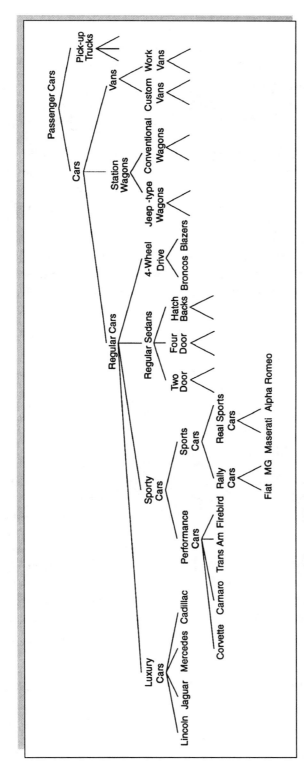

Figure 13.6 Part of Jack's Taxonomy of Cars and Trucks

didn't understand it. Of course, after expressing my ignorance, I learned that "utes" is short for "sport utility vehicles."

(3) There are those covert categories I mentioned—categories for which people have no label at all, or at least not one they find easily accessible. Some people insist that Corvettes, Camaros, Maseratis, and MGs are contained in a single category, which they find difficult to name (one informant suggested "sporty cars" as a label). Others, like Jack, separate "performance cars" from "sports cars" and even subdivide sports cars into "real sports cars" and "rally cars." Be on the lookout for unlabeled categories (that is, unlabeled nodes in a branching tree diagram) in any folk taxonomy.

(4) Even when there are consistent labels for categories, the categories may represent multiple dimensions, each of which has its own levels of contrast. For example, many native speakers of American English recognize a category of "foreign cars" that cuts across the taxonomy in Figure 13.6. There are foreign sports cars, foreign luxury cars, and foreign regular cars.

Folk taxonomies can be very, very complex. One way to get at the complexity is through a technique known as componential analysis. (Another is multidimensional scaling, which we'll get to in Chapter 16.)

COMPONENTIAL ANALYSIS

Componential analysis is a formal, qualitative technique for studying meaning. There are two objectives: (1) to specify the conditions under which a native speaker of a language will call something (like a plant, a kinsman, a car) by a particular term, and (2) to understand the cognitive process by which native speakers decide which of several possible terms they should apply to a particular thing.

The first objective is descriptive, but the second is a kind of *causal analysis* and is what the developers of the technique had in mind in the 1950s and 1960s (see Conklin 1955; Goodenough 1956; Frake 1962; Wallace 1962). Charles Frake, for example, described componential analysis as a step toward "the analysis of terminological systems in a way which reveals the conceptual principles that generate them" (1962:74).

Componential analysis is based on the principle of *distinctive features* in phonology, the branch of linguistics devoted to the study of the sounds of a language. To understand the principle, think about the difference in the sounds represented by P and B in English. Both are made by twisting your mouth into the same shape. This is a *feature* of the P and B sounds called "bilabial" or "two-lipped."

Another feature is that they are both "stops." That is, they are made by stopping the flow of air for an instant as it moves up from your lungs, and releasing the flow suddenly. An S sound, by contrast, also requires that you restrict the air flow, but not completely. You kind of let the air slip by in a hiss. The only difference between a P and a B sound is that the P is voiceless while the B is voiced—you vibrate your vocal cords while making a P.

If you add up all the phonological features of the words "bit" and "pit," the only feature that differentiates them is voicing on the first sound in each word. The "pitness" of a pit and the "bitness" of a bit are clearly not in the voicelessness

TABLE 13.5 A Componential Analysis of Four Things with Two Features

	Feature 1	Feature 2
Thing 1	+	+
Thing 2	+	−
Thing 3	−	+
Thing 4	−	−

or voicedness of the sounds P and B, but any native speaker of English will distinguish the two words, and their meanings, and can trace the difference between them to that little feature of voicing if you push them a bit.

There is a unique little bundle of features that defines each of the consonantal sounds in English. The only difference between the words "mad" and "bad" is that the bilabial sound M is nasal, and not a stop. These distinctive features carry meaning for native speakers of a language.

This principle can be adapted to the study of other domains of culture. Any two "things" (sounds, kinship terms, names of plants, names of animals, etc.) can be distinguished by exactly one binary feature that either occurs (+) or doesn't occur (−). Table 13.5 shows that with two features you can distinguish four things: Thing 1 can be ++, thing 2 can be +−, thing 3 can be −+, and thing 4 can be − −. Each bundle of features is different and defines each of the four things.

With three binary features, you can distinguish 8 things; with four, 16; with five, 32; and so on. (And yes, this is the same principle we used in Chapter 4 when we talked about factorial designs for experiments.)

When componential analysis was introduced into cultural anthropology, it was applied to the set of English kinship terms (Goodenough 1956), and it continues to be used for understanding kinship systems (Rushforth 1982; Kendall 1983; Hedican 1986). A "daughter" in English, for example, is a *consanguineal, female, descending-generation* person. So is a niece, but a niece is *through a sibling or a spouse.*

Table 13.6 shows the distinctive feature principle applied to a list of six kinds of horses. Stallions are male horses and foals are baby horses, but there is no column in Table 13.6 labeled "male" and no column labeled "juvenile." A parsimonious set of features for distinguishing among these kinds of horses does not require all that information. A stallion is a nonfemale, gendered (that is, not neuter), adult horse. Any horse that is not female and gendered and not an adult must be a colt.

Componential analysis can be applied to any domain of a language where you are interested in understanding the semantic features that make up the domain. Table 13.7 shows a componential analysis of seven cars, using three features elicited from Jack (he of the taxonomy shown in Figure 13.6). A Corvette is an expensive car, not very practical, and not foreign; a Mercedes is an expensive, practical, foreign car; and so on. Each of the seven cars is uniquely defined by the three features Jack mentioned.

There are two problems with componential analysis. First of all, it seems a bit shallow to say that a Corvette is an expensive, impractical, American car and nothing more, or that a Mercedes is an expensive, practical, foreign car and nothing more. You can get so caught up in finding the minimal analytic combination of features in this type of analysis that you forget you're interested in the meaning that people assign to differ-

TABLE 13.6 A Componential Analysis of Six Kinds of Horses

Name	Female	Neuter	Adult
Mare	+	−	+
Stallion	−	−	+
Gelding	−	+	+
Foal	−	+	−
Filly	+	−	−
Colt	−	−	−

SOURCE: Adapted from R. G. D'Andrade, *The Development of Cognitive Anthropology*, p. 31. Copyright © 1995, Cambridge University Press. Reprinted by permission.

TABLE 13.7 Minimal Componential Analysis for Seven Cars, According to Jack

Car	Expensive	Practical	Foreign
Corvette	+	−	−
Firebird	−	−	−
MG	−	−	+
Maserati	+	−	+
Mercedes	+	+	+
Jeep	−	+	−
Dodge van	+	+	−

ent objects in a domain. On the other hand, if you know the most parsimonious set of distinctive features for an item in a domain, you can predict how someone will label new things in the domain that they haven't encountered before.

The second problem with componential analysis is the same one we run into with all cognitive research methods: We have no idea if it reflects how people actually think. This problem was raised early in the development of cognitive studies by Robbins Burling (1964), who noted that, in a folk taxonomy of trees, he could not tell the essential cognitive difference between hemlock and spruce. "Is it gross size, type of needle, form of bark, or what?" If an ethnographer could not answer this question, Burling observed, then no componential analysis could claim to be "more than an exercise of the analyst's imagination" (p. 27).

Of course, this same critique could apply to any social research that "imputes the presence of something inside people" (like values and attitudes) and must be balanced with a positive perspective on what *can* be done (Hymes 1964:119).

In fact, what can be done is impressive, intuitively compelling analysis of the meanings that people attach to terms in their languages: Decision analysis allows us to predict which of several behavioral options people will take, under specific circumstances; taxonomic analysis lets us predict which class of things some new thing will be assigned to; componential analysis lets us predict what classification label will be assigned to some object. These methods produce effective knowledge that finds application in practical fields like health care delivery and advertising.

ANALYTIC INDUCTION AND BOOLEAN TESTS

Analytic induction is a formal, qualitative method for building up causal explanations of phenomena from a close examination of cases. The method involves the following steps:

(1) Define a phenomenon that requires explanation and propose an explanation.

(2) Examine a single case to see if the explanation fits.

(3) If it does, then examine another case. An explanation is accepted until a new case falsifies it.

When you find a case that doesn't fit, then, under the rules of analytic induction, the alternatives are to change the explanation to include the new case or redefine the phenomenon to exclude the nuisance case. Ideally, the process continues until a universal explanation for all known cases of a phenomenon is attained. (Explaining cases by declaring them all unique is not an option of the method. That's a convenient way out, but it doesn't get us anywhere.)

Charles Ragin (1987, 1994) formalized the logic of analytic induction, using an approach based on *Boolean analysis* (a branch of formal logic). Boolean variables are **dichotomous: true or false, present or absent,** and so on. This seems simple enough, but it's going to get very complicated, very quickly, so pay attention. Remember, there is no math in this. It's entirely qualitative.

Suppose you have four dichotomous variables, including three independent, or causal, variables, and one independent, or outcome, variable. With one dichotomous variable, *A,* there are 2 possibilities: *A* and not-*A*. With two dichotomous vari-

ables, *A* and *B,* there are 4 possibilities: *A* and *B, A* and not-*B,* not-*A* and *B,* and not-*A* and not-*B.* With three dichotomous variables, there are 8 possibilities; with four there are 16; and so on.

We've seen all this before: in the discussion about factorial designs of experiments (Chapter 4), in the discussion of how to use the number of subgroups to figure out sample size (Chapter 5), in the discussion of how to determine the number of focus groups you need in any particular study (Chapter 6), and in the discussion of factorial questionnaires (Chapter 7). The same principle is involved.

Thomas Schweizer (1991, 1996) applied this Boolean logic in his analysis of conflict and social status in Chen Village, China. In the 1950s, the village began to prosper with the application of technology to agriculture. The Great Leap Forward and the Cultural Revolution of the 1960s, however, reversed the village's fortunes. Chan et al. (1984) reconstructed the recent history of Chen Village, focusing on the political fortunes of key actors there.

Schweizer coded the Chan et al. text for whether each of 13 people in the village experienced an increase or a decrease in status after each of 14 events (such as the Great Leap Forward, land reform and collectivization, the collapse of Red Brigade leadership, and an event known locally as "the great betrothal dispute"). Schweizer wound up with a 13-actor-by-14-event matrix, where a 1 in a cell meant that an actor had success in a particular event and a 0 meant a loss of status in the village.

TABLE 13.8 Outcome of 17 Cases from Schweizer's (1996) Text Analysis

Success	External Ties	Proletarian Background	Urban Origin	No. of Cases
0	0	0	0	2
0	0	0	1	2
0	0	1	0	1
0	0	1	1	0
0	1	0	0	0
0	1	0	1	0
0	1	1	0	2
0	1	1	1	0
1	0	0	0	1
1	0	0	1	3
1	0	1	0	0
1	0	1	1	0
1	1	0	0	0
1	1	0	1	1
1	1	1	0	4
1	1	1	1	1

When Schweizer looked at this actor-by-event matrix he found that, over time, nine of the actors consistently won or consistently lost. That means that for nine of the villagers, there was just one outcome, a win or a loss. But four of the actors lost *sometimes* and won other times. For each of these four people, there could be a win or a loss, which means there are 8 possible outcomes.

In total, then, Schweizer needed to account for 17 unique combinations of actors and outcomes. He partitioned the 17 unique cases according to three binary independent variables (whether a villager was originally from a city or had been raised in the village, whether a villager had a proletarian or a nonproletarian background, and whether a villager had ties to people outside the village or not) and one dependent variable (whether the person was an overall success). There are a total of four variables. Table 13.8 shows the 16 outcomes that are possible with four binary variables, and the number of actual cases, out of 17, for each of those outcomes.

By setting up the logical possibilities in Table 13.8, Schweizer was able to test several hypotheses about success and failure in Chen Village. You can see, for example, that just two people who were originally from a city (people who had been sent to the village to work during the Cultural Revolution) turned out to be failures, but five people from the city turned out to be successful. People from an urban background have an advantage, but you can also see from Table 13.8 that it's not enough. To ensure success, you should come from a proletarian family OR have good external ties (which provide access to information and power at the regional level).

Failure is predicted even better: If an actor has failed in the Chen Village disputes, then he or she is of rural origin (comes from the village) OR comes from a nonproletarian family AND has no ties to authorities beyond the village. The Boolean formula for this statement is: Lack of success $\rightarrow$ nonurban v (nonproletarian and lack of ties).

Box 13.2
The Boolean Logic Used in Schweizer's Study of Chen Village

Here are the details of the logic of Schweizer's (1996) analysis. Three possible hypotheses can be derived from two binary variables: "if A then B," "if B then A," and "if A then and only then, B." In the first hypothesis, A is a sufficient condition to B and B is necessary to A. This hypothesis is falsified by all cases having A and not B. In the second hypothesis, B is a sufficient condition to A and A is necessary to B. The second hypothesis is falsified by all cases of B and not A. These two hypotheses are *implications* or *conditional statements.* The third hypothesis, an *equivalence* or *biconditional statement,* is the strongest: Whenever you see A, you also see B and vice versa; the absence of A implies the absence of B and vice versa. This hypothesis is falsified by all cases of A and not B, and all cases of B and not A.

Applied to the data from Chen Village, the strong hypothesis is falsified by many cases, but the sufficient condition hypotheses (urban origin implies success; proletarian background implies success; having external ties implies success) are true in 86% of the cases (this is an average of the three sufficient condition hypotheses). The necessary condition hypotheses (success implies urban origin; success implies proletarian background; success implies external ties) are true in just 73% of the cases (again, an average). (There are 7 disconfirming cases in 51 possible outcomes of the 12 *sufficient condition* possibilities: 4 possible outcomes for each of 3 independent variables and one dependent variable. There are 14 disconfirming cases in 51 possible outcomes of the 12 *necessary condition* possibilities.) To improve on this, Schweizer tested multivariate hypotheses, using the logical operators OR and AND.

The substantive conclusions from this analysis are intuitively appealing: In a communist revolutionary environment, it pays over the years to have friends in high places; people from urban areas are more likely to have those ties; and it helps to have been born into a politically correct (that is, proletarian) family.

Analytic induction helps identify the simplest model that logically explains the data. Like classic content analysis and cognitive mapping, human coders have to read and code the text into an event-by-variable matrix. The object of the analysis, however, is not to show the relations between all codes but to *find the minimal set of logical relations* among the concepts that accounts for a single dependent variable.

With three binary independent variables (as in Schweizer's data), two *logical operators* (OR and

AND), and three *implications* ("if A then B," "if B then A," and "if A, then and only then, B"), there are 30 multivariate hypotheses: 18 when all three independent variables are used, plus 12 when two variables are used. With more variables, the analysis becomes much more difficult. Fortunately, there are now computer programs, like QCA (Drass 1980) and ANTHROPAC (Borgatti 1992a, 1992b), that test all possible multivariate hypotheses and find the optimal solution (see Box 13.2).

These are not easy analyses to do, and some people I talk to about this kind of work wonder how qualitative analysis ever got so complicated. It just goes to show that qualitative doesn't mean wimpy.

KEY CONCEPTS

Ethnographic decision models, 474-483
Tree diagram, or dendrogram, 474, 475, 489
Decision table, 478-480
Postdiction vs. prediction, 483
Folk taxonomies, or taxonomic analysis, 483-490
Ethnoscience, 483
Covert categories, 483, 485-486
Nonaffiliated generics, 486
Cultural domain, 486
Frame elicitation, 487-488
Levels of contrast, 488

Interinformant variation, 488
Componential analysis, 490-492
Causal analysis, 490
Distinctive feature, 490
Analytic induction, 492-495
Boolean analysis, 492-495
Logical operators, 495
Implications, or conditional statements, 495
Equivalence, or biconditional statements, 495
Sufficient condition, 495
Necessary condition, 495

SUMMARY

- ❖ Ethnographic decision models are qualitative, causal analyses that predict what kinds of choices people will make under specific circumstances.
  - ◆ The first thing to do is decide which decision you are studying and what the alternatives are in that decision. Every alternative becomes a question you can ask the next respondent.
  - ◆ You can always build a model that accounts for the actual decisions of a group of people. The real test is whether the model works on a new group of people.
  - ◆ Complicated models can be represented with tables and IF-THEN charts.

- ❖ Folk taxonomies are hierarchical graphs that represent how people organize their knowledge of plants, animals, and other cultural domains. The object is to understand cultural knowledge on its own terms. We use folk taxonomies all the time to order our experience and guide our behavior.
  - ◆ Scientific taxonomies for plants and animals recognize six primary levels of distinction. Folk taxonomies of plants and animals across the world are generally limited to five or, at most, six levels.
  - ◆ The process of building a folk taxonomy involves getting a list of the items in a domain and then using the frame elicitation technique to sort out the hierarchical arrangement of the items in the domain.
  - ◆ Interinformant variation is common in folk taxonomies: Different people may use different words to refer to the same category of things. Some domains have covert categories, and category labels may be complex phrases, not just simple lexical items.

- ❖ Componential analysis is a formal technique for studying meaning. The objectives are to specify the conditions under which a native speaker of a language will call something by a particular term and to understand how people choose among alternative terms.
  - ◆ Componential analysis is based on the principle of distinctive features in phonology, the branch of linguistics devoted to the study of the sounds of a language. The principle was first extended to kinship terminology, but can be applied to many cultural domains.

- ❖ Analytic induction is a formal, qualitative method for building up causal explanations of phenomena from a close examination of cases. The method involves developing an explanation for something and examining cases until the explanation doesn't fit. As cases are added, the explanation becomes more inclusive.
  - ◆ The method of analytic induction can be formalized in terms of Boolean logic. Boolean variables are dichotomous: true or false, present or absent.
  - ◆ With three dichotomous variables, there are 8 possibilities; with four there are 16, and so on. Using logical operators, complex phenomena can often be explained with just a few well-chosen binary variables.

EXERCISES

1. This exercise can be done by individuals, but it's more productive if you get several students to work together. Replicate the study reported here on the decision to attend an early-morning class. Begin by asking students who have an early class if they went to the most recent one of those classes. Whatever their answer, ask for the reason: Why did they go or why did they not go? Keep asking people and continue to build a list of reasons until two people in a row give you *no new reasons*—that is, reasons you haven't heard before.

   Next, ask a sample of 40 students who have an early class if they went to the most recent of those classes. (If you have five students in your group, that's only eight interviews each.) Whatever their answer, ask them *all* the questions that can be based on the list of reasons you've accumulated for going or not going to an early-morning class. Use data *from 20 of the interviews* to build a decision model—one of those tree diagrams—and then use the data from the other 20 interviews to test the model.

2. Choose any cultural domain and build a folk taxonomy of that domain. Some interesting domains include things you can major in as an undergraduate; kinds of music; kinds of sports; tools you're likely to find in somebody's garage; things that students eat for lunch. Here again, the first thing to do is get several people to free list the items in the domain. Then, use the frame elicitation technique to find the taxonomic relations among the items in the domain.

3. Make a list of all the kinship terms in English. The basic set of terms is shared by most speakers of American English, but there are regional differences and ethnic differences in the content of this domain. Using a small set of distinctive features, do a componential analysis of this list of terms. Consult Romney and D'Andrade (1964) or D'Andrade (1995) for hints about the components of meaning in the list of English kin terms.

   Try to get lists of kin terms in several other languages. Some dialects of Spanish have a word (*concuñado, concuñada*) for "the nonblood relation between the two men who marry a pair of sisters or two women who marry a pair of brothers." There is no analog for this kinship term in English, where the men in this structural relation optionally refer to one another as a brother-in-law—if they use any kin term at all.

FURTHER READING

Ethnographic decision modeling. The cognitive psychology of decision making—that is, trying to understand the process of decision making inside people's heads—is a very important arena of research. For leads into this literature, consult Bell et al. (1988), Kahneman et al. (1982), Tversky (1972), and Tversky and Kahneman (1974). Use the *Social Sciences Citation Index* to move out from these classics to current research. Also see Zsambok and Klein (1997).

For more examples of ethnographic decision modeling, see Bauer and Wright (1996), on understanding the decision of Navajo women to breast-feed or to give formula to their babies; and Mathews and Hill (1990), on the choice of treatment for illness in villages in Costa Rica.

Folk taxonomies. The problem of how people think about sets of things (animals, people, emotions, concepts, movies, etc.) is of interest to scholars across the social sciences. See Bruner et al. (1956), Miller (1956), and Rosch (1975) for fundamental work on the concept of prototypes and how people manage to store and retrieve information about things in the natural world. See Atran (1990, 1996), Berlin (1992), Keil (1989), Raven et al. (1971), Rips (1975), and Rips et al. (1973) for work on cognition about plants and animals.

Componential analysis. For reviews of early work on componential analysis, as well as on folk taxonomies, see Sturtevant (1964) and Wallace (1962). The prototype descriptions of componential analysis for the study of kinship are Goodenough (1956) and Lounsbury (1956); Spradley (1987 [1972]) applied ethnoscience techniques, including componential analysis, to the study of "flops"—places to crash for the night—among tramps in Seattle. Hage (1987 [1972]) did a componential analysis of types of beer in Munich. And Taub and Leger (1984) used componential analysis to understand the meaning of a list of 22 terms used by young, gay men in the U.S. in the early 1980s—terms that refer to types of homosexual men and women or to types of people who associate with homosexual men and women.

Analytic induction and Boolean tests. Analytic induction was proposed as an alternative to statistical analysis by Znaniecki (1934) and is discussed by Bulmer (1979), Denzin (1978), Manning (1982), and Romme (1995). For applications of analytic induction to real research problems, see Wickham-Crowley (1991) on explaining the success of the Cuban and Nicaraguan revolutions and the failure of other late-twentieth-century revolutions in Latin America; Hicks et al. (1995) on the emergence of the social security state; and Williams and Farrell (1990) on explaining why certain cases of alleged child abuse in day care centers elicit a formal, legal response, while other cases do not.

14 | UNIVARIATE ANALYSIS

IN THIS CHAPTER:

❖ INTRODUCTION

The next three chapters are about quantitative data analysis. We begin here with descriptive and inferential univariate analysis and move on, in Chapters 15 and 16, to bivariate and multivariate analysis. Descriptive analysis involves understanding data through graphic displays, through tables, and through summary statistics.

Descriptive analysis is about the data you have in hand. Inferential analysis involves making statements—inferences—about the world beyond the data you have in hand. When you say that the average age of a group of telephone survey respondents is 44.6 years, that's a descriptive analytic statement. When you say that there is a 95% statistical probability that the true mean of the population from which you drew your sample of respondents is between 42.5 and 47.5 years, that's an inferential statement. You infer something about the rest of world from data in your sample.

Univariate analysis involves getting to know data intimately by examining variables precisely and in detail. Bivariate analysis involves looking at associations between pairs of variables and trying to understand how those associations work. Multivariate analysis involves, among other things, understanding the effects of more than one independent variable at a time on a dependent variable.

Suppose you're interested in the causes of variation in the income of women. You measure income as the dependent variable and some independent variables like age, marital status, employment history, number of children, ages of children, education, and so on. The first thing to do is examine carefully the data about all the variables. That's the univariate part of the analysis.

Next, you'd look at the association between each independent variable and the dependent variable—age and income, education and income, number of children and income, and so on. You'd also look at the association between pairs of independent variables—education and number of children, age and marital status, and so on. That's the bivariate part.

Finally, you'd look at the simultaneous effect of the independent variables on the dependent variables. That's the multivariate part.

You can see that there's no way to get to the multivariate part of analysis without having a real grip on the relations between pairs of variables. And there's no way to get to the bivariate part of the analysis without a solid understanding of what you've got in your data in the first place. So, on to univariate analysis.

MANAGING RAW DATA

The first thing to do, before you try any fancy statistical operations on your data, is to lay them out and get a feel for them. How many cases are there of people over age 70? What is the average number of children in each household? How many people in your sample have extreme views on some key attitude questions?

TABLE 14.1 30 Records from Bernard et al.'s (1999) Study of Green Attitudes

			Variable		
Respondent	GENDER	REDUCE	GUNGHO	AGE	EDUC
1	2	5	1	46	18
2	2	4	2	56	12
3	1	4	3	25	18
4	1	5	4	24	12
5	1	4	2	60	5
6	1	2	4	51	18
7	1	2	4	53	14
8	2	5	4	25	13
9	1	2	4	21	15
10	2	4	4	67	13
11	2	2	1	34	16
12	1	5	3	47	18
13	1	4	1	35	12
14	2	4	3	67	12
15	1	4	4	20	12
16	2	4	2	24	15
17	1	5	2	38	16
18	2	5	2	53	14
19	1	4	2	38	12
20	2	4	3	31	14
21	1	5	4	54	15
22	2	5	4	52	14
23	1	4	2	37	14
24	1	2	1	53	14
25	1	5	5	49	18
26	1	3	3	46	16
27	2	5	4	78	14
28	2	5	2	41	12
29	1	4	2	57	12
30	1	4	4	69	10

Table 14.1 shows the raw data for five variables and 30 respondents. These data come from a telephone survey that Gery Ryan, Stephen Borgatti, and I did of 609 adults in the United States (Bernard et al. 1999). Part of the survey was about people's attitudes toward environmental activism. (The 30 respondents in Table 14.1 are a random sample of the 609.)

The first variable, gender, is a nominal variable, or *qualitative variable.* The respondents were men and women over the age of 18, selected randomly from across the 48 continental states of the U.S. Men were coded as 1 (GENDER = male), and women were coded as 2 (GENDER = female). (For more on naming variables, see Box 14.1.)

Box 14.1
On Codes and Codebooks and Naming Variables

Naming variables is something of an art. Computer programs will handle long variable names, but I recommend keeping the variables down to 8-10 characters so that you don't wind up with big wide columns and gobs of white space in tables.

Variables are named in capital letters. Here are some variable names you might see in social research: AGE, INCOME, EDUC, HOUSETYPE, OWNCAR (does the respondent own a car?), LONGMIGR (how long has it been since the respondent immigrated here?), and PQOL (perceived quality of life).

Research projects typically have dozens, even hundreds, of variables. You can be as clever as you like with variable names; just be sure to include a good, verbose description of each variable in your codebook so that you'll know what all those clever names mean a year later. Here's an example:

PQOL = perceived quality of life. This was measured using an index consisting of the six items that follow. Each item is scored separately, but the items were tested and can be added to form an index. Since each item is scored from 1 to 5, the index of perceived quality of life can vary from 6 to 30 for any respondent.

Specify carefully the values that each variable can take. For example:

MARSTAT = marital status. 1 = married, 2 = divorced, 3 = separated, 4 = widowed, 5 = never married, 6 = unknown.

If you use an established index or scale, then name it and provide a citation to the source. If you adapt a published technique to meet your particular needs, be sure to mention that, too, in the codebook.

Always file a copy of any survey instrument with your codebook.

In statistics, qualitative description entails assigning numbers to classes of things. Those numbers, though—like 1 for male and 2 for female—are just substitute names for "male" and "female." They are not quantities. You can count the number of 1s and 2s, but you can't add up the numbers and take their average. The average of the 1s and 2s in the column for GENDER in Table 14.1 is 1.4, but that's no more helpful than knowing the average telephone number in New York City.

The second two variables are ordinal. They are responses, on a scale of 1 to 5, to two statements. Here are the two items from the survey:

Americans are going to have to drastically reduce their level of consumption over the next few years.

1. Strongly disagree
2. Disagree
3. Neutral
4. Agree
5. Strongly agree

Environmentalists wouldn't be so gung ho if it were their jobs that were threatened.

1. Strongly disagree
2. Disagree
3. Neutral
4. Agree
5. Strongly agree

These are items that Kempton et al. (1995) used in their study of environmental values in America. My colleagues and I wanted to see if we could replicate their results.

I've labeled the responses to the two items REDUCE and GUNGHO in Table 14.1. Notice that these two items are sort of opposites. The more you agree with REDUCE, the stronger your support for environmentalist issues is likely to be. But the more you agree with GUNGHO, the weaker your support for environmentalist issues is likely to be. If we want bigger numbers, like 4 and 5, always to stand for support of environmentalism and smaller numbers, like 1 and 2, always to stand for lack of support, then we have to transform the data for GUNGHO so that they run in the same direction as the data for REDUCE. We can easily do that in any statistics package.

This is a very important part of univariate analysis—getting the data into the computer in just the right form.

Variables 4 and 5, AGE (the respondent's age) and EDUC (the respondent's level of education), are interval. (They are really ratio variables, but recall from Chapter 2 that ratio variables are conventionally referred to as "interval.") For AGE, we simply asked respondents, "How old are you?" Here is the question from the survey that produced the data for EDUC:

What is the highest grade of school or year in college you yourself completed?

None	0
Elementary	01
Elementary	02
Elementary	03
Elementary	04
Elementary	05
Elementary	06
Elementary	07
Elementary	08
High school	09
High school	10
High school	11
High school	12
College-one year	13
College-two years	14
College-three years	15
College-four years	16
Some graduate school	17
Graduate/prof. degree	18

FREQUENCY DISTRIBUTIONS

Table 14.2a-e shows the raw data from Table 14.1 transformed into a set of *frequency distributions*. I used SYSTAT® to produce Table 14.2, but any program will do.

Using a Distribution Table

One thing to look for in a frequency distribution is variability. If a variable has no variability, then it is simply not of any further interest.

Looking carefully at the frequency distribution is your first line of defense against wasting a lot of time on variables that don't vary.

If everyone in this sample of respondents were the same gender, for instance, we wouldn't use GENDER in any further analysis. Looking care-

TABLE 14.2 Frequency Distribution for the Raw Data on the Five Variables in Table 14.1

a. Frequency Table of the Variable GENDER

Count	Cum. Count	Percentage	Cum. Percentage	Variable GENDER
18	18	60.0	60.0	Male
12	30	40.0	100.0	Female

b. Frequency Table of the Variable REDUCE

Count	Cum. Count	Percentage	Cum. Percentage	Variable REDUCE
5	5	16.7	16.7	2
1	6	3.3	20.0	3
13	19	43.3	63.3	4
11	30	36.7	100.0	5

c. Frequency Table of the Variable GUNGHO

Count	Cum. Count	Percentage	Cum. Percentage	Variable GUNGHO
4	4	13.3	13.3	1
9	13	30.0	43.3	2
5	18	16.7	60.0	3
11	29	36.7	96.7	4
1	30	3.3	100.0	5

d. Frequency Table of the Variable AGE

Count	Cum. Count	Percentage	Cum. Percentage	Variable AGE
1	1	3.3	3.3	20
1	2	3.3	6.7	21
2	4	6.7	13.3	24
2	6	6.7	20.0	25
1	7	3.3	23.3	31
1	8	3.3	26.7	34
1	9	3.3	30.0	35
1	10	3.3	33.3	37
2	12	6.7	40.0	38
1	13	3.3	43.3	41
2	15	6.7	50.0	46
1	16	3.3	53.3	47
1	17	3.3	56.7	49
1	18	3.3	60.0	51
1	19	3.3	63.3	52
3	22	10.0	73.3	53
1	23	3.3	76.7	54
1	24	3.3	80.0	56
1	25	3.3	83.3	57
1	26	3.3	86.7	60
2	28	6.7	93.3	67
1	29	3.3	96.7	69
1	30	3.3	100.0	78

TABLE 14.2 Continued

e. Frequency Table of the Variable EDUC

Count	Cum. Count	Percentage	Cum. Percentage	Variable EDUC
1	1	3.3	3.3	5
1	2	3.3	6.7	10
8	10	26.7	33.3	12
2	12	6.7	40.0	13
7	19	23.3	63.3	14
3	22	10.0	73.3	15
3	25	10.0	83.3	16
5	30	16.7	100.0	18

fully at the frequency distribution is your first line of defense against wasting a lot of time on variables that don't vary.

We see from Table 14.2a that 60% of the sample are men. Table 14.2d shows that age is pretty evenly distributed. Table 14.2e shows that two-thirds of the sample (20 out of 30) had more than a high school education and that 5 of the 30 had graduate degrees. Most people (24 out of 30) agreed or strongly agreed with the statement that Americans are going to have to reduce consumption drastically in the coming years (Table 14.2b).

People were pretty evenly split, though, on whether environmentalists would be so gung ho if their jobs were threatened (Table 14.2c): 13 people either disagreed or strongly disagreed with that sentiment, and 12 people either agreed or strongly agreed (5 were neutral).

Frequency distributions give you hints about how to collapse variables. With 609 respondents in the full survey, we had plenty of responses to all possible answers for the question about reducing consumption. But with a sample of just 30 responses, we didn't get anyone who said they strongly disagreed with the statement that Americans are going to have to drastically reduce their consumption in the coming years.

If all we had were these 30 cases, we'd want to create a three-category variable—*disagree, neutral,* and *agree*—by collapsing the data for RE-DUCE into (1) the 5 people who answered 2 (*disagree*); (2) the one person who answered 3 (*neutral*), and (3) the 24 people who answered 4 or 5 (*agree* and *strongly agree*). Notice that in collapsing this variable from five categories to three, we haven't changed the level of measurement. It's still an ordinal variable (for more on grouped data, see Box 14.2).

MEASURES OF CENTRAL TENDENCY

Once we have the data laid out and have a feel for what's in there, we can start describing the variables. The first thing to do is get some overall measure of the "typical" value for each variable. This is called a measure of *central tendency*.

Box 14.2
More about Grouped Data

It's not always obvious how to group data. In fact, it's often better not to. Look at Table 14.2e. Only two people in our sample of 30 had fewer than 12 years of education. We could conveniently group those two people into a category called "less than high school." There is a bulge of eight people who had 12 years of education (they completed high school), but then we see just two people who reported a year of college and seven people who reported two years of college. That bulge of seven respondents might be people who went to a community college. We might group those two sets of people into a category called "up to two years of college."

Those three people in Table 14.2e who reported four years of college form an obvious class ("finished college"), and so do the five people who reported having a graduate or professional degree that required more than four years of college. But what do we do with those three people who reported three years of college? We could lump them together with the three respondents who finished college, but we could also lump them with the nine people who reported one or two years of college.

The problem is, we don't have any iron-clad decision rule that tells us how to lump data into categories. We don't want to maintain a separate category of just three respondents (the people who reported three years of college), but we don't know if they "belong" (in some socially important sense) with those who had some college or with those who completed college.

I recommend not grouping interval-level data unless you really have to. No matter which decision you make about those three people who reported three years of college in Table 14.2e, you're turning an interval variable (years of education) into an ordinal variable (less than high school, high school, etc.). There are times when this might be a good idea, but trading interval-level for ordinal-level measurement means throwing away data. You need a really good reason to do that.

The three most widely used measures of central tendency are the *mode,* the *median,* and the *mean.* All these get packaged together in everyday speech as some kind of "average," but we have to be more precise in data analysis. Each measure of central tendency carries important information about the values of a variable.

Here are the definitions for each of these measures of central tendency:

(1) **The mode is the attribute of a variable that occurs most frequently.** The mode can be found for nominal, ordinal, and interval variables, but it is the only measure of central tendency available for nominal variables.

(2) **The median is the point in a distribution above and below which there is an equal number of scores in a distribution.** The median can be found for ordinal and interval variables.

(3) **The mean, or the average, is the sum of the individual scores in a distribution, divided by the number of scores.** The mean can be found for ordinal and interval variables.

Central Tendency: The Mode

The *mode* is the attribute of a variable that occurs most frequently. Technically, the mode is not calculated; it is observed. You find it by simply looking at the data and seeing which attribute of a variable occurs the most.

In Table 14.2d, we see that 3 out of 30 respondents said they were 53 years old, so 53 is the modal age. This doesn't tell us much, but in Table 14.2e we see that the modal value for education is 12 years (there are 8 out of 30 cases), and this does tell us something: Finishing high school is the most common level of education in our sample of 30 respondents.

All variables (nominal, ordinal, and interval) have modal values, but nominal variables can *only* have modal values. In Table 14.2a, for example, we see that there are 18 men (GENDER = 1) and 12 women (GENDER = 2). The mode, then, is male for this sample of 30. (The mode, by the way, was female for the full survey of 609 respondents. When you work with small samples, fluctuations of this magnitude are normal.)

Many distributions have more than one mode, and bimodal distributions are quite common. In a rural community that has experienced a lot of out-migration, for example, the age structure is likely to be bimodal: There are young people hanging around who aren't old enough to leave, and old people who can't find work in the city because of their age.

The age at onset of obsessive-compulsive disorder is bimodal: Very few people—probably less than 3%—*ever* experience obsessive-compulsive disorder, but the *probability* of developing it peaks at around 10 years of age and then again at around 21 (Geller et al. 1998).

Using the Mode

The mode is often said to be the weakest measure of central tendency, but it's very useful when you want to make a statement about a prominent qualitative attribute of a group. "More people profess to be Buddhist in this prefecture of Japan than profess any other religion" is such a statement.

The mode is also a good commonsense alternative to the sometimes unrealistic quality of the mean. Saying that "the modal family size is 4 people" makes a lot more sense than saying that the "average family size is 3.81 people"—even if both statements are true.

You'll often see the mode reported as a percentage: "In this survey, 60% of the respondents were men."

The mode can also be reported in terms of *ratios*. Of the 30 respondents in Table 14.1, 12 were women and 18 were men, so the modal value for the variable GENDER in Table 14.1 is male. The ratio of men to women among these respondents is $18/12 = 1.5$, while the ratio of women to men is $12/18 = .67$. Reporting that "there were 1.5 men for every woman in this survey" is the same as saying that "60% of the respondents were men." Reporting that "there were .67 women for every man in this survey" is the same as saying that "40% of the respondents were women."

Central Tendency: The Median

The *median* is the point in a distribution above and below which there is an equal number of scores in a distribution. It can be used with ranked or ordinal-level data and with interval- or ratio-level data. For an odd number of unique observations on a variable, the median score is $(N + 1)/2$, where N is the number of cases in a distribution.

Suppose we ask 9 people to tell us how many brothers and sisters they have and we get the following answers:

0   0   1   1   1   1   2   2   3

The median observation is 1 because it is the middle score—there are four scores on either side of it. ($(N + 1)/2 = 5$, and we see that the median is the fifth case in the series, once the data are arranged in order.

Often as not, of course, as with the data on those 30 respondents in the green survey, you'll have an *even number* of cases. Then the median is the average of $N/2$ and $N/2 + 1$, or the midpoint between the *two* middle observations. I asked 16 undergraduate students, "How long do you think you'll live?" Here are the responses:

70 73 75 75 79 80 80 83 85 86 86 87 87 90 95 96
              ▲ ▲

$N/2 = 8$ and $N/2 + 1 = 9$, so the median is midway between 83 and 85, or 84. (By the way, if the two middle observations had been, say, 83, then the "midpoint" between them would be 83.5)

The Median of Grouped Data

———————❖———————

A lot of data in the social sciences are reported in intervals, or groups. For example, some people are uncomfortable with a straightforward question like "How much money do you make?" so researchers often ask something like

Now we'd like to get an idea of about how much you earn each year. Do you earn:

1. less than $10,000 per year?
2. $10,000 or more but less than $20,000 per year?
3. $20,000 or more but less than $30,000 per year?
4. $30,000 or more but less than $40,000 per year?
5. $40,000 or more but less than $50,000 per year?

and so on. This produces *grouped data* (see Box 14.2). Table 14.3 shows the data on AGE from Table 14.2d, grouped into 10-year intervals. To find the median in grouped data, use the formula for finding *percentiles*.

The formula for finding *any* percentile score in a distribution of grouped data scores is

$$PS = L + i \left\{ \frac{n - C}{f} \right\} \quad \text{(Formula 14.1)}$$

where

PS is the percentile score you want to calculate;

L is the real lower limit of the interval in which the percentile score lies;

n is the case number that represents the percentile score;

C is the cumulative frequency of the cases up to the interval before the one in which the percentile score lies;

i is the interval size; and

f is the count, or *frequency,* of the interval in which the median lies.

TABLE 14.3 Frequency Table of the Grouped Variable AGE

Count	Cum. Count	Variable AGE
6	6	20-29
6	12	30-39
5	17	40-49
8	25	50-59
5	30	60+

Ten percent of scores in a list are below the 10th percentile, and 90% are above it.

If you've ever taken a standardized test like the ACT, SAT, or Graduate Record Exam (GRE), you might have been told that you scored in the 14th percentile, or the 31st percentile, or whatever. If you scored in the 14th percentile, then 86% of the scores were lower than yours (1.0 − .14 = .86).

The 25th percentile is called the *first quartile* and the 75th percentile is the *third quartile*. The difference between the values for the 25th and 75th percentiles is known as the *interquartile range* and is a measure of dispersion for ordinal and interval variables. (More on measures of dispersion later.) *The median is the 50th percentile.*

In applying Formula 14.1 to the data in Table 14.3, the first thing to do is calculate *n*. There are 30 cases and we are looking for the score at the 50th percentile (the median), so *n* is $(30)(.50) = 15$. We are looking, in other words, for a number *above which* there are 15 cases and *below which* there are 15 cases. Looking at the data in Table 14.3, we see that there are 12 cases up to 39 years of age and 17 cases up to 49 years of age. So, C is 12, and the median case lies somewhere in the 40-49 range.

The real lower limit, *L*, of this interval is 39.5 (midway between 39 and 40, the boundary of the two groups) and the interval, *i*, is 10 years. Putting all this into the formula, we get

$$PS = 39.5 + 10 \left\{ \frac{15 - 12}{5} \right\} =$$

$$39.5 + 10(.6) = 45.5$$

So, the median age for this group of 30 people is 45.5 years. Notice that none of the respondents actually got a score of 45.5. Still, 15 of the 30 scores are above 45.5 and 15 are below it.

I've given you this grand tour of the median as a specific percentile score because I want you to understand the conceptual basis for this statistic. I'm going to do the same thing for all the statistical procedures I introduce here and in the next two chapters. You only need to work through these detailed examples once, though. When you understand the concepts behind the median, the standard deviation, z-scores, chi-square, *t*-tests, and regression, you need never again calculate these statistics by hand. Once you understand a statistic, you can do all the calculations by computer.

In fact, even for small data sets, it's best to use a computer to handle statistical chores. It's not just easier to do—it's more accurate. You're less likely to make mistakes in recording data on a computer and when you do make mistakes (it happens all the time, even to the most experienced researchers), it's easier to find and fix them. Just think of how easy it is to find spelling errors in a document when you use a word processor. It's the same with checking and correcting mistakes in statistical analysis.

Central Tendency: The Mean

The arithmetic *mean,* or the average, is the sum of the individual scores in a distribution, divided by the number of scores. Means are everywhere. We see statistics on the average age at marriage, on the average price of a gallon of gas, on the average mortgage rate, on the average number of days people miss work because of illness each year, and so on.

The formula for calculating the mean is

$$\bar{x} = \Sigma\, x/N \qquad \text{(Formula 14.2)}$$

where $\bar{x}$ (read: x bar) is the mean, Σx means "sum all the values of x," and N is the number of values of x. To calculate the mean, or average age of the 30 respondents whose data are shown in Table 14.1, we add up the 30 ages and divide by 30. The mean age of these 30 respondents is 45.033 years. (We use $\bar{x}$ when we refer to the mean of a sample of data; we use the Greek letter μ when we refer to the mean of an entire population.)

The formula for calculating the *mean of a frequency distribution* is

$$\bar{x} = \Sigma\, f\, x/N \qquad \text{(Formula 14.3)}$$

where $\Sigma f x$ is the sum of the attributes of the variable, times their frequencies.

Table 14.4 shows the calculation of the mean age for the frequency distribution shown in Table 14.2d.

Table 14.5 shows the calculation of the mean for the grouped data on AGE in Table 14.3. When variable attributes are presented in ranges, as in the case here, we take the midpoint of the range (see Box 14.3).

A Mathematical Feature of the Mean

The arithmetic mean has an important feature: *The sum of the deviations from the mean of all the scores in a distribution is zero.* Table 14.6 shows this feature with data from 10 U.S. states on the percentage of people who are on welfare. These data are a random sample of the data in Table 14.7, showing some *social indicators* for the 50 U.S. states and Washington, D.C., during the mid-1990s. These data are from various editions of the *Statistical Abstract of the United States* (*SAUS*). We'll be using the data in Table 14.7, as well as some other data from the *SAUS* on things like suicide rates, motor vehicle deaths, energy consumption, and income, as we go along in the next few chapters.

Thus, while both the median and the mean are midpoints in sets of scores, the mean has the additional feature: It is the point in a distribution at which the two halves balance each other out. Table 14.8 shows that the sum of the differences between the scores and the mean of a set of scores is zero.

This feature of the mean figures prominently in the calculation of variance, which is coming right up in the section on measures of dispersion.

The Outlier Problem

The mean is one of the all-time great statistics, but it has one very important drawback: In small samples, it's heavily influenced by special cases, called *outliers,* and even in large samples, it's

TABLE 14.4	Calculating the Mean for the Data in Table 14.2d	

Count f	AGE x	f x
1	20	20
1	21	21
2	24	48
2	25	50
1	31	31
1	34	34
1	35	35
1	37	37
2	38	76
1	41	41
2	46	92
1	47	47
1	49	49
1	51	51
1	52	52
3	53	159
1	54	54
1	56	56
1	57	57
1	60	60
2	67	134
1	69	69
1	78	78

$$\Sigma\, fx = 1,351$$
$$\Sigma\, fx/N =$$
$$1,351/30 = 45.033$$

TABLE 14.5	Frequency Table of the Grouped Variable AGE		

AGE x	Midpoint	f	fx
20-29	25	6	150
30-39	35	6	210
40-49	45	5	225
50-59	55	8	440
60+	65	5	325

$$N = 30 \quad \Sigma\, fx = 1,350$$
$$\bar{x} = 1,350/30$$
$$= 45.00$$

two people who die at 1 year of age and at 79 years of age is 40.

You can see this problem yourself by calculating the mean rate of violent crimes in the U.S. in 1995. From the data in Table 14.7 (VIOL95), there were, on average, 581.039 violent crimes per 100,000 people that year in the U.S. But if you take away Washington, D.C., the mean for the rest of the U.S. was 539.440 violent crimes per 100,000 population. The data from D.C. raise the mean rate of violence for the entire U.S. by about 8%, even though D.C. has only two-tenths of 1% of the population of the U.S. (To put this in some perspective, though, the rate in Japan for 1995 was about 29 violent crimes per 100,000 population.)

The *median* rate of violent crime in 1995 was 522 per 100,000 population, *including* the data from Washington, D.C. When data are normally distributed, the mean is the best indicator of central tendency. When interval-level data are highly skewed, the median is often a better indicator of central tendency. You absolutely must get a feel for the *shape* of distributions to understand what's going on.

heavily influenced by big gaps in the distribution of cases.

For example, in Mozambique, lots of people live to 75 or 80 years of age. The mean life expectancy of people in Mozambique, however, is about 47 years, partly because Mozambique has one of the highest rates of infant mortality in the world. Of every 1,000 babies born, about 110 of them die in their first year of life. The average of

Box 14.3
And Still More about Grouped Data: Why It's Better
to Collect Interval-Level Data as Intervals

Note the problem in taking the mean of the grouped data in Table 14.5. If you go back to Table 14.2d, you'll see that all six of the people who are between 20 and 29 are really between 20 and 25. Counting them all as being 25 obviously distorts the mean. Also, there are 5 people over 60 in this data set: one who is 60, two who are 67, and one each who are 69 and 78. Their average age is 68.2, but they are all counted as being just 60+ in Table 14.3.

In calculating the mean for these grouped data, I've assigned the midpoint to be 65, *as if the range were 60-69,* even though the actual range is 60-78, and the real midpoint of the 60+ category is

$$(60 + 67 + 67 + 69 + 78)/5 = 68.2$$

If you have grouped data, however, it will almost certainly be because the data were collected in grouped form to begin with. In that case, there is no way to know what the real range or the real midpoint is for the 60+ category, so we have to assign a midpoint that conforms to the midpoints of the other ranges. Applying the midpoint for all the other classes, the midpoint for the 60+ category would be 65, which is what I've done in Table 14.5.

Obviously, all this distorts the mean: The grouped data have a mean of 45.00, while the ungrouped data have a calculated mean of 45.033. In this case, the difference is tiny, but it won't always be that way. If you collect data in groups about interval variables like age, you can never go back and see how much you've distorted things. It's always better to collect interval data at the interval level, if you can, rather than in grouped form. You can always group the data later, during the analysis, but you can't "ungroup" them if you collect data in grouped form to begin with.

TABLE 14.6 Data on Welfare in 10 U.S. States (from Table 14.7) Showing How the Sum of the Deviations from the Mean of a Distribution Is Zero

State	WELF94 x	Score – Mean $(x - \bar{x})$
Alabama	6.8	6.8 – 7.62 = –0.82
California	11.7	11.7 – 7.62 = 4.08
Colorado	4.7	4.7 – 7.62 = –2.92
Washington, D.C.	16.7	16.7 – 7.62 = 9.08
Idaho	3.4	3.4 – 7.62 = –4.22
Minnesota	5.4	5.4 – 7.62 = –2.22
New York	10.0	10.0 – 7.62 = 2.38
North Dakota	3.9	3.9 – 7.62 = –3.72
Washington	7.1	7.1 – 7.62 = –0.52
Wisconsin	6.5	6.5 – 7.62 = –1.12
	Σx = 76.2	$\Sigma (x - \bar{x})$ = 0.00
	$\bar{x}$ = 76.2/10 = 7.62	

TABLE 14.7 Some Social Indicators for the 50 U.S. States and Washington, D.C.

State	VIOL95	WELF94	OV6595	URB94	SCH94	DOC94	OWNHOME
AL	632	6.8	13.0	67.5	94.3	175	71.3
AK	771	7.4	4.9	42.1	90.3	143	67.2
AZ	714	6.5	13.3	87.2	99.6	201	63.0
AR	553	6.6	14.5	45.0	92.3	166	66.7
CA	966	11.7	11.0	96.8	91.4	241	55.7
CO	440	4.7	10.0	84.3	91.5	226	64.1
CN	406	6.4	14.3	95.7	90.4	325	68.1
DE	725	5.2	12.6	82.5	86.3	214	69.2
DC	2661	16.7	13.9	100.0	100.6	641	42.5
FL	1071	6.8	18.6	92.9	91.7	219	66.9
GA	657	8.2	10.0	68.1	94.6	187	70.9
HI	296	6.9	12.6	74.2	87.6	245	50.2
ID	322	3.4	11.4	30.7	95.5	136	72.3
IL	996	8.3	12.5	84.0	88.5	235	68.1
IN	525	5.2	12.6	71.7	91.2	173	74.1
IA	354	5.4	15.2	44.0	92.1	160	72.7
KS	421	4.7	13.7	55.0	91.0	188	66.5
KY	365	9.3	12.6	48.3	92.5	185	75.0
LA	1007	9.7	11.4	75.1	87.1	210	66.4
ME	131	7.4	13.9	35.9	94.5	196	74.9
MD	987	5.9	11.3	92.8	89.5	341	70.5
MA	687	7.5	14.2	96.1	89.7	373	62.3
MI	688	9.1	12.4	82.6	87.9	200	73.3
MN	356	5.4	12.4	69.4	90.5	237	75.4
MS	503	10.9	12.3	35.0	91.7	132	73.7
MO	664	7.0	13.9	68.0	85.9	213	70.5
MT	171	5.6	13.1	23.8	92.0	171	67.5
NE	382	4.0	13.9	50.7	87.9	192	66.7
NV	945	3.8	11.4	85.0	96.0	159	61.2
NH	115	3.5	11.9	59.6	88.1	212	66.8
NJ	600	6.0	13.7	100.0	86.9	269	63.1
NM	819	8.7	10.9	56.3	88.2	196	69.6
NY	842	10.0	13.4	91.8	89.2	343	52.6
NC	646	7.2	12.5	66.6	92.0	205	70.2
ND	87	3.9	14.5	42.1	92.6	192	68.1
OH	483	8.1	13.4	81.2	88.2	213	69.0
OK	664	6.2	13.5	60.2	95.1	155	68.5
OR	522	5.1	13.6	70.0	91.0	212	61.0
PA	427	7.2	15.9	84.6	84.8	262	73.3
RI	368	8.6	15.7	94.0	87.4	278	58.7
SC	982	6.7	12.0	70.1	94.6	179	74.1
SD	208	4.4	14.4	32.9	92.9	160	67.6
TN	772	9.0	12.5	67.8	93.0	218	70.2
TX	664	6.3	10.2	83.9	98.3	183	61.5
UT	329	3.6	8.8	77.3	96.1	190	72.5
VT	118	7.0	12.0	27.2	99.6	266	69.1

TABLE 14.7 Continued

State	VIOL95	WELF94	OV6595	URB94	SCH94	DOC94	OWNHOME
VA	362	4.8	11.1	77.7	93.4	220	68.4
WA	484	7.1	11.6	82.9	92.2	225	62.9
WV	210	9.6	15.3	41.8	96.5	190	74.6
WI	281	6.5	13.3	67.9	86.0	205	68.3
WY	254	4.5	11.1	29.8	97.2	141	67.6

SOURCE: Data are from various editions of the *Statistical Abstract of the United States* (U.S. Census Bureau), indicated by year.

NOTE:

VIOL95   The violent crime rate in 1995, per 100,000 population (1997, Table 315)

WELF94   Total recipients of Aid to Families with Dependent Children and of federal Supplemental Security Income as a percentage of the resident population in 1994 (1996, Table 599)

OV6595   Percentage of the resident population 65 years and older in 1995 (1996, Table 34)

URB94   Percentage of the resident population in metropolitan areas in 1994 (1996, Table 42)

SCH94   Percentage of persons 5-17 years old in public elementary and secondary schools in 1994. D.C. has slightly more than 100% of its 5- to 17-year-olds in school because pupils under 5 and over 17 are counted (1996, Table 251)

DOC94   Number of physicians per 100,000 population in 1994 (1996, Table 181)

OWNHOME   Percentage of families that owned their own home in 1997 (1998, Table 12.16)

TABLE 14.8 The Sum of the Differences between the Scores and the Mean of a Set of Scores Is Zero

Scores below the mean of 7.62 in Table 14.6	Scores above the mean of 7.62 in Table 14.6
−0.82	
−2.92	
−4.22	
−2.22	
−3.72	4.08
−0.52	9.08
−1.12	2.38
Total below the mean	Total above the mean
−15.54	15.54

−15.54 and +15.54 sum to 0

SHAPE: VISUALIZING DISTRIBUTIONS

A really good first cut at understanding whether data are normal or skewed is to lay them out graphically. This is easy to do with any of the full-featured statistics programs out there these days. I'll show you six ways to lay out your data: bar graphs and pie charts for nominal and ordinal variables; stem-and-leaf plots, box plots, histograms, and frequency polygons for interval variables.

Bar Graphs and Pie Charts

Bar graphs and *pie charts* are two popular ways to graph the distribution of nominal and ordinal variables. Figure 14.1 shows bar graphs for two of the variables in Table 14.1: GENDER and GUNGHO. Figure 14.2 shows the pie charts for the same variables. Notice that in the bar graphs, the bars don't touch one another. This indicates that the data are nominal or ordinal and not continuous.

The categories of the variables are shown along the horizontal axis of the bar graph. **The horizontal axis, or x-axis, is also called the** *abscissa*. The number of each category is shown on the left vertical axis. **The vertical axis, or y-axis, is also called the** *ordinate*. You can, of course, show the percentage of each category on the y-axis.

In Figure 14.1a, men are labeled 1 and women are labeled 2. Notice that it makes no difference whether we put the bar for men or the bar for women on the left or the right when we graph GENDER. There is no order implied in the attributes of a nominal variable. When we graph ordinal variables, however, like GUNGHO, the order of the bars becomes important. The bars don't touch, however, reflecting the fact that ordinal variables are not continuous.

Stem-and-Leaf Plots

I like to start visualizing interval-level data by running *stem-and-leaf plots*. Figure 14.3 shows a stem-and-leaf plot for the variable DOC94 in Table 14.7.

Inspection of Table 14.7 confirms that the lowest value for this variable is 132 doctors per 100,000 population (in Mississippi). The "stem" in the stem-and-leaf plot is 13 (the first two digits of 132) and the first "leaf" is 2. There are two cases in the 130s. The other is Idaho, with 136 doctors per 100,000 population, so the second leaf in this stem is 6. The M in Figure 14.3 stands for the median, or the 50th percentile (it's 205), and the Hs indicate the *upper hinge* and the *lower hinge*, or the 25th and the 75th percentiles.

Box Plots

Next, I like to produce *box plots* (also called box-and-whisker plots) for interval variables. Figure 14.4a-d shows the box-and-whisker plots for four of the variables in Table 14.7. Box-and-whisker plots are chock-full of information. The boxes themselves show you the middle 50% of the cases—that is, the interquartile range. The vertical line that marks off the box at the left is the 25th percentile (the lower hinge) of the plot; the vertical line that marks off the box at the right is the 75th percentile (the upper hinge).

The vertical line inside the box is the median, or the 50th percentile. Fifty percent of the cases in the distribution fall to the right of the median line and 50% fall to the left.

The whiskers in these box plots extend one and a half times the interquartile range from the lower

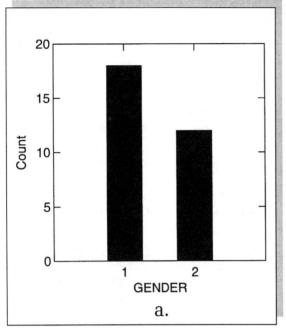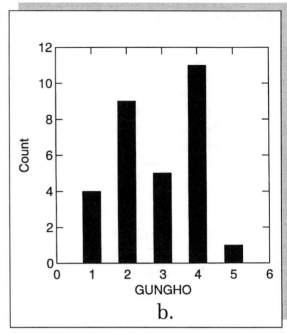

Figure 14.1 Bar Graphs for the Variables GENDER and GUNGHO in Table 14.1

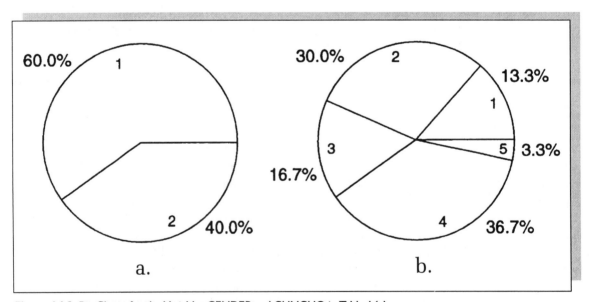

Figure 14.2 Pie Charts for the Variables GENDER and GUNGHO in Table 14.1

NOTE: a, on the left, is the proportion of men (1) and women (2) in the data from Table 14.1; b, on the right, is the proportion of people who answered 1, 2, 3, 4, or 5 to the GUNGHO question in Table 14.1.

```
Stem and Leaf Plot of variable:     DOC94, N = 51
    Minimum:      132.000
    Lower hinge:     181.000
    Median:      205.000
    Upper hinge:     230.500
    Maximum:      641.000
       13    26
       14    13
       15    59
       16    006
       17    1359
       18  H 3578
       19    002266
       20  M 0155
       21    02233489
       22    056
       23  H 57
       24    15
       25
       26    269
       27    8
   * * * Outside Values * * *
       32    5
       34    13
       37    3
       64    1
```

Figure 14.3 Stem-and-Leaf Plot for the Variable DOC94 in Table 14.7

and the upper hinges of the box. When data are normally distributed, this will be about 2.7 standard deviations from the mean. Cases outside that range are outliers and are marked by an asterisk. Cases that are more than *three times the interquartile range* from the hinges are marked by a little circle. Outliers can be quite instructive, as we'll see in a minute.

Figure 14.4a shows that the percentage of urban population is pretty evenly distributed across the United States. If you were to apply Formula 14.1 to the data for URB94 in Table 14.7 (or run a stem-and-leaf plot for those data), you'd find the 25th percentile (the lower hinge in Figure 14.1a) to be 49.5% and the 75th percentile (the upper hinge in Figure 14.1a) to be 84.15%. That is, half the states in the U.S. had between 49.5% and 84.15% urban population in 1994.

Notice, though, that *none* of the states in Table 14.7 is exactly 49.5% or exactly 84.15% urban. Just as the median is an abstract concept, so is every single percentile. Montana, with 23% of its population concentrated in urban areas, is the least urbanized of the states. Washington, D.C., is 100% urbanized, of course, but so is New Jersey, and California is 98.6% urbanized. There's plenty of rural land in New Jersey and California, but, compared to the concentration of people in the urban areas, hardly anyone lives in the rural zones. ("Urban," by the way, as far as the U.S. Census is concerned, means concentrations of at least 2,500 people in a town.)

Now look at Figure 14.4b. This, too, is pretty evenly distributed. In 50% of the states, the percentage of people over age 65 was between 11.5% and 13.9% in 1995—a pretty tight interquartile range. The full range, however, with the whiskers, is between 8.8% and 15.9%. And there are two relative outliers: Just 4.9% of the population of Alaska was over 65 and fully 18.6% of the population of Florida was over 65 in the mid-1990s.

Figure 14.4c shows that 50% of the states had between 355.0 and 719.5 violent crimes for every 100,000 people in 1995. North Dakota had the lowest violent crime rate—87 per 100,000. Except for one really isolated outlier, Florida had the highest rate of violent crime in the U.S., with 1,071 crimes per 100,000 population. The true outlier is Washington, D.C., with an astounding 2,661 violent crimes per 100,000 people.

Figure 14.4d shows that half the states had between 181.0 and 230.5 physicians per 100,000 population in 1994. Including the whiskers, all but five states had between 132 and 278 physicians per 100,000. Four states—Connecticut, Maryland, New York, and Massachusetts—are relative outliers; they had 325, 341, 343, and 373 physicians per 100,000 population, respectively.

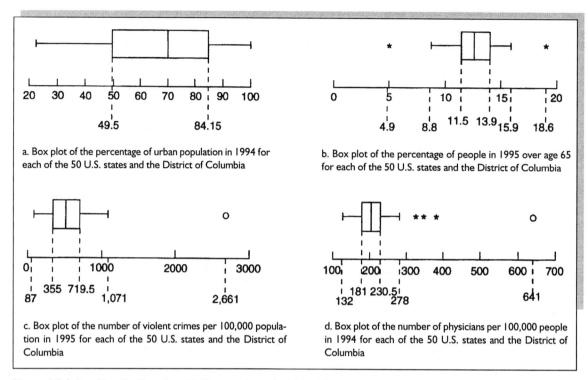

a. Box plot of the percentage of urban population in 1994 for each of the 50 U.S. states and the District of Columbia

b. Box plot of the percentage of people in 1995 over age 65 for each of the 50 U.S. states and the District of Columbia

c. Box plot of the number of violent crimes per 100,000 population in 1995 for each of the 50 U.S. states and the District of Columbia

d. Box plot of the number of physicians per 100,000 people in 1994 for each of the 50 U.S. states and the District of Columbia

Figure 14.4 Box Plots for Four Social Indicators about the United States

(There are only three asterisks in Figure 14.4d even though there are four relative outliers because Maryland and New York had practically the same number of physicians per 100,000 and two of the asterisks overlap.) And then there's that true outlier again, Washington, D.C., with 641 physicians per 100,000 population.

❖————

Histograms and Frequency Polygons

Two other graphic methods are useful in univariate analysis: *histograms* and *frequency polygons* (frequency polygons are also called frequency curves). Frequency polygons are line drawings made by connecting the tops of the bars of a histogram and displaying the result without the bars. What you get is a pure shape, but remember: The shape of a frequency polygon depends on how many bars you use for the underlying histogram.

These particular graphical methods actually give you less information than box plots or stem-and-leaf plots, but histograms and frequency polygons have a certain appeal because they are easily interpreted. Figure 14.5 shows the histogram and frequency polygon for the variable SCH94 in Table 14.7. Figure 14.6 shows the histogram and frequency polygon for WELF94 in Table 14.7. And Figure 14.7 shows the histogram and frequency polygon for OWNHOME in Table 14.7.

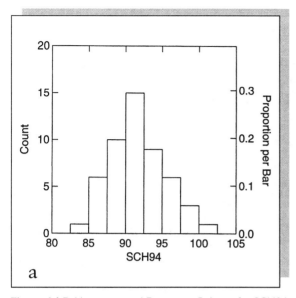

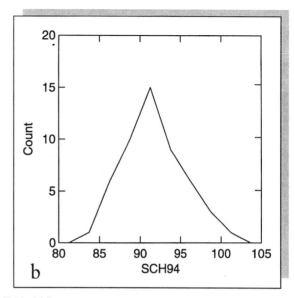

Figure 14.5 Histogram and Frequency Polygon for SCH94 in Table 14.7

NOTE: The percentage of school-age children attending school is normally distributed.

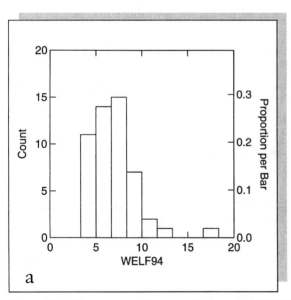

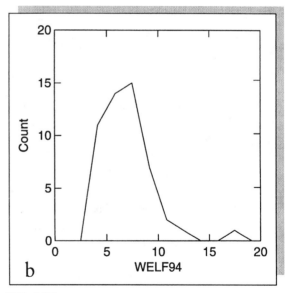

Figure 14.6 Histogram and Frequency Polygon for WELF94 in Table 14.7

NOTE: The percentage of people on welfare is positively skewed.

In Figure 14.5, we see that the variable SCH94 (the percentage of 5- to 17-year-olds who are in school) is evenly distributed: Between 84.8% and 100% of children 5-17 are in school across the U.S. and the distribution is symmetric, approaching the normal distribution (see Box 14.4).

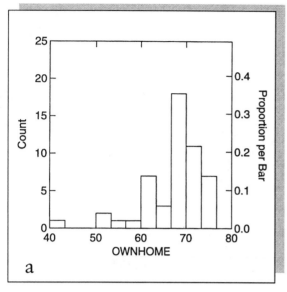
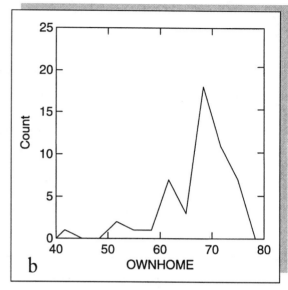

Figure 14.7 Histogram and Frequency Polygon for OWNHOME in Table 14.7
NOTE: The percentage of people who own their own homes is negatively skewed.

Figure 14.6 shows that the percentage of people on welfare in the U.S. is **skewed to the right, or *positively skewed*.** There is a bulge on the left and a tail of cases trailing off to the right.

Figure 14.7 shows that the percentage of people across the U.S. who owned their own homes in 1997 is **skewed to the left, or *negatively skewed*.**

Getting a visual understanding of distributions is a great first step, but we need more information to decide whether variables are more normally distributed or less normally distributed. As we saw in Chapter 5, the use of statistics like the z-score and Student's t depends on the population from which samples are drawn being normal. In a normal distribution, the mean, the median, and the mode are the same and the shape of the curve is perfectly symmetrical on both sides of the mean (see Figure 5.4 from Chapter 5).

> *Since virtually all distributions of real data are skewed, what really matters is how much.*

On the other hand, you won't find many perfectly normal distributions in the messy world of real social science data. Since virtually all distributions of real data are skewed, what really matters is *how much*. If the amount of skew is slight, then we can still use statistics that assume normality in the population distributions.

Figure 14.5 looks more or less like a normal distribution, but we can do better and actually check. Figure 14.8 shows the box plot and basic univariate statistics for SCH94. The plot confirms that there are no outliers and that the distribution of cases is more or less normal. The clincher is that the median (91.70) and the mean (91.714) are practically identical.

Box 14.4
Distribution Again

Back in Chapter 5, on sampling, we looked at some basic shapes of distributions: skewed to the right, skewed to the left, bimodal, and normal. Here they are again, but this time notice the mode, the median, and the mean:

  (1) the mode, the median, and the mean are the same in the normal distribution;
  (2) the mean is pulled to the left of the median in negatively skewed distributions; and
  (3) the mean is pulled to the right of the median in positively skewed distributions.

  The mean for WELF94, for example, is 6.873, while the median is 6.700; this is a slight positive skew. The mean for women's life expectancy across the world (see Figure 14.10) is 68.392, but the median 72.150; this shows strong negative skew.

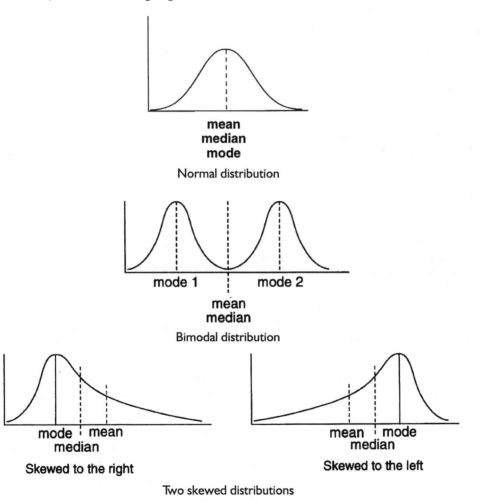

mean
median
mode
Normal distribution

mode 1   **mode 2**
mean
median
Bimodal distribution

mode ⋮ mean   **mean ⋮ mode**
median   **median**

Skewed to the right   **Skewed to the left**

Two skewed distributions

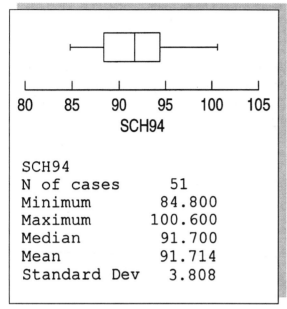

Figure 14.8 Box Plot for SCH94

NOTE: SCH94, the percentage of children ages 5-17 in school in each of the 50 states and Washington, D.C., in 1994, was more or less normally distributed. (D.C. shows more than 100% because pupils under 5 and over 17 are counted.)

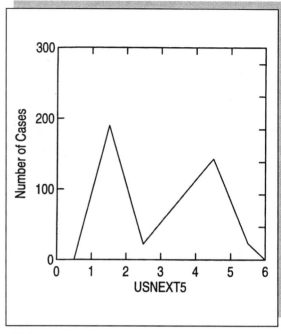

Figure 14.9 The Bimodal Distribution of Responses to a Survey Question

Bimodal Distributions

Be on the lookout for *bimodal distributions*. If you try to calculate the median or mean for a bimodal variable, you won't get a realistic picture of the central tendency in your data.

Here's an example. In late 1996, just after the U.S. presidential election, the Bureau of Economic and Business Research at the University of Florida ran a survey of 461 Floridians. One of the questions on that survey went like this:

Looking ahead, which would you say is more likely—that in the country as a whole we'll have continuous good times during the next five years or so, or that we will have periods of widespread unemployment or depression, or what?

1. Good times
2. Good with qualifications
3. Uncertain; good and bad
4. Bad with qualifications
5. Bad times

The mean response for this question was 3.32—that is, just slightly above the middle value of *uncertain*. The median, however was 4.00, which means that half the responses were *bad times* (4 or 5) and half the responses were *good times* (1 and 2) plus all the *uncertain* responses (3).

Figure 14.9 shows the frequency polygon for this variable, and the bimodal distribution is clear. Lots of people (190 of them, in fact) said they were looking forward to unambiguously good times; lots of other people (143 of them) said they

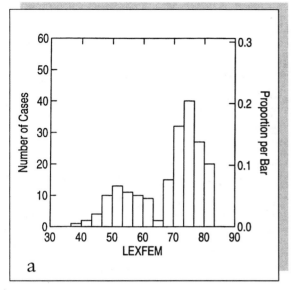

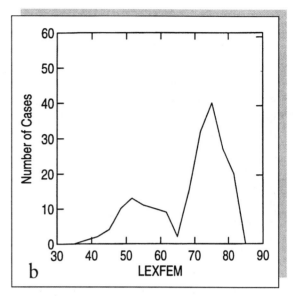

Figure 14.10 Histogram and Frequency Polygon for Female Life Expectancy in 196 Countries of the World
NOTE: Female life expectancy is bimodally distributed.

were looking forward to unambiguously bad times. The other 128 respondents were distributed across the other three possible answers: 23 answered "good with qualifications," 83 answered "uncertain," and 23 answered "bad with qualifications."

In other words, neither the mean nor the median tell us the real story here. Of the 190 people who said they were looking forward to solid good times, 137 (72%) had voted for Bill Clinton—who had won the election. Of the 143 who were looking forward to bad times, 90 (63%) had voted for Bob Dole or Ross Perot—who had lost the election. Those who voted for Clinton had a mean score of 2.13 on the good-times-or-bad-times-ahead question. Those who voted for Dole or Perot had a mean score of 3.02. There are two means here: one for the Clinton voters and one for supporters of Dole and Perot.

And take a look at Figure 14.10a-b. It shows the distribution of female life expectancy for 196 countries around the world. The mean for the distribution is 68.39 years, but the distribution is bimodal. The big leptokurtic bulge on the right is a more or less normal distribution of countries in which women live to be at least 65. The mean for these 135 countries is about 75 years. The platykurtic bulge on the left is another more or less normal distribution of countries in which women live fewer than 65 years. The mean for these 61 countries is just 53.7.

The moral is: Examine the frequency distribution for each of your variables. For interval and ordinal variables, find out if the distributions around the mean or median are symmetrical. If the distributions are symmetrical, then the mean is the measure of choice for central tendency. If the distributions are skewed, then the median is the measure of choice. And if the distributions are bimodal (or multimodal), then do a much closer examination and find out what's going on.

MEASURES OF DISPERSION I: RANGE AND INTERQUARTILE RANGE

After central tendency and shape, the next thing we want to know about data is something about how homogeneous or heterogeneous they are— that is, something about their dispersion. For example, from the data in Table 14.7 we can calculate that there were, on average, 219.57 physicians in the U.S. in 1994 for every 100,000 people in the population, but we'd like some measure of the variation in mean number of physicians across the 50 states and Washington, D.C.

One measure is the *range*. Inspecting the next-to-last column on the right of Table 14.7, we see that Mississippi had a low of 132 physicians per 100,000 people in 1994, while Washington, D.C., had a high of 641. The range is 641 – 132 = 509. The range is a useful statistic, but it is affected strongly by extreme scores. After Wash-

ington, D.C., the next-highest concentration of physicians in 1994 was 373 in Massachusetts, and the range is 373 – 132 = 241, a drop of more than 50%.

The *interquartile range* avoids extreme scores, either high or low. The 75th percentile is 230 for DOC94 in Table 14.7, and the 25th percentile is 181, so the interquartile range is 230 – 181 = 49. This tightens the range of scores, but it is often the extreme scores that are of greatest interest. The interquartile range of freshmen SAT scores at major universities tells you about the majority—the middle 50%—of students' scores. It doesn't tell you if the university is recruiting athletes whose SAT scores are more likely to be in the bottom 25%, the middle 50%, or the top 25% of scores at those universities (see Klein 1999).

MEASURES OF DISPERSION II: VARIANCE AND THE STANDARD DEVIATION

The best known and most useful measure of dispersion for a sample of interval-level data is the *standard deviation,* usually written just s or SD. The SD is a **measure of how much, on average, the scores in a distribution deviate from the mean score.** It gives you a feel for how homogeneous or heterogeneous a population is. (We use s or SD for the standard deviation of a sample; we use the lowercase Greek sigma, σ, for the standard deviation of a population.)

The SD is calculated from the *variance,* written s^2, which is the **average squared deviation from the mean** of the measures in a set of data. To find the variance in a distribution:

(1) Subtract the mean of the set of observations from each observation.
(2) Square the difference, thus getting rid of negative numbers.
(3) Sum the differences.
(4) Divide that sum by the sample size minus one.

Here is the formula for calculating the variance:

$$s^2 = \frac{\Sigma (x - \bar{x})^2}{N - 1} \qquad \text{(Formula 14.4)}$$

where s^2 is the variance, x represents the raw scores in a distribution of interval-level observa-

Box 14.5
Variance Is What You Want to Explain

Variance is an important concept in statistics. It describes in a single statistic how homogeneous or heterogeneous a set of data is, and by extension, how similar or different are the units of analysis described by those data.

Variance is so important that many researchers see it as the thing you want to explain when you do statistical analysis of data. I'll explain in detail what "accounting for variance" means when we get to Chapter 15. If you can explain 100% of the variance in a distribution, that means you can predict 100% of the scores on a dependent variable by knowing the scores on some independent variable.

Consider the original set of scores in Table 14.1 on the variable REDUCE. These scores show people's support for the idea that "Americans are going to have to drastically reduce their consumption over the next few years." Suppose that for each level of education you could predict the level of support for that attitudinal item about cutting back on consumption. If you could do this in 100% of all cases, then you would speak of "explaining all the variance" in the dependent variable.

I've never encountered this strength of association between two variables in the social sciences, but some things come pretty close, and in any event, the principle is what's important.

It's important to understand Formula 14.4 on calculating variance. Variance is the basis for many of the statistics coming in Chapter 15 on bivariate analysis.

---

tions, $\bar{x}$ is the mean of the distribution of raw scores, and N is the total number of observations.

Notice that we need to square the difference of each observation from the mean and *then* take the square root later. As we saw in calculating the mean, $\sum (x - \bar{x}) = 0$. That is, the simple sum of all the deviations from the mean is zero. Squaring each $(x - \bar{x})$ gets rid of the negative numbers (see Box 14.5).

The standard deviation, s, is the square root of the variance, s^2. The formula for the standard deviation is

$$s = \sqrt{\frac{\sum (x - \bar{x})^2}{N - 1}}$$

(Formula 14.5)

Table 14.9 shows how to calculate the standard deviation for the data on WELF94 in Table 14.6.

Substituting in the formula for standard deviation, we get

$$SD = \sqrt{152.056/9} = \sqrt{16.8951} = 4.11$$

If we were reporting these data, we would say that "the average percentage of adults on welfare is 7.62, with SD 4.11."

For grouped data, we take the midpoint of each interval as the raw score. Table 14.10 shows the procedure for calculating the standard deviation for the grouped data in Table 14.3. We know from Table 14.5 that $\bar{x} = 45$ for the data in Table 14.3.

TABLE 14.9 Calculating the Standard Deviation for the Data in Table 14.6

State	WELF94 x	x – x̄	(x – x̄)²
Alabama	6.8	6.8 – 7.62 = –0.82	0.6724
California	11.7	11.7 – 7.62 = 4.08	16.6464
Colorado	4.7	4.7 – 7.62 = –2.92	8.5264
Washington, D.C.	16.7	16.7 – 7.62 = 9.08	82.4464
Idaho	3.4	3.4 – 7.62 = –4.22	17.8084
Minnesota	5.4	5.4 – 7.62 = –2.22	4.9284
New York	10.0	10.0 – 7.62 = 2.38	5.6644
North Dakota	3.9	3.9 – 7.62 = –3.72	13.8384
Washington	7.1	7.1 – 7.62 = –0.52	0.2704
Wisconsin	6.5	6.5 – 7.62 = –1.12	1.2544
$N = 10$	$\Sigma x = 76.2$ $\bar{x} = 76.2/10$ $= 7.62$	$\Sigma x - \bar{x} = 0.00$	$\Sigma (x - \bar{x})^2 = 152.056$ $SD = \sqrt{152.056/9} = 4.11$

TABLE 14.10 Calculating the Standard Deviation for the Grouped Data in Table 14.3

AGE x	f x	Midpoint	x – x̄	(x – x̄)²
20-29	6	25	25 – 45 = –20	400
30-39	6	35	35 – 45 = –10	100
40-49	5	45	45 – 45 = 0	0
50-59	8	55	55 – 45 = 10	100
60+	5	65	65 – 45 = 20	400
	$\Sigma x = 30$		$\Sigma x - \bar{x} = 0$	$\Sigma (x - \bar{x})^2 = 1,000$

Substituting in the formula for *SD*, we get

$$\sqrt{1,000/29} = \sqrt{34.483} = 5.872$$

and we report that "the mean age is 45.00, *SD* 5.872." For comparison, the mean and *SD* of the 30 ages (the ungrouped data) in Table 14.2d are 45.033 and 15.52. Close, but not dead on.

❖——————

Are these numbers describing ages and welfare rates large, small, or about normal? There is no way to tell except by comparison across cases. By themselves, numbers such as means and standard deviations simply describe a set of data. But in comparative perspective, they help us produce theory; that is, they help us develop ideas about what causes things, and what those things, in turn, cause.

THE LOGIC OF HYPOTHESIS TESTING

One thing we can do, however, is test whether the *mean of a sample of data,* $\bar{x}$, is likely to represent the *mean of the population,* μ, from which the sample was drawn. We'll test whether the mean of WELF94 in Table 14.9 is likely to represent the mean of the population of 50 states and Washington, D.C. To do this, we will use the logic of hypothesis testing. This logic is used very widely, not just in the social sciences but in all probabilistic sciences, including meteorology and genetics, for example.

The key to this logic is the statement that we can test whether the mean of the sample *is likely to represent* the mean of the population. Here's how the logic works.

Step 1. First, we set up a *null hypothesis,* written H_0, which states that **there is no difference between the sample mean and a population mean, except for chance.**

Step 2. Then we set up the *research hypothesis* (also called the *alternative hypothesis*), written H_1, which states that, in fact, **there is a difference, not due to chance, between the sample mean and the popualtion mean.**

Step 3. Next, we decide whether the research hypothesis is only about *magnitude* or is also about *direction*. If H_1 is only about magnitude—that is, it's *nondirectional*—then it can be stated just as it was in (2) above: The sample mean and the mean of the population from which the sample was drawn are different. Period.

If H_1 is directional, then it has to be stated differently: The sample mean is [bigger than] or [smaller than] the mean of the population from which the sample was drawn.

This decision determines whether we will use a *one-tailed* or a *two-tailed test* of the null hypothesis.

To understand the concept of one-tailed and two-tailed tests, suppose you have a bell curve that represents the distribution of means from many samples of a population. Sample means are like any other variable. Each sample has a mean, and if you took thousands of samples from a population you'd get a distribution of means (or proportions). Some would be large, some small, and some exactly the same as the true mean of the population. The distribution would be normal and form a bell curve like the one in Box 14.4 (and Figure 5.4 from Chapter 5).

The unlikely means (the very large ones and the very small ones) show up in the narrow area under the tails of the curve, while the likely means (the ones closer to the true mean of the population) show up in the fat, middle part. In research, the question you want to answer is whether the means of variables from one, particular sample (the one *you've* got) probably represent the tails (that is, rare events) or the middle part (that is, common events) of the curve.

Hypothesis tests are two-tailed when you are interested only in whether the magnitude of some statistic is significant (i.e., whether you would have expected that magnitude by chance). When the direction of a statistic is not important, then a two-tailed test is called for.

As we'll see in Chapter 15, when you predict that one of two means will be higher than the other (like two tests taken a month apart), you would use a one-tailed test. After all, you'd be asking only whether the mean was likely to fall in one tail of the normal distribution. Look at

> ## Box 14.6
> ## On Being Significant
>
> By custom—and only by custom—social researchers generally accept as *statistically significant* any outcome that is not likely to occur by chance more than five times in a hundred tries. This **p-*value***, or ***probability value,*** is called the *.05 level of significance*. A *p*-value of .01 is usually considered *very* significant, and .001 is often labeled *highly* significant.
>
> But remember: Statistical significance is one thing, and substantive significance is another matter entirely. In exploratory research, you might be satisfied with a .10 level of significance. In evaluating the side effects of a medical treatment, you might demand a .001 level—or even more.
>
> More and more social researchers are using asterisks instead of *p*-values in their writing. A single asterisk signifies a *p*-value of .05, a double asterisk signifies a value of .01 or less, and a triple asterisk signifies a value of .001 or less. If you read: "Men were more likely than women** to report dissatisfaction with local schoolteacher training," you'll know that the double asterisk means that the difference between men and women on this variable was significant at the .01 level or better.

Appendix C carefully. Scores significant at the .10 level for a two-tailed test are significant at the .05 level for a one-tailed test.

Step 4. Finally, we determine the *alpha level,* written α, which is the *level of significance* for the hypothesis test. Typically, alpha is set at the .05 level or at the .01 level of significance (see Box 14.6 and the discussion on significance tests at the end of Chapter 15). What this means is that if a mean or a proportion from a sample is likely to occur more than alpha—say, more than 5% of the time—then we *cannot reject the null hypothesis.*

And conversely: If the mean or a proportion of a sample is likely to occur by chance less than alpha, then we *reject the null hypothesis.* Alpha defines the *critical region* of a sampling distribution—that is, **the fraction of the sampling distribution small enough to reject the null hypothesis.**

In neither case do we prove the research hypothesis, H_1. We either reject or we fail to reject the null hypothesis. Failing to reject the null hypothesis is the best we can do, since, in a probabilistic science, we can't ever really prove any research hypothesis beyond any possibility of being wrong.

Type I and Type II Errors

There is one more piece to the logic of hypothesis testing. The choice of an alpha level lays us open to making mistakes—one of two kinds of error, called, conveniently, *Type I errors* and *Type II errors.*

If we reject the null hypothesis when it's really true, that's a Type I error. If we fail to reject the null hypothesis when it is, in fact, false, that's a Type II error.

Suppose we set alpha at .05 and make a Type I error. Our particular sample produced a mean or a proportion that happened to fall in one of the 2.5% tails of the distribution (2.5% on either side accounts for 5% of all cases), but 95% of all cases would have resulted in a mean that let us reject the null hypothesis.

———————❖

Consider a program to teach restaurant workers to wash their hands after going to the bathroom and before returning to work. A successful program would increase public safety by decreasing the probability of transmitting disease.

We'll set this up as a field experiment, assigning some restaurants in a large chain to the experimental condition (the workers get the new program) and some to the control condition (the workers are not exposed to the new program). We'll use a chain because chains tend to hire workers at the same level of education. This will keep education from being a confound to the validity of our findings. We'll take some before and after measures for both groups. We might, for example, use an unobtrusive trace measure, like whether the paper towel dispenser had been used after each employee returned from the bathroom.

The null hypothesis is that the proposed program is useless. If you try the program out and the results show, at the .05 level of significance, that you can reject the null hypothesis, that would be great news. But suppose that H_0 is true (the program is useless) but is rejected at the .05 level. This Type I error sets off a flurry of activity: The health department proposes regulations, the city passes legislation requiring restaurant owners to shell out for the program, and so on. And for what?

The obvious way to guard against this Type I error is to raise the bar and set alpha at, say, .01. That way, a Type I error would be made once in a hundred tries, not five times in a hundred. But you see immediately the cost of this little ploy: It increases dramatically the probability of making a Type II error—not rejecting H_0 when we should do exactly that. We run that field test on the clean-hands program. Failing to reject the null hypothesis, we conclude that the program is useless. This places the public at greater risk.

In a probabilistic science, we are always in danger of making one or the other of these errors. Do we try to avoid one kind more than the other? It depends on what's at stake. A Type I error in testing the clean-hands program protects the public, but puts strain on employers and the health department for increased oversight. A Type II error does more or less the opposite.

The correct choice here is not so obvious. Suppose the clean-hands program works, but costs, say, $1 million to eliminate 6 additional cases per year of low-level food poisoning in a city of half a million people. How about $10,000 to eliminate 50 cases? A Type I error at the .01 level for an HIV test means that one person out of a hundred is declared HIV free when that person is really HIV positive. How many dollars are you willing to spend to get that level down to one out of thousand?

❖———————

SO, WHAT ABOUT THE MEAN OF WELF94?

As you know from Chapter 5, statistics (like the mean) vary from sample to sample and how much they vary depends on (1) the size of the sample and (2) the amount of actual variation in the population from which you take your sample. The average amount of error we make in estimating a parameter from sample statistics is called the *standard error,* or *SE,* of the statistic. The *SEM,* or standard error of the mean, is the standard deviation, *SD,* divided by the square root of the sample size, *N*:

$$SEM = SD/\sqrt{N}$$ (Formula 14.6)

We can calculate the *SEM* for the sample of 10 states on the variable WELF94. From Table 14.9, we know that

$$\bar{x} = 7.62\% \quad \text{and}$$

$$SD = 4.11$$

so

$$SEM = 4.11/\sqrt{10} = 1.30$$

Now, knowing the *SEM,* we can ask whether the random sample of 10 cases in Table 14.9 represents the total population (shown in Table 14.7) from which it was drawn. In other words: Does $\bar{x} = 7.62\%$ in Table 14.9 represent the real mean of the population in Table 14.7?

Since this is a small sample, we can test this using Student's *t* distribution, which I introduced in Chapter 5 (see Figure 5.8). If we use all 51 data points in Table 14.7, we can calculate the true mean of WELF94: In 1994, on average, 6.87% of the people across the U.S. were on welfare.

This produces a strong null hypothesis: Based on our sample of data, the mean of the population (those 50 states, plus Washington, D.C.) from which we drew the sample *is, in fact,* 7.62%.

And here is the equally strong alternative, or research hypothesis: Based on our sample of data, the mean of the population (those 50 states, plus

Washington, D.C.) from which we drew the sample is *not* 7.62%.

The formula for calculating *t,* when the parameter, μ, is known, is

$$t = \frac{\bar{x} - \mu}{SEM}$$ (Formula 14.7)

So, for the sample of 10 states on WELF94, *t* = (7.62 − 6.87)/1.30 = .58.

Test whether *t* is statistically significant by referring to the *t* table in Appendix C. To use Appendix C, you need to know two things: how many degrees of freedom you have and whether you want a one-tailed test or a two-tailed test.

———————❖

To understand the concept of *degrees of freedom,* suppose I give you a jar filled with thousands of beans numbered from 1 to 9 and ask you to pick two that sum to 10. If you pick a 4 on the first draw, then you must pick a 6 on the next; if you pick a 5 on the first draw, then you must pick another 5; and so on. This is an example of 1 degree of freedom, because after the first draw you have no degrees of freedom left.

Suppose, instead, that I ask you to pick four beans that sum to 25. In this example, you have 3 degrees of freedom. No matter what you pick on the first draw, there are lots of combinations you can pick on the next three draws and still have the beans sum to 25. But if you pick a 6, a 9, and a 7 on the first *three* draws, then you must pick a 3 on the last draw. You've run out of degrees of freedom.

For a one-sample, or univariate, *t-test,* the degrees of freedom, or *df,* is simply *N* − 1. For the sample of 10 representing WELF94, there are $10 - 1 = 9$ degrees of freedom.

Testing the Value of t

We'll use a two-tailed test for the problem here because we are only interested in whether our sample mean, 7.62, is significantly different from, not bigger than, the population mean of 6.87. Looking at the values in Appendix C, we see that any t-value above 2.262 is statistically significant at the .05 level with 9 degrees of freedom. With a t-value of .58, we can not reject the null hypothesis that the mean of the population (those 50 states, plus Washington, D.C.) from which we drew the sample is 6.87.

In other words, reaching in and grabbing samples of 10 from the 51 cases of WELF94 in Table 14.7, we could get the sample mean of 7.62 more than five times out of a hundred tries just by chance. (In fact, a lot more. With a t-value of .58, the mean will fall between 4.7 and 10.6 in 95% of samples of 10, and you can expect a mean of about 7.62 in 58% of all samples of 10 when the actual mean of the population is 6.87. The fact that the t-value is .58 and that you'd expect a mean of 7.62 in 58% of samples is just a coincidence.)

Testing the Mean of Large Samples

Another way to see this is to apply what we learned about the normal distribution in Chapter 5. We know that in any normal distribution for a large population, 68.26% of the statistics for estimating parameters will fall within 1 standard error of the actual parameter, 95% of the estimates will fall between the mean and 1.96 standard errors, and 99% of the estimates will fall between the mean and 2.58 standard errors.

In Table 14.1, I showed you a small sample of the data from the study that Ryan, Borgatti, and I did on attitudes about environmental activism. In that study, we interviewed a random sample of 609 adults from across the United States. The mean age of respondents in our sample was 44.21, SD 15.75. Only 591 respondents agreed to tell us their age, so the standard error of the mean is

$$15.75/\sqrt{591} = 0.648$$

Since we have a large sample, we can calculate the 95% confidence limits using the z distribution (Appendix B):

$$44.21 \pm 1.96 \, (0.648) =$$

$$44.21 - 1.27 = 42.94$$

$$\text{and} \quad 44.21 + 1.27 = 45.48$$

In other words, we expect that 95% of all samples of 591 taken from the 89 million adults in the U.S. will fall between 42.94 and 45.48. As we saw in Chapter 5, these numbers are the 95% *confidence limits* of the mean. As it happens, we know from the U.S. Census Bureau that the real average age of the adult (over-18) population in the U.S. in 1997 (when the survey was done) was 44.98.

Thus: (1) the sample statistic ($\overline{x} = 44.21$) and (2) the parameter ($\mu = 44.98$) *both* fall within the 95% confidence limits, and we *cannot reject the null hypothesis* that our sample comes from a population whose average age is equal to our sample mean.

MORE ABOUT z-SCORES

As we saw also in Chapter 5 on sampling, every real score in a distribution has a *z-score,* also called a *standard score.* A z-score tells you how far, in standard deviations, a real score is from the mean of the distribution. The formula for finding a z-score is

Raw score – $\bar{x}$/standard deviation   (Formula 14.8)

The mean for the welfare data in Table 14.9 is 7.62 and the standard deviation is 4.11. To find the z-scores of the data on welfare in Table 14.9, subtract 7.62 from each raw score and divide the result by 4.11. Table 14.11 shows these z-scores.

Why Use Standard Scores?

There are several advantages to using standard scores rather than raw scores. First of all, while raw scores are always in specialized units (percentages of people, kilos of meat, hours of time, etc.), standard scores measure the difference, in standard deviations, between a raw score and the mean of the set of scores. A z-score close to 0 means that the raw score was close to the average. A z-score that is close to plus-or-minus 1 means that the raw score was about 1 standard deviation from the mean, and so on.

What this means, in practice, is that when you standardize a set of scores, you create a scale that lets you make comparisons *within* chunks of your data.

❖

For example, we see from Table 14.11 that the welfare rates for Minnesota and Washington, D.C., are 5.4% and 16.7%, respectively. One of these raw numbers (16.7%) is about three times the other (5.4%). And similarly, the welfare rate for California (11.7%) is three times the rate for North Dakota (3.9%). These raw numbers (welfare rates) tell us something, but the z-scores tell us more: The rate for Minnesota is about half a *SD* below the mean, while the rate for Washington, D.C., is more than 2 *SD* above the mean; the rates for North Dakota and California are about 1 *SD* below and 1 above the mean, respectively.

A second advantage of standard scores over raw measurements is that standard scores are independent of the units in which the original measurements are made. This means that you can compare the relative position of cases across different variables.

Medical social scientists measure variables called "weight for length" and "length for age" in the study of nutritional status of infants across cultures. Linda Hodge and Darna Dufour (1991) studied the growth and development of Shipibo Indian children in Peru. They weighed and measured 149 infants, from newborns to 36 months in age.

By converting all measurements for height and weight to z-scores, they were able to compare their measurements of the Shipibo babies against standards set by the World Health Organization (Frisancho 1990) for healthy babies. The result: By the time Shipibo children are 12 months old, 77% of boys and 42% of girls have z-scores of –2 or more on length for age. In other words, by a year old, Shipibo babies are more than 2 *SD* under the mean for healthy babies on this measure.

By contrast, only around 10% of Shipibo babies (both sexes) have z-scores of –2 or worse on weight for length. By a year, then, most Shipibo babies are clinically "stunted" but they are not clinically "wasted." This does not mean that Shipibo babies are just small but healthy. Infant

TABLE 14.11 z-Scores for the Data in Table 14.9 on Welfare Rates

State	WELF94 x	z-Score
Alabama	6.8	–0.1995
California	11.7	0.9927
Colorado	4.7	–0.7105
Washington, D.C.	16.7	2.2093
Idaho	3.4	–1.0268
Minnesota	5.4	–0.5402
New York	10.0	0.5791
North Dakota	3.9	–0.9051
Washington	7.1	–0.1265
Wisconsin	6.5	–0.2725

mortality is as high as 50% in some villages, and the z-scores on all three measures are similar to scores found in many developing countries where children suffer from malnutrition.

There is one disadvantage to z-scores: They can be downright unintuitive. Imagine trying to explain to people who have not had any instruction in statistics why you are so proud of scoring a 1.96 on one of the SAT tests. That z-score—not quite 2 standard deviations above the average— means that just 2.5% of all test takers scored higher than you did. The fact that z-scores are negative as well as positive doesn't make things any easier. A z-score of –.50 on an SAT test means that about 33% of all test takers scored lower than you did.

This is why T-scores were invented. T-scores are *linear transformations* of z-scores. The mean of a set of z-scores is always 0 and its standard deviation is always 1. For the SAT, GRE, and some other achievement tests, the mean is set at 500 and the standard deviation is set at 100. A score of 400 on these tests, then, is 1 standard deviation below the mean; a score of 740 is 2.4 standard deviations above the mean (Friedenberg 1995:85).

THE UNIVARIATE CHI-SQUARE TEST

Finally, chi-square (often written χ^2) is an important part of univariate analysis. It is a test of whether the distribution of a series of counts is likely to be a chance event. The formula for χ^2 is

$$\chi^2 = \Sigma \frac{(O - E)^2}{E} \qquad \text{(Formula 14.9)}$$

where O represents the observed number of cases and E represents the number of cases you'd expect, ceteris paribus, or "all other things being equal."

Suppose that among 14 families there are a total of 42 children. If children were distributed

TABLE 14.12 Chi-Square for a Univariate Distribution

							Family No.							
1	*2*	*3*	*4*	*5*	*6*	*7*	*8*	*9*	*10*	*11*	*12*	*13*	*14*	

Expected number of children per family

| 3 | 3 | 3 | 3 | 3 | 3 | 3 | 3 | 3 | 3 | 3 | 3 | 3 | 3 | Total = 42 |

Observed number of children per family

| 0 | 0 | 5 | 5 | 5 | 6 | 6 | 0 | 0 | 3 | 1 | 0 | 6 | 5 | Total = 42 |

(Observed – Expected)^2

| 9 | 9 | 4 | 4 | 4 | 9 | 9 | 9 | 9 | 0 | 4 | 9 | 9 | 4 | |

$$\frac{(\text{Observed} - \text{Expected})^2}{\text{Expected}}$$

| 3 | 3 | 1.33 | 1.33 | 1.33 | 3 | 3 | 3 | 3 | 0 | 1.33 | 3 | 3 | 1.33 | |

$$\chi^2 = \Sigma \frac{(O-E)^2}{E} = 3 + 3 + 1.33 + 1.33 \ldots 1.33 = 30.65$$

equally among the 14 families, we'd expect each family to have three of them. Table 14.12 shows what we would expect and what we might find in an actual set of data. The χ^2 value for this distribution is 30.65.

Finding the Significance of χ^2

To determine whether this value of χ^2 is significant, first calculate the degrees of freedom (abbreviated *df*) for the problem. For a univariate table: *df* = the number of cells minus one, or 14 – 1 = 13 in this case.

Next, go to Appendix D, which is the distribution for χ^2, and read down the left-hand margin to 13 degrees of freedom and across to find the *critical value* of χ^2 for any given level of significance. The levels of significance are listed across the top of the table.

The greater the significance of a χ^2 value, the less likely it is that the distribution you are testing is the result of chance.

In exploratory research, you might be satisfied with a .10 level of significance. In evaluating the side effects of a medical treatment, you might demand a .001 level—or even more. Considering the χ^2 value for the problem in Table 14.12, the results look pretty significant. With 13 degrees of freedom, a χ^2 value of 22.362 is significant at the .05 level, a χ^2 value of 27.688 is significant at the .01 level, and a χ^2 value of 34.528 is significant at the .001 level.

In exploratory research, you might be satisfied with a .10 level of significance. In evaluating side effects of a medical treatment, you might demand a .001 level—or even more.

With a χ^2 of 30.65, we can say that the distribution of the number of children across the 14 families is statistically significant at better than the .01 level, but not at the .001 level.

Statistical significance here means only that the distribution of number of children for these 14 families is not likely to be a chance event. Perhaps half the families happen to be at the end of their fertility careers, while half are just starting. Perhaps half the families are members of an ethnic group that traditionally has large families and half are not. The *substantive* significance of these data requires interpretation, based on your knowledge of what's going on, on the ground.

Univariate numerical analysis—frequencies, means, distributions, and so on—and univariate graphical analysis—histograms, box plots, frequency polygons, and so on—tell us a lot. Begin all analysis this way and let all your data and your experience guide you in their interpretation. It is not always possible, however, to simply scan your data and use univariate, descriptive statistics to understand the subtle relations that they harbor. That will require more complex techniques that we'll take up in the next two chapters.

Chapter 14 Review

KEY CONCEPTS

SUMMARY

❖ Quantitative data analysis involves univariate, bivariate, and multivariate analysis.
  ◆ Univariate analysis involves getting to know data intimately by examining variables precisely and in detail.
  ◆ Bivariate analysis involves looking at associations between pairs of variables and trying to understand how those associations work.
  ◆ Multivariate analysis involves understanding the effects of more than one independent variable at a time on a dependent variable.

❖ The first thing to do in dealing with quantitative data is to lay them out in tables and in graphs and get a feel for them.

❖ Good codebooks are indispensable.
  ◆ Naming variables is something of an art, but research projects typically have dozens, even hundreds, of variables. You can be as clever as you like with variable names, but include a verbose description of each variable in your codebook so you'll know what all those clever names mean a year later.

❖ Frequency distributions show the frequency of each attribute of a variable.
  ◆ If a variable has no variability, then it is of no further interest for data analysis.
  ◆ Frequency distributions give you hints about how to collapse variables.

❖ The first thing to do is get some overall measure of the "typical" value for each variable. This is called a measure of central tendency. Social researchers rely on three main measures of central tendency: the mode, the median, and the mean.
  ◆ The mode is the attribute of a variable that occurs most frequently. The mode can be found for nominal, ordinal, and interval variables, but it is the only measure of central tendency available for nominal variables. The mode is often reported in terms of percentages or ratios.
  ◆ The median is the point in a distribution above and below which there is an equal number of scores in a distribution. The median can be found for ordinal and interval variables. The median is the 50th percentile in a distribution.
  ◆ The mean, or the average, is the sum of the individual scores in a distribution, divided by the number of scores. The mean can be found for ordinal and interval variables. The sum of the deviations from the mean of all the scores in a distribution is zero.

- The mean is heavily influenced by special cases, called outliers, and even in large samples, it's heavily influenced by big gaps in the distribution of cases. When data are normally distributed, the mean is the best indicator of central tendency. When interval-level data are highly skewed, the median is often a better indicator of central tendency.

❖ A good first cut at understanding whether data are normally distributed or skewed is to lay them out graphically. Among the most widely used methods for graphing data are bar graphs and pie charts for nominal and ordinal variables; stem-and-leaf plots, box plots, histograms, and frequency polygons for interval variables.
  - In the bar graphs, the bars do not touch one another. This indicates that the data are nominal or ordinal and not continuous.
  - Stem-and-leaf plots and box plots show the median (the 50th percentile) and the lower and upper hinges (the 25th and 75th percentiles). The whiskers in box plots extend one and a half times the interquartile range from the lower and the upper hinges of the box. When data are normally distributed, this will be about 2.7 standard deviations from the mean. Cases outside that range are outliers.
  - Histograms are bar graphs, but the bars touch one another, indicating that the data are continuous. Frequency polygons are continuous line drawings of the same data that produce histograms. You connect the tops of the bars of a histogram and display the result without the bars. Frequency polygons and box plots help you see whether a distribution is normal or skewed to the right or to the left.
  - Bimodal distributions are everywhere. Be on the lookout for them.

❖ After central tendency and shape, the next thing we want to know about data is something about how homogeneous or heterogeneous they are—that is, something about their dispersion.
  - For interval-scale variables, the most important measures of dispersion are variance and the standard deviation.
  - The standard deviation is calculated from the variance, written s^2, which is the average squared deviation from the mean of the measures in a set of data.

❖ Testing whether a sample mean is likely to represent the true mean of a population involves testing a hypothesis.
  - The logic of hypothesis testing involves setting up a null hypothesis, H_0, and an alternative hypothesis, H_1, and then trying to falsify the null hypothesis.
  - This, in turn, involves establishing a probability level—the so-called critical region—for rejecting the null hypothesis, and deciding whether to use a one-tailed or a two-tailed test.

EXERCISES

1. Here is a list of the suicide rates for the 50 states of the U.S. and Washington, D.C.

Deaths by Suicide per 100,000 for the United States, 1994

State	Suicide Rate	State	Suicide Rate	State	Suicide Rate
Washington, D.C.	5.1	Nebraska	11.6	Kentucky	13.5
New Jersey	7.3	Hawaii	11.7	Oklahoma	13.8
New York	8.2	Mississippi	11.8	Missouri	13.8
Rhode Island	8.2	California	11.8	West Virginia	14.2
Massachusetts	8.5	Georgia	11.8	Washington	14.2
Illinois	9.1	New Hampshire	12.1	Arkansas	14.8
Ohio	9.9	Virginia	12.5	Florida	14.9
Connecticut	9.9	North Dakota	12.5	Utah	15.3
Vermont	10.0	Indiana	12.5	Oregon	16.6
Maryland	10.5	Alabama	12.6	Colorado	16.8
Minnesota	10.8	North Carolina	12.7	Idaho	17.7
Michigan	10.9	Texas	12.7	New Mexico	18.3
Pennsylvania	11.0	South Carolina	12.8	Montana	18.5
Delaware	11.3	Louisiana	12.8	Arizona	18.8
Kansas	11.4	Tennessee	12.8	Alaska	20.0
Iowa	11.4	Maine	13.5	Wyoming	22.5
Wisconsin	11.6	South Dakota	13.5	Nevada	23.4

SOURCE: *Statistical Abstract of the United States* (U.S. Census Bureau 1997, Table 132).

— What is the mode for these data?

— Calculate the median for these data.

— Group these data into four chunks: (1) less than 10 per 100,000; (2) 10-12 per 100,000; (3) 12.1-15 per thousand; and (4) more than 15 per 100,000. Calculate the median and the mean of these grouped data.

— Calculate the mean and standard deviation for these data. What happens if you don't count the data for Nevada? How much does that change the mean and the standard deviation?

— Draw a histogram and a frequency polygon (you can do this by hand or use a computer program) for the 51 data points. If you have a statistics program, draw a stem-and-leaf plot and a box plot for these data. What is the range and the interquartile range?

— Take a random sample of 15 data points and calculate the mean for the sample. Using alpha = .05, test whether the mean of the sample reflects the mean of the population of 51 elements.

2. These data show the number of seats in the lower house of parliament for each of the 15 countries in the European Union (EU) and the percentage of women elected to those seats. Are women equally represented in the governments of the EU?

Percentage of Women in the Parliaments of the European Union

Country	No. of Seats in Parliament	Percentage of Women in Parliament
Austria	183	26.8
Belgium	150	12.0
Denmark	179	33.0
Finland	200	33.5
France	577	6.4
Germany	672	26.2
Greece	300	6.3
Ireland	166	13.9
Italy	630	11.1
Luxembourg	60	20.0
Netherlands	150	31.3
Portugal	230	13.0
Spain	350	24.6
Sweden	349	40.4
United Kingdom	651	9.5

SOURCE: *The World's Women 1995: Trends and Statistics*, New York: United Nations Publications. http://www.un.org/Depts/ unsd/ gender/intro.htm.

3. Suppose you are participating in the development of a new program to prepare prison inmates for parole into the community. The null hypothesis is that the program doesn't work. Discuss the consequences of making a Type I or a Type II error in assessing the null hypothesis. Consider the consequences if the recipients of the program were originally incarcerated for violent or for nonviolent crimes.

4. Use the t distribution to find the 95% and 99% confidence limits for $\bar{x} = 30$, $SD = 6$, $N = 18$. What happens to the confidence limits if $N = 40$?

FURTHER READING

Basic descriptive statistics. All the methods described in this chapter and the next two chapters are treated more fully in texts on statistical methods.

Visualizing data. For more on graphical methods of statistics, see Jacoby (1997). Wallgren et al. (1996) is an excellent step-by-step introduction for creating charts and figures.

If you want to go further, the two volumes by Tufte (1983, 1997) are required reading (well, not really reading, since they are mostly pictures) for all scientists. You'll find examples of every type of graph you can think of—and many you couldn't think of.

Statistical significance. For more on current thinking about statistical tests, see Chow (1996) and Harlow et al. (1997).

Data management. For a general discussion of problems in data management, see chapters in Bickman and Rog (1998).

15 | BIVARIATE ANALYSIS
TESTING RELATIONS

IN THIS CHAPTER:

❖ INTRODUCTION

This chapter is about describing relations between pairs of variables—covariations—and testing the significance of those relations.

The *qualitative* concept of covariation creeps into ordinary conversation all the time: "If kids weren't exposed to so much TV violence, there would be less crime." Ethnographers also use the concept of covariation in statements like "Many people in the neighborhood say that when more cops are on the street, crime goes down." Here the rate of crime is said to covary negatively with the rate of cops on the street.

The concept of *statistical* covariation, however, is more precise than that used in ordinary conversation. There are two primary and two secondary things we want to know about a statistical relation between two variables.

The primary questions are these:

1. How big is it? In other words, how much better could we predict the score of a dependent variable in our sample if we knew the score of some independent variable? Correlation coefficients answer this question.
2. Is the covariation due to chance, or is it likely to exist in the overall population to which we want to generalize? In other words, is it statistically significant? Statistical tests answer this question.

For many problems, we also want to know:

3. What is its direction? Is it positive or negative?
4. What is its shape? Is it linear or nonlinear?

Answers to these questions about qualities of a relationship come best from looking at graphs.

Testing for statistical significance is a mechanical affair—you look up, in a table, whether a statistic showing covariation between two variables is or is not significant. I'll discuss how to do this for several of the commonly used statistics that I introduce in this chapter. Statistical significance, however, does not necessarily mean substantive or theoretical importance. Interpreting the substantive and theoretical importance of statistical significance is anything but mechanical. It requires thinking, and that's *your* job.

THE *t*-TEST: COMPARING TWO MEANS

We begin our exploration of bivariate analysis with the two-sample *t*-test. In Chapter 14, we saw how to use the one-sample *t*-test to evaluate the probability that the mean of a sample reflects the mean of the population from which the sample was drawn. The two-sample *t*-test evaluates whether the means of two independent groups differ on some variable. Table 15.1 shows some

TABLE 15.1 Number of Children Wanted (CW) by College Students in the United States and in Liberia

No.	CW	REGION	SEX	No.	CW	REGION	SEX	No.	CW	REGION	SEX
1	1	US	M	29	0	US	F	57	12	LI	M
2	3	US	M	30	0	US	F	58	12	LI	M
3	3	US	M	31	0	US	F	59	8	LI	M
4	3	US	M	32	0	US	F	60	6	LI	M
5	3	US	M	33	1	US	F	61	4	LI	M
6	3	US	M	34	1	US	F	62	4	LI	M
7	2	US	M	35	2	US	F	63	2	LI	M
8	2	US	M	36	2	US	F	64	3	LI	M
9	2	US	M	37	2	US	F	65	3	LI	M
10	2	US	M	38	2	US	F	66	4	LI	M
11	2	US	M	39	2	US	F	67	4	LI	M
12	2	US	M	40	2	US	F	68	4	LI	M
13	1	US	M	41	2	US	F	69	4	LI	M
14	6	US	M	42	2	US	F	70	3	LI	F
15	1	US	M	43	2	US	F	71	3	LI	F
16	1	US	M	44	6	LI	M	72	3	LI	F
17	4	US	M	45	4	LI	M	73	3	LI	F
18	0	US	M	46	4	LI	M	74	7	LI	F
19	5	US	F	47	4	LI	M	75	2	LI	F
20	4	US	F	48	5	LI	M	76	4	LI	F
21	4	US	F	49	5	LI	M	77	6	LI	F
22	4	US	F	50	5	LI	M	78	4	LI	F
23	3	US	F	51	5	LI	M	79	4	LI	F
24	2	US	F	52	5	LI	M	80	4	LI	F
25	3	US	F	53	7	LI	M	81	4	LI	F
26	0	US	F	54	12	LI	M	82	4	LI	F
27	2	US	F	55	6	LI	M	83	4	LI	F
28	0	US	F	56	6	LI	M	84	4	LI	F

SOURCE: Data were provided by W. P. Handwerker.

data that Penn Handwerker collected from American and Liberian college students on how many children those students wanted.

Here are the relevant statistics for the data in Table 15.1 (I generated these with SYSTAT®, but you can use any statistics package):

```
                    CW-USA    CW-W.A.
N of cases           43         41
Minimum            0.000      2.000
Maximum            6.000     12.000
Mean               2.047      4.951
95% CI Upper       2.476      5.705
95% CI Lower       1.617      4.198
Std. Error         0.213      0.373
Standard Dev       1.396      2.387
```

There are 43 American students and 41 Liberian students. The Americans wanted, on average, 2.047 children, *SD* 1.396, *SEM* 0.213. The Liberians wanted, on average, 4.951 children, *SD* 2.387, *SEM* 0.373.

The null hypothesis, H_0, is that these two means, 2.047 and 4.951, come from random samples of the *same* population—that there is no difference, except for sampling error, between the two means. Stated another way, these two means come from random samples of two populations with identical averages. The research hypothesis, H_1, is that these two means, 2.047 and 4.951, come from random samples of truly different populations.

The formula for calculating *t* for two independent samples is

$$t = \frac{\bar{x}_1 - \bar{x}_2}{\sqrt{\sigma^2(1/N_1 + 1/N_2)}} \qquad \text{(Formula 15.1)}$$

That is, *t* is the difference between the means of the samples, divided by the fraction of the standard deviation σ, of the total population, that comes from each of the two separate populations from which the samples were drawn. (Remember, we use Roman letters, like *s,* for sample statistics, and Greek letters, like σ, for parameters.) Since the standard deviation is the square root of the variance, we need to know the variance, σ^2, of the *parent population.*

The parent population is **the general population from which the two samples were pulled.** Our best guess at σ^2 is to pool the standard deviations from the two samples:

$$\sigma^2 = \frac{(N_1 - 1)s_1^2 + (N_2 - 1)s_2^2}{N_1 + N_2 - 2} \qquad \text{(Formula 15.2)}$$

which is very messy, but just a lot of arithmetic. For the data on the two groups of students, the *pooled variance* is

$$\sigma^2 = \frac{(43 - 1)\,1.396^2 + (41 - 1)\,2.387^2}{43 + 41 - 2}$$

$$= \frac{81.85 + 227.91}{82} = 3.778$$

Now we can solve for *t*:

$$t = \frac{2.047 - 4.951}{\sqrt{3.777(.0477)}} = \frac{-2.904}{\sqrt{.180}} = \frac{-2.904}{.4243} = -6.844$$

Testing the Significance of *t*

We can evaluate the statistical significance of *t* using Appendix C. Recall from Chapter 14 that we need to calculate the degrees of freedom and decide whether we want a one-tailed or a two-tailed test to find the critical region for rejecting the null hypothesis. For a two-sample *t*-test, the degrees of freedom equals

$$(N_1 + N_2) - 2$$

so there are $43 + 41 - 2 = 82$ degrees of freedom in this particular problem.

If you test the possibility that one mean will be higher than another, then you need a one-tailed test. After all, you're only asking whether the mean is likely to fall in one tail of the *t* distribution (see Figure 5.8). If you want to test only whether the two means are different, and not that one will be higher than the other, then you need a two-tailed test. Notice in Appendix C that scores significant at the .10 level for a two-tailed test are significant at the .05 level for a one-tailed test; scores significant at the .05 level for a two-tailed

TABLE 15.2 A Typical Experiment in Education

	Average Score on the Pretest	Average Score on the Posttest
Classes using the new program	x_1	x_2
Classes using the old program	x_3	x_4

test are significant at the .025 level for a one-tailed test, and so on.

We'll use a two-tailed test for the problem here because we are interested only in the magnitude of the difference between the means, not its direction or sign (plus or minus). We are interested here, then, only in the *absolute value* of *t*, 6.844.

Looking at the values in Appendix C, we see that any *t*-value above 3.291 is significant for a two-tailed test at the .001 level. Assuming that our samples represent the populations of American students and Liberian students, we'd expect the observed difference in the means of how many children they want to occur by chance less than once every thousand times we run this survey.

An Example

Sandra Bem (1974) used the simple *t*-test to select items for the famous BSRI (Bem Sex Role Inventory). She compiled a list of about 400 personality traits: about 100 positive traits that seemed feminine in tone, according to normative standards at the time (expressive, nurturing, etc.); another 100 positive traits that seemed masculine in tone (instrumental, take charge, etc.); about 100 positive gender-neutral traits; and about 100 negative gender-neutral traits.

Bem asked 100 Stanford University undergraduates to rate each of the 400 traits on a scale of 1 to 7, from *not at all desirable* to *extremely desirable*. For example, two of the items were: "In American society, how desirable is it for a woman to be sincere?" and "In American society, how desirable is it for a man to be truthful?" If a trait was judged by both men and women to be significantly more desirable for a man than for a woman, then the trait was selected as a masculine trait. And, similarly for feminine traits.

Bem used two-tailed *t*-tests to assess whether traits were significantly (alpha = .05) more masculine or more feminine and selected 10 positive and 10 negative traits, all of which scored high as either appropriately masculine or appropriately feminine, for the BSRI.

ANALYSIS OF VARIANCE: A TEST FOR TWO OR MORE MEANS

A *t*-test measures the difference between two means. *Analysis of variance,* or *ANOVA,* is a technique that applies to a set of *K* means.

Suppose you want to know whether a new method for teaching reading skills to fifth graders really makes a difference. You divide the fifth-

---

Box 15.1
A Shortcut for Calculating the Variance in a Set of Scores

There's an easier way to calculate the variance than the way I've explained in the text. Here's the formula:

$$s^2 = \frac{\sum x^2 - [(\sum x)^2 / N]}{N - 1}$$

(Formula 5.4)

In other words, you square each value of x and take the sum. Then you square the sum of the values of x and divide by N. Subtract the second quantity from the first and divide by $N - 1$. This makes calculation easy but it doesn't make obvious the fact that the variance involves substracing each observation from the mean of the set of observations on a variable.

---

grade classes in a school district into two groups—one group that uses the new teaching method and one group that does not. Both groups get tested before the program gets under way, and after the program is finished. (You'll recognize this method from Chapter 4 on experimental design.) Then the scores are compared. Table 15.2 is a schematic of the scores you'd be working with.

x_1, x_2, x_3, and x_4 are average scores. The question is: Are all the differences in these scores significant? Put another way (the null hypothesis): Despite differences in the scores, are they really from identical populations? Does it make any real difference in their reading skills if fifth graders are exposed to the new program?

This is where ANOVA comes in. Recall the formula for variance from Chapter 14. Here it is again:

$$s^2 = \frac{\sum (x - \bar{x})^2}{N - 1}$$

(Formula 15.3)

where s^2 is the variance, x represents the raw scores in a distribution of interval-level observations, $\bar{x}$ is the mean of the distribution of raw scores, and N is the total number of observations. In other words, to find the variance in a distribu-

tion: (1) subtract each observation from the mean of the set of observations, (2) square the difference (thus getting rid of negative numbers), (3) sum the squared differences, and (4) divide that sum by the sample size. (See Box 15.1 for a shortcut in calculating the variance.)

Variance, then, is **a measure of how much the scores of individual units of analysis are different from one another.** This is what we called *within-group variance* in Chapter 5 on sampling. We also discussed *between-group variance,* which expresses **the amount that the scores between groups are different from one another.** How can we measure between-group variance?

Table 15.3 shows the scores for four groups of states in the U.S. on the percentage of teenage births.

We have four groups of states and each *group* has a mean. (Note that N is different for each of the four groups. One important feature of analysis of variance is that the Ns don't have to be the same for each of the groups.) The question we want to answer is: Are the differences among the means significantly different at, say, the .05 level?

To find whether the means of the four groups are significantly different from each other—that is, whether they represent different popula-

TABLE 15.3 Percentage of Teenage Births in the 50 U.S. States

	Northeast			Midwest			South			West	
	x_1	x_1^2		x_2	x_2^2		x_3	x_3^2		x_4	x_4^2
NY	9.2	84.64	KS	13.1	171.61	FL	13.4	179.56	NM	17.9	320.41
VT	8.9	79.21	SD	11.5	132.25	AR	19.8	392.04	OR	13.2	174.24
NJ	7.7	59.29	WI	10.6	112.36	KY	17.0	289.00	ID	13.5	182.25
PA	10.6	112.36	IA	11.0	121.00	LA	18.9	357.21	HI	10.3	106.09
MA	7.3	53.29	IN	14.5	210.25	MD	10.3	106.09	NV	13.3	176.89
NH	7.4	54.76	OH	13.3	176.89	MS	21.3	453.69	CO	11.9	141.61
ME	9.7	94.09	ND	9.6	92.16	AL	18.3	334.89	UT	10.6	112.36
CN	8.2	67.24	MI	12.2	148.84	DE	13.7	187.69	CA	12.0	144.00
RI	10.3	106.09	MN	8.5	72.25	GA	15.9	252.81	WY	14.4	207.36
			MO	14.4	207.36	OK	17.2	295.84	WA	11.3	127.69
			NB	10.6	112.36	VA	11.0	121.00	AZ	15.0	225.00
			IL	12.7	161.29	NC	15.0	225.00	AK	11.2	125.44
						WV	16.8	282.24	MT	12.5	156.25
						TN	16.8	282.24			
						SC	16.8	282.24			
						TX	16.2	262.44			

$$\Sigma x_1 = 79.3 \qquad \Sigma x_2 = 142 \qquad \Sigma x_3 = 258.4 \qquad \Sigma x_4 = 167.1$$

$$\Sigma x_1^2 = 710.97 \qquad \Sigma x_2^2 = 1718.62 \qquad \Sigma x_3^2 = 4303.98 \qquad \Sigma x_4^2 = 2199.59$$

$$N = 9 \qquad N = 12 \qquad N = 16 \qquad N = 13$$

$$\bar{x}_1 = 8.811 \qquad \bar{x}_2 = 11.833 \qquad \bar{x}_3 = 16.150 \qquad \bar{x}_4 = 12.854$$

$$s_1^2 = 1.531 \qquad s_2^2 = 3.481 \qquad s_3^2 = 8.721 \qquad s_4^2 = 4.309$$

tions—we will calculate the ratio between the mean of the between-group variance and the mean of the within-group variance.

The between-group and within-group variances sum to the **total variance,** so the next thing we do is find the total variance and subtract the within-group variance.

The formula for the total variance is

$$\text{Total variance} = \Sigma x^2 - \frac{(\Sigma x)^2}{N} \qquad \text{(Formula 15.5)}$$

At the bottom of Table 15.3, I've calculated the four separate, or within-group, variances, using the shortcut formula in Box 15.1. Applying Formula 15.5, the total variance for the data in Table 15.3 is

$$710.97 + 1{,}718.62 + 4{,}303.98 + 2{,}199.59 -$$

$$\frac{(79.3 + 142 + 258.4 + 167.1)^2}{50} =$$

$$8{,}933.16 - \frac{418{,}350.24}{50} = 8{,}933.16 -$$

$$8{,}367.005 = 556.16$$

The formula for calculating the between-group variance (that is, the sum of the squares between groups) is

Between-group variance =

$$\Sigma \; \frac{(\Sigma \, x_{1\ldots2\ldots n})^2}{N_{1\ldots2\ldots n}} - \frac{(\Sigma \, x_{\text{total}})^2}{N_{\text{total}}} \qquad \text{(Formula 15.6)}$$

So, the between-group variance here is

$(79.3^2/9) + (142^2/12) + (258.4^2/16) +$
$(167.1^2/13) - 8,367.005 = 698.72 + 1,680.33$
$+ 4,173.16 + 2,147.88 - 8,367.005 = 333.09$

And since

Within-group variance =
Total variance − Between-group variance

we can now calculate the within-group variance as

$$556.16 - 333.09 = 223.07$$

Analysis of variance involves comparing the mean between-group variance and the mean within-group variance. The mean of the between-group variance is

$$\frac{\text{Total between-group variance}}{\text{Degrees of freedom between groups}}$$

and the mean within-group variance is

$$\frac{\text{Total within-group variance}}{\text{Degrees of freedom within groups}}$$

We compute the degrees of freedom between groups and the degrees of freedom within groups as follows:

df between groups = Number of groups − 1

df within groups = N − Number of groups

So, for the data in Table 15.3, the *df* between groups is 4 − 1 = 3, and the *df* within groups is 50 − 4 = 46.

Then:

The mean between-group variance =
333.09/3 = 111.03

and

The mean within-group variance =
223.07/46 = 4.85

We now have all the information we need to calculate the *F* ratio, which is **the ratio of the mean between-group variance and the mean within-group variance.** (The *F* statistic was named for Sir Ronald Fisher, who developed the idea for the ratio of the between-group and the within-group variances as a general method for comparing the relative size of means across many groups.) We calculate the ratio of the means:

$$F = 111.03/4.85 = 22.89$$
(see Box 15.2 on rounding)

Well, is 22.89 a statistically significant number? To find out, we go to Appendix E, which shows the values of *F* for the .05 and the .01 levels of significance. The values for the between-group *df* are shown across the top of Appendix E, and the values for the within-group *df* are shown along the left side. Looking across the top of the table, we find the column for the between-group *df*. We come down that column to the value of the within-group *df*. In other words, we look down the column labeled 3 and come down to the row for 46.

Since there is no row for exactly 46 degrees of freedom for the within-group value, we use the nearest value, which is for 40 *df*. We see that any

Box 15.2
About Rounding Error

If you run the ANOVA on a computer, using SYSTAT or SPSS, for instance, you'll get a slightly different answer: 21.914. The difference (0.98) is due to rounding in all the calculations we just did.

Computer programs may hold on to 12 decimal places all the way through before returning an answer. In doing these calculations by hand, I've rounded each step of the way to just two decimal places. Rounding error doesn't affect the results of the ANOVA calculations in this particular example because the value of the F statistic is so big. But when the value of the F statistic is below 5, then a difference of .98 either way can lead you to make serious errors of interpretation.

The moral is: Do these calculations with at least six decimal places if you work them by hand, or use a computer program to do the drudge work for you, once you know what you're doing.

F value greater than 2.84 is statistically significant at the .01 (that is, the 1%) level. The F value we got for the data in Table 15.3 was a colossal 22.69. As it turns out, this is statistically significant at beyond the .001 level.

An Example of ANOVA

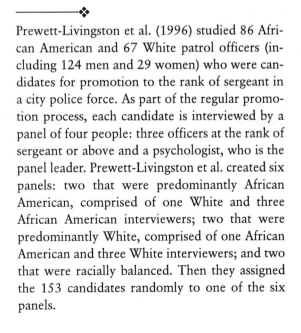

Prewett-Livingston et al. (1996) studied 86 African American and 67 White patrol officers (including 124 men and 29 women) who were candidates for promotion to the rank of sergeant in a city police force. As part of the regular promotion process, each candidate is interviewed by a panel of four people: three officers at the rank of sergeant or above and a psychologist, who is the panel leader. Prewett-Livingston et al. created six panels: two that were predominantly African American, comprised of one White and three African American interviewers; two that were predominantly White, comprised of one African American and three White interviewers; and two that were racially balanced. Then they assigned the 153 candidates randomly to one of the six panels.

Each panelist rated each candidate from 0 to 10 on 14 items (knowledge of procedure, communication skills, etc.). The 14 items were summed to form a single score for each candidate by each panelist. Then, the scores of the White panelists were averaged together and the scores of the African American panelists were averaged. Each candidate then had (1) an average score by Whites on his or her panel, and (2) an average score by African Americans on his or her panel.

Prewett-Livingston et al. tested each of the three pairs of panels to make sure that the overall ratings were not statistically different from one another. Since the panels were reliable, Prewett-Livingston et al. combined the data from the two panels in each panel type. This set up a $3 \times 2 \times 2$ analysis of variance test: There are three panel types (primarily White; primarily African American; racially balanced); two races for the candidates (African American and White); and two races for the interviewers (African American and White). Panel type and race of candidate are between-group variables, while race of interviewer is a within-group variable (see Box 15.3).

Analysis of variance showed evidence that the rated performance of candidates is affected by the

---

Box 15.3
More Complex Forms of ANOVA

Dependent variables in which social scientists are interested, and that are amenable to ANOVA, are things like scores on tests of knowledge or attitudes, scores on personality tests, number of interpersonal contacts, blood pressure, number of minutes per day spent in various activities, and number of grams of various nutrients consumed per day, to name just a few.

When there is one dependent variable (such as a test score) and one independent variable (a single intervention like the reading program), then no matter how many groups or tests are involved, a *one-way* analysis of variance is needed.

If more than one independent variable is involved (say, several competing new housing programs, and several socioeconomic backgrounds) and a single dependent variable (the fraction of income that people get from welfare, or scores on tests of attitudes toward welfare), then ***multiple-way ANOVA,*** or ***factorial ANOVA,*** is called for.

If there are multiple dependent variables, then ***MANOVA*** is called for. When two or more dependent variables are correlated with one another, then ***analysis of covariance (ANCOVA)*** techniques are used.

Multiple-way ANOVA allows you to determine if there are interaction effects among independent variables. That is, with interval-level scores on independent variables, we can use ANOVA to measure the interaction effects among variables—to determine if a variable has different effects under different conditions.

Analysis of variance is one of the most widely use methods for analyzing data across the social sciences. Like all popular multivariate techniques, ANOVA is available in the packaged computer programs that you are likely to deal with.

---

race of the candidate and the racial composition of the panels. The effects, however, were not stereotypical. White and African American raters on majority White panels *both* tended to score White candidates higher than they scored African American candidates. Similarly, White and African American raters on majority African American panels *both* tended to score African American candidates higher than they scored White candidates.

DIRECTION AND SHAPE OF COVARIATIONS

As you can tell from my discussion of box plots and frequency polygons and such in Chapter 14, I like to look at things like shape and direction—qualitative things—in connection with numerical results. The concept of *direction* refers to **whether a covariation is positive or negative**. The concept of *shape* refers to **whether a relation is *linear* or *nonlinear*.**

For example, the amount of cholesterol you have in your blood and the probability that you will die of a heart attack at any given age are *positive covariants*: The *more* cholesterol, the *higher* the probability. Similarly, the *more violence* that children are exposed to on television, the *more aggressive* they are likely to be (see Wood et al. 1991; Hogben 1998). These two variables are also positive covariants.

By contrast, the *more education* you have, the *lower the probability that you smoke cigarettes.* Education and the probability of smoking cigarettes are *negative covariants*.

Some shapes and directions of bivariate relations are shown in the five *scattergrams* of Figure 15.1. Figure 15.1a is a plot of the percentage of children, ages 5-17, in each of the 50 states in the U.S. (without Washington, D.C.) who were in public schools in 1994, and the percentage of adults in each of the 50 states who were in prison the following year. The dots are scattered haphazardly, and it's pretty obvious that there is *no relation* between these two variables.

Linear and Nonlinear Relations

Figure 15.1b is a plot of the infant mortality rate (the number of babies, per thousand, who die before they are a year old) by the life expectancy of women, for each of 194 countries in the world in the period 1995-2000. This is a clear case of a *linear and negative relation* between two variables: **The higher the score on one variable, the lower the score tends to be on the other.** So, in countries where the life expectancy is high, infant mortality tends to be low, and vice versa.

The third scattergram, Figure 15.1c, is a plot of the number of physicians per hundred thousand population in 1994 in each of the 50 states in the U.S. (without Washington, D.C.), by the average per capita income in those states in 1996. This is a clear case of a *linear and positive relation:* **The higher the score on one variable, the higher the score tends to be on the other.** So, across the U.S., the higher the per capita income, the higher the availability of physicians.

Figure 15.1d is a plot, for 194 countries of the world, of the relation between infant mortality in 1995 and per capita GDP that year. The GDP, or gross domestic product, is the total value of the goods and services produced in a country. The per capita GDP in 1995 ranged from less than $100 per person, for Sudan and Ethiopia, to over $40,000 person, for Japan and Switzerland. The dots in Figure 15.1d are not scattered around randomly—*something* is clearly going on between these two variables. As the per capita GDP rises, the rate of infant mortality falls, but the *shape* of the relation is *nonlinear.*

Figure 15.1e shows another kind of nonlinear relation. The relation between age and the number of people one knows has this peaked shape. Early in life the number of friends, kin, and acquaintances is small, but that number grows as you get older. This relation is linear and positive. The longer you live, the more people you get to know.

Up to a point. If you live long enough, a lot of the people you know start dying, and your network shrinks. There is a strong, negative relation between age and number of people in your network after age 70. A special kind of correlation coefficient, called eta, measures the strength of this kind of nonlinear covariation, and I'll discuss it at the end of this chapter when we deal with regression.

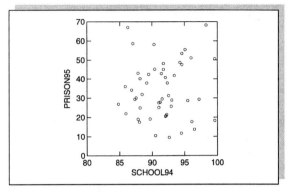

a. A random plot. There is no relation between the proportion of the adult population in prison and the proportion of the school-age children enrolled in school in the 50 states of the U.S.

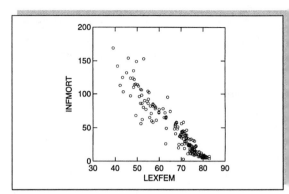

b. A linear, negative relation between the life expectancy for women and the rate of infant mortality in 194 countries, 1995-2000.

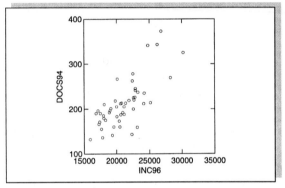

c. A linear, positive relation between the average per capita income and the number of physicians per hundred thousand population for the 50 states of the U.S.

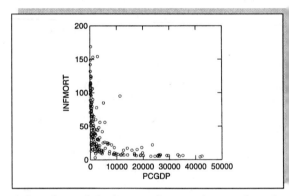

d. A nonlinear relation between the per capita gross domestic product and the rate of infant mortality for 194 countries, 1995-2000.

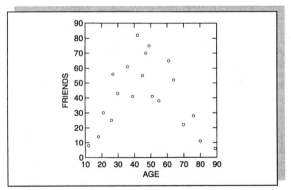

e. A nonlinear relation between age and the number of friends or acquaintances people have.

Figure 15.1 Scattergrams Showing the Common Shapes of Bivariate Relations

TABLE 15.4 Distribution of Family Types, by Race, in the United States in 1996

	White	African American	Row Total
Two parents	22,178 (74%)	1,942 (36%)	24,120
Single parent	7,769 (26%)	3,493 (64%)	11,262
Column total	29,947 (100%)	5,435 (100%)	35,382

a. A 2 × 2 table of household type by race (in thousands)

	White	African American	Row Total
Two parents	22,178 (74%)	1,942 (36%)	24,120
Female head of household	6,329 (21%)	3,171 (58%)	9,500
Male head of household	1,440 (5%)	322 (6%)	1,762
Column total	29,947 (100%)	5,435 (100%)	35,382

b. A 3 × 2 table of household type by race (in thousands)

SOURCE: *Statistical Abstract of the United States* (U.S. Census Bureau 1997, Table 75).

CROSS-TABS OF NOMINAL VARIABLES

Now that we've looked at shape and direction, let's get down to actually looking for relations between variables. We begin with nominal variables and move on to ordinal and then interval variables.

Table 15.4a is an example of a *cross-tab,* or *cross-tabulation table* of two nominal variables. It's a 2 × 2 (two-by-two) cross-tabulation of household types (married couples with children, and single parents with children) by so-called racial groups (White and African American) in the United States in 1996 (see Box 15.4).

A 2 × 2 table is also called a *fourfold table.* Any table comparing data on two variables is called a *bivariate table.* Not all bivariate tables are 2 × 2, since variables can take more than just two values. Table 15.4b shows a 3 × 2 (three-by-three) table. This time, the family type is broken into three types instead of just two: married couples with children, female-headed households with children, and male-headed households with children.

In these tables, the numbers in parentheses are the *column percentages* for each cell. The numbers in these tables are in thousands, so, in Table 15.4a, we see that there were 29,947,000 households in the U.S., with children under the age of 18, classified by the Bureau of the Census as White. Of those, 22,178,000, or 74% of the 29,947,000, had two parents and 7,769,000 (26%) had one parent.

Table 15.4a also shows that, in 1996, there were 5,435,000 households in the U.S. with children under the age of 18 classified by the Bureau of the Census as African American. Of those households, 1,942,000 (36%) had two parents and 3,493,000 (64%) had one parent.

Many researchers display only the column percentages in a bivariate table, along with the column totals, or *Ns,* and a summary statistic that describes the table. This convention is shown in Table 15.5. Tables are less cluttered this way, and you get a better understanding of what's going on.

Box 15.4
About the Social Concept of "Race"

I say so-called "race" here because, as an anthropologist, I know how problematic that word "race" is. For most English speakers, the word race has a thoroughly biological meaning, even though it is essentially a social concept, with hardly any biological utility when applied to humans.

I'm tempted to use the phrase "ethnic group" to refer to African Americans and Whites, but there are serious problems associated with that seemingly innocuous phrase, too. Applied to people whom the U.S. Census calls African Americans and Whites, the term ethnic group implies that people who have similar skin color and who share common historical roots (their ancestors either arrived in North America from Africa or came from Europe) share an ethnicity. Italian Americans from New York, Hasidic Jews from Denver, Mennonites from rural Minnesota, Polish Americans from Detroit . . . do all these people really share the same ethnicity because they are White skinned and have ancestors who came from some place in Europe?

Consider the differences in the cultural content of people who are black-skinned, Cajun-English bilinguals from rural Louisiana; black-skinned, Gullah-English bilinguals of coastal South Carolina; and black-skinned residents of, say, New York City. Do all these people really share an ethnicity because they are black skinned and have ancestors who came from some place on the continent of Africa? The mind boggles at the thought of trying to force all these cultural groups into some kind of cookie-cutter mold because of such arbitrary characteristics as skin color and historical ancestry.

I use the word "race," then, with all the qualifications it deserves. The data in Table 15.4 show pretty clearly that there is an association between skin color and family type. What that association is really about is worthy of serious investigation by social scientists.

---

from percentages than from raw numbers in a bivariate table. As long as the column Ns are given, the interested reader can easily reconstruct the Ns for each cell.

Numbers along the right side and below a table—that is, the numbers in the margins—are called, unsurprisingly, the *marginals*. The marginal in the lower-right-hand corner of Tables 15.4 and 15.5 (35,382) is the total frequency of elements in the table. The sum of the marginals down the right-hand side and the sum of the marginals across the bottom are identical.

CORRELATION AND CAUSE: ANTECEDENT AND INTERVENING VARIABLES

Note that the column percentages sum to 100% and that since we have percentaged the table down the columns, it makes no sense to total the percentages in the right margin. In constructing bivariate tables, no matter what size (2 × 2, 3 × 2, or larger tables), we put the dependent variable in the rows and the independent variable in the columns. Then there's an easy rule to follow in

TABLE 15.5 A 2 × 2 Table of Household Type by Race in the United States in 1996 (in thousands), with Percentages in the Cells and Ns in the Margins

	White	African American	Row Total
Two parents	74%	36%	24,120
Single parent	26%	64%	11,262
Column total	29,947 (100%)	5,435 (100%)	35,382

Box 15.5
Where Do X and Y Go?

By convention, the values of dependent variables make up the rows of tables and the values of independent variables make up the columns. Also by convention, the values of dependent variables are plotted on the y-axis, or *ordinate,* of a scattergram, and the values of independent variables are plotted on the x-axis, or *abscissa.* It is important to be consistent in data analysis, and it's much easier to be consistent if you follow a convention in setting up tables and scattergrams.

There are, of course, exceptions to these conventions in the literature—they are, after all, conventions and not laws—for example, when the independent variable (the columns) has too many categories to fit on a narrow page.

reading a table: *percentage down the columns and interpret across the rows* (see Box 15.5).

Try doing this for Table 15.5. I've put the independent variable (White, African American) in the columns and the dependent variable (single-parent and two-parent families) in the rows. *Percentaging down,* see that 74% of White households had two parents and 26% had one parent. For African American households, 36% had two parents and 64% had one parent. *Interpreting across,* we see that 74% of White households had two parents compared to 36% of African American households, and that 26% of White households had single parents compared to 64% for African American households.

In a bivariate cross-tab, one variable is the dependent and the other is the independent variable. In Table 15.5, then, household type is the dependent variable and race is the independent

variable. There's no getting around it: When we do cross-tab analysis, we're trying to *understand* something about cause and effect. But as I explained in Chapter 2, there is absolutely *no assumption* that an independent variable actually *causes* a dependent variable.

I know this sounds a little convoluted, but look at Table 15.5 carefully and you can see how it works. Clearly, the probability in 1996 of belonging to a one-parent family was much higher for African Americans than it was for Whites in the U.S. It was, in fact, two and a half times more likely (26% compared to 64%). Clearly, the dependent variable here is family type, and not race. Nobody's skin color (which is, after all, what the so-called race variable is about) depends on whether they are a member of a two-parent or a one-parent family.

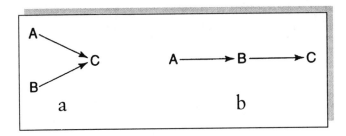

Figure 15.2 Antecedent and Intervening Variables

And clearly—and I mean absolutely, positively, no-fooling, clearly—*being* an African American did not cause anyone, not one single person, to be part of a single-parent household.

There is definitely a relation between the independent and dependent variables, but it's not a cause-and-effect relation. To understand the relation between these variables, we need to ask some questions about *antecedent variables* and *intervening variables*: (1) Is there some variable that is *related to, and prior to,* both the independent and dependent variables? and (2) Is there some variable that enters the picture *between* the independent and independent variables?

Figure 15.2a shows how antecedent variables work. Two variables are correlated, but it turns out that a third variable is related to, and prior to, both of them. The association between the first two variables—the independent and dependent variables—is not an illusion. It's a real association, but both variables are related to an antecedent.

We know, for example, that drivers under the age of 25 have more accidents than do drivers age 26 and older. The bivariate relation between age and the risk of wrecking a car is strong, but it is even stronger when we look at the data for men and for women separately. Men under 25 have far more accidents than do women under 25. Logi-

cally, gender is antecedent to the relation between age and the risk of wrecking a car.

The average age at which women in the U.S. get married is about 23. But women who were married in 1975, were, on average, about 22 years old, while women married in 1995 were about 25 years old. The age cohort is a variable that is antecedent to the relation between gender and age at marriage.

Figure 15.2b shows how intervening variables work. We've known for a very long time that women who graduate from women's colleges are more likely to turn up in lists like *Who's Who of American Women* than are women who graduate from coed schools (Tidball 1973). This correlation has been attributed to the fact that women's self-esteem is enhanced in the supportive environment of an all-women's school.

Ledman et al. (1995) found provisional support for the existence of an intervening variable: Women who graduate from all-women's schools are more likely to go on for graduate work and advanced degrees, which are pretty good predictors of success. The conclusion was tentative, but it's the sort of thing that makes good, incremental social science. Someone notices a relation between two variables; someone else improves our understanding of the relation.

Covariation and Cause

———❖

Go back to Table 15.5. Now, 74% of the White families are headed by two parents, compared to 36% of African American families. Clearly, race is somehow related to whether a family is headed by one parent or two. The question is: *How* are these variables related?

This is as good an example as I've ever seen of why you never use covariation alone to support a theory of cause and effect. As it turns out, race and family type are both related to (but once again, not caused by) a common, third variable: poverty. Poverty is the consequence of discrimination in many area of life, and single-family households—particularly female-headed ones—are one consequence of poverty.

In other words, for the data in Table 15.5, we know that being African American doesn't cause single-parent families. However, being an African American man does mean a high probability of attending poorly funded schools, and poor schooling produces severe disadvantage in the labor market. When men in the U.S. don't provide financial support, poor women—who have even worse prospects than men for finding stable, well-paying employment—are likely to turn to welfare.

> *Some of the most interesting puzzles in social science involve understanding the role of intervening and antecedent variables— and figuring out which is which.*

Historically, welfare systems have punished women who have a live-in husband by lowering the size of the women's allotment. Some women respond by maintaining single-parent households and some fraction of African American, single-parent families are caused by this sequence of intervening variables. There are, then, several intervening variables at work that link being counted as African American by the U.S. Census and being part of a single-parent household.

Some of the most interesting puzzles in social science involve understanding the role of intervening and antecedent variables—and figuring out which is which. Middle-aged men who drink a lot of coffee (six cups a day and more) are more likely to have a heart attack than are men who don't drink coffee. Men who drink a lot of coffee, however, are more likely than non-coffee drinkers to smoke, not to exercise, and to consume more alcohol, more saturated fats, and more cholesterol than men who don't drink coffee (Puccio et al. 1990; Schwarz et al. 1994).

Coffee may play a relatively small role in heart attacks for men, relative to the role of all those other behaviors. (Women's chances of coronary disease, by the way, are unaffected by drinking lots of coffee [Willett et al. 1996].) It may be Type A personality (impatient, aggravated people are Type A) that causes coffee consumption and heart attacks. Or coffee consumption may be an intervening variable between Type A personality and heart attacks (Ketterer and Maercklein 1991; James 1997). Lots of researchers are trying to disentangle this interesting problem.

❖———

LAMBDA AND THE PRE PRINCIPLE

Look at Table 15.4a. Suppose that, for each of the 35,382,000 households with children under 18, you were asked to guess whether they were single-parent families or two-parent families and that you didn't know anything about their race. Since the mode for the dependent variable in this table is "two parents" (that is, 24,120,000 two-parent families compared to 11,262,000 single-parent families), you should guess that all families have two parents.

If you did that, you'd make 11,262,000 mistakes out of the 35,382,000 choices, for an error rate of 11,262,000/35,382,000, or 31.8%. Call this the *old error.*

Now suppose you knew the mode for each independent variable (each column) in Table 15.4a. The mode for African Americans is single-parent households and the mode for Whites is two-parent households. Knowing this, your best guess would be that *every* White household has two parents and *every* African American household has one parent. You would still make some mistakes, but fewer than if you just guessed that all families have two parents.

How many fewer? When you guess that every one of the 5,435,000 African American families in the U.S. has one parent, you make 1,942,000 mistakes. And when you guess that every one of the 29,947,000 White families in the U.S. has two parents, you make 7,769,000 mistakes. The total *new error* is

$$1,942,000 + 7,769,000 = 9,711,000 \text{ mistakes}$$

which is 27.4% of 35,382,000.

The *difference* between the old error (31.8%) and the new error (27.4%), divided by the old error (31.8%), is the *proportionate reduction of error,* or *PRE.* Thus,

$$PRE = \frac{\text{Old error} - \text{New error}}{\text{Old error}} \quad \text{(Formula 15.7)}$$

$$PRE = \frac{11,262,000 - 9,711,000}{11,262,000} =$$

13.8% reduction in error

This **PRE measure of association for nominal variables** is called *lambda,* written either L or λ. A lambda of .138 (or 13.8%) means that if you know the distribution of the independent variable, you can guess the scores on the dependent variable 13.8% more of the time than if you didn't know the distribution of the independent variable.

The PRE principle is the basis for many of the most commonly used measures of association. (The PRE principle is well described by Freeman [1965] and Mueller et al. [1970].)

The Problems with Lambda

Lambda is a useful measure of the relation between nominal variables, but it has an unfortunate property: It can be zero (indicating no relation between the variables), even when there is an intuitively clear association between nominal variables.

Go back to Table 15.4a and reverse the dependent and independent variables. Without any information about family type, guess whether each of the 35,382,000 households is White or African American. If you guess that all families with children in the U.S. are White, you'd make 5,435,000 mistakes. Now add the information about family type. If you guess that all two-parent families are White and that all one-parent families are African American, you'd *still* make 5,435,000 mistakes, and lambda would be zero.

CHI-SQUARE

With bivariate data on nominal variables, many researchers use a statistic called *chi-square,* often written as χ^2, to **test the null hypothesis that differences in the table exist solely by chance.** As we saw in Chapter 14, χ^2 is easy to compute, and there are standardized tables for determining whether a particular χ^2 value is statistically significant.

Chi-square tells you whether or not a relation *exists* between or among variables. It tells you the *probability* that a relation is the result of chance. But it is not a PRE measure of correlation, so it doesn't tell you the strength of association among variables.

The principal use of χ^2 is for testing the null hypothesis that there is *no relation* between two nominal variables. If we look at the distribution of numbers in Table 15.4, it seems like there is some relation between race and household type. Using the null-hypothesis strategy, we try as hard as we can to prove that our suspicion is dead wrong—that, in fact, no such relation exists at all.

If, after a really good faith effort, we *fail to accept* the null hypothesis, we can reject it. Using this approach, we never prove anything using statistical tests like χ^2. We just fail to disprove things. As it turns out, that's quite a lot.

Calculating χ^2

The formula for calculating χ^2 for a bivariate table is the same as the one we saw in Chapter 14 for a univariate distribution. Here it is again:

$$\chi^2 = \Sigma \frac{(O - E)^2}{E} \qquad \text{(Formula 15.8)}$$

where O represents the observed number of cases in a particular cell of a bivariate table, and E represents the number of cases you'd expect for that cell *if there were no relation* between the variables in that cell.

For each cell in a bivariate table, simply subtract the expected frequency from the observed and square the difference. Then divide by the expected frequency and sum the calculations for all the cells. Clearly, if all the observed frequencies equal all the expected frequencies, then χ^2 will be zero; that is, there will be no relation between the variables.

While χ^2 can be zero, it can never have a negative value. The more the Os differ from the Es (that is, something nonrandom is going on), the bigger χ^2 gets.

Calculating the Expected Frequencies for χ^2 in Bivariate Tables

The expected frequencies are calculated *for each cell* with the formula

$$F_e = \frac{(R_t)\,(C_t)}{N} \qquad \text{(Formula 15.9)}$$

where F_e is the expected frequency for a particular cell in a table, R_t is the frequency total for the row in which that cell is located, C_t is the frequency total for the column in which that cell is located, and N is the total sample size (the lower-right-hand marginal).

Remember: It is inappropriate to use χ^2 if F_e for any cell is less than 5, and be sure to run χ^2 on tables of raw frequencies, not on tables of percentages (for more about low cell counts, see Box 15.6, later in the chapter).

The test for χ^2 can be applied to any size bivariate table. Table 15.6 shows a hypothetical census of observed adherents, in four Native

TABLE 15.6 A Hypothetical Census of Religious Belief in Four Groups of Native Americans

	Observed Frequencies			
Tribe	Catholic	Protestants	Native American Church	Total
1	150	104	86	340
2	175	268	316	759
3	197	118	206	521
4	68	214	109	391
Total	590	704	717	2,011
	Expected Frequencies			
1	99.75	119.03	121.22	
2	222.68	265.71	270.61	
3	152.85	182.39	185.76	
4	114.71	136.88	139.41	

American tribes, of three competing religions, and the expected number of adherents to each religion. Reading across the top of the table, in tribe 1, there are 150 Catholics, 104 Protestants, and 86 members of the Native American Church. For tribe 1, we expect

$$\frac{(340)\,(590)}{2{,}011} = 99.75$$

Catholics (the cell in the upper-left-hand corner of Table 15.6). We expect 119.03 Protestants and 121.22 members of the Native American Church for tribe 1, and so on.

Chi-square for this table is a walloping 162.08. To determine the number of degrees of freedom for a bivariate χ^2 table, we calculate

$$df = (r-1)\,(c-1) \qquad \text{(Formula 15.10)}$$

which means: Multiply the number of rows, minus one, by the number of columns, minus one. For Table 15.6, there are

$$(4-1 \text{ rows})\,(3-1 \text{ columns}) =$$
$$6 \text{ degrees of freedom}$$

Without even looking it up in Appendix D (the χ^2 distribution), it's clear that the competing religions are not evenly distributed across the groups. If you had collected these data, you'd now be faced with the problem of interpreting them—that is, telling the story of how the various religions gain adherents at the expense of the others in various places.

Suppose that instead of a census, we take a 10% random sample of the groups—one that turns out to reflect almost perfectly the religious preferences of the population. The results, and the expected frequencies, would look like Table 15.7.

Chi-square for Table 15.7 is 15.44. This is about 10% of the $\chi^2 = 162.08$ that we got for Table 15.6. (The difference between 15.44 and 16.2 is the result of rounding in the 10% sample. For example, we got 18 Catholics in tribe 2 instead of 17.5.) Chi-square for Table 15.7 is still

TABLE 15.7 Observed and Expected Frequencies for a 10% Sample of the Data in Table 15.6

| Tribe | Observed Frequencies | | | |
	Catholic	Protestants	Native American Church	Total
I	15	10	9	34
2	18	27	32	77
3	20	12	21	53
4	7	21	11	39
Total	60	70	73	203

Tribe	Expected Frequencies		
I	10.04926	11.72414	121.22
2	22.75862	26.55172	270.61
3	15.66502	18.27586	185.76
4	11.52709	11.52709	139.41

significant at the .02 level, but if we'd taken a 5% sample, χ^2 would be around 7 or 8, and with 6 degrees of freedom it would no longer be statistically significant, even at the .10 level. Sample size makes a real difference here.

Chi-Square for Multiple Comparisons

Like ANOVA, you can use χ^2 to make multiple comparisons across complex tables.

Table 15.8 is an example. Researchers have identified five value orientations among physical education teachers: disciplinary mastery (DM), learning process (LP), self-actualization (SA), social responsibility (SR), and ecological integration (EI) (Chen et al. 1997:136).

So, for example, teachers who score high on the DM scale focus their attention on helping students gain proficiency with sports skills. SA-oriented teachers believe that their job is to help students attain personal growth. Teachers who

score high on the SR scale believe that their job is to help children recognize the needs of society and to become team players. Teachers with a high LP value orientation focus on helping children "learn how to learn," with the expectation that this is what does children the most good. And the EI-oriented folks believe in an approach that integrates the other four values into the curriculum.

Ang Chen and his colleagues (1997) wanted to see if there were strong differences in these value perspectives among physical education teachers in the U.S. and China. The 854 participants in the study came from six American school districts ($n = 495$) and four Chinese school districts ($n = 359$). All the participants took the Revised Ennis Value Orientation Inventory (Ennis et al. 1992), which was designed to measure educational value orientations. (For details on how these researchers translated the scale into Chinese, see the section on back translation in Chapter 7.) The 90 items in the inventory are divided into five subscales of 18 items each. Each item is ranked on a scale of 1 to 5, where 5 = *most valued* and 1 = *least valued*.

TABLE 15.8 Five Value Orientations among Teachers in the United States and China

Value	DM USA	DM China	LP USA	LP China	SA USA	SA China	EI USA	EI China	SR USA	SR China
Low										
N	337	242	374	202	332	253	384	193	259	243
%	68.1	67.4	75.6	56.3	67.1	70.5	77.6	53.8	52.3	95.5
High										
N	158	117	121	157	163	106	111	166	236	16
%	31.9	32.6	24.4	43.7	32.9	29.5	22.4	46.2	47.7	4.5
Chi-square	0.02		28.85		0.74		43.79		147.08	
p	.89		.001		.39		.001		.001	

SOURCE: A. Chen et al., "Universality and Uniqueness of Teacher Educational Value Orientations: A Cross-Cultural Comparison between the USA and China." Copyright © 1997, *Journal of Research and Development in Education.* Reprinted with permission.

A teacher is given a score of "high value orientation" on a subscale if she or he scores 0.6 standard deviations above the mean, across all respondents, for that 18-item subscale. Chen et al. calculated the mean, *across all 854 respondents,* in both countries for each of the five value orientations. If a teacher's score on a particular value orientation was ≥ (equal to or greater than) 0.6 standard deviations above the mean for all teachers (irrespective of country), then they counted that teacher's score on that value orientation as "high." Otherwise, the teacher's score was "low." Table 15.8 shows the distribution of the results, and the χ^2 scores, for both countries on all five subscales.

There are five two-by-two tables in Table 15.8. Each of the five has a χ^2 value, shown in the next-to-last row, and a *p*-value, or probability, shown in the last row. The data for the first table, regarding the DM scale, show that about two-thirds of American and Chinese teachers think disciplinary mastery is very important in the physical education curriculum. The difference between them (68.1% vs. 67.4%) is insignificant. Chi-square is .02 and the *p*-value for this χ^2 is .89. If you ran this particular test a thousand times, you'd expect to get a distribution like the one in this table about 89% of the time.

Just because a χ^2 value is statistically insignificant doesn't mean it's uninteresting. The third χ^2 table across Table 15.8 is for SA, or self-actualization. There is no difference between the Chinese and American teachers on valuing self-actualization. Now, this is a trait that we usually associate with the "rugged individualist" American culture, so finding no real difference between Americans and Chinese on this value orientation captures our attention.

The real shocker, though, is in the subtable on social responsibility (labeled SR over on the right of Table 15.8). This is a trait we associate with the "collective mentality" of schooling in communist countries, yet it is valued far more by Americans in the physical education curriculum than by their Chinese counterparts. What's going on here?

According to Chen (personal communication), the Chinese education system, along with other components of the communist society, does, indeed, emphasize the value of aligning one's individual needs with those of the society. Chen speculates that by the time children get to high school, they have acquired this norm so completely (and their social behavior is under so much control) that physical education teachers don't need to give it any priority in the curriculum.

THE SPECIAL CASE OF THE 2 × 2 TABLE

When you have a 2 × 2 cross-tab of nominal data, there is an easy formula to follow for computing χ^2. Here it is:

$$\chi^2 = \frac{N(\mid ad - bc \mid - N/2)^2}{(a + b)\,(c + d)\,(a + c)\,(b + d)} \quad \text{(Formula 15.11)}$$

where a, b, c, and d are the individual cells shown in Figure 15.3, and N is the total of all the cells (the lower-right-hand marginal).

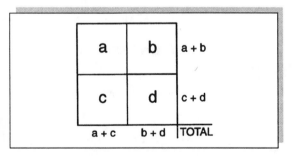

Figure 15.3 Cells in a 2 × 2 Table

The straight bars inside the parentheses mean that you take the absolute value of the operation $ad - bc$ (that is, you ignore a negative sign, if bc is bigger than ad), and you subtract $N/2$ from it. Then you square that number and multiply it by N and divide that by the denominator.

It takes a little practice to keep track of all the numbers, but this formula is easy to implement with just a simple calculator. Of course, any statistics program will calculate χ^2 for you, but spend the time to do this calculation once by hand, just so you understand it.

Carol Boyd and her colleagues (1993) in the school of nursing at the University of Michigan examined a random sample of 80 medical records for African American men and women who were enrolled in an urban community-based drug abuse treatment facility. The idea was to take gender differences into account in developing therapeutic programs for men and for women in recovery from drug abuse. There were no differences among the 37 men and 43 women in mean age, sibling order, or marital status.

There was, however, one variable on which men and women appeared to differ a lot: the probability of having experienced sexual abuse as a child. Table 15.9 shows the distribution of self-reported data from the sample. Chi-square for the data in Table 15.9 is 24.74, which is statistically significant at better than the $p < .001$ level. (About the low cell counts in Table 15.9, see Box 15.6.)

Table 15.10 shows the traditional calculation of χ^2 for Boyd's data. Notice that the numerator

TABLE 15.9 Data from Boyd et al.'s (1993) Study of Child Abuse

	Men	Women	Total
Reported having been sexually abused as a child	2	25	27
Reported not having been sexually abused as a child	35	18	53
Total	37	43	80

SOURCE: C. J. Boyd et al., "Gender Differences among African-American Substance Abusers." *Journal of Psychoactive Drugs* 25. Copyright © 1993. Used with permission.

Box 15.6
About Low Cell Counts

The conclusion we should draw from Table 15.9 seems pretty clear: Women are more likely to have experienced childhood sexual abuse than are men. Notice that there are only two cases in one of the cells in Table 15.9. When there are fewer than five cases *expected* in any cell, χ^2 can be distorted and there is a danger of drawing the wrong conclusion from the data. In this case, that would mean concluding incorrectly that women are more likely than are men to experience childhood sexual abuse.

But notice from Table 15.10 that there are 12.49 cases *expected* of men who report having been sexually abused as a child. The fact that only 2 cases actually turned up in this cell is thus strong evidence, not a cause for worry. Also, in this particular case, the researchers had a lot more to go on than just the χ^2 value. There are hundreds of studies, statistical and ethnographic, documenting the fact that women take the brunt of childhood sexual abuse.

Watch out, however, for situations in which the expected number of cases falls below 5. When this is the case, consider using Fisher's exact test, which is described next.

TABLE 15.10 Calculating χ^2 for the Data in Table 15.9

Observed	Expected	O − E	(O − E)²	(O − E)²/E
2	27 × 37/80 = 12.49	−10.49	110.04	8.81
25	27 × 43/80 = 14.51	10.49	110.04	7.58
35	53 × 37/80 = 24.51	10.49	110.04	4.49
18	53 × 43/80 = 28.49	−10.49	110.04	3.86
				S = 24.74
				p < .001

Box 15.7
Cramér's *V* and Phi

Cramér's V is based on χ^2 and is a measure of the association between two nominal variables. The formula is

$$V = \sqrt{\chi^2/N(\kappa - 1)}$$
(Formula 15.12)

where κ is the number of rows or columns in your table, whichever is less. If you have three rows and four columns, then $\kappa = 3$ and $\kappa - 1 = 2$. Multiply the number of cases in your sample by $\kappa - 1$. Next, divide χ^2 by that number. Finally, take the square root of *that* number. Cramér's *V* will give you an idea of how strong the association is between nominal variables.

For a 2×2 table, $\kappa - 1 = 1$, and so the denominator becomes, simply, *N*. This is the phi coefficient, sometimes written with the Greek letter, ϕ. Thus:

$$\phi = \sqrt{\chi^2/N}$$

---

in each of the four above calculations is the same, $(2 - 12.49)^2 = 110.04$. So is $25 - 14.51^2$ and so are the rest of the numerators. It is this property that allows computation of χ^2 for 2×2 tables using Formula 15.11. (Cramér's *V* and Phi are statistics based on χ^2. See Box 15.7.)

FISHER'S EXACT TEST

Fisher's exact test is used for 2×2 tables whenever the *expected* number of frequencies for any cell is less than 5. With fewer than 5 expected occurrences in a cell, χ^2 values are generally not trustworthy.

Table 15.11 shows hypothetical data on the attitudes of 14 American students toward spending a year overseas as part of their undergraduate program. Seven of the students grew up in families where at least one parent had served in the military; the other 7 grew up in families where neither parent had ever served in the military.

Of the 7 students who had at least one parent who had served in the military, 6 were positive toward the idea of a year abroad and 1 was negative. Of the 7 students who had no parent who had served in the military, 2 were positive about the study-abroad option and 5 were negative. The *expected* values for each cell are shown in brackets in Table 15.11.

Since the cells have expected values of less than 5, we apply Fisher's exact text. There are thousands of ways to throw the expected cases (4, 3, 4, 3) into four cells, but there are fewer ways to do it if you have to make the right-hand marginals add up to the observed values. Given a set of fixed marginals in a 2×2 table, the probability of seeing any distribution of cases is

TABLE 15.11 Hypothetical Data on Students' Attitudes toward Studying Abroad

Attitude	Parent(s) in Military	Parent(s) Not in Military	Total
Positive	6 [4]	2 [4]	8
Negative	1 [3]	5 [3]	6
Total	7	7	14

$$p = \frac{(a+b)!(c+d)!(a+c)!(b+d)!}{N!\,a!\,b!\,c!\,d!} \quad \text{(Formula 15.13)}$$

where a, b, c, and d are the actual contents of the four cells in the 2×2 table (see Figure 15.3) and N is the total number of cases. (An exclamation point signifies the factorial of a number, or the product of sequence of numbers. So, 5! is five-factorial, or $5 \times 4 \times 3 \times 2 \times 1 = 120$.) The exact probability of observing the particular distribution of cases in Table 15.11 is

$$p = \frac{(40,320)\,(720)\,(5,040)\,(5,040)}{(87,178,291,200)\,(720)\,(2)\,(1)\,(120)} = .04895$$

For a one-tailed test of the null hypothesis, we need to add this probability to the probability of finding any other distributions that are more extreme than the one in the actual data. There is one configuration of these data that is more extreme: $a = 7$, $b = 1$, $c = 0$, and $d = 6$ (where a, b, c, and d are the cells in Figure 15.3). The exact probability of that distribution is .0025. For a one-tailed test, we add these probabilities:

$$.0025 + .04895 = .05145$$

A two-tailed test is simply twice this probability, or .1029. There is a strong hint in these data that students who have at least one parent who served in the military are more favorably disposed toward study abroad, but the case is tentative and awaits further tests on larger samples.

The best way to calculate Fisher's test is with a computer program like SPSS®, SAS®, or SYSTAT®. Those programs automatically calculate Fisher's exact test along with χ^2.

THE ODDS RATIO

Table 15.12 shows the distribution, for a representative sample of 499 men and women in Florida, of voting choice by gender in the 1996 U.S. presidential election.

The χ^2 value for this table is 8.590, which, with 1 degree of freedom, is highly significant ($p < .003$). But statistics like χ^2 don't measure the strength of relationships. PRE coefficients are one kind of measure of strength. Another, very direct and intuitive measure of strength for understanding the relation between nominal variables is the odds ratio. The odds of voting for Clinton over Bush in this sample are $269/230 = 1.17$. That is, people in general were 1.17 times more likely to vote for Clinton than for either Bush or Perot. Recall from Chapter 14 that this is the same thing as saying that 54% of the voters went for Clinton ($269/499 = .54$).

TABLE 15.12 A 2 × 2 Table of Voting Choices

	Men	Women	Total
Clinton	112	157	269
Bush or Perot	126	104	230
Total	238	261	499

SOURCE: Bureau of Economic and Business Research, University of Florida.

We can go further. The odds of voting for Clinton over Bush or Perot *among men* are 112/126 = .89. When the odds of something happening are less than 1.0, of course, this indicates a negative association. Sure enough, we see in Table 15.12 that more men than women voted for Bush or Perot. (If we look at the reciprocal, we find that the odds among men of voting for Bush or Perot over Clinton are positive: 126/112 = 1.13.)

The odds among women of voting for Clinton over Bush or Perot are even greater: 157/104 = 1.51. The χ^2 statistic of 8.590 ($p < .003$) tells us, further, that we could expect to find these odds, or any larger odds, just by chance less than 3 times in 1,000.

For 2 × 2 tables, the two primary odds are a/c and b/d. The odds ratio is

$$\frac{a/c}{b/d}$$ (Formula 15.14)

which can be collapsed to simply ad/bc. The odds ratio for the data in Table 15.12 is

$$.89/1.51 = .589$$

This measure has a lot of appeal because it can be generalized for looking at the interactions among complex sets of nominal variables.

GAMMA: THE ALL-PURPOSE PRE MEASURE OF ASSOCIATION FOR ORDINAL VARIABLES

Once you understand the PRE principle, a lot of things in statistics fall into place. Kempton et al. (1995) surveyed intentionally selected samples of people in the U.S. whom they thought would show pro- and anti-environmentalist attitudes. (Members of the Sierra Club, for example, are people you'd anticipate would be pro-environmental activism, while loggers are people you'd think would be against that kind of activity.) Here are two questions from Kempton et al.'s study:

TABLE 15.13 Distribution of Responses on Two Ecological Attitude Items

Force Change in Lifestyle	Gung Ho		
	Disagree	Neutral	Agree
Disagree	16	7	61
Neutral	7	7	7
Agree	13	4	27
Total	36	18	95

You shouldn't force people to change their lifestyle for the sake of the environment.

   1. Disagree   2. Neutral   3. Agree

Environmentalists wouldn't be so gung ho if it were their jobs that were threatened.

   1. Disagree   2. Neutral   3. Agree

Gery Ryan, Stephen Borgatti, and I used these items in a survey we ran, and Table 15.13 shows the results. Notice that these items are reverse scored. That is, when respondents agree with a statement, they get a score of 1 and when they disagree, they get a score of 3. That way, higher scores consistently indicate support for environmentalism.

If the two variables were perfectly related, then every respondent who agreed with one statement would agree with the other, every respondent who disagreed with one statement would disagree with the other, and so on. Of course, things never work out so neatly, but if you knew the *proportion of matching pairs* among your respondents, you'd have a PRE measure of association for ordinal variables. The measure would tell you how much more correctly you could guess the rank of one ordinal variable for each respondent if you knew the score for the other ordinal variable in a bivariate distribution.

What we would like is a PRE measure of association that tells us whether knowing the ranking of pairs of people on one variable increases our ability to predict their ranking on a

second variable, and by how much. To do this, we need to understand the ways in which pairs of ranks can be distributed. This will not appear obvious at first, but bear with me.

The number of possible pairs of observations (on any given unit of analysis) is

$$\text{No. of pairs of observation} = \frac{N(N-1)}{2} \quad \text{(Formula 15.15)}$$

where N is the sample size. There are $(149)(148)/2 = 11{,}026$ pairs of observations in Table 15.13.

There are several ways that pairs of observations can be distributed if they are ranked on two ordinal variables.

(1) They can be ranked in the same order on both variables. We'll call these "same."
(2) They can be ranked in the opposite order on both variables. We'll call these "opposite."
(3) They can be tied on either the independent or dependent variables, or on both. We'll call these "ties."

In fact, in almost all bivariate tables comparing ordinal variables, there are going to be a lot of pairs with tied values on both variables. *Gamma* **is a popular measure of association between two**

In Table 15.13,
the number of same-ranked pairs is:

16 (7 + 7 + 4 + 27)	=	720
+ 7 (7 + 27)	=	238
+ 7 (4 + 27)	=	217
+ 7 (27)	=	189
Total		1,364

The number of opposite-ranked pairs is:

61 (7 + 7 + 13 + 4)	=	1,891
+ 7 (7 + 13)	=	140
+ 7 (4 + 13)	=	119
+ 7 (13)	=	91
Total		2,241

Figure 15.4 Calculating Gamma

NOTE: To calculate the same-ranked pairs in this 3 × 3 table, multiply each score by the sums of all scores below it and to the right. Then sum the totals. To calculate the opposite-ranked pairs, multiply each score by the sums of the scores below it and to the left. Then sum the totals.

ordinal variables because it ignores all the tied pairs. Gamma is the Greek letter γ, but it's usually written as G in statistics. The formula for gamma is

$$G = \frac{\text{No. of same-ranked pairs} - \text{No. of opposite-ranked pairs}}{\text{No. of same-ranked pairs} + \text{No. of opposite-ranked pairs}}$$

Gamma is an intuitive statistic; it ranges from −1.0 (for a perfect negative association) to +1.0 (for a perfect positive association), through 0 in the middle for complete independence of two variables.

If there are just two ordinal ranks in a measure, and if the number of opposite-ranked pairs is 0, then gamma would equal 1. Suppose we measured income and education ordinally, such that (1) anyone with less than a high school diploma is counted as having low education, and anyone with at least a high school diploma is counted as having high education; and (2) anyone with an income of less than $25,000 dollars a year is counted as having low income, while anyone with at least $25,000 a year is counted as having high income.

Now suppose that *no one* who had at least a high school diploma earned less than $30,000 dollars a year. There would be no pair of observations, then, in which low income and high education (an opposite pair) co-occurred.

If the number of same-ranked pairs is zero, then gamma would equal −1.0. Suppose that *no*

one who had high education also had a high income. This would be a perfect negative association, and gamma would be −1.0. Both +1.0 and −1.0 are perfect correlations.

Calculating the Pairs for Gamma

The number of same-ranked pairs in a bivariate table is calculated by multiplying each cell by the sum of all cells *below it and to its right*. The number of opposite-ranked pairs is calculated by multiplying each cell by the sum of all cells *below it and to its left*. This is diagrammed in Figure 15.4.

Gamma for Table 15.13, then, is

$$G = \frac{1,364 - 2,241}{1,364 + 2,241} = \frac{-877}{3,605} = -.24$$

Gamma tells us that the variables are associated negatively—people who agree with either of the statements tend to disagree with the other, and vice versa—but it also tells us that the association is relatively weak.

Is Gamma Significant?

How weak? If you have more than 50 elements in your sample, you can test for the probability that gamma is due to sampling error using a procedure developed by Goodman and Kruskal (1963). A useful presentation of the procedure is given by Loether and McTavish (1993:598, 609).

First, the gamma value must be converted to a z-score, or standard score. The formula for converting gamma to a z-score is

$$z = (G - g) \sqrt{(N_s + N_0)/2N(1 - G^2)} \quad \text{(Formula 15.17)}$$

where G is the *sample* gamma, γ is the gamma for the *population*, N is the size of your sample, N_s is the number of same-ranked pairs, and N_o is the number of opposite-ranked pairs.

As usual, we proceed from the null hypothesis and assume that γ for the entire population is zero—that is, that there really is no association between the variables we are studying. If we can reject that hypothesis, then we can assume that the gamma value for our sample probably approximates the gamma value, γ, for the population. Using the data from Figure 15.4 and the gamma value for Table 15.13:

$$z = (-.24 - 0)\sqrt{(1,364 + 2,241/2(149)(1 - .24^2)} = -.86$$

You'll recall that Appendix B—the z-score table—lists the proportions of area under a normal curve that are described by various z-score values. To test the significance of gamma, look for the z-score in column 1 of the table. Column 2 shows the area under a normal curve between the mean (assumed to be zero for a normal curve) and the z-score. We're interested in column 3, which shows the area under the curve that is *not* accounted for by the z-score.

A z-score of –.86 accounts for all but .1977 of the area under a normal curve. This means that we can *not* reject the null hypothesis. The gamma score of –.24 is not sufficiently strong to confirm that there is a significant association between responses to the two attitudinal questions about environmental activism (see Box 15.8).

YULE'S Q

Yule's Q is the equivalent of gamma for 2 × 2 tables of ordinal variables, like high vs. low prestige, salary, education, religiosity, and so on. Yule's Q can be calculated on frequencies or on percentages. The formula is

$$Q = \frac{(ad) - (bc)}{(ad) + (bc)} \quad \text{(Formula 15.19)}$$

Yule's Q is another of those handy, easy-to-use statistics. A good rule of thumb for interpreting Q is given by Davis (1971): When Q is 0, the interpretation is naturally that there is no association between the variables. When Q ranges from 0 to –.29, or from 0 to +.29, you can interpret this as a negligible or small association. Davis interprets a Q value of ±.30 to ±.49 as a "moderate" association; a value of ±.50 to ±.69 as a "substantial" association; and a value of ±.70 or more as a "very strong" association.

Rutledge (1990) was interested in the effect of one-parent or two-parent families on children's relations with their mothers and fathers. She surveyed African American, college-aged women, mostly from Chicago. One of the questions she asked was: "When you were growing up, how close were you to your father? Were you considerably close, moderately close, or not close at all?" I've collapsed Rutledge's data into two response categories, close and not close, in Table 15.14.

Here is the calculation of Yule's Q for these data:

Box 15.8
Kendall's Tau-b

Some researchers prefer a statistic called *Kendall's tau-b* (written T_b or τ_b) instead of gamma for bivariate tables of ordinal-level data because gamma ignores tied pairs in the data. The formula for τ_b is

$$\tau_b = \frac{N_S - N_O}{\sqrt{(N_S + N_O + N_{\tau d})(N_S + N_O + N_{\tau i})}}$$ (Formula 15.18)

where N_S is the number of same-ranked pairs, N_O is the number of opposite-ranked pairs, $N_{\tau d}$ is the number of pairs tied on the dependent variable, and $N_{\tau i}$ is the number of pairs tied on the independent variable. You can calculate the tied pairs as follows:

$$N_{\tau d} = \Sigma\, R(R - 1)/2$$
$$N_{\tau i} = \Sigma\, C(C - 1)/2$$

where R refers to the row marginals (the dependent variable) and C refers to the column marginals (the independent variable). In Table 15.13:

$$N_{\tau d} = 84(83) + 21(20) + 44(43)/2 = 4{,}642$$
$$N_{\tau i} = 36(35) + 18(17) + 95(94)/2 = 5{,}248$$

We already have the numerator for τ_b in this case (we calculated the number of same-ranked and opposite-ranked pairs in Figure 15.4), so:

$$\tau_b = \frac{1{,}364 - 2{,}241}{\sqrt{(1{,}364 + 2{,}241 + 4{,}642)(1{,}364 + 2{,}241 + 5{,}248)}} = -.10$$

This confirms the weak, negative association we saw from the results of the gamma test. Kendall's τ_b will usually be smaller than gamma because *gamma ignores tied pairs,* while τ_b uses almost all the data (*it ignores the relatively few pairs that are tied* on both variables).

$$Q = \frac{(135)(31) - (36)(13)}{(135)(31) + (36)(13)} = \frac{4185 - 468}{4185 + 468} = \frac{3717}{4653} = .80$$

Yule's Q for these data is .80. Most of the women who come from two-parent homes are close to their fathers, while 46% (31/67) who come from one-parent homes are not. The reason is obvious: Overwhelmingly, one-parent homes are headed by mothers, not by fathers.

TABLE 15.14 Family Structure and Self-Reported Closeness to Parents

Close to Father?	Two Parents	One Parent	Total
Yes	135	36	171
No	13	31	44
Total	148	67	215

SOURCE: E. M. Rutledge, "Black Parent-Child Relations: Some Correlates." Abstracted from data in Table 2. Copyright © 1998, *Journal of Comparative Family Studies*. Reprinted with permission.

WHAT TO USE FOR NOMINAL AND ORDINAL VARIABLES

In general:

(1) Use χ^2 to see how often you could expect to find the differences you see in the table just by chance. In appropriate situations, calculate odds ratios to measure the strength of relationships.

(2) Use gamma (or tau, or—in the case of 2 × 2 tables—Yule's Q) to measure the association between two ordinal variables.

In actual practice, ordinal variables with seven ranks are treated if they were interval variables. In fact, many researchers treat ordinals with just five ranks as if they were intervals, because association between interval variables can be analyzed by the most powerful statistics—which brings us to correlation and regression.

CORRELATION: THE POWERHOUSE STATISTIC FOR COVARIATION

When at least one of the variables in a bivariate relation is interval or ratio level, we use a measure of correlation: *Spearman's* r, written r_s, when the data are *rank ordered; Pearson product-moment correlation,* written simply as *r,* to measure the strength of linear relations; or *eta-squared* (the Greek letter η, pronounced either eat-a or ate-a), to measure the strength of certain kinds of non-linear relations. (Go back to the Direction and Shape of Covariations section at the beginning of this chapter if you have any doubts about the concept of a nonlinear relation.)

SPEARMAN'S r

Brenner and Tomkiewicz (1982) studied expectations among young African Americans and Whites entering the labor force out of college.

They surveyed 342 graduating business majors about the importance (on a scale of 1 to 5) of 25 job characteristics. The sample comprised 51

TABLE 15.15 Mean Scores and Item Rank by Race and Sex of 25 Job Characteristics

Job Characteristics: How important is it to you to have a job which:	White (n = 238)		Black (n = 104)		Male (n = 172)		Female (n = 170)	
	Mean	Rank	Mean	Rank	Mean	Rank	Mean	Rank
1. Requires originality and creativity	3.91	12	3.98	11	4.00	10.5	3.84	9
2. Makes use of your specific educational background	3.89	11	4.48	22.5	4.00	10.5	4.13	15
3. Encourages continued development of knowledge skills	4.40	23.5	4.48	22.5	4.33	22.5	4.52	23
4. Is respected by other people	4.17	18	4.26	17	4.15	17.5	4.26	17
5. Provides job security	4.40	23.5	4.60	24	4.44	24	4.47	22
6. Provides the opportunity to earn a high income	4.22	19	4.27	18.5	4.33	22.5	4.14	16
7. Makes a social contribution by the work you do	3.52	6	4.22	15	3.77	8	3.68	6
8. Gives you the responsibility for taking risks	3.42	5	3.48	4	3.59	5	3.27	4
9. Requires working on problems of central importance to the organization	3.70	8	3.89	7	3.83	9	3.69	7
10. Involves working with congenial associates	4.24	20.5	3.97	10	4.03	12	4.29	19
11. Provides ample leisure time off the job	3.99	13	3.94	9	4.07	14	4.87	25
12. Provides change and variety in duties and activities	4.24	20.5	4.27	18.5	4.18	19	4.31	20
13. Provides comfortable working conditions	4.31	22	4.47	21	4.28	21	4.44	21
14. Permits advancement to high administrative responsibility	4.16	17	4.24	16	4.26	20	4.11	14
15. Permits working independently	3.80	9.5	4.06	12	4.09	15	3.96	11
16. Rewards good performance with recognition	4.13	15	4.12	13	4.15	17.5	4.10	13
17. Requires supervising others	3.37	3	3.39	2	3.56	4	3.18	3
18. Is intellectually stimulating	4.14	16	4.21	14	4.06	13	4.27	18
19. Satisfies your cultural and aesthetic interests	3.40	4	3.93	8	3.48	3	3.63	5
20. Has clear-cut rules and procedures to follow	2.80	1	3.41	3	3.00	1	2.95	1
21. Permits you to work for superiors you admire and respect	3.80	9.5	3.72	5	3.63	6	3.93	10
22. Permits a regular routine in time and place of work	2.86	2	3.37	1	3.02	2	3.01	2
23. Requires meeting and speaking with many other people	3.68	7	3.88	6	3.75	7	3.74	8
24. Permits you to develop your own methods of doing the work	4.01	14	4.28	20	4.14	16	4.04	12
25. Provides a feeling of accomplishment	4.74	25	4.72	25	4.68	25	4.79	24

SOURCE: O. C. Brenner and J. Tomkiewicz, "Job Orientation of Black and White College Graduates in Business," Table 1. Copyright © 1982, *Personnel Psychology*. Reprinted with permission.

African American men, 53 African American women, 121 White men, and 117 White women. The results are shown in Table 15.15.

Notice that only two of the job characteristics (No. 20: Has clear-cut rules and procedures to follow and No. 22: Permits a regular routine in

TABLE 15.16 Computing Spearman's Rank-Order Correlation Coefficient for the Data on Men and Women in Table 15.15

Rank for Men	Rank for Women	Difference in the Ranks	d^2
10.5	9	1.5	2.25
10.5	15	−4.5	20.25
22.5	23	−.5	.25
17.5	17	.5	.25
24	22	2	4
22.5	16	6.5	42.25
8	6	2	4
5	4	1	1
9	7	2	4
12	19	−7	49
14	25	−11	121
19	20	−1	1
21	21	0	0
20	14	6	36
15	11	4	16
17.5	13	4.5	20.25
4	3	1	1
13	18	−5	25
3	5	−2	4
1	1	0	0
6	10	−4	16
2	2	0	0
7	8	−1	1
16	12	4	16
25	24	1	1

Total = 385.5

$$\text{Spearman's } r = 1 - \frac{6(385.5)}{25(25^2 - 1)} = 1 - 2,313/15,600 = .852$$

time and place of work) have mean scores below 3.0. Virtually all the characteristics are at least moderately desirable, but some are much more desirable than others.

The scale is ordinal (1-5), so, strictly speaking, you can't tell if a score of 4 is one-third greater than a score of 3 or twice as big as a score of 3. Pearson's correlation coefficient is designed specifically to take advantage of the information in interval variables, so with ordinal scales, you need some other measure of correlation. Spearman's coefficient of rank-ordered correlation is an excellent choice for sets of 30 or fewer rank-ordered objects.

Brenner and Tomkiewicz ranked the job characteristics and applied the following formula:

$$\text{Spearman's } r = 1 - \frac{6 \, \Sigma \, d^2}{n(n^2 - 1)} \qquad \text{(Formula 15.20)}$$

TABLE 15.17 Skruppy's (1993) Data on the Daily Activity Skills of 30 Elderly Men

Respondent	Self-Report	Observed	Respondent	Self-Report	Observed
1	40	40	16	40	40
2	45	30	17	45	30
3	45	40	18	45	40
4	70	70	19	70	70
5	70	70	20	60	25
6	70	70	21	60	60
7	70	70	22	45	40
8	45	40	23	70	70
9	60	60	24	45	40
10	60	25	25	40	40
11	70	70	26	45	40
12	70	70	27	60	60
13	70	70	28	45	30
14	45	40	29	45	40
15	60	60	30	45	35

SOURCE: Adapted from M. Skruppy, "Activities of Daily Living Evaluations: Is There a Difference in What the Patient Reports and What Is Observed?" *Physical and Occupational Therapy in Geriatrics* 11:13-25. Copyright © 1993, The Haworth Press, Inc. Reprinted with permission.

where d is the difference between the ranks on all pairs of objects. Table 15.16 shows the computation of d^2 for the data on men and women.

For these graduating business majors, at least, men and women have essentially the same (rather high) expectations for the jobs they hope to land. The Spearman correlation for African Americans and Whites is nearly as strong (.829), with just a couple of items accounting for most of the difference in ranks. Item 10 (Involves working with congenial associates) is ranked much higher by Whites, and item 19 (Satisfies your cultural and aesthetic interests) is ranked much higher by African Americans.

Skruppy (1993) interviewed 30 elderly men at the Veteran Affairs Medical Center in Minneapolis, Minnesota. She asked each of the patients a series of questions to assess their independence—whether they could drink from a cup, walk around unaided, wash their hands and face, and

so on. Then she asked each patient to show her how they actually do those things. This gave her two sets of scores: one for the 30 self-reports of the patients (their answers to the questions during the interview) and one for the patients' actual behavior. A perfect score on the index was 70. Table 15.17 shows the results.

The first thing you notice about these data is that 16 of the 30 patients got identical scores on both tests. This should make any correlation between the two sets of scores pretty high, and, in fact, r_s for these data is .75.

But notice, too, that 9 of those 16 patients who got identical scores on both tests also got perfect 70s. Skruppy removed these 9 patients and reran Spearman's correlation on the 21 remaining patients. Now the Spearman's correlation is just .18. So, when these patients had no limitations in their daily living activities (as measured by the test that Skruppy used), they reported their abilities accu-

TABLE 15.18 Spearman's Rank-Order Correlation of Favorite Activities between Groups Defined by Gender, Race, and Self-Defined Social Class

Lower-class Black women	—						
Middle-class Black women	.71	—					
Lower-class Black men	.54	.54	—				
Middle-class Black men	.35	.45	.61	—			
Lower-class White women	.23	.52	.17	.55	—		
Middle-class White women	.29	.66	.20	.52	.77	—	
Lower-class White men	.20	.33	.51	.87	.54	.41	—
Middle-class White men	.11	.07	.25	.81	.51	.26	.74

SOURCE: K. J. Shinew et al., "Gender, Race and Subjective Social Class and Their Association with Leisure Preferences." *Leisure Studies* 17, Table 2, p. 83, 1995.

rately. But when they had some disabilities (that is, less than perfect scores on the test), they tended to overestimate their abilities in their self-reports.

Another example of the use of Spearman's *r* is from Shinew et al.'s (1995) study of preferences for leisure activities among adults in the U.S., ages 18-65. This example illustrates the use of a *matrix of correlation scores*.

Shinew et al. analyzed data from a national, random telephone survey of 1,711 adults in the U.S. Respondents were asked, "How do you think of yourself? Would you say you are poor, in the working class, the middle class, the upper middle class, or the upper class?" Almost nobody said they were upper class, so Shinew et al. combined the data into two respondent-identified groups, lower class (combining poor and working class) and middle class (combining middle and upper middle class).

Respondents were also asked, "What is your favorite leisure or free-time activity?" Shinew et al. grouped these responses into 14 categories based on earlier research in this field (Noe 1974). For example, they lumped things like resting, loafing, and watching TV into a category called "immobile activities." They lumped woodwork-

ing, sewing, gardening, and cooking into a category called "popular arts," and so on.

Next, Shinew et al. used a simple frequency count and ranked the 14 activities in order, by race (Black/White), subjective social class (middle/lower), and gender (male/female). There were thus 8 rankings of preference for 14 leisure activities: a ranking for middle-class Black women; another ranking for lower-class White men; another for middle-class White women; and so on. With three dichotomous variables (race, class, gender), there are $2^3 = 8$ groups.

Now, with 8 rankings, there are $8 \times 7/2 = 28$ pairs of rankings, and each pair can be correlated. (Remember, there are $N(N - 1)/2$ pairs of any list of N things.) Table 15.18 shows the matrix of 28 Spearman's rank-order correlations for the Shinew et al. data.

The data in Table 15.18 are symmetrical, so we only need half the table. This simple table of rank-order correlations shows the complex interplay of race, gender, and social class on preferences for leisure activities.

There's a lot of information here. In row 2, we see that the correlation between the rank order of preferences among middle-class Black women and lower-class Black women for the 14 leisure activities is .71. In row 8, we see that the correla-

TABLE 15.19 Physicians and Per Capita Income for 10 U.S. States in 1994

State	x Per Capita Income in Thousands of Dollars	y Physicians/100,000 Population
Mississippi	15.838	132
South Carolina	17.695	179
North Dakota	18.546	192
Iowa	20.265	160
Kansas	20.896	188
Michigan	22.333	200
Delaware	22.828	214
Maryland	24.933	341
Oklahoma	17.744	155
Arizona	19.001	201

Mean of x = 20.008; mean of y = 196.2

SOURCE: *Statistical Abstract of the United States* (U.S. Census Bureau 1997, Tables 179, 713).

tion between middle-class White men and middle-class Black women is .07. The correlation for middle-class Black men and middle-class White men was .81. For middle-class White women and poor White women, Spearman's *r* was .77.

Middle-class White and Black women correlated at .66. Poor White men correlated .74 with middle-class White men.

PEARSON'S *r*

Pearson's r measures how much of the time changes in one variable correspond with equivalent changes in the other variables. It can also be used as a measure of association between an interval and an ordinal variable, or between an interval and a *dummy variable*. (Dummy variables are nominal variables coded as 1 or 0, present or absent. See Chapter 12 on text analysis.) The square of Pearson's *r* is a PRE measure of association for linear relations between interval variables. r^2 (read: *r* squared) tells us how much better we could predict the scores of a dependent variable, if we knew the scores of some independent variable.

Table 15.19 shows data for two interval variables for a random sample of 10 of the states in the U.S. in 1994: (1) the average number of physicians per 100,000 population, and (2) the average per capita income.

To give you an idea of where we're going with this example, the correlation between per capita income and the availability of physicians across the U.S. is around .77, and this is reflected in the sample of 10 states, for which the correlation is $r = .8179$, or about .82.

Now, suppose you had to predict the number of doctors per 100,000 population for each of the

10 states in Table 15.19 *without knowing anything about the average per capita income for those states.* Your best guess would be the mean, 196.2 physicians per 100,000 population.

In other words, if you have to make a wild guess on the particular scores of any interval variable, your prediction error will always be smallest if you pick the mean for each and every unit of analysis. You can see this in Figure 15.5. I have plotted the distribution of physician availability per 100,000 population and per capita income for the 10 states shown in Table 15.19.

The Sums of the Squared Distances to the Mean

Each dot in Figure 15.5 is physically distant from the dotted mean line by a certain amount. The sum of the squares of these distances to the mean line is the smallest sum possible (that is, the smallest cumulative prediction error you could make), given that you *only* know the mean of the dependent variable. The distances from the dots above the line to the mean are positive; the distances from the dots below the line to the mean are negative. The sum of the actual distances is zero. Squaring the distances gets rid of the negative numbers.

But suppose you *do* know the data in Table 15.19 regarding the per capita income of people in those 10 states. Can you reduce the prediction error in guessing the availability of physicians for

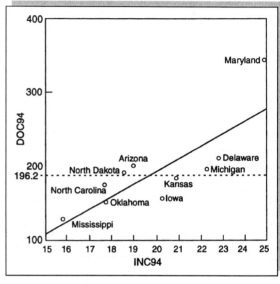

Figure 15.5 A Plot of the Data in Table 15.19
NOTE: The dotted line is the mean. The solid line is drawn from the regression equation $y = -137.147 + 16.661(x)$.

those 10 states? Could you draw another line through Figure 15.5 that "fits" the dots better and reduces the sum of the distances from the dots to the line?

You bet you can. The solid line that runs diagonally through the graph in Figure 15.5 minimizes the prediction error for these data. This line is called the **best-fitting line,** the **least squares line,** or the **regression line.** When you understand how this regression line is derived, you'll understand how correlation works.

REGRESSION

The formula for the regression line is

$$y = a + bx \quad \text{(Formula 15.21)}$$

where y is the variable value of the dependent variable, a and b are some constants (which you'll

learn how to derive in a moment), and x is the variable value of the independent variable. The constant, a, is computed as

$$a = \bar{y} - b(\bar{x}) \quad \text{(Formula 15.22)}$$

TABLE 15.20 Computation of Pearson's r Directly from Data in Table 15.19

State	x Per Capita Income in Thousands of Dollars	y Physicians/ 100,000 Population	xy	x²	y²
Mississippi	15.838	132	2090.616	250.842	17424
South Carolina	17.695	179	3167.405	313.113	32041
North Dakota	18.546	192	3560.832	343.954	36864
Iowa	20.265	160	3242.4	410.67	25600
Kansas	20.896	188	3928.448	436.643	35344
Michigan	22.333	200	4466.6	498.763	40000
Delaware	22.828	214	4885.192	521.118	45796
Maryland	24.933	341	8502.153	621.654	116281
Oklahoma	17.744	155	2750.32	314.85	24025
Arizona	19.001	201	3819.201	361.038	40401

Mean of $x = 20.008$; mean of $y = 196.2$

$\Sigma x = 200.079$; $\Sigma y = 1962$; $\Sigma xy = 40413.17$

$\bar{x} = 20.008$; $\bar{y} = 196.200$; $\Sigma x^2 = 4072.645$; $\Sigma y^2 = 413,776$

$$r_{xy} = \frac{N\Sigma xy - \Sigma x \Sigma y}{\sqrt{[N\Sigma x^2 - (\Sigma x)^2][N\Sigma y^2 - (\Sigma y)^2]}}$$ (Formula 15.24)

$$r_{xy} = \frac{10(40,413.17) - (200.079)(1962)}{\sqrt{[10(4072.645) - (200.079)^2][10(413,776) - (1962)^2]}} = .8179$$

and b is computed as

$$b = \frac{N(\Sigma xy) - (\Sigma x)(\Sigma y)}{N(\Sigma x^2) - (\Sigma x)^2}$$ (Formula 15.23)

Table 15.20 shows the data needed for finding the regression equation for the raw data in Table 15.19.

The constant b is

$$b = \frac{10(40,413.17) - (200.079)(1962)}{10(4072.645) - (200.079)^2} = \frac{11576.67}{694.843} = 16.661$$

and the constant a is then

$$a = 196.200 - 16.661(20.008) = -137.149$$

The regression equation for any pair of scores on income (y) and physician availability (x), then, is

$$y = a + bx = -137.149 + 16.661(x)$$

Drawing the Regression Line

To draw the regression line in Figure 15.5, find the expected y coordinate for two of the actual data points on the independent variable, x. For example:

(1) For Mississippi in Table 15.19, the expected number of physicians per 100,000 population is

$$y = -137.149 + 16.661(15.838) = 126.728$$

(2) For Kansas, the expected number of physicians is

$$y = -137.149 + 16.661(20.896) = 210.999$$

Put a dot on Figure 15.5 at the intersection of

$$x = 15.838, y = 126.728$$

and

$$x = 20.896, y = 210.999$$

and connect the dots. Extend the line through the entire graph. That's the regression line.

The squared deviations (the distances from any dot to the line, squared) add up to less than they would for any other line we could draw through that graph. The mean, then, is the least squares point for a *single* variable. The regression line is the least squares line for a plot of *two* variables. That's why the regression line is also called the "best-fitting" line.

Suppose we want to predict the dependent variable y (physician availability) when the independent variable x (per capita income) is $22,500 dollars per year. In that case,

$$y = -137.149 + 16.661(22.5)$$
$$= 374.873 - 137.149$$

or 237.724 physicians per 100,000 population. In other words, the regression equation lets us estimate the availability of physicians for income levels that are not even represented in our sample.

How Regression Works

To give you an absolutely clear idea of how the regression formula works, Table 15.21 shows all the predictions along the regression line for the data in Table 15.19.

We now have two predictors of the availability of physicians: (1) the mean number of physicians available, which is our best guess when we have no data about some independent variable like per capita income; and (2) the values produced by the regression equation when we *do* have information about something like per capita income.

Each of these predictors produces a certain amount of error, or *variance,* which is the difference between the predicted number for the dependent variable and the actual measurement. This is also called the **residual—that is, what's left over after making your prediction using the regression equation.** To anticipate the discussion of multiple regression in Chapter 16: The idea is to use two or more independent variables to reduce the size of the residuals.

You'll recall from Chapter 14, in the section on variance and the standard deviation, that in the case of the mean, the total variance is the average of the squared deviations of the observations from the mean, $1/N \ [\Sigma \ (x - \bar{x})^2]$. In the case of the regression line predictors, the variance is the sum of the squared deviations from the regression line.

TABLE 15.21 Regression Predictions for the Dependent Variable in Table 15.19

For the state of	Where the average per capita income in thousands of dollars in 1994 was	Predict that the number of physicians per 100,000 population will be	And compare that to the actual number of physicians that year
Mississippi	15.838	−137.149 + 16.661 (15.838) = 126.728	132
South Carolina	17.695	−137.149 + 16.661 (17.695) = 157.667	179
North Dakota	18.546	−137.149 + 16.661 (18.546) = 171.846	192
Iowa	20.265	−137.149 + 16.661 (20.265) = 200.486	160
Kansas	20.896	−137.149 + 16.661 (20.896) = 210.999	188
Michigan	22.333	−137.149 + 16.661 (22.333) = 234.941	200
Delaware	22.828	−137.149 + 16.661 (22.828) = 243.188	214
Maryland	24.933	−137.149 + 16.661 (24.933) = 278.260	341
Oklahoma	17.744	−137.149 + 16.661 (17.744) = 158.484	155
Arizona	19.001	−137.149 + 16.661 (19.001) = 179.427	201

TABLE 15.22 Comparison of the Error Produced by Guessing the Mean Number of Physicians per 100,000 Population in Table 15.19 and the Error Produced by Applying the Regression Equation for Each Guess

State	y Physicians	Old Error $(y - \bar{y})^2$	Prediction Using the Regression Equation	New Error (y − The prediction using the regression equation)^2
Mississippi	132	4121.64	126.728	27.794
South Carolina	179	295.84	157.667	455.097
North Dakota	192	17.64	171.846	406.184
Iowa	160	1310.44	200.486	1639.116
Kansas	188	67.24	210.999	528.954
Michigan	200	14.44	234.941	1220.873
Delaware	214	316.84	243.188	851.939
Maryland	341	20967.04	278.260	3936.308
Oklahoma	155	1697.44	158.484	12.138
Arizona	201	23.04	179.427	465.394
		$\Sigma = 28{,}831.6$		$\Sigma = 9{,}543.797$

Table 15.22 compares these two sets of errors, or variances, for the data in Table 15.19.

We now have all the information we need for a true PRE measure of association between two interval variables. Recall the formula for a PRE measure: the old error minus the new error, divided by the old error. For our example in Table 15.19:

$$\text{PRE} = \frac{28{,}831.6 - 9{,}543.797}{28{,}831.6} = .66896$$

In other words: The proportionate reduction of error in guessing the relative availability of physicians for the sample of states shown in Table 15.19—given that you know the distribution of per capita income for those states and can apply a regression equation—compared to just guessing the mean of physician availability is .66896, or about 67%.

This quantity is usually referred to as r^2 (read: r squared), or the **amount of variance accounted for by the independent variable.** It is also called the *coefficient of determination* because it tells us how much of the variance in the dependent variable is predictable from the scores of the independent variable. The Pearson product-moment correlation, written as r, is the square root of this measure, or, in this instance, .8179.

We calculated r in Table 15.20 by applying formula 15.24.

CALCULATING r AND r^2

I've given you this grand tour of regression and correlation because I want you to see that Pearson's r is not a direct PRE measure of association; its *square, r^2*, is.

> A correlation of .30 looks impressive until you square it and see that it explains just 9% of the variance in what you're studying.

So, what's better, Pearson's r or r^2 for describing the relation between interval variables? Pearson's r is easy to compute from raw data and it varies from –1 to +1, so it has direction and an intuitive interpretation of magnitude. It's also almost always bigger than r^2. By contrast, r^2 is a humbling statistic. A correlation of .30 looks impressive until you square it and see that it explains just 9% of the variance in what you're studying.

The good news is that if you double a correlation coefficient, you quadruple the variance accounted for. For example, if you get an r of .25, you've accounted for 6.25% of the variance, or error, in predicting the score of a dependent variable from a corresponding score on an independent variable. An r of .50 is twice as big as an r of .25, but four times as good, because $.50^2$ means that you've accounted for 25% of the variance.

Accounting for Variance

What does "accounting for variance" mean? It simply means being able to make a better prediction with an independent variable than we could without one. Recall from Chapter 14 that the total amount of variance in an observed set of scores is the sum of the squared deviations from the mean, divided by $N - 1$.

$$\text{Variance} = \frac{\Sigma (x - \bar{x})^2}{N - 1} \quad \text{(Formula 15.25)}$$

Well, if the correlation between the two variables in Table 15.19 is $r = 0.818$, and its square is $r^2 = 0.669$, then we can predict values of the dependent variable 66.9% better with the second variable than we can without it.

The mean number of physicians in the 10 states is 196.2 and the total variance is 3203.511. When

Box 15.9
Rounding Errors Again

Once again, just as we found in the calculation of the *F* ratio (see Box 15.2), there is rounding error. If you use a computer program, you'll find that the variance is 2315.342. This is because I've used only three *significant figures* in the calculations here. This means I've rounded to the nearest thousandth, or three places to the right of the decimal point, at each stage of the calculation. For example, I've used 16.661 as the value of *a* in the regression equation and –137.149 as the value for *b*.

At six significant figures instead of three, *a* is 16.660845 and *b* is –137.148530. If you go back to Table 15.21 and substitute 16.660845 for each of the 10 calculations where I've used 16.661 and –137.148530 for each of the calculations where I've used –137.149, you'll see that there is a change in each of the estimates of the dependent variable.

Major computer programs hold onto 12 decimal places during complex calculations. I've kept things down here to make the calculations more transparent. As it is, three significant figures is a lot of numbers floating around, but the accumulation of all the little differences along the way produces rounding error at the end.

we predict the number of physicians, using the regression formula, from the per capita income, the variance in the predicted scores will be 66.9% of 3203.511, or 2143.149 (see Box 15.9). This is what it means to say that "67% of the variance in the number of physicians per 100,000 population is [accounted for] [determined by] [predicted by] the mean per capita income of the states."

By the way, in case you're wondering, the correlation between the average per capita income and the availability of physicians has re-

mained steady at between $r = .75$ and $r = .77$ for the last several years in the U.S. Physicians earn a lot of money but there are very few of them, relative to the whole population, so their earnings have no noticeable effect on the average income of people across the 50 states in the U.S. Average state income predicts the number of physicians so well because physicians, like any other occupational group, go where the money is for their services.

TESTING THE SIGNIFICANCE OF *r*

Just as with gamma, it is possible to test whether or not any value of Pearson's *r* is the result of sampling error, or reflects a real covariation in the

larger population. In the case of *r*, the null hypothesis is that, within certain confidence limits, we should predict that the real coefficient of

TABLE 15.23 Confidence Limits for Pearson's r for Various Sample Sizes

Pearson's r	Sample Size 30	50	100	400	1,000
95% Confidence Limits					
.10	ns	ns	ns	ns	.04-.16
.20	ns	ns	.004-.40	.10-.29	.14-.26
.30	ns	.02-.54	.11-.47	.21-.39	.24-.35
.40	.05-.67	.14-.61	.21-.55	.32-.48	.35-.45
.50	.17-.73	.25-.68	.31-.63	.42-.57	.45-.54
.60	.31-.79	.39-.75	.45-.71	.53-.66	.56-.64
.70	.45-.85	.52-.82	.59-.79	.65-.75	.67-.73
.80	.62-.90	.67-.88	.72-.86	.76-.83	.78-.82
.90	.80-.95	.83-.94	.85-.93	.88-.92	.89-.91
99% Confidence Limits					
.10	ns	ns	ns	ns	.02-.18
.20	ns	ns	ns	.07-.32	.12-.27
.30	ns	ns	.05-.51	.18-.41	.23-.45
.40	ns	.05-.80	.16-.59	.28-.50	.33-.46
.50	.05-.75	.17-.72	.28-.67	.40-.59	.44-.56
.60	.20-.83	.31-.79	.41-.74	.51-.68	.55-.65
.70	.35-.88	.46-.85	.55-.81	.63-.76	.66-.74
.80	.54-.92	.62-.90	.69-.88	.75-.84	.77-.83
.90	.75-.96	.80-.95	.84-.94	.87-.92	.88-.91

correlation in the population of interest is actually zero. In other words, there is no relation between the two variables.

We need to be particularly sensitive to the possible lack of significance of sample statistics when we deal with small samples—which is a lot of the time, it turns out. The procedure for testing the confidence limits of r is a bit complex. To simplify matters, I have constructed Table 15.23, which you can use to get a ball-park reading on the significance of Pearson's r. The top half of Table 15.23 shows the 95% confidence limits for representative samples of 30, 50, 100, 400, and 1,000, where the Pearson's r values are .1, .2, .3, and so on. The bottom half of Table 15.23 shows the 99% confidence limits.

Reading the top half of Table 15.23, we see that at the 95% level, the confidence limits for a correlation of .20 in a random sample of 1,000 are .14 and .26. This means that in fewer than five tests in a hundred would we expect to find the correlation smaller than .14 or larger than .26. In other words, we are 95% confident that the true r for the population (written ρ, which is the Greek letter rho) is somewhere between .14 and .26.

By contrast, the 95% confidence limits for an r of .30 in a random sample of 30 is not significant at all; the true correlation could be 0, and our sample statistic of .30 could be the result of sampling error.

The 95% confidence limits for an r of .40 in a random sample of 30 is statistically significant.

We can be 95% certain that the true correlation in the population (ρ) is no less than .05 and no larger than .67. This is a statistically significant finding, but not much to go on insofar as external validity is concerned. You'll notice that with large samples (like 1,000), even very small correlations are significant at the .01 level. On the other hand, just because a statistical value is significant doesn't mean that it's important or useful in understanding how the world works.

Looking at the lower half of Table 15.23, we see that even an r value of .40 is statistically insignificant when the sample is as small as 30. If you look at the spread in the confidence limits for both halves of Table 15.23, you will notice something very interesting: A sample of 1,000 offers *some* advantage over a sample of 400 for bivariate tests, but the difference is small and the costs of the larger sample could be very high, especially if you're collecting all your own data.

Recall from Chapter 5, on sampling, that to halve the confidence interval you have to quadruple the sample size. Where the unit cost of data is high—as in research based on direct observation of behavior or on face-to-face interviews—the point of diminishing returns on sample size is reached quickly. Where the unit cost of data is low—as it is with mailed questionnaires or with telephone surveys—a larger sample is worth trying for.

NONLINEAR RELATIONS

And now for something different. All the examples I've used so far have been for linear relations where the best-fitting "curve" on a bivariate scattergram is a straight line. A lot of really interesting relations, however, are nonlinear. Consider political orientation over time. The Abraham Lincoln Brigade was a volunteer, battalion-strength unit of Americans who fought against the rightist forces of Francisco Franco during the Spanish Civil War, 1936-1939. The anti-Franco forces were supported by leftist groups, and by the Soviet Union. On the 50th anniversary of the start of the Spanish Civil War, surviving members of the Lincoln Brigade gathered at Lincoln Center in New York City.

Covering the gathering for the *New York Times* (April 7, 1986, p. B3), R. Shepard noted that "while some veterans might still be inspired by their youthful Marxism," many had "broken with early orthodoxies" and had become critical of the Soviet Union since their youth. There are many examples of leftist activists in modern society who are born into relatively conservative, middle-class homes; become radicals in their 20s; and become rather conservative after they "settle down" and acquire family and debt obligations. Later in life, when all these obligations are over, they may once again return to left-wing political activity.

This back-and-forth swing in political orientation probably looks something like Figure 15.6.

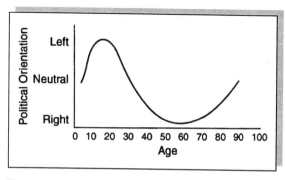

Figure 15.6 A Nonlinear Relation: Political Orientation through Time

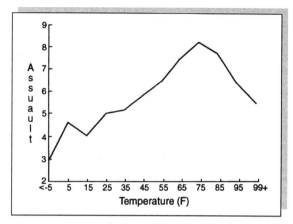

Figure 15.7 The Relation between Temperature and the Rate of Assault Is Nonlinear

SOURCE: E. G. Cohn and J. Rotton, "Assault as a Function of Time and Temperature: A Moderator-Variable Time-Series Analysis." *Journal of Personality and Social Psychology* 72:1322-34. Copyright © 1997 by the American Psychological Association. Reprinted with permission.

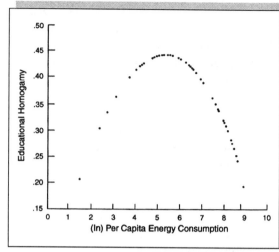

Figure 15.8 The Relation between Per Capita Energy Consumption and Educational Homogamy Is Nonlinear

SOURCE: J. Smits et al., "Educational Homogamy in 65 Countries: An Explanation of Differences in Openness Using Country-Level Explanatory Variables." *American Sociological Review* 63:264-85. Copyright © 1998 by the American Sociological Association. Reprinted with permission.

Nonlinear relations are everywhere, and you need to be on the lookout for them. Beginning with –5° F and continuing up to 75° F, the mean number of assaults rises steadily with the average daily temperature in U.S. cities. Then it begins to drop. Figure 15.7, from Cohn and Rotton (1997), shows the dramatic pattern. The reasons for this pattern are very complex, but it is clear from Figure 15.7 that a simple, linear correlation is inadequate to describe what's going on.

Smits et al. (1998) measured the strength of association between the educational level of spouses in 65 countries and how that relates to industrialization. Figure 15.8 shows what they found. It's the relation between per capita energy consumption (a measure of industrialization and hence of economic development) and the amount of educational homogamy in those 65 countries. (Homogamy means marrying someone who is similar to you, so educational homogamy means marrying someone who has the same level of education as you do.) The relation between the two variables is very clear: It's an inverted U.

You might think that the relation between these two variables would be linear—people of similar education would be attracted to each other—but it isn't. Here's how Smits et al. reckon the inverted U happens: People in nonindustrialized countries rely mostly on agriculture, so family background (which determines wealth) tends to be the main criterion for selecting mates. As industrialization takes off, education becomes more and more important and family background becomes less important for building wealth. Educated people seek each other out to maximize their life chances.

Eventually, though, when countries are highly industrialized, education is widespread, people have high wages, and there are social security

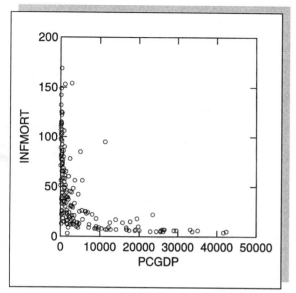

Figure 15.9 Infant Mortality by Per Capita Gross Domestic Product for 194 Countries

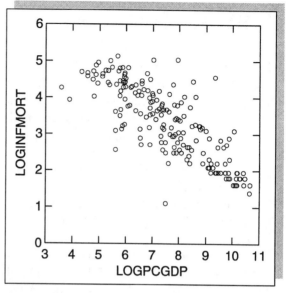

Figure 15.10 Log of Infant Mortality by Per Capita Gross Domestic Product for 194 Countries

systems. People in those countries don't have to rely on their children for support in old age, so romantic love becomes the dominant force in mate selection and the level of educational homogamy drops like a stone.

If you get a very weak r or r^2 for two variables that you believe, from theory or from field research, are strongly related, then draw a scattergram and check it out. Scattergrams are available in all the major statistical packages and they are, as you saw in Figure 15.1, packed with information. For sheer intuitive power, there is nothing like them.

Figure 15.9, for example, is the plot we saw in Figure 15.1d of infant mortality by per capita gross domestic product (PCGDP) for 194 countries around the world. (Recall that infant mortality is the number of babies who die before their first birthday and PCGDP is a measure of income, per person.) The correlation between these two

variables is −0.513, indicating a moderate negative relation, but the scattergram shows that the relation is not linear.

Figure 15.10 is a plot of the natural logarithm of infant mortality and PCGDP. Now, the correlation is −0.732 and the negative relation is linear: Per capita gross domestic product has to grow *proportionately* to lower infant mortality by a given amount. (Just to let you know how this works out: Countries at the bottom have to raise their per capita domestic product by a factor of 16 to cut their infant mortality rate in half. At $1,600 per year, countries only have to raise their per capita income by a factor of 4 to cut the infant mortality rate in half. After $6,400 per capita per year, each doubling of income results in a halving of the infant mortality rate.)

If a scattergram looks anything like Figure 15.9, consider transforming the data by "taking the logs" (that is, converting the data to their logarithms). If a scattergram looks like the shapes in Figure 15.6, 15.7, or 15.8, then consider using eta squared, a statistic for nonlinear regression.

CALCULATING ETA SQUARED

Eta squared, written η^2 or eta^2, is a PRE measure that tells you how much better you could do if you predicted the separate means for *chunks* of your data than if you predicted the mean for all your data. Figure 15.11 graphs the hypothetical data in Table 15.24. These data show, for a sample of 20 people, ages 12-89, their "number of close friends and acquaintances."

The dots in Figure 15.11 are the data points from Table 15.24. Respondent 10, for example, is 45 years of age and was found to have approximately 55 friends and acquaintances. The horizontal dashed line in Figure 15.11 is the global average for these data, 41.15. Clearly, (1) the global average is not of much use in predicting the dependent variable, (2) knowing a person's age *is* helpful in predicting the size of his or her social network, but (3) the linear regression equation is hardly any better than the global mean at reducing error in predicting the dependent variable. You can see this by comparing the mean line and the regression line (the slightly diagonal line running from lower left to upper right in Figure 15.11). They are very similar.

What that regression line depicts, of course, is the correlation between age and size of network, which is a puny $-.099$. But if we inspect the data visually, we find that there are a couple of natural "breaks." It looks like there's a break in the late 20s, and another somewhere in the 60s. We'll break these data into three age chunks, 12-26, 27-61, and 64-89; take separate means for each chunk; and see what happens. I have marked the three chunks and their separate means on Table 15.24.

Like r, which must be squared to find the variance accounted for, eta^2 is a measure of this and is calculated from the following formula:

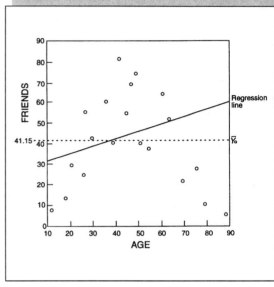

Figure 15.11 Number of Friends by Age

$$\eta^2 = 1 - \frac{\Sigma(y - \bar{y}_c)^2}{\Sigma(y - \bar{y})^2} \qquad \text{(Formula 15.26)}$$

where $\bar{y}_c$ is the average for each chunk and $\bar{y}$ is the overall average for your dependent variable. For Table 15.24, eta squared is

$$1 - \frac{3,871.55}{10,058.55} = .62$$

which is the proportionate reduction of error in predicting the number of friends people have from the three separate averages of their age rather than from the global average of their age. This shows a pretty strong relation between the two variables, despite the very weak Pearson's r.

TABLE 15.24 Hypothetical Data on Number of Friends by Age

Person	Age	Number of Friends	
1	12	8	
2	18	14	$\bar{y}_1 = 19.25$
3	21	30	
4	26	25	
5	27	56	
6	30	43	
7	36	61	
8	39	41	
9	42	82	$\bar{y}_2 = 57.00$
10	45	55	
11	47	70	
12	49	75	
13	51	41	
14	55	38	
15	61	65	
16	64	52	
17	70	22	
18	76	28	$\bar{y}_3 = 23.80$
19	80	11	
20	89	6	
		$\bar{y} = 41.15$	

STATISTICAL SIGNIFICANCE, THE SHOTGUN APPROACH, AND OTHER ISSUES

To finish this chapter, I want to deal with four thorny issues in social science data analysis: (1) measurement and statistical assumptions, (2) eliminating the outliers, (3) significance tests, and (4) the shotgun method of analysis.

Measurement and Statistical Assumptions

By now you are comfortable with the idea of nominal-, ordinal-, and interval-level measurement. This seminal notion was introduced into social science in a classic article by S. S. Stevens in 1946. Stevens said that statistics like t and r, because of certain assumptions that they made, required interval-level data, and this became an almost magical prescription.

Thirty-four years later, Gaito (1980) surveyed the (by then voluminous) mathematical statistics literature and found no support for the idea that measurement properties have anything to do with the selection of statistical procedures. Social scientists, said Gaito, confuse measurement (which focuses on the meaning of numbers) with statistics (which doesn't care about meaning at all) (p. 566). So, treating ordinal variables as if they were interval, for purposes of statistical analysis, is almost always a safe thing to do, especially with five or more ordinal categories (R. P. Boyle 1970; Labovitz 1971a).

The important thing is measurement, not statistics. As I pointed out in Chapter 2, many concepts, such as gender, race, and class, are much more subtle and complex than we give them credit for being. Instead of measuring them qualitatively (remember that assignment of something to a nominal category is a qualitative act of measurement), we ought to be thinking hard about how to measure them ordinally.

Émile Durkheim was an astute theorist. He noted that the division of labor became more complex as the complexity of social organization increased (Durkheim 1933 [1893]). But he, like other theorists of his day, divided the world of social organization into a series of dichotomous categories (*gemeinschaft* vs. *gesellschaft,* or mechanical vs. organic solidarity).

Today, social theorists want to know how degrees of differences in aspects of social organization (like the division of labor in society) are related to social complexity. This requires some hard thinking about how to measure these two variables with more subtlety. The meaning of the measurements is crucial.

Eliminating the Outliers

Another controversial practice in data analysis is called "eliminating the *outliers,*" that is, removing **extreme values** from data analysis. If there are clear indications of measurement error (a person with a score of 600 on a 300-point test turns up in your sample), you can throw out the data that are in error. If you decide to restrict the applicability of your sample, you can get rid of extreme cases—defining your population as "all cities in New York State under two million," for instance, eliminates New York City.

The problem is that outliers (so-called freak cases) are sometimes eliminated just to "smooth out" data and achieve better fits of regression lines to data. A single millionaire might be ignored in calculating the average net worth of a group of blue-collar workers on the theory that it's a "freak case." But what if it isn't a freak case? What if it represents a small, but substantively significant proportion of cases in the population under study? Eliminating it only prevents the discovery of that fact. It's better to use the median to describe the central tendency of the cases than to eliminate the case.

There were 2.3 television sets per household in the U.S. in 1995. A few households had 20 TVs. Just about everyone has phone service and just about everyone has one phone line. A few households have 20 lines. I have a line just for fax and e-mail. Anyway, if you do a consumer survey of 200 people in your home town, your sample might have one of those rare people who have 20 TVs or 20 phone lines. Do you remove them from the data because they mess up the averages?

Trivially, you can always achieve a perfect regression fit to a set of data if you reduce it to just 2 points. But is creating a good fit what you're after? Don't you really want to understand what makes the data messy in the first place? In general, you cannot achieve an understanding of messiness by cleaning things up. Still, as in all aspects of research, be ready to break this rule, too, when you think you'll learn something by doing so.

For example, Twenge (1997) did a meta-analysis of 71 studies, between 1970 and 1995, in which the Attitudes Toward Women Scale (AWS) was used. For the 63 studies in which respondents were undergraduate women the bivariate correlation of the mean score on the AWS and the year it was administered was $r = .78$. This strong, positive correlation (the later the year, the higher the score) means that undergraduate women became more feminist in their attitudes

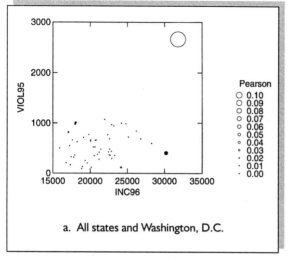

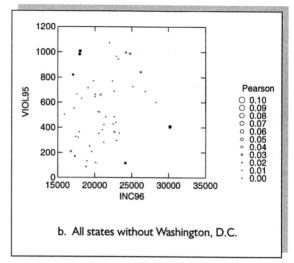

a. All states and Washington, D.C.

b. All states without Washington, D.C.

Figure 15.12 Violent Crimes in the United States per 100,000 Population in 1995, by Average Annual Pay, 1996

over time. The correlation for the 54 samples of men was $r = .60$. While men's attitudes also changed—and changed in the same direction—they did so more slowly than did women's.

Three of the large samples of men were from Texas A&M University, a traditionally more socially conservative school than, say, the University of Wisconsin. By removing these Texas A&M "outliers," the correlation of the men's mean scores on the AWS rose to $r = .73$. Twenge reported the results of her analysis when she left the outliers in and when she took the outliers out. This helps us understand the dynamics of the correlations—what's going on, and where the points of influence are.

I break the outlier rule myself once in a while. I've taught introduction to anthropology for about 35 years and I grade "on a curve." Grading on a curve means that you set the highest score in the class as 100% and grade everyone on the basis of that score. I give four exams, each with 60 questions, for a total of 240 points. Typically, the highest grade in the class is in the 200-210 range, or around 83%-88%. Every once in a while, I get a "curve breaker"—someone who scores, say, 225

or 230. When that happens, I'm stuck with a dilemma.

Here's one way to deal with it: "Well, that's the breaks. The world does have a few geniuses in it. One of them is bound to wind up in my class every so often. It's just a sampling issue. The students in this particular class will just have to live with that." What this means, of course, is that everyone in the class is held to a very high standard. Most people are going to get lower grades than they would have if they'd been lucky enough to enroll in a class that had no geniuses.

Here's the other way to deal with it: "This is a freakish incident. Students in this particular class should not have to pay the price for having enrolled in a class with a curve breaker. I'll set the highest grade in the class to be the modal high grade that I've seen over the years. That will still give the genius an A, but it will also ensure that others in the class get a shot at an A, too."

Figure 15.12a shows the relation between violent crime in the U.S. and the average pay for people in the 50 states plus Washington, D.C. Figure 15.12b shows exactly the same thing, but without including the data from Washington, D.C. The correlation between the two variables *with* D.C. is .62. When we leave out the data for D.C., the correlation sinks to .39.

That's because the violent crime rate in Washington, D.C., was an appalling 2,661 per 100,000 population and the average pay there was $42,453 a year in 1995. For the 50 states in the U.S., the next highest violent crime rate, in Florida, was less than half that of D.C. and the next highest average pay, in Connecticut, was 18% lower than that in D.C.

> *What to do with outliers?*
> *Report the results of your analysis*
> *with and without them.*

The actual sizes of the dots in Figures 15.12 indicate the amount of influence each data point has on the correlation. The legend for this little trick is over on the right of each of the figures. That huge circle in the upper-right-hand corner of Figure 15.12a is D.C. Now, *that's* an outlier.

What to do with outliers? Report the results of your analysis with and without them, like Twenge did.

Tests of Significance

This is a hot topic in social science. Some years ago, researchers began arguing that statistical tests of significance are virtually useless (Rozeboom 1960; Labovitz, 1971b; Carver 1978), and the drumbeat has continued ever since (Carver 1993; Cohen 1994). I wouldn't go that far, but tests of significance aren't magical, either.

If you do not have a representative sample, then a test of statistical significance doesn't allow you to generalize beyond your particular sample of data. On the other hand, if you get significant results on a nonrandom sample, at least you can

rule out the operation of random properties *in your sample* (Blalock 1979:239ff.).

Nor are the .01 and .05 levels of significance sacred. These numbers are simply conventions that have developed for convenience over the years. Greenwald et al. (1996:181-82) offer some useful advice about reporting p-values.

(1) Report p-values with an equal sign, $=$, not with a $<$ or $>$ sign. If a p-value is .042, don't report it as $p < .05$ ("the probability is less than .05"). Just report it as $p = .042$ and be done with it. Probability, just like the confidence we have in probabilistic results, is a continuous variable. Why cut out all that information with arbitrary cut-offs?

(2) A single p-value of .05 is an indicator of a relation, but is not convincing support for a hypothesis. By tradition, researchers almost never report probabilities that are greater than .05. Five *repeated results* of $p = .06$, or even .10, are more convincing than a single result of $p = .05$ that something's really going on.

The Bonferroni Correction

If you want to be especially cautious in reporting correlations, you can apply a test known as the **Bonferroni correction**. There are two kinds of spurious correlation. One happens when the correlation between two variables is caused by a third, independent, variable. Another occurs when two variables covary because of sheer accident. It happens all the time. In fact, it occurs with a known probability.

Take a random sample of, say, 30 variables in the world, measure them, and correlate all possible pairs of those variables. (There are $N[N-1]/2 = 435$ pairs of 30 anything.) According to the Bonferroni rule, you should get a correlation, significant at the $p = < .05$ level, in 5% of all cases—in 22 out of 435 pairs—just by chance. So, if you build a matrix with 435 pairs of correlations and find that 20 of them are significant at the .05 level or better, you can't be sure that this is not simply a random event.

Of course, you *always* have to explain why any two variables are correlated, since correlation, by itself, never implies cause and effect. But when you go fishing for significant correlations in a big matrix of them, and find fewer than you'd expect by chance alone, things are even tougher.

How tough? Pick a level of significance for reporting findings in your data—say, .05. If you have 30 variables in your analysis, and 435 tests of covariations in your matrix, divide .05 by 2,145 = .0001. If you report these correlations as significant at the 5% level (the level you chose originally), then, according to the Bonferroni rule, your report will be valid (see Koopmans 1981; Kirk 1982). This is a very, very conservative test, but it will prevent you from making those dreaded Type I errors, and reporting significant relations that aren't really there.

On the other hand, this will increase your chance of making Type II errors—rejecting some seemingly insignificant relations when they really are important. You might fail to show, for example, that certain types of exposure are related to contracting a particular disease, and this would have negative public health consequences. There's no free lunch.

Consider the study by Dressler (1980). He studied a sample of 40 people on the Caribbean island of St. Lucia, all of whom had high blood pressure. Dressler measured nine variables having to do with his respondents' ethnomedical beliefs and their compliance with a physician-prescribed treatment regimen. He reported the entire matrix of $(9 \times 8)/2 = 36$ correlations, 13 of which were significant at the 5% level or better.

Dressler might have expected just $36 \times .05 = 1.8$ such correlations by chance. Three of the 13 correlations were significant at the .001 level.

According to the Bonferroni inequality, correlations at the $.05/36 = .0014$ level would be reportable at the .05 level as valid. Under the circumstances, however (13 significant correlations with only about 2 expected by chance), Dressler was quite justified in reporting all his findings and was not being overly conservative.

My feeling is that if you are using small data sets, you can be comfortable with tests of significance at the $p < .10$ level, especially if you can repeat your finding in independent tests. Two or three repeated experiments that produce similar results in the same direction at the .10 level of significance are more convincing evidence of something going on than is one experiment that just barely pans out at the .05 level.

On the other hand, you can always find significant covariations in your data if you lower the level of significance level enough, so be careful. Remember, you're using statistics to get hints about things that are going on in your data. I cannot repeat often enough the rule that real analysis (building explanations and suggesting plausible mechanisms that make sense out of covariations) is what you do *after* you do statistics.

I also can't stress enough the difference between *statistical significance* and *practical significance*. If you have a large enough N (in the thousands), you will surely find significant statistical relations in your data. Each of those relations may account for a small amount of the variance in what you're interested in understanding, but that doesn't mean that the relations are of practical use.

Suppose you come up with a new curriculum for teaching high school students about the dangers of smoking cigarettes. You implement the program in a classic experimental design, so that, of the two thousand students in the district, a thousand are exposed to the curriculum and another thousand are exposed to the curriculum you hope to replace.

At the end of the experiment, students in the treatment group score significantly higher on their tests of knowledge about the dangers of smoking than do students who were exposed to the old curriculum. With that many students, a few points of difference on the test might be statistically significant, indicating that the new curriculum is better.

But suppose it costs $30 more per student to implement the new curriculum. Will the school board shell out $30 × 2,000 = $60,000 to put in the new curriculum and achieve a very small, but statistically significant, improvement in students' knowledge about smoking? The statistical level of significance in the results may play *some* role in the board's decision, but I'll bet that other things will weigh even more heavily in their deliberations.

Even if the difference in test results is spectacular—students who take the new curriculum learn, say, twice as much about the dangers of smoking than do the students who study the old curriculum—it doesn't mean that the board will implement the new curriculum. Someone on the board may have the audacity to ask you whether you can prove that a spectacular difference in knowledge among students translates into safer *behavior*.

Statistical Power

The *power* of a statistical test is the probability of correctly accepting your research hypothesis. If you're thinking: "You mean it's the probability of taking 'yes' for an answer?" then you're right on track. As you know, the way we usually conduct research—whether experiments or surveys—is by (1) formulating a hypothesis, (2) turning the hypothesis around into a null hypothesis, and then (3) trying as hard as we can to prove the null hypothesis.

This is *not* perverse. All of us positivists out here know that it's impossible to absolutely, positively, prove any hypothesis to be forever unfalsifiably true. So we do the next best thing. We try our very best to disprove our best ideas (our research hypotheses) and hope that we fail, leaving us with the right to say that our best guess is that we were right to begin with.

What this means in the real life of researchers is that statistical power is the probability of avoiding *both* Type I and Type II errors: rejecting the null hypothesis when it's really true (Type I error) or accepting a null hypothesis when it's really false (Type II error).

This probability depends on two things: (1) the minimum size of the difference between two outcomes that you will accept as a *real* difference, and (2) the size of the sample. So, to achieve a given amount of statistical power in any experiment, you need to calculate the size of the sample required, given the minimum size of the difference between two outcomes—the effect size—that you will accept as a real difference (Kraemer and Thiemann 1987; Cohen 1988).

This is a very important and subtle issue. Suppose you ask 100 men and 100 women, matched for socioeconomic status, race, and religion, to take the Attitudes Toward Women Scale. The null hypothesis is that there is no difference between the mean scores of the men and the mean scores of the women on this scale. How big a difference do you need between the mean of the men and the mean of the women on this scale to reject the null hypothesis and conclude that, in fact, the difference is real—that men and women really differ on their attitudes toward women as expressed in the AWS?

The answer depends on the power of the test of the difference in the means. Suppose you analyze the difference between the two means with a *t*-test, and suppose that the test is significant at the .05 level. Statistical power is the probability that you are wrong to report this result as an indicator that you can reject the null hypothesis. The result, at the $p = .05$ level, indicates that the difference you detected between the mean for the men and the mean for the women would be expected to occur by chance fewer than 5 times in 100 runs of the same experiment.

It does *not* indicate that you are $1 - p$, or 95% confident that you have correctly rejected the null hypothesis. The power of the finding of $p = .05$ depends on the size of the sample and on the size of the difference that you expected to find before you did the study.

In the case of the AWS, there are 25 years of data available. These data make it easy to say how big a difference you expect to find if the men and women in your sample are really different in their responses to the AWS. Many surveys are done without this kind of information available. You can offer a theory to explain the results from one experiment or survey. But you can't turn around and use those same data to *test* your theory. As replications accumulate for questions of importance in the social sciences, the question of statistical power becomes more and more important.

So, what's the right amount of statistical power to shoot for? Cohen (1992) recommends that researchers plan their work—that is, set the effect size they recognize as important, set the level of statistical significance they want to achieve (.05, for example, or .01), and calculate the sample size—to achieve a power of .80.

A power value of .80 would be an 80% chance of recognizing that our original hypothesis is really true and a 20% chance of rejecting our hypothesis when it's really true. If you shoot for a power level of much lower than .80, says Cohen, you run a big risk of making a Type II error.

On the other hand, power ratings much higher than .80 might require such large Ns that researchers couldn't afford them (ibid.:156). If you want 90% power for a .01 (1%) two-tailed test of, say, the difference between two Pearson's *r*s, then, you'd need 364 participants (respondents, subjects) to detect a difference of .20 between the scores of the two groups. If you were willing to settle for 80% power and a .05 (5%) two-tailed test, then the number of participants drops to 192.

The Shotgun Approach

A closely related issue concerns "shotgunning." This involves constructing a correlation matrix of all combinations of variables in a study, and then relying on tests of significance to reach substantive conclusions. It is quite common for field workers in anthropology or sociology to acquire measurements on as many variables as they have informants—and sometimes even *more* variables than informants.

There is nothing wrong with this. If you are doing field research, after a very short time in the field you will think up lots and lots of variables that appear potentially interesting to you. Include as many of them as you have time to ask on a survey without boring your informants.

The result of effective data collection is a large *matrix* of items-by-variables, like that in Figure 15.13a. The items are the units of analysis. Most of the time, these units are people, but they could just as easily be cultures or schools. (If this is unfamiliar to you, see the section on units of analysis in Chapter 2.)

The matrix in Figure 15.13a is called a *profile matrix*. (Profile and similarity matrices were introduced in Chapter 11; see also Figure 11.1.) Each row is a profile of a single unit of analysis. In Figure 15.13a, person 1 is profiled by the following facts: She is 27 years old, is female (recorded as a 2 under the variable sex), has completed high school, comes from a household that had 6 people in it, and is now part of a household that has 4 people in it.

For any profile matrix, you can compare pairs of rows or pairs of columns to see how similar they are. If you compare rows, you find out how similar the units of analysis are to one another. If

Respondent	Age	Sex	Education	Natal Household Size	Current Household Size	Ethnicity
1	27	2	3	6	4	3
2	31	1	2	3	2	1
3	.	.	.	.	.	.
4	.	.	.	.	.	.
.	.	.	.	.	.	.
.	.	.	.	.	.	.
.	.	.	.	.	.	.
.	.	.	.	.	.	.

a. Profile matrix of persons by variables

	Age	Sex	Education	Natal Household Size	Current Household Size	Ethnicity
Age	—					
Sex		—				
Education			—			
Natal Household Size				—		
Current Household Size					—	
Ethnicity						—

b. Similarity matrix of the variables (columns) in Figure 15.13a

Figure 15.13 Matrices

you compare columns, you find out how similar the variables are to one another.

Figure 15.13b shows a *similarity matrix* of variables. Imagine the list of variable names stretching several feet to the right, off the right-hand margin of the page, and several feet down, off the lower margin. That is what would happen if you had, say, 100 variables about each of your respondents. For each and every pair of variables in the matrix of data, you could ask: Are these variables related?

Now, if the matrix is symmetrical, then however much x and y covary, y and x covary in the same amount. That gets rid of half the pairs right there. We can also ignore the entries in the diagonal, since we're hardly interested in the covariation of variables with themselves. That still leaves $N(N-1)/2$ unique pairs of variables in a symmetric matrix. For 100 variables, there are 4,950 pairs to consider.

Even a small matrix of 20 variables contains 190 unique pairs. It would take forever to go through each pair and (1) decide whether it was worth spending the time to test for covariation in each case, (2) decide on the proper test to run (depending on the level of measurement involved in each case), (3) run the test, and (4) inspect and interpret the results.

There are two ways out of this fix. One way is to think hard about data and ask only those questions about covariation that seem plausible on theoretical grounds. It may not be important, for example, to test whether an informant's rank in a sibling set (first child, second child, etc.)

TABLE 15.25 Correlation Matrix of All 21 Variables in Kunitz et al.'s (1981) Study of Hospital Use on the Navajo Reservation

	1	2	3	4	5	6	7	8	9	10	11	12	13	14	15	16	17	18	19	20
1 Near hospital																				
2 Near surgery	.67																			
3 Wage work	−.24	−.09																		
4 Welfare	.52	.46	−.54																	
5 Education of men	−.42	−.43	.73	−.49																
6 Education of women	.01	−.21	.67	−.32	.81															
7 Hogans	.07	.37	−.26	.72	−.28	−.40														
8 Bathrooms	−.44	−.57	.63	−.63	.70	.64	−.47													
9 Household size	.01	−.16	−.48	.24	−.34	−.07	.04	.12												
10 Working women	−.35	−.36	.68	−.65	.65	.57	−.48	.62	−.22											
11 Working men	−.24	−.18	.73	−.37	.73	.63	−.16	.41	−.45	.45										
12 Vehicles	.34	−.08	.40	−.17	.22	.52	−.53	.29	−.06	.31	.40									
13 Median income	−.45	−.51	.66	−.60	.67	.60	−.38	.79	−.07	.83	.48	.27								
14 Per capita income	−.25	−.20	.68	−.46	.61	.40	−.15	.29	−.68	.48	.51	.30	.47							
15 Age of women	−.23	−.03	−.47	−.15	−.36	−.66	−.02	−.46	−.30	−.37	−.32	−.56	−.43	−.04						
16 Age of men	.28	.15	−.77	.31	−.60	−.55	.01	−.67	.06	−.51	−.68	−.35	−.63	−.45	.60					
17 Age of patients	.13	.47	.13	−.14	−.21	−.15	−.18	−.22	−.36	−.04	−.26	−.15	−.26	−.02	.29	.32				
18 Hysterectomies	−.41	−.48	.62	−.55	.57	.46	−.23	.75	−.09	.45	.46	.39	.62	.59	−.37	−.62	.28			
19 Appendectomies	−.31	−.40	.32	−.14	.44	.33	.16	.51	.13	.07	.27	.01	.42	.35	−.31	−.49	−.56	−.62		
20 Cholesystectomies	−.23	−.70	.15	−.43	.35	.34	−.46	.68	.22	.19	.12	.31	.40	.14	−.17	−.17	−.35	.70	.49	
21 Hospital rate	−.49	.24	.02	−.26	.02	−.25	−.09	.16	−.19	−.04	−.34	−.33	.01	.22	.43	.16	.45	.17	.10	.18

$N = 18$; 0.46, $p = .05$; 0.56 $p = .01$

SOURCE: Reprinted from *Social Science and Medicine*, 15B, S. J. Kunitz et al., "Determinants of Hospital Utilization and Surgery on the Navajo Indian Reservation, 1972-1978," 71-79. Copyright © 1981, with permission of Elsevier Science.

covaries with his or her blood pressure. On the other hand, maybe it is. You can decide whether to test the relation between these two particular variables based on your knowledge of prior research, theory, and hunches.

The other way out of the fix is the *shotgun strategy*. You simply use a computer to transform your profile matrix into a similarity matrix in which each cell is occupied by an appropriate measure of association—percentage of matched pairs, Pearson's *r*, gamma—depending on whether the variables were measured as nominals, ordinals, or intervals. Then you scan the similarity matrix in search of significant covariations.

❖

Kunitz et al. (1981) studied the determinants of hospital utilization and surgery in 18 communities on the Navajo Indian Reservation during the 1970s. They measured 21 variables in each community, including 17 independent variables (average education of adults, percentage of men and women who worked full time, average age of men and women, percentage of income from welfare, percentage of homes that had bathrooms, percentage of families living in traditional hogans, etc.) and 4 dependent variables (rate of hospital use and the rates for the three most common types of surgery). Table 15.25 shows the correlation matrix of all 21 variables in this study.

Kunitz et al. point out in the footnote to their matrix that, for $N = 18$, the .05 level of probability corresponds to $r = 0.46$ and the .01 level corresponds to $r = 0.56$. By the Bonferroni correction, they could have expected

$$(21 \times 20)/2 \times .05 = 10.5$$

correlations significant at the .05 level and

$$(21 \times 20)/2 \times .01 = 2.1$$

correlations significant at the .01 level by chance. There are 73 correlations significant at the .05 level in Table 15.25, and 42 of those correlations are significant at the .01 level.

Kunitz et al. examined these correlations and were struck by the strong association of the hysterectomy rate to all the variables that appear to measure acculturation. I'm struck by it, too. This interesting finding was not the result of deduction and testing; it was the result of shotgunning. The finding is not proof of anything, of course, but it sure seems like a strong clue to me. I'd want to follow this up with research on how acculturation affects the kind of medical care that women re-

ceive and whether all those hysterectomies are necessary.

The Problem with the Shotgun Approach

The problem with shotgunning is that you might be fooled into thinking that *statistically* significant correlations are also *substantively* significant. This is a real danger, and it should not be minimized (Labovitz 1972). It results from two problems.

1. *You have to be very careful about choosing a measure of association, depending on how the variables were measured.* A significant correlation in a matrix may be an artifact of the statistical technique used and not be of any substantive importance. Running a big correlation matrix of all your variables may produce some statistically significant results that would be insignificant if the proper test had been applied.

2. *There is a known probability that any correlation in a matrix might be the result of chance.* The number of expected significant correlations in a matrix is equal to the level of significance you choose, times the number of variables. If you are looking for covariations that are significant at the 5% level, then you only need 20 tests of covariation to find one such covariation by chance. If you are looking for covariations that are significant at the 1% level, you should expect to find one, by chance, in every 100 tries. In a matrix of 100 variables with 4,950 correlations, you might find around 50 significant correlations at the 1% level by chance.

This does not mean that 50 correlations at the 1% level in such a matrix *are* the result of chance. They just *might* be. There can easily be 100 or more significant correlations in a symmetric matrix of 100 variables. If 50 of them (4,950/100) might be the result of chance, then how can you decide which 50 they are? You can't. You can never know for sure whether any particular correlation is the result of chance. You simply have to be careful in your interpretation of *every* correlation in a matrix.

Use the shotgun. Be as cavalier as you can in looking for statistically significant covariations, but be very conservative in interpreting their substantive importance. Correlations are hints to you that something is going on between two variables. Just keep in mind that the leap from correlation to cause is often across a wide chasm.

If you look at Table 15.23 again, you can see just how risky things can be. A correlation of .60 is significant at the 1% level of confidence with a sample as small as 30. Notice, however, that the correlation in the population is 99% certain to fall between .20 and .83, which is a pretty wide spread. You wouldn't want to build too big a theory around a correlation that just might be down around the .20 level, accounting for just 4% of the variance in what you're interested in!

Remember these rules:

(1) Not all significant findings at the 5% level of confidence are equally important. A very weak correlation of .10 in a sample of millions of people would be statistically significant, even if it were substantively trivial. By contrast, in small samples, substantively important relations may show up as statistically insignificant.

(2) Don't settle for just one correlation that supports a pet theory; insist on several, and

be on the lookout for artifactual correlations.

Forty years ago, before statistical packages were available, it was a real pain to run any statistical tests. It made a lot of sense to think hard about which of the thousands of possible tests one really wanted to run by hand on an adding machine.

Computers have eliminated the drudge work in data analysis, but they haven't eliminated the need to think critically about your results. If anything, computers—especially those little ones that sit on your desk and have full-featured statistics packages that do everything from χ^2 to factor analysis—have made it more important than ever to be self-conscious about the interpretation of statistical findings. But if you are self-conscious about this issue and dedicated to thinking critically about your data, then I believe you should take full advantage of the power of the computer to produce a mountain of correlational hints that you can follow up.

Finally, by all means, use your intuition in interpreting correlations; common sense and your personal experience in research are powerful tools for data analysis. If you find a correlation between the number of times that men have been arrested for drug dealing and the number of younger siblings they have, you'd suspect that this correlation might be just a chance artifact.

On the other hand, maybe it isn't. There is just as much danger in relying slavishly on personal intuition and common sense as there is in placing ultimate faith in computers. What appears silly to you may, in fact, be an important signal in your data. The world is filled with self-evident truths that aren't true, and self-evident falsehoods that aren't false. The role of science, based on solid technique and the application of intuition, is to sort those things out.

KEY CONCEPTS

SUMMARY

❖ Statistical covariation involves four questions: (1) How much better can we predict the score of a dependent variable in our sample if we knew the score of some independent variable? (2) Is the covariation due to chance, or is it likely to exist in the overall population to which we want to generalize? (3) Is it positive or negative? (4) Is it linear or nonlinear?

❖ The two-sample t-test evaluates whether the means of two independent groups differ on some variable.
  ◆ The null hypothesis, H_0, is that the two means come from random samples of the *same* population—that there is no difference, except for sampling error, between the two means. The research hypothesis, H_1, is that the two means come from random samples of truly different populations.
  ◆ We evaluate the statistical significance of t using Appendix C. Testing the possibility that one mean is higher than another requires a one-tailed test. Use a two-tailed test when you are interested only in the magnitude of the difference between the means, not its direction or sign (plus or minus).

❖ A t-test measures the difference between two means. Analysis of variance, or ANOVA, is a technique that applies to a set of K means.
  ◆ Within-group variance is a measure of how much the scores of individual units of analysis are different from one another. Between-group variance expresses the amount that the scores between groups are different from one another.
  ◆ To find whether the means of several groups are significantly different from one another, calculate the ratio between the mean of the between-group variance and the mean of the within-group variance. Use Appendix E to determine the statistical significance of the ratio.

❖ The concept of direction refers to whether a covariation is positive or negative. The concept of shape refers to whether a relation is linear or nonlinear. Scattergrams help us see whether covariations are positive or negative, linear or nonlinear.

❖ Cross-tabulation tables, or cross-tabs, display the relations among two or more nominal or ordinal variables. The values for dependent variables are displayed in the rows and the values for independent variables are in the columns. Then the rule is: Percentage down the columns and interpret across the rows.

❖ Covariation does not necessarily mean cause and effect.
  ◆ To understand the relation between two variables, we need to ask about antecedent and intervening variables: (1) Is there some variable that is *related to, and prior to,* both the independent and dependent variables? and (2) Is there some variable that enters the picture *between* the independent and independent variables?

❖ The PRE (proportionate reduction of error) principle is the foundation for many statistical tests. A PRE measure tells you how much better you can guess the scores on a dependent variable by knowing the distribution of an independent variable.

❖ Chi-square tells you the probability that a relation between or among variables is the result of chance. But it is not a PRE measure of correlation, so it doesn't tell you the strength of association among variables. The principal use of χ^2 is for testing the hypothesis that there is no relation between two nominal variables—that is, for testing the null hypothesis.
  ◆ Fisher's exact test is used for 2 × 2 tables whenever the expected number of frequencies for any cell is less than five. With fewer than five expected occurrences in a cell, χ^2 values are generally not trustworthy.
  ◆ A direct and intuitive measure of strength for understanding the relation between nominal variables is the odds ratio.

❖ Gamma is a PRE measure for ordinal variables. Gamma tells you how much more correctly you could guess the rank of one ordinal variable for each unit of analysis if you knew the score for the other ordinal variable in a bivariate distribution.
  ◆ Some researchers prefer a statistic called Kendall's tau-b (written t_b or τ_b) instead of gamma for bivariate tables of ordinal-level data because gamma ignores tied pairs in the data.
  ◆ Yule's Q is the equivalent of gamma for 2 × 2 tables of ordinal variables.

❖ When at least one of the variables in a bivariate relation is interval or ratio level, we use a measure of correlation: Spearman's r, written r_s, when the data are rank ordered; Pearson product-moment correlation, written simply as r, to measure the strength of linear relations; or eta^2 (the Greek letter η) to measure the strength of certain kinds of nonlinear relations.
  ◆ Pearson's r measures how much of the time changes in one variable correspond with equivalent changes in the other variables. The square of Pearson's r is a PRE measure of association for linear relations between interval variables. r^2 tells us how much better we can predict the scores of a dependent variable, if we know the scores of some independent variable.

❖ Correlation is best understood in the context of regression. The regression equation for any pair of scores on two variables is $y = a + bx$. To draw the regression line, find the expected y coordinate for two of the actual data points on the independent variable, x, and connect the dots.
  ◆ The values produced by the regression equation produce a certain amount of error, which is the difference between the predicted number for the dependent variable and the actual measurement. This residual is what's left over after making your prediction using the regression equation.

- r^2, or the coefficient of determination, is the amount of variance accounted for by the independent variable. It tells us how much of the variance in the dependent variable is predictable from the scores of the independent variable. The Pearson product-moment correlation, written as r^2, is the square root of this measure.

❖ In linear relations, the best-fitting "curve" on a bivariate scattergram is a straight line. A lot of really interesting relations, however, are nonlinear. A few such relations include political orientation and age, the size of personal networks and age, the mean number of assaults and mean daily temperature, and the educational level of marriage partners and the mean level of industrialization.

❖ Data analysis is a complex intellectual exercise. Four important issues that continue to be debated are (1) measurement and statistical assumptions, (2) eliminating the outliers, (3) significance tests, and (4) the shotgun method of analysis.

- As I pointed out in Chapter 2, many concepts, such as gender, race, and class, are much more subtle and complex than we give them credit for being. Instead of measuring them qualitatively (remember that assignment of something to a nominal category is a qualitative act of measurement), we ought to be thinking hard about how to measure them ordinally.

- Eliminating the outliers is always a temptation because doing so produces higher correlations. But is creating a good statistical fit what you're after? Don't you really want to understand what makes the data messy in the first place? In general, you cannot achieve understanding of messiness by cleaning things up.

- Statistical tests of significance are not magical. In particular, the .05 and .01 levels of significance are entirely arbitrary. Test the power of any statistical test to guard against failing to see that your research hypothesis should be accepted.

- Shotgunning involves constructing a correlation matrix of all combinations of variables in a study, and then relying on tests of significance to reach substantive conclusions. The problem with shotgunning is that you might be fooled into thinking that statistically significant correlations are also substantively significant.

EXERCISES

1. Marlene Dobkin de Rios (1981) studied the clientele of a Peruvian folk healer. She suspected that women clients were more likely to have had personal experience with witchcraft (or to have a close family member who has had personal contact with witchcraft) than were men clients. The following table shows Dobkin de Rios's data.

Dobkin de Rios's Data on Experience with Witchcraft, by Gender			
	Personal Experience with Witchcraft or Close Family with Personal Contact	No Personal Experience with Witchcraft	Total
Male clients	12	15	27
Female clients	63	5	68
Total	75	20	95

SOURCE: Reprinted from *Social Science and Medicine*, 15B, M. Dobkin de Rios, "Socioeconomic Characteristics of an Amazon Urban Healer's Clientele," 51-63. Copyright © 1981, with permission of Elsevier Science.

In how many cases out of a thousand would you expect this distribution of cases by chance? To answer this question, find the value of χ^2 for this table. How many degrees of freedom does this table have? Using the proper number of *df*, consult Appendix D to find the level of significance for χ^2.

2. Hunfield et al. (1996) tested the level of grief in 13 couples in Rotterdam, Holland, six months after the couples had lost an infant. The couples were all relatively young and all the babies had died of major congenital anomalies less than a year after birth. Hunfield et al. tested the men and women separately on three separate measures of grief: amount of active grief, difficulty coping with the loss, and level of despair. For men, the mean total grief score was $\bar{x} = 72.8$, *SD* 11.2. For women, $\bar{x} = 73.6$, *SD* 16.1. Hunfield et al. report no significant difference between men and women on this grief scale. Test their conclusion using the *t* distribution.

3. Philipp (1998) asked 101 African American and 280 White high school students to rate their preferences for 20 leisure activities. Here are the results:

Preferences among 281 High School Students for 20 Leisure Activities								
	African American Males (n = 47)		African American Females (n = 54)		White Males (n = 140)		White Females (n = 140)	
Activity	Rank	Mean	Rank	Mean	Rank	Mean	Rank	Mean
Going to the beach	3	2.15	2	1.60	1	1.67	1	1.37
Playing basketball	1	1.41	5	2.36	4	2.41	13	3.29
Going to the mall	2	1.78	1	1.45	6	2.51	2	2.00
Reading for pleasure	15	4.30	10	3.55	18	4.50	14	3.37
Playing video games	5	2.76	9	3.21	9	3.09	17	3.62
Bowling	9	3.61	8	2.74	8	3.08	9	2.81
Watching TV	4	2.59	4	2.04	7	2.63	7	2.47
Playing soccer	20	4.98	18	4.44	15	3.88	11	3.15
Using a computer	10	3.63	7	2.72	12	3.39	10	3.08
Horseback riding	16	4.41	14	3.96	10	3.23	3	2.07
Waterskiing	14	4.26	17	4.30	5	2.42	5	2.13
Singing in a choir	13	4.07	6	2.37	19	4.51	16	3.47
Collecting stamps/coins	18	4.78	19	4.68	20	4.99	20	4.65
Camping	11	3.94	15	4.00	3	2.25	4	2.08
Jogging	8	3.49	11	3.57	11	3.31	8	2.74
Fishing	7	3.48	13	3.81	2	2.17	12	3.16
Playing a musical instrument	12	3.98	12	3.68	14	3.85	15	3.38
Golfing	19	4.89	20	4.92	16	4.15	19	4.58
Dancing	6	2.80	3	2.04	13	3.79	6	2.38
Going to a museum	17	4.52	16	4.02	17	4.47	18	3.68

SOURCE: S. F. Philipp, "Race and Gender Differences in Adolescent Peer Group Approval of Leisure Activities." *Journal of Leisure Research* 30:214-32. Copyright © 1998, National Recreation and Park Association. Reprinted by permission.

Use Spearman's rank-order correlation to test whether the leisure preferences of the White males are statistically different from those of the White females. What other comparisons can you make?

4. Rusting and Larsen (1998) used the experience sampling method to assess the mood of 19 men and 27 women, three times a day (morning, noon, and evening), for 60 days. At each rating time, participants rated, on a scale of 0 (*not at all*) to 6 (*extremely*), whether they felt depressed, unhappy, frustrated, worried, or angry. The also assessed, on a scale of 1 to 9: (1) whether they felt that *they* were responsible for their current mood or that others were responsible (this variable was scored 1 = *due to me* to 9 = *due to others* and is called EXTERNAL in the table below); (2) whether their moods were controllable or uncontrollable (1 = *controllable*, called CONTROLLABLE); (3) whether they felt their moods were unstable or stable (1 = *unstable*, and is called STABLE) ; and (4) whether their moods were the result of a particular situation or something that was a big part of their life in general (1 = *particular situation*, called GLOBAL).

Here are the results, across 46 people and 180 ratings. Test the hypothesis (using *t*-tests) that things get worse for people as the day goes along.

| | Assessment of Mood Changes across 60 Days | | | | | |
| | Morning | | Afternoon | | Evening | |
	M	SD	M	SD	M	SD
EXTERNAL	1.60	0.95	1.94	1.06	2.66	1.28
CONTROLLABLE	1.43	0.91	1.63	0.97	2.02	1.02
STABLE	1.29	0.68	1.51	0.72	2.06	0.96
GLOBAL	1.16	0.76	1.36	0.79	1.84	1.10

SOURCE: C. L. Rusting and R. J. Larsen, "Diurnal Patterns of Unpleasant Mood: Associations with Neuroticism, Depression, and Anxiety." *Journal of Personality* 66:85-103. Copyright © 1998, Blackwell Publishers. Reprinted by permission.

5. Make a list of 20 items that you normally buy at the supermarket (or use the list of 21 items from Titus and Everett's [1996] study; see Exercise 1, Chapter 10). The next time you go shopping, note the cost of these items. Ask two people who shop at markets other than yours to do the same. You should have a 15 × 3 table of items-by-supermarkets. Using ANOVA, test the hypothesis that there is no difference in the overall cost of shopping at the three markets. (If the brand is important in determining the price, then note the brand as well as the item. The price of soap, for example, is quite sensitive to brand differences, while the cost of bananas is much less so.)

As an alternative to this project, find the average price of renting an apartment in three or more different parts of your city and use ANOVA to test the hypothesis that it costs about the same to live anywhere.

6. Here are the average 1996 salaries of public school teachers for the 50 states of the U.S. Each state is identified as being in one of four regions: Northeast = 1, Midwest = 2, West = 3, and South = 4. Use ANOVA to test the hypothesis that, statistically speaking, there really isn't much difference in teachers' salaries across the United States.

Public Elementary and Secondary School Teachers' Average Salaries

State	Area	Salary ($)	State	Area	Salary ($)	State	Area	Salary ($)	State	Area	Salary ($)
CT	1	50,426	IL	2	42,125	AK	3	50,647	AL	4	32,549
ME	1	33,788	IN	2	38,845	AZ	3	33,300	AR	4	30,319
MA	1	42,650	IA	2	33,272	CA	3	43,031	DE	4	41,436
NH	1	36,029	KS	2	35,739	CO	3	36,271	FL	4	33,889
NJ	1	49,786	MI	2	48,238	HI	3	35,842	GA	4	35,596
NY	1	48,000	MN	2	38,281	ID	3	31,818	KY	4	33,797
PA	1	47,147	MO	2	33,155	MT	3	29,958	LA	4	29,025
RI	1	43,109	NB	2	31,768	NV	3	37,340	MD	4	41,148
VT	1	37,200	ND	2	27,711	NM	3	30,131	MS	4	27,720
			OH	2	38,676	OR	3	40,960	NC	4	31,167
			SD	2	26,764	UT	3	31,867	OK	4	30,369
			WI	2	39,057	WY	3	31,715	SC	4	32,830
						WA	3	37,815	TN	4	34,222
									TX	4	33,038
									VA	4	35,691
									WV	4	33,257

SOURCE: *Statistical Abstract of the United States* (U.S. Census Bureau 1998, Table 275).

FURTHER READING

Analysis of variance. R. A. Fisher, for whom the *F* ratio is named, was a pioneer in the development of ANOVA methods. See Fisher (1970), the 14th edition of his classic text on statistical methods, first published in 1925. See Iversen and Norpoth (1987) for an introduction and overview of analysis of variance. Bernieri (1993) is an instructive discussion of how to analyze hypothetical data from a typical social psychological experiment.

Antecedent, intervening, suppressor, and moderator variables. The logic for antecedent and other types of variables goes a long way back in the social sciences. Horst (1941) introduced the idea of suppressor variables—variables that actually make it seem like there's no relation between an independent and a dependent variable when there really is one. Rosenberg (1968) is the best source for a clear explanation of how survey researchers test for the effects of antecedent, intervening, and suppressor variables.

Visualizing direction and shape of relations. Two very good introductions to graphing data are Jacoby (1997) and Wallgren et al. (1996).

Outliers. For more about the problem of outliers, see Wilcox (1998). Also see Flowers et al. (1997).

Statistical power. Tables for statistical power are easily available in a really useful little book by Kraemer and Thiemann (1987).

Statistical significance. The pitfalls and benefits of using statistical tests of significance are among the most widely debated issues in the social sciences, particularly in psychology. For a thorough overview of the problem, see Harlow et al. (1997). For a general discussion of issues in data analysis, see Zuckerman et al. (1993).

16 MULTIVARIATE ANALYSIS

IN THIS CHAPTER:

❖ INTRODUCTION

Most of the really interesting dependent variables in the social world—things like personality type, amount of risk-taking behavior, level of wealth accumulation, attitudes toward women or men—appear to be caused by a large number of independent variables, some of which are dependent variables themselves. The goal of multivariate analysis is to explain *how* variables are related and to develop a theory of causation that accounts for the fact that variables are related to one another.

Multivariate analysis involves an array of statistical procedures. You will run into these procedures again and again as you read journal articles and monographs—things like multiple regression, partial regression, factor analysis, multidimensional scaling, analysis of variance, and so on. I'll introduce you to the conceptual basis of some of these methods here. I hope that this will give you an idea of the range of tools available and enough information so you can read and understand research articles in which these techniques are used. I also hope that this will arouse your curiosity enough so that you'll study these methods in more advanced classes. This is the fun part.

Once you have mastered the logic of multivariate analysis, seek out courses that take you more deeply into the use of these powerful tools. Courses on multivariate analysis are offered in statistics departments, of course, but many departments of sociology, psychology, education, and public health offer courses in multivariate analysis to their students. The examples used in those courses are usually from the academic discipline in which the instructor was trained, but by now, you must have gathered that *that* doesn't make much difference.

All multivariate techniques require caution in their use. It is easy to be impressed with the elegance of multivariate analysis and to lose track of the theoretical issues that motivated your study in the first place. On the other hand, multivariate techniques are important aids to research, and I encourage you to experiment and learn to use them. Try out several of these techniques; learn to read the computer output they produce when used on your data.

But don't be afraid to play and have a good time. If you hang around social scientists who use complex statistical tools in their research, you'll hear people talk about "massaging" their data with this or that multivariate technique, or about "teasing out signals" from their data, and "separating the signals from the noise." These are not the sort of phrases used by people who are bored with what they're doing.

THE ELABORATION METHOD

We begin with the *elaboration method* developed by Paul Lazarsfeld and his colleagues (1972) for analyzing data from surveys. This method involves **teasing out the complexities in a bivariate relation by *controlling for* the effects of a third (antecedent or intervening) variable.**

In 1996, just after the presidential election, the Bureau of Business and Economic Research at the

University of Florida conducted a statewide poll. Respondents were asked, among other things, whom they voted for plus some sociodemographic information (sex, age, income, marital status, race-ethnicity). Respondents were also asked the following questions:

Would you say that you (and your family living there) are better off or worse off financially than you were a year ago?

1. Better off
2. Same
3. Worse off
4. Don't know

Looking ahead, which would you say is more likely—that in the country as a whole we'll have continuous good times during the next five years or so, or that we will have periods of widespread unemployment or depression, or what?

1. Good times
2. Uncertain; good and bad
3. Bad times
4. Don't know

The first question is designed to measure current and personal financial optimism or pessimism. The second is designed to measure long-term and general optimism or pessimism. Table 16.1 shows the relation between the answers to the question about the short term (labeled YEAR-AGO) and income (labeled INCOME). Table 16.2 shows the relation between the answers to the question about the long term (labeled NEXT5) and income. Income was originally coded into nine categories, but I've cut it into two chunks: Low = up to $40,000 (which was the median for the sample) and High = above $40,000.

Table 16.1a shows that, across all 435 respondents (I've left out the respondents who did not answer one or both of the questions) the relation between current optimism and level of income is statistically very significant. Chi-square is 14.326 with 2 degrees of freedom (df) and $p = .001$. Not surprisingly, if you have high income, you are far more likely to see things as having gotten better over the past year.

When we control for sex, though, the picture changes. Table 16.1b shows that for women, the original relation continues to hold, but Table 16.1c shows that the statistically significant relation between current financial optimism and current income vanishes for men. The antecedent variable, sex, influences the relation between current financial optimism and current income.

Table 16.2 shows how the same antecedent variable—sex—can play a different role. Across the full sample of respondents (Table 16.2a), there is no statistically significant relation between long-term optimism/pessimism and current level of income. Controlling for sex, we see that the relation *remains* statistically nonsignificant for men (Table 16.2b) but *emerges* as significant for women (Table 16.2c).

In Table 16.1, controlling for the antecedent variable had the effect of trouncing a statistically significant relation in one of the **subtables**. In Table 16.2, controlling for the same antecedent variable had the effect of turning a statistically nonsignificant relation into a significant one in one of the subtables.

PARTIAL CORRELATION

Of course, I haven't proved anything by all this laying out of tables. Don't misunderstand me.

Elaboration tables are a great start—they test whether your ideas about some antecedent or

TABLE 16.1a Bivariate Relation between Current Financial Optimism and Current Income

	INCOME		
YEAR-AGO	Low	High	Total
Better off	74	102	176
Same	89	63	152
Worse off	67	40	107
Total	230	205	435
$\chi^2 = 14.326$ with 2 df, $p = .001$			

SOURCE: Bureau of Business and Economic Research, University of Florida.

TABLE 16.1b Same as 16.1a, But for Women Only

	INCOME		
YEAR-AGO	Low	High	Total
Better off	37	49	86
Same	51	23	74
Worse off	38	20	58
Total	126	92	218
$\chi^2 = 12.865$ with 2 df, $p = .002$			

TABLE 16.1c Same as 16.1a, But for Men Only

	INCOME		
YEAR-AGO	Low	High	Total
Better off	37	53	90
Same	38	40	78
Worse off	29	20	49
Total	104	113	217
$\chi^2 = 4.183$ with 2 df, $p = .124$ n.s.			

TABLE 16.2a   Bivariate Relation between Long-Term Optimism and Current Income

	INCOME		
NEXT5	Low	High	Total
Good times	107	85	192
Good and bad	31	36	67
Bad times	70	81	151
Total	208	202	410

$\chi^2 = 3.608$ with 2 df, $p = .165$

SOURCE: Bureau of Business and Economic Research, University of Florida.

TABLE 16.2b   Same as 16.2a, But for Men Only

	INCOME		
NEXT5	Low	High	Total
Good times	52	54	106
Good and bad	14	21	35
Bad times	34	36	70
Total	100	111	211

$\chi^2 = 0.924$ with 2 df, $p = .630$

TABLE 16.2c   Same as 16.2a, But for Women Only

	INCOME		
NEXT5	Low	High	Total
Good times	55	31	86
Good and bad	17	15	32
Bad times	36	45	81
Total	108	91	199

$\chi^2 = 6.417$ with 2 df, $p = .040$

TABLE 16.3 Correlation Matrix for Three Variables

	Variable 1: MVD	Variable 2: TEENBIRTH	Variable 3: INCOME
MVD	1.0	.778	–.662
TEENBIRTH	.778	1.0	–.700
INCOME	–.662	–.700	1.0

SOURCE: *Statistical Abstract of the United States:* MVD for 1995 (U.S. Census Bureau 1997, Table 1018); TEENBIRTH for 1996 (U.S. Census Bureau, 1997, Table 98); INCOME for 1996 (U.S. Census Bureau 1997, Table 706).

intervening variables are plausible by showing what *could* be going on—but they don't tell you *how things work* or *how much* those antecedent or intervening variables are contributing to a correlation you want to understand. For that, we need something a bit more . . . well, elaborate.

Partial correlation is a direct way to control for the effects of a third (or fourth or fifth, etc.) variable on a relation between two variables.

Here's an interesting case. Across the 50 states in the U.S., there is a stunning correlation ($r = .778$) between the percentage of live births to teenage mothers (15-19 years of age) and the number of motor vehicle deaths per hundred million miles driven. States that have a high rate of road carnage also have a high rate of births to teenagers.

This one's a real puzzle. Obviously, there's no *direct* relation between these two variables. There's no way that the volume of highway carnage causes the number of teenage mothers or vice versa, so we look for something that might cause both of them.

I have a hunch that these two variables are correlated because they are both the consequence of the fact that certain regions of the country are poorer than others. I know from my own experi-

ence, and from having read a lot of research reports, that the western and southern states are poorer, overall, than are the industrial and farming states of the Northeast and the Midwest. My hunch is that poorer states will have fewer miles of paved road per million people, poorer roads overall, and older vehicles. All this might lead to more deaths per miles driven.

Table 16.3 shows the *zero-order correlation* among three variables: motor vehicle deaths per hundred million miles driven (it's labeled MVD in Table 16.3), the percentage of live births to young women 15-19 years of age (TEENBIRTH), and average personal income (INCOME). Zero-order correlations do not take into account the influence of other variables (see Box 16.1). (The income and teenage birth rates are for 1996; the motor vehicle death rate is for 1995.)

With interval-scale variables we can use the formula for partial correlation to test directly what effect, if any, income has on the correlation between TEENBIRTH and MVD.

The formula for partial correlation is

$$r_{12 \cdot 3} = \frac{r_{12} - [r_{32} \times r_{13}]}{\sqrt{(1 - r_{32}^2)} \times \sqrt{(1 - r_{13}^2)}} \qquad \text{(Formula 16.1)}$$

where $r_{12 \cdot 3}$ means "the correlation between variable 1 (MVD) and variable 2 (TEENBIRTH), *controlling for* variable 3 (INCOME) is . . . ."

Box 16.1
Symmetry in Matrices

Table 16.3 is a *symmetrical matrix*. The correlation between variables A and B is the same as the correlation between variables B and A. Interpersonal preference matrices, by contrast, are typically *asymmetric*. For example, if you ask five children in a third-grade classroom whether they like each other (yes/no), you may get a matrix of 1s and 0s (1 = yes, 0 = no) like the following:

A Symmetric Matrix of Interpersonal Relation

Child	1	2	3	4	5
1	1	1	0	0	1
2	1	1	1	1	0
3	0	0	1	0	1
4	0	1	0	1	0
5	1	1	1	0	1

Notice that child 2 says she likes child 3, but child 3 says he doesn't like child 2. The relation of *liking,* then, is asymmetric. Notice the numbers down the diagonal in Table 16.3: In symmetric and asymmetric matrices alike, the correlation of any variable with itself is 1.

(Partial correlation can be done on ordinal variables by substituting a statistic like tau or gamma for r in the formula above.)

Table 16.4 shows the calculation of the partial correlations for the entries in Table 16.3.

So, the partial correlation between MVD and TEENBIRTH, controlling for INCOME is

$$\frac{.778 - (-.700 \times -.662)}{.714143 \times .749504} = \frac{.3146}{.535253} = .5877594$$

which we can round off to .59. (Remember, we have to use a *lot* of decimal places during the calculations to keep the rounding error in check. When we get through with the calculations, we can round off to two or three decimal places.) In other words, when we *partial out* the effect of income, the correlation between MVD and

TEENBIRTH drops from about .78 to about .59. That's because income is correlated with motor vehicle deaths ($r = -.662$) *and* with teenage births ($r = .49$).

If a partial correlation of .59 between the rate of motor vehicle deaths and the rate of teenage births still seems high, then perhaps other variables are at work. You can "partial out" the effects of two or more variables at once, but as you take on more variables, the formula naturally gets more complicated (see Box 16.2). Or you can work out and test a model of how several independent variables influence a dependent variable all at once. This is the task of multiple regression, which we'll take up next.

TABLE 16.4 Calculating the Partial Correlations for the Entries in Table 16.3

Pairs	Pearson's r	R^2	$1 - R^2$	$\sqrt{1 - R^2}$
r_{12} (MVD and TEENBIRTH)	.778	.605284	.394716	.628264
r_{13} (MVD and INCOME)	−.662	.438244	.561756	.749504
r_{32} (TEENBIRTH and INC)	−.700	.4900	.5100	.714143

Box 16.2
Higher-Order Partials

A simple correlation is referred to as a *zero-order correlation*. Formula 16.1 is for a *first-order correlation*. The formula for a *second-order correlation* (controlling for two variables at the same time) is

$$r_{12 \cdot 34} = \frac{r_{12 \cdot 3} - (r_{14 \cdot 3})(r_{24 \cdot 3})}{\sqrt{(1 - r_{14 \cdot 3}^2)} \times \sqrt{(1 - r_{24 \cdot 3}^2)}} \qquad \text{(Formula 16.2)}$$

For more on partial correlation, see Gujarati (1995).

MULTIPLE REGRESSION

Partial correlation tells us how much a third (or fourth, etc.) variable contributes to the relation between two variables. **Multiple regression** puts **all the information about a series of variables together into a single equation that takes account of the interrelation among independent variables.** The result of multiple regression is a statistic called **multiple R,** which is the **combined correlation of a set of independent variables with the dependent variable,** taking into account the fact that each of independent variables might be correlated with each of the *other* independent variables.

Even more interesting is R^2. Remember that r^2 —the square of the Pearson product-moment correlation coefficient—is the amount of variance in the dependent variable accounted for by the independent variable in a simple regression? Well R^2, or *multiple* R^2, is the amount of variance in the dependent variable accounted for by two or more independent variables simultaneously.

Now, if the predictors of a dependent variable were all uncorrelated with each other, we could just add together the pieces of the variance in the dependent variable accounted for by each of the independent variables. That is: $R^2 = r_1^2 + r_2^2 + r_3^2 \ldots$.

It's a real annoyance, but independent variables *are* usually correlated with one another. We need a method for figuring out how much variance in a dependent variable is accounted for by a series of independent variables after taking account of all the overlap in variances accounted for across the independent variables. That's what multiple regression does.

The Multiple Regression Equation

We covered basic regression in Chapter 15, but just to bring you back up to speed, remember that in simple regression we use an equation that expresses how an independent variable is related to a dependent variable. On the left-hand side of the equation, we have the unknown score for y, the dependent variable. On the right-hand side we have the y-intercept, called a. It's the score for y if the dependent variable were zero. We have another coefficient, called b, that tells by *how much* to multiply the score on the independent variable for each unit change in that variable.

The general form of the equation (from Chapter 15, Formula 15.21) is

$$y = a + bx$$

which means that the dependent variable, y, equals some constant plus another constant times the independent variable x. So, for example, a regression equation like

Starting annual income =

$22,000 + ($4,000 \times$ Years of college)

predicts that, on average, people with a high school education will start out earning $22,000 a year, people with a year of college will earn $26,000, and so on. A person with nine years of university education (say, someone who has a Ph.D.) would be predicted to start at $58,000:

Starting annual income =

$22,000 + ($4,000 \times 9) = $58,000

Now suppose that the average starting salary for someone who has a Ph.D. is $65,000. Several things could account for the discrepancy between our prediction and the reality. Sampling problems, of course, could be the culprit. Or it could be that there is just a lot of variability in starting salaries of people who have a Ph.D. English teachers who go to work in small, liberal arts colleges might start at $35,000, while chemists who go to work for major oil companies might start at $85,000.

No amount of fixing the sample will do anything to get rid of the variance of starting salaries. In fact, the better the sample, the better it will reflect the enormous variance in those salaries.

In simple regression, if starting salary and years of education are related variables, we want to know "how accurately can we predict a person's starting salary if we know how many years of education he or she has beyond high school?" In multiple regression, we build more complex equations that tell us how much each of *several* independent variables contributes to predicting the score of a single dependent variable.

A typical question for a multiple regression analysis might be "How well can we predict people's starting salary if we know how many years of college they have, *and* their major, *and* their gender, *and* their age, *and* their ethnic background?" Each of those independent variables contributes something to predicting a person's starting salary after high school.

The regression equation for two independent variables, called x_1 and x_2, and one dependent variable, called y, is

$$y = a + b_1x_1 + b_2x_2 \qquad \text{(Formula 16.3)}$$

TABLE 16.5 Correlation Matrix for Variables Associated with the Percentage of Teenage Births in the United States

	TEENBIRTH	INCOME	VIOLRATE	MVD
TEENBIRTH	1.000			
INCOME	−.700	1.000		
VIOLRATE	.340	.190	1.000	
MVD	.778	−.662	.245	1.000

which means that we need to find a separate constant—one called b_1 and one called b_2—by which to multiply each of the two independent variables. The general formula for multiple regression is

$$y = a + b_1x_1 + b_2x_2 \ldots b_nx_n \quad \text{(Formula 16.4)}$$

Recall that simple regression yields a PRE measure, r^2. It tells you how much better you can predict a series of measures of a dependent variable than you could by just guessing the mean for every measurement. Multiple regression is also a PRE measure. It, too, tells you how much better you can predict measures of a dependent variable than you could if you guessed the mean—but using all the information available in a series of independent variables.

The keys to regression are those b coefficients in Formula 16.4. We want weights that, when multiplied by the independent variables, produce the best possible prediction of the dependent variable—that is, we want predictions that result in the smallest possible *residuals*. Those coefficients, by the way, are not existential constants. They change with every sample you take and with the number of independent variables in the equation.

The MVD-TEENBIRTH Puzzle

Let's try to solve the puzzle of the relation between teenage births and the rate of motor vehicle deaths. We can take a stab at this using multiple regression by trying to predict the rate of teenage births *without* the data from motor vehicle deaths.

From our previous analyses with elaboration tables and with partial correlation, we already had an idea that income might have something to do with the rate of teen births. We know from the literature (Handwerker 1998) that poverty is associated with violence and with teenage pregnancy and that this is true across ethnic groups, so I've added a variable on violent crimes that I think might be a proxy for the amount of violence against persons in each of the states.

Table 16.5 shows the correlation matrix for four variables: TEENBIRTH (the percentage of births to teenagers in the 50 U.S. states during 1996); INCOME (the mean per capita income for each of the 50 states during 1996); VIOLRATE (the rate of violent crime—rape, murder, assault, and robbery—per 100,000 population in the 50 states in 1995); and MVD (the number of motor vehicle deaths per 100 million vehicle miles in each of the 50 states in 1995).

TABLE 16.6 Multiple Regression Output from SYSTAT®

```
Dep Var: TEENBIRTH  N: 50  Multiple R: 0.850  Squared multiple R: 0.722

Adjusted squared multiple R: 0.710  Standard error of estimate: 1.829

Effect Coefficient  Std Error  Std Coef  Tolerance     t      P(2 Tail)

CONSTANT  28.096    1.822      0.0                   15.423   0.000
VIOLRATE   0.006    0.001      0.491     0.964        6.269   0.000
INCOME    -0.001    0.000     -0.793     0.964      -10.130   0.000
```

We see right away that the mean per capita income predicts the rate of births to teenagers ($r = -.700$) almost as well as does the rate of motor vehicle deaths ($r = .778$) and that mean income also predicts the rate of motor vehicle deaths rather well ($r = -.662$).

This is a clue about what might be going on: An antecedent variable, the level of income, might be responsible for the rate of motor vehicle deaths *and* the rate of teenage births. (By the way, did you notice that the strong correlations above were negative? The greater the mean income in the state, the lower the rate of teenage births and the lower the rate of motor vehicle deaths. Remember, correlations can vary from -1.0 to $+1.0$ and that the strength of the correlation has nothing to do with its direction.)

And one more thing: The rate of violent crimes against people is moderately correlated with the rate of teenage births ($r = .340$), but is only weakly correlated with the mean income ($r = .190$) and with the rate of motor vehicle deaths ($r = .245$).

The task for multiple regression is to see how the independent variables predict the dependent variable *together*. If the correlation between mean per capita income and the rate of births to teenagers is $-.700$, that means that the independent variable accounts for 49% ($-.700^2$) of the variance in the dependent variable. And if the correlation between the rate of violent crimes and the rate of births to teenagers is .340, then the independent variable accounts for 11.56% ($.340^2$) of the variance in the dependent variable.

We can't just add these variances-accounted-for together, though, because the two independent variables are related to each other—each of the independent variables accounts for some variance in the other.

Table 16.6 shows what the output looks like from SYSTAT® when I asked the program to calculate the multiple correlation, called *R,* for INCOME and VIOLRATE on TEENBIRTH (see Box 16.3).

Table 16.6 tells us that the regression equation is

$$TEENBIRTH = 28.096 + (.006 \times VIOLRATE) + (-.001 \times INCOME)$$

For example, the violence rate for Wisconsin was 281 crimes per 100,000 residents in 1995 and the average income in Wisconsin was $21,184 in 1996. The regression equation predicts that the teenage birth rate for Wisconsin will be 8.6. The actual rate was 10.6 in 1996. The mean rate of teenage births for the 50 U.S. states was 12.9. The

Box 16.3
The Regression Coefficients

There are three coefficients in this regression equation. They are the a, b_1, and b_2 coefficients in Formula 16.3. Each of the b coefficients is the product of the standardized regression coefficient for each independent variable with the ratio of the standard deviation of the independent variable to the standard deviation of the dependent variable.

The standardized coefficient for the relation between x_1 (TEENBIRTH) and x_2 (INCOME) is

$$\beta\ (x_1\ x_2) = \frac{r_{12} - (r_{13})\ (r_{23})}{1 - (r_{23})^2}$$

for INCOME x_2, $\beta\ =\ -.793$
for VIOLRATE x_3, $\beta\ =\ -.491$

These figures are given in Table 16.6 as the standardized coefficients.

The standard deviation for the mean of INCOME is 3,074.969
The standard deviation for the mean of TEENBIRTH is 3.399
The standard deviation for the mean of VIOLRATE is 269.225

Thus, $b_1 = -.793 \times (3.399/3{,}074.969) = -.001$
and $b_2 = .491 \times (3.399/269.225) = .006$

These figures are given in Table 16.6 as the unstandardized regression coefficients. The method for calculating the value for a in the multiple regression equation is beyond the scope of this book. For details, see Pedhazur (1997).

multiple regression, then, makes a better prediction than the mean: The difference between 10.6 and 12.9 is 2.3, while the difference between 8.6 and 10.6 is 2.0.

If you work out all the differences between the predictions from the *multiple* regression equation and the predictions from the *simple* regression equation involving *just* the effect of income on teenage births, the difference in the predictions will be the difference between accounting for 49% of the variance vs. accounting for 72.2% of the variance in the dependent variable (see Box 16.4).

But there's more. If we add up the variances accounted for by the zero-order correlations of INCOME and VIOLRATE on TEENBIRTH, we get 49% + 11.56% = 60.56%. According to the results in Table 16.6 (and Box 16.3), however, the income in a state and the rate of violent crimes *together* account for 72.2% of the variance in teenage births. In other words, the two variables acting together account for *more* than they do separately, and this is the case despite the fact that the independent variables are moderately correlated ($r = .340$) with each other.

In fact, INCOME explains 43.82% of the variance in motor vehicle deaths ($r = -.662$ and r^2 is .4382) and VIOLRATE explains 6% of the variance in motor vehicle deaths ($r = .245$ and r^2 is .0600). *Together*, though, INCOME and

---

Box 16.4
Some Details about This Regression Example

In this example, y is TEENBIRTH, x_1 is INCOME, and x_2 is VIOLRATE. $R^2_{1 \cdot 23}$ is the relation of TEENBIRTH (the 1 in the subscript) to both INCOME and VIOLRATE (the 2 and 3 in the subscript). This relation is

$$R^2_{1 \cdot 23} = R^2_{12} + R^2_{1(3 \cdot 2)}$$

which is the relation between TEENBIRTH and VIOLRATE once you partial out the contribution of INCOME. Calculating $R^2_{1 \cdot 23}$, then:

$$R^2_{1 \cdot 23} = r_{13} - (r_{12})(r_{32}) = .340 - (-.700)(.19) = .473$$

Taking the partial contribution of this relation to the dependent variable:

$$\frac{.473}{\sqrt{1 - .19^2}} = .481776$$

The contribution of this correlation to the variance of TEENBIRTH is $.481776^2$, or $.23211$. INCOME accounts for 49% of the variance in TEENBIRTH. Adding contributions, we get $.49 + .23211$, or 72.2%, which is the squared multiple R in Table 16.6.

For more about deriving multiple regression equations, consult Pedhazur (1997) or Gujarati (1995).

VIOLRATE have a multiple R of .762 and an R^2 of .581. Here again, the two variables explain more variance working together than they explain working separately.

In other words, it's the complex association of per capita income *and* the level of violence that explains so much variance in *both* the rate of teenage births and the rate of motor vehicle deaths. It turns out that lots of things are best explained by a series of variables acting together (see Box 16.5).

TWO EXAMPLES OF MULTIPLE REGRESSION

Here are two examples of how multiple regression is actually used. John Poggie (1979) was interested in whether the beliefs of Puerto Rican fishermen about the causes of success in fishing were related to their actual success in fishing. He measured success by asking six key informants to

---

Box 16.5
Caution: Automated Regression Now Available Everywhere

Many computer programs in use today produce what is called a *stepwise multiple regression*. You specify a dependent variable and a series of independent variables that you suspect play some part in determining the scores of the dependent variable.

The program looks for the independent variable that correlates best with the dependent variable and then adds in the variables one at a time, accounting for more and more variance, until all the specified variables are analyzed, or until variables fail to enter because incremental explained variance is lower than a preset value, say, 1%. (There are even programs that test all possible path analysis equations.)

Stepwise multiple regression is another one of those controversial hot topics in data analysis. Some people feel strongly that it is mindless and keeps you from making your own decisions about what causes what in a complex set of variables. It's rather like the significance test controversy and the shotgun controversy I discussed in Chapter 15.

And my take on it is the same: Learn to use all the tools and make your own decisions about the meaning of your findings. It's *your* responsibility to do the data processing and it's *your* responsibility to determine the meaning of your findings. Don't let robots take over any of your responsibilities. And don't be afraid to use all the hot new tools, either.

---

rank 50 fishermen on this variable. Since his research was exploratory, he had a wide range of independent variables, three of which he guessed were related to fishing success: the fishermen's expressed orientation toward delaying gratification (measured with a standard scale), their boat size, and their years of experience at the trade.

The deferred gratification measure accounted for 15% of the variance in the dependent variable, years of experience accounted for another 10%, and boat size accounted for 8%. Together, these variables accounted for 33% of the variance in the success variable. Poggie's guess about which variables to test was pretty good.

Korsching et al. (1980) used a shotgun or shopping technique in their multivariate study of a group of families who were relocated when the land they lived on in Kentucky became part of a reservoir project. Their multiple regression found seven social and economic factors that accounted

for at least some of the variance in relative satisfaction with new and old residences among those relocated.

Those factors were: change in social activities (accounting for 18%), education (accounting for 4%), total family income before relocation (another 4%), change of financial situation (3%). Three other variables (satisfaction with resettlement payments, tenure status on the land, and length of residence in the old house) each accounted for 1% or less. All together, the seven independent variables accounted for 31% of the variance in satisfaction with the move.

On Explaining Just a Little of Something

In social science research, multiple regression (including path analysis, which is coming up next) typically accounts for between 30% and 50% of the variance in any dependent variable, using between two and eight independent variables. It is customary not to include independent variables that account for less than 1% of the variance in a multiple regression equation, but there is no law against doing so.

Does accounting for 30%-50% of the variance in what you're interested in seem feeble? Consider these two facts:

(1) In 1995, the average White male had a life expectancy at birth of 73.4 years in the U.S., or 26,809 days. The life expectancy at birth for the average African American male was 65.4 years, or 23,887 days. The *difference* is 2,922 days.

(2) There were approximately 2.5 million births in Mexico in 1997, and around 60,000 infant deaths—that is, about 24 infant deaths per 1,000 live births. Compare these figures to the United States, where there were 3.9 million births and approximately 30,000 infant deaths, or about 7.7 per 1,000 live births. If the infant mortality rate in Mexico were the same as that in the United States, the number of infant deaths would be about 20,000 instead of 60,000. The *difference* would be 40,000 infant deaths.

Suppose you could account for 10% of the *difference* in longevity among White and African American males in the United States (292 days) or 10% of the *difference* between the United States and Mexico in infant deaths (4,000 children). Would that be worthwhile? Because knowledge about phenomena leads to more effective control over those phenomena, the most important contribution a scientist can make to solving a human problem is to be right about what causes it. I'd try to account for every percentage I could.

PATH ANALYSIS

Path analysis is a particular application of multiple regression. In multiple regression, we know (1) which independent variables help to predict some dependent variable, and (2) how much variance in the dependent variable is explained by each independent variable. But multiple regression is an inductive technique: It does not tell us which are the antecedent variables, which are the intervening variables, and so on.

Path analysis is the application of multiple regression for testing conceptual models of multivariate relations—that is, for testing specific theories about how the independent variables in a multiple regression equation may be influencing each other—and how this ultimately leads to the dependent variable outcome.

The method was developed by the geneticist Sewall Wright in 1921 and became very popular in the social sciences in the 1960s (see Duncan 1966). It fell out of favor for a while (isn't it nice to know that there are fads and fashions even in statistics?), but it's making a strong comeback as full-featured statistics packages become more widely available.

I rather like the method because it depends crucially on the researcher's best guess about how a system of variables really works. It is, in other words, a nice combination of quantitative and qualitative methods. Here's an example.

Thomas (1981) studied leadership in Niwan Witz, a Mayan village. He was interested in understanding what causes some people to emerge as leaders, while others remain followers. From existing theory, Thomas thought that there should be a relation among leadership, material wealth, and social resources. He measured these

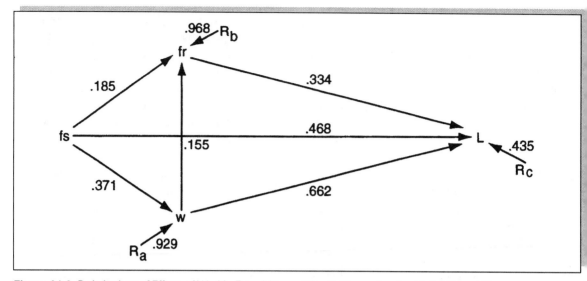

Figure 16.1 Path Analysis of Effects of Wealth, Friendship, and Family Size on Leadership in Niwan Witz
SOURCE: J. S. Thomas, "The Economic Determinants on Leadership on a Tojalabal Maya Community." Reproduced by permission of the American Anthropological Association from *American Ethnologist* 8:1, 1981. Not for further reproduction.

complex variables for all the household heads in Niwan Witz (using well-established methods) and tested his hypothesis using Pearson's *r*. Pearson correlations showed that indeed, in Niwan Witz, leadership is strongly and positively related to material wealth and control of social resources.

Since the initial hypothesis was supported, Thomas used multiple regression to look at the relation of leadership to *both* types of resources. He found that 56% of the variance in leadership was explained by just three variables in his survey: wealth (accounting for 46%), family size (accounting for 6%), and number of close friends (accounting for 4%). But, since multiple regression does not, as Thomas said, "specify the causal structure among the independent variables" (p. 132), he turned to path analysis.

From prior literature, Thomas conceptualized the relation among these three variables as shown in Figure 16.1. He felt that leadership, *L*, was caused by all three of the independent variables he had tested, that family size (*fs*) influenced both wealth (*w*) and the size of one's friendship net-

work (*fr*), and that wealth was a factor in determining the number of one's friends.

The *path coefficients* in Figure 16.1 are standardized values: They **show the influence of the independent variables on the dependent variables in terms of standard deviations.** The path coefficients in Figure 16.1, then, show that "a one standard deviation increase in wealth produces a .662 standard deviation increase in leadership; a one standard deviation increase in family size results in a .468 standard deviation increase in leadership; and so on" (Thomas 1981:133). (For details about how path coefficients are determined, consult Blalock [1979] or Kelloway [1998].)

Four things are clear from Figure 16.1.

(1) Among the variables tested, wealth is the most important cause of leadership in individuals.

(2) Family size has a moderate causal influence on wealth (making wealth a dependent, as

well as an independent, variable in this system).

(3) The size of a person's friendship network is only weakly related to either family size or wealth.

(4) The combined direct and indirect effects of family size, wealth, and friendship network on leadership account for 56.5% $(1 - .435)$ of the variance in leadership scores for the household heads of Niwan Witz.

Thomas concludes from this descriptive analysis that if you want to become a leader in the Mayan village of Niwan Witz, you need wealth, and the best way to get that is to start by having a large family.

Path analysis lets you test a particular theory about the relations among a system of variables, but it doesn't produce the theory; that's *your* job. In the case of Niwan Witz, for example, Thomas specified that he wanted his path analysis to test a particular model in which wealth causes leadership. The results were strong, leading Thomas to reject the null hypothesis that there really is no causal relation between wealth and leadership. But even the strong results that Thomas got don't prove anything. In fact, Thomas noted that an alternative theory is plausible. It might be that leadership in individuals (wherever they get it from) causes them to get wealthy rather than the other way around.

> *Path analysis lets you test a particular theory about the relations among a system of variables, but it doesn't produce the theory; that's your job.*

Path analysis often serves as reality therapy for social scientists. It's fun to build conceptual models—to think through a problem and hypothesize how variables are linked to each other—but our models are often much more complicated than they need to be. Path analysis can help us out of this fix.

Lockery et al. (1994) studied the rehospitalization of people over 60. These days, with managed care health plans, people are sent home from the hospital as quickly as possible. For old people in frail health, if they are discharged too quickly, or don't get the right posthospitalization therapy, they can quickly wind up back in the hospital.

Figure 16.2 shows Lockery et al.'s conceptual model of the process: Some sociodemographic factors associated with patients and their families influence the extent to which patients are involved in the decision about their own discharge from the hospital. This decision leads to patients being sent directly home or to some other, intermediate institution, like a nursing home or a rehabilitative hospital, for continued therapy. The dependent variable is whether the patient winds up back in the original hospital within 30 days of discharge.

The input variable ADL (the Activities of Daily Living scale) is a measure of how independent people are in feeding, bathing, and dressing themselves; going to the bathroom; and so on. The higher the ADL score, the less people can do for themselves. SES is socioeconomic class, with higher scores meaning lower SES. Marital status was coded as 1 = married and 0 = unmarried. Depression was measured with one of the standard checklists (Derogatis and Melisaratos 1983), so that the higher the score the higher the level of depression.

Locus of control is the famous scale developed by Rotter (1966) to measure how much people feel they are in control of their own lives. Higher scores mean higher internal control; lower scores

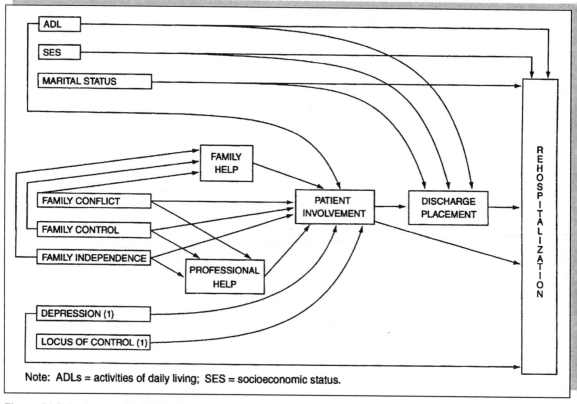

Figure 16.2 Lockery et al.'s (1994) Conceptual Model of Rehospitalization of Elders

SOURCE: S. A. Lockery et al., "Factors Contributing to the Early Rehospitalization of Elderly People." *Health and Social Work* 19:182-91. Copyright © 1994. Reprinted with permission of the National Association of Social Workers.

mean that people feel that others are in charge of their lives.

Family conflict, control, and independence refer to how much family members (1) discuss their feelings openly, (2) boss each other around, and (3) encourage each other to make their own decisions. These things were hypothesized to influence whether family members or hospital staff participated in the decision about where the patient would go after leaving the hospital and these, in turn, were thought to influence the extent of the patient's own involvement in the decision.

Patient involvement in the discharge was scored from 1 to 5, where 1 = *no involvement*

and 5 = *full involvement*. Patients were asked whether their families and/or the hospital staff had been involved in the process, and these were scored 1 or 0. Discharge placement was scored 1 if the patient went to another institution or 0 if the patient was sent home, and rehospitalization was scored 1 or 0, depending on whether the patient was back in the hospital 30 days later.

Of the 264 patients whom Lockery et al. interviewed, 45 wound up back in the hospital 30 days later. Figure 16.3 shows the path analysis from their data. Notice how much cleaner it is. Depression is gone. Locus of control is gone. Family help and professional help had no influence on patient involvement in the decision. Even more impor-

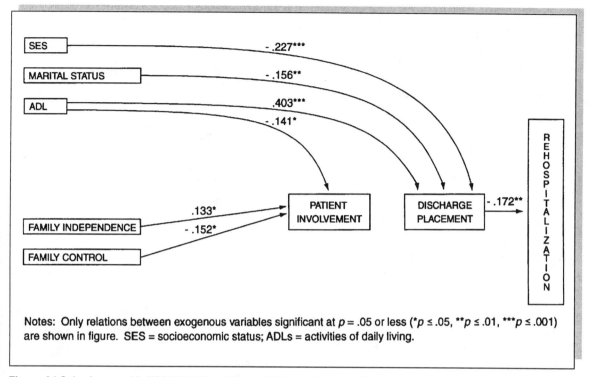

Figure 16.3 Lockery et al.'s (1994) Final Path Model of Rehospitalization of Elders

SOURCE: S. A. Lockery et al., "Factors Contributing to the Early Rehospitalization of Elderly People." *Health and Social Work* 19:182-91. Copyright © 1994. Reprinted with permission of the National Association of Social Workers.

tant, whether a patient was involved or not in the discharge decision had no impact on whether he or she was back in the hospital a month later.

The way it worked out was simply this: Lower-socioeconomic-status patients (those with higher scores on the SES variable) were more likely to be discharged directly to their homes (low-SES patients have less money to pay for expensive nursing and rehabilitative care); married patients were more likely to be sent home, but when they got there, they had someone to help take care of them; and patients who scored high on the ADL scale—that is, those who could not take care of themselves very well—were much more likely to be sent to a nursing home or a rehabilitation center.

In the end, those who wound up in nursing homes or in rehab care were less likely to be back in the hospital a month later. Home is nice, but frail elderly people—especially those who are poor and who have no spouse at home—need care and they won't get it there.

Path analysis is often used to test which of several plausible theories is most powerful, but in the end, you're left out there, all by yourself, defending your theory on the basis of whatever data are available right now.

TABLE 16.7 Zero-Order Correlations of Four Variables That Appear to Be Related

	SUICIDE	BTU	INCOME	OVER65
SUICIDE	1.00			
BTU	0.437	1.00		
INCOME	−0.52	−0.33	1.00	
OVER65	−0.367	−0.454	0.093	1.00

SOURCE: *Statistical Abstract of the United States:* SUICIDE in 1994 (U.S. Census Bureau 1995, Table 132); BTU in 1994 (U.S. Census Bureau 1997, Table 925); OVER65 in 1995 (U.S. Census Bureau 1996, Table 34).

MULTICOLLINEARITY

Multivariate models are subject to a problem that simply can't exist when you have one independent variable: Independent variables can be correlated. In fact, when two variables both strongly predict a third, you'd expect the first two to be correlated. This *multicollinearity* means that **you may not be able to tell the influence of one independent variable free from the influence of the independent variables with which it is correlated.**

One way to avoid this problem is to conduct true experiments and nothing but true experiments. By assigning research participants randomly to control and experimental groups, we ensure that any correlation between independent variables is the result of chance. Nice work if you can get it, but much of what we want to study in social science requires survey research, or ethnography, and simply isn't the stuff of lab experiments.

Fortunately, multicollinearity distorts the findings of multiple regression only occasionally, and multicollinearity problems show up very clearly. The most dramatic sign of a multicollinearity problem is when your statistical program tells you that it cannot solve the equation. Some statistical programs calculate *condition indexes* that **diagnose problematical multicollinearity.** Condition indexes higher than 30 signal a multicollinearity problem.

But basic regression output shows the most common sign of a multicollinearity problem: Low probabilities for zero-order correlations between a series of independent variables and one dependent variable remain low in multivariate models when the variables are entered separately, but the probabilities for all the variables rise when you put them in the model together.

For example, an old puzzle in the social sciences that remains of continuing interest is how to account for different rates of suicide across political units (countries, provinces, counties, cities). Table 16.7 shows the zero-order correlations among four variables for the 50 states of the U.S. plus Washington, D.C. SUICIDE is the number of deaths by suicide, per 100,000, in 1994; BTU is the average energy consumption, per person, in millions of BTUs in 1995; INCOME is the average personal income in 1995; and OVER65 is the percentage of people who were over age 65 in 1996.

TABLE 16.8 Separate Regressions of Three Independent Variables with SUICIDE

```
Dep Var: SUICIDE    N: 51    Multiple R: 0.520  Squared multiple R: 0.270

Adjusted squared multiple R: 0.255    Standard error of estimate: 3.112

Effect      Coefficient      Std Error      Std Coef  Tolerance      t    P(2 Tail)

CONSTANT        24.789          2.799          0.000       .        8.856    0.000
INCOME          -0.001          0.000         -0.520     1.000     -4.257    0.000


Dep Var: SUICIDE    N: 51    Multiple R: 0.437    Squared multiple R: 0.191

Adjusted squared multiple R: 0.174    Standard error of estimate: 3.277

Effect      Coefficient      Std Error      Std Coef  Tolerance      t    P(2 Tail)

CONSTANT         9.309          1.184          0.000       .        7.860    0.000
BTU              0.010          0.003          0.437     1.000      3.397    0.001


Dep Var: SUICIDE    N: 51    Multiple R: 0.372    Squared multiple R: 0.139

Adjusted squared multiple R: 0.121    Standard error of estimate: 3.381

Effect      Coefficient      Std Error      Std Coef  Tolerance      t    P(2 Tail)

CONSTANT        21.509          3.061          0.000       .        7.026    0.000
OVER65          -0.667          0.238         -0.372     1.000     -2.807    0.007
```

Notice that the rate of suicide (the ninth leading cause of death in the U.S.) is correlated with each of the three independent variables. The higher the level of energy consumption (i.e., the worse the weather), the higher the rate of suicide. The higher the average personal income, the lower the rate of suicide. And the higher the proportion of old people, the lower the rate of suicide. (Suicide is the third leading cause of death, after accidents and homicide, among Americans 15-24 years of age, but is hardly a factor among the elderly.)

Furthermore, each of these zero-order correlations is statistically very significant. Table 16.8 shows the regression between each of these independent variables separately and the rate of suicide. The *p*-value in each case is very low, indicating a highly significant statistical relation.

Table 16.9 shows what happens when we use multiple regression to check for spurious rela-

tions. If we put INCOME and BTU into the regression together, both variables remain statistically significant. If we put INCOME and OVER65 into the regression, both variables remain significant. Thus, both BTU and OVER65 show effects on suicide rates that are independent of the effects of INCOME.

But look what happens when we enter all three independent variables into the regression. Table 16.10 shows the result: INCOME remains statistically significant, but neither BTU nor OVER65 are.

If BTU remained statistically significant while OVER65 did not, we could conclude that OVER65 had no effect on suicide independently of INCOME and BTU. Likewise, if OVER65 remained statistically significant while BTU did not, we could conclude that BTU had no effect on suicide independently of INCOME and OVER65. In this instance, however, we can only

TABLE 16.9 Regressions of the Three Pairs of Independent Variables with SUICIDE

```
Dep Var: SUICIDE    N: 51   Multiple R: 0.591   Squared multiple R: 0.349

Adjusted squared multiple R: 0.322   Standard error of estimate: 2.969

Effect      Coefficient    Std Error    Std Coef Tolerance      t    P(2 Tail)

CONSTANT      20.038         3.318         0.000       .        6.038    0.000
INCOME        -0.000         0.000        -0.421     0.891     -3.417    0.001
BTU            0.007         0.003         0.298     0.891      2.413    0.020


Dep Var: SUICIDE    N: 51   Multiple R: 0.610   Squared multiple R: 0.372

Adjusted squared multiple R: 0.346   Standard error of estimate: 2.915

Effect      Coefficient    Std Error    Std Coef Tolerance      t    P(2 Tail)

CONSTANT      31.282         3.502         0.000       .        8.933    0.000
INCOME        -0.001         0.000        -0.490     0.991     -4.264    0.000
OVER65        -0.564         0.202        -0.321     0.991     -2.798    0.007
```

TABLE 16.10   Regression of All Three Independent Variables and SUICIDE

```
Dep Var: SUICIDE    N: 51   Multiple R: 0.630   Squared multiple R: 0.397

Adjusted squared multiple R: 0.358   Standard error of estimate: 2.889

Effect      Coefficient    Std Error    Std Coef Tolerance      t    P(2 Tail)

CONSTANT      26.898         4.806         0.000       .        5.597    0.000
INCOME        -0.000         0.000        -0.434     0.889     -3.613    0.001
BTU            0.004         0.003         0.183     0.714      1.362    0.180
OVER65        -0.439         0.228        -0.245     0.793     -1.927    0.060
```

conclude that we have a multicollinearity problem that obscures our findings. We can't tell if either BTU or OVER65 has effects on suicide independently of INCOME.

FACTOR ANALYSIS

Factor analysis is **a set of techniques for information packaging and data reduction.** The data are often about items for building scales (more about this in a minute), but can just as well be about artifacts (movies, songs, buildings, cars, brands of beer), people (movie stars, politicians, fashion models, criminals, classical musicians), or even countries.

Factor analysis is based on complex statistics, but the principle behind the method is simple and compelling. The idea is that if a bunch of things are correlated with each other, they must have something in common. That thing in common is called a *factor*. Factors are sort of "supervariables"—that is, **variables that incorporate a lot of variables.** If we can discover (or, more correctly, intuit) these underlying supervariables, then we can explain a lot of the variance in some dependent variable of interest by using a small number of independent variables.

This idea was first articulated by Charles E. Spearman (he for whom Spearman's rank-order correlation coefficient is named—see Chapter 15) in 1904. He noticed that the scores of students on various exams (classics, French, English, math, etc.) were correlated. He suggested that the exam scores were correlated with each other because they were all correlated with an underlying factor, which he labeled *g*, for general intelligence.

The single-factor theory of intelligence has been repudiated many times since then, as have been the IQ tests that were developed to measure intelligence as a single factor. But the idea of factors—supervariables—that underlie a set of correlated events became one of the most important developments in all the social sciences.

Look through recent issues of *Personality and Individual Differences, Behavior Research and Therapy,* and the *Journal of Personality and Social Psychology.* These are just three of the journals where scholars in clinical and experimental psychology publish the results of efforts to create useful measures of various psychological factors. Factor analysis figures in most of these efforts. A couple of recent examples include Cramer and Lake's (1998) test of a scale to measure a preference for solitude and Spence's (1998) test of a scale to measure children's anxiety.

Factor analysis is used across the social sciences in data reduction—to explore large data sets with dozens or even hundreds of variables to extract a few variables that tell a big story. In political science, for example, Lieske (1993) partitioned the 3,164 counties in the U.S. into 10 distinctive regional subcultures by looking for common, underlying factors in the correlations among 45 racial, ethnic, religious, and social structural variables. In social psychology, Stein et al. (1991) used factor analysis to test the influence of ethnicity, socioeconomic status, and various anxieties as barriers to the use of mammography among White, African American, and Hispanic women. Factor analysis confirmed the influence of five kinds of anxiety: fear of radiation, fear of pain, embarrassment about breast exams, anxiety about what might be found, and concerns about cost.

In multiple regression, there is one dependent variable and several independent, or predictor, variables. In factor analysis, all the variables in a matrix are considered together for their interdependence. The original, observed variables are thought of as reflections of some underlying dimensions—the so-called factors. The idea is to summarize the information contained in many variables (often dozens, or even hundreds) with a few underlying dimensions that covary with clumps of the variables in the original data. This reduces the original long list of variables to a shorter list that is easier to manipulate (e.g., to use in a regression analysis) and to interpret.

In other words, factors are extracted from a matrix of correlations among the variables in a study. The factors are new variables comprised of several old ones in a correlation matrix that are closely related to one another.

Factor Analysis and Scales

As I mentioned in Chapter 8, factor analysis is widely used across the social sciences in building reliable, compact scales for measuring social and psychological variables. Suppose, for example, you are interested in attitudes toward gender role changes among women. You suspect that the underlying forces of role changes are related to premarital sexuality, working outside the home, and the development of an independent social and economic life among women. You make up 50 attitudinal items and collect data on those items from a sample of respondents.

Factor analysis will help you decide whether the 50 items you made up really test for the underlying forces you think are at work. If they do, then you could use a few benchmark items—the ones that "load high" on the factors—and this would save you from having to ask every respondent about all 50 items you made up. You would still get the information you need—or much of it, anyway. How much? The amount would depend on how much variance in the correlation matrix each of your factors accounted for.

The notion of variance is very important here. Factors account for chunks of variance—the amount of dispersion or correlation in a correlation matrix. Factors are extracted from a correlation matrix in the order of the amount of variance that they explain in the matrix. Some factors explain a lot of variance, while others may be very weak and are discarded by researchers as not being useful. In a dense matrix, only one or a few factors may be needed to account for a lot of variance, while in a dispersed matrix, many factors may be needed.

The most common statistical solution for finding the underlying factors in a correlation matrix is called the **orthogonal solution**. In orthogonal factor analyses, **factors are found that have as little correlation with each other as possible.** Other solutions, that result in intercorrelated factors, are also possible (the various solutions are options that you can select in all the major statistical packages, like SAS®, SYSTAT, and SPSS®). Some researchers say that these solutions, al-

though messier than orthogonal solutions, are more like real life.

So-called factor loadings are the correlations between the new factors and the old variables that are replaced by factors. All the old variables "load" on each new factor. The idea is to establish some cutoff below which you would not feel comfortable accepting that an old variable "loaded onto" a factor. By convention, variables that load at least 0.60 on a factor unambiguously represent that factor, and variables between 0.30 and 0.59 are worth considering. Many researchers use 0.50 as the cutoff, and look at loadings of 0.30-0.49 as worth considering.

Once you have a list of variables that load high on a factor (irrespective of sign, plus or minus), you simply go through the list of old variables, you look at the list of variables that constitute each factor and decide what the factor *means*.

An example should make all this a lot clearer.

Handwerker's Domestic Activities Scale

Handwerker (1996a, 1998) used factor analysis to test whether the construct of "domestic cooperation" on Barbados was unidimensional. He asked a random sample of 428 Barbadian women whether their husbands or boyfriends helped with any of the following: cooking, washing clothes, washing dishes, bathing children, taking children places, and caring for children. To put these items of domestic cooperation in context, he also asked each woman whether her husband or boyfriend was *expected* to treat her as an equal and whether her husband or boyfriend *did, in fact,* treat her as an equal.

Table 16.11 is a schematic of Handwerker's data matrix. The eight variables are labeled

TABLE 16.11   Schematic of Handwerker's Profile Matrix

ID	COOK	WASH	DISH	BATHE	TAKE	CARE	EQUAL1	EQUAL2
1	1	0	1	1	1	0	1	0
2	0	1	0	0	1	0	1	1
3	1	0	0	0	1	1	1	0
.	.	.	.	.	.	.	.	.
.	.	.	.	.	.	.	.	.
.	.	.	.	.	.	.	.	.
428	1	1	0	1	1	0	1	1

SOURCE: Adapted from Handwerker (1996a:2). Reprinted with permission.

COOK, WASH, DISH, BATHE, TAKE, CARE, EQUAL1, and EQUAL2.

Table 16.11 is a profile matrix (see Figure 15.13a), but factor analysis is done on a similarity matrix (see Figure 15.13b). If Handwerker had asked the women: "On a scale of 1 to 5, how much does your husband or boyfriend help you with the cooking?" the entries in Table 16.11 would have been 1-5. With that kind of data, a factor analysis program would turn the profile matrix into a similarity matrix by calculating Pearson's *r* for all possible pairs of columns.

But Handwerker asked the women yes/no questions (that's why Table 16.11 contains only 0s and 1s).

One way to turn a 1/0 profile matrix into a similarity matrix is to calculate the percentage of matches for all possible pairs of columns. That is, when two columns have a 1 or a 0 in the same row, count that as a hit. When two columns have different entries in the same row, count that as a miss. Then, count up all the hits and divide by 428 (the number of possible hits for 428 respondents).

The result is an 8 × 8 similarity matrix. Table 16.12 shows the results of Handwerker's factor analysis of that matrix.

In reading the output from factor analysis, we look for items that load high—have scores of at least .60—on each factor.

From Table 16.12, it's clear that the domain of "domestic cooperation" is *not* unidimensional. In fact, it has three dimensions. Interpreting the results in Table 16.12, it seemed to Handwerker that Factor 1 had something to do with "household chores." He labeled that factor "Domestic." Factor 2, he thought, comprised "chores associated with children," so he labeled it "Children." In open-ended interviews, Barbadian women interpreted the third factor as being about affection and empowerment within families, so Handwerker labeled it "Affection."

Over the next few years, Handwerker had the opportunity to refine and test his scale on two more Caribbean islands, Antigua and St. Lucia. He dropped EQUAL1 because it was redundant with EQUAL2 and he dropped the question about "caring for children in other ways" (CARE) because respondents told him that it was ambiguous.

Handwerker also added four new questions— things that had come up in open-ended interviews as important to women: (1) Does your partner take responsibility for the children for an evening or an afternoon when you have something to do?

TABLE 16.12 Factor Loadings for Handwerker's Data

Variable	Factor 1: Domestic	Factor 2: Children	Factor 3: Affection
COOK	**.893**	.232	.161
WASH	**.895**	.121	.058
DISH	**.824**	.329	.191
BATHE	**.795**	.324	.194
TAKE	.291	**.929**	.159
CARE	.307	**.922**	.175
EQUAL1	.188	.203	**.734**
EQUAL2	.091	.066	**.854**
Explained variance	39.150	25.516	17.841

SOURCE: Handwerker (1996a:2). Reprinted with permission.

(2) Does your partner take time off from work to share responsibility for children who are sick? (3) Does your partner talk with you and respect your opinion? and (4) Does your partner spend his free time with you?

Table 16.13 shows the results for Antigua and St. Lucia.

There are at least four things to notice about Table 16.13:

(1) Despite the subtraction of some variables and the addition of others, the results from all three islands are very stable. COOK, WASH, and DISH are components of a single large factor across all three Caribbean countries.

(2) While BATHE loads high on the domestic chore factor across all three islands, it also loads high on the children factor for two of the islands. This item should be dropped in the future because it does not reliably distinguish the two factors.

(3) FREET loads on the children factor for St. Lucia, but it loads on the affection factor for Antigua. It turns out that Handwerker's assistant changed the wording

for the FREET question slightly when she did the interviews on Antigua. Instead of asking: "Does your partner spend his free time with you?" she asked: "Does your partner spend his free time with you or with your children?" (Handwerker 1996a:3). That little change apparently made enough of a difference in the responses to change the factor loading.

(4) Across all three replications, the three factors in Tables 16.12 and 16.13 account for 70%-80% of the variance in the original data matrix. That is, about three-fourths to four-fifths of the variance in the original data is accounted for by just three underlying variables (the three factors) rather than the full list of original variables. For women across the Caribbean, the construct of domestic cooperation is multidimensional and composed of three subconstructs: sharing of everyday domestic chores, sharing of responsibilities for children, and affection from men as defined by being treated as an equal.

TABLE 16.13 Handwerker's Data from Antigua and St. Lucia

| Variable | Antigua | | | St. Lucia | | |
	Domestic	Children	Affection	Domestic	Children	Affection
COOK	.793	.317	.106	.783	.182	.161
WASH	.845	.163	.090	.818	.056	.018
DISH	.791	.320	.203	.781	.197	.173
BATHE	.493	.654	.207	.596	.584	.090
TAKE	.271	.738	.289	.246	.790	.196
TIME	.253	.820	.258	.228	.833	.061
SICK	.210	.786	.151	.121	.742	−.067
FREET	.100	.299	.802	−.010	.691	.319
EQUAL	.147	.155	.898	.177	.117	.883
TALK	.142	.200	.883	.113	.112	.909
Explained variance	26.460	26.459	25.051	24.188	27.905	18.191

SOURCE: Handwerker (1996a:3). Reprinted with permission.

MULTIDIMENSIONAL SCALING

Multidimensional scaling analysis (MDS) is another multivariate data-reduction technique. Like factor analysis, it is used to tease out underlying relations among a set of observations. Also like factor analysis, MDS **requires a matrix of measures of associations**—for example, a correlation matrix based on things like *r*, tau, and gamma. But unlike factor analysis, MDS does not require metric data.

When you measure something like how strongly people feel about something, the numbers you assign to their feelings don't have the same meaning as, say, numbers that express distances in kilometers, weight in kilograms, or nutrition in grams of protein consumed per day. These latter numbers are called "metric" because they are grounded in well-understood units of measurement.

Most attitude and cognition data are nonmetric. MDS is an excellent way to analyze nonmetric data and to look for patterns and underlying commonalities. Also, MDS produces a graphic display of the relation among any set of items, whether those items are people, things, or questions about attitudes. (For more about the theory behind MDS, see Romney et al. [1972].)

How MDS Works

Suppose you measure the association among three variables, *A, B,* and *C,* using Pearson's *r.* The association matrix for these three variables is in the inside box of Table 16.14.

Clearly, variables *A* and *C* are more closely related to one another than are *A* and *B*, or *B*

TABLE 16.14 Matrix of Association among Four Variables

	A	B	C	D
A	X	.50	.80	.30
B		X	.40	.65
C			X	.35
D				X

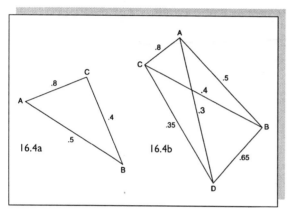

Figure 16.4 Two-Dimensional Plot of the Relation among Three Variables (a) and among Four Variables (b)

and C. You can represent this with a triangle, as in Figure 16.4a.

In other words, we can place points A, B, and C on a plane in some position relative to each other. The distance between A and B is longer than that between A and C (reflecting the difference between .50 and .80); and the distance between B and C is longer than that between A and C (reflecting the difference between .40 and .80). The numbers in this graph are *similarities*: The **lower the correlation, the longer the distance; the higher the correlation, the shorter the distance.**

With just three variables, it is easy to plot these distances in proper proportion to one another.

For example, the physical distance between B and C is twice that of A and C in Figure 16.4a. Figure 16.4a contains *precisely* the same information as the inside box of Table 16.14, but in graphic form.

With four variables, things get considerably more complicated. With four variables there are *six* relations to cope with. These relations are shown in the large box of Table 16.14. Only one two-dimensional graph (apart from rotations and enlargements) can represent the relative distances among the six relations in Table 16.14. The graph is shown in Figure 16.4b.

Figure 16.4b is a two-dimensional graph of six relations in *almost* proper proportions. It is often impossible to achieve perfect proportionality in a graph of six relations if we have only two dimensions to work with. One way out of this is to depict the six relations in Table 16.14 in three dimensions, instead of in only two. The extra dimension would give us plenty of room to move around and we could better adjust the proportionality of the distances between the various pairs of variables.

In principle, you can perfectly represent the relative relations among N variables in N – 1 dimensions, so that any graph of six variables can be perfectly represented in five dimensions. But even a three-dimensional graph is sometimes hard to read. What would you do with a five-dimensional graph?

TABLE 16.15 Distances between Nine U.S. Cities in Miles

	BOS	NY	DC	MIA	CHI	SEA	SF	LA	DEN
Boston	0								
NY	206	0							
DC	429	233	0						
Miami	1504	1308	1075	0					
Chicago	963	802	671	1329	0				
Seattle	2976	2815	2684	3273	2013	0			
SF	3095	2934	2799	3053	2142	808	0		
LA	2979	2786	2631	2687	2054	1131	379	0	
Denver	1949	1771	1616	2037	996	1037	1235	1059	0

SOURCE: Borgatti (1992a, 1992b). Reprinted with permission.

Most researchers specify a two-dimensional solution when they run an MDS computer analysis. MDS programs produce a statistic that measures the "stress" in the graph produced by the program. This is a measure of how far off the graph it is from one that would be perfectly proportional. The lower the stress, the better the solution. This means that a cluster of variables in an MDS graph with low stress is likely to reflect some reality about the cognitive world of the people being studied.

A Physical World Example

A physical example, based on metric data, will make this clearer. Afterward, we'll move on to a cognitive example, one based on nonmetric data.

Table 16.15 shows the road distance in miles between all pairs of nine cities in the United States. Note two things about the numbers in this table. First, the numbers are *dissimilarities*. **Bigger numbers mean that things are farther apart— less like each other. Smaller numbers mean that things are more similar.** Similarity and dissimilarity matrices are known collectively as *proximity matrices* because they **tell you how close or far apart things are.** The second thing to notice is that

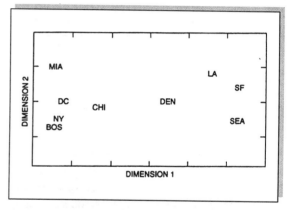

Figure 16.5 Two-Dimensional MDS Solution for the Numbers in Table 16.15

the numbers are reasonably accurate measures of a physical reality—distance between points on a map—so they are metric data.

In principle, there should be a two-dimensional solution with low stress that fits the numbers in this table. I used ANTHROPAC (Borgatti 1992a) to run MDS on these data, and the solution is shown in Figure 16.5.

Figure 16.5 looks suspiciously like a map of the United States. If you flip the figure left to right and turn it upside down, then Miami will wind up in the lower right and Seattle will be in the

TABLE 16.16 The Rokeach Value Survey

Terminal Values		Instrumental Values	
1. A comfortable life	10. Inner harmony	1. Ambitious	10. Imaginative
2. An exciting life	11. Mature love	2. Broadminded	11. Independent
3. A sense of accomplishment	12. National security	3. Capable	12. Intellectual
4. A world at peace	13. Pleasure	4. Cheerful	13. Logical
5. A world of beauty	14. Salvation	5. Clean	14. Loving
6. Equality	15. Self-respect	6. Courageous	15. Obedient
7. Family security	16. Social recognition	7. Forgiving	16. Polite
8. Freedom	17. True friendship	8. Helpful	17. Responsible
9. Happiness	18. Wisdom	9. Honest	18. Self-controlled

SOURCE: C. S. Johnston, "The Rokeach Value Survey: Underlying Structure and Multidimensional Scaling," *Journal of Psychology* 129:583-97. Reprinted with permission of the Helen Dwight Reid Education Foundation. Published by Heldref Publications, 1319 Eighteenth St., N.W., Washington, D.C. 20036-1802. Copyright © 1995.

upper right, where we expect them to be. All nine cities, in fact, are placed in proper juxtaposition to one another, but the map is upside-down and backward. MDS programs are notoriously unconcerned with details like this. So long as they get the juxtaposition right, they're finished. Figure 16.5 shows that the program got it right. You can rotate any MDS graph through 360 degrees in any dimension and it will still be the same graph.

A Cognitive World Example

Now that you understand the principle of MDS in metric data, we can apply the idea to nonmetric data. Think of this as moving from data about *physical space* to data about *cognitive space*.

Charles Johnston (1995) used MDS to examine the underlying structure of the Rokeach Value Survey (RVS). The RVS contains 18 *instrumental values* and 18 *terminal values*. "Instrumental" values are things that get you somewhere in life—things like being ambitious, courageous, forgiving, responsible, and so on. "Terminal" values are

desirable end states—like having a comfortable life, experiencing true friendship, having national security, and so on.

Table 16.16 shows the 36 values. In applying the RVS, you ask people to rank order the terminal values and then the instrumental ones "in order of importance to YOU, as guiding principles in YOUR life" (Rokeach 1973:27).

The RVS has been used in at least 400 studies, but attempts to reduce the 36 values to a smaller set with factor analysis have been inconclusive, so Johnston decided to try MDS. He asked 76 intro psych students (54 women and 22 men) at the University of Nebraska to pile sort the values. The values were printed on cards, one value to a card. Johnston spread the cards out on a table (first the terminal values, then the instrumental ones) and gave respondents this instruction: "Sort the value cards into groups based on how similar you find them."

That was it. No instructions on the number of piles to make or on the number of values per pile. It was a true, unconstrained pile sort of the kind we discussed in Chapter 7.

TABLE 16.17   One Person's Sorting

a. Of the Terminal Values in the RVS	b. Of the Instrumental Values in the RVS
Pile 1: 3, 9, 10, 11, 15, 18	Pile 1: 3, 8, 9, 15, 17, 18
Pile 2: 2, 5, 13	Pile 2: 1, 6, 10, 11
Pile 3: 14	Pile 3: 2, 12, 13
Pile 4: 1, 3, 16	Pile 4: 5
Pile 5: 6, 8	Pile 5: 4, 7, 14, 16
Pile 6: 4, 7, 12	

TABLE 16.18   Similarity Matrix from One Person's Pile Sorting of the 18 Instrumental Values of the RVS

	1	2	3	4	5	6	7	8	9	10	11	12	13	14	15	16	17	18
1	0																	
2		0																
3			0															
4				0														
5					0													
6	1					0												
7				1			0											
8			1					0										
9			1					1	0									
10	1					1				0								
11	1					1				1	0							
12		1										0						
13		1										1	0					
14				1			1							0				
15			1					1	1						0			
16				1			1							1		0		
17			1					1	1						1		0	
18			1					1	1						1		1	0

The result of a free, or unconstrained, pile sort is an ***individual similarity matrix***. I asked someone to pile sort the 36 values in the RVS. Table 16.17 shows the results. Table 16.17a shows the pile sort for the terminal values; Table 16.17b shows the pile sort for the instrumental values. And Table 16.18 shows the individual similarity matrix for the data in Table 16.17b.

Pile 1 for this respondent contains values 3, 8, 9, 15, 17, and 18. There are $N(N-1)/2$ unique pairs in any list of things, so there are $6(5)/2 = 15$ pairs of values in pile 1, $3(2)/2 = 3$ pairs of values for pile 2, and so on. The matrix in Table 16.18 shows a 1 in each cell that represents a pair of values placed together in any pile.

Johnston had 76 of these matrices, which he combined into one big matrix of similarities for analysis with MDS. To combine these matrices, you just stack them up, one on top of the other, and add up all the 1s in each cell down through the stack. That tells you how many people put, say, 18 and 3 (being self-controlled and capable), or 15 and 8 (being obedient and helpful), or 9 and 12 (being intellectual and honest) in the same pile.

If you have 76 respondents, like Johnston did, there would be 76 chances that any pair of values would wind up in the same pile together. So, after adding up the cells in the stack of matrices, you divide each result by 76 to find the percentage of times that any pair of values was placed together in a pile by the whole set of respondents.

Percentages are nice linear measures of similarity. A pair of items that occurs together 50% of the time (that is, half the respondents put the pair of items in a pile together) is twice as similar as a pair of items that occurs together 25% of the time. Figure 16.6 shows the two-dimensional MDS plot of Johnston's similarity matrix for the instrumental-values pile sort. The stress for this two-dimensional plot turned out to be .142 in Johnston's data. This is what most researchers agree is an acceptable level of stress for a matrix of this size, so the next step is to interpret the plot.

This is the fun part. Look at Figure 16.6. Keep looking at it. Think about the distribution of those values. Do you see any pattern? We're looking for *arrays,* or *dimensions,* of values across the plot and *clumps,* or *clusters,* of values scattered around the plot. Since the MDS program was able to plot the items in two dimensions with acceptably low stress, we are looking for two arrays. They don't have to be orthogonal (at right angles) to each other. And there can be any number of clumps. Interpretation means figuring out what the dimensions and the clumps are.

One array looks to me like it runs from imaginative, intellectual, and logical (10, 12, 13) in the upper-left quadrant, sort of diagonally to obedi-

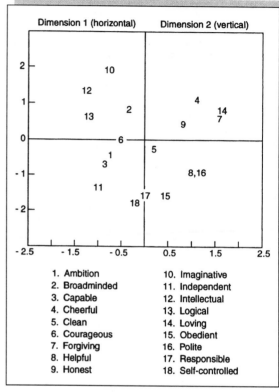

Figure 16.6 Two-Dimensional MDS Solution for Johnston's Study Using the Rokeach Value Survey

SOURCE: C. S. Johnston, "The Rokeach Value Survey," *Journal of Psychology* 129:583-97. Reprinted with permission of the Helen Dwight Reid Education Foundation. Published by Heldref Publications, 1319 Eighteenth St., N.W., Washington, D.C. 20036-1802. Copyright © 1995.

ent, responsible, and self-controlled (15, 17, 18) down in the lower-middle part of the graph. The other array seems to run from loving, forgiving, cheerful, and honest (14, 7, 4, 9) in the upper-right quadrant, sort of diagonally to ambitious, capable, and independent (1, 3, 11) in the lower-left quadrant.

Both of these dimensions look like they might represent components of affiliation orientation. That is, some people are more oriented toward individualistic values (and individual achievement), while others are more oriented toward collectivist values (and the success of the group, or groups, to which they belong). One of the dimensions (imaginative to self-controlled) might be a cognitive representation of this affiliation orientation. The other (loving to independent) might be an emotional representation.

As it turns out, my interpretation of Johnston's MDS plot is similar to his, but slightly different. He focused on the clumps in Figure 16.6. Johnston saw two broad clumps of values in Figure 16.6. One clump comprised imaginative, intellectual, broadminded, logical, courageous, ambitious, capable, and independent. Those are the values that run from 10 (imaginative) in the upper-left quadrant straight down to 11 (independent) in the lower-left quadrant. These represent, according to Johnston, individual or achievement-oriented values.

The other clump comprised loving, forgiving, cheerful, honest, clean, helpful, polite, obedient, responsible, and self-controlled. Those are the values that run from 14 and 7 (loving and forgiving) in the upper-right quadrant, diagonally down to 18 (self-controlled) just to the left of center in the lower-left quadrant. These, Johnston, said, seem to represent collective affiliation-oriented values (Johnston 1995:589).

In interpreting an MDS plot, you can focus on either the dimensions or the clumps, or both. As you can see, either way, interpretation is a brazen, flat-out qualitative exercise. It's a Rorschach test for social scientists—which is why I like it so much.

Think about sorting 18 items into piles with no constraints on the number of piles you can make. You have to decide if each item goes with each other item—or not. That means you are forced to make $18(17)/2 = 153$ decisions. When 76 people sort 18 cards, they make a total of 11,628 decisions. That's a fair amount of data.

If there are any patterns in all those decisions, MDS will find them. What those patterns mean is up to you. Fortunately, you can test your hunches about the clumps in an MDS plot using hierarchical cluster analysis, which comes next. (You can also test your ideas about dimensions, using a method called *property fitting analysis*. (See Further Reading at the end of this chapter.)

CLUSTER ANALYSIS

Like factor analysis and MDS, *cluster analysis* is a descriptive tool for exploring relations among items in a matrix—for finding what goes with what. You start with a similarity matrix, like a matrix of Pearson correlation coefficients. If you factor the matrix, you find underlying variables that may encompass the variables in the original data. If you scale the matrix (MDS), you get a map that shows you graphically the relations among the items. Clustering tells you which items go together and in what order. Thus, in the MDS example from Johnston (1995) above, a cluster analysis would let us check his guess about the clumps he labeled "individual achievement-oriented" and "collective affiliation-oriented" values.

To get an idea of where we're going with this, take another look at Figure 16.6. Johnston saw two big clumps, one of individualistic values and one of collectivistic values. There may, however, be more than two clumps of values. One clump might be 4, 7, and 14 (being cheerful, forgiving, and loving). Another might be 15, 17, and 18 (being obedient, responsible, and self-controlled). Yet another might be 1, 3, 6, and 11 (being ambitious, capable, courageous, and independent).

TABLE 16.19 Dissimilarity Matrix for Clustering

	1	3	7	9	14	20	21	25
1	0							
3	2	0						
7	6	4	0					
9	8	6	2	0				
14	13	11	7	5	0			
20	19	17	13	11	6	0		
21	20	18	14	12	7	1	0	
25	24	22	18	16	11	5	4	0

SOURCE: V. J. de Ghett, "Hierarchical Cluster Analysis." In *Quantitative Ethology,* ed. by P. W. Colgan. Copyright © 1978, John Wiley & Sons. Reprinted by permission of John Wiley & Sons.

And how do we know if the 15, 17, 18 clump goes with the values shooting off toward the upper right or with those shooting off toward the upper left? This is what we want a cluster analysis to help us determine.

> *Clustering is a technique for finding the similarity chunks. It doesn't label those chunks.*

I'm going to explain cluster analysis in some detail. It's a very important descriptive tool, but as we go through the next few paragraphs, keep in mind two things: First, clustering is just a technique for finding the similarity chunks. It doesn't label those chunks. That part is also a Rorschach test: You stare at the output and decide what the meaning is. Second, as with so many methods, different treatments of your data produce different outcomes. The next few pages will make it very clear just how much *you and only you* are responsible for every choice you make in data analysis.

How Cluster Analysis Works

Consider the following example from de Ghett (1978:121):

1 3 7 9 14 20 21 25

The distance between 1 and 3 is 2. The distance between 21 and 25 is 4. So, in a numerical sense, 1 and 3 are twice as similar to one another as 21 and 25 are to one another. Table 16.19 shows the *dissimilarity matrix* for these numbers.

There are several ways to find clusters in this matrix. Two of them are called *single-link* or *closest-neighbor analysis* and *complete-link* or *farthest-neighbor analysis* (there are others, but I won't go into them here). In single-link clustering, we use only the numbers adjacent to the diagonal: 2, 4, 2, 5, 6, 1, 4. The two clustering solutions (again, done with ANTHROPAC) are shown in Figure 16.7.

In the single-link solution, the two closest neighbors are 20 and 21. They are exactly one unit of distance apart, and there is a 1 adjacent to the diagonal of the original matrix where 20 and

A. SINGLE-LINK CLUSTERING

Level	1	3	7	9	14	20	21	25
1						x	x	x
2	x x x		x x x			x	x	x
4	x x x x x x x					x x x x x		
5	x x x x x x x x x					x x x x x		
6	x x x x x x x x x	x x x x x x x x						

B. COMPLETE-LINK CLUSTERING

Level	1	3	7	9	14	20	21	25
1						x	x	x
2	x x x		x x x			x	x	x
5	x x x		x x x			x x x x x		
7	x x x		x x x x x			x x x x x		
13	x x x x x x x x					x x x x x		
24	x x x x x x x x x	x x x x x x x x						

Figure 16.7 Cluster Analysis of Data in Table 16.19

21 come together. In Figure 16.7a, 20 and 21 are shown joined at level 1. The numbers 1,3 and the numbers 7,9 are the next closest neighbors. They are both two units apart. Figure 16.7a shows them joined at level 2.

Once a pair is joined, it is considered a unit. The pairs 1,3 and 7,9 are joined together at level 4 because they are four units apart (the nearest neighbor to the pair 1,3 is 7, which is four units from 3). The pair 21,25 are also four units apart. However, 20,21 are already joined, so 25 joins this pair at level 4. The connections are built up to form a tree.

Figure 16.7b shows the complete-link (or farthest-neighbor) clustering solution for the data in Table 16.19. In complete-link clustering, all the numbers in 1 are used. Once again, the pair 20,21 is joined at level 1 because the pair is just one unit apart. The pairs 1,3 and 7,9 join at level 2.

At this point, the complete-link and single-link solutions are identical. At the next level, though, things change. The neighbors of 20,21 are 14 and 25. The farthest neighbor from 14 to 20,21 is 21. The distance is seven units. The farthest neighbor from 25 to 20,21 is 20. The distance is five units. Since five is less than seven, 25 joins 20,21 at level 5. But the two pairs 1,3 and 7,9 are not joined at this level.

The only number not yet joined to some other number is 14. It is compared to its farthest neighbors in the adjacent clusters: 14 is 11 units away from 25 (which is now part of the 20,21,25 cluster) and it's 7 units away from the 7,9 cluster. So, at level 7, 14 is joined to 7,9. The same game is played out with all the clusters to form the tree in Figure 16.7b.

Clusters of Cities

The complete-link method tends to produce more clusters than the single-link method. The method you choose determines the results you get. Look at Figure 16.8a and 16.8b to see what happens when we use the single-link and complete-link clustering methods on the data in Table 16.15.

To me, the complete-link method seems better with these data. Denver "belongs" with San Francisco and Los Angeles more than it belongs with Boston and New York. But that may be my own bias. Coming from New York, I think of Denver as a western U.S. city, but I've heard people from San Francisco talk about "going back east to Denver for the weekend."

A. COMPLETE LINK

```
              B                 C           S
          M   O           C     H           E   D
          I   S           H     I           A   E
          A   T           I     C           T   N
          M   O   N   D   C     A   S   L   T   V
          I   N   Y   C   O     G   F   A   E   R
Level
 206      x x x
 379      x x x           x x x
 429      x x x x x       x x x
 963      x x x x x x x   x x x
1037      x x x x x x x   x x x       x x x
1235      x x x x x x x   x x x x x x x x
1504  x x x x x x x x x   x x x x x x x
3273  x x x x x x x x x x x x x x x x x x
```

B. SINGLE LINK

```
      S                   B               C
      E                   O               H       D
      A                   S               I       E
      T                   T               C       N
  M   T                   O   N   D       A       V
  I   L   S   L           N   Y   C       G       E
  A   E   F   A                               O   R
Level
 206                              x x x
 233                              x x x x x
 379          x x x               x x x x x
 671          x x x               x x x x x x x
 808      x x x x x               x x x x x x x
 996      x x x x x               x x x x x x x x x x
1037  x x x x x x x x x x x x x x x x x x x x
1075  x x x x x x x x x x x x x x x x x x x x x
```

Figure 16.8 Complete-Link and Single-Link Clustering for Data in Table 16.15

DISCRIMINANT FUNCTION ANALYSIS

Discriminant function analysis (DFA) is used to classify cases into categorical variables from ordinal and interval variables. For example, we may want to classify which of two (or more) groups an individual belongs to: male or female; those who have been labor migrants vs. those who have not; those who are high, middle, or low income; those in favor of something and those who are not; and so on.

DFA is a statistical method developed for handling this problem. It has been around for a long time (Fisher 1936) but, like most multivariate techniques, DFA has become more popular since user-friendly computer programs have made it easier to do.

Kelln et al. (1998), for example, used DFA to test how well some personality tests could postdict serious misbehavior in 128 prison inmates. Using prison records, they divided the sample into two groups: 21 men who had only been reprimanded for some infraction and 107 men who

had suffered some actual penalty (like time in segregation, or early lockup) for breaking the rules. A DFA model using age, sentence length, and type of offense correctly classified 46% of the cases. But when they put the scores for the personality tests scales into the model, they were able to classify 79% of the cases correctly.

Lambros Comitas and I used DFA in our study of two groups of people in Athens, Greece: those who had returned from having spent at least five years in (the former) West Germany as labor migrants and those who had never been out of Greece. We were trying to understand how the experience abroad might have affected the attitudes of Greek men and women about traditional gender roles (Bernard and Comitas 1978). Our sample consisted of 400 persons: 100 male migrants, 100 female migrants, 100 male nonmigrants, and 100 female nonmigrants. Using DFA, we were able to predict with 70% accuracy whether an informant had been a migrant on the basis of just five variables.

There are some things you need to be careful about in using DFA, however. Notice that our sample in the Athens study consisted of half migrants and half nonmigrants. That was because we used a disproportionate, stratified sampling design to ensure adequate representation of returned migrants in the study. Given our sample, we could have guessed whether one of our informants was a migrant with 50% accuracy, without any information about the informant at all.

Now, only a very small fraction of the population of Athens consists of former long-term labor migrants to West Germany. The chances of stopping an Athenian at random on the street and grabbing one of those returned labor migrants was less than 5% in 1977 when we did the study.

Suppose that, armed with the results of the DFA that Comitas and I did, I asked random Athenians five questions, the answers to which allow me to predict 70% of the time whether any respondent had been a long-term labor migrant to West Germany. No matter what the answers were to those questions, I'd be better off predicting that the random Athenian was *not* a returned migrant. I'd be right more than 95% of the time.

Furthermore, why not just ask the random survey respondent straight out: "Are you a returned long-term labor migrant from West Germany?" With such an innocuous question, presumably I'd have gotten a correct answer at least as often as our 70% prediction based on knowing five pieces of information.

DFA is a powerful classification device, but it is not really a prediction device. Still, many problems (like the one Comitas and I studied) are essentially about understanding things so you can classify them correctly. Livingstone and Lunt (1993) surveyed 217 people in Oxford, England, and divided them into six types, based on whether or not people were in debt, whether or not people had savings, and people who live exactly within their income (with neither savings nor debt). DFA, using a variety of variables (age, class, education, income, expenses, attitudes toward debt, etc.), correctly classified almost 95% of the cases into one of the six groups that Livingstone and Lunt had identified.

Gans and Wood (1985) used DFA technique for classifying Samoan women as "traditional" or "modern" with respect to their ideal family size. If women stated that they wanted three or fewer children, Gans and Wood placed them in a category they labeled "modern." Women who said they wanted four or more children were labeled "traditional." DFA showed that just six of the many variables that Gans and Wood had collected allowed them to classify correctly which category a woman belonged to in 75% of all cases. The variables were such things as age, owning a car, and level of education.

It would have been ridiculous for Gans and Wood to have asked women straight out: "Are you traditional or modern when it comes to the number of children you'd like?" DFA (combined with on-the-ground ethnography) gave them a good picture of the variables that go into Samoan women's desired family size.

Similarly, Comitas and I were able to describe the attitudinal components of gender role changes by using DFA, and our prediction rate of 70% was significantly better than the 50% we'd have gotten by chance, given our sampling design. If you're careful about how you interpret the results of a discriminant function analysis, then it can be a really important addition to your statistical tool kit.

AND FINALLY

In a world of thousands of variables and millions of combinations of variables, how do you decide what to test? There is no magic formula. My advice is to follow every hunch you get. Some researchers insist that you have a good theoretical reason for including variables in your design and that you have a theory-driven reason to test for relations among variables once you have data. They point out that anyone can make up an explanation for any relation or lack of relation after seeing a table of data or a correlation coefficient.

This is very good advice, but I think it's a bit too restrictive, for three reasons:

(1) I think that data analysis should be lots of fun, and it can't be unless it's based on following your hunches. Most relations are easy to explain, and peculiar relations beg for theories to explain them. You just have to be very careful not to conjure up support for every statistically significant relation, merely because it happens to turn up. There is a delicate balance between being clever enough to explain an unexpected finding and just plain reaching too far. As usual, there is no substitute for thinking hard about your data.

(2) It is really up to you during research design to be as clever as you can in thinking up variables to test. You're entitled to include some variables in your research just because you think they might come in handy. Of course, you can overdo it. There is nothing more tedious than an interview that drones on for hours without any obvious point other than that the researcher is gathering data on as many variables as possible.

(3) The source of ideas has no necessary effect on their usefulness. You can get ideas from an existing theory or from browsing through data tables—or from talking about research problems with your friends. The important thing is not how you get a hunch, it's whether you can test your hunches and create plausible explanations for whatever findings come out of those tests. If others disagree with your explanations, then let them demonstrate that you are wrong, either by reanalyzing your data or by producing new data. But stumbling onto a significant relation between some variables does nothing to invalidate the relation.

So, when you design your research, try to think about the kinds of variables that might be useful in testing your hunches. Use the principles in Chapter 3 and consider internal state variables (attitudes, values, beliefs); external state variables (age, height, gender, race, health status, occupation, wealth status, etc.); physical and cultural environmental variables (rainfall, socioeconomic class of a neighborhood, etc.); and time or space variables (Have attitudes changed over time? Do the people in one community behave differently from those in another otherwise similar community?).

In a world of thousands of variables and millions of combinations of variables, how do you decide what to test?

In applied research, important variables are the ones that let you "target" a policy—that is, focus intervention efforts on subpopulations of interest (the rural elderly, victims of violent crime, over-achieving third graders, etc.)—or that are more amenable to policy manipulation (knowledge is far more manipulable than attitudes or behavior, for example). No matter what the purposes of your research, or how you design it, the two principal rules of data analysis are

(1) If you have an idea, test it.
(2) You can't test it if you don't have data on it.

Chapter 16
Review

KEY CONCEPTS

Elaboration method, 614-615
Control variables, 614-619
Subtables, 615
Partial correlation, 615-620
Zero-order correlation, 618
Symmetrical and asymmetrical matrices, 619
Partialling out effects, 619
First-order, second-order correlation, 621
Multiple regression, 620-627
Multiple R, 620
Multiple R^2, 620
Residuals, 622
Regression coefficients, 624
Stepwise multiple regression, 626
Path analysis, 627-631
Path coefficients, 628
Multicollinearity, 632-634

Condition indexes, 632
Factor analysis, 634-639
Factors, 635
Orthogonal solution, 636
Multidimensional scaling, 639-645
Similarities, 640
Dissimilarities, 641
Proximity matrices, 641
Individual similarity matrix, 643
Arrays, or dimensions, 644
Clumps, or clusters, 644
Property fitting analysis, 645
Cluster analysis, 645-648
Dissimilarity matrix, 646
Single-link (closest-neighbor) solution, 646
Complete-link (farthest-neighbor) solution, 646
Discriminant function analysis, 648-649

SUMMARY

❖ Most social phenomena are complex. The goal of multivariate analysis is to explain *how* variables are related and to develop a theory of causation that accounts for the fact that variables are related to one another.

 ◆ Multivariate analysis is not a single method, but involves an array of statistical procedures.

❖ The elaboration method involves teasing out the complexities in a bivariate relation by controlling for the effects of antecedent or intervening variables.

 ◆ When we control for antecedent variables like sex, a bivariate relation may continue to hold, but it may also vanish for members of one sex.

 ◆ Alternatively, when we control for antecedent variables like sex, a nonexistent bivariate relation may emerge for members of one sex.

❖ Partial correlation is a direct way to control for the effects of a third (or fourth or fifth, etc.) variable on a relation between two variables.

 ◆ For example, when we partial out the effect of a third variable, a zero-order bivariate relation may change dramatically, one way or the other. And when we partial out the effect of income, the correlation between the rate of motor vehicle deaths and teenage births across the 50 states of the U.S. drops from about .78 to about .67. This is because income is correlated strongly with motor vehicle deaths and with teenage births.

❖ Multiple regression puts all the information about a series of variables together into a single equation that takes account of the interrelation among independent variables.

 ◆ The result of multiple regression is a statistic called multiple *R*, which is the combined correlation of a set of independent variables with the dependent variable, taking into account the fact that each of the independent variables might be correlated with each of the other independent variables.

 ◆ Multiple R^2 is the amount of variance in the dependent variable accounted for by two or more independent variables simultaneously.

 ◆ A typical question for a multiple regression analysis might be "How well can we predict people's starting salary if we know how many years of college they have, *and* their major, *and* their gender, *and* their age, *and* their ethnic background?"

 ◆ Multiple regression typically accounts for 30%–50% of the variance in any dependent variable, using between two and eight independent variables. This may seem like a small amount, but the implications, both theoretical and practical, of really understanding a piece of a complex social research puzzle can be very important.

❖ Path analysis is a method for testing theories about how the independent variables in a multiple regression equation may be influencing each other.

 ◆ Path analysis lets you test a particular theory about the relations among a system of variables, but it doesn't produce the theory. You have to do that.

 ◆ Path coefficients are standardized values. They show the influence of multiple independent variables on the dependent variables in terms of standard deviations.

❖ In multivariate models, independent variables can be correlated. This multicollinearity means that you can't tell the influence of an independent variable free from influence by other independent variables with which it is correlated.

❖ Factor analysis is a set of techniques for information packaging and data reduction. The idea is that if some things are correlated with each other, they must have something in common. That thing in common is called a factor.

 ◆ Factor analysis is used across the social sciences in the construction of personality and achievement tests and in exploring large data sets to extract a few variables that tell a big story.

 ◆ Factors account for chunks of variance in a data matrix. The most common method for finding the underlying factors in a matrix is called the orthogonal solution, in which factors are found that have as little correlation with each other as possible.

 ◆ Factor loadings are the correlations between the new factors and the old variables that are replaced by factors. All the old variables "load" on each new factor. By convention, variables that load at least 0.60 on a factor unambiguously represent that factor, and variables between 0.30 and 0.59 are worth considering.

❖ Multidimensional scaling (MDS) is another multivariate data-reduction technique. Like factor analysis, it is used to tease out underlying relations among a set of observations. Unlike factor analysis, MDS does not require metric data.

 ◆ The "stress" in an MDS solution is a measure of how far off the graph it is from one that would be perfectly proportional. The lower the stress, the better the solution. This means that a cluster of variables in an MDS graph with low stress is likely to reflect some reality about the cognitive world of the people being studied.

 ◆ Interpreting MDS graphs involves looking for dimensions and clusters. Dimensions do not have to be at right angles to each other. Interpretation means figuring out what the dimensions and the clumps are.

❖ Like factor analysis and MDS, cluster analysis is a descriptive tool for exploring relations among items in a matrix. Factoring explores how underlying variables may encompass the variables in the original data. MDS provides a graphic display of relations among items. Clustering tells you which items go together and in what order.

 ◆ Different algorithms for clustering produce different solutions. Interpreting these different solutions is the challenge for analysis.

❖ Discriminant function analysis (DFA) is used to classify cases into categorical variables from ordinal and interval variables.

  ◆ While DFA is a powerful classification device, it is not a prediction device. Still, many problems in the social sciences are essentially about understanding things so you can classify them correctly.

❖ Finally, it's good to remember that anyone can make up an explanation for any relation or lack of relation after seeing a table of data or a correlation coefficient.

  ◆ This means that you have to be very careful not to conjure up support for every statistically significant relation, merely because it happens to turn up.

  ◆ It doesn't mean that you have to back off. Conjuring up ideas and testing them is great fun and very productive.

EXERCISES

1. Immediately following the presidential election of 1996, the Bureau of Business and Economic Research at the University of Florida surveyed Florida's voters. Median annual income for the sample of 438 respondents was $40,000. In the following tables, INCOME = 1 is at or below the median. INCOME = 2 is above the median. VOTE = 1 means the respondent voted for Bill Clinton. VOTE = 2 means the respondent voted for George Bush or Ross Perot.

   Interpret the following tables:

TABLE A　Who People Voted for by Median Income

| | INCOME | | |
VOTE	Equal To or Less Than $40,000 Per Year	More Than $40,000 Per Year	Total
Clinton	141	94	235
Bush or Perot	92	111	203
Total	233	205	438

$\chi^2 = 9.427, p < .002$

TABLE B　Who People Voted for by Median Income, Men Only

| | INCOME | | |
VOTE	Equal To or Less Than $40,000 Per Year	More Than $40,000 Per Year	Total
Clinton	55	47	102
Bush or Perot	51	66	117
Total	106	113	219

$\chi^2 = 2.329, p < .127$

TABLE C　Who People Voted for by Median Income, Women Only

| | INCOME | | |
VOTE	Equal To or Less Than $40,000 Per Year	More Than $40,000 Per Year	Total
Clinton	86	47	133
Bush or Perot	41	45	86
Total	127	92	219

$\chi^2 = 6.187, p < .013$

SOURCE: Tables A, B, C: Bureau of Business and Economic Research, University of Florida.

Of the 499 original respondents, 438 provided data for both variables and were eligible for this cross-tab. Perot voters comprise 6.8% of the sample. How could you test whether combining them accounts for the results in these tables?

2. Here is the output of a multiple regression. The dependent variable, TFR, is the estimated total fertility rate for 1995-2000 of women in 187 countries around the world. The independent variables are the life expectancy of women in those countries (LEXFEM), the log of the per capita gross domestic product (LOGPCGDP), and the log of the informant mortality rate for those countries (LOGINFMORT). These data are from the United Nations Statistics Division Internet site on social indicators for countries of the world (http://www.un.org/Depts/unsd/social/main.htm).

Write the regression equation for predicting TFR. The standard coefficient for LEXFEM is negative. Explain what this means.

```
Dep Var: TFR  N: 187  Multiple R: 0.870  Squared multiple R: 0.757

Adjusted squared multiple R: 0.753  Standard error of estimate: 0.871

Effect      Coefficient Std Error Std Coef Tolerance   t    P(2 Tail)

CONSTANT       6.713     1.510     0.000              4.445   0.000
LEXFEM        -0.102     0.013    -0.643    0.196    -7.823   0.000
LOGPCGDP       0.196     0.068     0.185    0.328     2.907   0.004
LOGINFMORT     0.673     0.163     0.392    0.147     4.136   0.000
```

3. Here is a multidimensional scaling plot of similarity data about 15 animals. These data come from pile sorts. The stress in this two-dimensional plot is less than 0.10. Interpret this graph. Point out and name the clusters. Interpret the position of dog and cat and interpret the position of alligator.

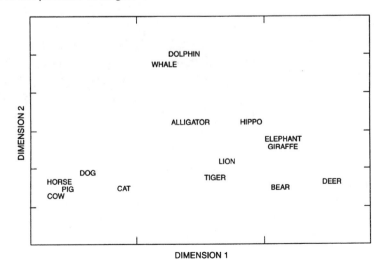

FURTHER READING

Multiple regression. For a general overview of multiple regression in the social sciences, see Pedhazur (1997). For details on regression diagnostics, see Belsley et al. (1980) and Fox (1991).

Path analysis. Pearson and Chong (1997) used path analysis to test a model of job satisfaction among Malaysian nurses. Their results show that Malaysian nurses rely more on the character of interpersonal relations on the job and less on characteristics of the job content than do Western workers. Opotow (1994) showed that our ideas about the "scope of justice" play an intermediary role between objective characteristics of animals (like how intelligent or how helpful to humans animals are) and our willingness to argue the case for protecting those animals. Aryee (1993) studied stress and burnout in 95 dual-earner couples in Singapore. He found that (1) burnout in wives was influenced significantly by work and nonwork stressors, but that (2) burnout in husbands is mostly due to on-the-job stressors. The wives, of course, are doing double duty as homemakers and by working full time at a paying job as well. Some things are apparently, and dismally, the same in Singapore as they are Western countries.

Factor analysis. For a general introduction to factor analysis, see Gorsuch (1983) and Kline (1994). See Mulaik (1987) on the philosophical foundations of factor analysis.

Factor analysis has a long history of use in the study of cognitive and personality variables. See Carroll (1993) and Cattell and Kline (1977). On the use of factor analysis in business research, see Heck (1998). Some examples of recent psychological tests developed with factor analysis include the Center for Epidemiological Studies-Depression Scale (Helmes and Nielson 1998) and a test of scales to measure social anxiety and social phobias (Safren et al. 1998).

Multidimensional scaling. For an overview of MDS, see Kruskal and Wish (1978) and Romney et al. (1972). MDS has long been used in marketing research (Green and Carmone 1970; Henderson et al. 1998) and in cognitive anthropology (Romney et al. 1972; Boster and Johnson 1989), and it is becoming more widely used in political science. After the collapse of the Soviet Union in 1991, there were important realignments of voting blocs at the United Nations. Holloway and Tomlinson (1995) used MDS and cluster analysis to plot changes in voting blocs at the United Nations between 1985 and 1991 (when the Soviet Union collapsed).

Researchers in psychology and social psychology have begun recently to use MDS instead of, or along with, factor analysis for building scales. Davison and Skay (1991) compare MDS and factor analysis in selecting items for an intelligence test. Popovich et al. (1997) used MDS to develop a scale of how obese people are judged in the workplace.

Property fitting analysis. PROFIT, or PROperty FITting analysis, is a method for testing hypotheses about dimensions in an MDS plot of similarity data. If data are collected by asking people to make direct similarity judgments (as is the case, for example, with pile sorts, triad tests, and paired comparisons; see Chapter 7), then PROFIT is a way to test ideas about what respondents must have been thinking when they made those judgments. For a detailed example, see Weller (1983).

Cluster analysis. For an overview of cluster analysis, see Aldenderfer and Blashfield (1984) and Lorr (1983). ENRICH is a set of scales used widely by counselors for evaluating marriages. Lavee and Olson (1993) used cluster analysis on data from a national sample of 8,385 married couples who had taken the ENRICH scales. The analysis sorts marriages into seven interesting clusters: devitalized couples (who are dissatisfied on all nine dimensions of marriage included in the analysis); financially focused couples (whose focus on financial management is the one great strength of their relationship); and so on.

Discriminant function analysis. Based on fine-grained observation of how 72 married couples talked to each other, Gottman and Levenson (1992) used DFA to classify the couples as having more positive than negative or more negative than positive interactions. Based on demographic data and data from a battery of psychological assessments, Anderson and Walsh (1998) were able to classify correctly 80% of juvenile offenders as either guilty or not guilty of a serious offense nine years after the youths were originally arrested.

APPENDIX A
TABLE OF RANDOM NUMBERS

10097	32533	76520	13586	34673	54876	80959	09117	39292	74945
37542	04805	64894	74296	24805	24037	20636	10402	00822	91665
08422	68953	19645	09303	23209	02560	15953	34764	35080	33606
99019	02529	09376	70715	28311	31165	88676	74397	04436	27659
12807	99970	80157	36147	64032	36653	98951	16877	12171	76833
66065	74717	34072	76850	36697	36170	65813	39885	11199	29170
31060	10805	45571	82406	35303	42614	86799	07439	23403	09732
85269	77602	02051	65692	68665	74818	73053	85247	18623	88579
63573	32135	05325	47048	90553	57548	28468	28709	83491	25624
73796	45753	03529	64778	35808	34282	60935	20344	35273	88435
98520	17767	14905	68607	22109	40558	60970	93433	50500	73998
11805	05431	39808	27732	50725	68248	29405	24201	52775	67851
83452	99634	06288	98083	13746	70078	18475	40610	68711	77817
88685	40200	86507	58401	36766	67951	90364	76493	29609	11062
99594	67348	87517	64969	91826	08928	93785	61368	23478	34113
65481	17674	17468	50950	58047	76974	73039	57186	40218	16544
80124	35635	17727	08015	45318	22374	21115	78253	14385	53763
74350	99817	77402	77214	43236	00210	45521	64237	96286	02655
69916	26803	66252	29148	36936	87203	76621	13990	94400	56418
09893	20505	14225	68514	46427	56788	96297	78822	54382	14598
91499	14523	68479	27686	46162	83554	94750	89923	37089	20048
80336	94598	26940	36858	70297	34135	53140	33340	42050	82341
44104	81949	85157	47954	32979	26575	57600	40881	22222	06413
12550	73742	11100	02040	12860	74697	96644	89439	28707	25815
63606	49329	16505	34484	40219	52563	43651	77082	07207	31790
61196	90446	26457	47774	51924	33729	65394	59593	42582	60527
15474	45266	95270	79953	59367	83848	82396	10118	33211	59466
94557	28573	67897	54387	54622	44431	91190	42592	92927	45973
42481	16213	97344	08721	16868	48767	03071	12059	25701	46670
23523	78317	73208	89837	68935	91416	26252	29663	05522	82562
04493	52494	75246	33824	45862	51025	61962	79335	65337	12472
00549	97654	64051	88159	96119	63896	54692	82391	23287	29529
35963	15307	26898	09354	33351	35462	77974	50024	90103	39333
59808	08391	45427	26842	83609	49700	13021	24892	78565	20106
46058	85236	01390	92286	77281	44077	93910	83647	70617	42941
32179	00597	87379	25241	05567	07007	86743	17157	85394	11838
69234	61406	20117	45204	15956	60000	18743	92423	97118	96338
19565	41430	01758	75379	40419	21585	66674	36806	84962	85207
45155	14938	19476	07246	43667	94543	59047	90033	20826	69541
94864	31994	36168	10851	34888	81553	01540	35456	05014	51176
98086	24826	45240	28404	44999	08896	39094	73407	35441	31880
33185	16232	41941	50949	89435	48581	88695	41994	37548	73043
80951	00406	96382	70774	20151	23387	25016	25298	94624	61171
79752	49140	71961	28296	69861	02591	74852	20539	00387	59579
18633	32537	98145	06571	31010	24674	05455	61427	77938	91936

(continued)

APPENDIX A   Continued

74029	43902	77557	32270	97790	17119	52527	58021	80814	51748
54178	45611	80993	37143	05335	12969	56127	19255	36040	90324
11664	49883	52079	84827	59381	71539	09973	33440	88461	23356
48324	77928	31249	64710	02295	36870	32307	57546	15020	09994
69074	94138	87637	91976	35584	04401	10518	21615	01848	76938
90089	90249	62196	53754	61007	39513	71877	19088	94091	97084
70413	74646	24580	74929	94902	71143	01816	06557	74936	44506
17022	85475	76454	97145	31850	33650	75223	90607	15520	39823
24906	46977	78868	59973	61110	13047	84302	15982	72731	82300
50222	97585	15161	11327	66712	76500	81055	43716	93343	02797
60291	56491	75093	71017	92139	21562	67305	33066	60719	20033
31485	66220	71939	23182	44059	00289	17996	05268	97659	02611
16551	13457	83006	43096	71235	29381	93168	46668	30723	29437
90831	40282	48952	90899	87567	14411	31483	78232	52117	57484
19195	94881	99625	59598	33330	34405	45601	39005	65170	48419
06056	81764	46911	33370	35719	30207	61967	08086	40073	75215
46044	94342	04346	25157	73062	41921	82742	70481	83376	28856
03690	95581	83895	32069	94196	93097	97900	79905	79610	68639
23532	45828	02575	70187	64732	95799	20005	44543	08965	58907
81365	88745	79117	66599	32463	76925	70223	80849	48500	92536
57660	57584	14276	10166	82132	61861	63597	91025	76338	06878
13619	18065	33262	41774	33145	69671	14920	62061	42352	61546
07155	33924	34103	48785	28604	75023	46564	44875	07478	61678
19705	73768	44407	66609	00883	56229	50882	76601	50403	18003
04233	69951	33035	72878	61494	38754	63112	34005	82115	72073
79786	96081	42535	47848	84053	38522	55756	20382	67816	84693
76421	34950	98800	04822	57743	40616	73751	36521	34591	68549
28120	11330	46035	36097	93141	90483	83329	51529	94974	86242
45012	95348	64843	44570	26086	57925	52060	86496	44979	45833
45251	99242	98656	72488	35515	08968	46711	56846	29418	15329
97318	06337	19410	09936	28536	08458	90982	66566	30286	27797
55895	62683	25132	51771	70516	05063	69361	75727	48522	89141
80181	03112	21819	10421	35725	92004	36822	18679	51605	48064
39423	21649	18389	01344	36548	07702	85187	75037	89625	39524
37040	87608	46311	03712	42044	33852	52206	86204	99714	82241
72664	17872	02627	65809	17307	97355	60006	18166	51375	79461
71584	11935	87348	22204	93483	37555	31381	23640	31469	92988
87697	30854	25509	22665	31581	12507	53679	26381	48023	47916
73663	27869	40208	40672	83210	48573	22406	46286	46987	12017
51544	01914	17431	97024	09620	54225	44529	90758	11151	98314
82670	82296	96903	45286	85145	60329	27682	64892	75961	19800
30051	16942	17241	93593	75336	48698	48564	76832	29214	84972
23338	01489	39942	06609	14070	07351	28226	51996	31244	10725
08739	21034	57145	25526	58145	72334	87799	95132	70300	88277
76383	52236	07587	14161	82994	22829	72713	70265	88650	56335

05933	81888	32534	56269	12889	05092	84159	40971	46430	86981
10347	07364	51963	31851	45463	41635	10195	18961	17515	34021
36102	55172	25170	81955	25621	25030	19781	48300	79319	34377
70791	56165	64310	28625	26760	82203	26535	99580	77676	91021
88525	67427	59554	42220	27202	18827	33362	90584	99516	72258
41221	71024	99746	77782	53452	52851	35104	20732	16072	72468
40771	10858	31707	46962	71427	85412	49561	93011	64079	38527
09913	14509	46399	82692	05526	19955	02385	85686	62040	39386
00420	06149	01688	72365	12603	83142	98814	66265	98583	93424
90748	19314	55032	64625	47855	32726	69744	54536	16494	33623

SOURCE: RAND Corporation, *A Million Random Digits with 100,000 Normal Deviates,* 1965,1985. New York: Free Press.

APPENDIX B
TABLE OF AREAS UNDER A NORMAL CURVE

(A) z	(B) area between mean and z	(C) area beyond z	(A) z	(B) area between mean and z	(C) area beyond z	(A) z	(B) area between mean and z	(C) area beyond z
0.00	.0000	.5000	0.40	.1554	.3446	0.80	.2881	.2119
0.01	.0040	.4960	0.41	.1591	.3409	0.81	.2910	.2090
0.02	.0080	.4920	0.42	.1628	.3372	0.82	.2939	.2061
0.03	.0120	.4880	0.43	.1664	.3336	0.83	.2967	.2033
0.04	.0160	.4840	0.44	.1700	.3300	0.84	.2995	.2005
0.05	.0199	.4801	0.45	.1736	.3264	0.85	.3023	.1977
0.06	.0239	.4761	0.46	.1772	.3228	0.86	.3051	.1949
0.07	.0279	.4721	0.47	.1808	.3192	0.87	.3078	.1922
0.08	.0319	.4681	0.48	.1844	.3156	0.88	.3106	.1894
0.09	.0359	.4641	0.49	.1879	.3121	0.89	.3133	.1867
0.10	.0398	.4602	0.50	.1915	.3085	0.90	.3159	.1841
0.11	.0438	.4562	0.51	.1950	-.3050	0.91	.3186	.1814
0.12	.0478	.4522	0.52	.1985	.3015	0.92	.3212	.1788
0.13	.0517	.4483	0.53	.2019	.2981	0.93	.3238	.1762
0.14	.0557	.4443	0.54	.2054	.2946	0.94	.3264	.1736
0.15	.0596	.4404	0.55	.2088	.2912	0.95	.3289	.1711
0.16	.0636	.4364	0.56	.2123	.2877	0.96	.3315	.1685
0.17	.0675	.4325	0.57	.2157	.2843	0.97	.3340	.1660
0.18	.0714	.4286	0.58	.2190	.2810	0.98	.3365	.1635
0.19	.0753	.4247	0.59	.2224	.2776	0.99	.3389	.1611
0.20	.0793	.4207	0.60	.2257	.2743	1.00	.3413	.1587
0.21	.0832	.4168	0.61	.2291	.2709	1.01	.3438	.1562
0.22	.0871	.4129	0.62	.2324	.2676	1.02	.3461	.1539
0.23	.0910	.4090	0.63	.2357	.2643	1.03	.3485	.1515
0.24	.0948	.4052	0.64	.2389	.2611	1.04	.3508	.1492
0.25	.0987	.4013	0.65	.2422	.2578	1.05	.3531	.1469
0.26	.1026	.3974	0.66	.2454	.2546	1.06	.3554	.1446
0.27	.1064	.3936	0.67	.2486	.2514	1.07	.3577	.1423
0.28	.1103	.3897	0.68	.2517	.2483	1.08	.3599	.1401
0.29	.1141	.3859	0.69	.2549	.2451	1.09	.3621	.1379
0.30	.1179	.3821	0.70	.2580	.2420	1.10	.3643	.1357
0.31	.1217	.3783	0.71	.2611	.2389	1.11	.3665	.1335
0.32	.1255	.3745	0.72	.2642	.2358	1.12	.3686	.1314
0.33	.1293	.3707	0.73	.2673	.2327	1.13	.3708	.1292
0.34	.1331	.3669	0.74	.2704	.2296	1.14	.3729	.1271
0.35	.1368	.3632	0.75	.2734	.2266	1.15	.3749	.1251
0.36	.1406	.3594	0.76	.2764	.2236	1.16	.3770	.1230
0.37	.1443	.3557	0.77	.2794	.2206	1.17	.3790	.1210
0.38	.1480	.3520	0.78	.2823	.2177	1.18	.3810	.1190
0.39	.1517	.3483	0.79	.2852	.2148	1.19	.3830	.1170

(A) z	(B) area between mean and z	(C) area beyond z	(A) z	(B) area between mean and z	(C) area beyond z	(A) z	(B) area between mean and z	(C) area beyond z
1.20	.3849	.1151	1.61	.4463	.0537	2.02	.4783	.0217
1.21	.3869	.1131	1.62	.4474	.0526	2.03	.4788	.0212
1.22	.3888	.1112	1.63	.4484	.0516	2.04	.4793	.0207
1.23	.3907	.1093	1.64	.4495	.0505	2.05	.4798	.0202
1.24	.3925	.1075	1.65	.4505	.0495	2.06	.4803	.0197
1.25	.3944	.1056	1.66	.4515	.0485	2.07	.4808	.0192
1.26	.3962	.1038	1.67	.4525	.0475	2.08	.4812	.0188
1.27	.3980	.1020	1.68	.4535	.0465	2.09	.4817	.0183
1.28	.3997	.1003	1.69	.4545	.0455	2.10	.4821	.0179
1.29	.4015	.0985	1.70	.4554	.0446	2.11	.4826	.0174
1.30	.4032	.0968	1.71	.4564	.0436	2.12	.4830	.0170
1.31	.4049	.0951	1.72	.4573	.0427	2.13	.4834	.0166
1.32	.4066	.0934	1.73	.4582	.0418	2.14	.4838	.0162
1.33	.4082	.0918	1.74	.4591	.0409	2.15	.4842	.0158
1.34	.4099	.0901	1.75	.4599	.0401	2.16	.4846	.0154
1.35	.4115	.0885	1.76	.4608	.0392	2.17	.4850	.0150
1.36	.4131	.0869	1.77	.4616	.0384	2.18	.4854	.0146
1.37	.4147	.0853	1.78	.4625	.0375	2.19	.4857	.0143
1.38	.4162	.0838	1.79	.4633	.0367	2.20	.4861	.0139
1.39	.4177	.0823	1.80	.4641	.0359	2.21	.4864	.0136
1.40	.4192	.0808	1.81	.4649	.0351	2.22	.4868	.0132
1.41	.4207	.0793	1.82	.4656	.0344	2.23	.4871	.0129
1.42	.4222	.0778	1.83	.4664	.0336	2.24	.4875	.0125
1.43	.4236	.0764	1.84	.4671	.0329	2.25	.4878	.0122
1.44	.4251	.0749	1.85	.4678	.0322	2.26	.4881	.0119
1.45	.4265	.0735	1.86	.4686	.0314	2.27	.4884	.0116
1.46	.4279	.0721	1.87	.4693	.0307	2.28	.4887	.0113
1.47	.4292	.0708	1.88	.4699	.0301	2.29	.4890	.0110
1.48	.4306	.0694	1.89	.4706	.0294	2.30	.4893	.0107
1.49	.4319	.0681	1.90	.4713	.0287	2.31	.4896	.0104
1.50	.4332	.0668	1.91	.4719	.0281	2.32	.4898	.0102
1.51	.4345	.0655	1.92	.4726	.0274	2.33	.4901	.0099
1.52	.4357	.0643	1.93	.4732	.0268	2.34	.4904	.0096
1.53	.4370	.0630	1.94	.4738	.0262	2.35	.4906	.0094
1.54	.4382	.0618	1.95	.4744	.0256	2.36	.4909	.0091
1.55	.4394	.0606	1.96	.4750	.0250	2.37	.4911	.0089
1.56	.4406	.0594	1.97	.4756	.0244	2.38	.4913	.0087
1.57	.4418	.0582	1.98	.4761	.0239	2.39	.4916	.0084
1.58	.4429	.0571	1.99	.4767	.0233	2.40	.4918	.0082
1.59	.4441	.0559	2.00	.4772	.0228	2.41	.4920	.0080
1.60	.4452	.0548	2.01	.4778	.0222	2.42	.4922	.0078

(continued)

APPENDIX B Continued

(A) z	(B) area between mean and z	(C) area beyond z	(A) z	(B) area between mean and z	(C) area beyond z	(A) z	(B) area between mean and z	(C) area beyond z
2.43	.4925	.0075	2.74	.4969	.0031	3.05	.4989	.0011
2.44	.4927	.0073	2.75	.4970	.0030	3.06	.4989	.0011
2.45	.4929	.0071	2.76	.4971	.0029	3.07	.4989	.0011
2.46	.4931	.0069	2.77	.4972	.0028	3.08	.4990	.0010
2.47	.4932	.0068	2.78	.4973	.0027	3.09	.4990	.0010
2.48	.4934	.0066	2.79	.4974	.0026	3.10	.4990	.0010
2.49	.4936	.0064	2.80	.4974	.0026	3.11	.4991	.0009
2.50	.4938	.0062	2.81	.4975	.0025	3.12	.4991	.0009
2.51	.4940	.0060	2.82	.4976	.0024	3.13	.4991	.0009
2.52	.4941	.0059	2.83	.4977	.0023	3.14	.4992	.0008
2.53	.4943	.0057	2.84	.4977	.0023	3.15	.4992	.0008
2.54	.4945	.0055	2.85	.4978	.0022	3.16	.4992	.0008
2.55	.4946	.0054	2.86	.4979	.0021	3.17	.4992	.0008
2.56	.4948	.0052	2.87	.4979	.0021	3.18	.4993	.0007
2.57	.4949	.0051	2.88	.4980	.0020	3.19	.4993	.0007
2.58	.4951	.0049	2.89	.4981	.0019	3.20	.4993	.0007
2.59	.4952	.0048	2.90	.4981	.0019	3.21	.4993	.0007
2.60	.4953	.0047	2.91	.4982	.0018	3.22	.4994	.0006
2.61	.4955	.0045	2.92	.4982	.0018	3.23	.4994	.0006
2.62	.4956	.0044	2.93	.4983	.0017	3.24	.4994	.0006
2.63	.4957	.0043	2.94	.4984	.0016	3.25	.4994	.0006
2.64	.4959	.0041	2.95	.4984	.0016	3.30	.4995	.0005
2.65	.4960	.0040	2.96	.4985	.0015	3.35	.4996	.0004
2.66	.4961	.0039	2.97	.4985	.0015	3.40	.4997	.0003
2.67	.4962	.0038	2.98	.4986	.0014	3.45	.4997	.0003
2.68	.4963	.0037	2.99	.4986	.0014	3.50	.4998	.0002
2.69	.4964	.0036	3.00	.4987	.0013	3.60	.4998	.0002
2.70	.4965	.0035	3.01	.4987	.0013	3.70	.4999	.0001
2.71	.4966	.0034	3.02	.4987	.0013	3.80	.4999	.0001
2.72	.4967	.0033	3.03	.4988	.0012	3.90	.49995	.00005
2.73	.4968	.0032	3.04	.4988	.0012	4.00	.49997	.00003

SOURCE: *Statistical Tables and Formulas*, Table 1, p. 3, 1981. New York: John Wiley. Reprinted by permission of A. Hald.

APPENDIX C
STUDENT'S t DISTRIBUTION

	Level of Significance for one-tailed test					
	.10	.05	.025	.01	.005	.0005
	Level of Significance for two-tailed test					
df	.20	.10	.05	.02	.01	.001
1	3.078	6.314	12.706	31.821	63.657	636.619
2	1.886	2.920	4.303	6.965	9.925	31.598
3	1.638	2.353	3.182	4.541	5.841	12.941
4	1.533	2.132	2.776	3.747	4.604	8.610
5	1.476	2.015	2.571	3.365	4.032	6.859
6	1.440	1.943	2.447	3.143	3.707	5.959
7	1.415	1.895	2.365	2.998	3.499	5.405
8	1.397	1.860	2.306	2.896	3.355	5.041
9	1.383	1.833	2.262	2.821	3.250	4.781
10	1.372	1.812	2.228	2.764	3.169	4.587
11	1.363	1.796	2.201	2.718	3.106	4.437
12	1.356	1.782	2.179	2.681	3.055	4.318
13	1.350	1.771	2.160	2.650	3.012	4.221
14	1.345	1.761	2.145	2.624	2.977	4.140
15	1.341	1.753	2.131	2.602	2.947	4.073
16	1.337	1.746	2.120	2.583	2.921	4.015
17	1.333	1.740	2.110	2.567	2.898	3.965
18	1.330	1.734	2.101	2.552	2.878	3.922
19	1.328	1.729	2.093	2.539	2.861	3.883
20	1.325	1.725	2.086	2.528	2.845	3.850
21	1.323	1.721	2.080	2.518	2.831	3.819
22	1.321	1.717	2.074	2.508	2.819	3.792
23	1.319	1.714	2.069	2.500	2.807	3.767
24	1.318	1.711	2.064	2.492	2.797	3.745
25	1.316	1.708	2.060	2.485	2.787	3.725
26	1.315	1.706	2.056	2.479	2.779	3.707
27	1.314	1.703	2.052	2.473	2.771	3.690
28	1.313	1.701	2.048	2.467	2.763	3.674
29	1.311	1.699	2.045	2.462	2.756	3.659
30	1.310	1.697	2.042	2.457	2.750	3.646
40	1.303	1.684	2.021	2.423	2.704	3.551
60	1.296	1.671	2.000	2.390	2.660	3.460
120	1.289	1.658	1.980	2.358	2.617	3.373
∞	1.282	1.645	1.960	2.326	2.567	3.291

SOURCE: R. A. Fisher and F. Yates, *Statistical Tables for Biological, Agricultural and Medical Research*, 1974, Table III, London: Longman. Reprinted by permission of Pearson Education Limited.

APPENDIX D
CHI-SQUARE DISTRIBUTION TABLE

			Probabilities			
df	.99	.95	.90	.80	.70	.50
1	.000157	.00393	.0158	.0642	.148	.455
2	.0201	.103	.211	.446	.713	1.386
3	.115	.352	.584	1.005	1.424	2.366
4	.297	.711	1.064	1.649	2.195	3.357
5	.554	1.145	1.610	2.343	3.000	4.351
6	.872	1.635	2.204	3.070	3.828	5.348
7	1.239	2.167	2.833	3.822	4.671	6.346
8	1.646	2.733	3.490	4.594	5.527	7.344
9	2.088	3.325	4.168	5.380	6.393	8.343
10	2.558	3.940	4.865	6.179	7.267	9.342
11	3.053	4.575	5.578	6.989	8.148	10.341
12	3.571	5.226	6.304	7.807	9.034	11.340
13	4.107	5.892	7.042	8.634	9.926	12.340
14	4.660	6.571	7.790	9.467	10.821	13.339
15	5.229	7.261	8.547	10.307	11.721	14.339
16	5.812	7.962	9.312	11.152	12.624	15.338
17	6.408	8.672	10.085	12.002	13.531	16.338
18	7.015	9.390	10.865	12.857	14.440	17.338
19	7.633	10.117	11.651	13.716	15.352	18.338
20	8.260	10.851	12.443	14.578	16.266	19.337
21	8.897	11.591	13.240	15.445	17.182	20.337
22	9.542	12.338	14.041	16.314	18.101	21.337
23	10.196	13.091	14.848	17.187	19.021	22.337
24	10.865	13.848	15.659	18.062	19.943	23.337
25	11.524	14.611	16.473	18.940	20.867	24.337
26	12.198	15.379	17.292	19.820	21.792	25.336
27	12.879	16.151	18.114	20.703	22.719	26.336
28	13.565	16.928	18.939	21.588	23.647	27.336
29	14.256	17.708	19.768	22.475	24.577	28.336
30	14.953	18.493	20.599	23.364	25.508	29.336

			Probabilities				
df	.30	.20	.10	.05	.025	.01	.001
1	1.074	1.642	2.706	3.841	5.024	6.635	10.827
2	2.408	3.219	4.605	5.991	7.378	9.210	13.815
3	3.665	4.624	6.251	7.815	9.348	11.345	16.268
4	4.878	5.989	7.779	9.488	11.143	13.277	18.465
5	6.064	7.289	9.236	11.070	12.832	15.086	20.517
6	7.231	8.558	10.645	12.592	14.449	16.812	22.457
7	8.383	9.803	12.017	14.067	16.013	18.475	24.322
8	9.524	11.030	13.362	15.507	17.535	20.090	26.125
9	10.656	12.242	14.684	16.919	19.023	21.666	27.877
10	11.781	13.442	15.987	18.307	20.483	23.209	29.588
11	12.899	14.631	17.275	19.675	21.920	24.725	31.264
12	14.011	15.812	18.549	21.026	23.337	26.217	32.909
13	15.119	16.985	19.812	22.362	24.736	27.688	34.528
14	16.222	18.151	21.064	23.685	26.119	29.141	36.123
15	17.322	19.311	22.307	24.996	27.488	30.578	37.697
16	18.418	20.465	23.542	26.296	28.845	32.000	39.252
17	19.511	21.615	24.769	27.587	30.191	33.409	40.790
18	20.601	22.760	25.989	28.869	31.526	34.805	42.312
19	21.689	23.900	27.204	30.144	32.852	36.191	43.820
20	22.775	25.038	28.412	31.410	34.170	37.566	45.315
21	23.858	26.171	29.615	32.671	35.479	38.932	46.797
22	24.939	27.301	30.813	33.924	36.781	40.289	48.268
23	26.018	28.429	32.007	35.172	38.076	41.638	49.728
24	27.096	29.553	33.196	36.415	39.364	42.980	51.179
25	28.172	30.675	34.382	37.652	40.646	44.314	52.620
26	29.246	31.795	35.563	38.885	41.923	45.642	54.052
27	30.319	32.912	36.741	40.113	43.194	46.963	55.476
28	31.391	34.027	37.916	41.337	44.461	48.278	56.893
29	32.461	35.139	39.087	42.557	45.722	49.588	58.302
30	33.530	36.250	40.256	43.773	46.979	50.892	59.703

SOURCE: R. A. Fisher and F. Yates, *Statistical Tables for Biological, Agricultural and Medical Research*, 1974, Table IV, London: Longman. Reprinted by permission of Pearson Education Limited.

APPENDIX E

F TABLE FOR THE .05 LEVEL OF SIGNIFICANCE

df_1 / df_2	Numerator Degrees of Freedom							
	1	2	3	4	5	6	8	10
1	161.4	199.5	215.7	224.6	230.2	234.0	238.9	241.9
2	18.51	19.00	19.16	19.25	19.30	19.33	19.37	19.40
3	10.13	9.55	9.28	9.12	9.01	8.94	8.85	8.79
4	7.71	6.94	6.59	6.39	6.26	6.16	6.04	5.96
5	6.61	5.79	5.41	5.19	5.05	4.95	4.82	4.74
6	5.99	5.14	4.76	4.53	4.39	4.28	4.15	4.06
7	5.59	4.74	4.35	4.12	3.97	3.87	3.73	3.64
8	5.32	4.46	4.07	3.84	3.69	3.58	3.44	3.35
9	5.12	4.26	3.86	3.63	3.48	3.37	3.23	3.14
10	4.96	4.10	3.71	3.48	3.33	3.22	3.07	2.98
11	4.84	3.98	3.59	3.36	3.20	3.09	2.95	2.85
12	4.75	3.89	3.49	3.26	3.11	3.00	2.85	2.75
13	4.67	3.81	3.41	3.18	3.03	2.92	2.77	2.67
14	4.60	3.74	3.34	3.11	2.96	2.85	2.70	2.60
15	4.54	3.68	3.29	3.06	2.90	2.79	2.64	2.54
16	4.49	3.63	3.24	3.01	2.85	2.74	2.59	2.49
17	4.45	3.59	3.20	2.96	2.81	2.70	2.55	2.45
18	4.41	3.55	3.16	2.93	2.77	2.66	2.51	2.41
19	4.38	3.52	3.13	2.90	2.74	2.63	2.48	2.38
20	4.35	3.49	3.10	2.87	2.71	2.60	2.45	2.35
21	4.32	3.47	3.07	2.84	2.68	2.57	2.42	2.32
22	4.30	3.44	3.05	2.82	2.66	2.55	2.40	2.30
23	4.28	3.42	3.03	2.80	2.64	2.53	2.37	2.27
24	4.26	3.40	3.01	2.78	2.62	2.51	2.36	2.25
25	4.24	3.39	2.99	2.76	2.60	2.49	2.34	2.24
26	4.23	3.37	2.98	2.74	2.59	2.47	2.32	2.22
27	4.21	3.35	2.96	2.73	2.57	2.46	2.31	2.20
28	4.20	3.34	2.95	2.71	2.56	2.45	2.29	2.19
29	4.18	3.33	2.93	2.70	2.55	2.43	2.28	2.18
30	4.17	3.32	2.92	2.69	2.53	2.42	2.27	2.16
40	4.08	3.23	2.84	2.61	2.45	2.34	2.18	2.08
60	4.00	3.15	2.76	2.53	2.37	2.25	2.10	1.99
80	3.96	3.11	2.72	2.48	2.33	2.21	2.05	1.95
120	3.92	3.07	2.68	2.45	2.29	2.17	2.02	1.91
∞	3.84	3.00	2.60	2.37	2.21	2.10	1.94	1.83

Degrees of Freedom for the Denominator

			Numerator Degrees of Freedom					
df_1 / df_2	12	15	20	30	40	60	120	∞
1	243.9	245.9	248.0	250.1	251.1	252.2	253.3	254.3
2	19.41	19.43	19.45	19.46	19.47	19.48	19.49	19.50
3	8.74	8.70	8.66	8.62	8.59	8.57	8.55	8.53
4	5.91	5.86	5.80	5.75	5.72	5.69	5.66	5.63
5	4.68	4.62	4.56	4.50	4.46	4.43	4.40	4.36
6	4.00	3.94	3.87	3.81	3.77	3.74	3.70	3.67
7	3.57	3.51	3.44	3.38	3.34	3.30	3.27	3.23
8	3.28	3.22	3.15	3.08	3.04	3.01	2.97	2.93
9	3.07	3.01	2.94	2.86	2.83	2.79	2.75	2.71
10	2.91	2.85	2.77	2.70	2.66	2.62	2.58	2.54
11	2.79	2.72	2.65	2.57	2.53	2.49	2.45	2.40
12	2.69	2.62	2.54	2.47	2.43	2.38	2.34	2.30
13	2.60	2.53	2.46	2.38	2.34	2.30	2.25	2.21
14	2.53	2.46	2.39	2.31	2.27	2.22	2.18	2.13
15	2.48	2.40	2.33	2.25	2.20	2.16	2.11	2.07
16	2.42	2.35	2.28	2.19	2.15	2.11	2.06	2.01
17	2.38	2.31	2.23	2.15	2.10	2.06	2.01	1.96
18	2.34	2.27	2.19	2.11	2.06	2.02	1.97	1.92
19	2.31	2.23	2.16	2.07	2.03	1.98	1.93	1.88
20	2.28	2.20	2.12	2.04	1.99	1.95	1.90	1.84
21	2.25	2.18	2.10	2.01	1.96	1.92	1.87	1.81
22	2.23	2.15	2.07	1.98	1.94	1.89	1.84	1.78
23	2.20	2.13	2.05	1.96	1.91	1.86	1.81	1.76
24	2.18	2.11	2.03	1.94	1.89	1.84	1.79	1.73
25	2.16	2.09	2.01	1.92	1.87	1.82	1.77	1.71
26	2.15	2.07	1.99	1.90	1.85	1.80	1.75	1.69
27	2.13	2.06	1.97	1.88	1.84	1.79	1.73	1.67
28	2.12	2.04	1.96	1.87	1.82	1.77	1.71	1.65
29	2.10	2.03	1.94	1.85	1.81	1.75	1.70	1.64
30	2.09	2.01	1.93	1.84	1.79	1.74	1.68	1.62
40	2.00	1.92	1.84	1.74	1.69	1.64	1.58	1.51
60	1.92	1.84	1.75	1.65	1.59	1.53	1.47	1.39
80	1.88	1.80	1.70	1.60	1.54	1.49	1.41	1.32
120	1.83	1.75	1.66	1.55	1.50	1.43	1.35	1.25
∞	1.75	1.67	1.57	1.46	1.39	1.32	1.22	1.00

Degrees of Freedom for the Denominator

(continued)

F TABLE FOR THE .01 LEVEL OF SIGNIFICANCE

	Numerator Degrees of Freedom							
df_1 / df_2	1	2	3	4	5	6	8	10
1	4052	4999.5	5403	5625	5764	5859	5982	6056
2	98.50	99.00	99.17	99.25	99.30	99.33	99.37	99.40
3	34.12	30.82	29.46	28.71	28.24	27.91	27.49	27.23
4	21.20	18.00	16.69	15.98	15.52	15.21	14.80	14.55
5	16.26	13.27	12.06	11.39	10.97	10.67	10.29	10.05
6	13.75	10.92	9.78	9.15	8.75	8.47	8.10	7.87
7	12.25	9.55	8.45	7.85	7.46	7.19	6.84	6.62
8	11.26	8.65	7.59	7.01	6.63	6.37	6.03	5.81
9	10.56	8.02	6.99	6.42	6.06	5.80	5.47	5.26
10	10.04	7.56	6.55	5.99	5.64	5.39	5.06	4.85
11	9.65	7.21	6.22	5.67	5.32	5.07	4.74	4.54
12	9.33	6.93	5.95	5.41	5.06	4.82	4.50	4.30
13	9.07	6.70	5.74	5.21	4.86	4.62	4.30	4.10
14	8.86	6.51	5.56	5.04	4.69	4.46	4.14	3.94
15	8.68	6.36	5.42	4.89	4.56	4.32	4.00	3.80
16	8.53	6.23	5.29	4.77	4.44	4.20	3.89	3.69
17	8.40	6.11	5.18	4.67	4.34	4.10	3.79	3.59
18	8.29	6.01	5.09	4.58	4.25	4.01	3.71	3.51
19	8.18	5.93	5.01	4.50	4.17	3.94	3.63	3.43
20	8.10	5.85	4.94	4.43	4.10	3.87	3.56	3.37
21	8.02	5.78	4.87	4.37	4.04	3.81	3.51	3.31
22	7.95	5.72	4.82	4.31	3.99	3.76	3.45	3.26
23	7.88	5.66	4.76	4.26	3.94	3.71	3.41	3.21
24	7.82	5.61	4.72	4.22	3.90	3.67	3.36	3.17
25	7.77	5.57	4.68	4.18	3.85	3.63	3.32	3.13
26	7.72	5.53	4.64	4.14	3.82	3.59	3.29	3.09
27	7.68	5.49	4.60	4.11	3.78	3.56	3.26	3.06
28	7.64	5.45	4.57	4.07	3.75	3.53	3.23	3.03
29	7.60	5.42	4.54	4.04	3.73	3.50	3.20	3.00
30	7.56	5.39	4.51	4.02	3.70	3.47	3.17	2.98
40	7.31	5.18	4.31	3.83	3.51	3.29	2.99	2.80
60	7.08	4.98	4.13	3.65	3.34	3.12	2.82	2.63
80	6.96	4.88	4.04	3.56	3.25	3.04	2.74	2.55
120	6.85	4.79	3.95	3.48	3.17	2.96	2.66	2.47
∞	6.63	4.61	3.78	3.32	3.02	2.80	2.51	2.32

Degrees of Freedom for the Denominator

df_1	\multicolumn{8}{c}{Numerator Degrees of Freedom}
df_2	12	15	20	30	40	60	120	∞
1	6106	6157	6209	6261	6287	6313	6339	6366
2	99.42	99.43	99.45	99.47	99.47	99.48	99.49	99.50
3	27.05	26.87	26.69	26.50	26.41	26.32	26.22	26.13
4	14.37	14.20	14.02	13.84	13.75	13.65	13.56	13.46
5	9.89	9.72	9.55	9.38	9.29	9.20	9.11	9.02
6	7.72	7.56	7.40	7.23	7.14	7.06	6.97	6.88
7	6.47	6.31	6.16	5.99	5.91	5.82	5.74	5.65
8	5.67	5.52	5.36	5.20	5.12	5.03	4.95	4.86
9	5.11	4.96	4.81	4.65	4.57	4.48	4.40	4.31
10	4.71	4.56	4.41	4.25	4.17	4.08	4.00	3.91
11	4.40	4.25	4.10	3.94	3.86	3.78	3.69	3.60
12	4.16	4.01	3.86	3.70	3.62	3.54	3.45	3.36
13	3.96	3.82	3.66	3.51	3.43	3.34	3.25	3.17
14	3.80	3.66	3.51	3.35	3.27	3.18	3.09	3.00
15	3.67	3.52	3.37	3.21	3.13	3.05	2.96	2.87
16	3.55	3.41	3.26	3.10	3.02	2.93	2.84	2.75
17	3.46	3.31	3.16	3.00	2.92	2.83	2.75	2.65
18	3.37	3.23	3.08	2.92	2.84	2.75	2.66	2.57
19	3.30	3.15	3.00	2.84	2.76	2.67	2.58	2.49
20	3.23	3.09	2.94	2.78	2.69	2.61	2.52	2.42
21	3.17	3.03	2.88	2.72	2.64	2.55	2.46	2.36
22	3.12	2.98	2.83	2.67	2.58	2.50	2.40	2.31
23	3.07	2.93	2.78	2.62	2.54	2.45	2.35	2.26
24	3.03	2.89	2.74	2.58	2.49	2.40	2.31	2.21
25	2.99	2.85	2.70	2.54	2.45	2.36	2.27	2.17
26	2.96	2.81	2.66	2.50	2.42	2.33	2.23	2.13
27	2.93	2.78	2.63	2.47	2.38	2.29	2.20	2.10
28	2.90	2.75	2.60	2.44	2.35	2.26	2.17	2.06
29	2.87	2.73	2.57	2.41	2.33	2.23	2.14	2.03
30	2.84	2.70	2.55	2.39	2.30	2.21	2.11	2.01
40	2.66	2.52	2.37	2.20	2.11	2.02	1.92	1.80
60	2.50	2.35	2.20	2.03	1.94	1.84	1.73	1.60
80	2.41	2.28	2.11	1.94	1.84	1.75	1.63	1.49
120	2.34	2.19	2.03	1.86	1.76	1.66	1.53	1.38
∞	2.18	2.04	1.88	1.70	1.59	1.47	1.32	1.00

Degrees of Freedom for the Denominator

SOURCE: C. M. Thompson, "Tables of the Percentage Points of the Inverted Beta (F) Distribution," *Biometrika* 33, pp. 73-88, 1943. Reprinted by permission of Oxford University Press.

APPENDIX F

RESOURCES FOR RESEARCH

In what follows, I have not included e-mail addresses. The current e-mail address for each of the products listed below can be found at the appropriate Internet page.

Check with the individual companies about prices. Many colleges and universities have site licenses for one or more statistical packages or text analysis packages.

STATISTICAL PACKAGES

EPI-INFO is a statistical package from the Centers for Disease Control. It is available free at www.cdc.gov/epo/epi/software.htm. Several vendors sell the program along with a bound manual. A list of several vendors is available at www.cdc.gov/epo/epi/vendors.htm.

SAS. For information about SAS, go to www.sas.com or write to SAS Institute Inc., SAS Campus Drive, Cary, NC 27513-2414. Phone 919-677-8000, fax 919-677-4444.

SPSS. For information about SPSS, go to www.spss.com or write to SPSS Inc., 233 S. Wacker Drive, 11th Floor, Chicago, IL 60606-6307. Phone 800-543-2185, fax 800-841-0064.

STATA. For more information about STATA, go to www.stata.com or write to Stata Corporation, 702 University Drive East, College Station, TX 77840. Phone 800-782-8272, fax 409-696-4601.

STATISTICA is a product of StatSoft®. Go to www.statsoft.com/addition.html or write to Statsoft, 2300 East 14th Street, Tulsa, OK 74104. Phone 918-749-1119, fax 918-749-2217.

STATMOST. For more information about STATMOST, go to www.dataxiom.com/smost.htm or write to Dataxiom Software Inc., 3700 Wilshire Blvd., Suite 1000, Los Angeles, CA 90010. Phone 213-383-9973, fax 213-383-3542.

SYSTAT is a product of SPSS, Inc. (address and phone numbers above). For more information, go to www.spss.com/software/science/SYSTAT/index.html.

WINKS. For more information on WINKS, go to www.texasoft.com or write to TexaSoft, P.O. Box 1169, Cedar Hill, TX 75106-1169.

TEXT ANALYSIS PACKAGES

All of the following packages for the analysis of nonnumerical data (text, images, artifacts, etc.) are distributed by the Scolari division of Sage Publications. Go to www.scolari.com or write to Sage Publications, 2455 Teller Road, Thousand Oaks, CA 91320 for further information. Phone 805-499-0721, fax 805-499-0871.

ATLAS/ti

Q.S.R., NUD·IST 4.0, and Q.S.R. NVivo

The Ethnograph v5.0

HyperRESEARCH

Code-A-Text

WinMAX

The following two software packages are for text analysis and are available free from the Centers for Disease Control. Go to www.cdc.gov/nchstp/hiv_aids/software/ez-text.htm.

CDC EZ-TEXT and AnSWR

ANTHROPAC is a suite of programs for collecting and analyzing many kinds of data. It has tools for ratings data, rank-ordered data, triad tests, free lists, and pile sorts. It treats whole texts as elements of a free list and creates word-by-text matrices for analysis. The analysis tools include multidimensional scaling, property fitting, quadratic assignment, correspondence analysis, several kinds of cluster analysis, and consensus analysis. It also has tools for doing Boolean analyses of truth tables. For further information, go to www.analytictech.com or contact Analytic Technologies, Inc., 104 Pond Street, Natick, MA 01760. Phone 508-647-1903, fax 508-647-3154.

FIELD OBSERVATION PACKAGES

The Observer and The Observer Video-Pro are software products for collecting, analyzing, managing, and presenting direct observational data. These products work with both laptop and palmtop computers. For more information, go to www.noldus.com or write to Noldus Information Technology, P.O. Box 268, 6700 AG Wageningen, The Netherlands. Phone (31) 317-497677, fax (31) 317-424496.

INTERNET ADDRESSES FOR SOME PROFESSIONAL AND SCHOLARLY ASSOCIATIONS IN THE SOCIAL SCIENCES

American Anthropological Association: www.ameranthassn.org

American Association for Public Opinion Research: www.aapor.org

American Educational Research Association: www.aera.net

American Political Science Association: www.apsanet.org

American Psychological Association: www.apa.org

American Sociological Association: www.asanet.org

American Society of Criminology: www.asc41.com

American Statistical Association: www.amstat.org

Association of American Geographers: www.aag.org

The Law and Society Association: www.lawandsociety.org

Marketing Research Association: www.mra-net.org

National Association of Social Workers: www.naswdc.org

National Institute of Nursing Research: www.nih.gov/ninr

REFERENCES

Abdel-Khalek, A. M. 1998. Internal consistency of an Arabic adaptation of the Depression Inventory in four Arab countries. *Psychological Reports* 82:264-66.

Abel, M. H. 1997. Low birth weight and interactions between traditional risk factors. *Journal of Genetic Psychology* 158:443-56.

Abernethy, A. D., and C. Cox. 1994. Anger management training for law enforcement personnel. *Journal of Criminal Justice* 22:459-66.

Ackerman, R. J., and E. W. Gondolf. 1991. Adult children of alcoholics: The effects of background and treatment on ACOA symptoms. *International Journal of the Addictions* 26:1159-72.

Adams-Webber, J. 1997. Self-reflexion in evaluating others. *American Journal of Psychology* 110:527-41.

Addams, J. 1926. *Twenty years at Hull House*. New York: Macmillan.

Adorno, T. W., E. Frenkel-Brunswick, D. J. Levinson, and R. N. Sanford. 1950. *The authoritarian personality*. New York: Harper & Row.

Agar, M. 1973. *Ripping and running*. New York: Academic Press.

Agar, M. 1979. Themes revisited: Some problems in cognitive anthropology. *Discourse Processes* 2:11-31.

Agar, M. 1980a. Getting better quality stuff: Methodological competition in an interdisciplinary niche. *Urban Life* 9:34-50.

Agar, M. 1980b. *The professional stranger*. New York: Academic Press.

Agar, M. 1982. Toward an ethnographic language. *American Anthropologist* 84:779-95.

Agar, M. 1983. Microcomputers as field tools. *Computers and the Humanities* 17:19-26.

Agar, M. 1996. *The professional stranger: An informal introduction to ethnography*. 2d ed. San Diego: Academic Press.

Ahrentzen, S., D. W. Levine, and W. Michelson. 1989. Space, time, and activity in the home: A gender analysis. *Journal of Environmental Psychology* 9:89-101.

Aiello, J. R., and S. E. Jones. 1971. Field study of the proxemic behavior of young school children in three subcultural groups. *Journal of Personality and Social Psychology* 19:351-56.

Akhtar, S. 1996. Do girls have a higher school drop-out rate than boys? A hazard rate analysis of evidence from a third world city. *Urban Studies* 33:49-62.

Albas, C. 1991. Proxemic behavior: A study of extrusion. *Journal of Social Psychology* 131:697-702.

Aldenderfer, M. S., and R. K. Blashfield. 1984. *Cluster analysis*. Sage University Papers Series. Quantitative applications in the social sciences, no. 07-044. Beverly Hills, Calif.: Sage.

Algase, D. L., B. Kupferschmid, C. A. Beel-Bates, and E. R. A. Beattie. 1997. Estimates of stability of daily wandering behavior among cognitively impaired long-term care residents. *Nursing Research* 46:172-78.

Allen, W. R., R. A. Comerford, and J. A. Ruhe. 1989. Factor analytic study of Bales' interaction process analysis. *Educational and Psychological Measurement* 49:701-707.

Alm, J., and L. A. Whittington. 1996. The rise and fall and rise . . . of the marriage tax. *National Tax Journal* 49:571-89.

Al-Nuaim, A. A., E. A. Bamgboye, K. A. Al-Rubeaan, and Y. Al-Mazrou. 1997. Overweight and obesity in Saudi Arabian adult population: Role of sociodemographic variables. *Journal of Community Health* 22:211-23.

Altmann, J. 1974. Observational study of behavior: Sampling methods. *Behaviour* 49:227-67.

Altorki, S., and C. Fawzi El-Solh, eds. 1988. *Arab women in the field: Studying your own society*. Syracuse, N.Y.: Syracuse University Press.

Alvarado, N. 1994. Empirical validity of the Thematic Apperception Test. *Journal of Personality Assessment* 63:59-79.

Alvarado, N. 1996. New findings on the contempt expression. *Cognition and Emotion* 10:379-407.

American Statistical Association. 1974. Report on the ASA Conference on Surveys of Human Populations. *The American Statistician* 28:30-34.

Amidon, E. J., and N. Flanders. 1967. Interaction analysis as a feedback system. In *Interaction analysis: Theory, research, and application*, ed. by E. J. Amidon and J. B. Hough, 121-40. Reading, Mass.: Addison-Wesley.

Amidon, E. J., and J. B. Hough. 1967. *Interaction analysis: Theory, research, and application*. Reading, Mass.: Addison-Wesley.

Amundson, N. E. 1995. An interactive model of career decision making. *Journal of Employment Counseling* 32:11-21.

Andersen, K., and E. A. Cook. 1985. Women, work, and political attitudes. *American Journal of Political Science* 29:606-25.

Anderson, A. B., and E. S. Anderson. 1983. People and the Palm Forest. (Contract 51-07-79-07 to John Ewel). Final report to United States Department of Agriculture, Forest Service, Consortium for the Study of Man's Relationship with the Global Environment. Washington, D.C.: USDA. (Also available through NTIS.)

Anderson, C. A. 1989. Temperature and aggression: Ubiquitous effects of heat on occurrence of human violence. *Psychological Bulletin* 106:74-96.

Anderson, L. E., and J. A. Walsh. 1998. Predictions of adult criminal status from juvenile psychological assessment. *Criminal Justice and Behavior* 25:226-39.

Anderson, P. M., and B. D. Meyer. 1998. *Using a natural experiment to estimate the effects of the unemployment insurance payroll tax on wages, employment, claims, and denials*. Cambridge, Mass.: National Bureau of Economic Research.

Andrews, F. M., and S. B. Withey. 1976. *Social indicators of well-being: Americans' perceptions of life quality*. New York: Plenum.

Appell, G. N. 1978. *Ethical dilemmas in anthropological inquiry: A case book*. Waltham, Mass.: Crossroads.

Aquilino, W. S. 1994. Interview mode effects in surveys of drug and alcohol use: A field experiment. *Public Opinion Quarterly* 58:210-40.

Archer, D., and L. Erlich. 1985. Weighing the evidence: A new method for research on restricted information. *Qualitative Sociology* 8:345-58.

Aronson, E., and J. Mills. 1959. The effect of severity of initiation on liking for a group. *Journal of Abnormal and Social Psychology* 59:177-81.

Arp, W., III, and K. Boeckelman. 1997. Religiosity: A source of Black environmentalism and empowerment? *Journal of Black Studies* 28:255-67.

Aryee, S. 1993. Dual-earner couples in Singapore: An examination of work and nonwork sources of their experienced burnout. *Human Relations* 46:1441-68.

Asakawa, K., and M. Csikszentmihalyi. 1998. The quality of experience of Asian American adolescents in activities related to future goals. *Journal of Youth and Adolescence* 27:141-63.

Ashraf, J. 1996. Is gender pay discrimination on the wane? Evidence from panel data, 1968-1989. *Industrial and Labor Relations Review* 49:537-46.

Asimov, I. 1989. *Asimov's chronology of science and discovery.* New York: Harper & Row.

Atkinson, P. 1992. The ethnography of a medical setting: Reading, writing, and rhetoric. *Qualitative Health Research* 2:451-74.

Atran, S. 1990. *Cognitive foundations of natural history: Towards an anthropology of science.* New York: Cambridge University Press.

Atran, S. 1996. From folk biology to scientific biology. In *Handbook of education and human development: New models of learning, teaching, and schooling,* ed. by D. R. Olson and N. Torrance, 646-82. Oxford, U.K.: Basil Blackwell.

Aunger, R. 1992. Sources of variation in ethnographic interview data: The case of food avoidances in the Ituri forest, Zaire. Paper presented at the annual meeting of the American Anthropological Association, San Francisco.

Axinn, W. G. 1991. The influence of interviewer sex on responses to sensitive questions in Nepal. *Social Science Research* 20:303-19.

Axinn, W. G., T. E. Fricke, and A. Thornton. 1991. The microdemographic community-study approach. *Sociological Methods & Research* 20:187-217.

Ayres, I. 1991. Fair driving: Gender and race discrimination in retail car negotiations. *Harvard Law Review* 104:817-72.

Baert, P. 1998. *Social theory in the twentieth century.* New York: New York University Press.

Bahr, H. M., and B. A. Chadwick. 1974. Conservatism, racial intolerance, and attitudes toward racial assimilation among Whites and American Indians. *Journal of Social Psychology* 94:45-56.

Bainbridge, W. S. 1978. *Satan's power: A deviant psychotherapy cult.* Berkeley: University of California Press.

Bainbridge, W. S. 1992. *Social research methods and statistics: A computer-assisted introduction.* Belmont, Calif.: Wadsworth.

Bakeman, R., and J. M. Gottman. 1997. *Observing interaction. An introduction to sequential analysis.* Cambridge, U.K.: Cambridge University Press.

Bakeman, R., and V. Quera. 1995. *Analyzing interaction. Sequential analysis with SDIS and GSEQ.* Cambridge, U.K.: Cambridge University Press.

Baker, J., M. Levy, and D. Grewal. 1992. An experimental approach to making retail store environmental decisions. *Journal of Retailing* 68:445-60.

Bales, R. F. 1950. *Interaction process analysis: A method for the study of small groups.* Cambridge, Mass.: Addison-Wesley.

Bales, R. F., and S. P. Cohen. 1979. *SYMLOG: A system for the multiple level observation of groups.* New York: Free Press.

Bandura, A., C. Barbaranelli, G. V. Caprara, and C. Pastorelli. 1996. Mechanisms of moral disengagement in the exercise of moral agency. *Journal of Personality and Social Psychology* 71:364-74.

Barash, D. P. 1972. Human ethology: The snack-bar security syndrome. *Psychological Reports* 31:577-78.

Barash, D. P. 1973. Human ethology: Personal space reiterated. *Environment and Behavior* 5:67-72.

Barash, D. P. 1974. Human ethology: Displacement activities in a dental office. *Psychological Reports* 34:947-49.

Barash, D. P. 1977. Human ethology: Exchanging cheetahs for Chevrolets? *Environment and Behavior* 9:487-90.

Barber, N. 1998. Ecological and psychosocial correlates of male homosexuality: A cross-cultural investigation. *Journal of Cross-Cultural Psychology* 29:387-401.

Barker, R., and H. F. Wright. 1951. *One boy's day: A specimen record of behavior.* New York: Harper & Brothers.

Barnes, B. 1995. *The elements of social theory.* Princeton, N.J.: Princeton University Press.

Barnes, J. H., B. F. Banahan III, and K. E. Fish. 1995. The response effect of question order in computer-administered questioning in the social sciences. *Social Science Computer Review* 13:47-63.

Barroso, J. 1997. Reconstructing my life: Becoming a long-term survivor of AIDS. *Qualitative Health Research* 7:57-74.

Barry, H., III, and A. Schlegel. 1980. *Cross-cultural samples and codes*. Pittsburgh, Pa.: University of Pittsburgh Press.

Bartlett, F. C. 1937. Psychological methods and anthropological problems. *Africa* 10:401-19.

Bauer, M., and A. L. Wright. 1996. Integrating qualitative and quantitative methods to model infant feeding behavior among Navajo mothers. *Human Organization* 55:183-92.

Beardsworth, A., and T. Keil. 1992. The vegetarian option: Varieties, conversions, motives and careers. *Sociological Review* 40:253-93.

Bechtel, R. B. 1977. *Enclosing behavior*. Stroudsburg, Pa.: Dowden, Hutchinson, & Ross.

Beck, A. T., C. H. Ward, M. Mendelson, J. E. Mock, and J. Erbaugh. 1961. An inventory for measuring depression. *Archives of General Psychiatry* 4:561-71.

Becker, H. S., B. Geer, E. C. Hughs, and A. L. Strauss. 1961. *Boys in white: Student culture in medical school*. Chicago: University of Chicago Press.

Becker, H. S., and M. M. McCall, eds. 1990. *Symbolic interaction and cultural studies*. Chicago: University of Chicago Press.

Begley, S., H. Fineman, and V. Church. 1992. The science of polling. *Newsweek*, September 28, 38-39.

Behar, R. 1996. *The vulnerable observer: Anthropology that breaks your heart*. Boston: Beacon.

Belansky, E. S., and A. K. Boggiano. 1994. Predicting helping behaviors: The role of gender and instrumental/expressive self-schemata. *Sex Roles* 30:647-61.

Belk, R. W., J. F. Sherry, Jr., and M. Wallendorf. 1988. A naturalistic inquiry into buyer and seller behavior at a swap meet. *Journal of Consumer Research* 14:449-69.

Bell, D. E., H. Raiffa, and A. Tversky, eds. 1988. *Decision making: Descriptive, normative, and prescriptive interactions*. New York: Cambridge University Press.

Belsley, D. A., E. Kuh, and R. E. Welsch. 1980. *Regression diagnostics: Identifying influential data and sources of collinearity*. New York: John Wiley.

Belter, R. W., J. A. McIntosh, A. J. Finch, Jr., and C. F. Saylor. 1988. Preschoolers' ability to differentiate levels of pain: Relative efficacy of three self-report measures. *Journal of Clinical Child Psychology* 17:329-35.

Bem, S. 1974. The measurement of psychological androgyny. *Journal of Consulting and Clinical Psychology* 42:155-62.

Bem, S. L. 1979. Theory and measurement of androgyny: A reply to the Pedhazur-Tetenbaum and Locksley-Colten critiques. *Journal of Personality and Social Psychology* 37:1047-54.

Berg, D. N., and K. K. Smith, eds. 1985. *Exploring clinical methods for social research*. Beverly Hills, Calif.: Sage.

Berlin, B. 1992. *Ethnobotanical classification: Principles of categorization of plants and animals in traditional societies*. Princeton, N.J.: Princeton University Press.

Bermant, G. 1982. Justifying social research in terms of social benefit. In *Ethical issues in social science research*, ed. by T. L. Beauchamp et al., 125-43. Baltimore: Johns Hopkins University Press.

Bernard, H. R. 1967. Kalymnian sponge diving. *Human Biology* 39:103-30.

Bernard, H. R. 1974. Scientists and policymakers: A case study in the ethnography of communications. *Human Organization* 33:261-75.

Bernard, H. R. 1987. Sponge fishing and technological change in Greece. In *Technology and social change*. 2d ed. Ed. by H. R. Bernard and P. J. Pelto, 167-206. Prospect Heights, Ill.: Waveland.

Bernard, H. R. 1992. Preserving language diversity. *Human Organization* 41:82-88.

Bernard, H. R. 1994. *Research methods in anthropology*. Walnut Creek, Calif.: AltaMira.

Bernard, H. R., and S. Ashton-Vouyoucalos. 1976. Return migration to Greece. *Journal of the Steward Anthropological Society* 8:31-51.

Bernard, H. R., and L. Comitas. 1978. Greek return migration. *Current Anthropology* 19:658-59.

Bernard, H. R., and M. J. Evans. 1983. New microcomputer techniques for anthropologists. *Human Organization* 42:182-85.

Bernard, H. R., E. Johnsen, P. Killworth, and S. Robinson. 1989. Estimating the size of an average personal network and of an event population. In *The small world*, ed. by M. Kochen, 159-75. Norwood, N.J.: Ablex.

Bernard, H. R., and P. D. Killworth. 1973. On the social structure of an ocean-going research vessel and other important things. *Social Science Research* 2:145-84.

Bernard, H. R., and P. D. Killworth. 1974. Scientists and crew. *Maritime Studies and Management* 2:112-25.

Bernard, H. R., and P. D. Killworth. 1993. Sampling in time allocation research. *Ethnology* 32:207-15.

Bernard, H. R., P. D. Killworth, L. Sailer, and D. Kronenfeld. 1984. The problem of informant accuracy: The validity of retrospective data. *Annual Review of Anthropology* 13:495-517.

Bernard, H. R., G. Ryan, and S. Borgatti. 1999. Modeling some green behaviors: Why Americans do or don't recycle aluminum cans. Manuscript.

Bernard, H. R., and J. P. Salinas. 1989. *Native ethnography: A Mexican Indian describes his culture.* Newbury Park, Calif.: Sage.

Bernieri, F. J. 1993. Analysis of variance in the study of interpersonal expectations: Theory testing, interaction effects, and effect sizes. In *Interpersonal expectations: Theory, research, and applications*, ed. by P. D. Blanck, 379-99. New York: Cambridge University Press.

Berra, Y., and J. Garagiola. 1998. *The Yogi book: "I really didn't say everything I said."* New York: Workman.

Berreman, G. D. 1962. *Behind many masks.* Ithaca, N.Y.: Society for Applied Anthropology.

Berry, J. 1976. *Human ecology and cognitive style.* New York: John Wiley.

Bickel, R., S. Weaver, T. Williams, and L. Lange. 1997. Opportunity, community, and teen pregnancy in an Appalachian state. *Journal of Educational Research* 90:175-81.

Bickman, L., and D. J. Rog, eds. 1998. *Handbook of applied social research methods.* Thousand Oaks, Calif.: Sage.

Bieri, D., R. A. Reeve, D. Champion, L. Addicoat, and J. B. Ziegler. 1990. The faces scale for the self-assessment of the severity of pain experienced by children: Development, initial validation, and preliminary investigation for ratio scale properties. *Pain* 41:139-50.

Biernacki, P., and D. Waldorf. 1981. Snowball sampling: Problems, techniques, and chain referral sampling. *Sociological Methods & Research* 10:141-63.

Billiet, J., and G. Loosveldt. 1988. Improvement of the quality of responses to factual survey questions by interviewer training. *Public Opinion Quarterly* 52:190-211.

Bingham, W. Van Dyke, B. V. Moore, and J. W. Gustad. 1959. *How to interview.* 4th rev. ed. New York: Harper.

Birdwell-Pheasant, D. 1984. Personal power careers and the development of domestic structure in a small community. *American Ethnologist* 11:699-717.

Bishop, B., and G. J. Syme. 1995. The social costs and benefits of urban consolidation: A time budget/contingent valuation approach. *Journal of Economic Psychology* 16:223-45.

Black, J. K. 1991. *Development in theory and practice: Bridging the gap.* Boulder, Colo.: Westview.

Blair, E., S. Sudman, N. M. Bradburn, and C. B. Stocking. 1977. How to ask questions about drinking and sex: Response effects in measuring consumer behavior. *Journal of Marketing Research* 14:316-21.

Blalock, H. M., ed. 1974. *Measurement in the social sciences: Theories and strategies.* Chicago: Aldine.

Blalock, H. M. 1979. *Social statistics.* Rev. 2d ed. New York: McGraw-Hill.

Blalock, H. M. 1989. *Power and conflict: Toward a general theory.* Newbury Park, Calif.: Sage.

Blau, P. M. 1975. *Approaches to the study of social structure.* New York: Free Press.

Bloom, D. E. 1998. Technology, experimentation, and the quality of survey data. *Science* 280:847-48.

Blumer, H. 1969. *Symbolic interactionism: Perspective and method.* Englewood Cliffs, N.J.: Prentice Hall.

Blurton-Jones, N. G., ed. 1972. *Ethological studies of child behaviour.* Cambridge, U.K.: Cambridge University Press.

Blustein, D. L., S. D. Phillips, K. Jobin-Davis, S. L. Finkelberg, and A. E. Roarke. 1997. A theory-building investigation of the school-to-work transition. *The Counseling Psychologist* 25:364-402.

Bochner, S. 1971. The use of unobtrusive measures in cross-cultural attitudes research. In *A question of choice: An Australian Aboriginal dilemma,* ed. by R. M. Berndt, 107-15. Nedlands: University of Western Australia Press.

Bochner, S. 1972. An unobtrusive approach to the study of housing discrimination against Aborigines. *Australian Journal of Psychology* 24:335-37.

Bochner, S. 1980. Unobtrusive observation in cross-cultural experimentation. In *Handbook of cross-cultural psychology,* ed. by H. C. Triandis and J. W. Berry. Vol. 2, *Methodology,* 319-88. Boston: Allyn & Bacon.

Bogardus, E. S. 1925. Measuring social distances. *Journal of Applied Sociology* 9:299-308.

Bogdan, R. 1972. *Participant observation in organizational settings.* Syracuse, N.Y.: Syracuse University Press.

Bogdan, R., and S. K. Biklen. 1992. *Qualitative research for education: An introduction to theory and methods.* 2d ed. Boston: Allyn & Bacon.

Bolton, R. 1984. We all do it, but how? A survey of contemporary fieldnote procedure. In *Final report: Computers in ethnographic research* (Grant NIE-G-78-0062). Washington, D.C.: National Institute of Education (ERIC, no. ED 1. 310/2:248173).

Bonham, C., E. Fujii, E. Im, and J. Mak. 1992. The impact of the hotel room tax: An interrupted time series approach. *National Tax Journal* 45:433-41.

BonJour, L. 1985. *The structure of empirical knowledge.* Cambridge, Mass.: Harvard University Press.

Booth, C., ed. 1902. *Life and labor of the people of London.* New York: Macmillan.

Borgatti, S. 1992a. *ANTHROPAC 4.0.* Columbia, S.C.: Analytic Technologies.

Borgatti, S. 1992b. *ANTHROPAC 4.0 methods guide.* Columbia, S.C.: Analytic Technologies.

Borgerhoff-Mulder, M. B., and T. M. Caro. 1985. The use of quantitative observational techniques in anthropology. *Current Anthropology* 26:323-36.

Borich, G., and G. Klinzing. 1984. Some assumptions in the observation of classroom process with suggestions for improving low inference measurement. *Journal of Classroom Interaction* 20:36-44.

Boruch, R. F., and J. S. Cecil, eds. 1983. *Solutions to ethical and legal problems in social research.* New York: Academic Press.

Boserup, E. 1970. *Women's role in economic development.* London: Allen and Unwin.

Boster, J. S. 1985. Requiem for the omniscient informant: There's life in the old girl yet. In *Directions in cognitive anthropology,* ed. by J. Dougherty, 177-98. Urbana: University of Illinois Press.

Boster, J. S. 1986. Exchange of varieties and information between Aguaruna manioc cultivators. *American Anthropologist* 88:428-36.

Boster, J. S. 1987. Agreement between biological classification systems is not dependent on cultural transmission. *American Anthropologist* 89:914-20.

Boster, J. S., and J. C. Johnson. 1989. Form or function: A comparison of expert and novice judgments of similarity among fish. *American Anthropologist* 91:866-89.

Boster, J. S., J. C. Johnson, and S. C. Weller. 1987. Social position and shared knowledge: Actors' perceptions of status, role, and social structure. *Social Networks* 9:375-87.

Bourgois, P. I. 1995. *In search of respect: Selling crack in El Barrio.* New York: Cambridge University Press.

Boyd, C. J., F. Blow, and L. S. Orgain. 1993. Gender differences among African-American substance abusers. *Journal of Psychoactive Drugs* 25:301-305.

Boyle, E., Jr. 1970. Biological patterns in hypertension by race, sex, body weight, and skin color. *Journal of the American Medical Association* 213:1637-43.

Boyle, R. P. 1970. Path analysis and ordinal data. *American Journal of Sociology* 75:461-80.

Bradburn, N. M. 1983. Response effects. In *Handbook of survey research,* ed. by P. H. Rossi, J. D. Wright, and A. B. Anderson, 289-328. New York: Academic Press.

Bradburn, N. M., and S. Sudman et al. 1979. *Improving interview method and questionnaire design: Response effects to threatening questions in survey research.* San Francisco: Jossey-Bass.

Bradley, C. 1997. Doing fieldwork with diabetes. *Cultural Anthropology Methods Journal* 9:1-7.

Braunstein, M. S. 1993. Sampling a hidden population: Noninstitutionalized drug users. *AIDS Education and Prevention* 5:131-40.

Bravo, M., M. Woodbury-Farina, G. J. Canino, and M. Rubio-Stipec Maritza. 1993. The Spanish translation and cultural adaptation of the Diagnostic Interview Schedule for Children (DISC) in Puerto Rico. *Culture, Medicine and Psychiatry* 17:329-44.

Brenner, O. C., and J. Tomkiewicz. 1982. Job orientation of Black and White college graduates in business. *Personnel Psychology* 35:89-103.

Brent, J. S. 1994. Leaving Protestant fundamentalism: A qualitative analysis of a major life transition. *Counseling and Values* 38:205-14.

Bridgman, P. W. 1927. *The logic of modern physics.* New York: Macmillan. (Reprinted 1980, New York: Arno.)

Brief, A. P., and L. Roberson, 1989. Job attitude organization: An exploratory study. *Journal of Applied Social Psychology* 19:717-27.

Briere, J., A. Downes, and J. Spensley. 1983. Summer in the city: Weather conditions and psychiatric emergency room visits. *Journal of Abnormal Psychology* 92:77-80.

Brink, P. J., and M. J. Wood, eds. 1998. *Advanced design in nursing research.* 2d ed. Thousand Oaks, Calif.: Sage.

Brislin, R. W., W. J. Lonner, and R. M. Thorndike. 1973. *Cross-cultural research methods.* New York: John Wiley.

Broadbent, N. 1995. Accident claims lives of researchers in Russian Far East. *Anthropology Newsletter,* November, 39-40.

Broeder, A. 1998. Deception can be acceptable. *American Psychologist* 53:805-806.

Brogan, D. 1998. Software for sample survey data, misuse of standard packages. In *Encyclopedia of biostatistics,* ed. by P. Armitage and T. Colton. Vol. 5, 4167-74. New York: John Wiley.

Brown, W. H., S. L. Odom, and A. Holcombe. 1996. Observational assessment of young children's social behavior with peers. *Early Childhood Research Quarterly* 11:19-40.

Bruner, J. S., J. J. Goodnow, and G. A. Austin. 1956. *A study of thinking.* New York: John Wiley.

Bruyn, S. T. H. 1966. *The human perspective in sociology: The methodology of participant observation.* Englewood Cliffs, N.J.: Prentice Hall.

Bryant, C. 1985. *Positivism in social theory and research.* New York: St. Martin's.

Buchman, T. A., and J. A. Tracy. 1982. Obtaining responses to sensitive questions: Conventional questionnaire versus randomized response technique. *Journal of Accounting Research* 20:263-71.

Bulmer, M. 1979. Concepts in the analysis of qualitative data. *Sociological Review* 27:65-77.

Bulmer, M. 1984. *The Chicago school of sociology: Institutionalization, diversity, and the rise of sociological research.* Chicago: University of Chicago Press.

Burgess, R. G. 1989. *The ethics of educational research.* London: Falmer.

Burling, R. 1964. Cognition and componential analysis: God's truth or hocus-pocus? *American Anthropologist* 66:20-28.

Burling, R. 1984. *Learning a field language.* Ann Arbor: University of Michigan Press.

Burn, S. M., A. K. O'Neil, and S. Nederend. 1996. Childhood tomboyism and adult androgyny. *Sex Roles* 34:419-28.

Burnam, M. A., and P. Koegel. 1988. Methodology for obtaining a representative sample of homeless persons: The Los Angeles Skid Row study. *Evaluation Review* 12:117-52.

Burton, M. L., and S. B. Nerlove. 1976. Balanced design for triad tests. *Social Science Research* 5:247-67.

Bush, A. J., and J. F. Hair, Jr. 1985. An assessment of the mall intercept as a data collection method. *Journal of Marketing Research* 22:158-67.

Byers, B., and R. A. Zeller. 1998. Measuring subgroup variation in social judgment research: A factorial survey approach. *Social Science Research* 27:73-84.

Cahnman, W. J. 1948. A note on marriage announcements in the *New York Times. American Sociological Review* 13:96-97.

Caldwell, J. C. 1982. *Theory of fertility decline.* New York: Academic Press.

Calhoun, R. E. 1994. Flanders Interaction Analysis System compared with the Amidon Control Orientation Questionnaire for trained and untrained in-service teachers. Ph.D. diss. Dissertation Abstracts International: Section A: The Humanities and Social Sciences.

Callanan, M. A., A. N. Repp, M. G. McCarthy, and M. A. Latzke. 1994. Children's hypotheses about word meanings: Is there a basic level of constraint? *Journal of Experimental Child Psychology* 57:108-38.

Campbell, D. T. 1957. Factors relevant to the validity of experiments in social settings. *Psychological Bulletin* 54:297-312.

Campbell, D. T. 1979. Degrees of freedom and the case study. In *Qualitative and quantitative methods in evaluation research,* ed. by T. D. Cook and C. S. Reichart, 49-67. Beverly Hills, Calif.: Sage.

Campbell, D. T., and R. F. Boruch. 1975. Making the case for randomized assignment to treatments by considering the alternatives: Six ways in which quasi-experimental evaluations in compensatory education tend to underestimate effects. In *Evalu-ation and experiment: Some critical issues in assessing social programs,* ed. by C. A. Bennett and A. A. Lumsdaine, 195-296. New York: Academic Press.

Campbell, D. T., and D. W. Fiske. 1959. Convergent and discriminant validation by the multitrait-multimethod matrix. *Psychological Bulletin* 56:8-105.

Campbell, D. T., and E. S. Overman. 1988. *Methodology and epistemology for social science: Selected papers.* Chicago: University of Chicago Press.

Campbell, D. T., and H. L. Ross. 1968. The Connecticut crackdown on speeding: Time-series data in quasi-experimental analysis. *Law and Society Review* 3:33-53.

Campbell, D. T., and J. C. Stanley. 1963. *Experimental and quasi-experimental designs for research.* Boston: Houghton Mifflin.

Campostrini, S., and D. V. McQueen. 1993. Sexual behavior and exposure to HIV infection: Estimates from a general-population risk index. *American Journal of Public Health* 83:1139-43.

Cannell, C. F., G. Fisher, and T. Bakker. 1961. Reporting of hospitalization in the Health Interview Survey. *Health Statistics.* Series D, no. 4. USDHEW, PHS. Washington, D.C.: Government Printing Office.

Cannell, C. F., and F. J. Fowler. 1965. Comparison of hospitalization reporting in three survey procedures. In *Vital and Health Statistics.* Series 2, no. 8. Washington, D.C.: Government Printing Office.

Cannell, C. F., and R. L. Kahn. 1968. Interviewing. In *The handbook of social psychology.* 2d. ed. Ed. by G. Lindzey and E. Aronson. Vol. 2, *Research methods,* 526-95. Reading, Mass.: Addison-Wesley.

Cannell, C. F., S. Lawson, and D. Hausser. 1975. *A technique for evaluating interviewer performance.* Ann Arbor: Institute for Social Research, University of Michigan.

Cannell, C. F., L. Oksenberg, and J. M. Converse. 1979. Experiments in interview techniques: Field experiments in health reporting 1971-1977. Ann Arbor: Institute for Social Research, University of Michigan.

Cantril, H. 1965. *The pattern of human concerns*. New Brunswick, N.J.: Rutgers University Press.

Carey, J. W., M. Morgan, and M. J. Oxtoby. 1996. Intercoder agreement in analysis of responses to open-ended interview questions: Examples from tuberculosis research. *Cultural Anthropology Methods Journal* 8:1-5.

Carroll, J. B. 1993. *Human cognitive abilities: A survey of factor-analytic studies*. New York: Cambridge University Press.

Carver, R. P. 1978. The case against statistical significance testing. *Harvard Educational Review* 48:378-99.

Carver, R. P. 1993. The case against statistical significance testing, revisited. *Journal of Experimental Education* 61:287-92.

Caserta, M. S., D. A. Lund, and M. F. Dimond. 1985. Assessing interviewer effects in a longitudinal study of bereaved elderly adults. *Journal of Gerontology* 40:637-40.

Cassell, C., and G. Symon, eds. 1994. *Qualitative methods in organizational research: A practical guide*. Thousand Oaks, Calif.: Sage.

Cassell, J., ed. 1987. *Children in the field*. Philadelphia: Temple University Press.

Catania, J. A., D. Binson, J. Canchola, L. M. Pollack, W. Hauck, and T. J. Coates. 1996. Effects of interviewer gender, interviewer choice, and item wording on responses to questions concerning sexual behavior. *Public Opinion Quarterly* 60:345-75.

Cattell, R. B., and P. Kline. 1977. *The scientific analysis of personality and motivation*. New York: Academic Press.

Chadsey-Rusch, J., and P. Gonzalez. 1988. Social ecology of the workplace: Employers' perceptions versus direct observations. *Research in Developmental Disabilities* 9:229-45.

Chagnon, N. 1983. *Yanomamo: The fierce people*. 3rd ed. New York: Holt, Rinehart & Winston.

Chambers, R. 1991. Rapid (or relaxed) and participatory rural appraisal—Notes on practical approaches and methods. *Qualitative Research Methods Newsletter 2* (Tata Institute of Social Research, Deonar, Bombay, India), August, 11-16.

Chan, A., R. Madsen, and J. Unger. 1984. *Chen Village: The recent history of a peasant community in Mao's China*. Berkeley: University of California Press.

Chapman, P., R. B. Toma, R. V. Tuveson, and M. Jacob. 1997. Nutrition knowledge among adolescent high school female athletes. *Adolescence* 32:437-46.

Charmaz, K. 1990. "Discovering" chronic illness: Using grounded theory. *Social Science and Medicine* 30:1161-72.

Chen, A., Z. Liu, and C. D. Ennis. 1997. Universality and uniqueness of teacher educational value orientations: A cross-cultural comparison between the USA and China. *Journal of Research and Development in Education* 30:135-43.

Choldin, H. M. 1994. *Looking for the last percent: The controversy over census undercounts*. New Brunswick, N.J.: Rutgers University Press.

Chomsky, N. 1972. *Language and mind*. New York: Harcourt Brace Jovanovich.

Chow, S. L. 1996. *Statistical significance: Rationale, validity and utility*. Thousand Oaks, Calif.: Sage.

Christianson, G. E. 1984. *In the presence of the creator: Isaac Newton and his times*. New York: Free Press.

Chung, Y. B. 1996. The construct validity of the Bem Sex-Role Inventory for heterosexual and gay men. *Journal of Homosexuality* 30:87-97.

Chyba, M. M. 1993. *Questionnaires from the National Health Interview Survey, 1985-89*. U.S. Department of Health and Human Services, Public Health Service, Centers for Disease Control and Prevention, National Center for Health Statistics, Hyattsville, Md. Washington, D.C.: Government Printing Office.

Cialdini, R. B., et al. 1976. Basking in reflected glory: Three (football) field studies. *Journal of Personality and Social Psychology* 34:366-75.

Claiborne, W. 1984. Dowry killings show social stress in India. *Washington Post*, September 22, A1.

Clark, S. J., and R. A. Desharnais. 1998. Honest answers to embarrassing questions: Detecting cheating in the randomized response model. *Psychological Methods* 3:60-168.

Cochran, W. G. 1977. *Sampling techniques.* 2d ed. New York: John Wiley.

Cohen, J. 1960. A coefficient of agreement for nominal scales. *Educational and Psychological Measurement* 20:37-48.

Cohen, J. 1988. *Statistical power analysis for the behavioral sciences.* 2d ed. Hillsdale, N.J.: Lawrence Erlbaum.

Cohen, J. 1992. A power primer. *Psychological Bulletin* 112:155-59.

Cohen, J. 1994. The earth is round ($p < .05$). *American Psychologist* 49:997-1003.

Cohn, E. G. 1990. Weather and crime. *British Journal of Criminology* 30:51-64.

Cohn, E. G., and J. Rotton. 1997. Assault as a function of time and temperature: A moderator-variable time-series analysis. *Journal of Personality and Social Psychology* 72:1322-34.

Cole, D. 1983. The value of a person lies in his *herzenbildung*: Franz Boas' Baffin Island letter-diary, 1883-1884. In *Observers observed*, ed. by G. W. Stocking, 13-52. Madison: University of Wisconsin Press.

Collins, D. M., and P. F. Hayes. 1993. Development of a short-form conservatism scale suitable for mail surveys. *Psychological Reports* 72:419-22.

Comrey, A. L. 1992. *A first course in factor analysis.* 2d ed. Hillsdale, N.J.: Lawrence Erlbaum.

Comte, A. 1875-77. *System of positive polity.* 4 vols. Trans. by J. H. Bridges, F. Harrison, E. S. Beeseley, R. Gongreve, and H. D. Hutton. London: Longmans, Green.

Comte, A. 1974 [1855]. *The essential Comte.* Ed. by S. Andreski. Trans. by M. Clarke. New York: Barnes & Noble.

Comte, A. 1975. *Auguste Comte and positivism: The essential writings.* Ed. by G. Lenzer. New York: Harper & Row.

Comte, A. 1988. *Cours de philosophie positive. Introduction to positive philosophy.* Trans. by F. Ferre. Indianapolis, Ind.: Hackett.

Conklin, H. C. 1955. Hanunóo color categories. *Southwestern Journal of Anthropology* 11:339-44.

Connolly, M. 1990. Adrift in the city: A comparative study of children in Bogota, Colombia, and Guatemala City. *Child and Youth Services* 14:129-49.

Converse, J. M. 1984. Strong arguments and weak evidence: The open/closed question controversy of the 1940s. *Public Opinion Quarterly* 48:267-82.

Converse, J. M., and H. Schuman. 1974. *Conversations at random: Survey research as the interviewers see it.* New York: John Wiley.

Cook, S. W. 1975. A comment on the ethical issues involved in West, Gunn, and Chernicky's "Ubiquitous Watergate": An attributional analysis. *Journal of Personality and Social Psychology* 32:66-68.

Cook, T. D., and D. T. Campbell. 1979. *Quasi-experimentation: Design and analysis issues for field settings.* Chicago: Rand McNally College Publishing.

Cook, T. D., H. Cooper, and D. S. Cordray et al. 1992. *Meta-analysis for explanation: A casebook.* New York: Russell Sage.

Cooker, M., and W. F. White. 1993. Influence of personal beliefs and attitudes on certification of preservice teachers. *Education* 114:284-92.

Coombs, C. H. 1964. *A theory of data.* New York: John Wiley.

Cordella, P., and L. Siegel, eds. 1996. *Readings in contemporary criminological theory.* Boston: Northeastern University Press.

Corral-Verdugo, V. 1997. Dual "realities" of conservation behavior: Self-reports vs. observations of re-use and recycling behavior. *Journal of Environmental Psychology* 17:135-45.

Coser, L. A., ed. 1975. *The idea of social structure: Papers in honor of Robert K. Merton.* New York: Harcourt Brace Jovanovich.

Cottingham, J. 1988. *The rationalists.* Oxford, U.K.: Oxford University Press.

Cowan, G., and M. O'Brien. 1990. Gender and survival vs. death in slasher films—A content analysis. *Sex Roles* 23:187-96.

Crabb, P. B., and D. Bielawski. 1994. The social representation of material culture and gender in children's books. *Sex Roles* 30:69-79.

Craib, I. 1997. *Classical social theory.* New York: Oxford University Press.

Cramer, D. 1996. Job satisfaction and organizational continuance commitment: A two-wave panel study. *Journal of Organizational Behavior* 17:389-400.

Cramer, K. M., and R. P. Lake. 1998. The preference for solitude scale: Psychometric properties and factor structure. *Personality and Individual Differences* 24:193-99.

Crawford, C., and D. L. Krebs, eds. 1998. *Handbook of evolutionary psychology: Ideas, issues, and applications.* Mahwah, N.J.: Lawrence Erlbaum.

Crespi, T. D. 1993. SYMLOG: Clinical technology for therapist family of origin and family system appraisal. *Contemporary Family Therapy: An International Journal* 15:369-80.

Csikszentmihalyi, M., and R. Larson. 1987. Validity and reliability of the experience-sampling method. Special issue: Mental disorders in their natural settings: The application of time allocation and experience-sampling techniques in psychiatry. *Journal of Nervous and Mental Disease* 175:526-36.

Curtice, J., and N. Sparrow. 1997. How accurate are traditional quota opinion polls? *Journal of the Market Research Society* 39:433-48.

Dadds, M. R., R. M. Rapee, and P. M. Barrett. 1994. Behavioral observation. In *International handbook of phobic and anxiety disorders in children and adolescents: Issues in clinical child psychology,* ed. by T. H. Ollendick, N. King, and W. Yule, 349-64. New York: Plenum.

Dalton, D. R., J. C. Wimbush, and C. M. Daily. 1996. Candor, privacy, and "legal immunity" in business ethics research: An empirical assessment of the randomized response technique (RTT). *Business Ethics Quarterly* 6:87-99.

Daly, M., and M. Wilson. 1988. *Homicide.* New York: Aldine de Gruyter.

Dancy, J. 1985. *An introduction to contemporary epistemology.* Oxford, U.K.: Basil Blackwell.

D'Andrade, R. G. 1973. Cultural constructions of reality. In *Cultural illness and health,* ed. by L. Nader and T. W. Maretzki, 115-27. Washington, D.C.: American Anthropological Association.

D'Andrade, R. G. 1974. Memory and the assessment of behavior. In *Measurement in the social sciences,* ed. by H. M. Blalock, Jr., 159-86. Chicago: Aldine.

D'Andrade, R. G. 1995. *The development of cognitive anthropology.* Cambridge, U.K.: Cambridge University Press.

D'Andrade, R. G., N. Quinn, S. B. Nerlove, and A. K. Romney. 1972. Categories of disease in American English and Mexican Spanish. In *Multidimensional scaling,* ed. by A. K. Romney, R. Shepard, and S. B. Nerlove. Vol. 2, *Applications,* 9-54. New York: Seminar.

Davis, D. 1986. Changing self-image: Studying menopausal women in a Newfoundland fishing village. In *Self, sex and gender in cross-cultural fieldwork,* ed. by T. L. Whitehead and M. E. Conaway, 240-62. Urbana: University of Illinois Press.

Davis, D. W. 1997. The direction of race of interviewer effects among African-Americans: Donning the Black mask. *American Journal of Political Science* 41:309-23.

Davis, J. A. 1971. *Elementary survey analysis.* Englewood Cliffs, N.J.: Prentice Hall.

Davis, K., and S. Weller. Forthcoming. The effectiveness of condoms in reducing heterosexually transmitted HIV. *Family Planning Perspectives.*

Davis, N. Z. 1981. Printing and the people. In *Literacy and social development in the West,* ed. by H. J. Graf, 69-95. Cambridge, U.K.: Cambridge University Press.

Davison, M. L., and C. L. Skay. 1991. Multidimensional scaling and factor models of test and item responses. *Psychological Bulletin* 110:551-56.

de Ghett, V. J. 1978. Hierarchical cluster analysis. In *Quantitative ethology,* ed. by P. W. Colgan, 115-44. New York: John Wiley.

DeHart, S. S., and N. G. Hoffmann. 1997. Screening and diagnosis: Alcohol use disorders in older adults. In *Older adults' misuse of alcohol, medicines, and other drugs: Research and practice issues,* ed. by A. M. Gurnack et al., 25-53. New York: Springer.

Dehavenon, A. L. 1978. Superordinate behavior in urban homes: A video analysis of request-compliance and food control behavior in two Black and two White families living in New York City. Ph.D. diss., Columbia University.

De Leon, G., J. A. Inciardi, and S. S. Martin. 1995. Residential drug abuse treatment research: Are conventional control designs appropriate for assessing treatment effectiveness? *Journal of Psychoactive Drugs* 27:85-91.

Dellino, D. 1984. Tourism: Panacea or plight. Impacts on the quality of life on Exuma, Bahamas. Master's thesis, University of Florida, Gainesville.

Deloria, V. 1969. *Custer died for your sins: An Indian manifesto.* New York: Macmillan.

Denzin, N. K. 1978. *The research act: A theoretical introduction to sociological methods.* 2d ed. New York: McGraw-Hill.

Denzin, N. K., and Y. Lincoln, eds. 1994. *Handbook of qualitative research.* Thousand Oaks, Calif.: Sage.

Derogatis, L. R., and N. Melisaratos. 1983. The Brief Symptom Inventory: An introductory report. *Psychological Medicine* 13:595-605.

Descartes, R. 1960 [1637]. *Discourse on method; and meditations.* New York: Liberal Arts Press.

Descartes, R. 1993 [1641]. *Discourse on method and meditations on first philosophy.* Trans. by D. A. Cress. 3d ed. Indianapolis, Ind.: Hackett.

Deutscher, I. 1973. *What we say, what we do.* Glenview, Ill.: Scott, Foresman.

De Valck, C., and K. P. Van de Woestijne. 1996. Communication problems on an oncology ward. *Patient Education & Counseling* 29:131-36.

DeVellis, F. F. 1991. *Scale development: Theory and applications.* Newbury Park, Calif.: Sage.

Devet, B. 1990. A method for observing and evaluating writing lab tutorials. *Writing Center Journal* 10:75-83.

DeWalt, B. R. 1979. *Modernization in a Mexican ejido.* New York: Cambridge University Press.

DeWalt, K., B. R. DeWalt, and C. B. Wayland. 1998. Participant observation. In *Handbook of methods in cultural anthropology,* ed. by H. R. Bernard, 259-99. Walnut Creek, Calif.: AltaMira.

Dey, I. 1993. *Qualitative data analysis: A user-friendly guide for social scientists.* London: Routledge & Kegan Paul.

Diaz de Chumaceiro, C. L. 1996. The analyst's consulting room. *American Journal of Psychoanalysis* 56:237-38.

Dillman, D. A. 1978. *Mail and telephone surveys: The total design method.* New York: John Wiley.

Dillman, D. A. 1983. Mail and other self-administered questionnaires. In *Handbook of survey research,* ed. by P. H. Rossi, J. D. Wright, and A. B. Anderson, 359-78. New York: Academic Press.

Dilthey, W. 1989 [1883]. *Introduction to the human sciences.* Ed. by A. Makkreel and F. Rodi. Princeton, N.J.: Princeton University Press.

Dilthey, W. 1996. *Hermeneutics and the study of history.* Ed. by R. A. Makkreel and F. Rodi. Princeton, N.J.: Princeton University Press.

DiMaggio, P., J. Evans, and B. Bryson. 1966. Have Americans' social attitudes become more polarized? *American Journal of Sociology* 102:690-755.

Ditmar, H. 1991. Meanings of material possessions as reflections of identity: Gender and social-material position in society. *Journal of Social Behavior and Personality* 6:165-86.

Divale, W. T. 1976. Female status and cultural evolution: A study in ethnographer bias. *Behavior Science Research* 11:169-212.

Dobkin de Rios, M. 1981. Socioeconomic characteristics of an Amazon urban healer's clientele. *Social Science and Medicine* 15B:51-63.

Dohrenwend, B. S., and S. A. Richardson. 1965. Directiveness and nondirectiveness in research interviewing: A reformulation of the problem. *Psychology Bulletin* 63:475-85.

Doob, A. N., and A. E. Gross. 1968. Status of frustrator as an inhibitor of horn honking responses. *Journal of Social Psychology* 76:213-18.

Doughty, P. 1979. A Latin American specialty in the world context: Urban primacy and cultural colonialism in Peru. *Urban Anthropology* 8:383-98.

Drass, K. 1980. The analysis of qualitative data: A computer program. *Urban Life* 9:332-53.

Dressler, W. W. 1980. Ethnomedical beliefs and patient adherence to a treatment regimen: A St. Lucian example. *Human Organization* 39:88-91.

Drury, C. C. 1990. Methods for direct observation of performance. In *Evaluation of human work: A practical ergonomics methodology,* ed. by J. R. Wilson and E. N. Corlett, 35-57. New York: Taylor & Francis.

Dukes, R. L., J. B. Ullman, and J. A. Stein. 1995. An evaluation of DARE (Drug Abuse Resistance Education) using a Solomon four-group design with latent variables. *Evaluation Review* 19:409-35.

Duncan, O. D. 1966. Path analysis: Sociological examples. *American Journal of Sociology* 72:1-16.

Dundes, A., ed. 1982. *Cinderella: A folklore casebook.* New York: Garland.

Duranleau, D. 1999. Random sampling of regional populations: A field test. *Field Methods* 11:61-67.

Durkheim, É. 1933 [1893]. *The division of labor in society.* Trans. by G. Simpson. Glencoe, Ill.: Free Press.

Durkheim, É. 1958. *Socialism and Saint-Simon.* Ed. by A. Gouldner. Trans. by C. Sattler. Yellow Springs, Ohio: Antioch.

Dyl, J., and S. Wapner. 1996. Age and gender differences in the nature, meaning, and function of cherished possessions for children and adolescents. *Journal of Experimental Child Psychology* 62:340-77.

Easlea, B. 1980. *Witch hunting, magic, and the new philosophy.* Atlantic Highlands, N.J.: Humanities.

Ebby, D. W., F. M. Streff, and C. Christoff. 1996. A comparison of two direct-observation methods for measuring daytime safety belt use. *Accident Analysis and Prevention* 28:403-407.

Edgerton, R. B., and A. Cohen. 1994. Culture and schizophrenia: The DOSMD challenge. *British Journal of Psychiatry* 164:222-31.

Edinburg, G. M., N. E. Zinberg, and W. Kelman. 1975. *Clinical interviewing and counseling: Principles and techniques.* New York: Appleton-Century-Crofts.

Edmondson, B. 1988. This survey is garbage (analyzing trash to estimate populations). *American Demographics* 10:13-15.

Edmonston, B., and C. Schultze, eds. 1995. *Modernizing the U.S. Census.* Washington, D.C.: National Academy Press.

Eibl-Eiblsfeldt, I. 1989. *Human ethology.* New York: Aldine de Gruyter.

Eisenstein, E. 1979. *The printing press as an agent of change: Communications and cultural transformations in early modern Europe.* 2 vols. Cambridge, U.K.: Cambridge University Press.

Eissa, N. 1995. *Taxation and labor supply of married women: The Tax Reform Act of 1986 as a natural experiment.* Cambridge, Mass.: National Bureau of Economic Research.

Ekman, P., E. R. Sorenson, and W. V. Friesen. 1969. Pan-cultural elements in facial displays of emotion. *Science* 164:86-88.

Elder, G. H., E. K. Pavalko, and E. C. Clipp. 1993. *Working with archival data: Studying lives.* Newbury Park, Calif.: Sage.

Ember, C. R. 1975. Residential variation among hunter-gatherers. *Behavior Science Research* 9:199-207.

Ember, C. R. 1978. Myths about hunter-gatherers. *Ethnology* 17:439-48.

Emerson, R. M., R. I. Fretz, and L. L. Shaw. 1995. *Writing ethnographic fieldnotes.* Chicago: University of Chicago Press.

Ennis, C. D., A. Chen, and J. Ross. 1992. Educational value orientations as a theoretical framework for experienced urban teachers' curricular decision making. *Journal of Research and Development in Education* 25:156-64.

Ennis, C. D., L. K. Mueller, and L. M. Hooper. 1990. The influence of teacher value orientations on curriculum planning within the parameters of a theoretical framework. *Research Quarterly for Exercise and Sport* 61:360-68.

Erikson, K. T. 1967. A comment on disguised observation in sociology. *Social Problems* 14:366-73.

Evans-Pritchard, E. E. 1958 [1937]. *Witchcraft, oracles, and magic among the Azande.* Oxford, U.K.: Oxford University Press.

Evans-Pritchard, E. E. 1973. Some reminiscences and reflections on fieldwork. *Journal of the Anthropological Society of Oxford* 4:1-12.

Eyberg, S. 1992. Parent and teacher behavior inventories for the assessment of conduct problem behaviors in children. In *Innovations in clinical practice: A source book.* Vol. 11, ed. by L. VandeCreek, S. Knapp, and T. L. Jackson, 261-70. Sarasota, Fla.: Professional Resource Press/Professional Resource Exchange, Inc.

Fabrega, H., Jr. 1970. On the specificity of folk illness. *Southwestern Journal of Anthropology* 26:305-14.

Fahim, H. M. 1982. *Indigenous anthropology in non-Western societies: Proceedings of a Burg-Wartenstein symposium.* Durham: University of North Carolina Press.

Farley, J. U., and D. R. Lehmann. 1986. *Meta-analysis in marketing: Generalization of response models.* Lexington, Mass.: D. C. Heath.

Farmer, W. R. 1976. *The synoptic problem.* Dilsboro: Western North Carolina Press.

Farnell, B., and L. R. Graham 1998. Discourse-centered methods. In *Handbook of methods in cultural anthropology,* ed. by H. R. Bernard, 411-57. Walnut Creek, Calif.: AltaMira.

Feigl, H. 1980. Positivism. In *Encyclopaedia Britannica.* Vol. 14. Chicago: Encyclopaedia Britannica.

Feigl, H., and A. Blumberg. 1931. Logical positivism: A new movement in European philosophy. *Journal of Philosophy* 28:281-96.

Feldman, R. E. 1968. Response to compatriot and foreigner who seek assistance. *Journal of Personality and Social Psychology* 10:202-14.

Fenno, R. F. 1990. *Watching politicians: Essays on participant observation.* Berkeley: Institute of Governmental Studies, University of California.

Fenton, W. S., C. R. Blyler, and R. K. Heinssen. 1997. Determinants of medication compliance in schizophrenia: Empirical and clinical findings. *Schizophrenia Bulletin* 23:637-51.

Fermi, L., and B. Bernardini. 1961. *Galileo and the scientific revolution.* New York: Basic Books.

Ferriter, M. 1993. Computer aided interviewing and the psychiatric social history. *Social Work and Social Sciences Review* 4:255-63.

Festinger, L. A. 1957. *A theory of cognitive dissonance.* Stanford, Calif.: Stanford University Press.

Fetterman, D. 1989. *Ethnography step by step.* Newbury Park, Calif.: Sage.

Fetterman, D. 1998. *Ethnography step by step.* 2d ed. Thousand Oaks, Calif.: Sage.

Fettes, P. A., and J. M. Peters. 1992. A meta-analysis of group treatments for bulimia nervosa. *International Journal of Eating Disorders* 11:97-110.

Fielding, N. 1993. Ethnography. In *Researching social life,* ed. by N. Gilbert, 154-71. London: Sage.

Fielding, N., and R. M. Lee. 1998. *Computer analysis and qualitative research.* London: Sage.

Fine, G. A., and K. L. Sandstrom. 1988. *Knowing children: Participant observation with minors.* Newbury Park, Calif.: Sage.

Finkel, S. E., Guterbock, T. M., and M. J. Borg. 1991. Race-of-interviewer effects in a preelection poll: Virginia 1989. *Public Opinion Quarterly* 55:313-30.

Finkler, K. 1974. *Estudio comparativo de la economía de dos comunidades de México: El papel de la irrigación.* Mexico City: Instituto Nacional Indigenista.

Fisher, D. 1993. *Fundamental development of the social sciences: Rockefeller philanthropy and the United States Social Science Research Council.* Ann Arbor: University of Michigan Press.

Fisher, R. A. 1936. The use of multiple measurements in taxonomic problems. *Annals of Eugenics* 7:179-88.

Fisher, R. A. 1970. *Statistical methods for research workers.* 14th ed., rev. and enlarged. New York: Hafner.

Fiske, D. W. 1982. Convergent-discriminant validation in measurements and research strategies. *New Di-*

rections for *Methodology of Social and Behavioral Science* 12:77-92.

Fjellman, S. M., and H. Gladwin. 1985. Haitian family patterns of migration to South Florida. *Human Organization* 44:301-12.

Flanagan, T. J., and D. R. Longmire, eds. 1996. *Americans view crime and justice: A national public opinion survey.* Thousand Oaks, Calif.: Sage.

Flanders, N. A. 1970. *Analyzing teaching behavior.* Reading, Mass.: Addison-Wesley.

Fleisher, M. 1989. *Warehousing violence.* Newbury Park, Calif: Sage.

Fleisher, M. 1998. *Dead end kids: Gang girls and the boys they know.* Madison: University of Wisconsin Press.

Fleiss, J. L. 1971. Measuring nominal scale agreement among many raters. *Psychological Bulletin* 76:378-82.

Fleiss, J. L. 1981. *Statistical methods for rates and proportions.* 2d ed. New York: John Wiley.

Flowers, J. H., D. C. Buhman, and D. D. Turnage. 1997. Cross-modal equivalence of visual and auditory scatterplots for exploring bivariate data samples. *Human Factors* 39:341-51.

Fluehr-Lobban, C. 1996. Rejoinder to Wax and Herrera. *Human Organization* 55:240. (See also entries for Wax [1996] and for Herrera [1996].)

Foddy, W. 1993. *Constructing questions for interviews and questionnaires: Theory and practice in social research.* New York: Cambridge University Press.

Fortney, J., K. Rost, and M. Zhang. 1998. A joint choice model of the decision to seek depression treatment and choice of provider sector. *Medical Care* 36:307-20.

Foster, G. M., T. Scudder, E. Colson, and R. V. Kemper, eds. 1979. *Long-term field research in social anthropology.* New York: Academic Press.

Foster, S. L., D. J. Bell-Dolan, and D. A. Burge. 1988. Behavioral observation. In *Behavioral assessment: A practical handbook.* 3d ed. Ed. by A. S. Bellack and M. Hersen, 119-60. Elmsford, N.Y.: Pergamon.

Foster, S. L., and J. D. Cone. 1986. Design and use of direct observation. In *Handbook of behavioral assessment.* 2d ed. Ed. by A. R. Ciminero, K. S. Calhoun, and H. E. Adams, 253-324. New York: John Wiley.

Fowler, F. J. 1984. *Survey research methods.* Beverly Hills, Calif.: Sage.

Fowler, F. J., A. M. Roman, and Z. X. Di. 1998. Mode effects in a survey of Medicare prostate surgery patients. *Public Opinion Quarterly* 62:29-46.

Fox, J. 1991. *Regression diagnostics.* Sage University Papers Series. Quantitative applications in the social sciences, no. 79. Newbury Park, Calif.: Sage.

Fox, R. J., M. R. Crask, and J. Kim. 1988. Mail survey response rate. *Public Opinion Quarterly* 52:467-91.

Fox-Wolfgramm, S. J., K. B. Boal, and J. G. Hunt. 1998. Organizational adaptation to institutional change: A comparative study of first-order change in prospector and defender banks. *Administrative Science Quarterly* 43:87-126.

Frake, C. O. 1962. The ethnographic study of cognitive systems. In *Anthropology and human behavior,* 72-85. Washington, D.C.: Anthropological Society of Washington.

Frake, C. O. 1964. Notes on queries in anthropology. In *Transcultural studies in cognition,* ed. by A. K. Romney and R. G. D'Andrade. *American Anthropologist* 66 (Part II).

Frank, S. H., K. C. Stange, D. Langa, and M. Workings. 1997. Direct observation of community-based ambulatory encounters involving medical students. *Journal of the American Medical Association* 278:712-16.

Freeman, D. 1983. *Margaret Mead and Samoa: The making and unmaking of an anthropological myth.* Cambridge, Mass.: Harvard University Press.

Freeman, L. C. 1965. *Elementary applied statistics for students in behavioral science.* New York: John Wiley.

Freeman, L. C., A. K. Romney, and S. C. Freeman. 1987. Cognitive structure and informant accuracy. *American Anthropologist* 89:310-25.

Freidenberg, B. M., and R. S. Cimbalo. 1996. Human ethology: Eating, security, and curiosity. *Perceptual and Motor Skills* 83:489-90.

Freilich, M., ed. 1977. *Marginal natives at work: Anthropologists in the field.* 2d ed. Cambridge, Mass.: Schenkman.

Frey, J. H. 1989. *Survey research by telephone.* 2d ed. Newbury Park, Calif.: Sage.

Friedenberg, L. 1995. *Psychological testing: Design, analysis, and use.* Needham Heights, Mass.: Allyn & Bacon.

Friedson, E. 1984. The changing nature of professional control. *Annual Review of Sociology* 10:1-20.

Frisancho, A. R. 1990. *Anthropometric standards for the assessment of growth and nutritional status.* Ann Arbor: University of Michigan Press.

Fry, D. P. 1990. Play aggression among Zapotec children: Implications for the practice hypothesis. *Aggressive Behavior* 16:321-40.

Gaito, J. 1980. Measurement scales and statistics: Resurgence of an old misconception. *Psychological Bulletin* 87:564-67.

Galambos, N. L., A. C. Peterson, M. Richards, and I. B. Gitelson. 1985. The Attitudes Toward Women Scale for Adolescents (ATWSA): A study of reliability and validity. *Sex Roles* 13:343-56.

Galilei, Galileo. 1967 [1632]. *Dialogue concerning the two chief world systems, Ptolomaic and Copernican.* 2d ed. Trans. by S. Drake. Berkeley: University of California Press.

Gallmeier, C. P. 1991. Leaving, revisiting, and staying in touch: Neglected issues in field research. In *Experiencing fieldwork,* ed. by W. B. Shaffir and R. A. Stebbins, 224-31. Newbury Park, Calif.: Sage.

Gans, L. P., and C. S. Wood. 1985. Discriminant analysis as a method for differentiating potential acceptors of family planning: Western Samoa. *Human Organization* 44:228-33.

Garrett, A. M., and E. Zaki. 1982. *Interviewing: Its principles and methods.* 3d ed. rev. New York: Family Service Association of America.

Garro, L. C. 1986. Intracultural variation in folk medical knowledge: A comparison between curers and noncurers. *American Anthropologist* 88:351-70.

Gatewood, J. B. 1983a. Deciding where to fish: The skipper's dilemma in southeast Alaska's salmon seining. *Coastal Zone Management Journal* 10:347-67.

Gatewood, J. B. 1983b. Loose talk: Linguistic competence and recognition ability. *American Anthropologist* 85:378-86.

Gatewood, J. B. 1984. Familiarity, vocabulary size, and recognition ability in four semantic domains. *American Ethnologist* 11:507-27.

Gatz, M., and M. Hurwicz. 1990. Are old people more depressed? Cross-sectional data on center for epidemiological studies depression scale factors. *Psychology and Aging* 5:284-90.

Gaulin, S. C., and J. S. Boster. 1990. Dowry as female competition. *American Anthropologist* 92:994-1005.

Gearing, J. 1995. Fear and loving in the West Indies: Research from the heart. In *Taboo: Sex, identity, and erotic subjectivity in anthropological fieldwork,* ed. by D. Kulick and M. Willson, 186-218. London: Routledge.

Geertz, C. 1973. *The interpretation of cultures. Selected essays.* New York: Basic Books.

Geertz, C. 1983. *Local knowledge: Further essays in interpretive anthropology.* New York: Basic Books.

Gelardi, A. M. G. 1996. The influence of tax law changes on the timing of marriages: A two-country analysis. *National Tax Journal* 49:17-30.

Geller, D., J. Biederman, J. Jones, K. Park, S. Schwartz, S. Shapiro, and B. Coffey. 1998. Is juvenile obsessive-compulsive disorder a developmental subtype of the disorder? A review of the pediatric literature. *Journal of the American Academy of Child and Adolescent Psychiatry* 37:420-27.

Gerard, H. B., and G. C. Mathewson. 1966. The effects of severity of initiation on liking for a group: A replication. *Journal of Experimental Social Psychology* 2:278-87.

Gianfrancesco, F. D., A. P. Baines, and D. Richards. 1994. Utilization of prescription drug benefits in an aging population. *Health Care Financing Review* 15:113-26.

Gilbreth, F. B. 1911. *Motion study.* New York: D. Van Nostrand. (Reprinted 1972 by Hive Publishing Co., Easton, Pa.)

Gilly, M. C. 1988. Sex roles in advertising: A comparison of television advertisements in Australia, Mexico, and the United States. *Journal of Marketing* 52:75-85.

Gittelsohn, J., A. V. Shankar, K. P. West, R. M. Ram, and T. Gynwali. 1997. Estimating reactivity in direct observation studies of health behaviors. *Human Organization* 56:182-89.

Gladwin, C. H. 1976. A view of plan puebla: An application of hierarchical decision models. *Journal of Agricultural Economics* 59:881-87.

Gladwin, C. H. 1980. A theory of real life choice: Applications to agricultural decisions. In *Agricultural decision making,* ed. by P. Barlett, 45-85. New York: Academic Press.

Gladwin, C. H. 1983. Contributions of decision-tree methodology to a farming systems program. *Human Organization* 42:146-57.

Gladwin, C. H. 1989. *Ethnographic decision tree modeling.* Newbury Park, Calif.: Sage.

Gladwin, H. 1971. Decision making in the Cape Coast (Fante) fishing and fish marketing system. Ph.d. diss., Stanford University, Stanford, Calif.

Glaser, B. G., and A. Strauss. 1967. *The discovery of grounded theory: Strategies for qualitative research.* New York: Aldine.

Glaser, J. M. 1996. The challenge of campaign watching: Seven lessons of participant-observation research. *PS: Political Science and Politics* 29:533-37.

Glaser, J. M., and M. Gilens. 1997. Interregional migration and political resocialization: A study of racial attitudes under pressure. *Public Opinion Quarterly* 61:72-96.

Glass, G. V. 1976. Primary, secondary, and meta-analysis of research. *Educational Researcher* 5:3-8.

Glass, G. V., V. L. Willson, and J. M. Gottman. 1979. *Design and analysis of time-series experiments.* Boulder, Colo.: Associated University Press.

Glazer, M. 1975. Impersonal sex. In *Tearoom trade: Impersonal sex in public places,* ed. by L. Humphreys, 213-22. Enlarged ed. with a retrospect on ethical issues. Chicago: Aldine.

Goldberg, D., S. T. Green, A. Taylor, M. Frischer, and N. McKegancy. 1994. Comparison of four survey methods designed to estimated the prevalence of HIV among female prostitutes who inject drugs. *International Journal of STD and AIDS* 5:186-88.

Goldberg, J., M. S. Richards, R. J. Anderson, and M. B. Rodin. 1991. Alcohol consumption in men exposed to the military draft lottery: A natural experiment. *Journal of Substance Abuse* 3:307-13.

Golde, P., ed. 1986. *Women in the field: Anthropological experiences.* 2d ed. Berkeley: University of California Press.

Goldman, A. E., and S. S. McDonald. 1987. *The group depth interview: Principles and practice.* Englewood Cliffs, N.J.: Prentice Hall.

Goldman, L. K., and S. A. Glantz. 1998. Evaluation of antismoking advertising campaigns. *Journal of the American Medical Association* 279:772-77.

Goldsmith, T. H. 1991. *The biological roots of human nature: Forging links between evolution and behavior.* New York: Oxford University Press.

González, N. S. 1986. The anthropologist as female head of household. In *Self, sex and gender in cross-cultural fieldwork,* ed. by T. L. Whitehead and M. E. Conaway, 84-102. Urbana: University of Illinois Press.

Good, K. (with D. Chanoff). 1991. *Into the heart.* New York: Simon & Schuster.

Goodenough, W. 1956. Componential analysis and the study of meaning. *Language* 32:195-216.

Goodenough, W. 1965. Rethinking "status" and "role": Toward a general model of the cultural organization of social relationships. In *The relevance of models for social anthropology. Association of Social Anthropology Monographs I,* ed. by M. Banton, 1-24. London: Tavistock.

Goodman, L., and W. Kruskal. 1963. Measures of association for cross classifications III: Approximate sampling theory. *Journal of the American Statistical Association* 58:302-22.

Goodstadt, M. S., G. Cook, and V. Gruson. 1978. The validity of reported drug use: The randomized response technique. *International Journal of the Addictions* 13:359-67.

Gorden, R. L. 1975. *Interviewing: Strategy, techniques, and tactics.* Homewood, Ill.: Dorsey.

Gordon, S. 1993. *The history and philosophy of social science.* New York: Routledge.

Gorsuch, R. L. 1983. *Factor analysis.* 2d ed. Hillsdale, N.J.: Lawrence Erlbaum.

Gottman, J. M., and R. W. Levenson. 1992. Marital processes predictive of later dissolution: Behavior, physiology, and health. *Journal of Personality and Social Psychology* 63:221-33.

Gottschalk, L. A. 1997. The unobtrusive measurement of psychological states and traits. In *Text analysis for the social sciences: Methods for drawing statistical inferences from texts and transcripts,* ed. by C. W. Roberts et al., 117-29. Mahwah, N.J.: Lawrence Erlbaum.

Gottschalk, L. A., and R. J. Bechtel. 1993. *Psychologic and neuropsychiatric assessment: Applying the Gottschalk-Gleser content analysis method to verbal sample analysis using the Gottschalk-Bechtel computer scoring system.* Palo Alto, Calif.: Mind Garden.

Gould, R. A., and P. B. Potter. 1984. Use-lives of automobiles in America: A preliminary archaeological view. In *Toward an ethnoarchaeology of modern America,* ed. by R. A. Gould, 69-93. Brown University: Department of Anthropology, Research Papers in Anthropology (no. 4).

Grayling, A. C. 1996. Epistemology. In *The Blackwell companion to philosophy,* ed. by N. Bunnin and E. P. Tsui-James, 38-63. Oxford, U.K.: Basil Blackwell.

Green, B. L., and D. T. Kenrick, 1994. The attractiveness of gender-typed traits at different relationship levels: Androgynous characteristics may be desirable after all. *Personality and Social Psychology Bulletin* 20:244-53.

Green, P. E., and F. J. Carmone. 1970. *Multidimensional scaling and related techniques in marketing analysis.* Boston: Allyn & Bacon.

Greenbaum, T. L. 1998. *The handbook for focus group research.* 2d ed. rev. and expanded. Thousand Oaks, Calif.: Sage.

Greenwald, A. G., R. González, R. J. Harris, and D. Guthrie. 1996. Effect sizes and *p* values: What should be reported and what should be replicated? *Psychophysiology* 33:175-83.

Greenwood, C. R., J. C. Delquadri, S. O. Stanley, B. Terry, and R. V. Hall. 1985. Assessment of ecobehavioral interaction in school settings. *Behavioral Assessment* 7:331-47.

Griffin, J. H. 1961. *Black like me.* Boston: Houghton Mifflin.

Griffin, R. 1991. Effects of work redesign on employee perceptions, attitudes, and behaviors: A long-term investigation. *Academy of Management Journal* 34:425-35.

Gross, D. R. 1984. Time allocation: A tool for the study of cultural behavior. *Annual Review of Anthropology* 13:519-58.

Gross, D. R. 1992. *Discovering anthropology.* Mountain View, Calif.: Mayfield.

Grote, N. K., I. H. Frieze, and L. C. Schmidt. 1997. Political attitudes and the Vietnam war: A study of college-educated men of the Vietnam generation. *Journal of Applied Social Psychology* 27:1673-93.

Groves, R. M., and N. A. Mathiowetz. 1984. Computer assisted telephone interviewing: Effects on interviewers and respondents. *Public Opinion Quarterly* 48:356-69.

Gubrium, J. F. 1988. *Analyzing field reality.* Newbury Park, Calif.: Sage.

Gubrium, J. F., and J. A. Holstein. 1997. *The new language of qualitative method.* New York: Oxford University Press.

Guilmet, G. M. 1979. Instructor reaction to verbal and nonverbal-visual behavior in the urban classroom. *Anthropology and Education Quarterly* 10:254-66.

Gujarati, D. N. 1995. *Basic econometrics.* 3d ed. New York: McGraw-Hill.

Gummesson, E. 1991. *Qualitative methods in management research*. Newbury Park, Calif.: Sage.

Gunter, B., A. Furnham, and C. Beeson. 1997. Recall of television advertisements as a function of program evaluation. *Journal of Psychology* 131:541-43.

Guth, W., J. P. Krahnen, and C. Rieck. 1997. Financial markets with asymmetric information: A pilot study focusing on insider advantages. *Journal of Economic Psychology* 18:235-57.

Guttman, L. 1950. The basis for scalogram analysis. In *Studies in social psychology in World War II*, ed. by S. A. Stouffer et al. Vol. 4, *Measurement and prediction*, 60-90. Princeton, N.J.: Princeton University Press.

Guzzo, R. A., S. E. Jackson, and R. E. Katzell. 1987. Meta-analysis. In *Research in organizational behavior*. Vol. 9, ed. by B. M. Staw and L. L. Cummings. Greenwich, Conn.: JAI.

Hadaway, C. K., P. L. Marler, and M. Chaves. 1993. What the polls don't show: A closer look at U.S. church attendance. *American Sociological Review* 58:741-52.

Hadaway, C. K., P. L. Marler, and M. Chaves. 1998. Overreporting church attendance in America: Evidence that demands the same verdict. *American Sociological Review* 63:122-30.

Hage, P. 1987 [1972]. München beer categories. In *Culture and cognition*, ed. by J. P. Spradley, 263-78. Prospect Heights, Ill.: Waveland.

Hall, E. T. 1963. A system of notation of proxemic behavior. *American Anthropologist* 65:1003-26.

Hall, E. T. 1966. *The hidden dimension*. Garden City, N.Y.: Doubleday.

Hammel, E. A. 1962. Social rank and evolutionary position in a coastal Peruvian village. *Southwestern Journal of Anthropology* 18:199-215.

Hammersley, M. 1990. *Classroom ethnography: Empirical and methodological essays*. Philadelphia: Open University Press.

Handwerker, W. P. 1989. *Women's power and social revolution: Fertility transition in the West Indies*. Newbury Park, Calif.: Sage.

Handwerker, W. P. 1993. Simple random samples of regional populations. *Cultural Anthropology Methods* 5:12.

Handwerker, W. P. 1996a. Constructing Likert scales: Testing the validity and reliability of single measures of multidimensional variables. *Cultural Anthropology Methods Journal* 9:1-6.

Handwerker, W. P. 1996b. Power and gender: Violence and affection experienced by children in Barbados, W.I. *Medical Anthropology* 17:101-28.

Handwerker, W. P. 1998. Why violence? A test of hypotheses representing three discourses on the roots of domestic violence. *Human Organization* 57:200-208.

Handwerker, W. P., and D. F. Wozniak. 1997. Sampling strategy for the collection of cultural data: An extension of Boas's answer to Galton's problem. *Current Anthropology* 38:869-75.

Haney, C., C. Banks, and P. Zimbardo. 1973. Interpersonal dynamics in a simulated prison. *International Journal of Criminology and Penology* 1:69-97.

Hanks, W. F. 1989. Texts and textuality. *Annual Review of Anthropology* 18:95-127.

Hansen, A., and L. A. McSpadden. 1993. Self-anchoring scale, or ladder of life: A method used with diverse refugee populations. Unpublished manuscript.

Hansley, W. E. 1974. Increasing response rates by choice of postage stamps. *Public Opinion Quarterly* 38:280-83.

Harari, H., O. Harari, and R. V. White. 1985. The reaction to rape by American male bystanders. *Journal of Social Psychology* 125:653-58.

Harburg, E., L. Gleibermann, P. Roeper, M. A. Schork, and W. J. Schull. 1978. Skin color, ethnicity and blood pressure I: Detroit Blacks. *American Journal of Public Health* 68:1177-83.

Hare, S. E., and A. P. Hare, eds. 1997. *SYMLOG field theory: Organizational consultation, value differences, personality and social perception*. Westport, Conn.: Praeger.

Harlow, L. L., S. A. Mulaik, and J. H. Steiger, eds. 1997. *What if there were no significance tests?* Mahwah, N.J.: Lawrence Erlbaum.

Harrell, M. C., and L. L. Miller 1997. *New opportunities for military women: Effects on readiness, cohesion, and morale.* Santa Monica, Calif.: RAND.

Harris, A. C. 1997. Gender as a determinant of household purchase decisions: African Americans versus Anglo Americans. *Western Journal of Black Studies* 21:134-41.

Harris, M. 1968. *The rise of anthropological theory.* New York: Thomas Y. Crowell.

Harris, M. 1979. *Cultural materialism: The struggle for a science of culture.* New York: Random House.

Harris, M. 1980. *Culture, people, nature: An introduction to general anthropology.* 3d ed. New York: Harper & Row.

Harris, M., J. G. Consorte, J. Lang, and B. Byrne. 1993. Who are the Whites? Imposed census categories and the racial demography of Brazil. *Social Forces* 72:451-62.

Harrison, G. G. 1976. Sociocultural correlates of food utilization and waste in a sample of urban households. Ph.D. diss., University of Arizona.

Harshbarger, C. L. 1995. Farmer-herder conflict and state legitimacy in Cameroon. Ph.D. diss., University of Florida, Gainesville.

Hartman, J. J. 1978. Social demographic characteristics of Wichita, Sedwick County. In *Metropolitan Wichita—Past, present, and future,* ed. by G. Miller and J. Skaggs, 22-37. Lawrence: Kansas Regents Press.

Hartman, J. J., and J. Hedblom. 1979. *Methods for the social sciences: A handbook for students and nonspecialists.* Westport, Conn.: Greenwood.

Hartmann, D. P., and D. D. Wood. 1990. Observational methods. In *International handbook of behavior modification therapy.* 2d ed. Ed. by A. S. Bellack, M. Hersen, and A. E. Kazdin, 107-38. New York: Plenum.

Harvey, D. L., and M. H. Reed. 1996. The culture of poverty: An ideological analysis. *Sociological Perspectives* 39:465-95.

Hatch, D., and M. Hatch. 1947. Criteria of social status as derived from marriage announcements in the *New York Times. American Sociological Review* 12:396-403.

Hausman, D. B., and A. Hausman. 1997. *Descartes's legacy: Minds and meaning in early modern philosophy.* Toronto: University of Toronto Press.

Hays, J. A. 1984. Aging and family resources: Availability and proximity of kin. *Gerontologist* 24:149-53.

Hazan, A. R., H. L. Lipton, and S. A. Glantz. 1994. Popular films do not reflect current tobacco use. *American Journal of Public Health* 84:998-1000.

Heath, C. 1986. *Body movement and speech in medical interaction.* New York: Cambridge University Press.

Heath, S. B. 1972. *Telling tongues.* New York: Columbia University Press.

Heatherton, T. F., and J. Polivy. 1991. Development of a scale for measuring self-esteem. *Journal of Personality and Social Psychology* 60:895-910.

Heberlein, T. A., and R. Baumgartner. 1978. Factors affecting response rates to mailed questionnaires: A quantitative analysis of the published literature. *American Sociological Review* 43:447-62.

Heberlein, T. A., and R. Baumgartner. 1981. Is a questionnaire necessary in a second mailing? *Public Opinion Quarterly* 45:102-108.

Heck, R. H. 1998. Factor analysis: Exploratory and confirmatory approaches. In *Modern methods for business research: Methodology for business and management,* ed. by G. A. Marcoulides et al., 177-215. Mahwah, N.J.: Lawrence Erlbaum.

Hedges, L. V., and I. Olkin 1985. *Statistical methods for meta-analysis.* Orlando, Fla.: Academic Press.

Hedican, E. J. 1986. Sibling terminology and information theory: An hypothesis concerning the growth of folk taxonomy. *Ethnology* 25:229-39.

Helmes, E., and W. R. Nielson. 1998. An examination of the internal structure of the Center for Epidemiological Studies-Depression Scale in two medical samples. *Personality and Individual Differences* 25:735-43.

Henderson, G. R., D. Iacobucci, and B. J. Calder. 1998. *Brand constructs: The complementary of consumer* associative networks and multidimensional scaling. Cambridge, Mass.: Marketing Science Institute.

Henderson, J., and J. P. Harrington. 1914. *Ethnozoology of the Tewa Indians.* Smithsonian Institution, Bureau of American Ethnology, Bulletin 56. Washington, D.C.: Government Printing Office.

Henderson, S., D. G. Byrne, and P. Duncan-Jones. 1981. *Neurosis and the social environment.* New York: Academic Press.

Henley, N. M. 1969. A psychological study of the semantics of animal terms. *Journal of Verbal Learning and Verbal Behavior* 8:176-84.

Henry, G. T. 1990. *Practical sampling.* Newbury Park, Calif.: Sage.

Henry, S., and W. Einstadter, eds. 1998. *The criminology theory reader.* New York: New York University Press.

Herdt, G. 1992. "Coming out" as a rite of passage: A Chicago study. In *Gay culture in America: Essays from the field,* ed. by G. Herdt, 29-68. Boston: Beacon.

Herrera, C. D. 1996. Informed consent and ethical exemptions. *Human Organization* 55:235-37. (See entries for Wax [1996] and for Fluehr-Lobban [1996]).

Herzfeld, M. 1977. Ritual and textual structures: The advent of spring in rural Greece. In *Text and context,* ed. by R. K. Jain, 29-45. Philadelphia: Institute for the Study of Human Issues.

Herzog, A. R., and J. G. Bachman. 1981. Effects of questionnaire length on response quality. *Public Opinion Quarterly* 45:549-59.

Hicks, A., J. Misra, and T. N. Ng. 1995. The programmatic emergence of the social security state. *American Sociological Review* 60:329-49.

Hill, C. E. 1978. Development of a counselor verbal response category system. *Journal of Counseling Psychology* 25:461-68.

Hill, M. S. 1992. *The panel study of income dynamics: A user's guide.* Newbury Park, Calif.: Sage.

Hines, A. M. 1993. Linking qualitative and quantitative methods in cross-cultural survey research: Techniques from cognitive science. *American Journal of Community Psychology* 21:729-46.

Hirschman, E. C. 1987. People as products: Analysis of a complex marketing exchange. *Journal of Marketing* 51:98-108.

Hitchcock, J., and H. S. Wilson. 1992. Personal risking: Lesbian self-disclosure to health professionals. *Nursing Research* 41:178-83.

Hoagwood, K., P. S. Jensen, and C. B. Fisher, eds. 1996. *Ethical issues in mental health research with children and adolescents.* Mahwah, N.J.: Lawrence Erlbaum.

Hochstim, J. R. 1967. A critical comparison of three strategies of collecting data from households. *Journal of the American Statistical Association* 62:976-89.

Hodge, L. G., and D. Dufour. 1991. Cross-sectional growth of young Shipibo Indian children in eastern Peru. *American Journal of Physical Anthropology* 84:35-41.

Hogan, H. 1992. The 1990 Post-Enumeration Survey: An overview. *The American Statistician* 46:261-69.

Hogben, M. 1998. Factors moderating the effect of televised aggression on viewer behavior. *Communication Research* 25:220-47.

Hogg, R. V., and E. A. Tanis. 1997. *Probability and statistical inference.* 5th ed. Upper Saddle River, N.J.: Prentice Hall.

Holland, D., and D. Skinner. 1987. Prestige and intimacy: The cultural models behind Americans' talk about gender types. In *Cultural models in language and thought,* ed. by D. Holland and N. Quinn, 78-111. New York: Cambridge University Press.

Hollinger, R. 1994. *Postmodernism and the social sciences: A thematic approach.* Thousand Oaks, Calif.: Sage.

Hollis, M. 1996. Philosophy of social science. In *The Blackwell companion to philosophy,* ed. by N. Bunnin and E. P. Tsui-James, 358-87. Oxford, U.K.: Basil Blackwell.

Holloway, S. K., and R. Tomlinson. 1995. The new world order and the General Assembly: Bloc realignment at the UN in the post-Cold War world. *Canadian Journal of Political Science* 28:227-54.

Holmes, T. H., and R. H. Rahe. 1967. The Social Readjustment Rating Scale. *Journal of Psychosomatic Research* 11:213-18.

Holsti, O. R. 1969. *Content analysis for the social sciences and humanities.* Reading, Mass.: Addison-Wesley.

Honomichl, J. 1997. Real growth driven by overseas research. *Marketing News* 31:H2-H43.

Hopkins, T. K., and I. M. Wallerstein et al. 1982. *World-systems analysis: Theory and methodology.* Beverly Hills, Calif.: Sage.

Hops, H., B. Davis, and N. Longoria. 1995. Methodological issues in direct observation: Illustrations with the Living in Familial Environments (LIFE) coding system. *Journal of Clinical Child Psychology* 24:193-203.

Horn, W. 1960. Reliability survey: A survey on the reliability of response to an interview survey. *Het PTT-Bedriff* 10:105-156 (The Hague).

Hornik, J., and S. Ellis. 1988. Strategies to secure compliance for a mall intercept interview. *Public Opinion Quarterly* 52:539-51.

Horowitz, T., and G. J. Massey, eds. 1991. *Thought experiments in science and philosophy.* Savage, Md.: Rowman & Littlefield.

Horst, P. 1941. Mathematical contributions. *Social Science Research Council Bulletin* No. 48: 403-47.

House, J. S., W. Gerber, and A. J. McMichael. 1977. Increasing mail questionnaire response: A controlled replication and extension. *Public Opinion Quarterly* 41:95-99.

Howell, N. 1990. *Surviving fieldwork.* Washington, D.C.: American Anthropological Association.

Hughes, W. W. 1984. The method to our madness: The garbage project methodology. In *Household refuse analysis: Theory, method, and applications in social science,* ed. by W. L. Rathje and C. K. Rittenbaugh, 41-50. *American Behavioral Scientist* 28(1). (Special issue)

Hull, C. L. 1934. The rat's speed-of-locomotion gradient in the approach to food. *Journal of Comparative Psychology* 17:383-422.

Hume, D. 1978 [1739-40]. *A treatise on human nature.* 2d ed. Ed. by L. A. Selby-Bigge and P. N. Nidditch. New York: Oxford University Press.

Humphreys, L. 1975. *Tearoom trade: Impersonal sex in public places.* Enlarged ed. with a retrospect on ethical issues. Chicago: Aldine.

Hunfield, J. A. M., M. M. Mourik, J. Passcher, and D. Tibboel. 1996. Do couples grieve differently following infant loss? *Psychological Reports* 79:407-10.

Hunt, J. G., and A. Ropo. 1995. Multilevel leadership—Grounded theory and mainstream theory applied to the case of General Motors. *Leadership Quarterly* 6:379-412.

Hunt, M. G. 1993. Expressiveness does predict well-being. *Sex Roles* 29:147-69.

Hunt, M. M. 1997. *How science takes stock: The story of meta-analysis.* New York: Russell Sage.

Hunter, C., and K. McClelland. 1991. Honoring accounts for sexual harassment: A factorial survey analysis. *Sex Roles* 24:725-52.

Hunter, J. E., and F. L. Schmidt. 1990. *Methods of meta-analysis.* Newbury Park, Calif.: Sage.

Huntington, D., and S. R. Schuler. 1993. The simulated client method: Evaluating client-provider interactions in family planning clinics. *Studies in Family Planning* 24:187-93.

Hursh-César, G., and P. Roy, eds. 1976. *Third World surveys: Survey research in developing nations.* Delhi: Macmillan.

Husserl, E. 1964 [1907]. *The idea of phenomenology.* Trans. by W. P. Alston and G. Nakhnikian. The Hague: Nijhoff.

Hutt, S. J., and C. Hutt. 1970. *Direct observation and measurement of behavior.* Springfield, Ill.: Charles C Thomas.

Hyman, H. H. 1954. *Survey design and analysis.* New York: Free Press.

Hyman, H. H. (with W. J. Cobb et al.). 1975. *Interviewing in social research.* Chicago: University of Chicago Press.

Hymes, D. H. 1964. Discussion of Burling's paper. *American Anthropologist* 66:116-19.

Igun, U. A. 1986. Reported and actual prescription of oral rehydration therapy for childhood diarrhoeas by retail pharmacists in Nigeria. *Social Science and Medicine* 39:797-806.

Inkeles, A. 1974. *Becoming modern: Individual change in six developing countries.* Cambridge, Mass.: Harvard University Press.

Institute for Coastal and Marine Resources (ICMR) et al. 1993. *Final technical report for the coastal North Carolina socioeconomic study.* Submitted to the U.S. Department of the Interior, Minerals Management Service, by the ICMR and East Carolina University, Department of Sociology and Anthropology, in cooperation with Impact Assessment, Inc., La Jolla, Calif.

Irurita, V. F. 1996. Hidden dimensions revealed—Progressive grounded theory study of quality care in the hospital. *Qualitative Health Research* 6:331-49.

Iversen, G. R., and H. Norpoth. 1987. *Analysis of variance.* 2d ed. Sage University Papers Series. Quantitative applications in the social sciences, no. 07-001. Newbury Park, Calif.: Sage.

Ives, E. 1995. *The tape-recorded interview: A manual for fieldworkers in folklore and oral history.* 2d ed. Knoxville: University of Tennessee Press.

Ivis, F. J., S. J. Bondy, and E. M. Adlaf. 1997. The effect of question structure on self-reports of heavy drinking: Closed-ended versus open-ended questions. *Journal of Studies on Alcohol* 58:622-24.

Jackson, B. 1987. *Fieldwork.* Urbana: University of Illinois Press.

Jackson, D. N. 1984. *Personality research form manual.* Goshen, N.Y.: Research Psychologists Press.

Jackson, H., and R. L. Nuttall. 1997. *Childhood abuse: Effects on clinicians' personal and professional lives.* Thousand Oaks, Calif.: Sage.

Jackson, P. B., P. A. Thoits, and H. F. Taylor. 1995. Composition of the workplace and psychological well-being: The effects of tokenism on America's Black elite. *Social Forces* 74:543-57.

Jacoby, W. G. 1997. *Statistical graphics for univariate and bivariate data.* Sage University Papers Series.

Quantitative applications in the social sciences, no. 117. Thousand Oaks, Calif.: Sage.

Jaeger, R. M. 1984. *Sampling in education and the social sciences.* New York: Longmans, Green.

James, J. E. 1997. Is habitual caffeine use a preventable cardiovascular risk factor? *The Lancet* 349:279-81.

Jennings, M. K. 1987. Residues of a movement: The aging of the American protest generation. *American Political Science Review* 81:367-82.

Jennings, M. K., and G. Markus. 1984. Partisan orientations over the long haul: Results from the three-wave political socialization study. *American Political Science Review* 78:1000-18.

Jennings, M. K., G. Markus, and R. Niemi. 1991. Youth parent socialization panel study 1965-1982. Computer File. Ann Arbor, Mich.: Inter-University Consortium for Political and Social Research.

Jensen, P. M., and R. B. Coambs. 1994. Health and behavioral predictors of success in an intensive smoking cessation program for women. *Women and Health* 21:57-72.

Johns, G. 1994. How often were you absent? A review of the use of self-reported absence data. *Journal of Applied Psychology* 79:574-91.

Johnson, A. 1975. Time allocation in a Machiguenga community. *Ethnology* 14:310-21.

Johnson, J. C. 1990. *Selecting ethnographic informants.* Newbury Park, Calif.: Sage.

Johnson, R. K., P. Driscoll, and M. I. Goran. 1996. Comparison of multiple-pass 24-hour recall estimates of energy intake with total energy expenditure determined by the doubly labeled water method in young children. *Journal of the American Dietetic Association* 96:1140-44.

Johnston, C. S. 1995. The Rokeach Value Survey: Underlying structure and multidimensional scaling. *Journal of Psychology* 129:583-97.

Johnstone, B., K. Ferrara, and J. M. Bean. 1992. Gender, politeness, and discourse management in same-sex and cross-sex opinion-poll interviews. *Journal of Pragmatics* 18:405-30.

Jones, D. J. 1973. The results of role-playing in anthropological research. *Anthropological Quarterly* 46:30-37.

Jones, E., and T. Badger. 1991. Deaf children's knowledge of internal human anatomy. *Journal of Special Education* 25:252-60.

Jones, M., and M. A. Nies. 1996. The relationship of perceived benefits of and barriers to reported exercise in older African American women. *Public Health Nursing* 13:151-58.

Jones, W. T. 1965. *The sciences and the humanities; conflict and reconciliation.* Berkeley: University of California Press.

Joravsky, D. 1970. *The Lysenko affair.* Cambridge, Mass.: Harvard University Press.

Jordan, B. 1992a. *Birth in four cultures: A cross-cultural investigation of childbirth in Yucatan, Holland, Sweden, and the United States.* 4th expanded ed. Rev. by R. Davis-Floyd. Prospect Heights, Ill.: Waveland.

Jordan, B. 1992b. *Technology and social interaction: Notes on the achievement of authoritative knowledge in complex settings.* Technical report no. IRL92-0027. Palo Alto, Calif.: Institute for Research on Learning.

Jordan, B., and A. Henderson. 1993. Interaction analysis: Foundations and practice. Working paper, Xerox Palo Alto Research Center and Institute for Research on Learning.

Jorgensen, D. 1989. *Participant observation.* Newbury Park, Calif.: Sage.

Junker, B. H. 1960. *Field work: An introduction to the social sciences.* Chicago: University of Chicago Press.

Jurgens, U., T. Malsch, and K. Dohse. 1993. *Breaking from Taylorism: Changing norms of work in the automobile industry.* New York: Cambridge University Press.

Kadushin, A. 1972. *The social work interview.* New York: Columbia University Press.

Kadushin, C. 1968. Power, influence and social circles: A new methodology for studying opinion makers. *American Sociological Review* 33:685-99.

Kafle, K. K., J. M. Madden, A. D. Shresta, S. B. Karkee, P. L. Das, Y. M. S. Pradhan, and J. D. Quick. 1996. Can licensed drug sellers contribute to safe motherhood? A survey of the treatment of pregnancy-related anaemia in Nepal. *Social Science and Medicine* 42:1577-88.

Kahn, R. L., and C. F. Cannell. 1957. *The dynamics of interviewing.* New York: John Wiley.

Kahneman, D., P. Slovic, and A. Tversky, eds. 1982. *Judgment under uncertainty: Heuristics and biases.* New York: Cambridge University Press.

Kail, B. L., D. D. Watson, S. Ray, and the National AIDS Research Consortium. 1995. Needle-using practices within the sex industry. *American Journal of Drug and Alcohol Abuse* 21:241-55.

Kallan, J. E. 1998. Drug abuse-related mortality in the United States: Patterns and correlates. *American Journal of Drug and Alcohol Abuse* 24:103-17.

Kane, E. W., and L. J. Macaulay. 1993. Interviewer gender and gender attitudes. *Public Opinion Quarterly* 57:1-28.

Kant, I. 1966 [1787]. *Critique of pure reason.* Trans. by F. M. Muller. New York: Anchor.

Kanter, R. M. 1977. *Men and women of the corporation.* New York: Basic Books.

Kasl, S. V. 1996. The influence of the work environment on cardiovascular health: A historical, conceptual, and methodological perspective. *Journal of Occupational Health Psychology* 1:42-56.

Katz, D. 1942. Do interviewers bias polls? *Public Opinion Quarterly* 6:248-68.

Kazdin, A. E. 1998. *Methodological issues and strategies in clinical research.* 2d ed. Washington, D.C.: American Psychological Association.

Kearney, M. H., S. Murphy, K. Irwin, and M. Rosenbaum. 1995. Salvaging self—A grounded theory of pregnancy on crack cocaine. *Nursing Research* 44:208-13.

Kearney, M. H., S. Murphy, and M. Rosenbaum. 1994. Mothering on crack cocaine—A grounded theory analysis. *Social Science and Medicine* 38:351-61.

Kearney, R. 1996. *Paul Ricoeur: The hermeneutics of action.* Thousand Oaks, Calif.: Sage.

Keil, F. 1989. *Concepts, kinds, and cognitive development.* Cambridge: MIT Press.

Keil, J. E., S. H. Sandifer, C. B. Loadholt, and E. Boyle, Jr. 1981. Skin color and education effects on blood pressure. *American Journal of Public Health* 71:532-34.

Keil, J. E., H. A. Tyroler, S. H. Sandifer, and E. Boyle, Jr. 1977. Hypertension: Effects of social class and racial admixture. *American Journal of Public Health* 67:634-39.

Kelle, U., G. Prein, and K. Bird, eds. 1995. *Computer-aided qualitative data analysis: Theory, methods and practice.* London: Sage.

Kelln, B.R.C., D.J.A. Dozois, and I. E. McKenzie. 1998. An MCMI-III discriminant function analysis of incarcerated felons: Prediction of subsequent institutional misconduct. *Criminal Justice and Behavior* 25:177-89.

Kelloway, E. K. 1998. *Using LISREL for structural equation modeling: A researcher's guide.* Thousand Oaks, Calif.: Sage.

Kelloway, K. E., and J. Barling. 1993. Members' participation in local union activities: Measurement, prediction, and replication. *Journal of Applied Psychology* 78:262-69.

Kelly, E. F., and P. J. Stone. 1975. *Computer recognition of English word senses.* Amsterdam: North-Holland.

Kelly, G. A. 1955. *The psychology of personal constructs.* New York: Norton.

Kemph, B. T., and T. Kasser. 1996. Effects of sexual orientation of interviewer on expressed attitudes toward male homosexuality. *Journal of Social Psychology* 136:401-403.

Kempton, W. 1987. Two theories of home heat control. In *Cultural models in language and thought,* ed. by D. Holland and N. Quinn, 222-42. New York: Cambridge University Press.

Kempton, W., J. S. Boster, and J. A. Jartley. 1995. *Environmental values in American culture.* Cambridge: MIT Press.

Kendall, C. 1983. Loose structure of family in Honduras. *Journal of Comparative Family Studies* 16:257-72.

Kendall, C., E. Leontsini, E. Gil, F. Cruz, P. Hudelson, and P. Pelto. 1990. Exploratory ethnoentomology. *Cultural Anthropology Methods* 2:11.

Kenner, A. N., and G. Katsimaglis. 1993. Gender differences in proxemics: Taxi-seat choice. *Psychological Reports* 72:625-26.

Kent, R. N., J. Kanowitz, K. D. O'Leary, and M. Cheiken. 1977. Observer reliability as a function of circumstances of assessment. *Journal of Applied Behavioral Analysis* 10:317-24.

Ketterer, M. W., and G. H. Maercklein. 1991. Caffeinated beverage use among Type A male patients suspected of CAD/CHD: A mechanism for increased risk? *Stress Medicine* 7:119-24.

Kiecker, P., and J. E. Nelson. 1996. Do interviewers follow telephone instructions? *Journal of the Market Research Society* 38:16-176.

Kilbride, P. L. 1992. Unwanted children as a consequence of delocalization in modern Kenya. In *Anthropological research: Process and application,* ed. by J. J. Poggie, Jr. et al., 185-206. Albany: State University of New York Press.

Killoran, M. M. 1984. The management of tension: A case study of *Chatelaine* magazine 1939-1980. *Journal of Comparative Family Studies* 15:407-26.

Killworth, P. D., and H. R. Bernard. 1974. CATIJ: A new sociometric technique and its application to a prison living unit. *Human Organization* 33:335-50.

Killworth, P. D., and H. R. Bernard. 1976. Informant accuracy in social network data. *Human Organization* 35:269-96.

Killworth, P.R.P. 1997. Culture and power in the British army: Hierarchies, boundaries and construction. Ph.D. diss., University of Cambridge.

Kimball, S. T., and W. T. Partridge. 1979. *The craft of community study: Fieldwork dialogues.* Gainesville: University of Florida Press.

Kimmel, A. J. 1996. *Ethical issues in behavioral research: A survey.* Cambridge, Mass.: Blackwell.

Kimmel, A. J. 1998. In defense of deception. *American Psychologist* 53:803-805.

Kincaid, H. 1996. *Philosophical foundations of the social sciences: Analyzing controversies in social research*. New York: Cambridge University Press.

King, G. 1997. *A solution to the ecological inference problem: Reconstructing individual behavior from aggregate data*. Princeton, N.J.: Princeton University Press.

King, N. 1994. The qualitative research interview. In *Qualitative methods in organizational research: A practical guide*, ed. by C. Cassell and G. Symon, 14-36. Thousand Oaks, Calif.: Sage.

Kinsey, A. C., W. B. Pomeroy, and C. E. Martin. 1948. *Sexual behavior in the human male*. Philadelphia: Saunders.

Kirk, J., and M. Miller. 1986. *Reliability and validity in qualitative research*. Beverly Hills, Calif.: Sage.

Kirk, L., and M. I. Burton. 1977. Meaning and context: A study of contextual shifts in meaning of Maasai personality descriptors. *American Ethnologist* 4:734-61.

Kirk, R. E. 1982. *Experimental design*. 2d ed. Monterey, Calif.: Brooks/Cole.

Kirkpatrick, H., J. Younger, P. Links, and P. Saunders. 1996. Life after years in hospital: What does it hold? *Psychiatric Rehabilitation Journal* 19:75-78.

Kish, L. 1995 [1965]. *Survey sampling*. New York: John Wiley.

Klein, F. C. 1999. On sports: Academic dilemma. *Wall Street Journal*, April 2, W4.

Kline, P. 1994. *An easy guide to factor analysis*. London: Routledge.

Klockars, C. B., and F. W. O'Connor. 1979. *Deviance and decency: The ethics of research with human subjects*. Beverly Hills, Calif.: Sage.

Kluckhohn, K. 1945. The personal document in anthropological science. In *The use of personal documents in history, anthropology, and sociology*, ed. by L. Gottschalk, C. Kluckhohn, and R. Angell, 79-176. Bulletin 53. New York: Social Science Research Council.

Knodel, J., N. Havanon, and A. Pramualratana. 1984. Fertility transition in Thailand: A qualitative analysis. *Population and Development Review* 10:297-315.

Kockelmans, J. J. 1994. *Edmund Husserl's phenomenology*. West Lafayette, Ind.: Purdue University Press.

Koeske, G. F., and R. D. Koeske. 1989. Construct validity of the Maslach Burnout Inventory: A critical review and reconceptualization. *Journal of Applied Behavioral Science* 25:131-44.

Koocher, G. P. 1977. Bathroom behavior and human dignity. *Journal of Personality and Social Psychology* 35:120-21.

Koopmans, L. H. 1981. *An introduction to contemporary statistics*. Boston: Duxbury.

Korn, J. H. 1997. *Illusions of reality: A history of deception in social psychology*. Albany: State University of New York Press.

Kornblum, W. 1989. Introduction. In *In the field: Readings on the field research experience*, ed. by C. D. Smith and W. Kornblum, 1-8. New York: Praeger.

Korsching, P., J. Donnermeyer, and R. Burdge. 1980. Perception of property settlement payments and replacement housing among displaced persons. *Human Organization* 39:332-33.

Kortendick, O. 1996. *Drei Schwestern und ihre Kinder. Rekonstruktion von Familiengeschichte und Identitätstransmission bei Indischen Nederlanders mit Hilfe computerunterstützer Inhaltsanlyze*. Canterbury, U.K.: Center for Anthropology and Computing, University of Kent.

Kraemer, H. C., and S. Thiemann. 1987. *How many subjects? Statistical power analysis in research*. Newbury Park, Calif.: Sage.

Krieger, L. 1986. Negotiating gender role expectations in Cairo. In *Self, sex and gender in cross-cultural fieldwork*, ed. by T. L. Whitehead and M. E. Conaway, 117-28. Urbana: University of Illinois Press.

Krippendorf, K. 1980. *Content analysis: An introduction to its methodology*. Beverly Hills, Calif.: Sage.

Kronenfeld, D. B., J. Kronenfeld, and J. E. Kronenfeld. 1972. Toward a science of design for successful food service. *Institutions and Volume Feeding* 70(11):38-44.

Krueger, R. A. 1994. *Focus groups: A practical guide for applied research.* 2d ed. Thousand Oaks, Calif.: Sage.

Kruskal, J. B., and M. Wish. 1978. *Multidimensional scaling.* Sage University Papers Series. Quantitative applications in the social sciences, no. 07-011. Beverly Hills, Calif.: Sage.

Kuhn, T. S. 1970. *The structure of scientific revolutions.* 2d ed. Chicago: University of Chicago Press.

Kulick, D., and M. Willson, eds. 1995. *Taboo: Sex, identity, and erotic subjectivity in anthropological fieldwork.* London: Routledge.

Kunin, T. 1955. The construction of a new type of attitude measure. *Personnel Psychology* 8:65-77.

Kunitz, S. J., H. Temkin-Greener, D. Broudy, and M. Haffner. 1981. Determinants of hospital utilization and surgery on the Navajo Indian Reservation, 1972-1978. *Social Science and Medicine* 15B:71-79.

Kunovich, R. S., and R. G. Rashid. 1992. Mirror training in three dimensions for dental students. *Perceptual and Motor Skills* 75:923-28.

Kurasaki, K. S. 1997. Ethnic identity and its development among third-generation Japanese Americans. Ph.D. diss., Department of Psychology, DePaul University.

Kvale, S. 1996. *InterViews: An introduction to qualitative research interviewing.* Thousand Oaks, Calif.: Sage.

Kvalem, I. L., J. M. Sundet, K. I. Rivo, and D. E. Eilertsen. 1996. The effect of sex education on adolescents' use of condoms: Applying the Solomon four-group design. *Health Education Quarterly* 23:34-47.

Labovitz, S. 1971a. The assignment of numbers to rank order categories. *American Sociological Review* 35:515-24.

Labovitz, S. 1971b. The zone of rejection: Negative thoughts on statistical inference. *Pacific Sociological Review* 14:373-81.

Labovitz, S. 1972. Statistical usage in sociology. *Sociological Methods & Research* 3:14-37.

Ladd, E. C., and K. H. Bowman. 1997. *Public opinion about abortion.* Washington, D.C.: American Enterprise Institute.

La Pierre, R. T. 1934. Attitudes versus actions. *Social Forces* 13:230-37.

Lastrucci, C. L. 1963. *The scientific approach.* Cambridge, Mass.: Schenkman.

Latané, B., and J. M. Darley. 1968. Group inhibition of bystander intervention in emergencies. *Journal of Personality and Social Psychology* 10:215-21.

Lauer, Q. 1978. *The triumph of subjectivity: An introduction to transcendental phenomenology.* 2d ed. New York: Fordham University Press.

Lavee, Y., and D. H. Olson. 1993. Seven types of marriage: Empirical typology based on ENRICH. *Journal of Marital and Family Therapy* 19:325-40.

Lavrakas, P. J. 1993. *Telephone survey methods: Sampling, selection, and supervision.* 2d ed. Newbury Park, Calif.: Sage.

Lawler, J., and J. Hearn. 1997. The managers of social work: The experiences and identifications of third tier social services managers and the implications for future practice. *British Journal of Social Work* 27:191-218.

Lazarsfeld, P. F. 1993. *On social research and its language.* Ed. by R. Boudon. Chicago: University of Chicago Press.

Lazarsfeld, P. F., A. Pasanella, and M. Rosenberg, eds. 1972. *Continuities in the language of social research.* New York: Free Press.

Lazarsfeld, P. F., and M. Rosenberg. 1955. *The language of social research: A reader in the methodology of social research.* Glencoe, Ill.: Free Press.

Lazzari, M. M., H. R. Ford, and K. J. Haughey. 1996. Making a difference: Women of action in the community. *Social Work* 41:197-205.

Lea, K. L. 1980. Francis Bacon. *Encyclopaedia Britannica.* Vol. 2. Chicago: Encyclopaedia Britannica.

Leach, E. 1967. An anthropologist's reflection on a social survey. In *Anthropologists in the field,* ed. by

D. C. Jongmans and P. C. Gutkind, 75-88. Assen, The Netherlands: Van Gorcum.

Le Compte, M. D., and J. Preissle (with R. Tesch). 1993. *Ethnography and qualitative design in educational research.* 2d ed. San Diego, Calif.: Academic Press.

Ledman, R. E., M. Miller, and D. R. Brown. 1995. Successful women and women's colleges: Is there an intervening variable in the reported relationship? *Sex Roles* 33:489-97.

Lee, R. M. 1995. *Dangerous fieldwork.* Thousand Oaks, Calif.: Sage.

Lehner, P. N. 1996. *Handbook of ethological methods.* 2d ed. Cambridge, U.K.: Cambridge University Press.

Leith, L. M. 1988. Choking in sports: Are we our own worst enemies? *International Journal of Sport Psychology* 19:59-64.

Lennon, S. J., L. D. Burns, and K. L. Rowold. 1995. Dress and human behavior research: Sampling, subjects, and consequences for statistics. *Clothing and Textiles Research Journal* 13:262-72.

Lester, P. E., and L. K. Bishop. 1997. *Handbook of tests and measurement in education and the social sciences.* Lancaster, Pa.: Technomic.

Leunes, A., A. Bourgeois, and R. Grajales. 1996. The effects of two types of exposure on attitudes toward aspects of juvenile delinquency. *Journal of Social Psychology* 136:699-708.

Levine, R. V. 1997. *A geography of time.* New York: Basic Books.

Levine, R. V., and K. Bartlett. 1984. Pace of life, punctuality, and coronary heart disease in six countries. *Journal of Cross-Cultural Psychology* 15:233-55.

Levinson, D., ed. 1978. *A guide to social theory: Worldwide cross-cultural tests.* New Haven, Conn.: Human Relations Area Files.

Levinson, D. 1989. *Family violence in cross-cultural perspective.* Newbury Park, Calif.: Sage.

Levy, R., and D. Hollan. 1998. Person-centered interviewing and observation. In *Handbook of methods in cultural anthropology,* ed. by H. R. Bernard, 333-64. Walnut Creek, Calif.: AltaMira.

Lewin, E., and W. Leap, eds. 1996. *Out in the field: Reflections of lesbian and gay anthropologists.* Urbana: University of Illinois Press.

Lewis, O. 1961. *The children of Sánchez.* New York: Random House.

Lewis, O. 1965. *La vida: A Puerto Rican family in the culture of poverty—San Juan and New York.* New York: Random House.

Lewis, R. B. 1998. ATLAS and NUD*IST: A comparative review of two leading qualitative data analysis packages. *Cultural Anthropology Methods Journal* 10:41-47.

LEXIS-NEXIS. 1998. LEXIS-NEXIS Background. www.lexis-nexis.com/lncc/about/background.html.

Lieberman, D., and W. W. Dressler. 1977. Bilingualism and cognition of St. Lucian disease terms. *Medical Anthropology* 1:81-110.

Lieske, J. 1993. Regional subcultures of the United States. *Journal of Politics* 55:888-913.

Light, I., and C. Lee. 1997. And just who do you think you aren't? Americans' ethnic and racial identity. *Society* 34:28-30.

Light, R. J. 1971. Measures of response agreement for qualitative data: Some generalizations and alternatives. *Psychological Bulletin* 76:365-77.

Lightcap, J. L., J. A. Kurland, and R. L. Burgess. 1982. Child abuse: A test of some predictions from evolutionary theory. *Ethology and Sociobiology* 3:61-67.

Likert, R. 1932. A technique for the measurement of attitudes. *Archives of Psychology* Vol. 140.

Lincoln, Y. S., and E. G. Guba. 1985. *Naturalistic inquiry.* Beverly Hills, Calif.: Sage.

Lindman, R., P. Jarvinen, and J. Vidjeskog. 1987. Verbal interactions of aggressively and nonaggressively predisposed males in a drinking situation. *Aggressive Behavior* 13:187-96.

Liotta, R. F., L. A. Jason, W. L. Robinson, and V. LaVigne. 1985. A behavioral approach for measuring social support. *Family Therapy* 12:285-95.

Lippa, R. 1991. Some psychometric characteristics of gender diagnosticity measures: Reliability, validity, consistency across domains and relationship to the

Big Five. *Journal of Personality and Social Psychology* 61:1000-11.

Liu, J. H., B. Bonzon-Liu, and M. Pierce-Guarino. 1997. Common fate between humans and animals? The dynamical systems theory of groups and environmental attitudes in the Florida Keys. *Environment and Behavior* 29:87-124.

Livingstone, S., and P. Lunt. 1993. Savers and borrowers: Strategies of personal financial management. *Human Relations* 46:963-85.

Locke, J. 1996 [1690]. *An essay concerning human understanding*. Abridged. Ed. by K. P. Winkler. Indianapolis, Ind.: Hackett.

Locke, K. 1996. Rewriting the discovery of grounded theory—After 25 years. *Journal of Management Inquiry* 5:239-45.

Lockery, S. A., R. E. Dunkle, C. S. Kart, and C. J. Coulton. 1994. Factors contributing to the early rehospitalization of elderly people. *Health and Social Work* 19:182-91.

Lodge, M. 1981. *Magnitude scaling: Quantitative measurement of opinions*. Beverly Hills, Calif.: Sage.

Loether, H. J., and D. G. McTavish. 1993. *Descriptive and inferential statistics*. Boston: Allyn & Bacon.

Lofland, J. H. 1971. *Analyzing social settings: A guide to qualitative observation and analysis*. Belmont, Calif.: Wadsworth.

Lofland, J. H. 1976. *Doing social life*. New York: John Wiley.

Lofland, J. H., and L. H. Lofland. 1995. *Analyzing social settings*. 3d ed. Belmont, Calif.: Wadsworth.

Lofland, L. H. 1983. Understanding urban life: The Chicago legacy. *Urban Life* 11:491-511.

Loftus, E. F., and W. Marburger. 1983. Since the eruption of Mt. St. Helens, has anyone beaten you up? Improving the accuracy of retrospective reports with landmark events. *Memory and Cognition* 11:114-20.

Long, V. O., and E. A. Martinez. 1997. Masculinity, femininity, and Hispanic professional men's self-esteem and self-acceptance. *Journal of Psychology* 131:481-88.

Longabaugh, R. 1963. A category system for coding interpersonal behavior as social exchange. *Sociometry* 26:319-44.

Longabaugh, R. 1980. The systematic observation of behavior in naturalistic settings. In *Handbook of cross-cultural psychology*, ed. by H. C. Triandis and J. W. Berry. Vol. 2, *Methodology*, 57-126. Boston: Allyn & Bacon.

Lonkila, M. 1995. Grounded theory as an emerging paradigm for computer-assisted qualitative data analysis. In *Computer-aided qualitative data analysis*, ed. by U. Kelle, 41-51. Thousand Oaks, Calif.: Sage.

Lorr, M. 1983. *Cluster analysis for social scientists*. San Francisco: Jossey-Bass.

Lounsbury, F. 1956. A semantic analysis of the Pawnee kinship usage. *Language* 32:158-94.

Love, M. B., and Q. Thurman. 1991. Normative beliefs about factors that affect health and longevity. *Health Education Quarterly* 18:183-94.

Lowrey, T. M., and C. Otnes. 1994. Construction of a meaningful wedding: Differences in the priorities of brides and grooms. In *Gender issues and consumer behavior*, ed. by J. A. Costa, 164-83. Thousand Oaks, Calif.: Sage.

Lucretius, C. T. 1995. *De rerum natura. (On the nature of things)*. Ed. and trans. by A. M. Esolen. Baltimore: Johns Hopkins University Press.

Lueptow, L. B., S. L. Moser, and B. F. Pendleton. 1990. Gender and response effects in telephone interviews about gender characteristics. *Sex Roles* 22:29-42.

Lundberg, G. A. 1942. *Social research: A study in methods of gathering data*. 2d ed. New York: Longmans, Green.

Lundberg, G. A. 1964. *Foundations of sociology*. New York: David McKay.

Lyman, S. M. 1989. *The seven deadly sins: Society and evil*. Rev. and expanded ed. Dix Hills, N.Y.: General Hall.

Lynd, R. S., and H. M. Lynd. 1929. *Middletown: A study in contemporary American culture*. New York: Harcourt, Brace & Company.

MacColl, M. D. 1995. A model of Japanese corporate decision making. *International Journal of Organizational Analysis* 3:375-93.

Mach, E. 1976. *Knowledge and error: Sketches on the psychology of enquiry.* Ed. by B. McGuiness. Trans. by T. J. McCormack and P. Foulkes. Boston: D. Reidel.

Machamer, P., ed. 1998. *The Cambridge companion to Galileo.* New York: Cambridge University Press.

Mahaffy, K. A. 1996. Cognitive dissonance and its resolution: A study of lesbian Christians. *Journal for the Scientific Study of Religion* 35:392-402.

Mainieri, T., E. G. Barnett, R. R. Valdero, J. B. Unipan, and S. Oskamp. 1997. Green buying: The influence of environmental concern on consumer behavior. *Journal of Social Psychology* 137:189-204.

Malinowski, B. 1961 [1922]. *Argonauts of the western Pacific.* New York: Dutton.

Malinowski, B. 1967. *A diary in the strict sense of the term.* New York: Harcourt, Brace & World.

Manning, P. K. 1982. Analytic induction. In *Handbook of social science methods.* Vol. 2, *Qualitative methods,* ed. by R. Smith and P. K. Manning, 273-302. New York: Harper.

Manza, J., and C. Brooks. 1998. The gender gap in U.S. presidential elections: When? Why? Implications? *American Journal of Sociology* 103:1235-66.

Marcus, S. E., S. L. Emont, R. D. Corcoran, G. A. Giovino, J. P. Pierce, M. N. Waller, and R. M. Davis. 1994. Public attitudes about cigarette smoking: Results from the 1990 Smoking Activity Volunteer Executed Survey. *Public Health Reports* 109:125-34.

Margolis, M. 1984. *Mothers and such.* Berkeley: University of California Press.

Markie, P. J. 1986. *Descartes' gambit.* Ithaca, N.Y.: Cornell University Press.

Marquis, G. S. 1990. Fecal contamination of shanty town toddlers in households with non-corralled poultry, Lima, Peru. *American Journal of Public Health* 80:146-50.

Marquis, K. H., and C. Cannell. 1969. *A study of interviewer-respondent interaction in the urban employ-

ment survey.* Ann Arbor: Survey Research Center, University of Michigan.

Marriott, B. 1991. The use of social networks by naval officers' wives. Ph.D. diss., University of Florida, Gainesville.

Marsh, C., and E. Scarbrough. 1990. Testing nine hypotheses about quota sampling. *Journal of the Market Research Society* 32:485-506.

Matarazzo, J. 1964. Interviewer mm-humm and interviewee speech duration. *Psychotherapy: Theory, Research and Practice* 1:109-14.

Mathews, H. F. 1985. The Weeping Woman: Variation and homogeneity in folk theories of gender in a Mexican community. Paper read at the annual meetings of the American Anthropological Association, Washington, D.C.

Mathews, H. F. 1992. The directive force of morality tales in a Mexican community. In *Human motives and cultural models,* ed. by R. D'Andrade and C. Strauss, 127-62. New York: Cambridge University Press.

Mathews, H. F., and C. E. Hill. 1990. Applying cognitive decision theory to the study of regional patterns of illness treatment choice. *American Anthropologist* 92:155-70.

Mathiowetz, N., and C. Cannell. 1980. Coding interviewer behavior as a method of evaluating performance. In *Proceedings of the section on survey research methods,* 525-28. Washington, D.C.: American Statistical Association.

Matsumoto, D., P. Ekman, and A. Fridlund. 1991. Analyzing nonverbal behavior. In *Practical guide to using video in the behavior sciences,* ed. by P. W. Dowrick, 153-65. New York: John Wiley.

Matt, G. E., and A. M. Navarro. 1997. What meta-analyses have and have not taught us about psychotherapy effects: A review and future directions. *Clinical Psychology Review* 17:1-32.

Matthey, S., B. E. W. Barnett, and A. Elliott. 1997. Vietnamese and Arabic women's responses to the Diagnostic Interview Schedule (depression) and self-report questionnaires: Cause for concern. *Aus-

tralian and New Zealand Journal of Psychiatry 31:360-69.

Maxwell, J. A. 1996. *Qualitative research design: An interactive approach*. Thousand Oaks, Calif.: Sage.

Mayadas, N. S., T. D. Watts, and D. Elliott. 1997. *International handbook on social work theory and practice*. Westport, Conn.: Greenwood.

McAllister, I., and R. Moore. 1991. Social distance among Australian ethnic groups. *Social Science Research* 75:95-100.

McCall, G. 1978. *Observing the law: Field methods in the study of crime and the criminal justice system*. New York: Free Press.

McCann, J. J., D. W. Gilley, L. E. Hebert, L. A. Beckett, and D. A. Evans. 1997. Concordance between direct observation and staff rating of behavior in nursing home residents with Alzheimer's disease. *The Journals of Gerontology*, Series B 52:63-74.

McCarroll, J. E., A. S. Blank, and K. Hill. 1995. Working with traumatic material: Effects on Holocaust Memorial Museum staff. *American Journal of Orthopsychiatry* 65:66-75.

McClelland, D. C. 1967. *The achieving society*. New York: Free Press.

McCracken, G. D. 1988. *The long interview*. Newbury Park, Calif.: Sage.

McDermott, M.1993. On cruelty, ethics and experimentation: Profile of Philip G. Zimbardo. *The Psychologist*, October 1, 6(10).

McDonald, D. D., and R. G. Bridge. 1991. Gender stereotyping and nursing care. *Research in Nursing and Health* 14:373-78.

McDonald, L. 1993. *The early origins of the social sciences*. Montreal: McGill-Queen's University Press.

McDonald, L. 1994. *The women founders of the social sciences*. Ottawa: Carleton University Press.

McGovern, P. G., N. Lurie, K. L. Margolis, and J. S. Slater. 1998. Accuracy of self-report of mammography and Pap smear in a low-income urban population. *American Journal of Preventive Medicine* 14:201-208.

McGrew, W. C. 1972. *An ethological study of children's behavior*. New York: Academic Press.

McGue, M., A. Sharma, and P. Benson. 1996. The effect of common rearing on adolescent adjustment: Evidence from a U.S. adoption cohort. *Developmental Psychology* 32:604-13.

McKenna, R. J. 1995. *The undergraduate researcher's handbook: Creative experimentation in social psychology*. Boston: Allyn & Bacon.

McLain, S., and B. Sternquist. 1991. Ethnocentric consumers: Do they "buy American"? *Journal of International Consumer Marketing* 4:39-57.

Mead, M. 1986. Fieldwork in Pacific islands, 1925-1967. In *Women in the field: Anthropological experiences*. 2d ed. Ed. by P. Golde, 293-332. Berkeley: University of California Press.

Means, B., A. Nigam, and M. Zarrow et al. 1989. *Autobiographical memory for health related events*. National Center for Health Statistics, Vital and Health Statistics, Series 6, no. 2. Washington, D.C.: Government Printing Office.

Medley, D. M., and H. E. Mitzel. 1958. A technique for measuring classroom behavior. *Journal of Educational Psychology* 49:86-92.

Meh, C. C. 1996. SOCRATES streamlines lesson observations. *Educational Leadership* 53:76-78.

Mehta, R., and R. W. Belk. 1991. Artifacts, identity, and transition: Favorite possessions of Indians and Indian immigrants to the United States. *Journal of Consumer Research* 17:398-411.

Mein, S., and M. A. Winkleby. 1998. Concerns and misconceptions about cardiovascular disease risk factors: A focus group evaluation with low-income Hispanic women. *Hispanic Journal of Behavioral Sciences* 20:192-211.

Melnik, T. A., S. J. Rhoades, K. R. Wales, C. Cowell, and W. S. Wolfe. 1998. Food consumption patterns of elementary schoolchildren in New York City. *Journal of the American Dietetic Association* 98:159-64.

Merton, R. K. 1968. *Social theory and social structure*. Enlarged ed. New York: Free Press.

Merton, R. K. 1987. The focused interview and focus groups. *Public Opinion Quarterly* 51:550-66.

Merton, R. K., M. Fiske, and P. L. Kendall. 1956. *The focused interview: A manual of problems and procedures.* Glencoe, Ill.: Free Press.

Merton, R. K., and P. F. Lazarsfeld. 1950. *Continuities in social research: Studies in the scope and method of "The American soldier."* Glencoe, Ill.: Free Press.

Messerschmidt, D. A., ed. 1981. *Anthropologists at home in North America: Methods and issues in the study of one's own society.* New York: Cambridge University Press.

Metzger, D. G., and G. E. Williams. 1966. Procedures and results in the study of native categories: Tseltal firewood. *American Anthropologist* 68:389-407.

Meyer, M. A. 1992. How to apply the anthropological technique of participant observation to knowledge acquisition for expert systems. *IEEE Transactions on Systems, Man, and Cybernetics* 22(5):983-91.

Meyerhoff, B. 1989. So what do you want from us here? In *In the field: Readings on the field research experience,* ed. by C. D. Smith and W. Kornblum, 83-90. New York: Praeger.

Mian, M., P. Marton, and D. LeBaron. 1996. The effects of sexual abuse on 3- to 5-year-old girls. *Child Abuse & Neglect* 20:731-45.

Michaelson, W. 1985. *From sun to sun: Daily obligations and community structure in the lives of employed women and their families.* Totowa, N.J.: Rowman & Allanheld.

Middlemist, R. D., E. S. Knowles, and C. F. Matter. 1976. Personal space invasion in the lavatory: Suggestive evidence for arousal. *Journal of Personality and Social Psychology* 33:541-46.

Middlemist, R. D., E. S. Knowles, and C. F. Matter. 1977. What to do and what to report: A reply to Koocher. *Journal of Personality and Social Psychology* 35:122-24.

Mikolic, J. M., J. C. Parker, and D. G. Pruitt. 1997. Escalation in response to persistent annoyance: Group versus individuals and gender effects. *Journal of Personality and Social Psychology* 72:151-63.

Miles, M. B. 1983. *Qualitative data as an attractive nuisance: The problem of analysis.* Beverly Hills, Calif.: Sage.

Miles, M. B., and A. M. Huberman. 1994. *Qualitative data analysis.* 2d ed. Thousand Oaks, Calif.: Sage.

Mileski, M. 1971. Courtroom encounters: An observation study of a lower criminal court. *Law and Society Review* 5:473-538.

Milgram, S. 1963. Behavioral study of obedience. *Journal of Abnormal and Social Psychology* 67:371-78.

Milgram, S. 1967. The small-world problem. *Psychology Today* 1:60-67.

Milgram, S. 1969. The lost-letter technique. *Psychology Today* 3:30-33, 66-68.

Milgram, S. 1977a. Ethical issues in the study of obedience. In *The individual in a social world,* ed. by S. Milgram, 139-46. Reading, Mass.: Addison-Wesley.

Milgram, S. 1977b. Interpreting obedience: Error and evidence. In *The social psychology of psychological research,* ed. by S. Milgram, 124-38. Reading, Mass.: Addison-Wesley.

Milgram, S., L. Mann, and S. Harter. 1965. The lost-letter technique: A tool for social research. *Public Opinion Quarterly* 29:437-38.

Mill, J. S. 1866. *Auguste Comte and positivism.* Philadelphia: J. B. Lippincott.

Mill, J. S. 1869. *The subjection of women.* New York: D. Appleton.

Miller, A. S., and T. Nakamura. 1996. On the stability of church attendance patterns during a time of demographic change: 1965-1988. *Journal for the Scientific Study of Religion* 35:275-84.

Miller, D. C. 1991. *Handbook of research design and social measurement.* 5th ed. Newbury Park, Calif.: Sage.

Miller, E. M. 1986. Street woman: The social world of female street hustlers. Ph.D. diss., University of Chicago, 1985. Abstract in *Dissertation Abstracts International* 45(11-A): 3453-54.

Miller, G. A. 1956. The magical number seven, plus or minus two: Some limits on our capacity for processing information. *Psychological Review* 63:81-97.

Miller, J. L., P. H. Rossi, and J. E. Simpson. 1991. Felony punishments: A factorial survey of perceived justice in criminal sentencing. *Journal of Criminal Law and Criminology* 82:396-422.

Miller, K. W., L. B. Wilder, F. A. Stillman, and D. M. Becker. 1997. The feasibility of a street-intercept survey method in an African-American community. *American Journal of Public Health* 87:655-58.

Miller, L. L. 1997. Not just weapons of the weak: Gender harassment as a form of protest for Army men. *Social Psychology Quarterly* 60:32-51.

Miller, S., T. King, P. Lurie, and P. Choitz. 1997. Certified nurse-midwife and physician collaborative practice—Piloting a survey on the Internet. *Journal of Nurse-Midwifery* 42:308-15.

Milliman, R. 1986. The influence of background music on the behavior of restaurant patrons. *Journal of Consumer Research* 13:286-89.

Minadeo, R. 1969. *The lyre of science: Form and meaning in Lucretius' De Rerum Natura.* Detroit, Mich.: Wayne State University Press.

Minton, A. P., and R. L. Rose. 1997. The effects of environmental concern on environmentally friendly consumer behavior: An exploratory study. *Journal of Business Research* 40:37-48.

Mizes, J. S., E. L. Fleece, and C. Ross. 1984. Incentives for increasing return rates: Magnitude levels, response bias, and format. *Public Opinion Quarterly* 48:794-800.

Monaco, D. et al. 1997. *An analysis of total nonresponse in the 1993-94 Schools and Staffing Survey (SASS).* U.S. Department of Education, Office of Educational Research and Improvement. Washington, D.C.: Government Printing Office.

Moody, L. E. 1990. *Advancing nursing science through research.* Newbury Park, Calif.: Sage.

Mooney, C. Z., and M.-H. Lee. 1995. Legislating morality in the American states: The case of pre-*Roe* abortion regulation reform. *American Journal of Political Science* 39:599-627.

Morgan, D. L. 1989. Adjusting to widowhood: Do social networks make it easier? *The Gerontologist* 29:101-107.

Morgan, D. L. 1992. Designing focus group research. In *Tools for primary care research,* ed. by M. Stewart et al., 177-93. Thousand Oaks, Calif.: Sage.

Morgan, D. L. 1996. Focus groups: Using focus groups in research. *Annual Review of Sociology* 22:129-52.

Morgan, D. L. 1997. *Focus groups as qualitative research.* 2d ed. Thousand Oaks, Calif.: Sage.

Morgan, D. L., and R. Krueger. 1998. *The focus group kit.* 6 vols. Thousand Oaks, Calif.: Sage.

Morgan, P., and K. A. Joe. 1996. Citizens and outlaws: The private lives and public lifestyles of women in the illicit drug economy. *Journal of Drug Issues* 26:125-42.

Morgan, R., and J. Barton. 1988. *Biblical interpretation.* New York: Oxford University Press.

Morokoff, P. J., K. Quina, L. L. Harlow, L. Whitmire, D. M. Grimley, P. R. Gibson, and G. J. Burkholder. 1997. Sexual Assertiveness Scale (SAS) for women: Development and validation. *Journal of Personality and Social Psychology* 73:790-804.

Morris, M. 1993. Telling tales explain the discrepancy in sexual partner reports. *Nature* 365:437-40.

Morris, M. 1996. Culture, structure, and the underclass. In *Myths about the powerless: Contesting social inequalities,* ed. by M. B. Lykes, A. Banuazizi, R. Liem, and M. Morris, 34-49. Philadelphia: Temple University Press.

Morris, W. W., K. C. Buckwalter, T. A. Cleary, J. S. Gilmer, D. L. Hatz, and M. Studer. 1990. Refinement of the Iowa Self-Assessment Inventory. *The Gerontologist* 30:243-48.

Morrison, F. J., E. M. Griffith, and J. A. Frazier. 1996. Schooling and the 5 to 7 shift: A natural experiment. In *The five to seven year shift: The age of reason and responsibility,* ed. by A. J. Sameroff and M. M. Haith, 161-86. Chicago: University of Chicago Press.

Morrison, M., and T. Morrison. 1995. A meta-analytic assessment of the predictive validity of the quantitative and verbal components of the Graduate Record Examination with graduate grade point average representing the criterion of graduate success. *Educational and Psychological Measurement* 55:309-16.

Morse, J. M. 1994. Designing funded qualitative research. In *Handbook of qualitative research,* ed. by

N. K. Denzin and Y. S. Lincoln, 220-35. Thousand Oaks, Calif.: Sage.

Moustakas, C. E. 1994. *Phenomenological research methods*. Thousand Oaks, Calif.: Sage.

Mueller, J. H., K. F. Schuessler, and H. L. Costner. 1970. *Statistical reasoning in sociology*. 2d ed. Boston: Houghton Mifflin.

Muhr, T. 1991. Atlas/ti—A prototype for the support of text interpretation. *Qualitative Sociology* 14:349-71.

Mulaik, S. A. 1987. A brief history of the philosophical foundations of exploratory factor analysis. *Multivariate Behavioral Research* 22:267-305.

Murdock, G. P. 1996. *Outline of cultural materials*. 5th rev. ed. New Haven, Conn.: Human Relations Area Files.

Murdock, G. P., and D. R. White. 1969. Standard cross-cultural sample. *Ethnology* 8:329-69.

Murray, S. O. 1992. Components of the gay community in San Francisco. In *Gay culture in America: Essays from the field*, ed. by G. Herdt, 107-46. Boston: Beacon.

Murtagh, M. 1985. The practice of arithmetic by American grocery shoppers. *Anthropology and Education Quarterly* 16:186-92.

Mwango, E. 1986. The sources of variation in farmer adoption of government recommended technologies in the Lilongwe rural development program area of Central Malawi. Master's thesis, University of Florida, Gainesville.

Nachman, S. R. 1984. Lies my informants told me. *Journal of Anthropological Research* 40:536-55.

Narayan, S., and J. A. Krosnick. 1996. Education moderates some response effects in attitude measurement. *Public Opinion Quarterly* 60:58-88.

Naroll, R. 1962. *Data quality control*. New York: Free Press.

National Cancer Institute. 1997. *Changes in cigarette-related disease risks and their implication for prevention and control*. Smoking and Tobacco Control Program, NCI. D. M. Burns, L. Garfinkel, and J. M. Samet, eds. Bethesda, Md.: National Institutes of Health, National Cancer Institute.

Nave, A. 1997. Conducting a survey in a newly developed country. *Cultural Anthropology Methods Journal* 9:8-12.

Nederhof, A. J. 1985. A survey on suicide: Using a mail survey to study a highly threatening topic. *Quality and Quantity* 19:293-302.

Neurath, O. 1973. *Empiricism and sociology*. Ed. by M. Neurath and R. S. Cohen. Trans. by P. Foulkes and M. Neurath. Dordrecht, The Netherlands: Reidel.

Newman, K. S. 1986. Symbolic dialects and generations of women: Variations in the meaning of post-divorce downward mobility. *American Ethnologist* 13:230-52.

Nicks, S. D., J. H. Korn, and T. Mainieri. 1997. The rise and fall of deception in social psychology and personality research, 1921 to 1994. *Ethics and Behavior* 7:69-77.

Niebel, B. W. 1982. *Motion and time study*. 7th ed. Homewood, Ill.: Irwin.

Niemi, I. 1993. Systematic error in behavioural measurement: Comparing results from interview and time budget studies. *Social Indicators Research* 30:229-44.

Nightingale, F. 1871. *Introductory notes on lying-in institutions*. London: Longmans, Green.

Nisbet, R. A. 1980. *The history of the idea of progress*. New York: Basic Books.

Noe, F. P. 1974. Leisure life style and social class: A trend analysis 1900-1960. *Sociology and Social Research* 58:286-94.

Nordstrom, C., and A.C.G.M. Robben, eds. 1995. *Fieldwork under fire: Contemporary studies of violence and survival*. Berkeley: University of California Press.

Nunnally, J. C. 1978. *Introduction to psychological measurement*. Rev. ed. New York: McGraw-Hill.

Nyamongo, I. K. 1998. Lay people's responses to illness: An ethnographic study of anti-malaria behavior among the Abagusii of southwestern Kenya. Ph.d. diss., University of Florida, Gainesville.

Oberschall, A. 1972. The institutionalization of American sociology. In *The establishment of empirical so-*

ciology, ed. by A. Oberschall, 187-251. New York: Harper & Row.

Oboler, R. S. 1985. *Women, power, and economic change: The Nandi of Kenya.* Stanford, Calif.: Stanford University Press.

O'Brien, T. O., and V. Dugdale. 1978. Questionnaire administration by computer. *Journal of the Market Research Society* 20:228-37.

Oettingen, G., T. D. Little, U. Lindenberger, and P. B. Baltes. 1994. Causality, agency, and control beliefs in East versus West Berlin children: A natural experiment on the role of context. *Journal of Personality and Social Psychology* 66:579-95.

Ogburn, W. F. 1930. The folk-ways of a scientific sociology. *Publication of the American Sociological Society* 25:1-10.

Ohanian, R. 1990. Construction and validation of a scale to measure celebrity endorsers' perceived expertise, trustworthiness, and attractiveness. *Journal of Advertising* 19:39-52.

Oliansky, A.1991. A confederate's perspective on deception. *Ethics and Behavior* 1:253-58.

Oliver, R. L., and P. K. Berger. 1980. Advisability of pretest designs in psychological research. *Perceptual and Motor Skills* 51:463-71.

Olson, W. C. 1929. *The measurement of nervous habits in normal children.* Minneapolis: University of Minnesota Press.

Opotow, S. 1994. Predicting protection: Scope of justice and the natural world. *Journal of Social Issues* 50:49-63.

Orth, B., and B. Wegener. 1983. Scaling occupational prestige by magnitude estimation and category rating methods: A comparison with the sensory domain. *European Journal of Social Psychology* 13:417-31.

Ortmann, A., and R. Hertwig. 1997. Is deception acceptable? *American Psychologist* 52:746-47.

Ortmann, A., and R. Hertwig 1998. The question remains: Is deception acceptable? *American Psychologist* 53:806-807.

Osgood, C. E., D. J. Suci, and P. H. Tannenbaum. 1957. *The measurement of meaning.* Urbana: University of Illinois Press.

Oskenberg, L., L. Coleman, and C. F. Cannell. 1986. Interviewers' voices and refusal rates in telephone surveys. *Public Opinion Quarterly* 50:97-111.

Ostrander, S. A. 1980. Upper-class women: Class consciousness as conduct and meaning. In *Power structure research,* ed. by G. W. Domhoff, 73-96. Beverly Hills, Calif.: Sage.

Otani, H., and H. L. Whiteman. 1994. Cued recall hypermnesia is not an artifact of response bias. *American Journal of Psychology* 107:401-21.

Otterbein, K. 1969. Basic steps in conducting a cross-cultural study. *Behavior Science Notes* 4:221-36.

Owen, C. A., H. C. Eisner, and T. R. McFaul. 1981. A half-century of social distance research: National replication of the Bogardus studies. *Sociology and Social Research* 66:80-98.

Packer, M. J., and R. B. Addison. 1989. *Entering the circle—Hermeneutic investigation in psychology.* New Brunswick, N.J.: Rutgers University Press.

Packer, T., K. E. H. Race, and D. F. Hotch. 1994. Focus groups: A tool for consumer-based program evaluation in rehabilitation agency settings. *Journal of Rehabilitation* 60(3):30-33.

Paik, H., and G. Comstock. 1994. The effects of television violence on antisocial behavior: A meta-analysis. *Communication Research* 21:516-46.

Papineau, D. 1996. Philosophy of science. In *The Blackwell companion to philosophy,* ed. by N. Bunnin and E. P. Tsui-James, 290-324. Oxford, U.K.: Basil Blackwell.

Papini, D. R., N. Datan, and K. A. McCluskey-Fawcett. 1988. An observational study of affective and assertive family interactions during adolescence. *Journal of Youth and Adolescence* 17:477-92.

Paredes, J. A. 1974. The emergence of contemporary Eastern Creek Indian identity. In *Social and cultural identity: Problems of persistence and change,* ed. by T. K. Fitzgerald, 63-80. *Southern Anthropological Society Proceedings,* no. 8. Athens: University of Georgia Press.

Paredes, J. A. 1992. "Practical history" and the Poarch Creeks: A meeting ground for anthropologist and tribal leaders. In *Anthropological research: Process and application*, ed. by J. J. Poggie, Jr. et al., 211-26. Albany: State University of New York Press.

Park, R. E., E. W. Burgess, and R. D. McKenzie. 1925. *The city*. Chicago: University of Chicago Press.

Passin, H. 1951. The development of public opinion research in Japan. *International Journal of Opinion and Attitude Research* 5:20-30.

Pausewang, S. 1973. *Methods and concepts of social research in a rural and developing society*. Munich: Weltforum Verlag.

Payne, B. K., H. Harper, B. Quandt, and T. Campbell. 1995. Accuracy of college honors students' self-reported American Collegiate Test scores. *Perceptual and Motor Skills* 81:64-66.

Payne, S. L. 1951. *The art of asking questions*. Princeton, N.J.: Princeton University Press.

Pearson, C. A. L., and J. Chong. 1997. Contributions of job content and social information on organizational commitment and job satisfaction: An exploration in a Malaysian nursing context. *Journal of Occupational and Organizational Psychology* 70:357-74.

Pearson, J. 1990. Estimation of energy expenditure in Western Samoa, American Samoa, and Honolulu by recall interviews and direct observation. *American Journal of Human Biology* 2:313-26.

Pederson, J. 1987. Plantation women and children: Wage labor, adoption, and fertility in the Seychelles. *Ethnology* 26:51-62.

Pedhazur, E. J. 1997. *Multiple regression in behavioral research: Explanation and prediction*. 3d ed. Fort Worth, Tex.: Harcourt Brace College Publishers.

Pellegrini, A. D. 1996. *Observing children in their natural worlds: A methodological primer*. Mahwah, N.J.: Lawrence Erlbaum.

Pelto, G. H., P. J. Pelto, and E. Messer, eds. 1989. *Research methods in nutritional anthropology*. Tokyo: United Nations University.

Pelto, P. J. 1970. *Anthropological research: The structure of inquiry*. New York: Harper & Row.

Pelto, P. J., and G. H. Pelto. 1978. *Anthropological research: The structure of inquiry*. New York: Cambridge University Press.

Perchonock, N., and O. Werner. 1969. Navajo systems of classification: Some implications of food. *Ethnology* 8:229-42.

Petersen, L. R., and G. V. Donnenwerth. 1997. Secularization and the influence of religion on beliefs about premarital sex. *Social Forces* 75:1071-89.

Peterson, L., V. Johannsson, and S. G. Carlsson. 1996. Computerized testing in a hospital setting: Psychometric and psychological effects. *Computers in Human Behavior* 12:339-50.

Peterson, M., and B. M. Johnstone. 1995. The Atwood Hall health promotion program, Federal Medical Center, Lexington, Ky.: Effects on drug-involved federal offenders. *Journal of Substance Abuse Treatment* 12:43-48.

Peterson, R. A. 1984. Asking the age question. *Public Opinion Quarterly* 48:379-83.

Petroshius, S. M., P. A. Titus, and K. J. Hatch. 1995. Physician attitudes toward pharmaceutical drug advertising. *Journal of Advertising Research* 35:41-51.

Philipp, S. F. 1998. Race and gender differences in adolescent peer group approval of leisure activities. *Journal of Leisure Research* 30:214-32.

Piliavin, I. M., J. Rodin, and J. A. Piliavin. 1969. Good samaritanism: An underground phenomenon? *Journal of Personality and Social Psychology* 13:289-99.

Plattner, S. 1982. Economic decision making in a public marketplace. *American Ethnologist* 9:399-420.

Poggie, J., Jr. 1972. Toward quality control in key informant data. *Human Organization* 31:23-30.

Poggie, J., Jr. 1979. Small-scale fishermen's beliefs about success and development: A Puerto Rican case. *Human Organization* 38:6-11.

Pokorny, A. D., B. A. Miller, and M. B. Kaplan. 1972. The brief MAST: A shortened version of the Michigan Alcoholic Screening Test. *American Journal of Psychiatry* 129:342-45.

Pollard, R., and M. E. Tomlin. 1995. The use of expert teachers to improve education. *Education* 116:3-8.

Pollock, P. H., III. 1994. Issues, values and critical moments: Did "Magic" Johnson transform public opinion on AIDS? *American Journal of Political Science* 8:426-46.

Popovich, P. M., W. J. Everton, K. L. Campbell, R. M. Godinho, K. M. Kramer, and R. R. Mangan. 1997. Criteria used to judge obese persons in the workplace. *Perceptual and Motor Skills* 85:859-66.

Popper, K. R. 1966. *The open society and its enemies*. 5th ed. Princeton, N.J.: Princeton University Press.

Popper, K. R. 1968. *The logic of scientific discovery*. 2d ed. New York: Harper & Row.

Pound, P., P. Gompertz, and S. Ebrahim. 1993. Development and results of a questionnaire to measure career satisfaction after stroke. *Journal of Epidemiology and Community Health* 47:500-505.

Powdermaker, H. 1966. *Stranger and friend: The way of an anthropologist*. New York: Norton.

Pramualratana, A., H. Napaporn, and J. Knodel. 1985. Exploring the normative basis for age at marriage in Thailand: An example from focus group research. *Journal of Marriage and the Family* 47:203-10.

Prebisch, R. 1970. *Change and development: Latin America's great task*. Washington, D.C.: Inter-American Development Bank.

Presser, S., and L. Stinson. 1998. Data collection mode and social desirability bias in self-reported religious attendance. *American Sociological Review* 63:137-45.

Presser, S., and S. Zhao. 1992. Attributes of questions and interviewers as correlates of interviewing performance. *Public Opinion Quarterly* 56:236-40.

Prewett-Livingston, A. J., H. S. Feild, J. G. Veres, III, and P. M. Lewis. 1996. Effects of race on interview ratings in a situational panel interview. *Journal of Applied Psychology* 2:178-86.

Price, D. J. de Solla. 1975. *Science since Babylon*. New Haven, Conn.: Yale University Press.

Prickett, S. 1986. *Words and the word: Language, poetics, and biblical interpretation*. New York: Cambridge University Press.

Proctor, S. P., R. F. White, T. G. Robins, and D. Echeverria. 1996. Effect of overtime work on cognitive function in automotive workers. *Scandinavian Journal of Work, Environment and Health* 22:124-32.

Puccio, E. M., J. B. McPhillips, E. Barrett Connor, and T. G. Ganiats. 1990. Clustering of atherogenic behaviors in coffee drinkers. *American Journal of Public Health* 80:1310-13.

Pugh, G. M., and D. P. Boer. 1989. An examination of culturally appropriate items for the WAIS-R information subtest with Canadian subjects. *Journal of Psychoeducational Assessment* 7:131-40.

Quandt, S., M. Z. Vitolins, K. M. DeWalt, and G. Roos. 1997. Meal patterns of older adults in rural communities: Life course analysis and implications for undernutrition. *Journal of Applied Gerontology* 16:152-71.

Quételet, A. 1969 [1835]. *Physique sociale, ou, essai sur le développement des facultés de l'homme*. Paris: J.-B. Bailliere et fils. Reprinted in trans. in 1969 from the 1842 ed. as *A treatise on man and the development of his faculties*. Gainesville, Fla.: Scholars' Facsimiles and Reprints.

Quinn, N. 1978. Do Mfantse fish sellers estimate probabilities in their heads? *American Ethnologist* 5:206-26.

Rabinow, P., and W. M. Sullivan. 1987. *Interpretive social science: A second look*. Berkeley: University of California Press.

Radin, P. 1966 [1933]. *The method and theory of ethnology*. New York: Basic Books.

Ragin, C. C. 1987. *The comparative method: Moving beyond qualitative and quantitative strategies*. Berkeley: University of California Press.

Ragin, C. C. 1994. Introduction to qualitative comparative analysis. In *The comparative political economy of the welfare state*, ed. by T. Janowski and A. M. Hicks, 299-317. Cambridge, U.K.: Cambridge University Press.

RAND Corporation. 1965. *A million random digits with 100,000 normal deviates*. Glencoe, Ill.: Free Press.

Rappaport, R. 1990. Foreword. In *Surviving fieldwork,* ed. by N. Howell, pp. vii-viii. Washington, D.C.: American Anthropological Association.

Rathje, W. L. 1979. Trace measures: Garbage and other traces. In *Unobtrusive measurement today,* ed. by L. Sechrest, 75-91. San Francisco: Jossey-Bass.

Rathje, W. L. 1984. The garbage decade. In *Household refuse analysis: Theory, method, and applications in social science,* ed. by W. L. Rathje and C. K. Rittenbaugh, 9-29. *American Behavioral Scientist* 28(1). (Special issue)

Rathje, W. L. 1992. Garbage demographics. *American Demographics* 14:50-54.

Raven, P., B. Berlin, and D. Breedlove. 1971. The origins of taxonomy. *Science* 174:1210-13.

Raver, S. A., and A. M. Peterson. 1988. Comparison of teacher estimates and direct observation of spontaneous language in preschool handicapped children. *Child Study Journal* 18:277-84.

Redfield, R. 1948. The art of social science. *American Journal of Sociology* 54:181-90.

Reed, T. W., and R. J. Stimson, eds. 1985. *Survey interviewing: Theory and techniques.* Boston: Allen & Unwin.

Reese, S. D., W. A. Danielson, and P. J. Shoemaker et al. 1986. Ethnicity-of-interviewer effects among Mexican-Americans and Anglos. *Public Opinion Quarterly* 50:563-72.

Reichardt, C. S. and M. M. Mark. 1998. Quasi-experimentation. In *Handbook of applied social research methods,* ed. by L. Bickman et al., 193-228. Thousand Oaks, Calif.: Sage.

Reiss, A. J., Jr. 1971. *The police and the public.* New Haven, Conn.: Yale University Press.

Reiss, N. 1985. *Speech act taxonomy as a tool for ethnographic description: An analysis based on videotapes of continuous behavior in two New York households.* Philadelphia: John Benjamins.

Reiss, S., and N. Dyhdalo. 1975. Persistence, achievement, and open-space environments. *Journal of Educational Psychology* 67:506-13.

Rennie, D. L. 1994. Clients' deference in psychotherapy. *Journal of Counseling Psychology* 41:427-37.

Repp, A. C., G. S. Nieminen, E. Olinger, and R. Brusca. 1988. Direct observation: Factors affecting the accuracy of observers. *Exceptional Children* 55:29-36.

Ricci, J. A., N. W. Jerome, N. Megally, and O. Galal. 1995. Assessing the validity of information recall: Results of a time use pilot study in peri-urban Egypt. *Human Organization* 54:304-308.

Richards, T., and L. Richards. 1991. The NUD*IST qualitative data analysis system. *Qualitative Sociology* 14:307-25.

Richardson, L. 1988. Secrecy and status: The social construction of forbidden relationships. *American Sociological Review* 53:209-19.

Ricoeur, P. 1981. *Hermeneutics and the human sciences: Essays on language, action, and interpretation.* Trans. by J. B. Thompson. New York: Cambridge University Press.

Ricoeur, P. 1991. *From text to action.* Trans. by K. Blamey and J. B. Thompson. Evanston, Ill.: Northwestern University Press.

Riessman, C. K. 1993. *Narrative analysis.* Newbury Park, Calif.: Sage.

Rindfleisch, A., J. E. Burroughs, and F. Denton. 1997. Family structure, materialism, and compulsive consumption. *Journal of Consumer Research* 23:312-25.

Rips, L. J. 1975. Inductive judgments about natural categories. *Journal of Verbal Learning and Verbal Behavior* 14:665-81.

Rips, L. J., E. Shoben, and E. Smith. 1973. Semantic distance and the verification of semantic relations. *Journal of Verbal Learning and Verbal Behavior* 12:1-20.

Rittenbaugh, C. K., and G. G. Harrison. 1984. Reactivity of garbage analysis. In *Household refuse analysis: Theory, method, and applications in social science,* ed. by W. L. Rathje and C. K. Rittenbaugh, 51-70. *American Behavioral Scientist* 28(1). (Special issue)

Robbins, M. C., A. V. Williams, P. L. Kilbride, and R. B. Pollnac. 1969. Factor analysis and case selection in complex societies. *Human Organization* 28:227-34.

Roberts, J. M. 1965 [1956]. *Zuni daily life.* Behavior Science Reprints. New Haven, Conn.: Human Relations Area Files.

Roberts, J. M., and G. E. Chick. 1979. Butler County eight-ball: A behavioral space analysis. In *Sports, games, and play: Social and psychological viewpoints,* ed. by J. H. Goldstein, 65-100. Hillsdale, N.J.: Lawrence Erlbaum.

Roberts, J. M., T. V. Golder, and G. E. Chick. 1981. Judgment, oversight, and skill: A cultural analysis of P-3 pilot error. *Human Organization* 39:5-21.

Roberts, J. M., and S. Nattrass. 1980. Women and trap-shooting: Competence and expression in a game of physical skill with chance. In *Play and culture,* ed. by H. B. Schwartzman, 262-90. West Point, N.Y.: Leisure Press.

Roberts, L. J., D. A. Luke, J. Rappaport, E. Seidman, P. A. Toro, and T. M. Reischl. 1991. Charting uncharted terrain: A behavioral observation system for mutual help groups. *American Journal of Community Psychology* 19:715-37.

Robinson, D., and S. Rhode. 1946. Two experiments with an anti-Semitism poll. *Journal of Abnormal and Social Psychology* 41:136-44.

Robinson, M. B., and C. E. Robinson. 1997. Environmental characteristics associated with residential burglaries of student apartment complexes. *Environment and Behavior* 29:657-75.

Robinson, W. S. 1950. Ecological correlations and the behavior of individuals. *American Sociological Review* 15:351-57.

Robinson, W. S. 1957. The statistical measurement of agreement. *American Sociological Review* 22:17-25.

Rodgers, J. R., and J. L. Rodgers. 1993. Chronic poverty in the United States. *Journal of Human Resources* 28:25-54.

Rogoff, B. 1978. Spot observation: An introduction and examination. *Quarterly Newsletter of the Institute for Comparative Human Development* 2:21-26.

Rohner, R. 1969. *The ethnography of Franz Boas.* Chicago: University of Chicago Press.

Rohner, R., B. R. De Walt, and R. C. Ness. 1973. Ethnographer bias in cross-cultural research. *Behavior Science Notes* 8:275-317.

Rokeach, M. 1973. *The nature of human values.* New York: Free Press.

Romme, A. G. L. 1995. Boolean comparative analysis of qualitative data. *Quality and Quantity* 29:317-29.

Romney, A. K. 1989. Quantitative models, science and cumulative knowledge. *Journal of Quantitative Anthropology* 1:153-223.

Romney, A. K., and R. G. D'Andrade, eds. 1964. Cognitive aspects of English kin terms. *American Anthropologist* 66 (3, part 2): 146-70. (Special issue, Transcultural studies in cognition)

Romney, A. K., R. N. Shepard, and S. B. Nerlove, eds. 1972. *Multidimensional scaling.* Vol. 2, *Applications.* New York: Seminar.

Romney, A. K., S. C. Weller, and W. H. Batchelder. 1986. Culture as consensus: A theory of culture and informant accuracy. *American Anthropologist* 88:313-38.

Rooney, B. L., and D. M. Murray. 1996. A meta-analysis of smoking prevention programs after adjustment for errors in the unit of analysis. *Health Education Quarterly* 23:48-64.

Rosch, E. 1975. Cognitive representations of semantic categories. *Journal of Experimental Psychology* 104:192-233.

Rosenau, P. M. 1992. *Post modernism and the social sciences: Insights, inroads, and intrusions.* Princeton, N.J.: Princeton University Press.

Rosenberg, M. 1968. *The logic of survey analysis.* New York: Basic Books.

Rosenhan, D. L. 1973. On being sane in insane places. *Science* 179:250-58.

Rosenhan, D. L. 1975. The contextual nature of psychiatric diagnosis. *Journal of Abnormal Psychology* 84:462-74.

Rosenshine, B., and N. Furst. 1973. The use of direct observation to study teaching. In *Second handbook of research on teaching*, ed. by R. W. Travers. 122-83. Chicago: Rand McNally.

Rosenthal, R. 1984. *Meta-analytic procedures for social research*. Beverly Hills, Calif.: Sage.

Rosenthal, R., and L. Jacobson. 1968. *Pygmalion in the classroom*. New York: Holt, Rinehart & Winston.

Rosenthal, R., and D. B. Rubin. 1978. Interpersonal expectancy effects: The first 345 studies. *Behavioral and Brain Sciences* 3:377-415.

Rosnow, R. L., and R. Rosenthal. 1997. *People studying people: Artifacts and ethics in behavioral research*. New York: Freeman.

Rossi, P. H., and S. L. Nock. 1982. *Measuring social judgments: The factorial survey approach*. Beverly Hills, Calif.: Sage.

Rothbart, G. S., M. Fine, and S. Sudman. 1982. On finding and interviewing the needles in the haystack: The use of multiplicity sampling. *Public Opinion Quarterly* 46:408-21.

Rothschild, R. F. 1981. What happened in 1780? *Harvard Magazine* 83:20-27.

Rotter, J. B. 1966. Generalized expectancies for internal versus external control of reinforcement. *Psychological Monographs* 30 (whole No. 609).

Rotter, J. B. 1990. Internal versus external control of reinforcement: A case history of a variable. *American Psychologist* 45:489-93.

Rotton, J., and M. Shats. 1996. Effects of state humor, expectancies, and choice on postsurgical mood and self-medication: A field experiment. *Journal of Applied Social Psychology* 26:1775-94.

Rotton, J., M. Shats, and R. Standers. 1990. Temperature and pedestrian tempo: Walking without awareness. *Environment and Behavior* 22:650-74.

Rousseau, J.-J. 1988. *On the social contract*. Trans. and ed. by D. A. Cress. Indianapolis, Ind.: Hackett.

Rovegno, I., and D. Bandhauer. 1997. Norms of the school culture that facilitated teacher adoption and learning of a constructivist approach to physical education. *Journal of Teaching in Physical Education* 16:401-25.

Royal Anthropological Institute of Great Britain and Ireland (RAI). 1951. *Notes and queries on anthropology*. 6th ed., rev. London: Routledge & Kegan Paul.

Rozeboom, W. 1960. The fallacy of the null-hypothesis significance test. *Psychological Bulletin* 67:416-28.

Rubin, H. J., and I. S. Rubin. 1995. *Qualitative interviewing: The art of hearing data*. Thousand Oaks, Calif.: Sage.

Ruby, J., ed. 1982. *A crack in the mirror: Reflexive perspectives in anthropology*. Philadelphia: University of Pennsylvania Press.

Ruffing-Rahal, M. A. 1993. An ecological model of group well-being: Implications for health promotion with older women. *Health Care for Women International* 14:447-56.

Ruffing-Rahal, M. A., L. J. Barin, and C. J. Combs. 1998. Gender role orientation as a correlate of perceived health, health behavior, and qualitative well-being in older women. *Journal of Women and Aging* 10:3-19.

Rushforth, S. 1982. A structural semantic analysis of Bear Lake Athapaskan kinship classification. *American Ethnologist* 9:559-77.

Rusting, C. L., and R. J. Larsen. 1998. Diurnal patterns of unpleasant mood: Associations with neuroticism, depression, and anxiety. *Journal of Personality* 66:85-103.

Rutledge, E. M. 1990. Black parent-child relations: Some correlates. *Journal of Comparative Family Studies* 21:369-78.

Ryan, G. W., and H. Martínez. 1996. Can we predict what mothers do? Modeling childhood diarrhea in rural Mexico. *Human Organization* 55:47-57.

Ryan, G. W., and T. Weisner. 1996. Analyzing words in brief descriptions: Fathers and mothers describe their children. *Cultural Anthropology Methods Journal* 8:13-16.

Saarijarvi, S., M. T. Hyyppa, V. Lehtinen, and E. Alanen. 1990. Chronic low back pain patient and spouse. *Journal of Psychosomatic Research* 34:117-22.

Safren, S. A., C. L. Turk, and R. G. Heimberg. 1998. Factor structure of the Social Interaction Anxiety Scale and the Social Phobia Scale. *Behaviour Research and Therapy* 36:443-53.

Sagar, H. A., and J. W. Schofield. 1980. Racial and behavioral cues in Black and White children's perceptions of ambiguously aggressive acts. *Journal of Personality and Social Psychology* 39:590-98.

Sagberg, F., S. Fosser, and I.-A.F. Saetermo. 1997. An investigation of behavioural adaptation to airbags and antilock brakes among taxi drivers. *Accident Analysis and Prevention* 29:293-302.

Sahlins, M. D. 1976. *The use and abuse of biology: An anthropological critique of sociobiology.* Ann Arbor: University of Michigan Press.

Salant, P., and D. Dillman. 1994. *How to conduct your own survey.* New York: John Wiley.

Salazar, M. K., and C. de Moor. 1995. An evaluation of mammography beliefs using a decision model. *Health Education Quarterly* 22:110-126 .

Salisbury, C. L., M. M. Palombaro, and T. M. Hollowood. 1993. On the nature and change of an inclusive elementary school. *Journal of the Association for Persons with Severe Handicaps* 18(2):75-84.

Sandelowski, M. 1995. Qualitative analysis: What it is and how to begin. *Research in Nursing and Health* 18:371-75.

Sanjek, R. 1990. *Fieldnotes.* Ithaca, N.Y.: Cornell University Press.

Sankoff, G. 1971. Quantitative analysis of sharing and variability in a cognitive model. *Ethnology* 10:389-408.

Sarantokos, S. 1996. Same-sex couples: Problems and prospects. *Journal of Family Studies* 2:147-63.

Sarkar, N. K., and S. J. Tambiah. 1957. *The disintegrating village.* Colombo, Sri Lanka: Ceylon University Socio-Economic Survey of Pata Dumbara.

Sarkar, S., ed. 1996. *The emergence of logical empiricism: From 1900 to the Vienna Circle.* New York: Garland.

Sarton, G. 1935. Quételet (1796-1874). *Isis* 23:6-24.

Saudargas, R. A., and K. Zanolli. 1990. Momentary time sampling as an estimate of percentage time: A field validation. *Journal of Applied Behavior Analysis* 23:533-37.

Scaglion, R. 1986. The importance of nighttime observations in time allocation studies. *American Ethnologist* 13:537-45.

Scharff, L., D. C. Turk, and D. A. Marcus. 1995. The relationship of locus of control and psychosocial-behavioral response in chronic headache. *Headache* 35:527-33.

Schatzman, L., and A. Strauss. 1973. *Field research: Strategies for a natural sociology.* Englewood Cliffs, N.J.: Prentice Hall.

Scheaffer, R. L., W. Mendenhall, and L. Ott. 1990. *Elementary survey sampling.* 4th ed. Boston: PWS-KENT.

Scheers, N. J., and C. M. Dayton. 1987. Improved estimation of academic cheating behavior using the randomized response technique. *Research in Higher Education* 26:61-69.

Scheper-Hughes, N. 1983. Introduction: The problem of bias in androcentric and feminist anthropology. In *Confronting problems of bias in feminist anthropology,* ed. by N. Scheper-Hughes, 109-16. *Women's Studies* 10. (Special issue)

Scheper-Hughes, N. 1992. *Death without weeping: The violence of everyday life in Brazil.* Berkeley: University of California Press.

Scherer, S. E. 1974. Proxemic behavior of primary-school children as a function of the socioeconomic class and subculture. *Journal of Personality and Social Psychology* 29:800-805.

Schiller, F. C. S. 1969 [1903]. *Humanism: Philosophical essays.* Freeport, N.Y.: Books for Libraries Press.

Schlegel, A., and H. Barry III. 1986. The cultural consequences of female contribution to subsistence. *American Anthropologist* 88:142-50.

Schober M. F., and F. G. Conrad. 1997. Does conversational interviewing reduce survey measurement error? *Public Opinion Quarterly* 61:576-602.

Schoenberg, N. E. 1997. A convergence of health beliefs: An "ethnography of adherence" of African-American rural elders with hypertension. *Human Organization* 56:174-81.

Schofield, J. W., and K. Anderson. 1987. Combining quantitative and qualitative components of research on ethnic identity and intergroup relations. In *Children's ethnic socialization: Pluralism and development*, ed. by J. S. Phinney and M. J. Rotheram, 252-73. Newbury Park, Calif.: Sage.

Schuman, H., and J. M. Converse. 1971. Effects of Black and White interviewers on Black response in 1968. *Public Opinion Quarterly* 35:44-68.

Schuman, H., and S. Presser. 1979. The open and closed question. *American Sociological Review* 44:692-712.

Schuman, H., and S. Presser. 1981. *Questions and answers in attitude surveys.* San Diego, Calif.: Academic Press.

Schuster, J. A. 1977. *Descartes and the scientific revolution.* Princeton, N.J.: Princeton University Press.

Schutte, J. W., and H. M. Hosch. 1997. Gender differences in sexual assault verdicts: A meta-analysis. *Journal of Social Behavior and Personality* 12:759-72.

Schutz, A. 1962. *Collected papers I: The problem of social reality.* The Hague: Martinus Nijhoff.

Schutz, A. 1967. *The phenomenology of the social world.* Evanston, Ill.: Northwestern University Press.

Schwarz, B., H.-P. Bischof, and M. Kunze. 1994. Coffee, tea, and lifestyle. *Preventive Medicine* 23:377-84.

Schwarz, N. 1999. Self-reports. How the questions shape the answers. *American Psychologist* 54:93-105.

Schweizer, T. 1991. The power struggle in a Chinese community, 1950-1980: A social network analysis of the duality of actors and events. *Journal of Quantitative Anthropology* 3:19-44.

Schweizer, T. 1996. Actor and event orderings across time: Lattice representation and Boolean analysis of the political disputes in Chen Village, China. *Social Networks* 18:247-66.

Schweizer, T. 1998. Epistemology: The nature and validation of anthropological knowledge. In *Handbook of methods in cultural anthropology,* ed. by H. R. Bernard, 39-87. Walnut Creek, Calif.: AltaMira.

Science. 1972. Briefing: The Brawling Bent. March 24, vol. 175, pp. 1346-47.

Scott, W. A. 1955. Reliability of content analysis: The case of nomimal scale coding. *Public Opinion Quarterly* 19:321-25.

Scrimshaw, S. C. M., and E. Hurtado. 1987. *Rapid assessment procedures for nutrition and primary health care.* Los Angeles: University of California at Los Angeles, Latin American Center.

Sechrest, L., ed. 1979. *Unobtrusive measurement today.* San Francisco: Jossey-Bass.

Sechrest, L., and L. Flores. 1969. Homosexuality in the Philippines and the United States: The handwriting on the wall. *Journal of Social Psychology* 79:3-12.

Sechrest, L., and M. Phillips. 1979. Unobtrusive measures: An overview. In *Unobtrusive measurement today,* ed. by L. Sechrest, 1-17. San Francisco: Jossey-Bass.

Segre, C. 1988. *Introduction to the analysis of literary text.* Collab. by Tomaso Kemeny. Trans. by J. Meddemmen. Bloomington: Indiana University Press.

Sellers, R. M., T. M. Chavous, J. N. Shelton, and M. A. Smith. 1997. Multidimensional inventory of Black identity; A preliminary investigation of reliability and construct validity. *Journal of Personality and Social Psychology* 73:805-15.

Selzer, M. L. 1971. The Michigan Alcoholism Screening Test: The quest for a new diagnostic instrument. *American Journal of Psychiatry* 127:1653-58.

Shaffer, T. L., and J. R. Elkins. 1997. *Legal interviewing and counseling in a nutshell.* 3d ed. St. Paul, Minn.: West Group.

Shaner, W. W., P. F. Phillip, and W. R. Schmehl. 1982. *Farming systems research and development: Guidelines for developing countries.* Boulder, Colo.: Westview.

Sharff, J. W. 1979. Patterns of authority in two urban Puerto Rican households. Ph.D. diss., Columbia University.

Sharpe, R. 1998. EEOC backs away from filing race-bias suit. *Wall Street Journal,* June 24, A4.

Shaw, C. R. 1930. *The jack-roller: A delinquent boy's own story.* Chicago: University of Chicago Press.

Shaw, S. 1992. Dereifying family leisure: An examination of women's and men's everyday experiences and perceptions of family time. *Leisure Studies* 14:271-86.

Sheatsley, P. B. 1983. Questionnaire construction and item wording. In *Handbook of survey research,* ed. by P. H. Rossi, J. D. Wright, and A. B. Anderson, 195-230. New York: John Wiley.

Shelley, G. A. 1992. The social networks of people with end-stage renal disease: Comparing hemodialysis and peritoneal dialysis patients. Ph.D. diss., University of Florida, Gainesville.

Shelley, G. A., H. R. Bernard, P. D. Killworth, E. Johnsen, and C. McCarty. 1995. Who knows your HIV status? What HIV+ patients and their network members know about each other. *Social Networks* 17:189-217.

Sherkat, D. E. 1998. Counterculture or continuity? Competing influences on baby boomers' religious orientations and participation. *Social Forces* 76:1087-14.

Sherkat, D. E., and J. J. Blocker. 1994. The political development of sixties' activists: Identifying the influence of class, gender, and socialization on protest participation. *Social Forces* 72:821-42.

Sherman, E., A. Mathur, and R. B. Smith. 1997. Store environment and consumer purchase behavior: Mediating role of consumer emotions. *Psychology and Marketing* 14:361-78.

Sherry, J. F., Jr. 1995. *Contemporary marketing and consumer behavior: An anthropological sourcebook.* Thousand Oaks, Calif.: Sage.

Shih, F.-J. 1997. Perception of self in the intensive care unit after cardiac surgery among adult Taiwanese and American-Chinese patients. *International Journal of Nursing Studies* 34:17-26.

Shinew, K. J., M. F. Floyd, F. A. McGuire, and F. P. Noe. 1995. Gender, race and subjective social class and their association with leisure preferences. *Leisure Studies* 17:75-89.

Shore, B. A., D. C. Lerman, R. G. Smith, B. A. Iwata, and I. G. De Leon. 1995. Direct assessment of quality of care in a geriatric nursing home. *Journal of Applied Behavior Analysis* 28:435-48.

Shostack, A. L., and G. P. Campagna. 1991. Daily living patterns, human relations, and community services in a sample of New Jersey board and care homes: Report of an exploratory survey. *Adult Residential Care Journal* 5:7-28.

Shotland, L., and M. K. Straw. 1976. Bystander response to an assault: When a man attacks a woman. *Journal of Personality and Social Psychology* 34:990-99.

Shweder, R., and R. D'Andrade. 1980. The systematic distortion hypothesis. In *Fallible judgment in behavioral research,* ed. by R. Shweder, 37-58. San Francisco: Jossey-Bass.

Silver, B. L. 1998. *The ascent of science.* New York: Oxford University Press.

Simpson, J. A., and S. W. Gangestad. 1991. Individual differences in sociosexuality: Evidence for convergent and discriminant validity. *Journal of Personality and Social Psychology* 60:870-83.

Singer, E., and S. Presser. 1989. *Survey research methods: A reader.* Chicago: University of Chicago Press.

Sirken, M. G. 1972. *Designing forms for demographic surveys.* Chapel Hill: Laboratories for Population Statistics, University of North Carolina.

Skinner, B. F. 1957. *Verbal behavior.* New York: Appleton-Century-Crofts.

Skruppy, M. 1993. Activities of daily living evaluations: Is there a difference in what the patient reports and what is observed? *Physical and Occupational Therapy in Geriatrics* 11:13-25.

Smith, A. B., and P. M. Inder. 1993. Social interaction in same- and cross-gender pre-school peer groups: A participant observation study. *Educational Psychology* 13:29-42.

Smith, C. D., and W. Kornblum, eds. 1996. *In the field: Readings on the research experience.* New York: Praeger.

Smith, C. J., R. G. Nelson, S. A. Hardy, E. M. Manahan, P. H. Bennett, and W. C. Knowler. 1996. Survey of the diet of Pima Indians using quantitative food frequency assessment and 24-hour recall. *Journal of the American Dietetic Association* 96:778-84.

Smith, L. D. 1986. *Behaviorism and logical positivism.* Stanford, Calif.: Stanford University Press.

Smith, M. L., and G. V. Glass. 1977. Meta-analysis of psychotherapy outcome studies. *American Psychologist* 32:752-60.

Smith, P. B., F. Trompenaars, and S. Dugan. 1995. The Rotter Locus of Control Scale in 43 countries: A test of cultural relativity. *International Journal of Psychology* 30:377-400.

Smith, P. C., L. M. Kendall, and C. L. Hulin. 1969. *The measurement of satisfaction in work and retirement: A strategy for the study of attitudes.* Chicago: Rand McNally.

Smith, R. 1997. *The Norton history of the human sciences.* New York: Norton.

Smith, T. W. 1987. That which we call welfare by any other name would smell sweeter: An analysis of the impact of question wording on response patterns. *Public Opinion Quarterly* 51:75-83.

Smith, T. W. 1989. The hidden 25 percent: An analysis of nonresponse on the 1980 General Social Survey. In *Survey research methods,* ed. by E. Singer and S. Presser, 50-68. Chicago: University of Chicago Press.

Smith, T. W. 1998. A review of church attendance measures. *American Sociological Review* 63:131-36.

Smits, J., W. Ultee, and J. Lammers. 1998. Educational homogamy in 65 countries: An explanation of differences in openness using country-level explanatory variables. *American Sociological Review* 63:264-85.

Snider, J. G., and C. E. Osgood, eds. 1969. *Semantic differential technique.* Chicago: Aldine.

Snow, C. P. 1964. *The two cultures: And a second look.* Cambridge, U.K.: Cambridge University Press.

Snow, W. G., and J. Weinstock. 1990. Sex differences among non-brain-damaged adults on the Wechsler Adult Intelligence Scales: A review of the literature. *Journal of Clinical and Experimental Neuropsychology* 12:873-86.

Soderfeldt, B., M. Soderfeldt, K. Jones, P. O'Campo, Muntaner, C.-G. Ohlson, C. Warg, and L.-E. Warg. 1997. Does organization matter? A multilevel analysis of the demand-control model applied to human services. *Social Science and Medicine* 44:527-34.

Sohier, R. 1993. Filial reconstruction: A theory on development through adversity. *Qualitative Health Research* 3:465-92.

Solomon, R. L. 1949. An extension of control group design. *Psychological Bulletin* 46:137-50.

Solomon, R. L., and M. S. Lessac. 1968. A control group design for experimental studies of developmental processes. *Psychological Bulletin* 70:145-50.

Sonn, U., G. Grimby, and A. Svanborg. 1996. Activities of daily living studied longitudinally between 70 and 76 years of age. *Disability and Rehabilitation: An International Multidisciplinary Journal* 18:91-100.

Sorensen, R. A. 1992. *Thought experiments.* New York: Oxford University Press.

Soskin, W. F. 1963. *Verbal interaction in a young married couple.* Lawrence: University of Kansas Press.

Soskin, W. F., and V. John. 1963. The study of spontaneous talk. In *The stream of behavior: Explorations of its structure and content,* ed. by R. G. Barker, 228-82. New York: Appleton-Century-Crofts.

Spearman, C. 1904. "General intelligence," objectively determined and measured. *American Journal of Psychology* 15:201-93.

Spector, P. E. 1992. *Summated rating scale construction.* Newbury Park, Calif.: Sage.

Spence, J. T. 1991. Do the BSRI and the PAQ measure the same or different concepts? *Psychology of Women Quarterly* 15:141-65.

Spence, J. T., and E. D. Hahn. 1997. The Attitudes Toward Women Scale and attitude change in college students. *Psychology of Women Quarterly* 21:17-34.

Spence, J. T., and R. L. Helmreich. 1972. The Attitudes Toward Women Scale: An objective instrument to measure attitudes toward the rights and roles of women in contemporary society. *Catalog of Selected Documents in Psychology* 2:66-67.

Spence, J. T., and R. L. Helmreich. 1978. *Masculinity and femininity: Their psychological dimensions, correlates, and antecedents.* Austin: University of Texas Press.

Spence, J. T., R. L. Helmreich, and J. Stapp. 1973. A short version of the Attitudes Toward Women Scale (AWS). *Bulletin of the Psychonomic Society* 2:219-20.

Spence, J. T., R. L. Helmreich, and J. Stapp. 1974. The Personal Attributes Questionnaire: A measure of sex-role stereotypes and masculinity-femininity. *Catalog of Selected Documents in Psychology* 4:43-44.

Spence, S. H. 1998. A measure of anxiety symptoms among children. *Behaviour Research and Therapy* 36:545-66.

Spitzer, R. L. 1976. More on pseudoscience in science and the case for psychiatric diagnostics. *Archives of General Psychiatry* 33:459-70.

Spradley, J. P. 1979. *The ethnographic interview.* New York: Holt, Rinehart & Winston.

Spradley, J. P. 1980. *Participant observation.* New York: Holt, Rinehart & Winston.

Spradley, J. P. 1987 [1972]. Adaptive strategies of urban nomads. In *Culture and cognition,* ed. by J. P. Spradley, 235-62. Prospect Heights, Ill.: Waveland. Orig. pub. in 1972 in *The anthropology of urban environments,* ed. by T. Weaver and D. J. White. Boulder, Colo.: Society for Applied Anthropology. Monograph, no. 11.

Sproull, L. S. 1981. Managing education programs: A micro-behavioral analysis. *Human Organization* 40:113-22.

Sque, M., and S. A. Payne. 1996. Dissonant loss: The experiences of donor relatives. *Social Science and Medicine* 43:1359-70.

Squire, P. 1988. Why the 1936 "Literary Digest" poll failed. *Public Opinion Quarterly* 52:125-33.

Srinivas, M. N. 1979. The fieldworker and the field: A village in Karnataka. In *The fieldworker and the field,* ed. by M. N. Srinivas, A. M. Shah, and E. A. Ramaswamy, 19-28. Delhi: Oxford University Press.

Steblay, N. M. 1997. Social influence in eyewitness recall: A meta-analytic review of lineup instruction effects. *Law and Human Behavior* 21:283-97.

Stein, J., S. A. Fox, and P. J. Murata. 1991. The influence of ethnicity, socioeconomic status, and psychological barriers on the use of mammography. *Journal of Health and Social Behavior* 32:101-13.

Stein, R. H. 1987. *The synoptic problem.* Grand Rapids, Mich.: Baker Book House.

Stemmer, N. 1990. Skinner's *Verbal Behavior,* Chomsky's review, and mentalism. *Journal of the Experimental Analysis of Behavior* 54:307-16.

Stephenson, J. B., and L. S. Greer. 1981. Ethnographers in their own cultures: Two Appalachian cases. *Human Organization* 30:333-43.

Sterk, C. 1989. Prostitution, drug use, and AIDS. In *In the field: Readings on the field research experience,* ed. by C. D. Smith and W. Kornblum, 91-100. New York: Praeger.

Stevens, S. S. 1946. On the theory of scales and measurement. *Science* 103:677-80.

Stevens, S. S. 1957. On the psychophysical power law. *Psychological Review* 64:153-81.

Stewart, A. 1998. *The ethnographer's method.* Thousand Oaks, Calif.: Sage.

Stewart, A. L., A. C. King, and W. L. Haskell. 1993. Endurance exercise and health-related quality of life in 50-65 year old adults. *The Gerontologist* 33:782-89.

Stewart, D. W., and P. N. Shamdasani. 1990. *Focus groups: Theory and practice.* Newbury Park, Calif.: Sage.

Stewart, M. A. 1984. What is a successful doctor-patient interview? A study of interactions and outcomes. *Social Science and Medicine* 19:167-75.

Stinchcombe, A. L. 1968. *Constructing social theories.* New York: Harcourt, Brace & World.

Stitsworth, M. H. 1989. Personality changes associated with a sojourn in Japan. *Journal of Social Psychology* 129:213-24.

Stolzenberg, L., and S. J. D'Alessio. 1997. "Three strikes and you're out": The impact of California's new mandatory sentencing law on serious crime rates. *Crime & Delinquency* 43:457-69.

Stone, P. J., D. C. Dunphy, M. S. Smith, and D. M. Ogilvie, eds. 1966. *The General Inquirer: A computer approach to content analysis*. Cambridge, Mass.: MIT Press.

Storer, N. W. 1966. *The social system of science*. New York: Holt, Rinehart & Winston.

Stouffer, S. A. et al. 1947-50. *Studies in social psychology in World War II*. 4 vols. Princeton, N.J.: Princeton University Press.

Strauss, A. 1987. *Qualitative analysis for social scientists*. Cambridge, U.K.: Cambridge University Press.

Strauss, A., and J. Corbin. 1990. *Basics of qualitative research: Grounded theory procedures and techniques*. Newbury Park, Calif.: Sage.

Streib, G. F. 1952. Use of survey methods among the Navaho. *American Anthropologist* 54:30-40.

Stricker, L. J. 1988. Measuring social status with occupational information: A simple method. *Journal of Applied Social Psychology* 18:423-37.

Stunkard, A., and D. Kaplan. 1977. Eating in public places: A review of reports of the direct observation of eating behavior. *International Journal of Obesity* 1:89-101.

Sturtevant, W. C. 1959. A technique for ethnographic note-taking. *American Anthropologist* 61:677-78.

Sturtevant, W. C. 1964. Studies in ethnoscience. *American Anthropologist* 66 (3, part 2): 99-131. (Special issue, *Transcultural studies in cognition*, ed. by A. K. Romney and R. G. D'Andrade)

Stycos, J. M. 1955. *Family and fertility in Puerto Rico*. New York: Columbia University Press.

Stycos, J. M. 1960. Sample surveys for social science in underdeveloped areas. In *Human organization research*, ed. by R. N. Adams and J. J. Preiss, 375-88. Homewood, Ill.: Dorsey.

Sudman, S. 1976. *Applied sampling*. New York: Academic Press.

Sudman, S., and N. M. Bradburn. 1974. *Response effects in surveys: Review and synthesis*. Chicago: Aldine.

Sudman, S., and N. M. Bradburn. 1982. *Asking questions*. San Francisco: Jossey-Bass.

Sudman, S., N. M. Bradburn, and N. Schwarz. 1996. *Thinking about answers: The application of cognitive processes to survey methodology*. San Francisco: Jossey-Bass.

Sudman, S., and N. Schwarz. 1989. Contributions of cognitive psychology to advertising research. *Journal of Advertising Research* 29:43-53.

Sugarman, J. R., G. Brenneman, W. LaRoque, C. W. Warren, and H. I. Goldberg. 1994. The urban Indian oversample in the 1988 National Maternal and Infant Health Survey. *Public Health Reports* 109:243-50.

Sulfaro, V., and M. N. Crislip. 1997. How Americans perceive foreign policy threat: A magnitude scaling analysis. *Political Psychology* 18:103-26.

Sullivan, K. A. 1990. Daily time allocation among adult and immature yellow-eyed juncos over the breeding season. *Animal Behaviour* 39:380-88.

Sullivan, P., and K. Elifson. 1996. In the field with snake handlers. In *In the field: Readings on the research experience*, ed. by C. D. Smith and W. Kornblum, 33-38. New York: Praeger.

Sundvik, L., and M. Lindeman. 1993. Sex-role identity and discrimination against same-sex employees. *Journal of Occupational and Organizational Psychology* 66:1-11.

Suttles, G. D. 1968. *The social order of the slum: Ethnicity and territory in the inner city*. Chicago: University of Chicago Press.

Sykes, R. E., and E. E. Brent. 1983. *Policing: A social behaviorist perspective*. New Brunswick, N.J.: Rutgers University Press.

Sykes, R. E., R. D. Rowley, and J. M. Schaefer. 1993. The influence of time, gender and group size on heavy drinking in public bars. *Journal of Studies on Alcohol* 54:133-38.

Szalai, A., ed. 1972. *The use of time: Daily activities of urban and suburban populations in twelve countries*. The Hague: Mouton.

Tannen, D. 1994. *Gender and discourse*. New York: Oxford University Press.

Tanur, J. M. 1992. *Questions about questions: Inquiries into the cognitive bases of surveys.* New York: Russell Sage.

Taub, D. E., and R. G. Leger. 1984. Argot and the creation of social types in a young gay community. *Human Relations* 37:181-89.

Taylor, F. W. 1911. *The principles of scientific management.* New York: Harper.

Taylor, H. 1997. The very different methods used to conduct telephone surveys of the public. *Journal of the Marketing Research Society* 37:421-32.

Taylor, K. M., and J. A. Shepperd. 1996. Probing suspicion among participants in deception research. *American Psychologist* 51:886-87.

Taylor, S. J. 1991. Leaving the field: Relationships and responsibilities. In *Experiencing fieldwork: An inside view of qualitative research,* ed. by W. B. Shaffir and R. A. Stebbins, 238-45. Newbury Park, Calif.: Sage.

Taylor, S. J., and R. Bogdan. 1998. *Introduction to qualitative research methods.* 3d ed. New York: John Wiley.

Tedlock, D. 1985. *Popol Vuh: The Mayan book of the dawn of life and the glories of gods and kings.* New York: Simon & Schuster.

Tedlock, D. 1987. Hearing a voice in an ancient text: Quiché Maya poetics in performance. In *Native American discourse: Poetics and rhetoric,* ed. by J. Sherzer and A. Woodbury, 140-75. Cambridge, U.K.: Cambridge University Press.

Templeton, J. F. 1994. *The focus group: A strategic guide to organizing, conducting and analyzing the focus group interview.* Rev. ed. Chicago: Probus.

Tesch, R. 1990. *Qualitative research: Analysis types and software tools.* New York: Falmer.

Thakur, H. B. 1996. Practical steps towards saving the lives of 25,000 potential victims of dowry and bride-burning in India in the next four years. *Journal of South Asia Women Studies* 2(2). Available [online]: www1.shore.net/india/jsaws/issue3/

Thomas, J. R., A. M. Lee, L. McGee, and S. Silverman. 1987. Effects of individual and group contingencies on disruptive playground behavior. *Journal of Research and Development in Education* 20:66-76.

Thomas, J. S. 1981. The economic determinants on leadership on a Tojalabal Maya community. *American Ethnologist* 8:127-38.

Thurman, Q., S. Jackson, and J. Zhao. 1993. Drunk-driving research and innovation: A factorial survey study of decisions to drink and drive. *Social Science Research* 22:245-64.

Tidball, M. E. 1973. Perspectives on academic women and affirmative action. *Educational Record* 54:130-35.

Tiefenthaler, J. 1997. Fertility and family time allocation in the Philippines. *Population and Development Review* 23:377-97.

Tindale, R. S., and D. A. Vollrath. 1992. "Thought experiments" and applied social psychology. In *Methodological issues in applied social psychology,* ed. by F. B. Bryant et al., 219-38. New York: Plenum.

Titus, P. A., and P. B. Everett. 1996. Consumer wayfinding tasks, strategies, and errors: An exploratory field study. *Psychology and Marketing* 13:265-90.

Tobler, N. S., and H. H. Stratton. 1997. Effectiveness of school-based drug prevention programs: A meta-analysis of the research. *Journal of Primary Prevention* 18:71-128.

Tomita, S. K. 1998. The consequences of belonging: Conflict management techniques among Japanese Americans. *Journal of Elder Abuse and Neglect* 9:41-68.

Tooker, E. 1997. Introduction. In *Systems of consanguinity and affinity of the human family,* by L. H. Morgan. Lincoln: University of Nebraska Press.

Torgerson, W. S. 1958. *Theory and methods of scaling.* New York: John Wiley.

Toulmin, S. E. 1980. Philosophy of science. *Encyclopaedia Britannica.* Vol. 16. Chicago: Encyclopaedia Britannica.

Tremblay, M. 1957. The key informant technique: A non-ethnographical application. *American Anthropologist* 59:688-701.

Trent, R., and H. R. Bernard. 1985. Local support for an innovative transit system. *Journal of Advanced Transportation Research* 19:237-39.

Trost, J. E. 1986. Statistically nonrepresentative stratified sampling: A sampling technique for qualitative studies. *Qualitative Sociology* 9:54-57.

Trotter, R. T., II. 1981. Remedios caseros: Mexican-American home remedies and community health problems. *Social Science and Medicine* 15B:107-14.

Trotter, R. T., II, and J. M. Potter. 1993. Pile sorts, a cognitive anthropological model of drug and AIDS risks for Navajo teenagers: Assessment of a new evaluation tool. *Drugs and Society* 7:23-39.

Tufte, E. R. 1983. *The visual display of quantitative information*. Cheshire, Conn.: Graphics Press.

Tufte, E. R. 1997. *Visual explanations: Images and quantities, evidence and narrative*. Cheshire, Conn.: Graphics Press.

Turnbull, C. 1972. *The mountain people*. New York: Simon & Schuster.

Turnbull, C. 1986. Sex and gender: The role of subjectivity in field research. In *Self, sex and gender in cross-cultural fieldwork*, ed. by T. L. Whitehead and M. E. Conaway, 17-29. Urbana: University of Illinois Press.

Turner, C. F., L. Ku, S. M. Rogers, L. D. Lindberg, and J. H. Pleck. 1998. Adolescent sexual behavior, drug use, and violence: Increased reporting with computer survey technology. *Science* 280:867-73.

Turner, J. H. 1972. *Patterns of social organization. A survey of social institutions*. New York: McGraw-Hill.

Tversky, A. 1972. Elimination by aspects: A theory of choice. *Psychological Review* 79:281-99.

Tversky, A., and D. Kahneman. 1974. Judgment under uncertainty: Heuristics and biases. *Science* 185:1124-31.

Twenge, J. M. 1997. Attitudes towards women, 1970-1995. *Psychology of Women Quarterly* 21:35-51.

Undén, A.-L. and K. Orth-Gomér. 1989. Development of a social support instrument for use in population surveys. *Social Science and Medicine* 29:1387-92.

U.S. Census Bureau. 1995. *Statistical abstract of the United States*. Washington, D.C.: Government Printing Office.

U.S. Census Bureau. 1996. *Statistical abstract of the United States*. Washington, D.C.: Government Printing Office.

U.S. Census Bureau. 1997. *Statistical abstract of the United States*. Washington, D.C.: Government Printing Office.

U.S. Census Bureau. 1998. *Statistical abstract of the United States*. Washington, D.C.: Government Printing Office.

U.S. Senate. 1993. Adjustment again? The accuracy of the Census Bureau's population estimates and the impact on state funding allocations. Hearing before the Committee on Governmental Affairs, United States Senate, August 12, 1992. Washington, D.C.: Government Printing Office.

University of Michigan, Survey Research Center. 1976. *Interviewer's manual*. Rev. ed. Ann Arbor: Institute for Social Research, University of Michigan.

Uris, A. 1988. *88 mistakes interviewers make—And how to avoid them*. New York: AMACOM.

Van Maanen, J., M. Miller, and J. C. Johnson. 1982. An occupation in transition: Traditional and modern forms of commercial fishing. *Work and Occupations* 9:193-216.

Vannatta, R. A. 1996. Risk factors related to suicidal behavior among male and female adolescents. *Journal of Youth and Adolescence* 25:149-60.

Van Willigen, J., and V. C. Channa. 1991. Law, custom, and crimes against women: The problem of dowry death in India. *Human Organization* 50:369-77.

Vaughn, B. J., and R. H. Horner. 1997. Identifying instructional tasks that occasion problem behaviors and assessing the effects of student versus teacher choice among these tasks. *Journal of Applied Behavior Analysis* 30:299-312.

Vaughn, S., J. S. Shumm, and J. Sinagub. 1996. *Focus group interviews in education and psychology*. Thousand Oaks, Calif.: Sage.

Veatch, H. B. 1969. *Two logics: The conflict between classical and neoanalytic philosophy*. Evanston, Ill.: Northwestern University Press.

Vieth, A. Z., K. K. Hagglund, D. L. Clay, and R. G. Frank. 1997. The contribution of hope and affectivity to diabetes-related disability: An exploratory study. *Journal of Clinical Psychology in Medical Settings* 4:65-77.

Voltaire. 1967 [1738]. *The elements of Sir Isaac Newton's philosophy*. Trans. by J. Hanna. London: Cass.

Wagley, C. 1983. Learning fieldwork: Guatemala. In *Fieldwork: The human experience*, ed. by R. Lawless, V. H. Sutlive, and M. D. Zamora, 1-18. New York: Gordon & Breach.

Waitzkin, H., and T. Britt. 1993. Processing narratives of self-destructive behavior in routine medical encounters: Health promotion, disease prevention, and the discourse of health care. *Social Science and Medicine* 36:1121-36.

Waitzkin, H., T. Britt, and C. Williams. 1994. Narratives of aging and social problems in medical encounters with older persons. *Journal of Health and Social Behavior* 35:322-48.

Wallace, A. F. C. 1962. Culture and cognition. *Science* 135:351-57.

Wallerstein, I. M. 1974. *The modern world-system: Capitalist agriculture and the origins of the European world-economy in the sixteenth century*. New York: Academic Press.

Wallgren, A., B. Wallgren, R. Persson, U. Jorner, and J.-A. Haaland. 1996. *Graphing statistics and data: Creating better charts*. Thousand Oaks, Calif.: Sage.

Walmsley, D. J., and G. J. Lewis. 1989. The pace of pedestrian flows in cities. *Environment and Behavior* 21:123-50.

Wanous, J. P., A. E. Reichers, and M. J. Hudy. 1997. Overall job satisfaction: How good are single-item measures? *Journal of Applied Psychology* 82:247-52.

Ward, T., C. Fon, S. M. Hudson, and J. McCormack. 1998. A descriptive model of dysfunctional cognitions in child molesters. *Journal of Interpersonal Violence* 13:129-35.

Ward, V. M., J. T. Bertrand, and L. F. Brown. 1991. The comparability of focus group and survey results. *Evaluation Review* 15:266-83.

Waring, S. P. 1991. *Taylorism transformed: Scientific management theory since 1945*. Chapel Hill: University of North Carolina Press.

Wark, G. R., and D. L. Krebs. 1996. Gender and dilemma differences in real-life moral judgment. *Developmental Psychology* 1996 32:220-30.

Warner, S. L. 1965. Randomized response: A survey technique for eliminating evasive answer bias. *Journal of the American Statistical Association* 60:63-69.

Warner, W. L. 1937. *A Black civilization*. New York: Harper & Brothers.

Warner, W. L., ed. 1963. *Yankee City*. New Haven, Conn.: Yale University Press.

Warner, W. L., and P. S. Hunt. 1941. *The social life of a modern community*. New Haven, Conn.: Yale University Press.

Warren, C. A. B. 1988. *Gender issues in field research*. Newbury Park, Calif.: Sage.

Warriner, K., J. Goyder, H. Gjertsen, P. Hohner, and K. McSpurren. 1996. Charities, no; lotteries, no; cash, yes. Main effects and interactions in a Canadian incentives experiment. *Public Opinion Quarterly* 60:542-62.

Warwick, D. P., and C. A. Lininger. 1975. *The sample survey: Theory and practice*. New York: McGraw-Hill

Watson, O. M., and T. D. Graves. 1966. Quantitative research in proxemic behavior. *American Anthropologist* 68:971-85.

Watson, T. J. 1996. How do managers think? Identity, morality and pragmatism in managerial theory and practice. *Management Learning* 27:323-41.

Watt, J. D., and J. Ewing. 1996. Toward the development and validation of a measure of sexual boredom scale. *Journal of Sex Research* 33:57-66.

Watters, J. K., and P. Biernacki. 1989. Targeted sampling: Options for the study of hidden populations. *Social Problems* 36:416-30.

Wax, M. 1996. Reply to Herrera. *Human Organization* 55:238-39. (See also entries for Herrera [1996] and for Fluehr-Lobban [1996].)

Wax, R. 1971. *Doing fieldwork: Warnings and advice.* Chicago: University of Chicago Press.

Wax, R. 1986. Gender and age in fieldwork and fieldwork education: "Not any good thing is done by one man alone." In *Self, sex and gender in cross-cultural fieldwork,* ed. by T. L. Whitehead and M. E. Conaway, 129-50. Urbana: University of Illinois Press.

Webb, B. 1926. *My apprenticeship.* London: Longmans, Green.

Webb, C. 1984. Feminist methodology in nursing research . . . women's perceptions of having a hysterectomy. *Journal of Advanced Nursing* 9:249-56.

Webb, E. J., D. T. Campbell, R. D. Schwartz, and L. Sechrest. 1966. *Unobtrusive measures: Nonreactive research in the social sciences.* Chicago: Rand McNally.

Webb, E. J., and K. E. Weick. 1983. Unobtrusive measures in organizational theory: A reminder. In *Qualitative research,* ed. by J. van Mannen, 209-24. Beverly Hills, Calif.: Sage.

Webb, S., and B. P. Webb. 1910. *The state and the doctor.* New York: Longmans, Green.

Weber, M. 1978. *Economy and society: An outline of interpretive sociology.* Ed. by G. Roth and C. Wittich. Berkeley: University of California Press.

Weeks, M. F., and R. P. Moore. 1981. Ethnicity-of-interviewer effects on ethnic respondents. *Public Opinion Quarterly* 45:245-49.

Weick, K. E. 1995. *Sensemaking in organizations.* Thousand Oaks, Calif.: Sage.

Weinberger, J. 1985. *Science, faith, and politics: Francis Bacon and the utopian roots of the modern age.* Ithaca, N.Y.: Cornell University Press.

Weinberger, M., J. A. Ferguson, G. Westmoreland, L. A. Mamlin, D. S. Segar, G. J. Eckert, J. Y. Greene, D. K. Martin, and W. M. Tierney. 1998. Can raters consistently evaluate the content of focus groups? *Social Science and Medicine* 46:929-33.

Weisfeld, G. E., and K. de Olivares. 1992. A participant-observation course in applied adolescent development. *Teaching of Psychology* 19:180-82.

Weisstub, D., ed. 1998. *Research on human subjects: Ethics, law, and social policy.* Kidlington, Oxford, U.K.: Pergamon.

Weitzman, E. A., and M. Miles. 1995. *Computer programs for qualitative data analysis: A software sourcebook.* Thousand Oaks, Calif.: Sage.

Weller, S. C. 1983. New data on intracultural variability: The hot-cold concept of medicine and illness. *Human Organization* 42:249-57.

Weller, S. C., and C. I. Dungy. 1986. Personal preferences and ethnic variations among Anglo and Hispanic breast and bottle feeders. *Social Science and Medicine* 23:539-48.

Weller, S. C., and A. K. Romney. 1988. *Structured interviewing.* Newbury Park, Calif.: Sage.

Wellman, B., and S. D. Berkowitz. 1997 [1988]. *Social structures: A network approach.* Greenwich, Conn.: JAI.

Wentland, E. J., and K. W. Smith. 1993. *Survey responses: An evaluation of their validity.* San Diego: Academic Press.

Werblow, J. A., Fox, H. M., and A. Henneman. 1978. Nutrition knowledge, attitudes and patterns of women athletes. *Journal of the American Dietetic Association* 73:242-45.

Werner, D. 1985. Psycho-social stress and the construction of a flood-control dam in Santa Catarina, Brazil. *Human Organization* 44:161-66.

Werner, O. 1996. Short Take 20: Native outlines for ethnographies. *Cultural Anthropology Methods Journal* 8:9-10.

Werner, O., and J. Fenton. 1973. Method and theory in ethnoscience or ethnoepistemology. In *A handbook of method in cultural anthropology,* ed. by R. Naroll and R. Cohen, 537-78. New York: Columbia University Press.

Werner, O., and G. M. Schoepfle. 1987. *Systematic fieldwork.* 2 vols. Newbury Park, Calif.: Sage.

Wertz, R. T. 1987. Language treatment for aphasia is efficacious, but for whom? *Topics in Language Disorders* 8:1-10.

West, S. G., S. P. Gunn, and P. Chernicky. 1975. Ubiquitous Watergate: An attributional analysis. *Journal of Personality and Social Psychology* 32:55-65.

Westermeyer, J. 1996. Alcohol and older American Indians. *Journal of Studies on Alcohol* 57:117-18.

Westfall, R. S. 1993. *The life of Isaac Newton.* New York: Cambridge University Press.

White, K. R. 1980. Socio-economic status and academic achievement. *Evaluation in Education* 4:79-81.

White, M. B., S. A. Edwards, and C. S. Russell. 1997. The essential elements of successful marriage and family therapy: A modified Delphi study. *American Journal of Family Therapy* 25:213-31.

Whitehead, T. L., and M. E. Conaway, eds. 1986. *Self, sex and gender in cross-cultural fieldwork.* Urbana: University of Illinois Press.

Whiting, B. W., and J. W. M. Whiting. 1973. Methods for observing and recording behavior. In *Handbook of method in cultural anthropology,* ed. by R. Naroll and R. Cohen, 282-315. New York: Columbia University Press.

Whiting, B. W., and J. W. M. Whiting (with R. Longabaugh). 1975. *Children of six cultures: A psychocultural analysis.* Cambridge, Mass.: Harvard University Press.

Whiting, J. W. M., I. L. Child, and W. W. Lambert et al. 1966. *Field guide for a study of socialization.* New York: John Wiley.

Whyte, W. F. 1960. Interviewing in field research. In *Human organization research,* ed. by R. W. Adams and J. J. Preiss, 299-314. Homewood, Ill.: Dorsey.

Whyte, W. F. 1981 [1943]. *Street corner society: The social structure of an Italian slum.* 3d ed. Chicago: University of Chicago Press.

Whyte, W. F. 1989. Doing research in Cornerville. In *In the field: Readings on the field research experience,* ed. by C. D. Smith and W. Kornblum, 69-82. New York: Praeger.

Whyte, W. F., and K. A. Whyte. 1984. *Learning from the field: A guide from experience.* Beverly Hills, Calif.: Sage.

Wickham-Crowley, T. P. 1991. A qualitative comparative approach to Latin American revolutions. *International Journal of Comparative Sociology* 32:82-109.

Widom, C. S., and S. Morris. 1997. Accuracy of adult recollections of childhood victimization, Part 2: Childhood sexual abuse. *Psychological Assessment* 9:34-46.

Wiederman, M., D. Weis, and E. Algeier. 1994. The effect of question preface on response rates in a telephone survey of sexual experience. *Archives of Sexual Behavior* 23:203-15.

Wilcox, R. R. 1998. How many discoveries have been lost by ignoring modern statistical methods? *American Psychologist* 53:300-14.

Wilke, J. R. 1992. Supercomputers manage holiday stock. *Wall Street Journal,* December 23, B1:8.

Will, J. A. 1993. The dimensions of poverty: Public perceptions of the deserving poor. *Social Science Research* 22:312-32.

Willett, W. C., M. J. Stampfer, J. E. Manson, G. A. Colditz, B. A. Rosner, F. E. Speizer, and C. H. Hennekens. 1996. Coffee consumption and coronary heart disease in women: A ten-year followup. *Journal of the American Medical Association* 275:458-62.

Williams, B. 1978. *A sampler on sampling.* New York: John Wiley.

Williams, L. M., and R. A. Farrell. 1990. Legal response to child sexual abuse in day care. *Criminal Justice and Behavior* 17:284-302.

Williams, T. 1996. Exploring the cocaine culture. In *In the field: Readings on the research experience,* ed. by C. D. Smith and W. Kornblum, 27-32. New York: Praeger.

Willimack, D. K., H. Schuman, B.-E. Pennell, and J. M. Lepkowski. 1995. Effects of a prepaid nonmonetary incentive on response rates and response quality in face-to-face surveys. *Public Opinion Quarterly* 59:78-92.

Willms, D. G., J. A. Best, D. W. Taylor, J. R. Gilbert, D. M. C. Wilson, E. A. Lindsay, and J. Singer. 1990. A systematic approach for using qualitative methods in primary prevention research. *Medical Anthropology Quarterly* 4:391-409.

Wilson, G. D., and J. R. Patterson. 1968. A new measure of conservatism. *British Journal of Social and Clinical Psychology* 7:264-69.

Wilson, H. S., and S. A. Hutchinson. 1996. Methodologic mistakes in grounded theory. *Nursing Research* 45:122-24.

Wilson, R. P., M. Nxumalo, B. Magonga, Jr., G. A. Shelley, K. A. Parker, and Q. Q. Dlamini. 1993. Diagnosis and management of acute respiratory infections by Swazi child caretakers, healers, and health providers, 1990-1991. Working paper, Office of Analysis and Technical Reports, United States Agency for International Development.

Wimbush, J. C., and D. R. Dalton. 1997. Base rate for employee theft: Convergence of multiple methods. *Journal of Applied Psychology* 82:756-63.

Winch, P. 1990. *The idea of a social science and its relation to philosophy.* 2d ed. London: Routledge.

Wlezien, C., M. Franklin, and D. Twiggs. 1997. Economic perceptions and vote choice: Disentangling the endogeneity. *Political Behavior* 19:7-17.

Wodak, R., ed. 1997. *Gender and discourse.* Thousand Oaks, Calif.: Sage.

Wolcott, H. 1995. *The art of fieldwork.* Walnut Creek, Calif.: AltaMira.

Wolcott, H. 1999. *Ethnography: A way of seeing.* Walnut Creek, Calif.: AltaMira.

Wolf, D. R. 1990. *The Rebels: A brotherhood of outlaw bikers.* Toronto: University of Toronto Press.

Wolf, D. R. 1991. High-risk methodology: Reflections on leaving an outlaw society. In *Experiencing fieldwork,* ed. by W. B. Shaffir and R. A. Stebbins, 211-23. Newbury Park, Calif.: Sage.

Wolf, F. M. 1986. *Meta-analysis: Quantitative methods for research synthesis.* Beverly Hills, Calif.: Sage.

Wong, M.M.-H., and M. Csikszentmihalyi. 1991. Affiliation motivation and daily experience: Some issues on gender differences. *Journal of Personality and Social Psychology* 60:154-64.

Wood, W., F. W. Wong, and J. G. Chachere. 1991. Effects of media violence on viewers' aggression in unconstrained social interaction. *Psychological Bulletin* 109:371-83.

Woodgate, R., and L. J. Kristjanson. 1996. A young child's pain: How parents and nurses "take care." *International Journal of Nursing Studies* 33:271-84.

Woods, P. 1986. *Inside schools: Ethnography in educational research.* London: Routledge & Kegan Paul.

Woods, P. 1996. *Researching the art of teaching. Ethnography for educational use.* London: Routledge.

Woolhouse, R. S. 1996. Locke. In *The Blackwell companion to philosophy,* ed. by N. Bunnin and E. P. Tsui-James, 541-54. Oxford, U.K.: Basil Blackwell.

Wormald, B. H. G. 1993. *Francis Bacon: History, politics and science.* New York: Cambridge University Press.

Wright, K. B. 1997. Shared ideology in Alcoholics Anonymous: A grounded theory approach. *Journal of Health Communication* 2:83-99.

Wright, S. 1921. Correlation and causation. *Journal of Agricultural Research* 20:557-85.

Wuthnow, R. 1976. A longitudinal, cross-national indicator of societal religious commitment. *Journal for the Scientific Study of Religion* 16:87-99.

Yamamoto, N., and M. I. Wallhagen. 1998. Service use by family caregivers in Japan. *Social Science and Medicine* 47:677-91.

Yammarino, F. J., S. J. Skinner, and T. L. Childers. 1991. Understanding mail survey response behavior: A meta-analysis. *Public Opinion Quarterly* 55:613-39.

Young, H. M. 1998. Moving to congregate housing: The last chosen home. *Journal of Aging Studies* 12:149-65.

Young, J. C. 1978. Illness categories and action strategies in a Tarascan town. *American Ethnologist* 5:81-97.

Young, J. C. 1980. A model of illness treatment decisions in a Tarascan town. *American Ethnologist* 7:106-31.

Yu, X. 1995. Conflict in a multicultural organization: An ethnographic attempt to discover work-related cultural assumptions between Chinese and American co-workers. *International Journal of Conflict Management* 6:211-32.

Zehner, R. B. 1970. Sex effects in the interviewing of young adults. *Sociological Focus* 3:75-84.

Zimbardo, P. G. 1973. On the ethics of intervention in human psychological research: With special reference to the Stanford prison experiment. *Cognition* 2:243-56.

Zirkle, C. 1949. *The death of a science in Russia.* Philadelphia: University of Pennsylvania Press.

Znaniecki, F. 1934. *The method of sociology.* New York: Farrar & Rinehart.

Zorbaugh, H. W. 1929. *The Gold Coast and the slum: A sociological study of Chicago's near North Side.* Chicago: University of Chicago Press.

Zsambok, C. E., and G. Klein, eds. 1997. *Naturalistic decision making.* Mahwah, N.J.: Lawrence Erlbaum.

Zuckerman, M., H. S. Hodgins, A. Zuckerman, and R. Rosenthal. 1993. Contemporary issues in the analysis of data: A survey of 551 psychologists. *Psychological Science* 4:49-53.

Zuell, C., R. P. Weber, and P. Mohler, eds. 1989. *Computer-assisted text analysis for the social sciences: The General Inquirer III.* Mannheim: Germany Center for Surveys, Methods, and Analysis (ZUMA).

INDEX

ABOUT THE AUTHOR

H. RUSSELL BERNARD (Ph.D., University of Illinois, 1968) is Professor of Anthropology at the University of Florida. He has taught at Washington State University and West Virginia University, and he has also taught or done research at the University of Athens, the University of Cologne, the National Museum of Ethnology (Osaka), and Scripps Institution of Oceanography. Bernard works with indigenous people to develop publishing outlets for works in previously nonwritten languages. He does research in social network analysis, particularly on the problem of estimating the size of uncountable populations. His publications include *Native Ethnography: An Otomí Indian Describes His Culture* (Sage, 1989, with Jesús Salinas Pedraza), *Technology and Social Change* (1983, 2d ed., edited with Pertti Pelto), and *Research Methods in Anthropology* (AltaMira, 1994, 2d ed.). Bernard was editor of *Human Organization* and the *American Anthropologist*. He is currently editor of the journal *Field Methods*.